ADVANCED ACCOUNTING

FIFTH EDITION

ADVANCED ACCOUNTING

Floyd A. Beams

Virginia Polytechnic Institute and State University

PRENTICE HALL, Englewood Cliffs, New Jersey 07632

Library of Congress Cataloging-in-Publication Data

Beams, Floyd A.
    Advanced accounting / Floyd A. Beams. — 5th ed.
       p. cm.
    Includes index.
    ISBN 0-13-010489-2
    1. Accounting. I. Title.
  HF5835.B41517 1992   91-35225
  657'.046—dc20   CIP

Editorial/production supervision: *Robert C. Walters*
Interior design: *Susan Behnke*
Cover design: *Bruce Kenselaar*
Prepress buyer: *Trudy Pisciotti*
Manufacturing buyer: *Robert Anderson*
Acquisitions editor: *Joseph Heider*

Material from Uniform CPA Examination Questions and Unofficial Answers, Copyright © 1958, 1960, 1961, 1963, 1964, 1967, 1968, 1969, 1970, 1971, 1972, 1973, 1974, 1975, 1976, 1977, 1978, 1979, 1980, 1981, 1982, 1983, 1984, 1985, 1986, 1987 1988, 1989, 1990, by the American Institute of Certified Public Accountants, Inc., is adapted with permission.

 ©1992, 1988, 1985, 1982, 1979 by Prentice-Hall, Inc.
A Paramount Communications Company
Englewood Cliffs, New Jersey 07632

Printed in the United States of America

10 9 8 7 6 5 4 3

ISBN 0-13-010489-2

Prentice-Hall International (UK) Limited, *London*
Prentice-Hall of Australia Pty. Limited, *Sydney*
Prentice-Hall Canada Inc., *Toronto*
Prentice-Hall Hispanoamericana, S.A., *Mexico*
Prentice-Hall of India Private Limited, *New Delhi*
Prentice-Hall of Japan, Inc., *Tokyo*
Simon & Schuster Asia Pte. Ltd., *Singapore*
Editora Prentice-Hall do Brasil, Ltda., *Rio de Janeiro*

CONTENTS

Chapter 1 **Business Combinations 1**

Impact of Business Combinations 2
The Form of Business Combinations 3
Reasons for Business Combinations 4
The Accounting Concept of a Business Combination 5
Note to the Student 10
Application of the Pooling of Interests Method 11
Accounting for Business Combinations under the Purchase Method 17
Pooling and Purchase Methods Compared 23
Disclosure Requirements for a Pooling 27
Disclosure Requirements for a Purchase 27
Summary 27

Chapter 2 **Stock Investments—Investor Accounting and Reporting 42**

Accounting for Stock Investments 42
Equity Method of Accounting—A One-line Consolidation 46
Interim Acquisitions of an Investment Interest 53
Investment in a Step-by-Step Acquisition 54
Sale of an Equity Interest 55
Investee Corporation with Preferred Stock 56
Extraordinary Items, Cumulative-Effect-Type Adjustments
  and Other Considerations 57
Disclosures for Equity Investees 58
Summary 60
Note to the Student 60

Chapter 3 **An Introduction to Consolidated Financial Statements 72**

Business Combinations Consummated Through Stock Acquisitions 72
Consolidated Balance Sheet at Date of Acquisition 76
Consolidated Balance Sheets after Acquisition 80

Allocation of Excess to Identifiable Net Assets and Goodwill   82
Consolidated Income Statement   89
Consolidated Statement of Cash Flows   91
Push Down Accounting   97
Pooled Subsidiaries   98
Summary   102

Chapter 4   **Consolidation Techniques and Procedures   122**

Consolidation under the Equity Method   122
Consolidation under an Incomplete Equity Method   129
Consolidation under the Cost Method   135
Locating Errors   143
Excess Allocated to Identifiable Net Assets   144
Trial Balance Working Paper Format   149
Summary   152

Chapter 5   **Intercompany Profit Transactions—Inventories   172**

Intercompany Inventory Transactions   173
Downstream and Upstream Sales   178
Unrealized Profits from Downstream Sales   181
Unrealized Profits from Upstream Sales   184
Consolidation Example—Intercompany Profits
   from Downstream Sales   187
Consolidation Example—Intercompany Profits
   from Upstream Sales   195
Summary   202

Chapter 6   **Intercompany Profit Transactions—Plant Assets   219**

Intercompany Profits on Nondepreciable Plant Assets   219
Intercompany Profits on Depreciable Plant Assets   225
Plant Assets Sold at Other than Fair Value   234
Consolidation Example—Upstream and Downstream Sales
   of Plant Assets   236
Inventory Items Purchased for Use as Operating Assets   245
Summary   245

Chapter 7   **Intercompany Profit Transactions—Bonds   262**

Intercompany Profit Transactions   262
Constructive Gains and Losses on Intercompany Bonds   263
Parent Company Bonds Purchased by Subsidiary   266
Subsidiary Bonds Purchased by Parent   272
Consolidation in Years After Intercompany Bond Purchase
   under Different Assumptions   278
Summary   287

Chapter 8   **Consolidations—Changes in Ownership Interests   303**

Acquisitions During an Accounting Period   303
Pooling of Interests During an Accounting Period   307
Piecemeal Acquisitions   310

Sales of Ownership Interests   312
Changes in Ownership Interests from Subsidiary
    Stock Transactions   318
Stock Dividends and Stock Splits by a Subsidiary   323
Summary   325

Chapter 9   **Indirect and Mutual Holdings   346**

Affiliation Structures   346
Indirect Holdings—Father-Son-Grandson Structure   348
Indirect Holdings—Connecting Affiliates Structure   354
Mutual Holdings—Parent Stock Held by Subsidiary   359
Subsidiary Stock Mutually Held   369
Summary   372

Chapter 10   **Subsidiary Preferred Stock, Consolidated Earnings
Per Share, and Consolidated Income Taxation   389**

Subsidiaries with Preferred Stock Outstanding   389
Parent Company and Consolidated Earnings Per Share   396
Subsidiary with Convertible Preferred Stock   400
Subsidiary with Options and Convertible Bonds   401
Accounting for Income Taxes of Consolidated Entities   404
Income Tax Allocation   405
Separate Company Tax Returns with Intercompany Gain   408
Effect of Consolidated and Separate Company Tax Returns
    on Consolidation Procedures   412
Purchase Business Combinations   418
Financial Statement Disclosures for Income Taxes   420
Summary   421

Chapter 11   **Consolidation Theories, Push-Down Accounting,
and Corporate Joint Ventures   437**

Comparison of Consolidation Theories   438
Illustration—Consolidation under Parent Company
    and Entity Theories   441
Push-Down Accounting and Other Basis Considerations   450
Joint Ventures   457
Summary   461
Appendix: Consolidation under a Current Cost System   462

Chapter 12   **Accounting for Branch Operations   483**

Sales Agencies and Branches   483
Sales Agency Accounts   484
Branch Accounting Systems   486
Merchandise Shipments in Excess of Cost   492
Freight Costs on Shipments   494
Home Office—Branch Expense Allocation   496
Reconciliation of Home Office and Branch Accounts   497
Illustration of Home Office and Branch Accounting   498
Summary   503

Chapter 13 **Foreign Currency Concepts and Transactions 516**

Brief Background on Authoritative Accounting Pronouncements 517
Objectives of Translation and the Functional Currency Concept 518
Foreign Exchange Concepts and Definitions 519
Foreign Currency Transactions Other Than Forward Contracts 522
Forward Exchange Contracts and Similar Agreements 526
Summary 536

Chapter 14 **Foreign Currency Financial Statements 548**

Application of the Functional Currency Concept 549
Illustration—Translation under *Statement 52* 553
Illustration—Remeasurement under *Statement 52* 560
Illustration—Translation with Minority Interest and the Cash Flow
  Statement 567
Accounting for a Foreign Branch 580
Summary 583

Chapter 15 **Segment and Interim Financial Reporting 601**

Evolution of Segment Reporting Requirements 601
Scope of the Segment Reporting Standard 603
Identification of Segment Reporting Responsibilities 603
Disclosures Required for Operations in Different Industries 611
Disclosures for Operations in Different Geographic Areas 614
Disclosures for Export Sales 617
Disclosures for Major Customers 617
Consolidation Policy and Segment Disclosures 618
Interim Financial Reporting 618
Guidelines for Preparing Interim Statements 621
SEC Interim Financial Disclosures 622
Summary 625

Chapter 16 **Partnerships—Formation, Operations, and Changes
in Ownership Interests 639**

Nature of Partnerships 639
Initial Investments in a Partnership 641
Additional Investments and Withdrawals 643
Partnership Operations 644
Profit and Loss Sharing Agreements 646
Changes in Partnership Interests 653
Purchase of an Interest from Existing Partners 654
Investing in an Existing Partnership 658
Dissolution of a Continuing Partnership Through
  Death or Retirement 663
Summary 665
Appendix: Uniform Partnership Act 678

Chapter 17 **Dissolution and Liquidation of a Partnership 692**

The Liquidation Process 692
Safe Payments to Partners 696
Installment Liquidations 699

Cash Distribution Plans   706
Insolvent Partners and Partnerships   708
Summary   711

Chapter 18   **Corporate Liquidations, Reorganizations, and Debt Restructurings for Financially Distressed Corporations   722**

Bankruptcy Reform Act of 1978   722
Liquidation   725
Illustration of a Liquidation Case   727
Reorganization   737
Financial Reporting During Reorganization   741
Financial Reporting for the Emerging Company   743
Illustration of a Reorganization Case   744
Troubled Debt Restructurings   753
Illustration of a Troubled Debt Restructuring   754
Summary   757

Chapter 19   **Accounting for State and Local Governmental Units—Part I   771**

Historical Development of Accounting Principles for State and Local
   Governmental Units   772
Overview of Basic Governmental Accounting Principles   774
Budgeting   782
The General Fund and Special Revenue Funds   783
Accounting for the General Fund   783
Summary   795

Chapter 20   **Accounting for State and Local Governmental Units—Part II   812**

Capital Projects Funds   812
Debt Service Funds   818
Special Assessment Activities   821
Account Groups   822
General Fixed Asset Account Group   822
General Long-term Debt Account Group   824
Accounting for Leases in Governmental Funds   826
Proprietary Funds   827
Internal Service Funds   827
Enterprise Funds   833
Combining Financial Statements   834
Fiduciary Funds   836
Agency Funds   836
Trust Funds   838
Disclosures for Post Retirement Benefits
   Other than Pension Benefits   843
Combined Financial Statements   844
Governmental Funds—Into the Future with GASB
   Statement 11   851
Summary   852

Chapter 21   **Colleges and Universities, Hospitals, and Voluntary Health and Welfare Organizations   872**

Source of Accounting Principles for Nonprofits   872
Specialized Accounting and Reporting Principles   873
Colleges and Universities   874

Current Funds of Colleges and Universities   876
Other Fund Groupings of Colleges and Universities   884
Financial Statements of Colleges and Universities   886
Hospitals and Other Health Care Providers   886
Voluntary Health and Welfare Organizations   900
Summary   911

Appendix A   **SEC Influence on Accounting   925**

The 1933 Securities Act   925
The Securities Exchange Act of 1934   926
The Registration Statement for Security Issues   927
The Integrated Disclosure System   927
SEC Developments   929
Summary   930

Appendix B   **Estates and Trusts   931**

Creation of an Estate   931
Probate Proceedings   932
Administration of the Estate   932
Accounting for the Estate   934
Illustration of Estate Accounting   935
Accounting for Trusts   938

Glossary   941

Index   951

PREFACE

Advanced Accounting is designed for financial accounting courses above the intermediate level. This fifth edition has been updated to reflect recent business developments and changes in accounting standards and related regulatory requirements. The chapter content is revised for better sequencing, more efficient coverage, and improved readability. These changes are the result of suggestions received from users and reviewers of earlier editions.

An important feature of this book is its student orientation, and special effort has been expended to maintain that emphasis in this fifth edition. The student-oriented strategies include shading working paper entries, presenting working papers on single, upright pages, and integrating excerpts from business publications and corporate annual reports into the text. The text includes many exhibits that summarize complex material and both clarify and reinforce the underlying concepts. Students should read and review these exhibits in conjunction with the text. A student orientation is also reflected in the assignment material, which is varied and inventive. All assignment material, including items from past CPA examinations, is closely aligned with chapter coverage. Names of parent and subsidiary companies begin with P and S for convenient identification and reference.

CHANGES IN THE FIFTH EDITION

The important changes in this fifth edition of *Advanced Accounting* include:

- *Corporate joint ventures and other conceptual issues.* Corporate joint venture accounting is added in this edition. The consolidation theories chapter is restructured to include three major topics: consolidation theories, push-down accounting, and accounting for corporate joint ventures. Other conceptual issues relating to acquisition valuation bases are discussed, including the Emerging Issues Task Force (EITF) Consensus Issue 88–16 on leveraged buyouts, and an example of how businesses may structure corporate takeovers to avoid push-down accounting. Consolidation under a current cost system is presented in an appendix to Chapter 11.
- *Interim financial reporting.* Chapter 15 is restructured under the title "Segment and Interim Financial Reporting." The interim financial reporting section is new and

includes APB Opinion No. 28 and SEC 10–Q requirements for interim reports. This section complements Appendix A, "SEC Influence on Accounting."

- *Fresh-start reporting.* Chapter 18 has been expanded to cover the AICPA's *Statement of Position* (SOP) 90–7, "Financial Reporting by Entities in Reorganization under the Bankruptcy Code." The update includes an illustration of financial accounting and reporting practices under fresh-start reporting for a corporate reorganization under Chapter 11 of the Bankruptcy Code.
- *GASB pronouncements.* Rapid changes are taking place in accounting for state and local governmental units. Chapter 20 illustrates financial reporting under GASB 9, "Reporting Cash Flows of Proprietary and Nonexpendable Trust Funds and Governmental Entities that Use Proprietary Accounting." Financial reporting requirements for pension plans under GASB 5 have been added. Chapter 20 also provides an overview of GASB Statement 11, "Measurement Focus and Basis of Accounting—Governmental Fund Operating Statements," that is scheduled to become effective in 1994.
- *Nongovernmental nonprofit entities.* Chapter 21 is updated for the AICPA's Audit Guide, Audits of Providers of Health Care Services, and the FASB Exposure Draft, "Accounting for Contributions Received and Contributions Made and Capitalization of Works of Art, Historical Treasures, and Similar Assets."
- *SEC reporting requirements.* An overview of reporting practices of public companies under SEC requirements is presented as Appendix A, "SEC Influence on Accounting."
- *Estate and trust accounting.* Accounting and reporting practices of estates and trusts are reviewed and illustrated in Appendix B, "Estates and Trusts."
- *Glossary.* A glossary of key terms is new in this edition.

ORGANIZATION

The first eleven chapters cover business combinations, the equity and cost methods of accounting for investments in common stock, and consolidated financial statements. This emphasis reflects the importance of business combinations and consolidations in advanced accounting courses as well as in financial accounting and reporting practices.

Accounting standards for business combinations under the purchase and pooling of interests methods are introduced in Chapter 1, along with applicable accounting and reporting standards. Chapter 1 also provides relevant background material on the form and economic impact (including human costs) of business combinations.

The equity method of accounting as a one-line consolidation is discussed in Chapter 2 and integrated throughout subsequent chapters on consolidations. This parallel one-line consolidation/consolidation coverage permits alternate computations for such key concepts as consolidated net income and consolidated retained earnings, and helps the instructor explain the objectives of consolidation procedures. It also permits students to check their logic by trying alternative approaches to key computations.

The one-line consolidation is established as the standard of parent-company accounting for subsidiaries, but the coverage does not ignore situations in which the parent company uses the cost method or an incomplete equity method to account for its subsidiaries and other investees. These methods are illustrated in the text and included in assignment material so that students are prepared for consolidation assignments regardless of the method used by the parent company in accounting for its subsidiary investments.

Consolidated financial statements, including the consolidated statement of cash flows (SCF), are introduced in Chapter 3. Coverage of the consolidated SCF includes worksheet illustrations for both the indirect and the direct methods. The consolidated SCF is included in problem material in Chapter 3 and subsequent chapters on consolidations, including Chapter 14, which covers consolidations of foreign subsidiaries. Similarly, accounting and reporting matters related to pooled subsidiaries are integrated into Chapters 3 through 11. An illustration of push-down accounting has been added in Chapter 3.

Chapter 4 introduces the student to consolidation working paper techniques and procedures. The three-section financial statement working paper approach is presented as basic, but the trial balance approach is also illustrated and included in the problem material. Consolidation working papers for a parent company that uses the equity method as a one-line consolidation are presented first to set the standard. Subsequently, working papers are illustrated under an incomplete (or simple) equity method and under the cost method, for both the year of acquisition and the following year.

Consolidation under the cost and incomplete equity methods are illustrated using the traditional approach (alternate working paper entries) and the conversion to equity approach (adjust to the equity method through a schedule and a working paper entry).

Intercompany transactions involving inventories, plant assets, and bonds are covered in Chapters 5, 6, and 7. These chapters include changes for better organization and expanded coverage. The chapters illustrate both the traditional and the conversion-to-equity approaches when a one-line consolidation is not used. Chapter 8 covers ownership changes in subsidiaries, and has been updated for the SEC's Staff Accounting Bulletin (SAB) 84, which prohibits gain recognition on subsidiary sales of stock to the public when there is uncertainty about realization of the gain. An updated section of Chapter 8 deals with subsidiary sales of stock to its parent company, and subsidiary repurchases of its own stock from the parent.

Chapter 9 covers complex affiliation structures, and Chapter 10 covers subsidiary preferred stock, consolidated earnings per share, and income taxation for consolidated entities. Chapter 10 has been updated for tax law changes and the FASB's Exposure Draft to replace FAS 96 on accounting for income taxes.

Chapter 11 covers consolidation theories, leveraged buyouts, push-down accounting and corporate joint ventures. An appendix to the chapter discusses current cost implications for consolidations. Since Chapters 9, 10, and 11 cover specialized topics, their coverage is not essential background for assignment of subsequent chapters.

Chapter 12 covers accounting and reporting practices for branch operations, including the use of perpetual inventory practices in the combining working papers. The use of perpetual inventory procedures makes the combining working paper entries for branches compatible with those for consolidations.

Foreign currency issues continue to be important to American business enterprises. The survival of many American businesses depends on access to foreign markets, suppliers, and capital. Chapter 13 covers foreign currency transactions, including imports and exports and forward contracts. Chapter 14 covers translation and remeasurement of foreign entity financial statements, one-line consolidations of equity investees, consolidation of foreign subsidiaries for external reporting purposes, and combining foreign branch operations.

Chapter 15 covers disclosures for industry segments and interim financial reporting. Interim reporting is a new topic. Chapter 16 covers organization, operations and dissolution of partnership entities, and Chapter 17 covers partnership liquidations. Chapter 18 covers corporate liquidations, reorganizations, and debt restructurings for financially distressed companies. Restructuring under Chapter 11 of the Bankruptcy Code is illustrated using fresh-start reporting as described in the AICPA's SOP 90–7.

The last three chapters of the book include two chapters on governmental accounting (Chapters 19 and 20), and a final chapter that introduces accounting for colleges and universities, hospitals, and voluntary health and welfare organizations (Chapter 21). GASB Statements through 11 are integrated into

Chapters 19 and 20, and the AICPA's Audit and Accounting Guide, *Audits of Providers of Health Care Services,* is integrated into Chapter 21.

Appendix A provides an overview of SEC accounting requirements, and Appendix B surveys fiduciary accounting for estates and trusts.

SUPPLEMENTARY MATERIALS

- *Solutions Manual.* The Solutions Manual contains answers to questions and solutions to exercises and problems. It is developed with convenient tear-out pages for preparing transparencies.
- *Instructor's Resource Manual.* The Instructor's Resource Manual includes:
  problem descriptions with estimated solution times
  transparency mats for outlines of relevant accounting standards, class illustrations, and other lecture aids
  examination material
  student check figures for problems
- *Exam disk.* Examination material is available on diskette from Prentice Hall.
- *Lotus templates.* Lotus spreadsheet templates for consolidation and other working paper problems are available on request to adopters for personal computer applications.
- *Working Papers.* Partially completed working papers for consolidation and other working paper problems in the textbook are available to adopters on request.

ACKNOWLEDGMENTS

Many people have made valuable contributions to the fifth edition of *Advanced Accounting* and I am happy to recognize their contributions. I am indebted to the many users of prior editions for the helpful comments and constructive criticism. I also acknowledge the help and encouragement that I received from my students at Virginia Tech who, often unknowingly, participated in class testing various sections of the manuscript.

My sincere appreciation is extended to the reviewers of the fifth edition for their thoughtful comments and valuable suggestions: James Chiu, California State University, Northridge; S. Thomas A. Cianciolo, Eastern Michigan University; Abo-El-Yazeed T. Habid, Mankato State University; Patricia Healy, Pace University, Pleasantville/Briarcliff; Saleha B. Khumawala, University of Houston; Lola Rhodes, University of Texas at Arlington; Joanne Rockness, North Carolina State University; and James D. Stice, Brigham Young University.

Several other friends and colleagues have provided comments and materials that contribute significantly to this text. They are Roy E. Tuttle, University of Wisconsin–Madison; Joseph E. Hampton, The American University; Lewis F. Davidson, Florida International University; José A. González, Inter American University of Puerto Rico; Bernard H. Newman, Pace University; Jerrell W. Habegger, Susquehanna University; Delmer P. Hylton, Wake Forest University; Charles Werner, Loyola University–Chicago; Steven A. Zeff, Rice University; Manson P. Dillaway, New Mexico State University; Gary M. Cunningham, Midwestern State University; and Craig D. Shoulders of Virginia Tech. I also express my appreciation for the valuable support services that I received from Robert C. Walters, Editorial and Production Supervisor, Sally Ann Bailey, copy editor and the people at Prentice Hall, including Joe Heider, Editor-in-Chief, Accounting and Information Systems; Esther S. Koehn, Supervisory Production Editor for Accounting; Linda Albelli, Assistant to Joe Heider; and especially Susan Seuling, Development Editor, who kept this revision on track. Finally, I express my deepest gratitude to my wife, Thais, whose multiple contributions to this book have been immeasurable.

1

BUSINESS COMBINATIONS

A *business combination* is the union of business entities. Uniting separate business entities is an alternative to internal expansion through the acquisition or development of business property on a piecemeal basis, and it frequently offers advantages to all the combining entities and their owners. Although the overriding objective of business combinations must be profitability, the immediate concern of many combinations is to gain operating efficiencies through horizontal or vertical integration of operations or to diversify business risks through conglomerate operations.

Horizontal integration is the combination of firms in the same business lines and markets. The acquisition of Empire Bancorp, a bank holding company for Empire Bank NA, by California State Bank in December 1990 is an example of horizontal integration. California State Bank is a state-chartered commercial bank and member of the Federal Deposit Insurance Corporation (FDIC), and Empire Bank NA, also based in California, is a nationally-chartered commercial bank and member of FDIC.

Vertical integration is the combination of firms with operations in different, but successive, stages of production and/or distribution. For example, in 1991 Chrysler Corporation acquired Dynasty Express Corporation, parent of General Rent-A-Car. Chrysler also owns Dollar Rent A Car, Inc., Thrifty Rent-A-Car System, and Snappy Car Rental, Inc., which gives Chrysler several captive customers for its vehicles.

Conglomeration is the combination of firms with unrelated and diverse products and/or service functions. For example, for 140 years Philip Morris Cos., Inc., was a tobacco company. To improve its image and diversity into the food industry, the company acquired two food companies, General Foods and Kraft, Inc., in December 1988. In March 1991, Philip Morris named the chief executive officer of its Kraft General Foods division as the first Philip Morris chairman with no background in the tobacco industry.

Business combinations can seldom be classified neatly into one of these catagories. For example, the 1990 acquisition of Beatrice Foods by ConAgra, Inc., had several business purposes. The combination increased the number of products sold at supermarkets by adding Beatrice's Hunts tomato products and Wesson oils to ConAgra's frozen food brands which include Banquet, Chun King, and Healthy Choice. It provided ConAgra with some vertical integration by giving it access to Beatrice's strong supermarket distribution network. And it provided ConAgra with additional diversification in the food industry.[1]

Federal laws prohibit combinations that would be in restraint of trade or would impair competition. Proposed business combinations are scrutinized by governmental agencies such as the Justice Department, the Federal Trade Commission, the Federal Reserve Board, the Department of Transportation, and the Securities and Exchange Commission, and many are found to be in violation of federal law. For example, a proposed combination of the computerized ticket reservation systems of Delta Airlines, Inc., and American Airlines, Inc., was opposed by the Justice Department on antitrust grounds and by the Department of Transportation on grounds that it would reduce competition in marketing air travel and selling computerized ticket services to travel agents. When antitrust objections are made to a proposed business combination, the objections may be settled through negotiation with the appropriate federal agency, or the agency may argue its case in court with a federal judge rendering the final decision. When Kohlberg Kravis Roberts & Co., (KKR), acquired RJR Nabisco, Inc., in 1989, KKR also owned Beatrice Cos., which competed with RJR in three food lines— ketchup, oriental foods, and packaged nuts. In a negotiated agreement with the Federal Trade Commission, KKR agreed to sell one of the units in each of the three food lines within twelve months.

In addition to federal antitrust laws, many states also have statutes limiting certain mergers deemed anticompetitive. In 1990 American Stores Co. agreed to sell one of its grocery store chains in settlement of an antitrust suit brought against it by the state of California. The suit stemmed from the acquisition of Lucky Stores, which had been completed two years earlier.[2] Some recent state statutes are aimed at preventing or delaying hostile takeovers of their incorporated business enterprises.

IMPACT OF BUSINESS COMBINATIONS

Several periods of merger and acquisition activity in the United States have been identified as boom periods because of the increased number and dollar volume of transactions. These periods include the monopoly-building period in the late 1800s, the oligopoly period in the 1920s, and the 1955–1969 conglomerate period. The 1980s were sometimes referred to as the restructuring years, with mergers, acquisitions, recapitalizations, and leveraged buyouts contributing to record-high stock prices. During this period, many mergers and acquisitions were made by "financial buyers" (a term used to describe corporate raiders and buyout specialists whose deals were motivated more by quick profits from financial engineering than by business expansion). By the end of the 1980s, public attitude toward highly leveraged buyouts was turning unfavorable, the market for high-yield, high-risk junk bonds was weak, and acquisition candidates were becoming scarcer and more expensive. With financial buyers no longer dominating the market, there was an increase in "corporate strategic acquisitions" (in other words, acquisitions with a real business purpose). Robert H. Rock, publisher of *Mergers & Acquisitions,* summarized the 1980s as follows:

> During the decade of the 1980s $2 trillion was spent on shuffling assets through the acquisition and restructuring of 25,000 U.S. companies. The debate goes on as to whether these deals were good for any company in specific or for the nation in general. For many, the selling shareholders benefited; for some, the buying

---

[1]*The Wall Street Journal,* June 13, 1990, p. A1.

[2]In California vs. American Stores Co., the Supreme Court ruled that states may sue in federal court to dismantle mergers that state officials believe are anticompetitive.

ones did too. However, in only a few cases have all stakeholders, including stockholders, creditors, management, employees, and the company itself, come out ahead.

The true test for many of these corporate takeovers and makeovers won't come until the next recession. In the 1980s the ratio of corporate debt to net worth nearly doubled to an average of 52 percent. Some famous deals and many lesser known ones already are collapsing under the weight of their debt loads. In a downturn, many more restructured companies will be in serious trouble.[3]

For the economy as a whole, mergers reshuffle the ownership of corporate assets without increasing the nation's supply of productive resources.

The Human Cost of Business Combinations

Business combinations provide opportunities for people to gain power and make money. But business combinations almost always result in some people losing their jobs. In a survey of executive stress, 54 percent of the respondents listed "loss of job due to merger or acquisition" as their greatest anxiety.[4]

Insight into the human cost of business combinations is provided in an article describing the leveraged buyout of Safeway Stores, Inc.[5] When Herbert and Robert Haft offered to buy Safeway, the company escaped the takeover by selling instead to an investor group led by Kohlberg Kravis Roberts & Co. (KKR), and including Safeway's top management, in a $5.65 billion leveraged buyout. In a leveraged buyout (LBO), an investor group acquires a company from the public shareholders in a transaction financed almost entirely with debt.

Many people made money on this LBO. Safeway stockholders and the top management that participated in the LBO made money. The Hafts made $100 million by selling their shares of Safeway stock to KKR. They made another $59 million from an option they received as consolation for losing the takeover fight. Fees of $65 million went to three investment banks; $60 million to KKR; and $25 million to law and accounting firms.

Sixty-three thousand managers and workers lost their jobs with Safeway because of the leveraged buyout—some through the sale of stores and some through layoffs. Many of these workers were rehired by new store owners, but at lower wages. Thousands were forced to take part-time work (with no benefits); or they remained unemployed. In addition to the Safeway workers who lost their jobs, hundreds of employees of businesses dependent on Safeway (such as suppliers) were laid off.

The new LBO company instituted cost-cutting measures and high pressure quota systems. This in turn, created dissatisfaction among the remaining employees who often complained about being overworked. And there was the constant worry about job security. Labor unions were forced to make concessions to prevent further layoffs.

But these are not the costs that accountants measure.

THE FORM OF BUSINESS COMBINATIONS

Business combination is a general term that encompasses all forms of combining previously separate business entities. Such combinations are labeled ***acquisitions*** when one corporation acquires the productive assets of another business entity and integrates those assets into its own operations. Business combinations are

[3]Robert H. Rock, "Is the Party Over?" *Mergers & Acquisitions* (March/April 1990), p. 6.

[4]Robert Half International in *Journal of Accountancy* (December 1989), p. 22.

[5]Susan C. Faludi, "The Reckoning," *The Wall Street Journal*, May 16, 1990, pp. A1, A8, and A9. Ms. Faludi won the Pulitzer Prize for explanatory journalism for this story on the Safeway leveraged buyout. See Chapter 11 for additional information on leveraged buyouts.

also referred to as *acquisitions* when one corporation obtains operating control over the productive facilities of another entity by acquiring a majority of its outstanding voting stock. The acquired company need not be dissolved, that is, the acquired company does not have to go out of existence.

The terms **merger** and **consolidation** are often used as synonyms for business combinations and acquisitions. However, there is a difference. A merger entails the dissolution of all but one of the business entities involved. A consolidation entails the dissolution of all the business entities involved and the formation of a new corporation.

A *merger* occurs when one corporation takes over all the operations of another business entity and that entity is dissolved. For example, Company A purchases the *assets* of Company B directly from Company B for cash, other assets, or Company A securities (stocks, bonds, or notes). This business combination is an acquisition. It is not a merger unless Company B goes out of existence. Alternatively, Company A may purchase the *stock* of Company B directly from Company B's stockholders for cash, other assets, or Company A securities. This acquisition will give Company A operating control over Company B's assets. It will not give Company A legal ownership of the assets unless it acquires all of Company B stock and elects to dissolve Company B (a merger).

A *consolidation* occurs when a new corporation is formed to take over the assets and operations of two or more separate business entities and those previously separate entities are dissolved. For example, Company D, a newly formed corporation, may acquire the net assets of Companies E and F by issuing stock directly to Companies E and F. In this case, Companies E and F may continue to hold Company D stock for the benefit of their stockholders (an acquisition), or they may distribute the Company D stock to their stockholders and go out of existence (a consolidation). In either case, Company D acquires ownership of the assets of Companies E and F. Alternatively, Company D could issue its stock directly to the stockholders of Companies E and F in exchange for a majority of their shares. In this case, Company D controls the assets of Company E and Company F, but it does not obtain legal title unless Companies E and F are dissolved. Company D must acquire all the stock of Companies E and F and dissolve those companies if their business combination is to be a consolidation. If Companies E and F are not dissolved, Company D will operate as a *holding company* and Companies E and F will be its *subsidiaries*.

Future reference in this chapter will use the term *merger* in the technical sense of a business combination in which all but one of the combining companies go out of existence. Similarly, the term *consolidation* will be used in its technical sense to refer to a business combination in which all the combining companies are dissolved and a new corporation is formed to take over their net assets. *Consolidation* is also used in accounting to refer to the accounting process of combining parent and subsidiary financial statements, such as in the expressions "principles of consolidation," "consolidation procedures," and "consolidated financial statements." In future chapters, the meanings of the terms will depend upon the context in which they are found.

REASONS FOR BUSINESS COMBINATIONS

If expansion is a proper goal of business enterprise, why does a business expand through combination rather than by construction of new facilities? One analyst writes, "Mergers and acquisitions could increase market shares, net new products, technologies, and markets, secure new talent, bolster marketing and distribution capabilities, branch into new geographical territories at home and abroad, even remold companies trapped in shopworn businesses and outmoded strategies."[6]

---

[6]Martin Sikora, "The M&A Bonanza of the '80s...And Its Legacy," *Mergers & Acquisitions* (March/April 1990), p. 91.

Among the many possible reasons for electing business combinations as the vehicle for expansion are:

Cost Advantage. It is frequently less expensive for a firm to obtain needed facilities through combination than through construction. This is particularly true in periods of inflation.

Lower Risk. The purchase of established product lines and markets is usually less risky than developing new products and markets. Business combination is especially less risky when the objective is diversification. It is often pointed out that MBAs are well schooled in mergers and acquisitions, but know very little about production.

Fewer Operating Delays. Plant facilities acquired through a business combination can be expected to be operative and to meet environmental and other governmental regulations. But firms constructing new facilities can expect numerous and expensive delays in construction as well as in getting the necessary governmental approval to commence operations. Construction on the Tellico Dam in Tennessee was held up for five years in order to preserve a small fish known as the snail darter. Environmental impact studies alone can take months or even years to complete.

Avoidance of Takeovers. Some companies combine in order to avoid being acquired themselves. Time's acquisition of Warner Communications Inc. in 1989 was due in part to Paramount Communications, Inc.'s hostile tender offer for Time. Since smaller companies tend to be more vulnerable to corporate takeovers, many of them adopt aggressive buyer strategies as the best defense against takeover attempts by other companies. Companies with high debt-equity ratios usually are not attractive takeover candidates.

Acquisition of Intangible Assets. Business combination involves the combining of intangible, as well as tangible, resources. Thus, the acquisition of patents, mineral rights, or management expertise may be a primary motivating factor in a particular business combination.

Other Reasons. Firms may choose business combination over other forms of expansion for business tax advantages (for example, tax-loss carryforwards), for personal income and estate tax advantages, and for personal reasons. The egos of company management and takeover specialists play an important role in some business combinations.[7]

THE ACCOUNTING CONCEPT OF A BUSINESS COMBINATION

The accounting concept of a business combination is reflected in *Accounting Principles Board (APB) Opinion No. 16,* "Business Combinations," which became effective on November 1, 1970. According to the Accounting Principles Board:

A business combination occurs when a corporation and one or more incorporated or unincorporated businesses are brought together into one accounting entity. The single entity carries on the activities of the previously separate, independent enterprises.[8]

Note that the accounting concept of a business combination emphasizes the *single entity* and the *independence of the combining companies* prior to their union. Although one or more of the combining companies may lose their separate legal identities, dissolution of the legal entities is not necessary within the accounting concept.

---

[7]Many interesting and entertaining books have been written about corporate takeover battles. For example, *Barbarians at the Gate* by Bryan Burrough and John Helyar (Harper & Row, 1990) describes in detail the leveraged buyout of RJR Nabisco, and *Merger* by Peter F. Hartz (William Morrow and Company, 1985) describes the unsuccessful takeover attempt of Martin Marietta by Bendix Corporation.

[8]*APB Opinion No. 16,* paragraph 1.

Previously separate businesses are brought together into one entity when their business resources and operations come under the control of a single management team. Such control within one business entity is established in business combinations in which:

1 One or more corporations become subsidiaries,
2 One company transfers its net assets to another, or
3 Each company transfers its net assets to a newly formed corporation.[9]

A corporation becomes a **subsidiary** when another corporation acquires a majority (over 50 percent) of its outstanding voting stock. Thus, a business combination can be consummated through acquisition of less than 100 percent of the stock of another corporation. In business combinations in which less than 100 percent of the voting stock of other combining companies is acquired, the combining companies necessarily retain their separate legal identities and separate accounting records even though they have become one entity for primary reporting purposes.

Business combinations in which one company transfers its net assets to another can be consummated in a variety of ways, but the acquiring company must acquire substantially all the net assets in any case. Alternatively, each combining company can transfer its net assets to a newly formed corporation. Since the newly formed corporation has no net assets of its own, it issues its stock to the other combining companies or to their stockholders or owners.

Brief Background on Accounting for Business Combinations

Accounting for business combinations is one of the most important and interesting topics of accounting theory and practice. At the same time, accounting for business combinations is one of the most complex and controversial areas of accounting thought. Business combinations are important and interesting because they involve financial transactions of enormous magnitudes, business empires, success stories and personal fortunes, executive genius, and management fiascos. By their nature they necessarily involve the takeover of entire companies. Business combinations are complex because each one is unique and must be evaluated in terms of its economic substance, irrespective of its legal form.

Much of the controversy concerning accounting requirements for business combinations involves the pooling of interests method, which became generally accepted in 1950 when the Committee on Accounting Procedure issued *Accounting Research Bulletin (ARB) No. 40.* Although there are conceptual difficulties with the pooling method, the underlying problem that arose with *ARB No. 40* was the introduction of alternative methods of accounting for business combinations (pooling versus purchase). Numerous financial interests are involved in a business combination, and alternate accounting procedures may not be neutral with respect to different interests. That is, the individual financial interests and the final plan of combination may be affected by the method of accounting.

Current accounting requirements for business combinations are reflected in *APB Opinion No. 16,* which continues to recognize both the pooling and the purchase methods of accounting for business combinations, but not as alternative methods of accounting for the same business combination. Even so, two very different methods of accounting for business combinations continue to be generally accepted. Currently, the Financial Accounting Standards Board (FASB) has a number of projects related to business combinations and consolidations on its agenda.

---

[9]Ibid., paragraph 5.

Methods of Accounting for Business Combinations

There are two generally accepted methods of accounting for business combinations—the ***pooling of interests method*** and the ***purchase method***. But the two methods "are not alternatives in accounting for the same business combination."[10] A business combination that meets the criteria of *APB Opinion No. 16* for a pooling of interests must be accounted for under the pooling method. All other business combinations must be accounted for under the purchase method.

Pooling of Interests Method   The two methods are based on different assumptions about the nature of a business combination. Under the pooling of interests method, it is assumed that the ownership interests of the combining companies are united and continue relatively unchanged in the new accounting entity. Since none of the combining companies are considered to have acquired the other combining companies, there is no purchase, no purchase price, and, accordingly, no new basis of accountability. Under the pooling method, the assets and liabilities of the combining companies are carried forward to the combined entity at *book value.* Retained earnings of the combining companies is also carried forward to the "pooled" entity (subject to certain limitations to be explained later), and income of the pooled entity includes the incomes of the combining companies for the entire year regardless of the date on which the business combination is consummated.

Separate companies in a business combination may have used different accounting methods for recording assets and liabilities. In a pooling of interests combination, the amounts recorded by the separate companies under different accounting methods "may be adjusted to the same basis of accounting if the change would otherwise have been appropriate for the separate company. A change in accounting method to conform the individual methods should be applied retroactively, and the financial statements presented for prior periods should be restated."[11] For example, if one company in a pooling of interests business combination prices its inventories at LIFO cost and the other company at FIFO cost, the historical cost data may be adjusted to either LIFO or FIFO to conform accounting methods.

 Purchase Method   The purchase method is based on the assumption that a business combination is a transaction in which one entity acquires the net assets of the other combining companies. Under the purchase method, the acquiring corporation records the assets received and liabilities assumed at their *fair values.* The cost of the acquired company is determined in the same manner as for other transactions. This cost is allocated to identifiable assets and liabilities acquired according to their fair values at the date of combination. Any excess of cost over the fair value of net assets acquired is allocated to goodwill and amortized over a maximum period of forty years. The retained earnings of the acquiring corporation under the purchase method might be decreased as a result of the business combination, but it could never be increased. The income of the acquiring company includes its own income for the period, plus the income of the acquired companies that is earned after the date of the business combination.

The use of different accounting methods (for example, LIFO versus FIFO) by the separate companies in a purchase business combination is not a relevant factor in recording a combination accounted for as a purchase because all assets and liabilities of the acquired company are recorded at their fair values.

Although the descriptions of pooling and purchase methods are cursory, they do serve to introduce the two methods and to indicate the significant dif-

---

[10]Ibid., paragraph 43.
[11]Ibid., paragraph 52.

ferences in accounting that can result from using one method rather than the other. The two methods are covered in more detail in subsequent sections of this chapter.

Conditions for Pooling

The pooling of interests concept is based on the assumption that it is possible to unite ownership interests through the exchange of equity securities without an acquisition of one combining company by another.[12] Accordingly, application of the concept is limited to those business combinations that involve the exchange of equity securities and a continuity of the operations and ownership interests of the combining companies through a new accounting entity. In *APB Opinion No. 16*, the Accounting Principles Board seeks to prevent pooling of interests accounting for business combinations that are incompatible with the pooling concept. It does this by specifying twelve conditions in paragraphs 45 through 48 of *Opinion 16* that must be met in order for the pooling of interests method to be used. These conditions are summarized under the headings used by the Accounting Principles Board.

Attributes of Combining Companies Two of the conditions for a pooling of interests are classified as attributes of the combining companies. The first condition is that each of the combining companies is *autonomous* and has not been a subsidiary or division of another corporation within *two years* before the plan of combination is initiated. The date of initiation is the earlier of the date of a public announcement of the ratio of exchange of stock or the date the stockholders are notified of the exchange ratio. The second condition is that each of the combining companies is *independent* of the other combining companies. This is interpreted to mean that the other combining companies in total own no more than 10 percent of the voting stock of any combining company.

Manner of Combining Interests Seven conditions for poolings are classified under this heading. First, the combination must be effected in a *single transaction* or be completed in accordance with a specific plan within one year after the plan is initiated. But failure to meet the one-year requirement will not prevent the pooling treatment if consummation is delayed by lawsuits, regulatory agencies, or other factors beyond the control of management. Second, one corporation (the issuing corporation) *must offer and issue only common stock* in exchange for substantially all (90 percent or more) of the outstanding voting stock of another company (combining company) at the date the plan is consummated. The number of shares assumed to be exchanged excludes shares of the combining company held by the issuing company when the plan is initiated, shares acquired by the issuing company before the plan is consummated, and shares outstanding after the plan is consummated. If the combining company holds shares in the issuing company, these shares must be converted into an equivalent number of shares of the combining company and also deducted from outstanding shares to determine the number of shares assumed to be exchanged. The reason for this adjustment is that the issuing company is issuing its shares to reacquire its own shares. Such shares are not issued to acquire stock of the other combining company.[13]

---

[12]The underlying assumptions of pooling have been challenged by many writers in accounting. For example, see *Accounting Research Study No. 5*, "A Critical Study of Accounting for Business Combinations," by Arthur R. Wyatt (New York: American Institute of Certified Public Accountants, 1963).

[13]Paragraph 99 of *Opinion 16* provided certain exceptions to the test of minority stock held prior to combination and the 90 percent "substantially all" test. These exceptions, commonly referred to as the *grandfather clause*, were intended to provide a five-year period of transition to the rules of *Opinion 16*. Although the grandfather clause was initially scheduled to expire on October 31, 1975, it was extended indefinitely by *FASB Statement No. 10*.

The third condition for pooling under the "Manner of Combining Interests" heading is that *none of the combining companies changes the equity interest* of the voting common stock in contemplation of effecting the combination within two years before initiation of the plan of combination or between the dates of initiation and consummation. A fourth condition is that each of the combining companies reacquires shares of voting common stock only for purposes other than business combination, and no company reacquires more than a normal number of shares between the dates the plan is initiated and consummated. This restriction on treasury stock transactions generally does not apply to shares purchased for stock option or compensation plans.

The fifth condition requires that the proportionate interest of each individual common stockholder in each of the combining companies remains the same as a result of the exchange of stock to effect the combination. For example, if Stockholder A held 100 shares in the other combining company and Stockholder B held 200 shares, then Stockholder B's interest in the pooled entity would have to be twice that of A's for the combination to be a pooling of interests.

Condition six specifies that the voting rights in the combined corporation be immediately exercisable by the stockholders. A final condition in this section requires resolution of the combination at the date of consummation with no provisions pending that relate to the issue of securities or other consideration.

Absence of Planned Transactions   The last group of conditions for a pooling of interests relates to planned transactions of the combined entity. First, the combined corporation must *not* agree to retire or reacquire stock issued to effect the combination. Second, the combined corporation must *not* enter into financial arrangements (such as loan guarantees) for the benefit of former stockholders of a combining company. Finally, the combined corporation must *not* plan to dispose of a significant part of the assets of the combining companies within two years after the combination. Plans to dispose of assets that represent duplicate facilities are permissible.

If all twelve of these conditions are met, the business combination is accounted for as a pooling of interests. Otherwise, the purchase method must be used. Exhibit 1–1 reviews the twelve conditions for a pooling of interests using key words and phrases.

all – pooling

Attributes of Combining Companies

1 Autonomous (two-year rule) ✓
2 Independent (10% rule) ✓

Manner of Combining Interests

3 Single transaction (or completed in one year after initiation)
4 Exchange of common stock (90% "substantially all" rule) ✓
5 No equity changes in contemplation of combination (two-year rule)
6 Shares reacquired only for purposes other than combination
7 No change in proportionate equity interests
8 Voting rights immediately exercisable
9 Combination resolved at consummation (no pending provisions)

Absence of Planned Transactions

10 Issuing company does *not* agree to reacquire shares
11 Issuing company does *not* make deals to benefit former stockholders
12 Issuing company does *not* plan to dispose of assets within two years

Exhibit 1–1   *Twelve Conditions for Pooling (APB Opinion No. 16)*

Computations for the "Substantially All Test"

While most of the conditions for pooling are easily understood, the second condition (the substantially all test) under the "Manner of Combining Interests" heading requires illustration. Assume that Pat Corporation and Sam Corporation entered into a plan of business combination on May 1, 19X1 in which Pat was to acquire Sam's outstanding stock by issuing 1 share of Pat stock for each 2 shares of Sam. The agreed-upon exchange ratio was .5 to 1. When the plan of combination was initiated, Sam Corportion had 10,000 shares of voting common stock outstanding of which 200 shares were owned by Pat. After the plan of combination was initiated, Pat purchased for cash an additional 200 shares of Sam stock directly from Sam's stockholders, and Sam purchased 200 shares of Pat stock from Pat's stockholders for cash. The business combination was consummated on July 1, 19X1 with Pat issuing 4,500 shares of its own stock for 9,000 shares of Sam. Sam's former stockholders continued to hold 600 shares of Sam stock.

Computations are necessary to determine if Pat Corporation has issued its own stock for substantially all of Sam's outstanding stock. "Substantially all" is interpreted to mean 90 percent or more of Sam's stock. Although it appears that the 90 percent test for a pooling is met, the computation shown in Exhibit 1–2 indicates otherwise. The Sam shares held by Pat and the Pat shares held by Sam disqualify the business combination for the pooling treatment, even though Pat issued its own stock for 90 percent of Sam's outstanding shares on the date of consummation of the plan.

Shares Assumed to Be Exchanged	
Sam's outstanding shares on July 1, 19X1	10,000
Deduct:	
Combining company shares held by issuing company:	
Sam shares held by Pat on May 1, 19X1	−200
Sam shares acquired by Pat during May 19X1	−200
Equivalent number of issuing company shares held by combining company:	
Equivalent number of Sam shares represented by Sam's 200 shares of Pat (200/.5 exchange ratio)	−400
Sam shares outstanding after consummation	−600
Sam shares assumed to be exchanged in the combination	8,600
Shares Required to Be Exchanged	
10,000 outstanding shares of Sam on July 1, 19X1 × 90%	9,000
90% Test	
8,600 shares assumed exchanged is less than the 9,000 required to be exchanged. Thus, the business combination is not a pooling of interests.	

Exhibit 1–2 *"Substantially All" Test for a Pooling of Interests*

NOTE TO THE STUDENT

The exhibits in this book are an integral part of the learning experience, and they should be studied in conjunction with the related text. In other words, the exhibits should be reviewed as they are introduced in the text. Exhibits contain information and explanations that are essential for understanding the material, and this information is often not provided elsewhere.

APPLICATION OF THE POOLING OF INTERESTS METHOD

A business combination that meets the conditions for a pooling of interests must be accounted for as a pooling. The accounting, however, is affected by the form of the business combination. In the case of a merger or a consolidation, there is only one surviving entity for which accounting records must be maintained and for which financial reports must be issued. Similarly, when one entity in a business combination receives the net assets of other combining companies, that receiving entity is the relevant entity for accounting and reporting purposes. By contrast, business combinations in which the combining entities continue to operate in a parent company–subsidiary relationship involve more complex accounting problems. This is because the accounting records are maintained by the separate legal entities (parent company and subsidiaries), whereas the reporting for the combined entity requires the issuance of consolidated financial statements.

Combining Stockholders' Equities in a Pooling

In a pooling of interests, the recorded assets and liabilities of the separate companies become the assets and liabilities of the surviving (combined) corporation. The capital stock of the surviving corporation must equal the par or stated value of outstanding shares. Ordinarily, the retained earnings of the surviving corporation will be equal to the total retained earnings of the combining companies, but this is not possible when the par or stated value of outstanding shares of the surviving entity exceeds the paid-in capital of the combining companies. If total paid-in capital of the combining companies exceeds the par or stated value of outstanding shares of the surviving entity, the amount of the excess becomes the additional paid-in capital of the surviving entity, and the total retained earnings of the combining companies becomes the retained earnings of the surviving entity. Alternatively, if the par or stated value of outstanding shares of the surviving entity exceeds the total paid-in capital of the combining companies, the combined retained earnings balance is reduced by the excess, and the surviving entity has no additional paid-in capital.

These computational procedures are not necessary in a merger accounted for as a pooling, provided that the total paid-in capital of the other combining company exceeds the par value of stock issued. This is because the surviving entity will record (pool) the entire retained earnings, and it will record as additional paid-in capital any excess of total paid-in capital of the other combining company over the par value of stock issued. The computational procedures will be necessary when the capital stock issued exceeds the total paid-in capital of the other combining company.

These relationships can be shown through a series of illustrations. Assume that the stockholders' equity accounts for Jake Corporation and Kate Corporation immediately before their pooling of interests business combination are as follows:

	Jake Corporation	Kate Corporation	Total
Capital stock, $10 par	$100,000	$ 50,000	$150,000
Additional paid-in capital	10,000	20,000	30,000
Total paid-in capital	110,000	70,000	180,000
Retained earnings	50,000	30,000	80,000
Net assets and equity	$160,000	$100,000	$260,000

In cases 1, 2, and 3 that follow, the pooling is in the form of a *merger,* with Jake Corporation being the issuing corporation and the surviving entity. In cases 4, 5, and 6, the pooling is in the form of a *consolidation,* with Pete Corporation being formed to take over the net assets of Jake and Kate and with Jake and Kate going out of business.

Case 1 Merger: Paid-in Capital Exceeds Stock Issued   Jake, the surviving corporation, issues 5,000 shares of its stock for the net assets of Kate. In this case, the $180,000 total paid-in capital of the combining companies exceeds the $150,000 capital stock of Jake, the surviving entity, by $30,000. As a result of the merger, Jake has capital stock of $150,000, additional paid-in capital of $30,000, and retained earnings of $80,000 for a total equity of $260,000. The entry on Jake's books to record the pooling is:

Net assets	$100,000	
Capital stock—$10 par		$50,000
Additional paid-in capital		20,000
Retained earnings		30,000

To record issuance of 5,000 shares in a pooling of interests with Kate Corporation.

The summary designation *net assets* is used only to simplify this illustration. The actual asset and liability accounts are debited or credited in any real business situation.

Kate records its dissolution by closing out its ledger as follows:

Capital stock—$10 par	$50,000	
Additional paid-in capital	20,000	
Retained earnings	30,000	
Net assets		$100,000

To record merger with Jake Corporation and final dissolutlon.

Case 2 Merger: Paid-in Capital Exceeds Stock Issued   Jake, the surviving corporation, issues 7,000 shares of its stock for the net assets of Kate. In this case, the $180,000 total paid-in capital of the combining companies exceeds the $170,000 capital stock of Jake by $10,000. As a result, Jake has capital stock of $170,000, additional paid-in capital of $10,000, and retained earnings of $80,000 for a total equity of $260,000. Observe that the net assets of the surviving entity are still equal to the total recorded assets of the combining companies. Jake records the pooling as follows:

Net assets	$100,000	
Capital stock—$10 par		$70,000
Retained earnings		30,000

To record issuance of 7,000 shares in a pooling with Kate Corporation.

Case 3 Merger: Stock Issued Exceeds Paid-in Capital   Jake, the surviving entity, issues 9,000 shares of its stock for the net assets of Kate. In this case, the $190,000 capital stock of Jake exceeds the $180,000 total paid-in capital of the combining companies by $10,000. The result is that Jake will have capital stock of $190,000, no additional paid-in capital, and retained earnings of $70,000. Notice that the maximum retained earnings that can be combined ($80,000) has been reduced by the $10,000 excess of capital stock over paid-in capital. The entry on Jake's books is:

Net assets	$100,000	
Additional paid-in capital	10,000	
Capital stock—$10 par		$90,000
Retained earnings		20,000

To record issuance of 9,000 shares in a pooling with Kate Corporation.

The previous cases illustrated accounting procedures for a *merger* accounted for as a pooling of interests. Accounting procedures for *consolidation* of Jake and Kate are illustrated by assuming that Pete Corporation is formed to take over the net assets of Jake and Kate Corporations.

Case 4 Consolidation: Paid-in Capital Exceeds Stock Issued   Pete Corporation issues 15,000 shares of $10 par capital stock, 10,000 to Jake and 5,000 to Kate for their net assets. In this case, the stockholders' equity of Pete, the surviving entity, is the same as for Jake Corporation in Case 1. Pete, however, opens its books with the following entry:

Net assets	$260,000	
Capital stock—$10 par		$150,000
Additional paid-in capital		30,000
Retained earnings		80,000

    To record issuance of 10,000 shares to Jake and 5,000 shares to Kate in a business
    combination accounted for as a pooling of interests.

Since the $180,000 combined paid-in capital of Jake and Kate exceeds the $150,000 capital stock of Pete, the surviving entity, the $30,000 excess is the additional paid-in capital of the pooled entity. Also, the $80,000 maximum retained earnings is pooled.

Case 5 Consolidation: Paid-in Capital Exceeds Stock Issued   Pete corporation issues 17,000 shares of $10 par capital stock, 11,000 to Jake and 6,000 to Kate for their net assets. The stockholders' equity of Pete in this case is the same as Jake's stockholders' equity in Case 2. Pete records the consolidation as follows:

Net assets	$260,000	
Capital stock—$10 par		$170,000
Additional paid-in capital		10,000
Retained earnings		80,000

    To record issuance of 11,000 shares to Jake and 6,000 shares to Kate in a business
    combination accounted for as a pooling of interests.

Since the $180,000 total paid-in capital of the combining entities exceeds the $170,000 capital stock of Pete, the $10,000 excess is the additional paid-in capital of the pooled entity, and the $80,000 maximum retained earnings is pooled.

Case 6 Consolidation: Stock Issued Exceeds Paid-in Capital   Pete Corporation issues 19,000 shares of $10 par capital stock, 12,000 to Jake and 7,000 to Kate for their net assets. Pete's stockholders' equity in this case is the same as Jake's stockholders' equity in Case 3. The entry on Pete's books to record the pooling is as follows:

Net assets	$260,000	
Capital stock—$10 par		$190,000
Retained earnings		70,000

    To record issuance of 12,000 shares to Jake and 7,000 shares to Kate in a business
    combination accounted for as a pooling of interests.

Since the $190,000 capital stock of Pete, the surviving entity, exceeds the $180,000 total paid-in capital of Jake and Kate, the maximum pooled retained earnings is reduced by the $10,000 excess to $70,000, and the pooled entity has no additional paid-in capital.

Summary Balance Sheets   A summary balance sheet for the surviving entity in each of the six pooling of interests business combinations is shown in Exhibit 1–3.

	Merger Jake's Books			Consolidation Pete's Books		
	Case 1	Case 2	Case 3	Case 4	Case 5	Case 6
Net assets	$260,000	$260,000	$260,000	$260,000	$260,000	$260,000
Capital stock—$10 par	$150,000	$170,000	$190,000	$150,000	$170,000	$190,000
Additional paid-in capital	30,000	10,000	—	30,000	10,000	—
Retained earnings	80,000	80,000	70,000	80,000	80,000	70,000
Stockholders' equity	$260,000	$260,000	$260,000	$260,000	$260,000	$260,000

Exhibit 1–3   *Summary Balance Sheets for the Six Pooling of Interests Cases*

Treasury Stock in a Pooling   Under the provisions of *APB Opinion No. 16,* a corporation that distributes treasury stock in a pooling of interests should first account for those shares as retired so that their issuance will be recorded in the same manner as previously unissued stock.[14]

Stock of One Combining Company Held by Another Combining Company
Accounting for the stock of one combining company held by another combining company depends on whether the stock is stock of the surviving entity. An investment in the common stock of the surviving entity is returned to the surviving company in the combination and should be treated as treasury stock of the combined entity. Alternatively, an investment in another combining company by the surviving entity should be treated as stock retired as part of the combination.[15]

   This requirement is illustrated by assuming that Pam Corporation owns 200 shares of Sax Corporation common stock at the consummation of the Pam and Sax merger. Pam carries its investment in Sax account at its $3,000 cost. Summary data for Pam and Sax are as follows:

	Pam	Sax
Investment in Sax	$ 3,000	—
Other assets	197,000	$300,000
Total	$200,000	$300,000
Capital stock—$10 par	$100,000	$200,000
Additional paid-in capital	50,000	30,000
Retained earnings	50,000	70,000
Total	$200,000	$300,000

   If Pam is the surviving entity and issues 19,800 shares to Sax (a 1:1 exchange ratio), the pooling of interests merger is recorded on the books of Pam:

---

[14]*APB Opinion No. 16,* paragraph 54.
[15]Ibid., paragraph 55.

Net assets	$300,000	
Capital stock—$10 par		$198,000
Additional paid-in capital		29,000 *plus*
Retained earnings		70,000
Investment in Sax		3,000

To record merger with Sax Corporation.

If Sax is the surviving entity and issues 10,000 shares of its own stock for 10,000 shares of Pam (a 1:1 exchange ratio), the pooling of interests merger is recorded on the books of Sax:

Net assets	$197,000	
Treasury stock	3,000	
Capital stock—$10 par		$100,000
Additional paid-in capital		50,000
Retained earnings		50,000

To record merger with Pam Corporation.

In each of these examples, the net assets of the surviving entity are $3,000 less than the recorded assets of the combining companies. The related effect on the combined stockholders' equity is to reduce paid-in capital when the investment is in the combining company and to record treasury stock when the investment is in stock of the surviving entity.

Reporting Combined Operations in a Pooling of Interests

When a business combination is treated as a pooling of interests, the financial statements of the surviving (combined) entity are prepared as though the companies had been combined as of the beginning of the year. This means that the results of operations of a pooled company are the same regardless of whether the business combination is consummated at the beginning of the period, at midyear, or at year-end. The revenue and expenses of the combined entity prior to combination during an accounting period should be recorded in the records of the surviving entity when the business combination is consummated.

The accounting entries to record a midyear pooling are illustrated in Cases 1 and 2 below for the July 1, 19X5 pooling of interests of Tom and Mini Corporations. Trial balances for the two companies at June 30, 19X5 are as follows:

	Tom Corporation	Mini Corporation
Other assets	$750,000	$290,000
Expenses	150,000	60,000
Total debits	$900,000	$350,000
Capital stock—$10 par	$500,000	$200,000
Retained earnings	200,000	50,000
Revenues	200,000	100,000
Total credits	$900,000	$350,000

Case 1: Merger   Tom Corporation, the surviving entity, issues 22,000 shares of $10 par common stock for the net assets of Mini Corporation on July 1, 19X5. The entry on Tom's books to record the merger is:

July 1, 19X5

Other assets	$290,000	
Expenses	60,000	
Capital stock—$10 par		$220,000
Retained earnings		30,000
Revenues		100,000

To record issuance of 22,000 shares in a pooling merger with Mini Corporation.

Immediately after this entry has been recorded, Tom Corporation's trial balance will include the following:

	Debits	Credits
Other assets	$1,040,000	
Expenses	210,000	
Capital stock		$ 720,000
Retained earnings		230,000
Revenues		300,000
	$1,250,000	$1,250,000

Note that the $250,000 maximum amount of retained earnings that could be pooled has been reduced by $20,000, the excess of the $720,000 capital stock of the surviving corporation over the $700,000 paid-in capital of the combining corporations.

Case 2: Consolidation   Wall Corporation is formed to consolidate the operations of Tom and Mini Corporations. On July 1, 19X5 Wall issues 72,000 shares of $10 par common stock for the net assets of Tom and Mini, 50,000 shares to Tom and 22,000 shares to Mini. The entry on the books of Wall Corporation to record the pooling of interests is:

July 1, 19X5

Other assets	$1,040,000	
Expenses	210,000	
Capital stock—$10 par		$720,000
Retained earnings		230,000
Revenues		300,000

To record issuance of 72,000 shares in the Tom and Mini pooling of interests.

Since the par value of outstanding stock of Wall Corporation is the same as in Case 1 in which Tom was the surviving entity, the trial balance of Wall Corporation immediately after the combination will be the same as for Tom Corporation in Case 1.

Expenses Related to Pooling Combinations

The costs incurred to effect a business combination and to integrate the operations of the combining companies in a pooling are expenses of the combined corporation. This treatment is required by *APB Opinion No. 16* and is consistent with the pooling concept of combining operations and shareholders' interests without an acquisition and without raising new capital. For example, costs of registering and issuing securities, providing stockholders with information, paying accountants and consultants' fees, and paying finder's fees to those who discovered the "combinable" situation are recorded as expenses of the combined entity in the period in which they are incurred. If Tom or Mini Corporations in the preceding cases had incurred accountants' fees, consultants' fees, costs of security registration, and other costs of combining, the combined net assets of the surviving entity would have been less and combined expenses would have been greater. But the capital stock and pooled retained earnings recorded at July 1, 19X5 would have been the same.

As discussed previously, financial statements of a pooled entity for the year of combination should be presented as if the combination had been consummated at the beginning of the period. In addition, if comparative financial statements for prior years are presented, they must be restated on a combined basis with disclosure of the fact that the statements of previously separate companies have been combined.[16]

ACCOUNTING FOR BUSINESS COMBINATIONS UNDER THE PURCHASE METHOD

All business combinations that do not meet the conditions for pooling must be recorded under the **purchase method**. In general, the purchase method follows the same accounting principles for recording a business combination as are followed in accounting for assets and liabilities under generally accepted accounting principles. The cost to the purchasing entity of acquiring another company in a purchase business combination is measured by the amount of cash disbursed or the fair value of other assets distributed or securities issued. The cost of the acquired company also includes the direct costs of combination (such as accounting, legal, consulting, and finder's fees), other than those for the registration or issuance of equity securities.[17] Registration and issuance costs of equity securities issued in a purchase combination are charged against the fair value of securities issued, usually as a reduction of additional paid-in capital. Indirect costs such as management salaries, depreciation, and rent are expenses under both the pooling and purchase methods. Costs incurred to close duplicate facilities are indirect costs and should be expensed.[18]

To illustrate, assume that Poppy Corporation issues 100,000 shares of $10 par common stock for the net assets of Sunny Corporation in a purchase business combination on July 1, 19X5. The market price of Poppy common stock on this date is $16 per share. Additional direct costs of the business combination consist of SEC fees of $5,000, accountants' fees in connection with the SEC registration statement of $10,000, costs of printing and issuing the common stock certificates of $25,000, and finder's and consultants' fees of $80,000.

The issuance of the 100,000 shares is recorded on Poppy books as:

Investment in Sunny	$1,600,000	
Common stock—$10 par		$1,000,000
Additional paid-in capital		600,000

To record issuance of 100,000 shares of $10 par common stock with a fair value of $16 per share in a purchase business combination with Sunny Corporation.

Additional direct costs of the business combination are recorded as:

Investment in Sunny	$80,000	
Additional paid-in capital	40,000	
Cash (or other net assets)		$120,000

To record additional direct costs of combining with Sunny Corporation, $80,000 for finder's and consultants' fees and $40,000 for registering and issuing equity securities.

---

[16]*APB Opinion No. 20,* "Accounting Changes," paragraph 34. Restatement of all prior-period financial statements presented is required for a change in the reporting entity if the results are material.

[17]Direct costs of combination can be significant. Tracor, a defense company, was acquired in a leveraged buyout for $714 million. Total fees and expenses for all the bankers and lawyers amounted to $70 million, or 10% of the purchase price. *The Wall Street Journal,* August 3, 1989, C2.

[18]*FASB Technical Bulletin* No. 85–5.

Registration and issuance costs of $40,000 are treated as a reduction of the fair value of the stock issued and are charged to additional paid-in capital. Other direct costs of the business combination ($80,000) are added to the cost of acquiring Sunny Corporation. The total cost to Poppy of acquiring Sunny is $1,680,000, the amount entered in the investment in Sunny account. It is desirable to accumulate the total cost incurred in purchasing another company in a single investment account regardless of whether the other combining company is dissolved or the combining companies continue to operate in a parent-subsidiary relationship. If Sunny Corporation is dissolved, its identifiable net assets are recorded on Poppy's books at their fair values, and any excess of investment cost over fair value is recorded as goodwill. In this case, the balance recorded in the investment in Sunny account is allocated by means of an entry on Poppy's books. Such an entry might appear as follows:

Receivables	$XXX	
Inventories	XXX	
Plant assets	XXX	
Goodwill	XXX	
Accounts payable		$ XXX
Notes payable		XXX
Investment in Sunny		1,680,000

To record allocation of the $1,680,000 cost of acquiring Sunny Corporation to identifiable net assets according to their fair values, and to goodwill.

If Poppy and Sunny Corporations were to operate as parent company and subsidiary, the entry to allocate the investment in Sunny balance would not be recorded by Poppy. Instead, Poppy would account for its investment in Sunny by means of the investment in Sunny account, and the allocation of the investment cost to identifiable net assets acquired would be made in the consolidation process. Because of the additional complications of accounting for parent-subsidiary operations, the remainder of this chapter is limited to business combinations in which a single acquiring entity receives the net assets of the other combining companies. Subsequent chapters cover parent-subsidiary operations and the preparation of consolidated financial statements.

Cost Allocation in a Purchase Business Combination

The first step in allocating the cost of an acquired company is to determine the fair values of all identifiable tangible and intangible assets acquired and liabilities assumed. This can be a monumental task, but much of the work is done before and during the negotiating process of the proposed merger. Companies generally retain outside appraisers to determine fair market values. Guidelines for assigning amounts to specific categories of assets received and liabilities assumed in the purchase are provided in *APB Opinion No. 16,* paragraph 88. In general the guidelines are as follows:

- Marketable securities—net realizable value[19]
- Merchandise inventories and finished goods—net realizable value less a reasonable profit
- Work-in-process inventories—net realizable value less a reasonable profit
- Raw materials—current replacement costs
- Receivables—present values determined at current interest rates less an allowance for uncollectibility

---

[19]*Net realizable value* of assets is the estimated selling price in the ordinary course of business less reasonably predictable costs of completion and disposal. *ARB 43,* Chapter 4, "Inventory Pricing," paragraph 8.

Cost

- Plant and equipment—current replacement costs for similar capacity if the assets are to be used and net realizable value for assets to be sold
- Other assets, including land, natural resources, and nonmarketable securities—appraisal values
- Identifiable intangible assets—appraisal values
- Liabilities—present values determined at appropriate current interest rates

Fair values for all identifiable assets and liabilities are to be determined regardless of whether they are recorded on the books of the acquired company. For example, an acquired company may have expensed the costs of developing patents, blueprints, formulas, and the like under the provisions of *FASB Statement No. 2,* "Accounting for Research and Development Costs." But fair values should be assigned to such identifiable intangible assets of an acquired company in a business combination accounted for as a purchase.[20] Similarly, *FASB Statement No. 87,* "Employers' Accounting for Pensions," requires that when the acquired company is an employer with a defined benefit pension plan, the assignment of the purchase price at the date of combination should include either a liability (the amount of projected benefit obligation in excess of plan assets) or an asset (the amount of plan assets in excess of the projected benefit obligation).

FASB Statement No. 38, "Accounting for Preacquisition Contingencies of Purchased Enterprises," identifies the time needed to quantify the assets acquired and liabilities assumed in a purchase business combination as an *allocation period.* If the fair value of a preacquisition contingency, other than the tax benefit of a loss carryforward, can be determined in the allocation period, it is included in allocating the purchase price. Even if the fair value is not determinable during the allocation period, amounts that can be *reasonably estimated* for contingencies that are considered probable are included in the allocation.[21] After the allocation period (usually no more than one year after consummation), any adjustment from a preacquisition contingency is included in net income of the period.

Contingent Consideration in a Purchase Business Combination   Some purchase business combinations provide for additional payments to the previous stockholders of the acquired company, contingent on future events or transactions. Guidance for accounting for contingent consideration in a purchase business combination is provided in *APB Opinion No. 16.* (Recall that contingent consideration is prohibited under pooling of interests combinations.) The *contingent consideration* may involve the distribution of cash or other assets or the issuance of debt or equity securities. Contingent consideration that is *determinable* at the date of acquisition is recorded as part of the cost of combination. Contingent consideration that is *not determinable* at the date of acquisition is recognized when the contingency is resolved and the consideration is issued or becomes issuable.

When the contingency involves *future earnings levels,* the fair market value of the consideration distributed or issued is recognized as an additional cost (usually goodwill) of the acquired company. The additional cost should be amortized over the remaining life of the asset.[22]

---

[20]*FASB Interpretation No. 4,* "Applicability of FASB Statement No. 2 to Business Combinations Accounted for by the Purchase Method," February 1975, paragraph 4.

[21]Two critical risk factors associated with mergers and acquisitions that require extensive investigation by the acquiring company are product liabilities (liabilities for injuries caused by the predecessor company's defective product) and environmental costs (in other words, inheriting costs of an environmental cleanup).

[22]For example, Acme Steel Company included the following partial financial statement note relating to a 1989 acquisition: "The purchase agreement, as amended, provides for contingent payments of up to $8.8 million based on the annual adjusted pre-tax income of the steel tubing operations over the next four years. Any such payments, if earned, will be allocated to the assets acquired or, if applicable, recorded as goodwill . . ." *Accounting Trends & Techniques—1990* (New York: American Institute of Certified Public Accountants, 1990), p. 49.

If the contingency is based on *security prices,* the recorded cost of the acquired company should not change. Instead, when the contingency is resolved, the additional consideration that is distributed is recorded at its fair market value. Securities issued and recorded at the date of acquisition should be written down proportionately. When capital stock is issued, the write-down would usually be to other paid-in capital. A write-down of debt securities would result in recording a discount on debt. Such a discount would be amortized from the date of settlement of the contingency.

Cost and Fair Value Compared   After fair values have been assigned to all identifiable assets acquired and liabilities assumed, the investment cost is compared with the total fair value of identifiable assets less liabilities. If the investment cost exceeds net fair value, it is allocated first to identifiable net assets according to their fair values and the excess is allocated to goodwill. Amounts assigned to goodwill and to identifiable intangible assets should be amortized over the period to be benefited but not in excess of the maximum period of forty years (See *APB Opinion No. 17,* "Intangible Assets.") Straight-line amortization is required "unless a company demonstrates that another systematic method is more appropriate."

In some business combinations, the total fair value of identifiable assets acquired over liabilities assumed may exceed the cost of the acquired company. Accounting procedures to dispose of the excess fair value in this situation are explained in paragraph 91 of *APB Opinion No. 16:*

> An excess over cost should be allocated to reduce proportionately the values assigned to noncurrent assets (except long-term investments in marketable securities) in determining their fair values. If the allocation reduces the noncurrent assets to zero value, the remainder of the excess over cost should be classified as a deferred credit and should be amortized systematically to income over the period estimated to be benefited but not in excess of forty years.

Illustration of a Purchase Combination

Pitt Corporation acquires the net assets of Seed Company in a purchase combination consummated on December 27, 19X5. The assets and liabilities of Seed Company on this date, at their book values and at fair values, are as follows:

	Book Value	Fair Value
Assets		
Cash	$ 50,000	$ 50,000
Net receivables	150,000	140,000
Inventories	200,000	250,000
Land	50,000	100,000
Buildings—net	300,000	500,000
Equipment—net	250,000	350,000
Patents	—	50,000
Total assets	$1,000,000	$1,440,000
Liabilities		
Accounts payable	$ 60,000	$ 60,000
Notes payable	150,000	135,000
Other liabilities	40,000	45,000
Total liabilities	$ 250,000	$ 240,000
Net assets	$ 750,000	$1,200,000

Case 1 Goodwill   Pitt Corporation pays $400,000 cash and issues 50,000 shares of Pitt Corporation $10 par common stock with a market value of $20 per share

for the net assets of Seed Company. The entries to record the business combination on the books of Pitt Corporation on December 27, 19X5 are as follows:

Investment in Seed Company (50×30 + 400)	$1,400,000	
Cash		$ 400,000
Common stock—$10 par		500,000
Additional paid-in capital		500,000 *plug*

To record issuance of 50,000 shares of $10 par common plus $400,000 cash in a purchase business combination with Seed Company.

Cash	$ 50,000	
Net receivables	140,000	
Inventories	250,000	
Land	100,000	
Buildings	500,000	
Equipment	350,000	
Patents	50,000	
Goodwill (1400000 − 1200000)	200,000	
Accounts payable		$ 60,000
Notes payable		135,000
Other liabilities		45,000
Investment in Seed Company		1,400,000

To assign the cost of Seed Company to identifiable assets acquired and liabilities assumed on the basis of their fair values, and to goodwill.

The amounts assigned to the assets and liabilities are based on fair values, except for goodwill. Goodwill is determined by subtracting the $1,200,000 fair value of identifiable net assets acquired from the $1,400,000 purchase price for Seed Company's net assets.

Case 2 Negative Goodwill Pitt Corporation issues 40,000 shares of its $10 par common stock with a market value of $20 per share, and also gives a 10 percent, five-year note payable for $200,000 for the net assets of Seed Company. Journal entries on Pitt's books to record the Pitt/Seed business combination as a purchase on December 27, 19X5 are as follows:

Investment in Seed Company (40×20 + 200)	$1,000,000	
Common stock—$10 par		$ 400,000
Additional paid-in capital		400,000 *plug*
10% Note payable		200,000

To record issuance of 40,000 shares of $10 par common stock plus a $200,000, 10% note in a purchase business combination with Seed Company.

Cash	$ 50,000	
Net receivables	140,000	
Inventories	250,000	
Land	80,000	
Buildings	400,000	
Equipment	280,000	
Patents	40,000	
Accounts payable		$ 60,000
Notes payable		135,000
Other liabilities		45,000
Investment in Seed Company		1,000,000

handwritten: $\frac{200,000}{1,000,000}$ = red by 20%

To assign the cost of Seed Company to current assets and to liabilities on the basis of their fair value and to noncurrent assets on the basis of fair value less a proportionate share of the excess of the fair value over investment cost.

The amounts assigned to the individual asset and liability accounts in the above entry are determined in accordance with the provisions of *APB Opinion No. 16* for purchase business combinations. Since the $1,200,000 fair value of the identifiable net assets acquired exceeds the $1,000,000 purchase price by

$200,000, the amounts otherwise assignable to noncurrent assets are reduced by 20 percent ($200,000 excess/$1,000,000 fair value of noncurrent assets). The reduction in specific noncurrent assets is as follows:

	Fair Value of Noncurrent Assets	Less 20% Reduction for the Excess of Fair Value over Cost*	Amounts Assignable to Noncurrent Assets
Land	$ 100,000	$ 20,000	$ 80,000
Buildings	500,000	100,000	400,000
Equipment	350,000	70,000	280,000
Patents	50,000	10,000	40,000
Total	$1,000,000	$200,000	$800,000

*Alternatively, the reduction in individual noncurrent assets for the excess of fair value over cost could be computed as:

Land	$100,000/$1,000,000 × $200,000 =	$ 20,000
Buildings	$500,000/$1,000,000 × $200,000 =	100,000
Equipment	$350,000/$1,000,000 × $200,000 =	70,000
Patents	$ 50,000/$1,000,000 × $200,000 =	10,000
		$200,000

In some instances, the excess fair value over cost may be so large that a balance remains after noncurrent assets have been reduced to zero. The remaining excess in this case should be reported as a deferred credit with a descriptive title other than negative goodwill.

When the fair value of net assets acquired in a purchase business combination exceeds investment cost, the excess is commonly referred to as *negative goodwill*. The designation negative goodwill is a misnomer because a firm either has goodwill (excess earning power) or does not have goodwill, but it cannot have minus goodwill. Even so, the designation is widely used by accountants to describe the excess of fair value acquired over cost in a business combination.

The Goodwill Controversy

The excess of the investment cost over the fair value of assets received can be enormous. During the 1980s, it was not uncommon for some assets to change hands several times—each time at premium prices; each time increasing the asset "goodwill" that appeared on the resulting balance sheet. Beatrice Co. is a good example. The assets of Beatrice were acquired three times by various owners in less than ten years. After an $8.2 billion leveraged buyout in 1986, the company was able to sell many of its assets over the next two years. But it had difficulty selling the remaining assets at acceptable prices, partly because of the $1.9 billion goodwill remaining on its balance sheet. (These assets were finally sold to ConAgra in 1990.)

In view of the obsolescence factor in modern technology, many accountants believe that a 40 year amortization period for intangible assets acquired in a business combination is much too long. For example, the competitive advantage of high tech assets is generally assumed to be less than five years.

U.S. companies have long complained that the accounting rule for goodwill puts them at a disadvantage in competing against foreign companies for merger partners. In Great Britain, for example, the excess of cost over book value was immediately written off to stockholders' equity. This could leave companies with minus net worth, but they could begin showing income from the merged operations immediately. However, in 1990 Britian's Accounting Standards Committee proposed a rule that would require British companies to capitalize and amortize goodwill similar to U.S. companies. The proposal faces considerable opposition from many British companies at the time of this writing.

In 1988 Australia's standard setting body passed a similar accounting rule, requiring amortization of goodwill over a maximum of 20 years. This was not a popular rule. An article appearing in the *Melbourne Age,* concluded:

> Companies buying assets that fall within the general concept of this term in future will be expected to write them off out of profits after tax over a 20-year maximum period.
> As a result, their balance sheets will set out some meaningless figures and their published profit results will become positively misleading. Although sophisticated investors will no doubt make their own adjustments to overcome this statutory piece of nonsense, less well-informed shareholders may be induced to let their shares go too cheaply.[23]

The International Accounting Standards Committee The International Accounting Standards Committee (IASC) is a private-sector organization formed in 1973 to develop international accounting standards and promote harmonization of accounting standards worldwide. Although more than 95 accounting organizations from all over the world are members, the IASC does not have authority to require compliance with its standards.

The IASC is working to reduce the number of acceptable alternatives in existing international standards. In line with this objective, it proposed a standard that mandates the capitalization of goodwill with a maximum twenty-year amortization period.

POOLING AND PURCHASE METHODS COMPARED

An indication of the relative importance of the purchase and pooling methods of accounting for business combinations is found in the 1990 edition of *Accounting Trends & Techniques*.[24] Data on business combinations from the AICPA's annual survey of six hundred stockholders' reports are as follows:

	1989	1988	1987	1986
Pooling of interests	18	14	21	22
Purchase method	219	216	194	239
Total business combinations	237	230	215	261

Poolings of interests accounted for less than ten percent of the business combinations in the AICPA survey in each of the four years. The issuance of *APB Opinion No. 16* in 1970 restricted the application of the pooling method and the percentage of combinations accounted for as poolings has decreased in most years since then. The conditions for a pooling are difficult to interpret, particularly when applied to complex capital structures. Numerous interpretations and informal rulings by the Securities and Exchange Commission have resulted in it becoming ever more difficult to structure a business combination as a pooling.

Conceptually, the assumption that there is no acquisition in a pooling of interests is often challenged. For example, Richard Dieter writes "In almost all business combinations that are accounted for as poolings-of-interests, an economic event has taken place whereby one entity has acquired another. To not account for these very significant transactions at their economic value further erodes the credibility of the continuing financial statements."[25]

[23]Nick Renton, "New Goodwill Standard Is Ridiculous," *Melbourne Age,* January 5, 1989.

[24]*Accounting Trends & Techniques—1990,* p. 49.

[25]Richard Dieter, "Is Now the Time to Revisit Accounting for Business Combinations?" *The CPA Journal,* LIX, 7 (July 1989), p. 48.

IASC Proposal for Poolings The IASC has proposed an international accounting standard for poolings of interests that would permit only combinations between companies of approximately equal fair value to be accounted for by the pooling method. This would rule out many U.S. business combinations that are currently accounted for as poolings.

Comparative Illustration of the Pooling and Purchase Methods

Comparative trial balances for Black Corporation and White Corporation at December 30, 19X6, just before the Black and White merger, together with the fair value of White's identifiable assets and liabilities, are shown in Exhibit 1–4.

The Black and White merger was consummated on December 31, 19X6, with Black Corporation, the surviving entity, issuing 50,000 shares of $10 par common stock with a total market value of $885,000 for the net assets of White Corporation. The cost of registering and issuing the common stock was $20,000 and other direct costs of the business combination amounted to $40,000. These costs were paid by Black Corporation on December 31, 19X6.

COMPARATIVE TRIAL BALANCES
DECEMBER 30, 19X6

	Black Corporation per Books	White Corporation per Books	White Corporation Fair Values
Cash	$ 475,000	$ 125,000	$125,000
Receivables—net	600,000	300,000	300,000
Inventories	800,000	200,000	250,000
Plant and equipment—net	1,200,000	350,000	450,000
Cost of goods sold	1,000,000	325,000	
Other expenses	325,000	100,000	
Total debits	$4,400,000	$1,400,000	
Accounts payable	$ 300,000	$ 180,000	$180,000
Other liabilities	200,000	120,000	120,000
Capital stock, $10 par	1,500,000	500,000 ⎫	
Additional paid-in capital	200,000	40,000 ⎬ inv.	
Retained earnings	650,000	110,000 ⎭	
Sales	1,550,000	450,000	
Total credits	$4,400,000	$1,400,000	

Exhibit 1–4 *Premerger Book Value and Fair Value Information*

Journal Entries Journal entries to record the Black and White merger as a pooling of interests are compared with the entries necessary to record the merger as a purchase in Exhibit 1–5. The first set of entries compares the differences in recording the stock issued by Black Corporation in the merger. Under the pooling method, the investment in White is recorded at $650,000, the book value of White's net assets on January 1, 19X6 (capital stock plus additional paid-in capital plus retained earnings). Under the purchase method, the investment in White is recorded at the $885,000 market value of the shares issued by Black Corporation on December 31, 19X6, the date on which the business combination was consummated. The retained earnings of Black and White are combined in the entry to record the stock issuance under the pooling of interests method, but there is no change in Black Corporation's retained earnings when the combination is recorded as a purchase.

Journal entries to record additional costs of the business combination under the pooling and purchase methods are shown in a second section of Exhibit 1–5. All additional costs of combination are expenses when the combination is recorded as a pooling of interests. Under the purchase method, security registration and issuance costs ($20,000) are charged against additional paid-in capital, and the other direct costs of combination ($40,000) are added to the cost of acquiring White Corporation.

	Pooling of Interests		Purchase	
Issuance of Securities	BV		FMV	
Investment in White	$650,000		$885,000	
Capital stock—$10 par		$500,000		$500,000
Additional paid-in capital		40,000		385,000 plug
Retained earnings		110,000		—
Direct Costs of Combination				
Expenses	$ 60,000		$ —	
Investment in White	—		40,000	
Additional paid-in capital	—		20,000	
Cash		$ 60,000		$ 60,000
Allocation of Investment				
Cash	$125,000		$125,000	
Receivables—net	300,000		300,000	
Inventories	200,000		250,000	
Plant and equipment—net	350,000		450,000	
Goodwill	—		100,000	
Cost of goods sold	325,000		—	
Other expenses	100,000		—	
Accounts payable		$180,000		$180,000
Other liabilities		120,000		120,000
Sales		450,000		—
Investment in White RE		650,000		925,000 ($885 + 40)

Exhibit 1–5 *Differences in Recording the Black and White Merger under the Pooling of Interests and Purchase Methods*

A third set of comparative journal entries in Exhibit 1–5 shows assignment of the investment in White balance to specific assets and liabilities, and in the case of a pooling of interests, to sales and expenses. Assets and liabilities are recorded at their fair market values when the purchase method is applied and at their book values under the pooling method. The excess of investment cost ($925,000) over the fair value of identifiable net assets ($825,000) is recorded as goodwill under the purchase method. In subsequent years the $100,000 allocated to goodwill will be amortized over the period to be benefited, but not more than the maximum period of forty years. This amortization will increase expenses and decrease income under the purchase method in future years. The excess of fair value over historical cost to White, which was allocated to inventories ($50,000) and to plant and equipment ($100,000) under purchase accounting, will also increase future expenses and decrease future income as compared with the pooling method. Thus, income of Black Corporation in subsequent years will be lower if the Black and White merger is recorded as a purchase rather than a pooling of interests.

Financial Statements   The combined financial statements for Black Corporation for 19X6 are compared in Exhibit 1–6 for the purchase and pooling methods. The differences in the comparative income statements result from the combining of sales and expenses under the pooling method but not under purchase accounting. An additional difference is reflected in charging additional costs of combination to expense under the pooling method.

Total assets of Black Corporation at December 31, 19X6 are $4,240,000 under the purchase method and $3,990,000 under the pooling method. This $250,000 balance sheet difference is the result of allocating the excess of cost over book value acquired to inventories, plant and equipment, and goodwill under the purchase method.

BLACK CORPORATION
COMPARATIVE FINANCIAL STATEMENTS
FOR THE YEAR ENDED DECEMBER 31, 19X6

	Pooling of Interests Method	Purchase Method
Income Statement		
Sales	$2,000,000	$1,550,000
Cost of sales	1,325,000*	1,000,000*
Other expenses	485,000*	325,000*
Net income	$ 190,000	$ 225,000
Retained Earnings Statement		
Retained earnings January 1, 19X6 (as reported)	$ 650,000	$ 650,000
Increase from pooling	110,000	
Retained earnings January 1, 19X6 (as restated)	760,000	
Net income	190,000	225,000
Retained earnings December 31, 19X6	$ 950,000	$ 875,000
Balance Sheet		
Assets:		
Cash	$ 540,000	$ 540,000
Receivables—net	900,000	900,000
Inventories	1,000,000	1,050,000
Plant and equipment—net	1,550,000	1,650,000
Goodwill	—	100,000
Total assets	$3,990,000	$4,240,000
Liabilities and stockholders' equity:		
Accounts payable	$ 480,000	$ 480,000
Other liabilities	320,000	320,000
Capital stock—$10 par	2,000,000	2,000,000
Additional paid-in capital	240,000	565,000
Retained earnings	950,000	875,000
Total liabilities and stockholders' equity	$3,990,000	$4,240,000

* Deduct.

Exhibit 1–6 *Comparative Financial Statements for the Black and White Merger in the Year of Business Combination*

The comparative balance sheets in Exhibit 1–6 show additional paid-in capital of $240,000 and $565,000 under the pooling and purchase methods, respectively. Additional paid-in capital under the pooling method is equal to the excess of paid-in capital of the combining companies ($2,240,000) over the capital stock of the combined entity ($2,000,000). The $565,000 additional paid-in capital under purchase accounting is equal to the $200,000 beginning balance, plus $385,000 from the issuance of the 50,000 shares in excess of par value, less the $20,000 cost of registering and issuing the securities in the business combination.

The pooled retained earnings of Black Corporation exceed the retained earnings of Black under the purchase method by $75,000. This difference stems from combining retained earnings under the pooling method, as well as from the income differences discussed earlier. Note that significant differences in accounting for the retained earnings of a combined entity are possible under generally accepted accounting principles (GAAP). Accordingly, users of financial statements of combined entities should be careful not to interpret the reported retained earnings balances as amounts legally available for dividends. Such interpretations are questionable when the reports are for separate legal entities, and they are even more suspect when two or more entities are combined into one accounting entity.

DISCLOSURE REQUIREMENTS FOR A POOLING

The combined corporation must disclose that the business combination was accounted for as a pooling of interests. In addition, financial statement notes for the period of pooling should include the names of the combined companies, a description of the shares issued, the details of the results of operations of the separate companies prior to pooling, the nature of any asset adjustments to adopt the same accounting practices, the details of the effect on retained earnings of changing the fiscal period of a combining company, and a reconciliation of the issuing company's revenue and earnings with combined amounts after the pooling. When a new corporation is formed in a pooling, this last disclosure requirement can be met by disclosing the earnings of the separate companies that comprise the combined earnings for the period.[26]

DISCLOSURE REQUIREMENTS FOR A PURCHASE

Notes to the financial statements of the acquiring corporation must disclose that the business combination was accounted for by the purchase method. The notes should also provide the name and a brief description of the acquired company; the period for which results of operations of the acquired company are included in the income statement; the cost of the acquired company and if applicable, the number and valuation of shares of stock issued or issuable, and a description of any contingent payments. A description of the plan for amortization of acquired goodwill should also be included. Information relating to several minor acquisitions may be combined for disclosure purposes.

For material purchase acquisitions, the financial statement notes for the period of combination should include supplemental information on a pro forma basis as follows: (1) the results of operations for the current period as though the companies had combined at the beginning of the period and (2) the results of operations for the immediately preceding period as though the companies had combined at the beginning of that period if comparative financial statements are presented.[27] Disclosures of these pro forma results are not required for nonpublic enterprises.[28]

SUMMARY

A business combination occurs when two or more separate businesses are brought together into one accounting entity. There are two generally accepted methods of accounting for business combinations—purchase and pooling of interests—but these methods are not alternatives in accounting for the same business combination. All combinations that do not meet the conditions for the pooling of

---

[26]*APB Opinion No. 16,* paragraph 64.

[27]Ibid., paragraphs 95 and 96.

[28]*FASB Statement No. 79,* "Elimination of Certain Disclosures for Business Combinations by Nonpublic Enterprises," 1984, paragraph 4.

interests method must be accounted for as purchases. A pooling of interests involves an exchange of voting common shares, the combining of stockholders' equities, and the recording of assets and liabilities of the combining companies at their book values. Purchase accounting requires the recording of assets acquired and liabilities assumed at their fair values at the time of combination. The illustrations in this chapter are for business combinations for which there is only one surviving entity. Later chapters cover accounting and reporting for parent-subsidiary operations in which more than one of the combining companies continue to exist as separate legal entities.

SELECTED READINGS

Accounting Interpretations Nos. 1–39 of APB Opinion No. 16. New York: American Institute of Certified Public Accountants, 1970–73.

Accounting Principles Board Opinion No. 16. "Business Combinations." New York: American Institute of Certified Public Accountants, 1970.

Accounting Principles Board Opinion No. 17. "Intangible Assets." New York: American Institute of Certified Public Accountants, 1970.

ANDREWS, WESLEY T. "The Evolution of *APB Opinion No. 17*—Accounting for Intantible Assets: A Study of the U.S. Position on Accounting for Goodwill." *Accounting Historians Journal* (Spring 1981), pp. 37–49.

BERESFORD, DENNIS R., and BRUCE J. ROSEN. "Accounting for Preacquisition Contingencies." *The CPA Journal* (March 1982), pp. 39–42.

CATLETT, GEORGE R., and NORMAN O. OLSON. "Accounting for Goodwill." *Accounting Research Study No. 10.* New York: American Institute of Certified Public Accountants, 1968.

COLLEY, J. RON, and ARA G. VOLKAN. "Accounting for Goodwill." *Accounting Horizons* (March 1988), pp. 35–41.

DEMOVILLE, WIG, and GEORGE A. PETRIE, "Accounting for a Bargain Purchase in a Business Combination," *Accounting Horizons* (September 1989), pp. 38–43.

DIETER, RICHARD. "Is Now the Time to Revisit Accounting for Business Combinations?" *The CPA Journal* (July 1989), pp. 44–48.

GRINYER, J. R., A. RUSSELL, and M. WALKER. "The Rationale for Accounting for Goodwill." *The British Accounting Review* (September 1990), pp. 223–235.

HERMANSON, ROGER H., and HUGH P. HUGHES. "Pooling vs. Purchase and Goodwill: A Long-standing Controversy Abates." *Mergers & Acquisitions* (Fall 1980), pp. 15–22.

HUGHES, HUGH P. *Goodwill in Accounting: A History of the Issues and Problems.* Georgia: Atlanta Business Publishing Division, College of Business Administration, Georgia State University, 1982.

NURNBERG, HUGO, and JAN SWEENEY. "The Effect of Fair Values and Historical Costs on Accounting for Business Combinations." *Issues in Accounting Education* (Fall 1989), pp. 375–395.

ROCK, MILTON L., and MARTIN SIKORA. "Accounting for Merger Mania." *Management Accounting* (April 1987), pp. 20–26.

Statement of Financial Accounting Standards No. 38. "Accounting for Preacquisition Contingencies of Purchased Enterprises—an Amendment of *APB Opinion No. 16.*" Stamford, CT: Financial Accounting Standards Board, 1980.

Statement of Financial Accounting Standards No. 87. "Employers' Accounting for Pensions." Stamford, CT: Financial Accounting Standards Board, 1985.

WYATT, ARTHUR R. "A Critical Study of Accounting for Business Combinations." *Accounting Research Study No. 5.* New York: American Institute of Certified Public Accountants, 1963.

ASSIGNMENT MATERIAL

QUESTIONS

1 Describe the accounting concept of a business combination.
2 Is dissolution of all but one of the separate legal entities necessary in order to have a business combination? Explain.
3 What is the distinction between a business combination, a merger, and a consolidation?

4 Explain the basic differences between the purchase and pooling of interests methods of accounting for business combinations.

5 Identify the twelve conditions that must be met for a business combination to be accounted for as a pooling of interests.

6 Ordinarily the retained earnings of the surviving corporation in a pooling of interests will be equal to the combined retained earnings of the combining companies. Under what conditions would the combined retained earnings be less than or greater than the total retained earnings of the combining companies?

7 The term instant earnings has been cited as an undesirable feature of the pooling of interests method. In what sense does pooling of interests accounting give rise to the so-called instant earnings? Explain.

8 Compare the costs of effecting a business combination under the purchase and pooling of interests methods.

9 When does goodwill result from a business combination? How does goodwill affect reported net income subsequent to a business combination?

10 What is negative goodwill? Describe the accounting procedures necessary to record and account for negative goodwill.

11 Why are purchase and pooling of interests business combinations accounted for differently?

12 Explain how the direct and indirect costs of combination are recorded for purchase business combinations and for poolings of interests.

EXERCISES

E 1-1   1 Which one of the following items is a requirement for a pooling of interests?
  a Fair value accounting
  b Amortization of goodwill
  c Exchange of common shares
  d Dissolution of all but one of the combining entities

2 In a purchase business combination, the direct costs of registering and issuing equity securities are:
  a Added to the parent/investor company's investment account
  b Charged against other paid-in capital of the combined entity
  c Deducted from income in the period of combination
  d None of the above

3 Which of the following accounts would be adjusted to its fair market value in a merger accounted for under the purchase method, regardless of the price paid?
  a Inventories   b Goodwill
  c Patents   d Equipment

4 A pooling of interests was consummated with the stockholders of the other combining corporation exchanging two of their shares for each share of stock of the issuing company. The exchange ratio in this pooling is:
  a 2   b .5
  c 3   d 1.5

5 The issuing company in a pooling of interests may issue treasury shares for the stock of the other combining corporation if the treasury stock is:
  a Acquired for cash to effect the business combination
  b Accounted for on a cost basis
  c Reissued at its current market value
  d First retired and then reissued

6 Corporation A and Corporation B combine in 19X2 in a pooling of interests business combination. Which of the following dates is the date of initiation of the plan for this business combination?
  a A consulting firm arranges a meeting between the officers and directors of the two companies on January 5, 19X2.
  b A public announcement is made on March 1, 19X2 that the exchange ratio will be 1.2 to 1.
  c Stockholders are notified that the officers of the two companies have agreed upon the 1.2 to 1 exchange ratio on March 15, 19X2.
  d Stockholders of the two companies vote to accept the terms of the proposed business combination on May 15, 19X2.

7 Which one of the following criteria is *not* a condition for a pooling of interests?
  a Each of the combining firms must be autonomous.

    b The combination must be completed in a single transaction or in accordance with a specific plan that is completed within one year of its initiation.

    c Each combining corporation other than the issuing corporation must be dissolved as of the date on which the combination is consummated.

    d The proportionate interest of each individual common stockholder in each of the combining companies remains the same as a result of stock exchanged to effect the combination.

8 An excess of the fair value of net assets acquired in a purchase business combination over the price paid is:

    a Reported as a deferred credit and amortized over a maximum period of forty years

    b Applied to a reduction of noncash assets before a deferred credit may be reported

    c Applied to reduce noncurrent assets other than marketable securities to zero before a deferred credit may be reported

    d Applied to reduce goodwill to zero before a deferred credit may be reported

9 When retained earnings of a combining company in a pooling are adjusted to conform accounting principles with those of the pooled entity, the accounting change

    a Disqualifies the combination for pooling of interests treatment

    b Is recorded as an initial entry in the pooled firm's records

    c Is unacceptable if the effect is to increase retained earnings

    d Is acceptable if the change would have been appropriate for the separate company

E 1–2 **[AICPA adapted]**

1 A business combination is accounted for appropriately as a pooling of interests. Costs of furnishing information to stockholders related to effecting the business combination should be:

    a Capitalized and subsequently amortized over a period *not* exceeding forty years

    b Capitalized but *not* amortized

    c Deducted directly from retained earnings of the combined corporation

    d Deducted in determining net income of the combined corporation for the period in which the costs were incurred

2 Two companies that have merged or combined in 19X3 in accordance with pooling of interests accounting are contemplating the preparation of statements at year-end 19X3. It has been proposed to present 19X2 statements also on a comparative basis.

    a The 19X2 statements must remain as they were prepared originally.

    b The 19X2 statements must be restated so as to reflect what the results would have been had the merger occurred then or earlier.

    c The 19X2 statements must be dropped from consideration, as it is not possible to prepare statements to reflect a relationship that did not in fact exist in 19X2.

    d The 19X3 statements must be so prepared as not to reflect the combination.

3 In order to report a business combination as a pooling of interests, the minimum amount of an investee's common stock that must be acquired during the combination period in exchange for the investor's common stock is

    a 51 percent   **b** 80 percent

    c 90 percent   **d** 100 percent

4 In a business combination, how should plant and equipment of the acquired corporation generally be reported under each of the following methods?

	Pooling of Interests	*Purchase*
a	Fair value	Recorded value
b	Fair value	Fair value
c	Recorded value	Recorded value
d	Recorded value	Fair value

5 In a business combination accounted for as a purchase, the appraisal values of the identifiable assets acquired exceeds the acquisition price. The excess appraisal value should be reported as a:

    a Deferred credit

    b Reduction of the values assigned to current assets and a deferred credit for any unallocated portion

    c Reduction of the values assigned to noncurrent assets and a deferred credit for any unallocated portion

    d Pro rata reduction of the values assigned to current and noncurrent assets

6 On December 1, 19X6, Company B was merged into Company A, with Company B going out of existence. Both companies report on a calendar year basis. This business combination should have been accounted for as a pooling of interests, but it was mistakenly accounted for as purchase. What was the effect of this error upon Company A's asset valuations at December 1, 19X6?

   a Overstated under any circumstances

   b Understated under any circumstances

   c Overstated if the fair value of B's assets exceeded their book value

   d Understated if the fair value of B's assets exceeded their book value

7 Which of the following transactions related to a business combination would require that the combination be accounted for as a purchase?

   a The combination is to be completed within twelve months from the date the plan was initiated.

   b Ninety-two percent of one company's common stock is exchanged for only common stock in the other company.

   c The combined company is to retire a portion of the common stock exchanged to effect the combination within twelve months of the combination.

   d The combined company will dispose of numerous fixed assets representing duplicate facilities subsequent to the combination.

8 A business combination is accounted for appropriately as a purchase. Which of the following should be deducted in determining the combined corporation's net income for the current period?

	Direct Costs of Acquisition	*General Expenses Related to Acquisition*
a	Yes	No
b	Yes	Yes
c	No	Yes
d	No	No

E 1-3 Maloney Corporation and Kyle Company enter into a plan of business combination in which Maloney will issue 1 share of common stock for each 5 shares of Kyle common stock. On the date of initiation of the business combination, Maloney held 1,500 shares of Kyle's common stock, and Kyle held 100 shares of Maloney common stock. Between the date of initiation and the date of consummation, Maloney purchased an additional 500 shares of Kyle common in the stock market. Kyle had 50,000 shares of common stock outstanding throughout the period. On the date of consummation, Maloney issued 9,500 shares of common stock for 47,500 shares of Kyle's common stock. Kyle's old stockholders still hold 500 shares of Kyle common.

Required: How many shares of Kyle stock are assumed to be exchanged in the combination under the substantially all test for a pooling of interests?

E 1-4 Allen Corporation initiated a plan to acquire all the voting stock of Lorenzo Glass Company on October 1, 19X7. On this date Lorenzo Glass had 200,000 shares of common stock outstanding, 5,000 of which were held by Allen.

   Between October 1 and December 1, Allen acquired 4,000 additional shares of Lorenzo Glass, and Lorenzo acquired 5,000 shares of Allen stock and 10,000 shares of its own stock. These acquisitions were for cash consideration but were not in contemplation of effecting the business combination. The business combination was consummated on December 1, with Allen issuing 1 share of Allen common for each 2 outstanding shares of Lorenzo Glass.

Required

   1 How many shares of Lorenzo Glass stock must be exchanged for common stock of Allen, the issuing corporation, in order for the combination to qualify as a pooling of interests?

   2 How many shares of Lorenzo Glass stock will be considered to be exchanged for purposes of determining whether the combination meets the test for a pooling of interests?

E 1-5 [AICPA adapted]

   1 Dan Corporation offered to exchange 2 shares of Dan common stock for each share of Boone Company common stock. On the initiation date Dan held 3,000 shares of

Boone common and Boone held 500 shares of Dan common. In later cash transactions, Dan purchased 2,000 shares of Boone common and Boone purchased 2,500 shares of Dan common. At all times, the number of common shares outstanding was 1,000,000 for Dan and 100,000 for Boone. After consummation Dan held 100,000 Boone common shares. The number of shares considered exchanged in determining whether this combination should be accounted for by the pooling of interests method is:

a 190,000   b 95,000

c 93,500   d 89,000

2 Fast Corporation paid $50,000 cash for the net assets of Agge Company, which consisted of the following:

	Book Value	Fair Value
Current assets	$10,000	$14,000
Plant and equipment	40,000	55,000
Liabilities assumed	(10,000)	(9,000)
	$40,000	$60,000

The plant and equipment acquired in this business combination should be recorded at:

a $55,000   b $50,000

c $45,833   d $45,000

3 The business combination of Jax Company—the issuing company—and the Bell Corporation was consummated on March 14, 19X3. At the initiation date, Jax held 1,000 shares of Bell. If the combination is accounted for as a pooling of interests, the 1,000 shares of Bell held by Jax will be accounted for as:

a Retired stock

b 1,000 shares of treasury stock

c (1,000 ÷ the exchange rate) shares of treasury stock

d (1,000 × the exchange rate) shares of treasury stock

4 On April 1, 19X9 the Jack Company paid $800,000 for all the issued and outstanding common stock of Ann Corporation in a transaction properly accounted for as a purchase. The recorded assets and liabilities of Ann Corporation on April 1, 19X9 follow:

Cash	$ 80,000
Inventory	240,000
Property and equipment (net of accumulated depreciation of $320,000)	480,000
Liabilities	(180,000)

On April 1, 19X9 it was determined that the inventory of Ann had a fair value of $190,000, and the property and equipment (net) had a fair value of $560,000. What is the amount of goodwill resulting from the business combination?

a $0   b $50,000

c $150,000   d $180,000

E1-6 Carrier Corporation issued 100,000 shares of $20 par common stock for all the outstanding stock of Homer Corporation in a business combination consummated on July 1, 19X5. Carrier Corporation common stock was selling at $30 per share at the time the business combination was consummated. Out-of-pocket costs of the business combination were as follows:

Finder's fee	$50,000
Accountants' fee (advisory)	10,000
Legal fees (advisory)	20,000
Printing costs	5,000
SEC registration costs and fees	12,000
Total	$97,000

1 If the business combination is treated as a pooling of interests, the acquisition cost of the combination will be:

a $3,097,000

b $2,097,000

c $2,080,000

d None of the above

2 If the combination is treated as a purchase, the acquisition cost of the combination will be:

a $3,097,000

b $3,080,000

c $3,017,000

d None of the above

E1–7 Darsy Corporation was combined with Heller Corporation on September 1, 19X7 in a business combination in which Darsy Corporation was the only surviving entity. Earnings from the separate and combined operations for 19X7 were as follows:

Darsy's earnings January 1 to September 1, 19X7	$860,000
Heller's earnings January 1 to September 1, 19X7	160,000
Darsy's earnings September 1 to December 31, 19X7	320,000

1 If the business combination is accounted for as a pooling of interests, Darsy, the surviving corporation, will report income for 19X7 of:

a $1,340,000

b $1,260,000

c $1,180,000

d $1,100,000

2 If the business combination is accounted for as a purchase, Darsy, the surviving corporation, will report income for 19X7 of:

a $1,340,000

b $1,260,000

c $1,180,000

d $1,100,000

E 1–8 Patter Corporation issues 500,000 shares of its own $10 par common stock for all the outstanding stock of Simpson Corporation in a merger consummated on July 1, 19X7. On this date, Patter stock is quoted at $20 per share. Summary balance sheet data for the two companies at July 1, 19X7, just before combination, are as follows:

	Patter	Simpson
Current assets	$18,000,000	$1,500,000
Plant assets	22,000,000	6,500,000
Total assets	$40,000,000	$8,000,000
Liabilities	$12,000,000	$2,000,000
Common stock—$10 par	20,000,000	3,000,000
Additional paid-in capital	3,000,000	1,000,000
Retained earnings	5,000,000	2,000,000
Total equities	$40,000,000	$8,000,000

1 If the business combination is treated as a pooling of interests, the pooled retained earnings immediately after the combination will be:

a $5,000,000

b $6,000,000

c $7,000,000

d $8,000,000

2 If the business combination is treated as a pooling of interests, the additional paid-in capital immediately after the combination will be:

a $5,000,000

b $4,000,000

c $3,000,000

d $2,000,000

3 If the business combination is treated as a purchase and Simpson's identifiable net assets have a fair value of $9,000,000, Patter's balance sheet immediately after the combination will show goodwill of:

a $1,000,000

b $2,000,000

c $3,000,000

d $4,000,000

E 1–9 The stockholders' equities of Paddy Corporation and Data-bank Corporation at January 1, 19X7 were as follows:

	Paddy	Data-bank
Capital stock, $10 par	$1,500,000	$ 500,000
Other paid-in capital	200,000	400,000
Retained earnings	600,000	300,000
Stockholders' equity	$2,300,000	$1,200,000

On January 2, 19X7 Paddy issued 120,000 of its shares with a market value of $20 per share for all of Data-bank's shares, and Data-bank was dissolved. On the same date Paddy paid $5,000 to register and issue the shares and $10,000 other direct costs of combination.

Required
1 Prepare the stockholders' equity section of Paddy Corporation's balance sheet immediately after the business combination on January 3, 19X7 assuming that the business combination is a pooling of interests.
2 Prepare the stockholders' equity section of Paddy Corporation's balance sheet immediately after the business combination on January 3, 19X7 assuming that the business combination is *not* a pooling of interests.

E 1-10 Ginny Company issued 100,000 shares of $10 par common stock with a fair value of $2,450,000 for all the voting common stock of Hester Company. In addition, Ginny incurred the following additional costs:

Legal fees to arrange the business combination	$15,000
Cost of SEC registration including accounting and legal fees	12,000
Cost of printing and issuing new stock certificates	3,000
Indirect costs of combining, including allocated overhead and executive salaries	20,000

Immediately before the business combination in which Hester Company was dissolved, Hester's assets and equities were as follows:

	Book Value	Fair Value
Current assets	$1,000,000	$1,100,000
Plant assets	1,500,000	2,000,000
Liabilities	300,000	300,000
Common stock	2,000,000	2,800,000
Retained earnings	200,000	

Required
1 Assume that the business combination is a pooling of interests. Prepare all journal entries on Ginny's books to record the business combination.
2 Assume that Ginny's acquisition is a purchase business combination. Prepare all journal entries on Ginny's books to record the business combination.

E 1-11 On January 1, 19X2 Pattern Corporation held 1,000 shares of Silk Corporation common stock acquired at $15 per share several years earlier. On this date Pattern issued 1.5 of its $10 par shares for each of the other 99,000 outstanding shares of Silk in a pooling of interests in which Silk Corporation was dissolved. Silk Corporation's after-closing trial balance on December 31, 19X1 consisted of the following:

Current assets	$ 800,000	
Plant and equipment—net	1,500,000	
Liabilities		$ 200,000
Capital stock—$5 par		500,000
Additional paid-in capital		1,000,000
Retained earnings		600,000
	$2,300,000	$2,300,000

Required: Prepare a journal entry (or entries) on Pattern's books to account for the pooling of interests. (Hint: Do not forget to consider the 1,000 shares of Silk held by Pattern on January 1, 19X2.)

E 1-12 Vernon issues 1,000,000 shares of its treasury stock for all the shares of Willy Corporation on June 6, 19X3. The stockholders' equities of the two corporations immediately before the pooling of interests business combination in which Willy is dissolved are as follows:

	Vernon	Willy
Capital stock—$10 par	$40,000,000	$ 6,000,000
Other paid-in capital	6,000,000	1,000,000
Retained earnings	5,000,000	4,000,000
	51,000,000	11,000,000
Treasury stock, 1,000,000 shares	9,000,000	
Total stockholders' equity	$42,000,000	$11,000,000

Required: Prepare the stockholders' equity section of Vernon's balance sheet immediately after the business combination.

E 1-13 Pansy Corporation issues its own common stock for all the outstanding shares of Stober Corporation in a pooling of interests business combination on January 1, 19X2. The balance sheets of the two companies at December 31, 19X1 were as follows:

	Pansy	Stober
Current assets	$15,000,000	$3,000,000
Plant assets—net	40,000,000	6,000,000
Total assets	$55,000,000	$9,000,000
Liabilities	$10,000,000	$3,000,000
Common stock—$10 par	30,000,000	3,000,000
Additional paid-in capital	3,000,000	2,000,000
Retained earnings	12,000,000	1,000,000
Total equities	$55,000,000	$9,000,000

Required: Prepare balance sheets for Pansy Corporation on January 1, 19X2, immediately after the pooling of interest in which Stober is dissolved under the following assumptions.
  1 Pansy issues 700,000 of its common shares for all of Stober's outstanding shares.
  2 Pansy issues 900,000 of its common shares for all of Stober's outstanding shares.

E 1-14 On January 1, 19X2 Anderson Corporation pays $100,000 cash and also issues 18,000 shares of $10 par common stock with a market value of $330,000 for all the outstanding common shares of Carlisle Corporation. In addition, Anderson pays $30,000 for registering and issuing the 18,000 shares and $70,000 for the other direct costs of the business combination in which Carlisle Corporation is dissolved. Summary balance sheet information for the companies immediately before the merger is as follows:

	Anderson Book Value	Carlisle Book Value	Carlisle Fair Value
Cash	$250,000	$40,000	$ 40,000
Inventories	120,000	80,000	100,000
Other current assets	30,000	20,000	20,000
Plant assets—net	260,000	180,000	240,000
	$660,000	$320,000	$400,000

	Anderson Book Value	Carlisle Book Value	Carlisle Fair Value
Current liabilities	$ 60,000	$ 30,000	$ 30,000
Other liabilities	80,000	50,000	40,000
Common stock—$10 par	420,000	200,000	
Retained earnings	100,000	40,000	
	$660,000	$320,000	

Required: Prepare all journal entries on Anderson Corporation's books to account for the business combination.

PROBLEMS

P 1-1 Pantic Corporation issues 36,000 shares of its own $5 par common stock with a market value of $720,000 for all the outstanding stock of Shelter Corporation on July 1, 19X7. On this date Shelter's balance sheet and related fair value information is as follows:

	Historical Records	Fair Value
Cash	$ 40,000	$ 40,000
Inventories	80,000	100,000
Other current assets	100,000	120,000
Plant and equipment—net	300,000	500,000
Total assets	$520,000	$760,000
Current liabilities	$ 50,000	$ 50,000
Note payable	100,000	90,000
Capital stock	300,000	NA*
Retained earnings	70,000	NA
Total equities	$520,000	

* NA = Not applicable.

Additional out-of-pocket costs of the combination and stock issuance are as follows:

Legal fees for arranging the combination	$ 5,000
SEC registration costs	5,000
Accountants' fees for SEC registration statements	8,000
Costs of printing new stock certificates	1,000
Finder's fee for identifying Shelter	10,000

Required

1 Prepare the journal entry (entries) necessary to record Pantic Corporation's investment assuming the combination is accounted for as a purchase and Shelter's stock is retired.

2 Prepare the journal entry (entries) necessary to record Pantic Corporation's investment assuming that the combination is accounted for as a pooling of interests and that Shelter's stock is retired.

P 1-2 Maximal and Ryder Corporations enter into a plan of business combination on August 1, 19X2 at which time Maximal owns 100 shares of Ryder common stock and Ryder owns 200 shares of Maximal common stock. During the next three months, Maximal purchases an additional 100 shares of Ryder common. Ryder has 4,000 shares of common stock outstanding throughout the period from initiation to consummation of the business combination.

On November 1 the business combination is consummated with Maximal, the issuing company, exchanging 1,900 shares of its previously unissued common stock for the 3,800 shares of Ryder stock it does not own.

Required

1 Calculate the number of Ryder shares assumed to be exchanged in order to determine if the combination meets the substantially all test for a pooling of interests.
2 Determine the number of Ryder shares required to be exchanged to meet the pooling of interests requirement.

P 1-3 Pond Corporation initiated a plan to pool its interests with Rulo Corporation on January 1, 19X1, at which time Pond held 40,000 of Rulo's 650,000 shares of authorized and issued common stock, acquired by Pond at a cost of $600,000. At this time Rulo held 5,000 shares of Pond's $10 par common stock acquired at $60 per share and 50,000 shares of its own common stock (treasury shares) reacquired at $30 per share.

On October 1, 19X1, Pond issued 280,000 of its $10 par shares for 560,000 shares of Rulo. The stockholders' equity of Rulo on October 1, just before the exchange of shares in which Rulo was dissolved, consisted of the following:

Capital stock—$10 par	$6,500,000
Retained earnings	4,500,000
Less: Treasury shares	(1,500,000)
Total stockholders' equity	$9,500,000

The direct costs of the business combination consisted of $20,000 to register and issue the common stock and $380,000 other costs of combination. These costs were paid in cash by Pond.

Required

1 How many of Rulo's shares are required to be exchanged to meet the "substantially all" test for a pooling of interests?
2 How many of Rulo's shares will be assumed to be exchanged to determine if the "substantially all" test is met?
3 Prepare the journal entries on Pond's books in summary form to record the business combination as a pooling. (*Hint:* Use an "other net assets" account to record Rulo's net assets other than its investment in Pond, and make a separate entry to account for Pond's investment in Rulo and Rulo's investment in Pond.)

P 1-4 Summary information for Pat Corporation and Carol Company at July 1, 19X7 follows. The quoted market price of Pat common stock on July 1, 19X7 is $35 per share.

	Pat Corporation per Books	Carol Company per Books	Carol Company Fair Values
Current assets	$24,000,000	$ 8,000,000	$ 9,000,000
Plant assets	26,000,000	22,000,000	26,000,000
Total assets	$50,000,000	$30,000,000	$35,000,000
Liabilities	$15,000,000	$ 5,000,000	$ 5,000,000
Common stock—$10 par	20,000,000	10,000,000	
Additional paid-in capital	1,000,000	1,000,000	30,000,000
Retained earnings	14,000,000	14,000,000	
Total equities	$50,000,000	$30,000,000	$35,000,000

Part A: Assume that Pat Corporation issues 1,000,000 shares of its own stock for all the outstanding stock of Carol Company on July 1, 19X7 in a purchase business combination in which Carol Company is dissolved.

1 Calculate the goodwill from the business combination.
2 Prepare a journal entry to record the combination.
3 Determine total paid-in capital of Pat Corporation immediately after the business combination.

Part B: Assume that Pat Corporation issues 500,000 shares of its own stock for all the outstanding stock of Carol Company on July 1, 19X7 in a purchase business combination in which Carol Company is dissolved.

> **4** Determine the excess or deficiency of investment cost over the fair value of net assets acquired.
> **5** Prepare a journal entry to record the combination.
> **6** Determine the additional paid-in capital and retained earnings of Pat Corporation immediately after the business combination.

P 1–5 On January 2, 19X7 Pemrow Corporation issues its own $10 par common stock for all the outstanding stock of Sinco Corporation in a purchase business combination, and Sinco is dissolved. In addition, Pemrow pays $20,000 for registering and issuing securities and $30,000 for other costs of combination. The market price of Pemrow's stock on January 2, 19X7 is $30 per share. Relevant balance sheet information for Pemrow and Sinco Corporations on January 1, 19X7 just before the business combination, is as follows:

	Pemrow	Sinco	Sinco
	Historical Cost	Historical Cost	Fair Value
Cash	$ 120,000	$ 10,000	$ 10,000
Inventories	50,000	30,000	40,000
Other current assets	100,000	90,000	100,000
Land	80,000	20,000	100,000
Plant and equipment—net	650,000	200,000	300,000
	$1,000,000	$350,000	$550,000
Liabilities	$ 200,000	$ 50,000	$ 50,000
Capital stock—$10 par	500,000	100,000 ⎫ NA	
Additional paid-in capital	200,000	50,000 ⎬	500,000
Retained earnings	100,000	150,000 ⎭	
	$1,000,000	$350,000	$550,000

Part A: Assume that Pemrow issues 25,000 shares of its stock for all of Sinco's outstanding shares.

> **1** Prepare journal entries to record the business combination of Pemrow and Sinco.
> **2** Prepare a balance sheet for Pemrow Corporation immediately after the business combination.

Part B: Assume that Pemrow issues 15,000 shares of its stock for all of Sinco's outstanding shares.

> **3** Prepare journal entries to record the business combination of Pemrow and Sinco.
> **4** Prepare a balance sheet for Pemrow Corporation immediately after the business combination.

P 1–6 On January 2, 19X4 Douglas and Cornell Corporations merge their operations through a business combination accounted for as a pooling of interests. The $300,000 direct costs of combination are paid in cash by the surviving entity on January 2, 19X4. At December 31, 19X3 Douglas held 25,000 shares of Cornell stock acquired at $20 per share. Summary balance sheet information for Douglas and Cornell Corporations at December 31, 19X3 is as follows:

	Douglas Corporation	Cornell Corporation
Current assets	$ 6,000,000	$ 5,000,000
Plant and equipment—net	10,000,000	10,000,000
Investment in Cornell	500,000	
Total assets	$16,500,000	$15,000,000

	Douglas Corporation	Cornell Corporation
Liabilities	$ 1,500,000	$ 3,000,000
Common stock—$10 par	10,000,000	8,000,000
Additional paid-in capital	2,000,000	3,000,000
Retained earnings	3,000,000	1,000,000
Total equities	$16,500,000	$15,000,000

Part A: Assume that the surviving corporation is Douglas Corporation and that Douglas issues 1,000,000 shares of its own stock for 775,000 shares of Cornell Corporation.
  1 Prepare journal entries on the books of Douglas Corporation to record the business combination.
  2 Prepare a balance sheet for Douglas Corporation on January 2, 19X4, immediately after the business combination.

Part B: Assume that the surviving corporation is Cornell Corporation and that Cornell issues 1,200,000 shares of its own stock for all the outstanding shares of Douglas Corporation.
  3 Prepare journal entries on the books of Cornell Corporation to record the business combination.
  4 Prepare a balance sheet for Cornell Corporation on January 2, 19X4, immediately after the business combination.

P 1–7 Patio Corporation was formed on January 2, 19X3 to consolidate the operations of Builders Corporation and Raines Corporation. Summary balance sheets for the two companies at December 31, 19X2 are as follows:

	Builders Corporation	Raines Corporation
Assets		
Cash	$ 2,000,000	$ 1,000,000
Receivables—net	3,500,000	1,500,000
Inventories	6,000,000	7,000,000
Land	1,000,000	2,000,000
Buildings—net	7,500,000	3,000,000
Equipment—net	3,000,000	5,500,000
Total assets	$23,000,000	$20,000,000
Liabilities and Stockholders' Equity		
Accounts payable	$ 1,700,000	$ 2,300,000
Bonds payable	3,000,000	—
Capital stock	10,000,000	5,000,000
Additional paid-in capital	4,300,000	3,700,000
Retained earnings	4,000,000	9,000,000
Total liabilities and stockholders' equity	$23,000,000	$20,000,000

Additional Information
  1 The stockholders of the combining corporations agree to the following plan of combination:
    a Stockholders of Builders Corporation are to receive 1,300,000 common shares of $10 par stock of Patio Corporation for their 5,000,000 shares of $2 par capital stock.
    b Stockholders of Raines Corporation are to receive 1,200,000 common shares of Patio Corporation for their 1,000,000 shares of $5 stated value capital stock.
    c Both Builders Corporation and Raines Corporation are to be dissolved.
  2 The business combination is treated as a pooling of interests with January 2, 19X3 as the date of initiation and consummation of the plan.

3 The inventories of Patio are to be maintained on a FIFO basis. Accordingly, Raines's December 31, 19X2 LIFO inventory is adjusted to its $8,000,000 FIFO cost.
4 Costs of registering and issuing securities in the combination amount to $60,000, and other direct costs of combination amount to $140,000. These costs are paid by Patio on January 2, 19X3 from cash obtained from the other combining companies.

Required
1 Prepare journal entries on the books of Patio Corporation to:
   a Record the issuance of 1,300,000 shares to the stockholders of Builders Corporation
   b Record the issuance of 1,200,000 shares to the stockholders of Raines Corporation
   c Record payment of the costs of business combination
2 Prepare a balance sheet for Patio Corporation at January 2, 19X3, immediately after the business combination has been consummated.

P 1–8 The balance sheets of Poole Corporation and Sen Corporation at December 31, 19X2 are summarized together with fair value information as follows:

	Poole Corporation		Sen Corporation	
	Book Value	Fair Value	Book Value	Fair Value
Assets				
Cash	$115,000	$115,000	$ 10,000	$ 10,000
Receivables—net	40,000	40,000	20,000	20,000
Inventories	120,000	150,000	50,000	30,000
Land	45,000	100,000	30,000	50,000
Buildings—net	200,000	300,000	100,000	200,000
Equipment—net	180,000	245,000	90,000	150,000
Total assets	$700,000	$950,000	$300,000	$460,000
Equities				
Accounts payable	$ 90,000	$ 90,000	$ 30,000	$ 30,000
Other liabilities	100,000	90,000	60,000	70,000
Capital stock—$10 par	300,000		100,000	
Other paid-in capital	100,000	770,000	80,000	360,000
Retained earnings	110,000		30,000	
Total equities	$700,000	$950,000	$300,000	$460,000

On January 1, 19X3 Poole Corporation acquired all of Sen Corporation's outstanding stock for $300,000. Poole paid $100,000 cash and issued a five-year, 12 percent note for the balance and Sen Corporation was dissolved.

Required
1 Prepare a schedule to show how the investment cost is allocated to identifiable assets and liabilities.
2 Prepare a balance sheet for Poole Corporation on January 1, 19X3 immediately after the business combination.

P 1–9 On January 1, 19X7 Able Corporation issues 600,000 shares of its capital stock for all of Baker Corporation's outstanding shares and Baker is dissolved. The fair value of Able's common stock on this date is $20 per share. The book values and fair values of Able and Baker at December 31, 19X6 are as follows:

	Able Corporation		Baker Corporation	
	Book Value	Fair Value	Book Value	Fair Value
Assets				
Cash	$ 3,000,000	$ 3,000,000	$ 1,000,000	$ 1,000,000
Receivables—net	5,500,000	5,500,000	2,000,000	2,000,000
Inventories (LIFO)	6,000,000	7,000,000	3,500,000	4,000,000
Other current assets	1,500,000	1,500,000	500,000	600,000
Plant assets—net	16,000,000	19,000,000	5,000,000	7,400,000
Total assets	$32,000,000	$36,000,000	$12,000,000	$15,000,000
Equities				
Accounts payable	$ 5,000,000	$ 5,000,000	$ 1,800,000	$ 1,800,000
Other liabilities	3,800,000	4,000,000	3,200,000	3,000,000
Capital stock—$10 par	15,000,000 ⎫		3,000,000 ⎫	
Other paid-in capital	3,000,000 ⎬	27,000,000	1,200,000 ⎬	10,200,000
Retained earnings	5,200,000 ⎭		2,800,000 ⎭	
Total equities	$32,000,000	$36,000,000	$12,000,000	$15,000,000

Required: Prepare comparative balance sheets for Able Corporation immediately after the business combination assuming that (a) the combination is a pooling of interests and (b) the combination is a purchase.

P 1–10 Parade Corporation paid $2,400,000 for Delmar Corporation's voting common stock on January 2, 19X7 and Delmar was dissolved. The purchase price consisted of 100,000 shares of Parade's common stock with a market value of $2,000,000 plus $400,000 cash. In addition, Parade paid $50,000 for registering and issuing the 100,000 shares of common stock and $100,000 for other costs of combination. Balance sheet information for the companies immediately before the business combination is summarized as follows:

	Parade Book Value	Delmar Book Value	Delmar Fair Value
Cash	$ 3,000,000	$ 240,000	$ 240,000
Accounts receivable—net	1,300,000	360,000	360,000
Notes receivable—net	1,500,000	300,000	300,000
Inventories	2,500,000	420,000	500,000
Other current assets	700,000	180,000	200,000
Land	2,000,000	100,000	200,000
Buildings—net	9,000,000	600,000	1,200,000
Equipment—net	10,000,000	800,000	600,000
Total assets	$30,000,000	$3,000,000	$3,600,000
Accounts payable	$ 1,000,000	$ 300,000	$ 300,000
Mortgage payable—10%	5,000,000	700,000	600,000
Capital stock—$10 par	10,000,000	1,000,000 ⎫	2,700,000
Other paid-in capital	8,000,000	600,000 ⎬	
Retained earnings	6,000,000	400,000	
Total equities	$30,000,000	$3,000,000	$3,600,000

Required
1 Prepare journal entries for Parade Corporation to record its acquisition of Delmar Corporation, including all allocations to individual asset and liability accounts.
2 Prepare a balance sheet for Parade Corporation on January 2, 19X7, immediately after the acquisition and dissolution of Delmar.

2

STOCK INVESTMENTS— INVESTOR ACCOUNTING AND REPORTING

T he illustrations of business combinations in Chapter 1 were limited to those in which one surviving entity received the net assets of the other combining companies. In that chapter, the net assets and operations of all combining companies were integrated into those of a single legal and accounting entity with one recordkeeping system. When an investment account was used to record a business combination in Chapter 1, its balance was eliminated immediately through allocation to individual asset and liability accounts.

This chapter is concerned with equity investments in which the investment accounts are maintained on a continuous basis. It includes accounting for investments under the cost method where the investor company *does not have the ability to influence* the activities of the investee, as well as accounting under the equity method where the investor company *can exercise significant influence* over the investee's operations. The chapter also includes accounting under the equity method where the investor *is able to control* the operations of the investee through stock ownership. This latter situation involves ownership of over 50 percent of the voting stock of the investee company and is the result of a business combination in which "one or more companies become subsidiaries."[1]

This chapter covers parent company accounting for its subsidiaries under the purchase method, but it does *not* cover poolings of interests or consolidated financial statements. Consolidated financial statements for parent and subsidiary companies are covered in Chapter 3 and subsequent chapters.

ACCOUNTING FOR STOCK INVESTMENTS

Generally accepted accounting principles (GAAP) for recording common stock acquisitions require that the investment be recorded at its cost. The basic guidelines for measuring the cost of common stock acquired in a purchase business combination are also applicable to common stock investments of less than 50 percent of the voting stock of another corporation. Investment cost includes

---

[1] *APB Opinion No. 16,* "Business Combinations," p. 5.

cash disbursed, the fair value of other assets given or securities issued, and additional direct costs of obtaining the investment, other than the costs of registering and issuing equity securities which are charged to additional paid-in capital.

One of the two basic methods of accounting for noncurrent common stock investments generally applies—the *cost method* or the *equity method*. If the cost method is used and the stock is marketable, the investment should be accounted for at the lower of cost or market according to the provisions of *FASB Statement No. 12*, "Accounting for Certain Marketable Securities." If the equity method of accounting applies, the investment is accounted for under the provisions of *APB Opinion No. 18,* "The Equity Method of Accounting for Investments in Common Stock," as amended by *FASB Statement No. 94,* "Consolidation of All Majority-owned Subsidiaries."

Concepts Underlying Cost and Equity Methods

Under the *cost method*, investments in common stock are recorded at cost, and dividends from subsequent earnings are reported as dividend income. There is an exception. Dividends received in excess of the investor's share of earnings after the stock is acquired are considered returns of capital (or liquidating dividends) and are recorded as reductions in the investment account.[2] Also, the lower of cost or market procedure is applied if the stock is marketable.

The *equity method* of accounting is essentially accrual accounting for equity investments that enable the investor firm to exercise significant influence over the investee firm. Under the equity method, the investments are recorded at cost and are adjusted for earnings, losses, and dividends. The investor company reports its share of the investee's earnings (loss) as investment income (loss) increasing (decreasing) its investment account for the investment income (loss) reported. Dividends received from investees are disinvestments under the equity method, and they are recorded as decreases in the investment account. Thus, investment income under the equity method reflects the investor's share of the net income of the investee, and the investment account reflects the investor's share of the investee's net assets.

An investment in voting stock that gives the investor the ability to exercise significant influence over the financial and operating policies of the investee should be accounted for by the equity method of accounting. This is explained in paragraph 17 of *APB Opinion No. 18:*

> The Board concludes that the equity method of accounting for an investment in common stock should . . . be followed by an investor whose investment in voting stock gives it the ability to exercise significant influence over operating and financial policies of an investee even though the investor holds 50% or less of the voting stock.

The ability to exert significant influence is based on a 20 percent ownership test as provided by the Accounting Principles Board:

> An investment (direct or indirect) of 20% or more of the voting stock of an investee should lead to a presumption that in the absence of evidence to the contrary an investor has the ability to exercise significant influence over an investee. Conversely, an investment of less than 20% of the voting stock of an investee should lead to a presumption that an investor does not have the ability to exercise significant influence unless such ability can be demonstrated.[3]

---

[2]*APB Opinion No. 18,* "The Equity Method of Accounting for Investments in Common Stock," paragraph 6a.

[3]Ibid., paragraph 17.

The equity method should not be applied if the investor's ability to exert significant influence is temporary or if the investees are foreign companies operating under severe exchange restrictions or controls.[4] *FASB Interpretation No. 35* cites (1) opposition by the investee that challenges the investor's influence, (2) surrender of significant stockholder rights by agreement between investor and investee, (3) concentration of majority ownership, (4) inadequate or untimely information to apply the equity method, and (5) failure to obtain representation on the investee's board of directors as indicators of an investor's inability to exercise significant influence.[5] Application of the equity method should be discontinued when the investor's share of losses reduces the carrying amount of the investment to zero.

The Equity Method and *FASB* Statement No. 94   The equity method may be used by a parent company to account for its subsidary investments, even though the financial statements of the subsidiaries are subsequently included in the consolidated financial statements for the parent company and its subsidiaries. In other words, the parent company maintains the "investment in subsidiary account" by taking up its share of the subsidiary's income and reducing the investment account for its share of subsidiary dividends declared. Under the equity method, the parent company's income and consolidated net income are equal. They reflect the income of the parent company and its subsidiaries as a single economic entity.

Before the issuance of *Statement 94* in 1987, parent companies were able to determine their own consolidation policies, and they had broad discretion in deciding whether to consolidate particular subsidiaries. *Unconsolidated subsidiaries,* in other words, subsidiaries whose assets and liabilities were not consolidated with those of the parent company, were accounted for by the equity method and *reported* in the parent's financial statements as equity investments. However, the provisions of *Statement 94* require that all majority-owned subsidiaries be consolidated, except where control is likely to be temporary or where control does not lie with the majority interests. Examples of control of a subsidiary not resting with the parent include a subsidiary in legal reorganization or in bankruptcy or a subsidiary operating under severe foreign exchange restrictions or other governmentally imposed uncertainties. An investment in an unconsolidated subsidiary is reported in the parent's financial statements by either the cost or equity method, according to the significant influence provisions of *APB Opinion No. 18.* Chapter 3 discusses situations in which certain subsidiaries should not be consolidated.

Accounting Procedures under the Cost and Equity Methods

Basic procedures of accounting under the cost and equity methods can be illustrated by assuming that Pilzner Company acquires 2,000 of the 10,000 outstanding shares of Sud Corporation at $50 per share on July 1, equal to the book value and fair value of Sud's net assets. Sud Corporation's net income for the entire year is $50,000, and $20,000 of dividends are paid on November 1. If there is evidence of an inability to exercise significant influence, Pilzner should apply the cost method. Otherwise, the equity method is required. Accounting by Pilzner Company under the two methods is as follows:

---

[4]Ibid., footnotes 4 and 7. For example, the 1987 BFGoodrich Company Annual Report contained the following statement note: Effective January 1, 1987, BFGoodrich discontinued using the equity method of accounting for its 40 percent interest in Policyd S.A. de C.V. (Policyd), because of the uncertain economic conditions in Mexico. Dividends of $1.6 [million] received from Policyd in 1987 have been applied to reduce the carrying value of the investment. Had BFGoodrich continued using the equity method of accounting for Policyd, net income for 1987 would have been approximately $3.6 [million] higher.

[5]*FASB Interpretation No. 35*, 1981, paragraph 3.

ENTRY ON JULY 1 TO RECORD INVESTMENT

Cost Method			*Equity Method*		
Investment in Sud	$100,000		Investment in Sud	$100,000	
Cash		$100,000	Cash		$100,000

ENTRY ON NOVEMBER 1 TO RECORD DIVIDENDS

Cost Method			*Equity Method*		
Cash	$ 4,000		Cash	$ 4,000	
Dividend income		$ 4,000	Investment in Sud		$ 4,000

ENTRY ON DECEMBER 31 TO RECOGNIZE EARNINGS

Cost Method			*Equity Method*		
None (Assume that the stock is either			Investment in Sud	$ 5,000	
nonmarketable or has a market price $\geq$			Income from Sud		$ 5,000
$50 per share.)			($50,000 $\times$ ½ year $\times$ 20%)		

Under the cost method Pilzner recognizes income of $4,000 and reports its investment in Sud at its $100,000 cost. Under the equity method, Pilzner recognizes $5,000 income and reports the investment in Sud at $101,000, equal to $100,000 cost plus $5,000 income less $4,000 dividends received.

The entries to illustrate the cost method reflect the usual situation in which the investor records dividend income equal to dividends actually received. An exception to this usual cost method situation arises when dividends are received in excess of the investor's share of earnings after the investment is acquired. From the investor's point of view, dividends in excess of the investor's share of earnings since acquisition of the investment are a return of capital or liquidating dividends. For example, if Sud's net income for the year had been $30,000, Pilzner's share would have been $3,000 ($30,000 $\times$ ½ year $\times$ 20%). Since the $4,000 dividend received exceeds the $3,000 equity in Sud's income, the $1,000 excess would be considered a return of capital and credited to the investment in Sud account. Assuming that Pilzner records the $4,000 cash received on November 1 as dividend income, a year-end entry to adjust dividend income and the investment account would be needed. Such an entry would be recorded as follows:

Dividend income	$1,000	
Investment in Sud		$1,000

To adjust dividend income and investment accounts for dividends received in excess of earnings.

This entry reduces dividend income to Pilzner's $3,000 share of income earned after July 1 and reduces the investment in Sud to $99,000, the new cost basis for the investment.

Economic Consequences of Using the Cost and Equity Methods

The different methods of accounting (cost and equity) result in showing different investment amounts in the balance sheet of the investor corporation and different income amounts in the income statement. When the investor can significantly influence or control the operations of the investee, including dividend declarations, the cost method is unacceptable. By influencing or controlling investee dividend decisions, the investor corporation is able to manipulate its own investment income. The possibility of income manipulation does not exist when the financial statements of a parent company/investor are consolidated with the statements of a subsidiary/investee because the consolidated statements are the same regardless of whether the cost or the equity method of accounting is used.

Although the equity method is not a substitute for consolidation, the income reported by a parent company/investor in its separate income statement under the equity method of accounting is generally the same as the income reported in consolidated financial statements for a parent company and its subsidiary.

EQUITY METHOD OF ACCOUNTING—A ONE-LINE CONSOLIDATION

The equity method of accounting is frequently referred to as a *one-line consolidation*. This is because the investment is reported in a single amount on one line of the investor company's balance sheet and investment income is reported in a single amount on one line of the investor's income statement (except when the investee has extraordinary or other "below-the-line" items that require separate disclosure). *"One-line consolidation" also means that a parent company/investor's income and stockholders' equity are the same when a subsidiary company/investee is accounted for under a complete and correct application of the equity method as when the financial statements of parent company and subsidiary are consolidated.* Consolidated financial statements show the same income and the same net assets but include the details of revenues and expenses and assets and liabilities.

The equity method involves many complexities; in fact, it involves the same computational complexities as are encountered in the preparation of consolidated financial statements. For this reason, the equity method is established as the standard of parent company accounting for its subsidiaries, and the one-line consolidation is integrated throughout the consolidation chapters of this book. This parallel one-line consolidation/consolidation coverage permits students and practitioners alike to check their work through alternative computations of such key financial statement items as consolidated net income and consolidated retained earnings.

Basic accounting procedures for applying the equity method are the same whether the investor has the ability to exercise significant influence over the investee (20 to 50 percent ownership) or the ability to control the investee (over 50 percent ownership). This is important because investments of over 50 percent are business combinations and are subject to the provisions of *APB Opinion No. 16*. Thus, the accounting principles that apply to purchase business combinations also apply to accounting for investments of 20 to 100 percent under the equity method. The difference between the way *Opinion No. 16* provisions are applied in this chapter and the way they are applied in Chapter 1 arises because:

1 Both the investor and investee companies continue to exist as separate legal entities with their own accounting systems.
2 The equity method applies to only one of those entities—the investor company.
3 The investor's equity interest may range from 20 percent to 100 percent.

Equity Investments at Acquisition

Since equity investments in voting common stock of other entities are subject to the provisions of *APB Opinion No. 16*, the investment cost is measured by the cash disbursed or the fair value of other assets distributed or securities issued. Similarly, direct costs of registering and issuing equity securities are charged against additional paid-in capital, and other direct costs of acquisition are added to the acquisition cost. The total investment cost is entered in an investment account under the one-line consolidation concept.

Assume that Payne Company purchases 30 percent of Sloan Company's outstanding voting common stock on January 1, 19X2 from existing stockholders for $2,000,000 cash plus 200,000 shares of Payne Company $10 par common stock with a market value of $15 per share. Additional cash costs of the equity interest consist of $50,000 for registration of the shares and $100,000 for consulting and advisory fees. These events would be recorded by Payne Company with the following journal entries:

January 1, 19X2

Investment in Sloan	$5,000,000	
Common stock		$2,000,000
Additional paid-in capital		1,000,000
Cash		2,000,000

To record acquisition of a 30% equity investment in Sloan Company.

January 1, 19X2

Investment in Sloan	$ 100,000	
Additional paid-in capital	50,000	
Cash		$ 150,000

To record additional direct costs of purchasing a 30% equity interest in Sloan.

Under a one-line consolidation, these entries can be made without knowledge of book value or fair value of Sloan Company's assets and liabilities.

Assignment of Excess Cost over Underlying Equity

Information regarding the individual assets and liabilities of Sloan Company *at the time of the purchase* is important because subsequent accounting under the equity method entails accounting for any differences between the investment cost and the underlying equity in the net assets of the investee.

Assume that the following book value and fair value information for Sloan Company at December 31, 19X1 is available:

	Book Value	Fair Value
Cash	$ 1,500,000	$ 1,500,000
Receivables—net	2,200,000	2,200,000
Inventories	3,000,000	4,000,000
Other current assets	3,300,000	3,100,000
Equipment—net	5,000,000	8,000,000
Total assets	$15,000,000	$18,800,000
Accounts payable	$ 1,000,000	$ 1,000,000
Note payable, due January 1, 19X7	2,000,000	1,800,000
Common stock	10,000,000 ⎫	
Retained earnings	2,000,000 ⎬	16,000,000
Total liabilities and stockholders' equity	$15,000,000	$18,800,000

The underlying equity in the net assets of Sloan Company is $3,600,000 (30 percent of the $12,000,000 book value of Sloan Company's net assets), and the difference between the investment cost and the underlying equity is $1,500,000. This difference must be assigned to the identifiable assets and liabilities based on their fair values, and any remaining difference is allocated to goodwill. The assignment to identifiable net assets and goodwill is illustrated in Exhibit 2–1.

The asset and liability information reflected in Exhibit 2–1 is not recorded separately on the books of Payne Company. Instead, the $1,500,000 excess cost over underlying equity is included in Payne's investment in Sloan account. Under

PAYNE COMPANY AND ITS 30% OWNED EQUITY INVESTEE, SLOAN COMPANY

Investment in Sloan	$5,100,000
Book value of the interest acquired:	
30% × $12,000,000 equity of Sloan	3,600,000
Total excess of cost over book value acquired	$1,500,000

Assignment to Identifiable Net Assets and Goodwill

	Fair Value	−	Book Value	×	Interest Acquired	=	Amount Assigned
Inventories	$4,000,000		$3,000,000		30%		$ 300,000
Other current assets	3,100,000		3,300,000		30		(60,000)
Equipment	8,000,000		5,000,000		30		900,000
Note payable	1,800,000		2,000,000		30		60,000
Total assigned to identifiable net assets							$1,200,000
Remainder assigned to goodwill							300,000
Total excess of cost over book value acquired							$1,500,000

Exhibit 2–1   *Schedule for Allocating the Excess of Investment Cost over the Book Value of the Interest Acquired*

the equity method of accounting, this difference is eliminated by periodic charges (debits) and credits to income from the investment and by equal credits or charges to the investment account. Thus, the original difference between investment cost and book value acquired will disappear over the remaining lives of identifiable assets and liabilities or over a maximum period of forty years if assigned to goodwill. The one exception is amounts assigned to land which are not amortized.

The $300,000 assigned to goodwill in Exhibit 2–1 was determined as a remainder of the total excess over amounts assigned to identifiable assets and liabilities. But the amount could have been computed directly as the excess of investment cost of $5,100,000 over the $4,800,000 fair value of Sloan's net assets acquired (30 percent × $16,000,000). If the difference between cost and underlying book value cannot be related to identifiable assets and liabilities, it is considered to be goodwill (or negative goodwill).

Accounting for Excess of Investment Cost over Book Value Acquired

Assume that Sloan Company pays dividends of $1,000,000 on July 1, 19X2 and reports net income of $3,000,000 for the year. The excess cost over book value acquired is amortized as follows:

	19X2 Amortization Rates
Excess Allocated To:	
Inventories—sold in 19X2	100%
Other current assets—disposed of in 19X2	100
Equipment—depreciated over 20 years	5
Note payable—due in 5 years	20
Goodwill—40-year maximum	2.5

Payne Company makes the following entries under a one-line consolidation to record its dividends and income from Sloan:

July 1, 19X2

Cash	$300,000	
Investment in Sloan		$300,000

To record dividends received from Sloan ($1,000,000 × 30%).

December 31, 19X2

Investment in Sloan	$900,000	
Income from Sloan		$900,000

To record equity in income of Sloan ($3,000,000 × 30%).

December 31, 19X2

Income from Sloan	$300,000	
Investment in Sloan		$300,000

To record write-off of excess allocated to inventory items that were sold in 19X2.

December 31, 19X2

Investment in Sloan	$60,000	
Income from Sloan		$60,000

To record income credit for overvalued other current assets disposed of in 19X2.

December 31, 19X2

Income from Sloan	$45,000	
Investment in Sloan		$45, 000

To record depreciation on excess allocated to undervalued equipment with a 20-year remaining use life ($900,000 ÷ 20 years).

December 31, 19X2

Income from Sloan	$12,000	
Investment in Sloan		$12,000

To amortize the excess allocated to the overvalued note payable over the remaining life of the note ($60,000 ÷ 5 years).

December 31, 19X2

Income from Sloan	$ 7,500	
Investment in Sloan		$ 7,500

To amortize the excess allocated to goodwill ($300,000 ÷ 40 years).

Since the last six journal entries all involve the income and investment accounts, Payne could record its income from Sloan for 19X2 in a single entry at December 31, 19X2 as follows:

Investment in Sloan	$595,500	
Income from Sloan		$595,500

To record equity income from 30% investment in Sloan as follows:

Equity in Sloan's reported income ($3,000,000 × 30%)	$900,000
Amortization of excess cost over book value:	
Inventories sold in 19X2 ($300,000 × 100%)	(300,000)
Other current assets sold in 19X2 ($60,000 × 100%)	60,000
Equipment ($900,000 × 5% depreciation rate)	(45,000)
Note payable ($60,000 × 20% amortization rate)	(12,000)
Goodwill ($300,000 × 2½% amortization rate)	(7,500)
Total investment income from Sloan	$595,500

Payne Company reports its investment in Sloan at December 31, 19X2 on one line of its balance sheet at $5,395,500 ($5,100,000 cost + $595,500 income − $300,000 dividends), and its income from Sloan for 19X2 at $595,500 on one line of its income statement. Sloan's net assets (stockholders' equity) increased by $2,000,000 during 19X2 to $14,000,000, and Payne's share of this underlying equity is 30 percent, or $4,200,000. The $1,195,500 difference between investment balance and the underlying equity at December 31, 19X2 represents the unamortized excess of investment cost over book value acquired. This amount can be confirmed by subtracting the $304,500 net amortization for 19X2 from the original excess of $1,500,000.

When the full $1,500,000 excess has been amortized, the investment balance will be equal to its underlying book value—30 percent of the common stockholders' equity of Sloan. A summary of these observations follows:

	Stockholders' Equity of Sloan A	Underlying Equity (30% of Sloan's Equity) B	Investment in Sloan Account Balance C	Unamortized Cost–Book Value Differential C – B
January 1, 19X2	$12,000,000	$3,600,000	$5,100,000	$1,500,000
Dividends, July 19X2	(1,000,000)	(300,000)	(300,000)	
Income, 19X2	3,000,000	900,000	900,000	
Amortization, 19X2			(304,500)	(304,500)
December 31, 19X2	$14,000,000	$4,200,000	$5,395,500	$1,195,500

This illustration of Payne Company's accounting for its 30 percent investee is equally applicable to parent company accounting for subsidiaries (over 50 percent owned investees).

Excess of Book Value Acquired over Investment Cost

The book value of the interest acquired in an investee corporation may be greater than the investment cost. This situation indicates that the identifiable net assets of the investee corporation are overvalued or that the interest was acquired at a bargain price. If the total excess relates to overvalued assets (investment cost is equal to fair value), the excess is assigned to reduce the specific assets that are overvalued. But if identifiable net assets are recorded at their fair values, the excess of fair value (and book value) of the interest acquired over investment cost is negative goodwill. Negative goodwill is assigned to reduce noncurrent assets other than marketable securities, as explained in Chapter 1.

Amounts assigned to reduce specific assets are amortized over the assets' remaining useful lives. The income effect of such amortization under a one-line consolidation is the reverse of the goodwill situation that reduces income and investment account balances. That is, both the investment and investment income accounts of the investor corporation are increased when an excess of book value over cost is amortized.

To illustrate, assume that Post Corporation purchases 50 percent of the outstanding voting common stock of Taylor Corporation on January 1, 19X6 for $40,000. A summary of the changes in Taylor's stockholders' equity during 19X6 appears as follows:

Stockholders' equity January 1, 19X6	$100,000
Add: Income for 19X6	20,000
Deduct: Dividends paid July 1	− 5,000
Stockholders' equity December 31, 19X6	$115,000

The $10,000 excess of book value acquired over investment cost ($100,000 × 50% − $40,000) was due to inventory items and equipment that were overvalued on Taylor's books. Taylor's January 1, 19X6 inventory was overvalued by $2,000 and was sold in December 19X6. The remaining $18,000 overvaluation related to equipment with a ten-year remaining use life from January 1, 19X6. No goodwill or negative goodwill results because the $40,000 cost is equal to fair value acquired (50% × $80,000).

The assignment of the difference between book value acquired and investment cost is as follows:

Cost of the investment in Taylor	$ 40,000
Less: Underlying book value of Post's 50% interest in Taylor ($100,000 stockholders' equity × 50%)	(50,000)
Excess book value over cost	$(10,000)
Excess assigned to:	
Inventories ($2,000 overvaluation × 50% owned)	$ (1,000)
Equipment ($18,000 overvaluation × 50% owned)	(9,000)
Excess book value over cost	$(10,000)

Journal entries to account for Post Corporation's investment in Taylor Corporation during 19X6 are as follows:

January 1, 19X6

Investment in Taylor	$40,000	
Cash		$40,000

To record purchase of 50% of Taylor's outstanding voting stock.

July 1, 19X6

Cash	$ 2,500	
Investment in Taylor		$ 2,500

To record dividends received ($5,000 × 50%).

December 31, 19X6

Investment in Taylor	$10,000	
Income from Taylor		$10,000

To recognize equity in the income of Taylor ($20,000 × 50%).

December 31, 19X6

Investment in Taylor	$ 1,900	
Income from Taylor		$ 1,900

To amortize excess of book value over investment cost assigned to:

Inventory ($1,000 × 100%)	$ 1,000
Equipment ($9,000 × 10%)	900
Total	$ 1,900

Because assets were purchased at less than book value Post reports investment income from Taylor for 19X6 in the amount of $11,900 ($10,000 + $1,900) and an investment in Taylor balance at December 31, 19X6 of $49,400 ($40,000 + $11,900 − $2,500). Amortization of the excess of book value over investment cost increases Post's investment in Taylor balance by $1,900 during 19X6.

Negative Goodwill

Assume that Post Corporation also acquires a 25 percent interest in Saxon Corporation for $110,000 on January 1, 19X6, at which time Saxon's net assets consist of the following:

	Book Value	Fair Value	Excess Fair Value
Inventories	$240,000	$260,000	$20,000
Other current assets	100,000	100,000	
Equipment—net	50,000	50,000	
Buildings—net	140,000	200,000	60,000
	530,000	610,000	
Less: Liabilities	130,000	130,000	
Net assets	$400,000	$480,000	$80,000

Saxon's net income and dividends for 19X6 are $60,000 and $40,000, respectively. The undervalued inventory items were sold during 19X6 and the buildings and equipment each had four-year remaining use lives when Post acquired its 25 percent interest. Exhibit 2–2 illustrates the assignment of the excess cost over book value.

In reviewing Exhibit 2-2, notice that the excess cost over book value is first assigned to fair values of identifiable net assets, after which the negative goodwill is reassigned to reduce noncurrent assets other than marketable securities.

Journal entries for Post Corporation to account for its investment in Saxon Corporation during 19X6 follow:

January 1, 19X6
Investment in Saxon $110,000
     Cash $110,000
     To record purchase of a 25% interest in Saxon's voting stock.

19X6
Cash $ 10,000
     Investment in Saxon $ 10,000
     To record dividends received ($40,000 × 25%).

December 31, 19X6
Investment in Saxon $ 8,750
     Income from Saxon $ 8,750
     To recognize investment income from Saxon computed as follows:

25% of Saxon's $60,000 net income	$15,000
Excess allocated to inventories	(5,000)
Excess allocated to equipment ($2,000/4 years)	500
Excess allocated to buildings ($7,000/4 years)	(1,750)
	$ 8,750

POST CORPORATION AND ITS 25% OWNED EQUITY INVESTEE, SAXON CORPORATION

Investment cost			$110,000
Book value acquired ($400,000 × 25%)			100,000
Excess cost over book value acquired			$ 10,000

	Assignment to Fair Value	Reassignment of Negative Goodwill	Final Assignment
Inventory $20,000 × 25%	$ 5,000		$ 5,000
Equipment—net	—	$(2,000)*	(2,000)
Buildings—net $60,000 × 25%	15,000	(8,000)*	7,000
Negative goodwill	(10,000)	10,000	
Excess cost over book value acquired	$10,000	—	$10,000

* Based on fair values: $50,000/$250,000 to equipment
$200,000/$250,000 to buildings

Exhibit 2–2   *Schedule for Allocating Negative Goodwill*

Post Corporation's investment in Saxon balance at December 31, 19X6 is $108,750 and the underlying book value of the investment is $105,000 ($420,000 × 25%). The $3,750 difference consists of the $5,250 unamortized excess assigned to buildings less the $1,500 unamortized negative goodwill assigned to equipment.

INTERIM ACQUISITIONS OF AN INVESTMENT INTEREST

The detail of accounting for equity investments is increased when acquisitions are made within an accounting period (interim acquisitions). Additional computations are needed both in determining the underlying equity at the time of acquisition and in determining the investment income for the year. Stockholders' equity of the investee company is computed by adding income earned since the last statement date to the beginning stockholders' equity and subtracting dividends declared to the date of purchase. A basic assumption that is used in accounting for interim acquisitions is that income of the investee is earned proportionately throughout the year, in the absence of evidence to the contrary.

Assume that Petron acquires 40 percent of the voting common stock of Fairview Company for $80,000 on October 1, 19X8. Fairview's net assets (owners' equity) at January 1, 19X8 are $150,000, and it reports net income of $25,000 for 19X8 and declares $15,000 dividends on July 1. The book values of Fairview's assets and liabilities are equal to fair values on October 1, 19X8 except for a building worth $60,000 and recorded at $40,000. The building has a twenty-year remaining use life from October 1, and any goodwill is to be amortized over five years. Generally accepted accounting principles require application of the equity method and assignment of any difference between investment cost and book value acquired first to identifiable assets and liabilities and then to goodwill.

The excess of Petron's investment cost over the book value of its 40 percent interest in Fairview is computed and assigned to identifiable assets and goodwill, as shown in Exhibit 2–3.

PETRON CORPORATION AND ITS 40% OWNED EQUITY INVESTEE, FAIRVIEW CORPORATION		
Investment cost		$80,000
Less: Share of Fairview equity on October 1		
Beginning equity	$150,000	
Add: Income to October 1	18,750	
Less: Dividends	−15,000	
	153,750	
Times: Interest purchased	40%	−61,500
Excess cost over book value		$18,500
Excess assigned to:		
Buildings ($60,000 − $40,000) × 40%		$ 8,000
Goodwill (remainder)		10,500
Excess cost over book value		$18,500

Exhibit 2–3 *Schedule for Allocating the Excess of Investment Cost over Book Value Acquired*

Journal entries on Petron's books to account for the 40 percent equity interest in Fairview for 19X8 are as follows:

October 1, 19X8
Investment in Fairview $80,000
   Cash $80,000
   To record acquisition of 40% of Fairview's voting stock.

December 31, 19X8

Investment in Fairview	$ 2,500	
Income from Fairview		$ 2,500

    To record equity in Fairview's income (40% × $25,000 × ¼ year).

December 31, 19X8

Income from Fairview	$100	
Investment in Fairview		$100

    To record amortization of excess of cost over book value allocated
      to the undervalued building ($8,000 ÷ 20 years) × ¼ year.

Income from Fairview	$525	
Investment in Fairview		$525

    To record amortization of the excess of cost over book value allocated
      to goodwill ($10,500 ÷ 5 years) × ¼ year.

At December 31, 19X8, after the entries are posted, Petron's investment in Fairview account will have a balance of $81,875 ($80,000 cost + $1,875 income). This investment account balance is $17,875 more than the $64,000 underlying book value of Petron's interest in Fairview on that date (40% × $160,000). The $17,875 consists of the original excess cost over book value acquired of $18,500 less the $625 amortized in 19X8.

INVESTMENT IN A STEP-BY-STEP ACQUISITION

An investor may acquire an ability to exercise significant influence over the operating and financial policies of an investee corporation in a series of stock acquisitions rather than in a single purchase. For example, an investor may acquire a 10 percent interest in an investee and later acquire another 10 percent interest. The original 10 percent interest should be accounted for by the cost method until a 20 percent interest is attained. When the interest owned reaches 20 percent, however, the equity method is adopted and the investment and retained earnings accounts are adjusted retroactively.

Assume that Hop Corporation acquires a 10 percent interest in Skip Corporation for $750,000 on January 2, 19X2 and another 10 percent interest for $850,000 on January 2, 19X3. The stockholders' equity of Skip Corporation on the dates of these acquisitions is as follows:

	January 2, 19X2	*January 2, 19X3*
Capital stock	$5,000,000	$5,000,000
Retained earnings	2,000,000	2,500,000
Total stockholders' equity	$7,000,000	$7,500,000

Hop Corporation is not able to relate the excess of investment cost over book value acquired to identifiable net assets. Accordingly, it is assumed that the excess of cost over book value from each of the acquisitions is due to goodwill with a ten-year amortization period.

On January 2, 19X3 when the second 10 percent is acquired, Hop Corporation adopts the equity method of accounting for its 20 percent interest. This involves converting the carrying value of the original 10 percent interest from its $750,000 cost to its correct carrying value on an equity basis.[6] The entry to adjust the investment account of Hop Corporation is:

January 2, 19X3

Investment in Skip	$45,000	
Retained earnings		$45,000

> To adjust the investment in Skip account from a cost to an equity basis as follows: Share of Skip's retained earnings increase during 19X2 of $50,000 [$500,000 × 10% interest held during the year] less $5,000 goodwill amortization for 19X2 [($750,000 cost − $700,000 book value acquired)/10 years] equals the retroactive adjustment from accounting change of $45,000.

Skip's $500,000 retained earnings increase for 19X2 represents its income less dividends for 19X2. Since Hop reports its share of dividends received from Skip as income under the cost method, Hop's income for 19X2 under the equity method is greater by 10 percent of Skip's retained earnings increase for 19X2 and less by the $5,000 goodwill amortization that is not charged to income under the cost method.

SALE OF AN EQUITY INTEREST

When an investor sells a portion of an equity investment that reduces its interest in the investee below 20 percent or below a level necessary to exercise significant influence, the equity method of accounting is no longer appropriate for the remaining interest. The investment is accounted for under the cost method from this time forward, and the investment account balance after the sale becomes the new cost basis. No other adjustments are required, and the investor accounts for the investment under the cost method in the usual manner. Gain or loss from the equity interest sold is the difference between the selling price and the book value of the equity interest immediately before the sale.

To illustrate, Leighton Industries acquires 320,000 shares (a 40 percent interest) in Sergio Corporation on January 1, 19X1 for $580,000 when Sergio's stockholders' equity is $1,200,000 and the book values of its assets and liabilities equal their fair values. The $100,000 goodwill is amortized over 10 years at a rate of $10,000 a year. Leighton accounts for its investment in Sergio under the equity method during the years 19X1 through 19X3, and at December 31, 19X3 the balance of the investment account is $670,000 equal to 40 percent of Sergio's $1,500,000 stockholders' equity plus $70,000 unamortized goodwill.

On January 1, 19X4 Leighton sells 80 percent of its holdings in Sergio (256,000 shares) for $600,000, reducing its interest in Sergio to 8 percent (40% × 20%). The book value of the interest sold is $536,000, or 80 percent of the $670,000 balance of the investment in Sergio account. Leighton recognizes a gain on the sale of its interest in Sergio of $64,000 ($600,000 selling price less $536,000 book value of the interest sold). The balance of the investment in Sergio account after the sale is $134,000 ($670,000 less $536,000 interest sold). Leighton determines that it can no longer exercise significant influence over Sergio and, accordingly, it switches to the cost method and accounts for its investment under the lower-of-cost or market rule, with the $134,000 balance becoming the new cost basis of the investment.

STOCK PURCHASES DIRECTLY FROM THE INVESTEE

Previous illustrations have assumed that the investor corporation purchased its shares from existing stockholders of the investee corporation. In that situation, the interest acquired was equal to the shares acquired divided by the investee's

---

[6]Changes in the cost, equity, and consolidation methods of accounting for subsidiaries and investments are changes in the reporting entity and require restatement of prior-period financial statements if the effect is material. See *APB Opinion No. 20,* "Accounting Changes," paragraph 34.

outstanding shares. If shares are purchased directly from the issuing corporation, however, the investor's interest is determined by the shares acquired divided by the shares outstanding after the new shares are issued by the investee.

Assume that Karl Corporation purchases 20,000 shares of previously unissued common stock directly from Master Corporation for $450,000 on January 1, 19X8. Master's stockholders' equity at December 31, 19X7 consists of $200,000 of $10 par common stock and $150,000 retained earnings.

Karl's interest in Master Corporation is 50 percent, computed as follows:

A	Shares purchased by Karl		20,000 shares
B	Shares outstanding after new shares are issued:		
	Outstanding December 31, 19X7	20,000	
	Issued to Karl	20,000	40,000 shares
	Karl's interest in Master A/B = 50%		

The book value of the interest acquired by Karl is $400,000, determined by multiplying the 50 percent interest acquired by Master's $800,000 stockholders' equity immediately after the issuance of the additional 20,000 shares. Computations are as follows:

Master's stockholders' equity before issuance ($200,000 capital stock + $150,000 retained earnings)	$350,000
Sale of 20,000 shares to Karl	450,000
Master's stockholders' equity after issuance	800,000
Karl's percentage ownership	50%
Book value acquired by Karl	$400,000

INVESTEE CORPORATION WITH PREFERRED STOCK

The equity method applies to investments in common stock and some adjustments in applying the equity method are necessary when an investee has preferred as well as common stock outstanding. These adjustments require:

1 Allocation of the investee corporation's stockholders' equity into preferred and common equity components upon acquisition in order to determine the book value of the common stock investment
2 Allocation of the investee's net income into preferred and common income components to determine the investor's share of the investee's income to common stockholders

Assume that Tech Corporation's stockholders' equity is $6,000,000 at the beginning of 19X3 and $6,500,000 at the end of 19X3, and that its net income and dividends for 19X3 are $700,000 and $200,000, respectively.

	January 1, 19X3	December 31, 19X3
10% cumulative preferred stock–$100 par	$1,000,000	$1,000,000
Common stock–$10 par	3,000,000	3,000,000
Other paid-in capital	500,000	500,000
Retained earnings	1,500,000	2,000,000
	$6,000,000	$6,500,000

If Mornet Corporation pays $2,500,000 on January 2, 19X3 for 40 percent of Tech's outstanding common stock, the investment is evaluated as follows:

Cost of 40 percent common interest in Tech		$2,500,000
Book value (and fair value) acquired:		
Stockholders' equity of Tech	$6,000,000	
Less: Preferred stockholders' equity	1,000,000	
Common stockholders' equity	5,000,000	
Percent acquired	40%	2,000,000
Goodwill		$ 500,000

The equity of preferred stockholders is equal to the par value of outstanding preferred stock, increased by the greater of any call or liquidating premium and by preferred dividends in arrears.

Mornet's income from Tech for 19X3 from its 40 percent interest is computed:

Tech's net income for 19X3	$700,000
Less: Preferred income ($1,000,000 × 10%)	100,000
Income to common	$600,000
Share of Tech's common income ($600,000 × 40%)	$240,000
Less: Goodwill amortization ($500,000 ÷ 40 years)	12,500
Income from Tech for 19X3	$227,500

APB Opinion No. 18, paragraph 9k, provides that when an investee company has cumulative preferred stock outstanding, an investor in common stock computes its share of earnings or losses after deducting preferred dividends, whether or not preferred dividends are declared. Additional coverage of accounting matters related to investees with preferred stock outstanding is provided in Chapter 10.

EXTRAORDINARY ITEMS, CUMULATIVE-EFFECT-TYPE ADJUSTMENTS, AND OTHER CONSIDERATIONS

In accounting for a stock investment under the equity method, the investor corporation reports its share of the ordinary income of an investee on one line of its income statement. But the one-line consolidation does not apply to the reporting of investment income when the investee corporation's income consists of extraordinary items or cumulative-effect-type adjustments. In this case, the investment income must be separated into its ordinary, extraordinary, and cumulative-effect components and reported accordingly.

Assume that Carl Corporation owns 40 percent of the outstanding stock of Homer Corporation and that Homer's income for 19X5 consists of the following:

Income from continuing operations before extraordinary item	$500,000
Extraordinary item—casualty loss (less applicable income taxes of $25,000	50,000
Net income	$450,000

Carl records its investment income from Homer as follows:

Investment in Homer	$180,000	
Casualty loss—Investee	20,000	
Income from Homer		$200,000
To record investment income from Homer.		

The $200,000 income from Homer is reported as investment income by Carl, and the $20,000 casualty loss is reported along with any extraordinary items that Carl may have had during the year. If Homer had a cumulative-effect-type adjustment, it would be recorded in similar fashion and reported along with Carl's cumulative-effect-type adjustments, if any. A gain or loss on an investee's disposal of a segment of a business would be treated similarly.

Other Requirements of the Equity Method

In reporting its share of earnings and losses of an investee under the equity method, an investor corporation must eliminate the effect of profits and losses on transactions between the investor and investee corporations until they are realized. This involves adjusting the investment and investment income accounts in a manner similar to that illustrated previously for identifiable net assets and goodwill. Transactions of an investee that change the investor's share of the net assets of the investee corporation also involve adjustments under the equity method of accounting. These and other complexities of the equity method are covered in subsequent chapters along with related consolidation procedures. Chapter 10 covers preferred stock, earnings per share, and income tax considerations.

DISCLOSURES FOR EQUITY INVESTEES

The extent to which separate disclosure should be provided for equity investments depends on the significance (materiality) of such investments to the financial position and results of operations of the investor company. If equity investments are significant, the investor should disclose the following information, parenthetically or in financial statement notes or schedules:

1 The name of each investee and percentage of ownership in common stock
2 The accounting policies of the investor with respect to investments in common stock

---

EXXON CORPORATION, 1990 ANNUAL REPORT
NOTES TO CONSOLIDATED FINANCIAL STATEMENTS
10. EQUITY COMPANY INFORMATION

The summarized financial information below includes those less than majority-owned companies for which Exxon's share of net income is included in consolidated net income. . . . These companies are primarily engaged in natural gas production and distribution in the Netherlands and Germany, refining and marketing operations in Japan and several chemical operations.

	1988		1989		1990	
			(millions of dollars			
	Total	*Exxon Share*	*Total*	*Exxon Share*	*Total*	*Exxon Share*
Total revenues[1]	$22,629	$7,411	$18,962	$6,206	$22,943	$7,522
Net income before income taxes	$ 3,471	$1,425	$ 2,431	$1,057	$ 2,531	$1,149
Less: Related income taxes	(1,547)	(582)	(867)	(337)	(827)	(369)
Net income	$ 1,924	$ 843	$ 1,564	$ 720	$ 1,704	$ 780
Current assets	$ 8,548	$2,780	$ 7,222	$2,356	$ 8,488	$2,791
Property, plant and equipment, less accumulated depreciation	12,062	4,569	12,510	4,696	11,560	4,800
Other long-term assets	3,096	1,008	2,112	782	2,208	835
Total assets	23,706	8,357	21,844	7,834	22,256	8,426
Short-term debt	1,026	306	1,516	426	2,430	725
Other current liabilities	5,052	1,829	4,857	1,795	5,766	2,191
Long-term debt	3,464	1,145	3,088	989	2,571	903
Other long-term liabilities	5,217	1,827	3,712	1,433	3,247	1,429
Advances from shareholders	1,269	637	1,161	570	756	382
Net assets	$ 7,678	$2,613[2]	$ 7,510	$2,621[2]	$ 7,486	$2,796[2]

[1]Includes sales to companies in the Exxon consolidation which amounted to 14% in 1988, 16% in 1989 and 15% in 1990.
[2]Includes $529 million in 1988, $688 million in 1989 and $1,091 million in 1990 of liabilities guaranteed by consolidated affiliates.

Exhibit 2–4 *Financial Statement Disclosures for Equity Investments*

3 The difference, if any, between the amount at which an investment is carried and the amount of underlying equity in net assets, including the accounting treatment of the difference

Additional disclosures for material equity investments include the aggregate value of each identified investment for which quoted market prices are available and summarized information regarding the assets, liabilities, and results of operations of the investees. Firms that made these disclosures for nonconsolidated subsidiaries under *APB Opinion No. 18* are required to continue the disclosures under *FASB Statement No. 94*, even though the subsidiaries are now consolidated.

An excerpt from the 1990 Annual Report of Exxon Corporation is presented in Exhibit 2–4 to illustrate the disclosure requirements. Financial information is summarized for all significant equity investees as a group. Exxon's share of underlying net assets of these investees is included in "investments and advances" in the balance sheet and its share of the investees net income is included in the income statement as "earnings from equity interests and other revenue." The consolidated statement of cash flows shows "dividends received which were in excess of/(less than) equity in current earnings of equity companies" as a deduction from net income.

Related Party Transactions

FASB Statement No. 57, "Related Party Disclosures," explains that there is no presumption of arms-length bargaining between related parties. The statement identifies material transactions between affiliated companies as related party transactions requiring financial statement disclosure. The required disclosures include:

1 The nature of the relationship
2 A description of the transaction
3 The dollar amounts of the transaction and any change from the previous period in the method used to establish the terms of the transaction for each income statement presented
4 Amounts due to or due from related parties at the balance sheet date for each balance sheet presented

---

CHEVRON CORPORATION ANNUAL REPORT 1990, p. 54.
NOTE 12. INVESTMENTS AND ADVANCES [PARTIAL]
(*in millions of dollars*)

The company's transactions with affiliated companies, primarily for the purchase of Indonesian crude oil from Caltex and the sale of crude oil and products to Caltex's refining and marketing companies are as follows:

	Year Ended December 31		
	1990	*1989*	*1988*
Sales to Caltex Group	$1,470	$692	$356
Sales to other affiliates	92	155	179
Total sales to affiliates	$1,562	$847	$535
Purchases from Caltex Group	$ 858	$528	$575
Purchases from other affiliates	223	187	69
Total purchases from affiliates	$1,081	$715	$644

Accounts and notes receivable in the Consolidated Balance Sheet include $261 and $158 at December 31, 1990 and 1989, respectively, of amounts due from affiliated companies. Accounts payable include $101 and $72 at December 31, 1990 and 1989, respectively, of amounts due to affiliated companies.

Exhibit 2–5 *Related Party Disclosures for Affiliates*

Related party disclosures for affiliated companies are illustrated in Exhibit 2–5 for Chevron Corporation. Chevron's 1990 Annual Report identifies the Caltex Group of Companies as Chevron's largest equity affiliate.

SUMMARY

Investments in the voting common stock of an investee corporation are accounted for under the cost method if the investment does not give the investor an ability to exercise significant influence over the investee. Otherwise, the equity method (a one-line consolidation) should normally be used. In the absence of evidence to the contrary, a 20 percent ownership test is used to determine if the investor has the ability to exercise significant influence over the investee.

The equity method is referred to as a one-line consolidation because its application produces the same net income and stockholders' equity for the investor as would result from consolidation of the financial statements of the investor and investee corporations. Under the one-line consolidation, the investment is reflected in a single amount on one line of the investor's balance sheet, and the investor's income from the investee is reported on one line of the investor's income statement except when the investee's income includes extraordinary or cumulative-effect-type items.

A flow chart summary of accounting procedures for business investments is presented in Exhibit 2–6. As indicated in the flow chart, the equity method is equally applicable to investments accounted for under the pooling and purchase methods, even though the initial recording of a stock investment under the two methods is different. The flow chart also indicates that consolidated statements are generally required for investments in excess of 50 percent of the voting stock of the investee and that the one-line consolidation (equity method) is used in reporting investments of 20 to 50 percent in the investor's financial statements and in consolidated financial statements.

NOTE TO THE STUDENT

In solving problems in the areas of business combinations, equity investments, and consolidations, it is frequently necessary to make assumptions about the nature of the difference between investment cost and book value of the net assets acquired, the amortization period for goodwill, the timing of income earned within an accounting period, the period in which inventory items affecting intercompany investments are sold, and the source from which an equity interest is acquired. *In the absence of evidence to the contrary,* you should make the following assumptions:

1 An excess of investment cost over book value of the net assets acquired is goodwill.
2 Goodwill is amortized over forty years (which is the maximum allowable amortization period).
3 Income is earned evenly throughout each accounting period.
4 Inventory items on hand at any date are sold in the immediately succeeding fiscal period.
5 An equity interest is purchased from the stockholders of the investee company rather than directly from the investee corporation (that is, the total outstanding stock of the investee corporation does not change).

SELECTED READINGS

Accounting Interpretations Nos. 1 and 2 of APB Opinion No. 17. New York: American Institute of Certified Public Accountants, 1971 and 1973.

Accounting Interpretation No. 1 of APB Opinion No. 18. New York: American Institute of Certified Public Accountants, 1971.

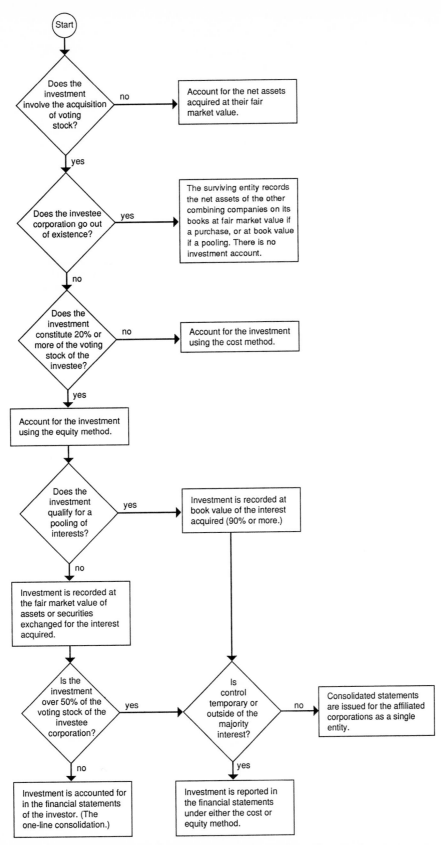

Exhibit 2-6 *Accounting for Equity Investments Generally*

Accounting Principles Board Opinion No. 18. "The Equity Method of Accounting for Investments in Common Stock." New York: American Institute of Certified Public Accountants, 1971.

FASB Interpretation No. 35. "Criteria for Applying the Equity Method of Accounting for Investments in Common Stock." An Interpretation of *APB Opinion No. 18.* Stamford, CT: Financial Accounting Standards Board, May 1981.

Statement of Financial Accounting Standards No. 94. "Consolidation of All Majority-owned Subsidiaries." Stamford, CT: Financial Accounting Standards Board, 1986.

ASSIGNMENT MATERIAL

QUESTIONS

1 How are the accounts of investor and investee companies affected when the investor acquires stock from stockholders of the investee company (for example, a New York Stock Exchange purchase)? When the investor acquires previously unissued stock directly from the investee?

2 Would goodwill arising from an equity investment of over 20 percent be recorded separately on the books of the investor corporation? Explain.

3 Under the cost method of accounting for stock investments, an investor records dividends received from earnings accumulated after the investment is acquired as dividend income. How does an investor treat dividends received from earnings accumulated before an investment is acquired?

4 Describe the equity method of accounting.

5 Why is the equity method of accounting for equity investments frequently referred to as a one-line consolidation?

6 Is there a difference between the amount of a parent company's net income under the equity method and the consolidated net income for the same parent company and its subsidiaries?

7 What is the difference in reporting income from a subsidiary in the parent company's separate income statement and in consolidated financial statements?

8 How does a parent company/investor record amortization of goodwill on its separate books?

9 Cite the conditions under which you would expect the balance of an equity investment account on a balance sheet date subsequent to acquisition to be equal to the underlying book value represented by that investment.

10 What accounting procedures or adjustments are necessary when an investor uses the cost method of accounting for an investment in common stock, and increases the investment such that the equity method is required?

11 Ordinarily, the income from an investment accounted for by the equity method is reported on one line of the investor company's income statement. When would more than one line of the income statement of the investor be required to report such income?

12 Describe the accounting adjustments needed when a 25 percent equity interest in an investee company is decreased to a 15 percent equity interest.

13 Does cumulative preferred stock in the capital structure of an investee affect the way that an investor company accounts for its 30 percent common stock interest? Explain.

EXERCISES

E 2-1 [AICPA adapted]

1 Under the equity method of accounting for investments, an investor recognizes its share of earnings in the period in which the:
   a Investor sells the investment
   b Investee declares a dividend
   c Investee pays a dividend
   d Earnings are reported by the investee in its financial statements

2 When the equity method of accounting for an investment in a subsidiary is used, dividends from the subsidiary should be accounted for by the parent corporation as:
   a Revenue unless paid from retained earnings of the subsidiary earned before the date of acquisition

b Revenue so long as the dividends were declared from retained earnings

c A reduction of the carrying value of the investment account

d A deferred credit

3 Investor Inc., owns 40 percent of Alimand Corporation. During the calendar year 19X5, Alimand had net earnings of $100,000 and paid dividends of $10,000. Investor mistakingly recorded these transactions using the cost method rather than the equity method of accounting. What effect would this have on the investment account, net earnings, and retained earnings, respectively?

a Understate, overstate, overstate   **b** Overstate, understate, understate

c Overstate, overstate, overstate   **d** Understate, understate, understate

4 The corporation exercises control over an affiliate in which it holds 40 percent common stock interest. If its affiliate completed a fiscal year profitably but paid *no* dividends, how would this affect the investor corporation?

a Result in an increased current ratio

b Result in increased earnings per share

c Increase several turnover ratios

d Decrease book value per share

5 An investor uses the cost method to account for an investment in common stock. A portion of the dividends received this year were in excess of the investor's share of investee's earnings subsequent to the date of investment. The amount of dividend revenue that should be reported in the investor's income statement for this year would be:

a Zero

b The total amount of dividends received this year

c The portion of the dividends received this year that were in excess of the investor's share of investee's earnings subsequent to the date of investment

d The portion of the dividends received this year that were *not* in excess of the investor's share of investee's earnings subsequent to the date of investment

E 2-2   Ivan Corporation's stockholders' equity at December 31, 19X1 consisted of the following:

Capital stock—$10 par	
45,000 shares issued and outstanding	$450,000
Additional paid-in capital	150,000
Retained earnings	200,000
Total stockholders' equity	$800,000

On January 1, 19X2 Henry Corporation purchased 15,000 previously unissued shares of Ivan stock directly from Ivan for $400,000.

Required

    1 Calculate Henry Corporation's percentage ownership in Ivan.

    2 Determine the goodwill from Henry's investment in Ivan.

E 2-3   Parsons Corporation pays $500,000 for a 30 percent interest in Shelby Corporation on July 1, 19X2 when the book value of Shelby's net assets equals fair value. Parsons amortizes any goodwill from this investment over 20 years. Information relating to Shelby follows:

	December 31, 19X1	December 31, 19X2
Capital stock—$1 par	$ 600,000	$ 600,000
Retained earnings	400,000	500,000
Total stockholders' equity	$1,000,000	$1,100,000

Shelby's net income earned evenly throughout 19X2	$200,000
Shelby's dividends for 19X2 (paid $50,000 on March 1 and $50,000 on September 1)	$100,000

Required: Calculate Parsons' income from Shelby for 19X2.

E 2-4   Martin Company acquired a 40 percent interest in Oakley Mills on January 1, 19X1 for $2,000,000 cash. Martin assigned the $500,000 cost over book value of the investment acquired to the following assets:

Inventories	$100,000 (sold in 19X1)
Building	$200,000 (4 year remaining life at January 1, 19X1)
Goodwill	$200,000 (40 year amortization period)

During 19X1 Oakley reported net income of $800,000 and paid $200,000 dividends.

Required
1 Determine Martin's income from Oakley Mills for 19X1.
2 Determine the December 31, 19X1 balance of the investment in Oakley Mills account.

E 2-5   Jersey Corporation purchased a 40 percent interest in Kelly Corporation for $500,000 on January 1, 19X1 at book value when Kelly's assets and liabilities were recorded at their fair values. During 19X1, Kelly reported net income of $200,000 as follows:

Income from continuing operations	$250,000
Less: Loss from discontinued operations	50,000
Net income	$200,000

Required: Prepare the journal entry on Jersey Corporation's books to recognize income from the investment in Kelly for 19X1.

E 2-6   Ardel Corporation acquired 25 percent of Baker Corporation's outstanding common stock on October 1, 19X2 for $500,000. A summary of Baker's adjusted trial balances on this date and at December 31, 19X2 follows:

	December 31, 19X2	October 1, 19X2
Debits		
Current assets	$ 500,000	$ 250,000
Plant assets—net	1,500,000	1,550,000
Expenses (including cost of goods sold)	800,000	600,000
Dividends (paid in July)	200,000	200,000
	$3,000,000	$2,600,000
Credits		
Current liabilities	$ 300,000	$ 200,000
Capital stock (no change during 19X2)	1,000,000	1,000,000
Retained earnings January 1, 19X2	500,000	500,000
Sales	1,200,000	900,000
	$3,000,000	$2,600,000

Ardel uses the equity method of accounting in accordance with GAAP. No information is available concerning the fair values of Baker's assets and liabilities.

Required
1 Determine Ardel's investment income from Baker Corporation for the year ended December 31, 19X2.
2 Compute the correct balance of Ardel's investment in Baker account at December 31, 19X2.

E 2-7   **[AICPA adapted]**

Use the following information in answering questions 1 and 2.

On January 1, 19X8 Avow, Inc. purchased 30 percent of the outstanding common stock of Depot Corporation for $129,000 cash. Avow is accounting for this investment by the equity method. On the date of acquisition, the book value of Depot's net assets was $310,000. Avow has determined that the excess of the cost of the investment over its share of Depot's net assets has an indeterminate life.

Depot's net income for the year ended December 31, 19X8 was $90,000. During 19X8 Depot declared and paid cash dividends of $10,000. There were no other transactions between the two companies.

1 On January 1, 19X8 the investment in Depot should have been recorded as:

a $ 93,000   b $120,000
c $129,000   d $165,000

2 Avow's statement of income for the year ended December 31, 19X8 should include "equity in net income of Depot Corporation" in the amount of:

a $17,000   b $26,100
c $27,000   d $27,900

3 On January 1, 19X8 Grade Company paid $300,000 for 20,000 shares of Medium Company's common stock, which represents a 15 percent investment in Medium. Grade does not have the ability to exercise significant influence over Medium. Medium declared and paid a dividend of $1 per share to its stockholders during 19X8. Medium reported net income of $260,000 for the year ended December 31, 19X8. The balance in Grade's balance sheet account "Investment in Medium Company" at December 31, 19X8 should be

a $280,000   b $300,000
c $319,000   d $339,000

4 On January 2, 19X1 Troquel Corporation bought 15 percent of Zafacon Corporation's capital stock for $30,000. Troquel accounts for this investment by the cost method. Zafacon's net income for the years ended December 31, 19X1 and December 31, 19X2 were $10,000 and $50,000, respectively. During 19X2 Zafacon declared a dividend of $70,000. No dividends were declared in 19X1. How much should Troquel show on its 19X2 income statement as income from this investment?

a $1,575   b $ 7,500
c $9,000   d $10,500

E 2–8 Poon Corporation purchased a 70 percent interest in Sperry Company's outstanding common stock on July 1, 19X6 for $260,000 in cash and other property. The entries in Sperry's retained earnings account from January 1, 19X6 to December 31, 19X9 are summarized below. Sperry had $200,000 of total paid-in capital throughout the 19X5–19X9 period. Assume that Sperry's income is earned proportionately throughout each year and that any excess of cost over book value is allocated to goodwill having a ten-year amortization period.

RETAINED EARNINGS

April 1, 19X6	Dividends	$10,000	Balance January 1, 19X6	$110,000
April 1, 19X7	Dividends	15,000	Earnings 19X6	20,000
April 1, 19X8	Dividends	15,000	Earnings 19X7	40,000
19X9	Net loss	20,000	Earnings 19X8	30,000

1 Poon should report income from its investment in Sperry for 19X6 under the equity method of accounting at:

a $14,000   b $9,700
c $7,000   d $4,850

2 Poon's investment in Sperry account at December 31, 19X6, after adjusting entries have been made and assuming the equity method of accounting, should have a balance of:

a $274,000   b $269,700
c $267,000   d $264,850

3 The balance of Poon's investment in Sperry account at December 31, 19X9, after adjusting entries and assuming the equity method of accounting, should be:

a $260,000   b $265,950
c $281,000   d $315,950

4 Poon should report income or loss from its investment in Sperry for 19X9, under the equity method of accounting, at:

a $24,300   b $18,300
c $17,010   d $14,000

5 Unamortized goodwill from Poon's investment in Sperry at December 31, 19X9 should be:

    a $38,700   **b** $27,950

    c $25,800   **d** $24,310

E 2–9   The stockholders' equity of Short Corporation at December 31, 19X1 was $380,000, consisting of the following:

Capital stock—$10 par (24,000 shares outstanding)	$240,000
Additional paid-in capital	60,000
Retained earnings	80,000
Total stockholders' equity	$380,000

On January 1, 19X2, Short Corporation, which was in a tight working capital position, sold 8,000 shares of previously unissued stock to Patriot Corporation for $160,000. All of Short's identifiable assets and liabilities were recorded at their fair values on this date except for a building with a ten-year remaining use life that was undervalued by $60,000. During 19X2 Short Corporation reported net income of $120,000 and paid dividends of $80,000.

Required: Prepare all journal entries necessary for Patriot Corporation to account for its investment in Short for 19X2.

E 2–10   BIP Corporation paid $195,000 for a 30 percent interest in Crown Corporation on December 31, 19X3 when Crown's equity consisted of $500,000 capital stock and $200,000 retained earnings. The price paid by BIP reflected the fact that Crown's inventory (on a FIFO basis) was overvalued by $50,000. The overvalued inventory items were sold in 19X4.

During 19X4 Crown paid dividends of $100,000 and reported income as follows:

Income before extraordinary items	$170,000
Extraordinary loss (net of tax effect)	20,000
Net income	$150,000

Required

  1 Prepare all journal entries necessary to account for BIP's investment in Crown for 19X4.

  2 Determine the correct balance of BIP's investment in Crown account at December 31, 19X4.

  3 Assume that BIP's net income for 19X4 consists of $1,000,000 sales, $700,000 expenses, and its investment income from Crown. Prepare an income statement for BIP Corporation for 19X4.

E 2–11   Federal Corporation paid $290,000 for 50 percent of the outstanding common stock of Wilson Corporation on January 2, 19X3. During 19X3 Wilson paid dividends of $48,000 and reported net income of $108,000. A summary of Wilson's stockholders' equity at December 31, 19X2 and 19X3 follows:

December 31,	19X3	19X2
8% cumulative preferred stock—$100 par	$100,000	$100,000
Common stock—$10 par	300,000	300,000
Premium on preferred stock	10,000	10,000
Other paid-in capital	90,000	90,000
Retained earnings	160,000	100,000
Total stockholders' equity	$660,000	$600,000

Required: Calculate Federal Corporation's income from Wilson for 19X3 and its investment in Wilson account balance at December 31, 19X3.

PROBLEMS

P 2-1 Mince Corporation acquired a 60 percent interest in the voting stock of Thor Corporation for $120,000 on January 2, 19X8 when Thor's capital stock and retained earnings totaled $150,000. Thor's assets were recorded at their fair values except for inventory items that were overvalued by $10,000.

Thor Corporation reported net income of $40,000 and paid dividends of $20,000 during 19X8. The overvalued inventory items were sold and their realization reflected in the $40,000 reported income of Thor. Mince Corporation amortizes goodwill over a ten-year period.

Required: Compute Mince Corporation's income from its investment in Thor for 19X8.

P 2-2 Prestige Company paid $110,000 for a 90 percent interest in Regal Company on July 1, 19X8 when Regal Company had total equity of $110,000. Regal Company reported earnings of $10,000 for 19X8 and declared dividends of $8,000 on November 1, 19X8.

Required: Give the entries to record these facts on the books of Prestige Company:
1 Assuming that Prestige Company uses the cost method of accounting for its subsidiaries.
2 Assuming that Prestige Company uses the equity method of accounting for its subsidiaries. (Any difference between investment cost and book value acquired is to be amortized over a ten-year period.)

P 2-3 Patterson Company acquired a 30 percent interest in the voting stock of Zelda Company for $331,000 on January 1, 19X2, when Zelda's stockholders' equity consisted of capital stock of $600,000 and retained earnings of $400,000. At the time of Patterson's investment, Zelda's assets and liabilities were recorded at their fair values, except for inventories that were undervalued by $20,000 and a building with a 10-year remaining use life that was overvalued by $50,000. Any goodwill from the investment is amortized over forty years.

Zelda has income for 19X2 of $100,000 and pays dividends of $50,000.

Required
1 Compute Patterson's income from Zelda for 19X2.
2 What is the balance of Patterson's investment in Zelda account at December 31, 19X2?
3 What is Patterson's share of Zelda's recorded net assets at December 31, 19X2?

P 2-4 Phyllis Corporation paid $300,000 for 40 percent of Sally Corporation's outstanding voting common stock on July 1, 19X7. Sally's stockholders' equity on January 1, 19X7 was $500,000, consisting of $300,000 capital stock and $200,000 retained earnings.

During 19X7 Sally had net income of $100,000, and on November 1, 19X7 Sally declared dividends of $50,000.

Sally's assets and liabilities were stated at their fair values on July 1, 19X7 except for land that was undervalued by $30,000 and equipment with a five-year remaining use life that was undervalued by $50,000.

Required: Prepare all the journal entries (other than closing entries) on the books of Phyllis Corporation during 19X7 to account for the investment in Sally.

P 2-5 Palm Corporation acquired 30 percent of the voting stock of Seatrain Corporation for $60,000 on January 2, 19X8 when Seatrain's stockholders' equity consisted of capital stock of $100,000 and retained earnings of $50,000. All of Seatrain's assets and liabilities were recorded at their fair values on January 2, 19X8 except for land that had a fair value of $5,000 greater than its book value and a building that had a fair value of $10,000 greater than its undepreciated cost. The remaining use life of the building on January 2, 19X8 was five years.

Seatrain Corporation reported net income for 19X8 of $30,000 and paid dividends of $20,000. Palm Corporation uses the equity method of accounting for all its investments that provide it with an ability to exercise significant influence over the operations of its investees.

Palm uses a ten-year amortization period for goodwill from its investments.

Required: Compute the correct amounts for each of the following items relevant to Palm's investment in Seatrain:

1 Palm's income from its investment in Seatrain for 19X8
2 The balance of Palm's investment in Seatrain account at December 31, 19X8
3 Palm's share of Seatrain Corporation's recorded net assets at December 31, 19X8

P 2-6 Lowe Corporation purchased 6,000 shares of voting common stock of Stapleton Corporation at $15 per share cash on July 1, 19X7. On this date, Stapleton's equity consisted of $100,000 of $10 par capital stock, $20,000 retained earnings from prior periods, and $10,000 current earnings (for one-half of 19X7).

Stapleton's income for the entire year 19X7 was $20,000, and it paid dividends of $12,000 on November 1, 19X7.

All of Stapleton's assets and liabilities were stated at their fair values at July 1, 19X7, and any difference between investment cost and book value acquired should be amortized over a ten-year period.

Required: Compute the correct amounts for each of the following items using the equity method of accounting for Lowe's investment.

1 Lowe Corporation's income from its investment in Stapleton for the year ended December 31, 19X7
2 The balance of Lowe's investment in Stapleton account at December 31, 19X7
3 Lowe's unamortized goodwill from its investment in Stapleton at December 31, 19X9

(*Note:* Assumptions on page 60 are needed for this problem.)

P 2-7 Tulip Corporation acquired 30 percent of the voting stock of Larken Company at book value on July 1, 19X1. During 19X3 Larken paid dividends of $80,000 and reported income of $200,000 as follows:

Income before extraordinary item	$150,000
Extraordinary gain (tax credit from operating loss carryforward)	50,000
Net income	$200,000

Required: Show how Tulip's income from Larken should be reported for 19X3 by means of a partial income statement for Tulip Corporation.

P 2-8 Hazelton Corporation purchased a 10 percent interest in Wilmot Company on January 1, 19X1 for $20,000 and an additional 20 percent interest for $50,000 on July 1, 19X3. Wilmot had total stockholders' equity of $150,000 when the 10 percent interest was acquired and $235,000 when the 20 percent interest was acquired. Any difference between investment cost and book value acquired is to be amortized over a ten-year period. Wilmot reported net income and paid dividends for the years 19X1 through 19X4 as follows:

	19X1	*19X2*	*19X3*	*19X4*
Net income for the year	$50,000	$60,000	$70,000	$90,000
Dividends paid in November	30,000	30,000	30,000	40,000

Hazelton accounts for its investment in Wilmot in accordance with generally accepted accounting principles.

Required

1 Determine Hazelton's investment income from Wilmot for the year 19X3.
2 Determine Hazelton's prior period adjustment for 19X3 relating to this investment.
3 Calculate the balance of Hazelton's investment in Wilmot account at December 31, 19X4 for its 30 percent interest.
4 On January 1, 19X5 Wilmot increases its outstanding shares from 10,000 to 12,000 by selling 2,000 shares to Hazelton for $70,000. What adjustment should Hazelton make in its investment in Wilmot account on this date?

P 2-9 Sigma Corporation became a subsidiary of Provo Corporation on July 1, 19X4 when Provo paid $1,980,000 cash for 90 percent of Sigma's outstanding common stock. The price paid by Provo reflected the fact that Sigma's inventories were undervalued by $50,000 and its plant assets were overvalued by $500,000. Sigma sold the undervalued inventory items during 19X4 but continues to hold the overvalued plant assets that had a remaining use life of nine years from July 1, 19X4.

During the years 19X4 through 19X6, Sigma's paid-in capital consisted of $1,500,000 capital stock and $500,000 additional paid-in capital. Sigma's retained earnings statements for the years 19X4, 19X5, and 19X6 were as follows:

	Year Ended December 31, 19X4	Year Ended December 31, 19X5	Year Ended December 31, 19X6
Retained earnings January 1	$525,000	$600,000	$700,000
Add: Net income	250,000	300,000	200,000
Deduct: Dividends (declared in December)	175,000	200,000	150,000
Retained earnings December 31	$600,000	$700,000	$750,000

Provo uses the equity method in accounting for its investment in Sigma.

Required
  1 Compute Provo Corporation's income from its investment in Sigma for 19X4.
  2 Determine the balance of Provo Corporation's investment in Sigma account at December 31, 19X5.
  3 Prepare the journal entries necessary for Provo to account for its investment in Sigma for the year 19X6.

P 2-10 Probst Corporation paid $36,000 for a 50 percent interest in Shelor Corporation on January 1, 19X6 when Shelor's net assets were as follows:

	Book Value	Fair Value	Comment
Inventories	$ 12,000	$ 10,000	Sold in 19X6
Other current assets	50,000	50,000	
Equipment—net	48,000	30,000	10-year life
Buildings—net	20,000	20,000	4-year life
	130,000	110,000	
Liabilities	30,000	30,000	
Net assets	$100,000	$ 80,000	

Shelor's net income for 19X6 was $30,000, and the company paid dividends of $10,000 on October 1.

Required
  1 Prepare a schedule to assign the cost–book value differential
  2 Calculate Probst Corporation's income from Shelor for 19X6
  3 Determine the balance of Probst Corporation's investment in Shelor account at December 31, 19X6.

P 2–11   Preston Corporation made three investments in Spencer during 19X5 and 19X6 as follows:

Date Acquired	Shares Acquired	Cost
July 1, 19X5	3,000	$ 48,750
January 1, 19X6	6,000	99,000
October 1, 19X6	9,000	162,000

Spencer Corporation's stockholders' equity on January 1, 19X5 consisted of 20,000 shares of $10 par common stock and retained earnings of $100,000.

Spencer had net income of $40,000 and $60,000 in 19X5 and 19X6 respectively, and paid dividends of $15,000 on May 1 and November 1 of 19X5 and 19X6 ($60,000 total for the two years).

Preston Corporation accounts for its investment in Spencer using the equity method of accounting. It amortizes differences between investment cost and book value acquired over a ten-year period from the date of acquisition.

Required: Computer the following amounts:

1 Preston's income from its investment in Spencer for 19X5
2 The correct balance of Preston's investment in Spencer account at December 31, 19X5
3 Preston's income from its investments in Spencer for 19X6
4 The correct balance of Preston's investment in Spencer account at December 31, 19X6

P 2–12   Pilot Corporation purchased 40 percent of the voting stock of Sassy Corporation on July 1, 19X5 for $300,000. On that date Sassy's stockholders' equity consisted of capital stock of $500,000, retained earnings of $150,000, and current earnings (just half of 19X5) of $50,000. Income is earned proportionately throughout each year.

The investment in Sassy account of Pilot Corporation and the retained earnings account of Sassy Corporation for the years 19X5 through 19X8 are summarized as follows:

RETAINED EARNINGS (SASSY)

November 1, 19X5	Dividends	$40,000	Balance January 1, 19X5	$150,000
November 1, 19X6	Dividends	40,000	Earnings 19X5	100,000
November 1, 19X7	Dividends	50,000	Earnings 19X6	80,000
November 1, 19X8	Dividends	50,000	Earnings 19X7	130,000
			Earnings 19X8	120,000

INVESTMENT IN SASSY (PILOT)

July 1, 19X5	40% Investment	$300,000	19X5	Dividends	$16,000
19X5	Income	40,000	19X6	Dividends	16,000
19X6	Income	32,000	19X7	Dividends	20,000
19X7	Income	52,000	19X8	Dividends	20,000
19X8	Income	48,000			

Required

1 Determine the correct amount of the investment in Sassy that should appear in Pilot's December 31, 19X8 balance sheet (assume a ten-year period for any difference between investment cost and book value acquired).
2 Prepare any journal entry (entries) on Pilot's books to bring the investment in Sassy account up to date on December 31, 19X8, assuming that the books have not been closed at year-end 19X8.

P 2-13   Penny Corporation acquired a 70 percent interest in Steve Corporation on April 1 19X3, when it purchased 14,000 of Steve's 20,000 outstanding shares in the open market at $12 per share. Additional costs of acquiring the shares consisted of $5,000 brokerage fees and $5,000 legal and consulting fees. Steve Corporation's balance sheets on January 1 and April 1, 19X3 are summarized as follows:

	January 1, 19X3 (per books)	April 1, 19X3 (per books)	April 1, 19X3 (fair values)
Cash	$ 40,000	$ 45,000	$ 45,000
Inventories	35,000	60,000	50,000
Other current assets	25,000	20,000	20,000
Land	30,000	30,000	50,000
Equipment—net	100,000	95,000	135,000
Total assets	$230,000	$250,000	$300,000
Accounts payable	$ 45,000	$ 40,000	$ 40,000
Other liabilities	15,000	20,000	20,000
Capital stock, $5 par	100,000	100,000	
Retained earnings January 1	70,000	70,000	240,000
Current earnings		20,000	
Total liabilities and equity	$230,000	$250,000	$300,000

Additional Information
1 The overvalued inventory items were sold in September 19X3.
2 The undervalued items of equipment had a remaining use life of four years on April 1, 19X3.
3 Steve's net income for 19X3 was $80,000 ($60,000 from April 1 to December 31, 19X3).
4 On December 1, 19X3 Steve declared dividends of $2 per share, payable on January 10, 19X4
5 Any unidentified assets of Steve are to be amortized over a period of ten years.

Required
1 Prepare a schedule showing how the difference between Penny's investment cost and book value acquired should be allocated to identifiable and/or unidentifiable assets.
2 Calculate Penny's investment income from Steve for 19X3.
3 Determine the correct balance of Penny's investment in Steve account at December 31, 19X3.

P 2-14   Use the information in Problem 2–13, except change the per share market price to $8 per share.

Required
1 Prepare a schedule showing how the difference between Penny's investment cost and book value acquired should be allocated to identifiable and/or unidentifiable assets.
2 Calculate Penny's investment income from Steve for 19X3.
3 Determine the correct balance of Penny's investment in Steve account at December 31, 19X3.

3

AN INTRODUCTION
TO CONSOLIDATED
FINANCIAL STATEMENTS

This chapter contains background material necessary for understanding consolidated financial statements and provides an overview of the procedures involved in the consolidation process. The purchase method of accounting for business combinations is applied in the first part of the chapter, and pooled subsidiaries are covered at the end of the chapter. The parent company/investor is assumed to use the equity method of accounting for subsidiary investments. Further discussions of business combinations in this textbook assume purchase accounting unless the pooling of interests method is specifically identified.

BUSINESS COMBINATIONS CONSUMMATED THROUGH STOCK ACQUISITIONS

The accounting concept of a business combination, as described in *APB Opinion No. 16,* clearly includes those combinations in which one or more companies become subsidiaries of a common parent corporation. A corporation becomes a subsidiary when another corporation acquires a controlling interest in its outstanding voting stock. Ordinarily, a controlling interest in another corporation is obtained directly by acquiring a majority (over 50 percent) of its voting stock, but there are exceptions. These exceptions usually involve indirect stock ownership situations, and they are covered in Chapter 9 of this book.[1] Until Chapter 9, assume that direct ownership of a majority of the voting stock of another corporation is required for control and in order to have a parent-subsidiary relationship.

A business combination is consummated when one corporation acquires over 50 percent of the voting stock of another corporation, but once a parent-subsidiary relationship is established, the purchase of additional subsidiary shares is not a business combination. In other words, separate entities can combine only once. Increasing a controlling interest is simply an additional investment. The acquisition of additional shares of a subsidiary is accounted for by the purchase method as explained in paragraph 43 of *APB Opinion No. 16:*

---

[1]See *ARB No. 51,* "Consolidated Financial Statements," paragraph 2.

The acquisition after the effective date of this Opinion of some or all of the stock held by minority stockholders of a subsidiary—whether acquired by the parent, the subsidiary itself, or another affiliate—should be accounted for by the purchase method rather than by the pooling of interests method.

The Reporting Entity

A business combination brings two previously separate corporations under the control of a single management team (the officers and directors of the parent company). Although both corporations continue to exist as separate legal entities, the purchase creates a new reporting entity that encompasses all operations controlled by the management of the parent company.

When an investment in voting stock creates a parent-subsidiary relationship, the purchasing entity (parent company) and the entity acquired (subsidiary) continue to function as separate entities and to maintain their accounting records on a separate legal basis. Financial statements for the combined entity are constructed by converting the separate parent company and subsidiary statements into consolidated financial statements that reflect the financial position and the results of operations of the combined entity. The new reporting entity is responsible for reporting to the stockholders and creditors of the parent company and to other interested parties.

The Parent-Subsidiary Relationship

A corporation that owns over 50 percent of the voting stock of another corporation is able to control that corporation through its stock ownership, and a ***parent-subsidiary relationship*** exists between two corporations. When parent-subsidiary relationships exist, the companies are *affiliated*. Often the term ***affiliate*** is used to mean *subsidiary,* and the two terms are used interchangeably in this book and throughout much of the literature of accounting. The *Paramount Communications Inc. 1990 Annual Report* includes this note: "The consolidated financial statements include the accounts of Paramount Communications Inc. . . . and its majority-owned affiliates" (page 36). In many annual reports, however, the term *affiliate* is used to include all investments accounted for by the equity method. The following excerpt from the *1990 Sun Company Annual Report* is an example of this latter usage of the term affiliate: "Affiliated companies (20 to 50 percent owned but not controlled) are accounted for by the equity method" (page 21).

Other companies have adopted the term *associated* to refer to equity investments of 20 to 50 percent of the voting interests in other companies. For example, the *Quantum Chemical Corporation 1990 Annual Report* includes the following note: "Associated companies (50% owned) are accounted for under the equity method, i.e., at cost, increased or decreased by the Company's share of earnings or losses, less distributions" (page 29). The *Kimberly-Clark Corporation 1990 Annual Report* explains that "investments in significant nonconsolidated companies which are at least 20 percent owned are stated at cost plus equity in undistributed net income. These latter companies are referred to as equity companies" (page 17).

An affiliation structure with two subsidiaries is illustrated in Exhibit 3–1 which shows Percy Company owning 90 percent of the voting stock of San Del Corporation and 80 percent of the voting stock of Saltz Corporation. Percy Company owns 90 percent of the voting stock of San Del, and stockholders outside the affiliation structure own the other 10 percent. These outside stockholders are the minority stockholders, and their interest is referred to as a ***minority interest.*** Outside stockholders have a 20 percent minority interest in Saltz Corporation.

Percy Company and each of its subsidiaries are separate legal entities for which separate accounting records are maintained. In its separate records Percy Company uses the equity method described in Chapter 2 to account for its investments in San Del and Saltz Corporations. For reporting purposes, however, the equity method of reporting usually does not result in the most meaningful financial statements. This is because the parent, through its stock ownership, is able to elect subsidiary directors and control all subsidiary decisions, including dividend declarations. Although affiliated companies are separate legal entities, there is really only one economic entity because all resources are under control of a single management—the directors and officers of the parent company.

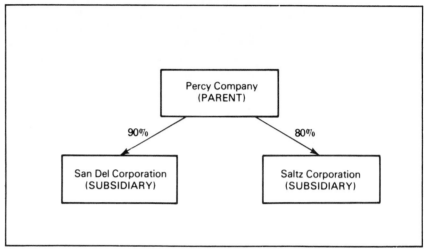

Exhibit 3–1   *Affiliation Structure*

The opening paragraph of *ARB No. 51,* "Consolidated Financial Statements," states that:

> the purpose of consolidated statements is to present, primarily for the benefit of stockholders and creditors of the parent company, the results of operations and the financial position of a parent company and its subsidiaries essentially as if the group were a single company with one or more branches or divisions.

Thus, consolidated statements are intended primarily for the parent company's investors rather than for the minority stockholders and subsidiary creditors. (The subsidiary, as a separate legal entity, continues to report the results of its own operations to the minority shareholders.)

Consolidation Policy

Consolidated financial statements provide much information that is not included in the separate statements of the parent corporation, and they are usually required for fair presentation of the financial position and results of operations for a group of affiliated companies. The usual condition for consolidation is ownership of over 50 percent of the voting stock of another company.[2] Under the provisions of *FASB Statement No. 94,* "Consolidation of All Majority-owned Subsidiaries," a subsidiary can be excluded from consolidation in only two situations: (1) where control is likely to be temporary or (2) where control does not rest with the majority owner. Control does not rest with the majority owner if the subsidiary is in legal reorganization, or in bankruptcy, or operating under severe foreign exchange restrictions, controls, or other governmentally imposed uncertainties.

---

[2]The Financial Accounting Standards Board is considering a consolidation policy based on control, rather than majority ownership, and expects to develop a position on this issue in 1991 (*FASB Status Report 216,* January 3, 1991).

History   *ARB No. 51,* issued in 1959, allowed parent company management broad discretion in determining consoidation policy as long as the objective was to provide the most meaningful financial presentation in the circumstances. Many firms adopted a policy of excluding from consolidation those subsidiaries whose operations differed greatly from those of the parent company. Manufacturing and merchandising companies routinely excluded their finance, insurance, and real estate subsidiaries. These "nonhomogeneous" subsidiaries were included in the financial statements as unconsolidated subsidiaries and accounted for by the equity method. As you learned in Chapter 2, accounting for an investee by the equity method provides the same net income as consolidating the accounts of the parent and subsidiary corporations. However, the assets, liabilities, revenues, and expenses of the unconsolidated subsidiary are not included in the financial statements under the equity method. It was concern over the possible omission of significant amounts of debt from the balance sheet that prompted the issuance of *FASB Statement No. 94* in 1987.

Disclosure of Consolidation Policies   A description of significant accounting policies is required for financial reporting under *APB Opinion No. 22,* "Disclosure of Accounting Policies," and traditionally, consolidation policy disclosures were among the most frequent of all policy disclosures. Since *FASB Statement No. 94* eliminates acceptable alternative consolidation policies, consolidation policy disclosures under *APB Opinion No. 22* are only needed to report exceptions (temporary control or inability to control) to the *Statement 94* requirement for consolidation of all majority-owned subsidiaries. Even so, the disclosure of consolidation policies in annual reports is not likely to decline significantly because the Securities and Exchange Commission (SEC) requires publicly held companies to report their consolidation policies under Regulation S–X, Rule 3A–03. The consolidation policy is usually presented under a heading such as "principles of consolidation" or "basis of consolidation." The 1990 edition of *Accounting Trends & Techniques* reports that 582 out of 600 companies surveyed for 1989 included the consolidation basis in their accounting policy disclosures.[3]

Parent and Subsidiary with Different Fiscal Periods

When the fiscal periods of the parent company and its subsidiaries are different, consolidated statements are prepared for and as of the end of the parent's fiscal period. If the difference in fiscal periods is not in excess of three months, it usually is acceptable to use the subsidiary's statements for its fiscal year for consolidation purposes, with disclosure of "the effect of intervening events which materially affect the financial position or results of operations.[4] Otherwise, the statements of the subsidiary should be adjusted so that they correspond as closely as possible to the fiscal period of the parent company. The Upjohn Company included the following note in its 1990 annual report: "Subsidiaries' fiscal years end November 30, with few exceptions, to facilitate consolidation of financial statements." Similarly, General Cinema Corporation reported: "All majority-owned subsidiaries are included in the consolidated financial statements. The financial statements of The Neiman Marcus Group, Inc. (NMG) are consolidated with a lag of one fiscal quarter."

---

[3]*Accounting Trends & Techniques—1990* (New York: American Institute of Certified Public Accountants, 1990), p. 27.

[4]*ARB No. 51,* paragraph 5.

CONSOLIDATED BALANCE SHEET AT DATE OF ACQUISITION

A consolidated entity is a fictitious (conceptual) reporting entity that is based on the assumption that the financial statements of separate legal and accounting entities of the parent and subsidiaries can be combined into a single meaningful set of financial statements for external reporting purposes. It is important to note that the consolidated entity does not have transactions and it does not maintain a ledger of accounts.

Parent Acquires 100 Percent of Subsidiary at Book Value

The basic differences between separate company and consolidated balance sheets can be seen by examining Exhibit 3–2. Penn Corporation acquires 100 percent of Skelly Corporation at its book value and fair value of $40,000 in a purchase business combination on January 1, 19X1. The balance sheets shown in Exhibit 3–2 are prepared immediately after the investment. Penn's "investment in Skelly" appears in the separate balance sheet of Penn, but not in the consolidated balance sheet for Penn and Subsidiary. When the balance sheets are consolidated, the investment in Skelly account (Penn's books) and the stockholders' equity accounts (Skelly's books) are eliminated because they are *reciprocal*—both representing the net assets of Skelly Corporation at January 1, 19X1. The nonreciprocal accounts of Penn and Skelly are combined and included in the consolidated balance sheet of Penn Corporation and Subsidiary. Note

	Separate Balance Sheets		Consolidated Balance Sheet:
	Penn	*Skelly*	*Penn and Subsidiary*
Assets			
Current assets			
Cash	$ 20,000	$10,000	$ 30,000
Other current assets	45,000	15,000	60,000
Total current assets	65,000	25,000	90,000
Plant assets	75,000	45,000	120,000
Less: Accumulated depreciation	(15,000)	(5,000)	(20,000)
Total plant assets	60,000	40,000	100,000
Investment in Skelly—100%	40,000	—	—
Total assets	$165,000	$65,000	$190,000
Liabilities and Stockholders' Equity			
Current liabilities			
Accounts payable	$ 20,000	$15,000	$ 35,000
Other current liabilities	25,000	10,000	35,000
Total current liabilities	45,000	25,000	70,000
Stockholders' equity			
Capital stock	100,000	30,000	100,000
Retained earnings	20,000	10,000	20,000
Total stockholders' equity	120,000	40,000	120,000
Total liabilities and stockholders' equity	$165,000	$65,000	$190,000

Exhibit 3–2 *100 Percent Ownership Acquired at Book Value*

that the consolidated balance sheet is not merely a summation of account balances of the affiliated corporations. *Reciprocal accounts are eliminated in the process of consolidation, and only nonreciprocal accounts are combined.* The capital stock that appears in a consolidated balance sheet is the capital stock of the parent company, and the consolidated retained earnings is the retained earnings of the parent company.

Parent Acquires 100 Percent of Subsidiary—with Goodwill

The consolidated balance sheet presented in Exhibit 3–2 was prepared for a parent company that purchased all the stock of Skelly Corporation at book value. If, instead, Penn purchases all of Skelly's stock for $50,000, there will be an excess of investment cost over book value acquired of $10,000 ($50,000 investment cost less $40,000 stockholders' equity of Skelly). The $10,000 appears in the consolidated balance sheet at acquisition as an asset of $10,000. In the absence of evidence that identifiable net assets are undervalued, this asset is assumed to be goodwill. Procedures for preparing a consolidated balance sheet are illustrated in Exhibit 3–3 for Penn Corporation, assuming that Penn pays $50,000 for all the stock of Skelly.

PENN CORPORATION AND SUBSIDIARY
CONSOLIDATED BALANCE SHEET WORKING PAPERS
JANUARY 1, 19X1

	Penn	100% Skelly	Adjustments and Eliminations Debits	Credits	Consolidated Balance Sheet
Assets					
Cash	$ 10,000	$10,000			$ 20,000
Other current assets	45,000	15,000			60,000
Plant assets	75,000	45,000			120,000
Accumulated depreciation	15,000*	5,000*			20,000*
Investment in Skelly	50,000			a 50,000	
Goodwill			a 10,000		10,000
Total assets	$165,000	$65,000			$190,000
Liabilities and Equity					
Accounts payable	$ 20,000	$15,000			$ 35,000
Other current liabilities	25,000	10,000			35,000
Capital stock—Penn	100,000				100,000
Retained earnings—Penn	20,000				20,000
Capital stock—Skelly		30,000	a 30,000		
Retained earnings—Skelly		10,000	a 10,000		
Total liabilities and stockholders' equity	$165,000	$65,000			$190,000

* Deduct.
a To eliminate reciprocal investment and equity accounts and to assign the excess of investment cost over book value acquired to goodwill.

Exhibit 3–3   *100 Percent Ownership: Cost $10,000 Greater than Book Value*

Only one working paper entry is required to consolidate the balance sheets of Penn and Skelly at acquisition. The entry is reproduced in general journal form for convenient reference:

a	Capital stock	$30,000	
	Retained earnings	10,000	
	Goodwill	10,000	
	Investment in Skelly		$50,000

To eliminate reciprocal investment and equity accounts and to assign the excess of investment cost over book value acquired to goodwill.

Entries such as those shown in Exhibit 3–3 are only working paper adjustments and eliminations and are not recorded in the accounts of the parent or subsidiary corporations. The entries will never be journalized or posted. Their only purpose is to facilitate completion of the working papers to consolidate a parent and subsidiary at and for the period ended at a particular date. In this book, working paper entries are shaded to avoid confusing them with actual journal entries that are recorded in the accounts of the parent and subsidiary companies.

In future periods the difference between the investment account balance and the subsidiary equity will decline as goodwill is amortized. If goodwill is amortized over a ten-year period, the difference between the balance in the investment in Skelly account and total stockholders' equity of Skelly at December 31, 19X1 will be $9,000; at December 31, 19X5, $5,000; and so on.

Parent Acquires 90 Percent of Subsidiary—with Goodwill

Assume that instead of acquiring all of Skelly's outstanding stock, Penn acquires 90 percent of Skelly's stock for $50,000. In this case, the excess of investment cost over book value acquired is $14,000 ($50,000 cost less $36,000 book value acquired), and there is a minority interest in Skelly of $4,000 ($40,000 equity × 10% minority interest). Procedures for preparing the consolidated balance sheet for Penn and Skelly under the 90 percent ownership assumption are illustrated in the working papers that appear in Exhibit 3–4.

The working paper entry to consolidate the balance sheets of Penn and Skelly and recognize the minority interest in Skelly at the date of acquisition is:

a	Capital stock—Skelly	$30,000	
	Retained earnings—Skelly	10,000	
	Goodwill	14,000	
	Investment in Skelly		$50,000
	Minority interest		4,000

To eliminate reciprocal investment and equity accounts, to assign the $14,000 excess of investment cost ($50,000) over book value acquired ($36,000) to goodwill, and to recognize a $4,000 minority interest in the net asets of Skelly ($40,000 equity × 10% minority interest).

Classification of Minority Interest

Since working papers provide the basis of preparing formal financial statements, the question arises as to how the $4,000 minority interest that appears in Exhibit 3–4 would be reported in a formal balance sheet. Although practice varies with respect to classification, the minority interest in subsidiaries is generally shown in a single amount in the liability section of the consolidated balance sheet, frequently under the heading of noncurrent liabilities.[5] Conceptually, classi-

---

[5]*Accounting Trends & Techniques—1990* shows that 130 of the 600 reporting corporations reported minority interest in the "Other Noncurrent Liabilities" section of the balance sheet in 1989 (p. 179).

PENN CORPORATION AND SUBSIDIARY
CONSOLIDATED BALANCE SHEET WORKING PAPERS
JANUARY 1, 19X1

	Penn	90% Skelly	Adjustments and Eliminations		Consolidated Balance Sheet
			Debits	Credits	
Assets					
Cash	$ 10,000	$10,000			$ 20,000
Other current assets	45,000	15,000			60,000
Plant assets	75,000	45,000			120,000
Accumulated depreciation	15,000*	5,000*			20,000*
Investment in Skelly	50,000			a 50,000	
Goodwill			a 14,000		14,000
Total assets	$165,000	$65,000			$194,000
Liabilities and Equity					
Accounts payable	$ 20,000	$15,000			$ 35,000
Other current liabilities	25,000	10,000			35,000
Capital stock—Penn	100,000				100,000
Retained earnings—Penn	20,000				20,000
Capital stock—Skelly		30,000	a 30,000		
Retained earnings—Skelly		10,000	a 10,000		
	$165,000	$65,000			
Minority interest				a 4,000	4,000
Total liabilities and stockholders' equity					$194,000

* Deduct.
a To eliminate reciprocal investment and equity accounts, to assign the $14,000 excess of investment cost ($50,000) over book value acquired ($36,000) to goodwill, and to recognize a $4,000 minority interest in the net assets of Skelly ($40,000 equity × 10% minority interest).

Exhibit 3–4   90 Percent Ownership; Cost $14,000 Greater than Book Value

fying minority stockholders' interests as liabilities or deferred credits is inconsistent because the interests of minority stockholders represent equity investments in the consolidated net assets by stockholders outside the affiliation structure. The alternatives are to include the minority interest in consolidated stockholders' equity or in a separate minority interest section. When classified as stockholders' equity, the minority interest should be separated from the equity of majority stockholders, that is, stockholders of the parent company. (See Chapter 11 for more discussion on the presentation of minority interests.)

Comparison of Equity Method and Consolidation

The following example illustrates the difference between consolidation and the equity method. In 1988 a new company, Qualex, Inc., was formed when Fuqua Industries combined its photofinishing operations with the domestic photofinishing operations of Eastman Kodak Co. A financial statement note in Fuqua's annual report describes the ownership interests in Qualex as follows:

In accordance with the shareholders' agreement, Fuqua received 51% of the voting stock of Qualex represented by 50% of the common stock and 100% of the voting preferred stock. Kodak received 49% of the voting stock of Qualex represented by the remaining common stock and, in addition, received nonvoting preferred stock. The board of directors is composed of seven members, four of whom are representatives of Fuqua. Certain decisions, which are specified in the agreement, require the concurrence of Kodak's representatives on the board.

Fuqua has consolidated the accounts of Qualex as Fuqua has a controlling interest in the new company. Kodak's portion of ownership and equity in the income of Qualex are reflected in Fuqua's consolidated financial statements as a minority interest.

Fuqua reported the assets, liabilities, revenues, and expenses of Qualex in its consolidated financial statements, and it reported "minority interest in Photofinishing Subsidiary" at $185,000,000 as the last item in the liability section of its balance sheet. Eastman Kodak, on the other hand, reported its equity investment in Qualex on one line of its balance sheet and its income from Qualex on one line of its income statement.

CONSOLIDATED BALANCE SHEETS AFTER ACQUISITION

The account balances of both parent and subsidiary corporations change to reflect their separate operations after the parent-subsidiary relationship is established, and additional adjustments may be necessary to eliminate other reciprocal balances in preparing consolidated balance sheets. If a consolidated balance sheet is prepared between the time a subsidiary declares and the time it pays dividends, the parent's books will show a dividend receivable account that is the reciprocal of a dividends payable account on the books of the subsidiary. Since such balances do not represent amounts receivable or payable outside the affiliated grouping, they are reciprocals and are eliminated in preparing consolidated statements. Other intercompany receivables and payables such as accounts receivable and accounts payable are reciprocal items that require elimination in preparing consolidated statements.

The balance sheets of Penn and Skelly Corporations at December 31, 19X1, one year after affiliation, contain the following:

	Penn	Skelly
Cash	$ 22,400	$15,000
Dividends receivable	9,000	—
Other current assets	41,000	28,000
Plant assets	75,000	45,000
Accumulated depreciation	(20,000)	(8,000)
Investment in Skelly (90%)	57,600	—
Total assets	$185,000	$80,000
Accounts payable	$ 30,000	$15,000
Dividends payable	—	10,000
Other current liabilities	20,000	5,000
Capital stock	100,000	30,000
Retained earnings	35,000	20,000
Total equities	$185,000	$80,000

Assumptions

1 Penn acquired a 90 percent interest in Skelly for $50,000 on January 1, 19X1 when Skelly's stockholders' equity was $40,000 (see Exhibit 3–4).
2 The accounts payable of Skelly include $5,000 owed to Penn.
3 Goodwill is amortized over a ten-year period.
4 During 19X1 Skelly had net income of $20,000 and declared dividends of $10,000.

Consolidated balance sheet working papers reflecting the above information are shown in Exhibit 3–5. The balance in the investment in Skelly account at December 31, 19X1 is determined using the equity method of accounting. Calculations of the December 31, 19X1 investment account balance are as follows:

Original investment January 1, 19X1	$50,000
Add: 90% of Skelly's $20,000 net income for 19X1	18,000
Deduct: 90% of Skelly's $10,000 dividends for 19X1	(9,000)
Deduct: Goodwill amortization ($14,000/10 years)	(1,400)
Investment account balance December 31, 19X1	$57,600

PENN CORPORATION AND SUBSIDIARY
CONSOLIDATED BALANCE SHEET WORKING PAPERS
DECEMBER 31, 19X1

	Penn	90% Skelly	Adjustments and Eliminations Debits	Adjustments and Eliminations Credits	Consolidated Balance Sheet
Assets					
Cash	$ 22,400	$15,000			$ 37,400
Dividends receivable	9,000			b 9,000	
Other current assets	41,000	28,000		c 5,000	64,000
Plant assets	75,000	45,000			120,000
Accumulated depreciation	20,000*	8,000*			28,000*
Investment in Skelly	57,600			a 57,600	
Goodwill			a 12,600		12,600
Total assets	$185,000	$80,000			$206,000
Liabilities and Equity					
Accounts payable	$ 30,000	$15,000	c 5,000		$ 40,000
Dividends payable		10,000	b 9,000		1,000
Other current liabilities	20,000	5,000			25,000
Capital stock—Penn	100,000				100,000
Retained earnings—Penn	35,000				35,000
Capital stock—Skelly		30,000	a 30,000		
Retained earnings—Skelly		20,000	a 20,000		
	$185,000	$80,000			
Minority interest				a 5,000	5,000
Total liabilities and stockholders' equity					$206,000

* Deduct.
a To eliminate reciprocal investment and equity accounts, to record unamortized goodwill ($14,000 less $1,400 amortization), and to enter the minority interest ($50,000 × 10%).
b To eliminate reciprocal dividends receivable and payable amounts (90% of $10,000 dividends payable of Skelly).
c To eliminate intercompany accounts receivable and accounts payable.

Exhibit 3–5   90 Percent Ownership; Consolidation One Year after Acquisition.

Even though the amounts involved are different, the *process* of consolidating balance sheets after acquisition is basically the same as for consolidating at acquisition. In all cases, the amount of the subsidiary investment account is eliminated and the equity accounts of the subsidiary are eliminated. The excess of the investment account balance over the book value of the interest owned (goodwill in this illustration) is entered in the working papers during the process of eliminating reciprocal investment and equity balances. Goodwill does not appear on the books of the parent and is added to the asset listing when the working papers are prepared. The minority interest is equal to the percentage of minority ownership times the equity of the subsidiary at the balance sheet date. Consolidated retained earnings is equal to the retained earnings of the parent.

The working paper entries necessary to consolidate the balance sheets of Penn and Skelly are reproduced in general journal form for convenient reference:

a	Capital stock—Skelly	$30,000	
	Retained earnings—Skelly	20,000	
	Goodwill	12,600	
	Investment in Skelly		$57,600
	Minority interest		5,000

To eliminate reciprocal investment and equity accounts, to record unamortized goodwill ($14,000 less $1,400 amortization for 19X1), and to enter the minority interest ($50,000 × 10%).

b	Dividends payable	$ 9,000	
	Dividends receivable		$ 9,000

To eliminate reciprocal dividends receivable and payable amounts (90% of $10,000 dividends payable of Skelly).

c	Accounts payable	$ 5,000	
	Accounts receivable		$ 5,000

To eliminate intercompany accounts receivable and accounts payable.

ALLOCATION OF EXCESS TO IDENTIFIABLE NET ASSETS AND GOODWILL

The excess of investment cost over book value of the interest acquired in the Penn-Skelly illustration was assigned to goodwill. An underlying assumption of that assignment of the excess is that the book values and fair values of identifiable assets and liabilities are equal. When the evidence indicates that fair values exceed book values or book values exceed fair values, however, the excess must be allocated accordingly. For example, when Fedders Corporation acquired an operating division from Camco, Inc., the $11,387,000 excess of the purchase price over the fair value of tangible assets was assigned to a non-compete agreement ($8,562,000), goodwill ($1,636,000), and other items including sales backlog and patents ($1,189,000).

Effect of Allocation on Consolidated Balance Sheet at Acquisition

In acquisitions involving parent–subsidiary relationships, the cost–book value differentials are *not* recorded on the books of the parent companies or subsidiaries. Therefore, the amounts that appear in a consolidated balance sheet of a parent company and its subsidiary are entered through working paper procedures that adjust the subsidiary book values to reflect the cost–book value differential. The amount of adjustment to individual asset and liability accounts is determined by means of the approach illustrated in Chapter 2 for one-line consolidations.

Accounting procedures for a purchase business combination consummated through stock acquisition are illustrated in this section for the combination of Pilot and Sand Corporations. Comparative book value and fair value information for Pilot and Sand immediately before their combination on December 31, 19X1 is presented in Exhibit 3–6.

	Pilot Corporation		Sand Corporation	
	Per Books	Fair Values	Per Books	Fair Values
Assets				
Cash	$ 6,600,000	$ 6,600,000	$ 200,000	$ 200,000
Receivables—net	700,000	700,000	300,000	300,000
Inventories	900,000	1,200,000	500,000	600,000
Other current assets	600,000	800,000	400,000	400,000
Land	1,200,000	11,200,000	600,000	800,000
Buildings—net	8,000,000	15,000,000	4,000,000	5,000,000
Equipment—net	7,000,000	9,000,000	2,000,000	1,700,000
Total assets	$25,000,000	$44,500,000	$8,000,000	$9,000,000
Liabilities and Equity				
Accounts payable	$ 2,000,000	$ 2,000,000	$ 700,000	$ 700,000
Notes payable	3,700,000	3,500,000	1,400,000	1,300,000
Common stock—$10 par	10,000,000 ⎫		4,000,000 ⎫	
Additional paid-in capital	5,000,000 ⎬	39,000,000	1,000,000 ⎬	7,000,000
Retained earnings	4,300,000 ⎭		900,000 ⎭	
Total liabilities and stockholders' equity	$25,000,000	$44,500,000	$8,000,000	$9,000,000

Exhibit 3–6 *Preacquisition Book and Fair Value Balance Sheets*

On December 31, 19X1 Pilot purchases 90 percent of Sand Corporation's outstanding voting common stock directly from Sand Corporation's stockholders for $5,000,000 cash plus 100,000 shares of Pilot Corporation $10 par common stock with a market value of $5,000,000. Additional costs of combination consist of $100,000 for registering and issuing the common stock and $200,000 for other costs of combination. These additional costs are paid in cash by Pilot. Pilot and Sand must continue to operate as parent company and subsidiary because 10 percent of Sand's shares are outstanding and held by minority stockholders.

Pilot records the business combination on its books with the following journal entries:

```
Investment in Sand                        $10,000,000
    Common stock                                          $1,000,000
    Additional paid-in capital                             4,000,000
    Cash                                                   5,000,000
```
To record acquisition of 90% of Sand Corporation's outstanding stock for $5,000,000 in cash and 100,000 shares of Pilot common stock with a value of $5,000,000.

```
Investment in Sand                         $200,000
Additional paid-in capital                  100,000
    Cash                                                   $300,000
```
To record additional costs of combining with Sand.

These are the only entries necessary on Pilot's books to record the business combination of Pilot and Sand. No entries are recorded by Sand because Pilot acquired its 90 percent interest directly from Sand's stockholders. The balance sheet information given in Exhibit 3–6 is not used in recording the business combination on Pilot's books, but it is used in preparing the consolidated balance sheet for the combined entity immediately after combination.

Allocating the Cost–Book Value Differential   The adjustments necessary to combine the balance sheets of parent and subsidiary corporations are determined by *assigning the difference between investment cost and the book value acquired to identifiable assets and liabilities and then to goodwill for any remainder.* The schedule to determine the adjustments necessary to consolidate the balance sheets of Pilot and Sand at December 31, 19X1 is presented in Exhibit 3–7.

Although the book values of assets and liabilities are not used in determining fair values for individual assets and liabilities (these are usually determined by management), book values are used in the mechanical process of combining the balance sheets of parent and subsidiary.

The underlying book value of the 90 percent interest acquired in Sand Corporation is $5,310,000 (as shown in Exhibit 3–7), and the excess of investment cost over book value acquired is $4,890,000. This excess is allocated first to the identifiable assets acquired and liabilites assumed, and the remainder is assigned to goodwill. The amounts assigned to identifiable assets and liabilities are only 90 percent of the differences between the fair values and the book values. This is because the price paid by Pilot Corporation is for 90 percent of the identifiable assets less liabilities of Sand Corporation. The other 10 percent of Sand's identifiable net assets relates to the interests of minority stockholders, which are not adjusted to their fair values on the basis of the price paid by Pilot for its 90 percent interest.[6] The cost–book value differences are determined by and allocated to the interest acquired by the parent/investor.

PILOT CORPORATION AND ITS 90% OWNED SUBSIDIARY, SAND CORPORATION

Investment in Sand—cost	$10,200,000
Book value of interest acquired	
90% × $5,900,000 equity of Sand	5,310,000
Total excess of cost over book value acquired	$ 4,890,000

Allocation of Identifiable Assets and Liabilities

	Fair Value	−	Book Value	×	Interest Acquired	=	Excess Allocated
Inventories	$ 600,000		$ 500,000		90%		$ 90,000
Land	800,000		600,000		90		180,000
Buildings	5,000,000		4,000,000		90		900,000
Equipment	1,700,000		2,000,000		90		(270,000)
Notes payable	1,300,000		1,400,000		90		90,000
Total allocated to identifiable net assets							$ 990,000
Remainder allocated to goodwill							3,900,000
Total excess of cost over book value acquired							$ 4,890,000

Exhibit 3–7   *Schedule for Allocating the Excess of Investment Cost over the Book Value of the Interest Acquired*

---

[6]Revaluation of all assets and liabilities of a subsidiary on the basis of the price paid by the parent for its majority interest is supported by the entity theory of consolidations. Entity theory is covered in Chapter 11.

Working Paper Procedures to Enter Allocations in Consolidated Balance Sheet

The allocation of the excess cost over book value as determined in Exhibit 3–7 is incorporated into a consolidated balance sheet through working paper procedures. These procedures are illustrated in Exhibit 3–8 for Pilot and Sand as of the date of their affiliation. The consolidated balance sheet working papers show two working paper entries for the consolidation. Entry a is reproduced in general journal form as follows:

a	Unamortized excess	$4,890,000	
	Common stock—$10 par Sand	4,000,000	
	Additional paid-in capital—Sand	1,000,000	
	Retained earnings—Sand	900,000	
	Investment in Sand		$10,200,000
	Minority interest—10%		590,000

This working paper entry eliminates reciprocal investment in Sand and stockholders' equity amounts for Sand, establishes the minority interest in Sand, and enters the total unamortized excess from Exhibit 3–7.

A second working paper entry allocates the unamortized excess to individual assets and liabilities and to goodwill.

b	Inventories	$ 90,000	
	Land	180,000	
	Buildings—net	900,000	
	Goodwill	3,900,000	
	Notes payable	90,000	
	Equipment—net		$ 270,000
	Unamortized excess		4,890,000

The *unamortized excess account* is used to simplify working paper entries when the investment cost-book value differential is allocated to numerous asset and liability accounts. But it is not needed when the total excess is allocated to goodwill, as in Exhibits 3–4 and 3–5. Since the two working paper entries enter equal debits and credits to the unamortized excess, the account has no final effect on the consolidated balance sheet.

Debit and credit working paper amounts are combined with the line items shown in the separate statements of Pilot and Sand to produce the amounts shown in the consolidated balance sheet column. Since Sand is a partially owned subsidiary, its assets and liabilities are not included in the consolidated balance sheet at either their fair values or their book values; that is, the consolidated assets and liabilities include Pilot's assets and liabilities at book value, plus Sand's assets and liabilities at book value, plus or minus unamortized cost–book value differentials from Pilot's investment in Sand.

Effect of Amortization on Consolidated Balance Sheet after Acquisition

In order to illustrate the effect of amortizing the $4,890,000 excess on Pilot and Sand's consolidated balance sheet at December 31, 19X2, it is necessary to make assumptions about the operations of Pilot and Sand during 19X2 and about the relevant amortization periods for the assets and liabilities to which the excess was allocated in Exhibit 3–7. These additional assumptions are:

Income for 19X2	
Sand's net income	$ 800,000
Pilot's income excluding income from Sand	2,523,500

PILOT CORPORATION AND SUBSIDIARY
CONSOLIDATED BALANCE SHEET WORKING PAPERS
AFTER COMBINATION ON DECEMBER 31, 19X1

	Pilot	90% Sand	Adjustments and Eliminations Debits	Adjustments and Eliminations Credits	Consolidated Balance Sheet
Assets					
Cash	$ 1,300,000	$ 200,000			$ 1,500,000
Receivables—net	700,000	300,000			1,000,000
Inventories	900,000	500,000	b 90,000		1,490,000
Other current assets	600,000	400,000			1,000,000
Land	1,200,000	600,000	b 180,000		1,980,000
Buildings—net	8,000,000	4,000,000	b 900,000		12,900,000
Equipment—net	7,000,000	2,000,000		b 270,000	8,730,000
Investment in Sand	10,200,000			a 10,200,000	
Goodwill			b 3,900,000		3,900,000
Unamortized excess			a 4,890,000	b 4,890,000	
Total assets	$29,900,000	$8,000,000			$32,500,000
Liabilities and Equity					
Accounts payable	$ 2,000,000	$ 700,000			$ 2,700,000
Notes payable	3,700,000	1,400,000	b 90,000		5,010,000
Common stock—Pilot	11,000,000				11,000,000
Other paid-in capital—Pilot	8,900,000				8,900,000
Retained earnings— Pilot	4,300,000				4,300,000
Common stock—Sand		4,000,000	a 4,000,000		
Other paid-in capital—Sand		1,000,000	a 1,000,000		
Retained earnings— Sand		900,000	a 900,000		
	$29,900,000	$8,000,000			
Minority interest				a 590,000	590,000
Total liabilities and stockholders' equity					$32,500,000

a To eliminate reciprocal subsidiary investment and equity accounts, establish minority interest, and enter the unamortized excess.

b To allocate the unamortized excess to identifiable assets, liabilities, and goodwill.

Exhibit 3–8 *90 Percent Ownership; Excess Allocated to Identifiable Net Assets and Goodwill*

Dividends Paid in 19X2

Sand	$ 300,000
Pilot	1,500,000

Amoritization of Excess

Undervalued inventories—sold in 19X2
Undervalued land—still held by Sand; no amortization
Undervalued buildings—use life 45 years from January 1, 19X2
Overvalued equipment—use life 5 years from January 1, 19X2
Overvalued notes payable—retired in 19X2
Goodwill—to be amortized over 40 years

At December 31, 19X2 Pilot's investment in Sand account has a balance of $10,406,500, consisting of the original $10,200,000 cost, increased by $476,500 investment income from Sand, and decreased by $270,000 dividends received from Sand. Pilot's income from Sand for 19X2 is calculated under a one-line consolidation as follows:

Equity in Sand's net income ($800,000 × 90%)		$720,000
Add: Amortization of overvalued equipment		
($270,000 ÷ 5 years)		54,000
Deduct: Amortization of excess allocated to:		
Inventories (sold in 19X2)	$90,000	
Land	—	
Buildings ($900,000 ÷ 45 years)	20,000	
Notes payable (retired in 19X2)	90,000	
Goodwill ($3,900,000 ÷ 40 years)	97,500	(297,500)
Income from Sand 19X2		$476,500

Pilot's net income for 19X2 is $3,000,000, consisting of income from its own operations of $2,523,500 plus $476,500 income from Sand. Sand's stockholders' equity increased $500,000 during 19X2, from $5,900,000 to $6,400,000. Pilot's retained earnings increased $1,500,000, from $4,300,000 at December 31, 19X1 to $5,800,000 at December 31, 19X2. This information is reflected in consolidated balance sheet working papers for Pilot and Subsidiary at December 31, 19X2 (see Exhibit 3–9). Working papers entries are reproduced as follows:

a	Common stock—Sand	$4,000,000	
	Other paid-in capital—Sand	1,000,000	
	Retained earnings—Sand	1,400,000	
	Unamortized excess	4,646,500	
	Investment in Sand		$10,406,500
	Minority interest		640,000

    To eliminate reciprocal subsidiary investment and equity accounts, establish minority interest, and enter the unamortized excess.

b	Land	$ 180,000	
	Buildings—net	880,000	
	Goodwill	3,802,500	
	Equipment—net		$ 216,000
	Unamortized excess		4,646,500

    To allocate the unamortized excess to identifiable assets and goodwill.

The differences in the adjustments and eliminations in Exhibits 3–8 and 3–9 result from changes that occurred between December 31, 19X1 when the investment was acquired and December 31, 19X2 after the investment had been held for one year. The following schedule provides the basis for the working paper entries that appear in Exhibit 3–9.

PILOT CORPORATION AND SUBSIDIARY
CONSOLIDATED BALANCE SHEET WORKING PAPERS
ON DECEMBER 31, 19X2

	Pilot	90% Sand	Adjustments and Eliminations Debits	Credits	Consolidated Balance Sheet
Assets					
Cash	$ 253,500	$ 100,000			$ 353,500
Receivables—net	540,000	200,000			740,000
Inventories	1,300,000	600,000			1,900,000
Other current assets	800,000	500,000			1,300,000
Land	1,200,000	600,000	b 180,000		1,980,000
Buildings—net	9,500,000	3,800,000	b 880,000		14,180,000
Equipment—net	8,000,000	1,800,000		b 216,000	9,584,000
Investment in Sand	10,406,500			a 10,406,500	
Goodwill			b 3,802,500		3,802,500
Unamortized excess			a 4,646,500	b 4,646,500	
Total assets	$32,000,000	$7,600,000			$33,840,000
Liabilities and Equity					
Accounts payable	$ 2,300,000	$1,200,000			$ 3,500,000
Notes payable	4,000,000				4,000,000
Common stock—Pilot	11,000,000				11,000,000
Other paid-in capital—Pilot	8,900,000				8,900,000
Retained earnings—Pilot	5,800,000				5,800,000
Common stock—Sand		4,000,000	a 4,000,000		
Other paid-in capital—Sand		1,000,000	a 1,000,000		
Retained earnings—Sand		1,400,000	a 1,400,000		
	$32,000,000	$7,600,000			
Minority interest				a 640,000	640,000
Total liabilities and stockholders' equity					$33,840,000

a To eliminate reciprocal subsidiary investment and equity accounts, establish minority interest, and enter the unamortized excess.
b To allocate the unamortized excess to identifiable assets and goodwill.

Exhibit 3–9   90 Percent Ownership; Unamortized Excess One Year after Acquisition

	Unamortized Excess December 31, 19X1	Amortization 19X2	Unamortized Excess December 31, 19X2
Inventories	$ 90,000	$ 90,000	$ —
Land	180,000	—	180,000
Buildings—net	900,000	20,000	880,000
Equipment—net	270,000*	54,000*	216,000*
Notes payable	90,000	90,000	—
Goodwill	3,900,000	97,500	3,802,500
	$4,890,000	$243,500	$4,646,500

*Excess book value over fair value.

The consolidated balance sheet working papers in Exhibit 3–9 show elimination of reciprocal stockholders' equity and investment in Sand accounts. This elimination, entry a, involves debits to Sand's stockholders' equity accounts of $6,400,000, a credit to the minority interest in Sand of $640,000, and a credit to the investment in Sand account of $10,406,500. The difference between these debit and credit eliminations totals $4,646,500, representing the unamortized excess of investment over book value acquired at December 31, 19X2, and is entered in the unamortized excess account.

Since the undervalued inventory items and the overvalued notes payable on Sand's books at December 31, 19X1 were fully amortized in 19X2 (the inventory was sold and the notes payable were retired), these items do not require balance sheet adjustments at December 31, 19X2. The remaining items—land, $180,000; buildings, $880,000; equipment, $216,000 (overvaluation); and goodwill, $3,802,500—account for the $4,646,500 unamortized excess and are entered in the consolidated balance sheet working papers through working paper entry b, which allocates the unamortized excess as of the balance sheet date. Technically, the working paper entries shown in Exhibit 3–9 are combination adjustment and elimination entries, since the investment in Sand and stockholders' equity accounts of Sand are eliminated, the minority interest is reclassified into a single amount representing 10 percent of Sand's stockholders' equity, and the asset accounts are adjusted.

CONSOLIDATED INCOME STATEMENT

Comparative separate company and consolidated income and retained earnings statements for Pilot Corporation and Subsidiary are shown in Exhibit 3–10. These statements reflect the previous assumptions and amounts that were used in preparing the consolidated balance sheet working papers for Pilot and Sand. Detailed revenue and expense items have been added in order to illustrate the consolidated income statement, but all assumptions and amounts are completely compatible with those already introduced. Adjustment and elimination entries have not been included in the illustration. These entries will be covered extensively in Chapter 4.

The difference between a consolidated income statement and an unconsolidated income statement of the parent company lies in the detail presented rather than the amount of net income. This can be seen in Exhibit 3–10 by comparing the separate income statement of Pilot with the consolidated income statement of Pilot and Subsidiary. Pilot's separate income statement shows the revenues and expenses from Pilot's own operations plus its investment income from Sand.[7]

---

[7]A parent company's income from subsidiary investments is referred to as income from subsidiary, equity in subsidiary earnings, investment income from subsidiary, or by other descriptive captions.

PILOT AND SAND CORPORATIONS
SEPARATE COMPANY AND CONSOLIDATED STATEMENTS
OF INCOME AND RETAINED EARNINGS
FOR THE YEAR ENDED DECEMBER 31, 19X2

	Separate Company		
	Pilot	Sand	Consolidated
Sales	$ 9,523,500	$2,200,000	$11,723,500
Investment income from Sand	476,500		
Total revenue	10,000,000	2,200,000	11,723,500
Less: Operating expenses			
Cost of sales	4,000,000	700,000	4,790,000
Depreciation expense—buildings	200,000	80,000	300,000
Depreciation expense—equipment	700,000	360,000	1,006,000
Goodwill amortization	—	—	97,500
Other expenses	1,800,000	120,000	1,920,000
Total operating expense	6,700,000	1,260,000	8,113,500
Operating income	3,300,000	940,000	3,610,000
Nonoperating item:			
Interest expense	300,000	140,000	530,000
Net income	**3,000,000**	**800,000**	
Total consolidated income			3,080,000
Less: Minority interest income			80,000
Consolidated net income			**3,000,000**
Retained earnings December 31, 19X1	4,300,000	900,000	4,300,000
	7,300,000	1,700,000	7,300,000
Deduct: Dividends	1,500,000	300,000	1,500,000
Retained earnings December 31, 19X2	$ 5,800,000	$1,400,000	$ 5,800,000

Exhibit 3–10   *Separate Company and Consolidated Income and Retained Earnings Statements*

By contrast, the consolidated income statement shows the revenues and expenses of both Sand and Pilot but does not show the investment income from Sand. The $476,500 investment income is excluded because the consolidated income statement includes the detailed revenues ($2,200,000), expenses ($1,400,000), net amortization of the excess ($243,500), and the minority interest deduction ($80,000) that account for the investment income. The net amortization is reflected in the consolidated income statement by increasing cost of goods sold for the $90,000 undervalued inventories that were sold in 19X2, increasing depreciation expense on buildings for the $20,000 amortization on the excess allocated to buildings, decreasing depreciation on equipment for the $54,000 amortization of the excess allocated to overvalued equipment, increasing interest expense for the $90,000 allocated to overvalued notes payable that were retired in 19X2, and adding a new expense category to reflect the $97,500 goodwill amortization.

Consolidated income statements, like consolidated balance sheets, are more than summations of the income accounts of affiliated companies. A summation of all income statement items for Pilot and Sand would result in a combined income figure of $3,800,000, whereas consolidated net income is only $3,000,000. The $800,000 difference between these two amounts lies in the investment income of $476,500, the $243,500 net amortization, and the $80,000 income allocated to minority stockholders.

It should be noted that consolidated net income represents income to the stockholders of the parent corporation. Income of minority stockholders is a deduction in the determination of consolidated net income.

If the parent company sells merchandise to its subsidiary or vice versa there will be intercompany purchases and sales on the separate books of the parent and its subsidiary. Intercompany purchases and sales balances are reciprocals that must be eliminated in preparing consolidated income statements because they do not represent purchases and sales to parties outside the consolidated entity. Adjustments for intercompany sales and purchases reduce revenue (sales) and expenses (cost of goods sold) by the same amount and therefore have no effect on consolidated net income. Reciprocal rent income and expense amounts are likewise eliminated without affecting consolidated net income.

Numerous other adjustments and eliminations arise in the preparation of consolidated income statements where the objective is to show the income for a parent company and its subsidiaries as if there were only one legal and accounting entity. Discussion of these additional complications is postponed until Chapter 4 and later chapters.

Observe that the amounts for Pilot's separate retained earnings are identical to those for consolidated retained earnings. As expected, the $5,800,000 ending consolidated retained earnings in Exhibit 3–10 is the amount of consolidated retained earnings that appears in the consolidated balance sheet for Pilot and Subsidiary at December 31, 19X2 (see Exhibit 3–9).

CONSOLIDATED STATEMENT OF CASH FLOWS

The consolidated statement of cash flows (SCF) is prepared from *consolidated* income statements and *consolidated* balance sheets rather than from the separate statements of parent companies and subsidiaries. With minor exceptions, the preparation of a consolidated SCF involves the same analysis and procedures that are used in preparing the SCF for separate entities.

Consolidated balance sheets at December 31, 19X5 and 19X6 and the 19X6 consolidated income statement for Polski Corporation and its 80 percent owned subsidiary, Seed Corporation, are presented in Exhibit 3–11. Consolidated balance sheets at the beginning and end of the year are used to calculate the year's changes which must be explained in the SCF. Other information pertinent to the preparation of Polski's consolidated SCF is as follows:

1 During 19X6 Seed sold land that cost $20,000 to outside entities for $10,000 cash.
2 Polski issued a $300,000, two-year note on January 8, 19X6 for new equipment.
3 Goodwill amortization from the Polski-Seed business combination is $10,000 per year.
4 Polski received $10,000 dividends from its investments in equity investees.
5 Changes in plant assets not explained above are due to provisions for depreciation.

The SCF is prepared using a single concept, cash and cash equivalents. Two presentations for reporting net cash flows from operations are permitted. The *indirect method* begins with consolidated net income and includes adjustments for items not providing or using cash to arrive at net cash flows from operations. Under the *direct method,* cash received from customers and investement income are offset against cash paid to suppliers, employees, governmental units, and so on in arriving at net cash flows from operations. Although the Financial Accounting Standards Board expressed a preference for the direct method of reporting net cash flows from operations,[8] the 1990 issue of *Accounting Trends & Techniques* reported that 17 of the 600 survey companies presenting a statement of cash flows used the direct method, while 583 used the indirect method.

---

[8]*FASB Statement No. 95,* "Statement of Cash Flows," paragraph 119.

POLSKI CORPORATION AND SUBSIDIARY
COMPARATIVE BALANCE SHEETS
AT DECEMBER 31

	19X6	19X5	Year's Change Increase (Decrease)
Cash	$ 255,000	$ 180,000	$ 75,000
Accounts receivable—net	375,000	270,000	105,000
Inventories	250,000	205,000	45,000
Equity investments	100,000	95,000	5,000
Land	80,000	100,000	(20,000)
Buildings—net	200,000	220,000	(20,000)
Equipment—net	800,000	600,000	200,000
Goodwill	90,000	100,000	(10,000)
	$2,150,000	$1,770,000	$380,000
Accounts payable	$ 250,000	$ 270,000	$ (20,000)
Dividends payable	20,000	20,000	—
Note payable due 19X8	300,000	—	300,000
Common stock	500,000	500,000	—
Other paid-in capital	300,000	300,000	—
Retained earnings	670,000	600,000	70,000
Minority interest—20%	110,000	80,000	30,000
	$2,150,000	$1,770,000	$380,000

CONSOLIDATED INCOME STATEMENT
FOR THE YEAR ENDED DECEMBER 31, 19X6

Sales		$750,000
Income from equity investees		15,000
Total revenue		765,000
Less expenses:		
Cost of goods sold	$300,000	
Depreciation expense	120,000	
Goodwill amortization	10,000	
Wages and salaries	54,000	
Other operating expenses	47,000	
Interest expense	24,000	
Loss on sale of land	10,000	(565,000)
Total consolidated income		200,000
Less: Minority interest income		(50,000)
Consolidated net income		150,000
Consolidated retained earnings January 1, 19X6		600,000
Less: Cash dividends paid		(80,000)
Consolidated retained earnings December 31, 19X6		$670,000

Exhibit 3–11 *Consolidated Balance Sheets and Income Statement for Polski and Subsidiary*

Consolidated Statement of Cash Flows— Indirect Method

A consolidated SCF is presented in Exhibit 3–12 for Polski Corporation and Subsidiary under the indirect method. This statement is based on the consolidated balance sheet changes and the 19X6 consolidated income statement shown in Exhibit 3–11 for Polski Corporation and Subsidiary. An SCF worksheet that organizes the information for statement preparation is presented in Exhibit 3–13

POLSKI CORPORATION AND SUBSIDIARY
CONSOLIDATED STATEMENT OF CASH FLOWS
FOR THE YEAR ENDED DECEMBER 31, 19X6

Cash Flows from Operating Activities		
Consolidated net income		$150,000
Adjustments to reconcile net income to cash provided by operating activities:		
Minority interest income	$ 50,000	
Undistributed income—equity investees	(5,000)	
Loss on sale of machinery	10,000	
Depreciation on equipment	100,000	
Depreciation on buildings	20,000	
Amortization of goodwill	10,000	
Increase in accounts receivable	(105,000)	
Increase in inventories	(45,000)	
Decrease in accounts payable	(20,000)	15,000
Net cash flows from operating activities		165,000
Cash Flows from Investing Activities		
Proceeds from sale of land	$ 10,000	
Net cash flows from investing activities		10,000
Cash Flows from Financing Activities		
Payment of cash dividends—majority	$ (80,000)	
Payment of cash dividends—minority	(20,000)	
Net cash flows from financing activities		(100,000)
Increase in cash for 19X6		75,000
Cash on January 1, 19X6		180,000
Cash on December 31, 19X6		$255,000

Listing of Non-cash Investing and Financing Activities

Equipment was purchased for $300,000 through the issuance of a two-year note payable.

Exhibit 3–12   *Consolidated Statement of Cash Flows—Indirect Method*

using the schedule approach. The consolidated SCF is prepared directly from the "cash flow from operations," "cash flow—investing activities," and "cash flow—financing activities" columns of the worksheet in Exhibit 3–13.

Minority interest income is an increase in the cash flow from operating activities because minority interest income increases consolidated assets and liabilities in exactly the same manner as consolidated net income. Similarly, minority interest dividends are deducted along with majority interest dividends in reporting the cash flows from financing activities.

Income and Dividends from Investees Under the Indirect and Direct Methods

Income from equity investees is an item that requires special attention in the consolidated SCF when the indirect method is used. Income from equity investees increases income without increasing cash because the increase is reflected in the investment account. Conversely, dividends received from equity investees increase cash but do not affect income because the decrease is reflected in the investment account. The net amount of these items (the change in the investment account) is deducted from (or added to) net income in the "cash flows from

POLSKI CORPORATION AND SUBSIDIARY
WORKING PAPERS FOR THE STATEMENT OF CASH FLOWS (INDIRECT METHOD)
FOR THE YEAR ENDED DECEMBER 31, 19X6

	Year's Change	Reconciling Items Debit		Reconciling Items Credit		Cash Flow from Operations	Cash Flow–Investing Activities	Cash Flow–Financing Activities
Asset Changes								
Cash	75,000							
Accounts receivable—net	105,000			k	105,000			
Inventories	45,000			l	45,000			
Equity investments	5,000			e	5,000			
Land	(20,000)	f	20,000					
Buildings—net	(20,000)	i	20,000					
Equipment—net	200,000	h	100,000	g	300,000			
Goodwill	(10,000)	j	10,000					
Total asset changes	380,000							
Equity Changes								
Accounts payable	(20,000)			m	20,000			
Dividends payable	0							
Note payable due 19X8*	300,000	g	300,000					
Common stock	0							
Other paid-in capital	0							
Retained earnings	70,000	a	150,000	b	80,000			
Minority interest	30,000	c	50,000	d	20,000			
Total equity changes	380,000							
Consolidated net income				a	150,000	150,000		
Minority interest income				c	50,000	50,000		
Income-equity investees		e	5,000			(5,000)		
Loss on sale of land				f	10,000	10,000		
Depreciation on equipment				h	100,000	100,000		
Depreciation on buildings				i	20,000	20,000		
Amortization of goodwill				j	10,000	10,000		
Increase in receivables		k	105,000			(105,000)		
Increase in inventories		l	45,000			(45,000)		
Decrease in accounts payable		m	20,000			(20,000)		
Proceeds from sale of land				e	10,000		10,000	
Payment of dividends—majority		b	80,000					(80,000)
Payment of dividends—minority		d	20,000					(20,000)
			925,000		925,000	165,000	10,000	(100,000)

Cash flows from operations	$ 165,000
Cash flows from investing activities	10,000
Cash flows from financing activities	(100,000)
Increase in cash for 19X6 = cash change above	$ 75,000

*Non-cash Investing and Financing Transaction: Equipment purchased for $300,000 by issuing a 2-year note payable.

Exhibit 3-13   *Worksheet for Consolidated SCF—Indirect Method*

operating activities" section of the SCF. An excess of dividends received over equity income would be added. When the direct method of reporting cash flows from operating activities is used, dividends received from equity investees are reported directly as cash flows from operating activities without the complications involved with the indirect method.

Consolidated Statement of Cash Flows— Direct Method

A consolidated SCF for Polski Corporation and Subsidiary under the direct method is presented in Exhibit 3–14. This statement is identical to the one presented in Exhibit 3–12 except for the presentation of cash flows from operating activities. Under the direct method, the consolidated income statement items that involve cash flows are converted from the accrual to the cash basis, and those items that do not involve cash are explained in notes or schedules supporting the cash flow statement. Exhibit 3–15 shows a worksheet that organizes infor-

---

POLSKI CORPORATION AND SUBSIDIARY
CONSOLIDATED STATEMENT OF CASH FLOWS
FOR THE YEAR ENDED DECEMBER 31, 19X6

Cash Flows from Operating Activities		
Cash received from customers		$645,000
Dividends received from equity investees		10,000
Less: Cash paid to suppliers	$365,000	
Cash paid to employees	54,000	
Paid for other operating items	47,000	
Cash paid for interest expense	24,000	(490,000)
Net cash flows from operating activities		165,000
Cash Flows from Investing Activities		
Proceeds from sale of land	$ 10,000	
Net cash flows from investing activities		10,000
Cash Flows from Financing Activities		
Payment of cash dividends—majority interests	$ (80,000)	
Payment of cash dividends—minority interests	(20,000)	
Net cash flows from financing activities		(100,000)
Increase in cash for 19X6		75,000
Cash on January 1, 19X6		180,000
Cash on December 31, 19X6		$255,000
Listing of Non-cash Investment and Financing Activities		
Equipment was purchased for $300,000 through the issuance of a 2-year note payable.		
Reconciliation of Consolidated Net Income to Operating Cash Flows		
Cash Flows From Operating Activities		
Consolidated net income		$150,000
Adjustments to reconcile net income to cash provided by operating activities:		
Minority interest income	$ 50,000	
Undistributed income-equity investees	(5,000)	
Loss on sale of machinery	10,000	
Depreciation on equipment	100,000	
Depreciation on buildings	20,000	
Amortization of goodwill	10,000	
Increase in accounts receivable	(105,000)	
Increase in inventories	(45,000)	
Decrease in accounts payable	(20,000)	15,000
Net cash flows from operating activities		$165,000

Exhibit 3–14 *Consolidated Statement of Cash Flows—Direct Method*

mation for the preparation of a consolidated statement of cash flows under the direct method. The SCF is prepared directly from the last three columns of the worksheet.

In comparing the cash flow statements in Exhibit 3–12 and 3–14, observe that the cash flows from investing and financing activities are identical. The significant differences lie in the presentation of cash flows from operating activities

POLSKI CORPORATION AND SUBSIDIARY
WORKING PAPERS FOR THE STATEMENT OF CASH FLOWS (DIRECT METHOD)
FOR THE YEAR ENDED DECEMBER 31, 19X6

	Year's Change	Reconciling Items Debit		Reconciling Items Credit		Cash Flow from Operations	Cash Flow– Investing Activities	Cash Flow– Financing Activities
Asset Changes								
Cash	75,000							
Accounts receivable—net	105,000			a	105,000			
Inventories	45,000			c	45,000			
Equity investments	5,000			b	5,000			
Land	(20,000)	h	20,000					
Buildings—net	(20,000)	f	20,000					
Equipment—net	200,000	e	100,000	d	300,000			
Goodwill	(10,000)	g	10,000					
Total asset changes	380,000							
Equity Changes								
Accounts payable	(20,000)			c	20,000			
Dividends payable	0							
Note payable due 19X8**	300,000	d	300,000					
Common stock	0							
Other paid-in capital	0							
Retained earnings*	70,000							
Minority interest	30,000	i	50,000	j	20,000			
Total equity changes	380,000							
Retained earnings changes								
Sales	750,000	a	105,000			645,000		
Income—equity investees	15,000	b	5,000			10,000		
Cost of goods sold	(300,000)	c	65,000			(365,000)		
Depreciation on equipment	(100,000)			e	100,000			
Depreciation on buildings	(20,000)			f	20,000			
Goodwill amortization	(10,000)			g	10,000			
Wage and salaries	(54,000)					(54,000)		
Other operating expenses	(47,000)					(47,000)		
Interest expense	(24,000)					(24,000)		
Loss on sale of land	(10,000)			h	10,000			
Minority interest income	(50,000)			i	50,000			
Dividends paid by Polski	(80,000)			k	80,000			
Change in retained earnings	70,000							
Payment of dividends—majority		k	80,000					(80,000)
Payment of dividends—minority		j	20,000					(20,000)
Proceeds from land sale				h	10,000		10,000	
			775,000		775,000	165,000	10,000	(100,000)

*Retained earnings changes replace the retained earnings account for reconciling purposes.
**Non-cash Investing and Financing Transaction: Equipment purchased for $300,000 by issuing a 2-year note payable.

Exhibit 3–15 *Worksheet for Consolidated SCF—Direct Method*

and the additional schedule to reconcile consolidated net income to operating cash flows under the direct method. Although the presentation in Exhibit 3–14 under the direct method may be less familiar, it is somewhat easier to interpret.

PUSH DOWN ACCOUNTING

In the Pilot and Sand illustration, the investment was recorded on the books of Pilot at cost, and allocation of the purchase price to identifiable assets and liabilities and goodwill was accomplished through working paper adjusting entries. In some instances, the allocation of the purchase price may be recorded in the subsidiary accounts, in other words, pushed down to the subsidiary records. Push down accounting relates to the books of the subsidiary and to separate subsidiary financial statements. It does not alter consolidated financial statements, and in fact, simplifies the consolidation process.

The SEC requires push down accounting for SEC filings when a subsidiary is substantially wholly owned with no publicly held debt or preferred stock outstanding.

Pack Corporation gives 5,000 shares of Pack $10 par common stock and $100,000 cash for all the capital stock of Simm Company, a closely held company, on January 3, 19X7. At this time Pack's stock is quoted on a national exchange at $55 a share. Simm's balance sheet and fair value information on January 3 is summarized as follows:

	Book Value	Fair Value
Cash	$ 30,000	$ 30,000
Accounts receivable—net	90,000	90,000
Inventories	130,000	150,000
Land	30,000	70,000
Buildings—net	150,000	130,000
Equipment—net	80,000	120,000
	$510,000	$590,000
Current liabilities	$100,000	$100,000
Long-term debt	150,000	150,000
Capital stock—$10 par	150,000	
Retained earnings	110,000	
	$510,000	

Under push-down accounting, Pack records its investment in Simm in the usual manner:

Investment in Simm	$375,000	
Cash		$100,000
Capital stock, $10 par		50,000
Paid-in capital		225,000

To record acquisition of Simm Company.

An entry must also be made on Simm's books on January 3 to record the new asset bases, including goodwill, in its accounts. Because Simm is considered similar to a new entity, it also has to reclassify retained earnings. Simm makes the following entry to record the push down values:

Inventories	$ 20,000	
Land	40,000	
Equipment—net	40,000	
Goodwill	35,000	
Retained earnings	110,000	
Building—net		$ 20,000
Push-down capital		225,000

A separate balance sheet prepared for Simm Company immediately following the business combination on January 3 includes the following accounts and amounts:

Cash	$ 30,000
Accounts receivable—net	90,000
Inventories	150,000
Land	70,000
Buildings—net	130,000
Equipment—net	120,000
Goodwill	35,000
	$625,000
Current liabilities	$100,000
Long-term debt	150,000
Capital stock—$10 par	150,000
Push-down capital	225,000
	$625,000

In consolidating the balance sheets of Pack and Simm at January 3, 19X7 after the push down entries are made on Simm's books, the investment in Simm account on Pack's book is eliminated against Simm's capital stock and push-down capital, and the other accounts are combined.

The arguments for and against push-down accounting and an illustration of push down accounting with minority interest are considered in more detail in Chapter 11.

POOLED SUBSIDIARIES

The pooling of interests method of accounting for business combinations was covered in Chapter 1, where the conditions for poolings of interests were discussed in some detail. It was assumed in that chapter that the combining corporations, other than the one issuing the stock, were dissolved. But neither merger nor consolidation is necessary in a pooling. This point was clearly established by the Accounting Principles Board in paragraph 49 of Opinion No. 16:

> Dissolution of a combining company is not a condition for applying the pooling of interests method of accounting for a business combination. One or more combining companies may be subsidiares of the issuing corporation after the combination is consummated if the other conditions are met.

If the other combining entities are not dissolved in a pooling of interests, the issuing corporation records the stock acquired as an investment at the book value of the net assets acquired. In this case, a parent-subsidiary relationship is established between the issuing corporation (parent) and the other combining corporations (subsidiaries), and consolidated financial statements are needed to combine the operations of the separate entities for external reporting.

The discussion in this chapter assumes that the combining corporations are not dissolved and that parent-subsidiary accounting and reporting procedures are appropriate. Except for initial differences in recording the investment in pooled companies and combining stockholders' equities in the year of combination, the parent company accounts for its investments in pooled corporations under the usual equity method. The investment account is increased for investment income and decreased for subsidiary dividends and losses.

Accounting for Subsidiary
Investments in Poolings of Interests

The parent company (issuer) records its investments in pooled companies at the book value of the net assets acquired in the other combining companies. In recording its investment in a pooled company, the parent company also combines its retained earnings with the retained earnings of the other combining company and adjusts its additional paid-in capital to reflect the paid-in capital of the pooled corporation. To illustrate the initial recording, assume that Pink Corporation issues its own capital stock for all the outstanding voting stock of Silver Corporation on January 1, 19X1. Immediately before the pooling, the stockholders' equity accounts for the combining corporations are as follows:

	Pink Corporation	Silver Corporation
Capital stock—$10 par	$1,500,000	$ 500,000
Additional paid-in capital	100,000	200,000
Retained earnings	400,000	300,000
Total stockholders' equity	$2,000,000	$1,000,000

If Pink Corporation issues 50,000 shares of its own stock for the outstanding stock of Silver, the investment is recorded:

Investment in Silver	$1,000,000	
Capital stock—Pink		$500,000
Additional paid-in capital		200,000
Retained earnings		300,000

Since the par value of stock issued by Pink is equal to the outstanding stock of Silver, all of Silver's retained earnings and additional paid-in capital is recorded on Pink Corporation's books.

This entry assumes that the parent will record the additional paid-in capital and retained earnings from the pooling in its existing equity accounts. This assumption is consistent with the pooling concept that a single entity emerges from the combining of previously separate companies. But the separate companies do continue to exist as separate legal entities when the combining companies are not dissolved. Since retained earnings and other capital accounts are affected by legal considerations, it may be desirable to maintain separate accounts for equity changes that result from a pooling without dissolution. If such separation is deemed necessary, it can be achieved by designating the accounts "Additional Paid-in Capital from Pooling" and "Retained Earnings from Pooling." This type of account separation is not reflected in the entries illustrated in the chapter.

The issuance of 90,000 shares of Pink Corporation in the pooling would be recorded:

Investment in Silver	$1,000,000	
Additional paid-in capital	100,000	
Capital stock		$900,000
Retained earnings		200,000

In this case, the par value of capital stock issued by Pink ($900,000) exceeds the paid-in capital of Silver ($700,000), plus the additional paid-in capital of Pink ($100,000). Accordingly, the retained earnings that would otherwise be combined has to be reduced by the $100,000 difference.

If Pink Corporation issues 40,000 shares for all of Silver Corporation's stock, its investment is recorded:

Investment in Silver	$1,000,000	
Capital stock		$400,000
Additional paid-in capital		300,000
Retained earnings		300,000

This entry combines the maximum retained earnings of Silver and credits Pink's additional paid-in capital for $300,000. This credit to additional paid-in capital consists of the additional paid-in capital of Silver ($200,000), plus the excess of capital stock of Silver ($500,000) over the par value of shares issued by Pink ($400,000).

In each of the three situations, the stockholders' equity of Pink Corporation is increased by $1,000,000, such that Pink's stockholders' equity reflects the $3,000,000 stockholders' equity of the pooled entity. In consolidating the balance sheets of Pink Corporation and Silver Corporation on the date of the pooling, the reciprocal investment in Silver and stockholders' equity of Silver amounts are eliminated, and the consolidated balance sheet shows the stockholders' equity accounts of Pink Corporation. The consolidation working paper entries are the same in all three situations:

Capital stock—Silver	$500,000	
Additional paid-in capital—Silver	200,000	
Retained earnings—Silver	300,000	
Investment in Silver		$1,000,000

Note that the investment account is equal to the equity of Silver such that there is no excess of investment balance over underlying equity of Silver.

After the pooling, Pink Corporation increases its investment in Silver account for 100 percent of Silver's income and decreases it for 100 percent of Silver's dividends, thereby maintaining the reciprocal relationship between the investment in Silver account and the total stockholders' equity of Silver. By using the equity method of accounting, Pink's net income is equal to consolidated net income, and Pink's retained earnings is equal to consolidated retained earnings.

Pooling of Interests with Minority Interest

The parent company in a pooling combination must acquire at least 90 percent of the outstanding shares of each combining subsidiary. Shares not acquired by the parent are accounted for as a minority interest. The minority interest can be no greater than 10 percent of the outstanding subsidiary shares prior to the pooling because additional holdings by minority interests would violate the 90 percent substantially all test for poolings. If the substantially all test is met, could a minority stockholder exchange some, but not all, of his or her shares for shares in the issuing corporation? The Accounting Principles Board responded to this question by stating that under the pooling method "each common stockholder of the combining company must either agree to exchange all of his shares for shares of the issuing corporation or refuse to exchange any of his shares."[9]

If Pink Corporation in the previous illustration had issued 50,000 shares of its own stock for 90 percent of the outstanding voting stock of Silver, the investment would have been recorded as follows:

---

[9]*AICPA Accounting Interpretations of APB Opinion No. 16, Interpretation No. 25,* November 1971.

Investment in Silver	$900,000	
Capital stock		$500,000
Additional paid-in capital		130,000
Retained earnings		270,000

This entry on Pink's books records the investment in Silver at 90 percent of the book value of Silver's net assets and combines $270,000 of Silver's retained earnings with Pink's retained earnings. Since only 90 percent of Silver's stock was acquired, a maximum of 90 percent of Silver's retained earnings can be combined. The $130,000 credit to additional paid-in capital is the excess of 90 percent of the paid-in capital of Silver over the par value of capital stock issued by Pink [($700,000 × 90%) − $500,000 = $130,000].

Total paid-in capital of the combining entities less the minority stockholders' share can also be compared with the parent's outstanding capital stock after the pooling. If total paid-in capital is greater, the excess is the parent's additional paid-in capital after the pooling. If capital stock is greater, additional paid-in capital of the parent will be zero, and the excess is the amount by which maximum pooled retained earnings must be reduced. To illustrate, Pink's $1,600,000 paid-in capital plus 90 percent of Silver's $700,000 paid-in capital exceeds Pink's $2,000,000 capital stock after the pooling by $230,000. This represents Pink's $100,000 additional paid-in capital before the pooling plus the $130,000 added here.

Issuance of 40,000 shares of Pink stock for the 90 percent interest would have been recorded as follows:

Investment in Silver	$900,000	
Capital stock		$400,000
Additional paid-in capital		230,000
Retained earnings		270,000

The effects of the 10 percent minority interest in Silver under the various assumptions discussed above are illustrated in Exhibit 3–15. The stockholders' equity

Stockholders' Equity	Pink	Silver	Consolidated (Pooled) Balance Sheet
A. Issuance of 50,000 Shares for a 90% Interest			
Capital stock—$10 par	$2,000,000	$ 500,000	$2,000,000
Additional paid-in capital	230,000	200,000	230,000
Retained earnings	670,000	300,000	670,000
Minority interest			100,000
Stockholders' equity	$2,900,000	$1,000,000	$3,000,000
B. Issuance of 90,000 Shares for a 90% Interest			
Capital stock—$10 par	$2,400,000	$ 500,000	$2,400,000
Additional paid-in capital	—	200,000	—
Retained earnings	500,000	300,000	500,000
Minority interest			100,000
Stockholders' equity	$2,900,000	$1,000,000	$3,000,000
C. Issuance of 40,000 Shares for a 90% Interest			
Capital stock—$10 par	$1,900,000	$ 500,000	$1,900,000
Additional paid-in capital	330,000	200,000	330,000
Retained earnings	670,000	300,000	670,000
MInority interest			100,000
Stockholders' equity	$2,900,000	$1,000,000	$3,000,000

Exhibit 3–15 *Comparison of Stockholders' Equity Pooling under Different Assumptions*

of Pink is $2,900,000 immediately after the pooling regardless of the number of shares issued. This $2,900,000 represents Pink's $2,000,000 stockholders' equity before the pooling, plus the $900,000 book value recorded in the investment in Silver account.

The $3,000,000 stockholders' equity shown in the consolidated or pooled balance sheets consists of Pink Corporation's stockholders' equity immediately after the pooling, plus $100,000 minority interest (10 percent of Silver's $1,000,000 stockholders' equity). In consolidation working papers, the following entry would be required to eliminate the reciprocal investment and equity amounts in each of the three situations:

Capital stock—Silver	$500,000	
Additional paid-in capital—Silver	200,000	
Retained earnings—Silver	300,000	
Investment in Silver		$900,000
Minority interest		100,000

This entry eliminates the equity accounts of Silver and the investment in Silver, and it establishes the 10 percent minority interest. Since net assets in a pooling are accounted for on the basis of book value, there is no excess of investment account balance over book value acquired to allocate to identifiable assets or goodwill.

Acquisition of Minority Shares

APB Opinion No. 16 specifically precludes firms from using the pooling method for acquisition of shares held by minority stockholders. If Pink Corporation acquires the remainder of Silver Corporation's outstanding shares after consummation of the business combination, the acquisition is not accounted for as a pooling of interests even if the transaction is consummated through an exchange of shares. Although not a business combination, the acquisition of the additional shares is accounted for under the purchase method, and the transaction is recorded on a fair value basis. The result is a revaluation of 10 percent of the net assets of Silver Corporation.

SUMMARY

Consolidated financial statements are usually required for the fair presentation of financial position and the results of operations of a parent company and its subsidiaries. Consolidated financial statements are not merely summations of parent company and subsidiary financial statement items. Reciprocal amounts are eliminated, and only nonreciprocal amounts are combined and included in consolidated statements. The investment in subsidiary and the subsidiary stockholders' equity accounts are eliminated in the preparation of consolidated financial statements because they are reciprocal, both representing the net assets of the subsidiary. Sales, borrowing, and leasing transactions between parent and subsidiaries also give rise to reciprocal amounts that must be eliminated in the consolidating process.

The stockholders' equity amounts that appear in the consolidated balance sheet are those of the parent company except for the equity of minority stockholders, which may be reported as a separate item within or outside of consolidated stockholders' equity. Consolidated net income is a measurement of income to the stockholders of the parent company. Any income accruing to the benefit of minority stockholders is a deduction in determination of consolidated net income. Parent company net income and retained earnings are equal to consolidated net income and consolidated retained earnings, respectively. Consolidated statements of cash flows are prepared from consolidated balance sheets and consolidated income statements, with adjustments for minority interest income and dividends and investment income and dividends from equity investees.

The pooling of interests method of accounting involves combination through the exchange of shares. If only the issuing corporation survives, the accounting is done as explained in Chapter 1. If the combining corporations continue to exist as separate legal entities, the companies are accounted for according to parent-subsidiary procedures with the following amendments:

1 The parent company/issuer records the subsidiary investment at its book value. Stock issued is credited for the par value of shares issued, retained earnings are combined to the extent possible, and additional paid-in capital is increased or decreased as necessary to account for differences between the par value of stock issued and paid-in capital of the other combining company.
2 Maximum retained earnings that can be combined with the parent's retained earnings is equal to the parent's ownership percentage times the subsidiary's retained earnings.
3 Earnings of combining companies are pooled for the entire year in which the business combination is consummated.

The equity method is used in accounting for investments in pooled subsidiaries. If it is correctly applied, the parent company's investment account will be equal to the underlying subsidiary equity, parent company income will be equal to consolidated (pooled) income, and parent company equity account balances will equal the consolidated (pooled) equity balances. These equalities are established in the year in which the pooling takes place. In subsequent years, the parent company accounts for its investments in pooled subsidiaries in the same manner as for purchased subsidiaries, and the consolidation procedures are the same as those for purchased subsidiaries.

SELECTED READINGS

Accounting Principles Board Opinion No. 16. "Business Combinations." New York: American Institute of Certified Public Accountants, 1970.

ANTHONY, JOSEPH H., and JOHN A. ELFRINK. "SFAS 94 Amends Consolidation Principles to Reduce Off Balance Sheet Financing." *The CPA Journal* (June 1989), pp. 58–60.

BLOCK, DIANE M., and PHILIP L. KINTZELE. "Implementing SFAS 95, *Statement of Cash Flows.*" *The CPA Journal* (February 1990), pp. 46–47.

BRILL, ROBERT J. "Redesigning the Accounting System for FASB 95." *Journal of Accountancy* (June 1989), p. 125–128.

BROWNLEE, E. RICHARD II, NORMAN S. SIEGEL, and KURT D. RASMUSSEN. "Mergers and Acquisitions: New Considerations." *The CPA Journal* (March 1989), pp. 12–20.

COLLEY, J. RON, and ARA G. VOLKAN. "Accounting for Goodwill." *Accounting Horizons* (March 1988), pp. 35–41.

Committee on Accounting Procedure. *Accounting Research Bulletin No. 51.* "Consolidated Financial Statements." New York: American Institute of Certified Public Accountants, 1959.

DeMOVILLE, WIG, and A. GEORGE PETRIE. "Accounting for a Bargain Purchase in a Business Combination." *Accounting Horizons* (September 1989), pp. 38–43.

DIETER, RICHARD. "Is Now the Time to Revisit Accounting for Business Combinations?" *The CPA Journal* (July 1989), pp. 44–48.

HEIAN, JAMES B., and JAMES B. THIES. "Consolidation of Finance Subsidiaries: $230 Billion in Off-Balance Sheet Financing Comes Home to Roost." *Accounting Horizons* (March 1989), pp. 1–9.

KRONQUIST, STACEY L., and NANCY NEWMAN-LIMATA. "Reporting Corporate Cash Flows." *Management Accounting* (July 1990), pp. 31–36.

LIVNAT, JOSHUA, and ASHWINPAUL C. SONDHI. "Finance Subsidiaries: Their Formation and Consolidation." *Journal of Business Finance & Accounting* (Spring 1986), pp. 137–147.

MAHONEY, JOHN J., MARK V. SEVER, and JOHN A. THEIS. "Cash Flow: FASB Opens the Floodgates." *Journal of Accountancy* (May 1988), pp. 26–38.

MOHR, ROSANNE M. "Unconsolidated Finance Subsidiaries: Characteristics and Debt/
Equity Effects." *Accounting Horizons* (March 1988), pp. 27–34.
RUE, JOSEPH C., and DAVID E. TOSH. "Should We Consolidate Finance Subsidiaries?"
Management Accounting (April 1987), pp. 45–50.
SEILER, MONA E., and STEVEN B. LILIEN. "A Simplified Approach for Converting Cash
Flows from Operating from Indirect to Direct Method." *The CPA Journal* (March
1990), pp. 38–39.
SHARP, ANDREW D., and JAMES H. THOMPSON. "SFAS 94: The Prodigal Son Becomes
Part of the Family." *The CPA Journal* (February 1989), pp. 40–44.
Statement of Financial Accounting Standards No. 94. "Consolidation of All Majority-owned
Subsidiaries.' Stamford, CT: Financial Accounting Standards Board, 1987.
Statement of Financial Accounting Standards No. 95. "Statement of Cash Flows." Stamford,
CT: Financial Accounting Standards Board, 1987.

ASSIGNMENT MATERIAL

QUESTIONS

1 When does a corporation become a subsidiary of another corporation?
2 In allocating the excess of investment cost over book value acquired of a subsidiary, are the amounts allocated to identifiable assets and liabilities (land and notes payable, for example) recorded separately in the accounts of the parent company? Explain.
3 If the fair value of a subsidiary corporation's land was $100,000 and its book value $90,000 when the parent company acquired its 100 percent interest for cash, at what amount would the land be included in the consolidated balance sheet of the two corporations immediately after the acquisition? Would your answer be different if the parent company had acquired an 80 percent interest?
4 Define or explain the terms *parent company, subsidiary company, affiliated companies,* and *associated companies.*
5 What is a minority interest?
6 Describe the circumstances under which the accounts of a subsidiary would not be included in the consolidated financial statements.
7 Who are the primary users for which consolidated financial statements are intended?
8 What amount of capital stock is reported in a consolidated balance sheet?
9 In what general ledger would you expect to find the account "goodwill from consolidation"?
10 How should the parent company's investment in subsidiary account be classified in a consolidated balance sheet? In the parent company's separate balance sheet?
11 Name some reciprocal accounts that might be found in the separate records of a parent company and its subsidiaries.
12 Why are reciprocal amounts eliminated in the preparation of consolidated financial statements?
13 How does the stockholders' equity of the parent company that uses the equity method of accounting differ from the consolidated stockholders' equity of the parent company and its subsidiaries?
14 Is there a difference in the amounts reported in the statement of retained earnings of a parent that uses the equity method of accounting and the amounts that appear in the consolidated retained earnings statement?
15 Is minority interest income an expense? Explain.
16 Describe how the total minority interest at the end of an accounting period is determined.
17 Explain why minority interest income is added to consolidated net income in determining cash flows from operating activities.
18 Since consolidated net income is a measurement of income to the stockholders of the parent company, does a change in cash as reflected in a statement of cash flows also relate to the stockholders of the parent company?
19 What special procedures are required to consolidate the statements of a parent company that reports on a calendar year basis and a subsidiary whose fiscal year ends on October 31?
20 When are parent-subsidiary accounting procedures applicable to a pooling business combination?

21 How does a parent company account for its investments in pooled subsidiaries?

22 Under what conditions does a parent company pool (or combine) all the retained earnings of its 100 percent owned subsidiaries?

23 Assume that a parent company makes the following journal entry to record its investment in a subsidiary under the pooling method:

Investment in Schwan	$1,300,000	
Capital stock—$10 par		$1,000,000
Additional paid-in capital		120,000
Retained earnings		180,000

Explain the components of the above entry in terms of what you would expect each of the amounts to represent.

24 Assume that the following entry is made by a parent company in recording its investment in a pooled subsidiary:

Investment in Starling	$1,250,000	
Additional paid-in capital	150,000	
Capital stock—$10 par		$1,000,000
Retained earnings		400,000

Did the parent company pool maximum retained earnings? Explain. Will the pooled additional paid-in capital be more or less than the parent company's additional paid-in capital before the pooling? Explain.

25 A parent company acquires 92 percent of the voting stock of a subsidiary in a pooling of interests that was consummated in 19X4 and an additional 4 percent of the subsidiary stock in 19X5. How should the acquisition of the additional 4 percent be accounted for by the parent company?

26 Does the acquisition of shares held by minority stockholders constitute a business combination? (Note: Don't forget the assumptions on page 60 when working exercises and problems in this chapter.)

EXERCISES

E 3-1

1 Which one of the following statements is correct?
  a A consolidated balance sheet encompasses all accounts found in the individual balance sheets of the parent and subsidiary.
  b Minority interest must be reported as a liability in the consolidated balance sheet.
  c The eliminations required on the working papers of the consolidated statements are not recorded in the ledgers of either the parent or the subsidiary companies.
  d Consolidated retained earnings several years after the parent company acquired an 80 percent interest in the subsidiary will include the entire amount of the subsidiary's earnings since the date of acquisition.

2 Minority interest, as it appears in a consolidated balance sheet, refers to:
  a Owners of less than 50 percent of the parent company stock
  b Parent's interest in subsidiary companies
  c Interest expense on subsidiary's bonds payable
  d Equity in the subsidiary's net assets held by stockholders other than the parent company

3 Dividends payable on December 31, 19X3 are as follows:
    Parent company—$120,000
    100% owned subsidiary—$30,000
  The amount of dividends payable in the consolidated balance sheet is:
  a $150,000   **b** $120,000
  c $90,000   **d** $30,000

4 On June 1, 19X3 P Company acquires 100 percent of the stock of S Company. On this date, P has retained earnings of $100,000 and S has retained earnings of $50,000. On December 31, 19X3 P Company has retained earnings of $120,000 and S Company has retained earnings of $60,000. The amount of retained earnings that should appear in the December 31, 19X3 consolidated balance sheet is:
  a $120,000   **b** $130,000
  c $150,000   **d** $180,000

5 On July 1, 19X4, when Sharkey Company's total stockholders' equity was $260,000, Pembroke, Inc., purchased 7,000 shares of Sharkey's common stock at $40 per share.

Sharkey Company had 10,000 shares of common stock outstanding both before and after the purchase by Pembroke, and the book value of Sharkey's net assets on July 1, 19X4 was equal to the fair value. On a consolidated balance sheet prepared at July 1, 19X4, goodwill would be shown at:

a $20,000   b $98,000
c $40,000   d $120,000

6 In computing consolidated cash flows from operations in the statement of cash flows, the following item is a deduction from consolidated net income from continuing operations:
a Depreciation
b Income from consolidated subsidiaries
c Undistributed income from equity investees
d Minority interest income

7 Which of the following would be added in converting consolidated net income to cash flows from operations in a consolidated cash flow statement?
a Amortization of premium on bonds payable
b Amortization of excess assigned to undervalued liabilities
c Minority interest dividends
d Minority interest's share of net earnings

8 The acquisition of minority shares that remain outstanding after a pooling of interests should be accounted for:
a At the book value of underlying equity
b At fair value of identifiable net assets
c As a pooling of interests
d As a purchase

E 3–2 1 Under *FASB Statement No. 94,* "Consolidation of All Majority-owned Subsidiaries," a parent company should exclude a subsidiary from consolidation if:
a It measures income from the subsidiary under the equity method
b The parent company is engaged in manufacturing operations and the subsidiary is an insurance company
c The subsidiary is a foreign entity whose books are recorded in a foreign currency
d The parent expects to sell the subsidiary investment within a year

2 The FASB's primary motivation for issuing *FASB Statement No. 94,* "Consolidation of All Majority-owned Subsidiaries," was to:
a Insure disclosure of all loss contingencies
b Prevent the use of off-balance sheet financing
c Improve comparability of the statements of cash flows
d Establish criteria for exclusion of finance and insurance subsidiaries from consolidation

3 Parent company and consolidated financial statement amounts would not be the same for
a Capital stock
b Retained earnings
c Investments in unconsolidated subsidiaries
d Investments in consolidated subsidiaries

4 If a 60 percent owned subsidiary cannot be consolidated under the provisions of *FASB Statement No. 94,* "Consolidation of All Majority-owned Subsidiaries," it must be accounted for
a Under the cost method
b Under the equity method
c Under the equity method if the parent can exercise significant influence over the subsidiary
d At market value if the subsidiary is in bankruptcy

5 In preparing a statement of cash flows, the cost of acquiring a subsidiary is reported:
a As an operating activity under the direct method
b As an operating activity under the indirect method
c As an investing activity
d As a financing activity

6 In computing cash flows from operating activities under the direct method, the following item is an addition:
a Cash dividends from equity investees
b Collection of principal on a loan made to a subsidiary

   c Minority interest dividends

   d Minority interest income

7 In computing cash flows from operating activities under the indirect method, the following item is an addition to consolidated net income:

   a Minority interest dividends

   b Minority interest income

   c Income from equity investees in excess of dividends received

   d Amortization of negative goodwill

8 A corporation is contemplating acquiring 90 percent of another corporation, either by (a) issuing common stock in exchange for 90 percent of the outstanding stock of the combining corporation in a pooling of interests or by (b) paying cash for 90 percent of the outstanding stock in a purchase business combination. Which of the following items would be reported in the consolidated financial statements at the same amount regardless of the accounting method used?

   a Minority interest

   b Goodwill

   c Retained earnings

   d Capital stock

E 3–3 **[AICPA adapted]**

1 The outstanding common stock of Mevlas, Inc., is owned 85 percent by the Airam Company and 15 percent by Nime, Inc. On Airam Company's consolidated statements Nime, Inc., should be considered:

   a An investor   **b** An unconsolidated subsidiary

   c An affiliate   **d** A minority interest

2 Presenting consolidated financial statements this year when statements of individual companies were presented last year is:

   a A correction of an error

   b An accounting change that should be reported prospectively

   c An accounting change that should be reported by restating the financial statements of all prior periods presented

   d *Not* an accounting change

3 In the preparation of financial statements, the accounts of a wholly owned subsidiary that exists primarily for the purpose of leasing property to the parent company should be:

   a Included in consolidated statements

   b Excluded from consolidated statements because inclusion would destroy interfirm comparability

   c Disclosed by the equity method of accounting for investments

   d Ignored if the parent company capitalizes the related leaseholds

4 What is the theoretically preferred method of presenting minority interest on a consolidated balance sheet?

   a As a separate item within the deferred credits section

   b As a deduction from (contra to) goodwill from consolidation, if any

   c By means of notes or footnotes to the balance sheet

   d As a separate item within the stockholders' equity section

5 How is the portion of consolidated earnings to be assigned to minority interest in consolidated financial statements determined?

   a The net income of the parent is subtracted from the subsidiary's net income to determine the minority interest.

   b The subsidiary's net income is extended to the minority interest.

   c The amount of the subsidiary's earnings recognized for consolidation purposes is multiplied by the minority's percentage ownership.

   d The amount of consolidated earnings determined on the consolidated working papers is multiplied by the minority interest percentage at the balance sheet date.

6 Which of the following would be subtracted in converting net earnings to cash flow from operations in the current period in a consolidated statement of cash flows?

   a Increase in accounts receivable

   b Amortization of goodwill

   c Increase in deferred income tax liability

   d Minority interest's share of net earnings

Use the following information in answering questions 1 and 2: Apex Company acquired 70 percent of the outstanding stock of Nadir Corporation. The separate balance sheet of Apex immediately after the acquisition and the consolidated balance sheet are as follows:

	Apex	Consolidated
Current assets	$106,000	$146,000
Investment in Nadir—cost	100,000	—
Goodwill	—	8,100
Fixed assets—net	270,000	370,000
	$476,000	$524,100
Current liabilities	$ 15,000	$ 28,000
Capital stock	350,000	350,000
Minority interest	—	35,100
Retained earnings	111,000	111,000
	$476,000	$524,100

Of the excess payment for the investment in Nadir, $10,000 was ascribed to under-valuation of its fixed assets; the balance of the excess payment was ascribed to good-will. Current assets of Nadir included a $2,000 receivable from Apex, which arose before they became related on an ownership basis.

The following two items relate to Nadir's separate balance sheet prepared at the time Apex acquired its 70 percent interest in Nadir.

1 What was the total of the current assets on Nadir's separate balance sheet immediately before Apex acquired its 70 percent interest?
a $38,000   b $40,000
c $42,000   d $104,000

2 What was the total stockholders' equity on Nadir's separate balance sheet at the time Apex acquired its 70 percent interest?
a $64,900   b $70,000
c $100,000   d $117,000

3 Cobb Company's current receivables from affiliated companies at December 31, 19X5 are (1) a $75,000 cash advance to Hill Corporation (Cobb owns 30 percent of the voting stock of Hill and accounts for the investment by the equity method), (2) a receivable of $260,000 from Vick Corporation for administrative and selling services (Vick is 100 percent owned by Cobb and is included in Cobb's consolidated financial statements), and (3) a receivable of $200,000 from Ward Corporation for merchandise sales on credit (Ward is a 90 percent owned, unconsolidated subsidiary of Cobb accounted for by the equity method). In the current assets section of its December 31, 19X5 consolidated balance sheet, Cobb should report accounts receivable from investees in the amount:
a $180,000   b $255,000
c $275,000   d $535,000

E 3-5   Pinto Corporation paid $900,000 for a 90 percent interest in Skeet Corporation on January 1, 19X1 at a price $20,000 in excess of underlying book value. The excess was allocated $12,000 to undervalued equipment with a three-year remaining use life and $8,000 to goodwill with a ten-year write-off period. The income statements of Pinto and Skeet for 19X1 are summarized as follows:

	Pinto	Skeet
Sales	$2,000,000	$800,000
Income from Skeet	90,000	
Cost of sales	(1,000,000)	(400,000)
Depreciation expense	(200,000)	(120,000)
Other expenses	(400,000)	(180,000)
Net income	$ 490,000	$100,000

Required
1 Calculate the unamortized goodwill that should appear in the consolidated balance sheet of Pinto and Subsidiary at December 31, 19X1.
2 Calculate consolidated net income for 19X1.

E 3–6 Pringle Corporation purchases a 90 percent interest in Roman Industries on January 1, 19X8, when Roman Industries has capital stock of $200,000 and retained earnings of $20,000. Roman Industries' net income for 19X8 is $20,000 and dividends declared are $16,000. Assume that the assets and liabilities of Roman Industries are stated at their fair values on January 1, 19X8.

Required: Prepare all journal entries during 19X8 to account for Pringle's investment in Roman Industries if Pringle pays:
1 $198,000
2 $220,000

E 3–7 On January 1, 19X2 Pascoe Corporation issues 50,000 previously unissued shares of $10 par common stock for 90 percent of Sonnet Corporation's outstanding common shares in a business combination accounted for as a pooling of interests. Balance sheet information for Pascoe and Sonnet at December 31, 19X1 follows:

	Pascoe Book Value	Sonnet Book Value	Sonnet Fair Value
Current assets	$ 4,000,000	$ 800,000	$ 900,000
Plant assets—net	6,000,000	1,200,000	1,300,000
	$10,000,000	$2,000,000	$2,200,000
Liabilities	$ 4,000,000	$ 800,000	$ 800,000
Capital stock—$10 par	3,000,000	600,000	
Additional paid-in capital	2,000,000	400,000	
Retained earnings	1,000,000	200,000	
	$10,000,000	$2,000,000	

Required
1 Prepare the journal entry on Pascoe's books to account for the business combination.
2 Prepare a consolidated balance sheet for Pascoe and Subsidiary on January 1, 19X2, immediately after the business combination.

E 3–8 Summary income statement information for Parade Corporation and its 80 percent owned subsidiary, Stanton Corporation, for the year 19X2 is as follows:

	Parade	Stanton
Sales	$1,000,000	$400,000
Income from Stanton	56,000	—
Cost of sales	(600,000)	(200,000)
Depreciation expense	(50,000)	(40,000)
Other expenses	(206,000)	(90,000)
Net income	$ 200,000	$ 70,000

Required
1 Assume that Parade acquired its 80 percent interest in Stanton at book value on January 1, 19X1 when Stanton's assets and liabilities were equal to their recorded book values. There were no intercompany transactions during 19X1 and 19X2. Prepare a consolidated income statement for Parade Corporation and Subsidiary for the year 19X2.
2 Assume that Parade acquired its 80 percent interest in Stanton on January 1, 19X1 at a price $20,000 in excess of book value and that $10,000 *was allocated* to a reduction of overvalued equipment with a five-year remaining use life and $30,000 to goodwill with a ten-year amortization period. There were no intercompany transactions during 19X1 and 19X2. Prepare a consolidated income statement for Parade Corporation and Subsidiary for the year 19X2.

E 3–9 Luball Corporation acquired an 80 percent interest in Tocurt Corporation on January 2, 19X2 for $700,000. On this date the capital stock and retained earnings of the two companies were as follows:

	Luball	Tocurt
Capital stock	$2,000,000	$500,000
Retained earnings	600,000	200,000

The assets and liabilities of Tocurt were stated at their fair values when Luball acquired its 80 percent interest. Luball uses the equity method to account for its investment in Tocurt.

Net income and dividends for 19X2 for the affiliated companies were:

	Luball	Tocurt
Net income	$300,000	$90,000
Dividends declared	180,000	50,000
Dividends payable December 31, 19X2	90,000	25,000

Required: Calculate the amounts at which the following items should appear in the consolidated balance sheet on December 31, 19X2:

1 Capital stock
2 Goodwill
3 Consolidated retained earnings
4 Minority interest
5 Dividends payable

E 3–10 Moslow and Kassen Corporations' balance sheets at December 31, 19X7 are summarized as follows:

	Moslow	Kassen
Cash	$255,000	$ 60,000
Other assets	200,000	100,000
Total assets	$455,000	$160,000
Liabilities	$ 70,000	$ 35,000
Capital stock, par $10	300,000	100,000
Additional paid-in capital	50,000	15,000
Retained earnings	35,000	10,000
Total equities	$455,000	$160,000

Moslow acquired 80 percent of the voting stock of Kassen on January 2, 19X8 at $15 per share. The fair value of Kassen's net assets was equal to their book value on January 2, 19X8.

During 19X8 Moslow reported earnings of $55,000 including income from Kassen of $16,000, and paid dividends of $25,000. Kassen's earnings for 19X8 were $20,000 and its dividends were $15,000.

Required: Prepare the stockholders' equity section of the December 31, 19X8 consolidated balance sheet for Moslow Corporation and Subsidiary.

E 3-11 Comparative income statements of Pokes Corporation and Slugger Corporation for the year ended December 31, 19X4 are as follows:

	Pokes	Slugger
Sales	$1,500,000	$500,000
Income from Slugger	129,000	—
Total revenue	1,629,000	500,000
Less: Cost of goods sold	900,000	200,000
Operating expenses	400,000	150,000
Total expenses	1,300,000	350,000
Net income	$ 329,000	$150,000

Additional Information
1 Slugger is a 90 percent owned subsidiary of Pokes, acquired by Pokes for $720,000 on January 1, 19X2 when Slugger's stockholders' equity was $700,000.
2 The excess of the cost of Pokes's investment in Slugger over book value acquired *was allocated* $30,000 to inventories that were sold in 19X2, $20,000 to equipment with a four-year remaining use life, and the remainder to goodwill.

Required: Prepare a consolidated income statement for Pokes Corporation and Subsidiary for the year ended December 31, 19X4.

E 3-12 On January 1, 19X7 Pedro Corporation issued 10,000 shares of its own $10 par common stock for 9,000 shares of the outstanding stock of Sisco Corporation in a business combination that met all the conditions for a pooling of interests. Pedro stock at January 1, 19X7 was selling at $80 per share. Just before the business combination, balance sheet information of the two corporations was as follows:

	Pedro: Historical Cost	Sisco Historical Cost	Sisco Fair Value
Cash	$ 20,000	$ 10,000	$ 10,000
Inventories	50,000	30,000	40,000
Other current assets	100,000	90,000	100,000
Land	80,000	20,000	100,000
Plant and equipment—net	750,000	200,000	300,000
	$1,000,000	$350,000	$550,000
Liabilities	$ 200,000	$ 50,000	$ 50,000
Capital stock—$10 par	500,000	100,000	
Additional paid-in capital	200,000	50,000	
Retained earnings	100,000	150,000	
	$1,000,000	$350,000	

Required
1 Prepare the journal entry or entries on Pedro Corporation's books to account for the business combination.
2 Prepare a consolidated balance sheet for Pedro Corporation and Subsidiary immediately after the business combination.

E 3-13 Selected information relevant to the "cash flow from operating activities" section of the statement of cash flows for Poker Corporation and Subsidiary for 19X8 is as follows:

Consolidated income statement information for 19X8

Revenue	$2,000,000	
Income from investee	200,000	$2,200,000
Less: Cost of sales	$1,200,000	
Depreciation expense	400,000	
Other expenses	100,000	(1,700,000)
Total consolidated income		500,000
Less: Minority interest income		(150,000)
Consolidated net income		$ 350,000

Other information for 19X8

Dividends from equity investees	$ 80,000
Increase in inventories	110,000
Increase in accounts payable	60,000
Decrease in accounts receivable	50,000

Required: Prepare the "cash flow from operating activities" section of the statement of cash flows for Poker Corporation and Subsidiary for 19X8
    1 Using the indirect method
    2 Using the direct method

PROBLEMS

P 3-1 On December 31, 19X2 Pendleton Corporation purchased 80 percent of the stock of Sutherland Sales Company at book value. The data reported on their separate balance sheets immediately after the acquisition follow. At December 31, 19X2 Pendleton Corporation owes Sutherland Sales $5,000 on accounts payable.

	Pendleton Corporation	Sutherland Sales
Assets		
Cash	$ 32,000	$ 8,000
Accounts receivable	45,000	24,000
Inventories	143,000	56,000
Investment in Sutherland	200,000	
Equipment—net	380,000	175,000
	$800,000	$263,000
Liabilities and Stockholders' Equity		
Accounts payable	$ 40,000	$ 13,000
Common stock—$10 par	460,000	150,000
Retained earnings	300,000	100,000
	$800,000	$263,000

Required
    1 Prepare a consolidated balance sheet for Pendleton Corporation and Subsidiary at December 31, 19X2.
    2 Compute consolidated net income for 19X3 assuming that Pendleton Corporation reported separate income of $150,000 and Sutherland Sales Company reported net income of $80,000. (Separate income does *not* include income from the investment in Sutherland Sales.)

P 3-2 Pope Corporation acquired 80 percent of the outstanding common stock of Specht Corporation on January 1, 19X3 for $168,000 cash. Immediately after this acquisition the balance sheet information for the two companies was as follows:

	Pope: Book Value	Specht Book Value	Specht Fair Value
Assets			
Cash	$ 42,000	$ 20,000	$ 20,000
Receivables—net	80,000	30,000	30,000
Inventories	70,000	30,000	50,000
Land	100,000	50,000	60,000
Buildings—net	110,000	70,000	90,000
Equipment—net	80,000	40,000	30,000
Investment in Specht	168,000	—	—
Total assets	$650,000	$240,000	$280,000
Liabilities and Stockholders' Equity			
Accounts payable	$ 90,000	$ 80,000	$ 80,000
Other liabilities	10,000	50,000	40,000
Capital stock—$10 par	500,000	100,000	160,000
Retained earnings	50,000	10,000	
Total equities	$650,000	$240,000	$280,000

Required

1 Prepare a schedule to allocate the difference between the cost of the investment in Specht and the book value of the interest acquired by Pope to identifiable and unidentifiable net assets.

2 Prepare a consolidated balance sheet for Pope Corporation and Subsidiary at January 1, 19X3.

P 3–3 Perrin Corporation acquired 80,000 shares of the $1 par value common stock of Salinas Company by paying $100,000 cash and issuing 5,000 shares of its own $2 par value common stock. At the time of the acquisition, Perrin's stock was selling for $10 per share and Salinas's for $15 per share.

Balance sheets and fair values of the two companies immediately before acquisition are as follows:

	Perrin Book Value	Perrin Fair Value	Salinas Book Value	Salinas Fair Value
Current assets	$ 200,000	$ 250,000	$ 50,000	$ 40,000
Plant assets	900,000	1,000,000	150,000	200,000
	$1,100,000		$200,000	
Liabilities	$ 500,000	$ 500,000	$ 50,000	$ 50,000
Capital stock	500,000		100,000	
Retained earnings	100,000		50,000	
	$1,100,000		$200,000	

Required: Prepare a consolidated balance sheet for Perrin Corporation and Subsidiary immediately after the acquisition. (*Hint:* It may be helpful to prepare the working paper adjustment and elimination entries as an approach to solution for problems and exercises of this nature.)

P 3–4 Paliti Corporation purchased a block of Stuart Company common stock for $250,000 cash on January 1, 19X8. Separate company and consolidated balance sheets prepared immediately after the acquisition are summarized as follows:

PALITI CORPORATION AND SUBSIDIARY
CONSOLIDATED BALANCE SHEET
AT JANUARY 1, 19X8

	Paliti	Stuart	Consolidated
Assets			
Current assets	$ 200,000	$100,000	$ 300,000
Investment in Stuart	250,000	—	—
Plant assets—net	550,000	200,000	758,000
Goodwill	—	—	34,000
Total assets	$1,000,000	$300,000	$1,092,000
Equities			
Liabilities	$ 400,000	$ 40,000	$ 440,000
Capital stock—$10 par	500,000	200,000	500,000
Retained earnings	100,000	60,000	100,000
Minority interest	—	—	52,000
Total equities	$1,000,000	$300,000	$1,092,000

Required: Reconstruct the schedule to allocate the cost–book value differential from Paliti's investment in Stuart.

P 3–5 Perry Corporation paid $400,000 cash for 90 percent of Sim Corporation's common stock on January 1, 19X6 when Sim had $300,000 capital stock and $100,000 retained earnings. The book values of Sim's assets and liabilities were equal to fair values. During 19X6 Sim reported net income of $20,000 and declared $10,000 dividends on December 31. Balance sheets for Perry and Sim at December 31, 19X6 are as follows:

	Perry	Sim
Assets		
Cash	$ 42,000	$ 20,000
Receivables—net	50,000	130,000
Inventories	400,000	50,000
Land	150,000	200,000
Equipment—net	600,000	100,000
Investment in Sim	408,000	—
	$1,650,000	$500,000
Equities		
Accounts payable	$ 410,000	$ 80,000
Dividends payable	60,000	10,000
Capital stock	1,000,000	300,000
Retained earnings	180,000	110,000
	$1,650,000	$500,000

Required: Prepare consolidated balance sheet working papers for Perry Corporation and Subsidiary for 19X6.

P 3–6 Port Corporation acquired 80 percent of the outstanding stock of Short Corporation for $240,000 cash on January 3, 19X5, on which date Short's stockholders' equity consisted of capital stock of $200,000 and retained earnings of $50,000.

There were no changes in the outstanding stock of either corporation during 19X5 and 19X6. At December 31, 19X6 the adjusted trial balances of Port and Short are as follows:

	Port Corporation	Short Corporation
Debits		
Current assets	$ 242,000	$ 75,000
Plant assets—net	400,000	300,000
Investment in Short—80%	298,000	—
Cost of goods sold	250,000	120,000
Other expenses	50,000	30,000
Dividends	60,000	25,000
	$1,300,000	$550,000
Credits		
Current liabilities	$ 161,000	$ 50,000
Capital stock	500,000	200,000
Retained earnings	200,000	100,000
Sales	400,000	200,000
Income from Short	39,000	—
	$1,300,000	$550,000

Additional Information
1 All of Short's assets and liabilities were recorded at their fair values on January 3, 19X5.
2 The current liabilities of Short at December 31, 19X6 include dividends payable of $10,000.

Required: Determine the amounts that should appear in the consolidated statements of Port Corporation and Subsidiary at December 31, 19X6 for each of the following:
1 Minority interest income
2 Current assets
3 Income from Short
4 Capital stock
5 Investment in Short
6 Excess of investment cost over book value acquired
7 Consolidated net income
8 Consolidated retained earnings, December 31, 19X5
9 Consolidated retained earnings, December 31, 19X6
10 Minority interest, December 31, 19X6

P 3-7   [AICPA adapted]

On January 1, 19X6 Todd Corporation made the following investments:
1 Acquired for cash, 80 percent of the outstanding common stock of Meadow Corporation at $70 per share. The stockholders' equity of Meadow on January 1, 19X6 consisted of the following:

Common stock, par value $50	$50,000
Retained earnings	20,000

2 Acquired for cash, 70 percent of the outstanding common stock of Van Corporation at $40 per share. The stockholders' equity of Van on January 1, 19X6 consisted of the following:

Common stock, par value $20	$60,000
Capital in excess of par value	20,000
Retained earnings	40,000

After these investments were made, Todd was able to exercise significant influence over the operations of both companies.
An analysis of the retained earnings of each company for 19X6 is as follows:

	Todd	Meadow	Van
Balance January 1, 19X6	$240,000	$20,000	$40,000
Net income (loss)	104,600	36,000	(12,000)
Cash dividends paid	(40,000)	(16,000)	(9,000)
Balance December 31, 19X6	$304,600	$40,000	$19,000

Required
1 What entries should have been made on the books of Todd during 19X6 to record the following?
  a Investments in subsidiaries
  b Subsidiary dividends received
  c Parent's share of subsidiary income or loss
2 Compute the amount of minority interest in each subsidiary's stockholders' equity at December 31, 19X6.
3 What amount should be reported as consolidated retained earnings of Todd Corporation and subsidiaries as of December 31, 19X6?
4 Compute the correct balances of Todd's investment in Meadow and investment in Van accounts at December 31, 19X6.

P 3–8 Pale Corporation purchased 90 percent of Sori Corporation's outstanding stock for $3,000,000 cash on January 1, 19X2 when Sori's stockholders' equity consisted of $2,000,000 capital stock and $500,000 retained earnings. The $750,000 excess *was allocated* $350,000 to undervalued equipment with a seven-year remaining useful life, and $400,000 to goodwill. Sori's net income and dividends for 19X2 were $500,000 and $200,000, respectively. Comparative balance sheet data for Pale and Sori Corporations at December 31, 19X2 are as follows:

	Pale	Sori
Cash	$ 300,000	$ 200,000
Receivables—net	600,000	400,000
Dividends receivable	90,000	
Inventory	700,000	600,000
Land	600,000	500,000
Buildings—net	2,000,000	1,000,000
Equipment—net	1,500,000	800,000
Investment in Sori	3,210,000	
	$9,000,000	$3,500,000
Accounts payable	$ 300,000	$ 600,000
Dividends payable	500,000	100,000
Capital stock	7,000,000	2,000,000
Retained earnings	1,200,000	800,000
	$9,000,000	$3,500,000

Required: Prepare consolidated balance sheet working papers for Pale Corporation and Subsidiary on December 31, 19X2.

P 3–9 The consolidated balance sheet of Patsy Corporation and its 80 percent subsidiary, Stub Corporation, contains the following items on December 31, 19X6:

Cash	$ 50,000
Inventories	180,000
Other current assets	70,000
Plant assets—net	270,000
Goodwill from consolidation	30,000
	$600,000

Liabilities	$120,000
Capital stock	400,000
Retained earnings	30,000
Minority interests	50,000
	$600,000

Patsy Corporation uses the equity method of accounting for its investment in Stub. Stub Corporation stock was acquired by Patsy on January 1, 19X2 when Stub's capital stock was $200,000 and its retained earnings was $20,000. The fair values of Stub's net assets were equal to their book values on January 1, 19X2, and there have been no changes in outstanding stock of either Patsy or Stub since January 1, 19X2.

Goodwill is being amortized over a twenty-year period.

Required: Determine the following:
1 The purchase price of Patsy's investment in Stub stock on January 1, 19X2.
2 The total of Stub's stockholders' equity on December 31, 19X6.
3 The balance of Patsy's investment in Stub account at December 31, 19X6.
4 The balances of Patsy's retained earnings and capital stock accounts on December 31, 19X6.

P 3-10 A summary of changes in Piper Corporation's investment in Satch account from January 1, 19X4 to December 31, 19X6 follows:

INVESTMENT IN SATCH (70%)

January 1, 19X4 Cost	$650,000		
Income—19X4	52,000	Dividends—19X4	$ 28,000
—19X5	66,000	—19X5	35,000
—19X6	80,000	—19X6	42,000
		to balance	743,000√
	$848,000		$848,000
December 31, 19X6			
Balance forward	$743,000		

Additional Information
1 Piper acquired its 70 percent interest in Satch Corporation when Satch had capital stock of $600,000 and retained earnings of $300,000.
2 Dividends declared by Satch Corporation in each of the years 19X4, 19X5, and 19X6 were equal to 50 percent of Satch Corporation's reported net income.
3 Satch Corporation's assets and liabilities were stated at their fair values on January 1, 19X4.

Required: Compute the following amounts:
1 Satch Corporation's dividends declared in 19X5
2 Satch Corporation's net income for 19X5
3 Unamortized goodwill at December 31, 19X5
4 Minority interest income for 19X6
5 Minority interest at December 31, 19X6
6 Consolidated net income for 19X6 assuming that Piper's separate income for 19X6 is $280,000

P 3-11 Separate balance sheets for Peyton Corporation and Sidney Corporation at December 31, 19X7 are as follows:

	Peyton	Sidney
Assets		
Cash	$ 50,000	$ 20,000
Other current assets	150,000	80,000
Land	300,000	50,000
Buildings	600,000	200,000
Less: Accumulated depreciation	200,000*	50,000*
	$900,000	$300,000

	Peyton	Sidney
Liabilities and Stockholders' Equity		
Current liabilities	$100,000	$ 50,000
Common stock—$10 par	600,000	100,000
Additional paid-in capital	60,000	75,000
Retained earnings	140,000	75,000
	$900,000	$300,000

* Deduct.

Peyton issued 10,000 shares of its own common stock with a market value of $300,000 on January 2, 19X8 in exchange for 80 percent of Sidney's outstanding stock. All of Sidney's assets and liabilities were recorded at their fair values except for buildings that had a fair value of $170,000 and a remaining use life of five years.

Required

Part A: At what amount would each of the following items appear in a consolidated balance sheet prepared on January 2, 19X8, immediately after the business combination?
1 Total current assets
2 Total plant and equipment (land and buildings less accumulated depreciation)
3 Common stock
4 Additional paid-in capital
5 Retained earnings

Part B: Assume that Sidney has net income of $40,000 and pays dividends of $20,000 during 19X8, and that Peyton has income from its own operations (does not include investment income) of $90,000 during 19X8 and pays dividends of $50,000. Determine the correct amounts for each of the following:
6 Peyton's income from Sidney for 19X8
7 Peyton's investment in Sidney account at December 31, 19X8
8 Consolidated net income for 19X8
9 Consolidated retained earnings at December 31, 19X8
10 Minority interest at December 31, 19X8

P 3-12 Prickett Corporation purchased 80 percent of the voting common stock of Sawyer Corporation for $2,660,000 cash on January 2, 19X3. On this date, before combination, the book values and fair values of Prickett and Sawyer were as follows:

	Prickett Corporation		Sawyer Corporation	
	Book Value	Fair Value	Book Value	Fair Value
Cash	$ 3,000,000	$ 3,000,000	$ 60,000	$ 60,000
Receivables—net	800,000	800,000	200,000	200,000
Inventories	1,100,000	1,200,000	400,000	500,000
Other current assets	900,000	900,000	150,000	200,000
Land	3,100,000	4,000,000	500,000	600,000
Buildings—net	6,000,000	8,000,000	1,000,000	1,800,000
Equipment—net	3,500,000	4,500,000	800,000	600,000
	$18,400,000	$22,400,000	$3,110,000	$3,960,000
Accounts payable	$ 400,000	$ 400,000	$ 200,000	$ 200,000
Other liabilities	1,500,000	1,600,000	610,000	560,000
Capital stock—$10 par	15,000,000	20,400,000	2,000,000	3,200,000
Retained earnings	1,500,000		300,000	
	$18,400,000	$22,400,000	$3,110,000	$3,960,000

Required
1 Prepare a schedule showing how the excess of Prickett's investment cost over book value acquired should be allocated.
2 Prepare a consolidated balance sheet.

P 3–13 Use the information in Problem 3–12, except change the amount of cash that Prickett Corporation paid for the 80 percent interest in Sawyer Corporation to $1,760,000.

Required
1 Prepare a schedule to allocate the cost–book value differential
2 Prepare a consolidated balance sheet immediately after the business combination.

P 3–14 The accountant for Panama Corporation collected the following information that he thought might be useful in the preparation of the company's consolidated statement of cash flows:

Cash paid for purchase of equipment	$ 250,000
Cash paid for other expenses	450,000
Cash paid to suppliers	600,000
Cash received from customers	1,500,000
Cash received from sale of land	400,000
Cash received from treasury stock sold	400,000
Dividends from equity investees	30,000
Dividends paid to minority stockholders	20,000
Dividends paid to Panama's stockholders	50,000
Gain on sale of land	200,000
Income from equity investees	60,000
Interest received from short-term loan	5,000
Minority interest income	50,000

Required: Prepare the "cash flows from operating activities" section of the consolidated statement of cash flows for Panama Corporation and Subsidiaries using the *direct method* of presentation.

P 3–15 Comparative consolidated financial statements for Percy Corporation and its 80 percent owned subsidiary at and for the years ended December 31, 19X7 and 19X6 are as follows:

PERCY CORPORATION AND SUBSIDIARY COMPARATIVE CONSOLIDATED FINANCIAL STATEMENTS

	Year 19X7	Year 19X6	Change 19X7–19X6
Income and Retained Earnings Statements for the Year			
Sales	$2,600,000	$2,400,000	$200,000
Cost of sales	1,450,000*	1,400,000*	50,000*
Depreciation expense	200,000*	150,000*	50,000*
Goodwill amortization	50,000*	50,000*	0
Other operating expenses	450,000*	430,000*	20,000*
Minority interest income	40,000*	30,000*	10,000*
Consolidated net income	410,000	340,000	70,000
Add: Beginning retained earnings	940,000	700,000	240,000
Less: Dividends	150,000*	100,000*	50,000*
Ending retained earnings	$1,200,000	$ 940,000	$260,000
Balance Sheets at December 31			
Assets			
Cash	$ 270,000	$ 400,000	$130,000*
Accounts receivable—net	730,000	650,000	80,000
Inventories	700,000	500,000	200,000
Plant and equipment—net	1,700,000	1,500,000	200,000
Goodwill	400,000	450 000	50 000*
Total assets	$3,800,000	$3,500,000	$300,000

	Year 19X7	Year 19X6	Change 19X7–19X6
Equities			
Accounts payable	$ 410,000	$ 360,000	$ 50,000
Dividends payable	70,000	100,000	30,000*
Capital stock	1,000,000	1,000,000	0
Other paid-in capital	900,000	900,000	0
Retained earnings	1,200,000	940,000	260,000
Minority interest—20%	220,000	200,000	20,000
Total equities	$3,800,000	$3,500,000	$300,000

* Deduct.

Required: Prepare a consolidated statement of cash flows for Percy Corporation and Subsidiary for the year ended December 31, 19X7. Assume that all changes in plant assets are due to asset acquisitions and depreciation.

P 3–16   [AICPA adapted]

The consolidated workpaper balances of Bush, Inc. and its subsidiary, Dorr Corporation, as of December 31, 19X6 and 19X5 are as follows:

	19X6	19X5	Net Change Increase (Decrease)
Assets			
Cash	$ 313,000	$ 195,000	$ 118,000
Marketable equity securities at cost (MES)	175,000	175,000	—
Allowance to reduce MES to market	(13,000)	(24,000)	11,000
Accounts receivable—net	418,000	440,000	(22,000)
Inventories	595,000	525,000	70,000
Land	385,000	170,000	215,000
Plant and equipment	755,000	690,000	65,000
Accumulated depreciation	(199,000)	(145,000)	(54,000)
Goodwill—net	57,000	60,000	(3,000)
Total assets	$2,486,000	$2,086,000	$ 400,000
Liabilities and Stockholders' Equity			
Note payable, current portion	$ 150,000	$ 150,000	$ —
Accounts and accrued payables	595,000	474,000	121,000
Note payable, long-term portion	300,000	450,000	(150,000)
Deferred income taxes	44,000	32,000	12,000
Minority interest in Dorr	179,000	161,000	18,000
Common stock—$10 par	580,000	480,000	100,000
Additional paid-in capital	303,000	180,000	123,000
Retained earnings	335,000	195,000	140,000
Treasury stock at cost	—	(36,000)	36,000
Total equities	$2,486,000	$2,086,000	$ 400,000

Additional Information
1 On January 20, 19X6 Bush, Inc., issued 10,000 shares of its common stock for land having a fair value of $215,000.
2 On February 5, 19X6 Bush reissued all of its treasury stock for $44,000.
3 On May 15, 19X6 Bush paid a cash dividend of $58,000 on its common stock.
4 On August 8, 19X6 equipment was purchased for $127,000.
5 On September 30, 19X6 equipment was sold for $40,000. The equipment cost $62,000 and had a carrying amount of $34,000 on the date of sale.

6 On December 15, 19X6 Dorr Corporation paid a cash dividend of $50,000 on its common stock.

7 Deferred income taxes represent timing differences relating to the use of accelerated depreciation methods for income tax reporting and the straight-line method for financial reporting.

8 Consolidated net income for 19X6 was $198,000. Dorr's net income was $110,000.

9 Bush, Inc. owns 70 percent of its subsidiary, Dorr Corporation. There was no change in the ownership interest in Dorr during 19X5 and 19X6. There were no intercompany transactions other than the dividend paid to Bush by its subsidiary.

Required: Prepare a consolidated statement of cash flows for Bush, Inc., and Subsidiary for the year ended December 31, 19X6. Use the *indirect method.*

P 3–17 Polski Corporation and Solomon Corporation consummate a business combination on December 31, 19X8 with Polski exchanging its previously unissued $10 par common shares for common stock held by Solomon's stockholders. The combination meets all the requirements for a pooling of interests, and the companies expect to continue their own operations in a parent company–subsidiary relationship. Summary balance sheet data for the two companies at December 31, 19X8 are as follows:

	Polski Corporation	Solomon Corporation
Assets		
Current assets	$ 8,000,000	$4,000,000
Plant assets	12,000,000	2,000,000
Total assets	$20,000,000	$6,000,000
Liabilities and Stockholders' Equity		
Current liabilities	$ 1,000,000	$2,000,000
Long-term liabilities	3,000,000	—
Common stock—$10 par	10,000,000	2,000,000
Additional paid-in capital	1,000,000	1,500,000
Retained earnings	5,000,000	500,000
Total equities	$20,000,000	$6,000,000

Required: Prepare a partial balance sheet showing consolidated stockholders' equity for Polski Corporation and Subsidiary at December 31, 19X8 immediately after the pooling of interests under each of the following assumptions:

1 Polski issues 300,000 shares of its common stock for all the outstanding shares of Solomon Corporation.

2 Polski issues 400,000 shares of its common stock for all the outstanding shares of Solomon Corporation.

3 Polski issues 300,000 shares of its common stock for 90 percent of the outstanding shares of Solomon Corporation.

4 Polski issues 400,000 shares of its common stock for 90 percent of the outstanding shares of Solomon Corporation.

CHAPTER

4

CONSOLIDATION TECHNIQUES AND PROCEDURES

This chapter examines procedures for consolidating the financial statements of parent and subsidiary companies. Some differences in the consolidation process result from different methods of parent company accounting for its subsidiary investments. Consolidation working papers for a parent company/investor that uses the equity method of accounting are illustrated first to set the standard for good consolidation procedures. Next, the illustrations are repeated for the incomplete equity and cost methods of parent company accounting. Subsequently, the chapter examines additional complexities that arise from errors and omissions in the separate company records and detailed allocations of cost–book value differentials. The final section of the chapter illustrates the trial balance working paper format, which is an alternative to the financial statement format used in other sections of the chapter.

Chapter 3 presented the balance sheet working papers used to organize the information needed for consolidated balance sheets. By contrast, this chapter presents working papers that develop the information needed for consolidated balance sheets and income and retained earnings statements.

CONSOLIDATION UNDER THE EQUITY METHOD

Basic procedures used to consolidate the financial statements of affiliated companies are explained in conjunction with the following example of a parent company that uses the equity method of accounting for its subsidiary. Subsequently, the example is changed to illustrate differences in consolidation procedures that arise when the parent company accounts for its subsidiary under the incomplete equity and cost methods.

Equity Method—Year of Acquisition

Prep Corporation pays $87,000 for 80 percent of the outstanding voting stock of Snap Corporation on January 1, 19X5 when Snap Corporation's stockholders' equity consists of $60,000 capital stock and $30,000 retained earnings. The $15,000 excess of investment cost over book value acquired [$87,000 − ($90,000 × 80%)]

PREP CORPORATION AND SUBSIDIARY
CONSOLIDATION WORKING PAPERS
FOR THE YEAR ENDED DECEMBER 31, 19X5

	Prep	80% Snap	Adjustments and Eliminations		Minority Interest	Consolidated Statements
Income Statement Revenue	$250,000	$ 65,000				$315,000
Income from Snap	18,500		a	18,500		
Expenses	200,000*	40,000*	c	1,500		241,500*
Minority interest income ($25,000 × 20%)					$ 5,000	5,000*
Net income	$ 68,500	$ 25,000				$ 68,500
Retained Earnings Retained earnings—Prep	$ 5,000					$ 5,000
Retained earnings—Snap		$ 30,000	b	30,000		
Add: Net income	68,500 ✓	25,000 ✓				68,500
Deduct: Dividends	30,000*	15,000*	a	12,000	3,000*	30,000*
Retained earnings December 31, 19X5	$ 43,500	$ 40,000				$ 43,500
Balance Sheet Cash	$ 40,000	$ 10,000				$ 50,000
Other current assets	90,000	50,000				140,000
Investment in Snap	93,500		a b	6,500 87,000		
Plant and equipment	300,000	100,000				400,000
Accumulated depreciation	50,000*	30,000*				80,000*
Goodwill			b 15,000	c 1,500		13,500
	$473,500	$130,000				$523,500
Liabilities	$ 80,000	$ 30,000				$110,000
Capital stock	350,000	60,000	b	60,000		350,000
Retained earnings	43,500 ✓	40,000 ✓				43,500
	$473,500	$130,000				
Minority interest January 1, 19X5 ($90,000 × 20%)			b	18,000	18,000	
Minority interest December 31, 19X5					$20,000	20,000
						$523,500

* Deduct.

Exhibit 4–1 Equity Method—Working Papers for Year of Acquisition

is allocated to goodwill with a ten-year amortization period, and Snap's net income and dividends are as follows:

	19X5	*19X6*
Net income	$25,000	$30,000
Dividends	15,000	15,000

Financial statements for Prep and Snap Corporations for 19X5 are presented in the first two working paper columns of Exhibit 4–1. Prep's $18,500 income from Snap for 19X5 consists of 80 percent of Snap's $25,000 net income for 19X5 less $1,500 goodwill amortization, and its $93,500 investment in Snap account at December 31, 19X5 consists of $87,000 investment cost plus $18,500 income from Snap, less $12,000 dividends received from Snap during 19X5.

Numerous consolidation approaches and any number of different adjustment and elimination combinations will result in correct amounts for the consolidated financial statements. The adjustment and elimination entries that appear in the working papers *do not affect the general ledger accounts of either the parent or its subsidiaries.* Adjusting or eliminating accounts or balances simply means that the amounts listed in the separate company columns of the working papers are either (1) adjusted before inclusion in the consolidated statement column, or (2) eliminated and do not appear in the consolidated statement column. A single working paper entry often adjusts some items and eliminates others. It is the objective of the working paper entry, not its classification as adjusting or eliminating, that is important in developing working paper skills and in understanding the consolidation process.

The check marks beside the net income and ending retained earnings amounts in the separate statement columns of Exhibit 4–1 are intended as reminders that these items are not subject to adjustment or elimination. This is because consolidated net income consists of consolidated revenues less consolidated expenses, and if adjustments are needed, they should relate to individual revenue and expense items rather than net income. Similarly, the retained earnings amount that appears in the consolidated balance sheet consists of beginning consolidated retained earnings plus consolidated net income less parent company dividends. If errors or omissions have occurred such that parent company retained earnings do not equal consolidated retained earnings, the amount of the parent company's beginning retained earnings is corrected through working paper entries to adjust it to *beginning* consolidated retained earnings. Since parent company net income and retained earnings amounts under the equity method are equal to consolidated net income and retained earnings, retained earnings adjustments are needed only when the parent company fails to apply the equity method as a one-line consolidation. Because Prep Corporation (Exhibit 4–1) has applied the equity method correctly, its net income of $68,500 is equal to consolidated net income, and both its beginning and ending retained earnings amounts are equal to the $5,000 and $43,500 consolidated retained earnings amounts, respectively.

The first entry in the Exhibit 4–1 working paper is journalized as:

a	Income from Snap	$18,500	
	Dividends		$12,000
	Investment in Snap		6,500

To eliminate income and dividends from Snap and return the investment account to its beginning of the period balance.

Recall that working paper entries are shaded to avoid confusion with journal entries that are recorded by parent companies and subsidiaries. Investment income is eliminated because the consolidated income statement shows the details of revenue and expense rather than the one-line consolidation reflected in the income from Snap account. Dividends received from the subsidiary are eliminated because they are mere transfers within the consolidated entity for which the statements are being prepared. The difference between income from subsidiary recognized on the books of the parent company and the dividends received represents the change in the investment account for the period. The $6,500 credit to the investment in Snap account reduces that account to its $87,000 beginning-of-the-period balance and thereby establishes reciprocity between the investment in Snap and Snap's stockholders' equity at January 1, 19X5.

Working paper entry b from Exhibit 4–1 is journalized as follows:

b	Retained earnings—Snap (beginning)	$30,000	
	Capital stock—Snap	60,000	
	Goodwill	15,000	
	Investment in Snap		$87,000
	Minority interest		18,000

To eliminate reciprocal equity and investment balances, establish beginning minority interest, and enter unamortized goodwill.

This entry eliminates reciprocal investment and equity balances, enters the unamortized excess of investment cost over book value acquired as of the beginning of the year, and constructs the beginning minority interest ($90,000 × 20%) as a separate item. Observe that entry b eliminates reciprocal investment and equity balances as of the *beginning* of the period and enters minority interest as of the *beginning* of the period. Therefore, the goodwill (cost–book value differential) portion of the entry is also a *beginning*-of-the-period unamortized amount.

Many accountants prefer to eliminate only the parent's percentage of the capital stock and retained earnings of the subsidiary and to transfer the amount not eliminated directly to the minority interest column. While the difference is solely a matter of preference, the approach used here emphasizes that *all* the individual stockholders' equity accounts of a subsidiary are eliminated in the process of consolidation.

Entry c in the working papers of Exhibit 4–1 enters the current year's goodwill amortization as an expense of the consolidated entity and reduces unamortized goodwill from its $15,000 unamortized balance at January 1 to its $13,500 unamortized balance at December 31, 19X5.

c	Expenses	$1,500	
	Goodwill		$1,500

To enter current amortization of goodwill.

This working paper entry to adjust consolidated expenses is needed even though Prep Corporation amortized goodwill on its separate books under the equity method. Prep's amortization of the goodwill is reflected in its income from Snap account, and working paper entry a eliminated that account for consolidation purposes in order to disaggregate the revenue and expense components in reporting consolidated income.

Sequence of Working Paper Entries

The *sequence* of the working paper entries in Exhibit 4–1 is both logical and necessary. Entry a adjusts the investment in Snap for changes during 19X5, and entry b eliminates the investment in Snap after adjustment to its beginning-of-the-period balance in entry a. Entry b also enters unamortized goodwill in the working papers as of the beginning of the period. Subsequently, entry c amortizes the goodwill for the current period and reduces the asset goodwill to its unamortized amount at the balance sheet date. As additional complexities of consolidation are encountered, the sequence of working paper adjustments and eliminations is expanded to the following:

1 Adjustments for *errors and omissions* in the separate parent company and subsidiary statements
2 Adjustments to eliminate *intercompany profits and losses*
3 Adjustments to eliminate *income and dividends* from subsidiary and adjust the investment in subsidiary to its beginning-of-the-period balance
4 Eliminations of *reciprocal investment in subsidiary and subsidiary equity balances*
5 *Allocation and amortization of cost–book value differentials* (from step 4)
6 Elimination of *other reciprocal balances* (intercompany receivables and payables, revenues and expenses, and so on)

Although other sequences of working paper entries may be adequate in a given consolidation, *the above sequence will always work. It is recommended that you learn it and apply it throughout your study of consolidation.*

After all adjustments and eliminations are entered in the working papers, the minority interest in subsidiary net income is computed and entered as an addition in the minority interest column (deduction for loss) and a deduction in the consolidated income statement (addition for loss). The $3,000 dividends of Snap that are not eliminated reflect dividends paid to minority stockholders and are carried to the minority interest column as a deduction. The minority interest reflected in the consolidated balance sheet is computed in the working papers as beginning minority interest plus minority interest income less minority interest dividends. In case the ownership in a subsidiary increases during a period, the minority interest computation will reflect the minority interest at the balance sheet date, with minority interest income and dividends also reflecting the ending minority interest percentages.

Some accountants prefer to use a working paper entry for inserting the minority interest income and dividend items into the consolidation worksheet. For exmaple, these items for the Prep–Snap consolidation could have been incorporated with the following working paper entry:

Minority interest income	$5,000	
Dividends		$3,000
Minority interest		2,000

This approach explains all minority interest components through consolidation working paper entries, but it tends to increase the size of the spreadsheet. Note that *the investment in subsidiary balances are always eliminated when a subsidiary is consolidated.* Although the investment in subsidiary account may be adjusted to establish reciprocity, it never appears in a consolidated balance sheet when the subsidiary accounts are consolidated. Likewise, *investment income from subsidiaries that are consolidated is always eliminated. Consolidated net income is computed by deducting consolidated expenses and minority interest income from consolidated revenues.* It is *not* determined by adjusting the separate net incomes of parent and subsidiary. Note the arrows from the consolidated income statement to the consolidated retained earnings statement and from the consolidated retained earnings statement to the consolidated balance sheet in Exhibit 4–1. These arrows simply indicate that consolidated net income is determined from consolidated revenue and expense and carried to the consolidated retained earnings statement, and the consolidated retained earnings is carried to the consolidated balance sheet.

Consolidated retained earnings at the end of the period is computed in the working papers as the sum of beginning consolidated retained earnings and consolidated net income less parent company dividends. If a complete equity method of accounting has been used, beginning consolidated retained earnings will equal beginning parent company retained earnings. In the absence of a correct equity method of accounting, the beginning retained earnings of the parent must be adjusted in years subsequent to the year of acquisition to convert it to beginning consolidated retained earnings. Capital stock and other paid-in capital accounts appearing in a consolidated balance sheet are those of the parent company.

Equity Method—Year Subsequent to Acquisition

Prep Corporation maintains its 80 percent ownership interest in Snap throughout 19X6, recording income from Snap of $22,500 for the year (80 percent of Snap's $30,000 net income less $1,500 goodwill amortization). At December 31, 19X6, Prep's investment in Snap account has a balance of $104,000, determined as follows:

Investment cost January 1, 19X5	$ 87,000
Income from Snap—19X5	18,500
Dividends from Snap—19X5	− 12,000
Investment in Snap December 31, 19X5	93,500
Income from Snap—19X6	22,500
Dividends from Snap—19X6	− 12,000
Investment in Snap December 31, 19X6	$104,000

The only intercompany transaction between Prep and Snap during 19X6 was a $10,000 noninterest-bearing loan to Snap during the third quarter of the year.

Consolidation working papers for Prep Corporation and Subsidiary for the year 19X6 are presented in Exhibit 4–2. Since there were no errors or omissions or intercompany profits relating to the consolidation, the first working paper entry is to eliminate income and dividends from Snap as follows:

a	Income from Snap	$22,500	
	Dividends		$12,000
	Investment in Snap		10,500

To eliminate income and dividends from Snap and return the investment account to its beginning of the period balance.

This entry adjusts the investment in Snap account to its $93,500 December 31, 19X5 balance and establishes reciprocity with Snap's stockholders' equity at December 31, 19X5.

Entry b eliminates investment in Snap and stockholders' equity of Snap as follows:

b	Retained earnings—Snap	$40,000	
	Capital stock—Snap	60,000	
	Goodwill	13,500	
	Investment in Snap		$93,500
	Minority interest		20,000

To eliminate reciprocal investment and equity balances, establish beginning minority interest, and enter unamortized goodwill.

PREP CORPORATION AND SUBSIDIARY
CONSOLIDATION WORKING PAPERS
FOR THE YEAR ENDED DECEMBER 31, 19X6

	Prep	80% Snap	Adjustments and Eliminations		Minority Interest	Consolidated Statements
Income Statement Revenue	$300,000	$ 75,000				$375,000
Income from Snap	22,500		a	22,500		
Expenses	244,000*	45,000*	c	1,500		290,500*
Minority interest income ($30,000 × 20%)					$ 6,000	6,000*
Net income	$ 78,500	$ 30,000				$ 78,500
Retained Earnings Retained earnings—Prep	$ 43,500					$ 43,500
Retained earnings—Snap		$ 40,000	b	40,000		
Net income	78,500✔	30,000✔				78,500
Dividends	45,000*	15,000*	a	12,000	3,000*	45,000*
Retained earnings December 31, 19X6	$ 77,000	$ 55,000				$ 77,000
Balance Sheet Cash	$ 46,000	$ 20,000				$ 66,000
Note receivable—Snap	10,000		d	10,000		
Other current assets	97,000	70,000				167,000
Investment in Snap	104,000		a b	10,500 93,500		
Plant and equipment	300,000	100,000				400,000
Accumulated depreciation	60,000*	40,000*				100,000*
Goodwill			b 13,500	c 1,500		12,000
	$497,000	$150,000				$545,000
Note payable—Prep		$ 10,000	d	10,000		
Liabilities	$ 70,000	25,000				$ 95,000
Capital stock	350,000	60,000	b	60,000		350,000
Retained earnings	77,000✔	55,000✔				77,000
	$497,000	$150,000				
Minority interest January 1, 19X6 ($100,000 × 20%)			b	20,000	20,000	
Minority interest December 31, 19X6					$23,000	23,000
						$545,000

* Deduct.

Exhibit 4–2   Equity Method—Working Papers for Year Subsequent to Acquisition

128

Since entry b eliminates the investment in Snap and stockholders' equity of Snap amounts at December 31, 19X5, and enters the minority interest at December 31, 19X5, the $13,500 investment cost–book value difference reflects unamortized goodwill at December 31, 19X5. Thus, entry c amortizes this amount to $12,000 at December 31, 19X6.

c	Expenses	$1,500	
	Goodwill		$1,500
	To enter current goodwill amortization.		

The final working paper entry eliminates intercompany notes payable and notes receivable balances because the amounts are not assets and liabilities of the consolidated entity.

d	Note payable—Prep	$10,000	
	Note receivable—Snap		$10,000
	To eliminate reciprocal receivable and payable balances.		

Since the intercompany loan was noninterest-bearing, the note receivable and the note payable are the only reciprocal balances created by the intercompany transaction. Additional eliminations for reciprocal interest income and interest expense and interest receivable and interest payable balances would have been needed if the intercompany loan had been interest bearing.

Compare the consolidation working papers of Exhibit 4–2 with those of Exhibit 4–1. Notice that the December 31, 19X5 minority interest from Exhibit 4–1 is the beginning minority interest in Exhibit 4–2. Also note that the unamortized goodwill in the consolidated balance sheet of Exhibit 4–1 is the beginning-of-the-period unamortized goodwill in Exhibit 4–2.

CONSOLIDATION UNDER AN INCOMPLETE EQUITY METHOD

When the equity method is correctly applied, the parent company's net income is equal to consolidated net income, and the parent company's retained earnings is equal to consolidated retained earnings. This equality of parent company and consolidated income and retained earnings amounts does not always exist. It does not exist when the equity method is applied incorrectly, or when the cost method of accounting for subsidiary investments is used. For example, a parent company, in applying the equity method of accounting, may not amortize the difference between investment cost and book value acquired on its separate books, or it may not eliminate intercompany profits or losses. Such omissions result in an incomplete application of the equity method of accounting.[1] Other errors in applying the equity method of accounting result in similar misstatements of parent company income and retained earnings.

The problem of a misapplication of the equity method of accounting or use of the cost method in accounting for subsidiary investments may not be as serious as it first appears. This is because *the accountant must prepare correct consolidated financial statements regardless of how the parent accounts for its subsidiary investment.* There is no violation of generally accepted accounting principles as

---

[1]*Incomplete applications of the equity method* are frequently encountered in textbook problems and illustrations and on CPA examinations.

long as the consolidated financial statements prepared for issuance to stockholders are correct and the parent/investor company issues no other audited financial statements. The continued use of either the cost method or an incomplete application of the equity method of accounting by many firms is based on the assumed issuance of consolidated financial statements as the only statements prepared for stockholders of the primary reporting entity. When bankers require audited parent company financial statements to support lines of credit and long-term loans, the statements should reflect the equity method as a one-line consolidation.

Incomplete Equity Method—Year of Acquisition

Exhibits 4–3 and 4–4 show consolidation working papers for Prep Corporation and Subsidiary for 19X5 and 19X6 based on the same assumptions and the same data as Exhibits 4–1 and 4–2, except that Prep Corporation has not amortized goodwill on its separate books. Thus, Prep's income statement for 19X5 (Exhibit 4–3) shows income from Snap of $20,000 and net income of $70,000, rather than $18,500 and $68,500, as shown under the equity method in Exhibit 4–1. The same $1,500 difference is reflected in Prep's investment in Snap account ($95,000 rather than $93,500) and Prep's retained earnings ($45,000 rather than $43,500) at December 31, 19X5.

One of the first things that the accountant does in consolidating the financial statements of affiliated companies is determine how the parent company has accounted for its subsidiary investment(s). A simple check of the relationship between the parent company's equity in the subsidiary's net income and the income recognized by the subsidiary will usually reveal the parent company's method of accounting. The fact that Prep's $20,000 income from Snap is equal to 80 percent of Snap's $25,000 net income for 19X5 provides evidence of an incomplete equity method. Further evidence lies in the fact that Prep's investment in Snap account of $95,000 at December 31, 19X5 is $15,000 greater than the underlying equity ($100,000 × 80%) on that date, indicating that no goodwill amortization has occurred.

The consolidation working paper entries for 19X5 (Exhibit 4–3) are reproduced in journal form as follows:

a	Income from Snap	$20,000	
	Dividends		$12,000
	Investment in Snap		8,000

To establish reciprocity as of the beginning of the period.

b	Retained earnings—Snap	$30,000	
	Capital stock—Snap	60,000	
	Goodwill	15,000	
	Investment in Snap		$87,000
	Minority interest		18,000

To eliminate reciprocal equity and investment amounts, establish minority interest at the beginning of the period, and set up the original goodwill at acquisition.

c	Expenses	$ 1,500	
	Goodwill		$ 1,500

To adjust expenses to reflect current goodwill amortization.

Compare the working paper entries in Exhibit 4–3 with those in Exhibit 4–1 under the equity method. Notice that the entries and amounts are the same except for entry a, where the $20,000 debit to income from Snap does not reflect goodwill amortization and the $8,000 credit to investment in Snap simply reflects

PREP CORPORATION AND SUBSIDIARY
CONSOLIDATION WORKING PAPERS
FOR THE YEAR ENDED DECEMBER 31, 19X5

	Prep	80% Snap	Adjustments and Eliminations		Minority Interest	Consolidated Statements
Income Statement Revenue	$250,000	$ 65,000				$315,000
Income from Snap	20,000		a	20,000		
Expenses	200,000*	40,000*	c	1,500		241,500*
Minority interest income ($25,000 × 20%)					$ 5,000	5,000*
Net income	$ 70,000	$ 25,000				$ 68,500 ⌐
Retained Earnings Retained earnings—Prep	$ 5,000					$ 5,000
Retained earnings—Snap		$ 30,000	b	30,000		
Add: Net income	70,000✔	25,000✔				68,500 ◄
Deduct: Dividends	30,000*	15,000*		a 12,000	3,000*	30,000*
Retained earnings December 31, 19X5	$ 45,000	$ 40,000				$ 43,500 ⌐
Balance Sheet Cash	$ 40,000	$ 10,000				$ 50,000
Other current assets	90,000	50,000				140,000
Investment in Snap	95,000		a 8,000 b 87,000			
Plant and equipment	300,000	100,000				400,000
Accumulated depreciation	50,000*	30,000*				80,000*
Goodwill			b 15,000	c 1,500		13,500
	$475,000	$130,000				$523,500
Liabilities	$ 80,000	$ 30,000				$110,000
Capital stock	350,000	60,000	b 60,000			350,000
Retained earnings	45,000✔	40,000✔				43,500 ◄
	$475,000	$130,000				
Minority interest January 1, 19X5 ($90,000 × 20%)			b 18,000		18,000	
Minority interest December 31, 19X5					$20,000	20,000
						$523,500

* Deduct.

Exhibit 4–3   Incomplete Equity Method—Working Papers for Year of Acquisition

the investment increase for 19X5 as reported on Prep's books. Even so, the objective of that entry is the same as the comparable working paper entry in Exhibit 4–1—to eliminate investment income and dividends received and adjust the investment account to its beginning-of-the-period balance.

Prep's failure to amortize goodwill in accounting for its investment in Snap for 19X5 has a minimal effect on the consolidation working papers for 19X5 because Prep's January 1, 19X5 investment in Snap ($87,000) and retained earnings ($5,000) are not affected by the omission. The omission does, of course, create an inequality between Prep's net income ($70,000) and consolidated net income ($68,500) and between Prep's retained earnings ($45,000) and consolidated retained earnings ($43,500) at December 31, 19X5. Since consolidated financial statements are unaffected by the parent company's method of accounting for its investment, the consolidated financial statements for the incomplete equity method (Exhibit 4–3) are identical with those prepared under a correct equity method (Exhibit 4–1).

Alternative Conversion to Equity Method

As an alternative to the working paper entries illustrated in Exhibit 4–3, the incomplete equity method may be considered a departure from the standard that requires (1) conversion to standard and (2) working paper entries as illustrated for the equity method in Exhibit 4–1. This alternative would entail the following *first* working paper entry in Exhibit 4–3.

Income from Snap	$1,500	
Investment in Snap		$1,500
To correct for the omission of goodwill amortization on Prep's books.		

This entry converts the parent company's accounts to the equity method, after which the other working paper entries for 19X5 would be the same as those illustrated in Exhibit 4–1 under the equity method. The working paper entry illustrated above could also be recorded on Prep's separate records to adjust to the equity method as a one-line consolidation. If Prep's books have been closed for 19X5, the correcting entry on Prep's books would be a debit to retained earnings and a credit to investment in Snap for $1,500.

Incomplete Equity Method—Year Subsequent to Acquisition

Application of the incomplete equity method has a greater effect on consolidation working paper procedures in years subsequent to the year of acquisition because beginning investment and retained earnings amounts on the parent company's books are affected by the omissions. Exhibit 4–4 shows Prep's investment in Snap account at December 31, 19X6 in the amount of $107,000, compared with $104,000 in Exhibit 4–2 under the equity method. This $3,000 difference reflects the omission of goodwill amortization for both 19X5 and 19X6. The omissions affect Prep's beginning retained earnings in 19X6 by $1,500 ($45,000 rather than $43,500 under the equity method) and ending retained earnings in 19X6 by $3,000 ($80,000 rather than $77,000 under the equity method). Although the consolidated financial statements presented in Exhibit 4–4 are identical with those shown in Exhibit 4–2 under the equity method, a working paper change is necessary.

PREP CORPORATION AND SUBSIDIARY
CONSOLIDATION WORKING PAPERS
FOR THE YEAR ENDED DECEMBER 31, 19X6

	Prep	80% Snap	Adjustments and Eliminations		Minority Interest	Consolidated Statements
Income Statement Revenue	$300,000	$ 75,000				$375,000
Income from Snap	24,000		a	24,000		
Expenses	244,000*	45,000*	c	1,500		290,500*
Minority interest income ($30,000 × 20%)					$ 6,000	6,000*
Net income	$ 80,000	$ 30,000				$ 78,500 ⌐
Retained Earnings Retained earnings—Prep	$ 45,000		c	1,500		$ 43,500
Retained earnings—Snap		$ 40,000	b	40,000		
Net income	80,000 ✓	30,000 ✓				78,500 ◄
Dividends	45,000*	15,000*		a 12,000	3,000*	45,000*
Retained earnings December 31, 19X6	$ 80,000	$ 55,000				$ 77,000 ⌐
Balance Sheet Cash	$ 46,000	$ 20,000				$ 66,000
Note receivable—Snap	10,000			d 10,000		
Other current assets	97,000	70,000				167,000
Investment in Snap	107,000			a 12,000 b 95,000		
Plant and equipment	300,000	100,000				400,000
Accumulated depreciation	60,000*	40,000*				100,000*
Goodwill			b 15,000	c 3,000		12,000
	$500,000	$150,000				$545,000
Note payable—Prep		$ 10,000	d 10,000			
Liabilities	$ 70,000	25,000				$ 95,000
Capital stock	350,000	60,000	b 60,000			350,000
Retained earnings	80,000 ✓	55,000 ✓				77,000 ◄
	$500,000	$150,000				
Minority interest January 1, 19X6 ($100,000 × 20%)				b 20,000	20,000	
Minority interest December 31, 19X6					$23,000	23,000
						$545,000

* Deduct.

Exhibit 4–4 *Incomplete Equity Method—Working Papers for Year Subsequent to Acquisition*

The working paper entries for 19X6 in journal form are as follows:

a	Income from Snap	$24,000	
	Dividends		$12,000
	Investment in Snap		12,000

To establish reciprocity as of the beginning of the period.

b	Retained earnings—Snap	$40,000	
	Capital stock—Snap	60,000	
	Goodwill	15,000	
	Investment in Snap		$95,000
	Minority interest		20,000

To eliminate reciprocal equity and investment amounts, establish minority interest at the beginning of the period, and set up the original goodwill at acquisition.

c	Expenses	$ 1,500	
	Retained earnings—Prep	1,500	
	Goodwill		$ 3,000

To adjust expenses to reflect current goodwill amortization and to charge Prep's retained earnings for goodwill amortization omitted in 19X5.

d	Note payable—Prep	$10,000	
	Note receivable—Snap		$10,000

To eliminate reciprocal note payable and receivable amounts.

Entry a eliminates the income from Snap (as recognized on Prep's books) and the dividends received from Snap and adjusts the investment in Snap to its beginning-of-the-year amount on Prep's books. Entry b eliminates Snap's beginning-of-the-period equity balances and the investment in Snap at the beginning of the year and enters minority interest at its beginning-of-the-year amount. Because the goodwill (cost–book value differential) was not amortized by Prep, the debit to goodwill reflects the original goodwill, a difference that will remain as long as Prep uses the incomplete equity method. The fact that goodwill is amortized for consolidation purposes does not affect this generalization because working paper entries are not recorded on parent company books.

Entry c for 19X6 includes an additional $1,500 adjustment for 19X5 amortization that was not recorded by Prep. The $1,500 debit in 19X6 to Prep's retained earnings converts Prep's beginning retained earnings to beginning *consolidated* retained earnings. That is, it reduces Prep's December 31, 19X5 retained earnings of $45,000 to reflect consolidated retained earnings of $43,500 as shown in the consolidated balance sheet at December 31, 19X5. The $3,000 credit to goodwill in working paper entry c reflects two years' amortization and reduces goodwill to its $12,000 unamortized balance at December 31, 19X6. The last working paper entry to eliminate reciprocal note payable and receivable balances is not affected by the method of parent company accounting for its subsidiaries.

Alternative Conversion to Equity Method

If the alternative working paper approach described at the end of the 19X5 illustration is used for the 19X6 working papers, the omissions on Prep's books can be corrected by a first working paper entry as follows:

a	Income from Snap	$1,500	
	Retained earnings—Prep	1,500	
	Investment in Snap		$3,000

To correct income from Snap for the omission of the current year's goodwill amortization and correct Prep's beginning retained earnings for prior years' goodwill amortization.

After this "conversion to equity" working paper entry, the other entries for Exhibit 4–4 would be the same as those illustrated in Exhibit 4–2. Assuming that Prep's books have been closed at December 31, 19X6, Prep could convert to the equity method as of January 1, 19X7 with a $3,000 correcting entry to debit retained earnings and credit the investment in Snap account.

CONSOLIDATION UNDER THE COST METHOD

The cost method of accounting for subsidiary investments emphasizes the concept of legal entity, as opposed to the equity method, which emphasizes the economic entity under control of a single management team. Under the cost method, income is recognized only when dividends are declared by the subsidiary. The investment account remains unchanged except when dividends reduce subsidiary retained earnings below retained earnings at the date of acquisition of the investment or when significant and permanent subsidiary losses impair subsidiary capital. Dividend income rather than investment income appears on the parent company's income statement when the cost method is used.

Differences from applying the cost, incomplete equity, and equity methods are reflected in the parent company's investment in subsidiary (assets) and retained earnings (equities) balances. No other balance sheet accounts are affected.

Consolidation under the cost method can be accomplished in either of two ways. The traditional set of working paper entries to consolidate a parent company and its investee accounted for by the cost method begins with an entry to adjust the investment in subsidiary account for the parent company's share of subsidiary retained earnings increases since acquisition, and to credit parent company retained earnings for the same amount to convert beginning parent company retained earnings to beginning consolidated retained earnings. This adjustment is not needed for consolidations in the period of acquisition since the parent's beginning investment and retained earnings balances will not have been affected. A second entry eliminates reciprocal dividend income and dividends paid amounts, and a third entry eliminates reciprocal investment and equity balances and enters beginning-of-the-period goodwill and minority interest. An alternative approach for consolidating a subsidiary accounted for by the cost method is to use the conversion to equity method. The conversion to equity is made in the first consolidation working paper entry, after which the remaining working paper entries are the same as under the equity method. The traditional method is easier to use for consolidations in the year of acquisition, but it gets quite complicated in years subsequent to acquisition, especially if there are intercompany transactions between the two affiliates. Both the traditional approach and the conversion to equity approach are illustrated for the Prep and Snap consolidation.

Cost Method—Traditional Approach

Year of Acquisition   Consolidation procedures for the cost method using the *traditional approach* are illustrated in Exhibits 4–5 and 4–6 for Prep Corporation and its 80 percent owned subsidiary, Snap Corporation. On the cost basis, Prep's investment in Snap remains at $87,000 throughout 19X5 and 19X6, and the only entries made by Prep are to record receipt of 80 percent of the dividends declared by Snap. The entry in 19X5 and again in 19X6 is:

Cash	$12,000	
Dividend income		$12,000

To record receipt of 80% of $15,000 dividends paid by Snap.

The consolidated financial statements that appear in the working papers in Exhibit 4–5 are exactly the same as those shown in Exhibits 4–1 and 4–3, but the working paper entries are slightly different. Entry a is journalized as follows:

a	Dividend income	$12,000	
	Dividends		$12,000
	To eliminate reciprocal dividend income and dividends paid to Prep.		

This working paper entry eliminates reciprocal dividend income and dividends paid amounts. The $3,000 subsidiary dividends not eliminated relate to the 20 percent minority interest and are deducted in the minority interest column. Entry b is reconstructed as follows:

b	Retained earnings—Snap (beginning)	$30,000	
	Capital stock—Snap	60,000	
	Goodwill	15,000	
	Investment in Snap		$87,000
	Minority interest		18,000
	To eliminate reciprocal investment and equity amounts and establish beginning minority interest and goodwill amounts.		

Reciprocity between the investment in Snap account on Prep's books and the capital stock and beginning retained earnings accounts on Snap's books exists since these items are stated at their January 1, 19X5 amounts. Entry b simply eliminates reciprocal investment and equity amounts and enters beginning of the period goodwill and minority interest.

Entry c for current amortization of goodwill is exactly the same as that for Exhibits 4–1 and 4–3.

c	Expenses	$1,500	
	Goodwill		$1,500
	To enter current goodwill amortization.		

Year Subsequent to Acquisition   More significant differences in traditional working paper procedures under the cost and equity methods of accounting for subsidiary investments occur in periods subsequent to the year in which the investment is acquired. These differences are illustrated in Exhibit 4–6 by extending the Prep/Snap illustration to the year 19X6.

Again, the consolidated statements that appear in Exhibit 4–6 are exactly the same as those in Exhibits 4–2 and 4–4, but the working paper entries are different. Entry a in Exhibit 4–6 establishes reciprocity between the investment in Snap at January 1, 19X6 and the subsidiary equity amounts at the same date.

a	Investment in Snap	$8,000	
	Retained earnings—Prep (beginning)		$8,000
	To establish reciprocity between the investment account and Snap's equity accounts.		

The $8,000 amount is Prep's share of the increase in Snap's retained earnings (undistributed income) from the January 1, 19X5 date of acquisition to the January 1, 19X6 beginning of the 19X6 period of consolidation. Alternatively, the $8,000 amount is 80 percent of Snap's $25,000 income for 19X5, less 80 percent of Snap's $15,000 dividends declared in 19X5 ($20,000 − $12,000). Observe that working

PREP CORPORATION AND SUBSIDIARY
CONSOLIDATION WORKING PAPERS
FOR THE YEAR ENDED DECEMBER 31, 19X5

	Prep	80% Snap	Adjustments and Eliminations		Minority Interest	Consolidated Statements
Income Statement Revenue	$250,000	$ 65,000				$315,000
Dividend income	12,000		a 12,000			
Expenses	200,000*	40,000*	c 1,500			241,500*
Minority interest income					$ 5,000	5,000*
Net income	$ 62,000	$ 25,000				$ 68,500
Retained Earnings Retained earnings—Prep	$ 5,000					$ 5,000
Retained earnings—Snap		$ 30,000	b 30,000			
Net income	62,000✔	25,000✔				68,500
Dividends	30,000*	15,000*		a 12,000	3,000*	30,000*
Retained earnings—ending	$ 37,000	$ 40,000				$ 43,500
Balance Sheet Cash	$ 40,000	$ 10,000				$ 50,000
Other current assets	90,000	50,000				140,000
Investment in Snap	87,000		b 87,000			
Plant and equipment	300,000	100,000				400,000
Accumulated depreciation	50,000*	30,000*				80,000*
Goodwill			b 15,000	c 1,500		13,500
	$467,000	$130,000				$523,500
Liabilities	$ 80,000	$ 30,000				$110,000
Capital stock	350,000	60,000	b 60,000			350,000
Retained earnings	37,000✔	40,000✔				43,500
	$467,000	$130,000				
Minority interest January 1, 19X5 ($90,000 × 20%)			b 18,000		18,000	
Minority interest December 31, 19X5					$20,000	20,000
						$523,500

* Deduct.

Exhibit 4–5 *Cost Method—Year of Acquisition (Traditional Approach)*

paper entry a adjusts for the omission of undistributed income under the cost method, but that it does not adjust for amortization of cost–book value differentials that are also omitted under the cost method. These latter items are adjusted in working paper entries c and d.

Entry b eliminates reciprocal dividend income and dividends paid amounts as follows:

	Prep	80% Snap	Adjustments and Eliminations				Minority Interest	Consolidated Statements
PREP CORPORATION AND SUBSIDIARY **CONSOLIDATION WORKING PAPERS** **FOR THE YEAR ENDED DECEMBER 31, 19X6**								
Income Statement Revenue	$300,000	$ 75,000						$375,000
Dividend income	12,000		b	12,000				
Expenses	244,000*	45,000*	d	1,500				290,500*
Minority interest income							$ 6,000	6,000*
Net income	$ 68,000	$ 30,000						$ 78,500
Retained Earnings Retained earnings—Prep	$ 37,000		d	1,500	a	8,000		$ 43,500
Retained earnings—Snap		$ 40,000	c	40,000				
Net income	68,000✓	30,000✓						78,500
Dividends	45,000*	15,000*			b	12,000	3,000*	45,000*
Retained earnings—ending	$ 60,000	$ 55,000						$ 77,000
Balance Sheet Cash	$ 46,000	$ 20,000						$ 66,000
Note receivable—Snap	10,000				e	10,000		
Other current assets	97,000	70,000						167,000
Investment in Snap	87,000		a	8,000	c	95,000		
Plant and equipment	300,000	100,000						400,000
Accumulated depreciation	60,000*	40,000*						100,000*
Goodwill			c	15,000	d	3,000		12,000
	$480,000	$150,000						$545,000
Note payable—Prep		$ 10,000	e	10,000				
Liabilities	$ 70,000	25,000						$ 95,000
Capital stock	350,000	60,000	c	60,000				350,000
Retained earnings	60,000✓	55,000✓						77,000
	$480,000	$150,000						
Minority interest January 1, 19X6 ($100,000 × 20%)					b	20,000	20,000	
Minority interest December 31, 19X6							$23,000	23,000
								$545,000

* Deduct.

Exhibit 4–6 *Cost Method—Year Subsequent to Acquisition (Traditional Approach)*

b	Dividend income	$12,000	
	Dividends		$12,000

To eliminate dividend income and dividends paid to Prep.

Entry c in the working papers is journalized as follows:

same →

c	Retained earnings—Snap (beginning)	$40,000	
	Capital stock—Snap	60,000	
	Goodwill	15,000	
	Investment in Snap		$95,000
	Minority interest		20,000

To eliminate reciprocal investment and equity accounts, establish beginning minority interest, and enter original goodwill.

This entry eliminates the reciprocal investment in Snap account, as adjusted in entry a, against Snap's capital stock and retained earnings balances at January 1, 19X6. It also enters the original $15,000 goodwill and the beginning-of-the-period minority interest.

Entry d adjusts expenses for the current amortization of goodwill, adjusts Prep's beginning retained earnings for the 19X5 goodwill amortization that was not recorded by Prep, and reduces the goodwill to $12,000, its correct unamortized balance at December 31, 19X6.

same →

d	Retained earnings—Prep (beginning)	$1,500	
	Expenses	1,500	
	Goodwill		$3,000

To enter current goodwill amortization and correct Prep's beginning retained earnings for prior years' amortization.

Entry e eliminates reciprocal note payable and note receivable accounts.

same →

e	Note payable—Prep	$10,000	
	Note receivable—Snap		$10,000

To eliminate reciprocal note payable and note receivable amounts.

Cost Method—Conversion to Equity Approach

Year of Acquisition   Consolidation under the cost method can be accomplished by converting to the equity method in the first entry in the working papers. The remaining working paper entries are then the same as under the equity method. This approach is illustrated for Prep and Snap in Exhibits 4–7 and 4–8. The cost-to-equity conversion in the year of acquisition is simplified by the fact that the investment is recorded at its cost. The entry on Prep's separate books in 19X5 to record dividend income of $12,000 fails to recognize its equity in Snap's undistributed income [80% × ($25,000 income − $15,000 dividends)] or to provide for the $1,500 goodwill amortization. Thus, Prep's income from Snap of $12,000 and net income of $62,000 under the cost method are each understated by Prep's $6,500 equity in Snap's undistributed income less amortization for 19X5.

PREP CORPORATION AND SUBSIDIARY
CONSOLIDATION WORKING PAPERS
FOR THE YEAR ENDED DECEMBER 31, 19X5

	Prep	80% Snap	Adjustments and Eliminations		Minority Interest	Consolidated Statements
Income Statement Revenue	$250,000	$ 65,000				$315,000
Dividend income	12,000		a 12,000			
Income from Snap			b 18,500	a 18,500		
Expenses	200,000*	40,000*	d 1,500			241,500*
Minority interest income ($25,000 × 20%)					$ 5,000	5,000*
Net income	$ 62,000	$ 25,000				$ 68,500
Retained Earnings Retained earnings—Prep	$ 5,000					$ 5,000
Retained earnings—Snap		$ 30,000	c 30,000			
Net income	62,000✓	25,000✓				68,500
Dividends	30,000*	15,000*		b 12,000	3,000*	30,000*
Retained earnings December 31, 19X5	$ 37,000	$ 40,000				$ 43,500
Balance Sheet Cash	$ 40,000	$ 10,000				$ 50,000
Other current assets	90,000	50,000				140,000
Investment in Snap	87,000		a 6,500	b 6,500 c 87,000		
Plant and equipment	300,000	100,000				400,000
Accumulated depreciation	50,000*	30,000*				80,000*
Goodwill			c 15,000	d 1,500		13,500
	$467,000	$130,000				$523,500
Liabilities	$ 80,000	$ 30,000				$110,000
Capital stock	350,000	60,000	c 60,000			350,000
Retained earnings	37,000✓	40,000✓				43,500
	$467,000	$130,000				
Minority interest January 1, 19X5 ($90,000 × 20%)				c 18,000	18,000	
Minority interest December 31, 19X5					$20,000	20,000
						$523,500

* Deduct.

Exhibit 4–7   *Cost Method—Year of Acquisition (Conversion to Equity)*

Conversion to the equity method requires the following working paper entry:

a	Dividend income	$12,000	
	Investment in Snap	6,500	
	Income from Snap		$18,500
	To correct income and investment account for the cost method.		

This entry enters income from Snap for 19X5 under the equity method, eliminates dividend income (distributed income from Snap), and adjusts the investment in Snap account for Prep's equity in undistributed income ($10,000 × 80%) less $1,500 goodwill amortization. If Prep chooses to adopt the equity method, this entry can be recorded in Prep's separate records to make the conversion.

The other working paper entries for 19X5 from Exhibit 4–7 are jouralized as follows:

b	Income from Snap	$18,500	
	Dividends		$12,000
	Investment in Snap		6,500
	To eliminate income and dividends of Snap and return the investment account to its beginning of the period balance.		
c	Retained earnings—Snap	$30,000	
	Capital stock—Snap	60,000	
	Goodwill	15,000	
	Investment in Snap		$87,000
	Minority interest		18,000
	To enter reciprocal investment and equity balances, establish beginning minority interest, and enter unamortized goodwill.		
d	Expenses	$ 1,500	
	Goodwill		$1,500
	To enter current goodwill amortization.		

A comparison of these last three working paper entries with those in Exhibit 4–1 shows that they are identical. Obviously, when the cost method is used, parent company net income and ending retained earnings ($62,000 and $37,000, respectively) are not equal to their consolidated financial statement counterparts because the parent has not taken up its share of the subsidiary's undistributed earnings, and it has not amortized the cost–book value differentials from the investment.

Year Subsequent to Acquisition   The cost-to-equity conversion in the consolidation working papers is more complex in periods after the year in which the subsidiary investment is acquired. This is because the parent's prior-year income will have been misstated by use of the cost method, which fails to recognize the parent's equity in any undistributed income of the subsidiary or to provide for amortization of cost–book value differentials. The balance sheet effect of the misstatement from using the cost method is to misstate the investment in subsidiary and retained earnings balances at year-end by equal amounts. Thus, the cost-to-equity conversion in years subsequent to acquisition requires adjustments for prior-year effects. It also requires adjustment for those effects occurring in the year of consolidation (current period). The cost-to-equity conversion in the working papers for the Prep/Snap example (Exhibit 4–8) for 19X6 is analyzed in terms of the components needed for conversion.

PREP CORPORATION AND SUBSIDIARY
CONSOLIDATION WORKING PAPERS—FOR THE YEAR ENDED DECEMBER 31, 19X6

	Prep	80% Snap	Adjustments and Eliminations		Minority Interest	Consolidated Statements
Income Statement Revenue	$300,000	$ 75,000				$375,000
Dividend income	12,000		a 12,000			
Income from Snap			b 22,500	a 22,500		
Expenses	244,000*	45,000*	d 1,500			290,500*
Minority interest income ($30,000 ×20%)					$ 6,000	6,000*
Net income	$ 68,000	$ 30,000				$ 78,500
Retained Earnings Retained earnings—Prep	$ 37,000			a 6,500		$ 43,500
Retained earnings—Snap		$ 40,000	c 40,000			
Net income	68,000✓	30,000✓				78,500
Dividends	45,000*	15,000*		b 12,000	3,000*	45,000*
Retained earnings December 31, 19X6	$ 60,000	$ 55,000				$ 77,000
Balance Sheet Cash	$ 46,000	$ 20,000				$ 66,000
Note receivable—Snap	10,000			e 10,000		
Other current assets	97,000	70,000				167,000
Investment in Snap	87,000		a 17,000	b 10,500 c 93,500		
Plant and equipment	300,000	100,000				400,000
Accumulated depreciation	60,000*	40,000*				100,000*
Goodwill			c 13,500	d 1,500		12,000
	$480,000	$150,000				$545,000
Note payable—Prep		$ 10,000	e 10,000			
Liabilities	$ 70,000	25,000				$ 95,000
Capital stock	350,000	60,000	c 60,000			350,000
Retained earnings	60,000✓	55,000✓				77,000
	$480,000	$150,000				
Minority interest January 1, 19X6 ($100,000 × 20%)				c 20,000	20,000	
Minority interest December 31, 19X6					$23,000	23,000
						$545,000

* Deduct.

Exhibit 4–8 *Cost Method—Year Subsequent to Acquisition (Conversion to Equity)*

	Prep's Retained Earnings 12/31/X5	Investment in Snap	Income from Snap	Dividend Income
Prior-Year Effect				
80% of Snap's $10,000 undistributed income for 19X5 (see note)	$ 8,000	$ 8,000		
Goodwill amortization— 19X5	(1,500)	(1,500)		
Current-Year Effect				
Reclassify dividend income as investment decrease ($15,000 dividend × 80%)		(12,000)		$(12,000)
Equity in 19X6 income of Snap ($30,000 × 80%)		24,000	$24,000	
Goodwill amortization— 19X6		(1,500)	(1,500)	
19X6 working paper adjustments	$ 6,500	$ 17,000	$22,500	$(12,000)

Note: A corporation's undistributed earnings are reflected in its retained earnings balances. Therefore, the changes in a subsidiary's retained earnings from the date of its acquisition to a subsequent evaluation date are ordinarily the changes in a subsidiary's undistributed earnings for cost-equity conversions. In this example, the computation is 80% × ($40,000 retained earnings at December 31, 19X5 – $30,000 retained earnings at January 1, 19X5).

This analysis provides the basis for working paper entry a in the consolidation working papers of Prep Corporation and Subsidiary for 19X6 (see Exhibit 4–8).

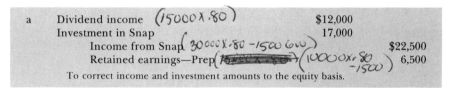

a	Dividend income (15000λ.80)		$12,000	
	Investment in Snap		17,000	
	Income from Snap (30000×.80 −1500 6w)			$22,500
	Retained earnings—Prep (10000×.80 −1500)			6,500

To correct income and investment amounts to the equity basis.

The other working paper entries for 19X6 are the same as those illustrated for the equity method in Exhibit 4–2. If the corporation chooses to convert from the cost to the equity method of parent company accounting, it can record entry a on its separate books before closing in 19X6. Alternatively, the entry to convert to the equity method after the books are closed at December 31, 19X6 would be a debit to the investment in Snap account and a credit to retained earnings for $17,000.

LOCATING ERRORS

The last part of consolidation working papers to be completed is the consolidated balance sheet section. Most errors made in consolidating the financial statements will show up when the consolidated balance sheet does not balance. If the consolidated balance sheet fails to balance after totals have been recomputed, individual items should be checked to ensure that all items have been included. Omissions involving the minority interest income in the consolidated income statement and minority interest equity in the consolidated balance sheet occur frequently because these items do not appear on the separate company statements. The equality of debits and credits in the working paper entries is checked by totaling the adjustment and elimination columns. Although proper coding of each working paper entry minimizes this type of error, many accountants prefer to total the adjustment and elimination columns as a regular working paper procedure.

EXCESS ALLOCATED TO IDENTIFIABLE NET ASSETS

Consolidation working paper procedures for allocating an excess of investment cost over underlying book value to specific assets and liabilities are similar to those illustrated for goodwill. The working paper entries are more complex, however, because more accounts are affected and additional allocation, amortization, and depreciation schemes are required. These additional working paper complexities are illustrated here for Pate Corporation and its 90 percent owned subsidiary, Solo Corporation.

Pate acquired its equity interest in Solo on December 31, 19X5 for $3,650,000 cash when Solo's stockholders' equity consisted of $2,000,000 capital stock and $500,000 retained earnings. On the date that Solo became a subsidiary of Pate, the following assets of Solo had book values different from their fair values:

	Fair Value	Book Value	Undervaluation (Overvaluation)
Inventories	$ 600,000	$ 500,000	$ 100,000
Land	600,000	300,000	300,000
Buildings	1,800,000	1,000,000	800,000
Equipment	700,000	900,000	(200,000)
	$3,700,000	$2,700,000	$1,000,000

Based on this information, Pate allocated the $1,400,000 excess cost over book value acquired [$3,650,000 cost − (90% × $2,500,000 equity of Solo)] to identifiable assets and goodwill, as shown in the following schedule:

	Undervaluation (Overvaluation)		Interest Acquired		Excess Allocation	Amortization Period
Inventories	$100,000	×	90%	=	$ 90,000	Sold in 19X6
Land	300,000		90		270,000	None
Buildings—net	800,000		90		720,000	36 years
Equipment—net	(200,000)		90		(180,000)	9 years
Goodwill—remainder					500,000	10 years
					$1,400,000	

The schedule also shows the amortization periods assigned to the undervalued and overvalued assets and goodwill.

Consolidation at Acquisition

Consolidated balance sheet working papers for Pate Corporation and Subsidiary immediately after the business combination on December 31, 19X5 are shown in Exhibit 4–9. Since the excess cost over book value allocation is reasonably complex, an unamortized excess account is used in the working papers. The first working paper entry eliminates reciprocal investment in Solo and stockholders' equity accounts of Solo, enters the 10 percent minority interest in Solo and debits the unamortized excess account for the $1,400,000 excess cost over book value acquired. A second working paper entry allocates the excess to identifiable net assets and goodwill. The amounts allocated in the second working paper entry are the original allocations because the accounts of Pate and Solo are being consolidated immediately after the business combination.

PATE CORPORATION AND SUBSIDIARY
CONSOLIDATED BALANCE SHEET WORKING PAPERS
ON DECEMBER 31, 19X5

	Pate	90% Solo	Adjustments and Eliminations		Consolidated Balance Sheet
Assets					
Cash	$ 200,000	$ 50,000			$ 250,000
Receivables—net	500,000	150,000			650,000
Inventories	800,000	500,000	b 90,000		1,390,000
Other current assets	400,000	100,000			500,000
Land	600,000	300,000	b 270,000		1,170,000
Buildings—net	2,000,000	1,000,000	b 720,000		3,720,000
Equipment—net	1,350,000	900,000		b 180,000	2,070,000
Investment in Solo	3,650,000			a 3,650,000	
Goodwill			b 500,000		500,000
Unamortized excess			a 1,400,000	b 1,400,000	
Totals	$9,500,000	$3,000,000			$10,250,000
Liabilities and Equity					
Accounts payable	$ 300,000	$ 100,000			$ 400,000
Other liabilities	1,000,000	400,000			1,400,000
Capital stock—Pate	7,000,000				7,000,000
Retained earnings—Pate	1,200,000				1,200,000
Capital stock—Solo		2,000,000	a 2,000,000		
Retained earnings—Solo		500,000	a 500,000		
Minority interest				a 250,000	250,000
Totals	$9,500,000	$3,000,000			$10,250,000

Exhibit 4-9   *Consolidation of Acquisition*

Consolidation after Acquisition

Solo reports net income for 19X6 in the amount of $600,000, and declares dividends of $100,000 on June 1 and December 1 ($200,000 total for 19X6). The June 1 dividend is paid on July 1, but the December 1 dividend remains unpaid at December 31, 19X6. During 19X6 Solo sells the undervalued inventory items, but the undervalued land and buildings and overvalued equipment are still in use by Solo at December 31, 19X6. On the date of business combination, the buildings had a remaining useful life of thirty-six years and the equipment, nine years. Goodwill is being amortized over ten years.

During 19X6 Solo borrows $200,000 from Pate on a noninterest-bearing note. Solo repays the note on December 30, but the repayment check to Pate was in transit and was not reflected in Pate's separate balance sheet at December 31, 19X6.

Pate made the following journal entries in 19X6 to account for its investment in Solo.

July 1, 19X6
Cash	$ 90,000	
Investment in Solo		$ 90,000

To record dividends from Solo ($100,000 × 90%).

December 31, 19X6
Investment in Solo	$400,000	
Income from Solo		$400,000

To record investment income from Solo determined as follows:

Share of Solo's net income ($600,000 × 90%)	$540,000
Amortization of excess allocated to:	
Inventories ($90,000 × 100% recognized)	−90,000
Buildings ($720,000 ÷ 36 years)	−20,000
Equipment ($180,000 ÷ 9 years)	+20,000
Goodwill ($500,000 ÷ 10 years)	−50,000
Income from Solo for 19X6	$400,000

These entries show that Pate has used a one-line consolidation in accounting for its $400,000 income from Solo for 19X6 but has failed to recognize Solo's December 1 dividend declaration. Accordingly, Pate's investment in Solo at December 31, 19X6 is overstated by $90,000 (90 percent of Solo's $100,000 December 1 dividend declaration). Consolidation working papers for Pate and Subsidiary for 19X6 in Exhibit 4–10 show Pate's investment in Solo at $3,960,000 ($3,650,000 cost plus $400,000 income less $90,000 dividends received), whereas the correct amount is $3,870,000. The overstatement is corrected in working paper entry a of Exhibit 4–10:

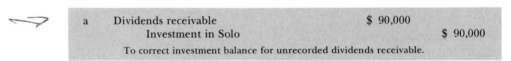

a	Dividends receivable	$ 90,000	
	Investment in Solo		$ 90,000
	To correct investment balance for unrecorded dividends receivable.		

This entry is different from previous working paper entries because it represents a *real adjustment* that should be recorded on Pate's books.

Working paper entry b adjusts for the $200,000 cash in transit from Solo to Pate at December 31, 19X6:

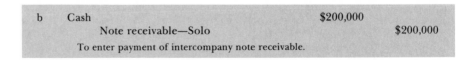

b	Cash	$200,000	
	Note receivable—Solo		$200,000
	To enter payment of intercompany note receivable.		

This working paper entry is also a real adjustment and one that should be recorded by Pate on its separate books. If entries a and b are not recorded as correcting entries on the separate books of Pate, however, they will be recorded in the normal course of events in 19X7 when Pate receives the $90,000 dividend and the $200,000 note repayment checks from Solo. Year-end transactions between affiliated companies always need to be examined to make sure that they are reflected in the records of both parent and subsidiary companies.

PATE CORPORATION AND SUBSIDIARY
CONSOLIDATION WORKING PAPERS—FOR THE YEAR ENDED DECEMBER 31, 19X6

	Pate	90% Solo	Adjustments and Eliminations		Minority Interest	Consolidated Statements
Income Statement Sales	$9,000,000	$3,000,000				$12,000,000
Income from Solo	400,000		c 400,000			
Cost of goods sold	6,000,000*	1,500,000*	e 90,000			7,590,000*
Operating expenses	1,900,000*	900,000*	f 20,000 h 50,000	g 20,000		2,850,000*
Minority interest income ($600,000 × 10%)					$ 60,000	60,000*
Net income	$1,500,000	$ 600,000				$ 1,500,000 ⌐
Retained Earnings Retained earnings—Pate	$1,200,000					$ 1,200,000
Retained earnings—Solo		$ 500,000	d 500,000			
Net income	1,500,000✓	600,000✓				1,500,000 ◄
Dividends	1,000,000*	200,000*		c 180,000	20,000*	1,000,000*
Retained earnings December 31, 19X6	$1,700,000	$ 900,000				$ 1,700,000 ⌐
Balance Sheet Cash	$ 80,000	$ 150,000	b 200,000			$ 430,000
Accounts receivable—net	260,000	200,000				460,000
Note receivable—Solo	200,000			b 200,000		
Inventories	900,000	600,000				1,500,000
Other current assets	500,000	50,000				550,000
Land	600,000	300,000	e 270,000			1,170,000
Buildings—net	1,900,000	1,100,000	e 720,000	f 20,000		3,700,000
Equipment—net	1,500,000	1,200,000	g 20,000	e 180,000		2,540,000
Investment in Solo	3,960,000			a 90,000 c 220,000 d 3,650,000		
Dividends receivable			a 90,000	i 90,000		
Goodwill			e 500,000	h 50,000		450,000
Unamortized excess			d 1,400,000	e 1,400,000		
	$9,900,000	$3,600,000				$10,800,000
Accounts payable	$ 200,000	$ 150,000				$ 350,000
Dividends payable		100,000	i 90,000			10,000
Other liabilities	1,000,000	450,000				1,450,000
Capital stock	7,000,000	2,000,000	d 2,000,000			7,000,000
Retained earnings	1,700,000✓	900,000✓				1,700,000 ◄
	$9,900,000	$3,600,000				
Minority interest January 1, 19X6				d 250,000	250,000	
Minority interest December 31, 19X6					$290,000	290,000
						$10,800,000

* Deduct.

Exhibit 4-10 Consolidation after Acquisition

Entry c eliminates the income from Solo and 90 percent of Solo's dividends, and it adjusts the investment in Solo account to its $3,650,000 beginning-of-the-period balance. Entry d eliminates the reciprocal investment in Solo account and the stockholders' equity accounts of Solo, records the 10 percent minority interest at the beginning of the period, and enters the $1,400,000 excess.

c	Income from Solo	$ 400,000	
	Dividends (200,000 × 90)		$ 180,000
	Investment in Solo		220,000

To eliminate income and dividends of Solo and return investment account to beginning of the period balance.

d	Retained earnings—Solo	$ 500,000	
	Capital stock—Solo	2,000,000	
	Unamortized excess	1,400,000	
	Investment in Solo		$3,650,000
	Minority interest—January 1		250,000

To eliminate reciprocal investment and equity amounts, establish beginning minority interest, and enter unamortized excess.

The unamortized excess entered in working paper entry d is allocated to identifiable assets and goodwill as of December 31, 19X5 in entry e and amortized in entries f, g, and h. A schedule to support these allocations and amortizations should be completed for convenience in preparing the working paper entries and to provide documentation for subsequent consolidations.

	Unamortized Excess December 31, 19X5	Amortization 19X6	Unamortized Excess December 31, 19X6
Inventories	$ 90,000	$ 90,000	$ —
Land	270,000		270,000
Buildings—net	720,000	20,000	700,000
Equipment—net	(180,000)	(20,000)	(160,000)
Goodwill	500,000	50,000	450,000
	$1,400,000	$140,000	$1,260,000

With the exception of the $90,000 excess allocated to cost of goods sold, the allocation in working paper entry e of Exhibit 4–10 is the same as the allocation in working paper entry b in the consolidated balance sheet working papers of Exhibit 4–9. The $90,000 excess assigned to inventories is allocated to cost of goods sold because the related undervalued inventories from December 31, 19X5 were sold in 19X6, thus increasing cost of goods sold in the 19X6 consolidated income statement. Working paper entry e is journalized as follows:

e	Cost of goods sold	$ 90,000	
	Land	270,000	
	Buildings—net	720,000	
	Goodwill	500,000	
	Equipment—net		$ 180,000
	Unamoritzed excess		1,400,000

To allocate unamortized excess to identifiable assets and goodwill.

Working paper entries f, g, and h are necessary to increase operating expenses for depreciation on the $720,000 excess allocated to undervalued buildings, to decrease operating expenses for excessive depreciation on the $180,000 assigned to overvalued equipment, and to increase operating expenses for amortization of the $500,000 originally assigned to goodwill, respectively. Entry h for amortizing goodwill has been illustrated previously and requires no further explanation. Entry f for recording depreciation on the excess allocated to buildings is procedurally the same as the adjustment for goodwill except that buildings—net of depreciation is credited. The credit is to accumulated depreciation or to buildings—net when the buildings are shown on a net of depreciation basis. The $20,000 debit to equipment—net and credit to operating expenses in working paper entry g corrects for excessive depreciation on the overvalued equipment. Procedurally, this adjustment is the exact opposite of entry f, which corrects for underdepreciation on the buildings:

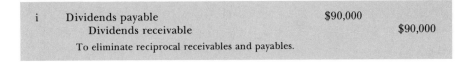

f	Operating expenses	$20,000	
	Buildings—net		$20,000
	To enter current depreciation on excess allocated to buildings.		
g	Equipment—net	$20,000	
	Operating expenses		$20,000
	To enter current depreciation on excess allocated to reduce equipment.		
h	Operating expenses	$50,000	
	Goodwill		$50,000
	To enter current amortization of goodwill.		

Working paper entry i eliminates reciprocal dividends payable and dividends receivable amounts:

i	Dividends payable	$90,000	
	Dividends receivable		$90,000
	To eliminate reciprocal receivables and payables.		

The $10,000 dividends payable of Solo that is not eliminated relates to the minority interest and is included among consolidated liabilities because it represents an amount payable outside the consolidated entity.

TRIAL BALANCE WORKING PAPER FORMAT

The trial balance approach to consolidation working papers brings together the adjusted trial balances for affiliated companies. Since both the financial statement approach and the trial balance approach generate the same information, the selection is based on user preference. If completed financial statements are available, the financial statement approach is easier to use because it provides measurements of parent and subsidiary income, retained earnings, assets, and equities that are needed in the consolidating process. If the accountant is given adjusted trial balances to consolidate, the trial balance approach may be more convenient.

Working paper entries illustrated in this chapter are designed for convenient switching between the financial statement and trial balance approaches for consolidation working papers. Recall that *only account balances are adjusted or eliminated*. Since net income is not an account balance, it is not subject to adjustment. *All nominal accounts are assumed to be open and to permit adjustment.* The only retained earnings amount that appears in an adjusted trial balance is the beginning retained earnings amount. Therefore, by working with beginning retained earnings amounts and by adjusting only actual accounts, the adjustments and eliminations are exactly the same whether the trial balance approach or the financial statement approach is used.

PIBB CORPORATION AND SUBSIDIARY
CONSOLIDATION WORKING PAPERS
FOR THE YEAR ENDED DECEMBER 31, 19X2

	Pibb	90% Shad	Adjustments and Eliminations	Income Statement	Retained Earnings	Minority Interest	Balance Sheet
Debits							
Cash	$ 6,800	$ 20,000					$ 26,800
Accounts receivable	30,000	15,000	e 5,000				40,000
Inventories	50,000	25,000					75,000
Plant and equipment	75,000	45,000					120,000
Investment in Shad	65,200		b 7,600 c 57,600				
Cost of goods sold	80,000	30,000	a 14,000	$96,000*			
Operating expenses	19,600	20,000	d 1,400	41,000*			
Dividends	15,000	10,000	b 9,000		$15,000*	$1,000*	
Goodwill			c 12,600 d 1,400				11,200
	$341,600	$165,000					$273,000
Credits							
Accumulated depreciation	$ 25,000	$ 11,000					$ 36,000
Accounts payable	45,000	34,000	e 5,000				74,000
Common stock	100,000	30,000	c 30,000				100,000
Retained earnings	35,000	20,000	c 20,000		35,000		
Sales	120,000	70,000	a 14,000	176,000			
Income from Shad	16,600		b 16,600				
	$341,600	$165,000					
Minority interest January 1, 19X2			c 5,000			5,000	
Minority interest income ($20,000 × 10%)				2,000*		2,000	
Consolidated net income				$37,000	37,000		
Consolidated retained earnings December 31, 19X2					$57,000		57,000
Minority interest December 31, 19X2						$6,000	6,000
							$273,000

*Deduct

Exhibit 4–11   *Trial Balance Approach for Working Papers*

Consolidation Example—Trial Balance Format and Equity Method

Consolidation working papers using the trial balance format are illustrated in Exhibit 4–11 for Pibb Corporation and its 90 percent owned subsidiary, Shad Corporation. Pibb acquired its interest in Shad on January 1, 19X1 at a price $14,000 in excess of underlying book value, and assigned the excess to goodwill with a ten-year amortization period. A summary of changes in Pibb's investment in Shad account from the date of acquisition to December 31, 19X2, the report date, is as follows:

Investment cost January 1, 19X1	$50,000
Add: Income—19X1 (90% of Shad's $10,000 net income less $1,400 amortization of goodwill)	7,600
Investment balance December 31, 19X1	57,600
Add: Income—19X2 (90% of Shad's $20,000 net income less $1,400 amortization of goodwill)	16,600
Deduct: Dividends received from Shad (90% × $10,000)	−9,000
Investment balance December 31, 19X2	$65,200

The working papers presented in Exhibit 4–11 reflect the additional assumptions that Pibb sold merchandise to Shad during 19X2 for $14,000 and that as of December 31, 19X2, Shad owed Pibb $5,000 from the sale. The merchandise was sold by Shad to its customers, so that all profit from the sale was realized by the consolidated entity during 19X2.

Separate adjusted trial balances are presented in the first two columns of Exhibit 4–11, which illustrates the trial balance approach for consolidated financial statements. As shown in the exhibit, debit balance accounts are presented first and totaled, and credit balance accounts are presented and totaled below the debit balance accounts.

The working paper entries to prepare consolidated financial statements using the trial balance format are the same as those for the financial statement approach. Since the accounts in a trial balance are classified according to their debit and credit balances, however, the locations of the accounts vary from those found in the financial statement format. Also, only beginning-of-the-period retained earnings amounts are found in a trial balance, and, accordingly, the checkmarks used in the financial statement format for net income and ending retained earnings amounts are not needed.

Working paper entries to consolidate the trial balances of Pibb and Subsidiary at December 31, 19X2 are as follows:

a	Sales	$14,000	
	Cost of goods sold		$14,000
	To eliminate reciprocal sales and cost of sales from intercompany purchases.		
b	Income from Shad	$16,600	
	Dividends		$ 9,000
	Investment in Shad		7,600
	To eliminate income and dividends from Shad and adjust the investment account to its beginning-of-the-year amount.		
c	Common stock—Shad	$30,000	
	Retained earnings—Shad	20,000	
	Goodwill	12,600	
	Investment in Shad		$57,600
	Minority interest (10%)		5,000
	To eliminate reciprocal investment in Shad and equity amounts of Shad, record beginning minority interest, and enter unamortized goodwill.		
d	Operating expenses	$ 1,400	
	Goodwill		$ 1,400
	To record current amortization of goodwill as an expense.		
e	Accounts payable	$ 5,000	
	Accounts receivable		$ 5,000
	To eliminate reciprocal accounts payable and receivable balances.		

After all adjustments and eliminations are entered in the working papers items not eliminated are carried to the Income Statement, Retained Earnings Statement, Minority Interest, or Balance Sheet columns. Next, minority interest income is computed independently and included in the Income Statement column as a deduction and in the Minority Interest column as an addition. An inconvenience of the trial balance approach can be seen at this point because Shad's $20,000 net income has to be computed from the revenue and expense data before it can be multiplied by the minority interest percentage. Subsidiary net income is shown directly when the financial statement approach is used.

The Consolidated Income Statement column is totaled and carried to the Consolidated Retained Earnings Statement column. The Consolidated Retained Earnings Statement column is totaled and carried to the Consolidated Balance Sheet column, and the Minority Interest column is totaled and carried to the Consolidated Balance Sheet column. Finally, Consolidated Balance Sheet debits and credits are totaled and the working papers are completed. Consolidated financial statements can be prepared directly from the Consolidated Income Statement, Consolidated Retained Earnings Statement, and Consolidated Balance Sheet columns.

SUMMARY

The objective of preparing working papers is to produce meaningful financial reports for a consolidated business entity. Working papers are merely tools for organizing and manipulating data. All the computations for consolidated financial statements can be determined independent of consolidation working papers if the objective is clearly understood.

The method of accounting for a subsidiary investment must be known before parent and subsidiary financial statements can be consolidated. Several approaches can be used to determine the method used by the parent company in accounting for its subsidiaries. For example, a dividend income account rather than an income from subsidiary account on the parent company's books suggests that the cost method is being used. Also, an investment in subsidiary account balance equal to the original cost of the interest acquired provides evidence that the cost method is being used. Alternatively, an income from subsidiary account equal to the parent company's share of subsidiary net income, or an investment in subsidiary account equal to underlying book value plus original cost–book value differentials provides evidence that the parent company is using an incomplete equity method.

Once the method of accounting is known, appropriate adjustments are made on the working papers to produce correct consolidated financial statements. Generally, the worksheet variations resulting from different methods of accounting for the same subsidiary investment are not great.

ASSIGNMENT MATERIAL

QUESTIONS

1 How are consolidated financial statements affected by the manner in which the parent company accounts for its subsidiary investments?
2 Is it ever acceptable for a parent company to use the cost method of accounting for its investments in subsidiary corporations? Explain.
3 If a parent company in accounting for its subsidiary investment amortizes goodwill on its separate books, why is it necessary to include an adjustment for goodwill amortization in the consolidation working papers?
4 How is minority interest income entered in consolidation working papers? Is there an alternative method?

5 How are the working paper procedures for the investment in subsidiary, income from subsidiary, and subsidiary's stockholders' equity accounts alike?

6 If a parent company uses the equity method but does not amortize the difference between investment cost and book value acquired on its separate books, its net income and retained earnings will not equal consolidated net income and consolidated retained earnings. How does this affect consolidation working paper procedures?

7 Are working paper adjustments and eliminations entered on the parent company books? The subsidiary books? Explain.

8 Since the financial statement and trial balance working paper approaches illustrated in the chapter generate comparable information, why learn both approaches?

9 Can the method used by a parent company in accounting for its subsidiary investments be determined by examining the separate financial statements of the parent and subsidiary companies?

10 How is reciprocity established between a parent company's investment account and the equity accounts of its subsidiary when the cost method is used?

11 In what way do the adjustment and elimination entries for consolidation working papers differ for the financial statement and trial balance approaches?

12 When is it necessary to adjust the parent company's retained earnings account in the preparation of consolidation working papers? In answering this question, explain the relationship between parent company retained earnings and consolidated retained earnings.

13 What approach would you use to check the accuracy of the consolidated retained earnings and minority interest amounts that appear in the balance sheet section of completed consolidation working papers?

(*Note:* Don't forget the assumptions on page 60 when working exercises and problems in this chapter.)

EXERCISES

E 4-1

1 Working paper entries normally:
 a Are posted to the general ledger accounts of one or more of the affiliated companies
 b Are posted to the general ledger accounts only when the financial statement approach is used
 c Are posted to the general ledger accounts only when the trial balance approach is used
 d Do not affect the general ledger accounts of any of the affiliated companies

2 Working paper techniques assume nominal accounts are:
 a Open when the financial statement approach is used
 b Open when the trial balance approach is used
 c Open in all cases
 d Closed

3 Most errors made in consolidating financial statements will appear when:
 a The consolidated balance sheet does not balance
 b Consolidated net income does not equal parent company net income
 c The retained earnings amount on the balance sheet does not equal the amount on the retained earnings statement
 d Adjustment and elimination column totals do not equal

4 Net income on consolidation working papers is:
 a Adjusted when the parent company uses the cost method
 b Adjusted when the parent company uses the equity method
 c Adjusted in all cases
 d Not an account balance and not subject to adjustment

5 On consolidation working papers, individual stockholders' equity accounts of a subsidiary are:
 a Added to parent company stockholders' equity accounts
 b Eliminated
 c Eliminated only to the extent of minority interest
 d Eliminated to the extent of the parent company's interest

6 On consolidation working papers, investment income from a subsidiary is:
 a Added to the investment account
 b Added to the parent company's beginning retained earnings

    c Allocated between majority and minority stockholders
    d Eliminated

7 On consolidation working papers, the investment in consolidated subsidiary account balances are:
    a Allocated between majority and minority interests
    b Always eliminated
    c Carried forward to the consolidated balance sheet
    d Eliminated when the financial statement approach is used

8 On consolidation working papers, consolidated net income is determined by:
    a Adding net income of the parent and subsidiary companies
    b Deducting consolidated expenses and minority interest income from consolidated revenues
    c Making adjustments to the parent company's income
    d Subtracting minority interest income from parent company net income

9 On consolidation working papers, consolidated end-of-the-period retained earnings is determined by:
    a Adding beginning consolidated retained earnings and consolidated net income and subtracting parent company dividends
    b Adding end-of-the-period retained earnings of the affiliated companies
    c Adjusting beginning parent company retained earnings for subsidiary profits and dividends
    d Adjusting the parent company's retained earnings account balance

10 Under the trial balance approach to consolidation working papers, which of the following is used?
    a Unadjusted trial balances
    b Adjusted trial balances
    c Postclosing trial balances
    d Either a or b, depending on the circumstances

E 4–2 Powell Corporation purchased 80 percent of the outstanding voting common stock of Sharon Corporation on January 2, 19X5 for $280,000 cash. Sharon's balance sheets on this date and on December 31, 19X5 are as follows:

SHARON CORPORATION BALANCE SHEETS

	January 2, 19X5	December 31, 19X5
Inventory	$ 50,000	$ 20,000
Other current assets	50,000	80,000
Plant assets—net	200,000	220,000
Total assets	$300,000	$320,000
Liabilities	$ 50,000	$ 60,000
Capital stock	150,000	150,000
Retained earnings	100,000	110,000
Total equities	$300,000	$320,000

Additional Information
    1 Powell uses the equity method of accounting for its investment in Sharon.
    2 Sharon's 19X5 net income and dividends were $70,000 and $60,000, respectively.
    3 Sharon's inventory, which was sold in 19X5, was undervalued by $12,500 at January 2, 19X5

Required
    1 What is Powell's income from Sharon for 19X5?
    2 What is the minority interest income for 19X5?
    3 What is the total minority interest at December 31, 19X5?
    4 What will be the balance of Powell's investment in Sharon account at December 31, 19X5 if investment income from Sharon is $50,000? *Ignore* your answer to 1.
    5 What is consolidated net income for Powell Corporation and Subsidiary if Powell's net income for 19X5 is $180,200? (Assume income from subsidiary is $50,000.)

E 4–3 Sarome Corporation is a 60 percent owned subsidiary of Prebenholm Corporation. Prebenholm paid $800,000 for its 60 percent interest on January 1, 19X1 when Sarome's stockholders' equity totaled $1,000,000. The cost–book value differential is being amortized over a forty-year period.

During 19X1 Sarome reports a net loss of $80,000 and passes its usual dividend declaration. Prebenholm's separate income for 19X1 is $400,000.

Required
1 Determine consolidated net income for 19X1.
2 Determine the balance of Prebenholm's investment in Sarome account at December 31, 19X1.

E 4–4 Pinto Corporation purchases a 75 percent interest in Saab Corporation for $2,000,000 cash on July 1, 19X8 when Saab Corporation has capital stock of $1,200,000, retained earnings of $400,000, and current earnings of $400,000. The $500,000 excess of investment cost over book value acquired is allocated $100,000 to undervalued inventory items (sold in 19X8) and $400,000 to goodwill with a ten-year write-off period.

Saab's total earnings for 19X8 are $800,000, and it pays dividends of $300,000 on December 1, 19X8. Pinto's income for 19X8 is $720,000, including investment income from Saab of $300,000. At December 31, 19X8 Pinto's investment in Saab account has a balance of $2,075,000.

Required: Compute the following amounts:
1 Minority interest income for 19X8
2 Minority interest on December 31, 19X8
3 Consolidated net income for 19X8
4 The correct balance of Pinto's investment in Saab account at December 31, 19X8
5 Goodwill at December 31, 19X8 to be included in the consolidated balance sheet

E 4–5 Abbreviated trial balances of Pardee and Sayers Corporations at December 31, 19X5 follow:

	Pardee	Sayers
Current assets	$ 240,000	$ 130,000
Land	300,000	50,000
Plant and equipment—net	1,000,000	450,000
Investment in Sayers—90%	410,000	
Cost of sales	1,000,000	300,000
Other expenses	250,000	120,000
Dividends	100,000	50,000
	$3,300,000	$1,100,000
Current liabilities	$ 255,000	$ 100,000
Common stock	1,000,000	300,000
Retained earnings	500,000	200,000
Sales	1,500,000	500,000
Dividend income	45,000	
	$3,300,000	$1,100,000

Pardee acquired a 90 percent interest in Sayers for $410,000 cash on January 1, 19X1 when Sayers's stockholders' equity consisted of $300,000 capital stock and $100,000 retained earnings. Any difference between investment cost and book value acquired relates to equipment with a ten-year life from January 1, 19X1. (*Hint:* Pardee uses the cost method.)

1 The amount of adjustment needed to convert the investment in Sayers account to an equity basis as of January 1, 19X5 is computed:
a   100%($200,000 − $100,000) − $5,000
b   90%($200,000 − $100,000) − $20,000
c   100%($200,000 − $100,000) + $20,000
d   90%($200,000 − $100,000) + $5,000

2 Consolidated net income for 19X5 is:

   a $322,000   **b** $317,000

   c $330,000   **d** $362,000

3 Minority interest in Sayers at December 31, 19X5 is:

   a $50,000   **b** $58,000

   c $53,000   **d** $68,000

4 Dividends to the minority stockholders for 19X5 are:

   a $50,000   **b** $20,000

   c $10,000   **d** $5,000

E 4–6   Shockley Corporation's outstanding capital stock (and paid-in capital) has been $200,000 since the company was organized in 19X4. Shockley's retained earnings account since 19X4 is summarized as follows:

RETAINED EARNINGS

Dividends December 1, 19X4	$20,000	Net Income 19X4	$50,000
Dividends December 1, 19X5	20,000	Net Income 19X5	70,000
Dividends December 1, 19X6	30,000	Net Income 19X6	10,000
Dividends December 1, 19X7	40,000	Net Income 19X7	60,000

Pickley Corporation purchased 80 percent of Shockley's outstanding stock on January 1, 19X6 for $300,000. During 19X7 Pickley's income, excluding its investment income from Shockley, was $90,000.

Required

  1 Prepare the journal entries, other than closing entries, on Pickley's books to account for its investment in Shockley during 19X7 under the *cost method.*

  2 Determine the balance of Pickley's investment in Shockley account at December 31, 19X7 under the *cost method.*

  3 Prepare the journal entries, other than closing entries, on Pickley's books to account for its investment in Shockley for 19X7 under the *equity method.*

  4 Determine the balance of Pickley's investment in Shockley account at December 31, 19X7 under the *equity method.*

  5 Compute consolidated net income for Pickley Corporation and Subsidiary for 19X7.

E 4–7   **[AICPA adapted]**

The following balance sheets as of the current date are for Parent Company and its subsidiary:

	Parent	Consolidated
Assets		
Current assets	$218,000	$363,000
Plant assets	93,000	154,000
Investment in subsidiary	145,000	—
	$456,000	$517,000
Equities		
Current liabilities	$ 83,000	$150,000
Minority interest	—	29,200
Capital stock	320,000	320,000
Retained earnings	53,000	17,800
	$456,000	$517,000

Parent Company uses the cost (legal-basis) method of accounting for its investment in 80 percent of the capital stock of the subsidiary.

A $7,000 excess of book value acquired over investment cost was allocated to reduce an overvaluation of the subsidiary's land account and is included in the above plant assets valuation.

1 The stockholders' equity of the subsidiary at the time Parent purchased its interest was:
  a $190,000   **b** $172,500
  c $159,000   **d** $152,000

2 The balance in the capital stock account of the subsidiary at the time Parent purchased its interest was:
  a $150,000   **b** $125,000
  c $100,000   **d** Indeterminable

3 The current stockholders' equity of the subsidiary is:
  a $173,000   **b** $159,000
  c $152,000   **d** $146,000

4 The current balance in the retained earnings account of the subsidiary is:
  a $152,000   **b** $150,000
  c $146,000   **d** Indeterminable

5 The current working capital of the subsidiary is:
  a $145,000   **b** $125,000
  c $78,000   **d** $67,000

E 4–8 Pastime Industries acquires an 80 percent interest in Saltine Corporation for $160,000 cash, its book value on January 1, 19X5. Saltine's capital stock and retained earnings on this date totaled $200,000.

Pastime reported net income for 19X5 at $120,000 and paid dividends during 19X5 of $60,000. Saltine's net income and dividends for 19X5 were $50,000 and $20,000, respectively.

Required
  1 Assume that Pastime uses the cost method of accounting for its investment in Saltine.
    a At what amount should the investment in Saltine appear on Pastime's books at December 31, 19X5?
    b Compute consolidated net income for 19X5.
  2 Assume that Pastime uses the equity method of accounting for its investment in Saltine.
    a At what amount should the investment in Saltine appear on Pastime's books at December 31, 19X5?
    b Compute consolidated net income for 19X5.
    c Compute minority interest at December 31, 19X5.

E 4–9 The stockholders' equity accounts of Parrot Corporation and Swan Corporation at December 31, 19X5 were as follows:

	Parrot Corporation	Swan Corporation
Capital stock	$1,200,000	$500,000
Retained earnings	500,000	100,000
Total	$1,700,000	$600,000

On January 1, 19X6 Parrot Corporation acquired an 80 percent interest in Swan Corporation for $560,000. The excess of cost over book value acquired was due to Swan Corporation's equipment being undervalued by $50,000, and the remainder due to goodwill. The undervalued equipment had a five-year remaining use life when Parrot acquired its interest. Goodwill is being amortized over a ten-year period.

The income and dividends of Parrot and Swan for 19X6 and 19X7 are as follows:

	Parrot		Swan	
	19X6	19X7	19X6	19X7
Net income	$340,000	$350,000	$120,000	$150,000
Dividends	240,000	250,000	80,000	90,000

Required

1 Assume that Parrot Corporation uses the equity method of accounting for its investment in Swan.

   a Determine consolidated net income for Parrot Corporation and Subsidiary for 19X6.

   b Compute the balance of Parrot's investment in Swan account at December 31 19X6.

   c Compute minority interest income for 19X6.

   d Compute minority interest at December 31, 19X7.

2 Compute consolidated net income for Parrot Corporation and Subsidiary for 19X6 assuming that Parrot uses the equity method of accounting except that it does not amortize the difference between cost and book value acquired on its separate books. (*Hint:* Determine separate income of Parrot Corporation as a first step in your computation.)

PROBLEMS

P 4–1   Pesic Corporation purchased 75 percent of the outstanding voting stock of Sable Corporation for $2,500,000 on January 1, 19X2. Sable's stockholders' equity on this date consisted of the following:

Capital stock—$10 par	$1,000,000
Additional paid-in capital	600,000
Retained earnings December 31, 19X1	400,000
Total stockholders' equity	$2,000,000

The excess of investment cost over book value of the net assets acquired was allocated 10 percent to undervalued inventory (sold in 19X2), 40 percent to plant assets with a remaining use life of eight years, and 50 percent to unidentifiable intangible assets with a ten-year write-off period.

Comparative trial balances of Pesic Corporation and Sable Corporation at December 31, 19X6 are as follows:

	Pesic	Sable
Other assets—net	$3,850,000	$2,600,000
Investment in Sable—75%	2,350,000	—
Expenses (including cost of sales)	3,150,000	600,000
Dividends	500,000	200,000
	$9,850,000	$3,400,000
Capital stock—$10 par	$3,000,000	$1,000,000
Additional paid-in capital	850,000	600,000
Retained earnings	1,800,000	800,000
Sales	4,000,000	1,000,000
Income from Sable	200,000	—
	$9,850,000	$3,400,000

Required: Determine the amounts that would appear in the consolidated financial statements of Pesic Corporation and Subsidiary for each of the following items:

   1 Goodwill at December 31, 19X6

   2 Minority interest income for 19X6

   3 Consolidated retained earnings at December 31, 19X5

   4 Consolidated retained earnings at December 31, 19X6

   5 Consolidated net income for 19X6

   6 Minority interest at December 31, 19X5

   7 Minority interest at December 31, 19X6

   8 Dividends payable at December 31, 19X6

P 4–2 Peter Company paid $79,000 for a 75 percent interest in Skippy Company on January 5, 19X1 when Skippy's capital stock was $60,000 and its retained earnings $40,000. Trial balances for the companies at December 31, 19X1 are as follows:

	Peter	Skippy
Cash	$ 11,000	$ 15,000
Accounts receivable	15,000	25,000
Other assets	120,000	100,000
Investment in Skippy	79,000	—
Cost of goods sold	50,000	30,000
Operating expenses	25,000	40,000
Dividends	20,000	10,000
	$320,000	$220,000
Liabilities	$ 80,000	$ 30,000
Capital stock	100,000	60,000
Paid-in excess	10,000	—
Retained earnings	22,500	40,000
Sales	100,000	90,000
Dividend income	7,500	—
	$320,000	$220,000

The only entries that Peter Company made in regard to the investment in Skippy Company are as follows:

January 5, 19X1
Investment in Skippy	$79,000	
Cash		$79,000

November 15, 19X1
Cash	$ 7,500	
Dividend income		$ 7,500

Goodwill is to be amortized over a ten-year period. Assets and liabilities of Skippy are stated at their fair values.

Required
1 Prepare a balance sheet for Peter Company at December 31, 19X1.
2 Prepare a consolidated income statement for Peter Company and Subsidiary for 19X1.
3 Prepare a consolidated balance sheet for Peter Company and Subsidiary at December 31, 19X1.

P 4–3 Photo Corporation acquired 80 percent of the outstanding voting stock of Snap Corporation for $520,000 cash on January 1, 19X8 when Snap's stockholders' equity was $650,000. All the assets and liabilities of Snap were stated at their fair values when Photo acquired its 80 percent interest.

Financial statements of the two corporations at and for the year ended December 31, 19X8 are summarized as follows:

	Photo	Snap
Combined Income and Retained Earnings Statement		
for the Year Ended December 31, 19X8		
Sales	$3,100,000	$1,000,000
Income from Snap	120,000	—
Cost of goods sold	2,000,000*	650,000*
Operating expenses	770,000*	200,000*
Net income	450,000	150,000
Add: Retained earnings January 1, 19X8	650,000	110,000
Deduct: Dividends	300,000*	100,000*
Retained earnings December 31, 19X8	$ 800,000	$ 160,000

	Photo	*Snap*
Balance Sheet at December 31, 19X8		
Cash	$ 400,000	$ 150,000
Receivables—net	600,000	300,000
Inventories	240,000	200,000
Plant and equipment—net	1,200,000	350,000
Investment in Snap	560,000	—
Total assets	$3,000,000	$1,000,000
Accounts payable	$ 300,000	$ 180,000
Other liabilities	200,000	120,000
Capital stock, $10 par	1,500,000	500,000
Other paid-in capital	200,000	40,000
Retained earnings	800,000	160,000
Total equities	$3,000,000	$1,000,000

* Deduct.

Required

1 Prepare consolidation working papers for Photo Corporation and Subsidiary for 19X8.
2 Prepare a consolidated income statement and a consolidated balance sheet for Photo Corporation and Subsidiary.

P 4–4 Pumo Corporation acquired 90 percent of Snow Corporation's common stock on January 1, 19X9 for $1,600,000 cash. The stockholders' equity of Snow at this time consisted of $1,000,000 capital stock and $200,000 retained earnings. The difference between the price paid by Pumo and the underlying equity acquired in Snow was *allocated* $20,000 to Snow's undervalued inventory, $100,000 to an undervalued building with a twenty-year remaining useful life, and the remainder to goodwill. The undervalued inventory items were sold by Snow during 19X9, and the building is being depreciated using the straight-line method.

Snow owed Pumo $20,000 on accounts payable at December 31, 19X9. Separate financial statements for Pumo and Snow Corporations for the year 19X9 are summarized as follows:

	Pumo	*Snow*
Combined Income and Retained Earnings Statements		
for the Year Ended December 31, 19X9		
Sales	$2,000,000	$1,200,000
Income from Snow	235,000	—
Cost of sales	(900,000)	(600,000)
Depreciation expense	(300,000)	(180,000)
Other expenses	(285,000)	(120,000)
Net income	750,000	300,000
Add: Retained earnings January 1, 19X9	250,000	200,000
Deduct: Dividends	(400,000)	(160,000)
Retained earnings December 31, 19X9	$ 600,000	$ 340,000
Balance Sheet at December 31, 19X9		
Cash	$ 203,000	$ 180,000
Accounts receivable—net	320,000	300,000
Dividends receivable	36,000	—
Inventories	400,000	200,000
Other current assets	100,000	120,000
Land	150,000	100,000
Buildings—net	600,000	300,000
Equipment—net	1,500,000	800,000
Investment in Snow	1,691,000	—
Total assets	$5,000,000	$2,000,000

	Pumo	Snow
Accounts payable	$ 400,000	$ 220,000
Dividends payable	1,000,000	40,000
Other liabilities	500,000	400,000
Capital stock—$10 par	2,500,000	1,000,000
Retained earnings	600,000	340,000
Total equities	$5,000,000	$2,000,000

Required: Prepare consolidation working papers for Pumo Corporation and Subsidiary for the year ended December 31, 19X9.

P 4–5 Paris Corporation acquired a 70 percent interest in Scot Corporation's outstanding voting common stock on January 1, 19X1 for $500,000 cash. The stockholders' equity of Scot on this date consisted of $500,000 capital stock and $100,000 retained earnings. The difference between the price paid by Paris and the underlying equity acquired in Scot was *allocated* $5,000 to Scot's undervalued inventory, $14,000 to undervalued buildings, $21,000 to undervalued equipment, and $40,000 to goodwill.

The undervalued inventory items were sold during 19X1, and the undervalued buildings and equipment had remaining useful lives of seven years and three years, respectively. Depreciation is straight line.

At December 31, 19X1 Scot's accounts payable include $10,000 owed to Paris. This $10,000 account payable is due on January 15, 19X2. Paris sold equipment with a book value of $15,000 for $25,000 on June 1, 19X1. This is not an intercompany sale transaction. Separate financial statements for Paris and Scot for 19X1 are summarized as follows:

	Paris	Scot
Combined Income and Retained Earnings Statements		
for the Year Ended December 31, 19X1		
Sales	$ 800,000	$700,000
Income from Scot	55,000	—
Gain on equipment	10,000	—
Cost of sales	(300,000)	(400,000)
Depreciation expense	(155,000)	(60,000)
Other expenses	(160,000)	(140,000)
Net income	250,000	100,000
Add: Retained earnings January 1, 19X1	300,000	100,000
Deduct: Dividends	(200,000)	(50,000)
Retained earnings December 31, 19X1	$ 350,000	$150,000
Balance Sheet at December 31, 19X1		
Cash	$ 86,000	$ 60,000
Accounts receivable—net	100,000	70,000
Dividends receivable	14,000	—
Inventories	150,000	100,000
Other current assets	70,000	30,000
Land	50,000	100,000
Buildings—net	140,000	160,000
Equipment—net	570,000	330,000
Investment in Scot	520,000	—
Total assets	$1,700,000	$850,000
Accounts payable	$ 200,000	$ 85,000
Dividends payable	100,000	20,000
Other liabilities	50,000	95,000
Capital stock—$10 par	1,000,000	500,000
Retained earnings	350,000	150,000
Total equities	$1,700,000	$850,000

Required: Prepare consolidation working papers for Paris Corporation and Subsidiary for the year ended December 31, 19X1. Use an unamortized excess account.

P 4–6 Separate company financial statements for Pen Corporation and its subsidiary, Syn Company, at and for the year ended December 31, 19X3 are summarized as follows:

	Pen	Syn
Combined Income and Retained Earnings Statement for the Year Ended December 31, 19X3		
Sales	$400,000	$100,000
Income from Syn	20,600	—
Cost of sales	250,000*	50,000*
Expenses	100,600*	26,000*
Net income	70,000	24,000
Add: Retained earnings January 1, 19X3	180,000	34,000
Deduct: Dividends	50,000*	16,000*
Retained earnings December 31, 19X3	$200,000	$ 42,000
Balance Sheet at December 31, 19X3		
Cash	$ 18,000	$ 15,000
Accounts receivable—net	80,000	20,000
Dividends receivable from Syn	7,200	—
Note receivable from Pen	—	5,000
Inventory	95,000	10,000
Investment in Syn	224,800	—
Land	65,000	30,000
Buildings—net	170,000	80,000
Equipment—net	130,000	50,000
Total assets	$790,000	$210,000
Accounts payable	$ 85,000	$ 10,000
Note payable to Syn	5,000	—
Dividends payable	—	8,000
Capital stock—$10 par	500,000	150,000
Retained earnings	200,000	42,000
Total equities	$790,000	$210,000

*Deduct

Additional Information
1 Pen Corporation acquired 13,500 shares of Syn Company stock for $15 per share on January 1, 19X2 when Syn's stockholders' equity consisted of $150,000 capital stock and $15,000 retained earnings.
2 Syn Company's land was undervalued when Pen acquired its interest, and accordingly, $14,000 of the cost-book value differential was allocated to land. Any remaining differential is goodwill.
3 Syn Company owes Pen $5,000 on account, and Pen owes Syn $5,000 on a note payable.

Required: Prepare consolidation working papers for Pen Corporation and Subsidiary for the year ended December 31, 19X3.

P 4–7 Prim Corporation acquired a 100 percent interest in Stan Corporation in a pooling of interests on January 1, 19X6 when Stan's equity consisted of $1,000,000 capital stock and $200,000 retained earnings. Prim exchanged 100,000 of its shares with a market value of $1,350,000 for all of Stan's outstanding shares.

Additional Information
1 Prim uses the equity method of accounting for Stan.
2 Stan's inventories were undervalued by $2,000 and its equipment by $10,000 on

January 1, 19X6. The inventory items were sold in 19X6 and the equipment had a ten-year remaining use life at the time.

3 Stan mailed a $10,000 check to Prim on December 31, 19X8 in settlement of an account receivable. Prim did not record the collection until 19X9. Accordingly, its December 31, 19X8 receivables are overstated.

4 In accounting for its investment in Stan for 19X8, Prim failed to record its share of Stan's dividends declared but not paid in 19X8.

5 Separate company financial statements for Prim Corporation and Stan Corporation at and for the year ended December 31, 19X8 are summarized as follows:

	Prim	Stan
Combined Income and Retained Earnings Statement for the Year Ended December 31, 19X8		
Sales	$1,900,000	$1,000,000
Income from Stan	200,000	—
Cost of sales	(800,000)	(400,000)
Depreciation expense	(200,000)	(100,000)
Interest expense	(200,000)	—
Operating expense	(400,000)	(300,000)
Net income	500,000	200,000
Add: Retained earnings January 1, 19X8	1,300,000	400,000
Deduct: Dividends	(400,000)	(150,000)
Retained earnings December 31, 19X8	$1,400,000	$ 450,000
Balance Sheet at December 31, 19X8		
Cash	$ 150,000	$ 60,000
Receivables—net	350,000	140,000
Inventories	1,000,000	150,000
Land	600,000	100,000
Buildings—net	1,500,000	500,000
Equipment—net	1,900,000	800,000
Investment in Stan	1,500,000	
Total assets	$7,000,000	$1,750,000
Accounts payable	$ 400,000	$ 250,000
Dividends payable	100,000	50,000
Bond interest payable	100,000	
10% bonds payable	2,000,000	
Common stock, $10 par	2,500,000	1,000,000
Other paid-in capital	500,000	
Retained earnings	1,400,000	450,000
Total equities	$7,000,000	$1,750,000

Required: Prepare working papers to consolidate the financial statements of Prim Corporation and Subsidiary at and for the year ended December 31, 19X8.

P 4–8   Pet Corporation acquired an 80 percent interest in Sun Corporation for $144,000 on January 2, 19X2 when Sun's stockholders' equity consisted of $100,000 capital stock, $10,000 other paid-in capital, and $25,000 retained earnings. The excess of the purchase price over the book value of the 80 percent interest acquired was due to goodwill and to undervalued plant assets with a remaining depreciable life of eight years (fair value $120,000 and book value $100,000).

Comparative financial statements for Pet and Sun Corporations for the year ended December 31, 19X2 are summarized as follows:

	Pet	Sun
Combined Income and Retained Earnings Statement for the Year Ended December 31, 19X2		
Sales	$405,300	$115,000
Income from Sun	4,700	—
Cost of sales	200,000*	70,000*
Depreciation expense	30,000*	12,000*
Other expenses	120,000*	24,000*
Net income	60,000	9,000
Add: Beginning retained earnings	130,000	25,000
Deduct: Dividends	40,000*	4,000*
Retained earnings December 31, 19X2	$150,000	$ 30,000
Balance Sheet at December 31, 19X2		
Cash	$ 9,300	$ 5,000
Accounts receivable—net	30,000	15,000
Dividends receivable	3,200	—
Inventories	50,000	22,000
Other current assets	12,000	11,000
Plant assets—net	300,000	107,000
Investment in Sun	145,500	—
Total assets	$550,000	$160,000
Accounts payable	$ 25,000	$ 10,000
Dividends payable	10,000	4,000
Other liabilities	40,000	6,000
Capital stock, $1 par	300,000	100,000
Other paid-in capital	25,000	10,000
Retained earnings	150,000	30,000
Total equities	$550,000	$160,000

* Deduct.

Required: Prepare consolidation working papers for Pet Corporation and Subsidiary for the year ended December 31, 19X2.

P 4-9 Pill Corporation paid $170,000 for an 80 percent interest in Stud Corporation on December 31, 19X1 when Stud's stockholders' equity consisted of $100,000 capital stock and $50,000 retained earnings. A summary of the changes in Pill's investment in Stud account from December 31, 19X1 to December 31, 19X5 follows:

Investment cost December 31, 19X1		$170,000
Increases		
80% of Stud's income 19X2 through 19X5		112,000
		282,000
Decreases		
80% of Stud's dividends 19X2 through 19X5	$56,000	
Amortization of excess cost over book value:		
Allocated to inventories, $7,000 (sold in 19X2)	7,000	
Allocated to plant assets, $18,000 (depreciated over a 9-year period) 19X2 through 19X5	8,000	
Allocated to goodwill, $25,000 (amortized over a 5-year period) 19X2 through 19X5	20,000	91,000
Investment balance December 31, 19X5		$191,000

Financial statements for Pill and Stud at and for the year ended December 31, 19X5 are summarized as follows:

	Pill	Stud
Combined Income and Retained Earnings Statement for the Year Ended December 31, 19X5		
Sales	$300,000	$200,000
Income from Stud	25,000	—
Cost of sales	180,000*	140,000*
Other expenses	50,000*	20,000*
Net income	95,000	40,000
Add: Retained earnings January 1, 19X5	255,000	100,000
Deduct: Dividends	50,000*	20,000*
Retained earnings December 31, 19X5	$300,000	$120,000
Balance Sheet at December 31, 19X5		
Cash	$ 41,000	$ 35,000
Trade receivables—net	60,000	55,000
Dividends receivable	8,000	—
Advance to Stud	25,000	—
Inventories	125,000	35,000
Plant assets—net	300,000	175,000
Investment in Stud	191,000	—
Total assets	$750,000	$300,000
Accounts payable	$ 50,000	$ 45,000
Dividends payable	—	10,000
Advance from Pill	—	25,000
Capital stock	400,000	100,000
Retained earnings	300,000	120,000
Total equities	$750,000	$300,000

* Deduct.

Additional Information
  1 The accounts payable of Stud at December 31, 19X5 include $5,000 owed to Pill.
  2 Pill advanced $25,000 to Stud during 19X3. This advance is still outstanding.
  3 Half of Stud's 19X5 dividends will be paid in January 19X6.

Required: Prepare working papers to consolidate the balance sheets only of Pill and Stud Corporations at December 31, 19X5.

P 4–10 Separate company and consolidated financial statements are presented for Powerhouse Corporation and its subsidiary, Starburst Corporation, at and for the year ended December 31, 19X9.

	Powerhouse	Starburst	Consolidated
Income Statement			
Sales	$1,000,000	$400,000	$1,400,000
Income from Starburst	85,000	—	—
Cost of goods sold	500,000*	150,000*	650,000*
Operating expenses	385,000*	150,000*	540,000*
Minority interest income	—	—	10,000*
Net income	$ 200,000	$100,000	$ 200,000

	Powerhouse	Starburst	Consolidated
Retained Earnings Statement			
Retained earnings January 1, 19X9	$ 350,000	$150,000	$ 350,000
Add: Net income	200,000	100,000	200,000
Deduct: Dividends	100,000*	50,000*	100,000*
Retained earnings December 31, 19X9	$ 450,000	$200,000	$ 450,000
Balance Sheet			
Cash	$ 138,000	$ 25,000	$ 163,000
Accounts receivable—net	155,000	50,000	200,000
Dividends receivable	27,000	—	—
Inventories	250,000	175,000	425,000
Plant assets—net	500,000	300,000	800,000
Investment in Starburst	430,000	—	—
Goodwill	—	—	25,000
Total assets	$1,500,000	$550,000	$1,613,000
Accounts payable	$ 150,000	$ 70,000	$ 215,000
Dividends payable	50,000	30,000	53,000
Capital stock—$10 par	700,000	100,000	700,000
Additional paid-in capital	150,000	150,000	150,000
Retained earnings	450,000	200,000	450,000
Minority interest	—	—	45,000
Total equities	$1,500,000	$550,000	$1,613,000

* Deduct.

Required: Reproduce in general journal form the working paper adjustments and eliminations that were made to consolidate the financial statements of Powerhouse and its subsidiary, Starburst, at December 31, 19X9. Include a working paper entry for minority interest income, dividends, and equity.

P 4–11 Comparative adjusted trial balances for Ply Corporation and Ski Corporation at December 31, 19X5, 19X6, and 19X7 are given here. Ply Corporation acquired an 80 percent interest in Ski Corporation on January 1, 19X6 for $800,000 cash. Except for inventory items that were undervalued by $10,000 and machinery that was undervalued by $40,000, all of Ski's identifiable assets and liabilities were stated at their fair values on December 31, 19X5.

Ski Corporation sold the undervalued inventory items during 19X6 but continues to own the machinery that had a four-year remaining use life as of December 31, 19X5.

	December 31, 19X5		December 31, 9X6		December 31, 19X7	
	Ply	*Ski*	*Ply*	*Ski*	*Ply*	*Ski*
Cash	$1,000,000	$ 300,000	$ 247,000	$ 150,000	$ 267,000	$ 200,000
Accounts receivable—net	300,000	150,000	250,000	200,000	450,000	300,000
Dividends receivable	—	—	40,000	—	40,000	–
Inventories	500,000	200,000	400,000	300,000	400,000	300,000
Plant and equipment—net	900,000	600,000	1,000,000	550,000	950,000	600,000
Investment in Ski	—	—	863,000	—	943,000	—
Cost of sales	1,000,000	400,000	1,050,000	350,000	1,100,000	350,000
Operating expenses	200,000	300,000	350,000	300,000	300,000	350,000
Dividends	100,000	50,000	100,000	50,000	150,000	100,000
	$4,000,000	$2,000,000	$4,300,000	$1,900,000	$4,600,000	$2,200,000

	December 31, 19X5		December 31, 9X6		December 31, 19X7	
	Ply	Ski	Ply	Ski	Ply	Ski
Accounts payable	$ 300,000	$ 350,000	$ 207,000	$ 150,000	$ 177,000	$ 250,000
Dividends payable	100,000	—	90,000	50,000	60,000	50,000
Capital stock	1,000,000	400,000	1,000,000	400,000	1,000,000	400,000
Additional paid-in capital	600,000	200,000	600,000	200,000	600,000	200,000
Retained earnings	500,000	250,000	700,000	300,000	903,000	400,000
Sales	1,500,000	800,000	1,600,000	800,000	1,700,000	900,000
Income from Ski	—	—	103,000	—	160,000	—
	$4,000,000	$2,000,000	$4,300,000	$1,900,000	$4,600,000	$2,200,000

Required: Prepare consolidation working papers for Ply Corporation and Subsidiary for 19X6 and 19X7 using the financial statement approach. (*Hint:* Ply Corporation's accountant applied the equity method correctly for 19X6 but misapplied the equity method for 19X7.)

P 4–12 Separate company financial statements for Pitt Corporation and its 80 percent owned subsidiary, Simm Corporation, at December 31, 19X8 are summarized as follows:

	Pitt	Simm
Combined Income and Retained Earnings Statement for the Year Ended December 31, 19X8		
Sales	$500,000	$100,000
Income from Simm	24,000	—
Cost of sales	240,000*	40,000*
Expenses	174,000*	30,000*
Net income	110,000	30,000
Add: Retained earnings January 1, 19X8	110,000	40,000
Deduct: Dividends	70,000*	20,000*
Retained earnings December 31, 19X8	$150,000	$ 50,000
Balance Sheet at December 31, 19X8		
Cash	$ 56,000	$ 30,000
Accounts receivable	40,000	20,000
Inventories	60,000	15,000
Plant assets—net	220,000	105,000
Investment in Simm	124,000	—
Total assets	$500,000	$170,000
Accounts payable	$ 50,000	$ 40,000
Capital stock	300,000	80,000
Retained earnings	150,000	50,000
Total equities	$500,000	$170,000

* Deduct.

Pitt acquired its interest in Simm on January 1, 19X6 for $100,000 when Simm's outstanding capital stock was $80,000 and its retained earnings, $20,000. Of the excess of cost over book value, $10,000 was allocated to inventories that were sold in 19X6 and the remainder to goodwill with a ten-year amortization period.

Required: Prepare consolidation working papers for Pitt Corporation and Subsidiary for the year ended December 31, 19X8.

P 4-13 Puff Corporation acquired an 80 percent interest in Scot Corporation for $240,000 on January 1, 19X5 when the stockholders' equity of Scot consisted of $200,000 capital stock and $25,000 retained earnings. The excess cost over book value acquired was allocated to machinery that was undervalued by $50,000 and to goodwill. The undervalued machinery is being depreciated over four years and goodwill is being amortized over 10 years.

Financial statements for Puff and Scot Corporations for 19X6 are summarized as follows:

	Puff	Scot
Combined Income and Retained Earnings Statement for the year 19X6		
Net sales	$900,000	$300,000
Dividends from Scot	8,000	—
Cost of goods sold	(600,000)	(150,000)
Operating expenses	(190,000)	(90,000)
Net income	118,000	60,000
Add: Retained earnings January 1, 19X6	112,000	50,000
Less: Dividends	(100,000)	(20,000)
Retained earnings December 31, 19X6	$130,000	$ 90,000
Balance Sheet at December 31, 19X6		
Cash	$ 6,000	$ 15,000
Accounts receivable—net	26,000	20,000
Inventories	82,000	60,000
Advance to Scot	20,000	—
Other current assets	80,000	5,000
Land	160,000	30,000
Plant and equipment—net	340,000	230,000
Investment in Scot	240,000	—
Total assets	$954,000	$360,000
Accounts payable	$ 24,000	$ 15,000
Dividends payable	—	10,000
Other liabilities	100,000	45,000
Capital stock	700,000	200,000
Retained earnings	130,000	90,000
Total equities	$954,000	$360,000

Additional Information
1 Scot mailed its check for $20,000 to Puff on December 30, 19X6 in settlement of the advance.
2 A $10,000 dividend was declared by Scot on December 30, 19X6 but not recorded by Puff.
3 Puff's accounts receivable includes $5,000 due from Scot.

Required: Prepare consolidation working papers for Puff Corporation and Subsidiary for the year ended December 31, 19X6.

P 4-14 Pam Industries acquired its interest in Sue Company for cash on July 1, 19X1 when Sue had capital stock of $50,000 and retained earnings of $31,000. Of the excess of investment cost over book value acquired, $15,000 was allocated to plant and equipment with a five-year remaining use life and the remainder to goodwill with a ten-year life as of the date of combination. No changes in the outstanding common stock of either company have occurred since July 1, 19X1.

Pam loaned Sue $100,000 at 8 percent interest on June 30, 19X4 with interest payable semiannually. All interest in the financial statements relate to this loan.

The separate company financial statements for Pam Industries and its subsidiary Sue Company at June 30, 19X5 are summarized as follows:

	Pam	Sue
Combined Income and Retained Earnings		
Statement for the Year Ended June 30, 19X5		
Sales	$500,000	$250,000
Dividend income	57,000	—
Interest income	8,000	—
Cost of sales	300,000*	120,000*
Interest expense	—	8,000*
Other expenses	150,000*	60,000*
Net income	115,000	62,000
Add: Beginning retained earnings	148,000	81,000
Deduct: Dividends	50,000*	60,000*
Retained earnings June 30, 19X5	$213,000	$ 83,000
Balance Sheet at June 30, 19X5		
Cash	$ 69,800	$ 22,000
Accounts receivable—net	60,000	30,000
Interest receivable	4,000	—
Dividends receivable	14,250	—
Other current assets	100,000	75,000
Plant and equipment	300,000	200,000
Less: Accumulated depreciation	72,000*	50,000*
Investment in Sue	101,950	—
Note receivable—8%	100,000	—
Total assets	$678,000	$277,000
Accounts payable	$ 40,000	$ 25,000
Dividends payable	25,000	15,000
Interest payable	—	4,000
Note payable—8%	—	100,000
Capital stock	400,000	50,000
Retained earnings	213,000	83,000
Total equities	$678,000	$277,000

* Deduct.

Required
1 Prepare a conversion to equity schedule for Pam's investment in Sue Company.
2 Prepare consolidation working papers for Pam Industries and Subsidiary for the year ended June 30, 19X5.

P 4–15 Pike Paper Company paid $100,000 for a 90 percent interest in Sean Mills on January 5, 19X2 when Sean Mills' capital stock was $60,000 and its retained earnings $20,000. Trial balances for the companies at December 31, 19X5 are as follows:

	Pike Paper	Sean Mills
Cash	$ 11,000	$ 15,000
Accounts receivable	15,000	25,000
Plant assets	220,000	180,000
Investment in Sean Mills	130,000	—
Cost of goods sold	50,000	30,000
Operating expenses	25,000	40,000
Dividends	20,000	10,000
	$471,000	$300,000

	Pike Paper	Sean Mills
Accumulated depreciation	$ 90,000	$ 50,000
Liabilities	80,000	30,000
Capital stock	100,000	60,000
Paid-in excess	20,000	—
Retained earnings	67,000	70,000
Sales	100,000	90,000
Income from Sean Mills	14,000	—
	$471,000	$300,000

The excess of investment cost over book value acquired was allocated $8,000 to undervalued inventory items that were sold in 19X2 and the remainder to undervalued machinery having a remaining use life of five years from January 1, 19X2.

Required
1 Summarize the changes in Pike Paper Company's investment in Sean Mills account from January 5, 19X2 through December 31, 19X5.
2 Prepare consolidation working papers for Pike Paper Company and Subsidiary for the year 19X5 using the trial balance approach for your working papers.

P 4-16 Peggy Corporation owns 90 percent of the voting stock of Super Corporation and 25 percent of the voting stock of Ellen Corporation.

The 90 percent interest in Super was acquired for $200,000 cash on January 1, 19X5 when Super's stockholders' equity was $200,000 ($180,000 capital stock and $20,000 retained earnings).

Peggy's 25 percent interest in Ellen was purchased for $70,000 cash on July 1, 19X5 when Ellen's stockholders' equity was $240,000 ($150,000 capital stock, $60,000 retained earnings, and $30,000 current earnings—first half of 19X5).

The difference between investment cost and book value acquired is considered goodwill and is being amortized over ten years.

Adjusted trial balances of the three associated companies at December 31, 19X5 are presented as follows:

	Peggy	Super	Ellen
Cash	$ 169,500	$ 40,000	$ 10,000
Other current assets	400,000	110,000	100,000
Plant and equipment—net	1,200,000	140,000	200,000
Investment in Super 90%	216,000	—	—
Investment in Ellen 25%	64,500	—	—
Cost of goods sold	600,000	160,000	150,000
Other expenses	250,000	70,000	90,000
Dividends (paid in November)	100,000	30,000	50,000
Total debits	$3,000,000	$550,000	$600,000
Current liabilities	$ 250,000	$ 70,000	$ 90,000
Capital stock	1,500,000	180,000	150,000
Retained earnings	200,000	20,000	60,000
Sales	1,000,000	280,000	300,000
Income from Super	43,000	—	—
Income from Ellen	7,000	—	—
Total credits	$3,000,000	$550,000	$600,000

Required
1 Reconstruct the journal entries that were made by Peggy Corporation during 19X5 to account for its investments in Super and Ellen Corporations.
2 Prepare an income statement, a retained earnings statement, and a balance sheet for Peggy Corporation at and for the year ended December 31, 19X5.

3 Prepare consolidation working papers (trial balance format) for Peggy and Subsidiary for 19X5.

4 Prepare consolidated financial statements other than the cash flows statement for Peggy Corporation and Subsidiary for the year ended December 31, 19X5.

P 4–17 Comparative consolidated financial statements for Pilgram Corporation and its 80 percent owned subsidiary at and for the year ended December 31, 19X7 and 19X6 are summarized as follows:

PILGRAM CORPORATION AND SUBSIDIARY
COMPARATIVE CONSOLIDATED FINANCIAL STATEMENTS
AT AND FOR THE YEAR ENDED DECEMBER 31

	Year 19X7	Year 19X6	Year's Change 19X7–19X6
Income and Retained Earnings			
Sales	$2,600,000	$2,400,000	$200,000
Income—equity investees	60,000	50,000	10,000
Cost of sales	(1,450,000)	(1,408,000)	(42,000)
Depreciation expense	(200,000)	(150,000)	(50,000)
Other operating expenses	(470,000)	(462,000)	(8,000)
Minority interest income	(40,000)	(30,000)	(10,000)
Net income	500,000	400,000	100,000
Retained earnings January 1	1,000,000	700,000	300,000
Dividends	(150,000)	(100,000)	(50,000)
Retained earnings December 31	$1,350,000	$1,000,000	$350,000
Balance Sheet			
Cash	$ 430,000	$ 360,000	$ 70,000
Accounts receivable—net	750,000	540,000	210,000
Inventories	700,000	700,000	0
Plant and equipment—net	1,800,000	1,500,000	300,000
Equity investments	430,000	400,000	30,000
Goodwill	190,000	200,000	(10,000)
Total assets	$4,300,000	$3,700,000	$600,000
Accounts payable	$ 492,000	$ 475,000	$ 17,000
Dividends payable	38,000	25,000	13,000
Long-term note payable	600,000	400,000	200,000
Capital stock	1,000,000	1,000,000	0
Other paid-in capital	600,000	600,000	0
Retained earnings	1,350,000	1,000,000	350,000
Minority interest—20%	220,000	200,000	20,000
Total equities	$4,300,000	$3,700,000	$600,000

Required: Prepare a consolidated statement of cash flows for Pilgram Corporation and Subsidiary for the year ended December 31, 19X7. Assume that all changes in plant assets are due to asset acquisitions and depreciation. Income and dividends from 20 percent to 50 percent owned investees for 19X7 were $60,000 and $30,000, respectively. Pilgram's only subsidiary reported $200,000 net income for 19X7 and declared $100,000 dividends during the year. Goodwill amortization for 19X7 is $10,000.

5

INTERCOMPANY PROFIT TRANSACTIONS— INVENTORIES

Consolidated statements are prepared to show the financial position and the results of operations of two or more affiliated companies as if they were one business enterprise. Therefore the effects of transactions between the affiliated companies (referred to as intercompany transactions) must be eliminated from consolidated financial statements. Intercompany transactions may result in reciprocal account balances on the books of the affiliated companies. For example, intercompany sales transactions produce reciprocal sales and purchases (or cost of goods sold) balances as well as reciprocal balances for accounts receivable and accounts payable. Intercompany loan transactions produce reciprocal notes receivable and notes payable balances as well as reciprocal interest income and interest expense balances. Since these intercompany transactions are intra-company transactions from the viewpoint of the consolidated entity, their effects must be eliminated in the consolidation process.

In addition to reciprocal account balances, gains and losses from inter-company transactions must be eliminated until realized through use or through sale outside of the consolidated entity. As stated in *Accounting Research Bulletin (ARB) No. 51*, consolidated statements "should not include gain or loss on trans-actions among the companies in the group. Accordingly, any intercompany profit or loss on assets remaining within the group shall be eliminated; the concept usually applied for this purpose is gross profit or loss."[1]

ARB No. 51 also notes in paragraph 14 that the amount of intercompany profit that should be eliminated is not affected by the existence of a minority interest and should be eliminated in its entirety. The reason for eliminating in-tercompany profits and losses is that the management of the parent company is able to control all intercompany transactions, including authorization and pricing, without arm's-length bargaining between the affiliated companies. In eliminating the effect of intercompany profits and losses from consolidated statements, however, the issue is not whether the intercompany transactions were or were not arm's length. *The objective is to show the income and financial position of the consolidated entity as it would have appeared if the intercompany transactions had*

---

[1]*ARB No. 51*, "Consolidated Financial Statements," paragraph 6.

never taken place, irrespective of the amounts involved in such transactions. The same reasoning applies to the measurement of the investment account and investment income under a one-line consolidation. In the case of a one-line consolidation, however, evidence that intercompany transactions were not arm's length may necessitate additional adjustments for fair presentation of the parent company's income and financial position in separate parent company financial statements. These additional adjustments are covered in *Accounting Interpretation No. 1 of APB Opinion No. 18,* "The Equity Method of Accounting for Investments in Common Stock."

Most intercompany transactions involving gains and losses can be grouped as inventory items, plant assets, and bonds. Consolidation procedures involving inventory items are discussed in this chapter, and those involving plant assets and bonds are covered in subsequent chapters. Although the discussion and illustrations in this chapter relate to intercompany profit situations, the examples also provide a basis for analyzing and accounting for intercompany losses. Tax considerations are covered in Chapter 10.

INTERCOMPANY INVENTORY TRANSACTIONS

Revenue is recognized (recorded as revenue) when it is realized, that is, when it is earned. In order for revenue to be earned from the viewpoint of the consolidated entity, there must be a sale to outside entities. Revenue on sales between affiliated companies cannot be recognized until merchandise is sold outside of the consolidated entity. No consolidated income results from transfers between affiliated companies. The sale of inventory items by one company to an affiliated company produces reciprocal sales and purchases accounts when the purchasing entity has a periodic inventory system and reciprocal sales and cost of goods sold accounts when the purchasing entity uses a perpetual inventory system. Such reciprocal accounts are eliminated in preparing a consolidated income statement in order to report sales and cost of goods sold for the consolidated entity. Eliminating equal sales and cost of goods sold amounts in preparing the consolidated income statement is important in that it reflects the merchandising activity of the consolidated entity accurately, but it has no effect on consolidated net income.

Elimination of Intercompany
Purchases and Sales

Intercompany sales and purchases of affiliated companies are eliminated in the consolidation process in order to report consolidated sales and purchases (or cost of goods sold) at amounts purchased from and sold to outside entities. When a periodic inventory system is used, the working paper entry to eliminate intercompany sales and purchases is simply a debit to sales and a credit to purchases. The working paper elimination under a perpetual inventory system, used throughout this book, is a debit to sales and a credit to cost of goods sold. The reason is that in a perpetual inventory system, intercompany purchases are included in the separate cost of goods sold account of the purchasing affiliate. These observations are illustrated for Pint Corporation and its subsidiary, Shep Corporation.

Pint Corporation formed a subsidiary, Shep Corporation, in 19X1 to retail a special line of Pint's merchandise. All Shep's purchases are made from Pint Corporation at 20 percent above Pint's cost. During 19X1 Pint sold merchandise that cost $20,000 to Shep for $24,000, and Shep sold all the merchandise to its customers for $30,000. Journal entries relating to the merchandise are recorded on the separate books of Pint and Shep as follows:

PINT'S BOOKS		
Inventory	$20,000	
Accounts payable		$20,000
To record purchases on account from other entities.		
Accounts receivable—Shep	$24,000	
Sales		$24,000
To record intercompany sales to Shep.		
Cost of sales	$20,000	
Inventory		$20,000
To record cost of sales to Shep.		

SHEP'S BOOKS		
Inventory	$24,000	
Accounts payable—Pint		$24,000
To record intercompany purchases from Pint.		
Accounts receivable	$30,000	
Sales		$30,000
To record sales to customers outside the consolidated entity		
Cost of sales	$24,000	
Inventory		$24,000
To record cost of sales to customers.		

At year-end 19X1, Pint's sales include $24,000 sold to Shep, and its cost of sales includes the $20,000 cost of merchandise transferred to Shep. Shep's sales consist of $30,000 merchandise sold to other entities, and its cost of sales consists of the $24,000 transfer price from Pint. Since Pint and Shep are considered one entity for reporting purposes, their combined sales and cost of sales are overstated by $24,000. That overstatement is eliminated in the consolidation working papers, where measurements for consolidated sales and cost of sales are finalized. The working paper elimination is as follows:

	Pint	100% Shep	Adjustments and Eliminations		Consolidated
Sales	$24,000	$30,000	a 24,000		$30,000
Cost of sales	20,000	24,000		a 24,000	20,000
Gross profit	$ 4,000	$ 6,000			$10,000

The working paper elimination has no effect on consolidated net income because equal sales and cost of sales amounts are eliminated and combined gross profit is equal to consolidated gross profit. But the elimination is necessary to reflect merchandising activity accurately for the consolidated entity that purchased merchandise for $20,000 (Pint) and sold it for $30,000 (Shep). The fact that Pint's separate records include $4,000 gross profit on the merchandise and Shep's records show $6,000 is irrelevant in reporting the consolidated results of operations. In addition to eliminating the intercompany profit items, it is necessary to eliminate intercompany receivables and payables in the consolidation process.

Elimination of Unrealized Profit in Ending Inventory

The full amount of intercompany profit on sales between affiliated companies is realized and recognized by the consolidated entity in the period in which the merchandise is resold to outside entities. But until the merchandise is resold, any profit or loss on intercompany sales is unrealized and its effect must be eliminated in the consolidation process. Any unrealized profit or loss on intercompany sales is reflected in the ending inventory of the purchasing affiliate because that inventory reflects the intercompany transfer price rather than cost to the consolidated entity. The elimination is a debit to cost of goods sold and a credit to the ending inventory for the amount of unrealized profit. The credit reduces the inventory to its cost basis to the consolidated entity; and the debit, when considered in conjunction with the elimination of intercompany purchases, reduces cost of goods sold to its cost basis. These relationships are illustrated by continuing the Pint and Shep example for 19X2.

During 19X2 Pint sold merchandise that cost $30,000 to Shep for $36,000 and Shep sold all but $6,000 of this merchandise to its customers for $37,500. Journal entries relating to the merchandise transferred intercompany during 19X2 are as follows:

PINT'S BOOKS

Inventory	$30,000	
Accounts payable		$30,000
To record purchase on account from other entities.		

Accounts receivable—Shep	$36,000	
Sales		$36,000
To record intercompany sales to Shep		

Cost of sales	$30,000	
Inventory		$30,000
To record cost of sales to Shep.		

SHEP'S BOOKS

Inventory	$36,000	
Accounts payable—Pint		$36,000
To record intercompany purchases from Pint.		

Accounts receivable	$37,500	
Sales		$37,500
To record sales to customers outside the consolidated entity.		

Cost of sales	$30,000	
Inventory		$30,000
To record cost of sales to outside entities.		

Pint's sales for 19X2 include $36,000 sold to Shep and its cost of sales reflects the $30,000 cost of merchandise transferred to Shep. Shep's $37,500 sales for 19X2 consist of merchandise acquired from Pint, and its $30,000 cost of sales is equal to 5/6, or $30,000/$36,000, of the $36,000 transfer price of merchandise acquired from Pint. The remaining merchandise acquired from Pint in 19X2 remains in Shep's December 31, 19X2 inventory at the $6,000 transfer price, which includes $1,000 unrealized profit. These intercompany merchandising activities can be analyzed as follows:

		Consolidated			
		Intercompany			
	Pint's Cost of Sales	*Pint's Gross Profit*	*Transfer Price*	*Shep's Gross Profit*	*Shep's Sales*
Goods transferred and sold in 19X2	$25,000	$5,000	$30,000	$7,500	$37,500
Goods inventoried in 19X2	5,000	1,000	6,000	—	—
Total	$30,000	$6,000	$36,000	$7,500	$37,500

From the viewpoint of the consolidated entity, merchandise that cost $30,000 was transferred intercompany: $25,000 of this merchandise was then sold outside the entity for $37,500, while $5,000 remains in inventory at year-end; and the consolidated entity has realized a gross profit of $12,500.

Working Paper Entries These consolidated results are accomplished through working paper entries that eliminate the effects of the intercompany transactions from sales, cost of sales, and inventory. While a single working paper entry can be made to reduce combined sales by $36,000, combined cost of sales by $35,000, and inventory by $1,000, two working paper entries are ordinarily used in order to separate the elimination of intercompany sales and purchases from the elimination (deferral) of unrealized profit. The working paper eliminations are as follows:

	Pint	Shep	Adjustments and Eliminations		Consolidated
Income Statement					
Sales	$36,000	$37,500	a 36,000		$37,500
Cost of sales	30,000	30,000	b 1,000	a 36,000	25,000
Gross profit	$ 6,000	$ 7,500			$12,500
Balance Sheet					
Inventory		$ 6,000		b 1,000	$ 5,000

The first working paper entry eliminates intercompany sales and purchases and is journalized as follows:

a	Sales	$36,000	
	Cost of sales		$36,000
	To eliminate intercompany sales and purchases.		

This entry is procedurally the same as the one made in 19X1 to eliminate intercompany purchases and sales.

A second entry defers the $1,000 intercompany profit that remains unrealized ($13,500 combined gross profit − $12,500 consolidated gross profit) and reduces the ending inventory from $6,000 to its $5,000 cost to the consolidated entity.

b	Cost of sales	$1,000	
	Inventory		$1,000
	To eliminate intercompany profit from cost of sales and inventory.		

The debit to cost of sales reduces profit by increasing consolidated cost of sales, and the credit reduces the valuation of inventory for consolidated statement purposes from the intercompany transfer price to cost. From the viewpoint of the consolidated entity, Shep's ending inventory is overstated by the $1,000 unrealized profit. Since an overstated ending inventory understates cost of sales and overstates gross profit, the error is corrected with working paper entry b that increases (debits) cost of sales and decreases (credits) the overstated ending inventory. This elimination entry reduces consolidated gross profit by $1,000 (income effect) and consolidated ending inventory by $1,000 (balance sheet effect).

These two working paper entries should be learned at this time because they are always the same, regardless of additional complexities that have yet to be introduced.

Equity Method On December 31, 19X2, Pint computes its investment income in the usual manner except that the $1,000 intercompany profit must be deferred. In Pint's one-line consolidation entry, income from Shep will be reduced by the $1,000 unrealized profits in the ending inventory, and accordingly, the investment in Shep account will also be reduced $1,000.

Recognition of Unrealized Profit in Beginning Inventory

Unrealized profit in an ending inventory is realized for consolidated statement purposes when the merchandise is sold outside the consolidated entity. Ordinarily, realization occurs in the immediately succeeding fiscal period, so that the recognition is simply deferred for consolidated statement purposes until the following year. Recognition of the previously unrealized profit requires a working paper credit to cost of goods sold because the amount of the beginning inventory is reflected in cost of goods sold when the perpetual system is used. The related working paper debits are complicated by the fact that the direction of the sale, minority ownership percentage, and parent company method of accounting for the subsidiary may affect the entry. These complications do not affect consolidated gross profit, and the previous example is extended to reflect 19X3 operations for Pint and Shep.

During 19X3 Pint Corporation sold merchandise that cost $40,000 to Shep for $48,000, and Shep sold 75 percent of the merchandise for $45,000. Shep also sold the items in the beginning inventory with a transfer price of $6,000 to its customers for $7,500. Journal entries relating to the merchandise transferred intercompany are as follows:

PINT'S BOOKS

| Inventory | $40,000 | |
| Accounts payable | | $40,000 |

To record purchase on account from other entities.

| Accounts receivable—Shep | $48,000 | |
| Sales | | $48,000 |

To record intercompany sales to Shep.

| Cost of sales | $40,000 | |
| Inventory | | $40,000 |

To record cost of sales to Shep.

SHEP'S BOOKS

| Inventory | $48,000 | |
| Accounts payable—Pint | | $48,000 |

To record intercompany purchases from Pint.

| Accounts receivable | $52,500 | |
| Sales | | $52,500 |

To record sales of $45,000 and $7,500 to outside entities.

| Cost of sales | $42,000 | |
| Inventory | | $42,000 |

To record cost of sales ($48,000 transfer price × 75% sold) and $6,000 from beginning inventory.

Since Shep sold 75 percent of the merchandise purchased from Pint, its ending inventory in 19X3 is $12,000 ($48,000 × 25%), and that inventory includes $2,000 unrealized profit [$12,000 − ($12,000/1.2 transfer price)]. The merchandising activity for 19X3 is analyzed as follows:

| | Pint's Cost of Sales | Consolidated Intercompany | | | Shep's Sales |
		Pint's Gross Profit	Transfer Price	Shep's Gross Profit	
Goods transferred in 19X2 and sold in 19X3	$ 5,000	$1,000	$ 6,000	$ 1,500	$ 7,500
Goods transferred and sold in 19X3	30,000	6,000	36,000	9,000	45,000
Goods inventoried in 19X3	10,000	2,000	12,000	—	—
Total	$45,000	$9,000	$54,000	$10,500	$52,500

From the viewpoint of the consolidated entity, merchandise that cost $40,000 was transferred intercompany, $30,000 of it plus $5,000 beginning inventory was sold for $52,500, $10,000 remained in inventory at year-end 19X3, and the consolidated entity realized a gross profit of $17,500.

These consolidated results are reflected in the consolidation working papers that eliminate the effects of intercompany transactions from sales, cost of sales, and inventory. Three working paper entries are used to eliminate intercompany purchases and sales, recognize previously deferred profit from beginning inventory, and defer unrealized profit in the ending inventory, as follows:

	Pint	Shep	Adjustments and Eliminations		Consolidated
Income Statement					
Sales	$48,000	$52,500	a 48,000		$52,500
Cost of sales	40,000	42,000	c 2,000	a 48,000 b 1,000	35,000
Gross profit	$ 8,000	$10,500			$17,500
Balance Sheet					
Inventory		$12,000		c 2,000	$10,000
Investment in Shep	XXX		b 1,000		

The working paper entries to eliminate the effects of intercompany transactions between Pint and Shep for 19X3 are journalized as follows:

a	Sales	$48,000	
	Cost of sales		$48,000
	To eliminate intercompany purchases and sales.		
b	Investment in Shep	$ 1,000	
	Cost of sales		$ 1,000
	To recognize previously deferred profit from beginning inventory.		
c	Cost of sales	$ 2,000	
	Inventory		$ 2,000
	To defer unrealized profit in ending inventory.		

Working paper entries a and c are procedurally the same as the entries for 19X2. Their purpose is to eliminate intercompany purchases and sales and defer unrealized profit in the ending inventory. From the consolidated viewpoint, the $1,000 overstated beginning inventory overstates cost of sales in 19X3. Entry b recognizes previously deferred profit from 19X2 by reducing consolidated cost of sales, and thereby increasing consolidated gross profit. The related debit to the investment in Shep account adjusts for the one-line consolidation entry that reduced the investment in Shep account in 19X2 to defer unrealized profit in the ending inventory of that year. While the credit side of this working paper entry is always the same, additional complexities sometimes arise with the debit side of the entry.

The Pint-Shep example illustrates the effects of intercompany inventory transactions on consolidated sales, cost of sales, and gross profit, and these effects are always the same. But the example did not cover the effects of intercompany inventory transactions on minority interest computations or on parent company accounting under the equity method. These ramifications are discussed and illustrated next.

DOWNSTREAM AND UPSTREAM SALES

A sale by a parent company to a subsidiary is designated as a *downstream sale*, and a sale by a subsidiary to its parent is designated as an *upstream sale*. The upstream and downstream designations relate to the usual diagram of affiliation structures which places the parent company at the top. Thus, sales from top to bottom are downstream, and sales from bottom to top are upstream.

Reciprocal sales and cost of goods sold (or purchases) amounts are eliminated in consolidated financial statements regardless of whether the sales are upstream or downstream. Likewise, any unrealized gross profit in inventories is eliminated in its entirety for both downstream and upstream sales. But the effect of unrealized profits on separate parent company statements (as investor) and on consolidated financial statements (which show income to the majority stockholders) is determined by both the direction of the intercompany sales activity and the percentage ownership of subsidiary companies, except for 100 percent owned subsidiaries that have no minority ownership.

In the case of downstream sales, the parent company's separate income includes the full amount of any unrealized profit (included in its sales and cost of sales accounts), and the subsidiary's income is not affected. When sales are upstream, the subsidiary company's net income includes the full amount of any unrealized profit (included in its sales and cost of sales accounts), and the parent company's separate income is not affected. The full amount of intercompany sales and cost of sales is eliminated in the consolidation process regardless of whether the sales are downstream or upstream. But the minority interest income *may be affected* if the subsidiary's net income includes unrealized profit (the upstream situation), while it *is not affected* if the parent company's separate income includes unrealized profit (the downstream situation). This is because the minority shareholders have an interest only in the income of the subsidiary. When subsidiary net income is overstated (from the viewpoint of the consolidated entity) because it includes unrealized profit, the income allocated to minority interests should be based on the *realized income of the subsidiary.* A subsidiary's realized income is its reported net income adjusted for intercompany profits from upstream sales.

Minority interest income *may be affected* by unrealized profit from upstream sales because accounting standards are not definitive with respect to the computation. *ARB No. 51,* paragraph 14, provides that "the elimination of intercompany profit or loss may be allocated proportionately between majority and minority interests," but does not require such allocation. The alternative to allocation is to eliminate intercompany profits and losses from upstream sales in the same manner as for downstream sales, charging (crediting) the full amount of unrealized gain (loss) to the parent's income.

The approach that allocates unrealized profits and losses from upstream sales proportionately between minority and majority interests is conceptually superior because it applies the viewpoint of the consolidated entity consistently to both majority and minority interests. That is, both consolidated net income and minority interest income are computed on the basis of income that is realized from the viewpoint of the consolidated entity. In addition, material amounts of unrealized profits and losses from upstream sales may be allocated between majority and minority interests in accounting practice. *Accordingly, unrealized profits and losses from upstream sales are allocated proportionately between consolidated net income (majority interests) and minority interest income (minority interests) throughout this book.* Consistent treatment between consolidation procedures and the equity method of accounting (the one-line consolidation) is accomplished by using the same allocation approach in accounting for the parent company/investor's interest under the equity method.

Downstream and Upstream Effects on Income Computations

Assume that the separate incomes of a parent company and its 80 percent owned subsidiary for 19X5 are as follows:

	Parent	Subsidiary
Sales	$600,000	$300,000
Cost of sales	300,000	180,000
Gross profit	300,000	120,000
Expenses	100,000	70,000
Parent's separate income	$200,000	
Subsidiary's net income		$ 50,000

Intercompany sales during the year are $100,000, and the December 31, 19X5 inventory includes $20,000 unrealized profit.

Minority Interest Income Computation   If the intercompany sales are downstream, the $20,000 unrealized profit is reflected in the parent company's sales and cost of sales accounts, and the subsidiary's $50,000 net income is equal to its realized income. In this case the minority interest income computation is unaffected by the intercompany transactions and is computed:

$$\$50,000 \text{ net income of subsidiary} \times 20\% = \underline{\$10,000}$$

If the intercompany sales are upstream, the $20,000 unrealized profit is reflected in the subsidiary's sales and cost of sales accounts and the subsidiary's realized income is $30,000. In this case the minority interest income computation is:

$$(\$50,000 \text{ net income of subsidiary} - \$20,000 \text{ unrealized}) \times 20\% = \underline{\$6,000}$$

Consolidated Net Income Computation   Comparative consolidated income statements for the parent and its 80 percent owned subsidiary under the two assumptions are shown in Exhibit 5–1. In examining the exhibit, note that the only difference in the computation of consolidated net income under the two assumptions lies in the computation of minority interest income. This is because the eliminations for intercompany purchases and sales and intercompany inventory profits are the same, regardless of whether the sales are downstream or upstream. Since parent company net income under the equity method is equal to consolidated net income, the approach used in computing income from subsidiary must be consistent with the approach used in determining consolidated net income. For downstream sales, the full amount of unrealized profit is charg-

---

PARENT CORPORATION AND SUBSIDIARY
CONSOLIDATED INCOME STATEMENTS
FOR THE YEAR ENDED DECEMBER 31, 19X5

	Downstream Sales	Upstream Sales
Sales ($900,000 − $100,000)	$800,000	$800,000
Cost of sales ($480,000 + $20,000 − $100,000)	400,000	400,000
Gross profit	400,000	400,000
Expenses ($100,000 + $70,000)	170,000	170,000
Total realized income	230,000	230,000
Less: Minority interest income	10,000	6,000
Consolidated net income	$220,000	$224,000

Exhibit 5–1   *Consolidated Income Effect of Downstream and Upstream Sales*

ed against income from subsidiary; but for upstream sales, only the parent's proportionate share is charged against its investment income from subsidiary. Computations are as follows:

	Downstream	Upstream
Parent's separate income	$200,000	$200,000
Add: Income from subsidiary		
Downstream		
Equity in subsidiary's reported income less unrealized profit ($50,000 × 80%) − $20,000	20,000	
Upstream		
Equity in subsidiary realized income ($50,000 − $20,000) × 80%		24,000
Parent (and consolidated) net income	$220,000	$224,000

UNREALIZED PROFITS FROM DOWNSTREAM SALES

Sales by a parent company to its subsidiaries increase parent company sales, cost of goods sold, and gross profit but do not affect the income of subsidiaries until the merchandise is resold to outside parties. Since the full amount of gross profit on merchandise sold downstream and remaining in subsidiary inventories increases parent company income, the full amount must be eliminated from the parent company income statement under the equity method of accounting. Consistent with the one-line consolidation concept, this is done by reducing investment income and the investment account. In consolidated financial statements, unrealized gross profit is eliminated by increasing consolidated cost of goods sold and reducing merchandise inventory to a cost basis to the consolidated entity. The overstatement of the ending inventory from the consolidated viewpoint understates consolidated cost of goods sold.

Deferral of Intercompany Profit in Period of Intercompany Sale

The following example illustrates the deferral of unrealized profits on downstream sales. Porter Corporation owns 90 percent of the voting stock of Sorter Corporation. Separate income statements of Porter and Sorter for 19X7, before consideration of unrealized profits, are as follows:

	Porter	Sorter
Sales	$100,000	$50,000
Cost of goods sold	60,000	35,000
Gross profit	40,000	15,000
Expenses	15,000	5,000
Operating income	25,000	10,000
Income from Sorter	9,000	—
Net income	$ 34,000	$10,000

Porter's sales include $15,000 to Sorter at a profit of $6,250, and Sorter's December 31, 19X7 inventory includes 40 percent of the merchandise from the intercompany transaction. The $2,500 unrealized profit in Sorter's inventory ($6,000 transfer price less $3,500 cost) is reflected in Porter's operating income. On its separate books, Porter takes up its share of Sorter's income and defers recognition of the unrealized profit with the following entries:

Investment in Sorter	$9,000	
Income from Sorter		$9,000
To record share of Sorter's income.		
Income from Sorter	$2,500	
Investment in Sorter		$2,500
To eliminate unrealized profit on sales to Sorter.		

The second entry on Porter's books reduces Porter's income from Sorter from $9,000 to $6,500. In consolidated financial statements reciprocal sales and cost of goods sold, as well as all unrealized profit, must be eliminated. These working paper adjustments are shown in the partial working papers in Exhibit 5–2.

The full amount of intercompany sales is deducted from sales and cost of goods sold in entry a. Working paper entry b then corrects cost of goods sold for the unrealized profit at year-end and reduces the inventory to its cost basis to the consolidated entity. Note that working paper entries a and b are equivalent to a single debit to sales for $15,000, a credit to cost of goods sold for $12,500, and a credit to inventory for $2,500.

In examining Exhibit 5–2, observe that Porter's net income on an equity basis is equal to consolidated net income. This equality would not have occurred without the one-line consolidation adjustment that reduced Porter's income from $34,000 to $31,500. The $1,000 minority interest income shown in Exhibit 5–2 is not affected by the unrealized profit on Porter's sales because minority

---

PORTER AND SUBSIDIARY, SORTER
PARTIAL WORKING PAPERS
FOR THE YEAR ENDED DECEMBER 31, 19X7

	Porter	90% Sorter	Adjustments and Eliminations				Consolidated
Income Statement							
Sales	$100,000	$50,000	a	15,000			$135,000
Income from Sorter	6,500		c	6,500			
Cost of goods sold	60,000*	35,000*	b	2,500	a	15,000	82,500*
Expenses	15,000*	5,000*					20,000*
Minority interest income ($10,000 × 10%)							1,000*
Net income	$ 31,500	$10,000					$ 31,500
Balance Sheet							
Inventory		$ 7,500			b	2,500	$ 5,000
Investment in Sorter	XXX				c	6,500	

* Deduct
a Eliminates reciprocal sales and cost of goods sold.
b Adjusts cost of goods sold and ending inventory to a cost basis to the consolidated entity.
c Eliminates investment income and adjusts the investment in Sorter account to the January 1, 19X7 balance.

Exhibit 5–2 *Inventory Profit on Downstream Sales in Year of Intercompany Sales*

stockholders share only in subsidiary profits and Sorter's reported income for 19X7 (equal to its realized income) is unaffected by the unrealized profit in its inventory. (Sorter's goods available for sale and its ending inventory are overstated by the amount of unrealized profit, but its cost of goods sold is not affected by the unrealized profit in its ending inventory.)

Recognition of Intercompany Profit upon Sale to Outside Entities

Now assume that the merchandise acquired from Porter during 19X7 is sold by Sorter during 19X8 and that there are no intercompany transactions between Porter and Sorter during 19X8. Separate income statements for 19X8 before consideration of the $2,500 unrealized profit in Sorter's beginning inventory are as follows:

	Porter	Sorter
Sales	$120,000	$60,000
Cost of goods sold	80,000	40,000
Gross profit	40,000	20,000
Expenses	20,000	5,000
Operating income	20,000	15,000
Income from Sorter	13,500	—
Net income	$ 33,500	$15,000

Porter's operating income for 19X8 is unaffected by the unrealized profit in Sorter's December 31, 19X7 inventory. But Sorter's 19X8 profit is affected because the $2,500 overstatement of Sorter's beginning inventory overstates cost of goods sold from a consolidated viewpoint. From Porter's viewpoint, the unrealized profit from 19X7 is realized in 19X8 and its investment income is recorded and adjusted as follows:

Investment in Sorter	$13,500	
Income from Sorter		$13,500

To record investment income from Sorter.

Investment in Sorter	$ 2,500	
Income from Sorter		$ 2,500

To record realization of profit from 19X7 intercompany sales to Sorter.

The effect of this entry is to increase Porter's investment income from $13,500 to $16,000 and Porter's net income from $33,500 to $36,000. These adjusted amounts are reflected in the partial working papers for Porter and Sorter for the year 19X8 as shown in Exhibit 5–3.

In examining the partial working papers in Exhibit 5–3, note that entry a debits the investment in Sorter account and credits cost of goods sold for $2,500. Since the beginning inventory of Sorter has already been closed to cost of goods sold under a perpetual inventory system, the inventory cannot be adjusted. The adjustment to the investment account is necessary to increase the investment account at the beginning of the year to reflect realization during 19X8 of the unrealized profit that was deferred at the end of 19X7. *This adjustment reestablishes reciprocity between the investment balance at January 1, 19X8 and the subsidiary equity accounts at the same date. It is important to record this adjustment before eliminating reciprocal investment and equity balances.* The computation of minority interest income in Exhibit 5–3 is not affected because the sales are downstream.

Unrealized inventory profits in consolidated financial statements are self-correcting over any two accounting periods and are subject to the same type

PORTER AND SUBSIDIARY, SORTER
PARTIAL WORKING PAPERS
FOR THE YEAR ENDED DECEMBER 31, 19X8

	Porter	90% Sorter	Adjustments and Eliminations		Consolidated
Income Statement					
Sales	$120,000	$60,000			$180,000
Income from Sorter	16,000		b 16,000		
Cost of goods sold	80,000*	40,000*		a 2,500	117,500*
Expenses	20,000*	5,000*			25,000*
Minority interest income ($15,000 × 10%)					1,500*
Net income	$ 36,000	$15,000			$ 36,000
Balance Sheet					
Investment in Sorter	XXX		a 2,500	b 16,000	

* Deduct.

a Adjusts cost of goods sold to a cost basis and adjusts the investment account balance to reestablish reciprocity with the beginning subsidiary equity accounts.
b Eliminates investment income and adjusts the investment account to January 1, 19X8 balance.

Exhibit 5–3 *Inventory Profit on Downstream Sales in Year after Intercompany Sales*

of analysis as inventory errors. Total consolidated net income for Porter and Sorter for 19X7 and 19X8 is unaffected by the $2,500 deferral in 19X7 and recognition in 19X8. The significance of the adjustments lies in the accurate statement of the income of the consolidated entity for each period.

UNREALIZED PROFITS FROM UPSTREAM SALES

Sales by a subsidiary to its parent company increase the sales, cost of goods sold, and gross profit of the subsidiary, but they do not affect the *operating income* of the parent until the merchandise is resold by the parent to other entities. The parent's *net income* is affected, however, because the parent recognizes its share of the subsidiary's income on an equity basis. If the selling subsidiary is a 100 percent owned affiliate, the parent defers 100 percent of any unrealized profit in the year of intercompany sale. If the subsidiary is a partially owned affiliate, the parent company defers only its proportionate share of the unrealized subsidiary profit.

Deferral of Intercompany Profit in Period of Intercompany Sale

Assume that Salt Corporation (subsidiary) sells merchandise that it purchased for $7,500 to Park Corporation (parent) for $20,000 during 19X7 and that Park Corporation sold 60 percent of the merchandise to outsiders during the year for $15,000. At year-end the unrealized inventory profit is $5,000 (cost $3,000 but included in Park's inventory at $8,000). If Salt reports net income of $50,000 for the year 19X7, Park's proportionate share is recognized as shown in Exhibit 5-4. The exhibit compares parent company accounting for a one-line consolidation of a 100 percent owned subsidiary and a 75 percent owned subsidiary.

As the illustration shows, if Park records 100 percent of Salt's income under the equity method, it must eliminate 100 percent of any unrealized profit included in that income. But if Park records only 75 percent of Salt's income under the equity method, it must eliminate only 75 percent of any unrealized profit included in Salt's income. In both cases, all the unrealized profit that is recorded by Park is eliminated from Park's income and investment accounts.

PART A IF SALT IS A 100% OWNED SUBSIDIARY			PART B IF SALT IS A 75% OWNED SUBSIDIARY		
Investment in Salt	$50,000		Investment in Salt	$37,500	
Income from Salt		$50,000	Income from Salt		$37,500
To record 100% of Salt's reported income as income from subsidiary.			To record 75% of Salt's reported income as income from subsidiary.		
Income from Salt	$ 5,000		Income from Salt	$ 3,750	
Investment in Salt		$ 5,000	Investment in Salt		$ 3,750
To defer 100% of the unrealized inventory profits reported by Salt until realized.			To defer 75% of the unrealized inventory profits reported by Salt until realized.		
A single entry for $45,000 [($50,000 − $5,000) × 100%] is equally acceptable.			A single entry for $33,750 [($50,000 − $5,000) × 75%] is equally acceptable.		

Exhibit 5–4   *Entries for a One-Line Consolidation on the Books of Park*

The elimination of unrealized inventory profits from upstream sales in consolidated financial statements results in the elimination of 100 percent of all unrealized inventory profits from consolidated sales and cost of goods sold accounts. But since consolidated net income is a measurement of income to the stockholders of the parent company, minority interest income is reduced for its proportionate share of any unrealized profit of the subsidiary. This involves deducting the minority interest's share of unrealized profits from the minority interest's share of the subsidiary's reported net income. Thus, the effect on consolidated net income of unrealized profits from upstream sales is the same as the effect on parent company income under the equity method of accounting.

Partial consolidation working papers for Park Corporation and its 75 percent owned subsidiary Salt Corporation are illustrated in Exhibit 5–5. Although the amounts for sales, cost of goods sold, and expenses are presented without prior explanation, the data provided are consistent with previous assumptions for Park and Salt Corporations.

The $33,750 income from Salt that appears in Park's separate income statement in Exhibit 5–5 is explained in Part B of Exhibit 5–4. Minority interest income is computed by subtracting unrealized profit from Salt's reported income and multiplying by the minority interest percentage. Failure to adjust the minority interest income for unrealized profit will result in a lack of equality between parent company net income on an equity basis and consolidated net income. This potential problem is, of course, absent in the case of a 100 percent owned subsidiary because there is no minority interest.

Recognition of Intercompany Profit upon Sale to Outside Entities

The effect of unrealized profits in a beginning inventory on parent company and consolidated net incomes is just the opposite of the effect of unrealized profits in an ending inventory. That is, the relationship between unrealized profits in ending inventories (year of intercompany sale) and consolidated net income is direct, whereas the relationship between unrealized profit in beginning inven-

PARK AND SUBSIDIARY, SALT (75% OWNED)
PARTIAL CONSOLIDATION WORKING PAPERS
FOR THE YEAR ENDED DECEMBER 31, 19X7

	Park	75% Salt	Adjustments and Eliminations		Consolidated
Income Statement					
Sales	$250,000	$150,000	a 20,000		$380,000
Income from Salt	33,750		c 33,750		
Cost of goods sold	100,000*	80,000*	b 5,000	a 20,000	165,000*
Expenses	50,000*	20,000*			70,000*
Minority interest income ($50,000 − $5,000) × 25%					11,250*
Net income	$133,750	$ 50,000			$133,750
Balance Sheet					
Inventory	$ 10,000			b 5,000	$ 5,000
Investment in Salt	XXX		c 33,750		

* Deduct.
a To eliminate reciprocal intercompany sales and cost of goods sold amounts.
b To adjust cost of goods sold and inventory to a cost basis.
c To eliminate investment income and to adjust the investment in Salt account to
  beginning-of-period balance.

Exhibit 5–5   *Inventory Profit on Upstream Sales in Year of Intercompany Sales*

tories (year of sale to outside entities) and consolidated net income is inverse.
This is illustrated by continuing the Park and Salt example to show realization
during 19X8 of the $5,000 unrealized profit in the December 31, 19X7 inven-
tories. Assume that there are no intercompany transactions between Park and
Salt during 19X8, that Salt is a 75 percent owned subsidiary of Park, and that
Salt reports income of $60,000 for 19X8. Park records its share of Salt's income
under the equity method as follows:

Investment in Salt	$45,000	
Income from Salt		$45,000

To record 75% of Salt's reported income as income from subsidiary.

Investment in Salt	$ 3,750	
Income from Salt		$ 3,750

To record realization during 19X8 of 75% of the $5,000 unrealized inventory profits of Salt
  from 19X7.

Consolidation procedures for unrealized profits in beginning inventories
from upstream sales are illustrated for Park and Subsidiary in Exhibit 5–6. Several
of the items in Exhibit 5–6 differ from those for upstream sales with unrealized
profit in the ending inventory (Exhibit 5–5). In particular, cost of goods sold
is overstated (because of the overstated beginning inventory) and requires a
worksheet adjustment to reduce it to a cost basis. This is shown in working paper
entry a, which also adjusts the investment account and beginning minority interest.
*The allocation between the investment balance (75 percent) and the minority interest (25
percent) is required for unrealized profits in beginning inventories from upstream sales to
correct for prior-year effects on the investment account and the minority interest.*

	Park	75% Salt	Adjustments and Eliminations	Consolidated
PARK AND SUBSIDIARY, SALT (75% OWNED) **PARTIAL CONSOLIDATION WORKING PAPERS** **FOR THE YEAR ENDED DECEMBER 31, 19X8**				
Income Statement Sales	$275,000	$160,000		$435,000
Income from Salt	48,750		b 48,750	
Cost of goods sold	120,000*	85,000*	a 5,000	200,000*
Expenses	60,000*	15,000*		75,000*
Minority interest income ($60,000 + $5,000) × 25%				16,250*
Net income	$143,750	$ 60,000		$143,750
Balance Sheet Investment in Salt	XXX		a 3,750 b 48,750	
Minority interest January 1, 19X8			a 1,250	

* Deduct.

a—To reduce cost of goods sold to a cost basis to the consolidated entity and adjust the investment in Salt account to establish reciprocity between it and subsidiary equity at January 1, 19X8, and eliminate intercompany profit from beginning minority interest.
b—To eliminate investment income and adjust the investment in Salt account to its January 1, 19X8 balance.

Exhibit 5–6   *Inventory Profit on Upstream Sales in Year after Intercompany Sales*

CONSOLIDATION EXAMPLE—INTERCOMPANY PROFITS FROM DOWNSTREAM SALES

Seay Corporation is a 90 percent owned subsidiary of Peak Corporation acquired for $945,000 cash on July 1, 19X1, when Seay's net assets consisted of $1,000,000 capital stock and $50,000 retained earnings. The cost of Peak's 90 percent interest in Seay was equal to book value and fair value of the interest acquired ($1,050,000 × 90 percent) and, accordingly, no allocation to identifiable and unidentifiable assets was necessary.

Peak sells inventory items to Seay on a regular basis, and the intercompany transaction data for 19X5 are as follows:

Sales to Seay in 19X5 (cost $150,000), selling price	$200,000
Unrealized profit in Seay's inventory at December 31, 19X4	20,000
Unrealized profit in Seay's inventory at December 31, 19X5	25,000
Seay's accounts payable to Peak December 31, 19X5	100,000

At December 31, 19X4, Peak's investment in Seay account had a balance of $1,285,000. This balance consisted of Peak's 90 percent equity in Seay's $1,450,000 net assets on that date less $20,000 unrealized profit in Seay's December 31, 19X4 inventory.

Equity Method

During 19X5 Peak made the following entries on its books to account for its investment in Seay under the equity method:

| Cash | $ 90,000 | |
| Investment in Seay | | $ 90,000 |

To record dividends from Seay ($100,000 × 90%).

| Investment in Seay | $265,000 | |
| Income from Seay | | $265,000 |

To record income from Seay for 19X5 computed as follows:

Equity in Seay's net income ($300,000 × 90%)	$270,000
Add: 19X4 inventory profit recognized in 19X5	20,000
Less: 19X5 inventory profit deferred at year-end	−25,000
	$265,000

Since the intercompany sales that led to the unrealized inventory profits were downstream, the full amount of profit deferred in 19X4 is recognized in 19X5, and the full amount of the unrealized inventory profit originating in 19X5 is deferred at December 31, 19X5. Peak's investment in Seay account increased from $1,285,000 at January 1, 19X5 to $1,460,000 at December 31, 19X5, the entire change consisting of $265,000 income less $90,000 dividends for the year. These amounts are shown in the separate company columns of the consolidation working papers of Peak Corporation and Subsidiary for the year ended December 31, 19X5 (see Exhibit 5–7).

The consolidation working papers reflect the previous information for Peak and Seay. The working paper entries in the exhibit are presented in journal form as follows:

a	Sales	$ 200,000	
	Cost of goods sold		$ 200,000

To eliminate intercompany sales and related cost of goods sold amounts.

b	Investment in Seay	$ 20,000	
	Cost of goods sold		$ 20,000

To adjust cost of goods sold and the beginning investment balance for unrealized profit in the beginning inventory.

c	Cost of goods sold	$ 25,000	
	Inventory		$ 25,000

To eliminate unrealized profit in the ending inventory and to increase cost of goods sold to a cost basis to the consolidated entity.

d	Income from Seay	$ 265,000	
	Dividends		$ 90,000
	Investment in Seay		175,000

To eliminate the investment income and 90% of the dividends of Seay and to reduce the investment account to its beginning-of-the-period balance, plus $20,000 from entry b.

e	Capital stock—Seay	$1,000,000	
	Retained earnings—Seay	450,000	
	Investment in Seay		$1,305,000
	Minority interest		145,000

To eliminate reciprocal investment and equity balances and record beginning minority interest.

f	Accounts payable	$ 100,000	
	Accounts receivable		$ 100,000

To eliminate reciprocal payables and receivables from intercompany sales.

In examining the working papers of Peak Corporation and Subsidiary in Exhibit 5–7, note that the net income of Peak ($1,265,000) is equal to consolidated net income, and the retained earnings of Peak ($2,705,000) are equal to consolidated retained earnings. These equalities are expected from a correct

PEAK CORPORATION AND SUBSIDIARY
CONSOLIDATION WORKING PAPERS—FOR THE YEAR ENDED DECEMBER 31, 19X5

	Peak	90% Seay	Adjustments and Eliminations				Minority Interest	Consolidated
Income Statement								
Net sales	$10,000,000	$3,000,000	a	200,000				$12,800,000
Income from Seay	265,000		d	265,000				
Cost of goods sold	5,500,000*	2,000,000*	c	25,000	b	20,000		
					a	200,000		7,305,000*
Other expenses	3,500,000*	700,000*						4,200,000*
Minority interest income ($300,000 × 10%)							$ 30,000	30,000*
Net income	$ 1,265,000	$ 300,000						$ 1,265,000
Retained Earnings								
Retained earnings—Peak	$1,940,000							$ 1,940,000
Retained earnings—Seay		$ 450,000	e	450,000				
Net income	1,265,000 ✓	300,000 ✓						1,265,000
Dividends	500,000*	100,000*			d	90,000	10,000*	500,000*
Retained earnings December 31, 19X5	$ 2,705,000	$ 650,000						$ 2,705,000
Balance Sheet								
Cash	$ 300,000	$ 50,000						$ 350,000
Accounts receivable	700,000	200,000			f	100,000		800,000
Inventories	900,000	450,000			c	25,000		1,325,000
Other current assets	640,000	100,000						740,000
Plant and equipment	8,000,000	1,200,000						9,200,000
Investment in Seay	1,460,000		b	20,000	d	175,000		
					e	1,305,000		
	$12,000,000	$2,000,000						$12,415,000
Accounts payable	$ 800,000	$ 150,000	f	100,000				$ 850,000
Other liabilities	495,000	200,000						695,000
Capital stock	8,000,000	1,000,000	e	1,000,000				8,000,000
Retained earnings	2,705,000 ✓	650,000 ✓						2,705,000
	$12,000,000	$2,000,000						
Minority interest December 31, 19X4					e	145,000	145,000	
Minority interest December 31, 19X5							$165,000	165,000
								$12,415,000

* Deduct.

Exhibit 5-7   *Intercompany Profits on Downstream Sales—Equity Method*

application of the equity method of accounting. Since the sales that gave rise to the intercompany profits in Seay's inventories were downstream, neither beginning minority interest ($145,000) nor minority interest income ($30,000) was affected by the intercompany transactions.

Incomplete Equity Method

Assume that Peak failed to consider its intercompany transactions in accounting for its investment in Seay during 19X4 and 19X5. In that case, both Peak's investment in Seay and its retained earnings account balances at December 31, 19X4 would be $20,000 greater than under the equity method. This $20,000 overstatement is the result of failing to reduce investment and investment income amounts for the $20,000 unrealized profit in 19X4. The amount of overstatement of Peak's investment in Seay and retained earnings balances would increase by $5,000 to $25,000 at December 31, 19X5 because the $20,000 unrealized profits deferred in 19X4 would not be recognized in Peak's 19X5 income and the $25,000 unrealized profit at year-end 19X5 would not be excluded from Peak's income. These observations can be summarized as follows:

	Incomplete Equity Method	− +	Overstated Understated	=	Equity Method
Investment balance at December 31, 19X4	$1,305,000		− $20,000		$1,285,000
Income from Seay in 19X5	270,000		+ 20,000 − 25,000		265,000
Dividends received in 19X5	(90,000)				(90,000)
Investment balance at December 31, 19X5	$1,485,000		− $25,000		$1,460,000

The errors of omitting the intercompany inventory profits affect the investment in Seay and retained earnings accounts of Peak by the same amount.

Conversion to Equity Method Approach   The working papers for Peak and Seay for 19X5 can be converted to the equity method with the following working paper entry to correct for the omissions on Peak's books:

a	Income from Seay	$ 5,000	
	Retained earnings—Peak (beginning)	20,000	
	Investment in Seay		$25,000

After this working paper correction is entered, the other working paper entries would be the same as those illustrated in the consolidation working papers of Exhibit 5–7. This entry could also be recorded on the separate books of Peak before closing in 19X5 to correct for all prior errors resulting from the misapplication of the equity method.

Traditional Working Paper Solution for Incomplete Equity Method   The initial approach to consolidating Peak and Seay financial statements under an incomplete equity method was to convert the income from subsidiary, investment in subsidiary, and retained earnings balances to a complete equity basis. Alternatively, the consolidation working paper entries can be adjusted to accommodate an incomplete equity method without conversion to the equity basis. This alternative working paper approach is illustrated in Exhibit 5–8.

PEAK CORPORATION AND SUBSIDIARY
CONSOLIDATION WORKING PAPERS—YEAR ENDED DECEMBER 31, 19X5

	Peak	90% Seay	Adjustments and Eliminations		Minority Interest	Consolidated Statements
Income Statement Sales	$10,000,000	$3,000,000	a	200,000		$12,800,000
Income from Seay	270,000		d	270,000		
Cost of goods sold	5,500,000*	2,000,000*	c 25,000	a 200,000 b 20,000		7,305,000*
Other expenses	3,500,000*	700,000*				4,200,000*
Minority interest income					$ 30,000	30,000*
Net income	$ 1,270,000 ✓	$ 300,000 ✓				$ 1,265,000
Retained Earnings Retained earnings—Peak	$1,960,000		b	20,000		$ 1,940,000
Retained earnings—Seay		$ 450,000	e	450,000		
Net income	1,270,000	300,000				1,265,000
Dividends	500,000*	100,000*		d 90,000	10,000*	500,000*
Retained earnings December 31	$ 2,730,000	$ 650,000				$ 2,705,000
Balance Sheet Cash	$ 300,000	$ 50,000				$ 350,000
Accounts receivable	700,000	200,000		f 100,000		800,000
Inventories	900,000	450,000		c 25,000		1,325,000
Other current assets	640,000	100,000				740,000
Plant and equipment	8,000,000	1,200,000				9,200,000
Investment in Seay	1,485,000			d 180,000 e 1,305,000		
	$12,025,000	$2,000,000				$12,415,000
Accounts payable	$ 800,000	$ 150,000	f 100,000			$ 850,000
Other liabilities	495,000	200,000				695,000
Capital stock	8,000,000	1,000,000	e 1,000,000			8,000,000
Retained earnings	2,730,000 ✓	650,000 ✓				2,705,000
	$12,025,000	$2,000,000				
Minority interest December 31, 19X4				e 145,000	145,000	
Minority interest December 31, 19X5					$165,000	165,000
						$12,415,000

* Deduct.

Exhibit 5-8   Incomplete Equity Method

   Only entries b and d are different from those appearing in Exhibit 5–7 under the equity method. These two working paper entries are reproduced for convenient reference:

b	Retained earnings—Peak January 1	$ 20,000	
	Cost of goods sold		$ 20,000

To adjust cost of goods sold and Peak's beginning-of-the-period retained earnings for unrealized profits in the beginning inventory.

d	Income from Seay	$270,000	
	Dividends		$ 90,000
	Investment in Seay		180,000

To eliminate investment income (as recorded by Peak) and 90% of Seay's dividends and to reduce the investment account to its beginning-of-the-period balance.

Beginning parent company retained earnings is overstated because Peak failed to eliminate the $20,000 unrealized profits in 19X4. The amount of the overstatement is the difference between the transfer price and historical cost of the merchandise sold downstream. Entry b decreases Peak's beginning retained earnings and cost of goods sold for realized profits in the beginning inventory. Entry d eliminates the investment income recognized on Peak's books and dividends received from Seay. The investment account is also adjusted to its beginning of the period balance in entry d.

Cost Method

If Peak had accounted for its investment in Seay using the cost method, the investment account and the December 31, 19X5 retained earnings would be understated by equal amounts in the parent's separate balance sheet. Also, instead of income from Seay, the income statement for 19X5 would show dividend income of $90,000. The investment in Seay account would be $945,000—the original amount paid by Peak for its investment.

Conversion to Equity Method Approach   The cost-to-equity conversion schedule in Exhibit 5–9 is based on the same data as under the equity method for Peak and Seay except that Peak maintains its investment in Seay account using the cost method. The objective of the schedule is to provide information necessary

	Retained Earnings 12/31/X4	Investment in Seay	Income from Seay	Dividend Income
Prior-Years' Effect				
90% of Seay's increase in undistributed earnings from July 1, 19X1 to December 31, 19X4 ($450,000 − $50,000) × 90%	$360,000	$360,000		
Unrealized profit in Seay's inventory at December 31, 19X4	(20,000)	(20,000)		
Current-Year's Effect				
Reclassify dividend income as investment decrease ($100,000 × 90%)		(90,000)		$(90,000)
Equity in Seay's income for 19X5 ($300,000 × 90%)		270,000	$270,000	
Unrealized profit in Seay's December 31, 19X4 inventory		20,000	20,000	
Unrealized profit in Seay's December 31, 19X5 inventory		(25,000)	(25,000)	
19X5 working paper adjustments to convert from cost to equity	$340,000	$515,000	$265,000	$(90,000)

Exhibit 5–9   *Peak and Subsidiary Cost-Equity Conversion Schedule*

to adjust the working paper accounts to what they would have been had the equity method been used. The following consolidation working paper entry is prepared from the schedule:

a	Dividend income		$ 90,000	
	Investment in Seay		515,000	
		Retained earnings—Peak		$340,000
		Income from Seay		265,000

To eliminate dividend income, enter income from Seay, adjust the investment in Seay account to an equity basis, and convert Peak's beginning retained earnings to beginning consolidated retained earnings.

After this working paper adjustment is entered, the other working paper entries are exactly the same as those in Exhibit 5–7 under the equity method. This entry may also be recorded on the parent company books before closing in 19X5 to convert the parent company records to an equity basis.

Traditional Working Paper Solution for Cost Method   When Peak accounts for its investment in Seay by the cost method, the financial statements of Peak and Seay can be consolidated without converting to the equity method. Exhibit 5–10 illustrates consolidation working papers when the parent company accounts for its investment under the cost method without a working paper entry for conversion to the equity method. Working paper entries from Exhibit 5–10 are reproduced for convenient reference:

a	Sales	$ 200,000	
	Cost of goods sold		$ 200,000

To eliminate intercompany sales and related cost of goods sold.

b	Retained earnings—Peak January 1	$ 20,000	
	Cost of goods sold		$ 20,000

To adjust cost of goods sold and Peak's beginning-of-the-period retained earnings for unrealized profits in the beginning inventory.

c	Cost of goods sold	$ 25,000	
	Inventories		$ 25,000

To eliminate unrealized profits in ending inventory.

d	Dividend income	$ 90,000	
	Dividends		$ 90,000

To eliminate dividend income and 90% of Seay's dividends.

e	Investment in Seay	$ 360,000	
	Retained earnings—Peak January 1		$ 360,000

To increase Peak's beginning retained earnings for its share of Seay's retained earnings increase between the date of acquisition and the beginning of the period.

f	Capital stock—Seay	$1,000,000	
	Retained earnings—Seay	450,000	
	Investment in Seay		$1,305,000
	Minority interest January 1		145,000

To eliminate reciprocal investment and equity balances.

g	Accounts payable	$ 100,000	
	Accounts receivable		$ 100,000

To eliminate reciprocal receivables and payables.

PEAK CORPORATION AND SUBSIDIARY
CONSOLIDATION WORKING PAPERS—FOR THE YEAR ENDED DECEMBER 31, 19X5

	Peak	90% Seay	Adjustments and Eliminations				Minority Interest	Consolidated Statements
Income Statement								
Sales	$10,000,000	$3,000,000	a	200,000				$12,800,000
Dividend income	90,000		d	90,000				
Cost of goods sold	5,500,000*	2,000,000*			a	200,000		
			c	25,000	b	20,000		7,305,000*
Other expenses	3,500,000*	700,000*						4,200,000*
Minority interest income†							$ 30,000	30,000*
Net income	$ 1,090,000	$ 300,000						$ 1,265,000
Retained Earnings								
Retained earnings—Peak	$1,600,000		b	20,000	e	360,000		$ 1,940,000
Retained earnings—Seay		$ 450,000	f	450,000				
Net income	1,090,000✓	300,000✓						1,265,000
Dividends	500,000*	100,000*			d	90,000	10,000*	500,000*
Retained earnings December 31, 19X5	$ 2,190,000	$ 650,000						$ 2,705,000
Balance Sheet								
Cash	$ 300,000	$ 50,000						$ 350,000
Accounts receivable	700,000	200,000			g	100,000		800,000
Inventories	900,000	450,000			c	25,000		1,325,000
Other current assets	640,000	100,000						740,000
Plant and equipment—net	8,000,000	1,200,000						9,200,000
Investment in Seay	945,000		e	360,000	f	1,305,000		
	$11,485,000	$2,000,000						$12,415,000
Accounts payable	$ 800,000	$ 150,000	g	100,000				$ 850,000
Other current liabilities	495,000	200,000						695,000
Capital stock	8,000,000	1,000,000	f	1,000,000				8,000,000
Retained earnings	2,190,000✓	650,000✓						2,705,000
	$11,485,000	$2,000,000						
Minority interest December 31, 19X4					f	145,000	145,000	
Minority interest December 31, 19X5							$165,000	165,000
								$12,415,000

* Deduct.
† Minority interest income $300,000 × 10% = $30,000.

Exhibit 5–10 *Intercompany Profits on Downstream Sales—Cost Method*

Entries a, b, and c are the same as those in Exhibit 5–8 under the incomplete equity method. Under the cost method, the balance of Peak's investment in Seay account remains at the $945,000 original cost. Peak recognizes dividend income but does not record its share of Seay's income or eliminate intercompany profits.

Entry d eliminates dividend income and 90 percent of Seay's dividends. Entry e establishes reciprocity between the investment in Seay account balance and Seay's equity balances at the beginning of the period ($1,450,000 × 90%). Entries f and g are the same as under the equity method.

CONSOLIDATION EXAMPLE—INTERCOMPANY PROFITS FROM UPSTREAM SALES

Smith Corporation is an 80 percent owned subsidiary of Poch Corporation acquired for $480,000 on January 2, 19X6 when Smith's stockholders' equity consisted of $500,000 capital stock and $100,000 retained earnings. Since the investment cost was equal to the book value and fair value of Smith's net assets acquired, no cost–book value differential resulted from the business combination.

Smith Corporation sells inventory items to Poch Corporation on a regular basis. The intercompany transaction data for 19X7 are as follows:

Sales to Poch in 19X7	$300,000
Unrealized profit in Poch's inventory December 31, 19X6	40,000
Unrealized profit in Poch's inventory December 31, 19X7	30,000
Intercompany accounts receivable and payable at December 31, 19X7	50,000

At December 31, 19X6, Poch's investment in Smith had an account balance of $568,000, consisting of $600,000 underlying equity in Smith's net assets ($750,000 × 80%) less 80 percent of the $40,000 unrealized profit in Poch's December 31, 19X6 inventory from upstream sales.

Equity Method

During 19X7 Poch made the following entries to account for its investment in Smith under the equity method:

Cash	$40,000	
Investment in Smith		$40,000
To record dividends from Smith ($50,000 × 80%).		
Investment in Smith	$88,000	
Income from Smith		$88,000

To record income from Smith for 19X7 computed as follows:

Equity in Smith's net income ($100,000 × 80%)	$80,000
Add: 80% of $40,000 unrealized profit deferred in 19X6	32,000
Less: 80% of $30,000 unrealized profit at December 31, 19X7	−24,000
	$88,000

The intercompany sales that led to the unrealized inventory profits in 19X6 and 19X7 were upstream and, accordingly, only 80 percent of the $40,000 unrealized profit from 19X6 is recognized by Poch in 19X7. Similarly, only 80 percent of the $30,000 unrealized profit from 19X7 sales is deferred by Poch at December 31, 19X7. Poch's investment in Smith account was increased by the $88,000 income from Smith during 19X7 and decreased by $40,000 dividends received from Smith. Thus, the $568,000 investment in Smith account at December 31, 19X6 increased to $616,000 at December 31, 19X7. These amounts are shown in the separate company columns of the consolidation working papers for Poch Corporation and Subsidiary in Exhibit 5–11.

Previous information for Poch Corporation and Smith Corporation is combined with other compatible information to provide complete separate company financial statements for the consolidation working papers. The working paper entries in Exhibit 5–11 are presented below in journal form for convenient reference.

a	Sales	$300,000	
	Cost of goods sold		$300,000

To eliminate reciprocal sales and cost of goods sold amounts.

b	Investment in Smith	$ 32,000	
	Minority interest	8,000	
	Cost of goods sold		$ 40,000

To adjust cost of goods sold for unrealized profit in beginning inventory and to allocate the unrealized profit 80% to the parent's investment account and 20% to minority interest.

c	Cost of goods sold	$ 30,000	
	Inventory		$ 30,000

To eliminate unrealized profit from ending inventory and cost of goods sold.

d	Income from Smith	$ 88,000	
	Dividends		$ 40,000
	Investment in Smith		48,000

To eliminate investment income and 80% of the dividends paid by Smith and to reduce the investment account to its beginning balance.

e	Retained earnings—Smith	$250,000	
	Capital stock—Smith	500,000	
	Investment in Smith		$600,000
	Minority interest		150,000

To eliminate reciprocal investment and equity balances and to enter beginning minority interest.

f	Accounts payable	$ 50,000	
	Accounts receivable		$ 50,000

To eliminate reciprocal accounts receivable and payable.

The consolidation working paper entries, as presented in Exhibit 5–11, are similar to those in the Peak/Seay illustration. Only entry b, which allocates the unrealized profit in Poch's beginning inventory between investment in Smith (80 percent) and minority interest (20 percent), is significantly different. Allocation is necessary because the unrealized profit arises from an upstream sale and was included in Smith's reported income for 19X6. Poch's share of the $40,000 unrealized profit is only 80 percent. The other 20 percent relates to minority interests and, accordingly, the $8,000 charge is necessary to reduce beginning minority interest from $150,000 (20 percent of Smith's reported equity of $750,000) to $142,000, in other words, 20 percent of Smith's realized equity of $710,000 ($750,000 − $40,000) at December 31, 19X6.

In computing minority interest income for 19X7, it is necessary to adjust Smith's reported net income for unrealized profits before multiplying by the minority interest percentage. The computation is:

Reported net income of Smith	$100,000
Add: Inventory profits from 19X6 realized in 19X7	+ 40 000
Deduct: Unrealized profits at December 31, 19X7	− 30 000
Smith's realized income for 19X7	110,000
Minority interest percentage	20%
Minority interest income	$ 22,000

The $154,000 minority interest at December 31, 19X7 is determined in the working papers by adding minority interest income of $22,000 to beginning minority interest of $142,000 and subtracting minority interest dividends. An alternative computation that may be used as a check is to deduct unrealized profit in the December 31, 19X7 inventory from Smith's equity at December 31, 19X7,

POCH CORPORATION AND SUBSIDIARY
CONSOLIDATION WORKING PAPERS—FOR THE YEAR ENDED DECEMBER 31, 19X7

	Poch	80% Smith	Adjustments and Eliminations				Minority Interest	Consolidated
Income Statement								
Sales	$3,000,000	$1,500,000	a	300,000				$4,200,000
Income from Smith	88,000		d	88,000				
Cost of goods sold	2,000,000*	1,000,000*	c	30,000	b	40,000		2,,690,000*
					a	300,000		
Other expenses	588,000*	400,000*						988,000*
Minority interest income†							$ 22,000	22,000*
Net income	$ 500,000	$ 100,000						$ 500,000
Retained Earnings								
Retained earnings—Poch	$1,000,000							$1,000,000
Retained earnings—Smith		$ 250,000	e	250,000				
Net income	500,000✓	100,000✓						500,000
Dividends	400,000*	50,000*			d	40,000	10,000*	400,000*
Retained earnings December 31, 19X7	$1,100,000	$ 300,000						$1,100,000
Balance Sheet								
Cash	$ 200,000	$ 50,000						$ 250,000
Accounts receivable	700,000	100,000			f	50,000		750,000
Inventories	1,100,000	200,000			c	30,000		1,270,000
Other current assets	384,000	150,000						534,000
Plant and equipment—net	2,000,000	500,000						2,500,000
Investment in Smith	616,000		b	32,000	d	48,000		
					e	600,000		
	$5,000,000	$1,000,000						$5,304,000
Accounts payable	$ 500,000	$ 150,000	f	50,000				$ 600,000
Other current liabilities	400,000	50,000						450,000
Capital stock	3,000,000	500,000	e	500,000				3,000,000
Retained earnings	1,100,000✓	300,000✓						1,100,000
	$5,000,000	$1,000,000						
Minority interest December 31, 19X6			b	8,000	e	150,000	142,000	
Minority interest December 31, 19X7							$154,000	154,000
								$5,304,000

* Deduct.
† Minority interest income ($100,000 + $40,000 − $30,000) × 20% = $22,000.

Exhibit 5–11 *Intercompany Profits on Upstream Sales—Equity Method*

and multiply the resulting realized equity of Smith by the 20 percent minority interest [that is, ($800,000 − $30,000) × 20% = $154,000]. The advantage of this approach is that only unrealized profits at the balance sheet date need to be considered in the computation.

Incomplete Equity Method

Now assume that Poch Corporation has failed to consider its intercompany transactions in accounting for its investment in Smith for 19X6 and 19X7. In that case, both Poch's investment in Smith and its retained earnings account balances at December 31, 19X6 would be $32,000 greater than under the equity method. This $32,000 overstatement is the result of Poch's failure to reduce investment and investment income accounts for 80 percent of the $40,000 unrealized inventory profit in 19X6. By December 31, 19X7, the overstatement would decrease to $24,000 because the $32,000 deferred from 19X6 would not be recognized in Poch's income for 19X7, and the $24,000 unrealized profit for 19X7 (80 percent of $30,000 unrealized profit at December 31, 19X7) would not be excluded from Poch's 19X7 income. These observations can be summarized by comparison with the equity method example already illustrated:

	Incomplete Equity Method	− +	Overstated Understated	=	Equity Method (see Exhibit 5–11)
Investment balance at December 31, 19X6	$600,000	− $32,000			$568,000
Income from Smith in 19X7	80,000	+ 32,000 − 24,000			88,000
Dividends received in 19X7	(40,000)				(40,000)
Investment balance at December 31, 19X7	$640,000	− $24,000			$616,000

Conversion to Equity Method Approach   The errors from omitting the intercompany profits in 19X6 and 19X7 affect the investment in Smith and retained earnings accounts of Poch by equal amounts.

A working paper entry to correct for the omissions on Poch's books in the 19X7 consolidation working papers of Poch and Subsidiary is as follows:

a	Retained earnings—Poch	$32,000	
	Income from Smith		$ 8,000
	Investment in Smith		24,000

This working paper entry converts the separate accounts of Poch from the incomplete equity to the equity method for working paper utilization. After the conversion is entered in the working papers, the other working paper entries will be the same as those illustrated in the consolidation working papers of Exhibit 5–11. The conversion entry could also be recorded in Poch's separate records before closing in 19X7 to correct for the 19X6 and 19X7 errors of omission.

Traditional Working Paper Solution for Incomplete Equity Method   The traditional approach to consolidating the financial statements of Poch and Smith under an incomplete equity method is illustrated in Exhibit 5–12. Beginning parent company retained earnings is overstated by Poch's share of the unrealized profits in Poch's December 31, 19X6 inventory of goods acquired from Smith. Entry b eliminates the $40,000 cost of goods sold effect of the intercompany profits in Poch's beginning inventory, and allocates it 80 percent to Poch's beginning-of-the-period retained earnings and 20 percent to beginning-of-the-period minority interest. Entry d eliminates income from Smith (as recorded

POCH CORPORATION AND SUBSIDIARY
CONSOLIDATION WORKING PAPERS—YEAR ENDED DECEMBER 31, 19X7

	Poch	80% Smith	Adjustments and Eliminations				Minority Interest	Consolidated Statements
Income Statement								
Sales	$3,000,000	$1,500,000	a	300,000				$4,200,000
Income from Smith	80,000		d	80,000				
Cost of sales	2,000,000*	1,000,000*	c	30,000	a	300,000		2,690,000*
					b	40,000		
Other expenses	588,000*	400,000*						988,000*
Minority interest income†							$ 22,000	22,000*
Net income	$ 492,000	$ 100,000						$ 500,000
Retained Earnings								
Retained earnings—Poch	$1,032,000		b	32,000				$1,000,000
Retained earnings—Smith		$ 250,000	e	250,000				
Net income	492,000✔	100,000✔						500,000
Dividends	400,000*	50,000*			d	40,000	10,000*	400,000*
Retained earnings December 31	$1,124,000	$ 300,000						$1,100,000
Balance Sheet								
Cash	$ 200,000	$ 50,000						$ 250,000
Accounts receivable	700,000	100,000			f	50,000		750,000
Inventories	1,100,000	200,000			c	30,000		1,270,000
Other current assets	384,000	150,000						534,000
Plant and equipment	2,000,000	500,000						2,500,000
Investment in Smith	640,000				d	40,000		
					e	600,000		
	$5,024,000	$1,000,000						$5,304,000
Accounts payable	$ 500,000	$ 150,000	f	50,000				$ 600,000
Other liabilities	400,000	50,000						450,000
Capital stock	3,000,000	500,000	e	500,000				3,000,000
Retained earnings	1,124,000✔	300,000✔						1,100,000
	$5,024,000	$1,000,000						
Minority interest December 31, 19X6			b	8,000	e	150,000	142,000	
Minority interest December 31, 19X7							$154,000	154,000
								$5,304,000

* Deduct.
† Minority interest income ($100,000 + $40,000 − $30,000) × 20% = $22,000.

Exhibit 5–12   Incomplete Equity Method

by Poch), 80 percent of Smith's dividends, and reduces the investment account to its beginning-of-the-period balance. Other entries in Exhibit 5–12 are the same as those under the equity method.

Cost Method

If Poch Corporation had used the cost method of accounting for its investment in Smith for 19X6 and 19X7, its investment in Smith account would remain at $480,000, the original cost of the investment. Assume the same facts for Poch and Smith as shown in Exhibit 5–11 under the equity method, except that Poch's investment in Smith is accounted for by the cost method.

Conversion to Equity Method Approach   Data for the working paper entry to convert Poch's cost-based accounting records to the equity basis are provided in the cost-equity conversion schedule that appears in Exhibit 5–13. The information in the cost-equity conversion schedule is used in constructing a consolidation working paper entry for Poch and Smith as follows:

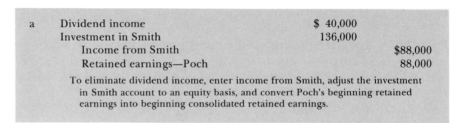

a	Dividend income	$ 40,000	
	Investment in Smith	136,000	
	Income from Smith		$88,000
	Retained earnings—Poch		88,000

To eliminate dividend income, enter income from Smith, adjust the investment in Smith account to an equity basis, and convert Poch's beginning retained earnings into beginning consolidated retained earnings.

This entry should be entered as the first working paper adjustment, after which other working paper entries are the same as those prepared when the equity method is used. The cost-equity conversion entry may be recorded on the parent company books before closing in 19X7 to convert the parent company records to an equity basis.

	Poch's Retained Earnings 12/31/X6	Investment in Smith	Income from Smith	Dividend Income
Prior-Years' Effect				
80% of increase in Smith's undistributed earnings from January 2, 19X6 to December 31, 19X6 ($250,000 − $100,000) × 80%	$120,000	$120,000		
80% of unrealized profit in Poch's December 31, 19X6 inventory ($40,000 × 80%)	(32,000)	(32,000)		
Current-Year's Effect				
Reclassify dividend income as investment decrease ($50,000 dividends × 80%)		(40,000)		$(40,000)
Equity in Smith's 19X7 income ($100,000 × 80%)		80,000	$ 80,000	
80% of unrealized profit in Poch's December 31, 19X6 inventory		32,000	32,000	
80% of unrealized profit in Poch's December 31, 19X7 inventory ($30,000 × 80%)		(24,000)	(24,000)	
19X7 working paper adjustments to convert from cost to equity	$ 88,000	$136,000	$ 88,000	$(40,000)

Exhibit 5–13   *Poch and Subsidiary Cost-Equity Conversion Schedule*

Traditional Working Paper Solution for the Cost Method   Exhibit 5–14 illustrates working paper procedures to consolidate the financial statements of Poch and Smith without converting to the equity method. Entries a, b, and c under

POCH CORPORATION AND SUBSIDIARY
CONSOLIDATION WORKING PAPERS—FOR THE YEAR ENDED DECEMBER 31, 19X7

	Poch	80% Smith	Adjustments and Eliminations				Minority Interest	Consolidated Statements
Income Statement								
Sales	$3,000,000	$1,500,000	a	300,000				$4,200,000
Dividend income	40,000		d	40,000				
Cost of goods sold	2,000,000*	1,000,000*	c	30,000	a	300,000		2,690,000*
					b	40,000		
Other expenses	588,000*	400,000*						988,000*
Minority interest income†							$ 22,000	22,000*
Net income	$ 452,000	$ 100,000						$ 500,000
Retained Earnings								
Retained earnings—Poch	$ 912,000		b	32,000	e	120,000		$1,000,000
Retained earnings—Smith		$ 250,000	f	250,000				
Net income	452,000 ✓	100,000 ✓						500,000
Dividends	400,000*	50,000*			d	40,000	10,000*	400,000*
Retained earnings December 31, 19X7	$ 964,000	$ 300,000						$1,100,000
Balance Sheet								
Cash	$ 200,000	$ 50,000						$ 250,000
Accounts receivable	700,000	100,000			g	50,000		750,000
Inventories	1,100,000	200,000			c	30,000		1,270,000
Other current assets	384,000	150,000						534,000
Plant and equipment—net	2,000,000	500,000						2,500,000
Investment in Smith	480,000		e	120,000	f	600,000		
	$4,864,000	$1,000,000						$5,304,000
Accounts payable	$ 500,000	$ 150,000	g	50,000				$ 600,000
Other current liabilities	400,000	50,000						450,000
Capital stock	3,000,000	500,000	f	500,000				3,000,000·
Retained earnings	964,000 ✓	300,000 ✓						1,100,000
	$4,864,000	$1,000,000						
Minority interest December 31, 19X6			b	8,000	f	150,000	142,000	
Minority interest December 31, 19X7							$154,000	154,000
								$5,304,000

* Deduct.
† Minority interest income ($100,000 + $40,000 − $30,000) × 20% = $22,000.

Exhibit 5–14   *Intercompany Profits on Upstream Sales—Cost Method*

the cost method are identical to those under an *incomplete equity method.* Entry d eliminates dividend income and 80 percent of Smith's dividends. Entry e takes up Poch's share of Smith's retained earnings increase between the date of acquisition of the investment and the beginning of 19X7, thereby establishing reciprocity between the investment account at the beginning of the period and

80 percent of Smith's $750,000 equity at the same date. Entries d and e are reproduced for convenient reference:

d	Dividend income	$40,000	
	Dividends		$40,000
	To eliminate dividend income and 80% of Smith's dividends.		
e	Investment in Smith	$120,000	
	Retained earnings—Poch January 1		$120,000
	To establish reciprocity between parent's beginning-of-the-period retained earnings and the investment account at the same date.		

Entry f eliminates reciprocal investment and equity balances and enters beginning minority interest the same as under the *equity method*. Entry g eliminates reciprocal accounts receivable and payable.

SUMMARY

Intercompany sales and purchases of inventory items result in reciprocal sales and cost of goods sold amounts that do not reflect merchandising activity of the consolidated entity. Such intercompany transactions also give rise to unrealized intercompany profits that are required to be deferred until they are realized by subsequent sales outside of the consolidated entity. Except for affiliation structures with only 100 percent owned subsidiaries, the direction of intercompany sales is important. The full amount of the unrealized intercompany profit from downstream sales is charged against parent company and consolidated net income. In the case of upstream sales, however, unrealized profits are charged to consolidated net income and minority interest income on the basis of majority and minority ownership. Intercompany profits that are deferred in one period are subsequently recognized in the period in which the related inventory items are sold to nonaffiliated entities. A summary illustration of the effect of intercompany profit eliminations on parent company and consolidated net income is presented in Exhibit 5–15.

SELECTED READINGS

Accounting Interpretation No. 1 of APB Opinion No. 18. New York: American Institute of Certified Public Accountants, 1971.

Accounting Principles Board Opinion No. 18. "The Equity Method of Accounting for Investments in Common Stock." New York: American Institute of Certified Public Accountants, 1971.

KING, THOMAS E., and VALDEAN C. LEMBKE. "Reporting Investor Income under the Equity Method." *Journal of Accountancy* (September 1976), pp. 65–71.

NEUHAUSEN, BENJAMIN S. "Consolidation and the Equity Method—Time for an Overhaul." *Journal of Accountancy* (February 1982), pp. 54–66.

Assumptions:

1 Parent Company's income, excluding income from subsidiary, is $100,000.
2 90 percent owned subsidiary reports net income of $50,000.
3 Unrealized profit in beginning inventory is $5,000.
4 Unrealized profit in ending inventory is $10,000.

	Downstream	Upstream
	Assume that P Sells to S	Assume that S Sells to P
P's Net Income—Equity Method		
P's separate income	$100,000	$100,000
P's share of S's reported net income:		
($50,000 × 90%)	45,000	45,000
Add: Unrealized profit in beginning inventory:		
($5,000 × 100%)	5,000	
($5,000 × 90%)		4,500
Deduct: Unrealized profit in ending inventory:		
($10,000 × 100%)	10,000*	
($10,000 × 90%)		9,000*
P's net income	$140,000	$140,500
Consolidated Net Income		
P's separate income plus S's net income	$150,000	$150,000
Adjustments for unrealized profits:		
Beginning inventory ($5,000 × 100%)	5,000	5,000
Ending inventory ($10,000 × 100%)	10,000*	10,000*
Total realized income	$145,000	$145,000
Less: Minority interest income:		
($50,000 × 10%)	5,000*	
($50,000 + $5,000 − $10,000) × 10%		4,500*
Consolidated net income	$140,000	$140,500

* Deduct.
Under the assumption that P sells to S, P's net income and consolidated net income are exactly the same as if the sales involving the unrealized profits had never taken place. In that case, P's separate income would have been $95,000 ($100,000 + $5,000 − $10,000), and P's income from S would have been $45,000 ($50,000 × 90%) for a total of $140,000.
Under the assumption that S sells to P, P's net income and consolidated net income are exactly the same as if the intercompany sales involving unrealized inventory profits had never taken place. In that case, P's separate income would have been $100,000 (as given), and S's net income would have been $45,000 ($50,000 + $5,000 − $10,000). P's $100,000 separate income plus P's income from S of $40,500 ($45,000 × 90%) is equal to P's net income and consolidated net income.

Exhibit 5-15 *Summary Illustration—Unrealized Inventory Profits*

ASSIGNMENT MATERIAL

QUESTIONS

1 The effect of unrealized profits and losses on sales between affiliated companies is eliminated in preparing consolidated financial statements. When are profits and losses on such sales realized for consolidated statement purposes?
2 In eliminating unrealized profit on intercompany sales of inventory items, should gross profit or net profit be eliminated?
3 Is the amount of intercompany profit to be eliminated from consolidated financial statements affected by the existence of a minority interest? Explain.

4 What effect does the elimination of intercompany sales and purchases (or cost of goods sold) have on consolidated net income?

5 What effect does the elimination of intercompany accounts receivable and accounts payable have on consolidated working capital?

6 Explain the designations *upstream sales* and *downstream sales*. Of what significance are these designations in computing parent company and consolidated net income?

7 Would failure to eliminate unrealized profit in inventories at December 31, 19X6 have any effect on consolidated net income in 19X7? 19X8?

8 Under what circumstances is minority interest income affected by intercompany sales activity?

9 How does a parent company adjust its investment income for unrealized profit on sales it makes to its subsidiaries (a) in the year of the sale and (b) in the year in which the subsidiaries sell the related merchandise to outsiders?

10 How is the combined cost of goods sold affected by unrealized profit in (a) the beginning inventory of the subsidiary and (b) the ending inventory of the subsidiary?

11 Is the effect of unrealized profit on consolidated cost of goods sold influenced by (a) the existence of a minority interest and (b) the direction of intercompany sales?

12 Unrealized profit in the ending inventory is eliminated in consolidation working papers by increasing cost of sales and decreasing the inventory account. How is unrealized profit in the beginning inventory reflected in the consolidation working papers?

13 Describe the computation of minority interest income in a year in which there is unrealized inventory profit from upstream sales in both the beginning and ending inventories of the parent company.

14 Consolidation working paper procedures are usually based on the assumption that any unrealized profit in the beginning inventory of one year is realized through sales in the following year. If the related merchandise is not sold in the succeeding period, would the assumption result in an incorrect measurement of consolidated net income?

(*Note:* Don't forget the assumptions on page 60 when working exercises and problems in this chapter.)

EXERCISES

E 5–1 Pannell Corporation acquired an 80 percent interest in Smittie Corporation on January 1, 19X1 at a cost equal to book value and fair value. Pannell regularly sells merchandise to Smittie at 120 percent of Pannell's cost. Intercompany sales information for 19X1 and 19X2 is as follows:

	19X1	19X2
Intercompany sales at selling price	$120,000	$180,000
Merchandise acquired from Pannell remaining unsold by Smittie on December 31	60,000	30,000

Smittie reported $200,000 net income for 19X1 and $250,000 for 19X2.

Required

1 Determine the unrealized profit in Smittie's inventories at December 31, 19X1 and 19X2.

2 Compute Pannell's income from Smittie for 19X1.

3 Compute Pannell's income from Smittie for 19X2.

E 5–2 The separate incomes (which do not include investment income) of Pycus Corporation and Sylvia Corporation, its 80 percent owned subsidiary, for 19X6 were determined as follows:

	Pycus	Sylvia
Sales	$400,000	$100,000
Less: Cost of sales	200,000	60,000
Gross profit	200,000	40,000
Other expenses	100,000	30,000
Separate incomes	$100,000	$ 10,000

During 19X6 Pycus sold merchandise that cost $20,000 to Sylvia for $40,000, and at December 31, 19X6 half of these inventory items remained unsold by Sylvia.

Required: Prepare a consolidated income statement for Pycus Corporation and Subsidiary for the year ended December 31, 19X6.

E 5–3 Income statement information for the year 19X3 for Penney Corporation and its 60 percent owned subsidiary, Shephard Corporation, is as follows:

	Penney	Shephard
Sales	$800,000	$300,000
Cost of sales	400,000	200,000
Gross profit	400,000	100,000
Operating expenses	250,000	50,000
Shephard's net income		$ 50,000
Penney's separate income	$150,000	

Intercompany sales for 19X3 are upstream (from Shephard to Penney) and total $100,000. Penney's December 31, 19X2 and December 31, 19X3 inventories contain unrealized profits of $5,000 and $8,000, respectively.

Required
  1 Compute minority interest income for 19X3.
  2 Compute consolidated cost of sales for 19X3.

E 5–4 Plate-G Corporation acquired a 90 percent interest in Shale Corporation for $180,000 on January 1, 19X1 when Shale's stockholders' equity consisted of $150,000 par capital stock and $50,000 retained earnings. Shale's assets and liabilities were recorded at their fair values on that date.
    Comparative income statements for 19X2 are as follows:

	Plate-G	Shale 90%
Sales	$750,000	$300,000
Income from Shale	45,000	
Cost of sales	500,000*	150,000*
Other expenses	105,000*	100,000*
Net income	$190,000	$ 50,000

* Deduct.

During 19X1 Plate-G sold merchandise to Shale for $60,000. Half of these goods were included in Shale's inventory on December 31, 19X1 at $30,000, even though the cost to Plate-G was only $20,000. These inventory items were sold by Shale during 19X2.
    During 19X2 Plate-G sold merchandise that cost $36,000 to Shale for $54,000. One-third of this merchandise remains unsold by Shale at December 31, 19X2.

Required: Prepare a consolidated income statement for Plate-G Corporation and Subsidiary for the year ended December 31, 19X2.

E 5–5 Steeple Corporation is a 90 percent owned subsidiary of Peake Corporation acquired by Peake at book value on January 1, 19X2. Peake uses the equity method of accounting for its investment in Steeple, but it does not make adjustments for intercompany profit transactions. Separate income statements for Peake and Steeple for 19X2 and 19X3 are as follows:

	Peake		Steeple	
	19X2	*19X3*	*19X2*	*19X3*
Sales	$1,000,000	$1,200,000	$500,000	$700,000
Income from Steeple	90,000	135,000		
Cost of sales	600,000*	720,000*	300,000*	350,000*
Other expenses	200,000*	250,000*	100,000*	200,000*
Net income	$ 290,000	$ 365,000	$100,000	$150,000

* Deduct.

Intercompany sales between the two affiliated companies were $80,000 during 19X2 and $120,000 during 19X3. Unrealized profits included in ending inventories from these intercompany sales amounted to $16,000 at December 31, 19X2 and $24,000 at December 31, 19X3.

Part A: Assume that all intercompany sales are from Peake to Steeple.
1 Consolidated sales for 19X2 should be:
  a $1,500,000   b $1,420,000
  c $1,370,000   d $1,354,000
2 Minority interest income for 19X2 should be:
  a $600   b $8,400
  c $10,000   d $29,000
3 Consolidated net income for 19X2 should be:
  a $290,000   b $275,600
  c $274,000   d $194,000

Part B: Assume that all intercompany sales are from Steeple to Peake.
4 Consolidated cost of sales for 19X3 should be:
  a $950,000   b $958,000
  c $942,000   d $926,000
5 Minority interest income for 19X3 should be:
  a $15,800   b $15,000
  c $14,200   d $12,600
6 Consolidated net income for 19X3 should be:
  a $373,000   b $372,200
  c $365,000   d $357,800

E 5–6 Sandy Corporation is an 80 percent owned subsidiary of Pinto Corporation. Comparative income and retained earnings statements for these affiliated companies for the year ended December 31, 19X1 are as follows:

	Pinto	Sandy
Sales	$500,000	$100,000
Dividend income from Sandy	16,000	
Cost of sales	300,000*	50,000*
Expenses	116,000*	20,000*
Net income	$100,000	$ 30,000
Retained earnings January 1, 19X1	500,000	210,000
Dividends	50,000*	20,000*
Retained earnings December 31, 19X1	$550,000	$220,000

* Deduct.

Part A: Assume that there are no intercompany transactions between these affiliated companies that affect their separate incomes.

1 Consolidated net income for Pinto Corporation and Subsidiary for 19X1 should be reported in the amount of:

    a $130,000   **b** $114,000

    c $108,000   **d** $100,000

Part B: Assume that Pinto sells merchandise to Sandy for $15,000 during 19X1, that the merchandise cost Pinto $10,000, and that half the merchandise remains unsold by Sandy at December 31, 19X1.

2 Under this assumption, consolidated net income for Pinto Corporation and Subsidiary for 19X1 should be reported in the amount of:

    a $125,000   **b** $111,500

    c $105,500   **d** $95,500

3 Consolidated cost of goods sold under the assumption in Part B should be reported in the amount of:

    a $352,500   **b** $347,500

    c $337,500   **d** $332,500

Part C: Assume that Sandy sells merchandise to Pinto at 120 percent of its cost and that Pinto's January 1, 19X1 inventory includes $4,800 of merchandise acquired from Sandy and its December 31, 19X1 inventory includes $6,000 of such merchandise.

4 Under this assumption, Pinto's investment income from Sandy for 19X1 under the equity method of accounting should be reported in the amount of:

    a $23,840   **b** $23,200

    c $22,800   **d** $18,000

5 Under the assumption of Part C, minority interest in Sandy Corporation's income for 19X1 should be reported in the amount of:

    a $6,960   **b** $6,160

    c $5,960   **d** $5,760

E 5–7 Piper Corporation recorded $65,000 investment income from Sneed Corporation, its 80 percent owned subsidiary, for the year 19X7 and $70,000 for the year 19X8. This investment income represented 80 percent of Sneed's reported income of $81,250 and $87,500 in 19X7 and 19X8, respectively. Piper's net income (including investment income) for 19X7 was $240,000, and for 19X8 it was $160,000.

    During 19X7 Piper sold merchandise to Sneed for $180,000. This merchandise cost Piper $130,000, and 50 percent of it was inventoried by Sneed at December 31, 19X7.

    Piper sold merchandise that cost $150,000 to Sneed for $210,000 during 19X8. The December 31, 19X8 inventory of Sneed included $84,000 of this merchandise.

Required

    1 Compute the following:

        a Piper's income from Sneed on a correct equity basis for 19X7 and 19X8

        b Consolidated net income for 19X7 and 19X8

    2 Prepare journal entries to correct Piper's books at December 31, 19X8, assuming that closing entries at December 31, 19X8 have not been made.

E 5–8 Specks Corporation is an 80 percent owned subsidiary of Pearl Corporation, acquired at book value on January 1, 19X2 when Specks's assets and liabilities were equal to their fair values. During 19X2 Specks sold $12,000 merchandise to Pearl at a 25 percent gross profit (cost to Specks was $9,000). At December 31, 19X2 Pearl included 40 percent of this merchandise in its inventory at its purchase price from Specks.

    Income statements for Pearl and Specks Corporations for 19X2 follow:

	Pearl	Specks
Sales	$300,000	$100,000
Income from Specks	12,000	
Cost of sales	200,000*	75,000*
Other expenses	50,000*	10,000*
Net income	$ 62,000	$ 15,000

* Deduct.

Required: Prepare a consolidated income statement for Pearl Corporation and Subsidiary for the year 19X2.

E 5–9 The consolidated income statement of Pullen and Swain for 19X2 was as follows:

Sales	$1,380,000
Cost of sales	920,000*
Operating expenses	160,000*
Income to 20% minority interest in Swain	40,000*
Consolidated net income	$ 260,000

* Deduct

After the consolidated income statement was prepared, it was discovered that intercompany sales transactions had not been considered and that unrealized profits had not been eliminated. Information concerning these items follows:

	Cost	Selling Price	Unsold at Year-end
19X1 Sales—Pullen to Swain	$160,000	$180,000	25%
19X2 Sales—Swain to Pullen	90,000	120,000	40

Required: Prepare a corrected consolidated income statement for Pullen and Swain for the year ended December 31, 19X2.

PROBLEMS

P 5–1 Paige Corporation acquired all the voting common stock of Sikora Corporation several years ago in a pooling of interests business combination. A summary of the separate income amounts of Paige and Sikora before consideration of any intercompany transactions for the year 19X2 is as follows:

	Paige	Sikora
Sales	$1,000,000	$600,000
Cost of sales	600,000	300,000
Gross profit	400,000	300,000
Operating expenses	200,000	200,000
Operating income	$ 200,000	$100,000

During 19X2 Paige sold merchandise that cost $140,000 to Sikora for $175,000. One-fifth of this merchandise remains in Sikora's inventory at December 31, 19X2. There were no other intercompany transactions during the year.

Required
1 Calculate consolidated cost of sales for 19X2.
2 Prepare the consolidated income statement for Paige Corporation and Subsidiary for the year 19X2.

P 5–2 Summary adjusted trial balances for Proctor Corporation and Samel Corporation at December 31, 19X8 follow:

	Proctor	Samel
Cash	$ 100,000	$ 20,000
Receivables—net	200,000	50,000
Inventories	240,000	100,000
Plant assets—net	250,000	480,000
Investment in Samel—90%	435,600	
Cost of sales	800,000	390,000
Other expenses	340,000	160,000
Dividends	100,000	50,000
	$2,465,600	$1,250,000
Accounts payable	$ 150,000	$ 90,000
Other liabilities	60,000	60,000
Capital stock—$10 par	500,000	300,000
Retained earnings	369,200	150,000
Sales	1,300,000	650,000
Income from Samel	86,400	
	$2,465,600	$1,250,000

Proctor acquired its 90 percent interest in Samel at its book value of $360,000 on January 1, 19X7 when Samel had capital stock of $300,000 and retained earnings of $100,000.

The December 31, 19X7 and 19X8 inventories of Proctor included merchandise acquired from Samel of $30,000 and $40,000, respectively. Samel realizes a gross profit of 40 percent on all merchandise sold. During 19X7 and 19X8, sales by Samel to Proctor were $60,000 and $80,000, respectively.

Required: Prepare a combined consolidated income and retained earnings statement for Proctor Corporation and Subsidiary for the year ended December 31, 19X8.

P 5–3 Sally is a 75 percent owned subsidiary of Pet Corporation, acquired by Pet at book value (also fair value) on January 2, 19X4. Comparative income statements for Pet and Sally for 19X6 are as follows:

	Pet	Sally
Net sales	$500,000	$200,000
Cost of goods sold	300,000	120,000
Gross profit	200,000	80,000
Operating expenses	60,000	30,000
Operating income	140,000	50,000
Income from Sally	37,500	—
Net income	$177,500	$ 50,000

Additional Information
   1 Sally made sales to Pet of $50,000 in 19X5 and $80,000 in 19X6.
   2 Pet's inventories at December 31, 19X5 and December 31, 19X6 included merchandise on which Sally reported profit of $15,000 and $22,000 during 19X5 and 19X6, respectively.
   3 Pet has not eliminated the effect of intercompany profits in accounting for its investment in Sally.

Required
   1 Prepare any entries necessary to adjust Pet's investment in Sally account at December 31, 19X6 and income from Sally for 19X6.

2 Determine the following:
  a Consolidated cost of goods sold for 19X6
  b Minority interest income for 19X6
  c Consolidated net income for 19X6

P 5-4 Comparative income statements for Probus Corporation and its 70 percent owned subsidiary, Shively Corporation, for 19X3 are summarized as follows:

	Probus	Shively
Sales	$1,000,000	$600,000
Cost of sales	480,000	310,000
Gross profit	520,000	290,000
Operating expenses	300,000	180,000
Separate income	220,000	110,000
Income from Shively	77,000	
Net income	$ 297,000	$110,000

Additional Information
  1 Probus acquired its interest in Shively on January 1, 19X2 at a price $360,000 in excess of the fair value of the interest acquired.
  2 Probus sells inventory items to Shively on a regular basis with intercompany sales data as follows:

	19X2	19X3
Probus's sales to Shively	$300,000	$420,000
Probus's cost of sales to Shively	200,000	280,000
Percent unsold at December 31	50%	40%

Required
  1 Prepare a corrected income statement for Probus Corporation for 19X3 with Shively Corporation being treated as an equity investee.
  2 Prepare a consolidated income statement for Probus Corporation and Subsidiary for 19X3.

P 5-5 Putt Corporation acquired a 90 percent interest in Slam Corporation at book value on January 1, 19X5. Intercompany purchases and sales and inventory data for 19X5, 19X6, and 19X7 are as follows:

	Sales by Slam to Putt	Intercompany Profit in Putt's Inventory at December 31
19X5	$200,000	$15,000
19X6	150,000	12,000
19X7	300,000	24,000

Selected data from the financial statements of Putt and Slam at and for the year ended December 31, 19X7 are as follows:

	Putt	Slam
Income Statement		
Sales	$900,000	$600,000
Cost of sales	625,000	300,000
Expenses	225,000	150,000
Income from Slam	124,200	—

	Putt	Slam
Balance Sheet		
Inventory	$150,000	$ 80,000
Retained earnings December 31, 19X7	425,000	220,000
Capital stock	500,000	300,000

Required: Prepare well-organized schedules showing computations for each of the following:
1. Consolidated cost of sales for 19X7
2. Minority interest income for 19X7
3. Consolidated net income for 19X7
4. Minority interest at December 31, 19X7

P 5-6 Potter Company owns controlling interests in Scan and Tray Corporations, having acquired an 80 percent interest in Scan in 19X1 and a 90 percent interest in Tray on January 1, 19X2. Potter's investments in Scan and Tray were at book value equal to fair value.

Inventories of the affiliated companies at December 31, 19X2 and December 31, 19X3 were as follows:

	December 31, 19X2	December 31, 19X3
Potter inventories	$60,000	$54,000
Scan inventories	38,750	31,250
Tray inventories	24,000	36,000

Potter sells to Scan at a 25 percent markup based on cost, and Tray sells to Potter at a markup based on cost of 20 percent. Potter's beginning and ending inventories for 19X3 consisted of 40 percent and 50 percent, respectively, of goods acquired from Tray. All of Scan's inventories consisted of merchandise acquired from Potter.

Required
1. Calculate the inventory that should appear in the December 31, 19X2 consolidated balance sheet.
2. Calculate the inventory that should appear in the December 31, 19X3 consolidated balance sheet.

P 5-7 Comparative income statements of Stoffel Corporation for the calendar years 19X7, 19X8, and 19X9 are as follows:

	19X7	19X8	19X9
Sales	$4,000,000	$4,250,000	$4,750,000
Cost of sales	2,100,000	2,200,000	2,500,000
Gross profit	1,900,000	2,050,000	2,250,000
Operating expenses	1,500,000	1,600,000	1,900,000
Net income	$ 400,000	$ 450,000	$ 350,000

Additional Information
1. Stoffel was a 75 percent owned subsidiary of Prowler Corporation throughout the 19X7–19X9 period. Prowler's separate income (income excuding income from Stoffel) was $1,800,000, $1,700,000, and $2,000,000 in 19X7, 19X8, and 19X9, respectively. Prowler acquired its interest in Stoffel at its underlying book value on July 1, 19X6.
2. Prowler sold inventory items to Stoffel during 19X7 at a gross profit to Prowler of $200,000. Half the merchandise remained in Stoffel's inventory at December 31, 19X7. Total sales by Prowler to Stoffel in 19X7 were $400,000. The remaining merchandise was sold by Stoffel in 19X8.

3 Prowler's inventory at December 31, 19X8 included items acquired from Stoffel on which Stoffel made a profit of $80,000. Total sales of Stoffel to Prowler during 19X8 were $300,000.

4 There were no unrealized profits in the December 31, 19X9 inventories of either Stoffel or Prowler.

5 Prowler uses the equity method of accounting for its investment in Stoffel.

Required

1 Prepare a schedule showing Prowler's income from Stoffel for each of the years 19X7, 19X8, and 19X9.

2 Compute Prowler's net income for each of the years 19X7, 19X8, and 19X9.

3 Prepare a schedule of consolidated net income for Prowler Corporation and Subsidiary for each of the years 19X7, 19X8, and 19X9, beginning with the separate incomes of the two affiliated corporations and including minority interest computations.

P 5–8 Comparative separate company and consolidated balance sheets for Phyllis Corporation and its 80 percent owned subsidiary, Sarah Corporation, at year end 19X2 are as follows:

	Phyllis	Sarah	Consolidated
Assets			
Cash	$ 180,000	$ 40,000	$ 220,000
Inventories	200,000	160,000	360,000
Other current assets	70,000	150,000	170,000
Plant assets—net	500,000	350,000	850,000
Investment in Sarah	630,000		
Goodwill			150,000
	$1,580,000	$700,000	$1,750,000
Equities			
Accounts payable	$ 80,000	$ 50,000	$ 120,000
Dividends payable	100,000	50,000	110,000
Capital stock—$10 par	1,000,000	500,000	1,000,000
Retained earnings	400,000	100,000	400,000
Minority interest			120,000
	$1,580,000	$700,000	$1,750,000

Investigation reveals that the consolidated balance sheet is in error because Phyllis Corporation has not amortized goodwill and because it has not eliminated unrealized inventory profits. The investment in Sarah was acquired on January 1, 19X1 at a price $150,000 in excess of the book value and fair value acquired. The original plan was to amortize goodwill over ten years. Unrealized profits in Sarah's December 31, 19X1 and 19X2 inventories of merchandise acquired from Phyllis were $25,000 and $40,000, respectively.

Required: Prepare a consolidated balance sheet at December 31, 19X2 for Phyllis Corporation and Subsidiary.

P 5–9 Pane Corporation acquired 100 percent of Seal Corporation's outstanding voting common stock on January 1, 19X1 for $660,000 cash. Seal's stockholders' equity on this date consisted of $300,000 capital stock and $300,000 retained earnings. The difference between the price paid by Pane and the underlying equity acquired in Seal was allocated $30,000 to Seal's undervalued inventory and the remainder to goodwill with a five-year write-off period. The undervalued inventory items were sold by Seal during 19X1.

Pane made sales of $100,000 to Seal at a gross profit of $40,000 during 19X1, and during 19X2 Pane made sales of $120,000 to Seal at a gross profit of $48,000. One-half the 19X1 sales were inventoried by Seal at year-end 19X1, and one-fourth the 19X2 sales were inventoried by Seal at year-end 19X2. Seal owed Pane $17,000 on account at December 31, 19X2.

The separate financial statements of Pane and Seal Corporations at and for the year ended December 31, 19X2 are summarized as follows:

	Pane	Seal
Combined Income and Retained Earnings Statements for the Year Ended December 31, 19X2		
Sales	$ 800,000	$400,000
Income from Seal	102,000	
Cost of sales	(400,000)	(200,000)
Depreciation expense	(110,000)	(40,000)
Other expenses	(192,000)	(60,000)
Net income	200,000	100,000
Beginning retained earnings	600,000	380,000
Less: Dividends	(100,000)	(50,000)
Retained earnings December 31, 19X2	$ 700,000	$430,000
Balance Sheet at December 31, 19X2		
Cash	$ 54,000	$ 37,000
Receivables—net	90,000	60,000
Inventories	100,000	80,000
Other assets	70,000	90,000
Land	50,000	50,000
Buildings—net	200,000	150,000
Equipment—net	500,000	400,000
Investment in Seal	736,000	
Total assets	$1,800,000	$867,000
Accounts payable	$ 160,000	$ 47,000
Other liabilities	340,000	90,000
Common stock—$10 par	600,000	300,000
Retained earnings	700,000	430,000
Total equities	$1,800,000	$867,000

Required: Prepare working papers to consolidate the financial statements of Pane Corporation and Subsidiary at and for the year ended December 31, 19X2.

P 5–10   Pary Corporation acquired a 90 percent interest in Sady Corporation for $280,000 on January 1, 19X7 when Sady's equity consisted of $150,000 capital stock and $50,000 retained earnings. The fair values of Sady's assets and liabilities were equal to their book values on this date, and any goodwill is to be amortized over a ten-year period. Pary uses the equity method of accounting for Sady.

During 19X7 Pary sold inventory items to Sady for $80,000, and at December 31, 19X7 Sady's inventory included items on which there were $10,000 unrealized profits. During 19X8 Pary sold inventory items to Sady for $100,000, and at December 31, 19X8 Sady's inventory included items on which there were $20,000 unrealized profits.

At December 31, 19X8 Sady owed Pary $15,000 on account for merchandise purchases.

The financial statements of Pary and Sady Corporations at and for the year ended December 31, 19X8 are summarized as follows:

	Pary	Sady
Combined Income and Retained Earnings Statements for the Year Ended December 31, 19X8		
Sales	$ 700,000	$300,000
Income from Sady	115,000	
Cost of sales	(270,000)	(130,000)
Operating expenses	(145,000)	(20,000)
Net income	400,000	150,000
Beginning retained earnings	70,000	90,000
Deduct: Dividends	(150,000)	(50,000)
Retained earnings December 31, 19X8	$320,000	$190,000

	Pary	Sady
Balance Sheet at December 31, 19X8		
Cash	$ 166,000	$ 30,000
Accounts receivable	180,000	100,000
Dividends receivable	18,000	
Inventories	60,000	80,000
Land	100,000	50,000
Buildings—net	280,000	100,000
Equipment—net	330,000	140,000
Investment in Sady	366,000	
Total assets	$1,500,000	$500,000
Accounts payable	$ 225,000	$100,000
Dividends payable	70,000	20,000
Other liabilities	150,000	40,000
Common stock—$10 par	735,000	150,000
Retained earnings	320,000	190,000
Total equities	$1,500,000	$500,000

Required: Prepare consolidation working papers for Pary Corporation and Subsidiary for the year ended December 31, 19X8.

P 5-11 **[AICPA adapted]**

On June 30, 19X6 Paul Corporation acquired for cash of $19 per share all the outstanding voting common stock of Sand Corporation. Both companies continued to operate as separate entities and both companies have calendar years.

On June 30, 19X6, after closing the nominal accounts, Sand's condensed balance sheet was as follows:

Assets	
Cash	$ 700,000
Accounts receivable—net	600,000
Inventories	1,400,000
Property, plant, and equipment—net	3,300,000
Other assets	500,000
Total assets	$6,500,000
Liabilities and Stockholders' Equity	
Accounts payable and other current liabilities	$ 700,000
Long-term debt	2,600,000
Other liabilities	200,000
Common stock, par value $1.00 per share	1,000,000
Additional paid-in capital	400,000
Retained earnings	1,600,000
Total liabilities and stockholders' equity	$6,500,000

On June 30, 19X6 Sand's assets and liabilities that had fair values that differed from the book values were as follows:

	Fair Value
Property, plant, and equipment—net	$16,400,000
Other assets	200,000
Long-term debt	2,200,000

The differences between fair values and book values resulted in a charge or credit to depreciation or amortization for the consolidated statements for the six-month period ended December 31, 19X6, as follows:

Property, plant, and equipment—net	$500,000 charge
Other assets	10,000 credit
Long-term debt	5,000 charge
	$495,000 charge

The amount paid by Paul in excess of the fair value of the net assets of Sand is attributable to expected future earnings of Sand and will be amortized over the maximum allowable period.

On June 30, 19X6 there were *no* intercompany receivables or payables. During the six-month period ending December 31, 19X6 Sand acquired merchandise from Paul at an invoice price of $500,000. The cost of the merchandise to Paul was $300,000. At December 31, 19X6 one half of the merchandise was not sold and Sand had not yet paid for any of the merchandise.

The 19X6 net income (loss) for both companies was as follows:

	Paul	Sand
January 1 to June 30	$ 250,000	$ (750,000)
July 1 to December 31	1,600,000	1,250,000

The $1,600,000 net income of Paul *includes* the equity in the net income of Sand.

On December 31, 19X6, after closing the nominal accounts, the condensed balance sheets for both companies were as follows:

	Paul	Sand
Assets		
Cash	$ 3,500,000	$ 600,000
Accounts receivable—net	1,400,000	1,500,000
Inventories	1,000,000	2,500,000
Property, plant, and equipment—net	2,000,000	3,100,000
Investment in subsidiary, at equity	20,250,000	—
Other assets	100,000	500,000
Total assets	$28,250,000	$8,200,000
Liabilities and Stockholders' Equity		
Accounts payable and other current liabilities	$ 1,500,000	$1,100,000
Long-term debt	4,000,000	2,600,000
Other liabilities	750,000	250,000
Common stock, par value $1.00 per share	10,000,000	1,000,000
Additional paid-in capital	5,000,000	400,000
Retained earnings	7,000,000	2,850,000
Total liabilities and stockholders' equity	$28,250,000	$8,200,000

Required

1 Prepare consolidated balance sheet working papers for Paul Corporation and Subsidiary at December 31, 19X6.
2 Prepare a condensed consolidated balance sheet of Paul Corporation and Subsidiary at December 31, 19X6.

P 5–12 Poly Corporation purchased a 90 percent interest in Susan Corporation on December 31, 19X4 for $275,000 cash when Susan had capital stock of $200,000 and retained earnings of $50,000. All Susan's assets and liabilities were recorded at their fair values when Poly acquired its interest. The excess of cost over book value is being amortized over a ten-year period.

The Poly/Susan affiliation is a vertically integrated merchandising operation with Susan selling all of its output to Poly Corporation at 140 percent of its cost. Poly sells the merchandise acquired from Susan at 150 percent of its purchase price from Susan.

All of Poly's December 31, 19X6 and December 31, 19X7 inventories of $28,000 and $42,000, respectively, were acquired from Susan. Susan's December 31, 19X6 and December 31, 19X7 inventories were $80,000 each.

Poly's accounts payable at December 31, 19X7 includes $10,000 owed to Susan from 19X7 purchases.

Comparative financial statements for Poly Corporation and Susan Corporation at and for the year ended December 31, 19X7 are as follows:

	Poly	Susan
Combined Income and Retained Earnings Statement for the Year Ended December 31, 19X7		
Sales	$819,000	$560,000
Income from Susan	81,400	—
Cost of sales	546,000*	400,000*
Other expenses	154,400*	60,000*
Net income	200,000	100,000
Add: Beginning retained earnings	120,000	70,000
Deduct: Dividends	100,000*	50,000*
Retained earnings December 31, 19X7	$220,000	$120,000
Balance Sheet at December 31, 19X7		
Cash	$ 75,800	$ 50,000
Inventory	42,000	80,000
Other current assets	60,000	20,000
Plant assets—net	300,000	300,000
Investment in Susan	312,200	—
Total assets	$790,000	$450,000
Current liabilities	$170,000	$130,000
Capital stock	400,000	200,000
Retained earnings	220,000	120,000
Total equities	$790,000	$450,000

* Deduct.

Required: Prepare consolidation working papers for Poly Corporation and Subsidiary for the year ended December 31, 19X7.

P 5-13 Sert is a 90 percent owned subsidiary of Phil Corporation, acquired by Phil in 19X1 at a price $5,000 in excess of fair value. The excess was amortized over a five-year period beginning with 19X1. Comparative financial statements for Phil and Sert for the year ended December 31, 19X8 are presented as follows:

	Phil	Sert
Combined Income and Retained Earnings Statement for the Year Ended December 31, 19X8		
Sales	$500,000	$100,000
Income from Sert	27,000	—
Cost of sales	240,000*	40,000*
Expenses	174,000*	30,000*
Net income	113,000	30,000
Add: Beginning retained earnings	110,000	40,000
Deduct: Dividends	70,000*	20,000*
Retained earnings December 31, 19X8	$153,000	$ 50,000
Balance Sheet at December 31, 19X8		
Cash	$ 63,000	$ 30,000
Accounts receivable	40,000	20,000
Inventories	60,000	15,000

	Phil	Sert
Plant assets—net	220,000	105,000
Investment in Sert	117,000	—
Total assets	$500,000	$170,000
Accounts payable	$ 47,000	$ 40,000
Capital stock	300,000	80,000
Retained earnings	153,000	50,000
Total equities	$500,000	$170,000

* Deduct.

During 19X8 Phil sold merchandise to Sert for $10,000. This merchandise cost Phil $6,000 and was not paid for or resold by Sert until 19X9. Phil's inventory at December 31, 19X7 included merchandise acquired from Sert on which Sert reported a profit during 19X7 of $5,000.

Required
1 Prepare correcting entries for Phil's investment in Sert.
2 Prepare consolidation working papers for 19X8 after adjusting the separate statements of Phil for prior errors and omissions.

P 5–14 Pandle and Stark Corporations were combined in a pooling of interests that was consummated on January 1, 19X7. Pandle issued 30,000 of its previously unissued common shares for all of Stark's outstanding shares and Stark became a 100 percent owned subsidiary of Pandle. Adjusted trial balances for the two companies at December 31, 19X6 immediately before the pooling and at December 31, 19X7, one year after the pooling, are as follows:

PANDLE CORPORATION AND STARK CORPORATION
ADJUSTED TRIAL BALANCES

	December 31, 19X6		December 31, 19X7	
	Pandle	Stark	Pandle	Stark
Cash	$ 180,000	$ 40,000	$ 155,000	$ 120,000
Accounts receivable	200,000	100,000	220,000	130,000
Dividends receivable			20,000	
Inventories	120,000	70,000	205,000	80,000
Land	100,000	50,000	100,000	50,000
Buildings—net	500,000	150,000	700,000	140,000
Equipment—net	400,000	160,000	470,000	200,000
Investment in Stark			530,000	
Cost of sales	550,000	200,000	600,000	240,000
Other expenses	250,000	150,000	300,000	160,000
Dividends	100,000	80,000	100,000	80,000
Total debits	$2,400,000	$1,000,000	$3,400,000	$1,200,000
Accounts payable	$ 225,000	$ 40,000	$ 300,000	$ 50,000
Dividends payable	25,000	20,000	25,000	20,000
Other liabilities	150,000	40,000	165,000	60,000
Capital stock, $10 par	500,000	200,000	800,000	200,000
Other paid-in capital	200,000	80,000	180,000	80,000
Retained earnings	300,000	120,000	590,000	190,000
Sales	1,000,000	500,000	1,200,000	600,000
Income from Stark			140,000	
Total credits	$2,400,000	$1,000,000	$3,400,000	$1,200,000

During 19X7 Stark sold inventory items to Pandle for $100,000, at a markup of 150 percent of cost to Stark. Pandle inventoried all of this merchandise at December 31, 19X7.

Required: Prepare a consolidated income statement, a consolidated retained earnings statement, and a consolidated balance sheet for Pandle Corporation and Subsidiary at and for the year ended December 31, 19X7.

6

INTERCOMPANY PROFIT TRANSACTIONS—PLANT ASSETS

Transactions between affiliated companies involving the sale and purchase of plant assets create unrealized profits and losses to the consolidated entity. Such profits and losses are eliminated (deferred) in reporting the results of operations and the financial position of the consolidated entity. They are also eliminated in reporting the financial position and results of operations of a parent company under the equity method of accounting. The adjustments involved in eliminating the effects of intercompany profits on plant assets are similar to, but not identical with, those for unrealized inventory profits. Unrealized inventory profits are self-correcting over any two accounting periods, but unrealized profits or losses on plant assets affect the financial statements until the related assets are sold outside the consolidated entity or are exhausted through use by the purchasing affiliate. This chapter covers concepts and procedures involved in eliminating the effect of unrealized profits on plant assets in one-line consolidations under the equity method of accounting and in consolidated statements.[1]

INTERCOMPANY PROFITS ON NONDEPRECIABLE PLANT ASSETS

The transfer of nondepreciable plant assets between affiliated companies at a price other than book value gives rise to unrealized profit or loss to the consolidated entity. An intercompany gain or loss appears in the income statement of the selling affiliate in the year of sale. However, such gain or loss is unrealized, and its effects must be eliminated from investment income in a one-line con-

---

[1]Most public utilities are subject to rate-of-return regulations. *FASB Statement No. 71,* "Accounting for the Effects of Certain Types of Regulations," states that "if rates are based on allowable costs that include reasonable intercompany profits, the company should not eliminate those intercompany profits in its financial statements." Thus, the *1990 Ameritech Annual Report* (page 37) includes the following note: "The original cost of telecommunications plant acquired from Ameritech Services, Inc., a wholly-owned centralized procurement and support subsidiary of the Ameritech Bell companies, includes a return on investment to Ameritech Services, Inc. which is not eliminated in consolidation."

solidation by the parent company. Its effects must also be eliminated in preparing consolidated financial statements.

The direction of intercompany sales of plant assets, like intercompany sales of inventory items, is important in evaluating the effect of unrealized profit on parent company and consolidated financial statements. Any gain or loss on sales downstream from parent to subsidiary is initially included in parent company income and must be eliminated. The amount of elimination is 100 percent regardless of the minority interest percentage. Any profit or loss from upstream sales from subsidiary to parent is initially included in subsidiary accounts. Since the parent company recognizes only its share of the subsidiary's income, only the parent's proportionate share of unrealized profits should be eliminated. The effect on consolidated net income is the same as for the parent.

This section of the chapter discusses and illustrates accounting practices for intercompany sales of land. Both downstream and upstream sales are covered.

Downstream Sale of Land

Stan Corporation is a 90 percent owned subsidiary of Park Corporation, acquired for $270,000 on January 1, 19X5. Investment cost was equal to book value and fair value of the interest acquired. Stan's net income for 19X5 was $70,000, and Park's income, excluding its income from Stan, was $90,000. Park's income includes a $10,000 unrealized gain on land that cost $40,000 and was sold to Stan for $50,000. Accordingly, Park makes the following entries in accounting for its investment in Stan at December 31, 19X5:

Investment in Stan	$63,000	
Income from Stan		$63,000
To record 90% of Stan's $70,000 reported income.		
Income from Stan	$10,000	
Investment in Stan		$10,000
To eliminate unrealized profit on land sold to Stan.		

Separate summary financial statements for Park and Stan at December 31, 19X5 are as follows:

	Park	Stan
Income Statement		
Sales	$380,000	$220,000
Income from Stan	53,000	—
Gain on land sale	10,000	—
Expenses (including cost of goods sold)	(300,000)	(150,000)
Net income	$143,000	$ 70,000
Retained Earnings		
Retained earnings January 1, 19X5	$207,000	$100,000
Net income	143,000	70,000
Retained earnings December 31, 19X5	$350,000	$170,000
Balance Sheet		
Other assets	$477,000	$350,000
Land	—	50,000
Investment in Stan	323,000	—
Total assets	$800,000	$400,000
Liabilities	$ 50,000	$ 30,000
Capital stock	400,000	200,000
Retained earnings	350,000	170,000
Total liabilities and stockholders' equity	$800,000	$400,000

Consolidation working papers for Park and Subsidiary are presented in Exhibit 6–1. Entry a eliminates the gain on sale of land and reduces the land account to $40,000—its cost to the consolidated entity. This is the only entry that is significantly different from adjustments and eliminations illustrated in previous chapters.

a	Gain on sale of land	$10,000
	Land	$10,000

To eliminate gain on intercompany sale of land and reduce land to its cost basis.

PARK CORPORATION AND SUBSIDIARY
CONSOLIDATION WORKING PAPERS
FOR THE YEAR ENDED DECEMBER 31, 19X5

	Park	90% Stan	Adjustments and Eliminations		Minority Interest	Consolidated Statements
Income Statement						
Sales	$380,000	$220,000				$600,000
Income from Stan	53,000		b	53,000		
Gain on sale of land	10,000		a	10,000		
Expenses (including cost of goods sold)	300,000*	150,000*				450,000*
Minority interest income ($70,000 × 10%)					$ 7,000	7,000*
Net income	$143,000	$ 70,000				$143,000
Retained Earnings						
Retained earnings—Park	$207,000					$207,000
Retained earnings—Stan		$100,000	c	100,000		
Add: Net income	143,000✓	70,000✓				143,000
Retained earnings December 31, 19X5	$350,000	$170,000				$350,000
Balance Sheet						
Other assets	$477,000	$350,000				$827,000
Land		50,000	a	10,000		40,000
Investment in Stan	323,000		b c	53,000 270,000		
	$800,000	$400,000				$867,000
Liabilities	$ 50,000	$ 30,000				$ 80,000
Capital stock	400,000	200,000	c	200,000		400,000
Retained earnings	350,000✓	170,000✓				350,000
	$800,000	$400,000				
Minority interest January 1, 19X5			c	30,000	30,000	
Minority interest December 31, 19X5					$37,000	37,000
						$867,000

* Deduct.
a Eliminates gain on sale of land and reduces land to a cost basis.
b Eliminates investment income and reduces the investment account to its January 1, 19X5 balance.
c Eliminates reciprocal equity and investment amounts and establishes beginning minority interest.

Exhibit 6–1 Intercompany Profit from Downstream Sale of Land

The overvalued land will continue to appear in the separate balance sheet of Stan in subsequent years until it is sold outside of the consolidated entity. But the gain on land does not appear in the separate income statements of Park in subsequent years. Therefore, entry a as shown in Exhibit 6-1 is applicable only in the year of the intercompany sale.

Years Subsequent to Intercompany Sale   The working paper adjustment to reduce land to its cost to the consolidated entity in years subsequent to the year of the intercompany sale is as follows for downstream sales:

Investment in Stan	$10,000	
Land		$10,000

To reduce land to its cost basis and adjust the investment account to establish reciprocity with Stan's equity accounts at the beginning of the period.

The debit to the investment account adjusts its balance to establish reciprocity with the subsidiary equity accounts at the beginning of each subsequent period in which the land is held. For example, the investment account balance at December 31, 19X5 is $323,000. This is $10,000 less than Park's underlying equity in Stan of $333,000 on that date ($370,000 × 90%). The difference arises from the entry on the parent company books to reduce investment income and the investment account for the intercompany profit in the year of sale.

Sale in Subsequent Year to Outside Entity

Assume that Stan uses the land for three years and sells it for $60,000 in 19X9. In the year of sale, Stan will report a $10,000 gain ($60,000 proceeds less $50,000 cost), but the gain to the consolidated entity is $20,000 ($60,000 proceeds less $40,000 cost to Park).

Park recognizes its gain on the land in 19X9 under the equity method of accounting by adjusting its investment income in that year. The entry on Park's books is:

Investment in Stan	$10,000	
Income from Stan		$10,000

To recognize previously deferred profit on sale of land to Stan.

This entry on Park's separate books reestablishes equality between the investment account and 90 percent of the equity of Stan on the same date.

The following working paper entry is required to adjust the $10,000 gain to Stan to the $20,000 consolidated gain on the land:

Investment in Stan	$10,000	
Gain on land		$10,000

To adjust gain on land to the $20,000 gain to the consolidated entity.

This entry in the year of sale is almost the same as the working paper entry in each of the years 19X6, 19X7, and 19X8 to eliminate the unrealized profit from the land account. The difference is that the credit is to gain because the land no longer appears on the separate books of Park or Stan.

Upstream Sale of Land

In order to illustrate the accounting for upstream sales of nondepreciable plant assets, assume that Park purchases the land referred to in the previous section during 19X5 from its 90 percent owned affiliate, Stan. As before, Stan's net income for 19X5 was $70,000 and Park's income, excluding its income from Stan, was $90,000. However, the $10,000 unrealized profit on the intercompany sale of land is now reflected in the income of Stan, rather than Park. In accounting for its investment in Stan at year-end 19X5, Park makes the following entries:

Investment in Stan	$63,000	
Income from Stan		$63,000
To record 90% of Stan's reported net income.		
Income from Stan	$ 9,000	
Investment in Stan		$ 9,000
To eliminate 90% of the $10,000 unrealized profit on land purchased from Stan.		

The combined effect of these entries is to record Park's investment income for 19X5 in the amount of $54,000 ($63,000 − $9,000). Note that the $54,000 investment income consists of 90 percent of Stan's $60,000 realized income for 19X5 ($70,000 reported income less $10,000 unrealized gain on land). Park's net income for 19X5 is $144,000 ($90,000 separate income plus $54,000 investment income) as compared with $143,000 in the case of the downstream sale (see page 220). The difference lies in the $1,000 unrealized gain attributed to minority interest and charged against minority interest income.

Consolidation working papers for Park Corporation and Subsidiary for 19X5 are presented in Exhibit 6–2. The working papers are based on the same information as the working papers in Exhibit 6–1 except for minor changes necessary to switch to the upstream sale situation.

The adjustments refected in the consolidation working papers in Exhibit 6–2 are the same as those in Exhibit 6–1 except for the amount of entry b, which is $54,000 rather than $53,000 in the previous consolidation working paper illustration.

Minority Interest Income One other difference in the consolidation working papers of Exhibits 6–1 and 6–2 needs to be explained. Minority interest is charged with its share of the unrealized gain on Stan's sale of land to Park. This is done in the consolidation working papers by converting Stan's reported net income into realized income and multiplying by the minority interest percentage. Thus, the $6,000 minority interest income is 10 percent of Stan's $60,000 realized income.

Year Subsequent to Intercompany Sale While Park continues to hold the land in subsequent years, the consolidation working papers will require an adjusting entry to reduce the land account to its cost basis to the consolidated entity. The working paper entry to eliminate unrealized profit from the land account is:

Investment in Stan	$9,000	
Minority interest	1,000	
Land		$10,000
To reduce land to its cost basis and adjust the investment account and beginning minority interest to establish reciprocity with Stan's equity accounts at the beginning of the period.		

Since minority interest is entered in the working papers at the minority interest share of *reported* subsidiary equity when reciprocal investment and subsidiary equity accounts are eliminated, the foregoing adjustment is needed to reduce minority interest to its *realized* amount each time consolidation working papers are prepared. In other words, this adjustment is necessary to make the beginning minority interest in 19X6 equal to ending minority interest in 19X5, and so on.

PARK CORPORATION AND SUBSIDIARY
CONSOLIDATION WORKING PAPERS
FOR THE YEAR ENDED DECEMBER 31, 19X5

	Park	90% Stan	Adjustments and Eliminations		Minority Interest	Consolidated Statements
Income Statement						
Sales	$390,000	$210,000				$600,000
Income from Stan	54,000		b	54,000		
Gain on sale of land		10,000	a	10,000		
Expenses (including cost of goods sold)	300,000*	150,000*				450,000*
Minority interest income ($70,000 − $10,000) × 10%					$ 6,000	6,000*
Net income	$144,000	$ 70,000				$144,000
Retained Earnings						
Retained earnings—Park	$207,000					$207,000
Retained earnings—Stan		$100,000	c	100,000		
Add: Net income	144,000 ✔	70,000 ✔				144,000
Retained earnings December 31, 19X5	$351,000	$170,000				$351,000
Balance Sheet						
Other assets	$427,000	$400,000				$827,000
Land	50,000		a	10,000		40,000
Investment in Stan	324,000		b	54,000		
			c	270,000		
	$801,000	$400,000				$867,000
Liabilities	$ 50,000	$ 30,000				$ 80,000
Capital stock	400,000	200,000	c	200,000		400,000
Retained earnings	351,000 ✔	170,000 ✔				351,000
	$801,000	$400,000				
Minority interest January 1, 19X5			c	30,000	30,000	
Minority interest December 31, 19X5					$36,000	36,000
						$867,000

* Deduct.
a Eliminates gain on sale of land and reduces land to a cost basis.
b Eliminates investment income and reduces the investment account to its January 1, 19X5 balance.
c Eliminates reciprocal equity and investment amounts and establishes beginning minority interest.

Exhibit 6–2   *Intercompany Profit from Upstream Sale of Land*

Sale in Subsequent Year to Outside Entity

Assume that Park uses the land for three years and sells it for $60,000 in 19X9. In the year of sale, Park will report a $10,000 gain ($60,000 proceeds less $50,000 cost), but the gain to the consolidated entity is $20,000, allocated $19,000 to majority stockholders (consolidated net income) and $1,000 to minority stockholders. Park adjusts its investment income from Stan in the year 19X9 with the following entry:

Investment in Stan	$9,000	
Income from Stan		$9,000

To recognize previously deferred intercompany profit on land.

The $10,000 gain on the sale of land plus the $9,000 increase in investment income on Park's books equals the $19,000 effect on consolidated net income in 19X9.

The adjustment of the $10,000 gain of Park to the $20,000 consolidated gain requires the following working paper entry:

Investment in Stan	$9,000	
Minority interest	1,000	
Gain on land		$10,000

To adjust gain on land to the $20,000 gain to the consolidated entity.

The $1,000 debit to minority interest in this working paper entry offsets the credit to the minority interest that arises when reciprocal investment and subsidiary stockholders' equity items are eliminated in the consolidation working papers. In other words, this $1,000 adjustment is necessary to make beginning minority interest in 19X6 equal to ending minority interest in 19X5, and so on.

INTERCOMPANY PROFITS ON DEPRECIABLE PLANT ASSETS

Intercompany sales of plant assets subject to depreciation, depletion, or amortization result in unrealized gains and losses that are reflected in the accounts of the selling affiliate. The effects of these gains and losses are eliminated from parent company and consolidated financial statements until they are realized by the consolidated entity *through sale to other entities or through use within the consolidated entity*. The adjustments to eliminate the effect of unrealized gains and losses on parent company and consolidated financial statements are more complex than in the case of nondepreciable assets. This additional complexity stems from the depreciation (or depletion or amortization) process that affects parent company and consolidated income in each year in which the related assets are held by affiliated companies.

The discussion of intercompany sales of plant assets in this section is limited to depreciable assets, but the analysis and procedures illustrated apply equally to assets subject to depletion or amortization. Intercompany gains and losses from downstream sales of depreciable plant assets are considered initially, and the upstream sale situation is covered next.

Downstream Sales of Depreciable Plant Assets

The initial effect of unrealized gains and losses from downstream sales of depreciable assets is the same as for nondepreciable assets. Gains or losses appear in the parent company accounts in the year of sale and must be eliminated by the parent company in determining its investment income under the equity method of accounting. Similarly, such gain or loss is eliminated from consolidated statements by removing the gain or loss and reducing the plant assets to their cost to the consolidated entity.

Downstream Sale at the End of a Year Assume that Perry Corporation sells machinery to its 80 percent owned subsidiary, Soper Corporation, at December 31, 19X2. The machinery has an undepreciated cost of $50,000 on this date (cost $90,000 and accumulated depreciation of $40,000) and is sold to Soper for $80,000. Journal entries to record the sale and purchase on Perry's and Soper's books are as follows:

PERRY'S BOOKS

Cash	$80,000	
Accumulated depreciation	40,000	
Machinery		$90,000
Gain on sale of machinery		30,000

SOPER'S BOOKS

Machinery	$80,000	
Cash		$80,000

The gain on Perry's books is unrealized at December 31, 19X2 and, accordingly, Perry adjusts its investment income for 19X2 under the equity method of accounting for the full amount of the unrealized gain:

Income from Soper	$30,000	
Investment in Soper		$30,000

The gain on machinery should not appear in the consolidated income statement for 19X2, and the machinery should be included in the consolidated balance sheet at $50,000, its depreciated cost to the consolidated entity. This effect is accomplished by a consolidation working paper adjustment as follows:

Gain on sale of machinery	$30,000	
Machinery		$30,000

Alternatively, the working paper entry could be recorded by debiting gain on sale of machinery for $30,000, debiting machinery for $10,000, and crediting accumulated depreciation—machinery for $40,000. Conceptually, this entry is superior because it results in reporting plant assets and accumulated depreciation at the amounts that would have been shown if the intercompany sale had not taken place. From a practical viewpoint, however, the additional detail is usually not justified by cost-benefit considerations, since the same net asset amounts are obtained without the additional recordkeeping costs. The examples in this book reflect the more practical approach.

No adjustment of the minority interest is necessary, since Soper's income is unaffected by the intercompany sale. Note that the analysis up to this point is equivalent to the one for the intercompany sale of land discussed earlier in this chapter.

Downstream Sale at the Beginning of a Year   If the sale from Perry to Soper had occurred on January 1, 19X2, the machinery would have been depreciated by Soper during 19X2, and any depreciation on the unrealized gain would be considered a piecemeal recognition of the gain during 19X2. Assume that on January 1, 19X2, the date of the intercompany sale, the machinery has a five-year remaining use life and no expected residual value at December 31, 19X6. Straight-line depreciation is used. The journal entries to record the sale and purchase are the same as for the December 31 sale; however, Soper also records depreciation expense of $16,000 for 19X2 ($80,000/5 years). Of this $16,000 depreciation, $10,000 is based on cost to the consolidated entity ($50,000 cost/5 years), and $6,000 is based on the $30,000 unrealized gain ($30,000/5 years). The $6,000 is considered a piecemeal recognition of one-fifth of the $30,000 unrealized gain on the intercompany transaction. Conceptually, this is equivalent to the sale to other entities of one-fifth of the services remaining in the machinery.[2]

In eliminating the effect of the intercompany sale from its investment in Soper account for 19X2, Perry Corporation makes the following entries:

Income from Soper	$30,000	
Investment in Soper		$30,000
Investment in Soper	$ 6,000	
Income from Soper		$ 6,000

Thus, elimination of the effect of the intercompany sale reduces Perry's investment income in 19X2 by $24,000 ($30,000 unrealized gain less $6,000 realized through depreciation). Although Soper's income is decreased by the $6,000 excess depreciation during 19X2, the $6,000 is considered realized through use and, accordingly, no adjustment of the minority interest income is necessary.

Effect of Downstream Sale on Consolidation Working Papers   The effect of the January 1 intercompany sale of machinery on the consolidated financial statements is illustrated in partial consolidation working papers as follows:

	Perry	80% Soper	Adjustments and Eliminations	Consolidated Statements
Income Statement				
Gain on sale of machinery	$30,000		a 30,000	
Depreciation expense		$16,000	b 6,000	$10,000
Balance Sheet				
Machinery		$80,000	a 30,000	$50,000
Accumulated depreciation		16,000	b 6,000	10,000

The first consolidation working paper entry eliminates the $30,000 unrealized gain on machinery and reduces machinery to its cost basis to the consolidated entity at the time of intercompany sale. Depreciation expense and accumulated depreciation are reduced in the second entry in order to adjust these items to the depreciated cost basis to the consolidated entity at December 31, 19X2. Minority interest computations are not affected by the working paper adjustments because the sale was downstream.

In each of the years 19X3 through 19X6, Perry Corporation adjusts its investment income for the piecemeal recognition of the previously unrecognized gain on the machinery with the following entry:

19X3, 19X4, 19X5, and 19X6		
Investment in Soper	$6,000	
Income from Soper		$6,000

Accordingly, by December 31, 19X6, the end of the useful life of the machinery, Perry will have recognized the full $30,000 gain as investment income. Its investment account balance will reflect the elimination and piecemeal recognition of the unrealized gain as follows:

---

[2]It is assumed that the machine services have entered the cost of goods delivered to customers during the current period. If, instead, they are included in inventory, realization has not yet occurred and appropriate adjustments should be made. This additional refinement is not justified when the amounts involved are immaterial.

Year	Elimination of Gain on Machinery	Piecemeal Recognition of Gain Through Depreciation	Effect on Investment Balance at December 31
19X2	$ − 30,000	$ + 6,000	$ − 24,000
19X3		+ 6,000	− 18,000
19X4		+ 6,000	− 12,000
19X5		+ 6,000	− 6,000
19X6		+ 6,000	0

In consolidation working papers, it is necessary to establish reciprocity between the investment and subsidiary equity accounts at the beginning of the period before eliminating reciprocal balances. Thus, the effect of the unrealized gain on the December 31, 19X2 investment account is eliminated in 19X3 consolidation working papers with the working paper entry:

Investment in Soper	$24,000	
Accumulated depreciation	6,000	
Machinery		$30,000

This entry for 19X3 is included in the partial consolidation working papers shown in Exhibit 6–3 for Perry and Soper. The exhibit shows consolidation eliminations for each subsequent year (after 19X2) in which the unrealized gain on machinery would require working paper adjustment.

The partial working papers in Exhibit 6–3 show two working paper adjustments for each of the years 19X3 through 19X6. Two entries for each year are used in order to isolate the effect on beginning-of-the-period balances and current-year changes. Since current-year changes only affect depreciation expense and accumulated depreciation in equal amounts, the entries can be combined and frequently are combined in subsequent illustrations and in problem solutions.

Upstream Sales of Depreciable Plant Assets

Upstream sales of depreciable assets from subsidiary to parent company result in unrealized gains or losses in the subsidiary accounts in the year of sale (unless the assets are sold at their book values). In computing its investment income in the year of sale, the parent company adjusts its share of the reported income of the subsidiary for (1) its share of any unrealized gain on the sale and (2) its share of any piecemeal recognition of such unrealized gain through the depreciation process.

Effect of Upstream Sale on the Affiliated Companies' Separate Books   The effect of a gain on an upstream sale is illustrated by the following example. Pruitt Corporation purchases a truck from its 80 percent owned subsidiary, Scott Corporation, on January 1, 19X4. Other information is as follows:

Scott's reported net income for 19X4	$50,000
Use life of the truck at January 1, 19X4	3 years
Depreciation method	straight-line
Trade-in value of the truck at December 31, 19X6	$ 3,000
Cost of truck to Scott	$14,000
Accumulated depreciation on truck at December 31, 19X3	$ 5,000

PERRY CORPORATION AND SUBSIDIARY
PARTIAL CONSOLIDATION WORKING PAPERS
FOR THE YEARS 19X3, 19X4, 19X5, and 19X6

	Perry	80% Soper	Adjustments and Eliminations	Consolidated Statements
19X3				
Income Statement—19X3				
Depreciation expense		$16,000	b 6,000	$10,000
Balance Sheet—December 31				
Machinery		80,000	a 30,000	50,000
Accumulated depreciation		32,000	a 6,000 / b 6,000	20,000
Investment in Soper	XXX*		a 24,000	
19X4				
Income Statement—19X4				
Depreciation expense		$16,000	b 6,000	$10,000
Balance Sheet—December 31				
Machinery		80,000	a 30,000	50,000
Accumulated depreciation		48,000	a 12,000 / b 6,000	30,000
Investment in Soper	XXX*		a 18,000	
19X5				
Income Statement—19X5				
Depreciation expense		$16,000	b 6,000	$10,000
Balance Sheet—December 31				
Machinery		80,000	a 30,000	50,000
Accumulated depreciation		64,000	a 18,000 / b 6,000	40,000
Investment in Soper	XXX*		a 12,000	
19X6				
Income Statement—19X6				
Depreciation expense		$16,000	b 6,000	$10,000
Balance Sheet—December 31				
Machinery		80,000	a 30,000	50,000
Accumulated depreciation		80,000	a 24,000 / b 6,000	50,000
Investment in Soper	XXX*		a 6,000	

*Whatever the balance of the investment account, it will be less than the underlying book value of the investment at the beginning of the year by the amount of the unrealized profit.

a Eliminates unrealized profit from machinery and accumulated depreciation as of the beginning of the year and adjusts the investment in Soper account to establish reciprocity with Soper's equity accounts at the beginning of the period.

b Eliminates the current year's effect of unrealized profit from depreciation expense and accumulated depreciation.

Exhibit 6–3 *Downstream Sale of Depreciable Asset—Years Subsequent to Sale*

If Scott sells the truck to Pruitt for $12,000 cash, Scott and Pruitt make the following journal entries on their separate books for 19X4:

SCOTT'S BOOKS

January 1, 19X4 (sale of truck)

Cash	$12,000	
Accumulated depreciation	5,000	
Trucks		$14,000
Gain on sale of truck		3,000

To record sale of truck.

PRUITT'S BOOKS

January 1, 19X4 (purchase of truck)

Trucks	$12,000	
Cash		$12,000

To record purchase of truck.

December 31, 19X4 (depreciation expense)

Depreciation expense	$ 3,000	
Accumulated depreciation		$ 3,000

To record depreciation for one year ($12,000 cost − $3,000 scrap)/3 years.

December 31, 19X4 (investment income)

Investment in Scott	$38,400	
Income from Scott		$38,400

To record investment income for 19X4 computed as follows:

Share of Scott's reported net income $50,000 × 80%	$40,000
Less: Unrealized gain on truck $3,000 × 80%	−2,400
Add: Piecemeal recognition of gain ($3,000 gain/3 years) × 80%	+800
Investment income for 19X4	$38,400

The deferral of the intercompany gain on the truck decreases Pruitt's investment income for 19X4 by $1,600 (from $40,000 to $38,400). This is 80 percent of the unrealized gain at December 31, 19X4 (($3,000 unrealized gain from sale − $1,000 piecemeal recognition through depreciation) × 80%. Pruitt will recognize the remaining $1,600 during 19X5 and 19X6 at the rate of $800 per year.

Effect of Upstream Sale on Consolidation Working Papers In order to illustrate the working paper procedures for Pruitt and Scott, the following investment and equity balances—and changes in them—are included as additional assumptions.

	Investment in Scott 80%	80% of the Equity of Scott	100% of the Equity of Scott
December 31, 19X3	$400,000	$400,000	$500,000
Income—19X4	+38,400	+40,000	+50,000
December 31, 19X4	438,400	440,000	550,000
Income—19X5	+40,800	+40,000	+50,000
December 31, 19X5	479,200	480,000	600,000
Income—19X6	+40,800	+40,000	+50,000
December 31, 19X6	$520,000	$520,000	$650,000

Pruitt's investment in Scott account at December 31, 19X4 is $1,600 below its underlying book value ($438,400 compared with $440,000), and at December

31, 19X5 it is $800 below its underlying book value ($479,200 compared with $480,000). By December 31, 19X6 the $3,000 gain on the truck has been realized through depreciation. Pruitt's share of that gain ($2,400) has been recognized at the rate of $800 per year in 19X4, 19X5, and 19X6. Thus, reciprocity between Pruitt's investment account and its underlying book value is reestablished at the end of 19X6.

Partial consolidation working papers for 19X4, the year of sale, appear below, followed by the working paper entries in journal form.

19X4: YEAR OF SALE

	Pruitt	80% Scott	Adjustments and Eliminations		Minority Interest	Consolidated Statements
Income Statement						
Income from Scott	$ 38,400		c	38,400		
Gain on sale of truck		$ 3,000	b	3,000		
Depreciation expense	3,000		a	1,000		$ 2,000
Minority interest income					$ 9,600	9,600
Balance Sheet						
Trucks	$ 12,000		b	3,000		$ 9,000
Accumulated depreciation	3,000		a	1,000		2,000
Investment in Scott	438,400		c	38,400		
			d	400,000		
Equity of Scott— January 1		$500,000	d	500,000		
Minority interest— January 1			d	100,000	100,000	
Minority interest— December 31					$109,600	109,600

a	Accumulated depreciation	$ 1,000	
	Depreciation expense		$ 1,000

To eliminate the current year's effect of unrealized gain from depreciation accounts.

b	Gain on sale of truck	$ 3,000	
	Trucks		$ 3,000

To eliminate unrealized gain and to reduce trucks to a cost basis.

c	Income from Scott	$ 38,400	
	Investment in Scott		$ 38,400

To eliminate investment income and to adjust the investment account to its beginning-of-the-period balance.

d	Equity of Scott January 1, 19X4	$500,000	
	Investment in Scott		$400,000
	Minority interest January 1, 19X4		100,000

To eliminate reciprocal investment and equity accounts and to establish beginning minority interest.

Note that minority interest income of $9,600 for 19X4 is computed as 20 percent of Scott's realized income of $48,000 [($50,000 − $3,000 + $1,000) × 20%].

Partial consolidation working papers and the working paper entries in journal form for 19X5, the first subsequent year after the upstream sale, are as follows:

19X5: FIRST SUBSEQUENT YEAR

	Pruitt	80% Scott	Adjustments and Eliminations		Minority Interest	Consolidated Statements
Income Statement						
Income from Scott	$ 40,800		c	40,800		
Depreciation expense	3,000			a 1,000		$ 2,000
Minority interest income					$ 10,200	10,200
Balance Sheet						
Trucks	$ 12,000			b 3,000		$ 9,000
Accumulated depreciation	6,000		b 1,000 a 1,000			4,000
Investment in Scott	479,200		b 1,600	c 40,800 d 440,000		
Equity of Scott— January 1		$550,000	d 550,000			
Minority interest— January 1			b 400	d 110,000	109,600	
Minority interest— December 31					$119,800	119,800

a	Accumulated depreciation		$ 1,000	
	Depreciation expense			$ 1,000
	To eliminate the effect of the 19X4 unrealized gain from current depreciation accounts.			
b	Accumulated depreciation		$ 1,000	
	Investment in Scott		1,600	
	Minority interest January 1, 19X5		400	
	Trucks			$ 3,000
	To eliminate the effect of 19X4 unrealized gain from the accumulated depreciation and truck accounts and to charge the unrealized gain of $2,000 at January 1 to the investment account (80%) and minority interest (20%).			
c	Income from Scott		$ 40,800	
	Investment in Scott			$ 40,800
	To eliminate investment income and to adjust the investment account to its beginning-of-the-period balance			
d	Equity of Scott January 1, 19X5		$550,000	
	Investment in Scott			$440,000
	Minority interest January 1, 19X5			110,000
	To eliminate reciprocal investment and equity accounts and to establish beginning minority interest.			

Minority interest income of $10,200 for 19X5 consists of 20 percent of Scott's reported net income of $50,000 plus 20 percent of the $1,000 gain realized through depreciation in 19X5. In 19X6 the computation of minority interest income is the same as in 19X5.

To explain further, minority interest income in 19X4 (the year of sale) is decreased by $400, the minority interest's share of the $2,000 gain not realized through depreciation in 19X4. Since the beginning equity of Scott is not affected by the intercompany sale in 19X4, beginning minority interest is unaffected and does not require adjustment. Depreciation expense for each of the years 19X4, 19X5, and 19X6 of $3,000 is reduced to $2,000 by a working paper adjustment of $1,000. The $2,000 depreciation expense that appears in the consolidated income statement is simply one-third of the book value less residual value of the truck at the time of intercompany sale [($9,000 − $3,000)/3 years].

Effect of Upstream Sale on Subsequent Years   In 19X5, the first subsequent year after the intercompany sale, both the beginning investment account and the beginning minority interest are affected by the unrealized gain. Working paper entry b allocates the $2,000 unrealized gain 80 percent to the investment in Scott account and 20 percent to beginning minority interest. The debit to the investment in Scott account adjusts for the $1,600 difference between the investment account and 80 percent of Scott's equity at December 31, 19X4. The $400 debit to minority interest is necessary to adjust beginning minority interest in 19X5 to $109,600, equal to the ending minority interest in 19X4.

Partial consolidation working papers and the working paper entries in journal form for 19X6, the second subsequent year after the upstream sale, follow:

19X6: SECOND SUBSEQUENT YEAR

	Pruitt	80% Scott	Adjustments and Eliminations		Minority Interest	Consolidated Statements
Income Statement						
Income from Scott	$ 40,800		c	40,800		
Depreciation expense	3,000		a	1,000		$ 2,000
Minority interest income					$ 10,200	10,200
Balance Sheet						
Trucks	$ 12,000		b	3,000		$ 9,000
Accumulated depreciation	9,000		b 2,000 a 1,000			6,000
Investment in Scott	520,000		b 800	c 40,800 d 480,000		
Equity of Scott— January 1		$600,000	d 600,000			
Minority interest— January 1			b 200	d 120,000	119,800	
Minority interest— December 31					$130,000	130,000

| a | Accumulated depreciation | $ 1,000 | |
| | Depreciation expense | | $ 1,000 |

To eliminate the effect of the 19X4 unrealized gain on current depreciation accounts.

b	Accumulated depreciation	$ 2,000	
	Investment in Scott	800	
	Minority interest January 1, 19X6	200	
	Trucks		$ 3,000

To eliminate the effect of 19X4 unrealized gain from the accumulated depreciation and truck accounts and to charge the $1,000 unrealized gain at January 1, 19X6 to the investment in Scott account (80%) and minority interest (20%).

| c | Income from Scott | $ 40,800 | |
| | Investment in Scott | | $ 40,800 |

To eliminate investment income and adjust the investment account to its beginning-of-the-period balance.

d	Equity of Scott January 1, 19X6	$600,000	
	Investment in Scott		$480,000
	Minority interest January 1, 19X6		120,000

To eliminate reciprocal investment and equity accounts and to establish beginning minority interest.

In the partial consolidation working papers for 19X6, the amounts allocated are $800 to the investment account and $200 to minority interest since only $1,000 of the initial $3,000 unrealized gain is unrealized at January 1, 19X6. No further adjustments are necessary in 19X7 because the full amount of the unrealized gain has been realized through depreciation. Observe that the truck account less accumulated depreciation at December 31, 19X6 is equal to the $3,000 residual value of the truck on that date (trucks, $9,000 less accumulated depreciation, $6,000).

PLANT ASSETS SOLD AT OTHER THAN FAIR VALUE

An intercompany sale of plant assets at a loss requires special evaluation to make sure that the loss is not one that the selling affiliate should have recognized on its separate books prior to the intercompany sale (or in the absence of an inter-company sale). For example, if a parent company sells a machine with a book value of $30,000 to its 90 percent owned subsidiary for $20,000 on January 1, 19X4, a question should arise as to the fair value of the asset at the time of sale. If the fair value is in fact $20,000, then the parent company should have written the asset down to its $20,000 fair value prior to the sale and recognized the actual loss on its separate company books. If the fair value is in fact $30,000, then the propriety of the parent company's action is suspect because the majority stockholders lose and the minority stockholders gain on the exchange. Parent company officers and directors may be charged with improper stewardship.

Similar suspicions arise if a subsidiary sells an asset to the parent at less than its fair value, because the transaction would have to have been approved by parent company officials who also serve as directors of the subsidiary. In March 1990, a court-appointed bankruptcy examiner for Eastern Airlines charged that Eastern's parent, Texas Air Corporation, had underpaid its subsidiary by as much as $403 million for assets acquired from Eastern between 1987 and 1989. In a negotiated settlement, Texas Air agreed to pay Eastern $280 million to help satisfy creditors' claims in the bankruptcy case.[3]

---

[3]Bridget O'Brian, "Texas Air Found to Underpay Its Eastern Unit," *The Wall Street Journal*, March 2, 1990, p. A3.

Intercompany sales at prices above fair value also create inequities. The Federal Trade Commission charged Nynex Corporation with overcharging its own telephone subsidiaries for equipment, supplies, and services. The telephone companies were fined $1.4 million for passing the costs of the overpayments along to their customers.[4]

Consolidation with Loss on Intercompany Sale

Consolidation procedures to recognize intercompany losses are essentially the same as those to eliminate unrealized gains. Assume that the machine referred to above had a remaining use life of five years when it was sold to the 90 percent owned subsidiary for $20,000. The parent company has a $10,000 unrealized loss that is recognized on a piecemeal basis over five years. If the subsidiary's net income for 19X4 is $200,000 and there are no other intercompany transactions, the parent records its income from subsidiary as follows:

Investment in Subsidiary	$188,000	
Income from Subsidiary		$188,000

To record income for 19X4 determined as follows:

Equity in subsidiary's income $200,000 × 90%	$180,000
Add: Unrealized loss on machine	10,000
Less: Piecemeal recognition of loss ($10,000/5 years)	− 2,000
	$188,000

Consolidation working paper entries relating to the intercompany loss for 19X4 would be as follows:

Machinery	$10,000	
Loss on sale of machinery		$10,000
To eliminate unrealized intercompany loss on downstream sale.		
Depreciation expense	$ 2,000	
Accumulated depreciation		$ 2,000
To increase depreciation expense to reflect depreciation on a cost basis.		

In the years 19X5 through 19X8, the parent company's income from subsidiary will be reduced by $2,000 each year under the equity method of accounting. Consolidated net income is also reduced by $2,000 each year through working paper entries to eliminate the effect of the intercompany loss. The elimination reduces consolidated income by increasing depreciation expense to a cost basis for consolidated statement purposes. In 19X5 the working paper entry would be:

Machinery	$10,000	
Depreciation expense	2,000	
Accumulated depreciation		$4,000
Investment in Subsidiary		8,000
To eliminate the effects of intercompany sale at a loss.		

An upstream sale of plant assets at a loss would be acounted for in similar fashion except that the intercompany loss and its piecemeal recognition would be allocated proportionately to majority stockholders (investment income and consolidated net income) and minority interests.

[4]Julie Amparano Lopez, "Nynex Launches Office Furniture Arm Amid Allegation It Overcharges Units," *The Wall Street Journal*, February 21, 1990, p. B8.

CONSOLIDATION EXAMPLE—UPSTREAM AND DOWNSTREAM SALES OF PLANT ASSETS

Comparative financial statements for Plank Corporation and its 90 percent owned subsidiary, Sharp Corporation, for 19X7 are shown in the separate company columns of the consolidation working papers in Exhibit 6–4. Plank acquired its 90 percent interest in Sharp at its underlying book value of $450,000 on January 3, 19X5.

Since Plank Corporation acquired its interest in Sharp, the two corporations have participated in the following transactions involving plant assets:

1 On July 1, 19X5 Plank sold land to Sharp at a gain of $5,000. Sharp resold the land to outside entities during 19X7 at a loss to Sharp of $1,000.
2 On January 2, 19X6 Sharp sold equipment with a five-year remaining useful life to Plank at a gain of $20,000. This equipment was still in use by Plank at December 31, 19X7.
3 On January 5, 19X7 Plank sold a building to Sharp at a gain of $32,000. The remaining useful life of the building on this date was eight years, and Sharp still owned the building at December 31, 19X7.

Equity Method

An examination of the consolidation working papers in Exhibit 6–4 shows that Plank Corporation uses the equity method of accounting. This is shown by the fact that Plank's net income of $300,000 is equal to consolidated net income as well as by the equality of Plank's retained earnings and consolidated retained earnings. A reconciliation of Plank's investment in Sharp account at December 31, 19X6 and December 31, 19X7 follows:

Underlying equity in Sharp December 31, 19X6 ($600,000 equity of Sharp × 90%)	$540 000
Less: Unrealized profit on land	− 5,000
Less: 90% of unrealized profit on equipment ($16,000 × 90%)	− 14,400
Investment in Sharp December 31, 19X6	520,600
Add: Income from Sharp 19X7 (90% of Sharp's $80,000 net income + $5,000 gain on land + $3,600 piecemeal recognition of gain on equipment − $28,000 unrealized profit on building)	52,600
Less: Dividends received 19X7	− 27,000
Investment in Sharp December 31, 19X7	$546,200

Plank Corporation sold land to Sharp in 19X5 at a gain of $5,000. This gain was realized in 19X7 when Sharp sold the land to another entity. But Sharp sold the land at a $1,000 loss based on the transfer price, and the net result is a $4,000 gain for the consolidated entity during 19X7. Working paper entry a converts the $1,000 loss included in Sharp's separate income to a $4,000 consolidated gain.

a	Investment in Sharp	$5,000	
	Gain on land		$5,000
	To recognize previously deferred gain on land.		

PLANK CORPORATION AND SUBSIDIARY
CONSOLIDATION WORKING PAPERS—FOR THE YEAR ENDED DECEMBER 31, 19X7

	Plank	90% Sharp	Adjustments and Eliminations		Minority Interest	Consolidated Statements
Income Statement						
Sales	$2,000,000	$700,000				$2,700,000
Gain on building	32,000		c 32,000			
Loss (or gain) on land		1,000*		a 5,000		4,000
Income from Sharp	52,600		d 52,600			
Cost of goods sold	1,000,000*	320,000*				1,320,000*
Depreciation expense	108,000*	50,000*	b 4,000 / c 4,000			150,000*
Other expenses	676,600*	249,000*				925,600*
Minority interest income					$ 8,400	8,400*
Net income	$ 300,000	$ 80,000				$ 300,000
Retained Earnings						
Retained earnings—Plank	$ 400,000					$ 400,000
Retained earnings—Sharp		$200,000	e 200,000			
Net income	300,000✓	80,000✓				300,000
Dividends	200,000*	30,000*		d 27,000	3,000*	200,000*
Retained earnings—ending	$ 500,000	$250,000				$ 500,000
Balance Sheet						
Cash	$ 131,800	$ 32,000				$ 163,800
Other current assets	200,000	150,000				350,000
Land	160,000	40,000				200,000
Buildings	500,000	232,000		c 32,000		700,000
Accumulated depreciation—buildings	200,000*	54,000*	c 4,000			250,000*
Equipment	620,000	400,000		b 20,000		1,000,000
Accumulated depreciation—equipment	258,000*	100,000*	b 8,000			350,000*
Investment in Sharp	546,200		a 5,000 / b 14,400	d 25,600 / e 540,000		
	$1,700,000	$700,000				$1,813,800
Current liabilities	$ 200,000	$ 50,000				$ 250,000
Capital stock	1,000,000	400,000	e 400,000			1,000,000
Retained earnings	500,000✓	250,000✓				500,000
	$1,700,000	$700,000				
Minority interest January 1, 19X7			b 1,600	e 60,000	58,400	
Minority interest December 31, 19X7					$63,800	63,800
						$1,813,800

*Deduct.

Exhibit 6–4 *Intercompany Sales of Plant Assets—Equity Method*

Entry b relates to the $20,000 intercompany profit on Sharp's sale of equipment to Plank at the beginning of 19X6. The working paper adjustment is:

b	Investment in Sharp	$14,400	
	Minority interest January 1	1,600	
	Accumulated depreciation—equipment	8,000	
	Depreciation expense		$ 4,000
	Equipment		20,000
	To eliminate unrealized profit on upstream sale of equipment.		

Depreciation on the unrealized gain is $4,000 per year ($20,000/5 years) and the portion unrealized at the beginning of 19X7 was $16,000, the original gain less piecemeal recognition of $4,000 through depreciation in 19X6. Since the sale was upstream, the $16,000 unrealized profit is allocated 90 percent and 10 percent to the investment in Sharp ($14,400) and beginning minority interest ($1,600), respectively. The $14,400 is debited to the investment in Sharp account because Plank used the equity method of accounting.

Working paper entry c eliminates intercompany profit on the buildings that Plank sold to Sharp in 19X7 at a gain of $32,000:

c	Gain on buildings	$32,000	
	Accumulated depreciation—buildings	4,000	
	Buildings		$32,000
	Depreciation expense		4,000
	To eliminate unrealized gain on the downstream sale of buildings.		

Since the transaction occurred at the beginning of the current year, prior period balances were not affected by the sale. The $32,000 gain is eliminated in the adjustment, and buildings are reduced to reflect their cost to the consolidated entity. Depreciation expense and accumulated depreciation amounts relating to the unrealized gain are also eliminated.

Entry d in the consolidation working papers eliminates income from Sharp and 90 percent of Sharp's dividends and credits the investment in Sharp for the $25,600 difference in order to establish reciprocity between investment and equity accounts at the beginning of the year. Entry e eliminates reciprocal investment and equity accounts and establishes the minority interest at the beginning of the year.

d	Income from Sharp	$ 52,600	
	Dividends		$ 27,000
	Investment in Sharp		25,600
	To eliminate income and dividends from subsidiary.		
e	Retained earnings—Sharp	$200,000	
	Capital stock—Sharp	400,000	
	Investment in Sharp		$540,000
	Minority interest—beginning		60,000
	To eliminate reciprocal investment and equity balances.		

The $8,400 deduction for minority interest income in the consolidated income statement of Exhibit 6–4 is equal to 10 percent of Sharp's reported income for 19X7 plus the piecemeal recognition of the gain in 19X7 from Sharp's sale of equipment to Plank [($80,000 + $4,000) × 10%]. At December 31, 19X7 the minority interest's share of the unrealized gain on the equipment is $1,200. This

$1,200 is reflected in the $63,800 minority interest that is shown in the consolidated balance sheet. If the effect of the unrealized gain applicable to minority interest had not been eliminated, minority interest in the consolidated balance sheet would be $65,000, 10 percent of Sharp's reported equity at December 31, 19X7.

Incomplete Equity Method

If Plank Corporation had used an incomplete equity method and failed to consider intercompany transactions in accounting for its investment in Sharp, its separate financial statements would show overstated amounts for beginning and ending retained earnings, investment income, net income, and the investment in Sharp.

Conversion to Equity Method Approach   The working paper entry to convert the separate accounts of Plank to the equity method is:

Retained earnings—Plank January 1	$19,400	
Income from Sharp	19,400	
Investment in Sharp		$38,800

The equality of these numbers is coincidental, since the retained earnings adjustment consists of overstatements from prior sales of land and equipment and the income adjustment consists of recognition of previously deferred gain on land, piecemeal recognition of the gain on equipment, and the gain on buildings less related piecemeal recognition. Computations to support the amounts in the working paper entry are shown in the following incomplete equity to equity conversion schedule:

	Plank's Beginning Retained Earnings	Investment in Sharp	Income from Sharp
Prior-Years' Effect			
Sale of land to Sharp in 19X5	$ −5,000	$ −5,000	
Purchase of equipment from Sharp on January 1, 19X6 ($20,000 gain × 90%)	−18,000	−18,000	
Piecemeal recognition through 19X6 depreciation of equipment ($20,000 gain/ 5 years) × 90%	+3,600	+3,600	
Current-Year's Effect			
Sharp's sale of land to outside entity		+5,000	$ +5,000
Sale of building to Sharp on January 5, 19X7		−32,000	−32,000
Piecemeal recognition of gain on equipment—19X7		+3,600	+3,600
Piecemeal recognition of gain on building through depreciation $32,000 gain/8 years		+4,000	+4,000
Working paper adjustment to convert to the equity method	$ −19,400	$ −38,800	$ −19,400

After entering the conversion to equity entry in the consolidation working papers, all other working paper entries should be the same as those in Exhibit 6–4 under the equity method.

Traditional Working Paper Solution for Incomplete Equity Method   Exhibit 6–5 illustrates working paper procedures to consolidate the financial statements of Plank and Sharp when Plank uses an incomplete equity method of accounting and consolidates without converting to the equity method.

Notice that the entries are similar to those in Exhibit 6–4 except that the debit amounts in entries a and b are to the parent's beginning retained earnings instead of the investment account. This is because the parent did not eliminate intercompany unrealized profits in prior years through a one-line consolidation of its investment in Sharp. The working paper entries from Exhibit 6–5 are reproduced for convenient reference as follows:

a	Retained earnings—Plank January 1	$ 5,000	
	Gain on land		$ 5,000
	To recognize previously deferred gain on land.		
b	Retained earnings—Plank January 1	$ 14,400	
	Accumulated depreciation—equipment	8,000	
	Minority interest January 1	1,600	
	Equipment		$ 20,000
	Depreciation expense		4,000
	To eliminate unrealized profit on upstream sale of equipment.		
c	Gain on building	$ 32,000	
	Accumulated depreciation	4,000	
	Buildings		$ 32,000
	Depreciation expense		4,000
	To eliminate unrealized gain on downstream sale of building.		
d	Income from Sharp	$ 72,000	
	Dividends		$ 27,000
	Investment in Sharp		45,000
	To eliminate investment income (as recorded by Plank) and dividends, and return investment account to its beginning of the period balance under an incomplete equity method.		
e	Retained earnings—Sharp	$200,000	
	Capital stock—Sharp	400,000	
	Investment in Sharp		$540,000
	Minority interest		60,000
	To eliminate reciprocal equity and investment balances and enter beginning minority interest.		

Cost Method

Now assume that Plank has used the cost method in accounting for its investment in Sharp. Under the cost method, Plank's investment in Sharp account remains at the $450,000 original investment. Net income and retained earnings are understated by Plank's share of Sharp's undistributed income plus or minus any unrealized intercompany profits.

Conversion to Equity Method Approach   Data to support a working paper entry to convert Plank's cost-based accounting records to the equity basis are provided in the following cost-equity conversion schedule:

PLANK CORPORATION AND SUBSIDIARY
CONSOLIDATION WORKING PAPERS—FOR THE YEAR ENDED DECEMBER 31, 19X7

	Plank	90% Sharp	Adjustments and Eliminations		Minority Interest	Consolidated Statements
Income Statement						
Sales	$2,000,000	$700,000				$2,700,000
Gain on building	32,000		c 32,000			
Loss (or gain) on land		1,000*		a 5,000		4,000
Income from Sharp	72,000		d 72,000			
Cost of goods sold	1,000,000*	320,000*				1,320,000*
Depreciation expense	108,000*	50,000*		b 4,000 c 4,000		150,000*
Other expenses	676,600*	249,000*				925,600*
Minority interest income					$ 8,400	8,400*
Net income	$ 319,400	$ 80,000				$ 300,000
Retained Earnings						
Retained earnings—Plank	$ 419,400		a 5,000 b 14,400			$ 400,000
Retained earnings—Sharp		$200,000	e 200,000			
Net income	319,400	80,000				300,000
Dividends	200,000*	30,000*		d 27,000	3,000*	200,000*
Retained earnings—ending	$ 538,800	$250,000				$ 500,000
Balance Sheet						
Cash	$ 131,800	$ 32,000				$ 163,800
Other current assets	200,000	150,000				350,000
Land	160,000	40,000				200,000
Buildings	500,000	232,000	c 32,000			700,000
Accumulated depreciation—buildings	200,000*	54,000*	c 4,000			250,000*
Equipment	620,000	400,000		b 20,000		1,000,000
Accumulated depreciation—equipment	258,000*	100,000*	b 8,000			350,000*
Investment in Sharp	585,000			d 45,000 e 540,000		
	$1,738,800	$700,000				$1,813,800
Current liabilities	$ 200,000	$ 50,000				$ 250,000
Capital stock	1,000,000	400,000	e 400,000			1,000,000
Retained earnings	538,800	250,000				500,000
	$1,738,800	$700,000				
Minority interest January 1, 19X7			b 1,600	e 60,000	58,400	
Minority interest December 31, 19X7					$63,800	63,800
						$1,813,800

*Deduct.

Exhibit 6–5 Incomplete Equity Method—Traditional Approach

	Plank's Beginning Retained Earnings	Investment in Sharp	Income from Sharp	Dividend Income
Prior-Years' Effect				
90% of Sharp's increase in undistributed income for 19X5 and 19X6 ($600,000 − $500,000) × 90%	$ + 90,000	$ + 90,000		
Gain on sale of land to Sharp	− 5,000	− 5,000		
Gain on purchase of equipment from Sharp	− 18,000	− 18,000		
Piecemeal recognition of gain on equipment through depreciation $4,000 × 90%	+ 3,600	+ 3,600		
Current-Year's Effect				
Reclassify dividend income as decrease in investment		− 27,000		$ − 27,000
Share of Sharp's reported income $80,000 × 90%		+ 72,000	$ + 72,000	
Sharp's sale of land to outside entity		+ 5,000	+ 5,000	
Gain from sale of building to Sharp		− 32,000	− 32,000	
19X7 piecemeal recognition of gain on equipment $4,000 × 90%		+ 3,600	+ 3,600	
19X7 piecemeal recognition of gain on buildilng $32,000/8 years		+ 4,000	+ 4,000	
Working paper entry to convert cost to equity method	$ + 70,600	$ + 96,200	$ + 52,600	$ − 27,000

The working paper entry to convert from the cost to the equity method in journal form is:

Investment in Sharp	$96,200	
Dividend income	27,000	
Income from Sharp		$52,600
Retained earnings—Plank January 1		70,600

To adjust Plank's account balances to an equity basis as a first step in consolidating its subsidiary.

As in the case of the conversion from incomplete equity to the equity method, after this first correcting entry is made in the working papers to convert Plank's accounting for its investment in Sharp to the equity method, the rest of the working paper entries are the same as those in Exhibit 6–4.

Traditional Working Paper Solution for Cost Method   Exhibit 6–6 illustrates working paper procedures to consolidate the financial statements of Plank and Sharp when Plank uses the cost method to account for its investment in Sharp and consolidates without converting to the equity method.

Working paper entries a, b, and c under the cost method are identical to those under an incomplete equity method. Entry d eliminates dividend income against dividends.

PLANK CORPORATION AND SUBSIDIARY
CONSOLIDATION WORKING PAPERS—FOR THE YEAR ENDED DECEMBER 31, 19X7

	Plank	90% Sharp	Adjustments and Eliminations				Minority Interest	Consolidated Statements
Income Statement								
Sales	$2,000,000	$700,000						$2,700,000
Gain on building	32,000		c	32,000				
Loss (or gain) on land		1,000*			a	5,000		4,000
Income from Sharp	27,000		d	27,000				
Cost of goods sold	1,000,000*	320,000*						1,320,000*
Depreciation expense	108,000*	50,000*	b	4,000				150,000*
			c	4,000				
Other expenses	676,600*	249,000*						925,600*
Minority interest income							$ 8,400	8,400*
Net income	$ 274,400	$ 80,000						$ 300,000
Retained Earnings			a	5,000	e	90,000		
Retained earnings—Plank	$ 329,400		b	14,400				$ 400,000
Retained earnings—Sharp		$200,000	f	200,000				
Net income	274,400	80,000						300,000
Dividends	200,000*	30,000*			d	27,000	3,000*	200,000*
Retained earnings—ending	$ 403,800	$250,000						$ 500,000
Balance Sheet								
Cash	$ 131,800	$ 32,000						$ 163,800
Other current assets	200,000	150,000						350,000
Land	160,000	40,000						200,000
Buildings	500,000	232,000			c	32,000		700,000
Accumulated depreciation—buildings	200,000*	54,000*	c	4,000				250,000*
Equipment	620,000	400,000			b	20,000		1,000,000
Accumulated depreciation—equipment	258,000*	100,000*	b	8,000				350,000*
Investment in Sharp	450,000		e	90,000	f	540,000		
	$1,603,800	$700,000						$1,813,800
Current liabilities	$ 200,000	$ 50,000						$ 250,000
Capital stock	1,000,000	400,000	f	400,000				1,000,000
Retained earnings	403,800	250,000						500,000
	$1,603,800	$700,000						
Minority interest January 1, 19X7			b	1,600	f	60,000	58,400	
Minority interest December 31, 19X7							$63,800	63,800
								$1,813,800

*Deduct.

Exhibit 6-6 *Cost Method—Traditional Approach*

Entry e takes up Plank's share of the increase in Sharp's retained earnings from the date of acquisition to the beginning of 19X7. In other words, entry e establishes reciprocity between the investment and equity balances to the beginning of the year. Entry f then eliminates the reciprocal investment and equity balances and enters beginning of the period minority interest. These last three working paper entries are journalized as follows:

d	Dividend income—Sharp	$27,000	
	Dividends		$27,000
	To eliminate dividend income.		
e	Investment in Sharp	$90 000	
	Retained earnings—Plank January 1		$90,000
	To increase parent's beginning retained earnings for its share of Sharp's retained earnings increase between date of acquisition and beginning of the period.		
f	Retained earnings—Sharp	$200,000	
	Capital stock—Sharp	400,000	
	Investment in Sharp		$540,000
	Minority interest		60,000
	To eliminate reciprocal investment and equity balances and enter beginning minority interest.		

Comparison of Results Under the Three Methods

Regardless of the method (equity, incomplete equity, or cost) used by the parent in accounting for its subsidiary, or the approach used in the working papers to consolidate the financial statements of the parent and subsidiary, the final consolidated financial statements will always be the same. A summary of the differences in the financial statement items of Plank under the equity, incomplete equity, and cost methods is as follows:

	Equity Method	Incomplete Equity Method	Cost Method
Income Statement			
Income from Sharp	$ 52,600	$ 72,000	—
Dividend income from Sharp	—	—	$ 27,000
Net income	300,000	319,400	274,400
Retained Earnings Statement			
Retained earnings January 1, 19X7	400,000	419,400	329,400
Net income	300,000	319,400	274,400
Dividends (no difference)	200,000*	200,000*	200,000*
Retained earnings December 31, 19X7	500,000	538,800	403,800
Balance Sheet			
Investment in Sharp	546,200	585,000	450,000
Retained earnings December 31, 19X7	500,000	538,800	403,800

* Deduct.

INVENTORY ITEMS PURCHASED FOR USE AS OPERATING ASSETS

Intercompany asset transactions do not always fall neatly into the categories of inventory items or plant assets. For example, inventory items may be sold for use in the operations of an affiliated company. In this case, any gross profit on the sale will be realized for consolidated statement purposes as the property is depreciated by the purchasing affiliate.

Assume that Premier Electronics Company sells a computer that it manufactures at a cost of $150,000 to Service Valley Corporation, its 100 percent owned subsidiary, for $200,000. The computer has a five-year expected use life and straight-line depreciation is used. Premier's separate income statement includes $200,000 intercompany sales, but Service Valley's cost of sales does *not* include intercompany purchases, since the purchase price is reflected in its plant assets and the $50,000 gross profit is reflected in its equipment account. Working paper entries to consolidate the financial statements of Premier and Service Valley in the year of sale are:

Sales	$200,000	
Cost of sales		$150,000
Equipment		50,000

To eliminate intercompany sales and to reduce cost of sales and equipment for the cost and gross profit, respectively.

Accumulated depreciation	$ 10,000	
Depreciation expense		$ 10,000

To eliminate depreciation on the gross profit from the sale ($50,000/5 years).

Recognition of the remaining $40,000 unrealized profit will occur as Service Valley depreciates the computer over its remaining four-year useful life. Assuming that Premier adjusts its investment in Service Valley account for the unrealized profit on the sale under the equity method, the working paper entry for the second year will be:

Investment in Service Valley	$40,000	
Accumulated depreciation—equipment	20,000	
Equipment		$50,000
Depreciation expense		10,000

To reduce equipment to its cost basis to the consolidated entity, to eliminate the effects of the intercomany sale from depreciation expense and accumulated depreciation, and to establish reciprocity between beginning-of-the-period equity and investment amounts.

Working paper entries for the remaining three years of the computer's useful life will include the same debit and credit items, but the accumulated depreciation debit will increase by $10,000 in each subsequent year to a maximum of $50,000 and the debits to investment in Service Valley will decrease by $10,000 in each subsequent year as the gross profit is realized. The credit amounts are the same in each year.

SUMMARY

The effects of intercompany gains and losses on plant assets must be eliminated from consolidated financial statements until the gains and losses are realized by the consolidated entity through use or through sale of the assets. Realization through use results from the depreciation recorded by the purchasing affiliate. Although all unrealized profit must be eliminated from the consolidated statements, consolidated net income is adjusted for all unrealized gains and losses in the case of downstream sales. For upstream sales, however, the total amount of unrealized gains and losses is allocated between consolidated net income and minority interest income. One-line consolidation procedures for parent company financial statements must be compatible with consolidation procedures in order to maintain the equality of parent company income under the equity method and consolidated net income. A summary illustration comparing the effect of intercompany sales of plant assets on parent company and consolidation income statements is presented in Exhibit 6–7.

Assumptions

1 Parent Company's income, excluding income from Subsidiary, is $100,000.
2 90 percent owned Subsidiary reported net income of $50,000.
3 An intercompany sale of land resulted in a gain of $5,000.
4 The land is still held within the consolidated entity.

	Downstream	Upstream
	Assume that P sells to S	Assume that S sells to P
P's Net Income—Equity Method		
P's separate income	$100,000	$100,000
P's share of S's reported net income	45,000	45,000
Deduct: Unrealized gain from land		
($5,000 × 100%)	5,000*	—
($5,000 × 90%)	—	4,500*
P's net income	$140,000	$140,500
Consolidated Net Income		
P's separate income plus S's net income	$150,000	$150,000
Less: Unrealized gain on land	5,000*	5,000*
Total realized income	145,000	145,000
Less: Minority interest income		
($50,000 × 10%)	5,000*	—
($50,000 − $5,000) × 10%	—	4,500*
Consolidated net income	$140,000	$140,500

* Deduct.

Note that P's net income and consolidated net income are the same as if the intercompany transaction had never taken place. In the downstream example, P's separate income would have been $95,000 ($100,000 − $5,000 gain) without the intercompany transaction, and S's reported income would have remained at $50,000. P's separate income of $95,000, plus P's $45,000 income from S ($50,000 × 90%), equals $140,000.

In the upstream example, P's separate income would have been unchanged at $100,000 in the absence of the intercompany transaction, but S's reported income would have been only $45,000 ($50,000 − $5,000 gain). P's separate income of $100,000, plus P's $40,500 income from S ($45,000 × 90%), equals $140,500. Although helpful in understanding the nature of accounting procedures, these assumptions concerning what the incomes would have been without the intercompany transactions lack economic realism because they ignore the productive use of the land.

Exhibit 6–7   *Summary Illustration—Unrealized Profit from Plant Assets*

ASSIGNMENT MATERIAL

QUESTIONS

1 What is the objective of eliminating the effects of intercompany sales of plant assets in the preparation of consolidated financial statements?

2 In accounting for unrealized profits and losses from intercompany sales of plant assets, does it make any difference if the parent company is the purchaser or the seller? Would your answer be different if the subsidiary were 100 percent owned?

3 When are unrealized gains and losses from intercompany sales of land realized from the viewpoint of the selling affiliate?

4 How is the computation of minority interest income affected by downstream sales of land? By upstream sales of land?

5 Consolidation working paper entries are made to eliminate 100 percent of the unrealized profit from the land account in downstream sales of land. Is 100 percent also eliminated for upstream sales of land?

6 How are unrealized gains and losses from intercompany transactions involving depreciable assets eventually realized?

7 Describe the computation of minority interest income in the year of an upstream sale of depreciable plant assets.

8 How does a parent company eliminate the effects of unrealized gains on intercompany sales of plant assets under the equity method?

9 What is the effect of intercompany sales of plant assets on parent company and consolidated net income in years subsequent to the year of sale?

10 Explain the sequence of working paper adjustments and eliminations when unrealized gains and losses on plant assets are involved. Is your answer affected by the method used by the parent company in accounting for its subsidiary investment? Is your answer affected by whether the intercompany transaction occurred in the current year or in prior years?

(*Note:* Don't forget the assumptions on page 60 when working exercises and problems in this chapter.)

EXERCISES

E 6-1 Selneck Corporation is a 100 percent owned subsidiary of Prinston Corporation, acquired at book value on January 1, 19X1 when Selneck's stockholders' equity consisted of $1,000,000 capital stock and $400,000 retained earnings. Selneck's net income and dividends for 19X1 are $150,000 and $80,000, respectively. During 19X1 Prinston sold land with a book value of $50,000 to Selneck for $100,000.

Required: Calculate (a) Prinston's income from Selneck for 19X1 and (b) Prinston's investment in Selneck at December 31, 19X1.

E 6-2 Samero Corporation is a 90 percent owned subsidiary of Parcon Corporation, acquired by Parcon in 19X2. During 19X5 Parcon sells land for which it paid $25,000 to Samero for $50,000. Samero owns this land at December 31, 19X5.

Required

1 How and in what amount will the sale of land affect Parcon's income from Samero and net income for the year 19X5, and the balance of Parcon's investment in Samero account at December 31, 19X5?

2 How will the consolidated financial statements of Parcon Corporation and Subsidiary for 19X5 be affected by the intercompany sale of land?

3 If Samero still owns the land at December 31, 19X6, how will Parcon's income from Samero and net income for 19X6 be affected and what will be the effect on Parcon's investment in Samero account at December 31, 19X6?

E 6-3 Silverman Corporation is a 90 percent owned subsidiary of Pruitt Corporation, acquired several years ago at book value equal to fair value. For the years 19X1 and 19X2, Pruitt and Silverman report the following:

	_19X1_	_19X2_
Pruitt's separate income	$300,000	$400,000
Silverman's net income	80,000	60,000

The only intercompany transaction between Pruitt and Silverman during 19X1 and 19X2 was the January 1, 19X1 sale of land. The land had a book value of $20,000 and was sold intercompany for $30,000, its appraised value at the time of sale.

1 Assume that the land was sold by Pruitt to Silverman and that Silverman still has the land at December 31, 19X2.
    a Calculate consolidated net income for 19X1 and 19X2.
    b Calculate minority interest income for 19X1 and 19X2.

2 Assume that the land was sold by Silverman to Pruitt and Pruitt still holds the land at December 31, 19X2.
    a Calculate consolidated net income for 19X1 and 19X2.
    b Calculate minority interest income for 19X1 and 19X2.

E 6-4 Income information for 19X2 taken from the separate company financial statements of Packman Corporation and its 80 percent owned subsidiary, Skyfall Corporation, is presented as follows:

	Packman	_Skyfall_
Sales	$1,000,000	$560,000
Gain on sale of building	20,000	
Income from Skyfall	160,000	
Cost of goods sold	(500,000)	(260,000)
Depreciation expense	(100,000)	(60,000)
Other expenses	(200,000)	(40,000)
Net income	$380,000	$200,000

Packman's gain on sale of building relates to a building with a book value of $40,000 and a ten-year remaining useful life that was sold to Skyfall for $60,000 on January 1, 19X2.

Required
    1 At what amount will the gain on sale of building appear on the consolidated income statement of Packman and Subsidiary for the year 19X2?
    2 Calculate consolidated depreciation expense for 19X2.
    3 Calculate consolidated net income for Packman and Subsidiary for 19X2.
    4 What entry should be made on Packman's books on December 31, 19X2 (after the books are closed) to correct the accounts to an equity basis?

E 6-5 Salmark is a 90 percent owned subsidiary of Pigwich Corporation, acquired at book value several years ago. Comparative separate company income statements for these affiliated corporations for 19X6 are as follows:

	Pigwich Corporation	_Salmark Corporation_
Sales	$1,500,000	$700,000
Income from Salmark	108,000	—
Gain on building	30,000	—
Income credits	1,638,000	700,000
Cost of sales	1,000,000	400,000
Operating expenses	300,000	150,000
Income debits	1,300,000	550,000
Net income	$ 338,000	$150,000

On January 5, 19X6 Pigwich sold a building with a ten-year remaining use life to Salmark at a gain of $30,000. Salmark paid dividends of $100,000 during 19X6.

Required

1 Reconstruct the journal entries made by Pigwich during 19X6 to account for its investment in Salmark. Explanations of the journal entries are required.

2 Prepare a consolidated income statement for Pigwich Corporation and Subsidiary for 19X6.

E 6–6 [AICPA adapted]

1 On January 1, 19X5 the Jonas Company sold equipment to its wholly owned subsidiary, Neptune Company, for $1,800,000. The equipment cost Jonas $2,000,000; accumulated depreciation at the time of sale was $500,000. Jonas was depreciating the equipment on the straight-line method over twenty years with no salvage value, a procedure that Neptune continued. On the consolidated balance sheet at December 31, 19X5 the cost and accumulated depreciation, respectively, should be:

a $1,500,000 and $600,000   b $1,800,000 and $100,000

c $1,800,000 and $500,000   d $2,000,000 and $600,000

2 In the preparation of consolidated financial statements, intercompany items for which eliminations will not be made are:

a Purchases and sales where the parent employs the equity method

b Receivables and payables where the parent employs the cost method

c Dividends received and paid where the parent employs the equity method

d Dividends receivable and payable where the parent employs the equity method

3 Dunn Corp. owns 100 percent of Grey Corp.'s common stock. On January 2, 19X6, Dunn sold to Grey for $40,000 machinery with a carrying amount of $30,000. Grey is depreciating the acquired machinery over a five-year life by the straight-line method. The net adjustments to compute 19X6 and 19X7 consolidated income before income tax would be an increase (decrease) of:

	19X6	19X7
a	$(8,000)	$2,000
b	$(8,000)	$0
c	$(10,000)	$2,000
d	$(10,000)	$0

E 6–7 Pepper Corporation owns 40 percent of the outstanding voting stock of Salt Corporation acquired for $100,000 on July 1, 19X4 when Salt's common stockholders' equity was $200,000. The excess of investment cost over book value acquired was due to valuable patents owned by Salt and expected to give Salt a competitive advantage until July 1, 19X9.

Salt's net income for 19X4 was $40,000 (for the entire year), and for 19X5 Salt's net income was $60,000. Pepper's December 31, 19X4 and 19X5 inventories included unrealized profit on goods acquired from Salt in the amounts of $4,000 and $6,000, respectively. At December 31, 19X4 Pepper sold land to Salt at a gain of $2,000. This land is still owned by Salt at December 31, 19X5.

Required

1 Compute Pepper's investment income from Salt for 19X4 on the basis of a one-line consolidation.

2 Compute Pepper's investment income from Salt for 19X5 on the basis of a one-line consolidation.

E 6–8 Plain Corporation has an 80 percent interest in Simple Corporation, its only subsidiary. The 80 percent interest was acquired on July 1, 19X3 for $400,000, at which time Simple's equity consisted of $300,000 capital stock and $100,000 retained earnings. The excess of cost over book value was allocated to buildings with a twenty-year remaining use life.

On December 31, 19X5 Simple sold equipment with a remaining use life of four years to Plain at a gain of $20,000. Plain Corporation had separate income for 19X5 of $500,000 and 19X6 of $600,000.

Income and retained earnings data for Simple Corporation for 19X5 and 19X6 are as follows:

	19X5	19X6
Retained earnings January 1	$150,000	$200,000
Add: Net income	100,000	110,000
Deduct: Dividends	−50,000	−60,000
Retained earnings December 31	$200,000	$250,000

Required

1 Compute Plain Corporation's income from Simple, net income, and consolidated net income for each of the years 19X5 and 19X6.

2 Compute the correct balances of Plain Corporation's investment in Simple at December 31, 19X5 and 19X6, assuming no changes in Simple's outstanding stock since Plain acquired its interest.

E 6–9 Pauley Corporation manufactures and sells heavy industrial equipment. On July 1, 19X8 Pauley sold equipment that it manufactured at a cost of $300,000 to its 100 percent owned subsidiary, Shanklin Company, for $400,000. Shanklin is depreciating the equipment over a five-year period using the straight-line method.

1 The equipment and accumulated depreciation that appear in the consolidated balance sheet for Pauley and Subsidiary at December 31, 19X8 will include amounts related to this transaction of:

a $300,000 and $30,000

b $300,000 and $60,000

c $400,000 and $40,000

d $400,000 and $80,000

2 If Pauley accounts for its investment in Shanklin as a one-line consolidation, working paper entries to consolidate the financial statements of Pauley and Shanklin for 19X8 will include which of the following entries:

a	Sales	$100,000	
	Cost of sales		$100,000
b	Sales	$100,000	
	Investment in Shanklin		$100,000
c	Sales	$400,000	
	Cost of sales		$300,000
	Equipment		100,000
d	Sales	$400,000	
	Cost of sales		$400,000

E 6–10 1 On January 1, 19X6 Portland Corporation sold land with a book value of $300,000 to its 90 percent owned subsidiary, Sheckler Corporation, for $500,000. In 19X8 Sheckler resold the land to the city of Whitethorn for $800,000. The consolidated income statement for the year 19X8 will show a gain from sale of land of:

a $270,000

b $300,000

c $450,000

d $500,000

2 On January 3, 19X8 Pella Corporation sells equipment with a book value of $90,000 to its 100 percent owned subsidiary, Satterman Corporation, for $120,000. The equipment has a remaining use life of three years with no salvage at the time of transfer. Satterman uses the straight-line method of depreciation. As a result of this intercompany transaction, Pella's investment in Satterman account balance at December 31, 19X8 will be:

a $20,000 greater than its underlying equity interest

b $20,000 less than its underlying equity interest

c $30,000 less than its underlying equity interest

d $10,000 greater than its underlying equity interest

3 Pentex Corporation sells equipment with a book value of $80,000 to Shirley Company, its 75 percent owned subsidiary, for $100,000 on January 1, 19X8. Shirley determines that the remaining useful life of the equipment is four years and that straight-line depreciation is appropriate. The December 31, 19X8 *separate* company financial

statements of Pentex and Shirley show equipment-net of $500,000 and $300,000, respectively. Consolidated equipment—net will be:

a $800,000   b $785,000

c $780,000   d $650,000

4 On January 1, 19X8 Sartin Corporation, a 60 percent owned subsidiary of Pollyparts Company, sells a building with a book value of $300,000 to its parent for $350,000. At the time of sale, the building has an estimated remaining life of ten years with no salvage value. Pollyparts uses straight-line depreciation. If Sartin reports net income of $1,000,000 for 19X8, minority interest income will be:

a $450,000   b $400,000

c $382,000   d $355,000

PROBLEMS

P 6–1 The separate income statements of Perdue Corporation and its 100 percent owned subsidiary, Spear Corporation, for 19X3 are summarized as follows:

	Perdue	Spear
Sales	$1,000,000	$600,000
Income from Spear	100,000	—
Gain on equipment	40,000	—
Cost of sales	600,000*	400,000*
Other expenses	200,000*	100,000*
Net income	$ 340,000	$100,000

* Deduct.

Investigation reveals that the effects of certain intercompany transactions are not included in Perdue's income from Spear. Information about those intercompany transactions is as follows:

Inventories

	19X2	19X3
Intercompany sales (Perdue to Spear)	$100,000	$150,000
Cost of intercompany sales	60,000	90,000
Percent unsold at year-end	50%	40%

Plant Assets

Perdue sold equipment with a book value of $60,000 to Spear for $100,000 on January 1, 19X3. Spear is depreciating the equipment on a straight-line basis (no scrap) over a four-year period.

Required
1 Determine the correct amount of Perdue's income from Spear for 19X3.
2 Prepare a consolidated income statement for Perdue Corporation and Subsidiary for 19X3.

P 6–2 Comparative balance sheets for Pontiac Corporation and its 90 percent owned subsidiary, Sioux Corporation, at December 31, 19X8 are as follows:

	Pontiac Corporation	Sioux Corporation
Assets		
Cash	$ 4,760,000	$ 1,200,000
Receivables—net	3,200,000	1,800,000
Inventories	4,040,000	2,000,000
Land	4,700,000	1,000,000
Building—net	7,000,000	3,000,000
Equipment—net	15,000,000	7,000,000
Investment in Sioux	11,300,000	—
Total assets	$50,000,000	$16,000,000
Liabilities and Stockholders' Equity		
Accounts payable	$ 3,500,000	$ 1,500,000
Other liabilities	8,500,000	2,500,000
Common stock	30,000,000	10,000,000
Retained earnings	8,000,000	2,000,000
Total equities	$50,000,000	$16,000,000

Pontiac acquired its 90 percent interest in Sioux for cash on December 31, 19X5 at a price $500,000 in excess of underlying book value. The excess was due to goodwill having a ten-year amortization period.

Sioux Corporation's inventories at December 31, 19X8 included merchandise acquired from Pontiac at a price $50,000 in excess of its cost to Pontiac. Unrealized profit in Sioux's December 31, 19X7 inventories acquired from Pontiac were $40,000.

During 19X8 Sioux sold land to Pontiac at a gain of $100,000. Pontiac's land account at December 31, 19X8 includes the full $700,000 paid for the land. Pontiac uses the equity method of accounting for its investment in Sioux but has applied the equity method without amortizing goodwill or adjusting for unrealized profits.

Required: Prepare a consolidated balance sheet for Pontiac Corporation and Subsidiary at December 31, 19X8.

P 6–3   Pine Corporation owns 80 percent of the outstanding voting stock of Spruce Corporation, having acquired its interest at book value when Spruce Corporation was incorporated on January 2, 19X5. Comparative income statements for Pine and Spruce for 19X5 and 19X6 are as follows:

	19X5		19X6	
	Pine	Spruce	Pine	Spruce
Sales	$500,000	$200,000	$600,000	$250,000
Gain on machinery	10,000	—	—	—
Dividend income	40,000	—	40,000	—
Total revenue	550,000	200,000	640,000	250,000
Inventory January 1	80,000	40,000	70,000	50,000
Purchases	300,000	100,000	400,000	120,000
Goods available for sale	380,000	140,000	470,000	170,000
Inventory December 31	70,000	50,000	90,000	60,000
Cost of goods sold	310,000	90,000	380,000	110,000
Gross profit	240,000	110,000	260,000	140,000
Operating expenses	80,000	60,000	100,000	80,000
Net income	$160,000	$ 50,000	$160,000	$ 60,000

Additional Information

1 Pine Corporation uses the cost method of accounting for its investment in Spruce.
2 The $10,000 gain relates to machinery sold to Spruce at the beginning of 19X5. Spruce still held the machinery on December 31, 19X6 and is depreciating it at the rate of 20 percent per year.
3 Intercompany sales and inventory data for 19X5 and 19X6 are as follows:

	19X5	19X6
Sales by Pine to Spruce	$40,000	—
Sales by Spruce to Pine	—	$50,000
Unrealized profit in Spruce's December 31 inventory	$ 8,000	—
Unrealized profit in Pine's December 31 inventory	—	$10,000

Required: Prepare comparative 19X5 and 19X6 consolidated income statements for Pine Corporation and Subsidiary. You may use a single line for cost of sales in your comparative income statements.

P 6–4 Page Corporation acquired a 90 percent interest in Sas Corporation's outstanding voting common stock on January 1, 19X1 for $630,000 cash. The stockholders' equity of Sas on this date consisted of $500,000 capital stock and $200,000 retained earnings.

The separate financial statements of Page and Sas Corporations at and for the year ended December 31, 19X1 are summarized as follows:

	Page	Sas
Combined Income and Retained Earnings Statements		
for the year ended December 31, 19X1		
Sales	$ 700,000	$500,000
Income from Sas	60,000	—
Gain on land	10,000	—
Gain on equipment	20,000	—
Cost of sales	(300,000)	(300,000)
Depreciation expense	(90,000)	(35,000)
Other expenses	(200,000)	(65,000)
Net income	200,000	100,000
Beginning retained earnings	600,000	200,000
Dividends	(100,000)	(50,000)
Retained earnings December 31, 19X1	$ 700,000	$250,000
Balance Sheet at December 31, 19X1		
Cash	$ 45,000	$ 20,000
Accounts receivable—net	90,000	110,000
Inventories	100,000	80,000
Other current items	70,000	40,000
Land	50,000	70,000
Buildings—net	200,000	150,000
Equipment—net	500,000	400,000
Investment in Sas	645,000	—
	$1,700,000	$870,000
Accounts payable	$ 160,000	$ 50,000
Other liabilities	340,000	70,000
Capital stock, $10 par	500,000	500,000
Retained earnings	700,000	250,000
	$1,700,000	$870,000

During 19X1 Page made sales of $50,000 to Sas at a gross profit of $15,000. One-third of these sales were inventoried by Sas at year-end. Sas owed Page $10,000 on open account at December 31, 19X1.

Page sold land that cost $20,000 to Sas for $30,000 on July 1, 19X1. Sas still owns the land. On January 1, 19X1 Page sold equipment with a book value of $20,000 and a remaining useful life of four years to Sas for $40,000. Sas uses straight-line depreciation and assumes no salvage value on this equipment.

Required: Prepare consolidation working papers for Page Corporation and Subsidiary for the year ended December 31, 19X1.

P 6–5 Sun Corporation is a 90 percent owned subsidiary of Part Corporation, acquired by Part for $405,000 cash on January 1, 19X5 when Sun had capital stock of $400,000 and retained earnings of $20,000. The excess cost over book value acquired was due to a $30,000 undervaluation of Sun's inventory that was sold in 19X5.

Sun sold merchandise to Part during 19X7 for $60,000. Half of this merchandise is included in Part's inventory at December 31, 19X7, and a $10,000 liability from intercompany purchases is reflected in Part's accounts payable at December 31, 19X7. Unrealized profit in Part's December 31, 19X6 inventory of goods acquired from Sun amounted to $5,000. All of Sun's sales, including intercompany sales, are made at 150 percent of their cost to Sun.

On January 2, 19X7 Part sold machinery with a remaining use life of four years to Sun for $60,000. This machinery had an undepreciated cost of $40,000 when sold by Part and continues to be used by Sun.

Part uses the equity method in accounting for its investment in Sun. Use the following financial statements of Part and Sun Corporations for the year ended December 31, 19X7 to prepare consolidation working papers:

	Part	Sun
Combined Income and Retained Earnings Statement for the Year Ended December 31, 19X7		
Sales	$ 800,000	$600,000
Income from Sun	52,500	—
Gain on machinery	20,000	—
Cost of sales	(500,000)	(400,000)
Operating expenses	(170,000)	(120,000)
Net income	202,500	80,000
Add: Beginning retained earnings	290,500	60,000
Deduct: Dividends	(100,000)	(40,000)
Retained earnings December 31, 19X7	$ 393,000	$100,000
Balance Sheet at December 31, 19X7		
Cash	$ 19,000	$ 8,000
Receivables—net	38,000	22,000
Inventories	250,000	150,000
Plant assets	600,000	400,000
Accumulated depreciation	(290,000)	(30,000)
Investment in Sun	426,000	—
Total assets	$1,043,000	$550,000
Accounts payable	$ 100,000	$ 40,000
Other liabilities	50,000	10,000
Capital stock	500,000	400,000
Retained earnings	393,000	100,000
Total equities	$1,043,000	$550,000

P 6-6 Financial statements for Phal Corporation and Sink Corporation for 19X6 are summarized as follows:

	Phal	Sink
Combined Income and Retained Earnings Statement		
for the Year Ended December 31, 19X6		
Sales	$210,000	$130,000
Income from Sink	32,500	—
Gain on sale of land	—	10,000
Depreciation expense	(40,000)	(30,000)
Other expenses	(110,000)	(60,000)
Net income	92,500	50,000
Add: Beginning retained earnings	138,000	50,000
Deduct: Dividends	(30,000)	—
Retained earnings December 31, 19X6	$200,500	$100,000
Balance Sheet at December 31, 19X6		
Current assets	$200,000	$170,000
Plant assets	550,000	350,000
Accumulated depreciation	(120,000)	(70,000)
Investment in Sink	320,500	—
Total assets	$950,500	$450,000
Current liabilities	$150,000	$ 50,000
Capital stock	600,000	300,000
Retained earnings	200,500	100,000
Total equities	$950,500	$450,000

Additional information

1 Phal acquired an 80 percent interest in Sink on January 2, 19X4 for $290,000 when Sink's stockholders' equity consisted of $300,000 capital stock and no retained earnings. The excess of investment cost over book value of the net assets acquired related 50 percent to undervalued inventories (subsequently sold in 19X4) and 50 percent to goodwill with a ten-year amortization period.

2 Phal sold equipment to Sink for $25,000 on January 2, 19X5, at which time the equipment had a book value of $10,000 and a five-year remaining useful life. (Included in plant assets in the financial statements.)

3 During 19X6 Sink sold land to Phal at a profit of $10,000. (Included in plant assets in the financial statements.)

4 Phal uses the equity method in accounting for its investment in Sink.

Required: Prepare consolidation working papers for Phal Corporation and Subsidiary for the year ended December 31, 19X6.

P 6-7 Port Corporation acquired all the outstanding stock of Skip Corporation on April 1, 19X1 for $15,000,000 when Skip's stockholders' equity consisted of $5,000,000 capital stock and $2,000,000 retained earnings. The purchase price reflected a $500,000 undervaluation of Skip's inventory on this date (sold in 19X1) and a $3,500,000 undervaluation of Skip's buildings (remaining use life seven years from April 1, 19X1). Goodwill from the acquisition is being amortized over forty years.

During 19X2 Skip sold land that cost $1,000,000 to Port for $1,500,000. Port resold the land for $2,200,000 during 19X5.

Port sells inventory items to Skip on a regular basis. Information relevant to such sales is as follows:

	Sales to Skip	Cost to Port	Percentage Unsold by Skip at Year-end	Percentage Unpaid by Skip at Year-end
19X1	$ 500,000	$300,000	0%	0%
19X2	1,000,000	600,000	30	50
19X3	1,200,000	720,000	18	30
19X4	1,000,000	600,000	25	20
19X5	1,500,000	900,000	20	20

Skip sold equipment with a book value of $800,000 to Port on January 3, 19X5 for $1,600,000. This equipment had a remaining use life of four years at the time of sale.

Port uses the equity method of accounting for its investment in Skip. The financial statements for Port and Skip Corporations are summarized as follows:

	Port	Skip
Combined Income and Retained Earnings Statement for the Year Ended December 31, 19X5		
Sales	$26,000,000	$11,000,000
Gain on land	700,000	—
Gain on equipment	—	800,000
Income from Skip	1,280,000	—
Cost of sales	(15,000,000)	(5,000,000)
Depreciation expense	(3,700,000)	(2,000,000)
Other expenses	(4,280,000)	(2,800,000)
Net income	5,000,000	2,000,000
Add: Beginning retained earnings	12,000,000	4,000,000
Deduct: Dividends	(3,000,000)	(1,000,000)
Retained earnings December 31, 19X5	$14,000.000	$ 5,000,000
Balance Sheet at December 31, 19X5		
Cash	$ 1,170,000	$ 500,000
Accounts receivable—net	2,000,000	1,500,000
Inventories	5,000,000	2,000,000
Land	4,000,000	1,000,000
Buildings—net	15,000,000	4,000,000
Equipment—net	10,000,000	4,000,000
Investment in Skip	13,930,000	—
Total assets	$51,100,000	$13,000,000
Accounts payable	$ 4,100,000	$ 1,000,000
Other liabilities	7,000,000	2,000,000
Capital stock	26,000,000	5,000,000
Retained earnings	14,000,000	5,000,000
Total equities	$51,100,000	$13,000,000

Required: Prepare consolidation working papers for Port Corporation and Subsidiary for the year ended December 31, 19X5.

P 6–8 Pic Corporation acquired an 80 percent interest in Sic Company on January 1, 19X5 for $136,000. Sic's capital stock and retained earnings on that date were $100,000 and $70,000, respectively.

At the beginning of 19X5, Sic sold a machine to Pic for $10,000. The machine had cost Sic $7,000, had depreciated $2,000 while being used by Sic, and had a remaining use life of five years from the date of sale.

Trial balances of the two companies at December 31, 19X5 and 19X6 are as follows:

	19X5		19X6	
	Pic	*Sic*	*Pic*	*Sic*
Debits:				
Cash and equivalents	$ 50,000	$ 30,000	$ 63,000	$ 30,000
Other current assets	130,000	70,000	140,000	80,000
Plant and equipment	400,000	200,000	440,000	245,000
Investment in Sic	160,000	—	192,000	—
Cost of sales	250,000	130,000	260,000	140,000
Depreciation expense	50,000	25,000	50,000	25,000
Other expenses	60,000	20,000	55,000	30,000
	$1,100,000	$475,000	$1,200,000	$550,000
Credits:				
Accumulated depreciation	$ 150,000	$ 50,000	$ 200,000	$ 75,000
Liabilities	100,000	50,000	48,000	40,000
Capital stock	300,000	100,000	300,000	100,000
Retained earnings	126,000	70,000	190,000	100,000
Sales	400,000	200,000	430,000	235,000
Gain on plant asset	—	5,000	—	—
Income from Sic	24,000	—	32,000	—
	$1,100,000	$475,000	$1,200,000	$550,000

Required: Prepare consolidation working papers for Pic Corporation and Subsidiary for the year ended December 31, 19X5 and the year ended December 31, 19X6.

P 6-9   Park Corporation acquired an 80 percent interest in Spin Corporation on January 1, 19X6 for $108,000 cash when Spin's capital stock was $100,000 and retained earnings, $10,000. The difference between investment cost and book value acquired is being amortized over a ten-year period.

Separate company financial statements for Park and Spin Corporations at December 31, 19X9 are summarized as follows:

	Park	Spin
Combined Income and Retained Earnings Statement		
for the Year Ended December 31, 19X9		
Sales	$650,000	$120,000
Income from Spin	42,000	—
Cost of sales	(390,000)	(40,000)
Other expenses	(170,000)	(30,000)
Net income	132,000	50,000
Add: Beginning retained earnings	95,600	20,000
Deduct: Dividends	(70,000)	(20,000)
Retained earnings December 31, 19X9	$157,600	$ 50,000
Balance Sheet at December 31, 19X9		
Cash	$ 58,000	$ 20,000
Accounts receivable	40,000	20,000
Inventories	60,000	35,000
Plant assets	290,000	205,000
Accumulated depreciation	(70,000)	(100,000)
Investment in Spin	121,600	—
Total assets	$499,600	$180,000
Accounts payable	$ 42,000	$ 30,000
Capital stock	300,000	100,000
Retained earnings	157,600	50,000
Total equities	$499,600	$180,000

Additional information

1 Spin's sales include intercompany sales of $8,000, and Park's December 31, 19X9 inventory includes $1,000 profit on goods acquired from Spin. Park's December 31, 19X8 inventory contained $2,000 profit on goods acquired from Spin.

2 Park owes Spin $4,000 on account.

3 On January 1, $9X8 Spin sold plant assets to Park for $60,000. These assets had a book value of $40,000 on that date and are being depreciated by Park over a five-year period.

4 Park uses the equity method to account for its investment in Spin.

Required: Prepare consolidation working papers for Park Corporation and Subsidiary for the year 19X9.

P 6–10 Pike Corporation issued 10,000 of its own $10 par shares for 90 percent of Shad Corporation's outstanding common shares on January 1, 19X7 in a pooling of interests business combination. Shad's stockholders' equity consisted of $100,000 capital stock, $50,000 other paid-in capital, and $50,000 retained earnings at the time of the pooling. Pike recorded the pooling as follows:

Investment in Shad (90%)	$180,000	
Capital stock, $10 par		$100,000
Other paid-in capital		35,000
Retained earnings		45,000

Separate company financial statements for Pike and Shad at December 31, 19X8 are summanzed as follows:

	Pike	Shad
Income Statement for 19X8		
Sales	$ 600,000	$200,000
Income from Shad	63,500	—
Gain on equipment	18,000	—
Cost of sales	270,000*	100,000*
Operating expenses	121,500*	20,000*
Net income	$ 290,000	$ 80,000
Retained Earnings for 19X8		
Retained earnings December 31, 19X7	$ 70,000	$ 90,000
Add: Net income	290,000	80,000
Deduct: Dividends	150,000*	40,000*
Retained earnings December 31, 19X8	$ 210,000	$130,000
Balance Sheet at December 31, 19X8		
Cash	$ 166,500	$ 23,000
Accounts receivable	180,000	100,000
Dividends receivable	18,000	—
Inventories	60,000	27,000
Land	100,000	30,000
Buildings—net	280,000	100,000
Equipment—net	330,000	120,000
Investment in Shad	215,500	—
Total assets	$1,350,000	$400,000
Accounts payable	$ 225,000	$ 60,000
Dividends payable	30,000	20,000
Other liabilities	150,000	40,000
Capital stock, $10 par	600,000	100,000
Other paid-in capital	135,000	50,000
Retained earnings	210,000	130,000
Total equities	$1,350,000	$400,000

* Deduct.

During 19X7 and 19X8, the intercompany transactions between these affiliated companies were as follows:

Inventory Items: During 19X7 Pike sold inventory items that cost $30,000 to Shad for $50,000. Half of these items were inventoried by Shad at December 31, 19X7. During 19X8 Pike sold inventory items that cost $20,000 to Shad for $40,000, and 40 percent of these items were inventoried by Shad at December 31, 19X8. Also, Shad owed Pike $5,000 at December 31, 19X8.

Plant Assets: On January 12, 19X7 Shad sold land with a book value of $10,000 to Pike for $15,000 and a building with a book value of $50,000 to Pike for $70,000. The building is being depreciated over a four-year period. On January 1, 19X8 Shad purchased equipment with a six-year remaining use life from Pike at a gain to Pike of $18,000.

Required: Prepare consolidation working papers for Pike Corporation and Subsidiary at and for the year ended December 31, 19X8.

P 6–11   **[AICPA adapted]**

Cain Corporation acquired all the outstanding $10 par value voting common stock of Frey, Inc. on January 1, 19X9 in exchange for 25,000 shares of its $10 par value voting common stock. On December 31, 19X8, Cain's common stock had a closing market price of $30 per share on a national stock exchange. The acquisition was appropriately accounted for as a purchase. Both companies continued to operate as separate business entities maintaining separate accounting records with years ending December 31.

On December 31, 19X9 the companies had condensed financial statements as follows:

	Cain	Frey
Income Statement for the Year Ended December 31, 19X9		
Net sales	$3,800,000	$1,500,000
Dividends from Frey	40,000	—
Gain on sale of warehouse	30,000	—
Cost of goods sold	(2,360,000)	(870,000)
Operating expenses (including depreciation)	(1,100,000)	(440,000)
Net income	$ 410,000	$ 190,000
Retained Earnings Statement for the Year Ended December 31, 19X9		
Retained earnings—beginning	$ 440,000	$ 156,000
Add: Net income	410,000	190,000
Less: Dividends paid	—	(40,000)
Retained earnings December 31, 19X9	$ 850,000	$ 306,000
Balance Sheet at December 31, 19X9		
Assets		
Cash	$ 570,000	$ 150,000
Accounts receivable—net	860,000	350,000
Inventories	1,060,000	410,000
Land, plant and equipment	1,320,000	680,000
Accumulated depreciation	(370,000)	(210,000)
Investment in Frey (at cost)	750,000	—
Total assets	$4,190,000	$1,380,000
Liabilities and Stockholders' Equity		
Accounts payable and accrued expenses	$1,340,000	$ 594,000
Common stock, $10 par	1,700,000	400,000
Additional paid-in capital	300,000	80,000
Retained earnings	850,000	306,000
Total equities	$4,190,000	$1,380,000

Additional information

1 There were no changes in the common stock and additional paid-in capital accounts during 19X9 except the one necessitated by Cain's acquisition of Frey.

2 At the acquisition date, the fair value of Frey's machinery exceeded its book value by $54,000. The excess cost will be amortized over the estimated average remaining life of six years. The fair values of all of Frey's other assets and liabilities were equal to their book values. Any goodwill resulting from the acquisition will be amortized over a 20-year period.

3 On July 1, 19X9 Cain sold a warehouse facility to Frey for $129,000 cash. At the time of the sale, Cain's book values were $33,000 for the land and $66,000 for the undepreciated cost of the building. Based on a real estate appraisal, Frey allocated $43,000 of the purchase price to land and $86,000 to building. Frey is depreciating the building over its estimated five-year remaining useful life by the straight-line method with no salvage value.

4 During 19X9, Cain purchased merchandise from Frey at an aggregate invoice price of $180,000, which included a 100 percent markup on Frey's cost. At December 31, 19X9, Cain owed Frey $86,000 on these purhases, and $36,000 of this merchandise remained in Cain's inventory.

Required: Prepare working papers to consolidate the financial statements of Cain and Frey for the year 19X9. (*Note:* Conversion to equity is an inefficient approach to the solution for this problem because the consolidation is in the year of acquisition.

P 6-12   Separate company and consolidated financial statements for Pape Corporation and its only subsidiary, Sach Corporation for 19X2 are summarized here. Pape acquired its interest in Sach on January 1, 19X1 at a price in excess of book value.

PAPE CORPORATION AND SUBSIDIARY
SEPARATE COMPANY AND CONSOLIDATED FINANCIAL STATEMENTS AT AND FOR THE YEAR ENDED DECEMBER 31, 19X2

	Pape	*Sach*	*Consolidated*
Income Statement			
Sales	$ 500,000	$300,000	$ 716,000
Income from Sach	17,000	—	—
Gain on equipment	20,000	—	—
Cost of sales	(200,000)	(150,000)	(275,000)
Depreciation expense	(60,000)	(40,000)	(95,000)
Other expenses	(77,000)	(60,000)	(141,000)
Minority interest income	—	—	(5,000)
Net income	$ 200,000	$ 50,000	$ 200,000
Retained Earnings			
Retained earnings	$ 250,000	$120,000	$ 250,000
Net income	200,000	50,000	200,000
Dividends	(100,000)	(30,000)	(100,000)
Retained earnings	$ 350,000	$140,000	$ 350,000
Balance Sheet			
Cash	$ 17,500	$ 35,000	$ 52,500
Accounts receivable—net	50,000	30,000	70,000
Dividends receivable	13,500	—	—
Inventories	90,000	60,000	136,000
Other current assets	70,000	40,000	110,000
Land	50,000	20,000	70,000
Buildings—net	100,000	50,000	150,000
Equipment—net	300,000	265,000	550,000
Investment in Sach	309,000	—	—
Goodwill	—	—	32,000
Total assets	$1,000,000	$500,000	$1,170,500

	Pape	Sach	Consolidated
Accounts payable	$ 60,000	$ 50,000	$ 100,000
Dividends payable	—	15,000	1,500
Other liabilities	90,000	95,000	185,000
Capital stock, $10 par	500,000	200,000	500,000
Retained earnings	350,000	140,000	350,000
Minority interest December 31, 19X2	—	—	34,000
Total equities	$1,000,000	$500,000	$1,170,500

Required: Answer the following questions about the financial statements of Pape and Sach.

1 What is Pape Corporation's percentage interest in Sach Corporation? Provide a computation to explain your answer.

2 Does Pape use a one-line consolidation in accounting for its investment in Sach? Explain your answer.

3 Were there intercompany sales between Pape and Sach in 19X2? If so, show computations.

4 Are there unrealized inventory profits at December 31, 19X2? If so, show computations.

5 Provide computations to explain the difference between the combined separate company cost of sales and consolidated cost of sales.

6 Explain the difference between combined separate company and the consolidated "equipment—net" line item by reconstructing the working paper entry(s) that was (were) apparently made.

7 Are there intercompany receivables and payables? If so, identify them and state their amounts.

8 Beginning with the minority interest at January 1, 19X2, provide calculations of the $34,000 minority interest at December 31, 19X2.

9 What was the amount of unamortized goodwill at December 31, 19X1? Show computations.

10 Provide computations to explain the $309,000 investment in Sach account balance at December 31, 19X2.

7

INTERCOMPANY PROFIT TRANSACTIONS— BONDS

Companies frequently hold the debt instruments of affiliated companies. Such intercompany borrowing and lending is justified on the basis of convenience, efficiency, and flexibility. Even though each affiliate is a separate legal entity, the management of the parent company is in a position to negotiate all loans between affiliated companies, and a decision to borrow from or loan directly to affiliated companies is really only a decision to transfer funds among affiliates. Direct loans among affiliates produce reciprocal receivable and payable accounts for both principal and interest, as well as reciprocal income and expense accounts. These reciprocal accounts are eliminated in the preparation of consolidated financial statements because the intercompany receivables and payables do not reflect assets or obligations of the consolidated entity.

Special problems of accounting for intercompany bonds and notes arise when one company purchases the debt instruments of an affiliate from outside entities. Such purchases constitute a retirement of debt from the viewpoint of the consolidated entity even though the debt remains outstanding from the viewpoint of the debtor corporation as a separate legal entity. That is, the issuing affiliate (debtor corporation) accounts for its debt obligations as if they were held by unaffiliated entities, and the purchasing affiliate accounts for its investment in the affiliate's obligations as if they were the obligations of unaffiliated entities. Subsequently, consolidated statements are prepared to show the financial position and results of operations that would have resulted if the issuing corporation had purchased and retired its own debt.

INTERCOMPANY BOND TRANSACTIONS

At the time a company issues bonds, its bond liability will reflect the current market rate of interest. But subsequent changes in the market rate will create a disparity between the book value and the market value of that liability. If the market rate increases, the market value of the liability will be less than book value and the issuing company will have *realized* a gain as a result. The gain is *not recognized* on the issuing company's books under generally accepted accounting principles.

Similarly, a decline in the market rate of interest gives rise to a *realized* loss that is *not recognized*.

Realized but unrecognized gains or losses on outstanding bonds of affiliated companies can be recognized by retiring the outstanding bonds. The parent company, which controls all debt retirement and other decisions for the consolidated entity, has the following options:

1 The *issuing company* (parent or subsidiary) can use its available resources to purchase and *retire its own bonds.*
2 The *issuing company* (parent or subsidiary) can borrow money from unaffiliated entities at the market rate of interest and use the proceeds to *retire its own bonds.* (This option constitutes refunding.)
3 The *issuing company* can borrow money from an affiliated company and use the proceeds to *retire its own bonds.*
4 An *affiliated company* (parent or subsidiary) can purchase the bonds of the issuing company, in which case the bonds are *constructively retired.*

The first three options result in an **actual retirement** of the bonds. The previously unrecognized gain or loss in these three situations is recognized by the issuing company and is appropriately included in measuring consolidated net income. The fourth option results in a **constructive retirement**. This means that the bonds are retired for consolidated statements purposes because the bond investment and the bonds payable items of the parent and the subsidiary are reciprocals that must be eliminated in the consolidation process. The difference between the book value of the bond liability and the purchase price of the bond investment is a gain or loss for consolidated statement purposes. It is also a gain or loss for parent company accounting under the equity method (one-line consolidation). The gain or loss is not recognized on the books of the issuing company whose bonds are held as an investment by the purchasing affiliate.

Although the constructive retirement is different in form, the substance of the debt extinguishment is the same as for the other three options from the viewpoint of the consolidated entity. And the effect of a constructive retirement on consolidated statements is the same as for an actual retirement. The gain or loss is a gain or loss of the issuing company that has been realized by changes in the market rate of interest after the bonds were issued, and it is recognized for consolidated statement purposes when the bonds are repurchased and held within the consolidated entity.

Several examples of parent companies offering to buy their subsidiary's bonds occurred during the junk bond market collapse in 1990. For example, Univision Holdings, Inc., a 63.5 percent owned subsidiary of Hallmark Cards, Inc., was in danger of defaulting on its $270 million junk bonds. Hallmark offered to buy the bonds from investors at about 40 percent of the face amount.[1] Similarly, Ingersoll Newspapers, Inc., offered to buy, at a deep discount, a majority of the $240 million junk bonds issued by its affiliate, Community Newspapers, Inc.[2]

CONSTRUCTIVE GAINS AND LOSSES ON INTERCOMPANY BONDS

If the price paid by one affiliate to acquire the debt of another is greater than the book value of the liability (par value plus unamortized premium or less unamortized discount and issuance costs), a constructive loss on the retirement of debt occurs. Alternatively, if the price paid is less than the book value of the

---

[1]*The Wall Street Journal*, April 2, 1990, p. B4.
[2]*The Wall Street Journal*, March 22, 1990, p. A3.

debt, a constructive gain results. The gain or loss is referred to as *constructive* because it is a gain or loss that is realized and recognized from the viewpoint of the consolidated entity, but it is not recorded on the separate books of the affiliated companies at the time of purchase.

Constructive gains and losses on bonds are (1) realized gains and losses from the consolidated viewpoint (2) that arise when a company purchases the bonds of an affiliate (3) from other entities (4) at a price other than the book value of the bonds. No gains or losses result from the purchase of an affiliate's bonds at book value or from direct lending and borrowing between affiliated companies.

Some accounting theorists argue that constructive gains and losses on intercompany bond transactions should be allocated between the purchasing and issuing affiliates according to the par value of the bonds. For example, if Parent Company pays $99,000 for $100,000 par of Subsidiary Company's outstanding bonds with $2,000 unamortized premium, the $3,000 constructive gain ($102,000 less $99,000) is allocated $1,000 to Parent and $2,000 to Subsidiary. The alternative to this **par value theory** is the **agency theory**, under which the affiliate that purchases the intercompany bonds acts as agent for the issuing company, under directions from Parent Company management. Under agency theory, the $3,000 constructive gain is assigned to Subsidiary Company (the issuing company), and the consolidated statement effect is the same as if Subsidiary Company had purchased its own bonds for $99,000. Although not supported by a separate theory, constructive gains and losses are sometimes assigned 100 percent to the parent company on the basis of expediency. That is, the accounting is less complicated.

Since changes in market interest rates generate gains and losses for the issuing company, accounting procedures should assign such gains and losses to the issuing affiliate, irrespective of the form of the transaction (direct retirement by the issuing company or purchase by an affiliate). Failure to assign the full amount of a constructive gain or loss to the issuing affiliate results in recognizing form over substance in debt retirement transactions. Since the substance of a transaction should be considered over its form (incidentally, this is what consolidation is all about), the agency theory is conceptually superior and, accordingly, constructive gains and losses are assigned to the issuing affiliate in this book.

Most corporate long-term debt is in the form of outstanding bonds, and accordingly, the analysis in this chapter relates to bonds even though it also applies to other types of debt instruments. Straight-line rather than effective interest amortization of premiums and discounts is used in the illustrations throughout the chapter. This is done to make the illustrations easier to follow and help students learn the concepts involved without the added complexity of effective interest computations. It should be understood that the effective interest method is generally superior to the straight-line method.[3] This discussion of intercompany bond transactions among affiliated companies also applies to companies associated through ownership of 20 percent or more of the voting stock of another company and accounted for under the equity method.

The first illustration in this section assumes that the subsidiary purchases parent company bonds (in other words, the parent company is the issuing affiliate) and the constructive gain or loss is assigned to the parent company. In the second illustration, the parent company purchases bonds issued by the subsidiary, and the constructive gain or loss is assigned to the subsidiary.

[3]*APB Opinion No. 21,* "Interest on Receivables and Payables," which generally requires the effective interest method of amortization, does not apply to "transactions between parent and subsidiary companies and between subsidiaries of a common parent." Paragraph 3f.

Acquisition of Parent Company Bonds

Assume that Sugar Corporation is an 80 percent owned affiliate of Peach Corporation and that Peach Corporation sells $1,000,000 par of 10 percent, ten-year mortgage bonds at par value to the public on January 2, 19X6. One year later, on December 31, 19X6, Sugar purchases $100,000 of these outstanding bonds for $104,500 through the bond market. The purchase by Sugar results in the constructive retirement of $100,000 of Peach bonds and a constructive loss of $4,500 ($104,500 paid to retire bonds with a book value of $100,000).

Peach adjusts its investment income and investment accounts at December 31, 19X6 to record the constructive loss under the equity method of accounting. The entry on Peach's books is:

Income from Sugar	$4,500	
Investment in Sugar		$4,500

    To adjust income from Sugar for the constructive loss on bonds.

Without this entry, the income of Peach on an equity basis would not equal consolidated net income.

The $4,500 constructive loss is charged against Peach's share of Sugar's reported income because Peach is the issuing company for the bonds. Under the agency theory, the full amount of any constructive gain or loss on bonds is assigned to the issuing affiliate. Since the parent company is the issuing affiliate, the analysis is similar to one for a downstream sale, and the full amount is charged to Peach and to consolidated net income.

The $4,500 constructive loss appears in the consolidated income statement of Peach Corporation and Subsidiary for 19X6, and the 10 percent mortgage bond issue is reported at $900,000 in the consolidated balance sheet at December 31, 19X6. This is accomplished through the following working paper adjustment:

Loss on constructive retirement bonds	$ 4,500	
10% mortgage bonds payable	100,000	
Investment in bonds		$104,500

    To enter loss and eliminate reciprocal bond investment and liability amounts.

Gains and losses on the extinguishment of debt, if material, are classified as extraordinary items under *FASB Statement No. 4,* "Reporting Gains and Losses from Extinguishment of Debt."

Acquisition of Subsidiary Bonds

Assume that Sugar sold $1,000,000 par of 10 percent, ten-year mortgage bonds to the public on January 2, 19X6 and that Peach acquires $100,000 par of these bonds for $104,500 at December 31, 19X6 in the bond market. The purchase by Peach results in a constructive retirement of $100,000 par of Sugar bonds and a constructive loss of $4,500 to the consolidated entity. Only 80 percent of the constructive loss is charged to majority stockholders because the purchase of subsidiary bonds is equivalent to an upstream sale situation, where the intercompany transactions affect minority interest income.

In accounting for its investment in Sugar under the equity method, Peach recognizes 80 percent of the constructive loss with the following entry:

Income from Sugar	$3,600	
Investment in Sugar		$3,600

The consolidation working paper adjustment in the year of the intercompany bond purchase is the same as that illustrated for the intercompany purchase of

Peach bonds. But the $3,600 decrease in consolidated net income (to equate it with the one-line consolidation effect) consists of the $4,500 constructive loss less the $900 minority interest share of the loss, which reduces minority interest income and thereby increases consolidated net income.

To summarize, when the parent company is the issuing affiliate, no allocation of gains and losses from intercompany bond transactions is necessary. But when the subsidiary is the issuing affiliate, intercompany gains and losses on bonds must be allocated between consolidated net income and minority interest income in the consolidated income statement. In a one-line consolidation, the parent company recognizes only its proportionate share of the constructive gain or loss on bonds issued by a subsidiary.

PARENT COMPANY BONDS PURCHASED BY SUBSIDIARY

A constructive retirement of parent company bonds occurs when the outstanding bonds of the parent are purchased by an affiliated company. The purchasing subsidiary records the amount paid as an investment in bonds. This is the only entry made by either the purchasing or the issuing affiliate at the time of intercompany purchase. Thus, any gain or loss that results from the constructive retirement is *not* recorded in the separate accounts of the affiliated companies, but rather is reflected in the difference between the bond liability and bond investment accounts on the books of the parent and subsidiary companies.

To illustrate assume that Sue is a 70 percent owned subsidiary of Pam acquired at its $56,000 book value on December 31, 19X2 when Sue had capital stock of $50,000 and retained earnings of $30,000. Pam had $100,000 par of 10 percent bonds outstanding with a $1,000 unamortized premium on January 1, 19X4 at which time Sue Company purchased $10,000 par of these bonds for $9,500 from an investment broker. This purchase results in a constructive retirement of 10 percent of Pam's bonds and a $600 constructive gain, computed as follows:

Book value of bonds purchased 10% × ($100,000 par + $1,000 premium)	$10,100
Purchase price	9,500
Constructive gain on bond retirement	$ 600

The only entry Sue makes at the time the Pam bonds are purchased is:

Investment in Pam bonds	$9,500	
Cash		$9,500

To record acquisition of Pam bonds at 95.

Equity Method

If consolidated financial statements were prepared immediately after the constructive retirement, the working paper entry to eliminate the intercompany bond investment and liability balances would include the $600 gain as follows:

January 1, 19X4		
10% bonds payable	$10,000	
Premium on bonds	100	
Investment in Pam bonds		$9,500
Gain on retirement of bonds		600

As a result of this working paper entry, the consolidated income statement reflects the gain, the investment in Pam bonds is eliminated, and the consolidated balance sheet shows the bond liability to holders outside the consolidated entity at $90,900 ($90,000 par plus $900 unamortized premium).

During 19X4 Pam will amortize the bond premium on its separate books and Sue will amortize the discount on its bond investment. Assuming that interest is paid on January 1 and July 1, that the bonds mature on January 1, 19X9 (five years after purchase), and that straight-line amortization is used, Pam will amortize 20 percent of the bond premium and Sue will amortize 20 percent of the discount as follows:

PAM'S BOOKS			SUE'S BOOKS		
July 1					
Interest expense	$5,000		Cash	$500	
Cash		$5,000	Interest income		$500
($100,000 par × 10% × ½ year)			($10,000 par × 10% × ½ year)		
December 31					
Interest expense	$5,000		Interest receivable	$500	
Interest payable		$5,000	Interest income		$500
($100,000 par × 10% × ½ year)			($10,000 par × 10% × ½ year)		
December 31					
Premium on bonds	$ 200		Investment in Pam bonds	$100	
Interest expense		$ 200	Interest income		$100
($1,000 premium/5 years)			($500 discount/5 years)		

At December 31, 19X4, after the foregoing entries are posted, the ledgers of Pam and Sue will show the following balances:

Pam's Books

10% bonds payable	$100,000
Premium on bonds	800
Interest expense	9,800

Sue's Books

Investment in Pam bonds	$9,600
Interest income	1,100

The difference between the bond investment ($9,600) and 10 percent of Pam's bond liability ($10,080) is now $480 rather than $600. The reason is that there has been a piecemeal realization and recognition of the constructive gain on the separate books of Pam and Sue. This piecemeal recognition occurred during 19X4 as Pam amortized $20 premium and Sue amortized $100 discount on bonds that were constructively retired on January 1, 19X4. This difference is reflected in interest expense and interest income accounts relating to the constructively retired bonds. That is, interest income of $1,100 less 10 percent of $9,800 interest expense equals $120, or 20 percent of the original constructive gain. The working paper entries to eliminate reciprocal bond accounts at December 31, 19X4 are:

10% bonds payable	$10,000	
Premium on bonds	80	
Investment in Pam bonds		$9,600
Gain on retirement of bonds		480

Interest income	$ 1,100	
Interest expense		$ 980
Gain on retirement of bonds		120
Interest payable	$ 500	
Interest receivable		$ 500

Since 19X4 is the year in which the bonds are constructively retired, the combined gain that is entered by these working paper entries is $600, the original gain. If the working paper entries were combined, the gain would appear as a single amount. Note that the amount of piecemeal recognition of a constructive gain or loss is always the difference between the intercompany interest expense and interest income amounts that are eliminated. The fact that the piecemeal recognition was 20 percent of the $600 gain is the result of straight-line amortization, a relationship that would not hold under the effective interest method.

Separate company financial statements for Pam and Sue are included in the first two columns of the consolidation working papers in Exhibit 7–1. Except for the investment in Sue and the income from Sue accounts, the amounts shown reflect all previous assumptions and computations.

Pam's investment income of $2,020 is computed:

70% of Sue's reported income of $2,200	$1,540
Add: Constructive gain on bonds	600
	2,140
Less: Piecemeal recognition of constructive gain	
($600/5 years)	120
Income from Sue	$2,020

Separate entries on the books of Pam to record the investment income from Sue under a one-line consolidation are:

Investment in Sue	$1,540	
Income from Sue		$1,540

    To record investment income from Sue ($2,200 × 70%).

Investment in Sue	$ 600	
Income from Sue		$ 600

    To adjust income from Sue for 100% of the $600 constructive gain on bonds.

Income from Sue	$ 120	
Investment in Sue		$ 120

    To adjust income from Sue for the piecemeal recognition of the constructive gain on bonds that occurred during 19X4. (Either $600 gain/5 years or $1,100 interest income—$980 interest expense.)

The $600 constructive gain is added to Pam's share of the reported income of Sue because it is realized from the consolidated viewpoint. This constructive gain is recognized on the separate books of the affiliated companies as they continue to account for the $10,000 par of bonds deemed to be constructively retired on January 1, 19X4.

Pam's investment income for 19X4 is increased by $480 from the constructive retirement of the bonds ($600 constructive gain less $120 piecemeal recognition of the gain). In the years 19X5, 19X6, 19X7, and 19X8, Pam's investment income will be reduced $120 each year as the constructive gain is recognized on the separate books of Pam and Sue. In other words, in addition to recording its share of the reported income of Sue in each of these four years, Pam makes the following entry to adjust its income from Sue for the piecemeal recognition of the constructive gain:

PAM CORPORATION AND SUBSIDIARY
CONSOLIDATION WORKING PAPERS
FOR THE YEAR ENDED DECEMBER 31, 19X4

	Pam	70% Sue	Adjustments and Eliminations		Minority Interest	Consolidated Statements
Income Statement						
Sales	$ 40,000	$ 20,000				$ 60,000
Income from Sue	2,020		c 2,020			
Gain on retirement of bonds			a	480		600
			b	120		
Interest income		1,100	b 1,100			
Expenses including cost of sales	19,100*	18,900*				38,000*
Interest expense	9,800*		b	980		8,820*
Minority interest income ($2,200 × 30%)					$ 660	660*
Net income	$ 13,120	$ 2,200				$ 13,120
Retained Earnings						
Retained earnings—Pam	$ 49,000					$ 49,000
Retained earnings—Sue		$ 40,000	d 40,000			
Add: Net income	13,120✓	2,200✓				13,120
Retained earnings December 31, 19X4	$ 62,120	$ 42,200				$ 62,120
Balance Sheet						
Other assets	$398,800	$191,000				$589,800
Interest receivable		500		e 500		
Investment in Sue	65,020			c 2,020		
				d 63,000		
Investment in Pam bonds		9,600		a 9,600		
	$463,820	$201,100				$589,800
Other liabilities	$ 95,900	$108,900				$204,800
Interest payable	5,000		e 500			4,500
10% bonds payable	100,000		a 10,000			90,000
Premium on bonds	800		a 80			720
Common stock	200,000	50,000	d 50,000			200,000
Retained earnings	62,120✓	42,200✓				62,120
	$463,820	$201,100				
Minority interest January 1, 19X4				d 27,000	27,000	
Minority interst December 31, 19X4					$27,660	27,660
						$589,800

*Deduct.

Exhibit 7–1 *Parent Company Bonds Held by Subsidiary*

Income from Sue $120
    Investment in Sue $120

At January 1, 19X9, the maturity date of the bonds, the full amount of the constructive gain will have been recognized and Pam's investment in Sue account will be equal to 70 percent of the equity of Sue.

The working paper entries to consolidate the financial statements of Pam Corporation and Subsidiary for 19X4 (see Exhibit 7–1) are reproduced in general journal form:

a	10 % bonds payable	$10,000	
	Premium on bonds	80	
	Gain on retirement of bonds		$ 480
	Investment in Pam bonds		9,600
	To enter gain and eliminate reciprocal bond investment and bond liability amounts.		
b	Interest income	$ 1,100	
	Interest expense		$ 980
	Gain on retirement of bonds		120
	To eliminate reciprocal interest income and interest expense amounts.		
c	Income from Sue	$ 2,020	
	Investment in Sue		$ 2,020
	To establish reciprocity.		
d	Retained earnings—Sue	$40,000	
	Common stock—Sue	50,000	
	Investment in Sue		$63,000
	Minority interest January 1, 19X4		27,000
	To eliminate reciprocal investment and equity accounts and set up beginning minority interest.		
e	Interest payable	$ 500	
	Interest receivable		$ 500
	To eliminate reciprocal interest payable and interest receivable amounts.		

The first working paper entry eliminates 10 percent of Pam's bond liability and Sue's bond investment and also enters $480 of the gain on retirement of bonds. This $480 is that part of the $600 constructive gain that has not been recognized on the separate books of Pam and Sue as of December 31, 19X4.

Reciprocal interest expense and interest income are eliminated in entry b. The difference between the interest expense and interest income amounts represents that part of the constructive gain that was recognized on the separate books of Pam and Sue through amortization in 19X4. This amount is $120, and when credited to the gain on retirement of bonds, brings the gain up to the original $600. As mentioned earlier, if entries a and b had been combined, the constructive gain would have been entered in the working papers as one amount.

Working paper entry c eliminates investment income and adjusts the investment in Sue account to its beginning-of-the-period balance. Entry d eliminates Pam's investment in Sue, and the equity accounts of Sue, and establishes the beginning-of-the-period minority interest.

Entry e of the consolidation working papers eliminates reciprocal interest payable and interest receivable amounts on the intercompany bonds. This results in showing interest payable in the consolidated balance sheet at $4,500, the nominal interest payable for one-half year on the $90,000 par of bonds held outside of the consolidated entity. Note that minority interest computations in Exhibit 7–1 are not affected by the intercompany bond holdings. This is because Pam issued the bonds and the full amount ol the constructive gain is assigned to the issuing company.

Incomplete Equity and Cost Methods

If an incomplete equity method of accounting or the cost method had been used by Pam in accounting for its investment in Sue, Pam's separate financial statements would show balances that differ from those illustrated under the equity method as follows:

	Equity Method	Incomplete Equity Method	Cost Method
Income Statement			
Income from Sue	$ 2,020	$ 1,540	—
Pam's net income	13,120	12,640	$11,100
Retained Earnings			
Retained earnings January 1, 19X4	49,000	49,000	42,000
Net income	13,120	12,640	11,100
Retained earnings December 31, 19X4	62,120	61,640	53,100
Balance Sheet			
Investment in Sue	65,020	64,540	56,000
Retained earnings December 31, 19X4	62,120	61,640	53,100

Assuming that Pam has used an incomplete equity method of accounting for its investment in Sue and has not adjusted for the constructive gain, the following working paper entry would adjust Pam's accounts to the equity method:

Incomplete Equity Method		
Investment in Sue	$480	
Income from Sue		$480

The conversion entry that would be required if the cost method had been used would be as follows:

Cost Method		
Investment in Sue	$9,020	
Retained earnings January 1, 19X4		$7,000
Income from Sue		2,020

After the conversion entry (incomplete equity to equity or cost to equity) is entered in the working papers, all other working paper entries to consolidate the financial statements of Pam and Sue for 19X4 are the same as those illustrated in Exhibit 7–1 under the equity method.

Effect on Consolidated Statements in Subsequent Years

In subsequent years until the intercompany bonds are retired, Pam and Sue will continue to account for the bonds on their separate books—reporting interest expense (Pam) of $980 and interest income (Sue) of $1,100. The $120 difference is recognized on Pam's separate books as an adjustment of investment income. In consolidated financial statements for 19X5 through 19X8, all balances related to the intercompany bonds are eliminated. The year-end balances related to the intercompany bonds on the separate books of Pam and Sue are shown in Exhibit 7–2.

PAM'S BOOKS

| | December 31, | | | |
	19X5	19X6	19X7	19X8
Interest expense	$ 9,800	$ 9,800	$ 9,800	$ 9,800
Interest payable	5,000	5,000	5,000	5,000
Bonds payable	100,000	100,000	100,000	100,000
Premium on bonds	600	400	200	—

SUE'S BOOKS

| | December 31, | | | |
	19X5	19X6	19X7	19X8
Interest income	$ 1,100	$ 1,100	$ 1,100	$ 1,100
Interest receivable	500	500	500	500
Investment in Pam bonds	9,700	9,800	9,900	10,000

Exhibit 7–2   Year-end Account Balances Relating to Intercompany Bonds

A single adjusting and eliminating entry in the consolidation working papers for 19X5 could be used for items relating to the intercompany bonds:

Interest income	$ 1,100	
Interest payable	500	
10% bonds payable	10,000	
Premium on bonds	60	
Interest expense		$ 980
Interest receivable		500
Investment in Pam bonds		9,700
Investment in Sue		480

This entry eliminates reciprocal interest income and interest expense amounts, reciprocal interest receivable and payable amounts, and reciprocal bond investment and bond liability amounts. The remaining difference of $480 is credited to the investment in Sue account to establish reciprocity between Pam's investment in Sue and the equity accounts of Sue at the beginning of 19X5. This is necessary because Pam increased its investment account in 19X4 when it adjusted its investment income account for the constructive gain. In other words, Pam's investment in Sue account exceeded its underlying book value in Sue by $480 at December 31, 19X4. The 19X5 working paper entry to adjust the investment in Sue account establishes reciprocity with the equity accounts of Sue and is entered in the consolidation working papers before reciprocal investment and equity amounts are eliminated.

Similar working paper adjustments are necessary in 19X6, 19X7, and 19X8. For example, the consolidation working paper credit to the investment in Sue account will be $360 in 19X6, $240 in 19X7, and $120 in 19X8.

SUBSIDIARY BONDS PURCHASED BY PARENT

The illustration in this section is similar to that for Pam and Sue, except that the subsidiary is the issuing affiliate and the constructive retirement of bonds results in a loss to the consolidated entity.

Pro Corporation owns a 90 percent interest in the voting common stock of Sky Corporation, having purchased its interest in Sky at its book value of $922,500 a number of years ago when Sky's capital stock was $1,000,000 and its retained earnings were $25,000. At December 31, 19X3 Sky had $1,000,000 par of 10 percent bonds outstanding with unamortized discount of $30,000. These bonds have interest payment dates of January 1 and July 1 and mature in five years, on January 1, 19X9.

On January 2, 19X4, Pro Corporation purchases 50 percent of Sky's outstanding bonds for $515,000 cash. This transaction results in a loss of $30,000 from the viewpoint of the consolidated entity because a liability of $485,000 (50 percent of $970,000 book value of the bonds) is constructively retired at a cost of $515,000. The loss is assigned to Sky Corporation under the theory that the management of the parent company acts as agent for Sky, the issuing company, in all intercompany bond transactions.

During 19X4 Sky records interest expense on the bonds of $106,000 [($1,000,000 par × 10%) + $6,000 discount amortization]. Of this interest expense, $53,000 relates to the intercompany bonds. Pro records interest income from its investment in bonds during 19X4 of $47,000 [($500,000 par × 10%) − $3,000 premium amortization]. The $6,000 difference between the interest expense and the interest income on the intercompany bonds reflects the recognition of one-fifth of the constructive loss during 19X4. At December 31, l9X4, $24,000 of the constructive loss has not been recognized on the books of Pro and Sky through premium amortization (Pro's books) and discount amortization (Sky's books).

Equity Method

Sky reports net income of $75,000 for 19X4, and Pro computes its $45,900 income from Sky as follows:

90% of Sky's $75,000 reported income	$67,500
Deduct: $30,000 constructive loss × 90%	− 27,000
Add: $6,000 recognition of constructive loss × 90%	+ 5,400
Investment income from Sky	$45,900

The journal entries that Pro makes to account for its investment in Sky during 19X4 are:

December 31, 19X4

Investment in Sky	$67,500	
Income from Sky		$67,500

   To record 90% of Sky's reported income for 19X4.

December 31, 19X4

Income from Sky	$27,000	
Investment in Sky		$27,000

   To adjust investment income from Sky for 90% of the loss on the constructive retirement of Sky's bonds. (This entry could be made on January 1, 19X4.)

December 31, 19X4

Investment in Sky	$ 5,400	
Income from Sky		$ 5,400

   To adjust investment income from Sky for 90% of the $6,000 piecemeal recognition of the constructive loss on Sky bonds during 19X4.

In future years until the bonds mature, Pro's income from Sky should be computed by adding $5,400 annually to its share of the reported income of Sky. Financial statements for Pro and Sky for 19X4 are presented in Exhibit 7–3. Pro Corporation's investment in Sky account at December 31, 19X4 has a balance of $1,058,400. This balance is equal to the underlying book value of Pro's investment in Sky at January 1, 19X4 plus $45,900 investment income from Sky for 19X4:

INCOME STATEMENTS
FOR THE YEAR ENDED DECEMBER 31, 19X4

	Pro	Sky
Sales	$2,575,000	$1,425,000
Income from Sky	45,900	—
Interest income	47,000	—
Total revenue	2,667,900	1,425,000
Expenses (including cost of sales)	2,167,900	1,244,000
Interest expense	—	106,000
Total expenses	2,167,900	1,350,000
Net income	$ 500,000	$ 75,000

RETAINED EARNINGS STATEMENTS
FOR THE YEAR ENDED DECEMBER 31, 19X4

Retained earnings January 1, 19X4	$1,300,000	$ 125,000
Add: Net income	500,000	75,000
Retained earnings December 31, 19X4	$1,800,000	$ 200,000

BALANCE SHEETS
AT DECEMBER 31, 19X4

Assets		
Other assets	$3,404,600	$2,500,000
Interest receivable	25,000	—
Investment in Sky (90%)	1,058,400	—
Investment in Sky bonds	512,000	—
Total assets	$5,000,000	$2,500,000
Liabilities and Stockholders' Equity		
Other liabilities	$1,200,000	$ 274,000
Interest payable	—	50,000
10% bonds payable	—	1,000,000
Discount on bonds	—	(24,000)
Capital stock	2,000,000	1,000,000
Retained earnings	1,800,000	200,000
Total liabilities and equity	$5,000,000	$2,500,000

Exhibit 7–3 *Comparative Financial Statements for Pro and Sky—19X4*

Investment in Sky January 1, 19X4 ($1,125,000 × 90%)	$1,012,500
Add: Income from Sky	45,900
Investment in Sky December 31, 19X4	$1,058,400

Consolidated financial statement working papers for Pro Corporation and Subsidiary are presented in Exhibit 7–4. The constructive loss of $30,000 on the intercompany bonds appears in the consolidated income statement for 19X4. Since $500,000 par of Sky bonds have been constructively retired, the consolidated balance sheet shows bonds payable of $500,000 and discount on bonds of $12,000 related to the bonds held outside of the consolidated entity.

Effect of Constructive Loss on Minority Interest Income and Consolidated Net Income   The minority interest income for 19X4 is $5,100 [($75,000 − $30,000 + $6,000) × 10%]. Since the constructive loss is assigned to Sky, the minority interest is charged for 10 percent of the $30,000 constructive loss and credited for 10 percent of the $6,000 piecemeal recognition of the constructive loss during 19X4. Accordingly, minority interest income for 19X4 is 10 percent of Sky's

PRO CORPORATION AND SUBSIDIARY
CONSOLIDATION WORKING PAPERS—FOR THE YEAR ENDED DECEMBER 31, 19X4

	Pro	90% Sky	Adjustments and Eliminations		Minority Interest	Consolidated Statements
Income Statement Sales	$2,575,000	$1,425,000				$4,000,000
Income from Sky	45,900		c	45,900		
Interest income	47,000		b	47,000		
Expenses including cost of sales	2,167,900*	1,244,000*				3,411,900*
Interest expense		106,000*	b	53,000		53,000*
Loss on retirement of bonds			a 24,000 b 6,000			30,000*
Minority interest income					$ 5,100	5,100*
Net income	$ 500,000	$ 75,000				$ 500,000
Retained Earnings Retained earnings—Pro	$1,300,000					$1,300,000
Retained earnings—Sky		$ 125,000	d	125,000		
Add: Net income	500,000✓	75,000✓				500,000
Retained earnings December 31, 19X4	$1,800,000	$ 200,000				$1,800,000
Balance Sheet Other assets	$3,404,600	$2,500,000				$5,904,600
Interest receivable	25,000		e	25,000		
Investment in Sky	1,058,400		c 45,900 d 1,012,500			
Investment in Sky bonds	512,000		a	512,000		
	$5,000,000	$2,500,000				$5,904,600
Other liabilities	$1,200,000	$ 274,000				$1,474,000
Interest payable		50,000	e 25,000			25,000
10% bonds payable		1,000,000	a 500,000			500,000
Discount on bonds		24,000*		a 12,000		12,000*
Capital stock	2,000,000	1,000,000	d 1,000,000			2,000,000
Retained earnings	1,800,000✓	200,000✓				1,800,000
	$5,000,000	$2,500,000				
Minority interest January 1, 19X4				d 112,500	112,500	
Minority interest December 31, 19X4					$117,600	117,600
						$5,904,600

* Deduct

Exhibit 7–4   Subsidiary Bonds Held by Parent

$51,000 realized income, and *not* 10 percent of Sky's $75,000 reported net income.

The effect of the constructive loss is to reduce consolidated net income for 19X4 by $21,600. This reduction is reflected in the consolidated income statement through the inclusion of the $30,000 loss on the constructive retirement of the bonds, through the elimination of interest income of $47,000 and interest expense of $53,000, and through the reduction of minority interest income by $2,400 (from $7,500 based on reported net income of Sky to $5,100 minority interest income for the year). The effect can be analyzed as follows:

CONSOLIDATED NET INCOME—19X4

Decreased by:	
Constructive loss	$30,000
Elimination of interest income	47,000
Total decreases	$77,000
Increased by:	
Elimination of interest expense	$53,000
Reduction of minority interest income	
($7,500 − $5,100)	2,400
Total increases	$55,400
Effect on consolidated net income for 19X4	$21,600

Observe that the reduction of minority interest income is similar to the reduction of expenses. A decrease in minority interest income increases consolidated net income and vice versa.

Consolidation Working Paper Entries   The entries shown in the consolidation working papers of Exhibit 7–4 are similar to those in the Pam/Sue illustration in Exhibit 7–1 except for amounts and the shift to a constructive loss situation. As in the previous illustration, working papers entries a and b are separated for illustrative purposes, but they could have been combined into a single entry as follows:

Loss on retirement of bonds	$ 30,000	
Interest income	47,000	
10% bonds payable	500,000	
Discount on bonds		$ 12,000
Investment in Sky bonds		512,000
Interest expense		53,000

Incomplete Equity and Cost Methods

If Pro had used an incomplete equity method or the cost method in accounting for its investment in Sky, its separate financial statements for 19X4 would contain amounts that differ from those under the equity method as follows:

	Equity Method	Incomplete Equity Method	Cost Method
Income Statement			
Income from Sky	$ 45,900	$ 67,500	—
Pro's net income	500,000	521,600	$ 454,100
Retained Earnings			
Retained earnings January 1	1,300,000	1,300,000	1,210,000
Net income	500,000	521,600	454,100
Retained earnings December 31	1,800,000	1,821,600	1,664,100

	Equity Method	Incomplete Equity Method	Cost Method
Balance Sheet			
Investment in Sky	1,058,400	1,080,000	922,500
Retained earnings December 31	1,800,000	1,821,600	1,664,100

An entry in the consolidation working papers to convert from an incomplete equity to the equity method of accounting for 19X4 would be as follows:

Income from Sky	$21,600	
Investment in Sky		$21,600

Since the only difference between the incomplete and complete equity methods lies in the constructive gain, the conversion entry only affects the year 19X4. The amount is 90 percent of the $30,000 constructive loss less 90 percent of the $6,000 piecemeal recognition of the loss.

If the cost method had been used by Pro, the cost-to-equity working paper conversion for the 19X4 consolidation would be:

Investment in Sky	$135,900	
Income from Sky		$45,900
Retained earnings January 1		90,000

When the conversion entry under the incomplete equity method or the cost method is entered in the working papers, the adjusted amounts of Pro will reflect the equity method of accounting as a one-line consolidation. Subsequently, the remaining working paper entries to consolidate the statements of Pro and Sky will be the same as those illustrated in Exhibit 7–4 under the equity method.

Effect on Consolidated Statements in Subsequent Years

The loss on the retirement of bonds appears in the consolidated income statement only in the year in which the bonds are constructively retired. In subsequent years the portion of the constructive loss that has not been recognized through premium and discount amortization on the separate books of Pro and Sky will be allocated between the investment account (the majority interest) and minority interest. For example, the combined working paper entry to eliminate the bond investment and bonds payable and the interest income and interest expense amounts in 19X5 would be as follows:

Investment in Sky	$ 21,600	
Minority interest—beginning	2,400	
Interest income	47,000	
10% bonds payable	500,000	
Discount on bonds		$ 9,000
Investment in Sky bonds		509,000
Interest expense		53,000

The allocation of the unrecognized loss between the investment in Sky ($21,600) and minority interest ($2,400) in the entry is dictated by the assignment of the constructive loss to Sky. Since the loss is a subsidiary loss, minority interest must share in the loss. In computing minority interest for 19X5, 10 percent of the

$6,000 constructive loss recognized in 19X5 is added to the minority interest share of income reported by Sky. This adjustment of minority interest income is required each year through 19X8. By December 31, 19X8 the bond investment will have been reduced to $500,000 through premium amortization, and the intercompany bond liability will have been increased to $500,000 through discount amortization.

The effect of the intercompany bond holdings on consolidated net income for 19X5 through 19X8 is to increase consolidated net income by $5,400 each year. Under the equity method of accounting, Pro's income from Sky and net income will also be increased by $5,400 in each of the years. Computations showing the effect on consolidated net income for the years 19X5 through 19X8 follow:

CONSOLIDATED NET INCOME—19X5 THROUGH 19X8

Increased by:	
Elimination of interest expense	$53,000
Decreased by:	
Elimination of interest income	$47,000
Increase in minority interest income	
($6,000 piecemeal recognition × 10%)	600
Total decreases	$47,600
Annual effect on consolidated net income	$ 5,400

Exhibit 7–5 summarizes the intercompany bond account balances that appear on the separate books of Pro and Sky at year-end 19X5 through 19X8. The exhibit also summarizes the consolidation working paper adjustments that are required to consolidate the financial statements of Pro and Sky for years subsequent to the year of intercompany purchase of Sky bonds. Since the investment in Sky account is involved, the working paper entries shown in Exhibit 7–5 are made before reciprocal investment and subsidiary equity amounts are eliminated.

The working paper entries shown in Exhibit 7–5 eliminate those amounts that would have been eliminated from the separate statements of Pro and Sky if the bonds had in fact been retired in 19X4. The objective is to produce the consolidated financial statements as they would have appeared if Sky had purchased and retired its own bonds.

CONSOLIDATION IN YEARS AFTER INTERCOMPANY BOND PURCHASE UNDER DIFFERENT ASSUMPTIONS

This section illustrates consolidation procedures in years after an intercompany bond purchase under several different parent company accounting assumptions. The first consolidation working paper (Exhibit 7–6) shows consolidation when the parent has accounted for its subsidiary by the equity method. The next two working paper exhibits show consolidation procedures when an incomplete equity method and a cost method of accounting are used and a conversion to equity is the first step in the working papers. This is followed with the same example using the traditional approach to consolidation working papers under an incomplete equity and a cost method of accounting.

Pima Corporation acquired an 80 percent interest in Sioux Corporation on January 1, 19X4 at its book value of $12,000,000 when the stockholders' equity of Sioux consisted of $10,000,000 common stock and $5,000,000 retained earnings. The only intercompany transactions between the two companies occurred on December 31, 19X4 when Sioux purchased 75 percent of Pima's $1,000,000 par, 10 percent outstanding bonds for $700,000. These bonds were issued at par

SUMMARY OF INTERCOMPANY BOND ACCOUNT BALANCES ON SEPARATE BOOKS

December 31,	19X5	19X6	19X7	19X8
Pro's Books				
Investment in Sky bonds	$ 509,000	$ 506,000	$ 503,000	$ 500,000
Interest income	47,000	47,000	47,000	47,000
Interest receivable	25,000	25,000	25,000	25,000
Sky's Books				
10% bonds payable	$1,000,000	$1,000,000	$1,000,000	$1,000,000
Discount on bonds	18,000	12,000	6,000	—
Interest expense	106,000	106,000	106,000	106,000
Interest payable	50,000	50,000	50,000	50,000

SUMMARY OF CONSOLIDATION WORKING PAPER ADJUSTMENTS

December 31,	19X5	19X6	19X7	19X8
Debits				
Investment in Sky (90%)*	$ 21,600	$ 16,200	$ 10,800	$ 5,400
Minority interest (10%)*	2,400	1,800	1,200	600
Interest income	47,000	47,000	47,000	47,000
10% bonds payable†	500,000	500,000	500,000	500,000
Interest payable	25,000	25,000	25,000	25,000
Credits				
Discount on bonds†	$ 9,000	$ 6,000	$ 3,000	$ —
Investment in Sky bonds	509,000	506,000	503,000	500,000
Interest expense†	53,000	53,000	53,000	53,000
Interest receivable	25,000	25,000	25,000	25,000

*The unrecognized portion of the constructive loss at the beginning of the year is charged 90% to the investment in Sky account and 10% to minority interest.
†Elimination of 50% ot Sky's bonds, 50% of the unamortized discount on the bonds, and 50% of the current interest expense on the bonds.

Exhibit 7–5 *Subsidiary Bonds Held by Parent—Years Subsequent to Year of Intercompany Purchase*

and mature in five years on December 31, 19X9. During 19X4 Sioux reported net income of $2,500,000 and paid $2,000,000 dividends. Comparisons of Pima's income from Sioux for 19X4 and its investment in Sioux at December 31, 19X4 under the equity, incomplete equity, and cost methods of accounting are as follows:

	Equity Method	Incomplete Equity Method	Cost Method
Income (dividends) from Sioux	$ 2,050,000	$ 2,000,000	$ 1,600,000
Investment in Sioux 80%	12,450,000	12,400,000	12,000,000

The $50,000 differences in Pima's income and investment in Sioux amounts under the equity and incomplete equity methods are due to the $50,000 constructive gain on the intercompany purchase of bonds [($1,000,000 × 75%) − $700,000]. Since Pima's bonds were constructively retired, no part of the gain is allocated to minority interests. Pima's dividend income under the cost method differs from income from Sioux under the incomplete equity method by $400,000, or 80 percent of Sioux's $500,000 undistributed income from 19X4. Under the

PIMA CORPORATION AND SUBSIDIARY
CONSOLIDATION WORKING PAPERS
FOR THE YEAR ENDED DECEMBER 31, 19X5

	Pima	80% Sioux	Adjustments and Eliminations		Minority Interest	Consolidated Statements
Income Statement						
Sales	$20,000,000	$ 9,915,000				$29,915,000
Income from Sioux	2,390,000		b	2,390,000		
Interest income		85,000	a	85,000		
Interest expense	100,000*			a	75,000	25,000*
Other expenses	14,290,000*	7,000,000*				21,290,000*
Minority interest income					$ 600,000	600,000*
Net income	$ 8,000,000	$ 3,000,000				$ 8,000,000
Retained Earnings						
Retained earnings—Pima	$10,000,000					$10,000,000
Retained earnings—Sioux		$ 5,500,000	c	5,500,000		
Net income	8,000,000✓	3,000,000✓				8,000,000
Dividends	6,000,000*	2,000,000*	b	1,600,000	400,000*	6,000,000*
Retained earnings December 31, 19X5	$12,000,000	$ 6,500,000				$12,000,000
Balance Sheet						
Investment in Sioux	$13,240,000		a 50,000 b 790,000 c 12,400,000			
Bond investment—Pima		$ 710,000	a	710,000		
Other assets	36,760,000	17,290,000				$54,050,000
	$50,000,000	$18,000,000				$54,050,000
10% bonds payable	$ 1,000,000		a	750,000		$ 250,000
Other liabilities	17,000,000	$ 1,500,000				18,500,000
Capital stock	20,000,000	10,000,000	c	10,000,000		20,000,000
Retained earnings	12,000,000✓	6,500,000✓				12,000,000
	$50,000,000	$18,000,000				
Minority interest January 1, 19X5			c	3,100,000	3,100,000	
Minority interest December 31, 19X5					$3,300,000	3,300,000
						$54,050,000

Exhibit 7–6 *Intercompany Bonds After Acquisition—Equity Method*

cost method, Pima's investment in Sioux remains at its $12,000,000 cost on January 1, 19X4.

During 19X5 Sioux reported $3,000,000 net income and paid $2,000,000 dividends, and the only intercompany transactions between Pima and Sioux relate to the $75,000 interest ($1,000,000 par × 10% interest × 75% owned) that Pima paid to Sioux and the $1,600,000 dividends that Sioux paid to Pima. Pima's total interest expense for 19X5 is $100,000 and Sioux's interest income is $85,000, consisting of $75,000 nominal interest plus $10,000 discount amortization. The changes in Pima's investment in Sioux from acquisition to December 31, 19X5 are compared under the equity, incomplete equity, and cost methods of parent company accounting as follows.

	Equity Method	Incomplete Equity Method	Cost Method
Investment balance January 1, 19X4	$12,000,000	$12,000,000	$12,000,000
Income from Sioux—19X4	2,050,000	2,000,000	—
Dividends received	(1,600,000)	(1,600,000)	—
Investment balance December 31, 19X4	12,450,000	12,400,000	12,000,000
Income from Sioux—19X5:			
Equity in Sioux's income	2,400,000	2,400,000	—
Piecemeal recognition of gain on bonds	(10,000)	—	—
Dividends	(1,600,000)	(1,600,000)	—
Investment balance December 31, 19X5	$13,240,000	$13,200,000	$12,000,000

This information is reflected in comparative consolidation working papers for Pima and Sioux for 19X5 in Exhibit 7–6 for the equity method, Exhibit 7–7 for the incomplete equity method, and Exhibit 7–8 for the cost method. Under the equity method consolidation illustrated in Exhibit 7–6, Pima's net income of $8,000,000 is equal to consolidated net income, and its beginning and ending retained earnings are equal to the respective consolidated retained earnings amounts. The first working paper entry in Exhibit 7–6 eliminates intercompany interest income and interest expense amounts, intercompany bond investment and bond liability amounts, and credits the investment in Sioux for the $50,000 constructive gain that had not been recognized on the separate books of Pima and Sioux at the beginning of the period.

a	Interest income	$ 85,000	
	10% bonds payable	750,000	
	Interest expense		$ 75,000
	Bond investment—Pima		710,000
	Investment in Sioux 80%		50,000

The second working paper entry in Exhibit 7–6 eliminates the income from Sioux and 80 percent of dividends paid by Sioux and returns the investment in Sioux to its beginning of the period amount:

b	Income from Sioux	$2,390,000	
	Dividends		$1,600,000
	Investment in Sioux 80%		790,000

The last working paper entry eliminates reciprocal investment and equity amounts and enters beginning minority interest.

c	Common stock—Sioux	$10,000,000	
	Retained earnings—Sioux	5,500,000	
	Investment in Sioux 80%		$12,400,000
	Minority interest		3,100,000

Conversion to Equity Approach   These three working paper entries are also used in consolidating the financial statements of Pima and Sioux under an incomplete equity method (Exhibit 7–7) and the cost method (Exhibit 7–8) after an initial conversion to equity entry is entered in the working papers. The working paper entry in Exhibit 7–7 to convert from an incomplete equity to the equity method is as follows:

PIMA CORPORATION AND SUBSIDIARY
CONSOLIDATION WORKING PAPERS
FOR THE YEAR ENDED DECEMBER 31, 19X5

	Pima	80% Sioux	Adjustments and Eliminations			Minority Interest	Consolidated Statements
Income Statement							
Sales	$20,000,000	$ 9,915,000					$29,915,000
Income from Sioux	2,400,000		a	10,000			
			c	2,390,000			
Interest income		85,000	b	85,000			
Interest expense	100,000*			b	75,000		25,000*
Other expenses	14,290,000*	7,000,000*					21,290,000*
Minority interest income						$ 600,000	600,000*
Net income	$ 8,010,000	$ 3,000,000					$ 8,000,000
Retained Earnings							
Retained earnings—Pima	$ 9,950,000			a	50,000		$10,000,000
Retained earnings—Sioux		$ 5,500,000	d	5,500,000			
Net income	8,010,000✓	3,000,000✓					8,000,000
Dividends	6,000,000*	2,000,000*		c	1,600,000	400,000*	6,000,000*
Retained earnings December 31, 19X5	$11,960,000	$ 6,500,000					$12,000,000
Balance Sheet							
Investment in Sioux	$13,200,000			b	50,000		
			a	40,000	c	790,000		
				d	12,400,000		
Bond investment—Pima		$ 710,000		b	710,000		
Other assets	36,760,000	17,290,000					$54,050,000
	$49,960,000	$18,000,000					$54,050,000
10% bonds payable	$ 1,000,000		b	750,000			$ 250,000
Other liabilities	17,000,000	$ 1,500,000					18,500,000
Capital stock	20,000,000	10,000,000	d	10,000,000			20,000,000
Retained earnings	11,960,000✓	6,500,000✓					12,000,000
	$49,960,000	$18,000,000					
Minority interest January 1, 19X5				d	3,100,000	3,100,000	
Minority interest December 31, 19X5						$3,300,000	3,300,000
							$54,050,000

Exhibit 7–7 *Intercompany Bonds After Acquisition—Incomplete Equity Method*

a	Income from Sioux	$10,000	
	Investment in Sioux 80%	40,000	
	Retained earnings—Pima		$50,000

This working paper entry corrects Pima's beginning retained earnings for the $50,000 constructive gain that was not recorded under an incomplete equity method, and it adjusts income from Sioux for the $10,000 piecemeal recognition of the constructive gain that was not charged to investment income under the incomplete equity method. The $40,000 debit to investment in Sioux cor-

PIMA CORPORATION AND SUBSIDIARY
CONSOLIDATION WORKING PAPERS
FOR THE YEAR ENDED DECEMBER 31, 19X5

	Pima	80% Sioux	Adjustments and Eliminations		Minority Interest	Consolidated Statements
Income Statement						
Sales	$20,000,000	$ 9,915,000				$29,915,000
Dividend income	1,600,000		a 1,600,000			
Income from Sioux			c 2,390,000	a 2,390,000		
Interest income		85,000	b 85,000			
Interest expense	100,000*			b 75,000		25,000*
Other expenses	14,290,000*	7,000,000*				21,290,000*
Minority interest income					$ 600,000	600,000*
Net income	$ 7,210,000	$ 3,000,000				$ 8,000,000
Retained Earnings						
Retained earnings—Pima	$ 9,550,000			a 450,000		$10,000,000
Retained earnings—Sioux		$ 5,500,000	d 5,500,000			
Net income	7,210,000✔	3,000,000✔				8,000,000
Dividends	6,000,000*	2,000,000*		c 1,600,000	400,000*	6,000,000*
Retained earnings December 31, 19X5	$10,760,000	$ 6,500,000				$12,000,000
Balance Sheet						
Investment in Sioux	$12,000,000		a 1,240,000	b 50,000		
				c 790,000		
				d 12,400,000		
Bond investment—Pima		$ 710,000		b 710,000		
Other assets	36,760,000	17,290,000				$54,050,000
	$48,760,000	$18,000,000				$54,050,000
10% bonds payable	$ 1,000,000		b 750,000			$ 250,000
Other liabilities	17,000,000	$ 1,500,000				18,500,000
Capital stock	20,000,000	10,000,000	d 10,000,000			20,000,000
Retained earnings	10,760,000✔	6,500,000✔				12,000,000
	$48,760,000	$18,000,000				
Minority interest January 1, 19X5				d 3,100,000	3,100,000	
Minority interest December 31, 19X5					$3,300,000	3,300,000
						$54,050,000

Exhibit 7–8 Intercompany Bonds After Acquisition—Cost Method

rects that account for the constructive gain for 19X4 less piecemeal recognition for 19X5, neither of which was recorded under the incomplete equity method. The other working paper entries in Exhibit 7–7 are the same as those illustrated for the equity method.

The consolidation illustrated in Exhibit 7–8 assumes that Pima uses the cost method in accounting for its investment in Sioux and that the balance of its investment in Sioux account is equal to the $12,000,000 cost at January 1, 19X4. Entry a in the working papers of Exhibit 7–8 converts the accounts of Pima to an equity basis for working paper purposes.

a	Dividend income	$1,600,000	
	Investment in Sioux 80%	1,240,000	
	Income from Sioux		$2,390,000
	Retained earnings—Pima (beginning)		450,000

A cost-equity conversion schedule is probably the best explanation of this working paper entry. After the conversion entry is entered in the working papers of Exhibit 7–8, the other working paper entries are the same as if the equity method had been used. Pima could also convert its separate accounts to the equity method by entering an equivalent entry before closing its books for 19X5. The conversion schedule is as follows:

	Pima's Beginning Retained Earnings	Investment in Sioux	Income from Sioux	Dividend Income
Prior-Year's Effect				
80% of $500,000 undistributed income from 19X4	$400,000	$ 400,000		
Constructive gain for 19X4	50,000	50,000		
Current-Year's Effect				
Reclassify dividend income as investment decrease		(1,600,000)		$(1,600,000)
80% share of Sioux's $3,000,000 net income		2,400,000	$2,400,000	
Piecemeal recognition of gain ($50,000/5 years, or $85,000 interest income − $75,000 interest expense)		(10,000)	(10,000)	
Conversion entry amounts	$450,000	$1,240,000	$2,390,000	$(1,600,000)

Traditional Approach The financial statements of Pima and Sioux can be consolidated without an initial conversion to equity. Procedures under the traditional approach are shown in Exhibits 7–9 and 7–10.

If Pima has accounted for its investment in Sioux using an incomplete equity method as shown in Exhibit 7–9, the financial statements can be consolidated using the following set of working paper entries:

a	10% bonds payable	$ 750,000	
	Bond investment—Pima		$ 710,000
	Retained earnings—Pima January 1		40,000

To eliminate intercompany bond investment and bond liability amounts and correct Pima's beginning of the period retained earnings for the constructive gain.

b	Interest income	$ 85,000	
	Interest expense		$ 75,000
	Retained earnings		10,000

To eliminate intercompany interest income and expense and adjust for piecemeal recognition of the constructive gain.

PIMA CORPORATION AND SUBSIDIARY
CONSOLIDATION WORKING PAPERS—NO CONVERSION TO EQUITY
FOR THE YEAR ENDED DECEMBER 31, 19X5

	Pima	80% Sioux	Adjustments and Eliminations		Minority Interest	Consolidated Statements
Income Statement						
Sales	$20,000,000	$ 9,915,000				$29,915,000
Income from Sioux	2,400,000		c	2,400,000		
Interest income		85,000	b	85,000		
Interest expense	100,000*			b 75,000		25,000*
Other expenses	14,290,000*	7,000,000*				21,290,000*
Minority interest income					$ 600,000	600,000*
Net income	$ 8,010,000	$ 3,000,000				$ 8,000,000
Retained Earnings						
Retained earnings—Pima	$ 9,950,000		a	40,000		$10,000,000
			b	10,000		
Retained earnings—Sioux		$ 5,500,000	d	5,500,000		
Net income	8,010,000	3,000,000				8,000,000
Dividends	6,000,000*	2,000,000*		c 1,600,000	400,000*	6,000,000*
Retained earnings December 31, 19X5	$11,960,000	$ 6,500,000				$12,000,000
Balance Sheet						
Investment in Sioux	$13,200,000			c 800,000		
				d 12,400,000		
Bond investment in Pima		$ 710,000		a 710,000		
Other assets	36,760,000	17,290,000				$54,050,000
	$49,960,000	$18,000,000				$54,050,000
10% bonds payable	$ 1,000,000		a	750,000		$ 250,000
Other liabilities	17,000,000	$ 1,500,000				18,500,000
Capital stock	20,000,000	10,000,000	d	10,000,000		20,000,000
Retained earnings	11,960,000	6,500,000				12,000,000
	$49,960,000	$18,000,000				
Minority interest January 1, 19X5				d 3,100,000	3,100,000	
Minority interest December 31, 19X5					$3,300,000	3,300,000
						$54,050,000

*Deduct

Exhibit 7–9 *Intercompany Bonds After Acquisition—Incomplete Equity Method (Traditional Approach)*

c	Income from Sioux	$ 2,400,000	
	Dividends		$ 1,600,000
	Investment in Sioux		800,000

To eliminate investment income (as recorded by Pima), 80% of Sioux's dividends, and return the investment account to its beginning of the period balance.

d	Retained earnings—Sioux	$ 5,500,000	
	Capital stock—Sioux	10,000,000	
	Investment in Sioux		$12,400,000
	Minority interest January 1		3,100,000

To eliminate reciprocal investment and equity accounts and enter beginning of the period minority interest.

PIMA CORPORATION AND SUBSIDIARY
CONSOLIDATION WORKING PAPERS—NO CONVERSION TO EQUITY
FOR THE YEAR ENDED DECEMBER 31, 19X5

	Pima	80% Sioux	Adjustments and Eliminations			Minority Interest	Consolidated Statements
Income Statement							
Sales	$20,000,000	$ 9,915,000					$29,915,000
Dividend income	1,600,000		d	1,600,000			
Interest income		85,000	c	85,000			
Interest expense	100,000*				c 75,000		25,000*
Other expenses	14,290,000*	7,000,000*					21,290,000*
Minority interest income						$ 600,000	600,000*
Net income	$ 7,210,000	$ 3,000,000					$ 8,000,000
Retained Earnings							
Retained earnings—Pima	$ 9,450,000		a 400,000				$10,000,000
			b 40,000				
			c 10,000				
Retained earnings—Sioux		$ 5,500,000	e 5,500,000				
Net income	7,210,000	3,000,000					8,000,000
Dividends	6,000,000*	2,000,000*			d 1,600,000	400,000*	6,000,000*
Retained earnings December 31, 19X5	$10,760,000	$ 6,500,000					$12,000,000
Balance Sheet							
Investment in Sioux	$12,000,000		a 400,000		e 12,400,000		
Bond investment in Pima		$ 710,000			b 710,000		
Other assets	36,760,000	17,290,000					$54,050,000
	$48,760,000	$18,000,000					$54,050,000
10% bonds payable	$ 1,000,000		b 750,000				$ 250,000
Other liabilities	17,000,000	$ 1,500,000					18,500,000
Capital stock	20,000,000	10,000,000	e 10,000,000				20,000,000
Retained earnings	10,760,000	6,500,000					12,000,000
	$48,760,000	$18,000,000					
Minority interest January 1, 19X5					e 3,100,000	3,100,000	
Minority interest December 31, 19X5						$3,300,000	3,300,000
							$54,050,000
* Deduct							

Exhibit 7–10   *Intercompany Bonds After Acquisition—Cost Method (Traditional Approach)*

Now assume that Pima has used the cost method in accounting for its investment in Sioux, and that it consolidates the financial statements under the traditional approach without a conversion to equity. The working paper entries from Exhibit 7–10 are reproduced for convenient reference:

a	Investment in Sioux	$ 400,000	
	Retained earning—Pima January 1		$ 400,000

To take up 80% of Sioux's increase in stockholders' equity between the date of acquisition and the beginning of the current period.

b	10% bonds payable	$ 750,000	
	Bond investment—Pima		$ 710,000
	Retained earnings—Pima January 1		40,000

To eliminate intercompany bond investment and bond liability amounts and increase Pima's beginning of the period retained earnings for the constructive gain on the bonds.

c	Interest income	$ 85,000	
	Interest expense		$ 75,000
	Retained earnings—Pima January 1		10,000

To eliminate intercompany interest income and expense and adjust for piecemeal recognition of the constructive gain.

d	Dividend income	$ 1,600,000	
	Dividends		$ 1,600,000

To eliminate dividend income and 80% of Sioux's dividends.

e	Retained earnings—Sioux	$ 5,500,000	
	Capital stock—Sioux	10,000,000	
	Investment in Sioux		$12,400,000
	Minority interest January 1		3,100,000

To eliminate reciprocal investment and equity accounts and enter beginning of the period minority interest.

SUMMARY

Transactions in which one corporation acquires the outstanding bonds of an affiliated company result in constructive gains and losses except when the bonds are purchased at their book value. Constructive gains and losses are realized from the viewpoint of the consolidated entity when the bonds are purchased by an affiliate, and they should be reflected in the income of the parent company and consolidated net income in the year of purchase. Gains and losses on parent company bonds are similar to unrealized gains and losses on downstream sales and do not require allocation between minority and majority interests. But constructive gains and losses on bonds in which a subsidiary is the issuing entity should be allocated between minority interest and consolidated net income. Constructive gains or losses on intercompany bonds are recognized on the books of the purchasing and issuing corporations as they amortize differences between the book value and par value of bonds.

A summary illustration comparing the effect of constructive gains and losses from intercompany bond transactions on parent company and consolidated net incomes is presented in Exhibit 7–11.

Assumptions

1 Parent Company's income, excluding income from Subsidiary, was $100,000 for 19X6.
2 90 percent owned Subsidiary reported net income of $50,000 for 19X6.
3 $100,000 of 10 percent bonds payable are outstanding with $6,000 unamortized premium as of January 1, 19X6.
4 $50,000 par of the bonds were purchased for $51,500 on January 2, 19X6.
5 The bonds mature on January 1, 19X9.

	S Acquires P's Bonds (similar to downstream)	P Acquires S's Bonds (similar to upstream)
P's Net Income—Equity Method		
P's separate income	$100,000	$100,000
P's share of S's reported net income	45,000	45,000
Add: Constructive gain on bonds		
($53,000 − $51,500) × 100%	1,500	
($53,000 − $51,500) × 90%		1,350
Deduct: Piecemeal recognition of constructive gain		
($1,500 gain/3 years) × 100%	500*	
($1,500 gain/3 years) × 90%		450*
P's net income	$146,000	$145,900
Consolidated Net Income		
P's separate income plus S's net income	$150,000	$150,000
Add: Constructive gain on bonds	1,500	1,500
Eliminate: Interest expense	4,000	4,000
Interest income	4,500*	4,500*
Total realized income	151,000	151,000
Less: Minority interest income		
($50,000 × 10%)	5,000*	
($50,000 + $1,500 − $500) × 10%		5,100*
Consolidated net income	$146,000	$145,900

* Deduct.

　　P's net income and consolidated net income of $146,000 when S acquires P's bonds are the same as if the bonds had actually been retired by P at the end of 19X6. In that case, P's separate income would have been $101,000 ($100,000 plus $1,000 constructive gain) and S's net income would have been unchanged. P's $101,000 plus P's $45,000 share of S's reported net income equal $146,000. An assumption of retirement at year-end is necessary because the interest expense of P and the interest income of S are both realized and recognized during 19X6. The amount of the gain is $1,000 ($1,500 less $500 realized and recognized during the current year).

　　P's net income and consolidated net income of $145,900 when P acquires S's bonds are the same as if the bonds had actually been retired by S at the end of 19X6. In that case, P's separate income would have been unchanged at $100,000 and S's reported net income would have been $51,000 ($50,000 plus $1,000 constructive gain). P's $100,000 separate income plus P's $45,900 share of S's reported income ($51,000 × 90%) equal $145,900. Again, the assumption of retirement at year-end is necessary because the interest income of P and the interest expense of S are realized and recognized during the current year.

Exhibit 7–11　*Summary Illustration—Constructive Gains and Losses on Intercompany Bonds*

ASSIGNMENT MATERIAL

QUESTIONS

1 What reciprocal accounts arise when one company borrows from an affiliated company?

2 Do direct lending and borrowing transactions between affiliated companies give rise to unrealized gains or losses? To unrecognized gains or losses?

3 What are constructive gains and losses? Describe a transaction involving a constructive gain.

4 A company has a $1,000,000 bond issue outstanding with unamortized premium of $10,000 and unamortized issuance cost of $5,300. What is the book value of its liability? If an affiliated company purchases half the bonds in the market at 98, what is the gain or loss? Is the gain or loss actual or constructive?

5 Compare a constructive gain on intercompany bonds with an unrealized gain on the intercompany sale of land.

6 Describe the process by which constructive gains on intercompany bonds are realized and recognized on the books of the separate affiliated companies. Does recognition of a constructive gain in consolidated financial statements precede or succeed recognition on the books of the affiliated companies?

7 If a subsidiary purchases parent company bonds at a price in excess of their recorded book value, is the gain or loss attributed to the parent company or the subsidiary? Explain.

8 The following information related to intercompany bond holdings was taken from the adjusted trial balances of a parent company and its 90 percent owned subsidiary four years before the bond issue matured:

	Parent	Subsidiary
Investment in S bonds, $50,000 par	$49,000	
Interest receivable	2,500	
Interest expense		$ 9,000
10% bonds payable, $100,000 par		100,000
Bond premium		4,000
Interest income	5,250	
Interest payable		5,000

Construct the consolidation working paper entries necessary to eliminate reciprocal balances (a) assuming that the parent acquired its intercompany bond investment at the beginning of the current year, and (b) assuming that the parent company acquired its intercompany bond investment two years prior to the date of the adjusted trial balance.

9 Prepare a journal entry (or entries) to account for the parent company investment income for the current year if the reported income of its 80 percent owned subsidiary is $50,000 and the consolidated entity has a $4,000 constructive gain from the subsidiary's acquisition of parent company bonds.

10 Calculate the parent company's income from its 75 percent owned subsidiary if the reported net income of the subsidiary for the period is $100,000 and the consolidated entity has a constructive loss of $8,000 from the parent's acquisition of subsidiary bonds.

11 If a parent company reports interest expense of $4,300 with respect to bonds held intercompany and the subsidiary reports interest income of $4,500 for the same bonds, (a) was there a constructive gain or loss on the bonds? (b) is the gain or loss associated with the parent company or the subsidiary? and (c) what does the $200 difference between interest income and interest expense represent?

12 How are intercompany receivables and payables of equity investees reported in parent company and consolidated financial statements?

EXERCISES

E 7–1   **1** A gain or loss resulting from the constructive retirement of intercompany bond holdings:
  a Is recorded in the separate accounts of the issuing affiliate.
  b Appears net of amortization on each successive consolidated income statement until the bonds reach maturity.
  c Is eliminated in the process of consolidation.
  d Is classified as an extraordinary item on the consolidated income statement, if material.

  2 No constructive gain or loss arises from the purchase of an affiliate's bonds if:
  a The affiliate is a 100 percent owned subsidiary.
  b The bonds are purchased at book value.
  c The bonds are purchased with arm's length bargaining from outside entities.
  d The gain or loss cannot be reasonably estimated.

  3 In years subsequent to the year of an intercompany bond purchase, the piecemeal recognition of a constructive gain or loss:
  a Is computed as the difference between the intercompany interest expense and interest income amounts that are eliminated.
  b Is allocated between majority and minority interests when a subsidiary holds bonds of its parent company.
  c Increases consolidated net income in the gain situation and decreases consolidated net income in the loss situation.
  d Does not affect consolidated net income.

E 7–2   Comparative income statements for Primrose Corporation and its 100 percent owned subsidiary, Sonder Corporation, for the year ended December 31, 19X9 are summarized as follows:

	Primrose	Sonder
Sales	$1,000,000	$500,000
Income from Sonder	236,000	—
Bond interest income (includes discount amortization)	—	32,000
Cost of sales	(670,000)	(200,000)
Operating expenses	(150,000)	(100,000)
Bond interest expense	(50,000)	—
Net income	$ 366,000	$232,000

Primrose purchased its interest in Sonder at book value on January 1, 19X1. On January 1, 19X2 Primrose sold $500,000 par of 10 percent, ten-year bonds to the public at par value, and on January 1, 19X9 Sonder purchased $300,000 par of the bonds at 98. Both companies use straight-line amortization. There are no other intercompany transactions between the affiliated companies.

Required: Prepare a consolidated income statement for Primrose Corporation and Subsidiary for the year ended December 31, 19X9.

E 7–3   Palmer Corporation's long-term debt on January 1, 19X5 consists of $400,000 par value of 10 percent bonds payable due on January 1, 19X9, with unamortized discount of $8,000. On January 2, 19X5 Scott Corporation, Palmer's 90 percent owned subsidiary, purchased $80,000 par of Palmer's 10 percent bonds for $76,000. Interest payment dates are January 1 and July 1, and straight-line amortization is used.
  1 On the consolidated income statement of Palmer Corporation and Subsidiary for 19X5, a gain or loss should be reported in the amount of:
  a $5,600   **b** $4,000
  c $2,400   **d** $2,000
  2 Bonds payable of Palmer less unamortized discount appears in the consolidated balance sheet at December 31, 19X5 in the amount of:
  a $392,000   **b** $394,000
  c $320,000   **d** $315,200

3 The amount of the constructive gain or loss that is unrecognized on the separate books of Palmer and Scott at December 31, 19X5 is:
  a $2,400
  c $1,800
  b $2,200
  d 0

4 Interest expense on Palmer bonds appears in the consolidated income statement for 19X5 at:
  a $42,000
  c $33,600
  b $40,000
  d $32,000

5 Consolidated net income for 19X6 will be affected by the intercompany bond transactions as follows:
  a Increased by 100% of the constructive gain from 19X5
  b Decreased by 25% of the constructive gain from 19X5
  c Increased by 25% of the constructive loss from 19X5
  d Decreased by (25% × 90%) of the constructive loss from 19X5

E 7-4 Comparative balance sheets of Pitt Corporation and Slick Corporation at December 31 19X4 follow:

	Pitt	Slick
Assets		
Accounts receivable—net	$ 1,024,300	$ 300,000
Interest receivable	10,000	—
Inventories	3,000,000	500,000
Other current assets	98,500	200,000
Plant assets—net	3,840,000	2,500,000
Investment in Slick stock	1,830,800	—
Investment in Slick bonds	196,400	—
Total assets	$10,000,000	$3,500,000
Liabilities and Stockholders' Equity		
Accounts payable	$ 400,000	$ 139,000
Interest payable	—	50,000
10% bonds payable	—	1,000,000
Premium on bonds payable	—	36,000
Capital stock	8,000,000	2,000,000
Retained earnings	1,600,000	275,000
Total equities	$10,000,000	$3,500,000

Pitt acquired 80 percent of Slick's capital stock for $1,660,000 on January 1, 19X2 when Slick's capital stock was $2,000,000 and its retained earnings was $75,000.

On January 1, 19X4 Pitt acquired $200,000 par of Slick 10 percent bonds in the bond market for $195,500, on which date the unamortized premium for bonds payable on Slick's books was $45,000. The bonds pay interest on January 1 and July 1 and mature on January 1, 19X9. (Assume straight-line amortization.)

1 The gain or loss on the constructive retirement of $200,000 of Slick bonds on January 1, 19X4 is reported in the 19X4 consolidated income statement in the amount of:
  a $13,500
  c $10,500
  b $11,500
  d $7,000

2 The portion of the constructive gain or loss on Slick bonds that remains unrecognized on the separate books of Pitt and Slick at December 31, 19X4 is:
  a $12,000
  c $10,500
  b $10,800
  d $9,200

3 Consolidated bonds payable at December 31, 19X4 should be reported at:
  a $1,036,000
  c $828,800
  b $1,000,000
  d $800,000

E 7-5 The consolidated balance sheet of Parise Corporation and Sasso Corporation (its 80 percent owned subsidiary) at December 31, 19X1 includes the following items related to an 8 percent, $1,000,000 outstanding bond issue:

Current Liabilities

Bond interest payable (6 months' interest due January 1, 19X2)	$ 40,000

Long-Term Liabilities

8% bonds payable (maturity date January 1, 19X7)	$1,000,000
Less: Unamortized discount	30,000
Total long-term liabilities	$ 970,000

Parise Corporation is the issuing corporation and straight-line amortization is applicable. Sasso purchases $500,000 par of the outstanding bonds of Parise on July 1, 19X2 for $477,500.

Required

1 Calculate the following:
   a The gain or loss on constructive retirement of the bonds
   b The consolidated bond interest expense for 19X2
   c The consolidated bond liability at December 31, 19X2
2 How would the amounts determined in 1 be different if Parise had purchased Sasso's bonds?

E 7-6   The balance sheets of Parker Pharmaceutical Company and Skadden Drug Corporation, an 80 percent owned subsidiary of Parker, at December 31, 19X3 are as follows:

	Parker	Skadden
Assets		
Cash	$ 2,440,000	$1,500,000
Accounts receivable—net	3,000,000	300,000
Other current assets	8,000,000	1,200,000
Plant assets—net	15,000,000	6,500,000
Investment in Skadden	6,560,000	
Total assets	$35,000,000	$9,500,000
Liabilities and Stockholders' Equity		
Accounts payable	$ 750,000	$ 230,000
Interest payable	250,000	50,000
10% bonds payable (due January 1, 19X9)	5,000,000	1,000,000
Discount on bonds payable	100,000*	
Premium on bonds payable		20,000
Capital stock	25,000,000	7,000,000
Retained earnings	4,100,000	1,200,000
Total liabilities and stockholders' equity	$35,000,000	$9,500,000

* Deduct.

Part A: Assume that Skadden Drug purchases $1,000,000 par of Parker Pharmaceutical's bonds for $950,000 on January 2, 19X4 and that semiannual interest is paid on July 1 and January 1. Determine the amounts at which the following items should appear in the consolidated financial statements of Parker and Skadden at and for the year ended December 31, 19X4.
   1 Gain or loss on bond retirement
   2 Interest payable
   3 Bonds payable at par value
   4 Investment in Parker bonds

Part B: Assume that Parker Pharmaceutical purchases $1,000,000 par of Skadden's bonds for $1,010,000 on January 2, 19X4, and that semiannual interest on the bonds is paid on July 1 and January 1. Determine the amounts at which the following items will appear in the consolidated financial statements of Parker and Skadden at and for the year ended December 31, 19X4.

5 Gain or loss on bond retirement
6 Interest expense (assume straight-line amortization)
7 Interest receivable
8 Bonds payable at book value

E 7–7 Perdue Corporation has $2,000,000 of 12 percent bonds outstanding on December 31, 19X2 with unamortized premium of $60,000. These bonds pay interest semiannually on July 1 and January 1 and mature on January 1, 19X8.

On January 1, 19X3 Shelly Corporation, an 80 percent owned subsidiary of Perdue, purchases $500,000 par of Perdue's outstanding bonds in the market for $490,000.

Additional Information
1 Perdue and Shelly use the straight-line method of amortization.
2 The financial statements are consolidated.
3 Perdue's bonds are the only outstanding bonds of the affiliated companies.
4 Shelly's net income for 19X3 is $200,000 and for 19X4, $300,000.

Required
1 Compute the constructive gain or loss that will appear in the consolidated income statement for 19X3.
2 Prepare a consolidation entry (entries) for 19X3 to eliminate the effect of the intercompany bondholdings.
3 Compute the amounts that will appear in the consolidated income statement for 19X4 for the following:
  a Constructive gain or loss   b Minority interest income
  c Bond interest expense   d Bond interest income
4 Compute the amounts that will show in the consolidated balance sheet at December 31, 19X4 for the following:
  a Investment in Perdue bonds   b Book value of bonds payable
  c Bond interest receivable   d Bond interest payable

E 7–8 Comparative income statements for Parrish Corporation and its 80 percent owned subsidiary, Sandwood Corporation, for the year ended December 31, 19X3 are summarized as follows:

	Parrish	*Sandwood*
Sales	$1,200,000	$600,000
Income from Sandwood	260,800	—
Bond interest income (includes discount amortization)	91,000	—
Cost of sales	(750,000)	(200,000)
Operating expenses	(200,000)	(200,000)
Bond interest expense	—	(60,000)
Net income	$ 601,800	$140,000

Parrish purchased its 80 percent interest in Sandwood at book value on January 1, 19X2 at which time Sandwood's assets and liabilities were equal to their fair values.

On January 1, 19X3 Parrish paid $783,000 to purchase all of Sandwood's $1,000,000, 6 percent outstanding bonds. The bonds were issued at par on January 1, 19X1, pay interest semiannually on June 30 and December 31, and mature on December 31, 19X9.

Required: Prepare a consolidated income statement for Parrish Corporation and Subsidiary for the year ended December 31, 19X3.

E 7–9 Provost Corporation acquires 50 percent of the outstanding bonds of its 90 percent owned subsidiary, Style Corporation, on July 1, 19X8. Information relevant to the outstanding bonds of Style and the price paid by Provost under four separate situations is as follows:

BONDS PAYABLE OF STYLE

	Par Value	Premium (discount)	Purchase Price by Provost
I	$200,000	$10,000	$105,000
II	300,000	(8,000)	150,000
III	800,000	16,000	390,000
IV	100,000	(5,000)	49,000

In each situation, assume that the intercompany purchase of bonds occurs five years before maturity, that Provost and Style are on a calendar-year basis, and that Provost uses a correct application of the equity method of accounting.

Required: For each case determine the following:
1 The gain or loss on the intercompany purchase of bonds
2 The effect of the intercompany bond purchase on investment income from Style and minority interest income for 19X8
3 The effect of the intercompany purchase of bonds on investment income from Style and minority interest income for 19X9
4 The difference in consolidated net income for 19X8 and 19X9 that results from the constructive retirement (as opposed to no constructive retirement)

E 7-10 Public Corporation, which owns an 80 percent interest in Spede Corporation, purchases $100,000 of Spede Corporation 8 percent bonds at 106 on July 1, 19X6. The bonds pay interest on January 1 and July 1 and mature on July 1, 19X9. Public uses the equity method of accounting for its investment in Spede. Selected data from the December 31, 19X6 trial balances of the two companies are as follows:

	Public	Spede
Interest receivable	$ 4,000	$ —
Investment in Spede 8% bonds	105,000	—
Bond discount	—	15,000
Interest payable	—	40,000
8% bonds payable	—	1,000,000
Interest income	3,000	—
Interest expense	—	86,000
Gain or loss on intercompany bonds		

Required
1 Determine the amounts for each of the foregoing items that will appear in the consolidated financial statements on or for the year ended December 31, 19X6.
2 Prepare in general journal form the working paper adjustments and eliminations related to the foregoing bonds that are required to consolidate the financial statements of Public and Spede Corporations for the year ended December 31, 19X6.
3 Prepare in general journal form the working paper adjustments and eliminations related to the bonds that are required to consolidate the financial statements of Public and Spede Corporations for the year ended December 31, 19X7.

E 7-11 Pappy Corporation acquired an 80 percent interest in Sonny Corporation at book value equal to fair value on January 1, 19X7, at which time Sonny's capital stock and retained earnings were $100,000 and $40,000, respectively. On January 1, 19X8, Sonny purchased $50,000 par of Pappy's 8 percent, $100,000 par bonds for $48,800 three years before maturity. Interest payment dates are January 1 and July 1. During 19X8 Sonny reports interest income of $4,400 in connection with the bonds and Pappy reports interest expense of $8,000.

Additional Information
1 Pappy's separate income for 19X8 is $200,000.
2 Sonny's net income for 19X8 is $50,000.
3 Pappy accounts for its investment by the equity method.
4 Straight-line amortization is applicable.

Required
1 Determine the gain or loss on the bonds.
2 Prepare the journal entries for Sonny to account for its bond investment during 19X8.
3 Prepare the journal entries for Pappy to account for its bonds payable during 19X8.
4 Prepare the journal entry for Pappy to account for its 80 percent investment in Sonny for 19X8.
5 Calculate minority interest income and consolidated net income for 19X8.

PROBLEMS

P 7–1   Partial adjusted trial balances for Panda Corporation and its 90 percent owned sub-sidiary, Xong Corporation, for the year ended December 31, 19X6 are as follows:

	Panda Corporation Debit (credit)	*Xong Corporation Debit (credit)*
Interest receivable	$ —	$ 1,000
Investment in Panda bonds	—	51,350
Interest payable	(2,000)	—
8% bonds payable, due April 1, 19X9	(100,000)	—
Discount on bonds payable	1,800	—
Interest income	—	(2,550)
Interest expense	8,800	—

Xong Corporation acquired $50,000 par of Panda bonds on April 1, 19X6 for $51,800. The bonds pay interest on April 1 and October 1 and mature on April 1, 19X9.

Required
1 Compute the gain or loss on the bonds that will appear in the 19X6 consolidated income statement.
2 Determine the amounts of interest income and interest expense that will appear in the 19X6 consolidated income statement.
3 Determine the amounts of interest receivable and interest payable that will appear in the December 31, 19X6 consolidated balance sheet.
4 Prepare in general journal form the consolidation working paper entries needed to eliminate the effect of the intercompany bonds for 19X6.

P 7–2   Intercompany transactions between Pewter Corporation and Steel Corporation, its 80 percent owned subsidiary, from January 19X1 when Pewter acquired its controlling interest to December 31, 19X4 are summarized as follows:

19X1   Pewter sold inventory items that cost $60,000 to Steel tor $80,000. Steel sold $60,000 of these inventory items in 19X1 and $20,000 of them in 19X2.

19X2   Pewter sold inventory items that cost $30,000 to Steel for $40,000. All of these items were sold by Steel during 19X3.

19X3   Steel sold land with a book value of $40,000 to Pewter at its fair market value of $55,000. This land is to be used as a future plant site by Pewter.

19X3   Pewter sold equipment with a four-year remaining use life to Steel on January 1 for $80,000. This equipment had a book value of $50,000 at the time of sale and was still in use by Steel at December 31, 19X4.

19X4   Steel purchased $100,000 par of Pewter's 10 percent bonds in the bond market for $106,000 on January 1, 19X4. These bonds had a book value of $98,000 when acquired by Steel and mature on January 1, 19X8.

The separate income of Pewter (does not include income from Steel) and the reported net income of Steel for the years 19X1 through 19X4 were:

	19X1	*19X2*	*19X3*	*19X4*
Separate income of Pewter	$500,000	$375,000	$460,000	$510,000
Net income of Steel	100,000	120,000	110,000	120,000

Required: Compute Pewter's net income (and consolidated net income) for each of the years 19X1 through 19X4. A schedular format with columns for the years 19X1, 19X2, 19X3, and 19X4 is suggested as the most efficient approach for solution of this problem. (Use straight-line depreciation and amortization and take a full year's depreciation on the equipment sold to Steel in 19X3.)

P 7–3   Comparative balance sheets for Phil Corporation and Sam Corporation at December 31, 19X4 follow:

COMPARATIVE BALANCE SHEETS AS OF DECEMBER 31, 19X4

	Phil Corporation	Sam Corporation
Assets		
Cash	$ 25,000	$19,400
Accounts receivable	32,200	25,000
Inventories	30,000	16,000
Plant and equipment	50,000	30,000
Accumulated depreciation	10,000*	4,000*
Bond discount	—	3,600
Investment in Sam stock (90%)	46,000	—
Investment in Sam bonds	20,800	—
	$194,000	$90,000
Liabilities and Equity		
Accounts payable	$ 25,500	$10,000
Bonds payable (10%)	—	40,000
Common stock	100,000	30,000
Retained earnings	68,500	10,000
	$194,000	$90,000

* Deduct.

Additional Information
1 Phil acquired its 90 percent interest in Sam Corporation on January 1, 19X1.
2 Phil uses the equity method of accounting but does not adjust for the excess of cost over book value acquired or for intercompany profits.
3 The difference between Phil's investment in Sam stock account and the underlying book value of Phil's equity interest relates to undervalued plant and equipment that had an expected use life of ten years on January 1, 19X1.
4 Sam's December 31, 19X4 inventory includes $2,000 profit on goods acquired from Phil.
5 Phil acquired $20,000 par of Sam bonds on January 1, 19X4. The bonds mature on December 31, 19X8, and the premium is amortized by the straight-line method.

Required: Prepare a consolidated balance sheet for Phil Corporation and Subsidiary at December 31, 19X4.

P 7–4   Pie Corporation acquired 100 percent of Sud Corporation's outstanding common stock at its underlying book value on January 1, 19X4 when Sud's equity consisted of $100,000 capital stock, $35,000 other paid-in capital, and $35,000 retained earnings. Sud's assets and liabilities were recorded at their fair values on this date.

Pie uses the equity method in accounting for Sud but has made no adjustment relative to the intercompany bond holdings of Pie and Sud. Sud's investment in Pie's bonds consists of $50,000 par value of Pie's 10 percent bonds that were purchased by Sud for $48,000 on January 2, 19X4. These bonds mature on January 1, 19X8 and have semiannual interest payment dates of July 1 and January 1. The combined income and retained earnings statements and balance sheets of Pie and Sud at and for the year ended December 31, 19X4 are summarized as follows:

	Pie	Sud
Combined Income and Retained Earnings Statements		
for the year ended December 31, 19X4		
Sales	$150,000	$ 55,000
Income from Sud	25,000	—
Interest income	—	5,500
Cost of sales	(72,000)	(20,000)
Depreciation expense	(28,000)	(9,000)
Interest expense	(10,000)	—
Other expenses	(30,000)	(6,500)
Net income	35,000	25,000
Add: Beginning retained earnings	65,000	35,000
Less: Dividends	(10,000)	(20,000)
Retained earnings December 31, 19X4	$ 90,000	$ 40,000
Balance Sheet at December 31, 19X4		
Cash	$ 15,000	$ 9,000
Accounts receivable	20,000	10,000
Interest receivable	—	2,500
Inventories	60,000	10,000
Land	70,000	20,000
Plant and equipment—net	140,000	100,000
Investment in Sud stock	175,000	—
Investment in Pie bonds	—	48,500
Total assets	$480,000	$200,000
Accounts payable	$ 45,000	$ 25,000
Interest payable	5,000	—
10% bonds payable	100,000	—
Capital stock, $10 par	200,000	100,000
Other paid-in capital	40,000	35,000
Retained earnings	90,000	40,000
Total equities	$480,000	$200,000

Required: Prepare consolidation working papers of Pie Corporation and Subsidiary for the year 19X4.

P 7–5   Paul Corporation acquired an 80 percent interest in Silas Corporation on January 1, 19X1 for $46,000 when Silas had capital stock of $26,000 and retained earnings of $6,500. The excess of investment cost over book value acquired was due to a $15,000 understatement of plant and equipment with a remaining useful life of fifteen years, and to goodwill, which is being amortized over a ten-year period.

Paul Corporation holds $25,000 par of Silas Corporation bonds acquired on January 1, 19X4 for $24,000. The bonds mature on January 1, 19X9.

Silas Corporation sells merchandise to Paul Corporation at a markup of 20 percent based on cost. Intercompany sales during 19X4 totaled $8,000. Paul's December 31, 19X4 inventory includes $4,500 of merchandise acquired from Silas, while the beginning inventory includes $2,250 of such merchandise. Accounts payable of Paul Corporation includes $1,500 owed to Silas on intercompany sales.

Separate company financial statements for Paul Corporation and its 80 percent owned subsidiary, Silas Corporation, for the year ended December 31, 19X4 are summarized on the next page.

Required: Prepare consolidated financial statement working papers for Paul Corporation and Subsidiary for the year ended December 31, 19X4.

	Paul	Silas
Combined Income and Retained Earnings Statement for the Year Ended December 31, 19X4		
Sales	$ 56,600	$ 20,000
Income from Silas	3,200	—
Interest income	2,700	—
Cost of goods sold	28,000*	7,000*
Operating expenses	12,000*	4,200*
Interest expense	—	4,800*
Net income	22,500	4,000
Add: Beginning retained earnings	42,000	14,000
Deduct: Dividends	15,000*	2,000*
Retained earnings December 31, 19X4	$ 49,500	$ 16,000
Balance Sheet at December 31, 19X4		
Cash	$ 15,000	$ 31,000
Accounts receivable	12,200	25,000
Inventories	30,000	8,000
Plant and equipment	50,000	40,000
Less: Accumulated depreciation	10,000*	4,000*
Investment in Silas stock	53,600	—
Investment in Silas bonds	24,200	—
Total assets	$175,000	$100,000
Accounts payable	$ 25,500	$ 7,200
Bonds payable, 10%	—	50,000
Premium on bonds	—	800
Common stock	100,000	26,000
Retained earnings	49,500	16,000
Total equities	$175,000	$100,000

* Deduct.

P 7–6 Peter Corporation acquired an 80 percent interest in Cher Corporation on January 1, 19X4 for $320,000, at which time Cher had capital stock of $200,000 outstanding and retained earnings of $100,000. The price paid by Peter reflected a $100,000 undervaluation of Cher's plant and equipment. This equipment had a remaining use life of eight years when Peter acquired its interest.

Separate company and consolidated financial statements for Peter Corporation and its subsidiary, Cher Corporation, for the year ended December 31, 19X6 are as follows:

	Peter	Cher	Consolidated
Combined Income and Retained Earnings Statement for the Year Ended December 31, 19X6			
Sales	$ 180,000	$100,000	$230,000
Income from Cher	20,000	—	—
Interest income	—	8,000	—
Cost of goods sold	110,000*	60,000*	110,000*
Operating expenses	30,000*	18,000*	58,000*
Interest expense	18,000*	—	9,000*
Loss	—	—	3,000*
Minority interest income	—	—	8,000*
Net income	42,000	30,000	42,000
Add: Beginning retained earnings	294,000	135,000	294,000
Deduct: Dividends	20,000*	15,000*	20,000*
Ending retained earnings	$ 316,000	$150,000	$316,000

	Peter	Cher	Consolidated
Balance Sheet at December 31, 19X6			
Cash	$ 60,000	$ 26,000	$ 86,000
Accounts receivable	120,000	60,000	165,000
Inventories	100,000	50,000	140,000
Plant and equipment	500,000	200,000	780,000
Accumulated depreciation	100,000*	50,000*	180,000*
Investment in Cher stock	320,000	—	—
Investment in Peter bonds	—	104,000	—
Total assets	$1,000,000	$390,000	$991,000
Accounts payable	$ 80,000	$ 40,000	$105,000
10% bonds payable	200,000	—	100,000
Premium on bonds	4,000	—	2,000
Common stock	400,000	200,000	400,000
Retained earnings	316,000	150,000	316,000
Minority interest	—	—	68,000
Total equities	$1,000,000	$390,000	$991,000

* Deduct.

Cher sells merchandise to Peter but never purchases from Peter.

On January 1, 19X6, Cher purchased $100,000 par of 10 percent Peter Corporation bonds for $106,000. These bonds mature on December 31, 19X8, and Cher expects to hold the bonds until maturity. Both Cher and Peter use straight-line amortization.

Required: Show computations for each of the following items:
1 The $3,000 loss in the consolidated income statement
2 The $230,000 consolidated sales
3 Consolidated cost of goods sold of $110,000
4 Intercompany profit in beginning inventories
5 Intercompany profit in ending inventories
6 Consolidated accounts receivable of $165,000
7 Minority interest income of $8,000
8 Minority interest at December 31, 19X6
9 Investment in Cher stock at December 31, 19X5
10 Investment income account of $20,000 (Peter's books)

P 7-7 Financial statements for Paar Corporation and its 75 percent owned subsidiary, Sahl Corporation, for 19X4 are summarized as follows:

	Paar	Sahl
Combined Income and Retained Earnings Statement for the Year Ended December 31, 19X4		
Sales	$630,000	$500,000
Gain on plant	30,000	—
Income from Sahl	52,000	
Cost of goods sold	350,000*	300,000*
Depreciation expense	76,000*	40,000*
Interest expense	20,000*	—
Other expenses	46,000*	60,000*
Net income	220,000	100,000
Add: Beginning retained earnings	150,000	100,000
Deduct: Dividends	160,000*	80,000*
Retained earnings, December 31, 19X4	$210,000	$120,000
Balance Sheet at December 31, 19X4		
Cash	$ 27,000	$ 81,000
Bond interest receivable	—	5,000
Other receivables—net	40,000	30,000
Inventories	80,000	50,000
Land	90,000	70,000

	Paar	Sahl
Buildings—net	150,000	180,000
Equipment—net	140,000	90,000
Investment in Sahl	343,000	—
Investment in Paar bonds	—	94,000
Total assets	$870,000	$600,000
Accounts payable	$ 50,000	$ 80,000
Bond interest payable	10,000	—
10% bonds payable	200,000	—
Common stock	400,000	400,000
Retained earnings	210,000	120,000
Total equities	$870,000	$600,000

* Deduct.

Paar Corporation acquired its interest in Sahl at book value during 19X1 when the fair values of Sahl's assets and liabilities were equal to their recorded book values.

Additional Information
1. Paar uses the equity method in accounting for its investment in Sahl.
2. Intercompany sales of merchandise between the two affiliated companies totaled $50,000 during 19X4. All intercompany balances have been paid except for $10,000 that was in transit from Sahl to Paar at December 31, 19X4.
3. Unrealized profits in Sahl's inventories of merchandise acquired from Paar were $12,000 at December 31, 19X3 and $15,000 at December 31, 19X4.
4. Sahl sold equipment with a six-year remaining use life to Paar on January 2, 19X2 at a gain of $24,000. The equipment is still in use by Paar.
5. Paar sold a plant to Sahl on July 1, 19X4. The land was sold at a gain of $10,000 and the building, which had a remaining use life of ten years, at a gain of $20,000.
6. Sahl purchased $100,000 par of Paar 10 percent bonds in the open market for $94,000 plus $5,000 accrued interest on December 31, 19X4. Interest is paid semi-annually on January 1 and July 1, and the bonds mature on January 1, 19X9.

Required: Prepare consolidation working papers for Paar Corporation and Subsidiary for the year ended December 31, 19X4.

P 7–8 Puter Corporation acquired a 90 percent interest in Surry Corporation in 19X4 in a pooling of interests business combination. The pooling was correctly recorded by Puter on the date of consummation. Financial statements for Puter and Surry Corporations at and for the year ended December 31, 19X7 are summarized as follows:

	Puter	Surry
Combined Income and Retained Earnings Statements for the Year Ended December 31, 19X7		
Sales	$300,000	$100,000
Income from Surry	50,300	—
Interest income	—	4,000
Cost of sales	(140,000)	(45,000)
Depreciation expense	(15,000)	(5,000)
Operating expense	(20,000)	(4,000)
Interest expense	(10,000)	—
Net income	165,300	50,000
Add: Beginning retained earnings	114,600	35,000
Deduct: Dividends	(60,000)	(20,000)
Retained earnings December 31, 19X7	$219,900	$ 65,000

	Puter	Surry
Balance Sheet at December 31, 19X7		
Cash	$ 90,000	$ 17,000
Accounts receivable—net	110,000	35,000
Interest receivable	—	2,500
Inventories	50,000	30,000
Land	70,000	15,000
Buildings—net	140,000	50,000
Equipment—net	160,000	90,000
Investment in Surry	174,900	—
Investment in Puter bonds	—	45,500
Total assets	$794,900	$285,000
Accounts payable	$120,000	$ 85,000
Interest payable	5,000	—
10% bonds payable	100,000	—
Capital stock, $10 par	300,000	100,000
Additional paid-in capital	50,000	35,000
Retained earnings	219,900	65,000
Total equities	$794,900	$285,000

Additional information

1 Surry purchased inventory items from Puter during 19X6 and 19X7 as follows:

	Sales	Cost of Sales	Gross Profit	Unsold December 31
19X6	$30,000	$20,000	$10,000	$15,000
19X7	40,000	25,000	15,000	16,000

2 Puter paid Surry $20,000 on January 5, 19X6 for equipment that had a book value of $12,000 on Surry's books and a four-year remaining useful life. Straight-line depreciation is used.

3 Surry paid $44,000 for $50,000 par of Puter's 10 percent bonds on July 1, 19X7. Puter issued the bonds at par in 19X1 and the bonds mature on July 1, 19X9. Interest payment dates are January 1 and July 1. Straight-line amortization is used.

4. Puter uses the equity method to account for its interest in Surry.

Required: Prepare consolidation working papers for Puter Corporation and Subsidiary at and for the year ended December 31, 19X7.

P 7–9   [AICPA adapted]

Madison, Inc., acquired all the outstanding $10 par voting common stock of Adams Corporation on December 31, 19X9, in exchange for 90,000 shares of its $10 par voting common stock in a business combination that meets all the conditions for a pooling of interests. On the acquisition date, Madison's common stock had a closing market price of $26 per share on a national stock exchange. Both corporations continued to operate as separate businesses maintaining separate accounting records with years ending December 31.

On December 31, 19X9, after nominal accounts were closed and immediately after acquisition, the condensed balance sheets for both corporations were as follows:

	Madison	Adams
Assets		
Cash	$ 750,000	$ 300,000
Accounts receivable, net	1,950,000	750,000
Inventories	2,100,000	950,000
Land	500,000	200,000
Depreciable assets, net	4,160,000	1,800,000
Investment in Adams Corporation	2,205,000	—
Long-term investments and other assets	785,000	350,000
Total assets	$12,450,000	$4,350,000
Liabilities and Stockholders' Equity		
Accounts payable and other current liabilities	$ 1,750,000	$ 945,000
Long-term debt	1,500,000	1,200,000
Common stock, $10 par	3,000,000	900,000
Additional paid-in capital	1,370,000	175,000
Retained earnings	4,830,000	1,130,000
Total liabilities and equity	$12,450,000	$4,350,000

Additional Information

1 Madison recorded its investment in Adams at the underlying equity in the net assets of Adams of $2,205,000.

2 On December 31, 19X9 Adams's assets and liabilities had fair values equal to the book balances with the exception of land, which had a fair value of $400,000.

3 Madison's accounting policy is to amortize excess cost over fair market value of net assets acquired over a forty-year period.

4 On December 15, 19X9 Adams paid a cash dividend of $3 per share on its common stock.

5 Adams's long-term debt consisted of 9 percent, ten-year bonds, issued at face value on June 30, 19X5, and due in ten years. Interest is paid semiannually on June 30 and December 31. Madison had purchased Adams's bonds at face value of $250,000. There was no change in Madison's ownership of Adams's bonds through December 31, 19X9.

6 During the three-month period ended December 31, 19X9, Madison purchased merchandise from Adams at an aggregate invoice price of $600,000. Madison had not paid for the merchandise as of December 31, 19X9. The amount of profit realized by Adams on these transactions was $120,000. At December 31, 19X9 one-half of the merchandise remained in Madison's inventory. There were no intercompany merchandise transactions prior to October 1, 19X9.

7 The 19X9 net income amounts per the separate books of Madison and Adams were $2,100,000 and $1,125,000, respectively.

8 The balances in retained earnings at December 31, 19X8 were $1,600,000 and $275,000 for Madison and Adams, respectively.

Required

1 Prepare a consolidated balance sheet working paper for Madison, Inc., and its subsidiary, Adams Corporation, as of December 31, 19X9.

2 Prepare a consolidated statement of retained earnings for the year ended December 31, 19X9.

8

CONSOLIDATIONS— CHANGES IN OWNERSHIP INTERESTS

This chapter considers several separate topics related to changes in parent company/investor ownership interests. These topics include parent/investor accounting and consolidation procedures for interim acquisitions of stock, midyear poolings, piecemeal acquisitions of a controlling interest, sales of ownership interests, and changes in ownership interests through investee stock issuances and treasury stock transactions.

ACQUISITIONS DURING AN ACCOUNTING PERIOD

Previous chapters in this book have illustrated consolidations for subsidiary acquisitions at the beginning of an accounting period. When a subsidiary is acquired during an accounting period, some consolidation adjustments have to be made in order to account for the income of the subsidiary that was earned prior to its acquisition and included in the purchase price. Such income is referred to as **preacquisition earnings** to distinguish it from income of the consolidated entity. Similarly, **preacquisition dividends** require consolidation adjustments in the period of acquisition.

Preacquisition Earnings

Conceptually, *preacquisition earnings* (also referred to as *purchased income)* can be eliminated from consolidated income by either of two methods. It can be eliminated by excluding the sales and expenses of the subsidiary prior to acquisition from consolidated sales and expenses. Or it can be eliminated by including the sales and expenses of the subsidiary in the consolidated income statement for the full year and deducting preacquisition income as a separate item.

Assume, for example, that Patter Corporation purchases a 90 percent interest in Sissy Company on April 1, 19X6 for $213,750. Sissy's income, dividends, and stockholders' equity for 19X6 are summarized as follows:

	January 1 to April 1	April 1 to December 31	January 1 to December 31
Income			
Sales	$ 25,000	$ 75,000	$100,000
Cost of sales and expenses	12,500	37,500	50,000
Net income	$ 12,500	$ 37,500	$ 50,000
Dividends	$ 10,000	$ 15,000	$ 25,000

	January 1	April 1	December 31
Stockholders' Equity			
Capital stock	$200,000	$200,000	$200,000
Retained earnings	35,000	37,500	60,000
Stockholders' equity	$235,000	$237,500	$260,000

Sissy's income from January 1, 19X6 to April 1, 19X6 is $12,500 ($25,000 sales − $12,500 expenses), and Sissy's equity at April 1, 19X6 is $237,500. Therefore, the book value acquired by Patter ($237,500 × 90% interest) is equal to the $213,750 purchase price of Sissy stock.

In recording income from its investment in Sissy at year-end, Patter makes the following entry:

Investment in Sissy	$33,750	
Income from Sissy		$33,750

To record income from the last three quarters of 19X6 ($37,500 × 90%).

Since the effect of recording investment income on an equity basis is to increase Patter's income by $33,750, the effect on consolidated net income must also be $33,750. Conceptually, the consolidated income statement is affected as follows:

Sales (last three quarters of 19X6)	$ 75,000
Expenses (last three quarters of 19X6)	− 37,500
Minority interest (last three quarters of 19X6)	− 3,750
Effect on consolidated net income	$ 33,750

This solution poses two practical problems. First, the income of the 10 percent minority interest for 19X6 is $5,000 for the full year, even though it is only $3,750 for the last nine months of 19X6. Second, by consolidating sales and expenses for only nine months of the year, the consolidated income statement does not provide a basis for projecting future annual sales and expenses for the consolidated entity. In considering these problems, the Committee on Accounting Procedure of the AICPA in *ARB No. 51* (paragraph 11) expressed the opinion that the most meaningful consolidated income statement presentation results from including the sales and expenses in the consolidated income statement for the full year and deducting preacquisition income as a separate item. The committee therefore recommended consolidating subsidiary accounts in the following manner:

Sales (full year)	$100,000
Expenses (full year)	− 50,000
Preacquisition income	− 11,250
Minority interest income	− 5,000
Effect on consolidated net income	$ 33,750

Preacquisition Dividends

Dividends paid on stock prior to its acquisition during an accounting period (preacquisition dividends) are eliminated in the consolidation process because they are not a part of the equity acquired. Sissy paid $25,000 dividends during 19X6, but $10,000 of this amount was paid prior to the acquisition by Patter. Accordingly, Patter makes the following entry in accounting for dividends actually received.

Cash	$13,500	
Investment in Sissy		$13,500
To record dividends received ($15,000 × 90%).		

The preacquisition dividends relating to the 90 percent interest acquired by Patter are eliminated in the consolidation process along with the preacquisition earnings. These eliminations are included in the working paper entry that eliminates reciprocal investment in subsidiary and subsidiary equity balances in order to compensate for the fact that subsidiary equity balances are eliminated as of the beginning of the period and the investment balance is eliminated as of the date of acquisition within the period. The allocations of income and dividends for Sissy can be summarized as follows:

	Majority Interest (Patter and Consolidated)	Minority Interest (10%)	Preacquisition Eliminations	Total
Sissy's net income	$33,750	$5,000	$11,250	$50,000
Sissy's dividends	13,500	2,500	9,000	25,000

Consolidation

Consolidation procedures for midyear acquisitions are illustrated in Exhibit 8–1 for Patter and Subsidiary. The $234,000 investment in Sissy balance in Patter's balance sheet consists of the $213,750 cost plus $33,750 income less $13,500 dividends received. While other amounts in the separate statements of Patter and Sissy are introduced for the first time in the consolidation working papers, they are entirely compatible with the previous assumptions and data for Patter and Sissy Corporations.

Working paper entry a eliminates the income from Sissy, dividends received from Sissy, and returns the investment in Sissy account to its $213,750 balance at acquisition on April 1, 19X6.

a	Income from Sissy	$ 33,750	
	Dividends—Sissy		$ 13,500
	Investment in Sissy		20,250
	To adjust the investment in Sissy to its cost on April 1, 19X6.		

This entry does not reflect new procedures, but care must be exercised to eliminate only dividends actually received (90% × $15,000), rather than the ownership percentage times dividends paid by the subsidiary for the year.

The second working paper entry in Exhibit 8–1 does reflect new working paper procedures because it contains items for preacquisition earnings and dividends. It is journalized as follows:

PATTER CORPORATION AND SUBSIDIARY
CONSOLIDATION WORKING PAPERS
FOR THE YEAR ENDED DECEMBER 31, 19X6

	Patter	90% Sissy	Adjustments and Eliminations		Minority Interest	Consolidated Statements
Income Statement Sales	$300,000	$100,000				$400,000
Income from Sissy	33,750		a	33,750		
Expenses including cost of goods sold	200,000*	50,000*				250,000*
Minority interest income ($50,000 × 10%)					$ 5,000	5,000*
Preacquisition income			b	11,250		11,250*
Net income	$133,750	$ 50,000				$133,750
Retained Earnings Retained earnings—Patter	$266,250					$266,250
Retained earnings—Sissy		$ 35,000	b	35,000		
Net income	133,750✓	50,000✓				133,750
Dividends	100,000*	25,000*	a 13,500 b 9,000		2,500*	100,000*
Retained earnings December 31, 19X6	$300,000	$ 60,000				$300,000
Balance Sheet Other assets	$566,000	$260,000				$826,000
Investment in Sissy	234,000		a 20,250 b 213,750			
	$800,000	$260,000				$826,000
Capital stock	$500,000	$200,000	b	200,000		$500,000
Retained earnings	300,000✓	60,000✓				300,000
	$800,000	$260,000				
Minority interest January 1, 19X6			b	23,500	23,500	
Minority interest December 31, 19X6					$26,000	26,000
						$826,000

* Deduct

Exhibit 8–1   *Preacquisition Income and Dividends in Consolidation Working Papers*

b	Preacquisition income	$ 11,250	
	Capital stock—Sissy	200,000	
	Retained earnings—Sissy	35,000	
	Dividends—Sissy		$ 9,000
	Investment in Sissy		213,750
	Minority interest—beginning		23,500

To eliminate reciprocal investment and equity balances, to record preacquisition income and beginning minority interest, and to eliminate preacquisition dividends.

In examining this entry, note that preacquisition income less preacquisition dividends of $2,250 is equal to the $213,750 investment cost on April 1, 19X6 less 90 percent of Sissy's equity on January 1, 19X6. Also note that beginning minority interest is 10 percent of Sissy's January 1, 19X6 equity. In case of increases in ownership interests during a period, minority interest is computed for the minority shares outstanding at year-end.

Preacquisition income is introduced in the working papers through a working paper entry. Subsequently, it is carried to the consolidated income statement as a deduction in measuring consolidated net income. The classification of preacquisition income in a consolidated income statement parallels the classification of minority interest income. Consolidation working papers in subsequent accounting periods are not affected by midyear acquisitions.

Since Sissy's 10 percent ending minority interest is held outside of the consolidated entity for the entire year, the minority interest computation is simply 10 percent of Sissy's equity at the beginning of the year plus 10 percent of Sissy's net income for the year less 10 percent of the dividends declared by Sissy during the year.

POOLING OF INTERESTS DURING AN ACCOUNTING PERIOD

When a pooling of interests takes place during an accounting period, the income of the combining companies is consolidated for the entire year irrespective of the date of combination. In addition, prior-period financial statements are restated to show the effect of the pooling for all prior periods reported. The requirement to pool the income of combining companies for the entire year of combination has important implications for recording investments in pooled companies within an accounting period and in accounting for such investments under the equity method of accounting. Income and retained earnings of the parent under the equity method of accounting should be equal to consolidated or pooled income and retained earnings. Therefore, the investment in a pooled company is recorded at the book value of the interest acquired at the beginning of the period of acquisition, adjusted downward for dividends paid prior to combination, but not adjusted upward for preacquisition earnings.

Accounting Procedures for Midyear Poolings

Assume that Pete Corporation acquires all the voting stock of Skag Corporation at July 1, 19X5 in a pooling of interests. Pete issues 10,000 shares of its own $10 par common stock for all the outstanding stock of Skag. Summary financial information for Skag Corporation at June 30, 19X5 and at December 31, 19X5 is as follows:

	Six Months Ended June 30, 19X5	Year Ended Dec. 31, 19X5
Net assets	$160,000	$170,000
Capital stock	$100,000	$100,000
Retained earnings, December 31, 19X4	50,000	50,000
Income	20,000	40,000
Dividends	(10,000)	(20,000)
Stockholders' equity	$160,000	$170,000

Pete Corporation records its investment in Skag on June 30, 19X5 as follows:

Investment in Skag	$160,000	
Capital stock, $10 par		$100,000
Retained earnings		40,000
Income from Skag		20,000

The $40,000 credit to retained earnings is equal to the December 31, 19X4 retained earnings less $10,000 dividends paid prior to the pooling. The entry for the pooling treatment provides for including a full year's earnings in investment income.

During the six months of 19X5, Pete records the receipt of $10,000 dividends from Skag, and at December 31, 19X5 it records income from Skag of $20,000. Pete's journal entries are:

Cash	$10,000	
Investment in Skag		$10,000

To record dividends received ($10,000 × 100%).

Investment in Skag	$20,000	
Income from Skag		$20,000

To record investment income ($20,000 × 100%) for the second six months.

The investment in Skag account at December 31, 19X5 is $170,000 ($160,000 + $20,000 − $10,000), equal to Skag's recorded net assets on that date.

Consolidation working papers for Pete and Skag for 19X5 are presented in Exhibit 8–2. Only three working paper entries are needed to consolidate the financial statements of the pooled companies. Entry a eliminates investment income and subsidiary dividends and credits the investment account for the difference. Entry b eliminates preacquisition dividends, and entry c eliminates reciprocal investment and equity balances. The working paper entries are reproduced for convenient reference.

a	Income from Skag	$ 40,000	
	Dividends		$ 10,000
	Investment in Skag		30,000

To eliminate income from Skag and dividends and credit investment account for the difference.

b	Retained earnings—Skag	$ 10,000	
	Dividends		$ 10,000

To eliminate preacquisition dividends.

c	Retained earnings—Skag	$ 40,000	
	Capital stock—Skag	100,000	
	Investment in Skag		$140,000

To eliminate reciprocal investment and equity balances.

The consolidated net income shown in Exhibit 8–2 is $140,000 and is equal to the net income of Pete. Consolidated retained earnings of $330,000 at December 31, 19X5 is also equal to Pete's retained earnings. Two items in the consolidation working papers are unusual and require some comment. Skag's dividends for the entire year ($20,000) are eliminated because there is no minority interest, and because the dividends to be reflected in the consolidated retained earnings statement are those paid by Pete, the parent company. Also, Pete's beginning retained earnings and beginning consolidated retained earnings of $240,000 is $10,000 less than the $250,000 combined retained earnings of the pooled com-

PETE CORPORATION AND SUBSIDIARY
CONSOLIDATION WORKING PAPERS
FOR THE YEAR ENDED DECEMBER 31, 19X5

	Pete	100% Skag	Adjustments and Eliminations			Consolidated Statements
Income Statement						
Income from Skag	$ 40,000		a	40,000		
Other income	100,000	$ 40,000				$140,000
Net income	$140,000	$ 40,000				$140,000
Retained Earnings						
Retained earnings—Pete	$240,000					$240,000
Retained earnings—Skag		$ 50,000	b	10,000		
			c	40,000		
Net income	140,000✓	40,000✓				140,000
Dividends	50,000*	20,000*	a	10,000		50,000*
			b	10,000		
Retained earnings December 31, 19X5	$330,000	$ 70,000				$330,000
Balance Sheet						
Investment in Skag	$170,000		a	30,000		
			c	140,000		
Other net assets	760,000	$170,000				$930,000
	$930,000	$170,000				$930,000
Capital stock	$600,000	$100,000	c	100,000		$600,000
Retained earnings	330,000✓	70,000✓				330,000
	$930,000	$170,000				$930,000
* Deduct						

Exhibit 8–2   Consolidation Working Papers for Pooling of Interests

panies at January 1, 19X5.[1] The difference is the result of eliminating the $10,000 dividends paid by Skag prior to the consummation of the pooling. Although other approaches for correcting the inconsistencies of the pooling requirements are available, the one illustrated was selected because it maintains a correct correspondence between the investment and underlying equity accounts, between parent company income and consolidated income and between parent company and consolidated retained earnings.

Reporting Pooled Retained Earnings

The reporting of consolidated retained earnings for 19X5 does not parallel the one-line consolidation entries presented above because reconciliation with Pete Corporation's $200,000 retained earnings at December 31, 19X4 is required. Therefore, consolidated retained earnings in the period of pooling would be presented as follows:

---

[1]Pete's retained earnings at December 31, 19X4 was $200,000. This amount was increased to $240,000 when the pooling was recorded.

PETE CORPORATION AND SUBSIDIARY CONSOLIDATED
(POOLED) RETAINED EARNINGS FOR THE YEAR ENDED
DECEMBER 31, 19X5

Retained earnings December 31, 19X4 as previously reported		$200,000
Pooling Adjustment		
Retained earnings of Skag December 31, 19X4		50,000
Retained earnings (pooled) December 31, 19X4		250,000
Net income (pooled income) 19X5		140,000
Dividends 19X5		
To Pete shareholders	$50,000	
To Skag shareholders before pooling	10,000	60,000
Retained earnings December 31, 19X5		$330,000

This presentation enables readers of Pete's financial statements to view the effect of the pooling from the perspective of amounts presented in prior years.

PIECEMEAL ACQUISITIONS

A corporation may acquire an interest in another corporation in a series of separate stock purchases over a period of time. This type of acquisition poses no new problems of analysis if the parent accounts for its investment on an equity basis. However, it does increase the details of computing investment income and consolidated net income. These details are discussed and accounting procedures for them are illustrated in this section.

Poca Corporation acquires a 90 percent interest in Sark Corporation in a series of separate stock purchases between July 1, 19X3 and October 1, 19X5. Data concerning the acquisitions and interests acquired are as follows:

Year	Date	Interest Acquired	Investment Cost	Equity January 1	Income for Year	Equity at Acquisition	Equity December 31
19X3	July 1	20%	$30,000	$100,000	$50,000	$125,000	$150,000
19X4	April 1	40%	$74,000	$150,000	$40,000	$160,000	$190,000
19X5	October 1	30%	$81,000	$190,000	$40,000	$220,000	$230,000

The net assets of Sark Corporation are stated at their fair values, and the excess of investment cost over book value acquired in each case is due to goodwill with a ten-year amortization period. Accordingly, the initial goodwill from each of the three acquisitions is computed:

Year	Investment Cost	Book Value and Fair Value Acquired	Goodwill
19X3	$30,000	($125,000 × 20%) = $25,000	$ 5,000
19X4	$74,000	($160,000 × 40%) = $64,000	$10,000
19X5	$81,000	($220,000 × 30%) = $66,000	$15,000

Since the interests are acquired within each accounting period, the consolidated income statements show preacquisition income in the years 19X4 and

19X5. Partial year amortization is necessary for the goodwill arising in each of the three accounting periods.

At December 31, 19X5 Poca's investment in Sark account balance is $233,625, consisting of $185,000 total cost, plus income of $48,625 (Poca's share of Sark's net income less goodwill amortization) during the period 19X3 through 19X5. For purposes of computing gain or loss on subsequent sales, Poca should keep a record for each of the investments. Such a record could be contained in a schedule such as the following:

		20% Interest	40% Interest	30% Interest	Total
Investment cost		$30,000	$ 74,000	$81,000	$185,000
Investment income	19X3	4,750	—	—	4,750
	19X4	7,500	11,250	—	18,750
	19X5	7,500	15,000	2,625	25,125
		$49,750	$100,250	$83,625	$233,625

When the financial statements of Poca and Sark are consolidated in the years 19X4 and 19X5, preacquisition income will appear in the consolidated income statements. Except for the preacquisition income item, no unusual consolidating procedures result from piecemeal acquisitions. Exhibit 8–3 shows consolidation working papers for Poca Corporation and Subsidiary for 19X5. Additional data, which are compatible with previous information for the Poca/Sark example, are provided for illustrative purposes. The working paper entries are reproduced for convenient reference:

a	Income from Sark	$ 25,125	
	Investment in Sark		$ 25,125

To eliminate investment income and return investment account to its beginning-of-the-period balance.

b	Preacquisition income	$ 9,000	
	Retained earnings—Sark	90,000	
	Capital stock—Sark	100,000	
	Goodwill	28,500	
	Investment in Sark		$208,500
	Minoirity interest January 1		19,000

To eliminate investment in Sark and Sark's equity balances, and enter preacquisition income, unamortized goodwill, and beginning of the period minority interest balances.

c	Expenses	$ 1,875	
	Goodwill		$ 1,875

To record current year's goodwill amortization.

Preacquisition income of $9,000 relates to the 30 percent interest acquired on October 1, 19X5 ($40,000 Sark's income × 30% interest × ¾ year). The income of the minority interest for 19X5 is computed on the basis of the 10 percent minority ownership at December 31, 19X5. Goodwill of $26,625 as shown in the consolidated balance sheet of Exhibit 8–3 is equal to the initial unamortized goodwill of $30,000 ($5,000 + $10,000 + $15,000) less amortization of $250 in 19X3, $1,250 in 19X4, and $1,875 in 19X5. Except for these three items, the consolidation working paper procedures are equivalent to those used in previous chapters.

POCA CORPORATION AND SUBSIDIARY
CONSOLIDATION WORKING PAPERS
FOR THE YEAR ENDED DECEMBER 31, 19X5

	Poca	90% Sark	Adjustments and Eliminations		Minority Interest	Consolidated Statements
Income Statement						
Sales	$274,875	$150,000				$424,875
Income from Sark	25,125		a	25,125		
Expenses including cost of goods sold	220,000*	110,000*	c	1,875		331,875*
Preacquisition income			b	9,000		9,000*
Minority interest income ($40,000 × 10%)					$ 4,000	4,000*
Net income	$ 80,000	$ 40,000				$ 80,000
Retained Earnings						
Retained earnings—Poca	$220,000					$220,000
Retained earnings—Sark		$ 90,000	b	90,000		
Net income	80,000✓	40,000✓				80,000
Retained earnings December 31, 19X5	$300,000	$130,000				$300,000
Balance Sheet						
Other assets	$466,375	$300,000				$766,375
Investment in Sark	233,625		a 25,125 b 208,500			
Goodwill			b 28,500	c 1,875		26,625
	$700,000	$300,000				$793,000
Liabilities	$100,000	$ 70,000				$170,000
Capital stock	300,000	100,000	b	100,000		300,000
Retained earnings	300,000✓	130,000✓				300,000
	$700,000	$300,000				
Minority interest January 1, 19X5			b	19,000	19,000	
Minority interest December 31, 19X5					$23,000	23,000
						$793,000

* Deduct.

Exhibit 8–3 *Piecemeal Acquisition of a Controlling Interest*

SALE OF OWNERSHIP INTERESTS

When a parent company/investor sells an ownership interest, the gain or loss on the sale is computed as the difference between the proceeds from the sale and the book value of the investment interest sold. The book value of the investment should, of course, reflect the equity method of accounting when the investor is able to exercise significant influence over the investee corporation. If a parent company acquires its interest in several different purchases, the shares sold must be identified with particular acquisitions. This is usually done on the basis of specific identification or the first-in, first out flow assumption.

The following information will be used to illustrate sale of ownership interests both at the beginning of the period and during the period. Sergio Corporation is a 90 percent owned subsidiary of Pablo Corporation. Pablo's investment in Sergio account at January 1, 19X7 has a balance of $288,000, consisting of its underlying equity in Sergio plus $18,000 unamortized goodwill with a remaining amortization period of two years. Sergio's stockholders' equity at January 1, 19X7 consists of $200,000 capital stock and $100,000 retained earnings. During 19X7, Sergio reports income of $36,000, earned proportionately throughout the year, and pays dividends of $20,000 on July 1.

Sale of an Interest at the Beginning of the Period

If Pablo Corporation sells a 10 percent interest in Sergio (one-ninth of its holdings) on January 1, 19X7 for $40,000, an $8,000 gain on sale will be recorded on Pablo's books and the investment in Sergio account will be reduced $32,000 ($288,000/9). The $8,000 gain is a gain for consolidated statement purposes as well as for Pablo as a separate entity. The sale of the 10 percent interest reduces Pablo's ownership percentage in Sergio to 80 percent and increases the minority interest to 20 percent.

During 19X7 Pablo accounts for its 80 percent interest under the equity method of accounting and records income of $20,800 ($36,000 net income of Sergio × 80% − $8,000 goodwill amortization) and a reduction in its investment account for dividends received. At December 31, 19X7 Pablo's investment in Sergio account has a balance of $260,800, computed as follows:

Investment balance January 1, 19X7	$288,000
Less: Book value of interest sold	32,000
	256,000
Add: Income less dividends ($20,800 − $16,000)	4,800
Investment balance December 31, 19X7	$260,800

The investment balance at year-end consists of Pablo's underlying equity in Sergio of $252,800 ($316,000 × 80%) plus $8,000 unamortized goodwill on the 80 percent interest still owned. Consolidation working papers for Pablo Corporation and Subsidiary as shown in Exhibit 8–4 illustrate the effect of a decrease in an ownership interest on working paper procedures.

Since the sale of the interest was at the beginning of the period, the effect of the sale on consolidation procedures for 19X7 is minimal. The working paper entries are as follows:

a	Income from Sergio	$ 20,800	
	Dividends—Sergio		$ 16,000
	Investment in Sergio		4,800
b	Capital stock—Sergio	$200,000	
	Retained earnings—Sergio	100,000	
	Goodwill	16,000	
	Investment in Sergio		$256,000
	Minority interest (20%)		60,000
c	Amortization of goodwill	$ 8,000	
	Goodwill		$ 8,000

Working paper entry a reduces the investment in Sergio to its $256,000 beginning-of-the-period balance after sale of the 10 percent interest and entry b enters goodwill and minority interest based on amounts immediately after the 10 percent interest was sold. The last entry simply reflects current period goodwill amortization related to the remaining 80 percent interest. The $8,000 gain

PABLO CORPORATION AND SUBSIDIARY
CONSOLIDATION WORKING PAPERS
FOR THE YEAR ENDED DECEMBER 31, 19X7

	Pablo	80% Sergio	Adjustments and Eliminations				Minority Interest	Consolidated Statements
Income Statement								
Sales	$600,000	$136,000						$736,000
Income from Sergio	20,800		a	20,800				
Gain on sale	8,000							8,000
Cost of sales and expenses	508,800*	100,000*	c	8,000				616,800*
Minority interest income ($36,000 ×20%)							$ 7,200	7,200*
Net income	$120,000	$ 36,000						$120,000
Retained Earnings								
Retained earnings—Pablo	$210,000							$210,000
Reatined earnings—Sergio		$100,000	b	100,000				
Net income	120,000✓	36,000✓						120,000
Dividends	80,000*	20,000*			a	16,000	4,000*	80,000*
Retained earnings December 31, 19X7	$250,000	$116,000						$250,000
Balance Sheet								
Other assets	$639,200	$350,000						$989,200
Investment in Sergio†	260,800				a b	4,800 256,000		
Goodwill			b	16,000	c	8,000		8,000
	$900,000	$350,000						$997,200
Liabilities	$150,000	$ 34,000						$184,000
Capital stock	500,000	200,000	b	200,000				500,000
Retained earnings	250,000✓	116,000✓						250,000
	$900,000	$350,000						
Minority interest January 1, 19X7					b	60,000	60,000	
Minority interest December 31, 19X7							$63,200	63,200
								$997,200

* Deduct.

† The $256,000 elimination in entry b is equal to the $288,000 beginning balance less the $32,000 book value of the 10% investment interest sold.

Exhibit 8–4 Sale of a 10 Percent Interest at Beginning of the Period

on sale is included in Pablo's income statement and is carried directly to the consolidated income statement without adjustment.

Sale of an Interest During an Accounting Period

If Pablo Corporation sells the 10 percent interest in Sergio Corporation on April 1, 19X7 for $40,000, the sale may be recorded as of April 1, 19X7 or, as an expedient, as of January 1, 19X7. Assuming that the sale is recorded as of January

1, 19X7, Pablo records the $8,000 gain on sale the same as in the beginning-of-the-year sale situation and makes the same one-line consolidation entries as those illustrated in the earlier example. Consistency with the one-line consolidation requires that the consolidated financial statements be prepared using the same beginning-of-the-period sale assumption. That is, minority interest income is computed for a 20 percent minority interest outstanding throughout 19X7, and beginning and ending minority interest amounts are based on a 20 percent minority interest. This alternative beginning-of-the-period sale assumption does not affect parent company or consolidated net income because any difference in the gain or loss on sale is exactly offset by differences in computing the income from subsidiary under a one-line consolidation, and in computing amortization and minority interest amounts in the consolidated financial statements.[2]

If the sale is recorded as of April 1, 19X7, the gain on sale will be $7,350, computed as:

Selling price of 10% interest		$40,000
Less: Book value of the interest sold:		
Investment balance January 1	$288,000	
Equity in income		
$36,000 × ¼ year × 90%	8,100	
Less: Amortization		
$18,000/2 years × ¼ year	(2,250)	
	293,850	
Portion of investment sold	× ⅑	32,650
Gain		$ 7,350

Journal entries on Pablo's books during 19X7 to account for the 10 percent interest sold and its investment in Sergio are as follows:

April 1, 19X7

Investment in Sergio	$ 5,850	
Income from Sergio		$ 5,850

To record income for first quarter 19X7. (See earlier computations.)

Cash	$40,000	
Investment in Sergio		$32,650
Gain on sale of investment		7,350

To record sale of a 10% interest in Sergio

July 1, 19X7

Cash	$16,000	
Investment in Sergio		$16,000

To record dividends received ($20,000 × 80%)

December 31, 19X7

Investment in Sergio	$15,600	
Income from Sergio		$15,600

To record income for last three quarters of 19X7 computed as follows:

Equity in income $36,000 × ¾ year × 80%		$21,600
Goodwill amortization:		
Unamortized January 1	$18,000	
Amortization January 1 to April 1	2,250	
Unamortized April 1 before sale	15,750	
Less: Goodwill on interest sold $15,750/9	1,750	
Unamortized April 1 after sale	14,000	
Amortization April 1 to December 31		
$14,000 ÷ ⅞ years × ¾ year		6,000
Income from Sergio		$15,600

---

[2]If recorded as of the beginning of the period, dividends actually received on the interest sold prior to sale must be considered in calculating the gain or loss on sale and consolidation procedures have to be adjusted accordingly.

The income from Sergio for 19X7 is $21,450, consisting of $5,850 the first quarter and $15,600 the last three quarters of the year. At year-end the investment in Sergio account has the same $260,800 balance as in the beginning-of-the-period sale illustration, but the balance involves different amounts:

Investment balance January 1	$288,000
Less: Book value of interest sold	32,650
	255,350
Add: Income less dividends	5,450
Investment balance December 31	$260,800

The investment balance at year-end is the same as before because Pablo holds the same ownership interest as under the beginning-of-the-year sale assumption. Further, Pablo has received the same cash inflow from the investment ($40,000 proceeds from the sale and $16,000 dividends), and therefore should report the same income. The income effects under the different assumptions are explained as follows:

	Sale at or Assumed at Beginning of Period	Sale within the Accounting Period
Gain on sale of investment	$ 8,000	$ 7,350
Income from Sergio	20,800	21,450
Total income effect	$28,800	$28,800

Since the total income effect on Pablo's net income is the same, the effect on the consolidated financial statements also has to be the same. Consolidation working papers for a sale within an accounting period are illustrated in Exhibit 8–5.

Working paper entries to consolidate the financial statements of Pablo and Sergio are journalized as follows:

a	Income from Sergio	$ 21,450	
	Dividends—Sergio		$ 16,000
	Investment in Sergio		5,450
b	Capital stock—Sergio	$200,000	
	Retained earnings—Sergio	100,000	
	Goodwill	16,250	
	Investment in Sergio		$255,350
	Minority interest January 1		30,000
	Minority interest April 1		30,900
c	Amortization of goodwill	$ 8,250	
	Goodwill		$ 8,250

The minority interest amounts that are entered in entry b are separated for illustrative purposes but do not have to be separated. One part of the minority interest calculation is based on the 10 percent minority interest at the beginning of the period ($300,000 equity of Sergio at January 1 × 10%) and the other part reflects the book value of the 10 percent increase in minority interest from the April 1 sale ($309,000 equity of Sergio on April 1 × 10%). Note that a dual calculation is also needed for minority interest income [($36,000 × 10%) + ($36,000 × 10% × ¾ year)] for midyear sale situations. Since the investment in Sergio was decreased when the interest was sold on April 1, the $255,350 credit in working

PABLO CORPORATION AND SUBSIDIARY
CONSOLIDATION WORKING PAPERS
FOR THE YEAR ENDED DECEMBER 31, 19X7

	Pablo	80% Sergio	Adjustments and Eliminations		Minority Interest	Consolidated Statements
Income Statement						
Sales	$600,000	$136,000				$736,000
Income from Sergio	21,450		a 21,450			
Gain on sale	7,350					7,350
Cost of sales and expenses	508,800*	100,000*	c 8,250			617,050*
Minority interest income†					$ 6,300	6,300*
Net income	$120,000	$ 36,000				$120,000
Retained Earnings						
Retained earnings—Pablo	$210,000					$210,000
Reatined earnings—Sergio		$100,000	b 100,000			
Net income	120,000 ✔	36,000 ✔				120,000
Dividends	80,000*	20,000*		a 16,000	4,000*	80,000*
Retained earnings December 31, 19X7	$250,000	$116,000				$250,000
Balance Sheet						
Other assets	$639,200	$350,000				$989,200
Investment in Sergio	260,800		a 5,450 / b 255,350			
Goodwill			b 16,250	c 8,250		8,000
	$900,000	$350,000				$997,200
Liabilities	$150,000	$ 34,000				$184,000
Capital stock	500,000	200,000	b 200,000			500,000
Retained earnings	250,000 ✔	116,000 ✔				250,000
	$900,000	$350,000				
Minority interest January 1, 19X7				b 30,000	30,000	
Minority interest April 1, 19X7				b 30,900	30,900	
Minority interest December 31, 19X7					$63,200	63,200
						$997,200

* Deduct.
† Minority interest income = ($36,000 × 10% × 1 year) + ($36,000 × 10% × ¾ year)

Exhibit 8–5   *Sale of a 10 Percent Interest Within an Accounting Period*

paper entry b reflects the $288,000 beginning investment balance less the $32,650 book value of the investment interest sold on April 1.

Except for the items discussed, the working papers in Exhibits 8–4 and 8–5 are comparable and the resulting consolidated financial statements are equivalent in all material respects. Because of the additional complexity involved when a sale is recorded as of the actual sale date, it is more efficient to use the beginning-of-the-period sale assumption. Use of a beginning-of-the-period assumption is also practical because current earnings information is usually not available during an accounting period.

CHANGES IN OWNERSHIP INTERESTS FROM SUBSIDIARY STOCK TRANSACTIONS

Subsidiary stock issuances provide a means of expanding the operations of a subsidiary through external financing. Both the expansion and the financing decisions are, of course, controlled by the parent company. Parent company management may decide to construct a new plant for the subsidiary and to finance the construction by selling additional subsidiary stock to the parent. For example, in February 1990 American Express Co. announced that it would assist its financially troubled 61 percent investee, Shearson Lehman Hutton Holdings, Inc. with an additional $750 million. The plan to transfer funds to Shearson involved a direct purchase of Shearson's preferred and common shares by American Express, thus increasing its ownership interest. (Subsequently, when this additional money appeared to be insufficient, American Express purchased the remainder of the Shearson stock it did not already own.) Subsidiary operations may also be expanded through the issuance of subsidiary stock to the public. In the case of a partially owned subsidiary, minority stockholders may exercise their preemptive rights to subscribe to additional stock issuances in proportion to their holdings.

Subsidiary operations may be curtailed if the parent company management decides to have the subsidiary reacquire its own shares.

A parent company/investor's ownership in a subsidiary/investee may change as a result of subsidiary sales of additional shares or through subsidiary purchases of its own shares. The effect of such activities on the parent company/investor depends on the price at which additional shares are sold or treasury stock is purchased, and on whether the parent company is directly involved in transactions with the subsidiary. In accounting for an equity investment under a one-line consolidation, *APB Opinion No. 18* stipulates that "a transaction of an investee of a capital nature that affects the investor's share of stockholders' equity of the investee should be accounted for as if the investee were a consolidated subsidiary."[3]

Sale of Additional Shares by a Subsidiary

Assume that Purdy owns an 80 percent interest in Stroh Corporation and that Purdy's investment in Stroh is $180,000 on January 1, 19X7, equal to 80 percent of Stroh's $200,000 stockholders' equity plus $20,000 unamortized goodwill. Stroh's equity on this date consists of:

Capital stock, $10 par	$100,000
Additional paid-in capital	60,000
Retained earnings	40,000
Total stockholders' equity	$200,000

Subsidiary Sells Shares to Parent If Stroh sells an additional 2,000 shares of stock to Purdy *at book value of $20 per share* on January 2, 19X7, Purdy's investment in Stroh will increase by $40,000 to $220,000, and its interest in Stroh will increase from 80 percent (8,000/10,000 shares) to 83⅓ percent (10,000/12,000 shares). Since the amount paid for the 2,000 additional shares is equal to book value, Purdy's investment in Stroh still reflects the $20,000 unamortized goodwill:

---

[3]*APB Opinion No. 18*, "The Equity Method of Accounting for Investments in Common Stock," paragraph 19e.

	January 1 *Before Sale*	January 2 *After Sale*
Stroh's stockholders' equity	$200,000	$240,000
Purdy's interest	80%	83⅓%
Purdy's equity in Stroh	160,000	200,000
Unamortized goodwill	20,000	20,000
Investment in Stroh balance	$180,000	$220,000

If Stroh sells the 2,000 shares to Purdy *at $35 per share*, Purdy's investment in Stroh will increase to $250,000 ($180,000 + $70,000 additional investment), and its ownership interest will increase from 80 percent to 83⅓ percent. Now Purdy's investment in Stroh reflects a $25,000 excess of investment balance over underlying book value. The additional $5,000 excess is the result of Purdy's $70,000 payment to increase its equity in Stroh by $65,000 and is analyzed as follows:

Price paid by Purdy (2,000 shares × $35)		$70,000
Book value acquired:		
Underlying book value after purchase ($200,000 + $70,000) × 83⅓%	$225,000	
Underlying book value before purchase ($200,000 × 80%)	160,000	
Book value acquired		65,000
Excess cost over book value acquired		$ 5,000

The $5,000 excess is assigned to identifiable assets or goodwill as appropriate and amortized over the remaining life of undervalued assets, or over a maximum of forty years if assigned to goodwill. Purdy should amortize the $20,000 unamortized goodwill at January 1, 19X1 without changing the initial amortization plan.

Now assume that Stroh sells the 2,000 shares to Purdy at *$15 per share* (or $5 per share below book value). Purdy's ownership interest increases from 80 percent to 83⅓ percent as before, and its investment in Stroh increases by $30,000 to $210,000. But as a result of paying less than book value for the shares, book value acquired exceeds investment cost:

Price paid by Purdy (2,000 shares × $15)		$30,000
Book value acquired:		
Underlying book value after purchase ($200,000 + $30,000) × 83⅓%	$191,667	
Underlying book value before purchase ($200,000 × 80%)	160,000	
Book value acquired		31,667
Excess book value acquired over cost		$ 1,667

Conceptually, the $1,667 excess book value acquired over cost should be assigned to reduce overvalued identifiable net assets. The practical solution however, is to charge the excess book value to any unamortized goodwill from investments in the same company's stock. In this example, reduce unamortized goodwill from $20,000 to $18,333.

Subsidiary Sells Shares to Outside Entities Assume that Stroh sells the 2,000 additional shares to other entities (minority stockholders). Purdy's ownership interest declines from 80 percent (8,000/10,000 shares) to 66⅔ percent

(8,000/12,000 shares) regardless of the selling price of the shares. But the effect on Purdy's investment in Stroh account depends upon the selling price of the shares. The effect of the sale on Purdy's underlying book value in Stroh under each of three issuance assumptions ($20, $35, and $15 per share) is:

	January 2, 19X1 after Sale		
	Sale at $20	*Sale at $35*	*Sale at $15*
Stroh's stockholders' equity	$240,000	$270,000	$230,000
Interest owned	66⅔%	66⅔%	66⅔%
Purdy's equity in Stroh after issuance	160,000	180,000	153,333
Purdy's equity in Stroh before issuance	160,000	160,000	160,000
Increase (decrease) in Purdy's equity in Stroh	0	$ 20,000	$ (6,667)

Sale to outside entities at $20 per share does not affect Purdy's equity in Stroh because the selling price is equal to book value. If the stock is sold at $35 per share (above book value), Purdy's equity in Stroh will increase by $20,000 and if it is sold at $15 per share (below book value), Purdy's equity in Stroh will decrease by $6,667.

Two methods of accounting for the effect of the decreased ownership percentage on the parent company's books are (1) to adjust the additional paid-in capital and the parent's investment account balances for the change in underlying equity and (2) to treat the decrease in ownership as a sale and recognize gain or loss for the difference between book value of the investment interest sold and the parent's share of the proceeds from the subsidiary's stock issuance.

The first approach is supported by *APB Opinion No. 9,* which excludes adjustments from transactions in a company's own stock from the determination of net income "under all circumstances."[4] From the viewpoint of the consolidated entity, the issuance of subsidiary shares to the public is a transaction in a company's own shares. Entries to record the changes in underlying equity on Purdy's books under this first method are:

Sale at $20 per Share (Book Value)
None

Sale at $35 per Share (Above Book Value)

Investment in Stroh	$20,000	
Additional paid-in capital		$20,000

Sale at $15 per Share (Below Book Value)

Additional paid-in capital[5]	$ 6,667	
Investment in Stroh		$ 6,667

Under this method, unamortized cost–book value differentials are not adjusted for the decreased ownership percentage.

Traditionally, the method just illustrated was the only one accepted by the accounting profession and the Securities and Exchange Commission (SEC). In 1980, however, the AICPA released an Issues Paper, "Accounting in Consolidation for Issuances of a Subsidiary's Stock," in which it recommended the recognition of gains or losses on subsidiary stock sales. Then, in 1983, the SEC issued

---

[4]*APB Opinion No. 9,* "Reporting the Results of Operations," paragraph 28.

[5]This debit is to retained earnings when the parent company's additional paid-in capital is insufficient to stand the charge.

Staff Accounting Bulletin (SAB) 51, which allows SEC companies to follow the recommendations of the Issues Paper for previously unissued shares, provided that the subsidiary shares are sold in a public offering and are not part of a broader reorganization that will involve other capital transactions. Subsequently, in 1989 the SEC, in *SAB 84* affirmed that a parent company can record a gain in the consolidated income statement on its subsidiary's sale of stock to the public if the per share offering price is greater than the carrying value of the subsidiary on the parent company's books. However, *SAB 84* restricts recognition of gain when there are concerns about realization of the gain. *SAB 84* prohibits gain recognition on subsidiary stock sales to the public if the registrant plans to repurchase the shares, if the subsidiary is a newly formed nonoperating entity or a research and development company, or if the subsidiary is a company whose continued existence is in question.

The argument in favor of gain or loss recognition is that there is no substantive difference between subsidiary stock sales that reduce a parent's investment and direct sales of stock by the parent. Since the FASB has not acted on the matter, neither the Issues Paper nor *SAB 51* constitutes generally accepted accounting principles at this time. And while *SAB 51* is permissive and not mandatory, it may help establish preferability for a firm that changes its accounting policy to recognize gains on subsidiary stock sales.

Under the second method of gain or loss recognition, Purdy is assumed to have sold 16⅔ percent of its interest in Stroh [(80% − 66⅔%)/80%] in exchange for 66⅔ percent of the proceeds from the subsidiary sale of stock. Thus, the entries on Purdy's books under the three selling price assumptions are:

Sale at $20 per Share (Book Value)

Loss on sale	$ 3,333	
Investment in Stroh		$ 3,333

  Computation: ($40,000 × 66⅔%) − ($180,000 × 16⅔%)

Sale at $35 per Share (Above Book Value)

Investment in Stroh	$16,667	
Gain on sale		$16,667

  Computation: ($70,000 × 66⅔%) − ($180,000 × 16⅔%)

Sale at $15 per Share (Below Book Value)

Loss on sale	$10,000	
Investment in Stroh		$10,000

  Computation: ($30,000 × 66⅔%) − ($180,000 × 16⅔%)

The different gain or loss amounts under this method and the amounts of adjustment to additional paid-in capital under the first method lie solely in the $3,333 unamortized goodwill [$20,000 × (80% − 66⅔%)/80%] applicable to the reduction in ownership percentage. Unamortized goodwill related to the interest assumed to be sold is only considered when gain or loss is recognized, and in the absence of unamortized cost–book value differences, the amounts are identical.

Summary of Subsidiary Stock Sales Concepts   Sales of stock by a subsidiary to its parent do not result in gain or loss recognition or adjustments to additional paid-in capital, but they do result in cost–book value differentials equal to the parent company's share of the difference in the subsidiary's stockholders' equity immediately before and immediately after the sale of stock.

Sales of stock by a subsidiary to outside parties are considered capital transactions under generally accepted accounting principles, and they require adjustment of the parent's investment and additional paid-in capital accounts except when the shares are sold at book value. The amount of adjustment is the difference between the underlying book value of the interest held immediately before and after the additional shares are issued to outsiders. The SEC permits recognition of gains or losses on subsidiary stock sales to the public-with certain restrictions. Such gain or loss is determined by comparing the parent's share of proceeds from the stock issue with the book value of the investment interest assumed to be sold. Alternatively, the gain or loss can be determined by adjusting the change in the parent's underlying book value in the subsidiary for any unamortized cost–book value differentials related to the interest assumed to be sold.

If a parent company and outside investors purchase shares of a subsidiary in relation to existing stock ownership (ratably), no adjustments to additional paid-in capital will be necessary regardless of whether the stock is sold at book value, below book value, or above book value. Similarly, no excess or deficiency of investment cost over book value for the parent company can result from this situation. This is true because the increased investment is necessarily equal to the parent's increase (or decrease) in underlying book value from the ratable purchase of additional shares.

Treasury Stock Transactions by a Subsidiary

The acquisition of treasury stock by a subsidiary decreases subsidiary equity and subsidiary shares outstanding. If the treasury stock is acquired from minority shareholders at book value, no change in the parent's share of subsidiary equity results even though the parent's percentage ownership increases. Purchase of its own shares from minority stockholders at an amount above or below book value decreases or increases the parent's share of subsidiary book value and at the same time increases the parent's ownership percentage. This latter situation requires an entry on the parent company's books to adjust the investment in subsidiary balance, and to charge or credit additional paid-in capital for the difference in the parent's share of subsidiary book value before and after the treasury stock transaction.

Assume that Shelly Company is an 80 percent subsidiary of Pointer Corporation and that Shelly has 10,000 shares of common stock outstanding at December 31, 19X7. On January 1, 19X8 Shelly purchases 400 shares of its own stock from minority stockholders. The effect of this treasury stock acquisition on Pointer's share of Shelly's book value is summarized in Exhibit 8–6 under three different assumptions regarding the purchase price of the treasury shares.

Pointer's equity in Shelly Company before the purchase of the 400 shares of treasury stock by Shelly was $160,000 and its ownership interest was 80 percent, as shown in the first column of Exhibit 8–6. The purchase of the 400 treasury shares by Shelly increases Pointer's ownership percentage to 83 ⅓ percent (or 8,000 of 9,600 outstanding shares) regardless of the price paid by Shelly to reacquire the shares. If Shelly purchases the 400 shares at their $20 per share book value, Pointer's share of Shelly's equity remains at $160,000, as shown in the second column of Exhibit 8–6, even though its interest increases to 83 ⅓ percent. In this case, no adjustment is required.

If Shelly purchases the 400 shares of treasury stock at $30 per share, Pointer's equity decreases by $3,333 to $156,667, as shown in column 3 of Exhibit 8–6. The decrease is recorded on Pointer's books with the following entry:

Additional paid-in capital	$3,333	
Investment in Shelly		$3,333

To record an investment decrease from Shelly's purchase of treasury stock in excess of book value.

This entry reduces Pointer's investment in Shelly to its share of the underlying book value in Shelly and also reduces additional paid-in capital. Since treasury stock transactions are of a capital nature, they do not affect gain or loss.

EQUITY OF SHELLY COMPANY

	Column 1	Column 2	Column 3	Column 4
	Before Purchase of Treasury Stock	*After Purchase of 400 Shares at $20*	*After Purchase of 400 Shares at $30*	*After Purchase of 400 Shares at $15*
Capital stock, $10 par	$100,000	$100,000	$100,000	$100,000
Retained earnings	100,000	100,000	100,000	100,000
	200,000	200,000	200,000	200,000
Less: Treasury stock (cost)	—	8,000	12,000	6,000
Total equity	$200,000	$192,000	$188,000	$194,000
Pointer's interest	4/5*	5/6†	5/6†	5/6†
Pointer's share of Shelly's book value	$160,000	$160,000	$156,667	$161,667

*8,000 out of 10,000 outstanding shares.
†8,000 out of 9,600 outstanding shares.

Exhibit 8-6 *Purchase of Treasury Stock by Subsidiary*

The third situation illustrated in Exhibit 8–6 (column 4) assumes that Shelly purchases 400 shares of treasury stock at $15 per share ($5 per share below book value). As a result of Shelly's acquisition of its own shares, Pointer's share of Shelly's equity increases from $160,000 to $161,667. This increase of $1,667 requires the following adjustment on Pointer's books:

Investment in Shelly	$1,667	
Additional paid-in capital		$1,667

    To record an investment increase from Shelly's purchase of treasury shares below book value.

The parent company adjustments illustrated here for changes resulting from subsidiary treasury stock transactions are supported by current accounting principles that prohibit the recognition of gain or loss from treasury stock transactions, but at the same time require the equity method of accounting with elimination of any differences between the investment and its underlying book value over a maximum period of forty years. The parent's accounting for subsidiary treasury stock transactions is based on the book value of the net assets. During the time the treasury shares are held, the book value of net assets would change due to the subsidiary's operations. If the treasury shares are eventually resold, the parent would account for this change on the basis of the book value of the assets at the time of sale. It should be understood, however, that *frequent and insignificant treasury stock transactions by a subsidiary tend to be offsetting with respect to purchases and sales and do not require the adjustments illustrated.*

STOCK DIVIDENDS AND STOCK SPLITS BY A SUBSIDIARY

Stock dividends and splits by substantially owned subsidiaries are not common unless the minority interest is actively traded in the security markets. This is because the management of the parent company controls such actions and there is ordinarily no advantage to the consolidated entity or the parent company from increasing the number of subsidiary shares outstanding through stock splits or stock dividends. Even if a subsidiary does split its stock or issue a stock dividend, the effect of such actions on consolidation procedures is minimal.

A stock split by a subsidiary increases the number of shares outstanding, but it does not affect either the net assets of the subsidiary or the individual equity accounts. Also, parent company and minority interest ownership percentages are unaffected by subsidiary stock splits and, accordingly, parent company accounting and consolidation procedures are unaffected. These same observations apply to stock dividends by subsidiaries except that the individual subsidiary equity accounts are changed in the case of stock dividends. This change occurs because retained earnings equal to par or stated value or to the market price of the additional shares issued is transferred to paid-in capital.[6] Although the capitalization of retained earnings does not affect parent company accounting for its subsidiaries, it does change the amounts of capital stock, additional paid-in capital, and retained earnings to be eliminated in the consolidation process.

Pictor Corporation owns 80 percent of the outstanding stock of Sorry Company acquired on January 1, 19X5 for $160,000. Sorry's stockholders' equity on that date was as follows:

Capital stock, $10 par	$100,000
Additional paid-in capital	20,000
Retained earnings	80,000
Total stockholders' equity	$200,000

During 19X5 Sorry had net income of $30,000 and paid cash dividends of $10,000. Pictor increased its investment in Sorry for its investment income of $24,000 ($30,000 × 80%) and decreased it for dividends received of $8,000 ($10,000 × 80%). Thus, Pictor's investment in Sorry account at December 31, 19X5 was $176,000.

On the basis of the information given, the consolidation working papers for Pictor Corporation and Subsidiary for 19X5 would include the following adjustments and eliminations:

Income from Sorry	$ 24,000		
Dividends			$ 8,000
Investment in Sorry			16,000
Capital stock—Sorry	$100,000		
Additional paid-in capital—Sorry	20,000		
Retained earnings—Sorry	80,000		
Investment in Sorry			$160,000
Minority interest—beginning			40,000

If Sorry had also declared and issued a 10 percent stock dividend on December 31, 19X5 when its stock was selling at $40 per share, the stock dividend would have been recorded by Sorry Corporation as follows:

Stock dividend on common	$40,000	
Capital stock, $10 par		$10,000
Additional paid-in capital		30,000

This stock dividend does not affect Pictor's accounting for its investment in Sorry, but it does affect the consolidation working papers, since Sorry's capital stock has increased to $110,000 ($100,000 + $10,000) and its additional paid-in capital

---

[6]See *ARB No. 43,* Chapter 7, paragraphs 10 through 14, for accounting procedures relating to stock dividends.

has increased to $50,000 ($20,000 + $30,000). Consolidation working paper adjustment and elimination entries for 19X5 would be as follows:

Income from Sorry	$ 24,000	
Dividends		$ 8,000
Investment in Sorry		16,000
Capital stock—Sorry	$110,000	
Additional paid-in capital—Sorry	50,000	
Retained earnings—Sorry	80,000	
Investment in Sorry		$160,000
Minority interest—beginning		40,000
Stock dividend on common		40,000

The $40,000 stock dividend account is eliminated along with the reciprocal investment and equity balances, since it is really an offset to $10,000 of the capital stock and $30,000 of the additional paid-in capital amounts. In 19X6 and subsequent years, the retained earnings account will reflect the $40,000 decrease from the stock dividend and no further complications will result.

SUMMARY

When a parent company purchases a subsidiary during an accounting period, the preacquisition earnings relating to the interest acquired are deducted in computing consolidated net income. Preacquisition dividends on an interest acquired during an accounting period are also eliminated in the consolidation process. Accounting for a midyear pooling of interests involves consolidating the incomes of the pooled affiliates for the entire year. The investment is recorded at its book value at the beginning of the period, adjusted for dividends paid prior to combination.

The acquisition of a controlling interest in another company through a series of separate stock purchases over a period of time increases the detail involved in accounting for the total investment under the equity method. It also complicates the preparation of consolidated financial statements because the investment cost–book value differential has to be related to each acquisition on the basis of the total interest held.

When a parent company/investor sells an ownership interest in a subsidiary/investee corporation, the gain or loss on sale is equal to the difference between the selling price and the book value of the investment interest sold. But if the investment is not accounted for on an equity basis, it has to be adjusted to an equity basis before gain or loss on sale is computed. The sale of an interest in a subsidiary during an accounting period increases the minority interest and necessitates some changes in the computation of minority interest income.

The sale of additional shares by a subsidiary changes the parent's percentage ownership in the subsidiary unless the shares are sold to the parent company and minority shareholders in proportion to their holdings. The direct sale of additional shares to the parent company increases the parent's interest and decreases the minority shareholders' interest. The issuance of additional shares to minority stockholders or outside entities by the subsidiary decreases the parent's percentage interest and increases the minority shareholders' interests. Similar changes in majority and minority ownership interests result from a subsidiary's treasury stock transactions. Such changes require special care in accounting for a parent company's investment under the equity method and in preparing consolidated financial statements.

Parent company accounting and consolidation procedures are not affected by subsidiary stock splits. However, subsidiary stock dividends may lead to changes in the consolidation working papers.

SELECTED READINGS

Accountants International Study Group. *Consolidated Financial Statements: Current Recommended Practices in Canada, the United Kingdom, and the United States.* Plainstow, England: Curwen Press Ltd., 1973.

CHILDS, WILLIAM HERBERT. *Consolidated Financial Statements: Principles and Procedures.* Ithaca, NY: Cornell University Press, 1949 (especially see Chapter 7, "Stock Transactions After Original Acquisition").

Committee on Accounting Procedure. *Accounting Research Bulletin No. 51.* "Consolidated Financial Statements." New York: American Institute of Certified Public Accountants, 1959.

NEMEC, MARILYN J. "Reporting in Consolidated Statements the Sale of Subsidiary Stock." *CPA Journal* (March 1973), pp. 214—217.

ASSIGNMENT MATERIAL

QUESTIONS

1 Explain the terms *preacquisition earnings* and *preacquisition dividends.*

2 How are preacquisition earnings accounted for by a parent company under the equity method? How are they accounted for in the consolidated income statement?

3 Assume that an 80 percent investor of Sub Company acquires an additional 10 percent interest in Sub halfway through the current fiscal period. Explain the effect of the 10 percent acquisition by the parent company on minority interest income for the period and on total minority interest at the end of the current period.

4 Isn't preacquisition income really minority interest income? If so, why separate preacquisition income and minority interest income in the consolidated income statement?

5 What modifications to the usual equity method of accounting are required on a parent company's books in accounting for a midyear pooling of interests? (In other words, how is equality established between parent company and consolidated net income for midyear poolings?)

6 Assume that Pam Corporation purchases plant and equipment from Sam Corporation in January 19X8 and that a pooling business combination between Pam and Sam is consummated in September 19X8. Is the plant asset transaction an intercompany transaction for which gains and losses must be eliminated in the consolidated statements for the year ended December 31, 19X8? Explain.

7 How is the gain or loss determined for the sale of part of an investment interest that is accounted for as a one-line consolidation? Is the amount of gain or loss affected by the accounting method used by the investor?

8 When a parent company sells a part of its interest in a subsidiary during an accounting period, is the income applicable to the interest sold up to the time of sale included in consolidated net income and parent company income under the equity method? Explain.

9 Assume that a subsidiary has 10,000 shares of stock outstanding, of which 8,000 shares are owned by the parent company. What equity method adjustment would be necessary on the parent company books if the subsidiary sells 2,000 additional shares of its own stock to outside interests at book value? At an amount in excess of book value?

10 Assume that a subsidiary has 10,000 shares of stock outstanding, of which 8,000 shares are owned by the parent company. If the parent company purchases an additional 2,000 shares of stock directly from the subsidiary at book value, how should the parent company record its additional investment? Would your answer have been different if the purchase of the 2,000 shares had been made above book value? Explain.

11 How do the treasury stock transactions of a subsidiary affect the parent company's accounting for its investment under the equity method?

12 Can gains or losses to a parent company (investor) result from a subsidiary's (investee's) treasury stock transactions? Explain.

13 Do common stock dividends and stock splits by a subsidiary affect the amounts that appear in the consolidated financial statements? Explain, indicating the items, if any, that would be affected.

(*Note:* Don't forget the assumptions on page 60 when working exercises and problems in this chapter.)

EXERCISES

E 8–1 A parent company increases its ownership interest in a subsidiary from 60 percent at January 1 to 90 percent at July 1 of the current year. The subsidiary's net income for the calendar year is $50,000, and it declares dividends of $30,000 ($7,500 each quarter of the year).

Required: Show the allocation of the subsidiary's net income and dividends among majority interests, minority interests, and preacquisition interests.

E 8–2 On January 1, 19X9 Pinnacle Industries purchased a 40 percent interest in Superstore, Inc. for $800,000 when Superstore's stockholders' equity consisted of $1,000,000 capital stock and $1,000,000 retained earnings. On September 1, 19X9 Pinnacle purchased an additional 20 percent interest in Superstore for $420,000. Both purchases were made at book value equal to fair value.

Superstore had income for 19X9 of $240,000, earned evenly throughout the year, and it paid dividends of $60,000 in April and $60,000 in October.

Required: Compute the following:
  1 Pinnacle's income from Superstore for 19X9
  2 Preacquisition income that will appear on the consolidated income statement of Pinnacle and Subsidiary for 19X9
  3 Minority interest income for 19X9

E 8–3 Pekin Corporation owns 100 percent (300,000 shares) of the outstanding shares of Script Corporation's common stock on January 1, 19X1. Its investment in Script account on this date is $4,400,000, equal to Script's $4,000,000 stockholders' equity plus $400,000 goodwill with a remaining write-off period of ten years. During 19X1 Script reports net income of $600,000 and pays no dividends.

On April 1, 19X1 Pekin sells a 10 percent interest (30,000 shares) in Script for $450,000, thereby reducing its holdings to 90 percent.

Required: Prepare the journal entries needed for Pekin to account for its investment in Script for 19X1, using a beginning-of-the-period sales assumption.

E 8–4 Pfizer Corporation owned an 80 percent interest in Savannah Corporation on January 1, 19X1 at which time its investment in Savannah balance was $840,000, consisting of 80 percent of Savannah's $1,000,000 net assets plus $40,000 unamortized goodwill with a remaining amortization period of five years. During 19X1, Savannah reported net income of $150,000 and declared no dividends. On April 1, 19X1 Pfizer reduced its interest in Savannah to 70 percent by selling a 10 percent interest for $132,000.

Part A: Assume that Pfizer uses a January 1, 19X1 date in accounting for the 10 percent interest sold. Compute the following:
  1 Gain or loss on sale
  2 Income from Savannah for 19X1
  3 Investment in Savannah, December 31, 19X1

Part B: Assume that Pfizer uses April 1, 19X1 (the actual sale date) in accounting for the 10 percent interest sold. Compute the following:
  4 Gain or loss on sale
  5 Income from Savannah for 19X1
  6 Investment in Savannah, December 31, 19X1

E 8–5 On October 1, 19X2 Presley Corporation issued 30,000 shares of $10 par common stock with a market value of $30 per share for a 90 percent interest in Solomon Corporation in a pooling of interests business combination. Direct costs of the combination which are paid by Presley total $30,000 for registering and issuing the shares and $35,000 for other items.

On January 1, 19X2 the book value (equal to fair value) of Solomon's net assets was $912,500. Solomon's net income for 19X2 is $100,000 earned evenly throughout the year, and Solomon declares dividends of $25,000 on June 1 and $25,000 on December 1. Presley's separate income for 19X2 is $300,000 *excluding* the direct costs of combination.

Required: Determine consolidated net income for Presley Corporation and Subsidiary for 19X2.

E 8-6 The stockholders' equities of Pecal Corporation and its 80 percent owned subsidiary, Socol Corporation, at December 31, 19X2 are as follows:

	Pecal	Socal
Common stock, $10 par	$10,000,000	$6,000,000
Retained earnings	4,000,000	3,000,000
Total stockholders' equity	$14,000,000	$9,000,000

Pecal's investment in Socal account balance on December 31, 19X2 is equal to its underlying book value. On January 2, 19X3 Socal issued 40,000 previously unissued common shares directly to Pecal at $25 per share.

Required
1 Calculate the balance of Pecal's investment in Socal account on January 2, 19X3 after the new investment is recorded.
2 Determine the goodwill, if any, from Pecal's purchase of the 40,000 new shares.

E 8-7 Prod Corporation holds 360,000 common shares of Soma Corporation, acquired at book value. The stockholders' equity of Soma on December 31, 19X1 and on January 1, 19X2 after Soma issues 100,000 common shares to the public at $20 per share are as follows:

	After Closing December 31, 19X1	After Issuance January 1, 19X2
Common stock, $10 par	$4,000,000	$5,000,000
Additional paid-in capital	2,000,000	3,000,000
Retained earnings	1,000,000	1,000,000
Total stockholders' equity	$7,000,000	$9,000,000

Required
1 Determine Prod's percentage ownership in Soma before and after the additional shares are issued.
2 Prepare any journal entries needed on Prod's books to account for the January 1, 19X2 stock issuance of Soma.

E 8-8 Pecko Corporation purchased a 20 percent interest in Schule Corporation for $72,000 on April 1, 19X7 and a 40 percent interest for $147,000 on October 1, 19X7.

Schule's stockholders' equity at January 1, 19X7 consisted of $200,000 capital stock and $100,000 retained earnings. During 19X7 Schule had income of $40,000, and in December 19X7 it declared dividends of $20,000.

Pecko Corporation amortizes any excess or deficiency of investment cost over book value acquired over a ten-year period.

Required: Compute the following:
1 Preacquisition earnings that will appear in the consolidated income statement of Pecko Corporation and Subsidiary for 19X7
2 Income from Schule from the 20 percent purchase for 19X7
3 Income from Schule from the 40 percent purchase for 19X7
4 Minority interest in Schule Corporation at December 31, 19X7
5 The balance of Pecko's investment in Schule account at December 31, 19X7 assuming that income from Schule for 19X7 is $8,875

E 8-9 Piccolo Corporation acquired a 90 percent interest in Sandridge Mines on July 1, 19X4 for $675,000. The stockholders' equity of Sandridge Mines at December 31, 19X3 was as follows:

Capital stock	$500,000
Retained earnings	200,000
Total	$700,000

During 19X4 and 19X5 Sandridge Mines reported income and declared dividends in the following amounts:

	19X4	19X5
Net income	$100,000	$80,000
Dividends (December)	50,000	30,000

On July 1, 19X5, Piccolo Corporation sold a 10 percent interest (or one-ninth of its investment) in Sandridge Mines for $85,000.

Required

1 Determine Piccolo's investment income for 19X4 and 19X5, and its investment balance at December 31, 19X4 and 19X5.
2 Determine minority interest income for 19X4 and 19X5, and the total of minority interest at December 31, 19X4 and 19X5.

E 8–10 Summarized adjusted trial balances for Pollock Corporation and Sequoia Corporation at August 31, 19X6, just prior to their *pooling of interests* on September 1, 19X6, are as follows:

	Pollock	Sequoia
Assets	$16,000,000	$5,500,000
Expenses	9,000,000	3,000,000
Dividends	2,000,000	500,000
	$27,000,000	$9,000,000
Liabilities	$ 3,000,000	$1,500,000
Common stock, $10 par	8,000,000	2,000,000
Other paid-in capital	1,000,000	500,000
Retained earnings	3,000,000	1,000,000
Sales	12,000,000	4,000,000
	$27,000,000	$9,000,000

Pollock's separate income for the year ended December 31, 19X6 was $4,500,000 and its dividends for 19X6 totaled $4,000,000. Sequoia Corporation's net income for 19X6 was $1,500,000 and its dividends were $1,000,000.

Required

1 Prepare journal entries on Pollock's books (a) to record its issuance of 300,000 common shares on September 1, 19X6 for all of the outstanding common stock of Sequoia, and (b) to account for its investment in Sequoia for 19X6 assuming that Pollock and Sequoia continue to exist as parent company and subsidiary.
2 Prepare the stockholders' equity section of the consolidated balance sheet of Pollock Corporation and Subsidiary at December 31, 19X6.

E 8–11 **[AICPA adapted]**

On June 30, 19X8, Purl Corp. issued 150,000 shares of its $20 par common stock for which it received all of Scott Corp.'s common stock. The fair value of the common stock issued is equal to the book value of Scott's net assets. Both corporations continued to operate as separate businesses, maintaining accounting records with years ending December 31. Net income from separate company operations and dividends paid were:

	Purl	*Scott*
Net income		
Six months ended June 30, 19X8	$750,000	$225,000
Six months ended December 31, 19X8	825,000	375,000
Dividends paid		
March 25, 19X8	950,000	—
November 15, 19X8	—	300,000

On December 31, 19X8, Scott held in its inventory merchandise acquired from Purl on December 1, 19X8 for $150,000, which included a $45,000 markup.

1 Assume that the business combination qualifies for treatment as a purchase. In the 19X8 consolidated income statement, net income should be reported at:

   a $1,650,000   **b** $1,905,000

   c $1,950,000   **d** $2,130,000

2 Assume that the business combination qualifies for treatment as a pooling of interests. In the 19X8 consolidated income statement, net income should be reported as:

   a $1,905,000   **b** $1,950,000

   c $2,130,000   **d** $2,175,000

E 8–12   **[AICPA adapted]**

On June 30, 19X7, Post, Inc., issued 630,000 shares of its $5 par common stock, for which it received 180,000 shares (90%) of Shaw Corp.'s $10 par common stock in a business combination appropriately accounted for as a pooling of interests. The stockholders' equities immediately before the combination were:

	Post	*Shaw*
Common stock	$ 6,500,000	$2,000,000
Additional paid-in capital	4,400,000	1,600,000
Retained earnings	6,100,000	5,400,000
	$17,000,000	$9,000,000

Both corporations continued to operate as separate businesses, maintaining accounting records with years ending December 31. For 19X7, net income and dividends paid from separate company operations were:

	Post	*Shaw*
Net income		
Six months ended June 30, 19X7	$1,000,000	$300,000
Six months ended December 31, 19X7	1,100,000	500,000
Dividends paid		
April 1, 19X7	1,300,000	—
October 1, 19X7	—	350,000

1 In the June 30, 19X7 consolidated balance sheet, common stock should be reported at:

   a $9,650,000   **b** $9,450,000

   c $8,500,000   **d** $8,300,000

2 In the June 30, 19X7 consolidated balance sheet, additional paid-in capital should be reported at:

   a $4,400,000   **b** $4,490,000

   c $5,840,000   **d** $6,000,000

3 In the June 30, 19X7 consolidated balance sheet, retained earnings should be reported at:

   a $6,100,000   **b** $9,660,000

   c $10,960,000   **d** $11,500,000

4 In the 19X7 consolidated income statement, net income should be reported at:
  a $2,550,000   **b** $2,600,000
  c $2,820,000   **d** $2,900,000

5 In the December 31, 19X7 consolidated balance sheet, total minority interest should be reported at:
  a $950,000   **b** $945,000
  c $915,000   **d** $900,000

E 8-13   Panda Corporation purchased a 75 percent interest in Sanyo Corporation in the open market on January 1, 19X3 for $700,000. A summary of Sanyo's stockholders' equity at December 31, 19X2 and 19X3 is as follows:

	December 31	
	19X2	19X3
Capital stock, $10 par	$400,000	$ 400,000
Additional paid-in capital	300,000	300,000
Retained earnings	100,000	300,000
Total stockholders' equity	$800,000	$1,000,000

On January 1, 19X4 Sanyo sold an additional 10,000 shares of its own $10 par stock for $30 per share. Panda amortizes any excess or deficiency of investment cost over book value acquired over a ten-year period.

Required: Compute the following:
  1 The underlying book value of the interest in Sanyo held by Panda on December 31, 19X3.
  2 Panda's percentage ownership interest in Sanyo on January 3, 19X4 assuming that Panda purchased the 10,000 additional shares directly from Sanyo
  3 Panda's investment in Sanyo on January 3, 19X4 assuming that Panda purchased the additional shares directly from Sanyo
  4 Panda's percentage ownership interest in Sanyo on January 3, 19X4 assuming that Sanyo sold the 10,000 additional shares to investors outside the consolidated entity
  5 Panda's investment in Sanyo on January 3, 19X4 assuming that Sanyo sold the 10,000 additional shares to investors outside the consolidated entity and no gain or loss is recognized

E 8-14   Puckett Corporation's investment in Saton Company account had a balance of $475,000 at December 31, 19X3. This balance consisted of unamortized goodwill of $35,000 (seven-year remaining amortization period) and 80 percent of Saton's $550,000 stockholders' equity.

On January 2, 19X4 Saton increased its outstanding shares from 10,000 to 12,000 shares by selling 2,000 additional shares directly to Puckett at $70 per share. Saton's net income for 19X4 is $90,000, and in December 19X4 it pays $60,000 dividends.

Required: Prepare all journal entries other than closing entries to account for Puckett's investment in Saton during 19X4. Any difference between investment cost and book value acquired is assumed to be goodwill with a ten-year amortization period.

E 8-15   Patrick Corporation paid $1,800,000 for 90,000 shares of Striper Corporation's 100,000 outstanding shares on January 1, 19X1 when Striper's stockholders' equity consisted of $1,000,000 of $10 par common stock and $500,000 retained earnings. The excess cost over book value acquired was assigned to goodwill with a ten-year amortization period. On January 2, 19X3 Striper sold an additional 20,000 shares to the public for $600,000 and its stockholders' equity before and after issuance of the additional 20,000 shares was as follows:

	January 1, 19X3 (before issuance)	January 2, 19X3 (after issuance)
$10 par common stock	$1,000,000	$1,200,000
Additional paid-in capital		400,000
Retained earnings	800,000	800,000
Total stockholders' equity	$1,800,000	$2,400,000

Required
1 Determine Patrick's investment in Striper account balance on January 1, 19X3.
2 Prepare the entry on Patrick's books to account for its decreased ownership interest if gain or loss is not recognized.
3 Prepare the entry on Patrick's books to account for its decreased ownership interest if gain or loss is recognized.

PROBLEMS

P 8-1 A summary of the changes in the stockholders' equity of Spence Corporation from January 1, 19X4 to December 31, 19X5 appears as follows:

	Capital Stock $10 Par	Additional Paid-in Capital	Retained Earnings	Total Equity
Balance January 1, 19X4	$500,000	—	$ 50,000	$550,000
Dividends, December 19X4	—	—	(50,000)	(50,000)
Income, 19X4	—	—	100,000	100,000
Balance December 31, 19X4	$500,000	—	$100,000	$600,000
Sale of stock January 1, 19X5	100,000	$50,000	—	150,000
Dividends, December 19X5	—	—	(60,000)	(60,000)
Income, 19X5	—	—	150,000	150,000
Balance December 31, 19X5	$600,000	$50,000	$190,000	$840,000

Pierre Corporation purchases 40,000 shares of Spence Corporation's outstanding stock on July 1, 19X4 in the open market for $580,000 and an additional 10,000 shares directly from Spence for $150,000 on January 1, 19X5. Any excess of investment cost over book value acquired is due to goodwill with a ten-year amortization period.

Required
1 Determine the balance of Pierre's investment in Spence account on December 31, 19X4.
2 Compute Pierre's investment income from Spence for 19X5.
3 Determine the balance of Pierre's investment in Spence account on December 31, 19X5.

P 8-2 Prince Corporation purchased 960,000 shares of Smithtown Corporation's common stock (an 80 percent interest) for $21,200,000 on January 1, 19X6. The $2,000,000 excess of investment cost over book value acquired was allocated to goodwill with a ten-year amortization period.

On January 1, 19X8 Smithtown sold 400,000 previously unissued shares of common stock to the public for $30 per share. Smithtown's stockholders' equity on January 1, 19X6, when Prince acquired its interest, and at January 1, 19X8 immediately before and after the issuance of additional shares, was as follows:

	January 1, 19X6	January 1, 19X8 Before Issuance	January 1, 19X8 After Issuance
Common stock, $10 par	$12,000,000	$12,000,000	$16,000,000
Other paid-in capital	4,000,000	4,000,000	12,000,000
Retained earnings	8,000,000	10,000,000	10,000,000
Total	$24,000,000	$26,000,000	$38,000,000

Required

1 Calculate the balance of Prince's investment in Smithtown account on January 1, 19X8 before the additional stock issuance.
2 Determine Prince's percentage interest in Smithtown on January 1, 19X8 immediately after the additional stock issuance.
3 Prepare a journal entry on Prince's books to adjust for the additional share issuance on January 1, 19X8 if gain or loss is not recognized.
4 Prepare a journal entry on Prince's books to adjust for the additional share issuance on January 1, 19X8 if the issuance is treated as a sale and gain or loss is recognized (as permitted by the SEC).

P 8-3 Patterson Corporation owned a 90 percent interest in Shawnee Corporation, and during 19X5 the following changes occurred in Shawnee's equity and Patterson's investment in Shawnee:

	Shawnee's Stockholders' Equity	Unamortized Goodwill	Investment in Shawnee (90%)
Balance January 1, 19X5	$1,000,000	$49,500	$ 949,500
Income 19X5	250,000	4,500*	220,500
Dividends 19X5	150,000*	—	135,000*
Balance December 31, 19X5	$1,100,000	$45,000	$1,035,000

* Deduct.

During 19X6 Shawnee Corporation's net income was $280,000, and it declared $40,000 dividends each quarter of the year.

Patterson reduced its interest in Shawnee to 80 percent on July 1, 19X6 by selling Shawnee shares for $120,000.

Required

1 Prepare the journal entry on Patterson's books to record the sale of Shawnee shares as of the actual date of sale.
2 Prepare the journal entry on Patterson's books to record the sale of Shawnee shares as of January 1, 19X6.
3 Prepare a schedule to reconcile the answers to (1) and (2).

P 8-4 Panama Corporation owns 300,000 of 360,000 outstanding shares of Shenandoah Corporation, and its $8,700,000 investment in Shenandoah account balance at December 31, 19X4 is equal to the underlying equity interest in Shenandoah. A summary of Shenandoah's stockholders' equity at December 31, 19X4 is as follows:

Common stock, $10 par, 500,000 shares authorized, 400,000 shares issued, of which 40,000 are treasury shares	$ 4,000,000
Additional paid-in capital	2,500,000
Retained earnings	5,500,000
	12,000,000
Less: Treasury shares at cost	1,560,000
Total stockholders' equity	$10,440,000

Because of a cash shortage, Panama has decided to reduce its ownership interest in Shenandoah from a 5/6 interest to a 3/4 interest and is considering the following options.

Option 1   Sell 30,000 of the 300,000 shares held in Shenandoah
Option 2   Instruct Shenandoah to issue 40,000 shares of previously unissued stock
Option 3   Instruct Shenandoah to reissue the 40,000 shares of treasury stock

Assume that the shares can be sold at the current market price of $50 per share under each of the three options and that any tax consequences can be ignored. Panama's stockholders' equity at December 31, 19X4 consists of $10,000,000 par value of common stock, $3,000,000 additional paid-in capital, and $7,000,000 retained earnings.

Required: Compare the consolidated stockholders' equity on January 1, 19X5 under each of the three options. (*Hint:* Prepare journal entries on Panama's books as an initial step to your solution.)

P 8-5   Pal Products Company purchased 9,000 shares of Solo Corporation's $50 par common stock at $90 per share on January 1, 19X5 when Solo had capital stock of $500,000 and retained earnings of $300,000. During 19X5 Solo Corporation had net income of $50,000 but declared no dividends.

On January 1, 19X6 Solo Corporation sold an additional 2,000 shares of stock at $100 per share. Solo's net income for 19X6 was $70,000 and no dividends were declared.

Required: Determine the following:
  1 The balance of Pal Products Company's investment in Solo account on December 31, 19X5. (Use a ten-year amortization period for goodwill.)
  2 The goodwill (or negative goodwill) that should appear in the consolidated balance sheet at December 31, 19X6 assuming that Pal Products Company purchased the 2,000 shares issued on January 1, 19X6.
  3 Additional paid-in capital from consolidation at December 31, 19X6 assuming that Solo sold the 2,000 shares issued on January 1, 19X6 to outside entities.
  4 Minority interest at December 31, 19X6 assuming that Solo sold the 2,000 shares issued on January 1, 19X6 to outsiders.

P 8-6   Post Corporation purchased a 70 percent interest in Stake Corporation on January 2, 19X6 for $94,000 when Stake had capital stock of $100,000 and retained earnings of $20,000. On June 30, 19X7 Post purchased an additional 20 percent interest for $38,000.

Comparative financial statements for Post and Stake at and for the year ended December 31, 19X7 are summarized as follows:

	Post	Stake
Combined Income and Retained Earnings Statement for the Year Ended December 31, 19X7		
Sales	$400,000	$200,000
Income from Stake	24,000	—
Cost of sales	250,000*	150,000*
Expenses	50,000*	20,000*
Net income	124,000	30,000
Add: Beginning retained earnings	200,000	50,000
Less: Dividends, December 1, 19X7	64,000*	10,000*
Retained earnings December 31, 19X7	$260,000	$ 70,000
Balance Sheet at December 31, 19X7		
Other assets	$432,000	$200,000
Investment in Stake	168,000	—
Total assets	$600,000	$200,000

	Post	Stake
Liabilities	$ 40,000	$ 30,000
Common stock	300,000	100,000
Retained earnings	260,000	70,000
Total equities	$600,000	$200,000

* Deduct.

Required

  1 Prepare a schedule explaining the $168,000 balance in Post's investment in Stake account at December 31, 19X7.

  2 Compute the amount of goodwill that should appear in the December 31, 19X7 consolidated balance sheet. Assume a ten-year amortization period.

  3 Prepare a schedule showing computations of the amount of consolidated net income for 19X7.

  4 Compute consolidated retained earnings at December 31, 19X7.

  5 Compute minority interest at December 31, 19X7.

P 8-7 Comparative separate company and consolidated balance sheets for Percy Corporation and its 70 percent owned subsidiary, Sawyer Corporation, at year-end 19X6 were as follows:

	Percy	Sawyer	Consolidated
Cash	$ 100,000	$ 70,000	$ 170,000
Inventories	800,000	100,000	900,000
Other current assets	500,000	130,000	630,000
Plant assets—net	3,500,000	800,000	4,300,000
Investment in Sawyer	600,000	—	—
Goodwill	—	—	40,000
Total assets	$5,500,000	$1,100,000	$6,040,000
Current liabilities	$ 500,000	$ 300,000	$ 800,000
Capital stock, $10 par	3,000,000	500,000	3,000,000
Other paid-in capital	1,000,000	100,000	1,000,000
Retained earnings	1,000,000	200,000	1,000,000
Minority interest	—	—	240,000
Total equities	$5,500,000	$1,100,000	$6,040,000

    Sawyer's net income for 19X7 was $150,000 and its dividends for the year were $80,000 ($40,000 on March 1 and $40,000 on September 1). On April 1, 19X7 Percy increased its interest in Sawyer to 80 percent by purchasing 5,000 shares in the market at $19 per share.

    Percy's goodwill from its 70 pecent interest is being amortized $8,000 per year, and any goodwill from the 10 percent interest will be amortized over a ten-year period.

    Separate incomes of Percy and Sawyer for the year 19X7 are computed as follows:

	Percy	Sawyer
Sales	$2,000,000	$1,200,000
Cost of sales	1,200,000*	700,000*
Gross profit	800,000	500,000
Depreciation expense	400,000*	300,000*
Other expenses	100,000*	50,000*
Separate incomes	$ 300,000	$ 150,000

* Deduct.

Required

1 Prepare a consolidated income statement for Percy Corporation and Subsidiary for the year ended December 31, 19X7.

2 Prepare a schedule to show how Sawyer's net income and dividends for 19X7 are allocated among minority interests, majority interests, and other interests.

P 8–8 Proctor Corporation issues 55,000 of its shares for 90 percent of Simon Corporation's outstanding common shares in a pooling of interests consummated on April 1, 19X5. Adjusted trial balances for these affiliated companies on April 1, 19X5 before the pooling and at December 31, 19X5 are summarized as follows:

| | April 1, 19X5 | | December 31, 19X5 | |
	Proctor	Simon	Proctor	Simon
Debits				
Cash	$ 100,000	$ 80,000	$ 278,000	$ 70,000
Other assets	2,000,000	550,000	2,400,000	650,000
Investment in Simon	—	—	522,000	—
Dividends	100,000	20,000	400,000	80,000
Expenses	800,000	300,000	2,300,000	1,200,000
	$3,000,000	$950,000	$5,900,000	$2,000,000
Credits				
Liabilities	$ 400,000	$ 50,000	$ 124,000	$ 140,000
Capital stock, $10 par	1,000,000	300,000	1,550,000	300,000
Other paid-in capital	100,000	200,000	—	200,000
Retained earnings	600,000	60,000	636,000	60,000
Sales	900,000	340,000	3,500,000	1,300,000
Income from Simon	—	—	90,000	—
	$3,000,000	$950,000	$5,900,000	$2,000,000

Required: Prepare consolidated balance sheet working papers for Proctor Corporation and Subsidiary as of December 31, 19X5.

P 8–9 Pump Corporation acquired 100 percent of Seel Corporation's outstanding voting common stock at its book value of $620,000 on May 1, 19X2. The stockholders' equity of Seel on January 1, 19X2 consisted of $400,000 capital stock and $200,000 retained earnings. Seel's dividends for 19X2 were $60,000, paid $30,000 on April 1 and $30,000 on October 1. The acquisition was paid for in cash.

During 19X2 Pump made sales of $100,000 to Seel at a gross profit of $30,000. One-half of this merchandise was inventoried by Seel at year end, and one-half of the 19X2 intercompany sales were not paid for at year end 19X2.

Pump sold equipment with a ten-year remaining useful life to Seel at a $20,000 gain on December 31, 19X2.

Financial statements of Pump and Seel Corporations for 19X2 are summarized as follows:

	Pump	Seel
Combined Income and Retained Earnings		
Statements for the Year Ended December 31, 19X2		
Sales	$ 800,000	$400,000
Income from Seel	65,000	—
Gain on sale of equipment	20,000	—
Cost of sales	(400,000)	(150,000)
Depreciation expense	(110,000)	(40,000)
Other expenses	(125,000)	(60,000)
Net income	250,000	150,000
Add: Beginning retained earnings	600,000	200,000
Less: Dividends	(100,000)	(60,000)
Retained earnings December 31, 19X2	$ 750,000	$290,000

	Pump	Seel
Balance Sheet at December 31, 19X2		
Cash	$ 35,000	$ 70,000
Receivables—net	190,000	160,000
Inventories	100,000	80,000
Other assets	70,000	70,000
Land	50,000	50,000
Buildings—net	200,000	150,000
Equipment—net	400,000	220,000
Investment in Seel	655,000	—
Total assets	$1,700,000	$800,000
Accounts payable	$ 160,000	$100,000
Other liabilities	190,000	10,000
Common stock, $10 par	600,000	400,000
Retained earnings	750,000	290,000
Total equities	$1,700,000	$800,000

Required: Prepare consolidation working papers for Pump Corporation and Subsidiary for the year ended December 31, 19X2.

P 8-10   Pal Corporation paid $175,000 for a 70 percent interest in Sid Corporation's outstanding stock on April 1, 19X6. Sid's stockholders' equity on January 1, 19X6 consisted of $200,000 capital stock and $50,000 retained earnings.

Accounts and balances taken from the financial statements for Pal and Sid at and for the year ended December 31, 19X6 are as follows:

	Pal	Sid
Combined Income and Retained Earnings Statement for the		
Year Ended December 31, 19X6		
Sales	$287,100	$150,000
Income from Sid	12,300	—
Gain	12,000	2,000
Interest income	—	5,850
Expenses (includes cost of goods sold)	200,000*	117,850*
Interest expense	11,400*	—
Net income	100,000	40,000
Add: Beginning retained earnings	250,000	50,000
Less: Dividends	50,000*	20,000*
Retained earnings December 31, 19X6	$300,000	$ 70,000
Balance Sheet at December 31, 19X6		
Cash	$ 17,000	$ 4,000
Interest receivable	—	6,000
Inventories	140,000	60,000
Other current assets	110,000	20,000
Plant assets—net	502,700	107,300
Investment in Sid common	180,300	—
Investment in Pal bonds	—	102,700
Total assets	$950,000	$300,000
Interest payable	$ 6,000	$ —
Other current liabilities	38,600	30,000
12% bonds payable	100,000	—
Premium on bonds	5,400	—
Common stock	500,000	200,000
Retained earnings	300,000	70,000
Total equities	$950,000	$300,000

* Deduct.

Additional Information

1 Sid Corporation paid $102,850 for all of Pal's outstanding bonds on July 1, 19X6. These bonds were issued on January 1, 19X6, bear interest at 12 percent, have interest payment dates of July 1 and January 1, and mature ten years from the date of issue. The $6,000 premium on the issue is being amortized under the straight-line method.

2 Other current liabilities of Sid Corporation on December 31, 19X6 include $10,000 dividends declared on December 15 and unpaid at year-end. Sid also declared $10,000 dividends on March 15, 19X6.

3 Pal Corporation sold equipment to Sid on July 1, 19X6 for $30 000. This equipment was purchased by Pal on July 1, 19X3 for $36,000 and is being depreciated over a six-year period under the straight-line method (no scrap).

4 Sid sold land that cost $8,000 to Pal for $10,000 on October 15, 19X6. Pal still owns the land.

5 Pal uses the equity method of accounting for its 70 percent interest in Sid.

Required: Prepare consolidation working papers for Pal Corporation and Subsidiary for the year ended December 31, 19X6.

P 8-11 Pure Corporation acquired an 80 percent interest in Sapo Corporation's outstanding common stock on January 1, 19X1 for $600,000 cash. The stockholders' equity of Sapo on this date consisted of $400,000 capital stock and $100,000 retained earnings. On October 1, 19X2 Pure acquired an additional 10 percent interest in Sapo at its $62,000 book value to bring its interest in Sapo to 90 percent.

During 19X1 Pure made sales to Sapo of $75,000 at a gross profit to Pure of $15,000, and during 19X2 Pure made sales to Sapo of $100,000 at a gross profit of $30,000. All of the 19X1 sales were inventoried by Sapo at year-end 19X1, and two-thirds of the 19X2 sales were inventoried by Sapo at year-end 19X2. Sapo owed Pure $20,000 on account at December 31, 19X2.

On January 1, 19X2 Pure sold equipment with a book value of $60,000 and a remaining useful life of 6 years to Sapo for $90,000. Sapo uses straight-line depreciation and assumes no salvage value on this equipment.

Pure uses a one-line consolidation in accounting for its investment in Sapo. Dividends of the affiliated companies were declared in December 19X2. Financial statements of Pure and Sapo for 19X2 are summarized as follows:

	Pure	Sapo
Combined Income and Retained Earnings Statement for the Year Ended December 31, 19X2		
Sales	$1,000,000	$600,000
Income from Sapo	64,000	—
Gain on sale of equipment	30,000	—
Cost of sales	(500,000)	(350,000)
Depreciation expense	(110,000)	(70,000)
Other expenses	(184,000)	(60,000)
Net income	300,000	120,000
Beginning retained earnings	300,000	130,000
Less: Dividends	(200,000)	(50,000)
Retained earnings December 31, 19X2	$ 400,000	$200,000
Balance Sheet at December 31, 19X2		
Cash	$ 55,000	$ 40,000
Accounts receivable—net	140,000	50,000
Inventories	130,000	90,000
Other current assets	90,000	90,000
Land	50,000	50,000
Buildings—net	150,000	100,000
Equipment—net	400,000	430,000
Investment in Sapo	685,000	—
Total assets	$1,700,000	$850,000

	Pure	Sapo
Accounts payable	$ 320,000	$140,000
Other liabilities	480,000	110,000
Capital stock, $10 par	500,000	400,000
Retained earnings	400,000	200,000
· Total equities	$1,700,000	$850,000

Required: Prepare consolidation working papers for Pure Corporation and Subsidiary for the year ended December 31, 19X2.

P 8–12 Pak Corporation acquired an 85 percent interest in Sly Corporation on August 1, 19X2 for $522,750, equal to 85 percent of the underlying equity of Sly on that date.

In August 19X2 Sly sold inventory items to Pak for $60,000 at a gross profit of $15,000. One-third of these items remained in Pak's inventory at December 31, 19X2.

On September 30, 19X2 Pak sold an inventory item (equipment) to Sly for $50,000 at a gross profit to Pak of $10,000. When this equipment was placed in service by Sly, it had a five-year remaining use life and no expected scrap value.

Sly's dividends were declared in equal amounts on June 15 and December 15, and its income was earned in relatively equal amounts throughout each quarter of the year. Pak applies the equity method of accounting, such that its net income is equal to consolidated net income. Financial statements for Pak and Sly are summarized as follows:

	Pak	Sly
Combined Income and Retained Earnings Statement for the Year Ended December 31, 19X2		
Sales	$ 910,000	$400,000
Income from Sly	7,500	—
Cost of sales	500,000*	250,000*
Operating expenses	200,000*	90,000*
Net income	217,500	60,000
Add: Beginning retained earnings	192,500	100,000
Deduct: Dividends	100,000*	40,000*
Retained earnings December 31, 19X2	$ 310,000	$120,000
Balance Sheet at December 31, 19X2		
Cash	$ 33,750	$ 10,000
Dividends receivable	17,000	—
Accounts receivable—net	120,000	70,000
Inventories	300,000	150,000
Plant assets—net	880,000	500,000
Investment in Sly—85%	513,250	—
Total assets	$1,864,000	$730,000
Accounts payable	$ 154,000	$ 90,000
Dividends payable	—	20,000
Capital stock	1,400,000	500,000
Retained earnings	310,000	120,000
Total equities	$1,864,000	$730,000

* Deduct.

Required: Prepare consolidation working papers for Pak Corporation and Subsidiary for the year ended December 31, 19X2.

P 8-13 Separate company financial statements for Pin Corporation (Pinco) and its 90 percent owned subsidiary, Sit Corporation (Sitco), for the year ended December 31, 19X8 are summarized as follows:

	Pinco	Sitco
Combined Income and Retained Earnings Statement for the Year Ended December 31, 19X8		
Sales	$1,265,000	$ 600,000
Income from Sitco	85,000	—
Cost of goods sold	800,000*	300,000*
Depreciation expense	180,000*	70,000*
Other expenses	120,000*	120,000*
Loss on plant assets	—	10,000*
Net income	250,000	100,000
Add: Beginning retained earnings	300,000	150,000
Deduct: Dividends	150,000*	50,000*
Retained earnings December 31, 19X8	$ 400,000	$ 200,000
Balance Sheet at December 31, 19X8		
Cash	$ 220,000	$ 160,000
Receivables	200,000	160,000
Inventory	170,000	140,000
Plant and equipment	1,417,500	720,000
Accumulated depreciation	272,500*	180,000*
Investment in Sitco	765,000	—
Total assets	$2,500,000	$1,000,000
Current liabilities	$ 300,000	$ 100,000
Other liabilities	300,000	200,000
Capital stock	1,500,000	500,000
Retained earnings	400,000	200,000
Total equities	$2,500,000	$1,000,000

* Deduct.

Additional Information

1 Pinco acquired an 80 percent interest in Sitco's common stock on January 5, 19X5 for $600,000 and an additional 10 percent interest on July 1, 19X8 for $82,500. These two acquisitions were made in the open market at regularly quoted exchange prices.
2 Sitco's capital stock and retained earnings on January 1, 19X5 were $500,000 and $100,000, respectively.
3 Any difference between investment cost and book value acquired relates to assets not specifically identifiable and is amortized over a ten-year period.
4 Sitco paid dividends of $25,000 on April 1 and October 1 of 19X8.
5 Pinco sold $50,000 merchandise to Sitco during 19X8. The gross profit of $10,000 on this merchandise is included in Sitco's December 31, 19X8 inventory. Sitco owed Pinco $20,000 from intercompany purchases at December 31, 19X8.
6 The amount of intercompany profit in Sitco's beginning inventory on goods acquired from Pinco amounted to $5,000.
7 Sitco sold machinery with a book value of $40,000 to Pinco for $30,000 on July 2, 19X8. At the time of sale the machinery had a remaining use life of five years and is being depreciated by Pinco on a straight-line basis.

Required: Prepare the consolidation working papers for Pinco and Subsidiary for the year ended December 31, 19X8.

P 8–14 Financial statements for Poe and Spy Corporations for 19X4 are summarized as follows:

	Poe	Spy
Combined Income and Retained Earnings		
Statement for the Year Ended December 31, 19X4		
Sales	$463,750	$130,000
Income from Spy	18,750	—
Gain on Spy stock	17,500	—
Cost of sales	(260,000)	(100,000)
Other expenses	(140,000)	(10,000)
Net income	100,000	20,000
Add: Beginning retained earnings	200,000	30,000
Deduct: Dividends	(50,000)	(10,000)
Retained earnings December 31, 19X4	$250,000	$ 40,000
Balance Sheet at December 31, 19X4		
Cash	$107,500	$ 20,000
Inventories	100,000	50,000
Other current assets	110,000	30,000
Plant assets	300,000	200,000
Investment in Spy	182,500	—
Total assets	$800,000	$300,000
Accounts payable	$150,000	$ 60,000
Capital stock	400,000	200,000
Retained earnings	250,000	40,000
Total equities	$800,000	$300,000

Due to a working capital shortage and other financial problems, Poe sold a 25 percent interest in Spy, its 100 percent owned subsidiary, on October 1, 19X4 for $75,000. Spy was formed by Poe in 19X1 to manufacture miscellaneous furniture for Poe, and all of Spy's sales are made to Poe at 130 percent of Spy's cost. A summary of Spy's sales to Poe from 19X1 through 19X4 follows:

	Sales for the Year	Spy's Cost of Sales for the Year	Percent Unsold by Poe at December 31	Percent of Sales Unpaid for at December 31
19X1	$ 91,000	$ 70,000	10%	20%
19X2	104,000	80,000	5	10
19X3	117,000	90,000	20	15
19X4	130,000	100,000	10	10

Additional Information

1 During 19X4 Spy declared dividends of $5,000 on April 1 and $5,000 on November 1.

2 The $182,500 balance of Poe's investment in Spy account is determined as follows:

Investment cost in 19X1 (when Spy was formed)	$200,000
Add: Income less dividends 19X1 through 19X3	30,000
	230,000
Less: Book value of investment sold ($230,000 × 25%)	(57,500)
	172,500
Add: Income from Spy 19X4	
($15,000 × 100%) + ($5,000 × 75%)	18,750
Less: Dividends from Spy in 19X4	
($5,000 × 100%) + ($5,000 × 75%)	(8,750)
Investment in Spy	$182,500

3 The auditor for Poe has determined that the correct balance of the investment in Spy account at December 31, 19X4 should be $177,750, computed as 75 percent of Spy's $237,000 *realized* equity. The auditor recommends that the following entry be made to correct the accounts because the books have been closed at December 31, 19X4:

Retained earnings	$4,750	
Investment in Spy		$4,750

The auditor further recommends that Poe adopt and use a correct equity method of accounting for 19X5 and subsequent years.

Required: Prepare consolidation working papers for Poe Corporation and Subsidiary for the year ended December 31, 19X4.

P 8-15 Polk Corporation issued 200,000 shares of its $10 par capital stock for 90 percent of the outstanding voting stock of Ski Company in a *pooling of interests* business combination on July 1, 19X5. On January 1, 19X5 Ski's stockholders' equity consisted of $1,500,000, $10 par capital stock, other paid-in capital of $1,000,000, and retained earnings of $600,000. Polk recorded the pooling correctly on July 1. Ski's net income for 19X5 was $400,000, earned evenly throughout the year, and dividends, paid on December 1, were $200,000.

On July 1, 19X6 Polk acquired an additional 5 percent interest in Ski for $195,000 cash. This acquisition is accounted for by the purchase method under the provisions of *APB Opinion No. 16.* Book values of Ski's net assets were equal to fair values at the time of purchase, and any excess of investment cost over book value acquired is to be amortized over a ten-year period.

Financial statements for the two companies at and for the year ended December 31, 19X6 are summarized as follows:

	Polk	Ski
Combined Income and Retained Earnings Statement for the Year Ended December 31, 19X6		
Sales	$ 6,138,400	$2,502,000
Income from Ski	361,600	—
Interest income	—	48,000
Cost of sales	4,000,000*	1,700,000*
Operating expenses	1,414,000*	450,000*
Interest expense	86,000*	—
Net income	1,000,000	400,000
Add: Beginning retained earnings	2,000,000	800,000
Deduct: Dividends	500,000*	200,000*
Retained earnings December 31, 19X6	$ 2,500,000	$1,000,000
Balance Sheet at December 31, 19X6		
Cash	$ 575,000	$ 86,000
Accounts receivable—net	882,400	670,000
Inventories	1,200,000	400,000
Investment in Ski stock	3,342,600	—
Investment in Polk bonds	—	494,000
Plant assets—net	5,000,000	2,000,000
Total assets	$11,000,000	$3,650,000
Accounts payable	$ 500,000	$ 110,000
Other current liabilities	92,000	40,000
9% bonds payable	1,000,000	—
Premium on bonds payable	8,000	—
Capital stock, $10 par	5,000,000	1,500,000
Other paid-in capital	1,900,000	1,000,000
Retained earnings	2,500,000	1,000,000
Total equities	$11,000,000	$3,650,000

* Deduct.

Additional Information

19X5

1 Ski sold merchandise that cost Ski $200,000 to Polk for $240,000 during 19X5. One-fourth of that merchandise remained in Polk's December 31, 19X5 inventory.

2 On December 31, 19X5, Ski acquired $500,000 par of Polk's 9 percent bonds for $491,000 cash. These bonds, which mature on December 31, 19X8 and pay interest on June 30 and December 31, had a book value of $506,000 when acquired by Ski.

19X6

3 Ski sold merchandise that cost $400,000 to Polk for $480,000 during 19X6. Polk sold 85 percent of this merchandise, and at December 31, 19X6 $72,000 of the merchandise remained in Polk's inventory.

4 At December 31, 19X6 Polk owed Ski $20,400 for merchandise purchased.

5 Ski's $400,000 net income for 19X6 was earned evenly throughout the year. Its $200,000 dividends were paid on December 1.

Required: Prepare consolidation working papers for Polk Corporation and Subsidiary for the year ended December 31, 19X6.

P 8–16   **[AICPA adapted]**

Presented here are the condensed financial statements (unconsolidated) of Royal Company and its subsidiary, Butler Company, for the year ended December 31, 19X5.

	Royal	Butler
Combined Income and Retained Earnings Statement for the Year Ended December 31, 19X5		
Sales	$4,000,000	$1,700,000
Cost of sales	2,982,000*	1,015,000*
Operating expenses	400,000*	377,200*
Dividend income	75,000	—
Subsidiary income	232,000	—
Interest expense	—	7,800*
Net income	925,000	300,000
Add: Retained earnings January 1, 19X5	2,100,000	640,000
Deduct: Dividends	170,000*	100,000*
Retained earnings December 31, 19X5	$2,855,000	$ 840,000
Balance Sheet at December 31, 19X5		
Cash	$ 486,000	$ 249,600
Accounts receivable	235,000	185,000
Inventories	475,000	355,000
Machinery and equipment	2,231,000	530,000
Investment in Butler stock	954,000	—
Investment in Butler bonds	58,000	—
Total assets	$4,439,000	$1,319,600
Accounts payable	$ 384,000	$ 62,000
Bonds payable	—	120,000
Unamortized discount on bonds payable	—	2,400*
Common stock	1,200,000	250,000
Contributed capital	—	50,000
Retained earnings	2,855,000	840,000
Total liabilities and owners' equity	$4,439,000	$1,319,600

* Deduct.

Additional Information

1 On January 3, 19X3 Royal acquired from John Roth, the sole stockholder of Butler Company, both a patent valued at $40,000 and 80 percent of the outstanding stock of Butler for $440,000 cash. The net book value of Butler's stock on the date of acquisition was $500,000, and the book values of the individual assets and liabilities were equal to their fair market values. Royal charged the entire $440,000 to the account "Investment in Butler Company." The patent, for which no amortization has been charged, had a remaining legal life of four years as of January 3, 19X3.

2 On July 1, 19X5 Royal reduced its investment in Butler to 75 percent of Butler's outstanding common stock, by selling shares for $70,000 to an unaffiliated company at a profit of $16,000. Royal recorded the proceeds as a credit to its investment account.

3 For the six months ended June 30, 19X5, Butler had net income of $140,000. Royal recorded 80 percent of this amount on its books of account prior to the time of sale.

4 During 19X4 Butler sold merchandise to Royal for $130,000, which was at a markup of 30 percent over Butler's cost. On January 1, 19X5 $52,000 of this merchandise remained in Royal's inventory. This merchandise was subsequently sold by Royal in February 19X5 at a profit of $8,000.

5 In November 19X5 Royal sold merchandise to Butler for the first time. Royal's cost for this merchandise was $80,000, and the sale was made at 120 percent of cost. Butler's inventory at December 31, 19X5 contained merchandise that was purchased from Royal at a cost to Butler of $24,000.

6 On December 31, 19X5 there was a $45,000 payment-in-transit from Butler Company to Royal Company. Accounts receivable and accounts payable include intercompany receivables and payables. In December 19X5 Butler declared and paid cash dividends of $100,000 to its stockholders.

7 On December 31, 19X5 Royal purchased 50 percent of the outstanding bonds issued by Butler for $58,000. The bonds mature on December 31, 19X9 and were originally issued at a discount. On December 31, 19X5 the balance in Butler's account "Unamortized Discount on Bonds Payable" was $2,400. It is the intention of the management of Royal to hold these bonds until their maturity.

Required: Prepare consolidated financial statement working papers for Royal Company and Subsidiary for the year ended December 31, 19X5.

P 8–17 Comparative consolidated financial statements for Poff Corporation and its subsidiary, Sato Corporation, at and for the years ended December 31, 19X4 and 19X3 are as follows:

POFF CORPORATION AND SUBSIDIARY COMPARATIVE CONSOLIDATED FINANCIAL STATEMENTS AT AND FOR THE YEARS ENDED DECEMBER 31, 19X4 AND 19X3

	Year 19X4	Year 19X3	Year's Change 19X4 – 19X3
Income Statement			
Sales	$30,500,000	$28,500,000	$2,000,000
Gain on 10% interest	57,000		57,000
Cost of sales	(17,507,000)	(16,900,000)	(607,000)
Depreciation expense	(5,280,000)	(5,080,000)	(200,000)
Other expenses	(4,550,000)	(3,920,000)	(630,000)
Minority income	(220,000)	(100,000)	(120,000)
Net income	$ 3,000,000	$ 2,500,000	$ 500,000
Retained Earnings			
Retained earnings—beginning	$10,000,000	$ 9,500,000	$ 500,000
Net income	3,000,000	2,500,000	500,000
Dividends	(2,000,000)	(2,000,000)	0
Retained earnings—ending	$11,000,000	$10,000,000	$1,000,000

	Year 19X4	Year 19X3	Year's Change 19X4 – 19X3
Balance Sheet			
Cash	$ 465,000	$ 505,000	$ (40,000)
Accounts receivable—net	875,000	900,000	(25,000)
Inventories	3,775,000	2,475,000	1,300,000
Prepaid expenses	680,000	880,000	(200,000)
Equipment	29,700,000	28,800,000	900,000
Accumulated depreciation	(15,420,000)	(10,440,000)	(4,980,000)
Land and buildings	9,600,000	9,600,000	0
Accumulated depreciation	(3,000,000)	(2,720,000)	(280,000)
Total assets	$26,675,000	$30,000,000	$(3,325,000)
Accounts payable	$ 1,400,000	$ 3,435,000	$(2,035,000)
Dividends payable	525,000	525,000	0
Long-term notes payable	2,450,000	5,450,000	(3,000,000)
Capital stock—$10 par	10,000,000	10,000,000	0
Retained earnings	11,000,000	10,000,000	1,000,000
Minority interest	1,300,000	590,000	710,000
Total equities	$26,675,000	$30,000,000	$(3,325,000)

Required: Prepare a consolidated statement of cash flows for Poff Corporation and Subsidiary for the year ended December 31, 19X4. The changes in equipment are due to a $1,000,000 equipment acquisition, current depreciation, and the sale of one-ninth of the cost–book value differential allocated to equipment [$100,000] and related accumulated depreciation [$20,000]. This reduction in the unamortized cost-book value differential results from selling a 10 percent interest in Sato for $727,000 and thereby reducing its interest from 90 percent to 80 percent. Sato's net income and dividends for 19X4 were $1,100,000 and $500,000, respectively. Use the indirect method.

9

INDIRECT AND MUTUAL HOLDINGS

The previous chapters of this book are concerned with stock ownership situations in which an investor or parent company directly owns some or all of the voting stock of an investee. The equity method of accounting is appropriate in those situations and equally appropriate when an investor indirectly owns 20 percent or more of an investee's voting stock. Consolidation is appropriate when one corporation, directly or indirectly, owns a majority of the outstanding voting stock of another corporation.[1] For example, Woolworth Corporation's 1991 Form 10–K indicated that Woolworth had a direct majority ownership interest in 14 subsidiaries and an indirect majority interest in about 100 subsidiaries as of April 10, 1991.

This chapter discusses parent company accounting and consolidation procedures for indirect ownership situations under the heading of "Indirect Holdings." The chapter also considers additional complexities that arise when affiliated corporations hold the voting stock of each other. Affiliation structures of this type are covered under the heading of "Mutual Holdings." Discussion of **mutual holding** relationships logically follows the coverage of **indirect holdings** because such relationships constitute a special type of indirect holdings—the type in which affiliates indirectly own themselves. Although consolidation procedures for indirectly held and mutually held affiliates are more complex than for directly held affiliates, the basic consolidation objectives remain the same. Most of the problems involve measuring the separate realized income of the separate entities and allocating it between majority and minority interests.

AFFILIATION STRUCTURES

The potential complexity of corporate affiliation structures is limited only by one's imagination. Even so, the general types of affiliation structures are not difficult to identify. The more basic types of affiliation structures are illustrated in Exhibit 9–1.

---

[1] *APB Opinion No. 18,* "The Equity Method of Accounting for Investments in Common Stock," paragraphs 3c and 17.

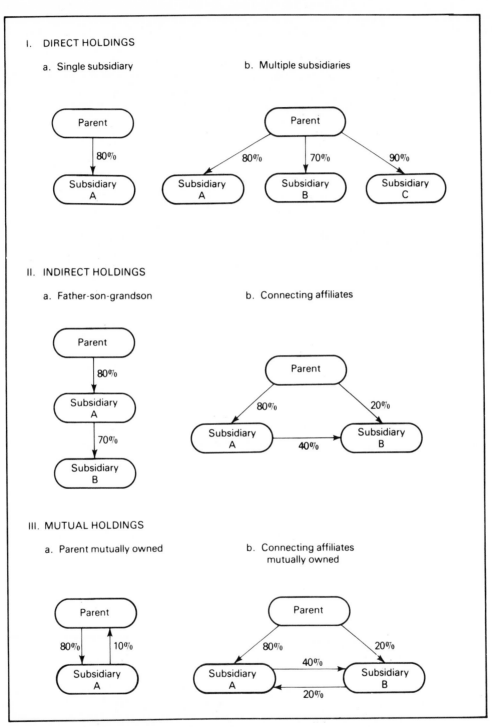

Exhibit 9–1 *Affiliation Structures*

Although Exhibit 9–1 illustrates affiliation structures for parent and subsidiary corporations, the diagrams are equally applicable to investor and investee
corporations associated through the direct or indirect ownership of 20 percent
or more of the voting stock of an investee corporation. **Direct holdings** result
from direct investments in the voting stock of one or more investees. Indirect
holdings are investments that enable the investor to control or significantly influence the decisions of an investee not directly owned through an investee that
is directly owned. Two types of indirect ownership structures are illustrated in
Exhibit 9–1—the **father-son-grandson relationship** and the **connecting affiliates
relationship**.

In the father-son-grandson diagram, the parent directly owns an 80 percent
interest in Subsidiary A and indirectly owns a 56 percent interest (80% × 70%)
in Subsidiary B. Minority shareholders own the other 44 percent of B—the 30
percent held directly by minority holders of B stock plus 14 percent held by the
20 percent minority holders of A stock (20% × 70%). Since the parent company indirectly holds 56 percent of Subsidiary B stock, consolidation of Subsidiary B is clearly appropriate. It is not the direct and indirect ownership of
the parent company, however, that determines whether an affiliate should be
consolidated. The decision to consolidate is based on whether a majority of the
stock of an affiliate is held within the affiliation structure, thus giving the parent
an ability to control the operations of the affiliate.

If Subsidiary A in the father-son-grandson diagram of Exhibit 9–1 had owned
60 percent of the stock of Subsidiary B, the parent's indirect ownership in
Subsidiary B would have been 48 percent (80% × 60%) and the minority shareholders' interest would have been 52 percent [40% + (20% × 60%)]. Consolidation of Subsidiary B would still be appropriate, since 60 percent of B's stock
is held within the affiliation structure.

In the illustration of connecting affiliates, the parent holds 20 percent of
Subsidiary B stock directly and 32 percent (80% × 40%) indirectly for a total
direct and indirect ownership of 52 percent. The other 48 percent of Subsidiary
B is held 40 percent by B's minority shareholders and 8 percent (20% × 40%)
indirectly by A's minority shareholders.

In the first affiliation diagram for mutual holdings, the parent owns 80 percent of the stock of Subsidiary A, and Subsidiary A owns 10 percent of the stock
of the parent. Thus, 10 percent of the parent's stock is held within the affiliation
structure and only 90 percent is outstanding. In Diagram b for mutual holdings
the parent is not a party to the mutual holding relationship, but Subsidiary A
owns 40 percent of Subsidiary B, and Subsidiary B owns 20 percent of Subsidiary
A. The complexity involved in this latter case requires the use of simultaneous
equations or other appropriate mathematical procedures to allocate incomes
and equities among the affiliated corporations.

INDIRECT HOLDINGS—FATHER-SON-
GRANDSON STRUCTURE

The major problems encountered in connection with indirect control situations
involve the determination of earnings and equities of the affiliated companies
on an equity basis. Once the income and equity accounts of the affiliated companies have been adjusted to an equity basis, the consolidation procedures are
the same for indirect as for direct ownership situations. The mechanics involved in the consolidation process may be cumbersome, however, because of the
additional detail required to consolidate the operations of multiple entities.

Assume that Poe Corporation acquires 80 percent of the stock of Shaw Corporation on January 1, 19X1, and that Shaw acquires 70 percent of the stock
of Turk Corporation on January 1, 19X2. Both Poe's investment in Shaw and
Shaw's investment in Turk are made at book value. Trial balances for the three

corporations on January 1, 19X2, immediately after Shaw acquires its 70 percent interest in Turk, are as follows:

	Poe	Shaw	Turk
Other assets	$400,000	$195,000	$190,000
Investment in Shaw (80%)	200,000	—	—
Investment in Turk (70%)	—	105,000	—
	$600,000	$300,000	$190,000
Liabilities	$100,000	$ 50,000	$ 40,000
Capital stock	400,000	200,000	100,000
Retained earnings	100,000	50,000	50,000
	$600,000	$300,000	$190,000

Separate earnings of the three corporations (that is, earnings excluding investment income) and dividends for 19X2 are:

	Poe	Shaw	Turk
Separate earnings	$100,000	$50,000	$40,000
Dividends	60,000	30,000	20,000

Equity Method of Accounting for Father-Son-Grandson Affiliates

In accounting for investment income for 19X2 on an equity basis, Shaw determines its investment income from Turk before Poe determines its investment income from Shaw. Shaw accounts for its investment in Turk for 19X2 with the following entries:

Shaw's Books

Cash	$14,000	
Investment in Turk		$14,000

To record dividends received from Turk ($20,000 × 70%).

Investment in Turk	$28,000	
Income from Turk		$28,000

To record income from Turk ($40,000 × 70%).

Shaw's net income for 19X2 is $78,000 ($50,000 separate income plus $28,000 income from Turk), and its investment in Turk account balance at December 31, 19X2 is $119,000 ($105,000 beginning balance, plus $28,000 income, less $14,000 dividends).

Poe's entries to account for its investment in Shaw for 19X2 are as follows:

Poe's Books

Cash	$24,000	
Investment in Shaw		$24,000

To record dividends received from Shaw ($30,000 × 80%).

Investment in Shaw	$62,400	
Income from Shaw		$62,400

To record income from Shaw ($78,000 × 80%).

Poe's net income for 19X2 is $162,400 ($100,000 separate income plus $62,400 income from Shaw), and its investment in Shaw account balance at December 31, 19X2 is $238,400 ($200,000 beginning balance plus $62,400 income less $24,000 dividends). Consolidated net income for Poe Corporation and Subsidiaries for 19X2 is $162,400, equal to Poe's net income on an equity basis.

Computational Approaches for Consolidated Net Income

Poe's income and consolidated net income can be determined independently by alternative methods. Computation in terms of the definition of consolidated net income is:

Poe's separate earnings	$100,000
Poe's share of Shaw's separate earnings ($50,000 × 80%)	40,000
Poe's share of Turk's separate earnings ($40,000 × 80% × 70%)	22,400
Poe's net income and consolidation net income	$162,400

Computation of parent and consolidated net income in terms of the consolidated income statement presentation involves the deduction of minority interest income from combined separate earnings:

Combined separate earnings:		
Poe	$100,000	
Shaw	50,000	
Turk	40,000	$190,000
Less: Minority interest incomes		
Direct minority interest in Turk's income ($40,000 × 30%)	$ 12,000	
Indirect minority interest in Turk's income ($40,000 × 70% × 20%)	5,600	
Direct minority interest in Shaw's income ($50,000 × 20%)	10,000	27,600
Poe's net income and consolidated net income		$162,400

Still another computational approach is to use a schedule such as the following:

	Poe	Shaw	Turk
Separate earnings	$100,000	$ 50,000	$ 40,000
Allocate Turk's income to Shaw: ($40,000 × 70%)	—	+28,000	−28,000
Allocate Shaw's income to Poe ($78,000 × 80%)	+62,400	−62,400	—
Consolidated net income	$162,400		
Minority interest income		$ 15,600	$ 12,000

Schedules are often helpful in making allocations for complex affiliation structures. This is particularly true when intercompany profits are involved and when the equity method of accounting is not used or is applied incorrectly. The schedule illustrated here shows parent company and consolidated net income as well as minority interest income. It also shows Shaw's investment income from Turk ($28,000) and Poe's investment income from Shaw ($62,400).

Consolidation Working Papers— Equity Method

Consolidation working papers for Poe Corporation and Subsidiaries for the year 19X2 are illustrated in Exhibit 9–2. The working papers show that no new con-

POE CORPORATION AND SUBSIDIARIES
CONSOLIDATION WORKING PAPERS FOR THE YEAR ENDED DECEMBER 31, 19X2

	Poe	80% Shaw	70% Turk	Adjustments and Eliminations		Minority Interests	Consolidated Statements
Income Statement Sales	$200,000	$140,000	$100,000				$440,000
Income from Shaw	62,400			c	62,400		
Income from Turk		28,000		a	28,000		
Expenses including cost of goods sold	100,000*	90,000*	60,000*				250,000*
Minority interest income— Shaw						$15,600	15,600*
Minority interest income— Turk						12,000	12,000*
Net income	$162,400	$ 78,000	$ 40,000				$162,400
Retained Earnings Retained earnings—Poe	$100,000						$100,000
Retained earnings—Shaw		$ 50,000		d	50,000		
Retained earnings—Turk			$ 50,000	b	50,000		
Net income	162,400 ✔	78,000 ✔	40,000 ✔				162,400
Dividends	60,000*	30,000*	20,000*	a	14,000	12,000*	60,000*
				c	24,000		
Retained earnings December 31, 19X2	$202,400	$ 98,000	$ 70,000				$202,400
Balance Sheet Other assets	$461,600	$231,000	$200,000				$892,600
Investment in Shaw	238,400			c	38,400		
				d	200,000		
Investment in Turk		119,000		a	14,000		
				b	105,000		
	$700,000	$350,000	$200,000				$892,600
Liabilities	$ 97,600	$ 52,000	$ 30,000				$179,600
Capital stock—Poe	400,000						400,000
Capital stock—Shaw		200,000		d	200,000		
Capital stock—Turk			100,000	b	100,000		
Retained earnings	202,400 ✔	98,000 ✔	70,000 ✔				202,400
	$700,000	$350,000	$200,000				
Minority interest in Turk January 1, 19X2				b	45,000	45,000	
Minority interest in Shaw January 1, 19X2				d	50,000	50,000	
Minority interest December 31, 19X2						$110,600	110,600
							$892,600

* Deduct.
Minority interest income—Shaw $78,000 × 20 percent = $15,600.
Minority interest income—Turk $40,000 × 30 percent = $12,000.

Exhibit 9–2 *Indirect Holdings—Father-Son-Grandson Type (Equity Method)*

solidation procedures have been introduced. Entries a and b eliminate investment income, dividends, investment and equity accounts for Shaw's investment in Turk; and entries c and d eliminate investment income, dividends, investment and equity accounts for Poe's investment in Shaw. Turk's $45,000 beginning minority interest is simply the 30 percent direct minority interest percentage times Turk's $150,000 equity at the beginning of 19X2. Minority interest income of Turk is 30 percent of Turk's $40,000 reported income. Similarly, the $50,000 beginning minority interest in Shaw is 20 percent of Shaw's $250,000 equity at January 1, 19X2, and the $15,600 minority interest income of Shaw is 20 percent of Shaw's reported net income. Consolidated net income and consolidated retained earnings of $162,400 and $202,400, respectively, are equal to Poe's net income and retained earnings.

Consolidation Working Papers— Cost Method

If Poe and Shaw Corporations had used the cost method of accounting, their investment incomes for 19X2 and their investment accounts at December 31, 19X2 would have appeared as follows (assume that Poe paid $192,000 for its investment in Shaw on January 1, 19X1 when Shaw's capital stock was $200,000 and retained earnings was $40,000):

Poe's Books	
Investment in Shaw (cost)	$192,000
Dividend income from Shaw	$ 24,000
Shaw's Books	
Investment in Turk (cost)	$105,000
Dividend income from Turk	$ 14,000

These amounts are shown in the separate company columns of the working papers for Poe and subsidiaries illustrated in Exhibit 9–3. Except for the first two working paper entries to convert from the cost to the equity method, the working paper procedures are the same as those shown in Exhibit 9–2. These first two working paper entries are explained shortly.

Because Turk is the lowest affiliate in the affiliation structure, Shaw's investment in Turk should be converted to the equity method first with the following working paper entry:

a	Investment in Turk	$14,000	
	Dividend income from Turk	14,000	
	Income from Turk		$28,000

Shaw's beginning-of-the-period retained earnings balance was not affected by the cost method, and accordingly, the cost-to-equity conversion merely involves reclassifying the $14,000 dividends as a decrease in the investment in Turk (debit dividend income and credit investment in Turk for $14,000) and taking up 70 percent of Turk's net income (debit investment in Turk and credit income from Turk for $28,000). After this adjustment, Shaw's realized net income on an equity basis is $78,000.

Poe's 80 percent investment in Shaw is converted to the equity method in a second working paper entry as follows:

b	Dividend income from Shaw	$24,000	
	Investment in Shaw	46,400	
	Income from Shaw		$62,400
	Retained earnings—Poe		8,000

POE CORPORATION AND SUBSIDIARIES
CONSOLIDATION WORKING PAPERS—FOR THE YEAR ENDED DECEMBER 31, 19X2

	Poe	80% Shaw	70% Turk	Adjustments and Eliminations		Minority Interests	Consolidated Statements
Income Statement Sales	$200,000	$140,000	$100,000				$440,000
Dividend income from Shaw	24,000			b 24,000			
Income from Shaw				e 62,400	b 62,400		
Dividend income from Turk		14,000		a 14,000			
Income from Turk				c 28,000	a 28,000		
Expenses (including cost of goods sold)	100,000*	90,000*	60,000*				250,000*
Minority income—Shaw						$15,600	15,600*
Minority income—Turk						12,000	12,000*
Net income	$124,000	$ 64,000	$ 40,000				$162,400
Retained Earnings Retained earnings—Poe	$ 92,000				b 8,000		$100,000
Retained earnings—Shaw		$ 50,000		f 50,000			
Retained earnings—Turk			$ 50,000	d 50,000			
Net income	124,000✓	64,000✓	40,000✓				162,400
Dividends	60,000*	30,000*	20,000*	c 14,000 e 24,000		12,000*	60,000*
Retained earnings December 31, 19X2	$156,000	$ 84,000	$ 70,000				$202,400
Balance Sheet Other assets	$461,600	$231,000	$200,000				$892,600
Investment in Shaw (cost)	192,000			b 46,400	e 38,400 f 200,000		
Investment in Turk (cost)		105,000		a 14,000	c 14,000 d 105,000		
	$653,600	$336,000	$200,000				$892,600
Liabilities	$ 97,600	$ 52,000	$ 30,000				$179,600
Capital stock—Poe	400,000						400,000
Capital stock—Shaw		200,000		f 200,000			
Capital stock—Turk			100,000	d 100,000			
Retained earnings	156,000✓	84,000✓	70,000✓				202,400
	$653,600	$336,000	$200,000				
Minority interest in Turk January 1, 19X2					d 45,000	45,000	
Minority interest in Shaw January 1, 19X2					f 50,000	50,000	
Minority interest December 31, 19X2						$110,600	110,600
							$892,600

* Deduct.

Exhibit 9–3   Indirect Holdings—Father-Son-Grandson Type (Cost Method)

353

This cost-equity working paper conversion entry involves both prior periods (19X1) and the current period (19X2) such that a regular cost-equity conversion schedule is needed.

	Poe's Beginning Retained Earnings	Investment in Shaw	Income from Shaw	Dividend Income
Prior-Year's Effect				
80% of Shaw's $10,000 undistributed income from 19X1	$8,000	$ 8,000		
Current-Year's Effect				
Reclassify dividend income as decrease in investment		(24,000)		$(24,000)
80% of Shaw's realized income on an equity basis ($78,000 × 80%)		62,400	$62,400	
Working paper adjustments	$8,000	$46,400	$62,400	$(24,000)

After the cost-equity conversion entries are entered in the working papers (entries a and b), the adjusted financial statement items are the same amounts as those shown in Exhibit 9–2 under the equity method. The remaining working paper entries in Exhibit 9–3 (entries c, d, e, and f) are the same as those illustrated in Exhibit 9–2 under the equity method.

INDIRECT HOLDINGS—CONNECTING AFFILIATES STRUCTURE

Pet Corporation owns a 70 percent interest in Sal Corporation and a 60 percent interest in Ty Corporation. In addition, Sal Corporation owns a 20 percent interest in Ty. The affiliation structure of Pet Corporation and Subsidiaries is diagrammed as follows:

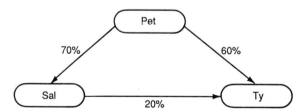

Data relevant to the investments of Pet and Sal are summarized as follows:

	Pet's Investment in Sal (70%) Acquired January 1, 19X5	Pet's Investment in Ty (60%) Acquired January 1, 19X4	Sal's Investment in Ty (20%) Acquired January 1, 19X1
Cost	$178,000	$100,000	$20,000
Less: Book value acquired	(168,000)	(90,000)	(20,000)
Goodwill	$ 10,000	$ 10,000	—

	Pet's Investment in Sal (70%) Acquired January 1, 19X5	Pet's Investment in Ty (60%) Acquired January 1, 19X4	Sal's Investment in Ty (20%) Acquired January 1, 19X1
Investment Balance December 31, 19X5			
Cost	$178,000	$100,000	$20,000
Add: Share of investees' pre–19X6 income less dividends	7,000	18,000	16,000
Deduct: Goodwill amortization at 10% per year	(1,000)	(2,000)	—
Balance December 31, 19X5	$184,000	$116,000	$36,000

During 19X6 Pet, Sal, and Ty had earnings from their own operations of $70,000, $35,000, and $20,000 and declared dividends of $40,000, $20,000, and $10,000, respectively. Pet's separate earnings of $70,000 included an unrealized gain of $10,000 from the sale of land to Sal during 19X6. Sal's separate earnings of $35,000 included unrealized profit of $5,000 on inventory items sold to Pet for $15,000 during 19X6 and remaining in Pet's December 31, 19X6 inventory. A schedule for the computation of consolidated net income and minority interest income for the Pet/Sal/Ty affiliation for 19X6 is shown in Exhibit 9–4.

	Pet	Sal	Ty
Separate earnings	$70,000	$35,000	$20,000
Deduct: Unrealized profit	− 10,000	− 5,000	—
Separate realized earnings	$60,000	$30,000	$20,000
Allocate Ty's income:			
20% to Sal	—	+ 4,000	− 4,000
60% to Pet	+ 12,000	—	− 12,000
Allocate Sal's income:			
70% to Pet	+ 23,800	− 23,800	—
Deduct goodwill amortization:			
from Pet's 70% investment in Sal	− 1,000	—	—
from Pet's 60% investment in Ty	− 1,000	—	—
Pet's net income and consolidated net income	$93,800		
Minority interest income		$10,200	$ 4,000

Exhibit 9–4 Income Allocation Schedule

Equity Method of Accounting for Connecting Affiliates

Before allocating the separate earnings of Sal and Ty to Pet, any unrealized profits included in such earnings should be eliminated. Exhibit 9–4 shows the allocation of Ty's income as 20 percent to Sal and 60 percent to Pet. This allocation must precede the allocation of Sal's income to Pet because Sal's income includes $4,000 investment income from Ty.

In accounting for its investment in Ty for 19X6, Sal makes the following entries:

Cash	$2,000	
Investment in Ty		$2,000

To record dividends received from Ty ($10,000 × 20%).

Investment in Ty	$4,000	
Income from Ty		$4,000

To record income from Ty ($20,000 × 20%).

Sal's investment in Ty account at December 31, 19X6 has a balance of $38,000, the $36,000 balance at December 31, 19X5, plus $4,000 investment income less $2,000 dividends. Sal's income from Ty is not reduced for the $5,000 unrealized profit on inventory items sold to Pet because Ty is not involved in the intercompany sale. Sal's $39,000 net income includes $5,000 unrealized profit, which is eliminated when Sal's realized income is allocated to Pet and Sal's minority stockholders.

Pet makes the following entries in accounting for its investments during 19X6:

Investment in Ty

Cash	$ 6,000	
Investment in Ty		$ 6,000

To record dividends received from Ty ($10,000 × 60%).

Investment in Ty	$11,000	
Income from Ty		$11,000

To record income from Ty computed as follows:

60% of Ty's $20,000 reported income	$12,000
Less: Goodwill amortization ($10,000 × 10%)	1,000
	$11,000

Investment in Sal

Cash	$14,000	
Investment in Sal		$14,000

To record dividends received from Sal ($20,000 × 70%).

Investment in Sal	$12,800	
Income from Sal		$12,800

To record income from Sal computed as follows:

70% of Sal's reported income of $39,000	$27,300
Less: 70% of Sal's unrealized inventory profit of $5,000	−3,500
Less: 100% of unrealized gain on land	−10,000
Less: Goodwill amortization ($10,000 × 10%)	−1,000
	$12,800

Pet's investment accounts at December 31, 19X6 show the following balances:

	Investment in Sal—70%	Investment in Ty—60%
Balance December 31, 19X5	$184,000	$116,000
Add: Investment income	12,800	11,000
Deduct: Dividends	−14,000	−6,000
Balance December 31, 19X6	$182,800	$121,000

Consolidation Working Papers— Equity Method

Consolidated statement working papers for Pet Corporation and Subsidiaries for 19X6 are presented in Exhibit 9–5. The adjustments and eliminations are reproduced in journal form for convenient reference.

PET CORPORATION AND SUBSIDIARIES
CONSOLIDATION WORKING PAPERS—FOR THE YEAR ENDED DECEMBER 31, 19X6

	Pet	Sal	Ty	Adjustments and Eliminations				Minority Interests	Consolidated Statements
Income Statement									
Sales	$200,000	$150,000	$100,000	a	15,000				$435,000
Income from Sal	12,800			g	12,800				
Income from Ty	11,000	4,000		d	15,000				
Gain on land	10,000			c	10,000				
Cost of sales	100,000*	80,000*	50,000*	b	5,000	a	15,000		220,000*
Other expenses	40,000*	35,000*	30,000*	f	1,000				107,000*
				i	1,000				
Minority income—Sal ($39,000 − $5,000) × .3								$10,200	10,200*
Minority income—Ty ($20,000 × .2)								4,000	4,000*
Net income	$ 93,800	$ 39,000	$ 20,000						$ 93,800
Retained Earnings									
Retained earnings—Pet	$220,000								$220,000
Retained earnings—Sal		$ 50,000		h	50,000				
Retained earnings—Ty			$ 80,000	e	80,000				
Net income	93,800 ✓	39,000 ✓	20,000 ✓						93,800
Dividends	40,000*	20,000*	10,000*	d	8,000			8,000*	40,000*
				g	14,000				
Retained earnings December 31, 19X6	$273,800	$ 69,000	$ 90,000						$273,800
Balance Sheet									
Other assets	$ 46,200	$ 22,000	$ 85,000						$153,200
Inventories	50,000	40,000	15,000			b	5,000		100,000
Plant assets—net	400,000	200,000	100,000			c	10,000		690,000
Investment in Sal 70%	182,800			g	1,200	h	184,000		
Investment in Ty 60%	121,000					d	5,000		
						e	116,000		
Investment in Ty 20%		38,000				d	2,000		
						e	36,000		
Goodwill				e	8,000	f	1,000		15,000
				h	9,000	i	1,000		
	$800,000	$300,000	$200,000						$958,200
Liabilities	$126,200	$ 31,000	$ 10,000						$167,200
Capital stock—Pet	400,000								400,000
Capital stock—Sal		200,000		h	200,000				
Capital stock—Ty			100,000	e	100,000				
Retained earnings	273,800 ✓	69,000 ✓	90,000 ✓						273,800
	$800,000	$300,000	$200,000						
Minority interest in Ty—January 1, 19X6						e	36,000	36,000	
Minority interest in Sal—January 1, 19X6						h	75,000	75,000	
Minority interest—December 31, 19X6								$117,200	117,200
									$958,200

Exhibit 9–5 *Connecting Affiliates with Intercompany Profits (Equity Method)*

a	Sales	$ 15,000	
	Cost of sales		$ 15,000

To eliminate reciprocal sales and cost of sales.

b	Cost of sales	$ 5,000	
	Inventory		$ 5,000

To eliminate intercompany profit from inventory at December 31, 19X6.

c	Gain on land	$ 10,000	
	Plant assets—net		$ 10,000

To eliminate intercompany profit from intercompany sale of land.

d	Income from Ty	$ 15,000	
	Dividends (Ty's)		$ 8,000
	Investment in Ty (60%)		5,000
	Investment in Ty (20%)		2,000

To eliminate income from Ty and dividends from Ty and to adjust the investment in Ty accounts.

e	Retained earning—Ty January 1, 19X6	$ 80,000	
	Goodwill	8,000	
	Capital stock—Ty	100,000	
	Investment in Ty (60%)		$116,000
	Investment in Ty (20%)		36,000
	Minority interests—Ty		36,000

To eliminate reciprocal investment and equity amounts of Ty and to establish goodwill and minority interest at January 1, 19X6.

f	Other expenses	$ 1,000	
	Goodwill		$ 1,000

To record amortization of goodwill from Pet's investment in Ty for 19X6.

g	Income from Sal	$ 12,800	
	Investment in Sal	1,200	
	Dividends (Sal's)		$ 14,000

To eliminate income from Sal and dividends from Sal and to adjust the investment in Sal account.

h	Retained earnings—Sal January 1, 19X6	$ 50,000	
	Goodwill	9,000	
	Capital stock—Sal	200,000	
	Investment in Sal		$184,000
	Minority interest—Sal		75,000

To eliminate reciprocal investment and equity amounts in Sal and to establish goodwill and minority interest at January 1, 19X6.

i	Other expenses	$ 1,000	
	Goodwill		$ 1,000

To record amortization of goodwill from Pet's investment in Sal for 19X6.

A check on the $117,200 minority interest at December 31, 19X6 as shown in Exhibit 9–5 may be helpful at this point. The minority interest can be confirmed as follows:

	Minority Interest in Sal 30%	Minority Interest in Ty 20%	Total Minority Interest
Book value at December 31, 19X6:			
Sal $269,000 × 30%	$80,700	—	$ 80,700
Ty $190,000 × 20%	—	$38,000	38,000
Less: Unrealized profit of Sal			
$5,000 × 30%	(1,500)	—	(1,500)
Minority interest December 31, 19X6	$79,200	$38,000	$117,200

Except for the deduction of 30 percent of the $5,000 unrealized inventory profit on Sal's upstream sale to Pet, the minority interest is stated at its underlying book value at December 31, 19X6.

MUTUAL HOLDINGS—PARENT STOCK HELD BY SUBSIDIARY

When affiliated companies hold ownership interests in each other, a mutual holding situation exists. Parent company stock held by the subsidiary is not outstanding from the consolidated viewpoint and should not be reported as outstanding stock in a consolidated balance sheet.[2] For example, if Pace Corporation owns a 90 percent interest in Salt Corporation, and Salt owns a 10 percent interest in Pace, the 10 percent interest held by Salt is not outstanding for consolidation purposes and neither is the 90 percent interest in Salt held by Pace. Consolidation practice requires the exclusion of both the 10 percent and the 90 percent interests from consolidated financial statements, and the question is not whether the 10 percent interest in Pace should be excluded, but rather how should it be eliminated in the consolidation process. The elimination procedures depend on the method used in accounting for the investment.

Two methods of accounting for parent company stock held by a subsidiary are generally acceptable—the treasury stock approach and the conventional approach. The **treasury stock approach** considers parent company stock held by a subsidiary to be treasury stock of the consolidated entity. Accordingly, the investment account on the books of the subsidiary is maintained on a cost basis and is deducted at cost from stockholders' equity in the consolidated balance sheet. The **conventional approach** is to account for the subsidiary investment in parent company stock on an equity basis and to eliminate the subsidiary investment account against the parent company equity accounts in the usual manner. Although both approaches are acceptable, they do not result in equivalent consolidated financial statements. In particular, the consolidated retained earnings and minority interest amounts are usually different under the two methods.

Treasury Stock Approach

Assume that Pace Corporation acquired a 90 percent interest in Salt Corporation on January 1, 19X5 for $270,000 when Salt's capital stock was $200,000 and its retained earnings, $100,000. In addition, Salt Corporation purchased a 10 percent interest in Pace Corporation on January 5, 19X5 for $70,000 when Pace's capital stock was $500,000 and its retained earnings, $200,000. Trial balances for Pace and Salt at December 31, 19X5, before either company recorded its investment income, were as follows:

	Pace	Salt
Debits		
Other assets	$480,000	$260,000
Investment in Salt (90%)	270,000	—
Investment in Pace (10%)	—	70,000
Expenses including cost of goods sold	70,000	50,000
	$820,000	$380,000
Credits		
Capital stock, $10 par	$500,000	$200,000
Retained earnings	200,000	100,000
Sales	120,000	80,000
	$820,000	$380,000

---

[2]*ARB No. 51*, "Consolidated Financial Statements," paragraph 13.

Consolidation in Year of Acquisition   If the treasury stock approach is used, Salt Corporation has no investment income for 19X5 and Pace's share of Salt's $30,000 income ($80,000 sales − $50,000 expenses) is $27,000 ($30,000 × 90%). Consolidation working papers for Pace Corporation and Subsidiary for 19X5 are shown in Exhibit 9–6. In examining the working papers, notice that Salt's investment in Pace is reclassified as treasury stock and deducted from stockholders' equity in the consolidated balance sheet.

Consolidation in Subsequent Years   During 19X6 the separate earnings and dividends of Pace and Salt Corporations are as follows:

	Pace	Salt
Separate earnings	$60,000	$40,000
Dividends	30,000	20,000

Under the treasury stock approach, Salt records dividend income of $3,000 from Pace (10 percent of Pace Corporation's $30,000 dividends) and reports its net income for 19X6 under the cost method in the amount of $43,000.

Pace Corporation accounts for its investment in Salt under the equity method as follows:

Cash	$18,000	
Investment in Salt		$18,000

To record 90% of $20,000 dividends paid by Salt.

Investment in Salt	$38,700	
Income from Salt		$38,700

To record 90% of Salt's $43,000 income for 19X6.

Income from Salt	$ 3,000	
Dividends		$ 3,000

To eliminate intercompany dividends of $3,000 (10% of Pace's $30,000 dividends paid to Salt) and to adjust investment income for Pace Corporation's dividends that are included in Salt's income.

Thus, Pace records investment income from Salt of $35,700 ($38,700 − $3,000) and an investment account increase of $20,700 during 19X6 ($38,700 − $18,000). The increase of $20,700 in Pace's investment in Salt account is equal to 90 percent of Salt's $40,000 separate earnings, plus 90 percent of the $3,000 dividends paid to Salt that accrued to the benefit of Pace, less 90 percent of Salt's $20,000 dividends. Pace Corporation's investment income from Salt consists of 90 percent of Salt's $40,000 separate earnings, less $300 (the part of the $3,000 dividends from Pace that accrues to the benefit of Salt Corporation's minority stockholders).

Consolidation working papers for Pace and Subsidiary for 19X6 are shown in Exhibit 9–7. The $317,700 balance in Pace's investment in Salt account is computed as follows:

Investment in Salt (90%) December 31, 19X5	$297,000
Add: 90% of Salt's reported income	38,700
Deduct: 90% of Salt's dividends	− 18,000
Investment in Salt (90%) December 31, 19X6	$317,700

Since Pace's investment in Salt was acquired at book value, the investment in Salt account balance can also be computed as 90 percent of Salt's equity at December 31, 19X6 ($353,000 × 90% = $317,700).

Entry a in the consolidation working papers shown in Exhibit 9–7 is affected by the $3,000 dividend adjustment under the equity method and is reproduced for convenient reference:

PACE CORPORATION AND SUBSIDIARY
CONSOLIDATION WORKING PAPERS
FOR THE YEAR ENDED DECEMBER 31, 19X5

	Pace	90% Salt	Adjustments and Eliminations		Minority Interests	Consolidated Statements
Income Statement						
Sales	$120,000	$ 80,000				$200,000
Investment income	27,000		a	27,000		
Expenses including cost of goods sold	70,000*	50,000*				120,000*
Minority interest income					$ 3,000	3,000*
Net income	$ 77,000	$ 30,000				$ 77,000
Retained Earnings						
Retained earnings—Pace	$200,000					$200,000
Retained earnings—Salt		$100,000	b	100,000		
Net income	77,000✔	30,000✔				77,000
Retained earnings December 31, 19X5	$277,000	$130,000				$277,000
Balance Sheet						
Other assets	$480,000	$260,000				$740,000
Investment in Salt (90%)	297,000		a b	27,000 270,000		
Investment in Pace (10%)		70,000	c	70,000		
	$777,000	$330,000				$740,000
Capital stock—Pace	$500,000					$500,000
Capital stock—Salt		$200,000	b	200,000		
Retained earnings	277,000✔	130,000✔				277,000
	$777,000	$330,000				
Treasury stock			c	70,000		70,000*
Minority interest January 1, 19X5			b	30,000	30,000	
Minority interest December 31, 19X5					$33,000	33,000
						$740,000

*Deduct.

Exhibit 9–6   Parent Stock Held by Subsidiary—Treasury Stock Approach

a	Income from Salt	$35,700	
	Dividend income	3,000	
	Dividends		$18,000
	Investment in Salt		20,700

This entry is unusual because both Pace Corporation's investment income from Salt, and Salt's dividend income from Pace, are eliminated in the process of adjusting the investment in Salt account to its $297,000 beginning-of-the-period balance. The other working paper adjustments are similar to those in Exhibit 9–6.

Although Pace Corporation paid dividends of $30,000 during 19X6, only $27,000 was paid to outside stockholders of Pace. Thus, the retained earnings statement of Pace and the consolidated retained earnings statement show $27,000

PACE CORPORATION AND SUBSIDIARY
CONSOLIDATION WORKING PAPERS
FOR THE YEAR ENDED DECEMBER 31, 19X6

	Pace	90% Salt	Adjustments and Eliminations		Minority Interests	Consolidated Statements
Income Statement						
Sales	$140,000	$100,000				$240,000
Income from Salt	35,700		a	35,700		
Dividend income		3,000	a	3,000		
Expenses including cost of goods sold	80,000*	60,000*				140,000*
Minority interest income $43,000 × 10%					$ 4,300	4,300*
Net income	$ 95,700	$ 43,000				$ 95,700
Retained Earnings						
Retained earnings—Pace	$277,000					$277,000
Retained earnings—Salt		$130,000	b	130,000		
Net income	95,700✓	43,000✓				95,700
Dividends	27,000*	20,000*	a	18,000	2,000*	27,000*
Retained earnings December 31, 19X6	$345,700	$153,000				$345,700
Balance Sheet						
Other assets	$528,000	$283,000				$811,000
Investment in Salt (90%)	317,700		a	20,700		
			b	297,000		
Investment in Pace (10%)		70,000	c	70,000		
	$845,700	$353,000				$811,000
Capital stock—Pace	$500,000					$500,000
Capital stock—Salt		$200,000	b	200,000		
Retained earnings	345,700✓	153,000✓				345,700
	$845,700	$353,000				
Treasury stock			c	70,000		70,000*
Minority interest January 1, 19X6			b	33,000	33,000	
Minority interest December 31, 19X6					$35,300	35,300
						$811,000

* Deduct.

Exhibit 9–7 Parent Stock Held by Subsidiary—Treasury Stock Approach (Year after Acquisition)

dividends rather than $30,000. The consolidated balance sheet shows a $70,000 equity deduction for the cost of Salt's investment in Pace. This amount is the same as was shown in the working papers in Exhibit 9–6.

Conventional Approach

The consolidated balance sheets in Exhibits 9–6 and 9–7 for the treasury stock approach consolidated 100 percent of Pace Corporation's capital stock and retained earnings, and deducted the cost of Salt's 10 percent investment in Pace from the consolidated stockholders' equity. Under the conventional approach, parent company stock held by a subsidiary is considered constructively retired, and the capital stock and retained earnings applicable to the interest held by the subsidiary do not appear in the consolidated financial statements.

Salt's acquisition of Pace stock under the conventional procedure is considered a constructive retirement of 10 percent of Pace's capital stock. A consolidated balance sheet for Pace and Subsidiary at the time of acquisition shows capital stock and retained earnings applicable to the 90 percent of Pace Corporation's equity held outside of the consolidated entity as follows:

| | *January 1, 19X5* | |
	Pace	*Consolidated*
Capital stock	$500,000	$450,000
Retained earnings	200,000	180,000
Total stockholders' equity	$700,000	$630,000

It is generally agreed that the consolidated balance sheet should show the capital stock and retained earnings applicable to majority stockholders outside the consolidated entity. But this treatment raises a question concerning the applicability of the equity method of accounting to mutual holdings involving parent company stock. Specifically, is the equity method of accounting applicable to affiliation structures that involve investments in the parent company? If so, the parent company's (investor's) "net income for the period and its stockholders' equity at the end of the period are the same regardless of whether an investment in a subsidiary is accounted for under the equity method or the subsidiary is consolidated."[3]

In spite of some reservations that have been expressed about the applicability of the equity method to mutually held parent company stock, the position taken in this book is that the equity method is applicable and, in fact required by *APB Opinion No. 18*. Paragraph 19e of that Opinion states that "a transaction of an investee of a capital nature that affects the investor's share of stockholders' equity of the investee should be accounted for as if the investee were a consolidated subsidiary." In accounting for Pace's investment in Salt, this requirement is applied as follows:

January 1, 19X5

| Investment in Salt (90%) | $270,000 | |
| Cash | | $270,000 |

To record acquisition of a 90% interest in Salt at book value.

January 5, 19X5

Capital stock ($10 par)	$ 50,000	
Retained earnings	20,000	
Investment in Salt		$ 70,000

To record the constructive retirement of 10% of Pace's outstanding stock as a result of Salt's purchase of Pace stock.

These entries reduce parent company capital stock and retained earnings to reflect amounts applicable to majority stockholders outside the consolidated entity. The reduction of the investment in Salt account is based on the theory that parent company stock purchased by a subsidiary is, in effect, returned to the parent company and constructively retired.

By recording the constructive retirement of the parent company stock on parent company books, parent company equity reflects the equity of stockholders outside the consolidated entity. These are the shareholders for which the con-

---

[3]*APB Opinion No. 18,* paragraph 19.

solidated statements are intended. In addition, recording the constructive retirement as indicated establishes consistency between capital stock and retained
earnings for the parent's outside stockholders (90 percent) and parent company
net income, dividends, and earnings per share which also relate to the 90 percent outside stockholders of the parent. Relevant financial statement notes should
explain the details of the constructive retirement.

Allocation of Mutual Income   When the conventional method of accounting
for mutually held stock is used, the income of the parent on an equity basis cannot be determined until the income of the subsidiary has been determined on
an equity basis, and vice versa. This is because the incomes are mutually related.
The solution to the problem of determining parent and subsidiary incomes lies
in the use of some mathematical procedure, the most common procedure being the use of simultaneous equations and substitution. The incomes of Pace
and Salt on a consolidated basis for 19X5 can be determined mathematically
as follows:

P = The income of Pace on a consolidated basis (includes mutual income)
S = The income of Salt on a consolidated basis (includes mutual income)

Then:

$$P = \text{Pace's separate earnings of } \$50,000 + 90\% \ S$$
$$S = \text{Salt's separate earnings of } \$30,000 + 10\% \ P$$

By substitution:

$$P = \$50,000 + .9 \ (\$30,000 + .1P)$$
$$P = \$50,000 + \$27,000 + .09P$$
$$P = \underline{\$84,615}$$
$$S = \$30,000 + (\$84,615 \times .1)$$
$$S = \underline{\$38,462}$$

These solutions are not final solutions because some of the income (mutual
income) has been double counted. The combined separate earnings of Pace and
Salt is only $80,000 ($50,000 + $30,000), but P plus S equals $123,077 ($84,615
+ $38,462). *Pace's net income on an equity basis is 90 percent of $84,615, or $76,154,
and the minority interest income is 10 percent of $38,462, or $3,846.* Pace's net income
(and consolidated net income) of $76,154, plus minority interest income of $3,846,
is equal to the $80,000 separate earnings of Pace and Salt.

Accounting for Mutual Income Under the Equity Method   Pace Corporation
records its investment income for 19X6 on an equity basis as follows:

Investment in Salt	$26,154	
Income from Salt		$26,154
To record income from Salt.		

The $26,154 is equal to 90 percent of Salt's $38,462 income on a consolidated
basis, less 10 percent of Pace's $84,615 income on a consolidated basis. This
represents Pace's 90 percent interest in Salt's income less Salt's 10 percent interest in Pace's income. An alternative calculation that gives the same result is
to deduct Pace's separate earnings from its net income ($76,154 − $50,000).

Assume that Salt Corporation accounts for its investment in Pace on a cost
basis because its interest in Pace is only 10 percent. Since Pace did not declare
dividends during 19X5, Salt would have no investment income for the year, and

its investment account would remain at the $70,000 original cost of the 10 percent interest.

Consolidation Under the Equity Method Consolidation working papers for Pace Corporation and Subsidiary under the conventional procedure for 19X5 are presented in Exhibit 9–8. The investment in Salt (90 percent) is shown in the working papers at $226,154 (the $270,000 initial investment, plus $26,154 investment income, less the $70,000 reduction for the constructive retirement of Pace's stock). Entry a in the working papers eliminates the $70,000 investment in Pace (Salt's books) and increases Pace's investment in Salt account to $296,154. This entry reflects the constructive retirement of Pace stock that was charged to Pace's investment in Salt account. Entry b eliminates investment income of $26,154 and reduces the investment account to its $270,000 cost at January 5, 19X5. Entry c eliminates the reciprocal investment in Salt and equity of Salt accounts and establishes the minority interest in Salt at $30,000 (10 percent of $300,000) at the beginning of 19X5.

In examining the working papers in Exhibit 9–8, observe that the net income, capital stock, and retained earnings in the separate statements of Pace Corporation are equal to consolidated net income, capital stock, and retained earnings. This equality would not have existed without the entry to record the constructive retirement of stock on Pace Corporation's books.

Consolidation in Subsequent Years The separate earnings and dividends of Pace and Salt for 19X6 are as follows:

	Pace	*Salt*
Separate earnings	$60,000	$40,000
Dividends	30,000	20,000

Application of the conventional method of accounting involves the following mathematical computations for Pace and Salt for 19X6:

P = Pace's income on a consolidated basis (includes mutual income)
S = Salt's income on a consolidated basis (includes mutual income)

Basic equations:

$$P = \$60,000 + .9S$$
$$S = \$40,000 + .1P$$

Substitution:

$$P = \$60,000 + .9 (\$40,000 + .1P)$$
$$.91P = \$96,000$$
$$P = \$105,495$$

$$S = \$40,000 + .1 (\$105,495)$$
$$S = \$50,549$$

The computed amounts for P and S are used in determining consolidated net income and minority interest income as follows:

Pace's net income (and consolidated net income)	
$105,495 × 90% outside ownership =	$ 94,945
Minority interest income $50,549 × 10% =	5,055
Total separate earnings of Pace and Salt	$100,000

PACE CORPORATION AND SUBSIDIARY
CONSOLIDATION WORKING PAPERS
FOR THE YEAR ENDED DECEMBER 31, 19X5

	Pace	90% Salt	Adjustments and Eliminations		Minority Interests	Consolidated Statements
Income Statement						
Sales	$120,000	$ 80,000				$200,000
Income from Salt	26,154		b	26,154		
Expenses including cost of sales	70,000*	50,000*				120,000*
Minority interest income (see equation)					$ 3,846	3,846*
Net income	$ 76,154	$ 30,000				$ 76,154
Retained Earnings						
Retained earnings—Pace	$180,000					$180,000
Retained earnings—Salt		$100,000	c	100,000		
Net income	76,154✓	30,000✓				76,154
Retained earnings December 31, 19X5	$256,154	$130,000				$256,154
Balance Sheet						
Other assets	$480,000	$260,000				$740,000
Investment in Salt (90%)	226,154		a 70,000 c 270,000	b 26,154		
Investment in Pace (10%)		70,000		a 70,000		
	$706,154	$330,000				$740,000
Capital stock—Pace	$450,000					$450,000
Capital stock—Salt		$200,000	c 200,000			
Retained earnings	256,154✓	130,000✓				256,154
	$706,154	$330,000				
Minority interest January 1, 19X5				c 30,000	30,000	
Minority interest December 31, 19X5					$33,846	33,846
						$740,000

*Deduct.

Exhibit 9–8   *Parent Stock Held by Subsidiary—Conventional Approach (Equity Basis)*

If Salt accounts for its investment in Pace under the cost method, it will record dividend income from Pace of $3,000 for 19X6 (10 percent of Pace's dividends). Alternatively, Salt will record income from Pace of $10,550 ($105,495 × 10%) if it uses the equity method.

Pace accounts for its investment in Salt on an equity basis as follows:

Cash	$18,000	
Investment in Salt		$18,000

To record 90% of Salt's $20,000 dividend for 19X6.

| Investment in Salt | $34,945 | |
| Income from Salt | | $34,945 |

To record investment income computed as follows: ($94,945 Pace's net income, less $60,000 Pace's separate earnings) or 90% of Salt's income on a consolidated basis ($50,549 × 90%), less 10% of Pace's income on a consolidated basis ($105,495 × 10%).

| Investment in Salt | $ 3,000 | |
| Dividends | | $ 3,000 |

To eliminate parent company dividends paid to Salt and to adjust the investment in Salt account.

Pace's investment in Salt account at December 31, 19X6 will have a balance of $246,099 under the equity method. This balance is computed:

Investment in Salt December 31, 19X5	$226,154
Add: Investment income	34,945
Add: Dividends paid to Salt	3,000
Deduct: Dividends received from Salt	− 18,000
Investment in Salt December 31, 19X6	$246,099

Consolidation working papers for Pace Corporation and Subsidiary for 19X6 are shown in Exhibit 9–9, which assumes that Salt accounts for its investment in Pace under the cost method. Since the equity method of accounting has been applied by Pace, parent company net income of $94,945 is equal to consolidated net income. Parent company capital stock and retained earnings amounts also are equal to their corresponding consolidated statement amounts. The working paper adjustments in Exhibit 9–9 are procedurally equivalent to those shown earlier in the chapter.

Conversion to Equity Method on Separate Company Books It is helpful at this point to consider the computations that would be necessary to correct consolidated retained earnings and minority interest if the equity method of accounting had not been used by Pace. First, it would be necessary to determine the separate net asset increases of the mutually held companies. This increase is computed for Pace and Salt from January 1, 19X5 to December 31, 19X6 as follows:

	Pace	*Salt*	*Total*
Separate earnings—19X5	$50,000	$30,000	$ 80,000
Separate earnings—19X6	+60,000	+40,000	+100,000
Less: Dividends declared	−30,000	−20,000	−50,000
Add: Dividends received from affiliates	+18,000	+ 3,000	+21,000
Increase in net assets	$98,000	$53,000	$151,000

Once the separate net asset increases were determined, the simultaneous equations used earlier for determining income allocations would be used in allocating the separate net asset increases to consolidated retained earnings and to minority interest. The computations for Pace and Salt would be:

P = Increase in net assets of Pace on a consolidated basis since acquired by Salt

S = Increase in net assets of Salt on a consolidated basis since acquired by Pace

PACE CORPORATION AND SUBSIDIARY
CONSOLIDATION WORKING PAPERS
FOR THE YEAR ENDED DECEMBER 31, 19X6

	Pace	90% Salt	Adjustments and Eliminations		Minority Interests	Consolidated Statements
Income Statement						
Sales	$140,000	$100,000				$240,000
Income from Salt	34,945		b	34,945		
Dividend income		3,000	b	3,000		
Expenses including cost of sales	80,000*	60,000*				140,000*
Minority interest income (see equation)					$ 5,055	5,055*
Net income	$ 94,945	$ 43,000				$ 94,945
Retained Earnings						
Retained earnings—Pace	$256,154					$256,154
Retained earnings—Salt		$130,000	c	130,000		
Net income	94,945✓	43,000✓				94,945
Dividends	27,000*	20,000*		b 18,000	2,000*	27,000*
Retained earnings December 31, 19X6	$324,099	$153,000				$324,099
Balance Sheet						
Other assets	$528,000	$283,000				$811,000
Investment in Salt (90%)	246,099		a 70,000	b 19,945 c 296,154		
Investment in Pace (10%)		70,000		a 70,000		
	$774,099	$353,000				$811,000
Capital stock—Pace	$450,000					$450,000
Capital stock—Salt		$200,000	c 200,000			
Retained earnings	324,099✓	153,000✓				324,099
	$774,099	$353,000				
Minority interest January 1, 19X6				c 33,846	33,846	
Minority interest December 31, 19X6					$36,901	36,901
						$811,000

*Deduct.

Exhibit 9-9 *Parent Stock Held by Subsidiary—Conventional Approach (Year After Acquisition)*

Basic equations:

$$P = \$98,000 + .9S$$
$$S = \$53,000 + .1P$$

By substitution:

$$P = \$98,000 + .9(\$53,000 + .1P)$$
$$P = \$98,000 + \$47,700 + .09P$$
$$.91P = \$145,700$$
$$\underline{P = \$160,110}$$

$$S = \$53,000 + (.1 \times \$160,110)$$
$$\underline{S = \$69,011}$$

These computations could be used to allocate the $151,000 net asset increase to consolidated retained earnings and minority interest as follows:

Pace's retained earnings increase (or increase in consolidated retained earnings) = $160,110 × 90% =	$144,099
Minority interest's retained earnings increase = $69,011 × 10% =	6,901
Total net asset increase	$151,000

At acquisition Pace's retained earnings were $200,000, and they were adjusted downward to $180,000 for the constructive retirement of 10 percent of Pace's stock. Thus, the correct amount of consolidated retained earnings at December 31, 19X6 can be computed independently as $180,000 + $144,099, or $324,099. This computation provides a convenient check on the $324,099 retained earnings shown in the consolidated balance sheet in Exhibit 9–9.

Minority interest in Salt Corporation at January 1, 19X5 was $30,000 ($300,000 equity × 10%). The minority interest at December 31, 19X6 is computed $30,000 + $6,901, or $36,901. This computation confirms the $36,901 minority interest that appears in the consolidation working papers of Exhibit 9–9.

SUBSIDIARY STOCK MUTUALLY HELD

Parent company stock that is held within an affiliation structure is not outstanding and must not be reported as outstanding stock either in the parent company statements under the equity method of accounting or in consolidated financial statements. Two generally accepted approaches for eliminating the effect of mutually held parent company stock—the treasury stock approach and the conventional approach—were explained and illustrated in the previous section of this chapter. In this section, *the mutually held stock involves subsidiaries holding the stock of each other, and the treasury stock approach is not applicable.*

Consider the following diagram of the affiliation structure of Poly, Seth, and Uno. Poly owns an 80 percent interest in Seth directly. Seth has a 70 percent interest in Uno, and Uno has a 10 percent interest in Seth. There is a 10 percent minority interest in Seth and a 30 percent minority interest in Uno.

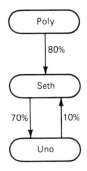

The acquisitions of Poly, Seth, and Uno were as follows:

1 Poly acquired its 80 percent interest in Seth Corporation on January 2, 19X5 for $260,000 when the stockholders' equity of Seth consisted of capital stock of $200,000 and retained earnings of $100,000 ($20,000 goodwill).
2 Seth acquired its 70 percent interest in Uno Corporation for $115,000 on January 3, 19X6 when the stockholders' equity of Uno consisted of $100,000 capital stock and $50,000 retained earnings ($10,000 goodwill).

3 Uno acquired its 10 percent interest in Seth for $40,000 on December 31, 19X6 when the stockholders' equity of Seth consisted of $200,000 capital stock and $200,000 retained earnings (no goodwill).

Accounting Prior to Mutual Holding Relationship

Assume that the recorded net assets from the investments described were equal to their fair values at the time of acquisition, and that any excess of investment cost over net assets acquired was allocated to goodwill with a ten-year amortization period. After-closing trial balances for Poly, Seth, and Uno at December 31, 19X6 are presented as follows:

	Poly	*Seth*	*Uno*
Cash	$ 64,000	$ 40,000	$ 20,000
Other current assets	200,000	85,000	80,000
Plant and equipment—net	500,000	240,000	110,000
Investment in Seth (80%)	336,000	—	—
Investment in Uno (70%)	—	135,000	—
Investment in Seth (10%)	—	—	40,000
	$1,100,000	$500,000	$250,000
Liabilities	$ 200,000	$100,000	$ 70,000
Capital stock	500,000	200,000	100,000
Retained earnings	400,000	200,000	80,000
	$1,100,000	$500,000	$250,000

The balance in Poly's investment in Seth account at December 31, 19X6 is $336,000, computed as follows:

Cost	$260,000
Add: 80% of Seth's $40,000 income less dividends—19X5	32,000
80% of Seth's $60,000 income less dividends—19X6	48,000
Deduct: Amortization of excess of cost over book value	
[$260,000 − ($300,000 × 80%)] × 10%: 19X5	−2,000
19X6	−2,000
	$336,000

The balance of Uno's 10 percent investment in Seth account at December 31, 19X6 is equal to the $40,000 cost of the investment on that date. Assume that this 10 percent investment in Seth is accounted for on a cost basis, even though the equity method might be used because absolute control lies with the parent company.

Seth's $135,000 investment in Uno at December 31, 19X6 is computed as follows:

Investment in Uno January 3, 19X6—cost	$115,000
Add: 70% of Uno's $30,000 income less dividends—19X6	21,000
Deduct: Amortization of excess of cost over book value acquired for 19X6:	
[$115,000 − ($150,000 × 70%)] × 10%	−1,000
	$135,000

Accounting for Mutually Held Subsidiaries

During 19X7 the three affiliated companies had income from their separate operations and dividends as follows:

	Income from Separate Operations	Dividends Declared
Poly	$112,000	$ 50,000
Seth	51,000	30,000
Uno	40,000	20,000
	$203,000	$100,000

The total separate incomes of the three companies are allocated under the conventional approach. An adjustment for goodwill amortization is necessary because goodwill amortization is not considered in determining income from separate operations, but is required for the determination of investment income on an equity basis.

Income Allocation Computations   Income allocation computations for the affiliated companies are as follows:

P = Separate income of Poly + .8S − $2,000 goodwill amortization
S = Separate income of Seth + .7U − $1,000 goodwill amortization
U = Separate income of Uno + .1S − 0 goodwill amortization
P = $112,000 + .8S − $2,000
S = $51,000 + .7U − $1,000
U = $40,000 + .1S

Solve for S (amounts are rounded to nearest $1):

$$S = \$51,000 + .7(\$40,000 + .1S) - \$1,000 = \$78,000 + .07S$$
$$.93\ S = \$78,000$$
$$S = \$83,871$$

$$U = \$40,000 + \$8,387$$
$$U = \$48,387$$

$$P = \$112,000 + .8(\$83,871) - \$2,000$$
$$P = \$177,097$$

Total income for the affiliated group is allocated to:

Consolidated net income (equal to Poly's net income)	$177,097
Minority interest in Seth's income ($83,871 × 10%)	8,387
Minority interest in Uno's income ($48,387 × 30%)	14,516
Total separate income less goodwill amortization	$200,000

Computations of Investment Account Balances   A summary of the investment account balances at December 31, 19X7 is as follows:

	Poly (Equity Method)	Seth (Equity Method)	Uno (Cost Method)*
Investment balances December 31, 19X6	$336,000	$135,000	$40,000
Add: Investment income			
Poly ($83,871 × .8) − $2,000	65,097	—	—
Seth ($48,387 × .7) − $1,000	—	32,871	—
Deduct: Dividends received:			
Poly ($30,000 × .8)	(24,000)	—	—
Seth ($20,000 × .7)	—	(14,000)	—
Investment balance December 31, 19X7	$377,097	$153,871	$40,000

*$3,000 dividend income and dividends received amounts for Uno's 10 percent investment in Seth do not affect the investment account because the cost method is used by Uno.

Consolidation Working Papers—Equity Method   The investment incomes and balances as summarized previously are reflected in the consolidation working papers that appear in Exhibit 9–10. Separate company financial statements of Poly, Seth, and Uno are shown in the first three columns of the consolidation working papers. Consolidation working paper entries a, b, and c eliminate investment income (including dividend income of Uno) and intercompany dividend balances and adjust the investment accounts to their beginning-of-the-period balances. Working paper entry d eliminates reciprocal equity and investment balances for Uno, records the $9,000 beginning-of-the-period unamortized goodwill from Seth's investment in Uno, and establishes the $54,000 beginning minority interest in Uno (computed as $180,000 × 30%). Entry e eliminates reciprocal equity and investment balances for Seth (both Poly's 80% and Uno's 10%), records the $16,000 beginning-of-the-period unamortized goodwill from Poly's investment in Seth, and establishes the $40,000 beginning minority interest in Seth (computed as $400,000 × 10%). Although there are two investment in Seth accounts and two elimination entries could have been made, *it is convenient to prepare one entry for each entity, Seth in this case, rather than for each investment account.* The final working paper entry records amortization of goodwill for the year.

Since Poly accounts for its investment in Seth as a one-line consolidation, consolidated net income of $177,097 for 19X7 and consolidated retained earnings of $527,097 at December 31, 19X7 are equal to the corresponding amounts in the separate financial statements of Poly. Minority interest income is determined by equation, as shown on page 371.

Summary

One corporation may control another corporation through direct or indirect ownership of its voting stock. Indirect holdings give the investor an ability to control or significantly influence the operations of the investee not directly owned through an investee that is directly owned. The major problem encountered in consolidating the financial statements of companies involved in indirect control situations lies in allocating income and equities among majority and minority stockholders. Several computational approaches are available for such allocations, but the schedule approach is probably the best overall approach because of its simplicity, and because it provides a step-by-step reference of all allocations made.

When affiliated companies hold the stock of each other, the stock is not outstanding from the viewpoint of the consolidated entity. The effect of mutually held parent company stock is eliminated from consolidated financial statements by either the treasury stock approach or the conventional approach. The treasury stock approach involves deducting the investment in parent company stock on

POLY CORPORATION AND SUBSIDIARIES
CONSOLIDATION WORKING PAPERS—FOR THE YEAR ENDED DECEMBER 31, 19X7

	Poly	Seth	Uno	Adjustments and Eliminations		Minority Interests	Consolidated Statements
Income Statement Sales	$ 412,000	$161,000	$100,000				$ 673,000
Income from Seth (80%)	65,097			c	65,097		
Income from Uno (70%)		32,871		b	32,871		
Dividend income (10%)			3,000	a	3,000		
Cost of sales	220,000*	70,000*	40,000*				330,000*
Expenses	80,000*	40,000*	20,000*	f	3,000		143,000*
Minority income—Seth†						$ 8,387	8,387*
Minority income—Uno†						14,516	14,516*
Net income	$ 177,097	$ 83,871	$ 43,000				$ 177,097
Retained Earnings Statement Retained earnings—Poly	$ 400,000						$ 400,000
Retained earnings—Seth		$200,000		e	200,000		
Retained earnings—Uno			$ 80,000	d	80,000		
Add: Net income	177,097✔	83,871✔	43,000✔				177,097
Deduct: Dividends	50,000*	30,000*	20,000*	a 3,000 b 14,000 c 24,000		9,000*	50,000*
Retained earnings December 31, 19X7	$ 527,097	$253,871	$103,000				$ 527,097
Balance Sheet Cash	$ 60,000	$ 30,000	$ 43,000				$ 133,000
Other current assets	250,000	80,000	70,000				400,000
Plant and equipment—net	550,000	300,000	130,000				980,000
Investment in Seth (80%)	377,097			c 41,097 e 336,000			
Investment in Uno (70%)		153,871		b 18,871 d 135,000			
Investment in Seth (10%)			40,000	e	40,000		
Goodwill—Poly				e 16,000	f 2,000		14,000
Goodwill—Seth				d 9,000	f 1,000		8,000
	$1,237,097	$563,871	$283,000				$1,535,000
Liabilities	$ 210,000	$110,000	$ 80,000				$ 400,000
Capital stock—Poly	500,000						500,000
Capital stock—Seth		200,000		e	200,000		
Capital stock—Uno			100,000	d	100,000		
Retained earnings	527,097✔	253,871✔	103,000✔				527,097
	$1,237,097	$563,871	$283,000				
Minority interest in Uno January 1, 19X7				d	54,000	54,000	
Minority interest in Seth January 1, 19X7				e	40,000	40,000	
Minority interest December 31, 19X7						$107,903	107,903
							$1,535,000

* Deduct.
† Minority income in Seth is 10% of $83,871 = $8,387; minority income in Uno is 30% of $48,387 = $14,516.

Exhibit 9–10   Consolidation Involving Mutually Held Subsidiary Stock

a cost basis from consolidated stockholders' equity. Under the conventional approach, the investment in parent company stock is treated as constructively retired by adjusting the parent's investment in subsidiary and parent's equity accounts to reflect a one-line consolidation. The subsidiary's investment in parent account is then eliminated against the parent's investment in subsidiary account.

Mutual investments by subsidiaries in the stock of each other are accounted for under the conventional method of eliminating reciprocal investment and equity balances. The treasury stock approach is not applicable to such mutually held investments because only parent company stock and retained earnings appear in the consolidated financial statements. Under the conventional method, simultaneous equations are used to allocate income and equities among mutually held companies.

SELECTED READINGS

CHILDS, WILLIAM HERBERT. *Consolidated Financial Statements: Principles and Procedures.* Ithaca, NY: Cornell University Press, 1949 (especially see Chapter 8, "Indirect and Reciprocal Relationships").

Committee on Accounting Procedure. *Accounting Research Bulletin No. 51.* "Consolidated Financial Statements." New York: American Institute of Certified Public Accountants, 1959.

MINCH, ROLAND A., and ENRICO PETRI. "Reporting Income for Reciprocal Parent-Subsidiary Stockholdings." *CPA Journal* (July 1975), pp. 36–40.

MOONITZ, MAURICE, "Mutual Stockholdings in Consolidated Statements." *Journal of Accountancy* (October 1939), pp. 227–35.

PETRI, ENRICO, and ROLAND A. MINCH. "The Treasury Stock Method and Conventional Method in Reciprocal Stockholdings—An Amalgamation." *Accounting Review* (April 1974), pp. 330–341.

WEIL, ROMAN L. "Reciprocal or Mutual Holdings: Allocating Earnings and Selecting the Accounting Method." *Accounting Review* (October 1973), pp. 749–58.

ASSIGNMENT MATERIAL

QUESTIONS

(Questions 1 through 8 relate to indirect holdings. Questions 9 through 17 relate to mutual holdings.)

1 What is an indirect holding of the stock of an affiliated company?
2 P owns a 60 percent interest in S and S owns a 40 percent interest in T. Should T be consolidated? If not, how should T be included in the consolidated statements of P Company and Subsidiaries?
3 Prepare diagrams of two types of affiliation structures involving indirect ownership. Compute the direct and indirect ownership held by majority and minority stockholders for each of your diagrams.
4 Distinguish between indirect holding affiliation structures and mutual holding affiliation structures.
5 Parent Company owns 70 percent of the voting stock of Subsidiary A, and Subsidiary A owns 70 percent of the stock of Subsidiary B. Is the inside ownership of Subsidiary B over 50 percent? Should Subsidiary B be included in the consolidated statements of Parent and Subsidiaries? Explain.
6 Pat Corporation owns 80 percent of the stock of Sam Corporation, and Sam Corporation owns 70 percent of the stock of Stan Corporation. Separate earnings of Pat, Sam, and Stan are $100,000, $80,000, and $50,000, respectively. Compute consolidated net income and minority interest income under two different approaches.
7 In using the schedule approach for allocating income of subsidiaries to majority and minority stockholders in an indirect holding affiliation structure, why is it necessary to begin with the lowest subsidiary in the affiliation tier?

8 P owns 80 percent of S1, and S1 owns 70 percent of S2. Separate incomes of P, S1, and S2 are $20,000, $10,000, and $5,000, respectively, for 19X1. During 19X1 S1 sold land to P at a gain of $1,000. Compute S1's income on an equity basis. Discuss why you did or did not adjust S1's investment in S2's account for the unrealized gain.

9 If a parent company owns 80 percent of the voting stock of a subsidiary, and the subsidiary in turn owns 20 percent of the stock of the parent, what kind of an affiliation structure is involved? Explain.

10 How is the treasury stock approach applied to the elimination of mutually held stock?

11 Are the treasury stock and conventional approaches equally applicable to all mutual holdings? Explain.

12 Under the treasury stock approach, a mutually held subsidiary accounts for its investment in the parent company on a cost basis. Are dividends received by the subsidiary from the parent company included in investment income of the parent under the equity method of accounting?

13 Describe the concept of a constructive retirement of parent company stock. Should the parent company adjust its equity accounts when its stock is constructively retired?

14 P's separate earnings are $50,000, and S's separate earnings are $20,000. P owns an 80 percent interest in S, and S owns a 10 percent interest in P. What is the amount of consolidated net income?

15 How do consolidation procedures for mutual holdings involving the father-son-grandson type of affiliation structure differ from those for mutually held parent company stock?

16 If all companies in an affiliation structure account for their investments on an equity basis, how can minority interests be determined without the use of simultaneous equations?

EXERCISES

(Exercises 9–1 through 9–6 relate to indirect holdings. Exercises 9–7 through 9–12 relate to mutual holdings.)

E 9–1 Price Corporation owns 80 percent of the voting common stock of Alex Corporation and 60 percent of the voting common stock of Baker Corporation. Alex owns 20 percent of the voting common stock of Baker. The separate incomes of these affiliated companies for 19X1 are:

Price	$150,000
Alex	80,000
Baker	60,000

There are no cost–book value differentials or unrealized profits to consider in measuring 19X1 income.

Required: Calculate consolidated net income for Price Corporation and Subsidiaries for 19X1.

E 9–2 The affiliation structure for Palace Corporation and its affiliates is as follows:

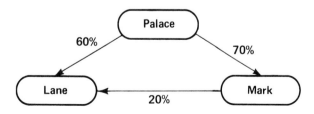

During 19X6 the separate incomes of these affiliated companies were as follows:

Palace	$200,000
Lane	90,000
Mark	70,000

Lane's income includes $10,000 unrealized profit on land sold to Mark during 19X6.

Required: Prepare a schedule that shows the allocation of income among the affiliated companies and also shows consolidated net income and minority interest income for the year 19X6.

E 9–3 Paul Corporation owns 80 percent each of the voting common stock of Sam and Tom Corporations. Sam owns 60 percent of the voting common stock of Utt Corporation and 10 percent of the voting stock of Tom Corporation. Tom owns 70 percent of the voting stock of Van Corporation and 10 percent of the voting stock of Utt.

The affiliated companies had separate incomes during 19X5 as follows:

Paul Corporation	$60,000
Sam Corporation	20,000
Tom Corporation	35,000
Utt Corporation	(10,000) loss
Van Corporation	40,000

The only intercompany profits included in the separate incomes of the affiliated companies consisted of $5,000 on merchandise that Paul acquired from Tom and which remained in Paul's December 31, 19X5 inventory.

Required
1 Prepare a diagram of the affiliation structure.
2 Compute consolidated net income and minority interest income for Paul Corporation and Subsidiaries.

E 9–4 Pete Corporation owns 90 percent of the stock of Mike Corporation and 70 percent of the stock of Nina Corporation. Mike owns 70 percent of the stock of Ople Corporation and 10 percent of the stock of Nina Corporation. Nina Corporation owns 20 percent of the stock of Ople Corporation.

Separate incomes for these corporations for the year ended December 31, 19X4 are as follows:

Pete	$65,000
Mike	18,000
Nina	28,000
Ople	9,000

During 19X4 Mike sold land to Nina at a profit of $4,000. Ople sold inventory items to Pete at a profit of $8,000, half of which remains in Pete's inventory. Pete purchased for $15,000 Nina's bonds, which had a book value of $17,000 on December 31, 19X4.

Required: Calculate consolidated net income and minority interest income for 19X4.

E 9–5 The affiliation structure for a group of interrelated companies is diagrammed as follows:

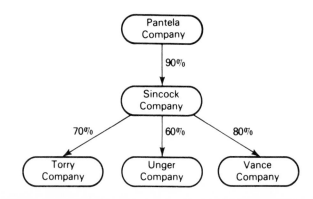

The investments in these companies were acquired at book value in 19X1, and there are no unrealized or constructive profits or losses.

Separate incomes and dividends for the companies for 19X4 are:

	Separate Income (Loss)	Dividends
Pantela	$620,000	$200,000
Sincock	175,000	100,000
Torry	200,000	80,000
Unger	(50,000)	none
Vance	120,000	60,000

1 The minority interest in Torry Company's net income for 19X4 is:
 a $60,000 **b** $74,000
 c $126,000 **d** $140,000

2 The income of the minority stockholders of Vance Company for 19X4 is:
 a $24,000 **b** $48,000
 c $55,200 **d** $72,000

3 The total minority interest income that should be shown in the consolidated income statement of Pantela Company and Subsidiaries for 19X4 is:
 a $122,100 **b** $105,100
 c $102,100 **d** $38,100

4 Consolidated net income for Pantela Company and Subsidiaries for 19X4 is:
 a $962,900 **b** $940,900
 c $620,000 **d** $342,900

5 Pantela Company's investment in Sincock account should reflect a net increase for the year 19X4 in the amount of:
 a $381,000 **b** $342,900
 c $312,900 **d** $252,900

E 9–6 Pasko Corporation owns an 80 percent interest in Savoy Corporation and a 70 percent interest in Trent Corporation. Trent also owns a 10 percent interest in Savoy. These investment interests were acquired at book value.

The net incomes of the affiliated companies for 19X1 were as follows:

Pasko	$240,000
Savoy	80,000
Trent	40,000

At December 31, 19X1 Pasko's inventory included $10,000 of unrealized profits on merchandise purchased from Savoy during 19X1, and Savoy's land account reflected $15,000 unrealized profit on land purchased from Trent during 19X1. These unrealized profits have not been eliminated from the net income amounts shown above. Except for adjustments related to unrealized profits, the net income amounts were determined on a correct equity basis.

1 The separate incomes of Pasko, Savoy, and Trent for 19X1 were:
 a $240,000, $80,000, and $32,000, respectively
 b $148,000, $80,000, and $32,000, respectively
 c $148,000, $72,000, and $40,000, respectively
 d $240,000, $72,000, and $40,000, respectively

2 The separate realized incomes of Pasko, Savoy, and Trent for 19X1 were:
 a $138,000, $80,000, and $25,000, respectively
 b $138,000, $70,000, and $25,000, respectively
 c $123,000, $80,000, and $17,000, respectively
 d $148,000, $70,000, and $17,000, respectively

3 Consolidated net income for Pasko Corporation and Subsidiaries for 19X1 was:
 a $220,800 **b** $215,900
 c $214,400 **d** $212,400

4 Minority interest income that should be shown in the consolidated income statement for Pasko Corporation and Subsidiaries for 19X1 is:

a $23,600   b $21,200
c $19,100   d $14,200

E 9-7 Polo Corporation owns an 80 percent interest in Sand Company acquired at book value, and Sand owns a 20 percent interest in Polo acquired at book value. Separate incomes (does not include investment income) of the two affiliates for 19X4 are:

Polo	$3,000,000
Sand	$1,000,000

Required: Compute consolidated net income for Polo Corporation and Subsidiary for the year 19X4 using the conventional (equation) approach.

E 9-8 Intercompany investment percentages and 19X1 separate earnings for three affiliated companies are as follows:

	Percentage Interest in Smedley	*Percentage Interest in Tweed*	*Separate Earnings*
Packard Corporation	70%		$200,000
Smedley Corporation		80%	120,000
Tweed Corporation	10%		80,000

Required
1 Construct a diagram of the affiliation structure.
2 Compute consolidated net income and minority interest income for Packard Corporation and Subsidiaries for 19X1.

E 9-9 [AICPA adapted]

D. Akron, Inc. owns 80 percent of the capital stock of Benson Co. and 70 percent of the capital stock of Cashin, Inc. Benson Co. owns 15 percent of the capital stock of Cashin, Inc. Cashin, Inc., in turn, owns 25 percent of the capital stock of Akron, Inc. These ownership interrelationships are illustrated in the following diagram:

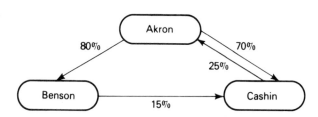

Income before adjusting for interests in intercompany income for each corporation follows:

Akron, Inc.	$190,000
Benson Co.	170,000
Cashin, Inc.	230,000

The following notations relate to the questions below:

A = Akron's consolidated income; that is, its separate income plus its share of the consolidated incomes of Benson and Cashin

B = Benson's consolidated income; that is, its separate income plus its share of the consolidated income of Cashin

C = Cashin's consolidated income; that is, its separate income plus its share of the consolidated income of Akron

1 The equation, in a set of simultaneous equations, that computes A is:
  a $A = .75(190,000 + .8B + .7C)$
  b $A = 190,000 + .8B + .7C$
  c $A = .75(190,000) + .8(170,000) + .7(230,000)$
  d $A = .75(190,000) + .8B + .7C$

2 The equation, in a set of simultaneous equations, that computes B is:
  a $B = 170,000 + .15C - .75A$
  b $B = 170,000 + .15C$
  c $B = .2(170,000) + .15(230,000)$
  d $B = .2(170,000) + .15C$

3 Cashin's minority interest in total consolidated income is:
  a $.15(230,000)$ **b** $230,000 + .25A$
  c $.15(230,000) + .25A$ **d** $.15C$

4 Benson's minority interest in total consolidated income is:
  a $34,316   **b** $25,500
  c $45,755   **d** $30,675

E 9–10 Separate incomes for three affiliated companies for the year ended December 31, 19X1 are as follows:

Police Corporation	$100,000
Marine Corporation	50,000
Navy Corporation	30,000

Police Corporation owns 80 percent of Marine Corporation's outstanding stock. Marine Corporation owns 80 percent of the outstanding stock of Navy Corporation, and Navy Corporation owns 10 percent of the outstanding stock of Marine Corporation.

1 Consolidated net income for Police Corporation and Subsidiaries for 19X1 is:
  a $180,435   **b** $164,348
  c $159,200   **d** $153,280

2 Total minority interest income that should be reflected in the consolidated income statement of Police Corporation and Subsidiaries for 19X1 is:
  a $23,696   **b** $16,000
  c $15,652   **d** $8,000

E 9–11 The affiliation structure of Pusan Corporation and Subsidiaries is diagrammed as follows:

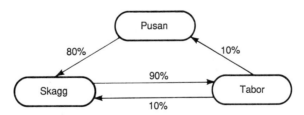

Each of the corporations uses the cost method of accounting for its investments. Separate earnings and dividends paid for 19X6 are as follows:

	Separate Earnings	*Dividends*
Pusan	$50,000	$20,000
Skagg	42,000	10,000
Tabor	20,000	none

Skagg sells merchandise to Pusan on which there is unrealized profit in Pusan's beginning inventory of $3,000 and in the ending inventory of $5,000.

Required: Compute consolidated net income and minority interest income for Pusan Corporation and Subsidiaries for the year ended December 31, 19X6.

E 9–12 Pulman Corporation acquired an 80 percent interest in Scover Corporation for $240,000 on January 2, 19X5 when Scover's equity consisted of $200,000 capital stock and $50,000 retained earnings. The excess is being amortized over a ten-year period and Pulman accounted for its investment in Scover during 19X5 as follows:

Investment cost January 2, 19X5	$240,000
Income from Scover ($40,000 × 80%) − $4,000	28,000
Dividends from Scover $20,000 × 80%	− 16,000
Investment balance December 31, 19X5	$252,000

On January 3, 19X6 Scover acquired a 10 percent interest in Pulman at its $60,000 book value. No intercompany profit transactions have occurred between these companies whose separate incomes and dividends for 19X6 were as follows:

	Pulman	*Scover*
Separate income 19X6	$120,000	$50,000
Dividends	60,000	30,000

Required

1 Determine the balance of Pulman's investment in Scover account at December 31, 19X6 if the treasury stock approach is used for Scover's investment in Pulman.
2 Compute consolidated net income and minority interest income if the conventional approach is used for Scover's investment in Pulman. Also determine the amount of Pulman's income from Scover and the balance in Pulman's investment in Scover account at December 31, 19X6.

PROBLEMS

(Problems 9–1 through 9–7 relate to indirect holdings. Problems 9–8 through 9–13 relate to mutual holdings.)

P 9–1 The investments of Perez Corporation and its affiliates were as follows throughout 19X3.

	Percentage Owned
Perez Corporation:	
Investment in Alice Company	60
Investment in Betty Company	80
Investment in Carol Company	70
Alice Company:	
Investment in Donna Company	70
Betty Company:	
Investment in Alice Company	20
Investment in Effie Company	90
Effie Company:	
Investment in Carol Company	10

Perez and all its affiliates account for their investments on a cost basis. All differences between investment costs and book values acquired were fully amortized for consolidated statement purposes in prior years, and the only unrealized profits within the affiliated grouping during 19X3 resulted from the sale of equipment by Alice to Effie at a gain of $15,000, of which $3,000 was depreciated during 19X3.

Net incomes as reported under the cost method and dividends for Perez and affiliates for 19X3 were as follows:

	Net Income (Loss)	Dividends
Perez Corporation	$110,000	$50,000
Alice Company	20,000	10,000
Betty Company	35,000	20,000
Carol Company	(15,000)	none
Donna Company	(20,000)	5,000
Effie Company	40,000	15,000

Required
1 Diagram the affiliation structure of Perez and affiliates.
2 Prepare a schedule of the allocation of income for Perez and Subsidiaries to consolidated net income and minority interest income.

P 9–2 Palmore Corporation owns an 80 percent interest in Summit Corporation and a 10 percent interest in Tonkin Corporation. Summit also owns a 70 percent interest in Tonkin Corporation. The investments were acquired at book value several years ago.

Both Palmore and Summit Corporations account for their investments by applying the equity method without eliminating the effects of intercompany profits. During 19X6 Tonkin sold merchandise that cost $30,000 to Palmore for $60,000. Half of this merchandise is included in Palmore's December 31, 19X6 inventory. Also, Palmore sold equipment with a book value of $50,000 and a remaining useful life of three years to Summit for $62,000 on January 2, 19X5. This equipment is expected to be in use by Summit until December 31, 19X7.

Comparative income statements for these affiliated companies for 19X6 follow:

COMPARATIVE INCOME STATEMENTS
FOR THE YEAR ENDED DECEMBER 31, 19X6

	Palmore	Summit	Tonkin	Total
Sales	$600,000	$200,000	$180,000	$980,000
Income from Summit	76,000	—	—	76,000
Income from Tonkin	5,000	35,000	—	40,000
Cost of sales	350,000*	80,000*	90,000*	520,000*
Other expenses	100,000*	60,000*	40,000*	200,000*
Net income	$231,000	$ 95,000	$ 50,000	$376,000

* Deduct.

Required: Prepare a consolidated income statement for Palmore Corporation and subsidiaries for 19X6.

P 9–3 The affiliation structure for Pida Corporation and subsidiaries is diagrammed as follows:

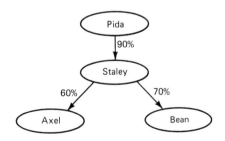

The separate incomes and dividends for the affiliated companies for 19X8 are:

	Pida	Staley	Axel	Bean
Separate income (loss)	$500,000	$300,000	$150,000	$(20,000)
Dividends	200,000	140,000	50,000	none

Additional Information
1 Axel sold land to Staley during 19X8 at a $20,000 gain. The land is still held by Staley.
2 Staley is amortizing the goodwill on its investment in Axel at the rate of $14,000 per year.

Required: Prepare a schedule to compute consolidated net income and minority interest income for the year 19X8.

P 9–4 A summary of the assets and equities of Posey Corporation and its 80 percent owned subsidiary, Seaton Corporation, at December 31, 19X1 is given as follows:

	Posey	Seaton
Assets	$ 800,000	$350,000
Investment in Seaton (80%)	200 000	—
Total assets	$1,000,000	$350,000
Liabilities	$ 150,000	$100,000
Capital stock	600,000	200,000
Retained earnings	250,000	50,000
Total equities	$1,000,000	$350,000

On January 2, 19X2 Seaton acquired a 70 percent interest in Thayer Corporation for $150,000. Thayer's net assets of $200,000 were recorded at their fair values on this date. The equity of Thayer on December 31, 19X1 consisted of $150,000 capital stock and $50,000 retained earnings.

Data concerning the operations of the three affiliated corporations for 19X2 are as follows:

	Separate Earnings	Dividends	Unrealized Profit Included in Separate Earnings
Posey	$150,000	$50,000	$10,000
Seaton	50,000	30,000	—
Thayer	30,000	10,000	5,000

Posey Corporation's $10,000 unrealized profit resulted from the sale of land to Thayer. Thayer's unrealized profit is from sales of merchandise items to Seaton and included in Seaton's inventory at December 31, 19X2.

Required
1 Prepare all journal entries required on the books of Posey and Seaton to account for their investments for 19X2 on an equity basis. Goodwill is to be amortized over a ten-year period.
2 Compute the net income of Posey, the net income of Seaton, and total minority interest income for 19X2.
3 Prepare a schedule showing the assets and equities of Posey, Seaton, and Thayer at December 31, 19X2, assuming liabilities of $150,000, $100,000, and $50,000 for Posey, Seaton, and Thayer, respectively.

P 9–5 Presley, Allen, Boone, and Clark Corporations have intercompany stock holdings acquired as follows:

1 January 19X1: Presley acquired 90 percent of Allen for $400,000 when Allen had capital stock of $300,000 and retained earnings of $100,000.
2 January 19X2: Allen acquired 80 percent of Boone for $200,000 when Boone had capital stock of $100,000 and retained earnings of $75,000.
3 January 19X2: Allen acquired 70 percent of Clark for $125,000 when Clark had capital stock of $100,000 and retained earnings of $50,000.

All the investments are maintained on a cost basis, and the differences between the investment costs and book values acquired are to be amortized over ten-year periods.

During 19X1 Allen had net income of $80,000 and paid dividends of $40,000. During 19X2 Allen had net income of $125,000 ($80,000 separate income, plus $24,000 dividend income from Boone, and $21,000 dividend income from Clark) and paid dividends of $60,000. During 19X2 Boone had net income of $50,000 and paid dividends of $30,000, and Clark had net income of $30,000 and paid dividends of $30,000.

Required
1 Prepare a schedule to show the correct balances of the investment accounts on an equity basis at December 31, 19X2.
2 Prepare journal entries to convert the investment accounts to an equity basis just before the books of Presley and Allen are closed on December 31, 19X2.

P 9-6 Potter Industries owns a 70 percent interest in Queen Company, an 80 percent interest in Rider Corporation, and a 90 percent interest in Style Company. Queen Company in turn owns a 60 percent interest in Thyme Corporation. Rider Corporation owns a 20 percent interest in Thyme and a 10 percent interest in Style. All the companies purchased their interests at book value several years ago and maintain their investment accounts on a cost basis.

During 19X7 the affiliated companies reported income and dividends as follows:

	Potter	Queen	Rider	Style	Thyme
Income	$180,000	$56,000	$46,000	$80,000	$30,000
Dividends	20,000	30,000	30,000	40,000	10,000

At December 31, 19X7 Queen held inventory items acquired from Potter on which Potter had made a profit of $6,000. Thyme held land acquired from Potter at a price $3,000 in excess of Potter's cost.

Required
1 Construct a diagram of the affiliation structure.
2 Compute realized income for each company.
3 Prepare a table showing separate realized income for each company divided into consolidated net income and minority interest income, and total consolidated net income and total minority interest income for the affiliated group.

P 9-7 Comparative financial statements for Pony Corporation and its subsidiaries, Star and Teel Corporations, at and for the year ended December 31, 19X9 are summarized as follows:

	Pony	Star	Teel
Income and Retained Earnings Statement for the Year Ended December 31, 19X9			
Sales	$ 500,000	$300,000	$100,000
Income from Star	72,000	—	—
Income from Teel	12,500	10,000	—
Cost of sales	240,000*	150,000*	60,000*
Other expenses	160,000*	70,000*	15,000*
Net income	184,500	90,000	25,000
Add: Beginning retained earnings	115,500	160,000	45,000
Deduct: Dividends	80,000*	40,000*	10,000*
Ending retained earnings	$ 220,000	$210,000	$ 60,000

	Pony	Star	Teel
Balance Sheet at December 31, 19X9			
Cash	$ 67,000	$ 36,000	$ 10,000
Accounts receivable—net	70,000	50,000	20,000
Inventories	110,000	75,000	35,000
Plant and equipment—net	250,000	425,000	115,000
Investment in Star (80%)	508,000	—	—
Investment in Teel (50%)	95,000	—	—
Investment in Teel (40%)	—	74,000	—
Total assets	$1,100,000	$660,000	$180,000
Accounts payable	$ 70,000	$ 40,000	$ 15,000
Other liabilities	110,000	10,000	5,000
Capital stock	700,000	400,000	100,000
Retained earnings	220,000	210,000	60,000
Total equities	$1,100,000	$660,000	$180,000

*Deduct

Additional Information
1 Pony acquired its 80 percent interest in Star Corporation for $420,000 on January 2, 19X7, when Star had capital stock of $400,000 and retained earnings of $100,000. The excess of cost over book value acquired relates to equipment that had a remaining use life of four years from January 1, 19X7.
2 Pony acquired its 50 pecent interest in Teel Corporation for $75,000 on July 1, 19X7 when Teel's equity consisted of $100,000 capital stock and $20,000 retained earnings. Star acquired its 40 percent interest in Teel on December 31, 19X8 for $68,000 when Teel's capital stock was $100,000 and its retained earnings, $45,000. The difference between investment costs and book value acquired is considered goodwill.
3 Although Pony and Star use the equity method in accounting for their investments, they do not apply the method to intercompany profits or to differences between investment cost and book value acquired.
4 At December 31, 19X8 the inventory of Star included inventory items acquired from Pony at a profit of $8,000. This merchandise was sold during 19X9.
5 Teel sold merchandise that had cost $30,000 to Star for $50,000 during 19X9. All of this merchandise is held by Star at December 31, 19X9. Star owes Teel $10,000 on this merchandise.
6 Goodwill is to be amortized ove a ten-year period.

Required: Prepare consolidation working papers for Pony Corporation and Subsidiaries for the year ended December 31, 19X9.

P 9-8 A schedule of intercompany investment interests and separate earnings for Parish Corporation, Swift Corporation, and Tolbert Corporation is presented as follows:

	Percentage Interest In Swift	Percentage Interest in Tolbert	Separate Earnings Current Year
Parish Corporation	80%	50%	$200,000
Swift Corporation	—	20	100,000
Tolbert Corporation	10	—	50,000

Required
1 Prepare a diagram of the affiliation structure of Parish Corporation and Subsidiaries.
2 Compute consolidated net income and minority interest income assuming no investment differences or unrealized profits.
3 Compute consolidated net income and minority interest income assuming $10,000

unrealized inventory profits on Tolbert's sales to Swift and a $20,000 gain on Parish's sale of land to Swift.

P 9–9 Consider the following intercompany relationships:

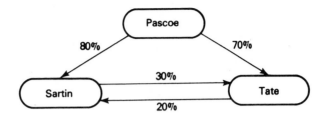

Separate trial balances at December 31, 19X6 are summarized as follows:

	Pascoe	Sartin	Tate
Other assets	$ 500,000	$400,000	$300,000
Investment in Sartin	350,000	—	90,000
Investment in Tate	300,000	100,000	—
	$1,150,000	$500,000	$390,000
Liabilities	$ 200,000	$150,000	$100,000
Capital stock	650,000	200,000	200,000
Retained earnings	300,000	150,000	90,000
	$1,150,000	$500,000	$390,000

All investment accounts are maintained on a cost basis. The investments in Sartin Corporation were made when Sartin had retained earnings of $115,000. The investments in Tate Corporation were made when Tate had retained earnings of $50,000.

Required
1 Prepare a consolidated balance sheet. You may ignore goodwill amortization for this problem.
2 Prepare a proof of consolidated retained earnings.

P 9–10 Punk Corporation paid $135,000 for a 90 percent interest in the voting common stock of Sub-one Corporation on January 1, 19X1 when Sub-one's equity was $150,000. At that time Sub-one owned an 80 percent interest in Sub-two, having acquired its interest at book value of $72,000 several years earlier when Sub-two's equity was $90,000. Sub-two owned a 10 percent interest in Punk Corporation at the time Sub-one acquired its interest in Sub-two Company.

Data from the financial statments of each of the affiliated companies at December 31, 19X1 are as follows:

	Net Income	Dividends	Subsidiary Investment (at cost)
Punk	$140,000	$70,000	$135,000
Sub-one	60,000	40,000	72,000
Sub-two	25,000	10,000	18,000

At December 31, 19X1, Punk holds inventory items acquired from Sub-one on which there are intercompany profits of $2,000. The investment accounts are maintained on a cost basis.

Required

1 Prepare a diagram of the affiliation structure of Punk Corporation and Subsidiaries. (The structure is referred to as a *circuit affiliation*.)

2 Prepare a schedule to compute separate earnings of each of the affiliated
companies.

3 Determine consolidated net income and minority interest income using the
treasury stock approach for holdings of parent company stock.

4 Determine consolidated net income and minority interest income using the conventional approach. (Use the same type of equations as for mutual holdings.)

P 9–11 Prill Company acquired a 90 percent interest in Skill Corporation for $355,000 cash
on January 2, 19X4 when Skill had capital stock of $200,000 and retained earnings of
$150,000. Skill purchased its 10 percent interest in Prill in 19X5 for $80,000. The excess
of Prill's investment cost over book value acquired is due to goodwill, which is being
amortized over eight years.

Comparative financial statements for Prill and Skill at and for the year ended
December 31, 19X8 are summarized as follows:

	Prill	Skill
Combined Income and Retained Earnings Statement for		
the Year Ended December 31, 19X8		
Sales	$400,000	$100,000
Investment income	27,000	—
Dividend income	—	10,000
Cost of goods sold	200,000*	50,000*
Expenses	50,000*	30,000*
Net income	177,000	30,000
Add: Beginning retained earnings	300,000	200,000
Deduct: Dividends	100,000*	20,000*
Retained earnings December 31, 19X8	$377,000	$210,000
Balance Sheet at December 31, 19X8		
Other assets	$491,000	$420,000
Investment in Skill 90%	409,000	—
Investment in Prill 10%	—	80,000
Total assets	$900,000	$500,000
Liabilities	$123,000	$ 90,000
Capital stock	400,000	200,000
Retained earnings	377,000	210,000
Total equities	$900,000	$500,000

*Deduct.

Required: Prepare consolidation working papers for Prill Company and Subsidiary using
the treasury stock approach for the mutual holding.

P 9–12 Pan Corporation (Panco) purchased an 80 percent interest in Stoker Corporation (Stoco)
for $170,000 on January 1, 19X1 when Stoco's equity was $200,000. The excess of cost
over book value is goodwill that is being amortized over a ten-year period.

At December 31, 19X2, the balance of Panco's investment in Stoco account is
$208,000, and the stockholders' equity of the two corporations is as follows:

	Panco	Stoco
Capital stock	$600,000	$150,000
Retained earnings	200,000	100,000
Total	$800,000	$250,000

On January 2, 19X3 Stoco acquires a 10 percent interest in Panco for $80,000. Separate earnings and dividends for 19X3 are:

	Panco	Stoco
Separate earnings	$100,000	$40,000
Dividends	50,000	20,000

Required
1. Compute consolidated net income and minority interest income for 19X3 using the conventional approach.
2. Prepare journal entries to account for Panco's investment in Stoco for 19X3 under the equity method (conventional approach).
3. Prepare journal entries on Stoco's books to account for its investment in Panco under the equity method (conventional approach).
4. Compute Panco's and Stoco's net incomes for 19X3.
5. Determine the balances of Panco's and Stoco's investment accounts at December 31, 19X3.
6. Determine the total stockholders' equity of Panco and Stoco at December 31, 19X3.
7. Compute the minority interest in Stoco at December 31, 19X3.
8. Prepare the adjustment and elimination entries that are needed to consolidate the financial statements of Panco and Stoco for the year ended December 31, 19X3.
9. Prepare the adjustment and elimination entries that are needed to consolidate the balance sheets of Panco and Stoco at December 31, 19X3.

P 9–13 Comparative adjusted trial balances for Pamol Corporation and its 90 percent owned subsidiary, Seward Corporation, at December 31, 19X8 are as follows:

ADJUSTED TRIAL BALANCES AT DECEMBER 31, 19X8

	Pamol	Seward
Debits		
Cash	$ 77,000	$ 60,000
Receivables—net	90,000	80,000
Inventory	100,000	70,000
Plant and equipment	800,000	340,000
Investment in Seward (90%)	473,000	—
Investment in Pamol (5%)	—	60,000
Cost of goods sold	400,000	150,000
Depreciation expense	100,000	40,000
Other expenses	50,000	60,000
Loss on sale of land	—	10,000
Dividends	60,000	30,000
Total debits	$2,150,000	$900,000
Credits		
Accumulated depreciation	$ 190,000	$ 90,000
Payables	200,000	50,000
Capital stock—$10 par	800,000	300,000
Retained earnings	215,000	150,000
Sales	700,000	307,000
Investment income	45,000	—
Dividend income	—	3,000
Total credits	$2,150,000	$900,000

Additional Information
1. Pamol acquired its 90 percent interest in Seward for $365,000 on January 1, 19X4 when Seward had capital stock of $300,000 and retained earnings of $50,000. The

excess of cost over book value acquired was allocated to goodwill and is being amortized over a ten-year period.

2 Seward's investment in Pamol was made on January 1, 19X8. The investment is accounted for on a cost basis and the financial statements are consolidated using the treasury stock approach.

3 Pamol's January 1, 19X8 inventory included merchandise acquired from Seward on which Seward had reported a $10,000 gross profit. Seward made sales of $50,000 to Pamol during 19X8, half of which were not paid for at December 31, 19X8. Intercompany profit in Pamol's December 31, 19X8 inventory of merchandise acquired from Seward amounted to $5,000.

4 On July 1, 19X7 Pamol sold equipment to Seward at a profit of $15,000. The equipment had a five-year remaining useful life on that date and is being depreciated on a straight-line basis.

5 On October 1, 19X8 Seward sold land to Pamol at a loss of $10,000.

Required: Prepare consolidation working papers for Pamol Corporation and Subsidiary for the year ended December 31, 19X8. Use the financial statement format and prepare a schedule to convert to the equity method.

SUBSIDIARY PREFERRED STOCK, CONSOLIDATED EARNINGS PER SHARE, AND CONSOLIDATED INCOME TAXATION

This chapter covers three miscellaneous topics relating to consolidation: consolidation of a subsidiary with preferred stock in its capital structure, consolidated earnings per share, and accounting for income taxes of consolidated entities. These topics tend to be detailed and technical, and the illustrations often use simplifying assumptions in order to minimize details and emphasize significant concepts and relationships. An intermediate accounting background in all three areas is assumed.

SUBSIDIARIES WITH PREFERRED STOCK OUTSTANDING

The existence of preferred stock in the capital structure of a subsidiary corporation complicates the consolidation process, but the basic procedures do not change. Parent company/investor accounting under the equity method is also affected when an investee company has preferred stock outstanding. The complications stem from the need to consider the contractual rights of preferred stockholders in allocating the investee company's equity and income between preferred and common stock components.

Most preferred stock issues are cumulative, nonparticipating, and nonvoting. In addition, preferred stock issues usually have preference rights in liquidation, and frequently are callable at prices in excess of the par or liquidating values. Net income of an investee corporation with preferred stock outstanding is allocated first to preferred stockholders based on the preferred stock contract, and the remainder is allocated to common stockholders. Similarly, the stockholders' equity of an investee is allocated first to preferred stockholders based on the preferred stock contract, and the remainder is allocated to common stockholders.

When preferred stock has a call or redemption price, this amount is used in allocating the investee's equity to preferred stockholders. In the absence of a redemption provision, the equity allocated to preferred would be based on par value of the stock plus any liquidation premium. In addition, any dividends in arrears on cumulative preferred stock must be included in the equity allocated

390

SUBSIDIARY PREFERRED
STOCK, CONSOLIDATED
EARNINGS PER SHARE,
AND CONSOLIDATED
INCOME TAXATION

to preferred stockholders. For nonparticipating preferred stock, income is assigned to preferred stockholders on the basis of the preference rate or amount. If the preferred stock is cumulative and nonparticipating, the current year's income assigned to the preferred stockholders is the current year's dividend requirement, irrespective of whether the directors declare only current-year dividends, current-year dividends plus prior-year arrearages, or no dividends at all. Income is assigned to noncumulative, nonparticipating preferred stock only if dividends are declared and only in the amount declared.

Subsidiary with Preferred Stock Not Held by Parent

Assume that Prix Corporation purchases 90 percent of Sol Corporation's outstanding common stock for $395,500 on January 1, 19X2 and that Sol Corporation's stockholders' equity on December 31, 19X1 was as follows:

$10 preferred stock, $100 par, cumulative, nonparticipating, callable at $105 per share	$100,000
Common stock, $10 par	200,000
Other paid-in capital	40,000
Retained earnings	160,000
Total stockholders' equity	$500,000

There were no preferred dividends in arrears as of January 1, 19X2. During 19X2 Sol reported net income of $50,000 and paid dividends of $30,000 ($20,000 on common stock and $10,000 on preferred stock). Sol's assets and liabilities were stated at their fair values when Prix acquired its interest and, accordingly, any excess of investment cost over book value acquired is goodwill to be amortized over a ten-year period.

In comparing the price paid for the 90 percent interest in Sol with the book value of the interest acquired, it is necessary to separate Sol's December 31, 19X1 equity into its preferred and common stock components:

Stockholders' equity of Sol	$500,000
Less: Preferred stockholders' equity (1,000 shares × $105 per share call price)	105,000
Common stockholders' equity	$395,000

The price paid for 90 percent of the common equity of Sol is compared with the book value (and fair value) acquired to determine goodwill:

Price paid for 90 percent common stock interest	$395,500
Less: Book value and fair value acquired ($395,000 × 90%)	355,500
Goodwill (10-year amortization period)	$ 40,000

Sol's $50,000 net income for 19X2 is allocated $10,000 to preferred stock (1,000 shares × $10 per share) and $40,000 to common stock. The entries to account for Prix Corporation's investment in Sol for 19X2 are:

January 1, 19X2

Investment in Sol common	$395,500	
Cash		$395,500

To record acquisition of 90% of Sol's common stock.

During 19X2

Cash	$ 18.000	
Investment in Sol common		$ 18,000

To reduce investment in Sol for dividends received ($20,000 × 90%).

December 31, 19X2

Investment in Sol common	$ 32,000	
Income from Sol		$ 32,000

To record equity in Sol's income less goodwill amortization [($40,000 × 90%)
  − $4,000 amortization].

In consolidating the financial statements of Prix and Sol for 19X2 (see Exhibit 10–1), Sol's $520,000 stockholders' equity at December 31, 19X2 is assigned to preferred and common components as follows:

Total stockholders' equity	$520,000
Less: Preferred stockholders' equity (1,000 shares × $105	
call price per share)	105,000
Common stockholders' equity	$415,000

Minority Interest in Preferred Stock   The *minority interest* in Sol at December 31, 19X2 (Exhibit 10–1) consists of 100 percent of the preferred stockholders' equity and 10 percent of the common stockholders' equity, or $146,500 [($105,000 × 100%) + ($415,000 × 10%)]. Similarly, *minority interest income* for 19X2 consists of 100 percent of the income to preferred stockholders and 10 percent of the income to common stockholders, or $14,000 [($10,000 × 100%) + ($40,000 × 10%)]. This information is reflected in the consolidation working papers for Prix Corporation and Subsidiary in Exhibit 10–1.

Except for working paper entry a, the working paper entries are the same as those encountered in earlier chapters. Entry a is reproduced in journal form as follows:

a	Preferred stock—Sol	$100,000	
	Retained earnings—Sol	5,000	
	Minority interest—preferred		$105,000

Entry a reclassifies the preferred stockholders' equity as a minority interest. Since the $105,000 preferred equity at the beginning of the period exceeded the $100,000 par value, the $5,000 excess is debited to Sol's retained earnings. This charge to Sol's retained earnings is made because the preferred stockholders have a maximum claim on Sol's retained earnings for the $5,000 call premium.

The consolidated income statement of Exhibit 10–1 shows separate deductions for minority interest income applicable to preferred ($10,000) and common stock ($4,000). This division is helpful in preparing working papers, but a consolidated income statement prepared from the working papers would ordinarily show minority interest income as one amount. Also, Exhibit 10–1 shows total minority interest in Sol at December 31, 19X2 on one line of the consolidated balance sheet in the single amount of $146,500. Although the consolidation working papers contain the information to separate this amount into preferred and common components, the separation is ordinarily not used for basic financial reporting, since all individual subsidiary equity accounts are typically eliminated in the consolidation process.[1] Consolidated financial statements are intended primarily for the stockholders and creditors of the parent company, and it is not expected that the minority stockholders could benefit significantly from the information contained in them.

---

[1]Minority interest in a subsidiary's preferred stock is sometimes reported as outstanding stock of the consolidated entity with notation of the name of the issuing corporation. This reporting practice is usually confined to regulated companies.

	Prix	90% Sol	Adjustments and Eliminations		Minority Interest	Consolidated Statements
PRIX CORPORATION AND SUBSIDIARY **CONSOLIDATION WORKING PAPERS** **FOR THE YEAR ENDED DECEMBER 31, 19X2**						
Income Statement Sales	$ 618,000	$300,000				$ 918,000
Income from Sol (cm)	32,000		b	32,000		
Expenses—including cost of goods sold	450,000*	250,000*	d	4,000		704,000*
Minority interest income (cm) ($40,000 × 10%)					$ 4,000	4,000*
Minority interest income (pf) ($10,000 × 100%)					10,000	10,000*
Net income	$ 200,000	$ 50,000				$ 200,000
Retained Earnings Retained earnings—Prix	$ 300,000					$ 300,000
Retained earnings—Sol		$160,000	a c	5,000 155,000		
Net income	200,000✓	50,000✓				200,000
Dividends (cm)	100,000*	20,000*		b 18,000	2,000*	100,000*
Dividends (pf)		10,000*			10,000*	
Retained earnings December 31, 19X2	$ 400,000	$180,000				$ 400,000
Balance Sheet Other assets	$1,290,500	$600,000				$1,890,500
Investment in Sol (cm)	409,500			b 14,000 c 395,500		
Goodwill			c 40,000	d 4,000		36,000
	$1,700,000	$600,000				$1,926,500
Liabilities	$ 200,000	$ 80,000				$ 280,000
Preferred stock—Sol		100,000	a 100,000			
Common stock	1,000,000	200,000	c 200,000			1,000,000
Other paid-in capital	100,000	40,000	c 40,000			100,000
Retained earnings	400,000✓	180,000✓				400,000
	$1,700,000	$600,000				
Minority interest (pf) January 1, 19X2				a 105,000	105,000	
Minority interest (cm) January 1, 19X2				c 39,500	39,500	
Minority interest December 31, 19X2					$146,500	146,500
						$1,926,500

* Deduct.

Exhibit 10–1 Preferred and Common Stock in the Affiliation Structure

Subsidiary Preferred Stock Acquired by Parent

A parent company's purchase of the outstanding preferred stock of a subsidiary results in a retirement of the stock purchased from the viewpoint of the consolidated entity. The stock is retired for consolidated statement purposes because its book value no longer appears as a minority interest in the consolidated balance sheet. But the retirement is really a constructive retirement because the investment in preferred (parent's books) and the preferred stock equity (subsidiary's books) are reported as outstanding in the separate financial statements of the parent and subsidiary companies.

The constructive retirement of a subsidiary's preferred stock through purchase by the parent company is reported as an actual retirement in the consolidated financial statements. That is, the equity related to the preferred stock held by the parent and the investment in preferred stock are eliminated, and any difference is charged or credited to the additional paid-in capital that would otherwise be reported in the consolidated balance sheet.[2] Since parent company stockholders' equity in a one-line consolidation is equal to consolidated stockholders' equity, comparable accounting requires that the parent company adjust its investment in subsidiary preferred stock to its book value at acquisition and charge or credit its additional paid-in capital for the difference between the price paid for the investment and its underlying book value. The investment in preferred stock is accounted for on the basis of its book value, not on the basis of the cost or equity method.

Constructive Retirement of Subsidiary Preferred Stock   Sol Corporation experiences a net loss of $40,000 in 19X3 and no dividends are paid. Its stockholders' equity decreases from $520,000 at December 31, 19X2 (see Exhibit 10–1) to $480,000 at December 31, 19X3, and Prix's 90 percent investment in Sol decreases from $409,500 at year-end 19X2 to $360,500 at year-end 19X3. The $49,000 decrease in Prix's investment in Sol common account is computed as follows:

Net loss of Sol	$40,000
Add: Income to preferred[3] (1,000 shares × $10)	10,000
Loss to common	50,000
Prix's ownership interest	90%
Decreased equity from Sol's loss	45,000
Add: Goodwill amortization ($40,000/10 years)	4,000
Loss from Sol for 19X3	$49,000

The $360,500 investment in Sol common at December 31, 19X3 can be checked as follows:

Stockholders' equity of Sol, December 31, 19X3	$480,000
Less: Preferred stockholders' equity [1,000 shares × ($105 per share call price + $10 per share dividend arrearage)]	115,000
Common stockholders' equity, December 31, 19X3	365,000
Prix's ownership interest	90%
Share of Sol's common stockholders' equity	328,500
Add: Unamortized goodwill ($40,000 − $8,000)	32,000
Investment in Sol common, December 31, 19X3	$360,500

---

[2]The parent company retained earnings are reduced when additional paid-in capital is insufficient to absorb an excess of purchase price over book value.

[3]A deduction of cumulative preferred dividends in computing income to common stockholders is required by *APB Opinion No. 18,* paragraph 19k, regardless of whether such dividends are declared.

394

SUBSIDIARY PREFERRED
STOCK, CONSOLIDATED
EARNINGS PER SHARE,
AND CONSOLIDATED
INCOME TAXATION

On January 1, 19X4 Prix responded to the depressed price of Sol's preferred stock and purchased 800 shares (an 80 percent interest) at $100 per share. Since the $80,000 price paid is less than the $92,000 book value of the stock that is constructively retired ($115,000 × 80%), Prix records the investment in Sol preferred as follows:

Investment in Sol preferred	$80,000	
Cash		$80,000

To record purchase of 80% of Sol's preferred stock.

Investment in Sol preferred	$12,000	
Other paid-in capital		$12,000

To adjust other paid-in capital to reflect the constructive retirement.

Assume that Sol reports net income of $20,000 for 19X4, but again passes dividends for the year. Prix accounts for its investments during 19X4 as follows:

Investment in Sol preferred	$8,000	
Income from Sol preferred		$8,000

To record 80% of the $10,000 increase in Sol's preferred dividend arrearage.

Investment in Sol common	$5,000	
Income from Sol common		$5,000

To record equity in Sol's income to common less goodwill amortization [($20,000 net income − $10,000 preferred income) × 90%] − $4,000 amortization.

A summary of Sol's preferred and common stockholders' equity and Prix's investment account balances at the end of 19X4 are:

Sol's Stockholders' Equity, December 31, 19X4

Total stockholders' equity ($480,000 on January 1, 19X4 plus $20,000 net income for 19X4)	$500,000
Less: Preferred stockholders' equity [1,000 shares × ($105 call price + $20 dividends in arrears)]	125,000
Common stockholders' equity	$375,000

Prix's Investment Accounts, December 31, 19X4

Investment in Sol preferred ($125,000 preferred equity × 80% owned)	$100,000
Investment in Sol common ($375,000 common equity × 90% owned + $28,000 unamortized goodwill)	$365,500

This information for 19X4 is reflected in consolidation working papers for Prix and Sol Corporations in Exhibit 10–2. The working paper entries for 19X4 are similar to those in Exhibit 10–1 for the year 19X2 except for items related to the investment in Sol's preferred stock. Procedures to eliminate the preferred equity and investment accounts parallel those for common stock. First, Prix's income from Sol preferred is eliminated against the investment in Sol preferred. This working paper entry (entry a) reduces the investment in Sol preferred to its $92,000 adjusted balance at January 1, 19X4. Next, the investment in Sol preferred and the preferred equity of Sol as of January 1, 19X4 are eliminated in working paper entry b. This entry also enters the preferred minority interest as of the beginning of the year. Entries a and b are reproduced in journal form as follows:

PRIX CORPORATION AND SUBSIDIARY
CONSOLIDATION WORKING PAPERS
FOR THE YEAR ENDED DECEMBER 31, 19X4

	Prix	90% Sol	Adjustments and Eliminations		Minority Interest	Consolidated Statements
Income Statement						
Sales	$ 690,000	$280,000				$ 970,000
Income from Sol (cm)	5,000		c	5,000		
Income from Sol (pf)	8,000		a	8,000		
Expenses—including cost of goods sold	583,000*	260,000*	e	4,000		847,000*
Minority interest income (cm) ($10,000 × 10%)					$ 1,000	1,000*
Minority interest income (pf) ($10,000 × 20%)					2,000	2,000*
Net income	$ 120,000	$ 20,000				$ 120,000
Retained Earnings						
Retained earnings—Prix	$ 450,000					$ 450,000
Retained earnings—Sol		$140,000	b 15,000 d 125,000			
Net income	120,000 ✔	20,000 ✔				120,000
Dividends	70,000*	—				70,000*
Retained earnings December 31, 19X4	$ 500,000	$160,000				$ 500,000
Balance Sheet						
Other assets	$1,334,500	$600,000				$1,934,500
Investment in Sol (pf)	100,000		a 8,000 b 92,000			
Investment in Sol (cm)	365,500		c 5,000 d 360,500			
Goodwill (cm)			d 32,000	e 4,000		28,000
	$1,800,000	$600,000				$1,962,500
Liabilities	$ 188,000	$100,000				$ 288,000
Preferred stock—Sol		100,000	b 100,000			
Common stock	1,000,000	200,000	d 200,000			1,000,000
Other paid-in capital	112,000	40,000	d 40,000			112,000
Retained earnings	500,000 ✔	160,000 ✔				500,000
	$1,800,000	$600,000				
Minority interest (pf) January 1, 19X4 ($115,000 × 20%)				b 23,000	23,000	
Minority interest (cm) January 1, 19X4 ($365,000 × 10%)				d 36,500	36,500	
Minority interest December 31, 19X4					$62,500	62,500
						$1,962,500

* Deduct.

Exhibit 10–2 Parent Company Holds Subsidiary's Common and Preferred Stock

396

SUBSIDIARY PREFERRED
STOCK, CONSOLIDATED
EARNINGS PER SHARE,
AND CONSOLIDATED
INCOME TAXATION

a	Income from Sol preferred	$ 8,000	
	Investment in Sol preferred		$ 8,000
b	Preferred stock—Sol	$100,000	
	Retained earnings—Sol	15,000	
	Investment in Sol preferred		$92,000
	Minority interest in Sol preferred		23,000

The remaining entries (c, d, and e) are the same as those for consolidations involving common stock only.

The working papers in Exhibit 10–2 show Prix Corporation's income equal to consolidated net income and its stockholders' equity equal to consolidated stockholders' equity. These equalities result from parent company entries to adjust the preferred stock investment account to its underlying equity at acquisition and to accrue dividend arrearages on cumulative preferred stock.

Preferred Stock Investment Maintained on Cost Basis   If the constructive retirement is *not* recorded by Prix at the time of purchase, the investment in Sol preferred would remain at its $80,000 cost throughout 19X4 and no preferred income would be recognized. In this case, the consolidation working paper entry to eliminate the preferred investment and equity amounts would be:

Retained earnings—Sol	$ 15,000	
Preferred stock—Sol	100,000	
Investment in Sol preferred		$80,000
Minority interest in Sol preferred		23,000
Other paid-in capital—Prix		12,000

To eliminate reciprocal preferred equity and investment amounts, establish minority interest at the beginning of the period (20% × $115,000 beginning book value of preferred), and adjust Prix's other paid-in capital account for the difference between the purchase price and underlying book value of the preferred stock.

Comparison of Cost Method and Constructive Retirement   The consolidated financial statements will be the same whether the investment in preferred stock remains at its original cost or is adjusted to book value in the parent company's books. However, by adjusting the parent company's additional paid-in capital for the constructive retirement of subsidiary preferred stock, further paid-in capital adjustments in the consolidation process are avoided. Under the cost method, a working paper entry to adjust additional paid-in capital is needed each time parent company and subsidiary statements are consolidated.

PARENT COMPANY AND CONSOLIDATED
EARNINGS PER SHARE

A parent company's net income and earnings per share (EPS) under the equity method are equal to consolidated net income and consolidated EPS. But the computational differences involved in determining parent company and consolidated net income (that is, one-line consolidation versus consolidation) do not extend to EPS calculations. Parent company and consolidated EPS calculations are identical. EPS procedures for equity investors that are able to exercise significant influence over their investees are the same as those for parent company investors. Although parent company and subsidiary relationships are addressed in this section, the discussion and illustrations are equally applicable to investments accounted for under the equity method.[4]

Parent company procedures for computing EPS depend on the subsidiary's capital structure. When the subsidiary (or equity investee) has *no* common stock equivalents[5] or other potentially dilutive securities, the procedures applied in computing consolidated EPS are the same as for separate entities. When the subsidiary does have common stock equivalents and other potentially dilutive securities outstanding, however, the potential dilution has to be considered in computing the parent company's primary and fully diluted EPS. The nature of the adjustment to parent company EPS calculations depends on whether the subsidiary's potentially dilutive securities are convertible into subsidiary or parent company common stock. If convertible into subsidiary common stock, the potential dilution is reflected in subsidiary EPS computations, which are then used in determining parent company (and consolidated) EPS. If the dilutive securities of the subsidiary are convertible into parent company stock, they are treated as parent company common stock equivalents or other dilutive securities and are included directly in computing the parent company's EPS.[6] In this latter case, subsidiary EPS computations are not needed (or used) in parent company EPS computations.

General formats for EPS calculations involving these situations are summarized in Exhibit 10–3 for primary EPS and in Exhibit 10–4 for fully diluted EPS. The first columns of Exhibits 10–3 and 10–4 show parent company computations for primary and fully diluted EPS when the subsidiary has no common stock equivalents or other potentially dilutive securities. In this case, the EPS computations are the same as those for unrelated entities, and no adjustments are necessary for subsidiary income included in parent company income provided that the equity method has been applied correctly.

Dilutive Securities of Subsidiary Convertible into Subsidiary Shares

The second column of Exhibits 10-3 and 10-4 summarizes parent company EPS computations when subsidiary common stock equivalents or other potentially dilutive securities are convertible into subsidiary common shares. Primary and fully diluted earnings of the parent company (the numerators of the EPS calculations) are adjusted by excluding the parent's **equity in subsidiary realized income**[7] and replacing that equity with the parent's share of primary or fully diluted earnings of the subsidiary. This adjustment to remove the potential dilution from the parent's primary and fully diluted earnings is based on separate EPS computations for the subsidiary. These computations of subsidiary EPS are made only for the purpose of calculating the parent's EPS and they are not necessarily the same as those prepared by the subsidiary for its own external reporting.

---

[4]The provisions of *APB Opinion No. 15,* "Earnings per Share," that apply to subsidiaries also apply to investments accounted for by the equity method. See *APB Opinion No. 18,* "The Equity Method of Accounting for Investments in Common Stock," footnote 8.

[5]*FASB Statement No. 85,* "Yield Test for Determining Whether a Convertible Security Is a Common Stock Equivalent," changes the yield test from a cash yield test to an effective yield test. Common stock equivalency results if the effective yield is less than two-thirds of the average Aa corporate bond yield at the time of issuance.

[6]*APB Opinion No. 15,* paragraphs 65–69.

[7]Equity in subsidiary realized income is the parent's percentage interest in reported income of the subsidiary adjusted for the effects of intercompany profits from upstream sales and constructive gains or losses of the subsidiary.

	Subsidiary Does Not Have Common Stock Equivalents	Subsidiary Has Common Stock Equivalents Convertible into Subsidiary Common Stock	Subsidiary Has Common Stock Equivalents Convertible into Parent Company Common Stock
Numerator in Dollars ($)			
Income to parent's common stockholders	$$$	$$$	$$$
Add: Adjustments for parent's common stock equivalents	+$	+$	+$
Add: Adjustments for subsidiary common stock equivalents convertible into parent company stock	NA	NA	+$
Replacement calculation (*must result in a net decrease*):			
Deduct: Parent's equity in subsidiary's realized income	NA	−$	NA
Add: Parent's equity in subsidiary's primary earnings	NA	+$	NA
Parent's primary earnings = a	$$$	$$$	$$$
Denominator in Shares (Y)			
Parent's common shares outstanding	YYY	YYY	YYY
Add: Shares represented by parent's common share equivalents	+Y	+Y	+Y
Add: Shares represented by subsidiary's common stock equivalents convertible into parent company common shares	NA	NA	+Y
Parent's common shares and common share equivalents = b	YYY	YYY	YYY
Parent Company and Consolidated Primary EPS	a/b	a/b	a/b

NA—Not applicable

Exhibit 10–3   *Parent Company and Consolidated Primary EPS Calculations*

Note that Parent's Equity in Subsidiary's Realized Income in column 2 of Exhibits 10–3 and 10–4 differs from Parent's Income from Subsidiary which includes amortization of goodwill and other valuation differentials and the income effects of all intercompany transactions. Since the parent company's investment valuation differentials, unrealized profits from downstream sales, and constructive gains and losses assigned to the parent do not affect the equity of the subsidiary's security holders, these items are not considered in the replacement calculation. In other words, the replacement calculation relates only to the parent's equity in subsidiary realized income.

Since the subsidiary's primary and fully diluted EPS are used in determining the primary and fully diluted earnings of the parent company (see column 2 of Exhibits 10–3 and 10–4), EPS computations for the subsidiary (based on subsidiary realized income) are made as a first step in computing the parent company's EPS. In computing the subsidiary's primary and fully diluted earnings, unrealized profits of the subsidiary are eliminated and constructive gains and losses of the subsidiary are included. The resulting EPS calculations of the subsidiary are reflected in parent company EPS calculation, by replacing the Parent's Equity in Subsidiary's Realized Income with the Parent's Equity in Subsidiary's Primary (or fully diluted) Earnings. The parent company's equity in the subsidiary's primary or fully diluted earnings is determined by multiplying the sub-

	Subsidiary Does Not Have Other Potentially Dilutive Securities Outstanding	Subsidiary Has Potentially Dilutive Securities Convertible into Subsidiary Common Stock	Subsidiary Has Potentially Dilutive Securities Convertible into Parent Company Common Stock
Numerator in Dollars ($)			
Income to parent's common stockholders	$$$	$$$	$$$
Add: Adjustment for parent's common stock equivalents and other dilutive securities	+$	+$	+$
Add: Adjustment for subsidiary's common stock equivalents and other potentially dilutive securities convertible into parent company common stock	NA	NA	+$
Replacement calculation (*must result in a net decrease*)			
Deduct: Parent's equity in subsidiary's realized income	NA	–$	NA
Add: Parent's equity in subsidiary's fully diluted earnings	NA	+$	NA
Parent's fully diluted earnings = a	$$$	$$$	$$$
Denominator in Shares (Y)			
Parent's common shares outstanding	YYY	YYY	YYY
Add: Shares represented by parent's common stock equivalents and other potentially dilutive securities	+Y	+Y	+Y
Add: Shares represented by subsidiary's common stock equivalents and other potentially dilutive securities convertible into parent company common shares	NA	NA	+Y
Parent's common shares and common share equivalents = b	YYY	YYY	YYY
Parent Company and Consolidated Fully Diluted EPS	a/b	a/b	a/b
NA—Not applicable			

Exhibit 10–4 *Parent Company and Consolidated Fully Diluted EPS Calculations*

sidiary shares owned by the parent by the subsidiary's primary or fully diluted EPS. This replacement allocates the subsidiary's realized income for EPS purposes to holders of the subsidiary's common stock, common stock equivalents, and other potentially dilutive securities, rather than only to the subsidiary's common stockholders.

Dilutive Securities of Subsidiary Convertible into Parent Company Shares

Parent company common shares and common share equivalents (the denominators of EPS computations) are identical in columns 1 and 2 of the two exhibits but are increased in column 3 for subsidiary securities that are convertible into parent company common stock. This adjustment in column 3 is

400

SUBSIDIARY PREFERRED
STOCK, CONSOLIDATED
EARNINGS PER SHARE,
AND CONSOLIDATED
INCOME TAXATION

necessary when the subsidiary's potentially dilutive securities are common stock equivalents or other potentially dilutive securities of the parent company, rather than of the subsidiary. When potentially dilutive securities of a subsidiary are convertible into parent common stock, income attributable to these securities under the "if converted" method must be added back in calculating the parent's primary or fully diluted earnings. Thus, column 3 of Exhibits 10–3 and 10–4 includes the item "Adjustment for Subsidiary's Common Stock Equivalents (and other dilutive securities) Convertible into Parent Common Stock," which is not applicable when the subsidiary does not have potentially dilutive securities (column 1), or such securities are convertible into subsidiary common stock (column 2).

SUBSIDIARY WITH CONVERTIBLE PREFERRED STOCK

Plant Corporation purchases 90 percent of Seed Corporation's outstanding voting common stock for $328,000 on January 1, 19X2. On this date the stockholders' equity of the two corporations consists of the following:

	Plant	Seed
Common stock, $5 par, 200,000 shares issued and outstanding	$1,000,000	
Common stock, $10 par, 20,000 shares outstanding		$200,000
10% cumulative, convertible preferred stock, $100 par, 1,000 shares outstanding		100,000
Retained earnings	500,000	120,000
Total stockholders' equity	$1,500,000	$420,000

During 19X2 Seed reports $50,000 net income and pays $25,000 dividends, $10,000 to preferred and $15,000 to common. Plant's net income for 19X2 is $182,000, determined as follows:

Income from Plant's operations		$150,000
Income from Seed ($50,000 net income − $10,000 preferred income) × 90%	$36,000	
Less: Goodwill amortization [$328,000 cost − ($320,000 common equity × 90%)] ÷ 10 years	(4,000)	32,000
Plant's net income		$182,000

Subsidiary Preferred Convertible into Subsidiary Common

Assume that Seed's preferred stock is a common stock equivalent that is convertible into 12,000 shares of Seed's common stock and that neither Plant nor Seed has other common stock equivalents or potentially dilutive securities outstanding. Seed's primary EPS is $1.5625 [$50,000 primary earnings ÷ (20,000 common shares + 12,000 common share equivalents)] and Plant's primary EPS is $.87, computed as follows:

Net income of Plant (equal to income to common)	$182,000
Replacement of Plant's equity in Seed's realized income ($40,000 × 90%)	(36,000)
with Plant's equity in Seed's primary earnings (18,000 shares of Seed × Seed's $1.5625 primary EPS)	28,125
Plant's primary earnings = a	$174,125
Plant's outstanding shares = b	200,000
Plant's primary EPS = a/b	$.87

The $7,875 potential dilution reflected in Plant's primary earnings results from replacing Plant's equity in Seed's realized income with Plant's equity in Seed's primary earnings. Since no other dilutive securities are outstanding, Plant's fully diluted EPS is equal to its primary EPS. Note that Plant's equity in Seed's realized income is $36,000, while Plant's income from Seed is $32,000. The $4,000 difference is goodwill amortization that relates to the parent company and is not subject to replacement in EPS computations.

Subsidiary Preferred Convertible into Parent Company Common

Assume that Seed's preferred stock is a common stock equivalent convertible into 24,000 shares of Plant's common stock and that neither Plant nor Seed has other common stock equivalents or other potentially dilutive securities outstanding. Seed's primary EPS (not used in Plant's EPS computations) is $2 per share ($40,000 income to common ÷ 20,000 common shares outstanding), since the preferred stock is not a common stock equivalent of Seed Corporation. Plant's primary EPS is computed as follows:

Net income of Plant (equal to income to common)	$182,000
Add: Income to preferred stockholders of Seed assumed to be converted	10,000
Plant's primary earnings = a	$192,000
Plant's outstanding shares	200,000
Add: Seed's preferred shares assumed converted	24,000
Plant's common shares and common stock equivalents = b	224,000
Plant's primary EPS = a/b	$.86

Preferred income is added to Plant's net income because no income is allocated to the preferred stock assumed to be converted.

SUBSIDIARY WITH OPTIONS AND CONVERTIBLE BONDS

Paddy Corporation has $1,500,000 income from its own operations for 19X3 and $300,000 income from Syd Corporation, its 80 percent owned subsidiary. The $300,000 income from Syd consists of 80 percent of Syd's $450,000 net income for 19X3, less 80 percent of a $50,000 unrealized gain on land purchased from Syd, less $20,000 amortization of the excess of investment cost over the book value acquired in Syd. Outstanding securities of the two corporations throughout 19X3 are:

Paddy: Common stock, 1,000,000 shares

Syd: Common stock, 400,000 shares

Options to purchase 60,000 shares of stock at $10 per share (average and year-end market price is $15 per share)

7% convertible bonds, $1,000,000 par outstanding, convertible into 80,000 shares of common stock, not common stock equivalents

Options and Bonds Convertible into Subsidiary Common Stock

Assume that the options and bonds are convertible into Syd's common stock. Computations for Syd's primary and fully diluted EPS are shown in Exhibit 10-5. Options to purchase common stock are always common stock equivalents, and they are used in EPS computations whenever their inclusion dilutes EPS. Under

	Syd's Primary EPS	Syd's Fully Diluted EPS
Syd's income to common stockholders	$450,000	$450,000
Less: Unrealized profit on sale of land	(50,000)	(50,000)
Add: Net-of-tax interest expense assuming subsidiary bonds converted into subsidiary shares ($1,000,000 × 7% × 66% assumed net-of-tax effect)	NA	46,200
Subsidiary adjusted earnings = a	$400,000	$446,200
Syd's common shares outstanding	400,000	400,000
Incremental shares assuming exercise of options [60,000 shares − ($600,000 proceeds from exercise of options ÷ $15 market price)]	20,000	20,000
Additional shares assuming bonds converted into subsidiary shares	NA	80,000
Syd's adjusted shares = b	420,000	500,000
Syd's EPS = a/b	$.95	$.89

Exhibit 10–5   Subsidiary's EPS Computations

the treasury stock approach for options and warrants, the effect on EPS is dilutive when the average market price of the common shares to which the options apply exceeds the exercise price. If holders of Syd's options had exercised their rights to acquire 60,000 shares of Syd's common stock at $10 per share, Syd would have received $600,000 cash. Under the treasury stock approach, Syd is assumed to use this cash to reacquire 40,000 shares of its own stock ($600,000 ÷ $15 average market price). This assumed exercise and repurchase of treasury shares increases Syd's outstanding common stock for EPS computations by 20,000 shares. The 20,000 incremental shares apply to both primary and fully diluted computations in this illustration because both average and year-end market prices of Syd's common stock are $15 per share.

Syd's primary EPS is not affected by the convertible bonds because the bonds are not common stock equivalents. The convertible bonds are potentially dilutive securities, however, and must be included in Syd's fully diluted EPS computations. Under the *if converted* method, $46,200 net-of-tax interest is included in Syd's fully diluted earnings, and the 80,000 shares issuable upon conversion are included in calculating Syd's fully diluted common shares and common share equivalents.

Syd's $.95 primary EPS and $.89 fully diluted EPS are used in the EPS computations for Paddy Corporation. Exhibit 10–6 shows computations for Paddy's primary and fully diluted EPS.

The replacement of Paddy's equity in Syd's realized income ($320,000) in computing Paddy's primary earnings with Paddy's share of Syd's primary earnings ($304,000) dilutes Paddy's primary earnings by $16,000. This dilution results from reallocating Syd's $400,000 realized income ($450,000 less $50,000 unrealized profit) to holders of Syd's common shares and common share equivalents (total of 420,000 common shares and common share equivalents), rather than just to Syd's 400,000 outstanding common shares. Similarly, the $320,000 exclusion and $284,800 replacement dilutes Paddy's fully diluted earnings by $35,200. This effect results from allocating Syd's $400,000 realized income plus $46,200 net-of-tax interest effect from the convertible bonds to holders of Syd's common shares, options, and convertible bonds (total of 500,000 common shares and common share equivalents) rather than just to Syd's common stockholders.

	Paddy's Primary EPS	Paddy's Fully Diluted EPS
Paddy's income to common stockholders	$1,800,000	$1,800,000
Replacement of Paddy's $320,000 equity in Syd's realized income [($450,000 − $50,000 unrealized profit) × 80%]	(320,000)	NA
with Paddy's $304,000 equity in Syd's primary earnings (320,000 shares × Syd's $.95 primary EPS)	304,000	
Replacement of Paddy's $320,000 equity in Syd's realized income [($450,000 − $50,000 unrealized profit) × 80%]	NA	(320,000)
with Paddy's $284,800 equity in Syd's fully diluted EPS (320,000 shares × Syd's $.89 fully diluted EPS)		284,800
Paddy's adjusted earnings = a	$1,784,000	$1,764,800
Paddy's outstanding common shares = b	1,000,000	1,000,000
Paddy's EPS = a/b	$1.78	$1.76

Exhibit 10–6 *Parent's EPS Computations—Dilution Relates to Subsidiary Shares*

Options and Bonds Convertible into Parent's Common Stock

Computations for Paddy's primary and fully diluted EPS are presented in Exhibit 10–7 under the assumption that Syd Corporation's options are convertible into 60,000 shares of Paddy Corporation's common stock and that Syd Corporation's bonds are convertible into 80,000 shares of Paddy Corporation's common stock. Under these assumptions, Syd's primary and fully diluted EPS are not needed or used in determining Paddy's EPS. This is because subsidiary EPS computations are only used for replacement computations when subsidiary dilutive securities are convertible into subsidiary shares. Since the subsidiary dilutive securities are convertible into parent company shares in this example, only parent company EPS computations are needed.

	Paddy's Primary EPS	Paddy's Fully Diluted EPS
Paddy's income to common stockholders	$1,800,000	$1,800,000
Add: Net-of-tax interest assuming subsidiary bonds converted into parent's common stock ($1,000,000 × 7% × 66% net-of-tax effect)	NA	46,200
Parent's adjusted earnings = a	$1,800,000	$1,846,200
Paddy's outstanding shares	1,000,000	1,000,000
Incremental shares assuming options converted into parent's shares [60,000 shares − ($600,000 proceeds from exercise of options ÷ $15 market price)]	20,000	20,000
Additional shares assuming subsidiary bonds are converted into parent shares	NA	80,000
Parent's adjusted shares = b	1,020,000	1,100,000
Parent's EPS = a/b	$1.76	$1.68

Exhibit 10–7 *Parent's EPS Computations—Dilution Relates to Parent Shares*

ACCOUNTING FOR INCOME TAXES OF CONSOLIDATED ENTITIES

This section of the chapter on accounting for income taxes of consolidated entities begins with a discussion of which companies may file consolidated tax returns, the advantages and disadvantages of filing consolidated tax returns, and the status of accounting pronouncements on income taxes. Temporary differences in consolidated and separate tax returns are discussed, and income tax allocation procedures are illustrated for a parent company and subsidiary that file separate tax returns. Next, four cases compare consolidation procedures when a parent company and subsidiary file separate tax returns with those necessary when a consolidated tax return is filed. A final section looks at the tax basis of assets and liabilities acquired in a purchase business combination.

Some consolidated entities prepare consolidated income tax returns and pay taxes on consolidated taxable income. Others prepare separate income tax returns for each affiliate and pay taxes on the taxable income included in those separate returns. The right of a consolidated entity to file a consolidated income tax return is contingent upon classification as an *affiliated group* under Sections 1501 through 1505 of the Internal Revenue Code. An affiliated group exists when a common parent corporation owns at least 80 percent of the voting power of all classes of stock and 80 percent or more of the total value of all outstanding stock of each of the includable corporations. The common parent must meet the 80 percent requirements directly for at least one includable corporation (USIRC 1504 [a]).

A consolidated entity that is an affiliated group may elect to file consolidated income tax returns. All other consolidated entities *must* file separate income tax returns for each affiliated company.

Advantages of Filing Consolidated Tax Returns

The primary advantages of filing a consolidated return are:

1 Losses of one affiliate are offset against income of other members of the affiliated group.[8]
2 Intercorporate dividends are excluded from taxable income.
3 Intercompany profits are deferred from income until realized (but unrealized losses are also deferred until realized).

Exclusion of intercorporate dividends is not a unique advantage of filing a consolidated tax return because a consolidated entity that is classified as an affiliated group is allowed a 100 percent exclusion on dividends received from members of the same group even if it elects not to file consolidated tax returns. In addition, the advantage of the 100 percent exclusion is mitigated by the right of corporate taxpayers to deduct 80 percent of the dividends received from domestic corporations that are 20 to 80 percent owned and to deduct 70 percent of the dividends received from domestic corporations that are less than 20 percent owned.

Disadvantages of Filing Consolidated Tax Returns

Consolidated entities that file consolidated tax returns lose some of the flexibility of entities that file separate returns. For example, each subsidiary included

---

[8]Loss carryforwards at the time of acquisition of an acquired affiliate can be offset only against taxable income of the affiliate.

in a consolidated tax return must use the parent's taxable year. Different years can be used when separate returns are filed. The election to file a consolidated return commits an entity to consolidated returns year after year. It is difficult to get permission to stop filing consolidated returns. Also, deconsolidated corporations cannot rejoin the affiliated group for five years. According to a March 1990 IRS regulation, a loss on the sale of stock of a subsidiary that has been included in the corporation's consolidated tax return is not an allowable deduction. The rule is controversial and may not become a permanent regulation.[9]

INCOME TAX ALLOCATION

FASB Statement No. 109, "Accounting for Income Taxes," is the primary source of GAAP for accounting for income taxes. Its issuance in February 1992 ended five years of controversy and uncertainty—the period in which *FASB Statement No. 96,* also entitled "Accounting for Income Taxes," was almost, but not quite, effective. In December 1987, the Financial Accounting Standards Board issued *Statement 96* to supersede essentially all previously issued income tax accounting statements.[10] *Statement 96* was to have become effective for fiscal years beginning after December 15, 1988, but many firms asked for more time to implement the complex provisions of the new standard. The Board granted a delay and *FAS 100* deferred the effective date of *FAS 96* to fiscal years beginning after December 15, 1989.

Implementation problems with *Statement 96* persisted, and the Board issued *FAS 103* to defer the effective date again, this time until fiscal years beginning after December 15, 1991. But before the new effective date, an Exposure Draft, "Accounting for Income Taxes," was issued to supersede *Statement 96. FAS 108* again deferred the effective date of *Statement 96,* and finally, in February 1992, *FAS 109,* "Accounting for Income Taxes," was adopted to supersede *FAS 96. Statement 109* became effective for fiscal years beginning after December 31, 1992.

The objectives of accounting for income taxes under *Statement 109* are to recognize the amount of taxes payable or refundable for the current year and to recognize deferred tax liabilities and assets for the future tax consequences of events that have been recognized in the financial statements or tax returns. Events that have future tax consequences are designated *temporary differences* to separate them from events such as interest on municipal obligations that do not have tax consequences. The tax consequences of temporary differences must be considered in the measurement of income for a period. Some accounting/income tax differences are the same regardless of whether separate entity or consolidated income tax returns are filed, whereas others depend on the kind of return filed. For example, unrealized and constructive gains and losses from intercompany transactions are temporary differences when separate returns are filed because the individual entities are taxed on the income included in their separate returns. But these items are *not* temporary differences when consolidated returns are filed because adjustments to defer intercompany profits until realized are reflected in both the consolidation working papers and the consolidated tax return. Dividends received from members of an affiliated group are excluded from taxation regardless of whether separate or consolidated returns are filed, but dividends received from affiliates that are not members of an affiliated group are taxed currently, subject to the 80 percent dividends received deduction. Goodwill amortization is not deductible for tax purposes in either separate or consolidated income tax returns and is not a temporary difference.

[9]*The Wall Street Journal,* March 27, 1990, p. A2.

[10]The one notable exception was *APB Opinion No. 23* "Accounting for Income Taxes—Special Areas."

406

SUBSIDIARY PREFERRED
STOCK, CONSOLIDATED
EARNINGS PER SHARE,
AND CONSOLIDATED
INCOME TAXATION

Temporary Differences from Undistributed
Earnings of Subsidiaries and Equity Investees

Accounting requirements under the equity method of accounting are generally the same for investments of 20 to 50 percent of the voting stock of an investee as for subsidiary investments. Equity investees and subsidiaries that are not members of an affiliated group pay income taxes currently on dividends received (distributed income) and are required to provide for deferred income taxes on their shares of undistributed income of their investees. That is, a temporary difference results when an investor's equity in its investees' income exceeds dividends received. Under *APB Opinion No. 23,* the parent company-investor could avoid the general presumption that all undistributed earnings will be transferred to the parent company by showing that undistributed earnings of the subsidiary had been invested indefinitely. *Statement 109* amends *APB Opinion No. 23* to remove the exception and require the parent company-investor to treat the undistributed income of their domestic subsidiaries as temporary differences unless the tax law provides a means by which the investment can be recovered tax free. (*The Opinion 23* exception is continued for undistributed earnings of foreign subsidiaries and foreign joint ventures and undistributed earnings of domestic subsidiaries that arose before the effective date of *Statement 109.*)

In accounting for the *tax effect* of a temporary difference relating to income from equity investees, the one-line consolidation concept is *not* used, since investment income is included in the investor's income *before* income taxes, in other words, on a pretax basis. If undistributed earnings of an investee is the only temporary difference, a parent company or equity investor provides for income taxes on its share of undistributed income by debiting income tax expense and crediting deferred income taxes. The temporary difference related to undistributed earnings is, of course, only one of several possible differences that interact to produce the combined tax impact.

Accounting for Distributed and Undistributed Income Assume that Parson Corporation owns a 30 percent interest in Seaton Corporation, a domestic corporation. Seaton reports $600,000 net income for the current year and pays dividends of $200,000. An income tax rate of 34 percent is applicable. (The 34 percent tax rate is the *only* enacted tax rate applicable throughout this illustration.) Parson's share of Seaton's distributed and undistributed income is analyzed as follows:

Share of distributed earnings (dividends) $200,000 × 30%	$ 60,000
Share of undistributed earnings (retained earnings increase) $400,000 × 30%	120,000
Equity in Seaton's earnings $600,000 × 30%	$180,000

Parson is taxed currently on 20 percent of the $60,000 dividends received because Seaton is a domestic corporation that qualifies for the 80 percent dividends received deduction. The income tax expense equals income tax liability for this part of Parson's income from Seaton. The current tax liability is $4,080 ($60,000 dividends received × 20% taxable × 34% tax rate). No income tax is due currently on Parson's share of Seaton's undistributed earnings, but accounting standards require that income taxes attributable to that temporary difference be recognized as if the earnings had been remitted as dividends during the current period. Assuming that undistributed earnings is the only temporary difference, Parson makes the following entry to provide for income taxes on its share of Seaton's undistributed earnings:

December 31, 19XX

Income tax expense	$8,160	
Deferred income taxes		$8,160

To provide for taxes on undistributed earnings of Seaton ($120,000 × 20% taxable × 34% tax rate).

The same procedures for income taxes on undistributed earnings apply to parent company investors, but not to dividends received from members of an affiliated group because 100 percent of those dividends are excluded from taxable income of the group.

Unrealized Gains and Losses from Intercompany Transactions

Unrealized and constructive gains and losses from intercompany transactions create temporary differences that may affect deferred tax calculations when separate income tax returns are filed. (This is *not* true when consolidated tax returns are filed.) In the case of an unrealized gain, the selling entity includes the gain in its separate tax return and pays the tax due on the transaction. Since the unrealized gain is eliminated in the consolidation process, the income taxes related to the gain should be deferred. Similarly, an unrealized loss may reduce deferred tax expense or add to a deferred tax asset.

The tax effects of temporary differences from unrealized gains and losses on intercompany transactions are included in measuring the income tax expense of the selling affiliate. Under this approach, the consolidated income tax expense is equal to the combined income tax expense of the consolidated entities, and intercompany profit items are eliminated on a gross basis. Similarly, this approach permits the parent company-investor to eliminate intercompany profits on a gross, rather than a net-of-tax basis. (When intercompany profits are eliminated on a net-of-tax basis by the parent company-investor, a consolidation working paper entry is needed to convert the combined income tax expense of the affiliated companies into consolidated income tax expense, and to adjust the deferred tax asset or liability amounts to a consolidated basis.)

Assume that Petit Corporation sells merchandise that cost $100,000 to Sellman Corporation, its 75 percent owned subsidiary, for $200,000, and that 70 percent of this merchandise is inventoried by Sellman at year-end. A 34 percent tax rate is applicable, and Petit pays $34,000 income tax on the transaction during the current year. Because Sellman is a 75 percent owned subsidiary, separate tax returns are required. (Again, assume that the intercompany transaction is the only temporary difference and that the 34 percent tax rate is the only enacted rate.) Relevant consolidation and one-line consolidation entries are as follows:

Consolidation Working Paper Entries—Year of Sale

Sales	$200,000	
Cost of sales		$200,000

To eliminate intercompany sales and purchases.

Cost of sales	$ 70,000	
Inventory		$ 70,000

To eliminate unrealized profit on intercompany merchandise remaining in inventory ($200,000 − $100,000) × 70%.

Petit's One-Line Consolidation Entry—Year of Sale

Income from Sellman	$ 70,000	
Investment in Sellman		$ 70,000

To eliminate unrealized profit on sales to Sellman ($70,000 unrealized profit × 100%).

408

SUBSIDIARY PREFERRED
STOCK, CONSOLIDATED
EARNINGS PER SHARE,
AND CONSOLIDATED
INCOME TAXATION

If Sellman sells the merchandise in the next period, the consolidation and one-line consolidation entries in that year will be:

Consolidation Working Paper Entry—Year of Realization		
Investment in Sellman	$ 70,000	
Cost of sales		$ 70,000

To recognize previously deferred profit on inventory and to adjust Petit's beginning investment in Sellman account to reflect realization.

Petit's One-Line Consolidation Entry—Year of Realization		
Investment in Sellman	$ 70,000	
Income from Sellman		$ 70,000

To reinstate previously deferred profit on intercompany sales.

If the sale had been upstream from Sellman to Petit, the $34,000 tax on the intercompany profit would have been paid by Sellman, but Sellman would show $23,800 ($70,000 × 34%) of that amount as a deferred tax asset, rather than as income tax expense for the year. The consolidation working paper entry to eliminate the intercompany profit in the year of sale would be for $70,000, the same amount as in the downstream example. Minority interest income in the year of sale would be decreased $17,500 (25% × $70,000 unrealized gain), and the amount of the one-line consolidation entry to eliminate the effect of the unrealized profit on Petit's books would be for $52,500 (75% × $70,000), rather than $70,000 as in the downstream example.

SEPARATE COMPANY TAX RETURNS WITH INTERCOMPANY GAIN

This section provides an extended illustration of income tax allocation for a parent company and its subsidiary that file separate income tax returns. Paco Corporation paid $400,000 cash for a 75 percent interest in Step Corporation on January 1, 19X1 when Step's equity consisted of $300,000 capital stock and $200,000 retained earnings. The $25,000 excess cost over book value acquired is goodwill with a ten-year amortization period.

On January 8, 19X1 Paco sold equipment to Step at a gain of $20,000. Step is depreciating the equipment on a straight-line basis over five years. Taxes on Paco's share of the $24,800 undistributed earnings of Step are required to be provided for under *Statement 109,* and the 80 percent dividends received deduction is applicable to dividends received from Step. At the beginning of 19X1, Paco has a deferred income tax liability of $6,800, consisting of $20,000 tax–book depreciation differences that reverse in equal amounts over the years 19X2 through 19X5. A flat 34 percent income tax rate is assumed for Paco and Step. Comparative income and retained earnings data for the year 19X1 are as follows:

	Paco	Step
Sales	$380,000	$300,000
Gain on equipment sale	20,000	—
Income from Step	21,100	—
Cost of sales	(200,000)	(180,000)
Operating expenses	(100,000)	(40,000)
Income tax expense	(31,253)	(27,200)
Net income	89,847	52,800
Add: Beginning retained earnings	360,153	200,000
Deduct: Dividends (December)	(50,000)	(28,000)
Retained earnings December 31, 19X1	$400,000	$224,800

One-Line Consolidation

Paco makes the following journal entries to account for its investment in Step during 19X1:

January 1, 19X1

Investment in Step	$400,000	
Cash		$400,000

    To record purchase of a 75% interest in Step.

December 19X1

Cash	$ 21,000	
Investment in Step		$ 21,000

    To record dividends received from Step ($28,000 × 75%).

December 31, 19X1

Investment in Step	$ 21,100	
Income from Step		$ 21,100

To record income from Step computed as follows:

Paco's share of Step's net income ($52,800 × 75%)	$ 39,600
Less: Goodwill amortization ($25,000/10 years)	(2,500)
Less: Unrealized profit ($20,000 gain − $4,000 depreciation)	(16,000)
Income from Step	$ 21,100

At December 31, 19X1 Paco's investment in Step account has a balance of $400,100 ($400,000 beginning balance + $21,100 income from Step − $21,000 dividends), and Paco's share of Step's equity is $393,600 ($524,800 × 75%). The $6,500 difference ($400,100 − $393,600) consists of $22,500 unamortized goodwill less $16,000 unrealized profit from the downstream sale of equipment.

Income Tax Expense Based on Separate Returns

Step's $27,200 income tax expense is simply 34 percent of Step's $80,000 pretax accounting income, but Paco's income tax expense of $31,253 requires further analysis. In accordance with the provisions of *FASB Statement No. 109,* Paco's income tax expense of $31,253 is calculated as follows:

Tax on Paco's operating income ($380,000 sales − $200,000 cost of sales − $100,000 operating expenses) × 34%		$27,200
Tax on gain from sale of equipment ($20,000 × 34%)		6,800
Tax on dividends received ($21,000 × 20% taxable) × 34%		1,428
Income taxes currently payable		35,428
Deferred tax at January 1, 19X1	$6,800	
Deferred tax at December 31, 19X1	2,625	(4,175)
Income tax expense		$31,253

A schedule to support the computation of Paco's income tax expense is provided in Exhibit 10–8. Because only one tax rate (34%) is applicable, the schedule approach is not necessary, but it may be helpful.

    Since Paco's interest in Step is only 75 percent, separate tax returns are required and income taxes are payable on the $20,000 intercompany gain on the equipment sold to Step. Paco also pays income taxes on dividends received from Step, less an 80 percent dividends received deduction. The multiplication of dividends received and undistributed income by 20 percent in calculating Paco's income tax expense effectively takes the 80 percent dividends received deduction into account without calculating the amount of the deduction and subtracting it from distributed (dividends) or undistributed earnings.

    Step's $27,200 income tax expense is equal to the tax liability indicated on its separate return, since it has no temporary differences. Paco's income tax

410

SUBSIDIARY PREFERRED
STOCK, CONSOLIDATED
EARNINGS PER SHARE,
AND CONSOLIDATED
INCOME TAXATION

Temporary Difference	19X1	19X2	19X3	19X4	19X5	Future Years
Depreciation		$5,000	$5,000	$5,000	$5,000	
Gain on equipment	$20,000					
Piecemeal recognition	(4,000)	(4,000)	(4,000)	(4,000)	(4,000)	
Future dividends*	(3,720)	—	—	—	—	$3,720
Taxable in future years		1,000	1,000	1,000	1,000	3,720
Enacted tax rate		34%	34%	34%	34%	34%
Deferred tax liability		$ 340	$ 340	$ 340	$ 340	$1,265

* The calculation is $52,800 net income − $28,000 dividends × 75% owned × 20% taxable.

Exhibit 10–8 *Schedule of Deferred Income Tax Liability at December 31, 19X1*

expense of $31,253 consists of $35,428 currently payable less a $4,175 decrease ($6,800 − $2,625) in deferred income taxes for the year. Step and Paco record their income tax expenses as follows:

Step's Books—December 31, 19X1

Income tax expense	$27,200	
Income taxes currently payable		$27,200
To accrue income taxes for 19X1.		

Paco's Books—December 31, 19X1

Income tax expense	$31,253	
Deferred income taxes	4,175	
Income taxes currently payable		$35,428
To accrue income taxes for 19X1.		

Consolidation Working Papers

Consolidation working papers for Paco Corporation and Subsidiary are presented in Exhibit 10–9. The working paper entries are the same as those encountered in earlier chapters except for the inclusion of income tax considerations. Observe that Paco's income tax expense plus Step's income tax expense equal the $58,453 consolidated income tax expense.

Paco paid income taxes on the $20,000 gain on the intercompany sale of equipment. This gain is not recognized for consolidated statement purposes and, accordingly, a temporary difference exists for which income tax allocation procedures are required.

Working Paper Entry for 19X2

The working paper entry for 19X2 to eliminate the effect of the unrealized profit from the intercompany sale of equipment is as follows:

Investment in Step	$16,000	
Accumulated depreciation	8,000	
Equipment		$20,000
Depreciation expense		4,000
To eliminate unrealized profit from downstream sale of equipment.		

The income tax expense in 19X2 will be equal to the income tax currently payable, adjusted for the change in the deferred tax asset or liability that occurs in 19X2.

PACO CORPORATION AND SUBSIDIARY
CONSOLIDATION WORKING PAPERS
FOR THE YEAR ENDED DECEMBER 31, 19X1

	Paco	Step	Adjustments and Eliminations		Minority Interest	Consolidated Statements
Income Statement						
Sales	$380,000	$300,000				$680,000
Gain on equipment	20,000		a 20,000			
Income from Step	21,100		c 21,100			
Cost of sales	200,000*	180,000*				380,000*
Operating expense	100,000*	40,000*	e 2,500	b 4,000		138,500*
Income tax expense	31,253*	27,200*				58,453*
Minority interest income					$ 13,200	13,200*
Net income	$ 89,847	$ 52,800				$ 89,847
Retained Earnings						
Retained earnings—Paco	$360,153					$360,153
Retained earnings—Step		$200,000	d 200,000			
Net income	89,847✔	52,800✔				89,847
Dividends	50,000*	28,000*		c 21,000	7,000*	50,000*
Ending retained earnings	$400,000	$224,800				$400,000
Balance Sheet						
Other assets	$339,900	$432,000				$771,900
Equipment	120,000	200,000		a 20,000		300,000
Accumulated depreciation	60,000*	50,000*	b 4,000			106,000*
Investment in Step	400,100			c 100 d 400,000		
Goodwill			d 25,000	e 2,500		22,500
	$800,000	$582,000				$988,400
Deferred tax liability	$ 2,625					$ 2,625
Income tax liability	35,428	$ 27,200				62,628
Other liabilities	61,947	30,000				91,947
Capital stock	300,000	300,000	d 300,000			300,000
Retained earnings	400,000✔	224,800✔				400,000
	$800,000	$582,000				
Beginning minority interest				d 125,000	125,000	
Ending minority interest					$131,200	131,200
						$988,400

* Deduct.

Exhibit 10-9   *Consolidation Working Papers with Separate Tax Returns*

EFFECT OF CONSOLIDATED AND SEPARATE COMPANY TAX RETURNS ON CONSOLIDATION PROCEDURES

This section compares consolidation procedures for a parent company and its subsidiary when separate company and consolidated tax returns are filed. Under the provisions of *FASB Statement 109*, the income tax expense as well as the income from subsidiary are the same in both cases. When consolidated tax returns are filed, the tax liability is allocated among the parent company and its subsidiaries.

Allocation of Consolidated Income Tax to Affiliates

A subsidiary that is part of a group filing a consolidated tax return is required to disclose its current and deferred income tax expense amounts and also any tax-related balances due to or from affiliates in its separately issued financial statements. Although no single method of allocating consolidated income tax expense among affiliates is prescribed, the method used must be disclosed.

Four methods currently used in the allocation of consolidated income taxes to affiliates are:[11]

- **Separate return method.** Each subsidiary computes income taxes as if it were filing a separate return.
- **Agreement method.** Tax expense is allocated by agreement between parent and subsidiaries.
- **With-or-without method.** The income tax provision is computed for the group with and without the pretax income of the subsidiary. The subsidiary's income tax expense is the difference.
- **Percentage allocation method.** Consolidated income tax expense is allocated to a subsidiary on the basis of its pretax income as a percentage of consolidated pretax income.

The percentage allocation method is the one used for illustrations in this book.

Background Information for Consolidated and Separate Tax Return Illustrations

The following illustrations for Pool Corporation, and its 90 percent owned subsidiary, Sal Corporation, compare consolidation procedures used when consolidated tax returns are filed, with consolidation procedures necessary when separate company tax returns are filed. The income tax effects of intercompany profits from both upstream and downstream inventory sales are also illustrated. Pool owns 90 percent of the outstanding voting stock of Sal, acquired in 19X2 at a price $50,000 in excess of book value (and fair value). The $50,000 excess is goodwill with a ten-year amortization period and it is not deductible for tax purposes. Additional information follows:

1. A flat 34 percent enacted income tax rate applies to all years.
2. Pool and Sal are an affiliated group entitled to the 100 percent dividend exclusion.
3. Sal pays dividends of $20,000 during 19X3.
4. Intercompany sales are $40,000, of which $10,000 represents unrealized profits at year-end 19X3.
5. Pretax operating incomes for the two affiliates are:

---

[11]Terry E. Allison and Paula Bevels Thomas, "Uncharted Territory: Subsidiary Financial Reporting," *Journal of Accountancy* (October 1989), p. 80.

	Pool	Sal
Sales	$1,000,000	$500,000
Cost of sales	(600,000)	(350,000)
Expenses	(250,000)	(100,000)
Pretax operating income	$ 150,000	$ 50,000

Cases 1 and 2 illustrate a temporary difference for unrealized profits from downstream sales that originates in the current year and reverses in the succeeding year. Subsequently, cases 3 and 4 repeat illustrations 1 and 2 using an upstream sale assumption as the only temporary difference.

Case 1: Consolidated Tax Return with Downstream Sales

Assume that a consolidated tax return is filed and that the intercompany sales are downstream. The consolidated income tax return will include the $200,000 combined operating income (Pool's $150,000 operating income plus Sal's $50,000 operating income) less $10,000 unrealized profit, and the consolidated income tax expense will be $64,600 ($190,000 × 34%). No tax is assessed on the $18,000 dividends that Pool receives from Sal, nor is a deduction allowed for the $5,000 goodwill amortization from the purchase price differential.

The $64,600 consolidated income tax liability is allocated to Pool and Sal based on the amounts of their income that are included in the $190,000 consolidated taxable income. Since the intercompany sales are downstream in this case, the allocation is:

$$Pool = \frac{(\$150,000 - \$10,000)}{\$190,000} \times \$64,600 = \$47,600$$

$$Sal = \frac{\$50,000}{\$190,000} \times \$64,600 = \$17,000$$

The income tax expense amounts determined in this allocation are recorded by Pool and Sal as follows:

Pool's books—December 31, 19X3

Income tax expense	$47,600	
Income taxes currently payable		$47,600
To record 14/19 of the consolidated income tax liability.		

Sal's books—December 31, 19X3

Income tax expense	$17,000	
Income taxes currently payable		$17,000
To record 5/19 of the consolidated income tax liability.		

After this tax allocation is entered, Sal's net income will be $33,000 ($50,000 − $17,000 income tax), and Pool's income from Sal is recorded as follows:

December 31, 19X3

Investment in Sal	$14,700	
Income from Sal		$14,700
To record investment income from Sal computed as follows:		
Share of Sal's net income ($33,000 × 90%)		$29,700
Less: Goodwill amortization		(5,000)
Less: Unrealized profit in inventory		(10,000)
Income from Sal		$14,700

POOL CORPORATION AND SUBSIDIARY
PARTIAL CONSOLIDATION WORKING PAPERS
FOR THE YEAR ENDED DECEMBER 31, 19X3

	Pool	Sal	Adjustments and Eliminations				Consolidated
Sales	$1,000,000	$500,000	a	40,000			$1,460,000
Income from Sal	14,700		c	14,700			
Cost of goods sold	600,000*	350,000*	b	10,000	a	40,000	920,000*
Expenses (excluding income taxes)	250,000*	100,000*	d	5,000			355,000*
Income tax expense	47,600*	17,000*					64,600*
Minority interest income							3,300*
Net income	$ 117,100	$ 33,000					$ 117,100

* Deduct.

Related working paper entries in general journal form:

a   Sales $40,000
           Cost of goods sold $40,000
           To eliminate intercompany sales and purchases.

b   Cost of goods sold $10,000
           Inventory $10,000
           To eliminate intercompany profits from downstream sale.

c   Income from Sal $14,700
    Investment in Sal   3,300
           Dividends $18,000
           To eliminate investment income and dividends and adjust the investment in Sal account to its beginning-of-the-period balance.

d   Expenses $ 5,000
           Goodwill $ 5,000
           To enter current amortization of goodwill.

Exhibit 10–10   *Consolidated Tax Return—Unrealized Profit from Downstream Sales*

The full amount of the unrealized inventory profit is deducted because the sale is downstream and because no tax is assessed on unrealized profits when consolidated returns are used. Partial consolidation working papers for Pool and Subsidiary are presented in Exhibit 10–10, with the relevant working paper entries shown in general journal form.

Case 2: Separate Tax Returns with Downstream Sales

Assume that the intercompany sales are downstream (from Pool to Sal) and that separate income tax returns are filed. Sal has an income tax liability of $17,000 and reports net income of $33,000. Pool records income from Sal of $14,700, computed as follows:

Share of Sal's net income ($33,000 × 90%)	$29,700
Less: Goodwill amortization ($50,000/10 years)	(5,000)
Less: Unrealized profit	(10,000)
Income from Sal	$14,700

	Pool	Sal	Adjustments and Eliminations		Consolidated Statements
Sales	$1,000,000	$500,000	a 40,000		$1,460,000
Income from Sal	14,700		c 14,700		
Cost of goods sold	600,000*	350,000*	b 10,000	a 40,000	920,000*
Expenses (other than taxes)	250,000*	100,000*	d 5,000		355,000*
Income tax expense	47,600*	17,000*			64,600*
Minority interest income					3,300*
Net income	$ 117,100	$ 33,000			$ 117,100

* Deduct.

Related working paper entries in general journal form:

a   Sales $40,000
         Cost of goods sold $40,000
      To eliminate intercompany sales and purchases.

b   Cost of goods sold $10,000
         Inventory $10,000
      To eliminate intercompany profits from downstream sales.

c   Income from Sal $14,700
      Investment in Sal   3,300
         Dividends $18,000
      To eliminate investment income and dividends and adjust the investment
      in Sal account to its beginning-of-the-period balance.

d   Expenses $ 5,000
         Goodwill $ 5,000
      To enter current amortization of goodwill.

Exhibit 10–11   *Separate Tax Return—Unrealized Profit from Downstream Sales*

Since goodwill (included in income from Sal) is not deductible for tax purposes, and dividends are not taxable, Pool's income tax currently payable is 34 percent of its $150,000 operating income, or $51,000. Pool's income tax expense is $47,600 computed as follows:

Income tax currently payable	$51,000
Less: Increase in deferred tax asset from temporary difference ($10,000 unrealized profit × 34% tax rate)	(3,400)
Income tax expense	$47,600

These observations are reflected in the partial consolidation working papers in Exhibit 10–11. Relevant working paper entries are shown in general journal form.

Income taxes currently payable that will appear in the consolidated balance sheet is $68,000 ($51,000 for Pool plus $17,000 for Sal). The difference between the consolidated income tax expense ($64,600) and income taxes currently payable ($68,000) is the $3,400 deferred income taxes on the $10,000 unrealized profit. The $64,600 income tax expense appearing in the consolidated income statement can be computed independently as follows:

416

SUBSIDIARY PREFERRED
STOCK, CONSOLIDATED
EARNINGS PER SHARE,
AND CONSOLIDATED
INCOME TAXATION

Consolidated income before income taxes and minority income ($1,460,000 sales − $920,000 cost of goods sold − $355,000 expenses)	$185,000
Add back: Nondeductible goodwill	5,000
Consolidated pretax accounting income	190,000
Tax rate	34%
Income tax expense	$64,600

Compare Exhibits 10–10 and 10–11. Note that there is no difference in the two working papers. Income tax expense and income from subsidiary are the same whether separate tax returns or consolidated tax returns are filed. However, there is a difference in income tax currently payable and in the deferred income tax liability.

When the consolidated tax return is filed, income tax expense is equal to income tax currently payable because no tax is assessed on the unrealized intercompany profit. When separate tax returns are filed, the consolidated income tax expense is the same as when a consolidated return is filed, but Pool's income tax expense consists of $51,000 income tax currently payable less the $3,400 deferred tax asset related to the $10,000 temporary difference.

Case 3: Consolidated Tax Return with Upstream Sales

Now assume that the intercompany sales are upstream (from Sal to Pool). If a consolidated return is filed, the consolidated income tax expense will be $64,600, the same as in the downstream example, but the allocation to Pool and Sal will be changed because $10,000 of Sal's $50,000 pretax income is not included in consolidated taxable income. The allocation is:

$$Pool = \frac{\$150,000}{\$190,000} \times \$64,600 = \$51,000$$

$$Sal = \frac{\$50,000 - \$10,000)}{\$190,000} \times \$64,600 = \$13,600$$

These amounts are recorded in the separate company books as follows:

Pool's books—December 31, 19X3

Income tax expense	$51,000	
Income taxes currently payable		$51,000

    To record share of consolidated income taxes (15/19 × $64,600).

Sal's books—December 31, 19X3

Income tax expense	$13,600	
Income taxes currently payable		$13,600

    To record share of consolidated income taxes (4/19 × $64,600).

Sal's net income is $36,400 ($50,000 pretax income less $13,600 income tax expense), and Pool's income from Sal is determined as follows:

Share of Sal's net income ($36,400 × 90%)	$32,760
Less: Goodwill amortization ($50,000/10 years)	(5,000)
Less: Unrealized profit from upstream sales ($10,000 × 90%)	(9,000)
Income from Sal	$18,760

Partial consolidation working papers to illustrate the effect of this upstream sales example appear in Exhibit 10–12. Minority interest income of $2,640 is computed as 10 percent of Sal's realized income of $26,400 ($36,400 net income

POOL CORPORATION AND SUBSIDIARY
PARTIAL CONSOLIDATION WORKING PAPERS
FOR THE YEAR ENDED DECEMBER 31, 19X3

	Pool	Sal	Adjustments and Eliminations		Consolidated
Sales	$1,000,000	$500,000	a 40,000		$1,460,000
Income from Sal	18,760		c 18,760		
Cost of goods sold	600,000*	350,000*	b 10,000	a 40,000	920,000*
Expenses (other than income taxes)	250,000*	100,000*	d 5,000		355,000*
Income tax expense	51,000*	13,600*			64,600*
Minority income					2,640*
Net income	$ 117,760	$ 36,400			$ 117,760
* Deduct.					

Exhibit 10–12 Consolidated Tax Return—Unrealized Profit from Upstream Sale

– $10,000 unrealized profit). The consolidated income tax expense of $64,600 is the same as in the downstream sale example, but consolidated net income is $660 greater because the $10,000 unrealized gain and the related $3,400 tax allocation effect are attributed to subsidiary operations. Thus, minority interest income is $660 less than in the downstream sale examples and consolidated net income is $660 more ($117,760 instead of $117,100 in Exhibits 10–10 and 10–11). The minority interest income computation in Exhibit 10–12 eliminates 100 percent of the $10,000 unrealized profit because no tax is paid on unrealized profits when consolidated returns are filed.

Case 4. Separate Tax Returns with Upstream Sales

Assume that the intercompany sales are upstream (from Sal to Pool) and that separate income tax returns are filed. Sal's income tax currently payable, as determined from its separate income tax return is $17,000 because income taxes are assessed on Sal's $50.000 pretax income, which includes the $10,000 unrealized profit. But Sal's income tax expense is only $13,600, computed as follows:

Income tax currently payable	$17,000
Less: Increase in deferred tax asset from temporary difference ($10,000 unrealized profit × 34% tax rate)	(3,400)
Income tax expense	$13,600

Sal's net income is $36,400, as in Case 3, and Pool records its income from Sal at $18.760, determined as follows:

Pool's share of Sal's net income ($36,400 × 90%)	$32,760
Less: Goodwill amortization ($50,000/10 years)	(5,000)
Less: Unrealized profit from upstream sales ($10,000 × 90% owned)	(9,000)
Pool's income from Sal	$18,760

This information is reflected in Exhibit 10–13, which shows partial working papers when separate returns are filed and unrealized inventory profit results from upstream sales.

417

POOL CORPORATION AND SUBSIDIARY
PARTIAL CONSOLIDATION WORKING PAPERS
FOR THE YEAR ENDED DECEMBER 31, 19X3

	Pool	Sal	Adjustments and Eliminations		Consolidated
Sales	$1,000,000	$500,000	a 40,000		$1,460,000
Income from Sal	18,760		c 18,760		
Cost of goods sold	600,000*	350,000*	b 10,000	a 40,000	920,000*
Expenses (other than income taxes)	250,000*	100,000*	d 5,000		355,000*
Income tax expense	51,000*	13,600*			64,600*
Minority income					2,640*
Net income	$ 117,760	$ 36,400			$ 117,760

* Deduct.

Exhibit 10–13   Separate Tax Returns—Unrealized Profit from Upstream Sale

Note that there is no difference in the two working papers shown in Exhibits 10–12 and 10–13. The income tax expense and the income from the subsidiary are the same whether separate or consolidated tax returns are filed. There is, however, a difference in income tax currently payable and in the deferred income tax liability. When separate tax returns are filed, the consolidated income tax expense consists of the following:

	Pool	Sal	Consolidated
Income taxes currently payable	$51,000	$17,000	$68,000
Deferred income tax asset	—	(3,400)	(3,400)
Income tax expense	$51,000	$13,600	$64,600

Thus, the consolidated income statement will show income tax expense of $64,600, and the consolidated balance sheet will show a current liability for income tax currently payable of $68,000 and a current asset for the $3,400 deferred income tax asset.

PURCHASE BUSINESS COMBINATIONS

FASB Statement No. 109 requires that a deferred tax liability or deferred tax asset be recognized for the difference between the book value (tax basis) and the assigned values of the assets and liabilities (except goodwill, negative goodwill, and leveraged leases) acquired in a purchase business combination.[12] In other words, the assets and liabilities acquired are recorded at their gross fair values, and a deferred tax asset or liability is recorded for the related tax effect. The business combination of Platt and Shad is used to illustrate the computation of a deferred tax liability for the book value/fair value differentials, and for the determination of goodwill.

On January 1, 19X2 Platt Corporation paid $400,000 for 60 percent of the outstanding voting stock of Shad Corporation when Shad's stockholders' equity

---

[12]Under *APB Opinion No. 11*, the amounts assigned to the assets and liabilities in a purchase business combination were net-of-tax amounts.

consisted of $300,000 capital stock and $200,000 retained earnings. Book values were equal to fair values of Shad's assets and liabilities except for a building with a book value of $80,000, a fair value of $120,000, and a remaining useful life of eight years and land with a book value of $50,000 and a fair value of $150,000. Any goodwill is to be amortized over 40 years. The tax rate applicable to both companies is 34 percent, and an 80 percent dividends deduction applies.

The $100,000 excess of cost over book value acquired [$400,000 cost − ($500,000 book value of net assets × 60% interest)] is allocated as follows:

	Book Value	Pretax Fair Value	Difference	Platt's 60% Interest × the Difference
Building	$80,000	$120,000	$ 40,000	$ 24,000
Land	50,000	150,000	100,000	60,000
Revaluation of assets (gross amount)				84,000
Less: Deferred tax on revaluation ($84,000 × 34%)				(28,560)
Net differential from revaluation of assets				55,440
Goodwill				44,560
Excess cost over book value acquired				$100,000

The $24,000 assigned to the building and the $8,160 related deferred tax ($24,000 × 34%) will be written off over the building's remaining eight-year useful life at the annual amounts of $3,000 and $1,020, respectively. Thus, consolidated net income will be decreased by $1,980 each year on an after-tax basis. The $60,000 revaluation of the land and the $20,400 deferred tax on the revalued land will remain on the books until the land is sold to outside entities. There is, of course, no tax effect of the goodwill since it is not deductible for tax purposes.

Equity Method of Accounting for Purchase Business Combinations

During 19X2 Shad has net income of $100,000 and pays dividends of $40,000. Platt makes the following entries on its separate books to account for its investment in Shad.

Investment in Shad	$400,000	
Cash		$400,000

To record purchase of a 60% interest in Shad Corporation.

Cash	$ 24,000	
Investment in Shad		$ 24,000

To record receipt of dividends from Shad ($40,000 × 60%). Note that Platt must also provide for income taxes on its share of the $60,000 undistributed earnings of Shad ($36,000 × 20% taxable × 34% tax rate = $2,448 deferred taxes).

Investment in Shad	$ 56,906	
Income from Shad		$ 56,906

To record income from Shad related to amortization of deferred tax liability on the building computed as follows:

Share of Shad's income ($100,000 × 60%)	$60,000
Less: Goodwill amortization ($44,560/40 years)	(1,114)
Less: Depreciation on excess allocated to building	(3,000)
Add: Amortization of deferred taxes on building	1,020
Income from Shad	$56,906

420

SUBSIDIARY PREFERRED
STOCK, CONSOLIDATED
EARNINGS PER SHARE,
AND CONSOLIDATED
INCOME TAXATION

The stockholders' equity of Shad at December 31, 19X2 consists of $300,000 capital stock and $260,000 retained earnings, and the balance of Platt's investment in Shad account is $432,906. An analysis of the investment account balance shows the following:

	January 1, 19X2	19X2 Change	December 31, 19X2
Book value of investment	$300,000	$36,000	$336,000
Unamortized excess:			
Building	24,000	(3,000)	21,000
Land	60,000		60,000
Deferred income taxes	(28,560)	1,020	(27,540)
Goodwill	44,560	(1,114)	43,446
Investment balance	$400,000	$32,906	$432,906

Working Paper Entries

When Platt prepares consolidation working papers at December 31, 19X2, the investment in Shad account will have a balance of $432,906 ($400,000 original investment + $56,906 income from Shad − $24,000 dividends). The working paper entries are shown in general journal form as follows:

a	Income from Shad	$ 56,906	
	Dividends		$ 24,000
	Investment in Shad		32,906

To eliminate income and dividends from Shad and adjust the investment in Shad account to its beginning-of-the-period balance.

b	Capital stock—Shad	$300,000	
	Retained earnings—Shad	200,000	
	Building	24,000	
	Land	60,000	
	Goodwill	44,560	
	Investment in Shad		$400,000
	Deferred taxes on revaluation		28,560
	Minority interest—beginning		200,000

To eliminate reciprocal investment and equity accounts, establish beginning minority interest, enter beginning-of-the-period cost–book value differentials, and enter deferred taxes on revaluation.

c	Depreciation expense	$ 3,000	
	Accumulated depreciation—building		$ 3,000

To record depreciation on excess allocated to building.

d	Deferred income taxes on revaluation	$ 1,020	
	Income tax expense		$ 1,020

To record amortization of deferred taxes.

e	Goodwill amortization	$ 1,114	
	Goodwill		$ 1,114

To record amortization of goodwill.

FINANCIAL STATEMENT DISCLOSURES FOR INCOME TAXES

Deferred tax assets or liabilities are divided into two categories, a current amount and a noncurrent amount, for balance sheet presentation. Under *FASB Statement No. 109,* deferred tax liabilities and assets are classified as current or noncurrent based on the classification of the related asset or liability for financial reporting. If the deferred item is not related to an asset or liability for financial reporting, its classification depends on the reversal date of the temporary difference. In addition, the significant components of income tax expense or benefit are required to be disclosed in the financial statements or notes to the financial statements.

Disclosures are also required for income tax expense and benefits allocated to continuing operations, discontinued operations, extraordinary items, cumulative-effect-type items, and prior-period adjustments.

SUMMARY

When the capital structure of a subsidiary or equity investee includes outstanding preferred stock, the investee's equity and income are allocated to the preferred stockholders based on the preferred contract, and then to common stockholders. If the subsidiary's preferred stock is not held by the parent company, the preferred income and equity are included in minority interest. From the viewpoint of the consolidated entity, any of the subsidiary's preferred stock held by the parent is considered retired for consolidated statement purposes.

Consolidated and parent company earnings-per-share computations are identical, and the procedures used in computing parent company earnings per share also apply to investor accounting under the equity method. Parent company (investor) relationships do not affect EPS computations unless the subsidiary (investee) has outstanding common stock equivalents or other potentially dilutive securities. When a subsidiary has potentially dilutive securities outstanding, the computational adjustments for EPS differ according to whether the subsidiary's potentially dilutive securities are convertible into subsidiary common stock or parent company common stock.

A consolidated entity that is classified as an affiliated group may elect to file consolidated tax returns. All other consolidated entities file separate income tax returns. In determining taxable income, consolidated entities that are members of an affiliated group can exclude all dividends received from members of the group. Those affiliated groups that elect to file consolidated tax returns also avoid paying taxes on unrealized profits, and can offset losses of one group member against income of other group members.

SELECTED READINGS

Accounting Principles Board Opinion No. 15. "Earnings per Share." New York: American Institute of Certified Public Accountants, 1969.

Accounting Principles Board Opinion No. 18. "The Equity Method of Accounting for Investments in Common Stock." New York: American Institute of Certified Public Accountants, 1971.

ALLISON, TERRY E., and PAULA BEVELS THOMAS. "Uncharted Territory: Subsidiary Financial Reporting." *Journal of Accountancy* (October 1989), pp. 76–84.

BILLINGS, B. ANTHONY, and LEONARD G. WELD. "Taxable Business Acquisitions: Issues and Answers." *The CPA Journal* (June 1990), pp. 42–48.

KNECHEL, W. ROBERT, and CHARLES L. MCDONALD. "Accounting for Income Taxes Related to Assets Acquired in a Purchase Business Combination." *Accounting Horizons* (September 1989), pp. 44–52.

LAIBSTAIN, SAMUEL. "Income Tax Accounting for Business Combinations." *The CPA Journal* (December 1988), pp. 32–40.

READ, WILLIAM J., and ROBERT BARTSCH. "How to Account for Acquisitions Under FASB 96." *Journal of Accountancy* (May 1989), pp. 54–60.

REINHARDT, U. E. "Conglomerate Earnings per Share: Immediate and Post-Merger Effects." *Accounting Review* (April 1972), pp. 360–370.

Statement of Financial Accounting Standards No. 109. "Accounting for Income Taxes." Stamford, CT: Financial Accounting Standards Board, 1992.

WOLK, HARRY I., DALE R. MARTIN, and VIRGINIA A. NICHOLS. "Statement of Financial Accounting Standards No. 96: Some Theoretical Problems." *Accounting Horizons* (June 1989), pp. 1–5.

ASSIGNMENT MATERIAL

QUESTIONS

1 Arom Corporation has 100,000 outstanding shares of no par common stock and 5,000 outstanding shares of $100 par, cumulative, 10 percent preferred stock. Arom Corporation's net income for the current year is $300,000, and its stockholders' equity at the end of the current year is as follows:

10% cumulative preferred stock, $100 par	$ 500,000
Common stock, $10 par	1,000,000
Additional paid-in capital	600,000
Retained earnings	400,000
Total stockholders' equity	$2,500,000

Flora Corporation owns 60 percent of the outstanding common stock of Arom, acquired at book value several years ago. Compute Flora's investment income for the current year and the balance of its investment in Arom account at the end of the current year.

2 Refer to the information in question 1. Assume that Arom pays two years' preferred dividend requirements during the current year. Would this affect your computation of Flora's investment income for the current year? If so, recompute Flora's investment income.

3 How should preferred stock of a subsidiary be shown in a consolidated balance sheet in each case?
  a If it is held 100 percent by the parent company
  b If it is held 50 percent by parent company and 50 percent by outside interests
  c If it is held 100 percent by outside interests

4 Describe the computation of minority interest income for an 80 percent subsidiary with both preferred and common stock outstanding.

5 How does consolidated earnings per share differ from parent company earnings per share?

6 Do investments in nonconsolidated subsidiaries and 20 to 50 percent owned investees affect the nature of the investor company's earnings per share calculations?

7 Under what conditions will the procedures used in computing a parent company's earnings per share be the same as those for a company without equity investments?

8 It may be necessary to compute the earnings per share for subsidiaries and equity investees before parent company (and consolidated) earnings per share can be determined. When are the subsidiary earnings-per-share computations used in calculating parent company earnings per share?

9 The common stock equivalents and other potentially dilutive securities of a subsidiary may be converted into parent company common stock or subsidiary common stock. Describe how these situations affect the parent company's EPS procedures.

10 In computing primary or fully diluted earnings for a parent company, it may be necessary to replace the parent's equity in subsidiary realized income with the parent company's equity in the subsidiary's primary or fully diluted earnings. Does this replacement calculation involve the goodwill amortization and unrealized profits that are included in the parent company's income from subsidiary?

11 Are consolidated income tax returns required for all consolidated entities? Discuss.

12 Can a consolidated entity that is classified as an "affiliated group" under the IRS Code elect to file separate tax returns for each affiliate?

13 What are the primary advantages of filing a consolidated tax return?

14 Some or all of the dividends received by a corporation from domestic affiliated companies may be excluded from federal income taxation. When are all of the dividends excluded?

15 Describe the nature of the tax effect of temporary differences that arise from use of the equity method of accounting.

16 Does a parent company/investor provide for income taxes on the undistributed earnings of a subsidiary by adjusting investment and investment income accounts? Explain.

17 When do unrealized and constructive gains and losses create temporary differences for a consolidated entity?

EXERCISES

E 10-1 [Preferred stock]

Skinner Corporation's stockholders' equity on December 31, 19X8 was as follows:

10% cumulative preferred stock, $100 par (callable at 105, with one year's dividends in arrears)	$ 1,000,000
Common stock, $1 par	5,000,000
Excess issue price over par on common stock	15,000,000
Total paid-in capital	21,000,000
Retained earnings	16,000,000
Total stockholders' equity	$37,000,000

On January 1, 19X9 Poindexter Corporation purchases a 70 percent interest in Skinner's common stock for $30,000,000 cash. On this date the book values of Skinner's assets and liabilities are equal to fair values.

Required
1 Determine the goodwill or negative goodwill from Poindexter's investment in Skinner's common stock.
2 If a consolidated balance sheet for Poindexter Corporation and Subsidiary is prepared immediately after the stock investment, what minority interest will be shown?

E 10-2 [Preferred stock]

The stockholders' equity of Sommerfeld Corporation at December 31, 19X5 was as follows:

12% preferred stock, cumulative, nonparticipating, $100 par, callable at 105	$ 600,000
Common stock, $10 par	1,000,000
Other paid-in capital	140,000
Retained earnings	760,000
Total stockholders' equity	$2,500,000

Parnell Corporation purchased 80 percent of Sommerfeld's common stock on January 2, 19X6 for $1,536,000. During 19X6, Sommerfeld reported a $100,000 net loss and paid no dividends. During 19X7, Sommerfeld reported $500,000 net income and declared dividends of $344,000.

Required
1 Compute the cost–book value differential from Parnell's investment in Sommerfeld.
2 Determine Parnell's income (loss) from Sommerfeld for 19X6.
3 Determine Parnell's income (loss) from Sommerfeld for 19X7.
4 Compute the balance of Parnell's investment in Sommerfeld account at December 31, 19X7.

E 10-3 [Preferred stock]

Penzance Corporation owns 80 percent of Sandalwood Corporation's common stock, having acquired the interest at book value on December 31, 19X4. During 19X5 Penzance's separate income is $3,000,000 and Sandalwood's net income is $500,000. Penzance and Sandalwood declare dividends in 19X5 of $1,000,000 and $300,000, respectively.

The stockholders' equity of Sandalwood at December 31, 19X4 and 19X5 consists of the following:

424

SUBSIDIARY PREFERRED
STOCK, CONSOLIDATED
EARNINGS PER SHARE,
AND CONSOLIDATED
INCOME TAXATION

	December 31, 19X4	December 31, 19X5
12% cumulative preferred stock, $100 par, callable at 105 per share	$1,000,000	$1,000,000
Common stock, $10 par	2,000,000	2,000,000
Other paid-in capital	300,000	300,000
Retained earnings	700,000	900,000
Total stockholders' equity	$4,000,000	$4,200,000

Required

1 Determine the cost of Penzance's investment in Sandalwood at December 31, 19X4 if Sandalwood has one year's preferred dividends in arrears on that date.
2 Calculate Penzance's net income (and consolidated net income) and minority interest income for 19X5.
3 Calculate the underlying book value of Penzance's investment in Sandalwood at December 31, 19X5.

E 10-4   [Preferred stock]

Perry Corporation purchased 60 percent of Sketch Corporation's outstanding preferred stock for $6,500,000 and 70 percent of its outstanding common stock for $35,000,000 on January 1, 19X7. Sketch's stockholders' equity at December 31, 19X6 consisted of the following:

10% cumulative, $100 par preferred stock, callable at $105 (100,000 shares issued and outstanding with one year's dividends in arrears)	$10,000,000
Common stock, $10 par	30,000,000
Other paid-in capital	5,000,000
Retained earnings	15,000,000
Total stockholders' equity	$60,000,000

Required

1 Determine the cost–book value differentials from Perry's investments in Sketch.
2 Without bias on your part, assume that the cost–book value differential applicable to the preferred investment is a negative $400,000. Describe the accounting treatment of the preferred cost–book value differential if the preferred investment is treated as a constructive retirement for consolidation purposes.

E 10-5   [EPS]

1 The computation of primary EPS for a consolidated entity involves the use of subsidiary EPS if the subsidiary has:
   a Common stock equivalents convertible into parent common stock
   b Common stock equivalents convertible into subsidiary common stock
   c Convertible bonds or preferred stock outstanding
   d Potentially dilutive securities outstanding
2 A parent company and its 100 percent owned subsidiary have only common stock outstanding (10,000 shares for the parent and 3,000 shares for the subsidiary), and neither company has issued other potentially dilutive securities. The equation to compute consolidated EPS for the parent company and its subsidiary is:
   a (Net income of parent + net income of subsidiary)/13,000 shares
   b (Net income of parent + net income of subsidiary)/10,000 shares
   c Net income of parent/13,000 shares
   d Net income of parent/10,000 shares
3 A parent company has a 90 percent interest in a subsidiary that has no common stock equivalents or other potentially dilutive securities outstanding. In computing consolidated EPS:
   a Subsidiary common shares are added to parent company common shares and common share equivalents
   b Subsidiary EPS and parent company EPS amounts are combined
   c Subsidiary EPS computations are not needed
   d Subsidiary EPS computations are used in computing primary earnings

4 In computing a parent company's primary EPS, it may be necessary to subtract the parent's equity in subsidiary realized income and replace it with the parent's equity in subsidiary primary earnings. The subtraction in this replacement computation is affected by:

a Constructive gain from purchase of parent company bonds
b Current amortization of goodwill from investment in the subsidiary
c Unrealized profits from downstream sales
d Unrealized profits from upstream sales

E 10–6 **[EPS]**

Palor Corporation's net income for 19X9 is $316,000, including $160,000 income from Solaid Corporation, its 80 percent owned subsidiary. The income from Solaid consists of $176,000 equity in income less $16,000 goodwill amortization. Palor has 300,000 shares of $10 par common stock outstanding, and Solaid has 50,000 shares of $10 par common stock outstanding throughout 19X9. In addition, Solaid has 10,000 outstanding warrants to acquire 10,000 shares of Solaid common stock at $10 per share. The average market price of Solaid's common stock was $20 per share during 19X9 and the year-end market price was $25 per share.

1 For purposes of calculating Palor Corporation's (and consolidated) earnings per share, Solaid's primary earnings are:

a $220,000   **b** $200,000
c $176,000   **d** $160,000

2 For purposes of calculating Palor Corporation's (and consolidated) primary earnings per share, Solaid's outstanding common shares and common share equivalents are:

a 60,000 shares   **b** 56,000 shares
c 55,000 shares   **d** 50,000 shares

3 For purposes of calculating Palor Corporation's (and consolidated) earnings per share, assume that Solaid's primary EPS is $4 per share. Palor Corporation's (and consolidated) primary earnings will be:

a $316,000   **b** $300,000
c $156,000   **d** $140,000

4 If Solaid's primary earnings for 19X9 are $4 per share, Palor Corporation's (and consolidated) primary earnings per share will be:

a $1.64   **b** $1.59
c $1.04   **d** $1.00

E 10–7 [EPS] Stickly Corporation is an 80 percent owned subsidiary of Pecton Corporation. Throughout 19X8 Stickly had 10,000 shares of common stock outstanding and Pecton had 20,000 shares outstanding. Pecton has no potentially dilutive securities outstanding, and Stickly's only potentially dilutive securities consist of options to acquire 2,000 shares of Stickly common stock at $15 per share.

Income data for the affiliated companies are as follows:

	Pecton	Stickly
Separate incomes	$60,000	$45,000
Income from Stickly ($45,000 × 80%)		
− $6,000 goodwill amortization	30,000	
Net income	$90,000	$45,000

Required: Compute consolidated primary and fully diluted EPS for Pecton Corporation and Subsidiary assuming that the average and year-end market price of Stickly common stock is $30 and $40 per share, respectively.

E 10–8 **[EPS]**

The income statements of Prince Corporation and its 80 percent owned subsidiary, Stanley Corporation, for 19X6 are as follows:

426

SUBSIDIARY PREFERRED
STOCK, CONSOLIDATED
EARNINGS PER SHARE,
AND CONSOLIDATED
INCOME TAXATION

	Prince	Stanley
Sales	$1,270,000	$740,000
Income from Stanley (see note)	13,920	—
Cost of sales	(700,000)	(470,000)
Expenses	(462,000)	(230,000)
Income before taxes	121,920	40,000
Provision for income taxes	(41,453)	(13,600)
Net income	$ 80,467	$ 26,400

[*Note:* Income from Stanley is computed as ($26,400 reported income × 80%) − $2,000 goodwill amortization − $5,200 unrealized profit in Stanley's inventory.]

Prince had 10,000 shares of common stock and 1,200 shares of $100 par, 10 percent, cumulative preferred stock outstanding throughout 19X6. Stanley had 20,000 shares of common stock and warrants to purchase 5,000 shares of Stanley common stock at $24 outstanding throughout 19X6. The average and year-end market prices of Stanley common stock were $30 per share and $40 per share, respectively.

Required: Compute Prince's (and consolidated) primary and fully diluted EPS.

E 10–9 [EPS] Poway Corporation owns an 80 percent interest in Scony Corporation. Since Poway does not have common stock equivalents or other potentially dilutive securities outstanding, it calculated its EPS for 19X7 as follows:

$$\frac{\$1,000,000 \text{ separate income } + \$480,000 \text{ income from Scony}}{1,000,000 \text{ outstanding common shares of Poway}} = \$1.48$$

An examination of Poway's income from Scony shows that it is determined correctly as 80 percent of Scony's $630,000 net income less $24,000 goodwill amortization. Poway's EPS computation is in error, however, because it fails to consider outstanding warrants of Scony that permit their holders to acquire 10,000 shares of Scony common stock at $24 per share and increase Scony's outstanding common stock to 60,000 shares. The average price of Scony common stock during 19X7 was $40 per share and at year-end it was $48 per share.

Required
1 Compute Scony Corporation's primary and fully diluted EPS for use in the determination of consolidated EPS.
2 Compute consolidated EPS for 19X7 (both primary and fully diluted).

E 10–10 [Tax]

1 Income taxes are currently due on intercompany profits when
   a Profits originate from upstream sales
   b Separate company tax returns are filed
   c Consolidated tax returns are filed
   d Affiliates are accounted for as unconsolidated subsidiaries
2 The right of a consolidated entity to file a consolidated income tax return is contingent upon:
   a Ownership by a common parent of all the voting stock of group members
   b Ownership by a common parent of 90 percent of the voting stock of group members
   c Classification as an affiliated group
   d Direct or indirect ownership of a majority of the outstanding stock of all group members
3 When affiliates are classified as an affiliated group for tax purposes, the group:
   a Excludes unrealized profits from intercompany transactions from taxable income
   b Must file a consolidated income tax return
   c May file separate income tax returns
   d Pays lower income taxes
4 Deferred income taxes are provided for unrealized profits from intercompany transactions when:

    a A consolidated tax return is filed
    b Separate company tax returns are filed
    c The unrealized profits are from upstream sales
    d The consolidated entity is an affiliated group

E 10–11 |Tax|

1 When Petty Corporation acquired its 100 percent interest in Simon Corporation, Simon's equipment had a fair value of $6,000,000 and a book value and tax basis of $4,000,000. If Petty's effective tax rate is 34 percent, how much of the purchase price should be allocated to equipment and to deferred income taxes?
    a $4,000,000 and $0, respectively
    b $5,320,000 and $680,000, respectively
    c $6,000,000 and $680,000, respectively
    d $6,000,000 and $2,040,000, respectively

2 Carl Corporation, whose effective income tax rate is 34 percent, received $200,000 dividends from its 30 percent owned domestic equity investee during the current year and recorded $500,000 equity in the investee's income. Carl's income tax expense for the year should include taxes on the investment of:
    a $13,600   **b** $20,400
    c $34,000   **d** $68,000

3 During 19X1 Palmer Corporation reported $60,000 investment income from Springer Corporation, its 30 percent owned investee, and received $30,000 dividends from Springer. Palmer's effective income tax rate is 34 percent, and it is entitled to an 80 percent dividends received deduction on dividends received from Springer. On the basis of this information, Palmer should:
    a Report investment income from Springer of $57,960
    b Increase its investment in Springer for 19X1 in the amount of $27,960
    c Credit its deferred income taxes in the net amount of $2,040 for the year 19X1
    d Debit its deferred income taxes in the net amount of $2,040 for the year 19X1

4 Polines Corporation owns 35 percent of the voting stock of Sissy Corporation, a domestic corporation. During 19X1 Sissy reports net income of $100,000 and pays dividends of $50,000. Polines' effective income tax rate is 34 percent. What amounts should Polines record as income taxes currently payable and deferred income taxes from its investment in Sissy?
    a $17,000 and $0, respectively
    b $5,950 and $5,950, respectively
    c $3,400 and $3,400, respectively
    d $1,190 and $1,190, respectively

5 Pint Corporation and its 100 percent owned domestic subsidiary, Star Corporation, are classified as an affiliated group for tax purposes. During the current year Star pays $80,000 in cash dividends. Assuming a 34 percent income tax rate, how much income tax expense on this dividend should be reported in the consolidated income statement of Pint Corporation and Subsidiary?
    a $0   **b** $27,200
    c $5,440   **d** $2,720

E 10–12 |Tax|

The pretax accounting incomes of Pruit Corporation and its 100 percent owned subsidiary, Solo Company, for 19X1 are as follows:

	Pruit	Solo
Sales	$1,000,000	$500,000
Gain on land	200,000	
Total revenue	1,200,000	500,000
Cost of sales	500,000	300,000
Gross profit	700,000	200,000
Operating expenses	400,000	100,000
Pretax accounting income	$ 300,000	$100,000

428

SUBSIDIARY PREFERRED
STOCK, CONSOLIDATED
EARNINGS PER SHARE,
AND CONSOLIDATED
INCOME TAXATION

The only intercompany transaction during 19X1 was the gain on land sold to Solo. Assume a 34 percent flat income tax rate.

Required
1 What amount should be shown on the consolidated income statement as income tax expense if separate company tax returns are filed?
2 Compute the consolidated income tax expense if a consolidated tax return is filed.

E 10-13 **[Tax]**

Paxton Corporation and its 70 percent owned subsidiary, Sutter Corporation, have pretax operating incomes for 19X8 as follows:

	Paxton	Sutter
Sales	$8,000,000	$4,000,000
Gain on equipment	200,000	—
Cost of sales	(5,000,000)	(2,000,000)
Other expenses	(1,800,000)	(1,200,000)
Pretax income	$1,400,000	$ 800,000

Paxton received $280,000 dividends from Sutter during 19X8. Goodwill from Paxton's investment in Sutter is being amortized at a rate of $50,000 per year.

On January 1, 19X8 Paxton sold equipment to Sutter at a $200,000 gain. Sutter is depreciating the equipment at a rate of 20 percent per year. A flat 34 percent tax rate is applicable to both companies.

Required: Prepare a consolidated income statement for Paxton Corporation and Subsidiary for 19X8. (Assume no deferred tax balance at January 1, 19X1.)

E 10-14 [Tax] Sullivan Corporation is a 100 percent owned subsidiary of Peddicord Corporation. During the current year Peddicord sold merchandise that cost $50,000 to Sullivan for $100,000. A 34 percent income tax rate is applicable and 80 percent of the merchandise remains unsold by Sullivan at year-end.

Required
1 Prepare comparative one-line consolidation entries relating to the unrealized profit when separate and consolidated income tax returns are filed.
2 Prepare comparative consolidation working paper entries in general journal form relating to the intercompany sales transaction and the related income tax effect when separate and consolidated income tax returns are filed.

E 10-15 [Tax] Sweeney Corporation, an 80 percent owned subsidiary of Pioneer Corporation, sold equipment with a book value of $150,000 to Pioneer for $250,000 at December 31, 19X3. Separate income tax returns are filed, and a 34 percent income tax rate is applicable to both Pioneer and Sweeney.

Required
1 Prepare a one-line consolidation entry for Pioneer to eliminate the effect of the intercompany transaction.
2 Prepare working paper entries in general journal form to eliminate the unrealized profit.
3 Assume that the reported net income of Sweeney is $800,000 and that the sale of equipment is the only intercompany transaction between Pioneer and Sweeney. What is the minority interest's share of total consolidated income?

PROBLEMS

P 10-1 **[Preferred stock]**

Philip Corporation pays $15,000,000 for 80 percent of the outstanding voting stock of Sierra Corporation on December 31, 19X2 when Sierra's stockholders' equity consists of the following:

11% cumulative preferred stock, $100 par (10,000 shares issued and outstanding, callable at $105, with one year's dividends in arrears)	$ 1,000,000
Common stock, $10 par (1,000,000 shares issued and outstanding)	10,000,000
Additional paid-in capital	5,000,000
Retained earnings	3,000 000
Total stockholders' equity	$19,000,000

During 19X3 Philip's income from its own operations is $2,000,000 and Sierra's net income is $520,000. Philip and Sierra declare dividends during 19X3 of $1,200,000 and $320,000, respectively.

Required
1 Calculate the goodwill from Philip's investment in Sierra's common stock at December 31, 19X2.
2 Calculate Philip's income from Sierra for 19X3.
3 Determine the balance of Philip's investment in Sierra account at December 31, 19X3.

P 10–2 [Preferred stock] Pulsen Corporation acquired 80 percent of Starky Corporation's preferred stock for $175,000 and 90 percent of Starky's common stock for $650,000 on July 1, 19X7. Starky's stockholders' equity on December 31, 19X7 was as follows:

Stockholders' Equity	
9% preferred stock, cumulative, nonparticipating, $100 par, call price $105	$200,000
Common stock, $10 par	500,000
Paid-in capital in excess of par	40,000
Retained earnings	160,000
Total stockholders' equity	$900,000

Starky Corporation had net income of $24,000 in 19X6 and $46,000 in 19X7, but it declared no dividends in either year. Assume that preferred dividends accrue ratably throughout each year and that Starky's net assets were fairly valued on July 1, 19X7.

Required
1 Determine the account balances of Pulsen Corporation's investments in Starky's preferred and common stocks at December 31, 19X7 on the basis of a one-line consolidation. Use a ten-year amortization period for any goodwill.
2 Prepare working paper entries to consolidate the balance sheets of Pulsen and Starky at December 31, 19X7.

P 10–3 [Preferred stock] Financial statements for Pat and Sal Corporations for 19X4 are summarized as follows:

	Pat	Sal
Combined Income and Retained Earnings Statements for the Year Ended December 31, 19X4		
Sales	$1,233,000	$700,000
Income from Sal	67,000	—
Cost of sales	(610,000)	(400,000)
Other expenses	(390,000)	(210,000)
Net income	300,000	90,000
Add: Retained earnings January 1, 19X4	500,000	200,000
Less: Dividends	(200,000)	(50,000)
Retained earnings December 31, 19X4	$ 600,000	$240,000

430

SUBSIDIARY PREFERRED
STOCK, CONSOLIDATED
EARNINGS PER SHARE,
AND CONSOLIDATED
INCOME TAXATION

	Pat	Sal
Balance Sheet at December 31, 19X4		
Cash	$ 181,000	$ 50,000
Other current assets	200,000	300,000
Plant assets—net	900,000	600,000
Investment in Sal	719 000	—
Total assets	$2,000,000	$950,000
Current liabilities	$ 200,000	$ 60,000
$10 preferred stock	—	100,000
Common stock	1,200,000	500,000
Other paid-in capital	—	50,000
Retained earnings	600,000	240,000
Total equities	$2,000,000	$950,000

Pat owns 90,000 shares of Sal's outstanding voting common stock at December 31, 19X4. These shares were acquired in two lots as follows:

	Date	*Shares*	*Purchase Price*
Lot 1	January 1, 19X3	70,000	$500,000
Lot 2	April 1, 19X4	20,000	152,000

The stockholders' equity of Sal at year-end 19X2, 19X3, and 19X4 is as follows:

December 31,	*19X2*	*19X3*	*19X4*
$10 preferred stock, $100 par, cumulative with no dividends in arrears	$100,000	$100,000	$100,000
Common stock, $5 par	500,000	500,000	500,000
Other paid-in capital	50,000	50,000	50,000
Retained earnings	150,000	200,000	240,000
Total stockholders' equity	$800,000	$850,000	$890,000

Sal's net income for 19X4 is $90,000 earned proportionately throughout the year, and its quarterly dividends of $12,500 are declared on March 15, June 15, September 15, and December 15. Any goodwill from Pat's stock acquisitions is to be amortized over ten years. There are no intercompany receivables or payables at December 31, 19X4, and there have been no intercompany transactions other than dividends.

Required: Prepare consolidation working papers for Pat Corporation and Subsidiary for 19X4.

P 10-4 [Preferred stock] Pari Corporation acquired an 80 percent interest in Sak Corporation common stock for $240,000 on January 1, 19X5 when Sak's stockholders' equity consisted of $200,000 common stock, $100,000 preferred stock, and $25,000 retained earnings. The excess was allocated to goodwill with a five-year amortization period.

Intercompany sales of inventory items from Pari to Sak were $50,000 in 19X5 and $60,000 in 19X6. The cost of these items to Pari was 60 percent of the selling price to Sak, and Sak inventoried $30,000 of the intercompany sales items at December 31, 19X5 and $40,000 at December 31, 19X6. Intercompany receivables and payables from these sales were $10,000 at December 31, 19X5 and $5,000 at December 31, 19X6.

Sak sold land that cost $10,000 to Pari for $20,000 during 19X5. During 19X6 Pari resold the land outside the consolidated entity for $30,000.

On July 1, 19X6 Pari purchased all of Sak's bonds payable in the open market for $91,000. These bonds were issued at par, have interest payment dates of June 30 and December 31, and mature on June 30, 19X9.

Sak declared and paid dividends of $10,000 on its cumulative preferred stock and $10,000 on its common stock in each of the years 19X5 and 19X6.

Financial statements for Pari and Sak Corporations at and for the year ended December 31, 19X6 are summarized as follows:

	Pari	Sak
Combined Income and Retained Earnings Statement for the Year Ended December 31, 19X6		
Sales	$900,000	$300,000
Gain on land	10,000	—
Interest income	6,500	—
Income from Sak	38,000	—
Cost of sales	600,000*	140,000*
Operating expenses	208,500*	90,000*
Interest expense	—	10,000*
Net income	146,000	60,000
Add: Beginning retained earnings	120,000	50,000
Deduct: Dividends	100,000*	20,000*
Retained earnings December 31, 19X6	$166,000	$ 90,000
Balance Sheet at December 31, 19X6		
Cash	$ 5,500	$ 15,000
Accounts receivable	26,000	20,000
Inventories	80,000	60,000
Other current assets	100,000	5,000
Land	160,000	30,000
Plant and equipment—net	268,000	420,000
Investment in Sak—bonds	92,500	—
Investment in Sak—stock	258,000	—
Total assets	$990,000	$550,000
Accounts payable	$ 24,000	$ 15,000
10% bonds payable	—	100,000
Other liabilities	100,000	45,000
10% preferred stock	—	100,000
Common stock	700,000	200,000
Retained earnings	166,000	90,000
Total equities	$990,000	$550,000

* Deduct.

Required: Prepare consolidation working papers for Pari Corporation and Subsidiary for the year ended December 31, 19X6.

P 10–5 [EPS] Palace corporation has $108,000 income from its own operations for 19X3 and $42,000 income from Skinner Corporation, its 70 percent owned subsidiary. Skinner's net income of $60,000 consists of $66,000 operating income less $6,000 net-of-tax interest on its outstanding 10 percent convertible debenture bonds. Throughout 19X3 Palace has 100,000 shares of common stock outstanding, and Skinner has 50,000 outstanding common shares.

Required
1 Compute Palace's primary earnings per share for 19X3 assuming that Skinner's convertible bonds are common stock equivalents that are convertible into 10,000 shares of Skinner's common stock.
2 Compute Palace's fully diluted earnings per share for 19X3 assuming that Skinner's convertible bonds are *not* common stock equivalents but are convertible into 10,000 shares of Palace's common stock.

P 10-6 [EPS] Data relating to earnings per share computations for Paris Corporation and its 50 percent owned equity investee, Salem Corporation, for 19X3 follow:

	Paris	Salem
Net income for 19X3	$1,020,000	$960,000
Income from Salem	$ 480,000	
Securities outstanding:		
Common stock	100,000 shares	46,000 shares
Warrants to purchase 10,000 additional shares of Salem common stock at $24 per share		10,000 warrants

Required: Compute Paris Corporation's primary and fully diluted earnings per share if the average price of Salem's common stock is $30 per share during 19X3 and the year-end price if $40 per share.

P 10-7 [EPS] Protein Corporation owns 80 percent of Starch Corporation's outstanding common stock. The 80 percent interest was acquired in 19X2 at $40,000 in excess of book value due to undervalued equipment with an eight-year remaining use life. Outstanding securities of the two companies throughout 19X3 and at December 31, 19X3 are:

	Protein	Starch
Common stock, $5 par	20,000 shares	—
Common stock, $10 par	—	6,000 shares
14% cumulative convertible preferred stock, $100 par	—	1,000 shares

Starch Corporation's net income is $50,000 for 19X3 and Protein's net income consists of $70,000 separate income and $23,800 income from Starch.

Required

1 Compute consolidated primary and fully diluted earnings per share assuming that the preferred stock is convertible into 4,000 shares of Starch Corporation's common stock but is *not* a common equivalent.
2 Compute consolidated primary and fully diluted earnings per share assuming that the preferred stock is convertible into 5,000 shares of Protein's common stock but is *not* a common stock equivalent.

P 10-8 [EPS] Premble Company owns 40,000 of 50,000 outstanding shares of Smithfield Company, and during 19X6 it recognizes income from Smithfield as follows:

Share of Smithfield's net income ($500,000 × 80%)	$400,000
Goodwill amortization	(50,000)
Unrealized profit—downstream sales	(40,000)
Unrealized profit—upstream sales ($60,000 × 80%)	(48,000)
Income from Smithfield	$262,000

Premble's net income (and consolidated net income) for 19X6 is $1,262,000, consisting of separate income from Premble of $1,000,000 and $262,000 income from Smithfield. Premble has 100,000 shares of common stock outstanding, but does not have common stock equivalents or other potentially dilutive securities.

Smithfield has $100,000 par of 10 percent convertible bonds outstanding that are common stock equivalents and are convertible into 10,000 shares of Smithfield common stock. The net-of-tax interest on the bonds is $6,400 and Smithfield's primary earnings per share for purposes of computing consolidated earnings per share is determined as follows:

Net income	$500,000
Add: Net-of-tax interest on convertible bonds	6,400
Less: Unrealized profit on upstream sales	(60,000)
a Primary earnings	$446,400
Common shares outstanding	50,000
Shares issuable upon conversion of bonds	10,000
b Common shares and equivalents	60,000
Primary earnings per share a/b	$7.44

Required: Compute Premble Company's and consolidated primary earnings per share for 19X6.

P 10–9   [EPS] Pike Corporation's net income for 19X6 consists of the following:

Separate income		$320,000
Income from Sim Corporation:		
80% of Sim's income to common	$160,000	
Less: Goodwill amortization	−4,000	
Less: Unrealized profits on equipment sold to Sim	−10,000	
Less: 80% of unrealized profit on land purchased from Sim	−16,000	130,000
Net income for 19X6		$450,000

Additional Information
1   Pike has 100,000 shares of common stock and Sim has 50,000 shares of common and 10,000 shares of $10 cumulative, convertible preferred stock outstanding throughout 19X6. The preferred stock is convertible into 30,000 shares of Sim stock but is not a common stock equivalent.
2   Sim has warrants outstanding that permit their holders to purchase 10,000 shares of Sim Corporation common stock at $15 per share (average market price $20 and year-end market price $25).
3   Sim's reported net income for 19X6 is $300,000, allocated $100,000 to preferred stockholders and $200,000 to common stockholders.
4   Pike owned 40,000 shares of Sim common stock throughout 19X6.

Required: Compute Pike Corporation's (and consolidated) primary and fully diluted EPS.

P 10–10   [Tax] Pactor Corporation and its 100 percent owned subsidiary, Shram Corporation are members of an affiliated group with pretax accounting incomes as follows:

	Pactor	*Shram*
Sales	$1,200,000	$700,000
Gain	50,000	
Cost of sales	600,000*	300,000*
Operating expenses	350,000*	250,000*
Pretax accounting income	$ 300,000	$150,000

* Deduct.

The gain reported by Pactor relates to land sold to Shram during the current year. A flat 34 percent income tax rate is applicable.

Required: Prepare income statements for Pactor Corporation assuming (a) that separate income tax returns are filed and (b) that a consolidated income tax return is filed. (*Note:* Pactor applies the equity method as a one-line consolidation.)

P 10–11   [Tax] Panama Corporation paid $600,000 cash for a 70 percent interest in Silky Corporation's outstanding common stock on January 2, 19X5 when the equity of Silky consisted of $500,000 common stock and $300,000 retained earnings. The excess cost over book value acquired is goodwill with a ten-year amortization period.

434

SUBSIDIARY PREFERRED
STOCK, CONSOLIDATED
EARNINGS PER SHARE,
AND CONSOLIDATED
INCOME TAXATION

In December 19X5 Silky sold inventory items to Panama at a gross profit of $50,000 (selling price $120,000 and cost $70,000) and all of these items were included in Panama's inventory at December 31, 19X5.

Silky paid dividends of $50,000 in 19X5, and an 80 percent dividends received deduction is applicable. A flat 34 percent income tax rate is applicable to both companies.

Separate pretax incomes of Panama and Silky for 19X5 are as follows:

	Panama	Silky
Sales	$4,000,000	$1,000,000
Cost of sales	(2,000,000)	(550,000)
Operating expenses	(1,500,000)	(250,000)
Pretax income	$ 500,000	$ 200,000

Required:
1 Determine income tax expense for Panama and Silky for 19X5.
2 Calculate Panama's income from Silky for 19X5.
3 Prepare a consolidated income statement for Panama and Silky for 19X5.

P 10–12 [Tax] Taxable incomes for Pulaski Corporation and Stewart Corporation, its 70 percent owned subsidiary, for 19X3 are as follows:

	Pulaski	Stewart
Sales	$500,000	$300,000
Dividends received from Stewart	28,000	
Total revenue	528,000	300,000
Cost of sales	250,000	120,000
Operating expenses	78,000	80,000
Total deductions	328,000	200,000
Taxable income	$200,000	$100,000

Additional Information
1 Pulaski acquired its interest in Stewart at book value on December 31, 19X2.
2 Stewart paid dividends of $40,000 in 19X3.
3 Pulaski sold $90,000 merchandise to Stewart during 19X3, and there was $10,000 unrealized profit from the sales at year-end.
4 A flat 34 percent income tax rate is applicable.
5 Pulaski is eligible for the 80 percent dividends received deduction.

Required: Prepare consolidation income statement working papers for Pulaski Corporation and Subsidiary for 19X3.

P 10–13 [Tax] Pac Corporation acquired a 90 percent interest in Shy Corporation at book value on January 1, 19X1. Pac uses the equity method to account for its investment in Shy. A 34 percent income tax rate is applicable and income taxes currently payable are $105,400. Partial consolidation working papers for Pac and Shy for 19X1 are as follows:

PAC CORPORATION AND SUBSIDIARY
CONSOLIDATED INCOME STATEMENT WORKING PAPERS
FOR THE YEAR ENDED DECEMBER 31, 19X1

	Pac	90% Shy	Adjustments and Eliminations		Minority Interest	Consolidated Statements
Sales	$900,000	$400,000				$1,300,000
Income from Shy	49,400		b	49,400		
Gain on land sale	10,000		a	10,000		
Cost of sales	500,000*	200,000*				700,000*
Operating expenses	200,000*	100,000*				300,000*
Income taxes	68,000*	34,000*				102,000*
Minority interest income					$6,600	6,600*
Net income	$191,400	$66,000				$ 191,400

Required
1 Do Pac and Shy Corporations file separate company or consolidated income tax returns? Explain.
2 Illustrate the computation of Pac's income tax expense for 19X1.
3 Explain Pac's income from Shy for 19X1.

P 10–14 [Tax] The pretax operating incomes of Pommer Corporation and Sooner Corporation, its 70 percent owned subsidiary, for the year 19X8 are as follows:

	Pommer	*Sooner*
Sales	$8,000,000	$4,000,000
Gain on equipment	500,000	—
Cost of sales	5,000,000*	2,000,000*
Other expenses	2,100,000*	1,200,000*
Pretax income (excluding Pommer's income from Sooner)	$1,400,000	$ 800,000

* Deduct.

Additional Information
1 Pommer received $280,000 dividends from Sooner during 19X8.
2 Goodwill from Pommer's investment in Sooner is being amortized at $50,000 per year.
3 Pommer sold equipment to Sooner at a gain of $500,000 on January 1, 19X8. Sooner is depreciating the equipment at a rate of 20 percent per year.
4 A flat 34 percent tax rate is applicable.
5 Pommer provides for income taxes on undistributed income from Sooner.

Required
1 Determine the separate income tax expenses for Pommer and Sooner.
2 Determine Pommer's income from Sooner on an equity basis.
3 Prepare a consolidated income statement for Pommer Corporation and Subsidiary for the year ended December 31, 19X8.

P 10–15 [Tax] On January 3, 19X7 Phoenix Corporation purchased a 90 percent interest in Selica Corporation at a price $120,000 in excess of book value and fair value. The excess is goodwill with a ten-year amortization period. During 19X7 Phoenix sold inventory items to Selica for $100,000 and $15,000 profit from the sale remained unrealized at year-end. Selica sold land to Phoenix during the year at a gain of $30,000.

Additional Information
1 The companies are an affiliated group for tax purposes.
2 Selica declared and paid dividends of $100,000 in 19X7.
3 Phoenix and Selica file separate income tax returns and a 34 percent tax rate is applicable to both companies.
4 Phoenix uses a correct equity method in accounting for its investment in Selica.
5 Pretax accounting incomes excluding Phoenix's income from Selica are as follows:

	Phoenix	*Selica*
Sales	$3,815,000	$2,000,000
Gain on land	—	30,000
Cost of sales	(2,200,000)	(1,200,000)
Other expenses	(1,000,000)	(400,000)
Pretax accounting income	$ 615,000	$ 430,000

Required: Calculate the following:
1 Selica's net income
2 Phoenix's income from Selica
3 Phoenix's net income

P 10–16 [Tax] The 19X3 consolidated income tax return of Peabody Corporation and Subsidiary, Sylvester Company (90 percent owned), is summarized as follows:

436

SUBSIDIARY PREFERRED
STOCK, CONSOLIDATED
EARNINGS PER SHARE,
AND CONSOLIDATED
INCOME TAXATION

Sales		$390,000
Cost of sales		180,000
Gross profit		210,000
Operating expenses:		
Depreciation expense	$40,000	
Other expenses	20,000	60,000
Consolidated taxable income		$150,000
Tax rate		× 34%
Income taxes payable (equal to income tax expense)		$ 51,000

Pretax accounting incomes for Peabody, Sylvester, and Peabody and Sylvester Consolidated are as follows:

	Peabody	Sylvester	Consolidated
Sales	$300,000	$150,000	$390,000
Cost of sales	150,000*	70,000*	180,000*
Goodwill amortization (valuation differential)			10,000*
Depreciation expense	25,000*	15,000*	40,000*
Other expense	15,000*	5,000*	20,000*
Pretax accounting income	$110,000	$ 60,000	$140,000

* Deduct.

The $10,000 differential between consolidated taxable income and consolidated pretax accounting income lies in Peabody's goodwill amortization that is not deductible for tax purposes. Peabody sold inventory items to Sylvester for $60,000, and the $20,000 gross profit on the sale remains unrealized at December 31, 19X3.

Required
1 Show how the $51,000 consolidated income tax expense should be allocated to Peabody and Sylvester.
2 Compute Peabody's income from Sylvester on the basis of a one-line consolidation.
3 Prepare an income statement for Peabody Corporation for 19X3.
4 Prepare a consolidated income statement for Peabody Corporation and Subsidiary for 19X3.

11

CONSOLIDATION THEORIES, PUSH-DOWN ACCOUNTING, AND CORPORATE JOINT VENTURES

Previous chapters of this book have described practices used in the preparation of consolidated financial statements, and explained the rationale for those practices. The concepts and procedures discussed in earlier chapters reflect the **contemporary theory** of consolidated statements. This contemporary theory has evolved from accounting practice, and it does *not* reflect an interconsistent approach to the preparation of consolidated financial statements. Instead, contemporary theory reflects parts of both parent company theory (proprietary theory) and entity theory.[1]

Parent company theory is based on the assumption that consolidated financial statements are an extension of parent company statements and should be prepared from the viewpoint of parent company stockholders. Under parent company theory, consolidated statements are prepared for the benefit of the stockholders of the parent company, and it is not expected that minority stockholders can benefit significantly from the statements. Consolidated net income under parent company theory is a measurement of income to the parent company stockholders.

Certain problems and inconsistencies in accounting procedures under parent company theory arise in the case of less than 100 percent owned subsidiaries. For example, the minority interest is a liability from the viewpoint of parent company stockholders, and published statements frequently report the minority interest in the liability section of the consolidated balance sheet. Similarly, minority interest income is an expense from the viewpoint of majority stockholders. But shareholder interests, whether majority or minority, are not liabilities under any of the accepted concepts of a liability, and income to shareholders does not meet the requirements for expense recognition.[2] The problem lies in the majority shareholder viewpoint.

---

[1]Parent company theory is sometimes referred to as the *conventional theory* [for example, see Eldon S. Hendriksen, *Accounting Theory*, 4th ed. (Homewood, IL: Richard D. Irwin, 1982), p. 469]. As viewed here, however, the differences between parent company and contemporary theory are sufficiently important to merit separate identification.

[2]Hendriksen points out that probably the strongest justification for including minority interest with the liabilities or between the liabilities and capital is the fact that "the creditors of the parent have only a secondary claim against the assets of a subsidiary, on the same level as the claim of the minority interest." See *Accounting Theory*, p. 472.

438

CONSOLIDATION
THEORIES, PUSH-DOWN
ACCOUNTING, AND
CORPORATE JOINT
VENTURES

Entity theory represents an alternative view of consolidation. This theory was developed by Professor Maurice Moonitz and published by the American Accounting Association in 1944 under the title *The Entity Theory of Consolidated Statements.* The focal point of entity theory is that the consolidated statements reflect the viewpoint of the total business entity, under which all resources controlled by the entity are valued consistently. Under entity theory, the income of minority interests is a distribution of the total income of the consolidated entity, and the interests of minority stockholders are a part of consolidated stockholders' equity. Entity theory requires that the income and equity of a subsidiary be determined for all stockholders, so that the total amounts can be allocated between majority and minority shareholders in a consistent manner. This is accomplished under entity theory by imputing a total value for the subsidiary on the basis of the price paid by the parent company for its majority interest. The excess of total value of the subsidiary over the book value of subsidiary net assets is assigned 100 percent to identifiable assets and to goodwill. In this manner, subsidiary assets (including goodwill) and liabilities are consolidated at their fair values which are applicable to both minority and majority interests.

COMPARISON OF CONSOLIDATION THEORIES

The basic differences between parent company theory, entity theory, and contemporary theory are compared in Exhibit 11–1. Parent company theory adopts the viewpoint of parent company stockholders, and entity theory focuses on the total consolidated entity. By contrast, contemporary theory identifies the primary users of consolidated financial statements as the stockholders and creditors of the parent company, but assumes the objective of reporting financial position and results of operations of a single business entity. Thus, the viewpoint of contemporary theory, as reflected in *ARB No. 51,* appears to be a compromise between the parent company and entity theories.

Income Reporting

Consolidated net income is a measurement of income to parent company stockholders under both the parent company and contemporary theories. Entity theory, however, requires a computation of income to all equity holders, which is labeled "total consolidated net income." Total consolidated net income is then assigned to minority and majority stockholders, with appropriate disclosure on the face of the income statement. Consolidated net income under existing practice reflects parent company theory. This is evidenced by the practice of reporting minority interest income as an expense and the equity of minority stockholders as a liability. But the preferred accounting practices under contemporary theory are to show minority interest income as a separate deduction in the determination of consolidated net income, and to report the equity of minority shareholders as a single amount within the consolidated stockholders' equity classification.

Asset Valuation

Perhaps the greatest difference between parent company theory and entity theory lies in the valuation of subsidiary net assets. Under parent company theory, subsidiary assets are initially consolidated at their book values, plus the parent company's share of any excess of their fair values over their book values. In other words, subsidiary assets are revalued only to the extent of the net assets (including goodwill) acquired by the parent company. The minority interest in subsidiary assets is consolidated at book value. While this approach reflects the cost principle from the viewpoint of the parent company, it leads to inconsistent treatment of majority and minority interests in the consolidated financial statements, and

	Parent Company Theory	Entity Theory	Contemporary Theory
Basic purpose and users of consolidated financial statements:	Consolidated statements are an extension of parent company statements. They are prepared for the benefit and from the viewpoint of the stockholders of the parent company.	Consolidated statements are prepared from the viewpoint of the total consolidated entity and are intended for all parties having an interest in the entity.	Consolidated statements present the financial position and results of operations of a single business enterprise but are prepared primarily for the benefit of the stockholders and creditors of the parent company. (ARB No. 51, para. 2 and 7)
Consolidated net income:	Consolidated net income is income to the stockholders of the parent company.	Total consolidated net income is income to all equity holders of the consolidated entity.	Consolidated net income is income to the stockholders of the parent company.
Minority interest income:	Minority interest income is an expense from the viewpoint of the parent company stockholders. It is measured on the basis of the subsidiary as a separate legal entity.	Minority interest income is an allocation of total consolidated net income to minority stockholders.	Minority interest income is a deduction in determining consolidated net income, but not an expense. Instead, it is an allocation of realized income of the entity between majority and minority interests.
Equity of minority interests:	Equity of minority stockholders is a liability from the viewpoint of the parent company stockholders. Its measurement is based on the subsidiary's legal equity.	Equity of minority stockholders is a part of consolidated stockholders' equity. Its reporting is equivalent to the presentation accorded the equity of majority stockholders.	Equity of minority stockholders is a part of consolidated stockholders' equity. It is presented as a single amount because it is not expected that minority interests will benefit from the disclosure.
Consolidation of subsidiary net assets:	Parent's share of subsidiary net assets is consolidated on the basis of the price paid by the parent for its interest. The minority interest's share is consolidated at book value.	All net assets of a subsidiary are consolidated at their fair values imputed on the basis of the price paid by the parent for its interest. Thus, majority and minority interests in net assets are valued consistently.	Subsidiary net assets are consolidated at book value plus the excess of the parent company's investment cost over the book value of the interest acquired. The excess is required to be amortized over a maximum period of 40 years.
Unrealized gains and losses:	100% elimination from consolidated net income for downstream sales and elimination of the parent company's share for upstream sales.	100% elimination in determining total consolidated net income with allocation between majority and minority interests for upstream sales.	100% elimination from revenue and expense accounts with allocation between majority and minority interests for upstream sales. (ARB No. 51, para. 7 and 13)
Constructive gains and losses on debt retirement:	100% recognition in consolidated net income on retirement of parent company debt, and recognition of the parent company's share for retirement of subsidiary debt.	100% recognition in total consolidated net income with allocation between majority and minority interests for retirement of subsidiary debt.	100% recognition in revenue and expense accounts with allocation between majority and minority interests for retirement of subsidiary debt.

Exhibit 11-1 *Comparison of Consolidation Theories*

to a balance sheet valuation that reflects neither historical cost nor fair value. Under entity theory, subsidiary assets and liabilities are consolidated at their fair values, and the majority and minority interests in those net assets are accounted for consistently. But this consistent treatment is obtained through the questionable practice of imputing a total subsidiary valuation on the basis of the price paid by the parent company for its majority interest. Conceptually, this valuation approach has considerable appeal when the parent acquires essen-

440

CONSOLIDATION
THEORIES, PUSH-DOWN
ACCOUNTING, AND
CORPORATE JOINT
VENTURES

tially all of the subsidiary's stock for cash. It has much less appeal when the parent acquires a slim majority of subsidiary outstanding stock for noncash assets or through an exchange of shares. An investor may be willing to pay a premium for the right to *control* an investee (an investment of over 50 percent), but not willing to purchase the remaining stock at the inflated price.

Additional problems with the imputed total valuation of a subsidiary under entity theory develop after the parent company acquires its interest. *Once the parent is able to exercise absolute control over the subsidiary, the shares held by minority stockholders do not represent equity ownership in the usual sense.* What good is the right to vote when the outcome of the election is predetermined? For example, when Southmark Corp. filed for bankruptcy court protection on July 14, 1989, it owned 62.5 percent of National Heritage, Inc., a manager of nursing homes and retirement centers. At that time, National was planning a restructuring to spin off two subsidiaries to shareholders and to prevent Southmark from draining its cash. To prevent National's restructuring, Southmark (1) asked the bankruptcy judge to permanently enjoin National from completion of the restructuring without shareholder approval, (2) replaced National's board and named a Southmark director as the new chairman, (3) fired National's president and chief executive, and (4) changed National's corporate structure to merge the two subsidiaries into National so that they could not be spun off.[3] The vote of the 37.5 percent minority interest would have little effect on these actions.

When Shearson Lehman Hutton experienced financial difficulties in 1990, its 60 percent parent, American Express, announced a plan to buy back the minority shareholders' interest from the public. Although the price offered was fair in that it reflected the market value of the stock at the time, it may not have represented the real value of Shearson. As one reporter wrote, "Timing in such deals is everything. And American Express is choosing to buy shares of the country's second biggest brokerage firm at a time when Wall Street is undergoing its worst recession in years. . . . The plan to buy back the public's stock in Shearson shows the pitfalls of investing as a minority partner alongside a giant, majority shareholder."[4]

Typically, the stock of a subsidiary will be "delisted" after a business combination, leaving the parent company as the only viable purchaser for minority shares. In this case, minority shareholders are at the mercy of the parent company. A minority share does not have the same equity characteristics as a majority share.

Contemporary theory conforms to the practices of parent company theory in the consolidation of subsidiary assets and liabilities. Although a conceptual superiority for entity theory in this area is frequently granted, the practical disadvantages of entity theory are of more concern. The price paid by the parent company for its majority interest is not currently considered a valid basis for valuation of minority interests. Even the current practice of measuring the equity of minority shareholders at book value is criticized because it tends to overstate the value of the minority interest (primarily due to the restricted marketability of minority shares).

Unrealized Gains and Losses

A difference between the parent company and entity theories of consolidation also exists in the treatment of unrealized gains and losses from intercompany transactions (see Exhibit 11–1). Although there is general agreement that 100 percent of all unrealized gains and losses from downstream sales should be eliminated, gains and losses arising from upstream sales are accorded different treatment under parent company and entity theories. Under parent company theory, unrealized gains and losses from upstream sales are eliminated to the

---

[3]*The Wall Street Journal,* September 28, 1989, p. C10. Southmark's interest in National Heritage was later reduced to 22 percent. (July 31, 1990, p. B12)

[4]Roger Lowenstein, "Shearson Holders May Sing Buy-Back Blues Someday," *The Wall Street Journal,* March 6, 1990, p. C1.

extent of the parent company's ownership percentage in the subsidiary. The portion of unrealized gains and losses not eliminated relates to the minority interest and, from the parent company viewpoint, is considered to be realized by minority shareholders.

All unrealized gains and losses are eliminated in determining total consolidated net income under entity theory. In the case of upstream sales, however, the amounts eliminated are allocated between income to minority and majority stockholders according to their respective ownership percentages.

The elimination of unrealized gains and losses under contemporary theory follows the pattern and consistency of entity theory. All unrealized gains and losses are required to be eliminated under the provisions of *ARB No. 51,* paragraph 13, but "the elimination of the intercompany profit or loss may be allocated proportionately between the majority and minority interests." Presumably, the assignment of the full amount of unrealized gains and losses to majority interests would also be acceptable under *ARB No. 51.* This latter approach was not used in earlier chapters of this book because of its inherent inconsistency for consolidation purposes and because its use seems incompatible with requirements for the equity method of accounting. If unrealized gains and losses from upstream sales are not allocated between majority and minority interests, the parent company's income and equity will not equal consolidated net income and equity unless the same inconsistency is applied under the equity method.

Constructive Gains and Losses

The pattern of accounting for constructive gains and losses from intercompany debt acquisitions under the three theories parallels the pattern of accounting for unrealized gains and losses (see Exhibit 11–1). Gains and losses on the constructive retirement of debt under contemporary theory are accounted for in the same manner as under entity theory.

Many of the requirements of the contemporary theory of consolidation are specified by FASB Accounting Standards. As noted earlier in the chapter, these requirements do not constitute an interconsistent theory of consolidated financial statements, but rather they contain elements of both parent company theory and entity theory. Although the contemporary theory of consolidation lacks internal consistency, the theory does adhere reasonably well to other components of accounting theory, such as the cost principle and the basic elements of financial statements.

ILLUSTRATION—CONSOLIDATION UNDER PARENT COMPANY AND ENTITY THEORIES

Differences between the various consolidation theories may be more comprehensible when numerical examples are used. The following section relates to the purchase business combination of Pedrich and Sandy Corporations on December 31, 19X1. Assume that Pedrich Corporation acquires a 90 percent interest in Sandy Corporation for $2,160,000 cash on December 31, 19X1. Comparative balance sheets of the two companies immediately before the acquisition are as follows:

	Pedrich		Sandy	
	Book Value	*Fair Value*	*Book Value*	*Fair Value*
Cash	$2,200,000	$2,200,000	$ 50,000	$ 50,000
Accounts receivable—net	800,000	800,000	300,000	350,000
Inventory	900,000	1,000,000	400,000	500,000
Other current assets	200,000	200,000	100,000	100,000
Plant assets—net	2,200,000	3,000,000	600,000	800,000
Total assets	$6,300,000	$7,200,000	$1,450,000	$1,800,000

442

CONSOLIDATION
THEORIES, PUSH-DOWN
ACCOUNTING, AND
CORPORATE JOINT
VENTURES

	Pedrich		Sandy	
	Book Value	Fair Value	Book Value	Fair Value
Liabilities	$ 800,000	$ 800,000	$ 250,000	$ 250,000
Capital stock, $10 par	4,000,000 ⎫		1,000,000 ⎫	
Retained earnings	1,500,000 ⎬	6,400,000	200,000 ⎬	1,550,000
Total equities	$6,300,000	$7,200,000	$1,450,000	$1,800,000

The $2,160,000 purchase price for the 90 percent interest implies a $2,400,000 total value for Sandy Corporation's net assets ($2,160,000/90%). Under entity theory, all subsidiary assets and liabilities are revalued and reflected in the consolidated statements on the basis of the $2,400,000 implied total valuation. Under parent company theory, the total implied value is not reflected in the consolidated financial statements and, accordingly, only 90 percent of the subsidiary's net assets are revalued. Although *the different theories do not affect parent company accounting under the equity method,* they do result in different amounts for consolidated assets, liabilities, and minority interests.

In the Pedrich-Sandy example, the $1,200,000 excess of implied value over the $1,200,000 book value of Sandy's net assets under entity theory is assigned to identifiable net assets and goodwill as follows:

	Fair Value	Book Value	Excess Fair Value
Accounts receivable—net	$350,000 −	$300,000 = $	50,000
Inventories	500,000 −	400,000 =	100,000
Plant assets—net	800,000 −	600,000 =	200,000
Goodwill (remainder)	—	—	850,000
Total implied value over book value			$1,200,000

The amounts assigned to identifiable net assets and goodwill in accordance with parent company theory (and contemporary theory) would be 90 percent of the foregoing amounts:

Accounts receivable—net	$ 50,000 × 90% = $	45,000
Inventories	100,000 × 90% =	90,000
Plant assets—net	200,000 × 90% =	180,000
Goodwill	850,000 × 90% =	765,000
Total purchase price over book value acquired		$1,080,000

Goodwill under the two theories can be determined independently. Under entity theory, the $850,000 goodwill is equal to the total implied value of Sandy's net assets over the fair value of Sandy's net assets ($2,400,000 − $1,550,000). Under parent company theory, the $765,000 goodwill is equal to the investment cost less 90 percent of the fair value of Sandy's identifiable net assets ($2,160,000 − $1,395,000). The $120,000 additional amount assigned to identifiable assets and goodwill under entity theory ($1,200,000 − $1,080,000) is refleced in the minority interest classification in a consolidated balance sheet.

Consolidation at Acquisition

Consolidated balance sheet working papers for Pedrich Corporation and Subsidiary are compared in Exhibit 11–2 under parent company and entity theories. In examining the working papers, recall that contemporary theory is the same as parent company theory in matters relating to the initial consolidation of subsidiary assets and liabilities.

PEDRICH CORPORATION AND SUBSIDIARY
CONSOLIDATED BALANCE SHEET WORKING PAPERS
AT DECEMBER 31, 19X1

	Pedrich	90% Sandy	Adjustments and Eliminations		Consolidated
Parent Company Theory					
Assets					
Cash	$ 40,000	$ 50,000			$ 90,000
Accounts receivable—net	800,000	300,000	b 45,000		1,145,000
Inventories	900,000	400,000	b 90,000		1,390,000
Other current assets	200,000	100,000			300,000
Plant assets—net	2,200,000	600,000	b 180,000		2,980,000
Investment in Sandy	2,160,000			a 2,160,000	
Goodwill			b 765,000		765,000
Unamortized excess			a 1,080,000	b 1,080,000	
Total assets	$6,300,000	$1,450,000			$6,670,000
Liabilities and Equity					
Liabilities	$ 800,000	$ 250,000			$1,050,000
Capital stock	4,000,000	1,000,000	a 1,000,000		4,000,000
Retained earnings	1,500,000	200,000	a 200,000		1,500,000
Minority interest				a 120,000	120,000
Total equities	$6,300,000	$1,450,000			$6,670,000
Entity Theory					
Assets					
Cash	$ 40,000	$ 50,000			$ 90,000
Accounts receivable—net	800,000	300,000	b 50,000		1,150,000
Inventories	900,000	400,000	b 100,000		1,400,000
Other current assets	200,000	100,000			300,000
Plant assets—net	2,200,000	600,000	b 200,000		3,000,000
Investment in Sandy	2,160,000			a 2,160,000	
Goodwill			b 850,000		850,000
Unamortized excess			a 1,200,000	b 1,200,000	
Total assets	$6,300,000	$1,450,000			$6,790,000
Liabilities and Equity					
Liabilities	$ 800,000	$ 250,000			$1,050,000
Capital stock	4,000,000	1,000,000	a 1,000,000		4,000,000
Retained earnings	1,500,000	200,000	a 200,000		1,500,000
Minority interest				a 240,000	240,000
Total equities	$6,300,000	$1,450,000			$6,790,000

Exhibit 11–2 *Balance Sheet Working Paper Comparisons*

The comparative working papers in Exhibit 11–2 begin with separate balance sheets of the affiliated companies and use established procedures for consolidating the separate balance sheets. Although the working papers could be modified under parent company theory to reflect the minority interest among the liabilities, this modification does not seem necessary. Such classification differences can be reflected in the consolidated statements without changing working paper procedures. Under parent company theory, 90 percent of the excess of

444

CONSOLIDATION
THEORIES, PUSH-DOWN
ACCOUNTING, AND
CORPORATE JOINT
VENTURES

fair value over book value of identifiable net assets is allocated to identifiable assets and liabilities, and the $765,000 excess of investment cost over fair value acquired is allocated to goodwill. Minority interest of $120,000 for parent company theory is equal to 10 percent of the $1,200,000 book value of Sandy's net assets at the time of acquisition. Under entity theory, the full excess of fair value over book value is assigned to identifiable net assets, and the excess of implied value over fair value is entered as goodwill. The $240,000 minority interest is 10 percent of the implied value of Sandy's net assets.

Consolidated assets under parent company theory consist of the book value of combined assets plus 90 percent of the excess of the fair value of Sandy's assets over their book value. Under entity theory, consolidated assets consist of the book value of Pedrich's assets plus the fair value of Sandy's assets. Although all assets of Sandy are consolidated at their fair values, total consolidated assets do not reflect fair values under either theory. This is because the assets of the parent company are not revalued at the time of a business combination.

Consolidation After Acquisition

Differences between parent company theory and entity theory can be explained further by examining the operations of Pedrich Corporation and Sandy Corporation for 19X2. The following assumptions are made:

1 Sandy's net income and dividends for 19X2 are $350,000 and $100,000, respectively.
2 The excess of fair value over book value of Sandy's accounts receivable and inventories at December 31, 19X1 is realized during 19X2.
3 Sandy's plant assets are being depreciated at a 5 percent annual rate, and goodwill from consolidation is to be amortized over a forty-year period.

Under these assumptions, Pedrich records $151,875 investment income from Sandy for 19X2 computed under the equity method as follows:

Share of Sandy's net income ($350,000 × 90%)	$315,000
Less: Realization of excess allocated to receivables ($50,000 × 90%)	− 45,000
Realization of excess allocated to inventories ($100,000 × 90%)	− 90,000
Depreciation on excess allocated to plant assets ($200,000 × 90%)/20 years	− 9,000
Amortization of goodwill ($850,000 × 90%)/40 years	− 19,125
Income from Sandy for 19X2	$151,875

Pedrich's investment in Sandy account under the equity method has a balance of $2,221,875 at December 31, 19X2. This investment balance consists of the $2,160,000 investment cost plus $151,875 investment income for 19X2 less $90,000 dividends received from Sandy during 19X2. Accounting under the equity method is not affected by the viewpoint adopted for consolidating the financial statements of affiliated companies and, accordingly, *the separate statements of Pedrich and Sandy will be the same at December 31, 19X2 regardless of the theory adopted.* Also, consolidated net income under parent company theory is the same as the income allocated to parent company stockholders under entity theory. Therefore, the differences between parent company and entity theories lie solely in the manner of consolidating parent and subsidiary financial statements, and in reporting the financial position and results of operations in the consolidated financial statements. These differences are reflected in consolidation working papers for Pedrich Corporation and Subsidiary under parent company theory in Exhibit 11–3 and under entity theory in Exhibit 11–4. Again, the working paper procedures have not been modified to reflect differences in financial statement

PEDRICH CORPORATION AND SUBSIDIARY
CONSOLIDATION WORKING PAPERS—YEAR ENDED DECEMBER 31, 19X2

	Pedrich	90% Sandy	Adjustments and Eliminations			Minority Interests	Consolidated Statements
Income Statement Sales	$6,000,000	$2,000,000					$8,000,000
Income from Sandy	151,875		a	151,875			
Cost of sales	3,000,000*	1,200,000*	c	90,000			4,290,000*
Operating expenses	2,151,875*	450,000*	c d e	45,000 9,000 19,125			2,675,000*
Minority income†						$ 35,000	35,000*
Net income	$1,000,000	$ 350,000					$1,000,000
Retained Earnings Retained earnings	$1,500,000	$ 200,000	b	200,000			$1,500,000
Net income	1,000,000✔	350,000✔					1,000,000
Dividends	800,000*	100,000*			a 90,000	10,000*	800,000*
Retained earnings December 31, 19X2	$1,700,000	$ 450,000					$1,700,000
Balance Sheet Cash	$ 78,125	$ 130,000					$ 208,125
Accounts receivable—net	900,000	320,000					1,220,000
Inventories	1,000,000	480,000					1,480,000
Other current assets	300,000	170,000					470,000
Plant assets—net	2,000,000	570,000	c	180,000	d 9,000		2,741,000
Investment in Sandy	2,221,875				a 61,875 b 2,160,000		
Goodwill			c	765,000	e 19,125		745,875
Unamortized excess			b	1,080,000	c 1,080,000		
	$6,500,000	$1,670,000					$6,865,000
Liabilities	$ 800,000	$ 220,000					$1,020,000
Capital stock	4,000,000	1,000,000	b	1,000,000			4,000,000
Retained earnings	1,700,000✔	450,000✔					1,700,000
	$6,500,000	$1,670,000					
Minority interest January 1, 19X2					b 120,000	120,000	
Minority interest December 31, 19X2						$145,000	145,000
							$6,865,000

* Deduct.
† Minority interest income $350,000 × 10% = $35,000.

Exhibit 11–3 *Parent Company Theory*

classification. Differences in financial statement presentation for Pedrich Corporation and Subsidiary are illustrated in Exhibits 11–5 and 11–6, which show financial statements prepared from the working papers.

In comparing the consolidation working papers under parent company theory in Exhibit 11–3 with those under entity theory in Exhibit 11–4, note that the working paper adjustment and elimination entries have the same debit and

PEDRICH CORPORATION AND SUBSIDIARY
CONSOLIDATION WORKING PAPERS—YEAR ENDED DECEMBER 31, 19X2

	Pedrich	90% Sandy	Adjustments and Eliminations			Minority Interests	Consolidated Statements
Income Statement							
Sales	$6,000,000	$2,000,000					$8,000,000
Income from Sandy	151,875		a	151,875			
Cost of sales	3,000,000*	1,200,000*	c	100,000			4,300,000*
Operating expenses	2,151,875*	450,000*	c	50,000			2,683,125*
			d	10,000			
			e	21,250			
Minority income†						$ 16,875	16,875*
Net income	$1,000,000	$ 350,000					$1,000,000
Retained Earnings							
Retained earnings	$1,500,000	$ 200,000	b	200,000			$1,500,000
Net income	1,000,000✔	350,000✔					1,000,000
Dividends	800,000*	100,000*			a 90,000	10,000*	800,000*
Retained earnings December 31, 19X2	$1,700,000	$ 450,000					$1,700,000
Balance Sheet							
Cash	$ 78,125	$ 130,000					$ 208,125
Accounts receivable—net	900,000	320,000					1,220,000
Inventories	1,000,000	480,000					1,480,000
Other current assets	300,000	170,000					470,000
Plant assets—net	2,000,000	570,000	c 200,000		d 10,000		2,760,000
Investment in Sandy	2,221,875				a 61,875		
					b 2,160,000		
Goodwill			c 850,000		e 21,250		828,750
Unamortized excess			b 1,200,000		c 1,200,000		
	$6,500,000	$1,670,000					$6,966,875
Liabilities	$ 800,000	$ 220,000					$1,020,000
Capital stock	4,000,000	1,000,000	b 1,000,000				4,000,000
Retained earnings	1,700,000✔	450,000✔					1,700,000
	$6,500,000	$1,670,000					
Minority interest January 1, 19X2					b 240,000	240,000	
Minority interest December 31, 19X2						$246,875	246,875
							$6,966,875

* Deduct.
† Minority interest income ($350,000 − $181,250 amortization) × 10% = $16,875.

Exhibit 11–4 *Entity Theory*

credit items, but that the amounts are different for all working paper entries other than entry a. Since accounting for the subsidiary investment under the equity method is the same for both consolidation theories, the entry to eliminate investment income and intercompany dividends, and to adjust the investment account to its beginning-of-the-period balance (entry a), is exactly the same under parent company theory as under entity theory.

The remaining adjustment and elimination entries in Exhibit 11–3 under parent company theory are the same as under the contemporary theory used in earlier chapters. Entry b eliminates reciprocal subsidiary equity amounts, establishes beginning minority interest at book value ($1,200,000 × 10%) and enters the unamortized excess. Entry c then allocates the excess of investment cost over book value acquired: $90,000 to cost of sales (for undervalued inventory items realized during 19X2), $45,000 to operating expense (for undervalued receivables realized during 19X2), $180,000 to plant assets (for undervalued plant assets at the beginning of 19X2), and $765,000 to goodwill (for unamortized goodwill at the beginning of 19X2). Entries d and e reflect current depreciation on the excess allocated to plant assets ($180,000 × 5%) and current amortization on the amount allocated to goodwill ($765,000/40 years), respectively. Minority interest income of $35,000 is simply 10 percent of Sandy's $350,000 reported net income.

Entries b, c, d, and e in Exhibit 11–4 under entity theory have the same objective as those for the same items under parent company theory except for amounts that relate to the minority interest. Beginning minority interest under entity theory is $240,000, equal to 10 percent of the $2,400,000 implied total value of Sandy Corporation at December 31, 19X1. The additional $120,000 allocation to beginning minority interest under entity theory relates $10,000 to cost of sales for undervalued inventory items realized during 19X2 (total $100,000 rather than $90,000 under parent company theory), $5,000 to operating expenses for undervalued receivables realized during 19X2 (total $50,000 rather than $45,000 under parent company theory), $20,000 to undervalued plant assets at the beginning of 19X2 (total $200,000 rather than $180,000 under parent company theory), and $85,000 to goodwill (total $850,000 rather than $765,000 under parent company theory. These *additional* amounts under entity theory are illustrated in journal form as follows:

b	Unamortized excess	$120,000	
	Minority interest January 19X2		$120,000
c	Cost of sales	$ 10,000	
	Operating expenses	5,000	
	Plant assets—net	20,000	
	Goodwill	85,000	
	Unamortized excess		$120,000

In other words, working paper entry b under entity theory is equivalent to entry b under parent company theory plus the additional $120,000 unamortized excess applicable to minority interest. Similarly, entry c under entity theory is equivalent to entry c under parent company theory plus the additional amounts included in the preceding explanation of the difference.

Working paper entry d for depreciation on the excess allocated to plant assets is $10,000 under entity theory, compared with $9,000 under parent company theory. The $1,000 difference is simply the 5 percent depreciation rate applied to the additional $20,000 allocated to plant assets under entity theory. Current amortization of goodwill under entity theory (entry e) is $21,250 compared with $19,125 under parent company theory. The $2,125 difference is equal to one-fortieth of the additional $85,000 assigned to goodwill under entity theory.

Minority interest income under entity theory is $16,875 (Exhibit 11–4) compared with $35,000 under parent company theory (Exhibit 11–3). The $18,125 difference lies in the following greater expenses under entity theory:

448

CONSOLIDATION
THEORIES, PUSH-DOWN
ACCOUNTING, AND
CORPORATE JOINT
VENTURES

PEDRICH CORPORATION AND SUBSIDIARY
CONSOLIDATED INCOME STATEMENTS
FOR THE YEAR ENDED DECEMBER 31, 19X2

Parent Company Theory		
Sales		$8,000,000
Less: Cost of sales	$4,290,000	
Operating expenses	2,675,000	
Minority interest income	35,000	
Total expenses		7,000,000
Consolidated net income		$1,000,000
Entity Theory		
Sales		$8,000,000
Less: Cost of sales	$4,300,000	
Operating expenses	2,683,125	
Total expenses		6,983,125
Total consolidated net income		$1,016,875
Distribution: to minority stockholders	$ 16,875	
to majority stockholders	$1,000,000	
Contemporary Theory		
Sales		$8,000,000
Less: Cost of sales	$4,290,000	
Operating expenses	2,675,000	
Total expenses		6,965,000
Total consolidated income		1,035,000
Less: Minority interest income		35,000
Consolidated net income		$1,000,000

Exhibit 11–5   *Consolidated Income Statements Under Alternative Theories*

Cost of sales (for inventory)	$10,000
Operating expenses (for receivables)	5,000
Operating expenses (for depreciation)	1,000
Operating expenses (for goodwill)	2,125
Total difference	$18,125

Comparison of Consolidated Income Statements   The $18,125 additional expenses that are deducted in determining total consolidated net income under entity theory are exactly offset by the lower minority interest income. Thus, income to the parent company stockholders is the same under the two theories, even though there are differences in the amounts reported and in the way the amounts are disclosed in the consolidated income statements. These differences are shown in Exhibit 11–5, which compares consolidated income statements for Pedrich Corporation and Subsidiary under parent company theory, entity theory, and contemporary theory.

Consolidated net income under parent company theory is the same as under contemporary theory; however, contemporary theory does not show minority interest income as an expense. The reporting of income under entity theory shows a final amount for "Total Consolidated Net Income" of $1,016,875 and distribution of that income to minority and parent company stockholders. Although the amounts shown for Pedrich Corporation and Subsidiary are identical under parent company and contemporary theories, this equivalence would not have existed if there had been unrealized profits from upstream sales or constructive gains or losses from intercompany purchases of subsidiary debt. Consolidation procedures for these items are the same under contemporary theory as under entity theory.

PEDRICH CORPORATION AND SUBSIDIARY
CONSOLIDATED BALANCE SHEETS
AT DECEMBER 31, 19X2

	Parent Company Theory	Entity Theory	Contemporary Theory
Assets			
Cash	$ 208,125	$ 208,125	$ 208,125
Accounts receivable—net	1,220,000	1,220,000	1,220,000
Inventories	1,480,000	1,480,000	1,480,000
Other current assets	470,000	470,000	470,000
Total current assets	3,378,125	3,378,125	3,378,125
Plant assets—net	2,741,000	2,760,000	2,741,000
Goodwill	745,875	828,750	745,875
Total noncurrent assets	3,486,875	3,588,750	3,486,875
Total assets	$6,865,000	$6,966,875	$6,865,000
Liabilities and Equity			
Liabilities	$1,020,000	$1,020,000	$1,020,000
Minority interest	145,000	—	—
Total liabilities	1,165,000	1,020,000	1,020,000
Capital stock	4,000,000	4,000,000	4,000,000
Retained earnings	1,700,000	1,700,000	1,700,000
Minority interest	—	246,875	145,000
Total stockholders' equity	5,700,000	5,946,875	5,845,000
Total equities	$6,865,000	$6,966,875	$6,865,000

Exhibit 11–6   *Consolidated Balance Sheets Under Alternative Theories*

Although the reporting formats under the three consolidation theories vary somewhat, it may be helpful to note the following relationships:

1   If a subsidiary investment is made at book value and the book values of individual assets and liabilities are equal to their fair values, the income statement amounts should be the same under entity theory as under contemporary theory.
2   In the absence of intercompany transactions, the income statement amounts should be the same under parent company theory as under contemporary theory.
3   In the absence of minority interests, the income statement amounts should be the same under all three theories.

Comparison of Consolidated Balance Sheets   Comparative balance sheets for Pedrich Corporation and Subsidiary at December 31, 19X2 are illustrated in Exhibit 11–6 under each of the three theories. The amount of total assets is the same under parent company and contemporary theories but is greater under entity theory. The difference in total assets is $101,875 ($6,966,875 − $6,865,000) and consists of the unamortized excess of implied value over book value of Sandy's net assets. This difference relates to goodwill, $82,875 ($85,000 − $2,125) and plant assets of $19,000 ($20,000 − $1,000).

Total liabilities and equity are the same under parent company theory and contemporary theory, but liabilities are $145,000 greater under parent company theory, where minority interest is classified as a liability. Stockholders' equity is $145,000 greater under contemporary theory where minority interest is classified as a part of stockholders' equity.

The difference between total liabilities and equity under the entity and contemporary theories lies solely in the $101,875 ($246,875 − $145,000) greater minority interest under entity theory. As in the case of the income generalizations, balance sheet amounts under the parent company and contemporary

450

CONSOLIDATION
THEORIES, PUSH-DOWN
ACCOUNTING, AND
CORPORATE JOINT
VENTURES

theories will be the same in the absence of intercompany transactions, and under entity and contemporary theories in the absence of a difference between invest-ment cost and book value acquired. In the absence of minority interests, all balance sheet amounts should be identical under the three theories.

Other Views of Minority Interest Some accountants believe that minority interest should not appear as a separate line item in consolidated financial statements. One suggestion for eliminating minority interest from consolidated statements is to report total consolidated income as the bottom line in the con-solidated income statements with separate *footnote disclosure* of majority and minority interests in the income. Consistent treatment in the consolidated balance sheet would require total consolidated equity to be reported as a single line item with separate footnote disclosure of the equity of majority and minority interests.

Another suggestion for excluding reference to minority interest in con-solidated financial statements is to consolidate only the majority-owned portion of the revenues, expenses, assets, and liabilities of less than 100 percent owned subsidiaries. Proportional consolidation is discussed in the last section of this chapter under accounting for corporate joint ventures.

PUSH-DOWN ACCOUNTING AND OTHER BASIS CONSIDERATIONS

Under the contemporary, entity, and parent company theories discussed in the first section of this chapter, cost–book value differentials were allocated to the individual identifiable assets and liabilities and goodwill by working paper entries in the process of consolidating the financial statements of the parent and sub-sidiary. The books of the subsidiary were not affected by the price paid by the parent for its ownership interest.

In certain situations, the Securities and Exchange Commission (SEC) requires that the fair values of the acquired subsidiary's assets and liabilities, which represent the parent company's cost basis under the provisions of *APB Opinion No. 16*, be recorded in the separate financial statements of the purchased subsidiary. In other words, the values are "pushed down" to the subsidiary's statements.[5] The SEC requires the use of push-down accounting for SEC filings when a subsidiary is substantially wholly owned (usually 97 percent) with no substantial publicly held debt or preferred stock outstanding.

The SEC's argument is that when the parent controls the form of owner-ship of an entity, the basis of accounting for purchased assets and liabilites should be the same regardless of whether the entity continues to exist or is merged into the parent's operations. However, when a subsidiary has outstanding public debt or preferred stock, or when a significant minority interest exists, the parent com-pany may not be able to control the form of ownership. The SEC encourages push-down accounting in these circumstances, but does not require it.

The AICPA Issues Paper "Push-Down Accounting" (October 30, 1979) describes **push-down accounting** as:

> The establishment of a new accounting and reporting basis for an entity in its separate financial statements, based on a purchase transaction in the voting stock of the entity, that results in a substantial change of ownership of the outstanding voting stock of the entity.

When push-down accounting is not used in an acquisition, the allocation of the purchase price to identifiable net assets and goodwill is done in the con-solidation working papers. The consolidated financial statements reflect the pur-

---

[5]*SEC Staff Accounting Bulletin*, No. 54, 1983. For further clarification of the SEC's position, see *Staff Accounting Bulletin*, No. 73, 1987.

chase allocation. If the subsidiary records the allocation in its financial statements under push-down accounting, the consolidation process is simplified.

Push-down accounting is controversial only in the separate company statements of the subsidiary that are issued to minority interests, creditors, and other interested parties. Critics of push-down accounting argue that the purchase transaction between the parent company/investor and the subsidiary's old stockholders does not justify a new accounting basis for the subsidiary's assets and liabilities under historical cost principles. The subsidiary is not a party to the transaction—it receives no new funds; it sells no assets. Proponents counter that the price paid by the new owners provides the most relevant basis for measuring the subsidiary's assets, liabilities, and results of operations.

Push-down accounting is not consistently applied among the supporters of the concept although in practice a subsidiary's assets are usually revalued on a proportional basis. What percentage of minority interest constitutes a significant minority interest that would preclude the use of push-down accounting? Should the allocation be done on a proportional basis if less than a 100 percent change in ownership has occurred?[6] These are questions in need of authoritative answers. In the illustration that follows, the Pedrich-Sandy example is extended using both a proportional allocation for the purchase of a 90 percent interest in Sandy (a parent company theory approach) and a 100 percent allocation in which the entity's market value as a whole is imputed from the purchase of the 90 percent interest (an entity theory approach).

Push-Down Procedures in Year of Acquisition

Recall that Pedrich acquired its 90 percent interest for $2,160,000 cash on December 31, 19X1 (see page 441). If push-down accounting is used and only 90 percent of Sandy's identifiable net assets are revalued (parent company theory), the $1,080,000 cost-book value differential is allocated as follows:

	Book Value	Push-Down Adjustment	Book Value After Push Down
Cash	$ 50,000	—	$ 50,000
Accounts receivable—net	300,000	$ 45,000	345,000
Inventory	400,000	90,000	490,000
Other current assets	100,000	—	100,000
Plant assets—net	600,000	180,000	780,000
Goodwill	—	765,000	765,000
	$1,450,000	$1,080,000	$2,530,000
Liabilities	$ 250,000	—	$ 250,000
Capital stock	1,000,000	—	1,000,000
Push-down capital	—	$1,280,000	1,280,000
Retained earnings	200,000	(200,000)	—
	$1,450,000	$1,080,000	$2,530,000

---

[6]Colley and Volcan argue that once an entity controls another entity through stock ownership of over 50 percent, the minority stockholders are not owners in the usual sense. There is only one owner, the parent, and the minority holders are "investors." They contend that this argument supports the use of push-down accounting for all majority-owned subsidiaries and, further, that it supports a total revaluation approach (in other words, imputing values for 100 percent of the subsidiary's net assets). See J. Ron Colley and Ara G. Volcan, "Business Combinations: Goodwill and Push-Down Accounting," *Accounting Horizons* (September 1989), pp. 38–43.

452

CONSOLIDATION
THEORIES, PUSH-DOWN
ACCOUNTING, AND
CORPORATE JOINT
VENTURES

The push-down adjustment on Sandy's separate books is recorded as follows:

Accounts receivable	$ 45,000	
Inventory	90,000	
Plant assets	180,000	
Goodwill	765,000	
Retained earnings	200,000	
Push-down capital		$1,280,000

If a total value of $2,400,000 is imputed from the purchase price of the 90 percent interest in Sandy under entity theory ($2,160,000 cost/90%), the $1,200,000 excess is pushed down on Sandy's books as follows:

	Book Value	Push-Down Adjustment	Book Value After Push Down
Cash	$ 50,000	—	$ 50,000
Accounts receivable—net	300,000	$ 50,000	350,000
Inventory	400,000	100,000	500,000
Other current assets	100,000	—	100,000
Plant assets—net	600,000	200,000	800,000
Goodwill	—	850,000	850,000
	$1,450,000	$1,200,000	$2,650,000
Liabilities	$ 250,000	—	$ 250,000
Capital stock	1,000,000	—	1,000,000
Push-down capital	—	$1,400,000	1,400,000
Retained earnings	200,000	(200,000)	—
	$1,450,000	$1,200,000	$2,650,000

The entry to record the 100 percent push-down adjustment on Sandy's separate books is:

Accounts receivable	$ 50,000	
Inventory	100,000	
Plant assets	200,000	
Goodwill	850,000	
Retained earnings	200,000	
Push-down capital		$1,400,000

Observe that the balance of Sandy's retained earnings account is transferred to push-down capital regardless of whether the push down is for 90 percent or 100 percent of the fair value–book value differential. This treatment is basic to push-down accounting that requires a new accounting and reporting basis for the acquired entity. Push-down capital is an additional paid-in capital account that includes both the revaluation of subsidiary identifiable net assets and goodwill based upon the price paid to acquire the subsidiary, and the subsidiary's retained earnings account balance that is eliminated under the new entity concept of push-down accounting.

Consolidated balance sheet working papers to illustrate the effect of the push-down adjustments are presented in Exhibit 11–7. The balance sheet worksheet at the top of the exhibit reflects the 90 percent push-down adjustment that is compatible with parent company theory, and the worksheet at the bottom reflects the 100 percent push-down adjustment that is compatible with entity theory. Because the push-down adjustments are included in Sandy's separate balance sheets in Exhibit 11–7, the consolidation procedures are greatly simplified

PEDRICH CORPORATION AND SUBSIDIARY
CONSOLIDATED BALANCE SHEET WORKING PAPERS
AT DECEMBER 31, 19X1

	Pedrich	90% Sandy	Adjustments and Eliminations	Consolidated
Push Down 90%—Parent Theory				
Assets				
Cash	$ 40,000	$ 50,000		$ 90,000
Accounts receivable—net	800,000	345,000		1,145,000
Inventories	900,000	490,000		1,390,000
Other current assets	200,000	100,000		300,000
Plant assets—net	2,200,000	780,000		2,980,000
Investment in Sandy	2,160,000		a 2,160,000	
Goodwill		765,000		765,000
Total assets	$6,300,000	$2,530,000		$6,670,000
Equities				
Liabilities	$ 800,000	$ 250,000		$1,050,000
Common stock	4,000,000	1,000,000	a 1,000,000	4,000,000
Push-down capital—Sandy		1,280,000	a 1,280,000	
Retained earnings	1,500,000	0		1,500,000
Minority interest			a 120,000	120,000
Total equities	$6,300,000	$2,530,000		$6,670,000
Push Down 100%—Entity Theory				
Assets				
Cash	$ 40,000	$ 50,000		$ 90,000
Accounts receivable—net	800,000	350,000		1,150,000
Inventories	900,000	500,000		1,400,000
Other current assets	200,000	100,000		300,000
Plant assets—net	2,200,000	800,000		3,000,000
Investment in Sandy	2,160,000		a 2,160,000	
Goodwill		850,000		850,000
Total assets	$6,300,000	$2,650,000		$6,790,000
Equities				
Liabilities	$ 800,000	$ 250,000		$1,050,000
Common stock	4,000,000	1,000,000	a 1,000,000	4,000,000
Push-down capital—Sandy		1,400,000	a 1,400,000	
Retained earnings	1,500,000	0		1,500,000
Minority interest			a 240,000	240,000
Total equities	$6,300,000	$2,650,000		$6,790,000

Exhibit 11–7   Push-Down Accounting: Parent Company versus Entity Approach

in relation to those illustrated in Exhibit 11–2. The simplification results from not having to allocate unamortized cost–book value differentials in the working papers under push-down accounting. The consolidated balance sheet amounts, however, are identical in Exhibit 11–7 under push-down accounting and in Exhibit 11–2 where the subsidiary balance sheets are maintained on an original cost basis.

454

CONSOLIDATION
THEORIES, PUSH-DOWN
ACCOUNTING, AND
CORPORATE JOINT
VENTURES

Push-Down Procedures in Year After Acquisition

Consolidated financial statement working papers for Pedrich and Sandy Corporations under push-down accounting procedures are illustrated for the year ended December 31, 19X2 in Exhibits 11–8 and 11–9. Exhibit 11–8 reflects the 90 percent push-down adjustment of parent company theory, and Exhibit 11–9 reflects the 100 percent push-down adjustment under entity theory. In both exhibits, the consolidation procedures are greatly simplified in relation to the comparable working papers for Pedrich and Sandy shown in Exhibits 11–3 and 11–4. As in the case of consolidated balance sheets, however, the amounts shown in the consolidated financial statements are identical.

In the consolidation working papers of Exhibit 11–9 (entity theory), the minority interest income of $16,875 is equal to 10 percent of Sandy's $168,750 net income as measured under push-down accounting procedures. Similarly, the $246,875 minority interest at December 31, 19X2 is equal to 10 percent of Sandy's $2,468,750 stockholders' equity on that date. These minority interest items are determined under standard consolidation procedures. By contrast, the $35,000 minority interest income for 19X2 and the $145,000 minority interest at December 31, 19X2 in Exhibit 11–8 (parent company theory) do not have a direct reference to the $186,875 net income of Sandy or the $2,366,875 stockholders' equity of Sandy, as shown in Sandy's separate income statement and balance sheet under 90 percent push-down accounting. This is a problem that arises in the use of push-down accounting for less than a 100 percent owned subsidiary where only the parent's percentage interest is pushed down on the subsidiary's books. In this case, separate cost-based records must be maintained by the subsidiary. The minority interest amount in Exhibit 11–8 can be determined directly from Sandy's separate cost-based statements as shown in Exhibit 11–3 (page 445). Since minority shareholders are not expected to get meaningful information from consolidated financial statements, especially when the affiliated group has multiple partially owned subsidiaries, the 100 percent push-down approach under entity theory may be preferable.

Leveraged Buyouts

In a **leveraged buyout** (LBO), an investor group (often including company management, an investment banker, and financial institutions) acquires a company (Company A) from the public shareholders in a transaction financed with very little equity and very large amounts of debt. Usually, the investor group raises the money for the buyout by investing perhaps 10 percent of their own money and borrowing the rest. A holding company may be formed to acquire the shares of Company A. Usually debt raised by the investor group to finance the LBO is partially secured by Company A's own assets and is serviced with funds generated by Company A's operations and/or the sale of its assets. Because the loans are secured by Company A's assets, banks loaning money to the investor group often require that the debt appear on Company A's financial statements. If the previous owners were paid a high premium for their stock, which is often the case, and book values, rather than fair values, of the assets and liabilities are carried forward to the balance sheet of the new company (the acquired Company A), the debt incurred in the LBO may cause the new company's financial condition to look worse than it is. The popularity of LBOs is one reason many accountants support a change to push-down accounting for acquisitions, including LBOs, that would allow the assets of the acquired firm to be written up on its financial statements to reflect the purchase price.

For several years, the SEC and the FASB's emerging issues task force (EITF) wrestled with the question of whether fair values or book values (predecessor basis) should be carried forward in LBOs. Answers were finally provided in May

PEDRICH CORPORATION AND SUBSIDIARY
CONSOLIDATION WORKING PAPERS—YEAR ENDED DECEMBER 31, 19X2

	Pedrich	90% Sandy	Adjustments and Eliminations		Minority Interests	Consolidated Statements
Push Down 90%—Parent Theory						
Income Statement						
Sales	$6,000,000	$2,000,000				$8,000,000
Income from Sandy	151,875		a	151,875		
Cost of sales	3,000,000*	1,290,000*				4,290,000*
Operating expenses	2,151,875*	523,125*				2,675,000*
Minority income					$ 35,000	35,000*
Net income	$1,000,000	$ 186,875				$1,000,000
Retained Earnings						
Retained earnings	$1,500,000	$ 0				$1,500,000
Net income	1,000,000✓	186,875✓				1,000,000
Dividends	800,000*	100,000*	a	90,000	10,000*	800,000*
Retained earnings December 31, 19X2	$1,700,000	$ 86,875				$1,700,000
Balance Sheet						
Cash	$ 78,125	$ 130,000				$ 208,125
Accounts receivable—net	900,000	320,000				1,220,000
Inventories	1,000,000	480,000				1,480,000
Other current assets	300,000	170,000				470,000
Plant assets—net	2,000,000	741,000				2,741,000
Investment in Sandy	2,221,875		a	61,875		
			b	2,160,000		
Goodwill		745,875				745,875
	$6,500,000	$2,586,875				$6,865,000
Liabilities	$ 800,000	$ 220,000				$1,020,000
Capital stock	4,000,000	1,000,000	b	1,000,000		4,000,000
Push-down capital—Sandy		1,280,000	b	1,280,000		
Retained earnings	1,700,000✓	86,875✓				1,700,000
	$6,500,000	$2,586,875				
Minority interest January 1, 19X2			b	120,000	120,000	
Minority interest December 31, 19X2					$145,000	145,000
						$6,865,000

* Deduct.

Exhibit 11-8   *Push-Down Accounting—Parent Company Approach*

1989 in the EITF consensus Issue No. 88-16, "Basis in Leveraged Buyout Transactions." The structure of a buyout influences the accounting basis. For example, a holding company may be used to acquire the net assets of Company A, a holding company may be used to acquire the equity of Company A, or an investor group may acquire Company A without using a holding company. The EITF consensus applies to LBOs in which a holding company is used to acquire all the equity of an operating company in a highly leveraged acquisition and sets forth tests

PEDRICH CORPORATION AND SUBSIDIARY
CONSOLIDATION WORKING PAPERS—YEAR ENDED DECEMBER 31, 19X2

	Pedrich	90% Sandy	Adjustments and Eliminations		Minority Interests	Consolidated Statements
Push Down 100%—Entity Theory						
Income Statement						
Sales	$6,000,000	$2,000,000				$8,000,000
Income from Sandy	151,875		a	151,875		
Cost of sales	3,000,000*	1,300,000*				4,300,000*
Operating expenses	2,151,875*	531,250*				2,683,125*
Minority income					$ 16,875	16,875*
Net income	$1,000,000	$ 168,750				$1,000,000
Retained Earnings						
Retained earnings	$1,500,000	$ 0				$1,500,000
Net income	1,000,000✓	168,750✓				1,000,000
Dividends	800,000*	100,000*	a	90,000	10,000*	800,000*
Retained earnings December 31, 19X2	$1,700,000	$ 68,750				$1,700,000
Balance Sheet						
Cash	$ 78,125	$ 130,000				$ 208,125
Accounts receivable—net	900,000	320,000				1,220,000
Inventories	1,000,000	480,000				1,480,000
Other current assets	300,000	170,000				470,000
Plant assets—net	2,000,000	760,000				2,760,000
Investment in Sandy	2,221,875		a b	61,875 2,160,000		
Goodwill		828,750				828,750
	$6,500,000	$2,688,750				$6,966,875
Liabilities	$ 800,000	$ 220,000				$1,020,000
Capital stock	4,000,000	1,000,000	b	1,000,000		4,000,000
Push-down capital—Sandy		1,400,000	b	1,400,000		
Retained earnings	1,700,000✓	68,750✓				1,700,000
	$6,500,000	$2,688,750				
Minority interest January 1, 19X2			b	240,000	240,000	
Minority interest December 31, 19X2					$246,875	246,875
						$6,966,875

* Deduct.

Exhibit 11–9   Push-Down Accounting—Entity Approach

for determining whether the LBO results in a change of the controlling interest. If there has been a change in control, a change in accounting basis is generally appropriate. The consensus provides complex rules based on the residual interest of each continuing shareholder for determining the accounting basis for the assets and liabilities carried forward to the books of the new entity. The final valuation in the subsidiary's books may be pre-LBO book values, fair values, or something in between, for example, 95 percent fair value and 5 percent book (predecessor) value.

Criticism of the consensus generally centers on its complexity, but it has also been challenged on conceptual grounds. In particular, critics do not like the resulting accounting basis if it reflects part fair value and part book value. The EITF argues that the method puts substance ahead of form—the new entity has new controlling shareholders and is similar to a purchase business combination.

Another Accounting Basis Solution

In some situations in which goodwill from an acquisition is recorded in the subsidiary's accounts, the amortization can depress subsidiary earnings for years. But it may be possible to structure an acquisition to avoid this problem. For example, Dow Chemical Company wished to acquire Marion Laboratories, Inc., in 1989 but at the same time keep goodwill at a minimum. Dow accomplished this by becoming two-thirds owner of a new company, Marion Merrell Dow, Inc. Dow purchased 39 percent of Marion Laboratories' shares and gained a lockup of voting proxies on another 13 percent. This gave Dow control of 52 percent of Marion Laboratories. Then Dow contributed the stock of its subsidiary, Merrell Dow Pharmaceuticals, Inc., to Marion Laboratories for an additional 15 percent equity. Marion Laboratories and Merrell Dow were then merged into a new corporation, Marion Merrell Dow. This was a tax-free exchange between companies under common control, in other words, a book value transfer. The only goodwill that the new company, Marion Merrell Dow, will have on its balance sheet is that acquired by the two,combining companies before the merger. Dow (the parent) will reflect cost–book value differentials (including goodwill) on its balance sheet when it prepares consolidated financial statements with its 67 percent owned subsidiary.[7]

JOINT VENTURES

A **joint venture** is a form of partnership that originated with the maritime trading expeditions of the Greeks and Romans. The objective was to combine management participants and capital contributors in undertakings limited to the completion of specific trading projects. In recent times the joint venture has taken many different forms such as partnership and corporate, domestic and foreign, and temporary as well as relatively permanent.

A common type of joint venture of the temporary type is the formation of syndicates of investment bankers to purchase securities from an issuing corporation and market them to the public. The joint venture enables several participants to share in the risks and rewards of undertakings that would be too large or too risky for a single venturer. It also enables them to combine technology, markets, and human resources to enhance the profit potential of all participants. Other areas in which joint ventures are common are land sales, oil exploration and drilling, and major construction projects. Examples of some joint venture projects are as follows:

> Texaco, Inc. (a 35 percent participant) and British Petroleum Co. (a 65 percent participant) agreed to combine their Rotterdam refineries under the name of Rijnmond Raffinaderji BV.[8]

> General Mills, Inc., joined Nestlé SA (the world's largest food company) to sell cereals in all markets except the United States and Canada (where General Mills already has a 25 percent share of the cereal market). The joint venture agreement contains a standstill provision that neither partner will try to gain control of the other.[9]

---

[7]"The Dow-Marion Linkage: A Restructuring in Reverse," *Mergers & Acquisitions* (November/December 1989), pp. 8–9.

[8]*Mergers & Acquisitions* (January/February 1990), p. 20.

[9]*Merqers & Acquisitions* (March/April 1990), p. 20.

458

CONSOLIDATION
THEORIES, PUSH-DOWN
ACCOUNTING, AND
CORPORATE JOINT
VENTURES

Merck & Co., Inc., and Johnson & Johnson created a 50:50 venture called Johnson & Johnson Merck Consumer Pharmaceuticals Co. to develop and market new and current prescription drugs.[10]

Texas Instruments, Inc., and Kobe Steel Ltd. of Japan (majority interest) will manufacture customized chips in a joint venture company, KTI Semiconductor Ltd.[11]

USX Corporation (a 50 percent participant) and Kobe Steel Ltd. of Japan (a 50 percent participant) plan to build a steel processing facility in Leipsic, Ohio.[12]

National Broadcasting Company and Cablevision Systems Corporation joined in a $300 million, 50:50 joint venture to combine NBC's Consumer and Business News Channel and the Rainbow Programming unit of Cablevision.[13]

Nature of Joint Ventures

A **joint venture** is a business entity that is owned, operated, and jointly controlled by a small group of investors (**venturers**) for the conduct of a specific business undertaking that provides mutual benefit for each of the venturers. It is common for each venturer to be active in the management of the venture, and to participate in important decisions that typically require the consent of each venturer irrespective of ownership interest. Ownership percentages vary widely, and unequal ownership interests in a specific venture are commonplace.

Organizational Structures of Joint Ventures

Joint ventures may be organized as corporations, partnerships, or undivided interests. These forms are defined in the AICPA's Statement of Position "Accounting for Investment in Real Estate Ventures" (SOP 78-9) as follows:

> Corporate Joint Venture—A corporation owned and operated by a small group of venturers to accomplish a mutually beneficial venture or project.
> General Partnership—An association in which each partner has unlimited liability.
> Limited Partnership—An association in which one or more general partners have unlimited liability and one or more partners have limited liability. A limited partnership is usually managed by the general partner or partners, subject to limitations, if any, imposed by the partnership agreement.
> Undivided Interest—An ownership arrangement in which two or more parties jointly own property and title is held individually to the extent of each party's interest.

Financial reporting requirements for the investors in ventures differ according to the organizational structures.

Accounting for Corporate Joint Ventures

Investors that can participate in the overall management of a *corporate joint venture* should report their investments as equity investments (one-line consolidations) under the provisions of *APB Opinion No. 18*. The approach for establishing significant influence in corporate joint ventures is quite different from that for most common stock investments because *each venturer* usually has to consent to *each significant venture decision,* thus establishing an ability to exercise significant influence regardless of ownership interest. Even so, when a venturer cannot exercise

---

[10]*Mergers & Acquisitions* (July/August 1989), p. 20.
[11]*Mergers & Acquisitions* (July/August 1990), p. 23.
[12]*Mergers & Acquisitions* (July/August 1990), p. 23.
[13]*Mergers & Acquisitions* (March/April 1989), p. 14.

significant influence over its joint venture investee for whatever reason, its investment in the venture is accounted for by the *cost method.*

An investment in the common stock of a corporate joint venture that exceeds 50 percent of the venture's outstanding shares is a *subsidiary investment* for which parent-subsidiary accounting and reporting requirements are applicable. A corporate joint venture that is more that 50 percent owned by another entity is not considered a joint venture for purposes of applying the provisions of *APB Opinion No. 18,* even though it continues to be described as a joint venture in financial releases.

Corporate joint ventures are described in *Opinion 18,* paragraph 2d as follows:

> "Corporate joint venture" refers to a corporation owned and operated by a small group of businesses (the "joint venturers") as a separate and specific business or project for the mutual benefit of the members of the group. A government may also be a member of the group. The purpose of a corporate joint venture frequently is to share risks and rewards in developing a new market, product or technology; to combine complementary technological knowledge; or to pool resources in developing production or other facilitiies. A corporate joint venture also usually provides an arrangement under which each joint venturer may participate, directly or indirectly, in the overall management of the joint venture. Joint venturers thus have an interest or relationship other than as passive investors. An entity which is a subsidiary of one of the "joint venturers" is not a corporate joint venture. The ownership of a corporate joint venture seldom changes, and its stock is usually not traded publicly. A minority public ownership, however, does not preclude a corporation from being a corporate joint venture.

Note that a subsidiary (over 50 percent owned) of a joint venturer is *not* a corporate joint venture under *APB Opinion No. 18*. Instead, it would have to be consolidated under the provisions of *FAS 94,* "Consolidation of All Majority-Owned Subsidiaries."

The reporting requirement of *Opinion 18* for corporate joint ventures is described as follows:

> The board concludes that the equity method best enables investors in corporate joint ventures to reflect the underlying nature of their investment in those ventures. Therefore, investors should account for investments in common stock of corporate joint ventures by the equity method in consolidated financial statements.[14]

Investments in the common stock of joint ventures, or other investments accounted for by the equity method, may be material in relation to the financial position or results of operations of the joint venture investor. If so, it may be necessary for the investor to provide summarized information about the assets, liabilities, and results of operations of its investees in its own financial statements. The required disclosures should be presented *individually* for investments in joint ventures that are material in relation to the financial position or results of operations of the investor. Alternatively, the required disclosures can be *grouped* for investments that are material as a group, but are not material individually.

Accounting for Unincorporated Joint Ventures

Accounting Interpretation No. 2 of APB Opinion No. 18 addresses the applicability of *Opinion 18* to investments in partnerships and undivided interests in joint ventures. While the provisions of *Opinion 18* apply only to investments in common

---

[14]*APB Opinion No. 18,* "The Equity Method of Accounting for Investments in Common Stock," paragraph 16.

460

CONSOLIDATION
THEORIES, PUSH-DOWN
ACCOUNTING, AND
CORPORATE JOINT
VENTURES

stock, and, therefore, do not cover unincorporated ventures, *Interpretation 2* explains that many of the provisions of *Opinion 18* are appropriate in accounting for investments in unincorporated entities. For example, partnership profits and losses accrued by investor-partners are generally reflected in the partners' financial statements. Elimination of intercompany profit in accounting for a partnership interest also seems appropriate, as does providing for deferred income tax liabilities on profits accrued by partner-investors.

The previous discussion of the applicability of *Opinion 18* to partnerships also applies to undivided interests in joint ventures, where the investor-venturer owns an undivided interest in each asset and is proportionately liable for its share of each liability. But the provisions of *Opinion 18* do not apply in some industries that have specialized industry practices. For example, the established industry practice in oil and gas ventures is for the investor-venturer to account for its pro rata share of the assets, liabilities, revenues, and expenses of a joint venture in its own financial statements. This reporting procedure is referred to as **pro rata** or **proportionate consolidation**. Alternatively, SOP 78-9 recommends against proportionate consolidation for undivided interests in real estate ventures subject to joint control by the investors. A venture is subject to joint control if decisions regarding the financing, development, or sale of property require the approval of two or more owner-venturers. Subsequently, a 1979 AICPA Issues Paper entitled "Joint Venture Accounting" recommended that a joint venture that is not subject to joint control, because its liabilities are several rather than joint, should be required to use the proportionate consolidation method.

One-Line Consolidation and Proportionate Consolidation

To illustrate the reporting alternatives for unincorporated joint ventures, assume that Price Corporation has a 50 percent undivided interest in Shield Company, a merchandising joint venture. Comparative financial statements under the two assumptions (accounting under the equity method and proportionate consolidation) appear in Exhibit 11–10. Column 1 presents a summary of Price's income statement and balance sheet assuming that it uses the equity method of accounting for its investment in Shield, an unconsolidated joint venture company. Shield's income statement and balance sheet are summarized in column 2. In column 3 Price has consolidated its share (50 percent) of Shield's assets, liabilities, revenues and expenses (from column 2); in other words, a proportionate consolidation.

Note that Shield's $1,000,000 venture capital is eliminated in its entirety against the $500,000 investment in Shield balance, and against half of Shield's asset, liability, revenue, and expense account balances in the proportionate consolidation.

Accounting Policy Disclosure for Joint Ventures

Alcoa uses proportionate consolidation for investments in certain joint ventures. The 1990 annual report of Alcoa includes the following note under significant accounting policies:

> Principles of Consolidation. The consolidated financial statements include the accounts of Alcoa and companies more than 50% owned. Also included are joint ventures in which Alcoa has an undivided interest. Investments in other entities are accounted for principally on the equity basis.[15]

---

[15]*Alcoa Annual Report 1990*, p. 43.

	Equity Method Price Corporation	Shield Unincorporated	Proporationate Consolidation Price and Shield
Income Statement			
Revenues			
Sales	$2,000,000	$ 500,000	$2,250,000
Income from Shield	100,000	—	—
Total revenue	2,100,000	500,000	2,250,000
Expenses			
Cost of sales	1,200,000	200,000	1,300,000
Other expenses	400,000	100,000	450,000
Total expenses	1,600,000	300,000	1,750,000
Net income	$ 500,000	$ 200,000	$ 500,000
Balance Sheet			
Cash	$ 200,000	$ 50,000	$ 225,000
Accounts receivable	300,000	150,000	375,000
Inventory	400,000	300,000	550,000
Plant assets	800,000	800,000	1,200,000
Investment in Shield	500,000	—	—
Total assets	$2,200,000	$1,300,000	$2,350,000
Accounts payable	$ 400,000	$ 200,000	$ 500,000
Other liabilities	500,000	100,000	550,000
Capital stock	1,000,000	—	1,000,000
Retained earnings	300,000	—	300,000
Venture capital	—	1,.000,000	—
Total equities	$2,200,000	$1,300,000	$2,350,000

Exhibit 11–10   *The Equity Method and Proportionate Consolidation Compared*

Other financial statement disclosures for joint ventures generally include those that are applicable to equity investees.

SUMMARY

This chapter looks at several different theories related to consolidating the financial statements of a parent company and its subsidiaries. It also examines the establishment of a new accounting basis for assets and liabilities in a subsidiary's separate financial statements under push-down accounting, and it illustrates accounting for a corporate joint venture.

The concepts and procedures underlying current consolidation practices are identified as the contemporary theory of consolidation in order to distinguish current practices from accounting practices under the parent company and entity theories. The basic differences among the three theories are compared in a matrix in Exhibit 11–1. Nearly all of the differences disappear when the subsidiary is wholly owned.

Under push-down accountng, the cost–book value differentials determined in a purchase business combination are recorded in the separate books of the subsidiary. Push-down accounting is ordinarily required by the SEC for purchase business combinations in which all or substantially all of the ownership interests in the acquired company change hands. Some acquisitions can be structured to avoid push-down accounting.

A joint venture is a business entity that is owned, operated, and jointly controlled by a small group of investors for their mutual benefit. The joint venture investors are usually active in the management of the venture, and each venturer

462

CONSOLIDATION
THEORIES, PUSH-DOWN
ACCOUNTING, AND
CORPORATE JOINT
VENTURES

usually has the ability to exercise significant influence over the joint venture investee. Investors account for their investments in corporate joint ventures as one-line consolidations under the equity method. Similarly, investors account for investments in unincorporated joint ventures (partnerships and undivided interests) as one-line consolidations or proportionate consolidations, depending on the special accounting practices of the industries in which they operate.

APPENDIX: CONSOLIDATION UNDER A CURRENT COST SYSTEM

Many of the differences between the parent company, entity, and contemporary theories of consolidation arise because value changes are not recorded in the accounts of affiliated companies as they occur. Although entity theory is intended to provide a consistent valuation approach for majority and minority interests, it does not accomplish its objective because the net assets of the parent company are not revalued at the time of acquisition and because no revaluations occur after the date of a business combination.

This section of the chapter provides a brief digression from generally accepted accounting principles in order to consider how the consolidation process might be altered if a current cost approach were adopted. Conceivably the adoption of a current cost system would eliminate many of the inconsistencies and complexities that arise in the preparation of consolidated financial statements.

Current Cost Accounting

U.S. companies may supplement their financial statements with current cost information as specified in *FASB Statement No. 89*.[16] This supplementary information includes current cost of inventories and property, plant, and equipment, and the effect on income from continuing operations of measuring cost of sales and depreciation on a current cost basis. Since authoritative accounting bodies do not require business enterprises to issue current cost financial statements, this section is limited to examining possible changes that a current cost system would have on the preparation of consolidated financial statements. The discussion assumes that implementation of a current cost system would involve the revaluation of all identifiable assets and liabilities on a current cost basis at each statement date, and that unidentifiable assets (that is, goodwill) would continue to be recorded and amortized on a cost basis.[17] All changes in current costs of identifiable assets and liabilities are assumed to be included in the measurement of net income in the period of change. Also, goodwill or negative goodwill is assumed to be measured by the difference between the purchase price and the current cost of net assets acquired and amortized over a maximum period of forty years. Under these assumptions, most of the problem areas of consolidations could conceivably be avoided.

Few consolidation adjustments are needed to consolidate the accounts of a parent company and its subsidiaries if all affiliates value their identifiable assets and liabilities on a current cost basis. Reciprocal accounts must still be eliminated, but the elimination process is greatly simplified. Reciprocal receivable and payable balances, including accounts for intercompany bond investments and bond

---

[16]*FASB Statement No. 33,* which required certain large companies to disclose current cost information, was superseded by *FASB Statement No. 89* in December 1986. *Statement 89* encourages, but does not require, disclosure of supplementary current cost information.

[17]Most current cost systems are not designed for the valuation of a business as a whole, but rather for the valuation of identifiable assets and liabilities. Unidentifiable assets are recorded only where necessary to reflect the acquisitions of groups of assets or entire business enterprises. Once recorded, the accounts for unidentifiable assets are not adjusted for changes in current costs.

liabilities,[18] should be precisely reciprocal under a current cost system, such that no income or equity accounts would be involved in the elimination process. Further, there are no constructive gains or losses on intercompany bond purchases because the purchase price of intercompany bonds is equivalent to the current cost of the liability at the time of its constructive retirement.

Under the historical cost system of accounting, the basis of income recognition is the sale of goods and services to other entities. In such a system all gains and losses on intercompany transfers are deferred (unrealized) until subsequent sale outside the consolidated entity. Because changes in current cost form the basis for income recognition under a current cost accounting system, there is no need for deferring recognition of gains and losses on intercompany transfers. The assets are stated at their current costs, not their transfer prices, in both separate company and consolidated financial statements. Thus, under the current cost system assumed in this section, there are no unrealized gains or losses on intercompany purchase and sale transactions. This is because the basis for income recognition becomes changes in current cost, and any differences between intercompany transfer prices and current costs are recognized on the books of the purchasing affiliate during the period of the intercompany transactions.

Investment in subsidiary and underlying subsidiary equity amounts under a current cost system should be reciprocal except for any unamortized excess of purchase price over the current cost of net assets acquired. In other words, the initial difference between investment cost and current value of net assets acquired would lie solely in the goodwill or negative goodwill associated with a purchase business combination. In years subsequent to acquisition, this difference would be reduced through goodwill amortization and no additional differences would arise because there would be no unrealized or constructive gains or losses.

Identifiable assets and liabilities would be the same for a business combination accounted for under the pooling of interests method as under the purchase method, since all assets and liabilities would be recorded at their current costs. Thus, the only difference in the net assets under the two methods lies in the valuation of unidentifiable assets.

Minority interest computations under a current cost system would also be simplified. Income of minority stockholders under parent company or contemporary theory would be equal to the minority interest in subsidiary net income, and total minority interest at any date would be equal to the minority interest's share of the current cost of subsidiary net assets.

Consolidation Procedures under Current Cost Accounting

Assume that Podunk Corporation acquires 80 percent of the outstanding stock of Sickle Corporation on January 2, 19X1 in a purchase business combination. Balance sheets of the two companies on a current cost basis just prior to the combination are as follows:

	Podunk	Sickle
Assets		
Cash	$ 50,000	$ 20,000
Accounts receivable	100,000	50,000
Inventories	250,000	80,000
Plant assets—net	500,000	300,000
Total	$900,000	$450,000

---

[18]Current costs of bond liabilities and investments can be determined by reference to market prices if current quotations are available. Otherwise, they would be determined by imputing current interest rates and using present value computations.

464

CONSOLIDATION
THEORIES, PUSH-DOWN
ACCOUNTING, AND
CORPORATE JOINT
VENTURES

	Podunk	*Sickle*
Liabilities and Equity		
Accounts payable	$ 60,000	$ 30,000
9% bonds payable	—	100,000
Capital stock, $10 par	500,000	300,000
Retained earnings	340,000	20,000
Total	$900,000	$450,000

The identifiable net assets of both Podunk and Sickle are fairly valued at their current costs and require no adjustment for purposes of the business combination. If Podunk issues 20,000 shares of stock with a market value of $400,000 for 80 percent of Sickle's outstanding shares, the investment is recorded as follows:

Investment in Sickle	$400,000	
Capital stock, $10 par		$200,000
Additional paid-in capital		200,000

To record acquisition of an 80% interest in Sickle.

A consolidated balance sheet for Podunk and Sickle immediately after acquisition shows goodwill of $144,000, equal to the excess of investment cost over current cost of net assets acquired [$400,000 − ($320,000 × 80%)]. A consolidation working paper entry to consolidate the balance sheets of the two companies is:

Capital stock—Sickle	$300,000	
Retained earnings—Sickle	20,000	
Goodwill	144,000	
Investment in Sickle		$400,000
Minority interest		64,000

The consolidated balance sheet prepared on a current cost basis immediately after the business combination would appear as follows:

PODUNK CORPORATION AND SUBSIDIARY CONSOLIDATED BALANCE SHEET AT JANUARY 2, 19X1

Assets		
Current Assets:		
Cash	$ 70,000	
Accounts receivable	150,000	
Inventories	330,000	
Total current assets		$ 550,000
Plant assets—net		800,000
Goodwill		144,000
Total assets		$1,494,000
Liabilities and Equity		
Liabilities:		
Accounts payable	$ 90,000	
9% bonds payable (at par value)	100,000	
Total liabilities		$ 190,000
Stockholders' equity		
Capital stock, $10 par	$ 700,000	
Additional paid-in capital	200,000	
Retained earnings	340,000	
Majority interest	$1,240,000	
Minority interest	64,000	
Total stockholders' equity		1,304,000
Total liabilities and stockholders' equity		$1,494,000

Because the identifiable assets and liabilities of both parent and subsidiary are consolidated at their current costs, all assets and liabilities are valued consistently except for goodwill which relates only to the majority interest. Assuming that the goodwill is amortized over a five-year period, the inconsistency will disappear at the end of five years. [Under entity theory, goodwill would be $180,000 ($144,000/80%) and minority interest would be $100,000 (20 percent of $500,000 implied total valuation), and even this inconsistency would be eliminated.]

Intercompany Sales of Inventory Items in a Current Cost System

Assume that Podunk sold merchandise to Sickle for $20,000, that the merchandise was produced by Podunk during 19X2 at a cost of $12,000, and that it had a current cost of $15,000 at the time of sale. Podunk's profit of $8,000 on the sale would be realized during 19X2 regardless of whether Sickle resells the merchandise or inventories it at year-end. But if the goods have a current cost of $15,000 and remain unsold at year-end, Sickle would decrease its income for 19X2 in the amount of $5,000 by writing down the merchandise to its $15,000 year-end current cost. The entry on Sickle's books to record the write-down would be:

Cost of sales	$5,000	
Inventory		$5,000

To reduce inventory to its current replacement cost at year-end.

Although a separate account to record the $5,000 loss on the write-down to current cost could have been used, the adjustment to cost of sales was made in order to keep the illustration basic.

The net result of the intercompany sales transactions during 19X2 is to increase the combined income of Podunk and Sickle by $3,000—an $8,000 increase by Podunk and a $5,000 decrease by Sickle. Consolidated net income for 19X2 also increases $3,000 during 19X2; not as a result of the intercompany sale, but because the consolidated entity held merchandise during 19X2 while its current cost increased from $12,000 to $15,000.

A consolidation working paper entry to consolidate the accounts of Podunk and Sickle for the year would be necessary to eliminate intercompany purchases and sales as follows:

Sales	$20,000	
Cost of sales		$20,000

To eliminate intercompany sales.

This working paper elimination entry is needed in order to show the correct operating results of the consolidated entity, but it has no effect on consolidated net income. Notice that no working paper entry is needed to adjust the inventory. This is because the inventory is recorded on a current cost basis in the separate accounts of Sickle.

A brief analysis of the separate company and consolidated income statement effect of the $20,000 intercompany sale may be helpful. Consider the following partial consolidated income statement working papers in terms of increases (+) and decreases (−):

	Podunk	Sickle	Adjustments and Eliminations	Consolidated Income Statement
Sales	$+20,000	$ —	$−20,000	$ —
Cost of sales	+12,000	+5,000	−20,000	−3,000
Gross profit	$+ 8,000	$−5,000		$+3,000

466

CONSOLIDATION
THEORIES, PUSH-DOWN
ACCOUNTING, AND
CORPORATE JOINT
VENTURES

Separate company cost of sales consist of the $12,000 historical cost on Podunk's books and $5,000 on Sickle's books from adjusting the inventory from $20,000 to its $15,000 current cost. When the intercompany sales and purchases are eliminated through the working paper entry, the final effect is to decrease consolidated cost of sales by $3,000 and increase consolidated net income by $3,000. This $3,000 is simply the increase in the current cost of the goods produced by Podunk and held within the consolidated entity at December 31, 19X2. Although some theorists would classify the $3,000 increase as a separate consolidated income statement item rather than as a reduction of consolidated cost of sales, this type of refinement does not seem necessary in view of the broad and general treatment accorded in this section. The previous discussion of the $20,000 downstream sale from Podunk to Sickle is equally applicable to an upstream sale by subsidiary to parent company.

Intercompany Sales of Plant Assets in a Current Cost System

Assume that Sickle owned land with a current cost of $8,000 on January 2, 19X2, that it sold the land to Podunk for $10,000 during 19X2, and that the land had a current cost of $8,500 at December 31, 19X2. Under these assumptions, Sickle would record a $2,000 gain at the time of sale and Podunk would record a $1,500 loss at year-end when it adjusts its land account to a current cost basis. Podunk would record the write-down to current cost as follows:

Loss on adjustment of land to current cost	$1,500	
Land		$1,500

To adjust the land account to its current cost at year-end.

The combined effect of the intercompany land sale is to increase income for 19X2 by $500—a $2,000 gain to Sickle and a $1,500 loss to Podunk. These amounts are realized by Sickle and Podunk, respectively. For consolidated statement purposes, however, only the $500 net increase is included in consolidated net income. This $500 consists of the increase in the current cost of the land while it is being held within the consolidated entity (from $8,000 at the beginning of the year to $8,500 at year-end).

Since the land is adjusted on Podunk's books to its current cost at year-end, the only working paper entry needed is as follows:

Gain on land	$1,500	
Loss on adjustment of land to current cost		$1,500

To offset gain and loss accounts from intercompany sale of land.

The $500 gain not eliminated is included in the consolidated income statement as the only income statement effect of the intercompany sale of land. By this time, you should have discovered that the effect of intercompany transactions on consolidated net income is determined by changes in the current cost of assets held within the consolidated entity, and not by transfer prices.[19] A $500 increase in consolidated income would have resulted if the intercompany sale had occurred at $7,000, $9,000, or some other amount. As in the case of inventory items, the gain could be reflected in the consolidated income statement in various ways.

---

[19]Because no gains or losses are deferred under the current cost system visualized in this chapter, it makes no difference if the sales are upstream or downstream.

Constructive Retirement of Intercompany Bonds in a Current Cost System

If Podunk acquires 50 percent of Sickle's outstanding bonds (see page 464) for $48,000 on December 31, 19X2, there is no constructive gain on the bonds. This is because Sickle's bond liability on this date is $96,000—its current cost at December 31, 19X2 as established by Podunk's purchase of 50 percent of the bonds for $48,000. On its separate books, Sickle Corporation would recognize a $4,000 gain for 19X2 on the revaluation of its bond liability to a current cost basis. But this gain is considered an adjustment of Sickle's bond interest expense for the year rather than a separate income statement item. The $4,000 decrease in Sickle's interest expense is reflected in Sickle's separate income statement and in the consolidated income statement for 19X2. The only working paper entry necessary for the intercompany bond holdings is:

9% bonds payable	$48,000	
Investment in Sickle bonds		$48,000
To eliminate reciprocal bond amounts.		

Now assume that the bonds of Sickle are purchased on July 1 rather than on December 31, 19X2, and that Podunk pays $47,000 for 50 percent of Sickle's bonds. Also assume that all adjustments to current cost are made at year-end, at which time the current cost of the bonds was $96,000 ($48,000 for 50 percent of the bonds). Under these assumptions, Podunk and Sickle would make the following entries on their separate books during 19X2:

Podunk's Books
July 1, 19X2

Investment in Sickle bonds	$47,000	
Cash		$47,000
To record bond investment.		

December 31. 19X2

Cash (or accrued interest receivable)	$ 2,250	
Investment in Sickle bonds	1,000	
Interest income		$ 3,250
To record nominal interest on Sickle bonds and to adjust interest income for a $1,000 increase in the current cost of the bonds.		

Sickle's Books
December 31, 19X2

Interest expense	$ 5,000	
9% bonds payable	4,000	
Cash (or accrued interest payable)		$ 9,000
To record nominal interest for the year and to adjust interest expense for the $4,000 decrease in the current cost of the bond liability.		

After these entries are recorded, the separate books of Podunk show investment in Sickle bonds and interest income of $48,000 and $3,250, respectively. The separate books of Sickle show 9 percent bonds payable and interest expense of $96,000 and $5,000, respectively. The working paper entry to eliminate reciprocal bond investment and bond liability amounts will be for $48,000, just as in the previous example. But an additional working paper entry is necessary to eliminate reciprocal interest income and interest expense as follows:

Interest income	$3,250	
Interest expense		$3,250
To eliminate reciprocal interest income and interest expense.		

468

CONSOLIDATION
THEORIES, PUSH-DOWN
ACCOUNTING, AND
CORPORATE JOINT
VENTURES

This entry, which reduces the interest expense for the full amount of the intercompany interest income, results in interest expense of $1,750 ($5,000 − $3,250) in the consolidated income statement for the year. The $1,750 consists of the nominal interest of $6,750 on bonds outstanding during the year [($ 100,000 × 9% × 1/2 year) + ($50,000 × 9% × 1/2 year)] less $5,000 decline in the current cost of bonds payable. (Others may prefer to show interest expense at $6,750 and to treat the $5,000 adjustment as a separate income item.) The $5,000 decrease in the current cost consists of a $3,000 decrease in the current cost of bonds constructively retired ($50,000 − $47,000) plus a $2,000 net decrease in the current cost of the bonds held outside of the consolidated entity at December 31, 19X2 ($50,000 − $48,000).

This type of analysis would not be necessary for practical accounting applications, since the $1,750 net amount of interest expense results automatically from offsetting intercompany interest income against interest expense. It makes no difference whether it is the parent company's or subsidiary's bonds that are constructively retired, since the analysis and computations under the current cost system described are exactly the same in either case.

SELECTED READINGS

Accountants International Study Group. *Consolidated Financial Statements: Current Recommended Practices in Canada, the United Kingdom, and the United States.* Plainstow, England: Curwen Press Ltd., 1973.

Accounting Interpretation No. 2 of APB Opinion No. 18. "Investments in Partnerships and Ventures." New York: American Institute of Certified Public Accountants, November 1971.

Accounting Standards Executive Committee of the American Institute of Certified Public Accountants. Issues Paper. *Joint Venture Accounting.* New York: American Institute of Certified Public Accountants, 1979.

CAMPBELL, J. D. "Consolidation vs. Combination." *Accounting Review* (January 1969), pp. 99–102.

Committee on Accounting Procedure. *Accounting Research Bulletin No. 51.* "Consolidated Financial Statements." New York: American Institute of Certified Public Accountants, 1959.

Committee on Concepts and Standards of the American Accounting Association. *Supplementary Statement No. 7.* "Consolidated Financial Statements." Sarasota, FL: American Accounting Association, 1954.

COLLEY, J. RON, and ARA G. VOLKAN. "Accounting for Goodwill." *Accounting Horizons* (March 1988), pp. 35–41.

COLLEY, J. RON, and ARA G. VOLKAN. "Business Combinations: Goodwill and Push-Down Accounting." *Accounting Horizons* (September 1989), pp. 38–43.

CUNNINGHAM, MICHAEL E. "Push-Down Accounting: Pros and Cons." *Journal of Accountancy* (June 1984), pp. 72–77.

DeMOVILLE, WIG, and A. GEORGE PETRIE. "Accounting for a Bargain Purchase in a Business Combination." *Accounting Horizons* (September 1989), pp. 38–43.

GORMAN, JERRY. "LBO Accounting: Consensus at Last!" *Journal of Accountancy* (August 1989), pp. 68–78.

HOLLEY, CHARLES L., EDWARD C. SEDE, and MICHAEL C. CHESTER JR. "The Push-Down Accounting Controversy." *Management Accounting* (January 1987), pp. 39–42.

HUSBAND, GEORGE R. "The Corporate-Entity Fiction and Accounting Theory." *Accounting Review* (September 1938), pp. 241–53.

HYLTON, DELMER P. "On the Usefulness of Consolidated Financial Statements." *The CPA Journal* (October 1988), pp. 74–77.

International Accounting Standards Committee. Exposure Draft No. 28. *Accounting for Investments in Associates and Joint Ventures.* London: IASC, 1986.

MOONITZ, MAURICE. "The Entity Approach to Consolidated Statements." *Accounting Review* (July 1942), pp. 236–242.

MOONITZ, MAURICE. *The Entity Theory of Consolidated Statements.* American Accounting Association Monograph No. 4. Sarasota, FL: American Accounting Association, 1944.

NURNBERG, HUGO, and JAN SWEENEY. "The Effect of Fair Values and Historical Costs on Accounting for Business Combinations." *Issues in Accounting Education* (Fall 1989), pp. 375–395.

Statement of Financial Accounting Standards No. 33. "Financial Reporting and Changing Prices." Stamford, CT: Financial Accounting Standards Board, 1979.

Statement of Position 78-9. "Accounting for Investment in Real Estate Ventures." New York: American Institute of Certified Public Accountants, Accounting Standards Division, 1978.

THOMAS, PAULA B., and J. LARRY HAGLER. "Push Down Accounting: A Descriptive Assessment." *Accounting Horizons* (September 1988), pp. 26–31.

WYATT, ARTHUR R. "A Critical Study of Accounting for Business Combinations." *Accounting Research Study No. 5.* New York: American Institute of Certified Public Accountants, 1963 (especially see pp. 81–86 on the fair value pooling concept).

ASSIGNMENT MATERIAL

QUESTIONS

1 Compare the contemporary, parent company, and entity theories of consolidated financial statements.

2 Which, if any, of the consolidation theories would be changed by FASB pronouncements? (For example, assume that a new FASB Statement requires minority interest income to be computed as the minority interest share of subsidiary dividends declared.)

3 Under the entity theory of consolidation, a total valuation of the subsidiary is imputed on the basis of the price paid by the parent company for its controlling interest. Do you see any practical or conceptual problems with this approach to valuation?

4 Assume that Pabst Corporation acquires 60 percent of the voting common stock of Seller Corporation for $6,000,000 and that a consolidated balance sheet is prepared immediately after the business combination. Would total consolidated assets be equal to their fair values if the parent company theory were applied? If the entity theory were applied?

5 Why might the current practice of valuing the equity of minority shareholders at book value overstate the value of the minority interest?

6 Cite the conditions under which consolidated net income under parent company theory would be equal to income to majority stockholders under entity theory.

7 If investment income from a subsidiary is measured under the equity method and the statements are consolidated under the entity theory, will consolidated net income be equal to parent company net income?

8 Why are the income statement amounts under entity theory and contemporary theory the same if the subsidiary investment is made at book value? (Do not consider the different income statement presentations of majority and minority interests in responding to this question.)

9 Does contemporary practice correspond to parent company or entity theory in matters related to unrealized and constructive gains and losses on intercompany transactions?

10 To what extent does push-down accounting facilitate the consolidation process?

11 What is a joint venture and how are joint ventures organized?

12 What accounting and reporting methods are used by investor-venturers in accounting for their joint venture investments?

13 *Appendix* How are unrealized gains and losses eliminated in consolidating the financial statements of affiliated companies when current cost accounting is applied?

14 *Appendix* Describe the computation of the equity of minority shareholders when a current cost system of accounting is used (assume the contemporary theory of accounting except for the application of the current cost system).

15 *Appendix* How would the current cost of goodwill be determined under a current cost system of accounting?

16 *Appendix* How would different transfer prices for intercompany transactions affect consolidated assets and consolidated net income under a current cost system of accounting?

17 *Appendix* If a current cost system of accounting were used, would it still be necessary to eliminate intercompany sales and purchases? Intercompany receivables and payables? Discuss.

EXERCISES

E 11-1
1 The classification of minority interest income as an expense and minority interest as a liability is preferred under

  a Parent company theory   **b** Entity theory
  c Contemporary theory   **d** None of the above

2 Contemporary theory is most similar to parent company theory in matters relating to

  a Goodwill computations
  b Minority interest computations
  c Intercompany profit eliminations
  d Consolidated financial statement presentations

3 Contemporary theory is most similar to entity theory in matters relating to

  a Goodwill computations
  b Minority interest computations
  c Intercompany profit eliminations
  d Consolidated financial statement presentations

4 When "consolidated income allocated to majority stockholders" under entity theory is compared to "consolidated net income" under contemporary theory, one would expect consolidated net income under contemporary theory to be

  a Equal to consolidated income allocated to majority stockholders under entity theory
  b Greater than consolidated income allocated to majority stockholders under entity theory
  c Less than consolidated income allocated to majority stockholders under entity theory
  d Greater or less depending on the relationship of investment cost to book value acquired

5 Consolidated financial statement amounts and classifications should be identical under the contemporary, entity, and parent company theories of consolidation if

  a All subsidiaries are acquired at book value
  b Only 100 percent owned subsidiaries are consolidated
  c There are no intercompany transactions
  d All subsidiaries are acquired at book value and there are no intercompany transactions

6 When the fair values of an acquired subsidiary's assets and liabilities are recorded in the subsidiary's accounts (push-down accounting), the subsidiary's retained earnings will be

  a Adjusted for the difference between the push-down capital and goodwill from the acquisition
  b Credited for the amount of the push-down capital
  c Transferred in its entirety to push-down capital
  d Credited for the difference between the total imputed value of the entity and the purchase price of the interest acquired

7 The most consistent statement of assets in consolidated financial statements would result from applying

  a Contemporary theory
  b Parent company theory
  c Entity theory
  d A current cost system of accounting

E 11-2
1 Peterson Company pays $720,000 for an 80 percent interest in Smith Corporation on December 31, 19X1 when Smith's net assets at book value and fair value are $800,000. Under entity theory the minority interest at acquisition is

  a $144,000   **b** $160,000
  c $180,000   **d** $200,000

2 Seattle Corporation sold inventory items to its parent company, Portland Corporation, during 19X2, and at December 31, 19X2 Portland's inventory included items acquired from Seattle at a gross profit of $50,000. If Seattle is an 80 percent owned subsidiary of Portland, the amount of unrealized inventory profits to be eliminated in preparing the consolidated income statements of Portland and Subsidiary for 19X2 is $40,000 under

  a Parent company theory   **b** Contemporary theory
  c Entity theory   **d** The equity method of accounting

3 A parent company that applies the entity theory of consolidation in preparing its consolidated financial statements computed income from its 90 percent owned subsidiary under the equity method of accounting as follows:

Equity in subsidiary income ($200,000 × 90%)	$180,000
Goodwill amortization ($70,000/10 years × 90%)	(6,300)
Income from subsidiary	$173,700

Given the foregoing information, minority interest income is
a $20,000   **b** $19,300
c $18,000   **d** $17,300

Use the following information in answering questions 4 and 5:
Piedmont Corporation acquired an 80 percent interest in Swan Corporation on January 1, 19X1 when Swan's total stockholders' equity was $840,000. The book values and fair values of Swan's assets and liabilities were equal on this date. At December 31, 19X1 the consolidated balance sheet of Piedmont and Subsidiary shows unamortized goodwill from consolidation of $54,000, with a note that goodwill is being amortized over a ten-year period.

4 If the entity theory of consolidation was used, the purchase price of the 80 percent interest in Swan must have been
a $720,000   **b** $732,000
c $747,000   **d** $900,000

5 If the contemporary theory of consolidation was used, the purchase price of the 80 percent interest in Swan must have been
a $720,000   **b** $732,000
c $747,000   **d** $900,000

E 11-3 On January 1, 19X5 Perry Corporation pays $300,000 for an 80 percent interest in Shelly Company when Shelly's net assets have a book value of $275,000 and a fair value of $350,000. The $75,000 excess fair value is due to undervalued equipment with a five-year remaining use life. Any goodwill is to be written off over a ten-year period.
Separate incomes of Perry and Shelly for 19X5 are $500,000 and $50,000, respectively.

Required
1 Calculate consolidated net income and minority interest income under (a) parent company theory and (b) entity theory.
2 Determine unamortized goodwill at December 31, 19X5 under (a) parent company theory and (b) entity theory.

E 11-4 Stahl Corporation's recorded assets and liabilities are equal to their fair values on July 1, 19X1 when Polak Corporation purchases 72,000 shares of Stahl common stock for $1,800,000. Identifiable net assets of Stahl on this date are $1,710,000, and Stahl's stockholders' equity consists of $800,000 of $10 par common stock and $910,000 retained earnings. Any goodwill is to be amortized over ten years.
Stahl has net income for 19X1 of $80,000 earned evenly throughout the year and declares no dividends.

Required
1 Determine the total value of Stahl's net assets at July 1, 19X1 under entity theory.
2 Determine goodwill that would appear in a consolidated balance sheet of Polak Corporation and Subsidiary at July 1, 19X1 under (a) entity theory, (b) parent company theory, and (c) contemporary theory.
3 Determine Polak's investment income from Stahl on an equity basis for 19X1.
4 Determine minority interest in Stahl that will be reported in the consolidated balance sheet at December 31, 19X1 under entity theory.

E 11-5 Pastor Corporation acquired a 90 percent interest in Sabian Corporation at book value several years ago. During 19X2 the separate incomes of Pastor and Sabian Corporations were $200,000 and $80,000, respectively. Unrealized profits at December 31, 19X2 from intercompany sales of inventory items from Sabian to Pastor amounted to $8,000.

472

CONSOLIDATION
THEORIES, PUSH-DOWN
ACCOUNTING, AND
CORPORATE JOINT
VENTURES

Required

1 Compute the net income of Pastor Company under the equity method of accounting.
2 Determine consolidated net income for Pastor Corporation and Subsidiary if the parent company theory of consolidation is used.
3 Determine total consolidated net income for Pastor Corporation and Subsidiary if the entity theory of consolidation is used. Also, compute income to majority stockholders and minority stockholders.

E 11-6 On July 1, 19X1 Prudent Corporation acquired a 75 percent interest in Smoot Corporation for $150,000. The net assets of Smoot Corporation on this date had a book value of $140,000 and a fair value of $160,000. The excess of fair value over book value at acquisition was due to understated plant assets with a remaining use life of five years from July 1, 19X1. Goodwill is to be amortized over a ten-year period. Separate incomes of Prudent and Smoot for 19X2 were $400,000 and $20,000, respectively.

Required

1 Determine consolidated net income and minority interest income for 19X2 under (a) parent company theory, and (b) entity theory.
2 Compute unamortized goodwill at December 31, 19X2 under (a) parent company theory and (b) entity theory.

E 11-7 Penniwise Corporation acquired an 80 percent interest in Stark Corporation at book value a number of years ago.

Separate incomes of Penniwise and Stark for 19X1 were $100,000 and $50,000, respectively. The only transactions between Penniwise and Stark during 19X1 were as follows:

1 Penniwise sold inventory items to Stark for $100,000. These items cost Penniwise $60,000, and half the items were inventoried at $50,000 by Stark at December 31, 19X1.
2 Stark sold land that cost $150,000 to Penniwise for $200,000 during 19X1. The land was still held by Penniwise at December 31, 19X1.
3 Stark paid $32,000 in dividends to Penniwise during 19X1.

Required: Compute consolidated net income for Penniwise Corporation and Subsidiary for 19X1 under:

1 Contemporary theory
2 Parent company theory
3 Entity theory

E 11-8 Proffitt Corporation pays $9,000,000 for a 90 percent interest in Schimmer Corporation on January 1, 19X8. Proffitt has determined that Schimmer has unrecorded trademarks with a fair value of $2,000,000 and that Schimmer's other assets and liabilities have book values and fair values as follows:

	Book Value	Fair Value	Difference
Cash	$ 100,000	$ 100,000	$ —
Accounts receivable—net	1,000,000	1,000,000	—
Inventory	1,500,000	2,000,000	500,000
Land	200,000	1,400,000	1,200,000
Buildings—net	1,200,000	1,000,000	(200,000)
Equipment—net	2,000,000	2,500,000	500,000
Trademarks	—	2,000,000	2,000,000
	$6,000,000	$10,000,000	
Current liabilities	$ 800,000	$ 800,000	—
Long-term debt	2,000,000	1,800,000	200,000
Common stock, $10 par	2,500,000		
Retained earnings	700,000		
	$6,000,000		

Required

1 Prepare the journal entry on Schimmer's books to record the push-down values under *parent company theory*.

2 Compute the amount of goodwill that would be included in the entry to record the push-down values on Schimmer's books under *entity theory*.

E 11-9   Sun-Belt Land Development Corporation is a corporate joint venture that is jointly controlled and operated by five investor-venturers; four with 15 percent interests each and one with a 40 percent interest. Each of the five venturers are active in venture management. Land sales and other important venture decisions require the consent of each venturer. All venturers paid $15 per share for their investments on January 1, 19X1, and no changes in ownership interests have occurred since that time. During 19X2 Sun-Belt reported net income of $500,000 and paid dividends of $100,000. The stockholders' equity of Sun-Belt at December 31, 19X2 is as follows:

SUN-BELT LAND DEVELOPMENT CORPORATION
STOCKHOLDERS' EQUITY AT DECEMBER 31, 19X2

Common stock $10 par, 500,000 shares authorized, issued, and outstanding	$5,000,000
Additional paid-in capital	2,500,000
Total paid-in capital	7,500,000
Retained earnings	1,000,000
Total stockholders' equity	$8,500,000

Required: Determine the investment income for 19X2 and the investment account balance at December 31, 19X2, for the 40 percent venturer and for one of the 15 percent venturers.

E 11-10   *Appendix*   Assume that Seaside Company is a 90 percent owned subsidiary of Prescott and that a current cost system of accounting is applicable to the separate company and consolidated financial statements of these affiliated companies. During 19X1 the following intercompany transactions took place between Prescott and Seaside:

1 Prescott sold merchandise that cost $18,000 and had a $20,000 current cost at the time of sale to Seaside for $25,000. At December 31, 19X1, 25 percent of this merchandise with a current cost of $5,500 remained unsold by Seaside.

2 Prescott acquired 10 percent of Seaside Company's outstanding bonds at December 31, 19X1 for $99,000. The book value of Seaside's bond liability before year-end adjustments on this date was $1,000,000.

3 On July 1, 19X1 Seaside sold land with a book value (current cost at January 1, 19X1) of $40,000 to Prescott for $50,000. This land had a current cost of $45,000 both at the time of sale and at December 31, 19X1.

Required

1 Prepare journal entries to record:

a The foregoing transactions for 19X1 on the separate books of Prescott and Seaside. (Current cost adjustments are only made at year-end.)

b Year-end adjustments on the separate books of Prescott and Seaside at December 31, 19X1.

2 Prepare the working paper entries related to the foregoing transactions that would be necessary to consolidate the financial statements of Prescott and Seaside at December 31, 19X1.

PROBLEMS

P 11-1   Pelator Corporation acquired its 90 percent interest in Sam Corporation on January 1, 19X1. On that date, Sam's assets and liabilities were equal to their fair values except for a building with a ten-year remaining use life. The building had a depreciated cost of $120,000 and a fair value of $220,000 when Pelator acquired its interest. A summary of the book values of Pelator and Sam immediately after their combination follows:

474

CONSOLIDATION
THEORIES, PUSH-DOWN
ACCOUNTING, AND
CORPORATE JOINT
VENTURES

	Pelator	Sam
Cash	$ 100,000	$ 50,000
Receivables—net	150,000	80,000
Inventories	200,000	100,000
Plant assets—net	500,000	120,000
Investment in Sam—90%	450,000	—
Total assets	$1,400,000	$350,000
Liabilities	$ 100,000	$ 40,000
Capital stock	1,000,000	200,000
Retained earnings	300,000	110,000
Total equities	$1,400,000	$350,000

Required

1 Prepare comparative consolidated balance sheets for Pelator Corporation and Subsidiary at January 1, 19X1 under the parent company and entity theories of consolidation.

2 Prepare comparative consolidated income statements for Pelator Corporation and Subsidiary for 19X2 under parent company and entity theories assuming that their separate income statement amounts are:

	Pelator	Sam
Sales	$1,500,000	$500,000
Cost of sales	800,000	300,000
Expenses	450,000	100,000

Assume that goodwill is being amortized over a ten-year period.

P 11–2 Pisces Corporation acquires an 80 percent interest in Scorpio Company on January 3, 19X1 for $160,000. On this date Scorpio's stockholders' equity consists of $100,000 capital stock and $70,000 retained earnings. The cost–book value differential is assigned to goodwill with a six-year amortization period. Immediately after acquisition, Scorpio sells equipment with a ten-year remaining useful life to Pisces at a gain of $5,000.

Adjusted trial balances of Pisces and Scorpio at December 31, 19X1 are as follows:

	Pisces	Scorpio
Current assets	$ 151,600	$ 90,000
Plant and equipment	400,000	200,000
Investment in Scorpio	168,400	—
Cost of sales	250,000	130,000
Depreciation	50,000	25,000
Other expenses	60,000	20,000
Dividends	50,000	10,000
	$1,130,000	$475,000
Accumulated depreciation	$ 150,000	$ 50,000
Liabilities	100,000	50,000
Capital stock	300,000	100,000
Retained earnings	163,600	70,000
Sales	400,000	200,000
Gain on plant assets	—	5,000
Income from Scorpio	16,400	—
	$1,130,000	$475,000

Required

1 Prepare a consolidated income statement for 19X1 using entity theory.
2 Prepare a consolidated balance sheet at December 31, 19X1 using entity theory.

P 11-3 Palace Corporation paid $595,000 cash for 70 percent of the outstanding voting stock of Sign Corporation on January 2, 19X2 when Sign's stockholders' equity consisted of $500,000 of $10 par common stock and $250,000 retained earnings. The book values of Sign's assets and liabilities were equal to their fair values on this date.

During 19X2 Palace Corporation had separate income of $300,000 and paid dividends of $150,000. Sign's net income for 19X2 was $90,000 and its dividends were $50,000. At December 31, 19X2 the stockholders' equities of Palace and Sign were as follows:

	Palace	Sign
Common stock ($10 par)	$1,400,000	$500,000
Retained earnings	450,000	290,000
Total stockholders' equity	$1,850,000	$790,000

There were no intercompany transactions between Palace Corporation and Sign Corporation during 19X2. Palace uses the equity method of accounting for its investment in Sign and amortizes goodwill over a ten-year period.

Part A: Assume that Palace Corporation uses the parent company theory for preparing consolidated financial statements for 19X2. Determine the following amounts:
   1 Palace Corporation's income from Sign for 19X2
   2 Goodwill that will appear in the consolidated balance sheet at December 31, 19X2
   3 Consolidated net income for 19X2
   4 Minority interest income for 19X2
   5 Minority interest at December 31, 19X2

Part B: Assume that Palace Corporation uses the entity theory for preparing consolidated financial statements for 19X2. Determine the following amounts:
   6 Palace Corporation's income from Sign for 19X2
   7 Goodwill that will appear in the consolidated balance sheet at December 31, 19X2
   8 Total consolidated income for 19X2
   9 Minority interest income for 19X2
   10 Minority interest at December 31, 19X2

P 11-4 At December 31, 19X1 when the fair values of Smiley Corporation's net assets were equal to their book values of $240,000, Padre Corporation acquired an 80 percent interest in Smiley Corporation for $224,000. One year later at December 31, 19X2, the comparative adjusted trial balances of the two corporations appear as follows:

	Padre Corporation	Smiley Corporation
Cash	$ 60,800	$ 70,000
Accounts receivable	80,000	30,000
Inventory	150,000	40,000
Land	100,000	80,000
Buildings	1,000,000	200,000
Investment in Smiley	239,200	—
Cost of sales	400,000	200,000
Expenses	150,000	50,000
Dividends	120,000	30,000
Total debits	$2,300,000	$700,000
Accumulated depreciation	$ 200,000	$ 60,000
Accounts payable	200,800	100,000
Capital stock	800,000	200,000
Retained earnings	360,000	40,000
Sales	700,000	300,000
Income from Smiley	39,200	—
Total credits	$2,300,000	$700,000

476

CONSOLIDATION
THEORIES, PUSH-DOWN
ACCOUNTING, AND
CORPORATE JOINT
VENTURES

Additional Information

1 During 19X2 Smiley Corporation sold inventory items costing $15,000 to Padre for $23,000. Half of these inventory items remain unsold at December 31, 19X2.
2 Goodwill is to be amortized over a forty-year period.

Required: Prepare comparative consolidated financial statements for Padre Corporation and Subsidiary at and for the year ended December 31, 19X2 under

1 Contemporary theory
2 Parent company theory
3 Entity theory

P 11-5 Balance sheets for Packard Manufacturing Corporation and its 80 percent owned subsidiary, Studs Building Supply Company, at December 31, 19X4 are summarized as follows:

	Packard	Studs
Assets		
Cash	$ 50,000	$ 20,000
Receivables—net	75,000	35,000
Inventories	110,000	30,000
Plant assets—net	215,000	85,000
Investment in Studs Building Supply	136,000	—
Total assets	$586,000	$170,000
Liabilities and Stockholders' Equity		
Accounts payable	$ 80,000	$ 15,000
Other liabilities	20,000	5,000
Total liabilities	100,000	20,000
Capital stock	300,000	100,000
Retained earnings	186,000	50,000
Stockholders' equity	486,000	150,000
Total equities	$586,000	$170,000

Additonal Information

1 Packard Manufacturing Corporation paid $128,000 for its 80 percent interest in Studs on January 1, 19X3 when Studs had capital stock of $100,000 and retained earnings of $10,000.
2 Goodwill is being amortized over a ten-year period.
3 At December 31, 19X4 Packard's inventory included items on which Studs had recorded gross profit of $20,000.

Required: Prepare comparative consolidated balance sheets for Packard Manufacturing Corporation and Subsidiary at December 31, 19X4 under the contemporary and entity theories of consoiidation.

P 11-6 [AICPA adapted]

The individual and consolidated balance sheets and income statements of X and Y Companies for the current year are as follows:

X AND Y COMPANIES INDIVIDUAL AND CONSOLIDATED BALANCE SHEETS AS OF THE END OF THE CURRENT YEAR

	X Company	Y Company	Consolidated
Assets			
Cash and receivables	$ 35,000	$108,000	$ 97,400
Inventories	40,000	90,000	122,000
Plant (net)	460,000	140,000	600,000
Goodwill from consolidation	—	—	30,000
Investment in Y	245,000	—	—
X bonds owned	—	103,000	—
Total assets	$780,000	$441,000	$849,400

	X Company	Y Company	Consolidated
Liabilities and Equity			
Current payables	$ 70,000	$ 23,000	$ 53,000
Dividends payable	10,000	8,000	12,400
Mortgage bonds (5%)	200,000	50,000	150,000
Capital stock	300,000	200,000	300,000
Retained earnings	200,000	160,000	217,000
Minority interest	—	—	117,000
Total liabilities and equity	$780,000	$441,000	$849,400

INDIVIDUAL AND CONSOLIDATED INCOME STATEMENTS FOR THE CURRENT YEAR

	X Company	Y Company	Consolidated
Sales	$600,000	$400,000	$760,000
Cost of sales	360,000	280,000	403,000
Gross profit	240,000	120,000	357,000
Operating expenses	130,000	54,000	189,000
Operating profit	110,000	66,000	168,000
Interest revenue	1,800	5,000	1,800
Dividend revenue	11,200	—	—
	123,000	71,000	169,800
Interest expense	10,000	3,000	8,000
Provision for income tax	56,000	34,000	90,000
Nonrecurring loss	—	—	3,000
Minority share	—	—	8,700
Net income	$ 57,000	$ 34,000	$ 60,100
Dividends	20,000	16,000	24,800
Transfer to retained earnings	$ 37,000	$ 18,000	$ 35,300

Additional Information

1 X Company purchased its interest in Y Company several years ago.
2 X Company sells products to Y Company for further processing and also sells to firms outside the affiliated entity. The inventories of Y Company include an intercompany profit at both the beginning and the end of the year.
3 At the beginning of the current year, Y Company purchased bonds of X Company having a maturity value of $100,000. These bonds are held as a temporary investment, and it is intended that no amortization of purchase premium will be made on either individual or consolidated statements. The bonds are carried by Y Company at cost. Y Company has agreed to offer X Company the option of reacquiring the bonds at Y's cost before deciding to dispose of them on the open market.

Required: Answer the following questions on the basis of the preceding information.

1 Does X Company carry its investment in Y Company on the cost or equity basis? Explain the basis of your answer.
2 If Y Company's common stock has a stated value of $100 per share, how many shares does X Company own? How did you determine this?
3 When X acquired its interest in Y Company, the assets and liabilities of Y Company were recorded at their fair values. The $30,000 goodwill from consolidation represents unamortized goodwill at the end of the current year. The original goodwill was $50,000 under entity theory, and the amortization is over a ten-year period. What was the amount of Y's retained earnings at the date that X Company acquired its interest in Y Company?
4 What is the nature of the nonrecurring loss appearing on the consolidated income statement? Reproduce the consolidating entry from which this figure originated and explain.
5 What is the amount of intercompany sales during the current year by X Company to Y Company?

478

CONSOLIDATION
THEORIES, PUSH-DOWN
ACCOUNTING, AND
CORPORATE JOINT
VENTURES

6 Are there any intercompany debts other than the intercompany bondholdings? Identify any such debts, and state which company is the debtor and which is the creditor in each case. Explain your reasoning.

7 What is the explanation for the difference between the consolidated cost of goods sold and the combined cost of goods sold of the two affiliated companies? Prepare a schedule reconciling combined and consolidated cost of goods sold, showing the amount of intercompany profit in the beginning and ending inventories of Y Company and demonstrating how you determined the amount of intercompany profit. (Hint: A well-organized and labeled T-account for cost of goods sold will be an acceptable approach.)

8 Show how the $8,700 minority interest in total consolidated net income was determined.

9 Show how the total minority interest on the balance sheet ($117,000) was determined.

10 Beginning with the $200,000 balance in X Company's retained earnings at the end of the current year, prepare a schedule in which you derive the $217,000 balance of consolidated retained earnings at the end of the current year.

P 11-7 [Push-down accounting] Playmore Corporation paid $400,000 cash for a 100 percent interest in Solvay Corporation on January 1, 19X8 when Solvay's stockholders' equity consisted of $200,000 capital stock and $80,000 retained earnings. Solvay's balance sheet on December 31, 19X7 is summarized as follows:

	Book Value	Fair Value
Cash	$ 30,000	$ 30,000
Accounts receivable—net	70,000	70,000
Inventories	60,000	80,000
Land	50,000	75,000
Buildings—net	100,000	150,000
Equipment—net	90,000	75,000
Total assets	$400,000	$480,000
Accounts payable	$ 40,000	$ 40,000
Other liabilities	70,000	60,000
Capital stock	200,000	
Retained earnings	90,000	
Total equities	$400,000	

Playmore uses the equity method to account for its interest in Solvay. The amortization periods for the fair value–book value differentials at the time of acquisition were as follows:

$20,000	Undervalued inventories (sold in 19X8)
25,000	Undervalued land
50,000	Undervalued buildings (10-year use life remaining)
(15,000)	Overvalued equipment (5-year use life remaining)
10,000	Other liabilities (2 years before maturity)
20,000	Goodwill (10-year amortization period)

Required

1 Prepare a journal entry on Solvay's books to push down the values reflected in the purchase price.

2 Prepare a balance sheet for Solvay Corporation on January 1, 19X8.

3 Solvay's net income for 19X8 under the new push-down accounting system is $90,000. What is Playmore's income from Solvay for 19X8?

P 11-8 [Push-down accounting] Parker Corporation paid $3,000,000 for an 80 percent interest in Sanue Corporation on January 1, 19X9 when the book values and fair values of Sanue's assets and liabilities were as follows:

	Book Value	Fair Value
Cash	$ 300,000	$ 300,000
Accounts receivable—net	600,000	600,000
Inventories	800,000	2,400,000
Land	200,000	200,000
Buildings—net	600,000	600,000
Equipment—net	1,000,000	500,000
	$3,500,000	$4,600,000
Accounts payable	$ 500,000	$ 500,000
Long-term debt	1,000,000	1,000,000
Capital stock, $1 par	800,000	
Retained earnings	1,200,000	
	$3,500,000	

Required
1 Prepare a journal entry on Sanue's books to push down 80 percent of the values reflected in the purchase price (the parent company theory approach).
2 Prepare a journal entry on Sanue's books to push down 100 percent of the values reflected in the purchase price (the entity theory approach).
3 Calculate the minority interest in Sanue on January 1, 19X9 under parent company theory.
4 Calculate the minority interest in Sanue on January 1, 19X9 under entity theory.

P 11-9 [Push-down accounting] Power Corporation paid $180,000 cash for a 90 percent interest in Swing Corporation on January 1, 19X8 when Swing's stockholders' equity consisted of $100,000 capital stock and $20,000 retained earnings. Swing Corporation's balance sheet on December 31, 19X7 was as follows:

BALANCE SHEET

	Book Value	Fair Value
Cash	$ 20,000	$ 20,000
Accounts receivable—net	50,000	50,000
Inventories	40,000	30,000
Land	15,000	15,000
Buildings—net	30,000	50,000
Equipment—net	70,000	100,000
Total assets	$225,000	$265,000
Accounts payable	$ 45,000	$ 45,000
Other liabilities	60,000	60,000
Capital stock	100,000	
Retained earnings	20,000	
Total equities	$225,000	

Additional Information
1 The amortization periods for the fair value–book value differentials at the time of acquisition were as follows:

Overvalued inventories (sold in 19X8)	$10,000
Undervalued buildings (10-year useful lives)	$20,000
Undervalued equipment (5-year useful lives)	$30,000
Goodwill (10-year amortization period)	Remainder

2 Power uses the equity method to account for its interest in Swing.

480

CONSOLIDATION
THEORIES, PUSH-DOWN
ACCOUNTING, AND
CORPORATE JOINT
VENTURES

Required

1 Prepare a journal entry on Swing Corporation's books to push down the values reflected in the purchase price under parent company theory.

2 Prepare a journal entry on Swing Corporation's books to push down the values reflected in the purchase price under entity theory.

3 Prepare comparative balance sheets for Swing Corporation on January 1, 19X8 under the approaches of (1) and (2).

P 11-10 [Push-down accounting] Use the information and assumptions from Problem 11-9 for this problem. The accompanying financial statements are for Power and Swing Corporations, one year after the business combination. Note that Swing's statements are presented first under contemporary theory with no push-down accounting, then under 90 percent push-down accounting and finally, under 100 percent push-down accounting.

Swing mailed a check to Power on December 31, 19X8 to settle an account payable of $8,000. Power received the check in 19X9. The $8,000 amount is included in Power's December 31, 19X8 accounts receivable.

POWER CORPORATION AND SWING CORPORATION
COMPARATIVE FINANCIAL STATEMENTS
WITH AND WITHOUT PUSH-DOWN ACCOUNTING
AT AND FOR THE YEAR ENDED DECEMBER 31, 19X8

	Basic Accounting Power Corporation	Basic Accounting Swing Corporation	Push Down 90% Swing Corporation	Push Down 100% Swing Corporation
Income Statement				
Sales	$310,800	$110,000	$110,000	$110,000
Income from Swing	34,200			
Cost of sales	(140,000)	(42,000)	(33,000)	(32,000)
Depreciation expense	(29,000)	(17,000)	(24,200)	(25,000)
Other operating expenses	(45,000)	(11,000)	(14,600)	(15,000)
Net income	$131,000	$ 40,000	$ 38,200	$ 38,000
Retained Earnings				
Retained earnings—beginning	$147,000	$ 20,000	$ 0	$ 0
Add: Net income	131,000	40,000	38,200	38,000
Deduct: Dividends	(60,000)	(10,000)	(10,000)	(10,000)
Retained earnings—ending	$218,000	$ 50,000	$ 28,200	$ 28,000
Balance Sheet				
Cash	$ 63,800	$ 27,000	$ 27,000	$ 27,000
Accounts receivable	90,000	40,000	40,000	40,000
Dividends receivable	9,000			
Inventories	20,000	35,000	35,000	35,000
Land	40,000	15,000	15,000	15,000
Buildings—net	140,000	27,000	43,200	45,000
Equipment—net	165,000	56,000	77,600	80,000
Investment in Swing	205,200			
Goodwill			32,400	36,000
Total assets	$733,000	$200,000	$270,200	$278,000
Accounts payable	$125,000	$ 20,000	$ 20,000	$ 20,000
Dividends payable	15,000	10,000	10,000	10,000
Other liabilities	75,000	20,000	20,000	20,000
Capital stock	300,000	100,000	100,000	100,000
Push-down capital			92,000	100,000
Retained earnings	218,000	50,000	28,200	28,000
Total equities	$733,000	$200,000	$270,200	$278,000

Required: Prepare consolidation working papers for Power Corporation and Subsidiary for the year ended December 31, 19X8 under (a) 90 percent push-down accounting and (b) 100 percent push-down accounting.

P 11-11 [Joint ventures] Pepper Corporation owns a 40 percent interest in Jerry Company, a joint venture that is organized as an undivided interest. In its separate financial statements, Pepper accounts for Jerry under the equity method, but for reporting purposes, the proportionate consolidation method is used.

Separate financial statements of Pepper and Jerry at and for the year ended December 31, 19X2 are summarized as follows:

	Pepper Corporation	Jerry Company
Comparative Income and Retained Earnings Statements for the Year Ended December 31, 19X2		
Sales	$ 800,000	$300,000
Income from Jerry	20,000	—
Cost of sales	(400,000)	(150,000)
Depreciation expense	(100,000)	(40,000)
Other expenses	(120,000)	(60,000)
Net income	200,000	50,000
Beginning retained earnings	300,000	—
Beginning venture equity	—	250,000
Dividends	(100,000)	—
Retained earnings/venture equity	$ 400,000	$300,000
Comparative Balance Sheets at December 31, 19X2		
Cash	$ 100,000	$ 50,000
Receivables—net	130,000	30,000
Inventories	110,000	40,000
Land	140,000	60,000
Buildings—net	200,000	100,000
Equipment—net	300,000	180,000
Investment in Jerry	120,000	—
Total assets	$1,100,000	$460,000
Accounts payable	$ 120,000	$100,000
Other liabilities	80,000	60,000
Common stock, $10 par	500,000	—
Retained earnings	400,000	—
Venture equity	—	300,000
Total equities	$1,100,000	$460,000

Required: Prepare working papers for a proportionate consolidation of the financial statements of Pepper Corporation and Jerry Company at and for the year ended December 31, 19X2.

P 11-12 [Appendix] Separate financial statement on a current cost basis for Pringle and Slate at and for the year ended December 31, 19X2 are as follows:

	Pringle	Slate
Combined Income and Retained Earnings Statement for the Year Ended December 31, 19X2		
Sales	$8,000,000	$2,900,000
Income from Slate	130,000	—
Cost of sales	6,950,000*	2,000,000*
Expenses	530,000*	700,000*
Net income	650,000	200,000

482

CONSOLIDATION
THEORIES, PUSH-DOWN
ACCOUNTING, AND
CORPORATE JOINT
VENTURES

	Pringle	Slate
Add: Beginning retained earnings	2,150,000	600,000
Deduct: Dividends	300,000*	100,000*
Retained earnings December 31, 19X2	$2,500,000	$ 700,000

Balance Sheet at December 31, 19X2

	Pringle	Slate
Cash	$ 820,000	$ 400,000
Other current assets	1,800,000	700,000
Plant assets—net	4,900,000	1,900,000
Investment in Slate	1,980,000	—
Total assets	$9,500,000	$3,000,000
Liabilities	$1,000,000	$ 300,000
Capital stock	6,000,000	2,000,000
Retained earnings	2,500,000	700,000
Total equities	$9,500,000	$3,000,000

* Deduct.

Additional Information
1 Pringle acquired its 70 percent interest in Slate for $1,920,000 on December 31, 19X1.
2 Goodwill is being amortized over a ten-year period.
3 During 19X2 Pringle sold inventory items that cost $200,000 to Slate for $300,000. Half of these goods are inventoried by Slate at a current cost of $140,000 and are included in Slate's "other current assets" at December 31, 19X2.

Required: Prepare consolidation working papers for Pringle Corporation and Subsidiary at and for the year ended December 31, 19X2.

12

ACCOUNTING FOR BRANCH OPERATIONS

Previous chapters of this book have considered accounting and reporting procedures for consolidating the separate operations of parent companies and their subsidiaries. The objective of consolidation is to report the financial position and results of operations of separate legal entities as if there were only one economic entity. By contrast, branches are identifiable locations within a business entity for which separate accounting records are maintained. Branches are separate accounting entities, but they are not separate legal entities, and their financial statements are used only for internal reporting purposes. Financial statements for the business entity are prepared by combining the financial statements of the branches with those of the central reporting unit of the business.

This chapter distinguishes between sales agency and branch operations, describes accounting procedures for branch operations, and illustrates procedures for combining home office and branch financial statements in the preparation of financial statements for the business entity as a whole.

SALES AGENCIES AND BRANCHES

A technical distinction is commonly made between *sales agencies* and *branches*. **Sales agencies** are established to display merchandise and to take customers' orders, but they do not stock merchandise to fill customers' orders or pass on customer credit. The sales agency is not a separate accounting or business entity. Ordinarily, the only accounting records required for sales agencies are for cash receipts and disbursements, which are handled in essentially the same manner as petty cash systems. The central accounting system of the business maintains records of sales made through agency operations and related cost of sales and other expenses.

By contrast, a **branch operation** stocks merchandise, makes sales to customers, passes on customer credit, collects receivables, incurs expenses, and performs other functions normally associated with the operations of a separate business enterprise. Such activities are accounted for through separate branch accounting systems that parallel the systems of independent businesses except in the manner of accounting for ownership equities and in recording transactions between branches and the main office of the enterprise.

Many of the larger branch operations are the result of business combinations in which the surviving corporations establish branch entities to account for the operations of the combining corporations that are dissolved. In such cases, the existing information systems of the combining companies can be converted into home office and branch accounting systems with only minor adjustments. This method of combining accounting systems is often economical in that it avoids major changes in existing information systems and minimizes disruptions in normal business operations. This method also makes it easy to dispose of the new branch operations if they prove unprofitable.

While the technical distinctions for classifying sales agencies and branches may be important for marketing, advertising, and other business purposes, they are not particularly helpful for accounting purposes. Some sales agencies do carry stock in trade, and some branch operations have limited responsibility for maintaining customer records and approving credit. Many firms with branch operations have centralized customer credit and record and billing services on a regional or even a companywide basis. The accounting system for a remote business location, whether a branch or an agency, should be designed to accumulate information needed as economically and efficiently as possible.

SALES AGENCY ACCOUNTS

As explained, sales agencies do not require complete accounting systems to account for their limited activities. Ordinarily, cash receipts and disbursements records are sufficient for accounting at agency locations. Records for sales agency operations must be maintained in the central accounting system of the enterprise. The amount of data accumulated by the enterprise for agency operations may be limited to records of cash and display merchandise at agency offices, on one hand, or comprise relatively complete asset and income data, on the other.

If detailed information for a sales agency is not deemed necessary, the following entries may suffice to account for agency operations.

1 Creation of an agency working capital fund:

Agency working capital	$5,000	
Cash		$5,000

To record transfer of cash to sales agency.

2 Transfer of sample inventory to sales agency:

Sample inventory—agency	$9,000	
Merchandise inventory (or purchases)		$9,000

To transfer display merchandise to sales agency.

3 Replenishment of agency working capital at month or year-end:

Salaries expense	$2,200	
Utilities expense	700	
Advertising expense	1,200	
Miscellaneous expense	300	
Cash		$4,400

To record expenses incurred by sales agency and replenishment of agency working capital.

4 Adjustment of agency sample inventory at month or year-end:

Advertising expense	$3,000	
Sample inventory—agency		$3,000

To adjust agency sample inventory to net realizable value and to charge the write-down to advertising expense.

These entries serve to account for agency expense transactions and cash and merchandise in possession of agency personnel. But the system illustrated is not adequate for effective control over agency expenses or for measuring the contribution of agency operations to enterprise income; nor does it provide a basis for determining if agency operations are being performed efficiently.

An expansion of the system to accumulate agency sales and expense information provides a basis for comparing agency expenses over time and with expenses of similar sales agencies. It also enables profit evaluation of agency operations. The extent of detail accumulated for each sales agency depends upon the information needs of management.

Journal entries for an expanded agency accounting system follow. The entries identify plant assets of the Newport sales agency separately. They also show sales, cost of sales, and expense information on an agency basis.

1 Purchase of Newport sales agency land and buildings:

Land—Newport sales agency	$ 2,000	
Buildings—Newport sales agency	18,000	
Cash		$20,000

Purchase of facilities for sales agency.

2 Creation of a sales agency working capital fund:

Newport sales agency working capital	$ 4,000	
Cash		$ 4,000

To record transfer of cash to Newport sales agency.

3 Transfer of display merchandise to sales agency:

Newport sales agency sample inventory	$ 8,000	
Merchandise inventory		$ 8,000

To record transfer of sample merchandise to sales agency.

4 Payment of salaries to employees of sales agency:

Salaries expense—Newport sales agency	$ 3,000	
Cash		$ 3,000

To record payment of salaries to sales agency employees.

5 Sales orders from sales agency are filled and customers are billed:

Accounts receivable	$12,000	
Sales—Newport sales agency		$12,000

Credit sales made through Newport sales agency.

Cost of sales—Newport sales agency	$ 6,000	
Merchandise inventory		$ 6,000

Cost of merchandise delivered to customers of sales agency.

6 Replenishment of agency's working capital fund at end of period:

Advertising expense—Newport sales agency	$ 1,800	
Utilities expense—Newport sales agency	400	
Other expenses—Newport sales agency	300	
Cash		$ 2,500

To record replenishment of sales agency's working capital.

7 Depreciation recorded on sales agency's buildings:

Depreciation expense—Newport sales agency	$ 900	
Accumulated depreciation—Newport sales agency		$ 900

To record depreciation on sales agency's buildings.

8 Sample merchandise at sales agency adjusted to reflect shopwear:

Advertising expense—Newport sales agency	$ 1,000	
Newport sales agency sample inventory		$ 1,000

To record adjustment of sample inventory to net realizable value.

The entries illustrated are merely examples of how an accounting system can be expanded to provide separate information for agency operations. Accumulation of such information is both practical and inexpensive with the aid of modern computer technology, even when an enterprise has a large number of sales agency operations.

BRANCH ACCOUNTING SYSTEMS

Branch accounting involves segmenting the accounting system of an enterprise into separate accounting systems for home office and branch operations. The home office records constitute the central accounting unit for the enterprise and branch records constitute adjunct accounting systems for each branch operation. Separate home office and branch systems are used for accounting and internal reporting purposes, but the separate financial statements of the home office and branches have to be combined into a single set of financial statements for the enterprise in order to meet external reporting requirements.

The process of combining home office and branch financial statements is similar to the process of consolidating parent and subsidiary statements. Reciprocity is established between home office and branch records, reciprocal accounts are eliminated, and nonreciprocal accounts are combined. Unrealized profits from internal transfers between the home office and the branches must, of course, be eliminated in preparing combined financial statements for the enterprise.

Transactions Between the Home Office and the Branch

Transactions of the home office with external entities are recorded in the home office accounting records in the usual fashion. Similarly, transactions between a branch and unrelated entities are recorded on the branch books in accordance with established accounting procedures. Thus, the unique feature of home office and branch accounting lies in the manner of recording transactions between the home office and its branches.

The creation of a new branch requires entries on the books of both the home office and the branch. Assume that Expando Corporation creates a branch in Splinter, Montana, by transferring cash of $5,000 and equipment with a cost of $10,000 to the branch manager. Entries on the books of the home office and the branch are:

Home Office Books		
Splinter branch	$15,000	
Cash		$ 5,000
Equipment		10,000

To record transfer of cash and equipment to Splinter branch.

Branch Books		
Cash	$ 5,000	
Equipment	10,000	
Home office		$15,000

To record receipt of cash and equipment from home office.

The branch account on the home office books represents the investment of the home office in branch net assets. The home office account on the branch books represents the equity of the home office in branch net assets. Thus, the branch and home office accounts are reciprocal, each representing the net assets of the branch. This reciprocal relationship between home office and branch accounts is a continuous relationship. Whenever the home office increases (debits) its branch account, the branch should increase (credit) its home office account. Similarly, any decrease (debit) in the home office account on the branch books should be accompanied by a decrease (credit) in the branch account on the home office books. The only reasons that differences between home office and branch accounts occur are time lags in recording information on the two sets of books and errors.

A second type of transaction between home office and branches is for merchandise transfers. Typically, branches are established to sell merchandise that is manufactured or purchased through home office operations. A branch manager may or may not have authority to purchase from outside suppliers. If Expando Corporation ships merchandise to the Splinter branch at its $8,000 home office cost, the following journal entries are required:

Home Office Books
Splinter branch	$8,000	
Shipments to Splinter branch		$8,000

To record shipments at cost to Splinter branch.

Branch Books
Shipments from home office	$8,000	
Home office		$8,000

To record shipments received from home office.

Two additional reciprocal accounts result from recording the merchandise transfer from home office to branch. The home office's shipments to branch account is a "contra purchases" account on the home office books, and the shipments from home office account on the branch books is essentially a "branch purchases" account. These accounts are used to determine the separate cost of sales for home office and branch operations, but since they are reciprocal, they are eliminated in preparing combined financial statements for the enterprise.

Illustration of Home Office and Branch Accounting

Assume that Jiffy-Stop Corporation created a new branch outlet in Bee, Nebraska at the beginning of 19X1, and that the transactions of the Bee branch during 19X1 are as follows:

1　Received cash of $20,000 from the home office.
2　Purchased equipment with a five-year life for $10,000 cash.
3　Received merchandise shipments from home office at the $16,000 home office cost.
4　Purchased merchandise from outside suppliers for $4,000 cash.
5　Sold merchandise for $30,000 cash.
6　Returned $1,000 of the merchandise acquired from the home office.
7　Paid expenses as follows:

Salaries	$6,000
Utilities	1,000
Rent expense	3,000
Other expenses	2,000

8　Remitted $15,000 to the home office.
9　Salaries payable at year-end were $1,000 and depreciation for the year was $2,000.
10　Branch inventory at year-end consisted of $1,000 merchandise acquired from outside suppliers and $5,000 acquired from home office.

Journal Entries Journal entries to record these transactions and related year-end events on the books of Bee branch are illustrated in Exhibit 12–1. The exhibit also shows journal entries on the home office books to reflect reciprocal home office items. The closing entry of Bee branch contains a $2,000 credit to the home office account. This $2,000 is equal to branch income for the period and reflects the net asset increase from branch operations. A related adjusting entry on the home office books debits the Bee branch account for $2,000 and credits Bee branch profit for the period. This home office adjusting entry is roughly equivalent to a parent company entry to record its share of subsidiary income for a period under the equity method of accounting.

Cost of Sales Computations The journal entries illustrated in Exhibit 12–1 are based on periodic inventory procedures that provide detailed information about merchandise transfers between home office and branch locations. While this detailed information can be used in the working papers to combine the home office and branch accounts for external reporting, it is convenient to group the separate inventory, purchases, and the shipment data into individual cost of sales categories for efficient preparation of working papers. Separate cost of sales computations for the home office and branch of Jiffy-Stop are as follows:

	Home Office	Bee Branch
Inventory January 1, 19X1	$ 85,000	$ —
Purchases	150,000	4,000
Shipments to branch	(15,000)	—
Shipments from home office	—	15,000
Goods available for sale	220,000	19,000
Inventory December 31, 19X1	(80,000)	(6,000)
Cost of sales	$140,000	$13,000

Data for home office purchases and inventories are included in the cost of sales computations without prior explanation.

Working Papers Home office and branch accounting records may be combined, using either the trial balance or the financial statement working paper format. These approaches are illustrated in Exhibits 12–2 and 12–3 for the Jiffy-Stop Corporation. Data for the home office not previously introduced are included in the working papers to complete the illustrations.

Adjusted trial balances for Jiffy-Stop's home office and its Bee branch are shown in the first two columns of the trial balance working papers in Exhibit 12–2. The working paper procedures are comparable to those for the trial balance working papers used in preparing consolidated financial statements. Only two working paper entries are needed: one to establish reciprocity between the branch and home office accounts by eliminating the Bee branch profit and reducing the branch account to its preadjustment balance and a second entry to eliminate reciprocal home office and branch account balances. These entries are similar to the consolidation working paper entries to eliminate income from subsidiaries against the investment in subsidiary account and, subsequently, to eliminate reciprocal investment and equity balances.

The same working paper entries are used in combining the home office and branch accounts in Exhibit 12–3 when the financial statement format is used. Under the financial statement format, however, the absence of a retained earnings account in the ledger of the branch necessitates a change in the retained earnings section of the working papers. Since the equity account of a branch is its home office account, the branch column of the working papers shows changes in the home office account from current operations. Observe that working paper entry a of Exhibit 12–3 returns the Bee branch account on the home office books

Transaction	Home Office Books			Bee Branch Books		
1	Bee branch	$20,000		Cash	$20,000	
	Cash		$20,000	Home office		$20,000
	To transfer cash to Bee branch.			Receipt of cash from home office.		
2				Equipment	$10,000	
				Cash		$10,000
				To record purchase of equipment.		
3	Bee branch	$16,000		Shipments from home office	$16,000	
	Shipments to Bee branch		$16,000	Home office		$16,000
	To transfer merchandise to Bee branch at cost.			Receipt of merchandise from home office.		
4				Purchases	$ 4,000	
				Cash		$ 4,000
				To record cash purchases.		
5				Cash	$30,000	
				Sales		$30,000
				To record cash sales.		
6	Shipments to Bee branch	$ 1,000		Home office	$ 1,000	
	Bee branch		$ 1,000	Shipments from home office		$ 1,000
	Merchandise returned from Bee branch.			Merchandise returned to home office.		
7				Salaries expense	$ 6,000	
				Utilities expense	1,000	
				Rent expense	3,000	
				Other expenses	2,000	
				Cash		$12,000
				To record payment of expenses.		
8	Cash	$15,000		Home office	$15,000	
	Bee branch		$15,000	Cash		$15,000
	Cash received from Bee branch.			To record cash remittance to home office.		
9				*Adjusting Entries*		
				Salaries expense	$ 1,000	
				Salaries payable		$ 1,000
				Accrued salaries.		
				Depreciation expense—		
				equipment	$ 2,000	
				Accumulated depreciation—		
				equipment		$ 2,000
				Depreciation expense $10,000 ÷ 5 years.		
10	*Adjusting Entry*			*Closing Entry*		
	Bee branch	$ 2,000		Sales	$30,000	
	Bee branch profit		$ 2,000	Inventory	6,000	
	To record Bee branch profit for the period.			Shipments from home office		$15,000
				Purchases		4,000
				Salaries expense		7,000
				Depreciation expense		2,000
				Utilities expense		1,000
				Rent expense		3,000
				Other expenses		2,000
				Home office		2,000
				To close income accounts to home office.		

Exhibit 12–1   *Jiffy-Stop Corporation: Home Office and Branch Journal Entries*

JIFFY-STOP CORPORATION
HOME OFFICE AND BRANCH WORKING PAPERS
FOR THE YEAR ENDED DECEMBER 31, 19X1

	Home Office	Bee Branch	Adjustments and Eliminations	Income Statement	Retained Earnings	Balance Sheet
Debits						
Cash	$ 41,000	$ 9,000				$ 50,000
Accounts receivable	60,000					60,000
Inventories—ending	80,000	6,000				86,000
Land	20,000					20,000
Buildings—net	100,000					100,000
Equipment—net	52,000	8,000				60,000
Bee branch	22,000		a 2,000 b 20,000			
Cost of sales	140,000	13,000		$153,000*		
Salaries expense	43,000	7,000		50,000*		
Depreciation expense— buildings	5,000			5,000*		
Depreciation expense— equipment	8,000	2,000		10,000*		
Utilities expense	6,000	1,000		7,000*		
Rent expense		3,000		3,000*		
Other expenses	8,000	2,000		10,000*		
Dividends	10,000				$ 10,000*	
	$595,000	$51,000				$376,000
Credits						
Accounts payable	$ 50,000					$ 50,000
Salaries payable	4,000	$ 1,000				5,000
Capital stock	200,000					200,000
Retained earnings	110,000				110,000	
Home office		20,000	b 20,000			
Sales	229,000	30,000		259,000		
Bee branch profit	2,000		a 2,000			
	$595,000	$51,000				
Net income				$ 21,000	21,000	
Retained earnings—December 31, 19X1					$121,000	121,000
						$376,000

* Deduct.

Exhibit 12–2   Combining Working Papers—Trial Balance Approach

JIFFY-STOP CORPORATION
HOME OFFICE AND BRANCH WORKING PAPERS
FOR THE YEAR ENDED DECEMBER 31, 19X1

	Home Office	Bee Branch	Adjustments and Eliminations	Combined Statement
Income Statement Sales	$229,000	$30,000		$259,000
Bee branch profit	2,000		a 2,000	
Cost of sales	140,000*	13,000*		153,000*
Salaries expense	43,000*	7,000*		50,000*
Depreciation expense—buildings	5,000*			5,000*
Depreciation expense—equipment	8,000*	2,000*		10,000*
Utilities expense	6,000*	1,000*		7,000*
Rent expense		3,000*		3,000*
Other expenses	8,000*	2,000*		10,000*
Net income	$ 21,000	$ 2,000		$ 21,000
Retained Earnings—Home Office Retained earnings January 1	$110,000			$110,000
Home office (preclosing)		$20,000	b 20,000	
Net income	21,000	2,000		21,000
Dividends	10,000*			10,000*
Retained earnings—Home office	$121,000	$22,000		$121,000
Balance Sheet Cash	$ 41,000	$ 9,000		$ 50,000
Accounts receivable—net	60,000			60,000
Inventory	80,000	6,000		86,000
Land	20,000			20,000
Buildings—net	100,000			100,000
Equipment—net	52,000	8,000		60,000
Bee branch	22,000		a 2,000 b 20,000	
	$375,000	$23,000		$376,000
Accounts payable	$ 50,000			$ 50,000
Salaries payable	4,000	$ 1,000		5,000
Capital stock	200,000			200,000
Retained earnings	121,000			121,000
Home office		22,000		
	$375,000	$23,000		$376,000

* Deduct.

Exhibit 12-3 Combining Working Papers—Financial Statement Approach

to its $20,000 preadjusted balance to establish reciprocity with the $20,000 pre-closing balance of the home office account. Subsequently, entry b eliminates these reciprocal balances. Other aspects of the home office–branch working papers are the same as those for working papers of parent and subsidiary operations. Normally, only the combined financial statements that reflect the financial position and results of operations for the entity as a whole are used for external reporting purposes.

MERCHANDISE SHIPMENTS IN EXCESS OF COST

The procedures illustrated for Jiffy-Stop are based on merchandise shipments between the home office and Bee branch at home office cost. Many corporations, however, use transfer prices in excess of cost for internal shipments to their branches. Some corporations set transfer prices at normal sales prices while others use standard markups. Still other corporations develop complex formulas for determining transfer prices. Reasons commonly cited for internal transfers of merchandise above cost include equitable allocation of income between the various units of the enterprise, efficiency in pricing inventories, and concealment of true profit margins from branch personnel.

Shipments to Branch Recorded at Cost

When a home office ships merchandise to its branches at transfer prices in excess of cost, the accounting records of the home office are adjusted to permit measurement of actual cost of merchandise transferred. This is usually done through an inventory "loading" or unrealized profit account. For example, if Southern Fashion Mart's home office ships merchandise that costs $100,000 to its Tampa branch at a 20 percent markup based on cost, the home office and branch entries are:

Home Office Books

Tampa branch	$120,000	
Shipments to Tampa branch		$100,000
Loading in Tampa branch inventory		20,000

   To record shipments to Tampa branch at 120% of cost.

Tampa Branch Books

Shipments from home office	$120,000	
Home office		$120,000

   To record receipt of merchandise from home office.

Entries to record transfers of merchandise at prices in excess of cost do not change the reciprocal relationship between the home office and branch accounts, but they do affect the relationship between home office and branch shipment accounts, since the "shipments to branch" account is credited at cost and the "shipments from home office" account is debited at the transfer price. The difference between the shipment accounts lies in the markup that is reflected in the loading in branch inventories account. This loading account is frequently designated "unrealized profit in branch inventories."

When a branch receives merchandise at transfer prices that include a loading factor and sells that merchandise, its cost of goods sold is overstated and its income is understated. Since the home office increases its branch account and records branch profit or loss on the basis of income reported by the branch, any branch profit recorded by the home office is similarly understated. This understatement of branch profit on home office books is corrected by a year-end adjusting entry that reduces the loading account to reflect amounts realized during the period through branch sales to outside entities.

Assume that the following account balances appear on the books of Southern Fashion Mart's home office and branch at December 31, 19X1 before adjusting entries are recorded:

Home Office Books

Tampa branch	$200,000 debit
Shipments to Tampa branch	100,000 credit
Loading in Tampa branch inventory	20,000 credit

Tampa Branch Books

Sales	$160,000 credit
Shipments from home office	120,000 debit
Expenses	30,000 debit
Home office	200,000 credit

If the Tampa branch has $12,000 inventory at transfer prices on December 31, 19X1, it reports income for the period of $22,000 (sales of $160,000, less cost of sales of $108,000 and other expenses of $30,000). The branch closing entry for the period is:

Sales	$160,000	
Inventory December 31, 19X1	12,000	
Shipments from home office		$120,000
Expenses		30,000
Home office		22,000

To close nominal accounts and transfer the balance to the home office account.

This information is used by the home office to record branch profit for the period:

Tampa branch	$ 22,000	
Tampa branch profit		$ 22,000

To take up branch profit and to update the branch account.

The home office also adjusts its loading account to reflect the $2,000 unrealized profit in branch ending inventory [$12,000 − ($12,000/120%)]:

Loading in Tampa branch inventory	$ 18,000	
Tampa branch profit		$ 18,000

To adjust branch loading account ($20,000 − $2,000) and branch profit for the period.

After this entry is posted, the loading account will have a $2,000 balance equal to the $2,000 unrealized profit in the Tampa branch inventory, and the Tampa branch profit account will show a balance of $40,000. This $40,000 is the income of the branch on a cost basis, an amount that is subject to independent confirmation as follows:

Sales		$160,000
Shipments to branch (at cost)	$100,000	
Less: Inventory (at cost)	10,000	90,000
Gross profit		70,000
Other expenses		30,000
Branch income		$ 40,000

When the $40,000 branch profit is added to separate home office income for the period, the total equals combined net income for the enterprise. Although year-end entries for subsequent years are substantially the same as those illustrated, there will be a difference because the branch will have a beginning inventory stated at transfer prices, and the home office will have a beginning balance in its loading account equal to the unrealized profit in the branch beginning inventory. An example of branch accounting for Dasher Corporation at the end of this chapter illustrates accounting procedures for unrealized profits in both beginning and ending branch inventories.

Shipments to Branch Recorded at Billing Prices

Some firms enter merchandise shipments to their branches at billing prices and adjust the loading account only at the end of the accounting period. When this approach is used, the balance of the loading account during an accounting period will reflect unrealized profit in branch beginning inventories, and the shipments to branch account will include the loading factor on shipments for the current period. The shipments to branch account (home office books) and the shipments from home office account (branch books) are reciprocals under this method.

To illustrate, Southern Fashion Mart's shipments to the Tampa branch could have been recorded at billing prices as follows:

Home Office Books

Tampa branch	$120,000	
Shipments to Tampa branch		$120,000

With this entry the home office and branch shipment accounts have equal balances, but two year-end adjusting entries are needed:

Home Office Books

Shipments to Tampa branch	$ 20,000	
Loading in Tampa branch inventory		$ 20,000
To adjust shipments to a cost basis.		
Loading in Tampa branch inventory	$ 18,000	
Tampa branch profit		$ 18,000
To adjust branch profit for realization of markup on branch shipments.		

The first entry adjusts the shipments to branch and loading in branch inventory accounts to create balances of $100,000 and $20,000, respectively. The second entry to adjust branch profit for the loading factor is the same as the one shown earlier.

FREIGHT COSTS ON SHIPMENTS

The cost of transporting merchandise to its final sale location can be an important element of the cost of merchandise inventoried and sold. Accordingly, freight costs on merchandise shipped between home office and branch locations should be included in branch inventory and cost of goods sold measurements. Assume that merchandise is shipped from a home office to its branch at 125 percent of the $10,000 home office cost, and that the home office pays $500 freight costs. The following home office and branch journal entries are required:

Home Office Books

Branch	$13,000	
Shipments to branch		$10,000
Loading in branch inventory		2,500
Cash		500
To record shipments to branch.		

Branch Books

Shipments from home office	$12,500	
Freight-in on home office shipments	500	
Home office		$13,000

To record receipt of merchandise from home office.

If half the merchandise remains unsold at year-end, cost of branch sales is reported at $6,500 and the branch inventory is priced at its $6,250 home office cost, plus $250 freight-in. Branch inventory and cost of goods sold are reported in the same amount if the branch pays the transportation costs, but the freight transaction is not recorded on the home office books.

Merchandise cost should not include excessive freight charges from the transfer of merchandise between a home office and its branches or between branch locations. If the branch returns half the merchandise received from the home office because it is defective, or because of a shortage of inventory at the home office location, the home office cost of the merchandise should not include the freight charges to or from the branch. Assuming that the branch pays $250 to return half the merchandise to the home office, the branch and home office entries are:

Branch Books

Home office	$6,750	
Shipments from home office		$6,250
Freight-in on home office shipments		250
Cash		250

To record return of merchandise to the home office.

Home Office Books

Shipments to branch	$5,000	
Loading in branch inventory	1,250	
Loss on excessive freight charges	500	
Branch		$6,750

To record merchandise returned from branch location.

Total freight charges on the merchandise are charged to a home office "loss on excessive freight charges" account because the freight charges represent management mistakes or inefficiencies. Therefore, they are not considered normal operating or freight expenses.

A second example of excessive freight charges involves shipments between branches. Assume that the home office of Maxwell Industries ships merchandise at its $50,000 cost from Chicago to its St. Louis branch, and that it pays $2,000 freight charges on the merchandise. A few days later, the Omaha branch experiences a merchandise shortage and the merchandise is transferred from St. Louis to Omaha at a $1,200 cost paid by the St. Louis branch. The cost of shipping the merchandise from Chicago to Omaha would have been $1,800. Entries to record the initial shipment to the St. Louis branch and the subsequent transfer to the Omaha branch are shown in Exhibit 12–4.

In addition to adjusting shipment accounts and home office and branch accounts, the freight accounts must be adjusted. Total freight charges incurred were $3,200 ($2,000 + $1,200), but the cost of shipping merchandise from the home office directly to the Omaha branch would have been $1,800. Only $1,800 is recorded as an inventoriable cost on the books of the Omaha branch. Since the duplicate shipments are assumed to have resulted from home office management errors, the $1,400 excessive freight is recorded as a home office loss. This accounting treatment is consistent with the accounting principle that inventory costs include only those costs necessary to get merchandise ready for final sale to customers.

ENTRIES TO RECORD SHIPMENT TO ST. LOUIS BRANCH

Home Office Books

St. Louis branch	$52,000	
Shipments to St. Louis branch		$50,000
Cash		2,000

    To record shipment to St. Louis branch.

St. Louis Branch Books

Shipments from home office	$50,000	
Freight-in on home office shipments	2,000	
Home office		$52,000

    To record merchandise received from home office.

ENTRIES TO RECORD TRANSFER FROM ST. LOUIS TO OMAHA

Home Office Books

Omaha branch	$51,800	
Loss on excessive freight charges	1,400	
Shipments to St. Louis branch	50,000	
St. Louis branch		$53,200
Shipments to Omaha branch		50,000

    To record transfer of merchandise from St. Louis branch to Omaha branch.

St. Louis Branch Books

Home office	$53,200	
Shipments from home office		$50,000
Freight-in on home office shipments		2,000
Cash		1,200

    To record transfer of merchandise to Omaha branch.

Omaha Branch Books

Shipments from home office	$50,000	
Freight-in on home office shipments	1,800	
Home office		$51,800

    To record receipt of merchandise from home office via the St. Louis branch.

Exhibit 12–4 *Maxwell Industries Excessive Freight Charges*

HOME OFFICE—BRANCH EXPENSE ALLOCATION

The allocation of expenses among home office and branch operations is frequently necessary to provide an accurate measurement of income for the separate units of the enterprise. Advertising expense, for example, may relate to sales efforts of the home office and one or more branches. If such advertising is paid by the home office, that part related to branch sales should be allocated to the branches. Pension costs paid by the home office and home office general and administrative expenses may also be allocated to branch operations in order to provide complete profit information for each business unit. Another situation that requires expense allocation for complete profit information arises when plant asset records are centralized in the home office accounting system.

Some examples of accounting for these expense allocations follow. If a branch pays $5,000 for advertising that relates equally to branch and home office sales efforts, the $5,000 could be allocated as follows:

Branch Books

Advertising expense	$ 2,500	
Home office	2,500	
Cash		$ 5,000

    To allocate advertising expense 50% to home office.

Home Office Books

Advertising expense	$ 2,500	
Branch		$ 2,500

To record advertising expense paid by branch.

Pension and general home office expenses of $50,000 and $120,000, respectively, that are incurred by the home office and allocated 25 percent each to the Denver and Cheyenne branches, would be recorded:

Home Office Books

Denver branch	$42,500	
Cheyenne branch	42,500	
Pension expense		$25,000
General expenses		60,000

To allocate pension and general expenses to branch operations.

Denver Branch Books

Pension expense	$12,500	
General expenses	30,000	
Home office		$42,500

To record expense allocations from home office.

Cheyenne Branch Books

Pension expense	$12,500	
General expenses	30,000	
Home office		$42,500

To record expense allocations from home office.

These examples illustrate the basic approach to expense allocations among home office and branch operations. Other expense items are allocated in similar fashion.

RECONCILIATION OF HOME OFFICE AND BRANCH ACCOUNTS

Reciprocity between home office and branch accounts will not exist at year-end if errors have been made in recording reciprocal transactions either on the home office or the branch books, or if transactions have been recorded on one set of books but not on the other. The approach for reconciling home office and branch accounts at year-end is similar to the approach used for bank reconciliations. A home office–branch reconciliation is illustrated in Exhibit 12–5 for

---

EMPIRE CORPORATION
HOME OFFICE—ROCHESTER BRANCH RECONCILIATION
AT DECEMBER 31, 19X1

	Home Office Account (Branch Books)	Rochester Branch Account (Home Office) Books)
Balance per books, December 31, 19X1	$452,300	$492,000
Cash in transit—Rochester branch to home office	—	(12,000)
Shipments in transit to Rochester branch	25,000	—
Error correction: Advertising expenses of $8,500 were recorded as $5,800	2,700	—
Adjusted balances, December 31, 19X1	$480,000	$480,000

Exhibit 12–5   Reconciliation of Home Office and Branch Accounts

Empire Corporation's home office and its Rochester branch at December 31, 19X1 according to the following assumptions:

1 Balances on December 31, 19X1: Home office account (branch books), $452,300, Rochester branch account (home office books), $492,000.
2 The Rochester branch sent a check for $12,000 cash to the home office on December 31, 19X1. The home office did not receive the check until January 4, 19X2.
3 The home office shipped merchandise costing $20,000 to its Rochester branch on December 28, 19X1 at a transfer price of $25,000. The merchandise was not received by Rochester branch until January 8, 19X2.
4 Advertising expenses in the amount of $8,500 were allocated by the home office to the Rochester branch. The expenses were recorded at $5,800 by the branch.

The following entry is made on the home office books to reflect the cash in transit at December 31, 19X1:

Cash in transit	$12,000	
Rochester branch		$12,000
To record cash in transit on December 31, 19X1.		

Although it is desirable to use the title "cash in transit" in order to ensure proper recording of the actual cash receipt, the cash is not in transit from the viewpoint of the combined entity, and it should be reported as cash rather than cash in transit in the combined financial statements of the enterprise.

Correcting entries on the books of the Rochester branch to reflect the items in the reconciliation are as follows:

Shipments from home office—in transit	$25,000	
Home office		$25,000
To record merchandise in transit from the home office.		
Advertising expense	$ 2,700	
Home office		$ 2,700
To correct an error in recording advertising expense allocation from home office as $5,800 rather than $8,500.		

After the accounts are updated to reflect these correcting entries, the home office and branch accounts will again have reciprocal balances.

ILLUSTRATION OF HOME OFFICE AND BRANCH ACCOUNTING

Dasher Corporation of Philadelphia has operated a sales branch in Dot, Rhode Island, for a number of years. In order to conceal profit margins from branch employees, all merchandise shipped to the Dot branch is transferred at normal sales prices, which are 125 percent of home office cost. The Dot branch also purchases merchandise from outside suppliers. This merchandise is sold by Dot at a 25 percent markup based on invoice cost. Balance sheets for Dasher Corporation's home office and its Dot branch at December 31, 19X1 are as follows:

DASHER CORPORATION HOME OFFICE AND BRANCH
BALANCE SHEETS AT DECEMBER 31, 19X1

	Home Office	Dot Branch
Assets		
Cash	$ 250,000	$110,000
Accounts receivable—net	420,000	230,000
Inventory	200,000	160,000
Plant assets—net	700,000	—
Dot branch	430,000	—
Total assets	$2,000,000	$500,000

	Home Office	Dot Branch
Liabilities and Equity		
Accounts payable	$ 140,000	$ 50,000
Other liabilities	100,000	20,000
Loading—branch inventory	16,000	—
Home office	—	430,000
Capital stock	1,500,000	—
Retained earnings	244,000	—
Total liabilities and equity	$2,000,000	$500,000

All plant asset records for Dasher's home office and Dot branch are maintained on the home office books. Half of the $160,000 branch inventory at December 31, 19X1 was received from local suppliers, and the remaining $80,000 was received from the home office at established transfer prices. A summary of the transactions of Dasher's home office and Dot branch for 19X2 follows, and journal entries to record the transactions are presented in Exhibit 12–6.

1 Dasher's sales for 19X2 were $2,817,500, of which $2,000,000 were home office sales and $817,500 were sales made by the Dot branch. All sales were on account.

DASHER CORPORATION
HOME OFFICE AND DOT BRANCH JOURNAL ENTRIES
FOR THE YEAR 19X2

Item Number	Home Office Books			Dot Branch Books		
1	Accounts receivable	$2,000,000		Accounts receivable	$817,500	
	Sales		$2,000,000	Sales		$817,500
	To record sales on account.			To record sales on account.		
2	Purchases	$2,050,000		Purchases	$200,000	
	Accounts payable		$2,050,000	Accounts payable		$200,000
	To record purchases on account.			To record purchases on account.		
	Dot branch	$ 500,000		Shipments from home office	$500,000	
	Shipments to Dot office		$400,000	Home office		$500,000
	Loading-branch inventory		100,000			
	To transfer merchandise to Dot branch at 125% of cost.			Receipt of merchandise from home office.		
3	Cash	$1,950,000		Cash	$797,500	
	Accounts receivable		$1,950,000	Accounts receivable		$797,500
	To record collections on accounts receivable.			To record collections on accounts receivable.		
4	Cash	$ 550,000		Home office	$550,000	
	Dot branch		$ 550,000	Cash		$550,000
	To record receipt of cash from Dot branch.			To record cash remittance to home office.		
5	Accounts payable	$2,100,000		Accounts payable	$210,000	
	Cash		$2,100,000	Cash		$210,000
	To record payments on account.			To record payments on account.		
6	Operating expenses	$ 200,000		Operating expenses	$ 20,000	
	Cash		$ 200,000	Cash		$ 20,000
	To record payment of expenses.			To record payment of expenses.		
	Dot branch	$ 10,000		Operating expenses	$ 10,000	
	Operating expenses		$ 10,000	Home office		$ 10,000
	To record allocation of expenses to Dot branch.			To record expenses allocated from home office.		
7	Dot branch	$ 15,000		Operating expenses	$ 15,000	
	Operating expenses	65,000		Home office		$ 15,000
	Accumulated depreciation		$ 80,000	To record depreciation allocated from home office.		
	To record allocation of depreciation to Dot branch.					

Exhibit 12–6   *Comparative Journal Entries for Home Office and Branch*

2 Home office and branch purchases on account for 19X2 were $2,050,000 and $200,000, respectively. The home office shipped $400,000 of merchandise to Dot branch at a transfer price of $500,000.

3 The home office collected $1,950,000 on account during 19X2, and Dot branch collected $797,500.

4 The Dot branch transferred $550,000 cash to the home office during 19X2.

5 Payments on account were: Home office, $2,100,000; Dot branch, $210,000.

6 During 19X2 the home office paid operating expenses of $200,000, and Dot branch paid operating expenses of $20,000. Of the operating expenses paid by the home office, $10,000 was allocated to Dot branch.

7 Total depreciation for the year was $80,000, of which $15,000 was allocated to branch operations.

Year-end inventories are $250,000 for the home office, and $100,000 for Dot branch, with half of the branch inventory consisting of merchandise acquired from the home office. Thus, total inventories for Dasher Corporation on a cost basis are $340,000, computed as follows:

Home office inventory	$250,000
Branch inventory acquired through purchases	50,000
Branch inventory transferred from home office: $50,000/1.25	40,000
Total inventories	$340,000

Separate cost of sales calculations for inclusion in the combining working papers for the home office and the Dot branch are as follows:

	Home Office	Dot Branch
Inventory January 1, 19X2	$ 200,000	$160,000
Purchases	2,050,000	200,000
Shipments to branch	(400,000)	—
Shipments from home office	—	500,000
Goods available for sale	1,850,000	860,000
Inventory December 31, 19X2	(250,000)	(100,000)
Cost of sales	$1,600,000	$760,000

Trial balances prepared at December 31, 19X2 after the transactions summarized in Exhibit 12–6 were recorded, and inventory items grouped into cost of sales categories are shown in the first two columns of Exhibit 12–7. Since these trial balances were taken before the home office recorded income from Dot branch for the year, the home office and branch accounts have reciprocal balances.

The working paper entries needed to combine the accounts of the home office and branch are as follows:

a	Loading in branch inventory	$ 16,000	
	Cost of sales		$ 16,000
	To eliminate loading in beginning branch inventory now included in cost of sales.		
b	Loading in branch inventory	$100,000	
	Cost of sales		$100,000
	To eliminate loading in current year shipments to branch.		
c	Cost of sales	$ 10,000	
	Inventories		$ 10,000
	To eliminate loading in ending branch inventory.		
d	Home office	$405,000	
	Dot branch		$405,000
	To eliminate reciprocal home office and branch balances.		

DASHER CORPORATION
HOME OFFICE AND BRANCH WORKING PAPERS
FOR THE YEAR ENDED DECEMBER 31, 19X2

	Home Office	Dot Branch	Adjustments and Eliminations		Income Statement	Balance Sheet
Debits						
Cash	$ 450,000	$ 127,500				$ 577,500
Accounts receivable—net	470,000	250,000				720,000
Inventories	250,000	100,000	c 10,000			340,000
Plant assets—net	620,000					620,000
Dot branch	405,000		d 405,000			
Cost of sales	1,600,000	760,000	c 10,000	a 16,000 b 100,000	$2,254,000*	
Operating expenses	255,000	45,000			300,000*	
	$4,050,000	$1,282,500				$2,257,500
Credits						
Accounts payable	$ 90,000	$ 40,000				$ 130,000
Other liabilities	100,000	20,000				120,000
Loading in branch inventory	116,000		a 16,000 b 100,000			
Home office		405,000	d 405,000			
Capital stock	1,500,000					1,500,000
Retained earnings— beginning	244,000					244,000
Sales	2,000,000	817,500			2,817,500	
	$4,050,000	$1,282,500				
Net income					$ 263,500	263,500
						$2,257,500

* Deduct.

Exhibit 12–7   Combining Working Papers

The home office and branch working papers in Exhibit 12–7 do not contain a retained earnings column. Since Dasher's net income for the period is the only item affecting the ending retained earnings balance, it is convenient to omit the separate retained earnings column and to carry net income for the period directly to the balance sheet column.

Closing entries for the Dot branch, and home office entries to record branch profit, adjust the loading account, and close the home office books, are as follows:

Dot Branch Closing Entry

Sales	$ 817,500	
Inventory December 31, 19X2	100,000	
Inventory January 1, 19X2		$ 160,000
Purchases		200,000
Shipments from home office		500,000
Operating expenses		45,000
Home office		12,500

Home Office Adjusting and Closing Entries

Dot branch	$ 12,500	
Dot branch profit		$ 12,500
Loading in branch inventory	$ 106,000	
Dot branch profit		$ 106,000

    Unrealized profit per books of $116,000, less $10,000 unrealized profit in branch ending inventory = $106,000 adjustment.

Sales	$2,000,000	
Inventory December 31, 19X2	250,000	
Shipments to Dot branch	400,000	
Dot branch profit	118,500	
Inventory January 1, 19X2		$ 200,000
Purchases		2,050,000
Operating expenses		255,000
Retained earnings		263,500

    The $12,500 income reported by the branch does not include any margin on goods received from the home office. This element of branch profit is recorded by the home office when it adjusts its loading account at year-end. Branch in-

---

DASHER CORPORATION
COMPARATIVE FINANCIAL STATEMENTS
AT AND FOR THE YEAR ENDED DECEMBER 31, 19X2

	Home Office	Dot Branch	Combined
Balance Sheets—December 31, 19X2			
Assets			
Cash	$ 450,000	$127,500	$ 577,500
Accounts receivable—net	470,000	250,000	720,000
Inventories December 31, 19X2	250,000	100,000	340,000
Dot branch	417,500	—	—
Plant assets—net	620,000	—	620,000
Total assets	$2,207,500	$477,500	$2,257,500
Liabilities and Equity			
Accounts payable	$ 90,000	$ 40,000	$ 130,000
Other liabilities	100,000	20,000	120,000
Loading—branch inventory	10,000	—	—
Home office	—	417,500	—
Capital stock	1,500,000	—	1,500,000
Retained earnings	507,500	—	507,500
Total liabilities and equity	$2,207,500	$477,500	$2,257,500
Income Statements—for 19X2			
Sales	$2,000,000	$817,500	$2,817,500
Dot branch income	118,500	—	—
	2,118,500	817,500	2,817,500
Cost of sales	1,600,000*	760,000*	2,254,000*
Operating expenses	255,000*	45,000*	300,000*
Net income	$ 263,500	$ 12,500	$ 263,500

* Deduct.

Exhibit 12–8 *Separate Home Office and Branch and Combined Financial Statements*

come for the year on a cost basis to the business entity is $118,500, an amount that appears in the separate home office income statement for 19X2.

Comparative balance sheets and income statements for Dasher Corporation's home office, its Dot branch, and its home office and branch combined appear in Exhibit 12–8. These statements are presented to highlight differences between separate home office and branch statements and combined statements for the enterprise. Note that the cost of sales on the home office books is equal to 80 percent of home office sales ($1,600,000/$2,000,000), and that combined cost of sales is equal to 80 percent of combined sales ($2,254,000/$2,817,500) reflecting the companywide policy of setting sales prices at 25 percent above cost. This relationship does not exist between branch cost of sales and sales because branch shipments from the home office are recorded on the branch books at selling prices. Since all the items in the comparative statements have been covered individually, additional discussion is not provided.

SUMMARY

Enterprises frequently conduct activities at diverse business locations by means of branches and sales agencies. Separate accounting systems are not required for sales agency operations, but the accounting system of the business entity may be expanded in order to provide information about agency operations for purposes of planning, control, and evaluation. By contrast, home office and branch operations are accounted for through separate home office and branch accounting systems. The home office accounts for its investment in the net assets of its branches by means of "branch" accounts that are reciprocal to "home office" accounts on the books of the branches. Reciprocal home office and branch accounts are eliminated when home office and branch financial statements are combined into financial statements for the enterprise.

Transactions between a home office and its branches require journal entries that are unique to home office and branch accounting systems. Entries to account for other transactions are recorded in the usual manner. Merchandise shipments to branches and related transfer pricing strategies require special attention in order to avoid recognition of unrealized profits. Other areas of concern in home office–branch accounting include expense allocation, account reconciliation, and year-end accounting procedures. Separate home office and branch financial statements are used only for internal purposes. Financial statements for the enterprise as a whole are developed by combining the separate statements of the home office and its branches.

ASSIGNMENT MATERIAL

QUESTIONS

1 How does branch accounting differ from accounting for sales agencies?
2 Should a company maintain separate accounts or subsidiary records in order to identify the revenues and expenses associated with operations of each of its sales agencies? Discuss.
3 When are expenses paid by a sales agency recorded on the books of the central accounting unit of the enterprise?
4 Alternative account titles for the branch account on the books of the home office include "Tampa branch," "investment in Tampa branch," and "Tampa branch—current." Describe the nature and function of this account.
5 Explain the nature of the "shipments to branch" account on the home office books and the "shipments from home office" account on the branch books.
6 The accounts "shipments to branch" and "shipments from home office" may or may not have reciprocal balances. When should the account balances be reciprocal and when would they be different?

7 What advantages can you see for a firm to set transfer prices to its branches at normal sales prices?

8 Telestar Company ships merchandise to its Denver branch at 30 percent above cost. If the Denver branch has a beginning inventory of $39,000 and records shipments from home office of $780,000, what should be the year-end balance of the "loading" account on the books of the home office before adjusting entries? After adjusting entries, assuming that the ending inventory of the Denver branch is $58,500?

9 Topper Corporation's home office shipped merchandise to its Pine branch at a cost of $20,000 and also paid $1,000 shipping costs. Pine branch shipped this merchandise to Spruce branch a few days later and paid $500 shipping costs on the If Topper's home office had shipped the merchandise directly to Spruce branch, the shipping cost would have been $900. Prepare journal entries on the books of the home office to record these transactions.

10 Does the allocation of home office expenses to branch operations affect the income of an enterprise? If not, what is the advantage of such allocation? Discuss.

11 Does the income of a home office plus the income of its branches equal the combined net income of the enterprise? Explain.

12 In preparing working papers to combine the adjusted trial balances of a home office and its branches, what is the advantage of combining the home office adjusted trial balance before recording the entry for branch profit or loss for the period?

EXERCISES

E 12-1 Arnimal Corporation is located in Dallas, Texas, and its branch is located in Fort Worth, Texas. Transactions and events affecting the Fort Worth branch during 19X9 are summarized as follows:

1 Received shipments from the home office, billed at $10,000 home office cost.
2 Purchased merchandise from Alta Wholesalers, $4,000.
3 Sold merchandise to customers on account in the amount of $20,000.
4 Paid operating expenses, $3,000.
5 Returned 20 percent of the merchandise received in item 1 to the home office.
6 Paid $2,000 for advertising, 50 percent of which is a home office expense.
7 Received a debit memo from the home office for the following expenses allocated by the home office to the branch: depreciation expense, $500; other operating expenses, $200.
8 Remitted $5,000 to the home office.
9 Collected $14,000 on accounts receivable.
10 Collected a note for the home office in the amount of $3,000 plus $150 interest.
11 Received notice that the home office had collected $1,000 from a branch customer (assume that it was a customer included in item 3).
12 Closed the nominal accounts to the revenue and expense summary account. Branch beginning and ending inventories were $1,900 and $2,000, respectively.
13 Closed the balance of the revenue and expense summary account.

Required: Prepare journal entries to reflect the transactions and events in the accounts of the branch and the home office.

E 12-2 Diazo Corporation operates a main store at its home office and a branch store in another state. The branch purchases most of its merchandise from the home office at 10 percent above home office cost. All merchandise acquired from other suppliers is accounted for by the branch at original cost. At September 30, 19X7 the records of the branch indicated the following:

September sales	$70,000	
Inventory, September 1	17,600*	(50% from outside suppliers)
Shipments from home office	27,500	(at billed prices)
Purchases from outsiders	12,000	
Expenses	20,000	
Inventory, September 30	15,000*	($4,000 from outside suppliers)

* Merchandise acquired from the home office is inventoried at billed prices.

Required

1 Prepare all necessary adjusting and closing entries on the branch books at September 30, 19X7.
2 Prepare all necessary adjusting entries on the home office books at September 30, 19X7 to adjust the home office records for the branch operations for September.

E 12–3 Kelper Corporation's home office and branch preclosing trial balances on December 31, 19X6 contained the following accounts and amounts:

	Home Office Books	Branch Books
Branch	$72,000	—
Home office	—	$58,200
Shipments to branch	66,000	—
Shipments from home office	—	55,200

Additional Information: On December 31, 19X6 Kelper's home office sent a $3,000 check to its branch to replenish working capital.

Required

1 Compute the correct balance of the "branch" account on Kelper's home office books, before closing entries are made.
2 What adjustments should be made on the branch books as of December 31, 19X6 in view of the information given?

E 12–4 Alamo Company has two merchandise outlets, its main store and its Bonomo branch. All purchases are made by the main store and shipped to Bonomo branch at cost plus 10 percent. On January 1, 19X7, the main store and Bonomo inventories were $17,000 and $4,950, respectively. During 19X7 the main store purchased merchandise costing $50,000 and shipped 40 percent of it to Bonomo. At December 31, 19X7 Bonomo made the following closing entry:

Sales	$40,000	
Inventory	6,050	
Inventory		$ 4,950
Shipments from main store		22,000
Expenses		13,100
Main store		6,000

1 What was the actual branch income for 19X7 on a cost basis assuming generally accepted accounting principles?
 a $6,000   b $7,900
 c $8,100   d $8,550
2 If the main store inventory at December 31, 19X7 is $14,000, the combined main store and branch inventory that should appear in Alamo Company's December 31, 19X7 balance sheet is:
 a $18,950   b $19,500
 c $20,050   d $21,500
3 If the main store inventory at December 31, 19X7 is $14,000, the combined cost of goods sold that should appear in Alamo Company's income statement for 19X7 is:
 a $74,000   b $54,000
 c $52,000   d $33,000
4 Which of the following accounts should be closed by Alamo at December 31, 19X7? (There may be more than one correct answer.)
 a Shipments to Bonomo branch
 b Investment in Bonomo branch
 c Bonomo branch profit and loss
 d Unrealized profit in overvaluation of inventories—Bonomo branch

E 12–5   On December 3, 19X3 the home office of Platt Valley Office Supply Company recorded a shipment of merchandise to its Lincoln branch as follows:

Lincoln branch	$30,000	
Shipments to Lincoln branch		$25,000
Unrealized profit in Lincoln branch inventory		4,000
Cash [for freight charges]		1,000

The Lincoln branch sells 30 percent of the merchandise to outside entities during the rest of December 19X3. The books of the home office and Platt Valley branches are closed on December 31 of each year.

On January 5, 19X4, the Lincoln branch transfers half of the original shipment to the Fremont branch and the Lincoln branch pays $400 freight on the shipment.

Required:
1 Prepare the journal entry on the books of the Lincoln branch to record receipt of the shipment from the home office on December 3, 19X3.
2 At what amounts should the 70 percent of the merchandise remaining unsold at December 31, 19X3 be included in (a) the inventory of the Lincoln branch at December 31, 19X3 and (b) the published balance sheet of Platt Valley Office Supply Company at December 31, 19X3?
3 Prepare journal entries on the books of (a) the home office, (b) the Lincoln branch, and (c) the Fremont branch for the January 5, 19X4 transfer assuming that the freight cost of the merchandise from the home office to the Fremont branch would have been $600.

E 12–6   Home office and branch accounts for Michael Company showing activities for the month of July 19X7 follow:

HOME OFFICE ACCOUNT (BRANCH BOOKS)

Cash remitted to home office	$42,000	June 30, 19X7 balance	$15,000
Merchandise returned to home office	3,000	Shipment from home office (cost)	32,000
Machine charged to home office	5,000	Expenses allocated from home office	14,500
		Home office note collected with $100 interest	2,100

INVESTMENT IN BRANCH ACCOUNT (HOME OFFICE BOOKS)

June 30, 19X7 balance	$15,000	Cash received from branch	$36,000
Shipments to branch (cost)	37,000	Machine purchased by branch	5,000
Expenses allocated to branch	15,400		
Note collected by branch	2,000		

Except for a branch error in recording expense allocations and a home office error in not recording interest, all differences in the accounts are due to timing differences in recording reciprocal information.

Required
1 Prepare a reconciliation of the home office account (branch books) and the investment in branch account (home office books) as of July 31, 19X7.
2 Prepare a single correcting journal entry to bring the home office account on the branch books up to date on July 31, 19X7.
3 Prepare a single correcting journal entry to bring the investment in branch account on the home office books up to date on July 31, 19X7.

E 12–7   Summary adjusted trial balances for the home office and branch of Tanker Corporation at December 31, 19X3 are as follows:

	Home Office	Branch
Debits		
Other assets	$ 530,000	$165,000
Inventories (January 1, 19X3)	50,000	45,000
Branch	200,000	—
Purchases	500,000	—
Shipments from home office	—	240,000
Expenses	120,000	50,000
Dividends	100,000	—
Total debits	$1,500,000	$500,000
Credits		
Other liabilities	$ 90,000	$ 25,000
Capital stock	500,000	—
Retained earnings	100,000	—
Home office	—	175,000
Unrealized profit in branch inventory	10,000	—
Sales	537,500	300,000
Shipments to branch	200,000	—
Branch profit	62,500	—
Total credits	$1,500,000	$500,000

Other Information

1 The home office ships merchandise to its branch at 120 percent of home office cost.
2 Inventories at December 31, 19X3 are $70,000 for the home office and $60,000 for the branch. Branch inventory is at transfer prices.

Required

1 Journalize the closing entries for the branch at December 31, 19X3.
2 Journalize the closing entries for the home office at December 31, 19X3.
3 Prepare a combined balance sheet for Tanker Corporation at December 31, 19X3 in a form acceptable for external reporting.
4 Prepare a combined income statement for Tanker Corporation for the year ended December 31, 19X3 in a form acceptable for external reporting.

E 12–8 Comparative data for Dalton Corporation's home office and branches are summarized as follows:

	Home Office	Salina Branch	Wichita Branch
Cash	$ 67,000	$ 43,000	$ 46,000
Inventory January 1	83,000	22,000	33,000
Other current assets	50,000	20,000	25,000
Salina Branch	90,000	—	—
Wichita Branch	60,000	—	—
Shipments from home office	—	55,000	66,000
Purchases	150,000	—	—
Expenses	100,000	40,000	30,000
	$600,000	$180,000	$200,000
Current liabilities	$ 34,000	$ 10,000	$ 20,000
Capital stock	200,000	—	—
Retained earnings	40,000	—	—
Home office	—	90,000	60,000
Loading—Salina Branch	7,000	—	—
Loading—Wichita Branch	9,000	—	—
Sales	200,000	80,000	120,000
Shipments to Salina Branch	50,000	—	—
Shipments to Wichita Branch	60,000	—	—
	$600,000	$180,000	$200,000

Ending inventories are $40,000 for the home office, $27,500 for the Salina Branch, and $28,600 for the Wichita Branch.

Required: Prepare an income statement for the home office of Dalton Corporation for the year (*not* a combined income statement).

PROBLEMS

P 12-1 Isaac Corporation retails merchandise through its home office store and through a branch store in a distant city. Separate ledgers are maintained by the home office and the branch. The branch store purchases merchandise from the home office (at 120 percent of home office cost) as well as from outside suppliers. Selected information from the December 31, 19X7 trial balances of the home office and branch is as follows:

	Home Office	Branch
Sales	$120,000	$60,000
Shipments to branch	16,000	—
Purchases	70,000	11,000
Inventory, January 1, 19X7	40,000	30,000
Shipments from home office	—	19,200
Expenses	28,000	12,000
Unrealized profit in branch inventory	7,200	—

Additional Information

1 The entire difference between the shipment accounts is due to the practice of billing the branch at cost plus 20 percent.

2 December 31, 19X7 inventories are $40,000 and $20,000 for the home office and the branch, respectively. (*Note:* Sixteen percent of the branch ending inventory was purchased from outside suppliers.)

3 Branch beginning and ending inventories include merchandise acquired from the home office as well as from outside suppliers. Merchandise acquired from the home office is inventoried at 120 percent of home office cost.

Required

1 Prepare a single closing journal entry for the branch books at December 31, 19X7.

2 Prepare journal entries to adjust the home office books for branch activities for 19X7. (*Hint:* Two entries are required.)

3 Prepare a single closing journal entry for the home office books at December 31, 19X7.

4 Prepare an income statement for Isaac Corporation for the year ended December 31, 19X7 for issuance to stockholders.

P 12-2 Fast-Stop has three all-night grocery stores located in western Virginia. Each store has a branch manager with authority to accept inventory items at home office cost plus 10 percent or to purchase from outside wholesalers, at his or her discretion.
Inventories at December 31, 19X1 were as follows:

Home office	$110,900 cost
Dublin branch	26,400 transfer price
Radford branch	29,700 transfer price
Blacksburg branch	46,200 transfer price

Summary information for Fast-Stop and its branches at December 31, 19X1 includes the following accounts and amounts.

	Home Office	Dublin Branch	Radford Branch	Blacksburg Branch
Cash	$ 42,000	$ 6,000	$ 44,000	$ 8,000
Inventories	60,900	37,400	33,000	18,700
Other current assets	45,100	26,600	40,000	53,300
Plant assets—net	200,000	—	—	—
Dublin branch	40,000	—	—	—
Radford branch	92,000	—	—	—
Blacksburg branch	50,000	—	—	—
Purchases	1,000,000	—	—	—
Shipments from home office	—	330,000	275,000	440,000
Expenses	20,000	50,000	48,000	80,000
	$1,550,000	$450,000	$440,000	$600,000
Liabilities	$ 46,900	$ —	$ —	$ —
Capital stock	400,000	—	—	—
Retained earnings	50,000	—	—	—
Home office	—	40,000	92,000	50,000
Unrealized profit in branch inventories	103,100	—	—	—
Shipments to Dublin branch	300,000	—	—	—
Shipments to Radford branch	250,000	—	—	—
Shipments to Blacksburg branch	400,000	—	—	—
Sales	—	410,000	348,000	550,000
	$1,550,000	$450,000	$440,000	$600,000

Required
1 Prepare adjusting and closing entries for the home office of Fast-Stop.
2 Prepare an income statement for Fast-Stop for 19X1 for external reporting.
3 Prepare a balance sheet for Fast-Stop at December 31, 19X1 for external reporting.

P 12-3 Separate financial statements of Leonard Company's home office and branch for 19X3 are summarized as follows:

	Home Office	Branch
Income Statements for the Year Ended December 31, 19X3		
Sales	$1,650,000	$800,000
Income from branch	218,000	—
Total revenue	1,868,000	800,000
Less: Cost of goods sold		
Beginning inventory	$ 250,000	$104,000*
Purchases	800,000	120,000
Shipments to branch	(200,000)	—
Shipments from home office	—	240,000
Goods available for sale	850,000	464,000
Inventory, December 31	(200,000)	(114,000)†
Cost of goods sold	650,000	350,000
Gross profit	1,218,000	450,000
Expenses	(700,000)	(270,000)
Net income	$ 518,000	$180,000

	Home Office	Branch
Retained Earnings Statement		
for the Year Ended December 31, 19X3		
Retained earnings—beginning	$ 132,000	—
Home office—preclosing balance	—	$250,000
Add: Net income	518,000	180,000
Less: Dividends	(400,000)	—
Retained earnings/home office balance—ending	$ 250,000	$430,000
Balance Sheet at December 31, 19X3		
Cash	$ 66,000	$ 56,000
Accounts receivable—net	320,000	180,000
Inventories	200,000	114,000
Unrealized profit in branch inventory	(16,000)	—
Plant assets—net	800,000	200,000
Branch	430 000	—
Total assets	$1,800,000	$550,000
Accounts payable	$ 400,000	$ 80,000
Other liabilities	150,000	40,000
Capital stock	1,000,000	—
Retained earnings	250,000	—
Home office	—	430 000
Total equities	$1,800,000	$550,000

*Includes $84,000 acquired from home office at 120% of home office cost plus $20,000 acquired through purchases.
†Includes $96,000 acquired from home office at 120% of home office cost plus $18,000 acquired through purchases.

Required: Prepare working papers to combine the operations of Leonard's home office and branch using the cost of goods sold summary approach with supporting schedules.

P 12–4 The after-closing balances of Carler Corporation's home office and its branch at January 1, 19X1 were as follows:

	Home Office	Branch
Cash	$ 70,000	$ 20,000
Accounts receivable—net	100,000	35,000
Inventory	150,000	55,000
Plant assets—net	450,000	200,000
Branch	280,000	—
Total assets	$1,050,000	$310,000
Accounts payable	$ 45,000	$ 25,000
Other liabilities	30,000	5,000
Unrealized profit—branch inventory	5,000	—
Home office	—	280,000
Capital stock	800,000	—
Retained earnings	170,000	—
Total equities	$1,050,000	$310,000

A summary of the operations of the home office and branch for 19X1 follows:

   1 Home office sales, $1,000,000 including $330,000 to the branch. A standard 10 percent markup on cost applies to all sales to the branch. Branch sales to its customers totaled $500,000.

2 Purchases from outside entities: home office, $500,000; branch, $70,000.
3 Collections from sales: home office, $980,000 (including $300,000 from branch); branch collections, $510,000.
4 Payments on account: home office, $515,000; branch, $40,000.
5 Operating expenses paid: home office, $200,000; branch, $60,000.
6 Depreciation on plant assets: home office, $40,000; branch, $10,000.
7 Home office operating expenses allocated to the branch, $20,000.
8 At December 31, 19X1 the home office inventory is $110,000 and the branch inventory is $60,000, of which $10,500 was acquired from outside suppliers.

Required
1 Prepare journal entries to reflect the foregoing information in the accounts of the home office and the branch.
2 Post the journal entries to ledger accounts.
3 Prepare trial balances for the home office and branch.
4 Construct working papers to combine the activities of the home office and branch into financial statements for external reporting.
5 Prepare closing entries for the branch and adjusting and closing entries for the home office.

P 12-5 Trial balances for Bear Corporation and its two branches at December 31, 19X6 are as follows:

	Home Office	Branch A	Branch B
Debits			
Cash	$ 15,000	$ 1,300	$ 6,400
Inventory January 1, 19X6	34,000	5,500	8,800
Other assets	300,000	150,000	125,000
Branch A	100,000	—	—
Branch B	81,000	—	—
Purchases	350,000	—	—
Shipments from home office	—	68,200	41,800
Other expenses	120,000	35,000	38,000
	$1,000,000	$260,000	$220,000
Credits			
Liabilities	$ 60,000	$ 16,000	$ 25,000
Home office	—	94,000	75,000
Sales	500,000	150,000	120,000
Shipments to Branch A	73,700	—	—
Shipments to Branch B	46,200	—	—
Loading in December 31, 19X5 inventories	1,300	—	—
Capital stock	300,000	—	—
Retained earnings	18,800	—	—
	$1,000,000	$260,000	$220,000

Additional Information
1 Inventories on hand excluding all goods in transit on December 31, 19X6 are:

Home office (cost)	$31,000
Branch A (billing prices)	7,260
Branch B (billing prices)	8,250

2 All differences between home office and branch accounts are due to cash in transit and merchandise in transit. (All cash in transit is from branch to home office.)
3 Bear consistently uses a standard markup on all goods shipped to its branches.

Required: Prepare working papers to combine the operations of Bear Corporation's home office and its branches at and for the year ended December 31, 19X6.

P 12–6 Selected information from the trial balances for the home office and the branch of Certy Company at December 31, 19X8 is provided. These trial balances cover the period from December 1 to December 31, 19X8. The branch acquires some of its merchandise from the home office (which is billed at 20 percent above the cost to the home office) and some of it from outsiders. Differences in the shipments accounts result entirely from the home office policy of billing the branch at 20 percent above cost.

	Home Office	Branch
Sales	$60,000	$30,000
Shipments to branch	8,000	—
Shipments to branch—loading	3,600	—
Purchases (outsiders)	35,000	5,500
Shipments from home office	—	9,600
Merchandise inventory, December 1, 19X8	20,000	15,000
Expenses	14,000	6,000

Other Information: Merchandise inventory, December 31, 19X8—home office, $20,000; branch, $10,000.

Required
1. How much of the December 1 inventory of the branch represents purchases from outsiders and how much represents goods acquired from the home office?
2. The ending inventory of the branch consists of merchandise purchased from the home office of $8,400; and from outsiders of $1,600. What entry is necessary on the home office books to adjust the "shipments to branch—loading" account at December 31, 19X8?
3. Prepare the income statement to be submitted by the branch to the home office for the month of December 19X8.
4. Prepare the income statement for the home office for December 19X8 showing separately the results of home office and branch operations (*not* a combined or consolidated statement).

P 12–7 Eastman Corporation has three distribution centers—the main office, Buffalo branch, and Carson branch. All merchandise is purchased through the main office and billed to the branches at 20 percent above cost. Trial balances for the three locations at December 31, 19X5, are as follows:

	Main Office	Buffalo Branch	Carson Branch
Cash	$ 26,000	$ 14,500	$ 25,000
Inventory December 31, 19X4	82,000	12,000	15,600
Shipments from main office	—	48,000	55,200
Buffalo branch	62,000	—	—
Carson branch	72 000	—	—
Other assets	300,000	50,000	60,000
Purchases	220,000	—	—
Expenses	38,000	9,500	10,200
	$800,000	$134,000	$166,000
Liabilities	$ 95,400	$ 20,000	$ 27,800
Shipments to Buffalo branch	54,000	—	—
Shipments to Carson branch	66,000	—	—
Sales	160,000	60,000	80,000
Unrealized profit in beginning branch inventories	4,600	—	—
Main office	—	54,000	58,200
Capital stock	350,000	—	—
Retained earnings	70,000	—	—
	$800,000	$134,000	$166,000

Additional Information

1 At December 31, 19X5 Buffalo branch deposited $2,000 to the account of the main office.
2 On December 30, 19X5 the main office sent a $3,000 check to Carson branch to replenish Carson's working capital.
3 Inventories at December 31, 19X5 are as follows:

Home office (cost)	$86,000
Buffalo branch (billed prices)	8,400
Carson branch (billed prices)	7,200

These inventories do not include goods in transit.

Required

1 Prepare a reconciliation of the main office and branch accounts on December 31, 19X5 before closing entries are made.
2 Calculate the separate and the combined inventories of the main office and the two branches on a cost basis at December 31, 19X5.
3 Compute the combined income of Eastman Corporation for the year ended December 31, 19X5.
4 Prepare a combined balance sheet for Eastman Corporation at December 31, 19X5.

P 12-8 Control Products Corporation has two branches, A and B, to which merchandise is billed at 20 percent above cost. Unadjusted trial balances of the three entities at December 31, 19X7 are summarized as follows:

	Home Office	Branch A	Branch B
Cash	$ 33,000	$ 22,000	$ 13,000
Inventory	80,000	18,000	24,000
Other current assets	50,000	25,000	23,000
Branch A	45,000	—	—
Branch B	42,000	—	—
Shipments from home office	—	60,000	36,000
Purchases	160,000	—	—
Expenses	90,000	25,000	20,000
	$500,000	$150,000	$116,000
Current liabilities	$ 40,000	$ 15,000	$ 11,000
Capital stock	100,000	—	—
Retained earnings	50,000	—	—
Home office	—	45,000	30,000
Loading—Branch A	13,000	—	—
Loading—Branch B	12,000	—	—
Sales	195,000	90,000	75,000
Shipments to Branch A	50,000	—	—
Shipments to Branch B	40,000	—	—
	$500,000	$150,000	$116,000

Additional Information

1 Merchandise that cost $10,000 was in transit from the home office to Branch B at December 31, 19X7.
2 Physical inventories at December 31, 19X7 were as follows:

Home office	$70,000 at cost
Branch A	21,000 at billed prices
Branch B	15,000 at billed prices (does not include merchandise in transit)

Required

1 Prepare working papers to combine home office and branch accounts for the year ending December 31, 19X7.

2 Prepare a reconciliation of the branch and home office accounts starting with the balances given in the unadjusted trial balances and reconciling to the correct balances at December 31, 19X7, after all adjusting and closing entries have been made.

P 12–9   Trial balances for Homer Corporation and its two branches at December 31, 19X4 are as follows:

	Homer Home Office	Hampton Branch	Norfolk Branch
Debits			
Cash	$ 18,000	$ 5,000	$ 15,000
Receivables	30,000	12,000	26,000
Inventories January 1, 19X4	36,000	7,200	5,400
Other assets	200,000	42,800	47,600
Hampton branch	50,000	—	—
Norfolk branch	68,000	—	—
Shipments from home office	—	30,000	27,000
Purchases	120,000	—	—
Expenses	78,000	35,000	40,000
	$600,000	$132,000	$161,000
Credits			
Accounts payable	$ 40,000	$ 10,000	$ 30,000
Capital stock	200,000	—	—
Retained earnings	41,900	—	—
Home office	—	42,000	61,000
Sales	250,000	80,000	70,000
Shipments to Hampton branch	36,000	—	—
Shipments to Norfolk branch	30,000	—	—
Loading—branch inventories	2,100	—	—
	$600,000	$132,000	$161,000

Additional Information

1 All shipments are billed at 120 percent of cost.
2 Ending inventories are $32,000, $8,400, and $4,800 for the home office, the Hampton branch and the Norfolk branch, respectively. Ending inventories of the branches include the standard 20 percent loading factor but exclude goods in transit.
3 Goods in transit at billing prices on December 31, 19X4 are $6,000 to the Hampton branch and $3,000 to the Norfolk branch. Cash in transit from home office to the Hampton branch for operating expenses at December 31, 19X4 is $2,000. Cash in transit from the Norfolk branch to home office amounts to $4,000.
4 "Loading—branch inventories" represents unrealized profit in beginning inventories of the Hampton and Norfolk branches.

Required

1 Prepare all journal entries necessary to adjust and close the books of the Hampton branch.
2 Prepare all journal entries necessary to adjust and close the books of the Norfolk branch.
3 Prepare all journal entries necessary to adjust and close the books of the home office.
4 Prepare an income statement for 19X4 and a balance sheet on December 31, 19X4 for Homer Corporation in a form acceptable for external reporting, that is, report revenue and expense details rather than branch profit and loss.

P 12–10   Comparative trial balances of the home office and the two branches of Toller Corporation at December 31, 19X2 were as follows:

	Home Office	Roca Branch	Lane Branch
Debits			
Cash	$ 5,000	$ 15,000	$ 22,000
Accounts receivable (net)	80,000	30,000	40,000
Inventories	150,000	60,000	48,000
Roca branch	170,000	—	—
Lane branch	165,000	—	—
Plant assets (net)	730,000	250,000	200,000
Purchases	900,000	—	—
Shipments from home office	—	300,000	240,000
Expenses	300,000	75,000	50,000
Total debits	$2,500,000	$730,000	$600,000
Credits			
Accounts payable	$ 100,000	$ 45,000	$ 30,000
Other liabilities	80,000	15,000	5,000
Loading in branch inventories	108,000	—	—
Capital stock, $10 par	500,000	—	—
Retained earnings	262,000	—	—
Home office	—	170,000	165,000
Sales	1,000,000	500,000	400,000
Shipments to branches	450,000	—	—
Total credits	$2,500,000	$730,000	$600,000

Additional Information: Home office and branch inventories at December 31, 19X2 were:

Home office (at cost)	$120,000
Roca branch (at billing prices)	72,000
Lane branch (at billing prices)	96,000

All branch shipments are billed at 120 percent of home office cost.

Required
1 Compute the beginning inventory of Toller Corporation dated December 31, 19X1.
2 Compute the ending inventory of Toller Corporation at December 31, 19X2.
3 Prepare journal entries to close the books of the Roca branch and the Lane branch at December 31, 19X2.
4 Prepare journal entries to adjust and close the books of the home office at December 31, 19X2.
5 Prepare an income statement for the home office of Toller Corporation for the year ended December 31, 19X2 (*not* a combined income statement).
6 Prepare a combined balance sheet for Toller Coporation at December 31, 19X2, in a form acceptable for external reporting.

CHAPTER

13

FOREIGN CURRENCY CONCEPTS AND TRANSACTIONS

F oreign business activity by U.S. corporations has expanded rapidly over the years; 1990 alone saw imports of merchandise of $497.7 billion and exports of merchandise of $389.6 billion. In addition to import and export activities, U.S. corporations are heavily involved in foreign business operations through investments in foreign branches and foreign subsidiaries. For example, nearly 70 percent of General Motors Corp.'s 1989 profits were from non-U.S. operations. Other companies, such as IBM, Xerox, Dow Chemical, and Gillette, sell more of their products in other countries than they sell in the United States. Over half of Gillette's assets are located outside the United States.[1] *Survey of Current Business* reported in 1990 that U.S. direct investment abroad for the preceding year was $373.4 billion, while foreign direct investment in the United States was $400.8 billion.[2] International operations, in total, represent a sizable part of American business activity and a significant area of accounting for U.S. corporations.

This chapter and Chapter 14 provide an introduction to accounting for international operations and an exposure to generally accepted accounting principles for translating foreign currency transactions and financial statements. Chapter 13 covers foreign currency concepts and definitions and accounting for foreign currency transactions. Chapter 14 covers translating and remeasuring foreign currency financial statements into U.S. dollars, consolidating the financial statements of foreign subsidiaries with their U.S. parents,[3] and combining the operations of foreign branches with those of their U.S. home offices. A primary reference for these chapters is *FASB Statement No. 52*, "Foreign Currency Translation."

---

[1]"The Stateless Corporation," *Business Week,* May 14, 1990, p. 99.

[2]U.S. Department of Commerce, Bureau of Economic Analysis, *Survey of Current Business,* Vol. 70, no. 8 (August 1990).

[3]With the issuance of *FASB Statement No. 94,* "Consolidation of All Majority-Owned Subsidiaries," majority-owned foreign subsidiaries must be consolidated unless the parent's control of the subsidiary is in doubt or the parent's control is temporary.

BRIEF BACKGROUND ON AUTHORITATIVE ACCOUNTING PRONOUNCEMENTS

Accounting standards for foreign operations and foreign exchange transactions began in 1939 with the issuance of *Accounting Research Bulletin (ARB) No. 4*. This pronouncement, which was reissued in 1953 as Chapter 12 of *ARB No. 43*, called for current accounts of foreign operations to be translated into U.S. dollars at current exchange rates, and noncurrent accounts to be translated at historical rates (the current-noncurrent method of translation). The basic procedures of accounting for foreign operations remained unchanged until the Financial Accounting Standards Board was formed in 1973.

The FASB placed a project on "Accounting for Foreign Currency Translation" on its original agenda and in December 1973 issued *Statement No. 1*, "Disclosure of Foreign Currency Translation Information." *Statement No. 1* did not change the accounting methods used by firms to account for their foreign operations and transactions. However, it did require identification of the policies that were used and financial disclosure of foreign exchange adjustments reflected in income or deferred at year-end.

Both *FASB Statement No. 1* and Chapter 12 of *ARB No. 43* (except for a section on consolidation policies for foreign subsidiaries) were superseded by the issuance of *FASB Statement No. 8* in 1975. In developing *Statement No. 8* the FASB considered a number of approaches to translating foreign currency statement items into dollars, including:

1 The **current-noncurrent method**, specified in the 1939 pronouncement, which translates current accounts at current rates and noncurrent accounts at historical rates.
2 The **monetary-nonmonetary method**, which translates monetary items at current rates and nonmonetary items at historical rates.
3 The **temporal method,** which translates items carried at past, current, and future prices in a manner that retains the accounting principles used to measure them. For example, cash, receivables and payables, and assets and liabilities carried at present or future prices are translated at the current exchange rate, and assets and liabilities carried at past prices are translated at applicable historical exchange rates.
4 The **current rate method**, which translates all assets and liabilities at the current exchange rate.

Although the FASB expressed a preference for the temporal method in *Statement No. 8,* it did not completely accept any of the methods considered. The method that the FASB adopted in *Statement No. 8* required translation of foreign statements in a manner that retained the measurement bases, which was essentially the temporal method.

From the time of its issuance in 1975, *Statement No. 8* had many critics. Much of the disagreement surrounding foreign currency translation related to the temporal method of translating foreign currency financial statements and the recognition of translation adjustments and gains and losses from foreign currency transactions in the income statement. Criticism of *Statement No. 8* often arose because foreign operations of different U.S. companies vary dramatically. Foreign operations of some companies have the objective of producing dollar profits for ultimate remittance to the United States. For these operations, the *Statement No. 8* requirement to recognize translation gains and losses as they arose was appropriate. Other companies finance their foreign operations locally (that is, within the foreign country) and evaluate them in terms of the local currency. *Statement No. 8* requirements to translate local borrowings at current rates and the assets purchased at historical rates were said to distort economic reality for these companies because the debt was repaid from local operations and the translation gains and losses were never realized. Still other companies finance foreign operations in the United States, transfer U.S. equipment and personnel to the foreign localities, sell the output in the world markets, and account for the operations in U.S. dollars. The translation gains and losses arising under *Statement No. 8* for such companies were labeled "fictitious" because the functional currency was the U.S. dollar and translation only distorted the nature of the operations.

In response to these arguments and in recognition of the differing nature of foreign operations among U.S. companies, the FASB issued *Statement No. 52*, "Foreign Currency Translation," in 1981.

OBJECTIVES OF TRANSLATION AND THE FUNCTIONAL CURRENCY CONCEPT

The objectives of translation under *FASB Statement No. 52* are set forth in paragraph 4 as (a) providing "information that is generally compatible with the expected economic effects of a rate change on an enterprise's cash flows and equity" and (b) reflecting "in consolidated statements the financial results and relationships of the individual consolidated entities as measured in their *functional curriences* in conformity with U.S. generally accepted accounting principles."

Functional Currency Concept

The FASB seeks to meet the objectives of *Statement No. 52* through application of the functional currency concept. An entity's *functional currency* is the currency of the primary environment in which it operates. Normally, a foreign entity's functional currency is the currency in which it generates and expends cash. When the functional currency is not obvious from cash flows, other factors may be considered. Economic indicators in addition to cash flows that might aid in the determination of the functional currency include the following:

1 If *sales prices* of the foreign entity's products are determined by local competition or local government regulation, rather than by short-run exchange rate changes or worldwide markets, then the foreign entity's local currency may be the functional currency.
2 A *sales market* that is primarily in the parent company's country, or sales contracts that are normally denominated in the parent's currency, may indicate that the parent's currency is the functional currency.
3 *Expenses* such as labor and materials that are primarily local costs provide some evidence that the foreign entity's local currency is the functional currency.
4 If *financing* is denominated primarily in the foreign entity's local currency, and funds generated by its operations are sufficient to service existing and expected debt, then the foreign entity's local currency is likely to be the functional currency.
5 A high volume of *intercompany transactions and arrangements* indicates that the parent's currency may be the functional currency.

The FASB concluded that company management was in the best position to determine the functional currency of its foreign operations, and in the final analysis, the functional currency is based on management's judgment.

Statement No. 52 changed some traditional definitions by redefining foreign currency. Before the statement was issued, foreign currency meant a currency other than the currency of the country being referred to, or a currency other than the reporting currency of the enterprise being referred to. Local currency was the currency of a particular country being referred to or the reporting currency of a domestic or foreign operation being referred to. Under *Statement No. 52, foreign currency is a currency other than an entity's functional currency.* The statement provides no counterpart to local currency.

Assume for example that a U.S. company has a subsidiary in Germany, and the subsidiary's books of record are maintained in German marks. If the subsidiary's functional currency is the German mark, the U.S. dollar is a foreign currency from the viewpoint of the subsidiary. However, if the U.S. dollar is determined to be the subsidiary's functional currency, the mark would be a foreign currency from the subsidiary's viewpoint even though it is the local currency and the currency of its accounting records.

Statement No. 52 permits two different methods for converting the financial statements of foreign subsidiaries into U.S. dollars, based on the foreign entity's functional currency. If the functional currency is the U.S. dollar, the foreign financial statements are remeasured into U.S. dollars using procedures similar to the temporal method. If the functional currency is the local currency of the foreign entity, the foreign financial statements are translated into U.S. dollars using the current rate method. A company can select the method that best reflects the nature of its foreign operations. Remeasurement and translation of foreign financial statements into U.S. dollars is covered in Chapter 14.

FOREIGN EXCHANGE CONCEPTS AND DEFINITIONS

The objective of a currency is to provide a standard of value, a medium of exchange, and a unit of measure. Currencies of different countries perform the first two functions with varying degrees of efficiency, but essentially all currencies provide a unit of measure for the economic activities and resources of their respective countries. That is, the financial activities and resources of a country are measured in the currency of that country. A transaction is **measured** in a particular currency if its magnitude is expressed in that currency.

Assets and liabilities are **denominated** in a currency if their amounts are fixed in terms of that currency. Transactions within a country (local transactions) are ordinarily both measured and denominated in that country's currency, and in the United States, one seldom investigates the possibility that a purchase or sale could be denominated (fixed) in a currency other than the U.S. dollar. In the case of transactions between business entities of different countries, however, the amounts receivable and payable are ordinarily denominated in the local currency of either the buying entity or the selling entity.[4] For example, if a U.S. firm sells merchandise to a British firm, the transaction amount will be denominated (fixed) in either U.S. dollars or British pounds even though the U.S. firm will measure and record its account receivable and sales in U.S. dollars and the British firm will measure and record its purchase and account payable in British pounds. If the transaction is denominated in British pounds, the U.S. firm has to determine how many U.S. dollars the transaction represents in order to record it. If the transaction is denominated in U.S. dollars, the British firm has to determine how many British pounds the transaction represents. In order to measure the transaction in its own currency, businesses around the world rely on exchange rates negotiated on a continuous basis in world currency markets.

Direct and Indirect Quotation of Exchange Rates

An **exchange rate** is the ratio between a unit of one currency and the amount of another currency for which that unit can be exchanged (converted) at a particular time. The exchange rate can be computed directly or indirectly. Assume that $1.80 can be exchanged for one British pound:

---

[4]Sometimes the amounts are denominated in a currency of a third country whose currency is relatively more stable than the currency of either the buyer or the seller.

direct quotation (U.S. dollar equivalent):

$$\frac{\$1.80}{1} = \$1.80$$

indirect quotation (foreign currency per U.S. dollar):

$$\frac{1}{\$1.80} = .5556 \text{ British pounds}$$

The first approach is referred to as a *direct quotation* (from a U.S. viewpoint) because the rate is expressed in U.S. dollars. It means that $1.80 is equivalent to one British pound (one unit of the foreign currency). The second approach is referred to as an *indirect quotation* (from a U.S. viewpoint) because the rate is expressed in British pounds (the foreign currency). It means that .5556 British pounds is equivalent to one U.S. dollar. The Foreign Exchange section of *The Wall Street Journal* shows both direct (U.S. dollar equivalent) and indirect (currency per U.S. dollar) exchange rates on a daily basis.

Floating, Fixed, and Multiple Exchange Rates

Exchange rates may be fixed by a governmental unit or they may be allowed to fluctuate (float) with changes in currency markets. **Official**, or **fixed, exchange rates** are set by a government and do not change as a result of changes in world currency markets. **Free**, or **floating, exchange rates** are those that reflect fluctuating market prices for a currency based on supply and demand and other factors in the world currency markets.

Floating Exchange Rates   Theoretically, a currency's value should reflect its buying power in world markets. For example, an increase in a country's inflation rate indicates that its currency's purchasing power is decreasing. The currency's value should fall in relation to other currencies. A large trade surplus indicates an increased demand for a country's currency and should result in that currency strengthening against other currencies. Conversely, a large trade deficit should lead to a decrease in the currency's value. Although inflation and trade are basic to floating exchange rates, other factors have sometimes been more influential. Investors buy securities in the world market, and interest rates rather than trade deficits may determine supply and demand for a country's currency. For example, during the early 1980s the dollar was strong against most other currencies because of high interest rates. Speculative trading in currency movements also affects exchange rates.

To reduce its trade deficit, the U.S. government has occasionally asked other countries (Taiwan and Korea, for example) to let their currencies appreciate against the U.S. dollar. A decline in value of the dollar in relation to other major currencies should increase the price of foreign products in the United States and lead to a reduction of imports to this country. Similarly, U.S. goods can be sold in international markets for fewer foreign currency units. Even so, a weakening U.S. dollar has often done little to abate the U.S. consumers' demand for imported products, and changes in the exchange rates may have little effect on the trade deficit. Other factors that may affect a country's trade balance include interest rates[5] and tax rates.

Because floating exchange rates are not always in the best interests of the

---

[5]Domestic savings in the United States have not been sufficient to finance the country's deficit, and the United States has had to bid up interest rates in the world capital markets.

world economy, a Group of Seven (G–7) countries was formed to keep the U.S. dollar, the West German (now German) mark, and the Japanese yen within a secret range of exchange rates. The G–7 includes the United States, Japan, Germany, Britain, France, Italy, and Canada. Their purpose is to stabilize the dollar within the secret range "so it is low enough to help the U.S. correct its trade deficit, but not so low as to bring on inflation in the U.S."[6] Although the United States has a floating exchange rate, the G–7 hopes to "manage" the exchange rate through market intervention.

Fixed and Multiple Exchange Rates   When exchange rates are fixed, the issuing government is able to set (fix) different rates for different kinds of transactions. For example, it may set a preferential rate for imports or certain kinds of imports, and penalty rates for exports or certain kinds of exports, in order to promote the economic objectives of the country. Such rates are referred to as **multiple exchange rates**. Multiple exchange rates exist in Argentina and Uruguay and in some other countries.

U.S. Change from Fixed to Floating Rates   Foreign currency translation was a pressing issue when the FASB was formed in 1973, largely because the United States changed from fixed to floating exchange rates in 1971, and major devaluations of the dollar occurred in 1971 and 1973. The change to floating exchange rates had a major impact on U.S. business firms with significant international operations and, quite naturally, led to a reexamination of accounting and reporting principles for foreign currency translation.

Spot, Current, and Historical Exchange Rates

The exchange rates that are used in accounting for foreign operations and transactions (other than forward contracts[7]) are spot rates, current exchange rates, and historical exchange rates. Spot rate is a market term; current and historical rates are accounting terms. These are defined as follows:

> **Spot rate**—the exchange rate for immediate delivery of currencies exchanged
> **Current rate**—the rate at which one unit of currency can be exchanged for another currency at the balance sheet date or the transaction date
> **Historical rate**—the rate in effect at the date a specific transaction or event occurred

Spot, current, and historical rates may be either fixed or floating rates, depending upon the particular currency involved. Spot rates for foreign transactions between the United States and a country with fixed exchange rates will normally change in that foreign country as a result of governmental action, (except for transactions in the black market in the foreign country's currency). For example, the Argentine government can control the exchange rate in Buenos Aires, but not in New York. Spot rates for foreign transactions with a country that has floating exchange rates may change daily, or several times in a single day, depending on factors that influence the currency markets. But note that there is only one spot rate for a given transaction.

The current rate for foreign currency transactions is the spot rate in effect for immediate settlement of the amounts denominated in foreign currency at the transaction date or at the balance sheet date. The current rate for translating foreign statements is the same as for foreign currency transactions except where

---

[6]*The Wall Street Journal,* January 12, 1989, p. A2.

[7]A *forward exchange contract* is an agreement to exchange different currencies at a specified future date and at a specified rate.

multiple exchange rates exist, in which case the rate to be used should be the rate applicable to dividend remittances (*FASB Statement No. 52,* paragraph 27).

Historical rates are the spot rates that were in effect on the date that a particular event or transaction occurred.

Foreign Exchange Quotations

Major U.S. banks facilitate international trade by maintaining departments that provide bank transfer services between American and foreign companies, as well as currency exchange services. Selling prices at 3:00 P.M. on June 14, 1991 for bank transfers of $1,000,000 or more in the United States for payment abroad for selected currencies were as follows:

	U.S. $ *Equivalent*	*Currency* *per U.S. $*
Britain (pound)	$1.6350	0.6116 pounds
Canada (dollar)	$0.8751	1.1427 $ Canadian
Mexico (peso)	$0.0003317	3015.00 pesos
Germany (mark)	$0.5574	1.7940 marks

These rates indicate the prices for immediate delivery of the selected currencies. For example, a payment of $1,635,000 to a U.S. banker at 3:00 P.M. on June 14, 1991 would have entitled an American corporation to purchase British goods selling for 1,000,000 British pounds or to settle an account payable denominated at 1,000,000 British pounds. Similarly, an American company could have purchased merchandise selling for 10,000,000 Canadian dollars for $8,751,000 at that time.

The United States bankers that provide foreign exchange services are, of course, remunerated for their services. The remuneration is the difference between the amount that they receive from U.S. corporations and the amount that they pay out for the foreign currencies, or vice versa. For example, a bank that trades in foreign currency may offer to sell British pounds for $1.66 or buy them for $1.62 when the quoted rate for British bank notes is $1.64. Thus, a firm can buy 1,000,000 pounds for $1,660,000 or sell 1,000,000 pounds for $1,620,000 and the bank realizes a $20,000 gain in either case.

FOREIGN CURRENCY TRANSACTIONS OTHER THAN FORWARD CONTRACTS

Transactions within a country are **local transactions** that are measured and recorded in the currency of that country. The transactions of a British subsidiary would be recorded in British pounds, and its financial statements would be stated in British pounds. But its financial statements must be converted into U.S. dollars before consolidation with a U.S. parent company. Translation of foreign currency financial statements is covered in Chapter 14.

This discussion of foreign currency transactions assumes the point of view of a U.S. firm whose functional currency is the U.S. dollar (which is also its local currency). **Foreign transactions** are transactions between countries or between enterprises in different countries. **Foreign currency transactions** are transactions whose terms are stated (denominated) in a currency other than an entity's functional currency. Thus, a foreign transaction may or may not be a foreign currency transaction. The most common types of foreign transactions are imports and exports of goods and services. Import and export transactions are foreign transactions, but they are not foreign currency transactions unless their terms are denominated in a foreign currency—that is, a currency other than the entity's functional currency. An export sale by a U.S. company to a Canadian company is a foreign currency transaction from the viewpoint of the U.S. company only if the invoice is denominated (fixed) in Canadian dollars. Translation is required if the transaction is denominated in a foreign currency, but not if it is denominated in the entity's functional currency.

FASB Requirements

The provisions of *FASB Statement No. 52* apply only to foreign currency transactions and to foreign currency financial statements. *Statement No. 52* (paragraph 16) requirements for foreign currency transactions other than forward exchange contracts are:

1 At the date the transaction is recognized, each asset, liability, revenue, expense, gain, or loss arising from the transaction shall be measured and recorded in the functional currency of the recording entity by use of the exchange rate in effect at that date.

2 At each balance sheet date, recorded balances that are denominated in a currency other than the functional currency of the recording entity shall be adjusted to reflect the current exchange rate.

Translation at the Spot Rate The first requirement for foreign currency transactions is that they be translated into U.S. dollars at the spot rate in effect at the transaction date. Each asset, liability, revenue, and expense account arising from the transaction is translated into dollars. The unit of measurement is changed from the foreign currency to the U.S. dollar functional currency.

Assume that an American corporation imports inventory items from a Canadian firm when the spot rate for Canadian dollars is $.80. The invoice calls for payment of 10,000 Canadian dollars in thirty days. (*Note:* The $ sign used for the spot rate indicates direct quotation, or in other words, the U.S. dollar equivalent of one unit of foreign currency.)

The American importer records the transaction as follows:

Inventory	$8,000	
Accounts payable fc		$8,000

(Translation 10,000 Canadian dollars × $.80 spot rate.)

Except for the foreign currency (fc) notation, the entry is recorded in the usual manner. The notation is used to indicate that the account payable is denominated in foreign currency. Since the inventory is both measured and denominated in U.S. dollars, no subsequent adjustment is made to the inventory account.

If the account payable is settled when the spot rate is $.79, payment of the account is recorded:

Accounts payable (fc)	$8,000	
Exchange gain		$ 100
Cash		7,900

(Cash required equals 10,000 Canadian dollars × the $.79 spot rate.)

The $100 exchange gain results because a liability measured at $8,000 is settled for $7,900. This gain reflects a change in the exchange rate between the transaction date and the date of settlement. If the exchange rate had changed to $.82, a $200 exchange loss would have resulted. Under the provisions of *Statement No. 52*, transaction gains and losses are reflected in income in the period in which the exchange rate changes.

Exhibit 13–1 compares the accounting differences that arise when foreign transactions are denominated in an entity's functional currency (U.S. dollars) as opposed to foreign currency. In examining the exhibit, keep in mind that a transaction must be denominated in foreign currency to be a foreign currency

Sales Transaction

Assumption: U.S. Foods sells merchandise to London Industries Ltd. for $15,000 or 10,000 pounds when the exchange rate is $1.50, and receives payment when the exchange rate is $1.49.

If Billing is in U. S. Dollars

(Date of sale)

Accounts receivable	$15,000	
Sales		$15,000

To record sale to London Industries: invoice is $15,000

(Date of receipt)

Cash	$15,000	
Accounts receivable		$15,000

To record collection in full from London Industries.

If Billing is in British Pounds

Accounts receivable (fc)	$15,000	
Sales		$15,000

To record sale to London Industries; billing is for 10,000 British pounds. (10,000 pounds × $1.50 = $15,000)

Cash (fc)	$14,900	
Exchange loss	100	
Accounts receivable (fc)		$15,000

To record collection in full from London Industries. (10,000 pounds × $1.49 = $14,900)

Purchase Transaction

Assumption: U S. Foods purchases merchandise from London Industries Ltd. for $7,500 or 5,000 pounds when the exchange rate is $1.50, and pays the account when the exchange rate is $1.52.

If Billing is in U.S. Dollars

(Date of purchase)

Inventory	$ 7,500	
Accounts payable		$ 7,500

To record purchase from London Industries; billing is $7,500.

(Date of payment)

Accounts payable	$ 7,500	
Cash		$ 7,500

To record payment in full to London Industries.

If Billing is in British Pounds

Inventory	$ 7,500	
Accounts payable (fc)		$ 7,500

To record purchase from London Industries: billing is for 5,000 British pounds. (5,000 pounds × $1.50 = $7,500)

Accounts payable (fc)	$ 7,500	
Exchange loss	100	
Cash		$ 7,600

To record payment in full to London Industries. (5,000 pounds × $1.52 = $7,600)

Note that the exchange losses occurred only when the billing was in foreign currency, and that the losses were on settlement, not on initial recording.

Exhibit 13–1 *Comparison of Purchase and Sale Transactions Dominated in U.S. Dollars Versus British Pounds*

transaction. When billing for a U.S. company is denominated in U.S. dollars, no translation is required and the provisions of *Statement No. 52* are not applicable.

Adjustment to Current Exchange Rate The second requirement of *Statement No. 52* for foreign currency transactions is that cash and amounts owed by or to the enterprise that are denominated in foreign currency be adjusted to reflect the current exchange rate at the balance sheet date. This provision means that gains and losses on foreign currency transactions cannot be deferred until foreign currency is converted into U.S. dollars or until related receivables are collected or payables are settled. Instead, these amounts must be adjusted to reflect current exchange rates at the balance sheet date, and any exchange gains or losses that result from the adjustments must be reflected in current income.

Purchases Denominated in Foreign Currency

American Trading Company, a U.S. corporation, purchased merchandise from Kimetz Company of Switzerland on December 1, 19X8 for 10,000 Swiss francs when the spot rate for Swiss francs was $.6100. American Trading closed its books at December 31, 19X8 when the spot rate for Swiss francs was $.6050, and settled the account on January 30, 19X9 when the spot rate was $.6150. These transactions and events are recorded by American Trading as follows:

December 1, 19X8

Inventory	$6,100	
Accounts payable (fc)		$6,100

    To record purchase of merchandise from Kimetz Company (10,000 Swiss francs ×
    $.6100 spot rate).

December 31, 19X8

Accounts payable (fc)	$ 50	
Exchange gain		$ 50

    To adjust accounts payable to exchange rate at year-end (10,000 Swiss francs ×
    ($.6100 − $.6050)].

January 30, 19X9

Accounts payable (fc)	$6,050	
Exchange loss	100	
Cash		$6,150

    To record payment in full to Kimetz Company (10,000 Swiss francs × $.6150 spot rate).

The example shows that on December 1, 19X8 American Trading Company incurred a liability of $6,100 denominated in Swiss francs. On December 31, 19X8 the liability was adjusted to reflect the current exchange rate, and a $50 exchange gain was included in American Trading Company's 19X8 income statement. The exchange gain is the product of multiplying 10,000 Swiss francs by the change in the spot rate for Swiss francs between December 1 and December 31, 19X8. By January 30, 19X9 when the liability was settled, the spot rate for Swiss francs had increased to $.6150 and American Trading recorded a $100 exchange loss. The actual exchange loss is only $50 [10,000 francs × ($.6150 − $.6100)], but under *Statement No. 52* requirements, this loss is reported as a $50 exchange gain in 19X8 and a $100 exchange loss in 19X9.

Sales Denominated in Foreign Currency

On December 16, 19X8, American Trading Company sold merchandise to Kimetz Company for 20,000 Swiss francs when the spot rate for Swiss francs was $.6000. American Trading closed its books on December 31 when the spot rate was $.6050, collected the account on January 15, 19X9, when the spot rate was $.6100, and held the cash until January 20 when it converted the Swiss francs into U.S. dollars at the $.6125 spot rate in effect on that date. American Trading records the transactions as follows:

December 15, 19X8

Accounts receivable (fc)	$12,000	
Sales		$12,000

    To record sales to Kimetz (20,000 Swiss francs × $.6000 spot rate).

December 31, 19X8

Accounts receivable (fc)	$ 100	
Exchange gain		$ 100

    To adjust accounts receivable at year-end [20,000 Swiss francs × ($.6050 − $.6000)].

January 15, 19X9

Cash (fc)	$12,200	
Accounts receivable (fc)		$12,100
Exchange gain		100

    To record collection in full from Kimetz (20,000 Swiss francs × $.6100) and recognize
    exchange gain for 19X9 [20,000 Swiss francs × ($.6100 − $.6050)].

January 20, 19X9

Cash	$12,250	
Exchange gain		$ 50
Cash (fc)		12,200

To convert 20,000 Swiss francs into U.S. dollars (20,000 Swiss francs × $.6125).

To summarize, American Trading recorded a $12,000 receivable denominated at 20,000 Swiss francs on December 15, 19X8. It then recognized an exchange gain of $100 from holding the receivable as the exchange rate increased to $.6050 at year-end, and another $100 exchange gain as the rate increased from $.6050 at December 31, 19X8 to $.6100 at the January 15, 19X9 settlement date. Because American Trading did not convert the Swiss francs into U.S. dollars on January 15, it speculated in exchange rate changes until January 20 when the 20,000 Swiss francs were converted into U.S. dollars. This speculation resulted in an additional $50 exchange gain for American Trading. A company that holds foreign currency units is a speculator in that currency, and under *Statement No. 52,* it recognizes gains and losses from changes in exchange rates as they occur.

FORWARD EXCHANGE CONTRACTS AND SIMILAR AGREEMENTS

Firms can often avoid gains and losses on foreign exchange transactions by immediate settlement of accounts denominated in a foreign currency or by hedging operations. A **hedging operation** is the purchase or sale of foreign currency contracts to offset the risks of holding receivables and payables denominated in a foreign currency. The usual strategy for avoiding the risks of exchange rate fluctuations is through forward contracts. Under *Statement 52* (paragraph 17), a **forward exchange contract** is an agreement to exchange different currencies at a specified future date and at a specified rate (the forward rate). Currency swaps and other agreements that are essentially the same as forward contracts are considered forward contracts for accounting purposes. Although forward contracts are foreign currency transactions, *FASB Statement No. 52* contains different provisions for forward exchange contracts depending on their nature and purpose. The FASB identifies four situations in which forward exchange contracts (or forward contracts, or futures) are used:

1 To speculate in foreign currency exchange price movements
2 To hedge an exposed foreign currency net asset or net liability position
3 To hedge a foreign currency commitment
4 To hedge a net investment in a foreign entity

Speculation

Exchange gains or losses on forward contracts (futures) that are speculations in foreign currency price movements are included in income in the periods in which the forward exchange rates change. Forward or future exchange rates for 30-, 90-, and 180-day delivery are quoted on a daily basis for the leading world currencies. A forward contract that is a speculation is valued at forward rates throughout the life of the contract. The basic accounting for a forward contract that is a speculation is illustrated in the following example.

On November 2, 19X7, U.S. International enters into a ninety-day forward contract (future) to purchase 10,000 German marks when the current quotation for ninety-day futures in German marks is $.6150. The spot rate for German marks on November 2 is $.6190. Applicable exchange rates at December 31, 19X7 and January 30, 19X8 are as follows:

	December 31, 19X7	January 30, 19X8
30-day futures	$.6200	$.6230
Spot rate	.6250	.6280

Journal entries on the books of U.S. International to account for the speculation are:

November 2, 19X7

Contract receivable (fc)	$6,150	
Contract payable		$6,150

To record contract for 10,000 marks × $.6150 exchange rate for 90-day futures.

December 31, 19X7

Contract receivable (fc)	$ 50	
Exchange gain		$ 50

To adjust receivable from exchange broker and recognize exchange gain (10,000 marks × $.6200 forward exchange rate for 30-day futures − $6,150 per books).

January 30, 19X8

Cash (fc)	$6,280	
Exchange gain		$ 80
Contract receivable (fc)		6,200

To record receipt of 10,000 marks. The current spot rate for German marks is $.6280.

Contract payable	$6,150	
Cash		$6,150

To record payment of the liability to the exchange broker denominated in dollars.

The entry on November 2 records U.S. International's right to receive 10,000 German marks from the exchange broker in ninety days. It also records U.S. International's liability to pay $6,150 to the exchange broker in ninety days. Both the receivable and the liability are recorded at $6,150 (10,000 marks × $.6150 forward rate), but only the receivable is denominated in German marks and is subject to exchange rate fluctuations.

At December 31, 19X7 the forward contract has thirty days left until maturity. Under the provisions of *Statement No. 52*, the receivable denominated in German marks is adjusted to reflect the exchange rate of $.6200 for thirty-day futures on December 31, 19X7. The amount of the adjustment is reflected in U.S. International's income for 19X7.

On January 30, 19X8 U.S. International receives 10,000 German marks with a current value of $6,280 (10,000 marks × $.6280 spot rate). Since the translated value of the foreign currency received is $80 more than the recorded amount of the receivable, an additional exchange gain results. U.S. International also settles its liability with the exchange broker on January 30.

A speculation involving the sale of a foreign currency for future delivery is accounted for in a similar fashion except that the receivable is fixed in U.S. dollars, and the liability is denominated in foreign currency.

Hedging an Exposed Net Asset or Net Liability Position

A **foreign currency exposed net asset position** (exposed net asset position) is an excess of assets denominated in foreign currency over liabilities denominated in that foreign currency and translated at the current rate. A **foreign currency exposed net liability position** (exposed net liability position) is an excess of liabilities denominated in a foreign currency over assets denominated in that foreign currency and translated at the current rate. A forward contract to hedge an exposed net asset or exposed net liability position may be used by importers to hedge accounts payable, and by exporters to hedge accounts receivable, denominated in foreign currency.

Forward Contract to Sell Foreign Currency   In order to hedge an exposed net asset position, a firm enters into a forward contract to sell foreign currency for future delivery. For example, a U.S. exporter sells merchandise to a Canadian company and records an account receivable denominated in Canadian dollars. To avoid exposure to exchange rate changes between the date of the sale and the date payment is due, the U.S. firm enters a contract with an exchange broker to sell the anticipated number of Canadian dollars at a specified forward rate at a future date. The U.S. firm receives the Canadian dollars as payment of the account receivable, delivers the Canadian dollars to the exchange broker, and receives U.S. dollars in exchange. Any exchange gain or loss on the account receivable is offset by an exchange loss (or gain) on the forward contract denominated in the same currency.

Forward Contract to Purchase Foreign Currency   In order to hedge an exposed net liability position, a firm enters into a forward contract to purchase foreign currency for future receipt. For example, a U.S. firm buys merchandise from a British firm. The invoice is denominated in British pounds and due in 30 days. To avoid exposure to exchange rate changes between the date of the purchase and the date payment is due in British pounds, the U.S. firm buys British pounds at a specified forward rate for receipt in thirty days. In this way any gain (or loss) on the account payable denominated in British pounds is offset by a loss (or gain) on the contract receivable denominated in the same foreign currency.

Exchange Gains and Losses   If the forward contracts are for the same number of foreign currency units and for the same time periods as the exposed net asset or net liability positions, the exchange gains or losses on the forward contracts will offset the exchange gains or losses on the exposed net asset or net liability positions in each period for which financial statements are prepared. In other words, no net exchange gains or losses result when an exposed net asset or liability position is completely hedged.

Premium or Discount on Forward Contract   Generally, there is a cost of avoiding the risk of exchange rate changes, and that cost is the income effect of the hedging operation. The exchange broker ordinarily sets the forward rate at an amount different from the spot rate on the contract date to cover his or her own risk. The part of the firm's forward contract denominated in foreign currency is translated at the spot rate, and the part denominated in U.S. dollars is stated at the forward rate. Any difference between these rates creates a premium or discount on the forward contract (the cost of avoiding the risk of exchange rate fluctuations), and it is accounted for separately from any transaction gains or losses on the contract. *Statement No. 52* requires that the premium or discount be amortized over the life of the forward contract, with the amount of amortization being reflected in income. The income effect of a completely hedged foreign currency position is equal to the expense that results from amortizing the premium or discount on the forward contract. Amortization must be reported separately from the exchange gain or loss on the forward contract.

Illustration: Hedge Against Exposed Net Asset Position   U.S. Oil Company sells oil to Monato Company of Japan for 15,000,000 yen on December 1, 19X7. The billing date for the sale is December 1, 19X7, and payment is due in sixty days on January 30, 19X8. Concurrent with the sale, U.S. Oil enters into a forward contract to deliver 15,000,000 yen to its exchange broker in sixty days. Exchange rates for Japanese yen are as follows:

	December 1, 19X7	December 31, 19X7	January 30, 19X8
Spot rate	$.006150	$.006148	$.006147
30-day futures rate	$.006140	$.006139	$.006138
60-day futures rate	$.006140	$.006138	$.006136

The underscored rates are the relevant rates for accounting purposes.

Journal entries to record the sale, the forward contract, year-end adjustments, and final settlement of accounts on the books of U.S. Oil are shown below. The discount on the forward contract is the difference between the $92,100 receivable from the broker, which reflects the $.006140 forward rate, and the $92,250 liability to the broker, which reflects the $.006150 spot rate at the date of the forward contract. The liability to the exchange broker is denominated in foreign currency.

December 1, 19X7
Accounts receivable (fc)	$92,250	
Sales		$92,250

To record sales to Monato Company 15,000,000 yen × $.006150).

Contract receivable	$92,100	
Discount on forward contract	150	
Contract payable (fc)		$92,250

To record forward contract to deliver 15,000,000 yen in 60 days. Receivable: 15,000,000 yen × $.006140: Liability: 15,000,000 yen × $.006150.

At December 31, 19X7, the accounts receivable from the sale is adjusted to reflect the current exchange rate, and a $30 exchange loss is recorded. But the liability to the exchange broker is also adjusted to the current exchange rate, giving rise to a $30 exchange gain. Since the exchange gain and exchange loss are equal, the net exchange gains and losses are nil. The income of U.S. Oil for 19X7 is decreased by the $75 amortization of the discount on the forward contract.

December 31, 19X7
Exchange loss	$30	
Accounts receivable (fc)		$30

To adjust accounts receivable for current exchange rate [15,000,000 yen × ($.006150 − $.006148) = $30].

Contract payable (fc)	$30	
Exchange gain		$30

To adjust contract payable to exchange broker to the current exchange rate. Payable: 15,000,000 yen × $.006148 = $92,220.

Amortization of discount on forward contract	$75	
Discount on forward contract		$75

To record discount amortization of $150 × (30/60 days).

Equal exchange gains and losses of $15 each result from the settlement of the accounts denominated in foreign currency on January 30, 19X8, so that no net exchange gains and losses result. But amortization of the remaining unamortized discount on the forward contract in 19X8 reduces U.S. Oil's income in 19X8 by $75.

January 30, 19X8
Cash (fc)	$92,205	
Exchange loss	15	
Accounts receivable (fc)		$92,220

To record collection of receivable from Monato Company. Cash: 15,000,000 yen × $.006147.

Contract payable (fc)	$92,220	
Exchange gain		$ 15
Cash (fc)		92,205

To record delivery of 15,000,000 yen from Monato to foreign exchange broker in settlement of liability.

Cash	$92,100	
Contract receivable		$92,100

To record receipt of cash from exchange broker.

Amortization of discount on forward contract	$ 75	
Discount on forward contract		$ 75

To record amortization of discount on forward contract of $150 × (30/60 days).

In the final analysis, U.S. Oil Company makes a sale in the amount of $92,250, it takes a $150 discount on the transaction in order to avoid the risks of foreign currency price fluctuations, and it collects $92,100 in final settlement of the sale transaction. The $150 discount is charged to income over the term of the forward contract.

Hedge Against Exposed Net Liability Position   Accounting procedures for hedging an exposed net liability position are comparable to those illustrated for U.S. Oil Company except that the objective is to hedge a liability denominated in foreign currency, rather than a receivable. Normally a premium will arise from hedging an exposed liability position because the forward rate for buying foreign currency for future receipt is ordinarily greater than the spot rate. Such a premium has a debit balance, so that its amortization decreases income over the life of the forward contract. For example, a forward contract to acquire 10,000 British pounds for receipt in sixty days might have a forward rate of $1.515 when the spot rate is $1.50. The forward contract is recorded:

Contract receivable (fc)	$15,000	
Premium on forward contract	150	
Contract payable		$15,150

Result of Hedging   The point is that forward rates are ordinarily set so that there is a cost to the firm for its hedging operations. This cost is a discount if foreign currency is being sold and a premium if foreign currency is being purchased. Occasionally, the rates for futures are such that the hedging operations create credit balances, in which case amortization would increase income.

In summary, if the contract receivable is recorded at the forward rate as in a sales transaction, the contract payable is recorded at the spot rate. The situation is reversed when foreign currency is purchased. The spot rate sets the standard. One side of the transaction is recorded at the spot rate—the other side is recorded at the forward rate. If the spot rate is higher than the forward rate, the difference is a discount, and if the forward rate is greater than the spot rate, the difference is a premium.

If a firm enters a forward contract for foreign currency units in excess of the foreign currency units reflected in its exposed net asset or net liability position, the excess should be accounted for as a speculation under the provisions of *Statement No. 52.*

Hedging an Identifiable Foreign Currency Commitment

A **foreign currency commitment** is a contract or agreement denominated in foreign currency that will result in a foreign currency transaction at a later date. For example, a U.S. firm may contract to buy equipment from a Canadian firm at a future date with the invoice price denominated in Canadian dollars. The U.S. firm has an exposure to exchange rate changes because the future price in U.S. dollars may increase or decrease before the transaction is consummated. An identifiable foreign currency commitment differs from an exposed asset or liability position because the commitment does not meet the accounting tests for recording the related asset or liability in the accounts. The risk of the exposure may be avoided by hedging, but in this situation, a hedge of the commitment creates an exchange gain or loss that is not offset by an equal exchange gain or loss on a related receivable or payable denominated in foreign currency.

Because the hedge of a foreign currency commitment can result in the recording of an exchange gain or loss prior to recognition of the related foreign currency transaction, *Statement No. 52* contains special provisions for such forward contracts. A gain or loss on a forward contract is deferred and treated as an adjustment of the related foreign currency transaction if it is intended to hedge an identifiable foreign currency commitment and the following conditions are met:

1 The foreign currency transaction is designated as, and is effective as, a hedge of a foreign currency commitment.
2 The foreign currency commitment is firm.

The portion of the forward contract for which gains and losses may be deferred and included in measuring the related transaction is limited to the amount of the commitment. If the forward contract is intended to provide a hedge on an after-tax basis, however, additional gains or losses may be deferred and treated as an offset to income taxes related to the transaction. Any gains or losses on the portion of a forward contract in excess of amounts intended to provide a hedge on an after-tax basis are recognized in income currently as exchange gains or losses. Losses may not be deferred if deferral would lead to recognizing losses in later periods.

There is no requirement that the life of the forward contract has to begin at the foreign currency commitment date; however, the required accounting for the forward contract must begin at the designation date (in other words, when the forward contract is designated as a hedge of a foreign currency commitment).

Illustration: Hedge of an Identifiable Foreign Currency Purchase Commitment

On October 2, 19X7, American Stores Corporation contracts with Canadian Distillers for delivery of 1,000 cases of bourbon at a price of 60,000 Canadian dollars when the spot rate for Canadian dollars is $.85. The bourbon is to be delivered in March, and payment made in Canadian dollars on March 31, 19X8. In order to hedge this future commitment, American Stores purchases 60,000 Canadian dollars for delivery in 180 days at a forward exchange rate of $.875. Applicable spot rates on December 31, 19X7 and March 31, 19X8 are $.84 and $.83, respectively.

Assume that the conditions of *Statement No. 52* for a hedge of an identifiable foreign currency commitment are satisfied. In this case, the purchase of the forward contract on October 2, 19X7 is recorded in the same manner as for a hedge of an exposed net liability position:

October 2, 19X7		
Contract receivable (fc)	$51,000	
Premium on forward contract	1,500	
Contract payable		$52,500

To record purchase of 60,000 Canadian dollars for delivery in 180 days at a forward rate of $.875.

By December 31, 19X7, the exchange rate for Canadian dollars decreases to $.84, and American Stores adjusts its receivable to reflect the 60,000 Canadian dollars at the current exchange rate. This adjustment creates a $600 exchange loss, but the loss is deferred as follows:

December 31, 19X7

Deferred exchange loss	$600	
Contract receivable (fc)		$600

To record deferral of exchange loss: 60,000 Canadian dollars × ($.85 − $.84).

Under *Statement No. 52* the premium on the forward contract can be amortized over the term of the forward contract, as required in the case of a hedge of an exposed net asset or liability position, or it can be deferred and treated as an adjustment of the related foreign currency transaction. In this illustration, the premium is treated as an adjustment of the related transaction.[8]

Journal entries on March 31, 19X8 to account for the foreign currency transaction and related forward contract are as follows:

March 31, 19X8

1.   Purchases $49,800

      Accounts payable (fc) $49,800

    To record receipt of 1,000 cases of bourbon at a cost of 60,000 Canadian dollars × exchange rate of $.83.

2.   Contract payable $52,500

      Cash $52,500

    To record settlement of forward contract with the exchange broker (denominated in U.S. dollars).

3.   Cash (fc) $49,800

    Deferred exchange loss   600

      Contract receivable (fc) $50,400

    To record receipt of 60,000 Canadian dollars from the exchange broker when the exchange rate is $.83.

4.   Accounts payable (fc) $49,800

      Cash (fc) $49,800

    To record payment of 60,000 Canadian dollars to Canadian Distillers.

5.   Purchases $ 2,700

      Premium on forward contract $ 1,500

      Deferred exchange loss   1,200

    To reclassify the premium and the deferred exchange loss as adjustments to the cost of merchandise purchased.

The first entry on March 31 records receipt of the 1,000 cases of bourbon from Canadian Distillers and records the liability payable in Canadian dollars. Entry 2 records payment to the exchange broker for the 60,000 Canadian dollars at the contracted forward rate of $.875. The third entry reflects collection of the 60,000 Canadian dollars from the broker and records an additional exchange loss on the further decline of the exchange rate from $.84 at December 31, 19X7 to $.83 at March 31, 19X8. In entry 4 Canadian Distillers is paid the 60,000 Canadian dollars in final settlement of the account payable.

The final entry adjusts the purchases account for the total amount of the premium on the forward contract and for the deferred exchange loss. With adjustment, the total purchase cost of the bourbon is $52,500. This is equal to the $52,500 cash paid to the exchange broker on March 31, 19X8. If the premium on the

---

[8]The entry on October 2, 19X7 is recorded on a gross basis. Some accountants argue that the forward contract should be recorded on a net basis because the right of offset does exist for the two-sided contract. However, there is a difference between the two sides of the contract—one part is stated in foreign currency and the other part is stated in U.S. dollars. They will not be equal. On a net basis, the contract is recorded as a debit to premium on forward contract, $1,500, and a credit to contract payable, $1,500. On December 31 the loss from the rate change in Canadian dollars is recorded as a deferred exchange loss and the contract payable account is increased. When the liability to the exchange broker is recorded on a net basis, the gross amount at risk is disclosed in notes to the financial statements.

forward contract had been amortized, as permitted by *Statement No. 52,* the adjusted purchase cost of the bourbon would have been $51,000, and $750 amortization would have been charged to the income of American Stores in each of the years 19X7 and 19X8.

Hedge of an Identifiable Foreign Currency Sales Commitment   Accounting procedures for hedging an identifiable foreign currency sales commitment are comparable to those illustrated here for hedging a purchase commitment, except that the sales rather than the purchases account is adjusted for any deferred exchange gains or losses.

Hedging a Net Investment in a Foreign Entity

U.S. firms with foreign investees may enter into forward exchange contracts or other foreign currency transactions to offset the effects of foreign currency fluctuations on their net investments. Gains and losses that arise from foreign currency transactions designated as, and effective as, economic hedges of a net investment in a foreign entity are recorded as translation adjustments of stockholders' equity. Classification as a **translation adjustment** means that these transaction gains and losses are excluded from the determination of net income and, instead, are reported as a component of stockholders' equity. This treatment is necessary because translation of the financial statements of a foreign subsidiary *with a functional currency other than the U.S. dollar* also produces translation adjustments to stockholders' equity, rather than charges or credits to income. Thus, the equity adjustment from hedging a net investment in a foreign entity offsets the equity adjustment from translating the foreign investees' financial statements into U.S. dollars.

Procedures to hedge a net investment in a foreign entity are not applicable to investees with a U.S. dollar functional currency. Hedges of these investments are accounted for as speculations. The reason is that gains and losses from remeasuring the foreign investees' financial statements into U.S. dollars are included in net income for the period when the U.S. dollar is the investee's functional currency. Therefore, the gains and losses resulting from the hedge of the net investment must also be included in net income for the period. Translation and remeasurement of foreign currency financial statements are covered in the next chapter.

Illustration: Hedge of a Net Investment in a Foreign Entity   To illustrate the hedge of a net investment of a foreign entity, assume that Pinehurst Corporation, a U.S. company, has a 40 percent equity investment in a British company, Bennett Ltd., acquired at book value equal to fair value. The British pound is the functional currency. The British investee's assets and liabilities hedge each other, but the net assets are exposed to the risk of exchange rate fluctuations. In order to hedge the foreign currency exposure, the translation adjustment from the hedging transaction must move in a direction opposite to the translation adjustment from the net assets of the investee. Thus, Pinehurst borrows British pounds to hedge the equity investment. Any translation losses on the equity investment will be fully or partially offset by the translation gains on the loan and vice versa.

The balance in Pinehurst's investment in Bennett account at December 31, 19X2 is $1,280,000, equal to 40 percent of Bennett's net assets of 2,000,000 pounds times a $1.60 year-end current exchange rate. On this date, Pinehurst has no translation adjustment balance relative to its investment in Bennett. In order to hedge its net investment in Bennett, Pinehurst borrows 800,000 pounds for one year at 12 percent interest on January 1, 19X3 at a spot rate of $1.60. The loan is denominated in pounds with principal and interest payable on January 1, 19X4. Pinehurst records its loan as follows:

January 1, 19X3

Cash	$1,280,000	
Loan payable (fc)		$1,280,000

    To record loan denominated in British pounds (800,000 pounds × $1.60 spot rate).

On November 1, 19X3 Bennett declares and pays a 100,000 pound dividend. Pinehurst records receipt of the dividend at the $1.75 spot rate on this date.

November 1, 19X3

Cash	$ 70,000	
Investment in Bennett		$ 70,000

    To record receipt of dividends from Bennett (100,000 pounds × 40% × $1.75 spot rate).

For the year 19X3 Bennett reports net income of 400,000 pounds. The weighted average exchange rate for translation of Bennett's revenue and expense items for the year is $1.70, and the current exchange rate at December 31, 19X3 is $1.80. These changes in Bennett's net assets are included in the following summary:

	British Pounds		U.S. Dollars
Net assets on January 1, 19X3	2,000,000	× $1.60	$3,200,000
Add: Net income for 19X3	400,000	× $1.70	680,000
Less: Dividends	(100,000)	× $1.75	(175,000)
Equity adjustment—change	—		435,000
Net assets on December 31, 19X3	2,300,000	× $1.80	$4,140,000

Pinehurst makes the following entries to take up its share of Bennett's income, adjust the loan payable and the equity investment to the current rate at December 31, 19X3, and accrue interest on the loan.

December 31, 19X3

Investment in Bennett	$446,000	
Income from Bennett		$272,000
Equity adjustment from translation		174,000

    To record share of Bennett's income (400,000 pounds × $1.70 weighted average exchange rate × 40% interest) and to record 40% share of gain from exchange rate changes as translation adjustment ($435,000 × 40%).

Equity adjustment from translation	$160,000	
Loan payable (fc)		$160,000

    To adjust loan payable denominated in British pounds to the current rate at year end [800,000 pounds × ($1.80 − $1.60)].

Interest expense	$163,200	
Exchange loss	9,600	
Interest payable		$172,800

    To record interest expense (at weighted average exchange rates) and accrue interest payable denominated in pounds at the year-end current rate as follows: $172,800 interest payable (800,000 pounds × 12% interest × 1 year × $1.80 current exchange rate) less $163,200 interest expense (800,000 pounds × 12% interest × 1 year × $1.70 weighted average exchange rate) = $9,600 exchange loss.

On January 1, 19X4, Pinehurst pays the loan and interest at the $1.80 spot rate as follows:

January 1, 19X4

Interest payable (fc)	$ 172,800	
Loan payable (fc)	1,440,000	
Cash		$1,612,800

    To record payment of loan and interest denominated in British pounds when the spot rate is $1.80.

As a result of the hedging operation, the changes in Pinehurst's investment in Bennett that were due to changing exchange rates were partially offset by its loan in British pounds. The equity adjustment from translation balance that appears in the stockholders' equity section of Pinehurst's December 31, 19X3 balance sheet is a $14,000 credit ($174,000 credit from the equity investment from translation less $160,000 debit from adjustment of the loan denominated in British pounds).

Limit on Gain or Loss from Translation Adjustment   The gain or loss on an after-tax basis from the hedging operations that can be considered a translation adjustment is limited in amount to the *current* translation adjustment from the equity investment (see paragraph 129 of *Statement No. 52*). Any discount or premium on the forward contract may be combined with the translation adjustment or it may be amortized to net income over the life of the contract.

A reference to this type of hedging operation is found in the *Wang Laboratories, Inc., Annual Report 1990* (page 38), which includes the following note:

Classification	*Purpose*	*Recognition*	*Disposition of Premium or Discount on Forward Contract*	*Expected Effect of Hedge and Related Foreign Currency Item*
Speculation	To speculate in exchange rate changes.	Exchange gains and losses recognized currently, based on forward exchange rate changes.	None	Income effect equal to exchange gains and losses recognized.
Hedge of a net asset or liability position	To offset exposure to existing net asset or liability position.	Exchange gains and losses are recognized currently, but they are offset by related gains or losses on net asset or liability position.	Amortized to income over the term of the forward contract.	Income effect equal to amortization of premium or discount. (Gains and losses offset.)
Hedge of an identifiable commitment	To offset exposure to a future purchase or sale and thereby lock in the price of an existing contract in U.S. dollars.	Exchange gains and losses are deferred until the commitment becomes a transaction. Then deferred gains or losses are treated as an adjustment of the transaction price.	Choice: Premiums and discounts may be amortized to income currently or deferred and treated as adjustments of the transaction price.	Income effect equal to amortization of premium or discount if elected. (Gains or losses are adjustments of transaction price.)
Hedge of a net investment in a foreign entity	To offset exposure to an existing net investment in a foreign entity.	Exchange gains and losses are recognized as equity adjustments and will offset equity adjustments recorded on the net investment.	Choice: Premiums and discounts may be amortized to income currently or included in the amount of equity adjustment from translation.	Income effect equal to amortization of premium or discount if elected. (Equity adjustments on net investments and hedges are offsetting.)

Exhibit 13-2   Summary of Forward Contracts

"Notes payable to banks are principally multicurrency lines used to minimize the Company's exposure to foreign currency fluctuations."

Forward Contracts Summarized

The accounting required for a forward contract depends primarily on management's intent when entering into the transaction. In other words, the purpose of the transaction governs the accounting. Exhibit 13–2 summarizes the four types of forward contracts and the purpose, required accounting, and effect on income of each.

SUMMARY

International accounting is concerned with accounting for foreign currency transactions and operations. The current accounting standard for foreign exchange transactions and financial statements is *FASB Statement No. 52,* "Foreign Currency Translation." *Statement No. 52* develops a functional currency concept: an entity's functional currency is the currency of the primary environment in which the entity operates.

Foreign currency transactions are transactions whose terms are denominated in a currency other than an entity's functional currency. Foreign currency transactions (other than forward contracts) are measured and recorded in U.S. dollars at the spot rate in effect at the transaction date. A change in the exchange rate between the date of the transaction and the settlement date results in an exchange gain or loss that is reflected in income for the period. At the balance sheet date, any remaining balances that are denominated in a currency other than the functional currency are adjusted to reflect the current exchange rate, and the gain or loss is charged to income.

Corporations use forward exchange contracts to avoid the risks of exchange rate changes and to speculate on foreign currency exchange price movements. *Statement No. 52* prescribes different provisions for forward contracts, depending on their nature and purposes.

SELECTED READINGS

BINDON, KATHLEEN RANNEY, and EDWARD J. SCHNEE. "Forward Contracts: Accounting and Tax Implications." *The CPA Journal* (September 1986), pp. 38–50.

BRIDGES, TIM. "Foreign Exchange Exposure Management." *The CPA Journal* (August 1988), pp. 77–79.

NASH, RONALD. "Preparing Small and Middle Market Companies for Europe 1992." *The CPA Journal* (February 1990), pp. 11–20.

OLDFIELD, TIM. "ADRs: An Emerging Force in Cross-border Deals." *Mergers & Acquisitions* (January/February 1989), pp. 57–59.

ROLLINS, THERESA P., DAVID E. STOUT, and DANIEL J. O'MARA. "The New Financial Instruments." *Management Accounting* (March 1990), pp. 35–41.

Statement of Financial Accounting Standards No. 52. "Foreign Currency Translation." Stamford, CT: Financial Accounting Standards Board, 1981.

STEWART, JOHN E. "The Challenges of Hedge Accounting." *Journal of Accountancy* (November 1989), pp. 48–56.

ASSIGNMENT MATERIAL

QUESTIONS

1 Outline the evolution of accounting for foreign currency transactions and financial statements in terms of Professional Accounting Standards.
2 Distinguish between *measurement* and *denomination* in a particular currency.
3 Is the Canadian dollar a foreign currency? Explain.

4 Assume that one Canadian dollar can be exchanged for .92 U.S. dollars. What is the exchange rate if the exchange rate is quoted directly? Indirectly?

5 What is the difference between official and floating foreign exchange rates? Does the United States have floating exchange rates?

6 What is a spot rate with respect to foreign currency transactions? Could a spot rate ever be a historical rate? Could a spot rate ever be a fixed exchange rate? Discuss.

7 Describe the objectives of translation for purposes of preparing the financial statements of an enterprise.

8 Assume that a U.S. corporation imports electronic equipment from Japan in a transaction denominated in U.S. dollars. Is this transaction a foreign currency transaction? A foreign transaction? Explain.

9 How are assets and liabilities denominated in foreign currency measured and recorded at the transaction date? At the balance sheet date?

10 Criticize the following statement: "Exchange losses arise from foreign import activities, and exchange gains arise from foreign export activities."

11 When are exchange gains and losses reflected in the financial statements of a business enterprise?

12 A U.S. corporation imported merchandise from a British company for 1,000 British pounds when the spot rate was $1.45, it issued financial statements when the current rate was $1.47, and it paid for the merchandise when the spot rate was $1.46. What amount of exchange gain or loss will be included in the U.S. corporation's income statements in the period of purchase and in the period of settlement?

13 For what purpose or purposes might an enterprise enter into a "futures" contract? In answering this question, you are to begin by defining the term forward exchange contract.

14 Under what conditions would exchange gains or losses on a forward exchange contract be deferred? Explain the reason for deferring such gains or losses.

15 How are premiums and discounts on forward exchange contracts measured? Do premiums on forward contracts have debit or credit balances?

16 Do net exchange gains and losses arise from forward contracts that are designed to hedge a liability denominated in foreign currency?

17 Describe two acceptable ways of accounting for a discount on a forward contract that is intended as a hedge against an identifiable foreign currency commitment.

EXERCISES

E 13-1

1 A foreign exchange transaction from the viewpoint of a U.S. company is a transaction in which the amount is:
  a. Measured in a foreign currency
  b Denominated in a foreign currency
  c Measured in U.S. currency
  d Denominated in U.S. currency

2 The exchange rate for immediate delivery of currencies exchanged is the definition of a:
  a Current exchange rate
  b Historical exchange rate
  c Spot rate
  d Forward exchange rate

3 An exchange loss on foreign currency transactions would result from:
  a An increase in the exchange rate applicable to an asset denominated in a foreign currency
  b An increase in the exchange rate applicable to a liability denominated in a foreign currency
  c The import of merchandise when the transaction is denominated in a foreign currency
  d The export of merchandise when the transaction is denominated in a foreign currency

4 Foreign exchange gains and losses may be deferred if they meet the conditions of *FASB Statement No. 52* for a:
  a Speculation in foreign currencies
  b Hedge of an identifiable foreign currency commitment
  c Hedge of an exposed net asset position
  d Foreign exchange transaction

5 The forward exchange rate is used to account for a forward exchange contract throughout its term of existence if the contract:

a Extends beyond one year or the current operating cycle
b Constitutes a hedge of an identifiable foreign currency commitment
c Constitutes a hedge of an exposed net liability position
d Is classified as a speculation in foreign currency

6 A premium on a forward contract must be amortized if the contract is classified as a:

a Hedge of an identifiable foreign currency commitment
b Hedge of an exposed net asset or liability position
c Speculation in foreign currency
d Future

E 13-2 Donner Corporation, a U.S. firm, sold merchandise to Ballet Company of Paris on December 15, 19X8 for 20,000 French francs, payable on January 14, 19X9. Donner closed its books as of December 31, 19X8, and collected the 20,000 francs on January 14, 19X9. The exchange rates for francs were:

December 15, 19X8	$.1740
December 31, 19X8	$.1700
January 14, 19X9	$.1720

Required: Prepare the journal entries needed for Donner to account for the sale, recognition of gain or loss at year-end, and collection of the account.

E 13-3 Alliance Corporation, a U.S. company, sold inventory items to Royal Cabinets Ltd. of Great Britian for 124,000 British pounds on May 1, 19X2, when the spot rate was .6200 pounds. The invoice was paid by Royal on May 30, 19X2, when the spot rate was .6250 pounds.

Required: Prepare journal entries for the sale to Royal on May 1 and receipt of the 124,000 pounds on May 30.

E 13-4 **[AICPA adapted]**

1 On September 1, 19X7, Bain Corp. received an order for equipment from a foreign customer for 300,000 local currency units (LCU) when the U.S. dollar equivalent was $96,000. Bain shipped the equipment on October 15, 19X7 and billed the customer for 300,000 LCU when the U.S. dollar equivalent was $100,000. Bain received the customer's remittance in full on November 16, 19X7 and sold the 300,000 LCU for $105,000. In its income statement for the year ended December 31, 19X7, Bain should report a foreign exchange gain of:

a $0   **b** $4,000
c $5,000   **d** $9,000

2 On April 8, 19X7 Day Corp. purchased merchandise from an unaffiliated foreign company for 10,000 units of the foreign company's local currency. Day paid the bill in full on March 1, 19X8 when the spot rate was $.45. The spot rate was $.60 on April 8, 19X7 and was $.55 on December 31, 19X7. For the year ended December 31, 19X8, Day should report a transaction gain of:

a $1,150   **b** $1,000
c $500   **d** $0

3 On July 1, 19X4 Clark Company borrowed 1,680,000 local currency units from a foreign lender, evidenced by an interest-bearing note due on July 1, 19X5, which is denominated in the currency of the lender. The U.S. dollar equivalent of the note principal was as follows:

July 1, 19X4 (date borrowed)	$210,000
December 31, 19X4 (Clark's year-end)	240,000
July 1, 19X5 (date paid)	280,000

In its income statement for 19X5, what amount should Clark include as a foreign exchange gain or loss?

a $70,000 gain   **b** $70,000 loss
c $40,000 gain   **d** $40,000 loss

4 On July 1, 19X1 Stone Company lent $120,000 to a foreign supplier, evidenced by an interest-bearing note due on July 1, 19X2. The note is denominated in the currency of the borrower and was equivalent to 840,000 local currency units on the loan date. The note principal was appropriately included at $140,000 in the receivables section of Stone's December 31, 19X1 balance sheet. The note principal was repaid to Stone on the July 1, 19X2 due date when the exchange rate was 8 LCU to $1. In its income statement for the year ended December 31, 19X2, what amount should Stone include as a foreign currency transaction gain or loss?

    a $0   **b** $15,000 loss
    c $15,000 gain   **d** $35,000 loss

E 13-5 American TV Corporation had two foreign currency transactions during December 19X1 as follows:

> *December 12*   Purchased electronic parts from Toko Company of Japan at an invoice price of 50,000,000 yen when the spot rate for yen was $.006150. Payment is due on January 11, 19X2.
>
> *December 15*   Sold television sets to British Products Ltd. for 40,000 pounds when the spot rate for British pounds was $1.52. The invoice is denominated in pounds and is due on January 14, 19X2.

Required
    1 Prepare journal entries to record the foregoing transactions.
    2 Prepare journal entries to adjust the accounts of American TV Corporation at December 31, 19X1 if the current exchange rates are $.00620 and $1.50 for Japanese yen and British pounds, respectively.
    3 Prepare journal entries to record payment to Toko Company on January 11, 19X2 when the spot rate for Japanese yen is $.00621, and to record receipt from British Products Ltd. on January 14, 19X2 when the spot rate for British pounds is $1.51.

E 13-6 Hayes Corporation, a U.S. importer, purchased merchandise from Cavilier Company of France for 100,000 francs on March 1, 19X8 when the spot rate for French francs was $.1730. Since the account payable denominated in francs was not due until May 30, 19X8, Hayes immediately entered into a ninety-day forward contract to hedge the transaction against exchange rate changes. The contract was made at a forward exchange rate of $.1750. Hayes settled the forward contract and the account payable on May 30 when the spot rate for francs was $.1700.

Required: Prepare the journal entries needed for Hayes to account for the purchase and forward contract on March 1, 19X8 and the subsequent settlements on May 30, 19X8.

E 13-7 Trendy Corporation purchases merchandise from Benetton S.p.A. of Italy for 10,000,000 lira. The merchandise is received on December 1, 19X8, with payment due in sixty days on January 30, 19X9. Also on December 1, 19X8 Trendy enters into a sixty-day forward contract with the exchange broker to purchase the necessary 10,000,000 lira for delivery on January 30, 19X9 to hedge the Benetton transaction. Exchange rates for lira on selected dates are as follows:

	12/1/X8	*12/31/X8*	*1/30/X9*
Spot rate	$.00078	$.00079	$.00078
30-day futures	.00079	.00080	.00080
60-day futures	.00080	.00081	.00081

    1 What is the net exchange gain or loss from this transaction and hedge that will be reported on Trendy's 19X8 income statement?
    2 What effect will the transaction and hedge have on Trendy's income for 19X9?

E 13-8 The unadjusted trial balance of Electronic Importers at the end of its calendar year December 31, 19X8 included receivables and payables denominated in Japanese yen as follows:

Receivables
    Contract receivable dated December 1, 19X8 for
    20,000,000 yen to hedge a commitment to purchase
    computer hardware for 20,000,000 yen in 90 days
    ending on March 1, 19X9 $124,000

Payables
    Account payable for 70,000,000 yen for unpaid merchandise
    acquired on December 16, 19X8 and due on January 15,
    19X9 $427,000

    Contract payable dated December 16, 19X8 for 30,000,000
    yen to speculate in exchange rate changes and due on
    January 15, 19X9 $180,000

Exchange rates quoted in the U.S. for Japanese yen are:

	12/1/X3	12/16/X8	12/31/X8	1/15/X9	3/1/X9
Spot rate	$.00620	$.00610	$.00600	$.00590	$.00580
Purchase rates for 90-day forward	.00630	.00620	.00610	.00600	.00590
Selling rates for 30-day forward	.00610	.00600	.00590	.00580	.00570
Selling rates for 15-day forward	.00615	.00605	.00595	.00585	.00575

1 The contract receivable at December 31, 19X8 should be included in accounts receivable at:
  a $126,000   **b** $124,000
  c $120,000   **d** None of the above

2 The exchange gain or loss on the accounts payable should be reported in Electronic Importers' 19X8 income statement in the amount of:
  a $14,000   **b** $13,000
  c $7,000   **d** None of the above

3 The exchange gain or (loss) on the contract payable should be reported in Electronic Importers' 19X8 and 19X9 income statements in the amount of:
  a ($3,000) and $3,000, respectively
  b $3,000 and $0, respectively
  c $0 and $3,000, respectively
  d $1,500 and $1,500, respectively

4 Upon settlement of the contract receivable on March 1, 19X9, Electronic Importers should:
  a Record an $8,000 exchange gain
  b Record a $4,000 exchange loss
  c Adjust its purchases downward by $4,000
  d Adjust its purchases upward by $8,000

E 13–9   The accounts receivable of Bradley Corporation, a U.S. export company, include the following items denominated in foreign currency at December 31, 19X2 *before* adjusting entries are made:

	Foreign Currency Units	Exchange Rate on Transaction Date	Balance per Books in U.S. Dollars
British pounds	50,000	$1.60	$ 80,000
German marks	200,000	$0.50	100,000
Swiss francs	100,000	$0.60	60,000
Japanese yen	10,000,000	$0.0068	68,000

On December 31, 19X2 the current exchange rates for British pounds, German marks, Swiss francs, and Japanese yen were $1.57, $.55, $.58, and $.0070, respectively.

Required
1 Determine the amount at which the above receivables should be included in Bradley Corporation's December 31, 19X2 balance sheet.
2 Calculate the exchange gain or loss that should be included in Bradley's 19X2 income statement.

E 13-10 Kelly Corporation, a U.S. firm, had several foreign exchange transactions during 19X8. Prepare journal entries to record these transactions and year-end adjustments as described.

June 8	Purchased merchandise denominated at 10,000 British pounds when the spot rate was $1.60.
July 7	Paid the invoice of June 8 when the spot rate for British pounds was $1.61.
October 1	Sold merchandise to a Swiss firm for 30,000 Swiss francs when the spot rate for francs was $.660.
October 19	Settled the invoice of October 1 when the spot rate for francs was $.655.
November 16	Sold merchandise for 500,000 Swedish krona, payment to be received in krona in sixty days on January 16, 19X9. Spot rate for krona on this date was $.164.
November 16	Entered into a forward contract to deliver 500,000 krona to the exchange broker to hedge the sale of November 16 when the forward rate for 60-day futures in krona was $.1638 and the spot rate for krona was $.164.
December 31	Adjusted the accounts for the transactions of November 16 when the current exchange rate for krona was $.1643.

E 13-11 On April 1, 19X9 Windsor Ltd. of Canada ordered customized fittings from Ace Foundry, a U.S. firm, to be delivered on May 31, 19X9 at a price of 50,000 Canadian dollars. The spot rate for Canadian dollars on April 1, 19X9 was $.83. Also on April 1, in order to fix the sale price of the fittings at $41,500, Ace entered into a 60-day forward contract with the exchange broker to hedge the Windsor contract. This contract met the conditions set forth in *FASB Statement No. 52* for a hedge of a foreign currency commitment. Exchange rates for Canadian dollars are as follows:

	April 1	*May 31*
Spot rate	$.830	$.845
60-day forward	.825	.835

Required: Prepare all journal entries on Ace Foundry's books to account for the commitment and related events on April 1 and May 31, 19X9.

E 13-12 On November 2, 19X1 Import Bazaar, a U.S. retailer, ordered merchandise from Matsushita Company of Japan. The merchandise is to be delivered to Import Bazaar on January 30, 19X2 at a price of 1,000,000 yen. Also on November 2, Import Bazaar hedged the foreign currency commitment with Matsushita by contracting with its exchange broker to buy 1,000,000 yen for delivery on January 30, 19X2. Exchange rates for yen are:

	11/2/X1	*12/31/X1*	*1/30/X2*
Spot rate	$.0060	$.0061	$.0063
60-day forward rate	.0061	.0063	.0064
90-day forward rate	.0063	.0064	.0065

Required
1 Prepare the entry (or entries) on Import Bazaar's books on November 2, 19X1.
2 What two alternative year-end treatments may Import Bazaar use on its hedge of the foreign currency commitment?

E 13-13 Martin, Inc., a U.S. import-export firm, enters into a forward contract on October 2, 19X3 to speculate in Swiss francs. The contract requires Martin to deliver 1,000,000 Swiss francs to the exchange broker on March 31, 19X4.

Quoted exchange rates for Swiss francs are as follows:

	10/2/X3	*12/31/X3*	*3/31/X4*
Spot rate	$.6590	$.6500	$.6550
30-day forward	$.6580	$.6450	$.6500
90-day forward	$.6560	$.6410	$.6460
180-day forward	$.6530	$.6360	$.6400

Required: Prepare the journal entries on Martin's books to account for the speculation throughout the life of the contract.

PROBLEMS

P 13-1 The accounts of Lincoln International, a U.S. corporation, show $81,300 accounts receivable and $39,900 accounts payable at December 31, 19X1 before adjusting entries are made. An analysis of the balances reveals the following:

Accounts receivable	
Receivable denominated in U.S. dollars	$28,500
Receivable denominated in 20,000 German marks	11,800
Receivable denominated in 25,000 British pounds	41,000
Total	$81,300

Accounts payable	
Payable denominated in U.S. dollars	$ 6,850
Payable denominated in 10,000 Canadian dollars	8,600
Payable denominated in 15,000 British pounds	24,450
Total	$39,900

Current exchange rates for German marks, British pounds, and Canadian dollars at December 31, 19X1 are $.60, $1.65, and $.85, respectively.

Required
1 Determine the net exchange gain or loss that should be reflected in Lincoln's income statement for 19X1 from year-end exchange adjustments.
2 Determine the amounts at which the accounts receivable and accounts payable should be included in Lincoln's December 31, 19X1 balance sheet.
3 Prepare journal entries to record collection of the receivables in 19X2 when the spot rates for German marks and British pounds are $.61 and $1.63, respectively.
4 Prepare journal entries to record settlement of accounts payable in 19X2 when the spot rates for Canadian dollars and British pounds are $.86 and $1.62, respectively.

P 13-2 Shelton Corporation of New York is an international dealer in jewelry and engages in numerous import and export activities. Shelton's receivables and payables in foreign currency units before year-end adjustments on December 31, 19X7 are summarized as follows:

Foreign Currency	Currency Units	Rate on Date of Transaction	Per Books in U.S. Dollars	Current Rate on 12/31/X7
Accounts receivable denominated in foreign currency:				
British pounds	100,000	$1.6500	$165,000	$1.6600
German marks	250,000	$0.5900	147,500	$0.6000
Swiss francs	160,000	$0.6500	104,000	$0.6300
French francs	500,000	$0.1700	85,000	$0.1750
Japanese yen	2,000,000	$0.0065	13,000	$0.0066
			$514,500	
Accounts payable denominated in foreign currency:				
Canadian dollars	150,000	$0.8500	$127,500	$0.8400
German marks	50,000	$0.5800	29,000	$0.6000
Swedish krona	220,000	$0.1600	35,200	$0.1650
Japanese yen	4,500,000	$0.0064	28,800	$0.0066
			$220,500	

Required

1 Determine the amount at which the receivables and payables should be reported in Shelton's December 31, 19X7 balance sheet.
2 Calculate the individual gains and losses on each of the receivables and payables and the net exchange gain that should appear in Shelton's 19X7 income statement.
3 Assume that Shelton wants to hedge its exposure to amounts denominated in German marks. Should it buy or sell marks for future delivery, in what amount or amounts, and is a discount or premium likely to result?

P 13–3 Worldwide Corporation is an international firm that manufactures to the specifications of the purchaser and sells on a contract basis. The firm is headquartered in New York and its contracts are primarily with European firms.

The following transactions and events relate to one of its transactions and related hedging activities. Prepare all journal entries on Worldwide's books to account for the transactions and events.

November 16, 19X6	Contracted to deliver equipment to a British firm on February 14, 19X7. The contract is denominated in pounds, 400,000 pounds are due upon delivery, and the spot rate for pounds is $1.640 on November 16.
November 16, 19X6	Acquired a forward contract to sell 200,000 pounds for delivery on February 14, 19X7 at a forward rate of $1.630 in order to hedge 50% of the exposure.
December 31, 19X6	Current exchange rate for pounds on this date is $1.650 and the rate for a 45-day forward contract is $1.635. Worldwide elects not to amortize the discount currently.
February 14, 19X7	Worldwide delivers the equipment, collects the 400,000 pounds, delivers 200,000 pounds to the exchange broker, collects the amount due from the broker, and adjusts the sales account as appropriate. The spot rate for pounds on this date is $1.665.

P 13–4 On October 2, 19X1 Flex-American Corporation, a U.S. company, entered into a forward contract to purchase 50,000 German marks for delivery in 180 days at a forward rate of $.5750. The forward contract is a hedge of an identifiable foreign currency commitment as defined in *FASB Statement No. 52*. The spot rate for marks on this date was $.5650. Spot rates and forward rates for marks on December 31, 19X1 and March 31, 19X2 are:

	December 31, 19X1	March 31, 19X2
Spot rate	$.5790	$.5960
Forward rates: 30-day futures	.5810	.5975
90-day futures	.5820	.6015
180-day futures	.5850	.6080

Required: Prepare journal entries to:
1 Record the forward contract on October 2, 19X1
2 Adjust the accounts at December 31, 19X1
3 Account for settlement of the forward contract and record and adjust the related cash purchase on March 31, 19X2

P 13–5 Arvil Corporation, a U.S. manufacturer of personal computers, negotiated a contract on November 2, 19X5 to deliver 600 personal computers to Kramer Company Ltd. of London. The delivery date is January 30, 19X6, and the contract calls for payment of 300,000 British pounds upon delivery. In order to hedge the commitment, Arvil acquired a forward contract on November 2, 19X5 to sell 300,000 British pounds in 90 days. Exchange rates between U.S. dollars and British pounds on selected dates were as follows:

	11/2/X5	12/31/X5	1/30/X6
Spot rate	$1.6000	$1.6100	$1.6200
90-day futures	$1.5800	$1.5900	$1.6000

The forward contract meets all the requirements for the hedge of an identifiable foreign currency commitment.

Required: Prepare the necessary journal entries on Arvil Corporation's books to account for the forward contract on November 2, 19X5 and December 31, 19X5 and the delivery, collection, and settlement of the forward contract on January 30, 19X6. The discount on the forward contract is to be considered an adjustment of the selling price of the personal computers.

P 13–6 Marlington Corporation, a U.S. firm, purchased equipment for 400,000 British pounds from Thacker Company, Ltd. on December 16, 19X4. The terms were n/30, payable in British pounds.

On December 16, 19X4, Marlington also entered into a thirty-day forward contract to hedge the account payable to Thacker. Exchange rates for British pounds on selected dates are as follows:

	12/16/X4	12/31/X4	1/15/X5
Spot rate	$1.62	$1.60	$1.59
30-day forward rate	$1.63	$1.61	$1.61

Required
1 Prepare journal entries on December 16, 19X4 to record Marlington's purchase and the forward contract.
2 Prepare year-end journal entries for Marlington as needed on December 31, 19X4.
3 Prepare journal entries for Marlington's settlement of its accounts payable and the forward contract on January 15, 19X5.

P 13–7 Rontex Corporation recorded a $100,000 account receivable from Renault Corporation of Quebec on December 1, 19X1. This receivable is denominated in Canadian dollars and is due on March 1, 19X2. Also on December 1, 19X1, Rontex sold 125,000 Canadian dollars for delivery on March 1, 19X2 in order to hedge its exposed net asset position. The spot rate for Canadian dollars was $.800 on December 1, 19X1, and the forward rate for ninety-day delivery was $.790.

The following exchange rates were quoted for Canadian dollars on December

31, 19X1 when Rontex Corporation closed its books and on March 1, 19X2 when the receivable was collected and the accounts with the foreign exchange broker were settled.

	12/31/X1	3/1/X2
Spot rate	$.830	$.870
Forward rate for 60-day futures	$.825	$.865
Forward rate for 90-day futures	$.822	$.864

Required: Prepare journal entries to:
1 Recognize the forward contract on December 1, 19X1
2 Adjust Rontex's books for foreign currency transactions on December 31, 19X1
3 Record collection of the receivable from Renault Corporation and settlement with the foreign exchange broker on March 1, 19X2

P 13–8 The unadjusted accounts of Stuart-American Corporation at December 31, 19X1 that relate to its forward exchange contracts are summarized as follows:

	In U.S. Dollars
Debit Balances	
Contract receivable from exchange broker in U.S. dollars (to hedge foreign currency commitment to Bennett, Ltd of London)	$158,000
Contract receivable from exchange broker in German marks (for speculation to purchase 200,000 marks in 90 days from December 2, 19X1)	120,000
Contract receivable from exchange broker in yen (to hedge payable to Toyaki for 120 days from November 1, 19X1)	63,000
Discount on forward contract (for Bennett hedge)	2,000
Premium on forward contract (for Toyaki hedge)	1,000
Credit Balances	
Accounts payable to Toyaki Company of Japan (billing was for 10,000,000 Japanese yen)	$ 63,000
Contract payable to exchange broker in British pounds (to hedge a 100,000 pound sales commitment with Bennett, Ltd. of London)	160,000
Contract payable to exchange broker in U.S. dollars (for Toyaki hedge)	64,000
Contract payable to exchange broker in U.S. dollars (for speculation in German marks)	120,000

Exchange rates at December 31, 19X1 were as follows:

	Marks	Yen	Pounds
Current rate	$.590	$.0065	$1.615
Forward rates to purchase marks and yen and to sell pounds:			
30-day futures	$.610	$.0066	$1.600
60-day futures	$.620	$.0067	$1.590
90-day futures	$.630	$.0068	$1.580

Required
1 Prepare a schedule to show the amounts at which the above accounts will appear in Stuart-American's December 31, 19X1 balance sheet (also include any deferred gain or loss).
2 Compute the amount of exchange gain or loss that will appear in Stuart-American's

19X1 income statement.

3 Compute the effect on income of amortization of the premiums and discounts for 19X1.

P 13-9 The unadjusted accounts of Grandview International, Inc., at December 31, 19X8 that relate to its forward exchange contracts are summarized as follows:

	In U.S. Dollars
Debit Balances	
Accounts receivable from Nokia Co. of Finland (billing was for 100,000 markka)	$22,000
Contract receivable from exchange broker in U.S. dollars (to hedge the receivable from Nokia for 60 days from December 1, 19X8)	21,000
Contract receivable from exchange broker in won (to hedge the payable to Cheil Textile Co. for 120 days from November 1, 19X8)	12,000
Contract receivable from exchange broker in Canadian dollars (to hedge a 10,000 Canadian dollar purchase commitment from Sterling Corporation of Toronto for 60 days from December 1, 19X8)	8,200
Discount on forward contract (for Nokia hedge)	1,000
Premium on forward contract (for Cheil hedge)	1,000
Premium on forward contract (for Sterling hedge)	200
Credit Balances	
Accounts payable to Cheil Textile Co. of South Korea (billing was for 10,000,000 South Korean won)	12,000
Contract payable to exchange broker in markka (for Nokia hedge)	22,000
Contract payable to exchange broker in U.S. dollars (for Cheil hedge)	13,000
Contract payable to exchange broker in U.S. dollars (for Sterling hedge)	8,400

Exchange rates at December 31, 19X8 were as follows:

	Finnish Markka	South Korean Won	Canadian Dollars
Current rate	$.23	$.0014	$.81
Forward rates to sell markka and purchase won and Canadian dollars			
30-day futures	.22	.0015	.82
60-day futures	.21	.0016	.83

Required

1 At what amount will the contract receivable from the exchange broker to hedge the account receivable from Nokia Co. of Finland be included on Grandview's December 31, 19X8 balance sheet?

2 At what amounts will the account payable from Cheil Textile Co. and the related contract receivable from the exchange broker be included on Grandview's December 31, 19X8 balance sheet?

3 Determine the deferred exchange gain or loss for 19X8 on the forward contract to hedge the purchase commitment from Sterling.

4 Assume that Grandview allocates premiums and discounts on contracts to hedge foreign currency commitments as adjustments of the related transaction amounts. In this case, what is the income effect of amortization of the premiums and discounts for 19X8?

P 13-10 Phillip Corporation of Atlanta paid $1,920,000 for a 40 percent interest in Slusser Company, Ltd. of London on January 1, 19X1 when Slusser's net assets totaled 3,000,000 British pounds and the exchange rate for pounds was $1.60. A summary of changes in Slusser's net assets during 19X1 is as follows:

	British Pounds	Exchange Rate	U.S. Dollars
Net assets, January 1	3,000,000	$1.60	$4,800,000
Add: Net income 19X1	600,000	1.55	930,000
Less: Dividends 19X1	(200,000)	1.54	(308,000)
Less: Equity adjustment from translation			(322,000)
Net assets December 31, 19X1	3,400,000	1.50	$5,100,000

Phillip anticipated a strengthening of the U.S. dollar against the British pound during the last half of 19X1, and it borrowed 1,200,000 pounds from a London bank for one year at 10 percent interest on July 1, 19X1 to hedge its net investment in Slusser. The loan was made when the exchange rate for British pounds was $1.55 and the loan was denominated in British pounds. The current exchange rate at December 31, 19X1 was $1.50.

Required
1 Prepare journal entries to account for Phillip's investment in Slusser during 19X1.
2 Prepare journal entries for Phillip to:
   a Record the loan on July 1, 19X1.
   b Adjust the loan payable at December 31, 19X1.
   c Accrue interest on the loan at December 31, 19X1. (The interest, not a part of the hedge of the net investment, was incurred at a $1.525 average exchange rate.)

P 13-11 Pepperell Corporation, a U.S. firm, has a 25 percent interest in a German firm whose functional currency is the German mark. Its investment balance at December 31, 19X4 was $845,000, equal to 25 percent of the investee's net assets of 5,200,000 marks x $.65 current exchange rate on that date.

Because of anticipated strengthening of the U.S. dollar against the German mark, Pepperell negotiated a one-year, 15 percent loan of 1,300,000 marks on January 1, 19X5 to hedge its net investment in the German investee and immediately invested the money in 9 percent U.S. government securities. These transactions were conducted while the spot rate for marks was $.65.

During 19X5 the U.S. dollar strengthened against the mark and the current exchange rate and spot rate for marks at December 31, 19X5 stood at $.62, and the average exchange rate for 19X5 was $.625. A summary of the changes in equity of the German investee during 19X5 is as follows:

	Marks		U.S. Dollar
Net assets, January 1	5,200,000	× $.65	$3,380,000
Net income 19X5	832,000	× $.625	520,000
Equity adjustment-change			(160,160)
Net assets, December 31	6,032,000	× $.62	$3,739,840

Required: Prepare journal entries on Pepperell's books to:
1 Record the loan of 1,300,000 German marks
2 Invest the $845,000 from the loan in U.S. securities
3 Liquidate the U.S. securities at December 31, 19X5
4 Settle the German loan and interest at December 31, 19X5
5 Account for the foreign investee during 19X5

14

FOREIGN CURRENCY
FINANCIAL STATEMENTS

Since 1982, U.S. multinational corporations have applied the provisions of *FASB Statement No. 52* in converting the financial statements of their foreign subsidiaries and branches into U.S. dollars. *Statement No. 52* requires application of the functional currency concept under which *a foreign entity's functional currency is the currency of the primary economic environment in which it operates.* The foreign entity's functional currency affects (1) the procedures used to measure its financial position and results of operations and (2) whether exchange gains and losses will be included in consolidated net income or will be reported as a separate component of consolidated stockholders' equity.

A U.S. company may have operations located outside the United States in which the books of record are maintained in the U.S. dollar and, therefore, the financial statements are prepared in U.S. dollars. Because these statements are not foreign currency financial statements, they are combined or consolidated according to the procedures described in Chapters 3 through 12, and they are not considered in this chapter.

Several definitions from *Statement No. 52* are important to the functional currency concept. A **foreign currency** is a currency other than the entity's functional currency. If the functional currency of a German subsidiary is the German mark, the U.S. dollar is a foreign currency of the German subsidiary. If the functional currency of the German subsidiary is the U.S. dollar, the German mark is a foreign currency to the German subsidiary. The **local currency** is the currency of the country being referred to. Thus, the Canadian dollar is the local currency of a Canadian subsidiary of a U.S. firm. Note that the books of record and the subsidiary's financial statements will be prepared in the local currency in nearly all cases involving foreign currency financial statements, regardless of the determination of the functional currency. The **reporting currency** is the currency in which the consolidated financial statements are prepared, in other words, the currency of the parent company. The reporting currency for the consolidated statements of a U.S. firm with foreign subsidiaries is the U.S. dollar. **Foreign currency statements** are statements prepared in a currency that is *not* the reporting currency (the U.S. dollar) of the U.S. parent/investor.

APPLICATION OF THE FUNCTIONAL CURRENCY CONCEPT

Before the foreign currency statements of a foreign entity can be translated into U.S. dollars, they must be in conformity with generally accepted accounting principles, and all account balances on the balance sheet date that are denominated in a foreign currency (from the foreign entity's point of view) must be adjusted to reflect current exchange rates. (This is similar to the year-end adjustments illustrated in Chapter 13 for U.S. firms with account balances denominated in a foreign currency.)

Under the objectives of the functional currency concept, a foreign entity's assets, liabilities, and operations must be measured in its functional currency. Subsequently, the foreign entity's statement of financial position and results of operations have to be consolidated (subsidiary) or combined (branch) with those of the parent company in the currency of the reporting enterprise. The accounting procedures required to convert a foreign entity's financial statements into the currency of the U.S. parent depend on the functional currency of the foreign subsidiary or branch. Since the foreign entity's books are maintained in its local currency, which may be its functional currency or a foreign currency, the combining or consolidating may require translation, remeasurement, or both.

Translation   When the foreign entity's books are maintained in its functional currency (in other words, the local currency of the foreign entity is its functional currency), the statements are *translated* into the currency of the reporting entity. **Translation** *involves expressing functional currency measurements in the reporting currency.* A basic provision of *Statement No. 52* is that all elements of financial statements (assets, liabilities, revenues, and expenses) shall be translated using a current exchange rate. This is referred to as the **current rate method**. Since the functional currency is not the U.S. dollar, no direct impact on the reporting entity's cash flows is expected, and the effects of exchange rate changes are reported as stockholders' equity adjustments. The equity adjustments from translation are accumulated until sale or liquidation of the foreign entity investment, at which time they are reported as adjustments of the gain or loss on sale.

Remeasurement   When the foreign entity's books are not maintained in its functional currency, the foreign currency financial statements must be *remeasured* into the functional currency. Remeasurement obviates translation if the entity's functional currency is also the reporting currency. In other words, if the foreign currency financial statements are remeasured into a U.S. dollar functional currency, no translation is necessary because the reporting currency of the parent/ investor is the U.S. dollar. *The objective of remeasurement is to produce the same results as if the books were maintained in the functional currency.* In order to accomplish this objective, both historical and current exchange rates are used in the remeasurement process. Under this method (the **temporal method**), monetary assets and liabilities are remeasured at current exchange rates, while other assets and equities are remeasured at historical rates. **Monetary assets and liabilities** are those in which the amounts are fixed in currency units. **Nonmonetary items** are those in which the amounts change with changes in market prices. The remeasurement produces exchange rate adjustments which are included in income because a direct impact on the enterprise's cash flows is expected.

Translation and Remeasurement of Foreign Currency Financial Statements

Patriot Corporation, a U.S. company, has a wholly owned subsidiary, Romel Corporation, that operates in Germany. The translation-remeasurement possibilities for the accounts of Romel are as follows:

	Functional Currency	Currency of Accounting Records	Required Procedures for Consolidating or Combining
Case 1	German mark	German mark	Translation
Case 2	U.S. dollar	German mark	Remeasurement
Case 3	Swiss franc	German mark	Remeasurement and translation

Under Case 1, Romel Corporation keeps its books in the local currency, marks, which is also the functional currency, and no remeasurement is needed provided that the books reflect U.S. generally accepted accounting principles. The accounts do require translation to U.S. dollar amounts (the currency of the reporting enterprise) and *FASB Statement No. 52* requires translation under the *current rate method*. The current exchange rate at the balance sheet date is used to translate all assets and liabilities. Theoretically, the exchange rates in effect at transaction dates should be used to translate all revenues, expenses, and gains and losses. As a practical matter, it is expected that revenues and expenses will be translated at appropriate weighted average exchange rates for the period. The adjustments from translation are reported in consolidated stockholders' equity as "equity adjustment from foreign currency translation" or some equally descriptive title.

In Case 2, Romel's books are maintained in marks, but the functional currency is the U.S. dollar. Under *Statement No. 52* the accounts of Romel are remeasured into the functional currency, which is also the currency of the reporting entity. In this case, remeasurement into the reporting currency obviates translation. The objective of remeasurement is to obtain the results that would have been produced if Romel's books of record had been maintained in the functional currency. Thus, remeasurement requires the use of historical exchange rates for some items and current rates for others, and recognition of exchange gains and losses from remeasurement of all monetary assets and liabilities not denominated in the functional currency (the U.S. dollar in this case).

In Case 3, Romel's books are maintained in marks while the functional currency is Swiss francs. (This situation could arise if the subsidiary is a holding company for operations in Switzerland.) The consolidation requires a *remeasurement* of all assets, liabilities, revenues, expenses, and gains and losses into Swiss francs (the functional currency) and recognition of exchange gains and losses from remeasurement of the monetary assets and liabilities not denominated in Swiss francs. After the remeasurement is completed and Romel's financial statements are stated in Swiss francs, the statements are *translated* into U.S. dollars using the current rate method. This translation from the functional currency to the currency of the reporting entity will create translation adjustments, but such adjustments are not recognized in current income. Rather, they are reported in consolidated stockholders' equity as "equity adjustments from translation."

A summary of exchange rates to be used for remeasurement and translation is provided in Exhibit 14–1. Once the functional currency has been determined, it should be "used consistently unless significant changes in economic facts and circumstances" indicate that the functional currency has changed. A change in functional currency does not require restatement of previously issued financial statements because it is not a change in an accounting principle (*FASB Statement No. 52,* paragraph 45).

Intercompany Foreign Currency Transactions

Intercompany transactions between affiliated companies are foreign currency transactions if they produce receivable or payable balances denominated in a currency other than the entity's (parent's or subsidiary's) functional currency.

	Remeasurement to Functional Currency	Translation to Currency of Reporting Entity
Assets		
Cash, demand deposits, and time deposits	Current	Current
Marketable securities carried at cost:		
Equity securities	Historical	Current
Debt securities	Historical	Current
Accounts and notes receivable and related unearned		
discounts	Current	Current
Allowance for uncollectible accounts and notes	Current	Current
Inventories:		
Carried at cost	Historical	Current
Carried at lower of cost or market	*	Current
Prepaid insurance, advertising, and rent	Historical	Current
Refundable deposits	Current	Current
Property, plant, and equipment	Historical	Current
Accumulated depreciation on property, plant, and equipment	Historical	Current
Cash surrender value of life insurance	Current	Current
Unamortized policy acquisition costs of life insurance		
company	Current	Current
Deferred income tax assets	Current	Current
Patents, trademarks, licenses, and formulas	Historical	Current
Goodwill	Historical	Current
Other intangible assets	Historical	Current
Liabilities		
Accounts and notes payable and overdrafts	Current	Current
Accrued expenses	Current	Current
Deferred income tax liabilities	Current	Current
Deferred income	Historical	Current
Other deferred credits	Historical	Current
Bonds payable and other long-term debt	Current	Current
Stockholders' Equity		
Common stock	Historical	Historical†
Preferred stock carried at issuance price	Historical	Historical†
Other paid-in capital	Historical	Historical†
Retained earnings	Not remeasured	Not translated
Income Statement Items Related to Nonmonetary Items‡		
Cost of goods sold	Historical	Current
Depreciation on property, plant, and equipment	Historical	Current
Amortization of intangible items (patents, goodwill, etc.)	Historical	Current
Amortization of policy acquisition costs of life insurance		
companies	Current	Current
Amortization of deferred income taxes	Current	Current
Amortization of deferred charges and credits	Historical	Current

* When the books are not maintained in the functional currency and the lower of cost or market rule is applied to inventories, inventories at cost are remeasured using historical rates. Then the historical cost in the functional currency is compared to market in the functional currency.
† Translation at historical rates is necessary for elimination of reciprocal parent investment and subsidiary equity accounts. It should be noted that conversion of all asset, liability, and equity accounts at current exchange rates would obviate the "equity adjustment from translation" component.
‡ Income statement items related to monetary items are translated or remeasured at weighted average exchange rates to approximate the exchange rates in existence at the time of the related transactions. Intercompany dividends are converted at the rate in effect at the time of payment under both the remeasurement and translation approaches. Translation of income statement items at current rates is implemented by using weighted average exchange rates.

Exhibit 14–1   *Summary of Exchange Rates Used for Remeasurement and Translation*

Such intercompany foreign currency transactions result in exchange gains and losses that are included in income except when they produce intercompany balances of a long-term investment nature (that is, settlement is not expected in the foreseeable future), in which case the translation adjustments are reported as a separate stockholders' equity component (equity adjustment from translation).

An intercompany transaction requires analysis to see if it is a foreign currency transaction for one, both, or neither of the affiliates. To illustrate the variables involved, assume that a U.S. parent company borrows $1,500,000 (1,000,000 pounds) from its British subsidiary. The following analysis shows that either the parent or the subsidiary will have a foreign currency transaction if the subsidiary's local currency is its functional currency.

	Currency in Which Loan is Denominated	Functional Currency of Subsidiary	Foreign Currency Transaction of	
			Subsidiary?	Parent?
Case 1	British pound	British pound	No	Yes
Case 2	British pound	U.S. dollar	Yes	Yes
Case 3	U.S. dollar	British pound	Yes	No
Case 4	U.S. dollar	U.S. dollar	No	No

When the U.S. dollar is the functional currency of the subsidiary, either both affiliates have a foreign currency transaction with offsetting effects (Case 2), or the intercompany transaction is not a foreign currency transaction (Case 4). Thus, only the cases in which the functional currency is the local currency of the subsidiary (Cases 1 and 3) have the potential to affect consolidated income. In these cases, translation adjustments will be reported as equity adjustments from translation if the loan is of a long-term investment nature; otherwise, they will be reported as exchange gains and losses.

Foreign Entities Operating in Highly Inflationary Economies

In a highly inflationary economy, the local currency rapidly loses value against goods and services. Generally, it is weakening against other currencies as well. The lack of a stable measuring unit presents special problems for converting foreign currency statements into U.S. dollars. For example, assume that at the end of year 1, $1 can be exchanged for 50 local currency units (LCU), a $.02 exchange rate, but at the end of year 2, $1 can be exchanged for 200 LCU, a $.005 exchange rate. An equity investment of 9,000,000 LCU at the end of year 1 is translated at $180,000 using the current exchange rate, but one year later the same investment of 9,000,000 LCU is translated at $45,000 using the current exchange rate. Under the current rate method, translation gains and losses are accumulated and reported as a component of stockholders' equity. They are not recognized in income until the investment is sold.

The FASB recognized that the current rate method of translation would pose a problem for foreign entities operating in countries with high rates of inflation. Since price-level-adjusted financial statements are not basic financial statements under GAAP, the FASB prescribed a practical alternative. The reporting currency (the U.S. dollar) has to be used to remeasure the financial statements of foreign entities in highly inflationary economies because the inflationary currency is not a functional measuring unit. Exchange gains and losses from remeasuring the financial statements of the foreign entity are recognized in the income for the period.

Statement No. 52 defines a "highly inflationary economy" as one with a cumulative three-year inflation rate of approximately 100 percent or more. Consider a foreign country with inflation data for a three-year period as follows:

	Index	Change in Index	Annual Rate of Inflation
January 1, 1989	120		
January 1, 1990	150	30	30/120 (or 25%)
January 1, 1991	210	60	60/150 (or 40%)
January 1, 1992	250	40	40/210 (or 19%)

The three-year inflation rate is 108.3 percent [(250 − 120)/120], *not* 84 percent (25 + 40 + 19). Management applies judgment in the final determination to avoid frequent changes in the functional currency due to minor changes in the three-year inflation rate. Since the three-year inflation rate in this example exceeds 100 percent, the usual criteria for identifying the functional currency are ignored and the U.S. dollar (the functional currency of the reporting entity) is the functional currency for purposes of preparing consolidated financial statements.

Business Combinations

The assets and liabilities of a foreign entity are translated into U.S. dollars using the current exchange rate in effect on the date of the business combination. For a *pooling of interests business combination,* this involves translating the recorded assets and liabilities into U.S. dollars at book values.

In the case of a business combination accounted for as a *purchase,* the identifiable assets and liabilities of the foreign operations are adjusted to their fair values in local currency and translated at the exchange rate in effect at the date of the purchase business combination. Any difference between investment cost and translated net assets acquired is accounted for as goodwill or as an excess of net assets acquired over cost, as required by *APB Opinion No. 16.*

Cost–Book Value Differential   When the foreign entity's books are maintained in the functional currency, the excess of cost over book value acquired is assigned to assets, liabilities, and goodwill in local currency units and subsequently *translated* at current exchange rates under the current rate method. For example, assume that the excess is allocated 10,000 British pounds to equipment with a five-year life on January 1, 19X2 when the exchange rate is $1.50. If the average exchange rate for 19X2 is $1.45 and the year-end exchange rate is $1.40, depreciation on the excess for 19X2 will be $2,900 (2,000 pounds × $1.45), the undepreciated balance at December 31 will be $11,200 (8,000 pounds × $1.40), and the unrealized translation loss of $900 [$15,000 − ($2,900 + $11,200)] will be recorded as an equity adjustment from translation.

When the foreign entity's books are not maintained in the functional currency, *remeasurement* is required and the excess allocated to equipment is amortized at the historical exchange rates in effect at the time of the business combination. Thus, the depreciation expense would be $3,000 (2,000 pounds × $1.50) and the undepreciated balance would be $12,000 (8,000 pounds × $1.50).

Minority Interest   The computation of the amount of a minority interest in a foreign subsidiary must be based on the translated or remeasured financial statements of the subsidiary. Similarly, the financial statements of a foreign investee must be translated or remeasured before the equity method of accounting is applied.

ILLUSTRATION—TRANSLATION UNDER STATEMENT NO. 52

The following illustration will demonstrate the translation requirements of *Statement No. 52* in action.

Background Information

Assume that Patriot Corporation, a U.S. firm, paid $5,250,000 cash to acquire all the stock of the British firm, Sterling Company Ltd., when the book value of Sterling's net assets was equal to fair value. This purchase business combination was consummated on December 31, 19X1, at which time the exchange rate for British pounds (£) was $1.50. Sterling's assets and equities at acquisition on December 31, 19X1 were as follows:

	British Pounds	Exchange Rate	U.S. Dollars
Assets			
Cash	1,400,000	$1.50	2,100,000
Accounts receivable	400,000	1.50	600,000
Inventories (cost)	1,200,000	1.50	1,800,000
Plant assets	1,000,000	1.50	1,500,000
Less: Accumulated depreciation	(200,000)	1.50	(300,000)
Total assets	3,800,000		5,700,000
Equities			
Accounts payable	300,000	1.50	450,000
Bonds payable	1,000,000	1.50	1,500,000
Capital stock	2,000,000	1.50	3,000,000
Retained earnings	500,000	1.50	750,000
Total equities	3,800,000		5,700,000

During 19X2 the British pound weakened against the U.S. dollar, and at year-end the current exchange rate was $1.40. Average exchange rates for 19X2 were $1.45. Sterling paid 300,000 £ dividends on December 1, 19X2 when the exchange rate was $1.42 (U.S.) per British pound.

Intercompany Transaction

The only intercompany transaction between the firms was an $840,000 (560,000 £) noninterest-bearing advance by Sterling to Patriot that was made on January 4, 19X2 when the exchange rate was still $1.50. The advance is denominated in U.S. dollars. Under the assumption that Patriot determines Sterling's functional currency to be the British pound, the advance to Patriot is a foreign currency transaction to Sterling, but not to Patriot. Therefore, Sterling adjusts its advance to Patriot account at year-end 19X2 to reflect the $1.40 current exchange rate. Sterling records an exchange gain because there is no evidence that the advance is of a long-term investment nature. The entry on Sterling's books is:

Advance to Patriot	40,000 £	
Exchange gain		40,000 £

To adjust receivable denominated in dollars [($840,000/$1.40) − 560,000 £ per books].

Sterling's adjusted trial balance at December 31, 19X2 reflects the advance to Patriot in the amount of 600,000 £, and the exchange gain at 40,000 £.

Translating the Foreign Subsidiary's Adjusted Trial Balance

Patriot has to translate Sterling's adjusted trial balance at December 31, 19X2 into U.S. dollars before it can either account for its investment under the equity method or consolidate its financial statements with those of Sterling. The translation of Sterling's accounts into U.S. dollars is shown in Exhibit 14–2, which illustrates translation working paper procedures. Under the *current rate method* required for foreign subsidiaries whose functional currency is not the U.S. dollar, all assets and liabilities are translated at the current exchange rate at the balance sheet date and all income statement items are translated at average exchange rates during the accounting period. Average rates are applied so as to approximate the current exchange rates in effect when the revenue and expense transactions were consummated during the period. The exchange rates in effect when dividends are paid are used in translating the dividends of a foreign subsidiary.

STERLING COMPANY LTD.
TRANSLATION WORKSHEET FOR 19X2
(BRITISH POUNDS FUNCTIONAL CURRENCY)

	Trial Balance (in British Pounds)	Translation Rate	Trial Balance (in U.S. Dollars)
Debits			
Cash	1,100,000	$1.40	1,540,000
Accounts receivable	800,000	1.40	1,120,000
Inventories (FIFO)	1,200,000	1.40	1,680,000
Plant assets	1,000,000	1.40	1,400,000
Advance to Patriot	600,000	1.40	840,000
Cost of sales	2,700,000	1.45	3,915,000
Depreciation	100,000	1.45	145,000
Wages and salaries	1,200,000	1.45	1,740,000
Other expenses	600,000	1.45	870,000
Dividends	300,000	1.42	426,000
Equity adjustment on translation			286,000
	9,600,000		13,962,000
Credits			
Accumulated depreciation	300,000	1.40	420,000
Accounts payable	360,000	1.40	504,000
Bonds payable	1,000,000	1.40	1,400,000
Capital stock	2,000,000	1.50	3,000,000
Retained earnings	500,000	computed	750,000
Sales	5,400,000	1.45	7,830,000
Exchange gain (advance)	40,000	1.45	58,000
	9,600,000		13,962,000

Exhibit 14–2 *Translation of Foreign Subsidiary Accounts into U.S. Dollars*

The stockholders' equity accounts of a subsidiary are not translated at current exchange rates. Capital stock and other paid-in capital accounts are translated at the exchange rate in effect when the subsidiary (or investee) was acquired. Retained earnings are not translated after acquisition but, rather, *the retained earnings dollar amount consists of retained earnings at acquisition plus income less dividends after acquistion, all in translated dollar amounts.*

After all financial statement items have been translated into dollars, the trial balance debits and credits are totaled and *the amount needed to balance debits and credits is entered as an equity adjustment from translation.* For example, the $286,000 equity adjustment on translation in Exhibit 14–2 is measured by subtracting the $13,676,000 debits from the $13,962,000 credits in the U.S. dollar column. Financial statements in dollars for the foreign entity are prepared directly from the translated trial balance. These are illustrated in Exhibit 14–3 for Sterling Company at and for the year ended December 31, 19X2.

Equity Method of Accounting

Patriot records the investment in Sterling at its $5,250,000 cost on December 31, 19X1, and subsequently uses one-line consolidation procedures to account for its foreign subsidiary. Sterling's translated financial statements are used in applying the equity method. The entry to record receipt of the 300,000 £, or $426,000, dividend from Sterling on December 1, 19X2 is:

Cash	$426,000	
Investment in Sterling		$426,000

STERLING COMPANY LTD.
INCOME AND RETAINED EARNINGS STATEMENTS
FOR THE YEAR ENDED DECEMBER 31, 19X2
(IN U.S. DOLLARS)

Sales		$7,830,000
Less costs and expenses:		
Cost of sales	$3,915,000	
Depreciation	145,000	
Wages and salaries	1,740,000	
Other expenses	870,000	
Total costs and expenses		6,670,000
Operating income		1,160,000
Exchange gain		58,000
Net income		1,218,000
Retained earnings, January 1		750,000
		1,968,000
Dividends		426,000
Retained earnings, December 31, 19X2		$1,542,000

STERLING COMPANY LTD. BALANCE SHEET
AT DECEMBER 31, 19X2
(IN U.S. DOLLARS)

Assets	
Cash	$1,540,000
Accounts receivable	1,120,000
Inventories	1,680,000
Plant assets	1,400,000
Less: Accumulated depreciation	(420,000)
Advance to Patriot	840,000
	$6,160,000
Equities	
Accounts payable	$ 504,000
Bonds payable	1,400,000
Capital stock	3,000,000
Retained earnings	1,542,000
Equity adjustment from translation	(286,000)
	$6,160,000

Exhibit 14–3   *Translated Financial Statements—British Pounds Functional Currency*

Since Patriot received this dividend when the exchange rate was $1.42, the dividends paid by Sterling also have to be translated into dollars at the current exchange rate in effect when the dividends were paid, $1.42 (see Exhibit 14–2).

Patriot recognizes its equity in Sterling's income from 19X2 in an entry that also recognizes Sterling's unrecognized loss on translation. The entry for 19X2 is as follows:

Investment in Sterling	$932,000	
Equity adjustment on translation	286,000	
Income from Sterling		$1,218,000

This entry recognizes 100 percent of Sterling's net income for 19X2, in dollars, as investment income, and it also enters the $286,000 unrecognized loss from translation on Patriot's books. The recognized income of $1,218,000 less the

$286,000 unrecognized loss on translation is the $932,000 investment increase from Sterling's operations in 19X2.

Goodwill Amortization   Patriot's goodwill from its investment in Sterling is $1,500,000, equal to $5,250,000 investment cost less $3,750,000 book value and fair value of net assets acquired. Under the current rate method, the goodwill calculations are based on local currency units (British pounds) rather than U.S. dollar amounts. Thus, a first step in calculating goodwill amortization for Patriot's investment in Sterling is to convert the $1,500,000 goodwill at acquisition into 1,000,000 £ goodwill by dividing $1,500,000 by the $1.50 exchange rate at acquisition on December 31, 19X1.

Current amortization on Patriot's books is 1,000,000 £/10 years × $1.45 average exchange rate for 19X2, or $145,000. Goodwill amortization for 19X2 is recorded on Patriot's books as follows:

Income from Sterling	$145,000	
Equity adjustment from translation	95,000	
Investment in Sterling		$240,000

The equity adjustment on translation of goodwill that appears in the entry is the result of changes in exchange rates during 19X2, and the $240,000 credit to the investment in Sterling reflects the decrease in unamortized goodwill during the year, $1,500,000 − (900,000 £ × $1.40). These relationships are summarized as follows:

	In Pounds	Exchange Rate	In Dollars
Beginning goodwill	1,000,000	$1.50	$1,500,000
Less: Amortization	100,000	1.45	145,000
	900,000		1,345,000
Equity adjustment	—		95,000
Ending goodwill	900,000	1.40	$1,260,000

Alternatively, the $95,000 equity adjustment can be computed as follows:

100,000 £ amortization × ($1.50 − $1.45) exchange rate decline to midyear	$ 5,000
900,000 £ unamortized goodwill × ($1.50 − $1.40) exchange rate decline for the year	90,000
Equity adjustment	$95,000

Similar adjustments are required when an excess of cost over book value is allocated to identifiable assets and liabilities and the current rate method is used.

Investment in Foreign Subsidiary   At this point, it may be helpful to summarize the changes in Patriot's investment in Sterling account during 19X2:

Investment cost, December 31, 19X1		$5,250,000
Dividends received 19X2		(426,000)
Equity in Sterling's net income	$1,218,000	
Less: Unrealized loss on translation	(286,000)	932,000
Goodwill amortization	$ 145,000	
Add: Unrealized translation loss on goodwill	95,000	(240,000)
Investment balance, December 31, 19X2		$5,516,000

The translated amount of Sterling's net assets at December 31, 19X2 is $4,256,000, as shown in Exhibit 14–3. Patriot's $5,516,000 investment in Sterling balance on this date consists of the $4,256,000 equity in Sterling's net assets plus $1,260,000 unamortized goodwill. Patriot also has unrealized losses from translation of $381,000 at December 31, 19X2, consisting of $286,000 translation losses on Sterling's net assets plus a $95,000 translation loss on goodwill. These unrealized losses are reflected in Patriot's equity adjustment from translation account, which is reported as a deduction from stockholders' equity. The equity adjustment is increased or decreased to reflect translation gains or losses during each period that the investment is held, and the final balance is treated as an adjustment of any gain or loss on sale or other disposal of the investment. *FASB Statement No. 52* requires disclosure of beginning and ending balances and changes to the translation adjustment account.

The functional currency concept provides a way to recognize exchange rate changes without affecting the income statement. When the local currency of a foreign entity is its functional currency, net assets can change without impacting income, the FASB reasoned. This may be because "a change in the exchange rate between the dollar and the other currency produces a change in the dollar equivalent of the net investment, but there is no change in the net assets of the other entity measured in its functional currency."[1] Or it might be argued that "the translation adjustment is merely a mechanical by-product of the translation process and thus represents a restatement of previously reported equity."[2]

Consolidation

Working papers to consolidate the financial statements of Patriot Corporation and Sterling Company Ltd. for the year ended December 31, 19X2 are illustrated in Exhibit 14-4. Although the account balances for Patriot Corporation are introduced for the first time in the working papers, the amounts that appear are compatible with earlier assumptions. For example, the $1,073,000 income from Sterling ($1,218,000 equity in income less $145,000 goodwill amortization), the $5,516,000 investment in Sterling, and the $381,000 equity adjustment on translation appear in Patriot's separate financial statements. The financial statements of Sterling that appear in the consolidation working papers of Exhibit 14-4 are based on those presented in Exhibit 14-3.

The procedures to consolidate a foreign subsidiary are basically the same as the procedures needed to consolidate a domestic subsidiary, and the sequence of working paper entries is the same. When the current rate method is used, however, the appearance of the equity adjustment from translation account does require special interpretation. For example, working paper entry a in Exhibit 14-4 is as follows:

a	Income from Sterling	$1,073,000	
	Dividends		$426,000
	Investment in Sterling		647,000

While the objective of this working paper entry is the same as for similar entries encountered in earlier chapters, the $647,000 credit to the investment in Sterling account reduces the investment to $4,869,000 rather than to the $5,250,000 beginning-of-the-period balance. Actually, the $4,869,000 is the beginning-of-the-period balance less the $381,000 translation adjustments reflected in Patriot's equity adjustment from translation account.

Working paper entry b is reproduced in journal form as follows:

---

[1]Wig De Moville and Roben Hatami, "Nonowner Equity Transactions—A Review," *The CPA Journal* (June 1990), p. 50.

[2]Ibid.

**PATRIOT CORPORATION AND SUBSIDIARY
CONSOLIDATION WORKING PAPERS
TRANSLATION—FUNCTIONAL CURRENCY BRITISH POUND
FOR THE YEAR ENDED DECEMBER 31, 19X2**

	Patriot	Sterling	Adjustments and Eliminations		Consolidated Statements
Income Statement					
Sales	$12,183,000	$7,830,000			$20,013,000
Income from Sterling	1,073,000		a	1,073,000	
Cost of sales	6,000,000*	3,915,000*			9,915,000*
Depreciation	400,000*	145,000*			545,000*
Wages and salaries	3,000,000*	1,740,000*			4,740,000*
Other expenses	1,500,000*	870,000*	c	145,000	2,515,000*
Exchange gain		58,000			58,000
Net income	$ 2,356,000	$1,218,000			$ 2,356,000
Retained Earnings					
Retained earnings—Patriot	$ 2,455,000				$ 2,455,000
Retained earnings—Sterling		$ 750,000	b	750,000	
Net income	2,356,000 ✓	1,218,000 ✓			2,356,000
Dividends	1,000,000*	426,000*		a 426,000	1,000,000*
Retained earnings December 31, 19X2	$ 3,811,000	$1,542,000			$ 3,811,000
Balance Sheet					
Cash	$ 3,176,000	$1,540,000			$ 4,716,000
Accounts receivable	1,500,000	1,120,000			2,620,000
Inventories	3,000,000	1,680,000			4,680,000
Plant assets	4,000,000	1,400,000			5,400,000
Accumulated depreciation	1,000,000*	420,000*			1,420,000*
Advance to Patriot		840,000		d 840,000	
Investment in Sterling	5,516,000			a 647,000 b 4,869,000	
Goodwill			b 1,405,000	c 145,000	1,260,000
	$16,192,000	$6,160,000			$17,256,000
Accounts payable	$ 1,422,000	$ 504,000			$ 1,926,000
Advance from Sterling	840,000		d 840,000		
Bonds payable	2,500,000	1,400,000			3,900,000
Capital stock	8,000,000	3,000,000	b 3,000,000		8,000,000
Retained earnings	3,811,000 ✓	1,542,000 ✓			3,811,000
Equity adjustment	381,000*	286,000*		b 286,000	381,000*
	$16,192,000	$6,160,000			$17,256,000

* Deduct

Exhibit 14–4   Working Papers Under the British Pound Functional Currency Assumption

b	Retained earnings—Sterling	$ 750,000	
	Goodwill	1,405,000	
	Capital stock—Sterling	3,000,000	
	Investment in Sterling		$4,869,000
	Equity adjustment—Sterling		286,000

The objective of this entry is to eliminate reciprocal equity in Sterling and investment in Sterling balances and enter unamortized goodwill as of the beginning of the accounting period. Because of unrealized translation losses under the current rate method, the objective is modified to include "less unrecognized translation losses." Thus, Sterling's $3,464,000 beginning-of-the-period equity less unrecognized translation losses ($750,000 retained earnings and $3,000,000 capital stock less $286,000) is eliminated against the $4,869,000 beginning-of-the-period investment balance less unrecognized translation losses and $1,405,000 unamortized goodwill less unrecognized translation losses ($1,500,000 goodwill less $95,000 translation loss) is entered as the difference. Although less convenient, entry b may be divided into two working paper entries. The first entry eliminates reciprocal equity and investment balances at beginning-of-the-period amounts and enters beginning-of-the-period goodwill. A second entry adjusts the investment in Sterling account for unrealized translation losses, eliminates the unrealized translation loss from goodwill, and eliminates Sterling's remaining stockholders' equity account—the equity adjustment from translation account. These two entries would be journalized as follows:

Retained earnings—Sterling	$ 750,000	
Capital stock—Sterling	3,000,000	
Goodwill	1,500,000	
Investment in Sterling		$5,250,000
Investment in Sterling	$ 381,000	
Goodwill		$ 95,000
Equity adjustment from translation		286,000

Working paper entry c enters current goodwill amortization as an expense (100,000 £ × $1.45 average exchange rate) and reduces goodwill to its $1,260,000 unamortized amount at year-end (900,000 £ × $1.40 exchange rate).

The final working paper entry eliminates the reciprocal advance to Patriot and advance from Sterling balances. It should be noted that Patriot's stockholders' equity balances, including its equity adjustment from translation, are equal to consolidated stockholders' equity balances because the equity method of accounting is used.

Illustration—Remeasurement
Under *Statement* No. 52

When the functional currency of a foreign entity is the U.S. dollar, the foreign entity's accounts are *remeasured* into the U.S. dollar functional currency and the net exchange gains or losses that result from the remeasurement are recognized in current income. In order to enable you to compare remeasurement and translation procedures, remeasurement procedures are applied to the Patriot-Sterling example, assuming that Sterling's functional currency is the U.S. dollar and its books of record are maintained in British pounds. The objective of remeasurement is to produce the same results as if the books had been maintained in the U.S. dollar (see *FASB Statement No. 52,* paragraph 47).

Sterling's assets, liabilities, and stockholders' equity at acquisition on December 31, 19X1 are all remeasured using the $1.50 exchange rate in effect on that date. In other words, the remeasurement at acquisition is exactly the same as translation at acquisition. The $5,250,000 investment cost to Patriot over the $3,750,000 net assets acquired in Sterling results in $1,500,000 goodwill. Under remeasurement procedures, however, goodwill is not adjusted for subsequent changes in exchange rates, and annual amortization over a ten-year period will result in $150,000 amortization each year.

The 560,000 £ ($840,000) advance to Patriot is not a foreign currency transaction of either Patriot or Sterling because the advance is denominated in dollars and the functional currency of both Patriot and Sterling is the U.S. dollar. As a result, Sterling does not adjust its advance to Patriot to reflect the 600,000 British pound equivalent, but rather the 560,000 £ advance to Patriot is remeasured at its $840,000 reciprocal amount on Patriot's books. A remeasurement worksheet for Sterling Company Ltd. for 19X2 is illustrated in Exhibit 14–5. Except for the advance to Patriot and the resulting exchange gain, Sterling's December 31, 19X2 trial balance in British pounds is the same as the one shown under the British pound functional currency assumption in Exhibit 14–2.

Sterling's monetary items other than the intercompany advance are remeasured at current exchange rates. These monetary items include cash, accounts receivable, accounts payable, and bonds payable, and the remeasurement produces the same amounts as translation under the current rate method. The advance to Patriot and the dividends paid are translated at the reciprocal amounts in dollars that Patriot recorded on its own books.

The cost of sales and inventory remeasurements shown in the measurement worksheet assume first-in, first-out procedures and acquisition of the ending

---

STERLING COMPANY LTD.
REMEASUREMENT WORKSHEET FOR 19X2
(U.S. DOLLAR FUNCTIONAL CURRENCY)

	Trial Balance (in British Pounds)	Exchange Rate		Trial Balance (in U.S. Dollars)
Debits				
Cash	1,100,000	C	$1.40	1,540,000
Accounts receivable	800,000	C	1.40	1,120,000
Inventories (FIFO)	1,200,000	H	1.42	1,704,000
Plant assets	1,000,000	H	1.50	1,500,000
Advance to Patriot	560,000	R		840,000
Cost of sales	2,700,000	H		4,011,000
Depreciation	100,000	H	1.50	150,000
Wages and salaries	1,200,000	A*	1.45	1,740,000
Other expenses	600,000	A*	1.45	870,000
Dividends	300,000	R		426,000
Exchange loss				33,000
	9,560,000			13,934,000
Credits				
Accumulated depreciation	300,000	H	1.50	450,000
Accounts payable	360,000	C	1.40	504,000
Bonds payable	1,000,000	C	1.40	1,400,000
Capital stock	2,000,000	H	1.50	3,000,000
Retained earnings	500,000	Computed		750,000
Sales	5,400,000	A	1.45	7,830,000
	9,560,000			13,934,000

C Current exchange rate.	H Historical exchange rate.		
A Average exchange rate.	R Reciprocal of U.S. dollar amounts.		
* Assumed to be paid in cash during 19X2.			

Exhibit 14–5 *Remeasurement of Foreign Subsidiary Accounts into U.S. Dollars.*

inventory items on December 1, 19X2, when the exchange rate was $1.42. Historical exchange rates are used in the computations as follows:

	Pounds	Exchange Rate	Dollars
Inventory December 31, 19X1	1,200,000	$1.50 H	$1,800,000
Purchases 19X2	2,700,000	1.45 A	3,915,000
	3,900,000		5,715,000
Inventory December 31, 19X2	1,200,000	1.42 H	1,704,000
Cost of sales	2,700,000		$4,011,000

Special procedures are required when inventories are priced at the lower-of-cost-or-market rule. These procedures are explained later in this chapter.

All of Sterling's plant assets were owned by Sterling when it became a subsidiary of Patriot. Therefore, the plant assets, as well as the related depreciation expense and accumulated depreciation, are remeasured at the $1.50 exchange rate in effect at December 31, 19X1. If Sterling had acquired additional plant assets during 19X2, the additions and related depreciation would be remeasured at the exchange rates in effect when the additional assets were acquired.

Under *Statement No. 52*, expenses are remeasured at average rates during the period if they relate to monetary items (cash, receivables, and payables, and at historical exchange rates if they relate to nonmonetary items (such as plant assets, deferred charges, or intangibles). The wages and salaries and other expense items in Exhibit 14–5 are remeasured at average exchange rates assuming they are related to monetary items. When a single expense account includes amounts related to both monetary and nonmonetary items, the remeasurement involves computations rather than application of a single average rate. The same reasoning applies to the remeasurement of sales, even though it would be rather unusual for sales to relate to nonmonetary items.

Capital stock and other paid-in capital items are remeasured at historical exchange rates, and there is no difference between the amounts that result from remeasurement and translation for these items. As explained earlier, the retained earnings balance is computed but not remeasured or translated.

After all items in the remeasurement worksheet, other than the exchange loss, are remeasured into the U.S. dollar functional currency, the trial balance debits and credits are totaled and the difference between debits and credits is determined. If the credits are greater, the difference is entered in the remeasurement working papers as the exchange loss for the period. Thus, the $33,000 exchange loss in Exhibit 14–5 is computed by subtracting $13,901,000 debits excluding the exchange loss from $13,934,000 total credits. Exchange gains and losses on remeasurement are recognized in income currently under the provisions of *Statement No. 52*. Exchange gains and losses on remeasurement and those arising from foreign currency transactions are combined for external reporting purposes. Separate disclosure of transaction and remeasurement gains and losses is provided in financial statement notes.

The Equity Method and Consolidation

The U.S. dollar amounts determined in the remeasurement worksheet of Exhibit 14–5 are used to prepare Sterling's financial statements in U.S. dollars. These financial statements are included in the consolidation working papers of Exhibit 14–6. Since all remeasurement gains and losses are recognized in current income, the one-line consolidation entries under the U.S. dollar func-

PATRIOT CORPORATION AND SUBSIDIARY
CONSOLIDATION WORKING PAPERS
REMEASUREMENT—FUNCTIONAL CURRENCY U.S. DOLLAR
FOR THE YEAR ENDED DECEMBER 31, 19X2

	Patriot	Sterling	Adjustments and Eliminations				Consolidated Statements
Income Statement							
Sales	$12,183,000	$7,830,000					$20,013,000
Income from Sterling	876,000		a	876,000			
Cost of sales	6,000,000*	4,011,000*					10,011,000*
Depreciation	400,000*	150,000*					550,000*
Wages and salaries	3,000,000*	1,740,000*					4,740,000*
Other expenses	1,500,000*	870,000*	c	150,000			2,520,000*
Exchange loss		33,000*					33,000*
Net income	$ 2,159,000	$1,026,000					$ 2,159,000
Retained Earnings							
Retained earnings—Patriot	$ 2,455,000						$ 2,455,000
Retained earnings—Sterling		$ 750,000	b	750,000			
Net income	2,159,000 ✔	1,026,000 ✔					2,159,000
Dividends	1,000,000*	426,000*			a	426,000	1,000,000*
Retained earnings December 31, 19X2	$ 3,614,000	$1,350,000					$3,614,000
Balance Sheet							
Cash	$ 3,176,000	$1,540,000					$ 4,716,000
Accounts receivable	1,500,000	1,120,000					2,620,000
Inventories	3,000,000	1,704,000					4,704,000
Plant assets	4,000,000	1,500,000					5,500,000
Accumulated depreciation	1,000,000*	450,000*					1,450,000*
Advance to Patriot		840,000			d	840,000	
Investment in Sterling	5,700,000				a b	450,000 5,250,000	
Goodwill			b	1,500,000	c	150,000	1,350,000
	$16,376,000	$6,254,000					$17,440,000
Accounts payable	$ 1,422,000	$ 504,000					$ 1,926,000
Advance from Sterling	840,000		d	840,000			
Bonds payable	2,500,000	1,400,000					3,900,000
Capital stock	8,000,000	3,000,000	b	3,000,000			8,000,000
Retained earnings	3,614,000 ✔	1,350,000 ✔					3,614,000
	$16,376,000	$6,254,000					$17,440,000

Exhibit 14–6 *Working Papers Under the U.S. Dollar Functional Currency Assumption*

tional currency assumption are the same as those for a domestic subsidiary. The entries on Patriot's books to account for its investment in Sterling are as follows:

Investment in Sterling	$5,250,000	
Cash		$5,250,000

To record acquisition on December 31, 19X1.

Cash	$ 426,000	
Investment in Sterling		$ 426,000

To record dividends received on December 1, 19X2.

Investment in Sterling	$ 876,000	
Income from Sterling		$ 876,000

To record investment income for 19X2 equal to Sterling's $1,026,000 net income less $150,000 goodwill amortization.

Patriot's investment in Sterling account at December 31, 19X2 has a balance of $5,700,000 and is equal to Sterling $4,350,000 net assets on that date plus $1,350,000 unamortized goodwill. These amounts are shown in the consolidation working papers of Exhibit 14–6.

Consolidation of a foreign subsidiary with a U.S. dollar functional currency is essentially the same as for a domestic subsidiary, once the foreign entity's financial statements have been remeasured in U.S. dollars. Although the remeasurement process is more complex than translation, the consolidation process is less complex because remeasurement does not produce unrealized translation gains and losses or equity adjustments from translation. The content of Exhibit 14–6 is not discussed in detail because the procedures applied are the same as those encountered in earlier chapters.

Translation and Remeasurement Differences in Consolidated Statements

The differences between the consolidated financial statements of Patriot Corporation and Subsidiary under the translation and remeasurement procedures are easily discernible when they are presented in comparative form. Such a format is provided in Exhibit 14–7, which shows more income under translation ($2,356,000 compared with $2,159,000) and greater net assets under remeasurement ($11,614,000 compared with $11,430,000). A substantial part of these differences lies in the $381,000 unrecognized translation losses that are excluded from income when the statements are translated and subsequently deducted from consolidated stockholders' equity by means of the equity adjustment on translation account. In future years, however, unrecognized translation gains may result from the translation process and offset the unrecognized translation losses of 19X2, or even produce credit balances in the equity adjustment from translation account.

Since the Patriot-Sterling illustration involves consolidation in the year of acquisition, the impact of translation and measurement differences is relatively small. For many firms it can be substantial, however.

A section of the consolidated statement of changes in stockholders' equity for Woolworth Corporation for 1990 shows the following disclosure of changes in its foreign currency translation adjustment for the years 1990, 1989, and 1988:

	1990	1989	1988
	(amounts in millions)		
Foreign currency translation adjustment:			
Balance at beginning of year	$109	$102	$135
Effect of fluctuations in foreign currency translation rates	73	7	(33)
Balance at end of year	$182	$109	$102

PATRIOT CORPORATION AND BRITISH SUBSIDIARY
CONSOLIDATED INCOME AND RETAINED EARNINGS STATEMENTS
FOR THE YEAR ENDED DECEMBER 31, 19X2

	Translation	*Remeasurement*
Sales	$20,013,000	$20,013,000
Less costs and expenses:		
Cost of sales	9,915,000	10,011,000
Wages and salaries	4,740,000	4,740,000
Other expenses	2,370,000	2,370,000
Depreciation	545,000	550,000
Goodwill amortization	145,000	150,000
Total costs and expenses	17,715,000	17,821,000
Operating income	2,298,000	2,192,000
Exchange gain (loss)	58,000	(33,000)
Net income	2,356,000	2,159,000
Retained earnings January 1, 19X2	2,455,000	2,455,000
	4,811,000	4,614,000
Less: Dividends	1,000,000	1,000,000
Retained earnings December 31, 19X2	$ 3,811,000	$ 3,614,000

PATRIOT CORPORATION AND BRITISH SUBSIDIARY
CONSOLIDATED BALANCE SHEETS
AT DECEMBER 31, 19X2

	Translation	*Remeasurement*
Assets		
Cash	$ 4,716,000	$ 4,716,000
Accounts receivable	2,620,000	2,620,000
Inventories	4,680,000	4,704,000
Plant assets	5,400,000	5,500,000
Less: Accumulated depreciation	(1,420,000)	(1,450,000)
Goodwill	1,260,000	1,350,000
Total assets	$17,256,000	$17,440,000
Liabilities		
Accounts payable	$ 1,926,000	$ 1,926,000
Bonds payable	3,900,000	3,900,000
Total liabilities	5,826,000	5,826,000
Stockholders' Equity		
Capital stock	8,000,000	8,000,000
Retained earnings	3,811,000	3,614,000
Equity adjustment on translation	(381,000)	
Total stockholders' equity	11,430,000	11,614,000
Total liabilities and stockholders' equity	$17,256,000	$17,440,000

Exhibit 14–7 *Comparative Consolidated Financial Statements*

In addition, the financial review section of the report provides an analysis of the translation adjustment changes by country as follows (page 32):

	1990	1989	1988
	(amounts in millions)		
Germany	$220	$160	$137
Canada	(16)	(25)	(20)
Australia	(11)	(14)	(3)
Mexico	(12)	(12)	(12)
Other	1		
Total foreign currency translation adjustment	$182	$109	$102

The translation adjustment changes by country provides information not ordinarily included in corporate annual reports. At year end 1990, the equity adjustment from translation accounted for 7.8 percent of Woolworth's consolidated stockholders' equity.

Lower-of-Cost-or-Market Rule to Remeasure Inventories

Nonmonetary assets carried at cost are remeasured at historical rates and those carried at market are remeasured at current rates when the foreign entity's books of record are not maintained in the functional currency. Special care must be exercised in applying the lower-of-cost-or-market rule to inventories in remeasured statements because remeasured amounts are affected both by changes in exchange rates and by changes in replacement costs. Write-downs to market may be appropriate for both foreign currency statements and remeasured statements; for foreign currency statements, but not remeasured statements, or for remeasured statements, but not foreign currency statements. These three possibilities are illustrated as follows:

	Foreign Currency Units	Exchange Rate	U.S. Dollars
Case A: Inventory carried at market in both foreign currency statements and remeasured statements:			
Cost	1,000	$1.80 (H)	1,800
Replacement cost	950	1.85 (C)	1,758
Case B: Inventory carried at market in foreign currency statements, but cost in remeasured statements:			
Cost	1,000	$1.80 (H)	1,800
Replacement cost	950	1.92 (C)	1,824
Case C: Inventory carried at cost in foreign currency statements, but market in remeasured statements:			
Cost	950	$1.92 (H)	1,824
Replacement cost	1,000	1.80 (C)	1,800

The (H) and (C) designations represent historical rates and current rates, respectively. In each of the three cases, it is assumed that replacement cost falls between the ceiling and the floor as required by *ARB No. 43*, Chapter 4. The write-downs to market in Cases A and C are the result of applying the lower-of-cost-or-market rule in remeasurement statements and are reflected in cost of sales.

ILLUSTRATION—TRANSLATION WITH MINORITY INTEREST AND THE CASH FLOW STATEMENT

The Patriot and Sterling illustration provided an introduction to translation and consolidation procedures for foreign subsidiaries, but it omitted some important aspects of accounting for foreign subsidiaries. For example, intercompany profits, minority interests, long-term intercompany advances, and funds flow were not covered in that illustration. These areas are integrated into an extended translation and consolidation example in this section of the chapter.

Background Information

Pacific Corporation acquired a 90 percent interest in Sea Corporation, a French company, for $2,325,000 on January 1, 19X5. The exchange rate for French francs (frs) on that date was $.15, and Sea's stockholders' equity consisted of 10,000,000 frs capital stock and 5,000,000 frs retained earnings. Pacific designated Sea's functional currency to be the French franc.

Cost–Book Value Differential   The excess cost over book value from Pacific's investment in Sea Corporation is goodwill with a ten-year amortization period. Computations are as follows:

Investment in Sea	$2,325,000
Book value acquired	
(15,000,000 frs × $.15 exchange rate × 90%)	2,025,000
Goodwill in dollars	$ 300,000

Goodwill in francs ($300,000/$.15) = 2,000,000 frs

Exchange Rates   Relevant exchange rates for 19X5 are as follows:

Current exchange rate January 1, 19X5	$.150
Average exchange rate for 19X5	.160
Exchange rate for dividends	.160
Current exchange rate December 31, 19X5	.170

Translation and Consolidation in the Year of Acquisition

A translation worksheet based on Sea Corporation's adjusted trial balance in francs at December 31, 19X5 is presented in Exhibit 14–8. The translation is based on the background information provided and the procedures are comparable to those illustrated earlier in the chapter. In interpreting Sea's U.S. dollar financial statements, however, one must consider the existence of the 10 percent minority interest. For example, compare Sea's stockholders' equity at the beginning and end of 19X5:

	January 1	*December 31*
Capital stock	$1,500,000	$1,500,000
Retained earnings	750,000	830,000
Equity adjustment	—	305,000
Stockholders' equity	$2,250,000	$2,635,000

SEA CORPORATION TRANSLATION WORKSHEET
AT AND FOR THE YEAR ENDED DECEMBER 31, 19X5

	French Francs	Exchange Rate	U.S. Dollars
Cash	100,000	$0.170	17,000
Accounts receivable	400,000	0.170	68,000
Inventories	1,500,000	0.170	255,000
Land	2,500,000	0.170	425,000
Buildings	7,000,000	0.170	1,190,000
Equipment	10,000,000	0.170	1,700,000
Cost of sales	7,000,000	0.160	1,120,000
Depreciation expense	2,000,000	0.160	320,000
Operating expenses	1,500,000	0.160	240,000
Dividends	1,000,000	0.160	160,000
	33,000,000		5,495,000
Accumulated depreciation—buildings	1,000,000	0.170	170,000
Accumulated depreciation—equipment	3,000,000	0.170	510,000
Accounts payable	2,000,000	0.170	340,000
Capital stock	10,000,000	0.150	1,500,000
Retained earnings	5,000,000	0.150	750,000
Sales	12,000,000	0.160	1,920,000
Equity adjustment on translation			305,000
	33,000,000		5,495,000

Exhibit 14–8 *Translation Worksheet—19X5*

The $80,000 increase in Sea's retained earnings comes from Sea's $240,000 net income less $160,000 dividends for 19X5. Sea's stockholders' equity also increased by the $305,000 equity adjustment for a total stockholders' equity increase of $385,000. Sea's stockholders' equity at December 31, 19X5 can be allocated between majority and minority interests as follows:

	To Pacific 90%	To Minority Interests 10%	Total
Stockholders' equity January 1	$2,025,000	$225,000	$2,250,000
Net income	216,000	24,000	240,000
Dividends	(144,000)	(16,000)	(160,000)
Equity adjustment	274,500	30,500	305,000
Stockholders' equity December 31	$2,371,500	$263,500	$2,635,000

Pacific's underlying equity in Sea Corporation is $2,371,500 at December 31, 19X5, and its investment in Sea equals underlying equity plus $306,000 unamortized goodwill (2,000,000 francs × 90% unamortized × $.170 exchange rate)

One-Line Consolidation in Year of Acquisition Pacific Corporation makes the following one-line consolidation entries in accounting for its investment in Sea for 19X5:

Cash	$144,000	
Investment in Sea		$144,000
To record dividends ($160,000 × 90%).		

Investment in Sea	$496,500	
Equity adjustment		$312,500
Income from Sea		184,000

To record income from Sea ($240,000 × 90% – $32,000 goodwill amortization)
and equity adjustment computed as follows:

Equity adjustment from translation ($305,000 × 90%)		$274,500
Add: Equity adjustment from goodwill [$300,000		
beginning balance – $32,000 amortization –		
(1,800,000 frs ending balance × $.17 current rate)]		38,000
Equity adjustment		$312,500

The investment in Sea account at December 31, 19X5 has a balance of $2,677,500. This balance consists of the $2,325,000 cost on January 1 plus $496,500 equity adjustment plus income for 19X5, less $144,000 dividends received. Alternatively, the balance of the investment account can be checked by adding $306,000 unamortized goodwill at December 31, 19X5 (1,800,000 frs goodwill × $.17 current exchange rate) to 90 percent of Sea's $2,635,000 stockholders' equity on that date. Remember that the equity adjustment from translation account in the subsidiary's U.S. dollar financial statements is a stockholders' equity account. This account may have a positive (credit) balance or negative (debit) balance, depending upon the direction of exchange rate movements.

Consolidation in Year of Acquisition Working papers to consolidate the financial statements of Pacific Corporation and its French subsidiary at and for the year ended December 31, 19X5, are presented in Exhibit 14–9. In examining the consolidation worksheet, observe that the consolidated equity adjustment from translation is equal to Pacific Corporation's equity adjustment. That equity adjustment consists of 90 percent of Sea's $305,000 equity adjustment plus the $38,000 equity adjustment from goodwill. Under a one-line consolidation, the parent company equity adjustment balance is equal to the consolidated equity adjustment balance.

Entry a eliminates income and dividends from Sea and returns the investment account to its beginning balance plus the $312,500 equity adjustment.

a	Income from Sea	$184,000	
	Dividends		$144,000
	Investment in Sea		40,000

While working paper entry a is relatively unaffected by the existence of the minority interest, entry b is subject to some complications that require explanation. Entry b is reproduced in general journal form for convenient reference as follows:

b	Capital stock—Sea	$1,500,000	
	Retained earnings—Sea (beginning)	750,000	
	Equity adjustment—Sea	305,000	
	Goodwill	338,000	
	Investment in Sea		$2,637,500
	Minority interest (beginning)		255,500

The $338,000 goodwill amount in entry b is equal to beginning-of-the-period goodwill of $300,000 plus the $38,000 equity adjustment from goodwill for 19X5. The $2,637,500 investment in Sea amount in entry b is equal to the $2,325,000 beginning-of-the-period amount (cost) plus Pacific's $312,500 equity adjustment from translation. Finally, the $255,500 beginning minority interest amount is equal to Sea Corporation's $2,250,000 stockholders' equity at the beginning of

PACIFIC CORPORATION AND SUBSIDIARY
CONSOLIDATION WORKSHEET FOR THE YEAR ENDED DECEMBER 31, 19X5

	Pacific	Sea 90%	Adjustments and Eliminations		Minority Interest	Consolidated Statements
Income Statement						
Sales	$ 6,000,000	$1,920,000				$ 7,920,000
Income from Sea	184,000		a	184,000		
Cost of sales	(3,000,000)	(1,120,000)				(4,120,000)
Depreciation	(1,200,000)	(320,000)				(1,520,000)
Operating expense	(684,000)	(240,000)	c	32,000		(956,000)
Minority interest income					$ 24,000	(24,000)
Net income	$ 1,300,000	$ 240,000				$ 1,300,000
Retained Earnings						
Retained earnings	$ 1,200,000	$ 750,000	b	750,000		$ 1,200,000
Net income	1,300,000	240,000				1,300,000
Dividends	(500,000)	(160,000)	a	144,000	(16,000)	(500,000)
Retained earnings December 31, 19X5	$ 2,000,000	$ 830,000				$ 2,000,000
Balance Sheet						
Cash	$ 122,500	$ 17,000				$ 139,500
Accounts receivable	400,000	68,000				468,000
Inventories	800,000	255,000				1,055,000
Land	500,000	425,000				925,000
Buildings—net	1,500,000	1,020,000				2,520,000
Equipment—net	4,000,000	1,190,000				5,190,000
Investment in Sea	2,677,500		a 40,000 b 2,637,500			
Goodwill			b 338,000	c 32,000		306,000
	$10,000,000	$2,975,000				$10,603,500
Accounts payable	$ 687,500	$ 340,000				$ 1,027,500
Capital stock	7,000,000	1,500,000	b 1,500,000			7,000,000
Retained earnings	2,000,000	830,000				2,000,000
Equity adjustment*	312,500	305,000	b 305,000			312,500
	$10,000,000	$2,975,000				
Minority interest January 1, 19X5†			b	255,500	255,500	
Minority interest December 31, 19X5					$263,500	263,500
						$10,603,500

* Pacific's equity adjustment (90% × $305,000 equity adjustment) + $38,000 goodwill adjustment.
† Minority interest 10% × $2,555,000.

Exhibit 14–9   *Consolidation Working Papers—19X5*

the period plus Sea's $305,000 equity adjustment from translation times 10 percent.

To generalize, in the working paper entry to eliminate reciprocal invest-ment and stockholders' equity balances and enter beginning-of-the-period unamortized cost–book value differentials and minority interest, the amounts entered are the usual beginning-of-the-period amounts adjusted for end-of-the-period equity adjustments from translation. Since translation adjustments under the current rate method do not enter into the computation of minority interest income and consolidated net income, the complications are limited to balance sheet items.

Entry c provides for the current year's goodwill amortization at the average exchange rate [(2,000,000 frs × $.160)/10 years]:

c	Operating expenses	$32,000	
	Goodwill		$32,000

Translation and Consolidation in Year After Acquisition

Pacific Corporation held its 90 percent interest in Sea Corporation throughout 19X6, and the only stockholders' equity changes of the two affiliated entities resulted from income, dividends, and equity adjustments from translation. A translation worksheet based on Sea's adjusted trial balance in francs at December 31, 19X6, is presented in Exhibit 14–10. Other information related to the year 19X6 is summarized below.

Exchange Rates   Relevant exchange rates for 19X6 (and those from 19X5 for convenient reference) are as follows:

	19X5	*19X6*
Current exchange rate January 1	$.150	$.170
Exchange rate for intercompany sales	—	.175
Average exchange rate	.160	.180
Exchange rate for the advance	—	.180
Exchange rate for dividends	.160	.180
Current exchange rate December 31	.170	.190

Advance from Subsidiary   Sea Corporation made a 3,000,000 franc advance to Pacific on July 1, 19X6. This advance is long-term, denominated in francs, and bears interest at 10 percent per year. Pacific Corporation recorded the advance at $540,000 on July 1 but adjusted the advance to $570,000 to reflect current exchange rates at December 31, 19X6. The related debit of $30,000 was to Pacific's equity adjustment account, as required by *FASB Statement No. 52* for translation adjustments from long-term intercompany balances.

Plant Asset Acquisitions   Neither Pacific Corporation nor Sea Corporation had plant disposals during 19X5 and 19X6, but both companies had acquisi-tions during 19X6. Pacific purchased buildings for $800,000 and equipment for $1,500,000 during 19X6. Sea purchased equipment for 2,000,000 frs at December 31, 19X6, issuing a note payable for the purchase price that is denominated in francs. A summary of plant asset changes for Pacific Corporation and Sea Cor-poration for 19X6 is as follows:

19X6	Land Pacific	Land Sea	Buildings—Net Pacific	Buildings—Net Sea	Equipment—Net Pacific	Equipment—Net Sea
Balance January 1	$500,000	$425,000	$1,500,000	$1,020,000	$4,000,000	$1,190,000
Acquisitions	0	0	800,000	0	1,500,000	380,000
Depreciation	0	0	(500,000)	(90,000)	(1,000,000)	(270,000)
Exchange adjustment	0	50,000	0	115,000	0	125,000
Balance December 31	$500,000	$475,000	$1,800,000	$1,045,000	$4,500,000	$1,425,000

Intercompany Sales Pacific Corporation sold inventory items that cost $700,000 to Sea Corporation for $840,000, denominated in dollars, during 19X6 when the exchange rate for francs was $.175. Sea measured its purchases and accounts payable at 4,800,000 frs ($840,000/$.175), sold 3,600,000 frs of the merchandise during 19X6, and included 1,200,000 frs in its inventory at December 31, 19X6.

Translation The translation worksheet presented in Exhibit 14–10 repeats the 19X5 translation data and shows the translation for 19X6. The difference between the $588,000 translation adjustment at year-end 19X6 and the $305,000 translation adjustment at year-end 19X5 is $283,000, the increase in the equity adjustment from translation for 19X6. This increase is allocated 90 percent to Pacific and 10 percent to minority interest.

TRANSLATION WORKSHEETS FOR SEA CORPORATION

	December 31, 19X5 French Francs	December 31, 19X5 Exchange Rate	December 31, 19X5 U.S. Dollars	December 31, 19X6 French Francs	December 31, 19X6 Exchange Rate	December 31, 19X6 U.S. Dollars
Cash	100,000	$0.170	17,000	150,000	$0.190	28,500
Accounts receivable	400,000	0.170	68,000	250,000	0.190	47,500
Inventories	1,500,000	0.170	255,000	800,000	0.190	152,000
Inventories				1,200,000	0.175	210,000
Advance to Pacific				3,000,000	0.190	570,000
Land	2,500,000	0.170	425,000	2,500,000	0.190	475,000
Buildings	7,000,000	0.170	1,190,000	7,000,000	0.190	1,330,000
Equipment	10,000,000	0.170	1,700,000	10,000,000	0.190	1,900,000
Equipment (new)				2,000,000	0.190	380,000
Cost of sales	7,000,000	0.160	1,120,000	4,800,000	0.180	864,000
Cost of sales				3,600,000	0.175	630,000
Depreciation expense	2,000,000	0.160	320,000	2,000,000	0.180	360,000
Operating expenses	1,500,000	0.160	240,000	1,700,000	0.180	306,000
Dividends	1,000,000	0.160	160,000	1,000,000	0.180	180,000
	33,000,000		5,495,000	40,000,000		7,433,000
Accumulated depreciation—buildings	1,000,000	0.170	170,000	1,500,000	0.190	285,000
Accumulated depreciation—equipment	3,000,000	0.170	510,000	4,500,000	0.190	855,000
Accounts payable	2,000,000	0.170	340,000	2,500,000	0.190	475,000
Notes payable				2,000,000	0.190	380,000
Capital stock	10,000,000	0.150	1,500,000	10,000,000	0.150	1,500,000
Retained earnings	5,000,000	0.150	750,000	5,500,000		830,000
Sales	12,000,000	0.160	1,920,000	13,850,000	0.180	2,493,000
Interest income				150,000	0.180	27,000
Equity adjustment			305,000			588,000
	33,000,000		5,495,000	40,000,000		7,433,000

Exhibit 14–10 Translation Worksheets—19X6

One-Line Consolidation in Year After Acquisition Pacific Corporaon makes the following one-line consolidation entries in accounting for its investment in Sea for 19X6:

Cash	$162,000	
Investment in Sea		$162,000

To record dividends received ($180,000 × 90%).

Investment in Sea	$541,700	
Equity adjustment from translation		$288,700
Income from Sea		253,000

To record income from Sea ($360,000 × 90% − $36,000 goodwill amortization − $35,000 unrealized inventory profit) and equity adjustment ($283,000 × 90% + $34,000 from goodwill).

In addition, Pacific makes the following entry to adjust its advance from Sea account at year-end:

Equity adjustment	$ 30,000	
Advance from Sea		$ 30,000

To adjust the advance from $540,000 to $570,000 to recognize a $.01 exchange rate change on the 3,000,000 franc liability to Sea.

The balance of Pacific Corporation's investment in Sea account at December 31, 19X6 is $3,057,200, equal to 90 percent of Sea Corporation's $3,098,000 stockholders' equity on that date plus $304,000 unamortized goodwill less $35,000 unrealized inventory profit. Alternatively, the $3,057,200 investment in Sea account balance is equal to its $2,677,500 beginning balance less $162,000 dividends received plus $253,000 income from Sea plus $288,700 equity adjustment from translation.

Consolidation in Year After Acquisition Consolidation working papers for Pacific Corporation and Subsidiary are presented in Exhibit 14–11. These working papers are complicated by the existence of intercompany transactions and reciprocal items, but no new consolidation procedures are introduced.

Working paper entries a and b of Exhibit 14–11 eliminate intercompany profits from Pacific Corporation's sales to Sea Corporation.

a	Sales	$840,000	
	Cost of sales		$840,000
b	Cost of sales	$ 35,000	
	Inventories		$ 35,000

Entry a eliminates the $840,000 transfer price from sales and cost of sales, and entry b defers recognition of the $35,000 unrealized profit in Sea's ending inventory. The intercompany sales in dollars are analyzed as follows:

	Transfer Price		Cost	Intercompany Profit
	In Francs	*In Dollars*	*5/6*	*1/6*
Sold by Sea 75%	3,600,000	$630,000	$525,000	$105,000
Inventoried by Sea 25%	1,200,000	210,000	175,000	35,000
Total	4,800,000	$840,000	$700,000	$140,000

The translation worksheet in Exhibit 14–10 shows translation of the 1,200,000 frs inventory and 3,600,000 frs cost of sales at the $.175 historical exchange rate at the time of transfer. These items are separated from other

PACIFIC CORPORATION AND SUBSIDIARY
CONSOLIDATION WORKSHEET FOR THE YEAR ENDED DECEMBER 31, 19X6

	Pacific	Sea 90%	Adjustments and Eliminations				Minority Interest	Consolidated
Income Statement								
Sales	$ 7,000,000	$2,493,000	a	840,000				$ 8,653,000
Income from Sea	253,000		c	253,000				
Interest income		27,000	f	27,000				
Cost of sales	(4,000,000)	(1,494,000)	b	35,000	a	840,000		(4,689,000)
Depreciation	(1,500,000)	(360,000)						(1,860,000)
Operating expense	(726,000)	(306,000)	e	36,000				(1,068,000)
Interest expense	(27,000)				f	27,000		
Minority income							$ 36,000	(36,000)
Net income	$ 1,000,000	$ 360,000						$ 1,000,000
Retained Earnings								
Retained earnings	$ 2,000,000	$ 830,000	d	830,000				$ 2,000,000
Net income	1,000,000 ✓	360,000 ✓						1,000,000
Dividends	(500,000)	(180,000)			c	162,000	(18,000)	(500,000)
Retained earnings December 31, 19X6	$ 2,500,000	$1,010,000						$ 2,500,000
Balance Sheet								
Cash	$ 42,800	$ 28,500						$ 71,300
Accounts receivable	300,000	47,500			h	95,000		252,500
Inventories	1,000,000	362,000			b	35,000		1,327,000
Advance to Pacific		570,000			g	570,000		
Land	500,000	475,000						975,000
Buildings—net	1,800,000	1,045,000						2,845,000
Equipment—net	4,500,000	1,425,000						5,925,000
Investment in Sea	3,057,200				c	91,000		
					d	2,966,200		
Goodwill			d	340,000	e	36,000		304,000
	$11,200,000	$3,953,000						$11,699,800
Accounts payable	$ 558,800	$ 475,000	h	95,000				$ 938,800
Advance from Sea	570,000		g	570,000				
Note payable		380,000						380,000
Capital stock	7,000,000	1,500,000	d	1,500,000				7,000,000
Retained earnings	2,500,000 ✓	1,010,000 ✓						2,500,000
Equity adjustment*	571,200	588,000	d	588,000				571,200
	$11,200,000	$3,953,000						
Minority interest January 1, 19X6†					d	291,800	291,800	
Minority interest December 31, 19X6							$309,800	309,800
								$11,699,800

* Pacific's equity adjustment (90% × $588,000 equity adjustment) + $72,000 goodwill adjustment − $30,000 advance adjustment.

† Minority interest 10% × $2,918,000.

Exhibit 14–11   *Consolidation Working Papers—19X6*

inventory and cost of sales items that are translated at current and average exchange rates, respectively. Paragraph 25 of *FASB Statement No. 52* provides that

> the elimination of intercompany profits that are attributable to sales or other transfers between entities that are consolidated, combined, or accounted for by the equity method in the enterprise's financial statements shall be based on the exchange rates at the dates of the sales or transfers. The use of reasonable approximations or averages is permitted.

When the inventory and cost of sales accounts are translated at historical exchange rates, the inventory profit elimination for a foreign subsidiary is the same as for a domestic subsidiary and no complications arise in the working papers.

Entry c eliminates income and dividends and returns the investment account to its beginning-of-the-period balance of $2,677,500 plus the $288,700 equity adjustment for 19X6.

c	Income from Sea	$253,000	
	Dividends		$162,000
	Investment in Sea		91,000

Working paper entry d from Exhibit 14-11 is relatively complex and is reproduced in general journal form for convenient reference and analysis as follows:

d	Capital stock—Sea	$1,500,000	
	Retained earnings—Sea (beginning)	830,000	
	Equity adjustment—Sea	588,000	
	Goodwill	340,000	
	Investment in Sea		$2,966,200
	Minority interest (beginning)		291,800

The $340,000 debit to goodwill is equal to the $306,000 beginning-of-the-period unamortized goodwill plus $34,000 equity adjustment to goodwill for the period. For convenience, the $340,000 goodwill amount may be calculated as goodwill amortization for the period (200,000 frs × $.18) plus unamortized goodwill at year-end (1,600,000 frs × $.19).

The $291,800 minority interest at January 1, 19X6 is 10 percent of Sea Corporation's capital stock and retained earnings at January 1, 19X6, plus $588,000 equity adjustment at December 31, 19X6—in other words, 10% × ($1,500,000 + $830,000 + $588,000). The change in Sea's equity adjustment for the period is reflected in the beginning minority interest amount because neither minority interest income nor dividends reflect translation adjustments. The $309,800 minority interest at December 31, 19X6, can be confirmed by comparing it with 10 percent of Sea's $3,098,000 stockholders' equity at year-end 19X6.

Entry e enters the current year's amortization (2,000,000 frs × $.18 average exchange rate), and entry f eliminates interest on the intercompany advance.

e	Operating expenses	$36,000	
	Goodwill		$36,000
f	Interest income	$27,000	
	Interest expense		$27,000

Working paper entry g debits advance from Sea for $570,000 and credits advance to Pacific for $570,000. The elimination of these reciprocal items requires no change in working paper procedures even though both amounts reflect a $30,000 increase since the 3,000,000 frs ($540,000) advance was made on July 1, 19X6. The $30,000 increase in Sea's advance to Pacific is reflected in the $588,000 equity adjustment in Sea Corporation's U.S. dollar financial statements, and the $30,000 increase in Pacific's advance from Sea is recorded by Pacific as a direct debit to its equity adjustment account.

Pacific Corporation's $571,200 equity adjustment from translation at December 31, 19X6 is equal to the consolidated equity adjustment from translation on that date. The amount is calculated as follows:

Sea's $588,000 equity adjustment at December 31, 19X6 × 90%	$529,200
Equity adjustment from goodwill—19X5	38,000
Equity adjustment from goodwill—19X6	34,000
Equity adjustment from advance—19X6	(30,000)
Pacific's equity adjustment December 31, 19X6	$571,200

Comparative consolidated financial statements for Pacific Corporation and Subsidiary for the years 19X6 and 19X5 are presented in Exhibit 14–12. This

PACIFIC CORPORATION AND SUBSIDIARY
COMPARATIVE CONSOLIDATED FINANCIAL STATEMENTS
FOR THE YEARS ENDED DECEMBER 31, 19X6 and 19X5

	19X6	19X5	Year's Change 19X6 – 19X5
Income Statement			
Sales	$ 8,653,000	$ 7,920,000	$ 733,000
Cost of sales	(4,689,000)	(4,120,000)	(569,000)
Depreciation expense	(1,860,000)	(1,520,000)	(340,000)
Operating expense	(1,068,000)	(956,000)	(112,000)
Minority income	(36,000)	(24,000)	(12,000)
Net income	$ 1,000,000	$ 1,300,000	$ (300,000)
Retained Earnings			
Retained earnings January 1	$ 2,000,000	$ 1,200,000	$ 800,000
Net income	1,000,000	1,300,000	(300,000)
Dividends	(500,000)	(500,000)	0
Retained earnings December 31	$ 2,500,000	$ 2,000,000	$ 500,000
Balance Sheet			
Cash	$ 71,300	$ 139,500	$ (68,200)
Accounts receivable	347,500	468,000	(120,500)
Inventories	1,327,000	1,055,000	272,000
Land	975,000	925,000	50,000
Buildings—net	2,845,000	2,520,000	325,000
Equipment—net	5,925,000	5,190,000	735,000
Goodwill	304,000	306,000	(2,000)
Total assets	$11,794,800	$10,603,500	$1,191,300
Accounts payable	$ 1,033,800	$ 1,027,500	$ 6,300
Note payable	380,000	0	380,000
Capital stock	7,000,000	7,000,000	0
Retained earnings	2,500,000	2,000,000	500,000
Equity adjustment	571,200	312,500	258,700
Minority interest	309,800	263,500	46,300
Total equities	$11,794,800	$10,603,500	$1,191,300

Exhibit 14–12   *Comparative Financial Statements and Year's Change*

information provides a convenient summary and comparison of the consolidated financial statement amounts as well as information for the consolidated statement of cash flows.

Statement of Cash Flows

The consolidated statement of cash flows (SCF) for a foreign subsidiary is complicated somewhat by the existence of translation adjustments. Individual translation adjustments for the assets and liabilities have to be determined so that their effects can be eliminated in determining the cash flows for a period. As a first step in preparing the SCF, a reconciliation of the individual asset and liability translation adjustments for the year is needed, along with the change in the parent company (and consolidated) translation adjustment.

Translation Adjustments   Individual translation adjustments for cash and other balance sheet items are not needed in preparing the consolidation working papers, but they are needed in preparing the consolidated SCF. Since income statement items are translated at average exchange rates under the current rate method, and assets and liabilities at current exchange rates at the balance sheet date, each individual translation adjustment is ordinarily equal to the beginning balance of the account times the exchange rate change from the beginning to midpoint in the year, plus the ending balance of the account times the exchange rate change from midpoint in the year to year-end. For example, the $6,500 translation adjustment of accounts receivable for 19X6 (see Exhibit 14–13) is determined as follows:

	Account Balance	Exchange Rate Change	Translation Adjustment
January 1, 19X6	400,000 frs	$.180 avg. − $.170 beg.	$4,000
December 31, 19X6	250,000 frs	$.190 end. − $.180 avg.	2,500
Translation adjustment of accounts receivable			$6,500

The translation adjustments for most other asset and liability items can be determined by using the same procedure.

An exception to the usual procedure occurs when actual cash flows differ from cash flows expected under the assumption that all cash receipts and cash disbursements are made at average exchange rates for the year. For example, the use of the historical exchange rate for the 4,800,000 franc intercompany purchase transaction requires adjustment to reflect the fact that a 4,800,000 cash disbursement was made at the rate of $.175 rather than the $.180 average rate (otherwise a 133,333 frs exchange gain would have been recognized on the transaction). Thus, the $21,500 translation adjustment of cash is determined as follows:

	Account Balance	Exchange Rate Change	Translation Adjustment
January 1, 19X6	100,000 frs	$.180 avg. − $.170 beg.	$ 1,000
December 31, 19X6	150,000 frs	$.190 end. − $.180 avg.	1,500
Purchases adjustment:			
Cash payment	4,800,000 frs	$.180 avg. − $.175 actual	(24,000)
Translation adjustment of cash			$(21,500)

PACIFIC CORPORATION AND SUBSIDIARY
INDIVIDUAL ASSET AND LIABILITY TRANSLATION ADJUSTMENTS AND RECONCILIATION
AT AND FOR THE YEAR ENDED DECEMBER 31, 19X6

	12/31/ 19X5 Balance In Francs A	Rate* Change 1st Half B	$ Change 1st Half of 19X6 C	12/31/ 19X6 Balance In Francs D	Rate† Change 2nd Half E	$ Change 2nd Half of 19X6 F	Consolidated Translation Changes C + F
Cash	100,000	$0.010	$ 1,000	150,000	$0.010	$ 1,500	$ 2,500
Cash (adjustment)	4,800,000	$0.005	(24,000)				(24,000)
Accounts receivable	400,000	$0.010	4,000	250,000	$0.010	2,500	6,500
Inventories	1,500,000	$0.010	15,000	800,000	$0.010	8,000	23,000
Inventories				1,200,000			0
Land	2,500,000	$0.010	25,000	2,500,000	$0.010	25,000	50,000
Buildings—net	6,000,000	$0.010	60,000	5,500,000	$0.010	55,000	115,000
Equipment—net	7,000,000	$0.010	70,000	5,500,000	$0.010	55,000	125,000
Equipment (new)				2,000,000		0	0
Goodwill	1,800,000	$0.010	18,000	1,600,000	$0.010	16,000	34,000
			$169,000			$163,000	$332,000
Accounts payable	2,000,000	$0.010	$ 20,000	2,500,000	$0.010	$ 25,000	$ (45,000)
Notes payable				2,000,000			0
Effect of translation changes on consolidated net assets							$287,000

Reconciliation

Minority interest translation adjustment ($283,000 change during 19X6 × 10%)	$ 28,300
Equity adjustment of Pacific ($283,000 × 90% + $34,000 − $30,000)	258,700
Effect of translation changes on consolidated stockholders' equity	$287,000

* Average exchange rate of $.180—current exchange rate of $.170 at year-end 19X5.
† Current exchange rate of $.190 at year-end 19X6—average exchange rate of $.180 for the year 19X6.

Exhibit 14–13 *Individual Translation Adjustments*

A translation adjustment of cash is also needed for dividends except when they are translated at average exchange rates.

The calculation of the individual translation adjustment for inventories is an exception to the usual procedure because of the intercompany sales that are translated at historical rather than current exchange rates. Inventories are divided into the 1,200,000 portion that is translated at historical exchange rates and the 800,000 portion on which a $23,000 translation adjustment is determined using the basic procedure (see Exhibit 14–13). Also note that the calculation of individual translation adjustments for plant asset items requires special analysis for all acquisitions and disposals during a period.

The individual asset and liability items that are shown in Exhibit 14–13 are those that appear in the consolidated balance sheet and have individual translation adjustments for 19X6. Thus, the $34,000 goodwill translation adjustment appears because it is included in consolidated assets. The advance to Pacific and advance from Sea accounts do not appear, since they are eliminated in the consolidation process. Exhibit 14–13 shows a line item for the effect of translation adjustments on consolidated net assets for 19X6 of $287,000. This amount differs from the $283,000 equity change in Sea Corporation's balance sheet because it includes the 34,000 translation adjustment of goodwill but excludes the $30,000 translation of the advance to Pacific that was eliminated in the consolidation process. The translation effect on consolidated net assets for a period is necessarily equal to the effect on consolidated stockholders' equity for that period. A reconciliation of those equalities is included in Exhibit 14–13.

PACIFIC CORPORATION AND SUBSIDIARY
CONSOLIDATED STATEMENT OF CASH FLOWS WORKSHEET
FOR THE YEAR ENDED DECEMBER 31, 19X6

	Year's Change 19X6–19X5	Trnaslation Adjustments	Year's Change Less Translation Adjustments	Cash Flows from Operating Activities	Cash Flows from Investing Activities	Cash Flows from Financing Activities
Balance Sheet						
Cash	$ (68,200)	$ (21,500)*	$ (46,700)			
Accounts receivable	(120,500)	6,500	(127,000)	$ 127,000		
Inventories	272,000	23,000	249,000	(249,000)		
Land	50,000	50,000	0			
Buildings—net	325,000	115,000	210,000	590,000	(800,000)	
Equipment—net	735,000	125,000	610,000	1,270,000	(1,880,000)	
Goodwill	(2,000)	34,000	(36,000)	36,000		
Total assets	$1,191,300	$332,000	$859,300			
Accounts payable	$ 6,300	$ 45,000	$ (38,700)	(38,700)		
Note payable	380,000	0	380,000			380,000
Capital stock	0	0	0			
Retained earnings	500,000	0	500,000	1,000,000		(500,000)
Equity adjustment	258,700	258,700	0			
Minority interest	46,300	28,300	18,000	36,000		(18,000)
Total equities	$1,191,300	$332,000	$859,300	$2,771,300	$(2,680,000)	$(138,000)

*Presented in the SCF immediately below cash flows from financing activities.

Exhibit 14–14   *Worksheet for Consolidated Statement of Cash Flows*

Consolidated SCF Worksheet   A worksheet for the consolidated SCF using the indirect format is presented in Exhibit 14–14. The year's change column in that exhibit reflects consolidated balance sheet changes for Pacific Corporation and Subsidiary between December 31, 19X5 and 19X6. That information was presented earlier in Exhibit 14–12. A second column in the SCF worksheet shows the translation adjustments to individual balance sheet items as illustrated in Exhibit 14–13 and discussed in the preceding paragraph. The third column subtracts column 2 from column 1 to obtain the year's changes without translation adjustments. This information is pivotal in preparing a SCF for a consolidated entity with foreign subsidiaries. Once the translation effects are eliminated from the year's change information, preparation of the consolidated SCF is essentially the same as for a consolidated entity with only domestic subsidiaries.

Items in the "year's change less translation adjustments" column of Exhibit 14–14 are analyzed and carried to the "cash flows from operating activities," "cash flows from investing activities," or "cash flows from financing activities" column, as appropriate. Information for consolidated net income, minority interest income, dividends, and depreciation is obtained from the consolidated income and retained earnings statements. Other information relating to plant asset purchases, goodwill amortization, and minority interest dividends is found in the consolidated working papers for 19X6 and in the background information for the illustration.

The consolidated SCF of Pacific Corporation and Subsidiary for 19X6 is presented in Exhibit 14–15. This statement is developed directly from the completed worksheet in Exhibit 14–14. The $21,500 translation adjustment of cash is shown as a separate line item immediately below the "cash flows from financing activities" section of the SCF.

PACIFIC CORPORATION AND SUBSIDIARY
CONSOLIDATED STATEMENT OF CASH FLOWS
FOR THE YEAR ENDED DECEMBER 31, 19X6

Cash Flows from Operating Activities		
Consolidated net income	$1,000,000	
Add: Minority interest income	36,000	$1,036,000
Noncash expenses, revenues, losses and gains included in income:		
Depreciation	$1,860,000	
Goodwill amortization	36,000	
Decrease in accounts receivable	127,000	
Decrease in accounts payable	(38,700)	
Increase in inventories	(249,000)	1,735,300
Net cash flows from operating activities		2,771,300
Cash Flows from Investing Activities		
Purchase of buildings	$ (800,000)	
Purchase of equipment	(1,880,000)	
Net cash used in investing activities		(2,680,000)
Cash Flows from Financing Activities		
Long-term borrowing	$ 380,000	
Dividends to Pacific's stockholders	(500,000)	
Dividends to minority stockholders	(18,000)	
Net cash used in financing activities		(138,000)
Effect of exchange rate changes on cash		(21,500)
Net decrease in cash		(68,200)
Cash and cash equivalents at beginning of year		139,500
Cash and cash equivalents at end of year		$ 71,300

Exhibit 14–15   *Consolidated Statement of Cash Flows*

ACCOUNTING FOR A FOREIGN BRANCH

The conversion of the accounts of a foreign branch into the currency of the home office is similar to the conversion process for foreign subsidiaries. If the functional currency of the branch is the currency of the home office, the accounts are remeasured into the home office's reporting currency, and gains or losses on remeasurement are recognized currently in income. If the local currency of the branch is its functional currency, the branch accounts are translated into the reporting currency of the home office, using the current rate method, and gains and losses on translation are deferred through an equity adjustment from translation account. In accounting for foreign branches, the accounts that are unique to home office–branch accounting (reciprocal accounts) are converted into the currency of the reporting entity by reference to the reciprocal amounts that are recorded on the home office books.

Illustration of Accounting for a Foreign Branch[3]

Sun-Bud Corporation is a U.S. corporation with its home office in Detroit, Michigan. In addition to the Detroit operation, Sun-Bud has a branch in Toronto, Canada. All branch sales relate to merchandise acquired at cost from the home

---

[3]Both translation and remeasurement of foreign branch operations are illustrated, even though the very nature of branch operations implies a U.S. dollar functional currency.

office. The current exchange rate was $.90 in December 19X1 when the Canadian branch was established, and $.92 in January 19X2 when the plant assets of the Canadian branch were acquired. During 19X2 the Canadian dollar weakened against the U.S. dollar. Relevant exchange rates for 19X2 were:

Current exchange rate December 31, 19X2	$.80
Average exchange rate for 19X2	$.85

Working papers to illustrate the translation of the Canadian branch accounts into U.S. dollars as of December 31, 19X2 are shown in Exhibit 14–16 under alternative U.S. dollar and Canadian dollar functional currency assumptions. The working papers also include the accounts of Sun-Bud's home office for reference purposes.

The beginning branch inventory of 40,000 Canadian dollars was acquired when the exchange rate was $.90 and the year-end inventories were $100,000 for the home office and 42,500 Canadian dollars for the branch. The ending branch inventory was acquired when an $.82 exchange rate was in effect. Branch shipments in 19X2 were 335,500 Canadian dollars or $285,000 U.S.

SUN-BUD CORPORATION
TRIAL BALANCE WORKING PAPERS
FOR THE YEAR ENDED DECEMBER 31, 19X2

	Home Office U.S. Dollars	Branch Canadian Dollars	Functional Currency U.S. Dollar Exchange Rate	Functional Currency U.S. Dollar U.S. Dollars	Functional Currency Canadian Dollar Exchange Rate	Functional Currency Canadian Dollar U.S. Dollars
Debits						
Cash	$ 480,000	30,000	$.80 C	$ 24,000	$.80 C	$ 24,000
Accounts receivable	91,000	25,000	.80 C	20,000	.80 C	20,000
Inventory—ending	100,000	42,500	.82 H	34,850	.80 C	34,000
Land	100,000	22,000	.92 H	20,240	.80 C	17,600
Equipment	500,000	375,000	.92 H	345,000	.80 C	300,000
Canadian branch	394,600					
Cost of goods sold	255,000	333,000	Computed	286,150	.85 A	283,050
Depreciation expense	80,000	27,500	.92 H	25,300	.85 A	23,375
Bad debts expense	4,550	1,300	.85 A	1,105	.85 A	1,105
Other operating expenses	340,000	17,400	.85 A	14,790	.85 A	14,790
Exchange loss				19,965		
Equity adjustment from translation						66,880
	$2,345,150	873,700		$791,400		$784,800
Credits						
Allowance for bad debts	$ 5,550	1,500	$.80 C	$ 1,200	$.80 C	$ 1,200
Accumulated depreciation	230,000	55,000	.92 H	50,600	.80 C	44,000
Accounts payable	65,000	2,000	.80 C	1,600	.80 C	1,600
Home office		411,200	R	394,600	R	394,600
Capital stock	700,000					
Retained earnings	344,600					
Sales	1,000,000	404,000	.85 A	343,400	.85 A	343,400
	$2,345,150	873,700		$791,400		$784,800

A = average exchange rate
C = current exchange rate
H = historical exchange rate
R = reciprocal

Exhibit 14–16 Working Papers to Convert Branch Accounts into U.S. Dollars

The information from Exhibit 14–16 is used to prepare combined financial statements for Sun-Bud and its Canadian branch. These combined statements are presented in Exhibit 14–17. Because the cost of goods sold computations are not apparent from an inspection of the working papers, the following additional explanation is provided.

	Home Office U.S. Dollars	Branch Canadian Dollars			Branch Remeasured in U.S. Dollars
Inventory January 1	$170,000	40,000	× $.90	H	$ 36,000
Purchases	470,000				
Shipments (to branch) from home office	(285,000)	335,500		R	285,000
Goods available	355,000	498,500			321,000
Inventory December 31	100,000	42,500	× $.82	H	34,850
Cost of goods sold	$255,000	333,000			$286,150

SUN-BUD CORPORATION
COMPARATIVE INCOME AND RETAINED EARNINGS STATEMENTS
FOR THE YEAR ENDED DECEMBER 31, 19X2

	Remeasurement	Translation
Sales	$1,343,400	$1,343,400
Cost of goods sold	541,150	538,050
Gross profit	802,250	805,350
Depreciation expense	105,300	103,375
Bad debt expense	5,655	5,655
Other operating expenses	354,790	354,790
Exchange loss	19,965	
Total expenses	485,710	463,820
Net income	316,540	341,530
Retained earnings January 1, 19X2	344,600	344,600
Retained earnings December 31, 19X2	$ 661,140	$ 686,130

SUN-BUD CORPORATION
COMPARATIVE BALANCE SHEETS
AT DECEMBER 31, 19X2

	Remeasurement	Translation
Assets		
Cash	$ 504,000	$ 504,000
Accounts receivable—net	104,250	104,250
Inventories	134,850	134,000
Land	120,240	117,600
Equipment—net	564,400	526,000
Total assets	$1,427,740	$1,385,850
Equities		
Accounts payable	$ 66,600	$ 66,600
Capital stock	700,000	700,000
Retained earnings	661,140	686,130
Equity adjustment from translation		(66,880)
Total equities	$1,427,740	$1,385,850

Exhibit 14–17 *Comparative Financial Statements*

Under the U.S. dollar functional currency assumption, the combined cost of goods sold is $541,150 ($255,000 + $286,150) and under the Canadian dollar functional currency assumption, it is $538,050 [$255,000 + (333,000 Canadian dollars × $.85 average exchange rate)]. The elimination of reciprocal home office and shipment accounts has no effect on the combined financial statements.

SUMMARY

Before the results of foreign operations can be included in the financial statements of U.S. corporations, they have to be converted into U.S. dollars using procedures specified in *FASB Statement No. 52* that are based on the foreign entity's functional currency. If the U.S. dollar is determined to be the functional currency, the foreign entity's financial statements are remeasured into U.S. dollar financial statements using the temporal method, and the resulting exchange gain or loss is included in consolidated net income for the period. If the functional currency is determined to be the local currency of the foreign entity, the financial statements of that entity must be translated into U.S. dollars using the current rate method. The effects of the exchange rate changes from translation are accumulated in an equity adjustment from translation account and reported as a component of stockholders' equity.

Foreign currency financial statements of subsidiaries operating in highly inflationary economies are remeasured as if the functional currency were the U.S. dollar.

Intercompany transactions between affiliated companies will result in a foreign currency transaction for either the parent or the subsidiary if the subsidiary's local currency is its functional currency. Alternatively, if the subsidiary's functional currency is the U.S. dollar, the intercompany transaction will be a foreign currency transaction to both affiliates or to neither affiliate.

On the date of a business combination, assets and liabilities are translated into U.S. dollars using current exchange rates.

Before a consolidated statement of cash flows for a parent company and its foreign subsidiary can be prepared, the effects of individual translation adjustments for assets and liabilities must be identified. These translation adjustments are combined and reported as a separate line-item under the heading "effect of exchange rate changes on cash."

SELECTED READINGS

BRIDGES, TIM. "Foreign Exchange Exposure Management." *The CPA Journal* (August 1988), pp. 77–79.

HUEFNER, RONALD J., J. EDWARD KETZ, and JAMES A. LARGAY III. "Foreign Currency Translation and the Cash Flow Statement." *Accounting Horizons*, Vol. 3, no. 2. (June 1989), pp. 66–76.

MALLEY, SUSAN L. "Swaps: A 1990s Tool for Management of Financing." *Management Accounting* (March 1990), pp. 38–40.

ROLLINS, THERESA P., DAVID E. STOUT, and DANIEL J. O'MARA. "The New Financial Instruments." *Management Accounting* (March 1990), pp. 35–37, 40, 41.

Statement of Financial Accounting Standards No. 52. "Foreign Currency Translation." Stamford, CT: Financial Accounting Standards Board, 1981.

ASSIGNMENT MATERIAL

QUESTIONS

1 Do you agree that all financial statement items of a foreign entity are *translated* at current exchange rates under *FASB Statement No. 52*?

2 In the process of restructuring its manufacturing and distributions lines, a parent company changes its foreign subsidiary's functional currency. Does this accounting change require restatement of previously issued financial statements?

3 How does *Statement No. 52* define a highly inflationary economy?

4 What procedures may be required in accounting for a 60 percent interest in a foreign investee located in a highly inflationary economy?

5 Does the functional currency of the foreign subsidiary affect the initial recording of the business combination?

6 Explain how a pooling of interests business combination with a foreign subsidiary is recorded. What changes in recording the initial investment would be necessary if the business combination is accounted for under the purchase method?

7 Discuss the possible accounting problems that can arise in remeasuring inventory items that are accounted for under the lower-of-cost-or-market pricing procedure in the foreign operation's financial statements.

8 At what exchange rate would the retained earnings account of a foreign subsidiary be translated? Explain.

9 In consolidating the financial statements of a Canadian subsidiary that has a Canadian dollar functional currency with those of its U.S. parent, how are goodwill and goodwill amortization computed? Would the computation be different if the subsidiary had a U..S. dollar functional currency? Explain.

10 Is the equity adjustment from translation account ever eliminated? Explain.

11 How are expenses that relate to monetary items of a foreign subsidiary remeasured under *Statement No. 52*?

12 How is the effect of exchange rate changes in cash reported in a consolidated statement of cash flows?

EXERCISES

E 14–1

1 An objective of foreign currency translation is to:
   a Measure foreign operations in functional currencies in conformity with generally accepted accounting principles
   b Recognize exchange gains and losses as they occur
   c Record all foreign transactions at their dollar equivalents
   d Reflect assets and liabilities denominated in foreign currency at their current exchange values

2 In translating foreign financial statements into U.S. dollars, *FASB Statement No. 52* requires the use of the:
   a Current-noncurrent method
   b Current rate method
   c Monetary-nonmonetary method
   d Temporal method

3 Which one of the following items from the financial statements of a foreign subsidiary would be translated into dollars using the historical exchange rate?
   a Accounts payable
   b Amortization of bond premium
   c Common stock
   d Inventories priced at the lower of cost or market

4 Average exchange rates are used to translate certain items from foreign income statements into U.S. dollars. Such averages are used in order to:
   a Approximate the effects of using the current exchange rates in effect on the transaction dates
   b Avoid using different exchange rates for some revenue and expense accounts
   c Eliminate large and temporary fluctuations in exchange rates that may reverse in the near future
   d Smooth out large exchange gains and losses

5 An exchange gain from remeasurement of a foreign entity's financial statements should be:
   a Deferred and amortized over a period not to exceed 40 years
   b Deferred until a subsequent year when a loss occurs that can be offset against it
   c Included in net income in the period it occurs
   d Included as a separate item in the equity section of the balance sheet

6 The foreign currency financial statements of a subsidiary whose functional currency is its local currency are being converted into U.S. dollar financial statements. Which of the following items would be translated using the current exchange rates?
   a Capital stock
   b Dividends
   c Goodwill
   d Retained earnings

7 In remeasuring foreign currency financial statements into U.S. dollars, which of the following items would be remeasured using the historical exchange rate?

a Accrued expenses payable
b Deferred income
c Long-term debt
d Notes payable

8 A gain resulting from translating foreign currency financial statements into U.S. dollars should be reported as:
   a A deferred item in the balance sheet
   b An extraordinary item in the income statement for the period in which the rates change
   c An ordinary item in the income statement
   d A stockholders' equity adjustment from translation

9 The remeasurement of foreign currency financial statements into U.S. dollars entails application of the:
   a Current-noncurrent method
   b Current rate method
   c Monetary-nonmonetary method
   d Temporal method

10 The same exchange rate is used for translation as for remeasurement when the foreign entity account is classified as:
    a An asset
    b A liability
    c An expense
    d Paid-in capital

11 A U.S. parent company borrows money from a British subsidiary on a loan denominated in British pounds. The functional currency of the subsidiary is the U.S. dollar. This is a foreign currency transaction of the:

	Subsidiary	Parent
a	No	Yes
b	Yes	Yes
c	Yes	No
d	No	No

E 14-2 [AICPA adapted]

1 When preparing consolidated financial statements for a U.S. parent and its foreign subsidiary, the account balances expressed in foreign currency must be converted into the currency of the reporting entity. One objective of the translation process is to provide information that:
   a Reflects current exchange rates
   b Reflects current monetary equivalents
   c Is compatible with the economic effects of rate changes on the firm's cash flows
   d Reflects each translated account at its unexpired historical cost

2 A balance arising from the translation or remeasurement of a subsidiary's foreign currency financial statements is reported in the consolidated income statement when the subsidiary's functional currency is the:

	Foreign currency	U.S. dollar
a	No	No
b	No	Yes
c	Yes	No
d	Yes	Yes

3 A company is translating account balances from another currency into dollars for its December 31, 19X5 statement of financial position and its calendar year 19X5 earnings statement and statement of cash flows. The average exchange rate for the year 19X5 should be used to translate:
   a Cash at December 31, 19X5
   b Land purchased in 19X3
   c Retained earnings at January 1, 19X5
   d Sales for 19X5

4 If a parent company bills all sales to a foreign subsidiary in terms of dollars and is to be repaid in the same number of dollars, the purchases account on the subsidiary's trial balance will be converted to U.S. dollars by using:
   a The average exchange rate for the period
   b The exchange rate at the beginning of the period

c The exchange rate at the end of the period
d The amount showing in the parent's accounts for sales to the subsidiary
5 A subsidiary's functional currency is the local currency which has not experienced significant inflation. The appropriate exchange rate for translating the depreciation on plant assets in the income statement of the foreign subsidiary is the:
  a Exit rate
  b Historical exchange rate
  c Weighted average exchange rate over the economic life of each plant asset
  d Weighted average exchange rate for the current year
6 The year-end balance of accounts receivable on the books of a foreign subsidiary should be translated by the parent company for consolidation purposes at the:
  a Historical rate   **b** Current rate
  c Negotiated rate   **d** Spot rate
7 When translating foreign currency financial statements, which of the following accounts would be translated using current exchange rates?

	Property, plant and equipment	Inventories carried at cost
a	Yes	Yes
b	No	No
c	Yes	No
d	No	Yes

E 14–3 On January 1, 19X8 Paxton Company, a U.S. firm, purchases all the outstanding capital stock of Stanley Ltd., a British firm, for $1,080,000 when the exchange rate for British pounds (£) is $1.80. The book values of Stanley's assets and liabilities are equal to fair values on this date except for land which has a fair value of 200,000 £ and equipment with a fair value of 100,000 £.

Summarized balance sheet information for Paxton in U.S. dollars and for Stanley in pounds just before the business combination is as follows:

	Paxton	Stanley
Current assets	$3,000,000	100,000 £
Land	800,000	100,000
Buildings—net	1,200,000	250,000
Equipment—net	1,000,000	50,000
	$6,000,000	500,000 £
Current liabilities	$ 600,000	50,000 £
Notes payable	1,000,000	150,000
Capital stock	3,000,000	200,000
Retained earnings	1,400,000	100,000
	$6,000,000	500,000 £

Required: Prepare a consolidated balance sheet for Paxton Company and Subsidiary at January 1, 19X8, immediately after the business combination.

E 14–4 Hoogovens Corporation of the Netherlands is an 80 percent owned subsidiary of Porter Corporation, a U.S. firm, and its functional currency is the U.S. dollar. Hoogovens's books of record are maintained in guilders and its inventory is carried at the lower of cost or market.

The current exchange rate for guilders at December 31, 19X8 is $.58.
The historical cost of the inventory is 10,000 guilders.
The replacement cost of the inventory is 9,500 guilders.
The historical exchange rate is $.53.

Required: Determine the amount at which the inventory will be carried on (a) the foreign currency statements and (b) the remeasured statements.

E 14–5 Penny Company paid $2,400,000 for all the outstanding stock of Superior Corporation of Canada on January 1, 19X1. The book values of Superior's assets and liabilities were equal to fair values except for plant assets with a five-year remaining life that had a book value of 500,000 Canadian dollar (C$) and 1,000,000 C$ fair value. Superior's stockholders' equity at January 1, 19X1 consisted of 2,000,000 C$ capital stock and 500,000 C$ retained earnings.

Superior's functional currency is the Canadian dollar. Exchange rates for Canadian dollars in 19X1 are:

Spot rate on January 1, 19X1	$.80
Average rate for 19X1	.85
Current rate on December 31, 19X1	.90

Required: Determine the unrealized translation gain or loss at December 31, 19X1 related to the cost–book value differential assigned to plant assets.

E 14–6 Packer Corporation of the United States purchased all the outstanding stock of Swiss Products Company of Switzerland for $1,350,000 cash on January 1, 19X9. The book values of Swiss's assets and liabilities were equal to fair values on this date except for land, which was valued at 1,000,000 Swiss francs. Summarized balance sheet information in Swiss francs (SFr) at January 1, 19X9 is as follows:

Current assets	800,000 SFr	Current liabilities	400,000 SFr
Land	600,000	Bonds payable	500,000
Buildings—net	400,000	Capital stock	1,000,000
Equipment—net	500,000	Retained earnings	400,000
	2,300,000 SFr		2,300,000 SFr

The functional currency of Swiss Products Company is the Swiss franc. Exchange rates for Swiss francs for 19X9 are:

Spot rate January 1, 19X9	$.75
Average rate 19X9	.76
Current rate December 31, 19X9	.77

Required: Determine the unrealized translation gain or loss at December 31, 19X9 relating to the excess allocated to the undervalued land.

E 14–7 [AICPA adapted]

1 Fay Corp. had a realized foreign exchange loss of $15,000 for the year ended December 31, 19X8 and must also determine whether the following items will require year-end adjustment.

Fay had an $8,000 equity adjustment resulting from the translation of the accounts of its wholly owned foreign subsidiary for the year ended December 31, 19X8.

Fay had an account payable to an unrelated foreign supplier payable in the supplier's local currency. The U.S. dollar equivalent of the payable was $64,000 on the October 31, 19X8 invoice date, and it was $60,000 on December 31, 19X8. The invoice is payable on January 30, 19X9.

In Fay's 19X8 consolidated income statement, what amount should be included as foreign exchange loss?

a $11,000   b $15,000
c $19,000   d $23,000

2 On January 1, 19X8 the Ben Company formed a foreign subsidiary. On February 15, 19X8 Ben's subsidiary purchased 100,000 local currency units of inventory; 25,000 LCU of the original inventory purchased on February 15, 19X8 made up the entire inventory on December 31, 19X8. The subsidiary's functional currency is the U.S. dollar. The exchange rates were 2.2 LCU to $1 from January 1, 19X8 to June 30, 19X8; and 2 LCU to $1 from July 1, 19X8 to December 31, 19X8. The December 31, 19X8 inventory balance for Ben's foreign subsidiary should be remeasured into U.S. dollars in the amount of:

a $10,500 **b** $11,364
c $11,905 **d** $12,500

3 The Dease Company owns a foreign subsidiary with 3,600,000 local currency units of property, plant, and equipment before accumulated depreciation at December 31, 19X5. Of this amount, 2,400,000 LCU were acquired in 19X3 when the rate of exchange was 1.6 LCU to $1, and 1,200,000 LCU were acquired in 19X4 when the rate of exchange was 1.8 LCU to $1.

The rate of exchange in effect at December 31, 19X5 was 2 LCU to $1. The weighted average of exchange rates in effect during 19X5 was 1.92 LCU to $1. The subsidiary's functional currency is the U.S. dollar.

Assuming that the property, plant, and equipment are depreciated using the straight-line method over a ten-year period with no salvage value, how much depreciation expense relating to the foreign subsidiary's property, plant, and equipment should be charged in Dease's income statement for 19X5?
a $180,000 **b** $187,500
c $200,000 **d** $216,667

4 The Clark Company owns a foreign subsidiary that had net income for the year ended December 31, 19X5 of 4,800,000 local currency units, which was appropriately translated into $800,000.

On October 15, 19X5, when the rate of exchange was 5.7 LCU to $1, the foreign subsidiary paid a dividend to Clark of 2,400,000 LCU. The dividend represented the net income of the foreign subsidiary for the six months ended June 30, 19X5, during which time the weighted average of exchange rate was 5.8 LCU to $1.

The rate of exchange in effect at December 31, 19X5 was 5.9 LCU to $1. What rate of exchange should be used to translate the dividend for the December 31, 19X5 financial statements?
a 5.7 LCU to $1 **b** 5.8 LCU to $1
c 5.9 LCU to $1 **d** 6.0 LCU to $1

5 The Jem Company used the current rate method when translating foreign currency amounts at December 31, 19X5. At that time, Jem had foreign subsidiaries with 1,500,000 local currency units in long-term receivables and 2,400,000 LCU in long-term debt. The rate of exchange in effect when the specific transactions occurred involving those foreign currency amounts was 2 LCU to $1. The rate of exchange in effect at December 31, 19X5 was 1.5 LCU to $1. The translation of the above foreign currency amounts into U.S. dollars would result in long-term receivables and long-term debt, respectively, of:
a $750,000 and $1,200,000 **b** $750,000 and $1,600,000
c $1,000,000 and $1,200,000 **d** $1,000,000 and $1,600,000

6 Certain balance sheet accounts of a foreign subsidiary of Rowan, Inc., at December 31, 19X9, have been translated into U.S. dollars as follows:

	Translated at	
	Current Rates	Historical Rates
Note receivable, long term	$240,000	$200,000
Prepaid rent	85,000	80,000
Patent	150,000	170,000
	$475,000	$450,000

The subsidiary's functional currency is the currency of the country in which it is located. What total amount should be included in Rowan's December 31, 19X9 consolidated balance sheet for the three accounts?
a $450,000 **b** $455,000
c $475,000 **d** $495,000

7 On January 1, 19X2 Kiner Company formed a foreign branch. The branch purchased merchandise at a cost of 720,000 local currency units on February 15, 19X2. The purchase price was equivalent to $180,000 on this date. The branch's inventory at December 31, 19X2 consisted solely of merchandise purchased on February 15, 19X2 and amounted to 240,000 LCU. The exchange rate was 6 LCU to $1 on December 31, 19X2, and the average rate of exchange was 5 LCU to $1 for 19X2. Assume that the LCU is the functional currency of the branch. In Kiner's December 31, 19X2 balance sheet, the branch inventory balance of 240,000 LCU should be translated into U.S. dollars at:

a $40,000

b $48,000

c $60,000

d $84,000

E 14–8   Use the following information in answering questions 1 and 2.

Bradstreet Corporation has a 70 percent interest in Kasan Corporation of Switzerland, acquired in 19X5 at a price equal to book value and fair value of Kasan's net assets. Kasan's functional currency is the Swiss franc, and changes in Kasan's U.S. dollar translated stockholders' equity for 19X8 are summarized as follows:

	Balance 1/1/X8	Change 19X8	Balance 12/31/X8
Capital stock	$10,000,000	none	$10,000,000
Other paid-in capital	8,000,000	none	8,000,000
Retained earnings	4,000,000	$1,500,000	5,500,000
Equity adjustment from translation	(2,000,000)	500,000	(1,500,000)
Total	$20,000,000	$2,000,000	$22,000,000

1 Kasan's U.S. dollar net income for 19X8 is $1,500,000, and Bradstreet accounts for its investment in Kasan as a one-line consolidation. Bradstreet's income from Kasan for 19X8 is:

a $2,000,000

b $1,500,000

c $1,400,000

d $1,050,000

2 The change in Bradstreet's investment in Kasan account for 19X8 is:

a $2,000,000

b $1,500,000

c $1,400,000

d $1,050,000

Use the following information in answering questions 3 and 4.

Martin Corporation loaned its 90 percent Colombian subsidiary 10,000,000 pesos denominated as $19,000 on July 1, 19X9 when the exchange rate for Colombian pesos was $.0019. The subsidiary's functional currency is its local currency and the 19X9 average and year-end exchange rates are $.0018 and $.0016, respectively.

3 If the loan is short term, the subsidiary's separate financial statements denominated in pesos at and for the year ended December 31, 19X9 should reflect:

a An exchange gain of 555,556 pesos

b An exchange loss of 1,875,000 pesos

c An equity adjustment of 1,875,000 pesos

d None of the above

4 If the loan is long-term, the consolidated financial statements of Martin Corporation and Subsidiary at and for the year ended December 31, 19X9 should reflect:

a An exchange gain of $889

b An exchange loss of $3,000

c An equity adjustment of $2,700

d None of the above

5 Inflation data of a foreign country for three years are as follows:

	Index	Change in Index	Annual Rate of Inflation
January 1, 19X6	150		
January 1, 19X7	200	50	50/150 = 33%
January 1, 19X8	250	50	50/200 = 25%
January 1, 19X9	330	80	80/250 = 32%

The cumulative three-year inflation rate is:

a 45%

b 90%

c 120%

d 180%

E 14-9 Pender Corporation owns an 80 percent interest in Shinhan Ltd. of South Korea, purchased several years ago at book value equal to fair value. The functional currency of Shinhan is the U.S. dollar.

Shinhan uses the FIFO inventory method. Data in won relating to Shinhan's cost of sales and inventory are as follows:

Inventory January 1, 19X7	9,000,000 won
Inventory December 31, 19X7	5,000,000 won
Purchases 19X7	86,000,000 won

The rate of exchange for the won on November 30, 19X7 when the ending inventory items were acquired was $.00135. Other exchange rates for 19X7 are:

Exchange rate January 1, 19X7	$.0012
Exchange rate December 31, 19X7	.0014
Average exchange rate for 19X7	.0013

Required: Determine cost of sales and ending inventory amounts in U.S. dollars that will appear in Shinhan's remeasured financial statements.

E 14-10 [AICPA adapted]

Jay Company's 19X5 consolidated financial statements include two wholly owned subsidiaries, Jay Company of Australia (Jay A) and Jay Company of France (Jay F). Functional currencies are the U.S. dollar for Jay A and the franc for Jay F.

Required
   1 What are the objectives of translating a foreign subsidiary's financial statements?
   2 How are gains and losses arising from translating or remeasuring of each subsidiary's financial statements measured and reported in Jay's consolidated financial statements?
   3 *FASB Statement No. 52* identifies several economic indicators that are to be considered both individually and collectively in determining the functional currency for a consolidated subsidiary. List three of those indicators.
   4 What exchange rate is used to incorporate each subsidiary's equipment cost, accumulated depreciation, and depreciation expense in Jay's consolidated financial statements?

PROBLEMS

P 14-1 Parkway Corporation purchased a 40 percent interest in Scorpio Company of Switzerland for $1,080,000 on January 1, 19X6. The excess cost over book value is goodwill with a ten-year amortization period. A summary of Scorpio's net assets at December 31, 19X5 and at December 31, 19X6 after translation into U.S. dollars is as follows:

	Capital Stock	Retained Earnings	Equity Adjustment	Net Assets
December 31, 19X5	$2,000,000	$400,000		$2,400,000
Net income		310,000		310,000
Dividends		(192,000)		(192,000)
Translation adjustment			$212,000	212,000
December 31, 19X6	$2,000,000	$518,000	$212,000	$2,730,000

Exchange rates for Swiss francs were $.60 on January 1, 19X6, $.62 average for 19X6, $.64 when dividends were declared, and $.65 at December 31, 19X6. Scorpio had net assets of 4,000,000 francs at January 1, 19X6, 500,000 francs net income for 19X6, dividends of 300,000 francs, and ended the year with net assets of 4,200,000 francs.

Required
   1 Calculate Parkway's income from Scorpio for 19X6.
   2 Determine the balance of Parkway's investment in Scorpio account at December 31, 19X6.

3 Develop a proof of your calculation of the investment in Scorpio account balance at December 31, 19X6.

P 14–2 Penn Corporation purchased a 40 percent interest in Ferrier Company of France on January 1, 19X1 for $342,000 when Ferrier's stockholders' equity consisted of 3,000,000 francs capital stock and 1,000,000 francs retained earnings. Ferrier's functional currency is the French franc. The exchange rate at this time was $.18 for French francs. Any goodwill is to be amortized over ten years.

A summary of changes in the stockholders' equity of Ferrier during 19X1 (including relevant exchange rates) is as follows:

	French Francs	Exchange Rate	U.S. Dollars
Stockholders' equity January 1, 19X1	4,000,000	$.18 C	$720,000
Net income	800,000	$.17 A	136,000
Dividends	(400,000)	$.17 C	(68,000)
Equity adjustment			(84,000)
Stockholders' equity December 31, 19X1	4,400,000	$.16 C	$704,000

Required: Determine the following:

1 Goodwill from Penn's investment in Ferrier on January 1, 19X1
2 Goodwill amortization for 19X1
3 Unamortized goodwill at December 31, 19X1
4 Equity adjustment from goodwill for 19X1
5 Income from Ferrier for 19X1
6 Investment in Ferrier balance at December 31, 19X1

P 14–3 Peter Corporation acquired 80 percent of the common stock of Schultz Corporation, a German company, for $3,200,000 on January 2, 19X6 when the stockholders' equity of Schultz consisted of 5,000,000 German marks capital stock and 2,000,000 marks retained earnings. The spot rate for marks on this date was $.5000. Any cost–book value difference is goodwill to be amortized over a ten-year period, and Schultz's functional currency is the mark.

Accounts from Schultz's adjusted trial balance in marks at December 31, 19X6 are as follows:

Debits	
Cash	1,000,000 marks
Accounts receivable	2,000,000
Inventories	4,000,000
Equipment	8,000,000
Cost of sales	4,000,000
Depreciation expense	800,000
Operating expenses	2,700,000
Dividends	500,000
	23,000,000 marks

Credits	
Accumulated depreciation—equipment	2,400,000 marks
Accounts payable	3,600,000
Capital stock	5,000,000
Retained earnings January 1	2,000,000
Sales	10,000,000
	23,000,000 marks

Relevant exchange rates in U.S. dollars for German marks are as follows:

Current exchange rate December 31, 19X6	$.6000
Average exchange rate 19X6	.5500
Exchange rate applicable to dividends	.5400

Required

1 Prepare a translation worksheet for Schultz at December 31, 19X6.
2 Calculate Peter's income from Schultz for 19X6 on the basis of a one-line consolidation.
3 Determine the correct balance of Peter's investment in Schultz at December 31, 19X6.

P 14-4 Pence Corporation, based in San Francisco, purchased 90 percent of Sevin Company's outstanding capital stock on January 1, 19X7 for $7,680,000. Sevin is a British company and the exchange rate for British pounds (£) was $1.60 when Pence acquired its interest. Sevin's stockholders' equity on January 1, 19X7 consisted of 4,000,000 £ capital stock and 1,000,000 £ retained earnings. Sevin's functional currency is the British pound and its comparative adjusted trial balances in pounds at December 31, 19X7 and 19X8 are as follows:

SEVIN COMPANY
ADJUSTED TRIAL BALANCES IN BRITISH POUNDS
AT DECEMBER 31,

	19X7	19X8
Debits		
Cash	300,000	500,000
Accounts receivable	600,000	900,000
Inventories	800,000	1,500,000
Equipment	9,000,000	10,000,000
Cost of sales	3,000,000	3,600,000
Depreciation expense	1,000,000	1,100,000
Operating expenses	800,000	900,000
Dividends	500,000	500,000
	16,000,000	19,000,000
Credits		
Accumulated depreciation—equipment	2,000,000	3,100,000
Accounts payable	2,000,000	2,200,000
Advance from Pence	200,000	200,000
Capital stock	4,000,000	4,000,000
Retained earnings	1,000,000	2,500,000
Sales	6,800,000	7,000,000
	16,000,000	19,000,000

Cost–Book Value Differential: The cost–book value differential from the investment in Sevin is goodwill with a ten-year amortization period. The original goodwill is $480,000 [$7,680,000 − 90% (5,000,000 £ × $1.60 exchange rate)].

Advance to Pence: On January 2, 19X7 Pence made a $300,000 (200,000 pound) short-term advance to Sevin. The advance is noninterest bearing and is denominated in pounds.

Summary of exchange rates:

	19X7	19X8
Current exchange rate January 1	$1.600	$1.700
Average exchange rate	1.650	1.750
Exchange rate on the date of the advance	1.600	
Exchange rate for dividends	1.680	1.780
Current exchange rate December 31	1.700	1.800

Required: Prepare translation worksheets for Sevin Company for the years ended December 31, 19X7 and 19X8. Also, calculate Pence's income from Sevin for 19X7 and 19X8 and the investment in Sevin balance at year end 19X7 and 19X8.

P 14-5 Philip Corporation, based in El Paso, Texas, acquired 100 percent of Segovia Corporation's outstanding stock at book value on January 1, 19X8 for $112,000. Segovia is a Mexican company and its functional currency is the U.S. dollar. The exchange rate for pesos was $.0007 when Philip acquired its interest. Segovia's stockholders' equity on January 1, 19X8 consisted of 150,000,000 pesos capital stock and 10,000,000 pesos retained earnings. The adjusted trial balance for Segovia at December 31, 19X8 is as follows:

Debits	
Cash	15,000,000 pesos
Accounts receivable—net	60,000,000
Inventories	30,000,000
Prepaid expenses	10,000,000
Land	45,000,000
Equipment	60,000,000
Cost of sales	120,000,000
Depreciation expense	12,000,000
Other operating expenses	28,000,000
Dividends	20,000,000
	400,000,000 pesos

Credits	
Accumulated depreciation	22,000,000 pesos
Accounts payable	18,000,000
Capital stock	150,000,000
Retained earnings	10,000,000
Sales	200,000,000
	400,000,000 pesos

Additional Information

1 Prepaid expenses (supplies) of 18,000,000 pesos were on hand when Philip acquired Segovia. Other operating expenses include 8,000,000 pesos of these supplies that were used in 19X8, and the remaining 10,000,000 are on hand at year-end.

2 The 120,000,000 pesos cost of sales consists of 50,000,000 inventory on hand at January 1, 19X8 and 100,000,000 purchases during the year, less 30,000,000 pesos ending inventory that was acquired when the exchange rate was $.00045.

3 The 60,000,000 pesos of equipment consists of 50,000,000 pesos included in the business combination and 10,000,000 pesos purchased during 19X8, at which time the exchange rate was $.00055. A depreciation rate of 20 percent is applicable to all equipment for 19X8.

4 Exchange rates for 19X8 are summarized as follows:

Current exchange rate January 1, 19X8	$.00070
Exchange rate when new equipment was acquired	.00055
Average exchange rate for 19X8	.00050
Exchange rate for December 31, 19X8 inventory	.00045
Exchange rate for dividends	.00045
Current exchange rate December 31, 19X8	.00040

Required: Prepare a worksheet to remeasure the adjusted trial balance of Segovia Corporation into U.S. dollars at December 31, 19X8.

P 14-6 Paragon Corporation, a U.S. company, acquired a 90 percent interest in Freeman Corporation, an Australian company, on July 1, 19X4 when the exchange rate for Australian dollars (A$) was $.70. Paragon acquired its interest in Freeman at book value equal to fair value. Freeman's functional currency is the U.S. dollar. Relevant exchange rates for Australian dollars are:

Current rate December 31, 19X8	$.80
Current rate December 31, 19X7	.75
Average rate 19X8	.78

Freeman's adjusted trial balance in Australian dollars at December 31, 19X8 included the following accounts and amounts.

Debits	
Cash	50,000 A$
Accounts receivable	85,000
Inventories (at FIFO cost)	170,000
Land	200,000
Buildings	700,000
Equipment	230,000
Cost of sales	800,000
Depreciation expense—building	50,000
Depreciation expense—equipment	30,000
Other operating expenses	320,000
Dividends	200,000
Total debits	2,835,000 A$

Credits	
Allowance for bad debts	5,000 A$
Accumulated depreciation—buildings	200,000
Accumulated depreciation—equipment	80,000
Accounts payable	150,000
Advance from Paragon	300,000
Capital stock	400,000
Retained earnings	200,000
Sales	1,500,000
Total credits	2,835,000 A$

Information relevant to selected balance sheet items: Freeman's inventories at December 31, 19X8 are 170,000 A$ acquired during the last quarter of 19X8 when the exchange rate was $.79. Inventories at December 31, 19X7 were 250,000 A$ acquired during the last quarter of 19X7 when the exchange rate was $.74.

The land (200,000 A$) and buildings (700,000 A$) have been held since the subsidiary was acquired on July 1, 19X4.

The equipment on hand since July 1, 19X4 is 170,000 A$ less accumulated depreciation of 70,000 A$ for a net amount of 100,000 A$. The rest of the equipment was acquired on December 31, 19X7 for 60,000 A$ and has accumulated depreciation of 10,000 A$ for a book value of 50,000 A$.

There have been no changes in Freeman's capital stock since Paragon purchased its 90 percent interest on July 1, 19X4. Freeman's December 31, 19X7 retained earnings in the remeasured balance sheet was $144,000.

Other operating expenses (other than 2,000 A$ bad debt expense) were incurred proportionately throughout 19X8.

Reciprocal amounts include the following:

Dividends. Paragon credited its investment in Freeman account for $135,000 for dividends received from Freeman.

Advance. The advance is denominated in A$. It is reported by Paragon at December 31, 19X8 as an "advance to Freeman," $240,000 and it is not of a long-term nature.

Required
1 Remeasure Freeman's trial balance into U.S. dollars.
2 Prepare income and retained earnings statements and a balance sheet for Freeman in U.S. dollars.

P 14-7   PWA Corporation paid $17,100,000 for 100 percent of the stock of Salina Company Ltd., a British firm, on January 1, 19X5 when the stockholders' equity of Salina consisted of 5,000,000 pounds (£) capital stock and 3,000,000 £ retained earnings. Salina's functional currency is the British pound, and any cost–book value differential is goodwill with a ten-year amortization period.

On July 1, 19X5 PWA advanced $3,330,000 (1,800,000 £) to Salina when the exchange rate was $1.85. The advance is short-term and denominated in U.S. dollars.

Relevant exchange rates for British pounds for 19X5 are:

Rate at acquisition on January 1	$1.90
Rate applicable to the advance on July 1	1.85
Rate applicable to dividends on September 1	1.85
Average rate for the year	1.85
Current rate at December 31	1.80

A translation worksheet for Salina's adjusted trial balance at December 31, 19X5 is as follows:

	British £	Exchange Rate	U.S. $
Debits			
Cash	550,000	$1.80 C	$ 990,000
Accounts receivable—net	500,000	1.80 C	900,000
Inventories	1,500,000	1.80 C	2,700,000
Land	1,600,000	1.80 C	2,880,000
Equipment—net	3,000,000	1.80 C	5,400,000
Buildings—net	5,000,000	1.80 C	9,000,000
Expenses	4,000,000	1.85 A	7,400,000
Exchange loss (advance)	50,000	1.85 A	92,500
Dividends	1,000,000	1.85 R	1,850,000
Equity adjustment from translation			847,500
	17,200,000		$32,060,000
Credits			
Accounts payable	750,000	1.80 C	$ 1,350,000
Other liabilities	600,000	1.80 C	1,080,000
Advance from PWA (short term)	1,850,000	1.80 C	3,330,000
Capital stock	5,000,000	1.90 H	9,500,000
Retained earnings January 1	3,000,000	1.90 H	5,700,000
Sales	6,000,000	1.85 A	11,100,000
	17,200,000		$32,060,000

Financial statements for PWA and Salina at and for the year ended December 31, 19X5 are summarized as follows:

	PWA	Salina
Combined Income and Retained Earnings		
Statement for the Year Ended		
December 31, 19X5		
Sales	$ 5,695,000	$11,100,000
Income from Salina	3,422,500	—
Expenses	(4,000,000)	(7,400,000)
Exchange loss	—	(92,500)
Net income	5,117,500	3,607,500
Add: Beginning retained earnings	8,565,000	5,700,000
Less: Dividends	(3,000,000)	(1,850,000)
Retained earnings December 31	$10,682,500	$ 7,457,500
Balance Sheet at December 31, 19X5		
Cash	$ 907,200	$ 990,000
Accounts receivable—net	1,285,000	900,000
Advance to Salina	3,330,000	—
Inventories	1,200,000	2,700,000
Land	1,000,000	2,880,000
Equipment—net	6,000,000	5,400,000

	PWA	Salina
Buildings—net	3,000,000	9,000,000
Investment in Salina	17,730,000	—
	$34,452,200	$21,870,000
Accounts payable	$ 1,627,200	$ 1,350,000
Advance from PWA	—	3,330,000
Other liabilities	3,085,000	1,080,000
Common stock	20,000,000	9,500,000
Retained earnings	10,682,500	7,457,500
Equity adjustment from translation	(942,500)	(847,500)
	$34,452,200	$21,870,000

Required

1 Prepare journal entries on PWA's books to account for its investment in Salina for 19X5.

2 Prepare consolidation working papers for PWA Corporation and Subsidiary for the year ended December 31, 19X5.

P 14–8 Sante Corporation is a 90 percent owned Colombian subsidiary of Pulsar Corporation, acquired by Pulsar on January 1, 19X8 at book value equal to fair value when the exchange rate for Colombian pesos was $.0024. The peso is Sante's functional currency. Pulsar made a 20,000,000 peso loan to Sante on May 1, 19X8 when the exchange rate for Colombian pesos was $.0023. The loan is short term and denominated at $46,000. Adjusted trial balances of the affiliated companies at year-end 19X8 are as follows:

	Pulsar in U.S. Dollars	Sante in Pesos
Debits		
Cash	$ 347,000	15,000,000
Accounts receivable	200,000	18,000,000
Short-term loan to Sante	46,000	—
Inventories	200,000	23,000,000
Land	1,500,000	25,000,000
Buildings	3,000,000	60,000,000
Equipment	5,000,000	80,000,000
Investment in Sante (90%)	207,000	—
Cost of sales	5,000,000	20,000,000
Depreciation expense	800,000	10,000,000
Other expenses	3,000,000	12,000,000
Exchange loss	—	3,000,000
Dividends	600,000	10,000,000
Equity adjustment	39,600	—
	$19,939,600	276,000,000
Credits		
Accumulated depreciation—buildings	$ 1,200,000	30,000,000
Accumulated depreciation—equipment	1,500,000	40,000,000
Accounts payable	390,100	13,000,000
Short-term loan from Pulsar	—	23,000,000
Capital stock	5,000,000	80,000,000
Retained earnings, January 1	1,800,000	20,000,000
Sales	10,000,000	70,000,000
Income from Sante	49,500	—
	$19,939,600	276,000,000

Sante paid dividends in September when the exchange rate was $.0021. The exchange rate for Colombian pesos was $.0020 at December 31, 19X8 and the average exchange rate for 19X8 was $.0022.

Required

1 Prepare a worksheet to translate Sante's adjusted trial balance into U.S. dollars at December 31, 19X8.

2 Prepare the necessary journal entries for Pulsar to account for its investment in Sante for 19X8 under the equity method.

3 Prepare consolidation working papers for Pulsar Corporation and Subsidiary for the year ended December 31, 19X8.

P 14–9 Perry Corporation, based in New York, acquired 75 percent of the outstanding shares of Smithe Corporation, a foreign company, on January 1, 19X7 for $14,210,000 when the exchange rate for local currency units of Smithe's home country was $1.40. At that date, Smithe's stockholders' equity was 13,000,000 LCU, consisting of 10,000,000 LCU capital stock and 3,000,000 LCU retained earnings. Any cost–book value differential from the investment in Smithe is assigned to goodwill with a ten-year amortization period. The functional currency of Smithe is its local currency unit. On January 2, 19X7 Smithe made a 400,000 LCU long-term noninterest-bearing advance to Perry when the exchange rate was still $1.40. The advance is denominated in LCU. The adjusted trial balances of Smithe in LCU at December 31, 19X7 and 19X8 are as follows:

SMITHE COMPANY ADJUSTED TRIAL BALANCES AT DECEMBER 31

	19X7 in LCU	Exchange Rate	19X7 in Dollars	19X8 in LCU	Exchange Rate	19X8 in Dollars
Debits						
Cash	700,000	$1.45	1,015,000	800,000	$1.50	1,200,000
Accounts receivable	600,000	1.45	870,000	1,800,000	1.50	2,700,000
Inventories	1,500,000	1.45	2,175,000	2,000,000	1.50	3,000,000
Advance to Perry	400,000	1.45	580,000	400,000	1.50	600,000
Equipment	15,000,000	1.45	21,750,000	15,000,000	1.50	22,500,000
Cost of sales	6,000,000	1.43	8,580,000	7,000,000	1.48	10,360,000
Depreciation expense	1,500,000	1.43	2,145,000	1,500,000	1.48	2,220,000
Operating expenses	1,800,000	1.43	2,574,000	2,000,000	1.48	2,960,000
Dividends	500,000	1.42	710,000	500,000	1.47	735,000
	28,000,000		40,399,000	31,000,000		46,275,000
Credits						
Accumulated depreciation	3,000,000	1.45	4,350,000	4,500,000	1.50	6,750,000
Accounts payable	2,000,000	1.45	2,900,000	1,300,000	1.50	1,950,000
Capital stock	10,000,000	1.40	14,000,000	10,000,000	1.40	14,000,000
Retained earnings	3,000,000	1.40	4,200,000	3,200,000		4,491,000
Sales	10,000,000	1.43	14,300,000	12,000,000	1.48	17,760,000
Equity adjustment	—		649,000	—		1,324,000
	28,000,000		40,399,000	31,000,000		46,275,000

Relevant exchange rates for local currency units for 19X7 and 19X8 are summarized as follows:

	19X7	19X8
Current exchange rate January 1	$1.40	$1.45
Average exchange rate for year	1.43	1.48
Spot rate for dividends	1.42	1.47
Current exchange rate December 31	1.45	1.50

Financial statements for Perry Corporation for the two years ended December 31, 19X7 and 19X8 are summarized as follows:

PERRY CORPORATION

	19X7	19X8
Combined Income and Retained Earnings Statement for the Year Ended December 31		
Sales	$20,000,000	$21,000,000
Income from Smithe	693,550	1,605,800
Cost of sales	9,000,000*	9,000,000*
Depreciation expense	2,000,000*	2,500,000*
Operating expenses	6,693,550*	7,105,800*
Net income	3,000,000	4,000,000
Add: Retained earnings January 1	4,500,000	5,000,000
Deduct: Dividends	2,500,000*	2,500,000*
Retained earnings December 31	$ 5,000,000	$ 6,500,000
Balance Sheet at December 31		
Cash	$ 1,123,000	$ 595,000
Accounts receivable	1,500,000	1,950,000
Inventories	2,500,000	2,000,000
Equipment—net	20,000,000	21,000,000
Investment in Smithe	14,877,000	16,455,000
	$40,000,000	$42,000,000
Accounts payable	$ 3,934,050	$ 3,910,600
Advance from Smithe	580,000	600,000
Capital stock	30,000,000	30,000,000
Retained earnings	5,000,000	6,500,000
Equity adjustment	485,950	989,400
	$40,000,000	$42,000,000

* Deduct.

Required

   1 Prepare consolidation working papers for Perry Corporation and Subsidiary for the years ended December 31, 19X7 and December 31, 19X8.

   2 Prepare a consolidated statement of cash flows for the year ended December 31, 19X8.

P 14–10 Progress Corporation, a U.S. company based in New York, acquired 90 percent of the outstanding voting shares of Scheele Corporation, a foreign company, on January 1, 19X7 for $2,070,000. The functional currency of Scheele is its local currency unit. The exchange rate for LCUs at the time of the business combination was $.45. Also on January 1, 19X7 Progress made a $450,000 (1,000,000 LCU) short-term advance to Scheele. Adjusted trial balances of Progress and Scheele Corporations at December 31, 19X7 and 19X8 are as follows:

ADJUSTED TRIAL BALANCES AT DECEMBER 31

	Progress Corporation		Scheele Corporation	
	19X7 in $	19X8 in $	19X7 in LCU	19X8 in LCU
Cash	406,200	183,800	100,000	600,000
Accounts receivable	1,200,000	1,400,000	400,000	1,000,000
Advance to Scheele	450,000	450,000		
Inventories	1,100,000	1,950,000	500,000	1,500,000
Investment in Scheele	2,196,000	2,426,250		
Equipment	2,500,000	3,000,000	9,000,000	9,000,000
Equity adjustment	247,800	389,950		
Cost of sales	4,300,000	4,800,000	3,000,000	3,600,000
Depreciation expense	600,000	700,000	900,000	900,000

	Progress Corporation		Scheele Corporation	
	19X7 in $	19X8 in $	19X7 in LCU	19X8 in LCU
Operating expenses	2,000,000	2,200,000	975,000	1,325,000
Exchange loss			125,000	75,000
	15,000,000	17,500,000	15,000,000	18,000,000
Accumulated depreciation	1,200,000	1,900,000	1,800,000	2,700,000
Accounts payable	1,700,000	1,500,000	1,075,000	1,100,000
Advance from Progress			1,125,000	1,200,000
Capital stock	3,000,000	3,000,000	4,000,000	4,000,000
Retained earnings	1,200,000	2,200,000	1,000,000	2,000,000
Income from Scheele	373,800	372,400		
Sales	7,526,200	8,527,600	6,000,000	7,000,000
	15,000,000	17,500,000	15,000,000	18,000,000

Additional Information
1 The cost–book value difference is goodwill with ten-year amortization.
2 The advance to Scheele is a noninterest-bearing loan denominated in U.S. dollars and adjusted on Scheele's books for exchange losses.
3 Current exchange rates are $.40 at December 31, 19X7 and $.375 at December 31, 19X8. Average exchange rates are $.42 for 19X7 and $.38 for 19X8.

Required: Develop comparative consolidated financial statements for Progress Corporation and Subsidiary at and for the years ended December 31, 19X7 and 19X8. An income statement, a retained earnings statement, and a balance sheet are required for 19X7 and 19X8; and a statement of cash flows is required for 19X8.

P 14–11 Oil Well Services, Inc., of Houston has a branch in Calgary, Alberta, to service Canadian customers. The trial balance of the Calgary branch in Canadian dollars is as follows:

OIL WELL SERVICES, CALGARY BRANCH
TRIAL BALANCE—DECEMBER 31, 19X2

	Canadian Dollars
Debits	
Cash	5,000
Accounts receivable	50,000
Operating supplies	80,000
Equipment	600,000
Operating expenses	500,000
Depreciation expense	60,000
	1,295,000
Credits	
Accumulated depreciation	110,000
Accounts payable	5,000
Home office	380,000
Sales revenue	800,000
	1,295,000

Additional Information
1 The branch purchased equipment for $500,000 (Canadian) when it was formed on January 1, 19X1, and additional equipment on January 1, 19X2 for $100,000 (Canadian). Equipment is depreciated on a straight-line basis over ten years with no salvage value.
2 Operating supplies are purchased proportionately throughout the year.

3 Sales and operating expenses are incurred evenly throughout the year.

4 Exchange rates in U.S. dollars on selected dates are as follows:

January 1, 19X1	$1.05
Average 19X1	$1.00
January 1, 19X2	$ .95
Average 19X2	$ .87
December 31, 19X2	$ .85

5 The branch account on the home office books is correctly recorded at $375,000 U.S.

Required: Prepare working papers to convert the trial balance of Calgary Branch into U.S. dollars assuming (a) a U.S. dollar functional currency and (b) a Canadian dollar functional currency.

15

SEGMENT AND INTERIM FINANCIAL REPORTING

The purpose of this chapter is to discuss two forms of disaggregation of the information in financial reports. In the first part of the chapter, the consolidated financial data of an enterprise are disaggregated by product lines and geographic information under the provisions of *FASB Statement No. 14*, "Financial Reporting for Segments of a Business Enterprise." The second part of the chapter covers financial reporting for a firm's operations in periods of less than one year. Guidelines for the preparation of partial year reports are found in *APB Opinion No. 28*, "Interim Financial Reports."

Historically, the emphasis in financial reporting was on disclosure for the enterprise as a whole, with little concern for disaggregation of information reported for the business entity. With such an emphasis, it was not unusual for a small local business to disclose as much information about its operations and financial position as the largest national and multinational corporations disclosed about their financial affairs. This situation changed in the 1970s. Companies having significant operations in different industries and foreign countries are now required to disclose information about such operations.

About the same time that investors and others were asking for financial information broken down by lines of business or products, they were also asking for more timely financial information. Balance sheets are prepared annually at a specific date, but income is earned throughout the reporting period. Investors wanted earnings data accumulated for shorter periods, such as by quarter, to show the progress of the enterprise. Some firms issued interim financial reports to shareholders, but the information provided was not consistent. The guidelines established by *APB Opinion No. 28* are applicable whenever publicly traded companies issue interim financial information to their securityholders.

EVOLUTION OF SEGMENT REPORTING REQUIREMENTS

The origin of current segment reporting requirements has been traced to the 1964 hearings on economic concentration in American industry by the Subcommittee on Antitrust and Monopoly of the Senate Committee on the Judiciary.[1]

These hearings were particularly concerned with diversified companies or con-glomerates, that is, companies that diversify into different industries by acquisi-tions or mergers. Testimony from the hearings included a recommendation that the SEC "require corporations to disclose revenues and profits for each of the operations engaged in."[2]

Reporting requirements for conglomerates soon became a topic of primary concern throughout the financial community. Business people, financial analysts, and accountants alike became interested in the subject, and the issue was widely aired at professional business meetings, in business and accounting literature, and in news releases. By 1967 the conglomerate issue had reached such a high priority level that the Accounting Principles Board issued *Statement No. 2*, "Disclosure of Supplemental Financial Information by Diversified Companies." This statement did not establish a reporting requirement for diversified companies, but it did recommend that such companies "review their own cir-cumstances carefully and objectively with a view toward disclosing voluntarily supplemental financial information as to industry segments of the business."[3]

During 1968 two major studies concerning financial reporting for diver-sified companies were published. Both studies, *External Reporting for Segments of a Business* by Morton Backer and Walter McFarland[4] and *Financial Reporting by Diversifed Companies* by Robert K. Mautz,[5] recommended additional disclosures for diversified companies.

The first financial reporting requirement for diversified companies became effective in 1969 when the SEC adopted "line-of-business" reporting requirements for its registrants. SEC developments in the area are summarized by the FASB as follows:

> In 1969, the Securities and Exchange Commission issued requirements for reporting line-of-business information in registration statements. In 1970, those requirements were extended to annual reports filed with the SEC on Form 10-K, and in October 1974 they were extended to the annual reports to securityholders of companies filing with the SEC.[6]

The basic SEC requirement consisted of disclosure of total sales revenue and income (or loss) before income taxes and extraordinary items for the most recent five-year period for *each line of business* with 10 percent or more of the enterprise's revenue or income before income taxes and extraordinary items. Applicability of the SEC rules was, of course, limited to SEC registrants and did not apply to all companies issuing financial statements under generally accepted accounting principles (GAAP).

Reporting by diversified companies was one of the topics that appeared on the original agenda of the FASB in 1973, and by May 1974 the FASB had issued a Discussion Memorandum on the topic entitled "An Analysis of Issues Related to Financial Reporting for Segments of a Business Enterprise." Also, in 1974 the SEC made a commitment to reconsider its line-of-business disclosure requirements when the FASB adopted a statement on segment reporting.

An Exposure Draft on "Financial Reporting for Segments of a Business Enterprise" was issued by the FASB in 1975, and the standard on segment report-

---

[1]K. Fred Skousen, "Chronicle of Events Surrounding the Segment Reporting Issue," *Journal of Accounting Research*, 8 (Autumn, 1970), p. 294.

[2]Ibid.

[3]*APB Statement No 2*, paragraph 11.

[4]Backer and McFarland, *External Reporting for Segments of a Business* (New York: National Association of Accountants, 1968).

[5]Mautz, *Financial Reporting by Diversified Companies* (New York: Financial Executives Research Foundation, 1968).

[6]*FASB Statement No. 14*, paragraph 44.

ing, *FASB Statement No. 14,* was issued in 1976. The SEC did reconsider its line-of-business disclosure requirements in 1977, and it issued *Accounting Series Release (ASR) 236,* which adopted industry segment rather than line-of-business requirements and brought the SEC requirements closer to those in *Statement No. 14.* In 1980 the SEC reduced the reporting period for industry segment data and foreign operations from five years to three years as one of a number of changes in form 10-K.

SCOPE OF THE SEGMENT REPORTING STANDARD

The segment reporting standard as established by *FASB Statement No. 14* was initially applicable to all business enterprises that issue a complete set of financial statements in accordance with GAAP. But *Statement No. 14* was amended by *FASB Statement No. 21* to exclude nonpublic enterprises from its requirements.[7] Disclosure requirements include information about enterprise *operations in different industries, foreign operations and export sales, and major customers.* The financial statement disclosures for these areas are intended to "assist financial statement users in analyzing and understanding the enterprise's financial statements by permitting better assessment of the enterprise's past performance and future prospects."[8]

Statement No. 14 requirements are based on the accounting principles used for consolidated financial statements except that the *information is disaggregated* and *most intersegment transactions are included in the segment information.* Disaggregation is not required for unconsolidated subsidiaries, corporate joint ventures, and other investments accounted for by the equity method, but the geographic areas and industries in which these equity investees operate must be identified. Also, vertically integrated operations of equity investees do not have to be disaggregated, but additional disclosure is required.

Although segment reporting requirements of the FASB were originally applicable to interim financial statements, *Statement No. 14* was amended in 1977 to exclude interim reports. Segment information *may* be included in interim reports, and if included, the information disclosed must be consistent with the segment reporting requirements.[9]

IDENTIFICATION OF SEGMENT REPORTING RESPONSIBILITIES

All business enterprises except for nonpublic entities are subject to the segment reporting provisions of *Statement No. 14.* However, the reporting responsibilities for an individual enterprise are determined by its operations in different industries and geographic areas and by its sales to major customers, in other words, by the extent of its diversification. Under *Statement No. 14,* an enterprise may have to disclose information for one of the following areas but not for others:

Operations in different industries
Domestic and foreign operations
Export sales
Major customers

---

[7]*FASB Statement No. 21* defines *nonpublic enterprise* as "an enterprise other than one (a) whose debt or equity securities trade in a public market on a foreign or domestic stock exchange or in the over-the-counter market...or (b) that is required to file financial statements with the Securities and Exchange Commission."

[8]*FASB Statement No. 14,* paragraph 5.

[9]*FASB Statement No. 18,* "Financial Reporting for Segments of a Business Enterprise—Interim Financial Statements," paragraphs 7 and 8.

A firm's reporting responsibility in each of the four areas is determined by specific tests for that area.

Operations in Different Industries

To determine if information about operations in different industries must be reported, a firm first identifies its industry segments. **Industry segment** is defined as "a component of an enterprise engaged in providing a product or service or a group of related products or services primarily to unaffiliated customers... for a profit."[10] Industry segments are identified through an analysis of the products and services from which the enterprise derives its revenue and by grouping these products and services into industry segments.

Ordinarily, the starting point for determining the enterprise's industry segments is to identify the profit centers for which information about revenue and profitability is accumulated for internal planning and control purposes. If the profit centers cross industry lines, or if the enterprise does not accumulate information on a less than total enterprise basis, additional disaggregation along industry lines is necessary. Standard classification schemes such as the Standard Industrial Classification and the Enterprise Standard Industrial Classification may be helpful in determining industry segments, but no single classification scheme is applicable to all firms. Industry segmentation on a worldwide basis is required, but foreign operations for which disaggregation along industry lines is not practicable are aggregated and treated as a single industry segment.

A **reportable industry segment** is an industry segment or group of closely related industry segments for which information is required to be reported. Industry segments are designated as reportable segments on the basis of their significance to the enterprise as a whole. An industry segment is reportable if it meets a 10 percent revenue test, a 10 percent asset test, *or* a 10 percent operating profit test for each year for which financial statements are presented. These tests are included in Exhibit 15–1, which summarizes the tests for disclosure in each of the four reporting areas.

10 Percent Revenue Test   An industry segment is a reportable segment if its revenue is 10 percent or more of the combined revenue of all industry segments (see Exhibit 15–1). Revenue includes intersegment sales and transfers. Interest, including interest on intersegment trade receivables, is included in the revenue test if the asset on which the interest is earned is included in that segment's identifiable assets. But interest on intersegment loans and advances is not included in revenue except for interest of a segment whose operations are primarily of a financial nature.

10 Percent Asset Test   An industry segment is a reportable segment if its identifiable assets are 10 percent or more of the combined identifiable assets of all industry segments (see Exhibit 15–1). Identifiable assets of an industry segment are the tangible and intangible assets used by the segment. Assets used by more than one industry segment are allocated among those segments on a reasonable basis. Goodwill from an enterprise's investment in a segment is included in that segment's identifiable assets. Assets maintained for general corporate purposes (in other words, assets that are not used in the operations of any industry segment, such as corporate headquarters or marketable securities) and intersegment advances and loans are not included. (But intersegment loans and advances are included in the identifiable assets of a financial segment.) Asset valuation allowances for depreciation, bad debts, marketable securities, and so forth are considered in determining a segment's identifiable assets.

10 Percent Operating Profit Test   An industry segment is a reportable segment if the absolute amount of its operating profit or operating loss is 10 percent or

---

[10]*FASB Statement No. 14,* paragraph 10a.

	Revenue Tests		Asset Tests		Operating Profit Tests
Reportable Industry Segments An industry segment is a reportable segment if:	Its revenue from affiliated and unaffiliated customers ≥ 10 percent of the combined revenue from affiliated and unaffiliated customers of all industry segments.	*or*	Its identifiable assets ≥ 10 percent of the combined identifiable assets of all industry segments.	*or*	Its operating profit or loss ≥ 10 percent of the greater of (a) combined operating profit of all profitable industry segments or (b) combined operating losses of all unprofitable industry segments.
Additional industry segments must be identified as reportable segments if:	Combined revenue of reportable segments from sales to unaffiliated customers < 75 percent of the combined revenue from unaffiliated customers of all industry segments.				
Dominant Industry Segment A single industry segment is a dominant industry segment if:	Its revenue from affiliated and unaffiliated customers > 90 percent of the combined revenue from affiliated and unaffiliated customers of all industry segments.	*and*	Its identifiable assets > 90 percent of the combined identifiable assets of all industry segments.	*and*	Its operating profit or loss > 90 percent of the greater of (a) combined operating profit of all profitable segments or (b) combined operating losses of all unprofitable industry segments.
Domestic and Foreign Operations Information on domestic and foreign operations must be reported if:	Revenue generated by foreign operations to unaffiliated customers ≥ 10 percent of consolidated revenue as reported in the enterprise's income statement.	*or*	Identifiable assets of foreign operations ≥ 10 percent of consolidated assets as reported in the enterprise's balance sheet.		
Export Sales Information on export sales must be reported if:	Export sales from an enterprise's home country to unaffiliated customers in foreign countries ≥ 10 percent of the total revenue from unaffiliated customers as reported in the enterprise's consolidated income statement.				
Major Customers Information about major customers must be reported if:	Revenue from a single customer (or customers under common control) ≥ 10 percent of the revenue of the enterprise *or if* Revenue from the federal government, or a state, local, or foreign government ≥ 10 percent of the revenue of the enterprise.				

FASB Statement No. 14 uses the term *sales* to include "the sale of a product, the rendering of a service, and other types of transactions by which revenue is earned" (see footnote 4, page 5, of *FASB Statement No. 14*). References in this exhibit use the term *revenue* to avoid misinterpretation of the test bases. Although *FASB Statement No. 14* defines *segment revenue* rather precisely, it does not define *enterprise revenue*.

Exhibit 15–1   *Tests for Disclosure Under FASB Statement No. 14 and Related FASB Pronouncements*

more of the greater, in absolute amount, of (a) the combined operating profits of all industry segments that did not incur an operating loss, or (b) the combined operating loss of all industry segments that did incur an operating loss (see Exhibit 15–1). Operating profit includes expenses that relate to intersegment sales or transfers and expenses allocated among segments on a reasonable basis. However, revenue earned at the corporate level, general corporate expenses, interest expense (except for financial segments), domestic and foreign income taxes, income (loss) from equity investees, gain or loss on discontinued operations, extraordinary items, minority interest, and the cumulative effect of an accounting change are excluded from the computation of operating profit. Intersegment interest expense and interest revenue of an industry segment whose operations are principally of a financial nature are included in determining that segment's profit or loss.

PHIL-BROWN CORPORATION
SELECTED DATA IN THOUSANDS OF DOLLARS
AT OR FOR THE YEAR ENDED DECEMBER 31, 19X1

	Food	Paper	Copper	Finance	General Corporate	Total	Consolidated
Revenue							
Sales to unaffiliated customers	$135	$170	$ 40			$ 345	$345
Sales to Paper Segment	10					10	
Interest income— unaffiliated	5			$ 50		55	55
Interest income from Copper Segment		5				5	
Interest income from Paper Segment				10		10	
Total	$150	$175	$ 40	$ 60		$ 425	$400
Assets							
Loans and receivables— unaffiliated	$ 50	$100		$320		$ 470	$470
Loan to Copper Segment		50				50	
Advance to Paper Segment				100		100	
Other current assets	100	50	$ 20	50	$ 30	250	250
Plant assets	50	100	40	30	10	230	230
Total	$200	$300	$ 60	$500	$ 40	$1,100	$950
Income Before Income Taxes							
Total revenue (from revenue section above)	$150	$175	$ 40	$ 60		$ 425	$400
Cost of sales— unaffiliated	100*	80*	50*			230*	230*
Cost of sales—Food Segment		10*				10*	
Interest expense— outsiders	15*	20*		4*		39*	39*
Interest expense—to Finance Segment		10*				10*	
Interest expense—to Paper Segment			5*			5*	
Other expenses	25*	25*	10*	6*	$ 25*	91*	91*
Income (loss)	$ 10	$ 30	$(25)	$ 50	$(25)	$ 40	$ 40

* Deduct.

Exhibit 15–2 *Selected Data to Illustrate Segment Reporting Requirements*

Illustration of the 10 Percent Tests
for Reportable Industry Segments

Phil-Brown Corporation has four industry segments with revenue, asset, and income data at or for the year ended Decemer 31, 19X1 as shown in Exhibit 15–2.

Revenue Test   The 10 percent revenue test is applied by determining the amount of each industry segment's revenue and by comparing that amount with 10 percent of the combined revenue of all industry segments. This test is illustrated for the Phil-Brown Corporation as follows:

	Industry Segment Revenue		Test value (10% × $420,000)	Reportable Segment Under Revenue Test?
Food	$150,000	≥	$42,000	Yes
Paper	170,000	≥	42,000	Yes
Copper	40,000	<	42,000	No
Finance	60,000	≥	42,000	Yes
Total	$420,000			

Revenue of the Food Segment includes $10,000 intersegment sales to the Paper Segment, and revenue of the Finance Segment includes $10,000 intersegment interest income from the Paper Segment. But the Paper Segment's revenue does not include the $5,000 interest income from the Copper Segment. Only financial segments include interest income from intersegment loans and advances in their revenue. The Food, Paper, and Finance Segments are reportable segments under the revenue test. The Copper Segment is not a reportable segment under the revenue test.

Asset Test   The 10 percent asset test involves comparing the total amount of each industry segment's identifiable assets with 10 percent of the combined identifiable assets of all industry segments. Computations for the Phil-Brown Corporation follow:

	Industry Segments Identifiable Assets		Test value (10% × $1,010,000)	Reportable Segment Under Asset Test?
Food	$ 200,000	≥	$101,000	Yes
Paper	250,000	≥	101,000	Yes
Copper	60,000	<	101,000	No
Finance	500,000	≥	101,000	Yes
Total	$1,010,000			

Assume that all assets of Phil-Brown Corporation are assigned to industry segments other than those maintained for general corporate purposes. *Statement No. 14* specifies that intersegment loans and advances can only be included in the identifiable assets of financial segments. Thus, the $50,000 loan to Copper Segment (see Exhibit 15–2) is not included in the identifiable assets of the Paper Segment. Food, Paper, and Finance Segments all meet the 10 percent asset test for reportable industry segments.

Operating Profit Test   In applying the operating profit test to the identification of reportable segments, the absolute amount of each segment's operating profit or loss is compared with 10 percent of the greater of the combined operating profits of all profitable industry segments or the combined operating losses of all unprofitable industry segments. The test is illustrated as follows for the Phil-Brown example:

	Indusry Segments Operating Profit	*Industry Segments Operating Loss*		*Test Value (10% × $130,000)*	*Reportable Segment Under Operating Profit Test?*
Food	$ 25,000		≥	$13,000	Yes
Paper	55,000		≥	13,000	Yes
Copper		$(20,000)	≥	13,000	Yes
Finance	50,000		≥	13,000	Yes
Total	$130,000	$(20,000)			

The operating profits and losses are determined by adding interest expense (including intersegment interest) to the amount of income or loss shown in Exhibit 15–2 for the Food, Paper, and Copper Segments, and deducting the $5,000 intersegment interest income from the Paper Segment. Interest expense is not considered in computing the operating profit or loss of any segment other than a finance segment. After the $13,000 test value is determined, the test is applied to the absolute amounts of operating profit or loss for each segment. All the segments of Phil-Brown are reportable segments under the 10 percent operating profit test.

Reevaluation of Reportable Segments

The industry segments that meet one or more of the 10 percent tests for reportable segments are subject to further evaluation before the final determination of reportable segments is made. A segment that meets only one of the tests but is not expected to meet the test in future years should not be considered a reportable segment. Conversely, a segment that fails to meet any of the tests, but has been a reportable segment in prior years and is expected to meet one or more of the tests in future years, should be regarded as a reportable segment.

In addition, the reportable segments must represent a "substantial portion of the enterprise's total operations." If the combined revenue from sales to unaffiliated customers of all reportable segments is less than 75 percent of the combined revenue from sales to unaffiliated customers of all industry segments, additional segments must be identified as reportable segments to bring the total up to 75 percent (see Exhibit 15–1). Similarly, if the number of reportable segments is more than ten, it may be appropriate for the enterprise to combine the most closely related industry segments into broader reportable segments.

The 75 percent test for final determination of reportable industry segments can be illustrated for the Phil-Brown example by assuming that the Copper Segment was not a reportable segment under any of the 10 percent tests. Under this asumption, the 75 percent test would have to be applied to make sure that the Food, Paper, and Finance Segments account for a substantial portion of the enterprise's total operations. The test is applied as follows:

	Combined Revenue from Unaffiliated Customers by Reportable Industry Segments	Combined Revenue from Unaffiliated Customers of All Industry Segments
Food	$140,000	$140,000
Paper	170,000	170,000
Copper		40,000
Finance	50,000	50,000
Total	$360,000	$400,000

Since $360,000 is greater than 75 percent of $400,000, no additional industry segments have to be identified as reportable segments.

Dominant Industry Segments

If a single segment's revenue, identifiable assets, and operating profit or loss each constitute more than 90 percent of the combined totals for all industry segments, the segment is considered a dominant industry segment, and segment information disclosures are not required. The financial statements of the enterprise must, however, identify the industry in which the dominant segment operates. Exhibit 15–1 includes a summary of the 90 percent tests for classification of an industry segment as a dominant industry segment. In examining the requirements as shown in Exhibit 15–1, notice that *all three of the 90 percent tests have to be met for a segment to qualify as a dominant industry segment.*

The 1991 annual report of H. J. Heinz Company (page 50) indicates that the company operates principally in one line of business, processed food products, representing over 90 percent of consolidated sales. Although Heinz was not required to provide industry segment information, it did provide information by geographic area.

Domestic and Foreign Operations

Foreign operations are revenue-producing operations that are located outside of the enterprise's home country and that generate revenue from sales to unaffiliated customers or from intraenterprise sales or transfers between geographic areas (interarea sales or transfers). Operations of unconsolidated subsidiaries and equity investees are excluded from this requirement. In other words, their operations do not have to be disaggregated. Domestic operations are revenue-producing operations of the enterprise located in the enterprise's home country that generate revenue from sales to unaffiliated customers or from interarea sales or transfers. Foreign geographic areas are countries or groups of countries that are determined by an enterprise on the basis of its particular circumstances. Factors to be considered in identifying foreign geographic areas include "proximity, economic affinity, similiarities in business environments, and the nature, scale, and decree of interrelationship of the enterprise's operations in the various countries."[11]

An enterprise is required to include information about domestic and foreign operations in its financial statements if:

1 Revenue generated by its foreign operations from sales to unaffiliated customers is 10 percent or more of consolidated revenue as reported in the enterprises income statement, *or*
2 Identifiable assets of foreign operations are 10 percent or more of consolidated assets as reported in the enterprise's balance sheet.

---

[11]Ibid., paragraph 34.

If foreign operations are conducted in more than one geographic area, information is required to be reported separately for operations in each geographic area that meets either the revenue or the identifiable asset test. The tests for disclosure of domestic and foreign operations are included in the summary of tests for disclosure under *Statement No. 14* (see Exhibit 15–1).

Application of the tests based on summary data for Alex American Corporation is illustrated as follows:

ALEX AMERICAN CORPORATION
SUMMARY DATA IN THOUSANDS OF DOLLARS
AT AND FOR THE YEAR ENDED DECEMBER 31, 19X1

	Domestic	British Isles	Germany	France	Japan	Consolidated
Revenue						
Sales to unaffiliated customers	$ 920	$100	$160	$140	$180	$1,500
Transfers between geographic areas (affiliated interarea sales)	80	10	50	20	40	
	$1,000	$110	$210	$160	$220	$1,500
Assets						
Identifiable assets	$1,100	$110	$150	$140	$200	$1,700
Investment in unconsolidated subsidiaries	100					100
Corporate assets	50					50
	$1,250	$110	$150	$140	$200	$1,850

Alex American is required to report information about its domestic and foreign operations if revenue generated by its foreign operations from sales to unaffiliated customers is $150,000 or more (10 percent of $1,500,000 consolidated revenue). Since revenue from its foreign operations to unaffiliated customers is $580,000 ($100,000 + $160,000 + $140,000 + $180,000), Alex American is required to provide information about its domestic and foreign operations. The asset test is also met, since the $600,000 identifiable assets of foreign operations are greater than 10 percent of Alex American's $1,850,000 consolidated assets.

In addition to the overall requirement to report information about domestic and foreign operations, however, operations in each foreign geographic area must be tested to determine if separate disclosure is required. These tests are illustrated as follows:

REVENUE TEST

	Revenue from Unaffiliated Customers		10% of Consolidated Revenue	Separate Information Required for Geographic Area?
Area				
British Isles	$100,000	<	$150,000	No
Germany	160,000	≥	150,000	Yes
France	140,000	<	150,000	No
Japan	180,000	≥	150,000	Yes

ASSET TEST

Area	Identifiable Assets		10% of Total Consolidated Assets	Separate Information Required for Geographic Area?
British Isles	$110,000	<	$185,000	No
Germany	150,000	<	185,000	No
France	140,000	<	185,000	No
Japan	200,000	≥	185,000	Yes

Since the foreign operations in Germany and Japan meet at least one of the tests, separate disclosure is required for operations in these two foreign areas. Operations in the British Isles and France can be combined and disclosed as operations in "other foreign areas." The information required to be disclosed for domestic and foreign operations is covered in a later section of this chapter.

DISCLOSURES REQUIRED FOR OPERATIONS IN DIFFERENT INDUSTRIES

The disclosures required for operations in different industries are based on the identification of reportable segments as discussed in the previous section of this chapter. Once the reportable segments are identified, all other industry segments are combined into an "Other Industry Segments" category for reporting purposes. Required disclosures must be made for each year for which financial statements are presented. The information to be included *for reportable segments and other industry segments in the aggregate* is summarized as follows:

Revenue

1 Amount of revenue from unaffiliated customers.
2 Amount of revenue from affiliated customers.
3 Reconciliation of the amounts of revenue from all reportable segments with revenue reported in the income statement of the enterprise.
4 Basis of accounting for intersegment sales and transfers, including the effect of any changes in basis on the operating profit or loss of the segment.

Assets

1 Aggregate carrying amount of identifiable assets.
2 Reconciliation of identifiable assets for all reportable segments and other industry segments with total consolidated assets. Corporate assets are to be identified separately in the reconciliation.

Profitability

1 Amount of operating profit or loss.
2 Nature and amount of unusual or infrequently occurring items for each reportable segment and other industry segments.
3 Reconciliation of operating profit or loss for all reportable segments and other industry segments with pretax income from continuing operations as reflected in the consolidated income statement. Corporate expenses are to be disclosed separately. (The reconciliation is for pretax income before gain or loss on discontinued operations, extraordinary items, and cumulative effect type changes in accounting principles.)
4 Effect on operating profit or loss of reportable segments of any changes in allocating operating expenses among segments.
5 Effect on operating profit of each reportable segment of a change in accounting principle.

Other Disclosures

1 Aggregate amount of depreciation, depletion, and amortization expense for each reportable segment.
2 Amount of capital expenditures for each reportable industry segment.
3 Amount of investments in and income from unconsolidated subsidiaries and other equity investees whose operations are vertically integrated with the operations of the reportable industry segment.
4 Geographic areas in which vertically integrated equity method investees operate.
5 Products and services of each reportable industry segment and accounting policies relative to segment information to the exent not disclosed elsewhere in the financial report.

Retroactive Restatement of Segment Information Is Required For

1 Changes in the way enterprise products and services are grouped
2 Change in an accounting principle that requires restatement of prior financial statements (such as from a pooling of interests)

The information required to be disclosed can be presented in the body of the financial statements, in footnotes to the financial statements, or in a separate schedule that is included as an integral part of the financial statements. Information for the reportable industry segments and for all other industry segments in the aggregate must be reconciled to the related amounts that appear in the enterprise's financial statements. Revenue is reconciled to revenue reported in the consolidated income statement, and operating profit or loss is reconciled to pretax income from continuing operations in the consolidated income statement. Identifiable assets are reconciled to total consolidated assets, with separate identification of general corporate assets.

An example of the basic segment reporting requirements with disclosure in a separate schedule is presented in Exhibit 15-3 for Cardinal Corporation, a fictitious U.S. company. The schedule provides a convenient means of presenting comparative 19X2 and 19X1 segment information as well as reconciling this information to amounts shown in the consolidated financial statements. Exhibit 15-3 shows comparative segment data for two years. However, firms subject to SEC regulations are required to include segment information for at least three years in their annual reports to shareholders.[12]

Note that the information presented in Exhibit 15-3 includes essentially all the financial disclosures that are required by *Statement No. 14* for reporting operations in different industries. All the revenue, operating profit, and asset information are included in the illustration, along with required reconciliations to amounts shown in the consolidated financial statements. The nature of the products sold is reflected in the titles of the reportable industry segments, and even the basis for intersegment transfers (market) is reflected in the exhibit. Additional disclosures would be necessary, however, for changes in accounting principles, changes in procedures for allocating operating expenses among the segments, and changes in the way in which products or services are grouped. These types of changes are not expected to occur frequently.

Some firms present the required three-year industry segment information in one set of data. Exhibit 15-4 shows industry segment information from the Allied-Signal Inc., 1990 Annual Report. Note 23, "Segment Financial Data," identifies three industry segments—aerospace, automotive, and engineered materials—and provides a reconciliation of segment information to the related consolidated financial statement amounts.

---

[12]An excellent example of this format for presenting segment information is found in the *1990 Annual Report of Sun Company,* pages 30-33.

CARDINAL CORPORATION
NOTE TO CONSOLIDATED STATEMENTS

19X2	Building Materials	Custom Homes	Other Industries	Eliminations	Consolidated
Sales					
Sales to unaffiliated customers	$420,000	$180,000	$100,000		$ 700,000
Intersegment sales at market	40,000	35,000	25,000	$(100,000)	
Total sales	$460,000	$215,000	$125,000	$(100,000)	$ 700,000
Income					
Operating income	$ 72,000	$ 40,000	$ 28,000		$ 140,000
Income from equity investments					20,000
Corporate expenses					(12,000)
Interest expense					(38,000)
Income before income taxes					$ 110,000
Assets				Corporate*	
Identifiable assets	$500,000	$250,000	$110,000	$ 190,000	$1,050,000
Capital expenditures	$ 50,000	$ 40,000	$ 10,000	$ 10,000	$ 110,000
Depreciation and amortization	$ 30,000	$ 35,000	$ 8,000	$ 2,000	$ 75,000

19X1	Building Materials	Custom Homes	Other Industries	Eliminations	Consolidated
Sales					
Sales to unaffiliated customers	$410,000	$170,000	$ 80,000		$ 660,000
Intersegment sales at market	35,000	30,000	25,000	$ (90,000)	
Total sales	$445,000	$200,000	$105,000	$ (90,000)	$ 660,000
Income					
Operating income	$ 70,000	$ 40,000	$ 25,000		$ 135,000
Income from equity investments					10,000
Corporate expenses					(10,000)
Interest expense					(40,000)
Income before income taxes					$ 95,000
Assets				Corporate*	
Identifiable assets	$480,000	$245,000	$100,000	$ 175,000	$1,000,000
Capital expenditures	$ 40,000	$ 40,000	$ 5,000	$ 4,000	$ 89,000
Depreciation and amortization	$ 30,000	$ 35,000	$ 7,000	$ 3,000	$ 75,000

* Corporate assets include investment in nonconsolidated subsidiary of $126,000 in 19X2 and $119,000 in 19X1.

Exhibit 15–3   *Business Segment Information by Industry*

NOTE 23. SEGMENT FINANCIAL DATA (in millions)

		Aerospace	Automotive	Engineered Materials	Corporate and Unallocated(1)	Total
Net sales(2)	1990	$5,358	$4,181	$2,786	$ 18	$12,343
	1989	5,079	3,849	2,993	21	11,942
	1988	4,746	4,101	3,033	29	11,909
Research, development and engineering expense(3)	1990	384	170	139	28	721
	1989	306	149	122	26	603
	1988	311	174	120	42	647
Depreciation and amortization	1990	140	143	129	14	426
	1989	123	120	128	14	385
	1988	114	121	125	16	376
Income from operations(4)	1990	498	166	287	(221)	730
	1989	514	302	355	(225)	946
	1988	346	268	377	(310)	681
Net income (4)(5)	1990	235	34	228	(35)	462
	1989	225	114	245	(56)	528
	1988	119	99	222	23	463
Capital expenditures	1990	230	222	214	9	675
	1989	162	209	163	7	541
	1988	163	246	181	12	602
Identifiable assets	1990	4,224	2,794	1,896	1,542	10,456
	1989	4,335	2,619	1,879	1,509	10,342
	1988	4,351	2,582	1,839	1,297	10,069

Intersegment sales approximate market and are not significant.

(1) The "Corporate and Unallocated" column includes amounts for businesses sold, nonrecurring, discontinued and Corporate items. Net Income in 1988 includes nonrecurring gains relating to Automotive and Engineered Materials of $57 and $24 million, respectively. Also included in Net Income are amounts (including preferred dividends) for Union Texas, accounted for on the equity basis, of $59, $80 and $57 million for each of the respective years. Identifiable Assets include an investment in Union Texas of $509, $473 and $476 million, and other Corporate assets of $1,033, $1,036 and $821 million for each of the respective years.
(2) Sales to the U.S. government and its agencies, mainly for the Aerospace segment, were $1,373, $1,335 and $1,314 million for each of the respective years.
(3) Engineering activities totaled $295, $222 and $232 million for each of the respective years.
(4) Includes in 1988 a pre- and after-tax provision to cover streamlining and restructuring charges for Aerospace of $76 and $50 million, Automotive of $37 and $23 million, Engineered Materials of $23 and $14 million and Corporate and Unallocated of $61 and $38 million (including environmental expenditures of $22 and $14 million), respectively.
(5) An interest charge is made by Corporate Office to the segments on the basis of relative investment, taxes on income are generally included in the segments which gave rise to the tax effects and equity in income of affiliated companies is included in the segments in which these companies operate.
Source: *Allied-Signal Inc., 1990 Annual Report*, Note 23, page 37.

Exhibit 15–4   *Multiyear Business Segment Information*

DISCLOSURES FOR OPERATIONS IN DIFFERENT GEOGRAPHIC AREAS

Enterprises have to report information about their domestic and foreign operations on the basis of the revenue and asset tests discussed previously. If foreign operations are conducted in two or more geographic areas, disclosures are required for *each* foreign geographic area in which revenues from unaffiliated customers or identifiable assets are 10 percent or more of the related consolidated amounts. Information for all remaining geographic areas are reported in the aggregate. The disclosures for *domestic operations, each foreign geographic area that meets either of the tests, and all other foreign geographic areas in the aggregate* are as follows:

Revenue

1 Amount of revenue from unaffiliated customers.
2 Amount of interarea sales and transfers.

3 Reconciliation of revenue shown in 1 and 2 above with revenue shown in the income statement of the enterprise.
4 Basis of interarea sales and transfers including the effect of any change in basis on operating profit or loss.

Assets

1 Aggregate carrying amount of identifiable assets.
2 Reconciliation of identifiable assets with assets shown in the balance sheet of the enterprise.

Profitability

1 Amounts of operating profit or loss (or some other measure of profitability between operating profit and net income, but a common measure of profitability must be used for all geographic areas).
2 Reconciliation of operating profit or loss (or other profitability measure) to pretax income from continuing operations as reflected in the consolidated income statement.

Other Disclosures

1 The geographic areas into which foreign operations have been disaggregated.
2 Changes in the way foreign operations are grouped into geographic areas and how such changes affect the geographic area information.
3 Nature and effect of restatements of prior years' information that result from prior period adjustments.

Observe that the disclosure requirements do not correspond to the *tests* for reporting information about domestic and foreign operations. The revenue test relates to revenue from unaffiliated customers even though the reporting requirement includes interarea sales and transfers. In addition, there is a disclosure requirement for operating profit (or similar measure of profitability), but there is no operating profit test for reporting information on domestic and foreign operations.

Information about operations in different geographic areas may appear within the body of the financial statements with appropriate explanatory notes, entirely in footnotes, or in separate schedules. Exhibit 15–5 illustrates the presentation for domestic and foreign operations in a separate schedule similar to the one used in Exhibit 15–3 for operations in different industries. Although the schedule in Exhibit 15–5 includes reconciliation with related consolidated statement amounts, it is not necessary to repeat the reconciliations if they have been made in disclosing operations in different industries. Note, however, that an enterprise may operate in a dominant industry on a worldwide basis, in which case it would have to report operations in different geographic areas, but not in different industries.

Exhibit 15–5 illustrates the basic disclosure requirements for domestic and foreign operations of Cardinal Corporation, the fictitious U.S. company whose financial data were previously disclosed by industry segment. Exhibit 15–5 shows Cardinal's revenue, operating profit, and assets disaggregated by geographic area and reconciliation with related consolidated amounts for a two-year period. The basis for transfer pricing (market) is also disclosed.

A note on export sales is included in the schedule of business segment information by geographic area (Exhibit 15–5). Another note in Exhibit 15–5 provides information regarding the geographic area and industry in which equity investees and unconsolidated subsidiaries operate, as required by *FASB Statement No. 14.*

The Allied-Signal Inc., 1990 Annual Report summarized the company's operations in different geographic areas for the years 1990, 1989, and 1988 in a schedule shown in Exhibit 15–6.

CARDINAL CORPORATION
NOTE TO CONSOLIDATED STATEMENTS

19X2	United States	Europe	Other Foreign	Eliminations	Consolidated
Sales					
Sales to unaffiliated customers*	$350,000	$275,000	$ 75,000		$ 700,000
Interarea sales at market	60,000	20,000	30,000	$(110,000)	
Total sales	$410,000	$295,000	$105,000	$(110,000)	$ 700,000
Income					
Operating income	$ 65,000	$ 63,000	$ 12,000		$ 140,000
Income from equity investments					20,000
Corporate expenses					(12,000)
Interest expense					(38,000)
Income before income taxes					$ 110,000
Assets				*Corporate†*	
Identifiable assets	$450,000	$325,000	$ 85,000	$ 190,000	$1,050,000
Capital expenditures	$ 60,000	$ 25,000	$ 15,000	$ 10,000	$ 110,000
Depreciation and amortization	$ 40,000	$ 25,000	$ 8,000	$ 2,000	$ 75,000

19X1	United States	Europe	Other Foreign	Eliminations	Consolidated
Sales					
Sales to unaffiliated customers	$330,000	$250,000	$ 80,000		$ 660,000
Interarea sales at market	40,000	30,000	10,000	$ (80,000)	
Total sales	$370,000	$280,000	$ 90,000	$ (80,000)	$ 660,000
Income					
Operating income	$ 70,000	$ 55,000	$ 10,000		$ 135,000
Income from equity investments					10,000
Corporate expenses					(10,000)
Interest expense					(40,000)
Income before income taxes					$ 95,000
Assets				*Corporate**	
Identifiable assets	$425,000	$320,000	$ 80,000	$ 175,000	$1,000,000
Capital expenditures	$ 50,000	$ 24,000	$ 5,000	$ 10,000	$ 89,000
Depreciation and amortization	$ 40,000	$ 30,000	$ 2,000	$ 3,000	$ 75,000

*United States operations include export sales of $70,000 in 19X2 and $63,000 in 19X1. Over 90 percent of these sales were to Germany.
†Corporate assets include investment in an unconsolidated German subsidiary of $126,000 in 19X2 and $119,000 in 19X1.

Exhibit 15–5   *Business Segment Information by Geographic Area*

NOTE 21. GEOGRAPHIC AREAS—FINANCIAL DATA (in millions)

		United States (1)	Canada	Europe	Other International	Adjustments and Eliminations	Total
Net sales (2)	1990	$9,395	$341	$2,002	$605	$ —	$12,343
	1989	9,339	382	1,663	558	—	11,942
	1988	9,169	452	1,738	550	—	11,909
Net income	1990	399	13	48	2	—	462
	1989	391	21	88	28	—	528
	1988	340	18	70	35	—	463
Assets	1990	8,658	212	1,800	469	(683)	10,456
	1989	8,509	204	1,423	439	(233)	10,342
	1988	8,214	236	1,292	455	(128)	10,069
Liabilities	1990	6,124	149	1,253	233	(683)	7,076
	1989	5,992	129	840	202	(233)	6,930
	1988	5,778	127	817	224	(145)	6,801

Sales between geographic areas approximate market and are not significant.
(1) Corporate Office income, expenses, assets and liabilities are included in the United States column.
(2) Included in United States net sales are export sales of $1,838, $1,692 and $1,464 million for each of the respective years.
Source: Allied-Signal Inc., 1990 Annual Report, Note 21, page 36.

Exhibit 15–6   *Multiyear Geographic Area Information*

DISCLOSURES FOR EXPORT SALES

If a firm's export sales from its home country to unaffiliated customers in foreign countries are 10 percent or more of total revenue from unaffiliated customers as reported in the enterprise's consolidated income statement, the amount of such export sales must be reported in the aggregate and by geographic areas. Separate disclosure is required for each geographic area that meets the 10 percent test. This disclosure requirement is independent of the previous requirements to report information about operations in different industries and foreign operations. The information presented must be in U.S. dollar amounts and may be disclosed in financial statements, in notes, or in separate schedules. Depending upon the circumstances, a financial statement note such as the following may be adequate to disclose export sales:

> Of the $920 thousand U.S. sales to unaffiliated customers, $180 thousand was export sales, principally to Germany ($80 thousand) and Japan ($65 thousand). thousand).

DISCLOSURES FOR MAJOR CUSTOMERS

Statement No. 14 requires disclosure of the amount of sales to any single customer (or group of customers under common control) that constitutes 10 percent or more of the enterprise's total revenue. Also, the segment or segments making such sales must be identified. If sales to the federal government or to any state, local, or foreign governmental unit are 10 percent or more of an enterprise's revenue, that fact and the amount of such sales must be disclosed. Allied-Signal (Exhibit 15–4) included the following footnote: "Sales to the U.S. government and its agencies, mainly from the Aerospace segment, were $1,373, $1,335 and $1,314 million for each of the respective years."

The requirements for reporting sales to major customers are independent of the requirements for reporting operations in different industries and geographic areas and for disclosing export sales. The disclosures for sales to major customers are often made in a statement note such as the following from Whirlpool Corporation's annual report for 1990, page 46:

Percentages of consolidated net sales to Sears, Roebuck and Co. were 20% in 1990, 23% in 1989, and 38% in 1988. The 1988 percentage was higher primarily because Whirlpool International was first included in 1989.

Note that Whirlpool identifies Sears as its largest customer, even though this identification is not required by *Statement No. 14*. Companies that file Form 10–K with the SEC must disclose the names of customers that account for 10 percent or more of total enterprise revenue.

CONSOLIDATION POLICY AND SEGMENT DISCLOSURES

FASB Statement No. 94, "Consolidation of All Majority-Owned Subsidiaries," requires consolidation of all subsidiaries such that their assets, liabilities, revenues, and expenses are aggregated into one set of financial statements. The FASB believes that this aggregation of data improves comparability and completeness in financial reporting. However, in order to prevent the loss of information that was already being disclosed under the provisions of *ABP Opinion No. 18* about the assets, liabilities, and results of operations of previously unconsolidated subsidiaries, *Statement No. 94* requires that these disclosures be continued for subsidiaries consolidated as a result of the *Statement*. Some companies include the required disclosures of their previously unconsolidated subsidiaries in the segment information. For example, before *Statement No. 94* was adopted, Whirlpool Corporation operated predominantly in one business segment classified as Major Home Appliances, and its finance subsidiary, Whirlpool Acceptance Corporation, was reported under the equity method as an unconsolidated subsidiary. Condensed consolidated financial statements for Whirlpool Acceptance Corporation were included in notes to the financial statements. After *Statement No. 94* was adopted, Whirlpool consolidated its finance subsidiary and reported operations in two business segments—major home appliances and financial services. Whirlpool now presents the condensed consolidated financial statements for Whirlpool Acceptance Corporation in the segment note. Similarly, Talley Industries reports the financial position and results of operations of its previously unconsolidated real estate subsidiary in the segment note.

INTERIM FINANCIAL REPORTING

Interim financial reports provide information about a firm's operations for less than a full year. They are commonly issued on a quarterly basis, and typically include cumulative year-to-date information as well as comparative information for corresponding periods of the prior year. Before 1973, there was little uniformity in the content of interim financial reports issued to shareholders. This situation and the increasing importance of quarterly reports to investors subsequently led to the issuance of *APB Opinion No. 28,* "Interim Financial Reporting," in May 1973.

The segment disclosure requirements of *Statement No. 14* are not applicable to interim reports unless the interim reports are complete sets of financial statements that purport to present the financial position, results of operations, and changes in financial position in conformity with generally accepted accounting principles.[13]

The guidelines for interim reporting are particularly applicable to publicly traded companies that are required to prepare quarterly reports pursuant to Security and Exchange Commission (SEC) and New York Stock Exchange (NYSE) requirements. Even so, the guidelines of *Opinion 28* are applicable whenever

---

[13]*FASB Statement No. 18*—An amendment of *FASB Statement No. 14,* "Financial Reporting for Segments of a Business Enterprise—Interim Financial Statements," November 1977.

publicly traded companies issue interim financial information to their securityholders (*APB Opinion No. 28,* paragraph 7).

Nature of Interim Reports

Conceptually, **interim financial reports** provide more timely, but less complete, information than do annual financial reports. Interim reports reflect a trade-off between timeliness and reliability because estimates must replace many of the extensive reviews of receivables, payables, inventory, and the related income effects that support the measurements presented in annual financial reports that have to meet audit requirements. The minimum disclosure requirements of *Opinion 28* do not constitute fair presentations of financial position and results of operations in conformity with generally accepted accounting principles. Therefore, interim financial statements are usually labeled *unaudited.*

Under *APB Opinion No. 28,* each interim period is considered an integral part of each annual period, rather than a basic accounting period unto itself. Generally, interim period results should be based on the accounting principles and practices used in the latest annual financial statements. Some modifications may be needed, however, to relate the interim period to annual period results in a meaningful manner. For example, interim statements may modify the procedures used in annual statements for product costs and other expenses.

Product Costs

Gross Profit Method   When firms use the gross profit method for pricing interim inventories, disclosure of the method and reconciliation with the annual inventory amounts are necessary.

LIFO Inventories   If LIFO inventories are liquidated at an interim date but are expected to be replaced by year end, cost of sales should include the cost of replacing the LIFO base, instead of giving effect to the interim liquidation. For example, a firm that experiences a liquidation of 100 units of a LIFO inventory during the first quarter of a year would charge cost of sales for the current cost of the 100 units rather than the historical LIFO cost if the 100 units are expected to be replaced by year-end. The amount of current cost in excess of the historical cost may be shown as a current liability on an interim balance sheet.

In case of a change to the LIFO inventory method, the cumulative effect of the change at the beginning of the period cannot be computed. If the change is made in the first period, that fact, but not the pro forma amounts, is disclosed. If the change is made in other than the first interim period, the change will be disclosed together with the financial information of prechange interim periods.[14]

Inventory Market Declines   Inventory market declines are not deferred beyond the interim period unless they are considered temporary such that no loss is expected for the fiscal year as a whole.

Standard Cost System   Planned variances under a standard cost system that are expected to be absorbed by year end should usually be deferred at the interim date.

Expenses Other than Product Costs

Annual Expenses in Interim Reports   Amounts charged to expense for annual purposes should be allocated to the interim periods that are expected to be benefited. The allocation procedures should be consistent with those used for annual reports. Major annual repairs are an example of this kind of allocation.

---

[14]*FASB Statement No. 3,* "Reporting Accounting Changes in Interim Financial Statements," paragraphs 9–13.

Expenses arising in an interim period are not deferred unless they would be deferred at year end. For example, property taxes accrued or deferred for annual purposes are also accrued or deferred for interim periods.

Advertising Costs   Advertising costs are not deferred beyond an interim period unless the benefits clearly apply to subsequent interim periods.

Income Taxes   Income taxes for interim reporting are divided into (1) those applicable to income from continuing operations before income taxes, excluding unusual or infrequently occurring items, and (2) those applicable to significant unusual or infrequently occurring items, discontinued items, and extraordinary items.[15]

Income tax expense for an interim period is based on an estimated effective annual tax rate that is applied to taxable income from continuing operations excluding unusual and infrequently occurring items. The year-to-date tax expense less the tax expense recognized in earlier interim periods is the tax expense for the current interim period. The tax effects of unusual and infrequently occurring items are calculated separately and added to the tax expense of the interim period in which these items are reported. Gains and losses on discontinued operations and extraordinary items are reported on a net-of-tax basis as in annual reports.

Computation of the Estimated Annual Effective Tax Rate

The following illustration shows how Small Corporation, a fictitious company, estimates its annual effective tax rate for the purpose of preparing quarterly financial reports. Small Corporation bases its estimate on the following tax rate schedule for corporations for the current year:

If Taxable Income Is:		The Tax Is:			
Over	But Not Over	Pay	+	Excess	Of the Amount Over
0	$ 50,000			15%	0
$ 50,000	75,000	$ 7,500	+	25	$ 50,000
75,000	100,000	13,750	+	34	75,000
100,000	335,000	22,250	+	39*	100,000
335,000	—			34	0

*A 5% additional tax rate applies to phase out the benefits of the graduated rates between $100,000 and $335,000 of taxable income.

Small estimates quarterly income for the calendar year 19X2 as follows:

Quarter	Estimated Income		Rate	Estimated Tax
1st	$ 20,000	×	15%	$ 3,000
2nd	30,000	×	15	4,500
3rd	25,000	×	25	6,250
4th	25,000	×	34	8,500
Totals	$100,000			$22,250

The estimated quarterly income and income tax estimates assume that Small anticipates no accounting changes, discontinued operations, or extraordinary

[15]See *FASB Interpretation No. 18*, "An Interpretation of *APB Opinion No. 28*," (March 1977).

items for the year. Thus, the estimated annual effective tax rate is 22.25%, equal to the estimated tax divided by the estimated income ($22,250 ÷ $100,000 = 22.25%). Income tax for the first quarter is $20,000 × 22.25%, or $4,450. This computation reflects the *integral theory that each interim period is an essential part of an annual period, and not the discrete theory* that each interim period is a basic, independent accounting period. The integral theory is required by *APB Opinion No. 28.* If no changes in the estimates occur during the year, the income by quarter would be calculated as follows:

	First Quarter	Second Quarter	Third Quarter	Fourth Quarter	Fiscal
Income year to date	$20,000	$50,000	$75,000	$100,000	$100,000
Quarterly period income	20,000	30,000	25,000	25,000	100,000
Tax expense (22.25%)	(4,450)	(6,675)	(5,563)	(5,563)	(22,250)
Net income	$15,550	$23,325	$19,438	$ 19,438	$ 77,750

Note that the estimated annual effective tax rate is applied to the year-to-date income and prior quarter income taxes are deducted to get the current quarterly income tax expense. For example, the third quarter tax expense is calculated as follows: $75,000 × 22.25% − ($4,450 + $6,675) = $5,563. This procedure provides for revision of the estimated annual effective tax rate to reflect changes in estimated income levels during the year. For example, if the $100,000 estimated income for the year had included $5,000 dividend income subject to an 80 percent dividend-received deduction, the annual effective tax rate would have been 20.89%. The calculation entails a $1,360 deduction for the tax savings on the dividends-received deduction: ($5,000 × 80% × 34% tax rate) = $1,360. The estimated annual effective tax rate would have been calculated: ($22,250 − $1,360) ÷ $100,000 = 20.89%.

GUIDELINES FOR PREPARING INTERIM STATEMENTS

The Accounting Principles Board summarized the financial information to be disclosed in interim reports in *APB Opinion No. 28* guidelines. At a minimum, publicly traded companies should report:

1 **a** Sales or gross revenues
   b Provision for income taxes
   c Extraordinary items net of income taxes
   d Cumulative effect type changes in accounting principles
   e Net income
2 Primary and fully diluted earnings per share
3 Seasonal revenue, costs, or expenses
4 Significant changes in estimates of income tax expense
5 Disposal of a segment of a business, extraordinary items and unusual or infrequently occurring items
6 Contingent items
7 Changes in accounting principles and estimates
8 Significant changes in financial position

In addition, when interim data are reported on a regular basis, information should also be reported for the current year to date, or the last twelve months to date with comparable information for the preceding year (*APB Opinion No. 18,* paragraph 30). If fourth quarter reports are not issued, material disposals of business segments, extraordinary items, unusual and infrequently occurring items, and accounting changes for the quarter should be disclosed in notes to the annual report.[16]

---

[16]*FASB Statement No. 3,* paragraph 14.

SAMPLE CORPORATION, INC., AND SUBSIDIARIES
CONDENSED CONSOLIDATED STATEMENTS OF INCOME
(UNAUDITED)
DATA ARE IN THOUSANDS EXCEPT PER SHARE AMOUNTS.

	Three Months Ended September 30,		Nine Months Ended September 30,	
	1992	*1991*	*1992*	*1991*
Revenues	$2,469	$2,165	$6,725	$6,025
Cost and Expenses				
Cost of sales	1,624	1,409	4,412	3,936
Other operating expenses	691	613	1,969	1,763
Interest expense	26	29	76	77
	2,341	2,051	6,457	5,776
Income from continuing operations before income taxes	128	114	268	249
Income taxes	48	44	100	95
Income from continuing operations	80	70	168	154
Loss on discontinued operations*				34
Net income	$ 80	$ 70	$ 168	$ 120
Earnings per Common Share				
Continuing operations	$ 1.24	$ 1.08	$ 2.60	$ 2.38
Discontinued operations				(0.53)
Net earnings per common share	$ 1.24	$ 1.08	$ 2.60	$ 1.85
Cash Dividends per Common Share	$ 0.52	$ 0.50	$ 1.56	$ 1.50

*Earnings were negatively affected in the first six months of 1991 by discontinued furniture operations.

Exhibit 15–7   *Quarterly Report*

Exhibit 15–7 shows a quarterly report for Sample Corporation and Subsidiaries for the three months ended September 30, 1992. In addition to the 1992 quarterly data, the Sample report gives the quarterly data for the previous year and year-to-date information for 1991 and 1992.

SEC INTERIM FINANCIAL DISCLOSURES

The SEC requires that quarterly reports be prepared for the company's stockholders and for filing with the SEC. These reports are to be prepared in accordance with generally accepted accounting principles and are filed on Form 10-Q within 45 days from the end of a quarter. Fourth quarter reports are not required, but SEC Rule 14a-3 requires inclusion of selected quarterly data in the annual report to shareholders. Since the quarterly reports are not audited, the CPA's report states that a *review* rather than an audit has been made.

A company's Form 10-Q report to the SEC includes information in excess of the minimum reporting requirements under *APB Opinion No. 28,* as amended by *FASB Statement No. 3* and *FASB Interpretation No. 18.* In fact, financial information requirements for quarterly reporting are similar to the disclosures required in annual reports to the SEC. For example, Part I of Form 10-Q contains the following summary of contents:

Part 1—Financial Information
Item 1—Consolidated Balance Sheet
Consolidated Statement of Income

RALSTON PURINA COMPANY AND SUBSIDIARIES
STATEMENT OF EARNINGS
(IN MILIONS EXCEPT PER SHARE DATA—UNAUDITED)

	Three Months Ended March 31,		Six Months Ended March 31,	
	1990	*1989*	*1990*	*1989*
Net Sales	**$1,714.5**	$1,589.3	**$3,595.7**	$3,270.4
Cost and Expenses				
Cost of products sold	**932.9**	871.5	**1,952.1**	1,764.2
Selling, general and administrative	**367.4**	331.3	**715.2**	640.8
Advertising and promotion	**210.4**	182.0	**456.8**	387.0
Interest expense	**52.3**	55.6	**103.0**	114.1
	1,563.0	1,440.4	**3,227.1**	2.906.1
Earnings from Continuing Operations Before Income Taxes	**151.5**	148.9	**368.6**	364.3
Income Taxes	**59.9**	58.1	**146.7**	142.1
Earnings from Continuing Operations	**91.6**	90.8	**221.9**	222.2
Discontinued Seafood Operations				71.3
Net Earnings	**91.6**	90.8	**221.9**	293.5
Preferred Stock Dividend, Net of Taxes	**5.1**	3.4	**10.1**	3.4
Earnings Available to Common Shareholders	$ **86.5**	$ 87.4	$ **211.8**	$ 290.1
Earnings per Common Share— Primary:				
Continuing Operations	$ **1.47**	$ 1.39	$ **3.52**	$ 3.35
Discontinued Operations				1.09
Net Earnings	$ **1.47**	$ 1.39	$ **3.52**	$ 4.44
Fully Diluted:				
Continuing Operations	$ **1.39**	$ 1.33	$ **3.30**	$ 3.26
Discontinued Operations				1.06
Net Earnings	$ **1.39**	$ 1.33	$ **3.30**	$ 4.32
Cash Dividends Declared per Common Share	$ **.925**	$ .825	$ **.925**	$ .825

Exhibit 15–8 *Ralston Purina Quarterly Report*

Consolidated Statement of Cash Flows
Notes to Consolidated Financial Statements
Item 2—Management's Discussion of Financial Condition and Results of Operations

Comparative consolidated balance sheets are presented as of the end of the current quarter, and at the prior year end. The comparative consolidated income statements are presented for the current quarter and the same quarter of the prior year, as well as the current year to date and the prior year to date.

RALSTON PURINA COMPANY AND SUBSIDIARIES
BALANCE SHEET
(IN MILLIONS—UNAUDITED)

	March 31, 1990	Sept. 30, 1989
Assets		
Current Assets		
Cash	$ 37.2	$ 28.6
Marketable securities	202.7	352.0
Receivables, net	601.9	636.3
Inventories	702.8	677.8
Other current assets	96.3	126.3
Total Current Assets	1,640.9	1,821.0
Investments and Other Assets	788.7	795.1
Property at Cost	2,891.0	2,718.3
Accumulated depreciation	1,055.6	952.7
	1,835.4	1,765.6
Total	$4,265.0	$4,381.7
Liabilities and Shareholders Equity		
Current Liabilities		
Current maturities of long-term debt	$ 54.0	$ 225.6
Notes payable	275.9	142.0
Accounts payable	321.3	382.7
Other current liabilities	562.7	565.5
Total Current Liabilities	1,213.9	1,315.8
Long-Term Debt	1,943.0	1,790.7
Deferred Income Taxes	183.3	172.9
Other Liabilities	249.6	242.0
Redeemable Preferred Stock	500.0	500.0
Unearned ESOP Compensation	(453.9)	(471.4)
Shareholders Equity		
Common stock	47.8	47.8
Capital in excess of par value	261.7	261.8
Retained earnings	3,077.8	2,919.7
Cumulative translation adjustment	(30.8)	(33.3)
Common stock in treasury, at cost	(2,713.9)	(2,350.1)
Unearned portion of restricted stock	(13.5)	(14.2)
Total Shareholders Equity	629.1	831.7
Total	$4,265.0	$4,381.7

Exhibit 15–8   *Ralston Purina Quarterly Report (continued)*

Comparative consolidated statements of cash flows are presented for the current year to date and the prior year to date.

The information required in Form 10-Q in excess of that required by *APB Opinion No. 28* is available from the company to its shareholders upon request. Many companies, however, include essentially all the information from Form 10-Q in their regular quarterly reports. Exhibit 15–8 illustrates this extended disclosure for the Ralston Purina Company. In addition to the statements in the

RALSTON PURINA COMPANY AND SUBSIDIARIES
STATEMENT OF CASH FLOWS
(IN MILLIONS—UNAUDITED)

	Six Months Ended March 31,	
	1990	*1989*
Cash Flow from Operations		
Earnings from continuing operations	**$221.9**	$222.2
Non-cash items included in income	**122.9**	120.0
Changes in operating assets and liabilities used in continuing operations	**(21.4)**	(151.6)
Other, net	**9.9**	13.8
Net cash flow from continuing operations	**333.3**	204.4
Discontinued operations		14.5
Net cash flow from operations	**333.3**	218.9
Cash Flow from Investing Activities		
Acquisition of businesses	**(55.0)**	(124.0)
Property additions, net	**(120.5)**	(86.9)
Proceeds from the sale of discontinued operations		260.0
Other, net	**(11.7)**	(52.5)
Net cash used by investing activities	**(187.2)**	(3.4)
Cash Flow from Financing Activities		
Net cash flow provided (used) by debt	**141.9**	(73.1)
Cash proceeds from the sale of preferred stock		500.0
Treasury stock purchases	**(362.0)**	(528.5)
Dividends paid	**(68.9)**	(51.2)
Net cash used by financing activities	**(289.0)**	(152.8)
Effect of Exchange Rate Changes on Cash	**2.2**	(5.1)
Net (Decrease) Increase in Cash and Cash Equivalents	**(140.7)**	57.6
Cash and Cash Equivalents, Beginning of Year	**380.6**	360.9
Cash and Cash Equivalents, End of Period	**$239.9**	$418.5

Exhibit 15–8 *Ralston Purina Quarterly Report (continued)*

quarterly report that are reprinted in the exhibit, Ralston includes a review of the financial information, a letter to shareholders from the company's chairman, and additional corporate information.

SUMMARY

Concern about segment disclosures increased throughout the 1960s—approximately the same period as the merger and acquisition boom years in which huge conglomerates were formed. In 1967 the Accounting Principles Board recommended voluntary disclosures for diversified enterprises, and in 1969 the SEC adopted line-of-business disclosure requirements. It was not until 1977, however, that public firms issuing complete sets of financial statements in accordance with GAAP became subject to segment reporting requirements. That was the year in which *FASB Statement No. 14* became effective.

Under *Statement No. 14,* reporting responsibilities are determined by a series of tests. Firms other than nonpublic enterprises must disclose information on their operations in different industries unless more than 90 percent of their revenue, operating profit, and identifiable assets relate to a single dominant industry segment. Disclosures of operations in different geographic areas are required for all enterprises whose foreign operations account for 10 percent or more of the firm's identifiable assets or revenue from unaffiliated customers. The amount of a firm's export sales must be disclosed if such sales account for 10 percent or more of the firm's total revenue from unaffiliated customers. Also, business enterprises must disclose the amount of revenue from major customers when such revenue is equal to 10 percent or more of the total revenue of the enteprise. These reporting requirements are independent of each other, so a firm could be required to report information in one or more areas. Many firms have reporting responsibilities in all four areas.

Security analysts and other users of segment disclosures believe that segment information is important for effective analysis of financial statements because the operations in different industries and geographic areas vary with respect to risk, profitability, opportunities for expansion, and capital requirements.

Disclosure requirements for interim financial reports are found in *APB Opinion No. 28,* as amended by *FASB Statement No. 3,* and *FASB Interpretation No. 18.* Interim financial reports provide timely information. However, much of the information is based on estimates, and the reports are unaudited.

Each interim period is considered an integral part of the annual period. Interim period information should be based on the accounting principles used in the last annual report; however, some modifications at the interim reporting date may be necessary so that the interim period results complement the annual results of operations.

The Securities and Exchange Commission requires additional disclosures in interim reports filed on Form 10-Q. Information above the minimum requirements of *APB Opinion No. 28* that is issued to shareholders in quarterly reports varies from company to company.

SELECTED READINGS

Accounting Principles Board Opinion No. 28. "Interim Financial Reporting." New York: American Institute of Certified Public Accountants, 1973.

BACKER, MORTON, and WALTER MCFARLAND. *External Reporting for Segments of a Business.* New York: National Association of Accountants, 1968.

FASB Interpretation No. 18. "An Interpretation of *APB Opinion No. 28.*" Stamford, CT: Financial Accounting Standards Board, 1977.

MAUTZ, ROBERT K. *Financial Reporting by Diversified Companies.* New York: Financial Executives Research Foundation, 1968.

Statement of Financial Accounting Standards No. 3. "Reporting Accounting Changes in Interim Financial Statements." Stamford, CT: Financial Accounting Standards Board, 1974.

Statement of Financial Accounting Standards No. 14. "Financial Reporting for Segments of a Business Enterprise." Stamford, CT: Financial Accounting Standards Board, 1976.

STEEDLE, LAMONT F. "Disclosure of Segment Information—SFAS #14." *The CPA Journal* (October 1983), pp. 34–47.

ASSIGNMENT MATERIAL

QUESTIONS

1 Under the provisions of *FASB Statement No. 14,* what disclosures are made for an enterprise's equity investees?

2 What is an industry segment?

3 What is a reportable segment according to *FASB Statement No. 14*? What criteria are used in determining what industry segments are also reportable segments?

4 How are the industry segments that are not reportable segments handled in the required disclosures of *FASB Statement No. 14*?

5 Are foreign operations always aggregated and treated as a single industry segment? Explain.

6 Revenue information for Mahoney Corporation is as follows:

Consolidated revenue (from the income statement)	$400,000
Intersegment sales and transfers	80,000
Combined revenues of all industry segments	$480,000

Does the 10 percent revenue test for a reportable segment apply to 10 percent of the $400,000 or 10 percent of the $480,000?

7 Describe the 10 percent operating profit test for determining reportable segments.

8 Describe the 10 percent asset test for determining reportable segments.

9 Assume an enterprise has ten industry segments. Five industry segments qualify as reportable segments by passing one of the 10 percent tests; however, their combined revenues from sales to unaffiliated customers total only 70 percent of the combined revenues from all industry segments. Should the remaining five industry segments be aggregated and shown as an "other industries" category? Explain.

10 What disclosures are required for a "dominant industry segment" as defined in *FASB Statement No. 14*?

11 What disclosures are required for the reportable industry segments, and all remaining industry segments in the aggregate?

12 When is an enterprise required to include information in its financial statements about its foreign and domestic operations?

13 What are foreign geographic areas and how are they determined?

14 What disclosures are required for export sales?

15 Must a major customer be identified by name?

16 Do the requirements of *FASB Statement No. 14* apply to financial statements for interim periods?

17 Explain how a company estimates its annual effective tax rate for interim reporting purposes.

18 What is the difference between the integral theory and the discrete theory with respect to interim financial reporting?

19 Describe the minimum financial information to be disclosed in interim reports under the provisions of *APB Opinion No. 28*.

EXERCISES

E 15-1 **[AICPA adapted]**

1 In financial reporting for segments of a business enterprise, the revenue of a segment should include:
   a Intersegment billings for the cost of shared facilities
   b Intersegment sales of services similar to those sold to unaffiliated customers
   c Equity in income from unconsolidated subsidiaries
   d Extraordinary items

2 Selected data for a segment of a business enterprise are to be separately reported in accordance with *FASB Statement No. 14* when the revenues of the segment exceed 10 percent of the:
   a Combined net income of all segments reporting profits
   b Total revenues obtained in transactions with outsiders
   c Total revenues of all the enterprise's industry segments
   d Total combined revenues of all segments reporting profits

3 In financial reporting for segments of a business enterprise, the operating profit or loss of a segment should include:

	Expenses Related to Revenue from Intersegment Sales	Portion of General Corporate Expenses
a	Yes	Yes
b	Yes	No
c	No	No
d	No	Yes

4 In financial reporting for segments of a business enterprise, the operating profit or loss of a manufacturing segment should include:

	Interest Expense	Income Taxes
a	Yes	Yes
b	Yes	No
c	No	Yes
d	No	No

5 In financial reporting for segments of a business enterprise, which of the following should be taken into account in computing the amount of an industry segment's identifiable assets?

	Accumulated Depreciation	Allowance for Doubtful Accounts
a	No	No
b	No	Yes
c	Yes	Yes
d	Yes	No

6 In financial reporting of segment data, which of the following would be used to determine a segment's operating income?
a Gain or loss on discontinued operations
b General corporate expense
c Sales to other segments
d Income tax expense

E 15–2 Shoney, Inc. has operations in five industries. Each of the industry segments has an operating profit in 19X8. Information from the consolidated income statement for the year 19X8 follows. There were no intersegment sales or transfers.

Sales		$1,200,000
Equity in income of investees		100,000
		1,300,000
Cost of sales	$800,000	
General, selling, and administrative expenses including corporate expenses of $40,000	200,000	
Depreciation expense	80,000	
Interest	10,000	
Income taxes	100,000	
Minority interest income	10,000	1,200,000
Income before extraordinary item		100,000
Extraordinary loss net of $2,500 tax effect		2,500
Net income		$ 97,500

Required: Determine the combined operating profit of the industry segments of Shoney, Inc., according to the concept developed in *FASB Statment No. 14.*

E 15–3 The revenues, operating profits, and assets of the industry segments of Superior Corporation are presented as follows:

	Sales to Nonaffiliates	Intersegment Sales	Total Sales	Operating Profit (Loss)	Identifiable Assets
Food Service Industry	$300,000,000	$40,000,000	$340,000,000	$ 40,000,000	$200,000,000
Copper Mine	80,000,000	—	80,000,000	(10,000,000)	60,000,000
Information Systems	20,000,000	15,000,000	35,000,000	5,000,000	40,000,000
Chemical Industry	130,000,000	20,000,000	150,000,000	30,500,000	217,000,000
Agricultural Products	48,000,000	—	48,000,000	(15,500,000)	50,000,000
Pharmaceutical Products	20,000,000	—	20,000,000	8,000,000	18,000,000
Foreign Operations	15,000,000	—	15,000 000	5,000,000	20,000,000
Corporate Assets*					33,000,000
	$613,000,000	$75,000,000	$688,000,000	$ 63,000,000	$638,000,000

* Corporate assets include equity investees of $10,000,000 and general assets of $23,000,000.

Required: Determine the reportable segments of Superior Corporation.

E 15–4 The sales of the industry segments of Worldwide Corporation for 19X6 are as follows:

	Unaffiliated Sales	Interarea Sales	Total
United States	$50,000,000	$15,000,000	$ 65,000,000
Canada	18,000,000	8,000,000	26,000,000
Europe	10,000,000	1,000,000	11,000,000
Latin America	7,000,000	3,000,000	10,000,000
Japan	3,000,000	—	3,000,000
Korea	1,000,000	—	1,000,000
	$89,000,000	$27,000,000	$116,000,000

The $89,000,000 sales to unaffiliated customers is the amount of revenue reported in Worldwide's consolidated income statement.

Required: Illustrate the disclosure of Worldwide's domestic and foreign revenue in a form acceptable for external reporting, including reconciliation with consolidated revenue.

E 15–5 **[AICPA adapted]**

1 Correy Corp. and its divisions are engaged solely in manufacturing operations. The following data (consistent with prior years' data) pertain to the industries in which operations were conducted for the year ended December 31, 19X7:

Industry	Total Revenue	Operating Profit	Identifiable Assets at December 31, 19X7
A	$10,000,000	$1,750,000	$20,000,000
B	8,000,000	1,400,000	17,500,000
C	6,000,000	1,200,000	12,500,000
D	3,000,000	550,000	7,500,000
E	4,250,000	675,000	7,000,000
F	1,500,000	225,000	3,000,000
	$32,750,000	$5,800,000	$67,500,000

In its segment information for 19X7, how many reportable segments does Correy have?
a Three
b Four
c Five
d Six

2 Kee Co. has five manufacturing divisions, each of which has been determined to be a reportable segment. Common costs are appropriately allocated on the basis of each division's sales in relation to Kee's aggregate sales. Kee's Sigma Division comprised 40 percent of Kee's total sales in 19X2. For the year ended December 31, 19X2, Sigma had sales of $1,000,000 and traceable costs of $600,000. In 19X2 Kee incurred operating expenses of $100,000 that were not directly traceable to any of the five divisions. In addition, Kee incurred interest expense of $80,000 in 19X2. In reporting supplementary segment information, how much should be shown as Sigma's operating income in 19X2?

a $300,000   b $328,000
c $360,000   d $400,000

3 Kaycee Corporation's revenues for the year ended December 31, 19X1 were as follows:

Consolidated revenue per income statement	$1,200,000
Intersegment sales	180,000
Intersegment transfers	60,000
Combined revenues of all segments	$1,440,000

Kaycee has a reportable segment if that segment's revenues exceed:

a $6,000   b $24,000
c $120,000   d $144,000

4 The following information pertains to Aria Corp. and its divisions for the year ended December 31, 19X8:

Sales to unaffiliated customers	$2,000,000
Intersegment sales of products similar to those sold to unaffiliated customers	600,000
Interest earned on loans to other industry segments	40,000

Aria and all of its divisions are engaged solely in manufacturing operations. Aria has a reportable segment if that segment's revenue exceeds:

a $264,000   b $260,000
c $204,000   d $200,000

5 The following information pertains to revenue earned by Timm Company's industry segments for the year ended December 31, 19X2:

Segment	Sales to Unaffiliated Customers	Intersegment Sales	Total Revenues
Alo	$ 5,000	$ 3,000	$ 8,000
Bix	8,000	4,000	12,000
Cee	4,000	—	4,000
Dil	43,000	16,000	59,000
Combined	60,000	23,000	83,000
Elimination	—	(23,000)	(23,000)
Consolidated	$60,000	—	$60,000

In conformity with the revenue test, Timm's reportable segments were:

a Only Dil
b Only Bix and Dil
c Only Alo, Bix, and Dil
d Alo, Bix, Cee, and Dil

E 15–6 The following data relate to Dominion Corporation for 19X6 and were accumulated for use in preparing industry segment information.

	Food	Packing	Other	Corporate	Consolidated
Sales	$600,000	$400,000	$100,000		$1,100,000
Cost of sales	300,000	350,000	50,000		(700,000)
Operating expenses	120,000	60,000	20,000	$10,000	(210,000)
Interest expense					(30,000)
Income taxes					(64,000)
Net income					$ 96,000
Intercompany sales*			100,000		
Intercompany purchases*	100,000				

* Amounts were eliminated from the consolidated sales and cost of sales data as given.

Required: Prepare schedules for the required revenue and operating profit disclosures of Dominion Corporation for 19X6 together with reconciliations to consolidated statement amounts.

E 15-7 A summary of the domestic and foreign operations of the Johnson-Miller Corporation for the year ended December 31, 19X2 follows:

	United States	Canada	Germany	Japan	Mexico	Other Foreign	Consolidated
Sales to unaffiliated customers	$ 70,000	$12,000	$ 6,000	$ 7,000	$3,000	$2,000	$100,000
Interarea transfers	20,000			6,000			
Total revenue	$ 90,000	$12,000	$ 6,000	$13,000	$3,000	$2,000	$100,000
Operating profit	$ 16,000	$ 2,000	$ 3,000	$ 2,000	$1,000	$1,000	$ 25,000
Identifiable assets	$100,000	$15,000	$17,000	$18,000	$4,000	$3,000	$150,000
Total assets	$149,000	$15,000	$19,000	$18,000	$4,000	$3,000	$200,000

1 In deciding if Johnson-Miller is required to disclose information on its domestic and foreign operations, which of the following computations are appropriate?
 a $30,000 divided by $100,000 ≥ 10 percent
 b $36,000 divided by $100,000 ≥ 10 percent
 c $36,000 divided by $126,000 ≥ 10 percent
 d $30,000 divided by $126,000 ≥ 10 percent
2 For which of the following geographic areas would separate disclosures be required if only the 10 percent revenue test is considered?
 a United States, Canada, and Japan
 b United States and Canada
 c United States, Canada, and Germany
 d United States, Canada, Germany, and Japan
3 For which of the following geographic areas would separate disclosures be required if only the 10 percent asset test is considered?
 a United States
 b United States and Canada
 c United States, Canada, and Germany
 d United States, Canada, Germany, and Japan
4 For which of the following geographic areas would separate disclosures be required if *all* relevant tests are considered?
 a United States, Canada, Germany, and Japan
 b United States, Canada, and Germany
 c United States, Canada, and Japan
 d United States and Canada

E 15-8 The information presented here is for McCauley Corporation at and for the year ended December 31, 19X9. McCauley's industry segments are cost centers currently used for internal planning and control purposes. Amounts shown in the "total consolidated" column are amounts prepared under generally accepted accounting principles for external reporting.

	Drug Industry	Food Industry	Packing Industry	Textile Industry	Foreign Operations	All Other Industries	Corporate	Total Consolidated
Income Statement Sales to unaffiliated cusotmers	$350,000	$600,000	$500,000	$300,000	$250,000	$400,000		$2,400,000
Income from equity investees								100,000
Cost of sales to unaffiliated customers	200,000*	400,000*	350,000*	175,000*	125,000*	250,000*		1,500,000*
Operating expenses	100,000*	100,000*	75,000*	150,000*	75,000*	75,000*	$ 25,000*	600,000*
Interest expense								20,000*
Income taxes								150,000*
Minority interest income								30,000*
Income (loss)	$ 50,000	$100,000	$ 75,000	$(25,000)	$ 50,000	$ 75,000	$ (25,000)	$ 200,000
Assets Current assets	$100,000	$200,000	$100,000	$ 75,000	$100,000	$225,000	$ 25,000	$ 825,000
Plant assets—net	250,000	150,000	400,000	250,000	100,000	175,000	25,000	1,350,000
Advances		50,000		25,000			50,000	—
Equity investments							1,000,000	1,000,000
Total assets	$350,000	$400,000	$500,000	$350,000	$200,000	$400,000	$1,100,000	$3,175,000
Intersegment transfers Sales†	$ 20,000	$ 40,000	$ 60,000	$ 30,000	$ 50,000			
Purchases†		$100,000	$ 25,000		$ 75,000			

* Deduct.
† Amounts have been eliminated from the income data given.

1 McCauley must report information about its foreign and domestic operations if revenue generated by its foreign operations from sales to unaffiliated customers is equal to or greater than:
   a $200,000   **b** $220,000
   c $240,000   **d** $260,000
2 McCauley must report information about its foreign and domestic operations if iden-tifiable assets of its foreign operations are equal to or greater than:
   a $317,500   **b** $207,500
   c $167,500   **d** $147,500
3 McCauley must report the amount of its export sales in the aggregate and by geographic area if its sales to unaffiliated customers outside of the United States are equal to or greater than:
   a $200,000   **b** $240,000
   c $250,000   **d** $260,000
4 McCauley must report the fact and amount of revenue and the segments making such sales if sales to any single customer are equal to or greater than:
   a $200,000   **b** $240,000
   c $260,000   **d** $280,000

E 15–9   **[AICPA adapted]**

1 Farr Corp. had the following transactions during the quarter ended March 31, 19X2:
     Loss on early extinguishment of debt $ 70,000
     Payment of fire insurance premium for calendar year 19X2   100,000

What amount should be included in Farr's income statement for the quarter ended March 31, 19X2?

	Extraordinary loss	Insurance expense
a	$70,000	$100,000
b	$70,000	$ 25,000
c	$17,500	$ 25,000
d	$0	$100,000

2 An inventory loss from a permanent market decline of $360,000 occurred in May 19X1. Cox Co. appropriately recorded this loss in May 19X1 after its March 31, 19X1 quarterly report was issued. What amount of inventory loss should be reported in Cox's quarterly income statement for the three months ended June 30, 19X1?

a $0
b $90,000
c $180,000
d $360,000

3 On July 1, 19X5, Dolan Corp. incurred an extraordinary loss of $300,000, net of income tax saving. Dolan's operating income for the full year ending December 31, 19X5 is expected to be $500,000. In Dolan's income statement for the quarter ended September 30, 19X5, how much of this extraordinary loss should be disclosed?

a $300,000
b $150,000
c $75,000
d $0

4 In January 19X3, Pine Company paid property taxes of $80,000 covering the calendar year 19X3. Also in January 19X3 Pine estimated that its year-end bonuses to executives would amount to $320,000 for 19X3. What is the total amount of expense relating to these two items that should be reflected in Pine's quarterly income statement for the three months ended June 30, 19X3?

a $100,000
b $80,000
c $20,000
d $0

E 15-10 Trapper Manufacturing Co. records sales of $1,000,000 and cost of sales of $550,000 during the first quarter of 19X1. Trapper uses the LIFO inventory method, and its inventories are computed as follows:

Beginning LIFO inventory at January 1	10,000 units at $5	$50,000
Ending LIFO inventory at March 31	6,000 units at $5	$30,000

Before year-end, Trapper expects to replace the 4,000 units liquidated in the first quarter. The current cost of the inventory units is $8 each.

Required: At what amount will Trapper report cost of sales in its first quarter interim report?

PROBLEMS

P 15-1 The following data for 19X8 relate to Hawkeye Industries, a worldwide conglomerate:

Segments	Sales to Unaffiliated Customers	Intersegment Sales	Operating Profit (Loss)	Identifiable Assets
Food	$300,000	$ 50,000	$45,000	$310,000
Chemical	110,000	40,000	23,000	150,000
Textiles	65,000	5,000	(8,000)	60,000
Furniture	48,000	—	9,000	40,000
Beverage	62,000	10,000	18,000	60,000
Oil	15,000	—	(2,000)	25,000
Segment	600,000	105,000	85,000	645,000
Corporate	—	—	(7,000)	15,000
Consolidated	$600,000	0	$78,000	$660,000

Required: Answer the following questions relating to Hawkeye's required segment disclosures and show computations.

1 Which segments are reportable segments under (a) the revenue test, (b) the operating profit test, and (c) the asset test?

2 Do additional reportable segments have to be identified?

3 Will Hawkeye have to report on domestic and foreign operations:

   a If foreign sales are $58,000 to unaffiliated customers and $14,000 interarea sales?

   b If identifiable assets for foreign operations are $65,000?

   c If operating profit from foreign operations is $8,000?

4 If Hawkeye's exports from the United States to unaffiliated customers are $65,000, will it have to disclose export sales?

P 15-2 United Steel Company has operations in three industry segments—steel, iron ore, and coal. Summary information for these segments is as follows:

	Steel	Iron Ore	Coal
Information for Segments			
Sales to unaffiliated customers	$11,600,000	$ 900,000	$200,000
Sales to affilitated customers	150,000	400,000	100,000
Operating profit	600,000	(60,000)	20,000
Identifiable assets	11,800,000	1,600,000	400,000
Depreciation and depletion	1,300,000	150,000	100,000
Capital expenditures	1,500,000	100,000	200,000

Other Information for All Operations of United Steel Company

Total operating profit		$ 560,000
Less: General corporate expenses	$ 10,000	
Interest expense	40,000	
Minority interest income	5,000	
Income taxes	250,000	305,000
Net income		$ 255,000

Required

1 Which of the industry segments are reportable segments? (Show computations.)

2 Is the steel segment a dominant industry segment? (Show computations.)

3 What disclosures are required for a company that has one dominant industry segment?

P 15-3 Daton-Paulo Corporation's home country is the United States, but it also has opera-tions in Canada, Mexico, Brazil, and South Africa. Information relevant to Daton-Paulo's domestic and foreign disclosure requirement for the year ended December 31, 19X2 is presented in summary form as follows:

	United States	Canada	Mexico	Brazil	South Africa	Consolidated
Sales to unaffiliated customers	$120,000	$13,000	$20,000	$22,000	$15,000	$190,000
Interarea transfers	29,000	11,000			10,000	
Total revenue	$149,000	$24,000	$20,000	$22,000	$25,000	$190,000
Operating profit	$ 24,000	$ 6,000	$ 8,000	$ 5,000	$ 7,000	$ 50,000
Identifiable assets	$150,000	$30,000	$19,000	$20,000	$31,000	$250,000
Total assets	$197,000	$35,000	$20,000	$20,000	$33,000	$305,000

Required

1 Prepare schedules to show which, if any, of Daton-Paulo's foreign geographic areas require separate disclosure under (a) the 10 percent revenue test and (b) the 10 percent asset test.

2 Which of Daton-Paulo's foreign geographic areas meet at least one of the tests for reporting on foreign and dometic operations?

3 Prepare a schedule for disclosure of Daton-Paulo's domestic and foreign operations from the information given above. (Assume that reconciliations to related
consolidated statement amounts have been made in the related segment reporting disclosure.)

P 15-4 Mid-America Corporation has five major industry segments and operates in both
domestic and foreign markets. Information about its revenue from industry segments
and foreign operations for 19X1 is as follows:

SALES TO UNAFFILIATED CUSTOMERS

	Domestic	Foreign	Total
Foods	$ 150,000	$ 30,000	$ 180,000
Soft drinks	650,000	250,000	900,000
Distilled spirits	500,000	50,000	550,000
Cosmetics	200,000	—	200,000
Packaging	110,000	—	110,000
Other (four minor segments)	240,000	—	240,000
	$1,850,000	$330,000	$2,180,000

SALES TO AFFILIATED CUSTOMERS

	Domestic	Foreign	Total
Foods	$ 30,000	$ —	$ 30,000
Soft drinks	160,000	—	160,000
Distilled spirits	—	20,000	20,000
Cosmetics	—	—	—
Packaging	10,000	—	10,000
Other (four minor segments)	—	—	—
	$200,000	$20,000	$220,000

A Japanese subsidiary of Mid-America operates exclusively in the soft drink market.
All other foreign operations are carried out through European subsidiaries, none of
which are included in the soft drink business.

Only the soft drinks and distilled spirits segments are reportable segments under
the asset and operating profit tests for segments.

Required

1 Determine which industry segments are reportable segments under the revenue
test for segment reporting. (Show all computations.)
2 Prepare a schedule suitable for disclosing Mid-America's revenue by segment for
19X1.
3 Prepare a schedule suitable for dislosing Mid-America's revenue by geographic
area for 19X1.

P 15-5 Selected information for the five segments of Random Choice Company for the year
ended December 31, 19X1 is as follows:

	Food	Tobacco	Lumber	Textiles	Furniture	General Corporate	Consolidated
Revenue Data							
Sales to unaffiliated customers	$12,000	$10,000	$7,000	$18,000	$7,000		$ 54,000
Sales to affiliated customers	5,000	7,000		8,000			
Income from equity investees				3,000		$ 6,000	9,000
Total revenue	$17,000	$17,000	$7,000	$29,000	$7,000	$ 6,000	$ 63,000

	Food	Tobacco	Lumber	Textiles	Furniture	General Corporate	Consolidated
Expense Data							
Cost of sales	$10,000	$ 9,000	$4,000	$16,000	$4,000		$ 23,000
Depreciation expense	1,000	2,000	2,500	3,000	500		9,000
Other operating expenses	2,000	2,000	1,000	2,000	1,000		8,000
Interest expense	2,000			2,000		$ 3,000	7,000
Income taxes	1,000	2,000	(250)	3,000	750	1,500	8,000
Net income	$ 1,000	$ 2,000	$ (250)	$ 3,000	$ 750	$ 1,500	$ 8,000
Asset Data							
Identifiable assets	$18,000	$19,000	$6,000	$22,000	$7,000		$ 72,000
Investment in affiliates				20,000		$40,000	60,000
General corporate assets						4,000	4,000
Intersegment advances	1,000	2,000					
Total assets	$19,000	$21,000	$6,000	$42,000	$7,000	$44,000	$136,000

The lumber segment has not been a reportable segment in prior years and is not expected to be a reportable segment in future years.

Required
1 Prepare schedules to show which of the segments are reportable segments under:
  a The 10 percent revenue test
  b The 10 percent operating profit test
  c The 10 percent asset test
2 Which of the segments meet at least one of the tests for reportable segments?
3 Must additional reportable segments be identified?
4 Prepare a schedule for appropriate disclosure of the above segmented data in the financial report of Random Choice Company for the year ended December 31, 19X1.

P 15–6   The consolidated income statement of Truetest Corporation for 19X2 apears as follows:

TRUETEST CORPORATION CONSOLIDATED INCOME STATEMENT FOR THE YEAR ENDED DECEMBER 31, 19X2

Sales	$360,000
Interest income	10,000
Income from equity investee	30,000
Total revenue	400,000
Cost of sales	$180,000
General expenses	40,000
Selling expenses	50,000
Interest expense	10,000
Minority interest income	15,000
Income taxes	45,000
Total expenses	340,000
Income before extraordinary loss	$ 60,000
Extraordinary loss (net of income taxes)	10,000
Consolidated net income	$ 50,000

Truetest's operations are conducted through three domestic industry segments with sales, expenses, and assets as follows:

	Chemical Segment	Food Segment	Drug Segment	Corporate
Sales (including intersegment sales	$160,000	$140,000	$120,000	
Cost of sales (including intersegment cost of sales)	80,000	70,000	60,000	
General expenses	15,000	10,000	10,000	$ 5,000
Selling expenses	20,000	15,000	15,000	
Interest expense (unaffiliated)	5,000		5,000	
Identifiable assets	200,000	180,000	150,000	200,000
Investment in equity investee				300,000

The $10,000 interest income is not related to any industry segment. Consolidated total assets are $1,000,000. The chemical and food segments had intersegment sales of $35,000 and $25,000, respectively.

Required. Prepare a schedule of required disclosures for Truetest's industry segments in a form acceptable for reporting purposes.

P 15–7 The information given here is for Colby Company at and for the year ended December 31, 19X9. Colby's industry segments are cost centers currently used for internal planning and control purposes. Amounts shown in the "Total Consolidated" column are amounts prepared under generally accepted accounting principles for external reporting. (*Data are in thousands of dollars.*)

Required

1 Prepare a schedule to determine which of Colby's industry segments are reportable industry segments under (a) the 10 percent revenue test, (b) the 10 percent operating profit test, and (c) the 10 percent asset test.

2 Prepare a schedule to show how Colby's segment information would be disclosed under the provisions of *FASB Statement No. 14.*

	Food Industry	Packing Industry	Textile Industry	Foreign Operations	All Other Industries	Corporate	Total Consolidated
Income Statement							
Sales to unaffiliated customers	$950	$500	$300	$250	$400		$2,400
Income from equity investees							100
Cost of sales to unaffiliated customers	600*	350*	175*	125*	250*		1,500*
Operating expense	200*	75*	150*	75*	75*	$ 25*	600*
Interest expense							20*
Income taxes							150*
Minority interest income							30*
Income (loss)	$150	$ 75	$(25)	$ 50	$ 75	$ (25)	$ 200
Assets							
Current assets	$300	$100	$ 75	$100	$225	$ 25	$ 825
Plant assets—net	400	400	250	100	175	25	1,350
Advances	50		25			50	—
Equity investments						1,000	1,000
Total assets	$750	$500	$350	$200	$400	$1,100	$3,175
Intersegment Transfers							
Sales†	$ 60	$ 60	$ 30	$ 50			
Purchases†	$100	$ 25		$ 75			

* Deduct.

† Amounts have been eliminated from the income data given.

P 15–8   Trotter Corporation is subject to income tax rates of 20 percent of its first $50,000 pretax income and 34 percent on amounts in excess of $50,000. Quarterly pretax accounting income for the calendar year is estimated by Trotter to be:

Quarter	Estimated Pretax Income
1st	$ 20,000
2nd	30,000
3rd	60,000
4th	50,000
Total	$160,000

No changes in accounting principles, discontinued items, unusual or infrequently occurring items, or extraordinary items are anticipated for the year. The fourth quarter's pretax income is, however, expected to include $20,000 dividends from domestic corporations for which an 80 percent dividend received deduction is available.

Required
1 Calculate the estimated annual effective tax rate for Trotter Corporation for 19X2.
2 Prepare a schedule showing Trotter's estimated net income for each quarter and the calendar year 19X2.

16

PARTNERSHIPS— FORMATION, OPERATIONS, AND CHANGES IN OWNERSHIP INTERESTS

I n this and the succeeding chapter the focus is on accounting for partnership entities. This chapter describes general matters relating to the partnership form of business organization including partnership formation, accounting for partnership operations, and accounting for changes in ownership interests. Chapter 17 covers matters relating to the dissolution and liquidation of partnerships. Although partnership accounting for ownership equities differs from that of other types of business organizations, generally accepted accounting principles for asset, liability, and income accounting are usually applicable to partnership entities. In other words, the analysis and recording of transactions not affecting ownership interests are ordinarily the same for partnerships as for proprietorships and corporations.

NATURE OF PARTNERSHIPS

The advantages of the partnership over the proprietorship form of business organization include sharing the investment needed, the talents required, and the risks involved in a particular business venture. Thus, the partnership form of organization is found in many areas of business including service industries, retail trade, wholesale and manufacturing operations, and the professions, particularly the legal, medical, and public accounting professions. The popularity of partnerships in the professions stems from the frequent need to combine the talents and skills of professional people on the one hand and the inability of professionals to limit their professional liability through incorporation on the other.

Partnership Characteristics

Partnership is defined in Section 6 of the Uniform Partnership Act as "an association of two or more persons to carry on as co-owners a business for profit." Since most states have adopted the Act, its provisions generally apply to the formation, operation, and dissolution of partnerships in the United States. When the Uniform Partnership Act is cited in this chapter and in Chapter 17, the reference

640

PARTNERSHIPS—
FORMATION,
OPERATIONS AND
CHANGES IN
OWNERSHIP INTERESTS

will be to the Act (for example, Section 6 of the Act). The Uniform Partnership Act appears as an appendix to this chapter.

One legal feature of a partnership is its **limited life**. Under the Uniform Partnership Act, the legal life of a partnership terminates with the admission of a new partner, the withdrawal or death of an old partner, voluntary dissolution by the partners, or involuntary dissolution such as through bankruptcy proceedings. However, the termination of a partnership association does not necessarily terminate the partnership as a separate business and accounting entity. Business operations frequently continue without substantial interference in spite of the admission and withdrawal of partners.

Another legal feature of a partnership is **mutual agency**. Each partner is assumed to be an agent for all partnership activities with the power to bind all other partners by his or her actions on behalf of the partnership. The implications of mutual agency are particularly significant when considered in conjunction with the **unlimited liability** feature of partnerships. Each partner is liable for all partnership debts and, in case of insolvency, may be required to use personal assets to pay partnership debts authorized by any partner. In some states the unlimited liability characteristic may be circumvented by designating particular partners as limited partners whose risks are limited to partnership investments. Such action requires notification to partnership creditors. In addition, at least one partner (a *general partner*) must have unlimited liability for all partnership debts.

Articles of Partnership

A partnership may be formed by a simple oral agreement among two or more people to operate a business for profit. The *ease of formation* feature of partnerships should not, however, encourage unsound business practices. Even though oral agreements may be legal and binding, **partnership agreements** should be in writing and at a minimum should specify:

1 The nature of the business
2 The rights and duties of each of the partners
3 The initial investment of each of the partners, including the amounts at which noncash assets are to be recorded
4 Provisions for additional investments and withdrawals
5 The manner in which profits and losses are to be shared
6 Procedures for dissolving the partnership

In the absence of a specific agreement for dividing profits and losses, all partners share equally irrespective of investments made or time devoted to the business (Section 18 of the Act).

Partnership Financial Reporting

The accounting reports of partnerships are designed to meet the needs of three user groups—the partners, the partnership creditors, and the Internal Revenue Service. Partners need accounting information for planning and controlling partnership assets and activities and for making personal investment decisions with respect to their partnership investments. In the absence of an agreement to the contrary, every partner has access to the partnership books at all times (Section 19 of the Act). Credit grantors such as banks and other financial institutions frequently require financial reports in support of loan applications and other credit matters relating to partnerships.

Although partnerships do not pay federal income taxes, they are required to submit financial information returns to enable the Internal Revenue Service to check the income calculations of the partnership for assurance that each partner pays income taxes on his or her share of partnership income. Outside of these three specific user groups, there is no widespread or public interest in the financial reports of partnerships. Therefore partnerships are not expected to prepare annual reports for public circulation.

INITIAL INVESTMENTS IN A PARTNERSHIP

All property brought into the partnership or acquired by the partnership is partnership property (Section 8[1] of the Act). Initial investments in a partnership are recorded in capital accounts maintained for each partner. If Ashley and Becker each invest $20,000 cash in a new partnership, the investments are recorded:

Cash	$20,000	
Ashley capital		$20,000
To record Ashley's original investment of cash.		
Cash	$20,000	
Becker capital		$20,000
To record Becker's original investment of cash.		

Noncash Investments

When property other than cash is invested in a partnership, the cost of the noncash property is measured and recorded at the fair value of the property at the time of the investment. Conceptually, the fair value should be determined by independent valuations; but as a practical matter, the fair value of noncash property is determined by agreement of all partners, since agreement is essential to partnership formation. The amounts involved should be specified in the written partnership agreement. Assume, for example, that C. Cola and R. Crown enter into a partnership with the following investments:

	C. Cola (Fair Value)	R. Crown (Fair Value)
Cash	—	$ 7,000
Land (cost to C. Cola, $5,000)	$10,000	—
Building (cost to C. Cola, $30,000)	40,000	—
Inventory items (cost to R. Crown, $28,000)	—	35,000
Total	$50,000	$42,000

The valuations to be recorded must be agreed upon by both Cola and Crown and are recorded as follows:

Land	$10,000	
Building	40,000	
C. Cola capital		$50,000
To record C. Cola's original investment of land and building at fair value.		
Cash	$ 7,000	
Inventory	35,000	
R. Crown capital		$42,000
To record R. Crown's original investment of cash and inventory items at fair value.		

Partnership investments are recorded at fair value because all property brought into the partnership becomes partnership property, and any gains or losses from use or disposal of such property will be divided in the profit and loss sharing ratios of the partners. Thus, equitable treatment of the partners re-

642

PARTNERSHIPS—
FORMATION,
OPERATIONS AND
CHANGES IN
OWNERSHIP INTERESTS

quires that noncash property be recorded at its fair value. Assume that the investments of C. Cola and R. Crown are recorded at original cost to the individual partners, that the noncash assets are immediately sold at their fair values, and that the partnership is liquidated. C. Cola invests assets with a fair value of $50,000 but receives only $46,000 (half of the $92,000 fair value) in liquidation. Crown invests assets with a fair value of $42,000 and receives $46,000 in liquidation. Entries on the partnership books to reflect the accounting under these assumptions are shown in Exhibit 16–1.

Although immediate sale and liquidation of partnership investments is unusual, the computation of the $4,000 inequity is equally applicable when unrecorded gains (and losses) on property contributed by individual partners are realized through use in partnership operations. Recording partners' noncash investments at their fair value ensures that any gains and losses on subsequent disposition of the property through use or through sale will be equitable. Such gains or losses are correctly divided in the profit and loss sharing ratios provided in the partnership agreement.

Bonus or Goodwill on Initial Investments

A different problem of valuation arises when partners agree on relative capital interests that are not aligned with their investments of identifiable assets. For example, C. Cola and R. Crown could agree to divide initial partnership capital equally, even though C. Cola contributed $50,000 in identifiable assets and R. Crown contributed $42,000. Such an agreement implies that R. Crown is contributing an unidentifiable asset such as individual talent, established clientele, or banking connections to the partnership. The alternative interpretation that C. Cola is making a gift to R. Crown is unacceptable because it implies irrational conduct, and it conflicts with the accountant's assumption of rational and honest conduct of business affairs.

	Investment at Original Cost		Investment at Fair Value	
1. To record C. Cola's investment:				
Land	$ 5,000		$10,000	
Building	30,000		40,000	
C. Cola capital		$35,000		$50,000
2. To record R. Crown's investment:				
Cash	$ 7,000		$ 7,000	
Inventory	28,000		35,000	
R. Crown capital		$35,000		$42,000
3. To record sale of assets at fair value:				
Cash	$85,000		$85,000	
Land		$ 5,000		$10,000
Building		30,000		40,000
Inventory		28,000		35,000
Gain on sale		22,000		none
4. To distribute the gain on sale equally:				
Gain on sale	$22,000		none	
C. Cola capital		$11,000		none
R. Crown capital		11,000		none
5. To distribute cash in final liquidation of the partnership:				
C. Cola capital	$46,000		$50,000	
R. Crown capital	46,000		42,000	
Cash		$92,000		$92,000

Exhibit 16–1 *Comparison of Initial Investment Involving Noncash Assets*

Since the partnership agreement specifies equal capital interests, the capital account balances of C. Cola ($50,000) and R. Crown ($42,000) have to be adjusted to meet the conditions of the agreement. Either of two approaches may be used to adjust the capital accounts—the bonus approach or the goodwill approach. Under the **bonus approach**, the unidentifiable asset is not recorded on the partnership books and the only journal entry necessary is as follows:

C. Cola capital	$4,000	
R. Crown capital		$4,000

To establish equal capital interests of $46,000 by recording a $4,000 bonus from C. Cola to R. Crown.

When the **goodwill approach** is used, the unidentifiable asset contributed by Crown is measured on the basis of C. Cola's $50,000 investment for a 50 percent interest. C. Cola's investment implies total partnership capital of $100,000 ($50,000/50%) and goodwill of $8,000 ($100,000 total capital − $92,000 identifiable assets). The unidentifiable asset is recorded:

Goodwill	$8,000	
R. Crown capital		$8,000

To establish equal capital interests of $50,000 by recognizing R. Crown's investment of an $8,000 unidentifiable asset.

Both approaches are equally effective in aligning the capital accounts with the agreement and equitable in assigning capital interests to individual partners. A decision to use one approach over the other will depend on partner attitudes toward recording the $8,000 unidentifiable asset under the goodwill method and to C. Cola's reaction to receiving a $46,000 capital credit for a $50,000 investment under the bonus approach.

ADDITIONAL INVESTMENTS AND WITHDRAWALS

The partnership agreement should establish guidelines for additional investments and withdrawals made after partnership operations have begun. When additional investments are made, they are credited to the investing partner's capital account subject to the same rules of valuation as those discussed earlier for original investments. Withdrawals of large and irregular amounts are ordinarily charged directly to the withdrawing partner's capital account. The entry for such a withdrawal might be:

Smith capital	$20,000	
Cash		$20,000

To record the withdrawal of cash.

Drawings

Because the business rewards of partners are in the form of partnership profits, partners do not have take-home pay as do the employees of the partnership business. Instead, active partners commonly withdraw regular amounts of money on a weekly or monthly basis in anticipation of their share of partnership profits. Such withdrawals are called **drawings, drawing allowances,** or sometimes **salary allowances**, and they are usually charged to the partners' drawing accounts rather than directly to the capital accounts. For example, if Townsend and Lee withdraw $1,000 from the partnership each month, the monthly withdrawals would be recorded:

644

PARTNERSHIPS—
FORMATION,
OPERATIONS AND
CHANGES IN
OWNERSHIP INTERESTS

| Townsend drawing | $1,000 | |
| Cash | | $1,000 |

To record Townsend's drawing allowance for January.

| Lee drawing | $1,000 | |
| Cash | | $1,000 |

To record Lee's drawing allowance for January.

The drawing accounts should be closed to the capital accounts at the end of each accounting period. Thus, the final effect is the same as if direct charges had been made to the capital accounts. The use of drawing accounts does, however, provide a record of each partner's drawings during an accounting period. This record may be compared with drawings allowed in the partnership agreement in order to establish an accounting control over excessive drawings. (Drawings balances are also a factor in many profit and loss sharing agreements, and will be discussed in conjunction with such agreements.) If Townsend draws $1,000 each month during the year, his drawing account balance at year-end will be $12,000 and his drawing account will be closed by the following entry:

| Townsend capital | $12,000 | |
| Townsend drawing | | $12,000 |

To close Townsend's drawing account.

Regardless of the name given to regular withdrawals by partners, such withdrawals are disinvestments of essentially the same nature as large and irregular withdrawals, and the effect on the capital accounts after closing entries will be the same for each dollar withdrawn. Drawing accounts should be closed to capital accounts before a partnership balance sheet is prepared.

Loans and Advances

A partner may make a personal loan to the partnership. This situation is provided for in Section 18(c) of the Act, which specifies that "a partner, who in the aid of the partnership makes any payment or advance beyond the amount of capital which he agreed to contribute, shall be paid interest from the date of the payment or advance." Such loans or advances and accrued interest thereon are correctly regarded as liabilities of the partnership. Similarly, partnership loans and advances to an individual partner are considered partnership assets. Matters concerning loans and advances to or from partners should be covered in the partnership agreement.

PARTNERSHIP OPERATIONS

The operations of a partnership are similar in most respects to those of other forms of organization operating in the same line of business. In measuring partnership income for a period, however, the expenses should be scrutinized to make sure that personal expenses of the partners are not included among the business expenses of the partnership. If personal expenses of a partner are paid with partnership assets, the payment is charged to the drawing or capital account of the partner whose personal obligations have been settled. Drawings and salary allowances should be closed to the capital accounts of the partners, rather than to an income summary account. Salary allowances, whether debited to partner salary or drawing accounts, may be considered in allocating partnership net income to individual partners. (See the next section on profit and loss sharing agreements.)

General-purpose financial statements of a partnership include an income statement, a balance sheet, a statement of partnership capital, and a statement of cash flows. Since the statement of partnership capital is the only one of these statements that is unique to the partnership form of organization, it is the only statement that will be illustrated at this time.

Assume that Ratcliffe and Yancey are partners sharing profits in a 60:40 ratio, respectively. Data relevant to the partnership's equities for the year 19X2 are as follows:

Partnership net income, 19X2	$34,500
Ratcliffe capital, January 1, 19X2	40,000
Ratcliffe additional investment, 19X2	5,000
Ratcliffe drawing, 19X2	6,000
Yancey capital, January 1, 19X2	35,000
Yancey drawing, 19X2	9,000
Yancey withdrawal, 19X2	3,000

This information is reflected in the statement of partners' capital that appears in Exhibit 16–2. Although other forms of presentation are acceptable, the format illustrated in Exhibit 16–2 is used because it provides a comparison of capital changes before and after the division of partnership net income. An ability to compare beginning capital balances and net contributed capital is helpful to the partners in setting investment and withdrawal policies and in controlling abuses of the established policies. In the case of incomplete partnership records, the format illustrated also provides a convenient means of computing net income—which is simply the difference between net contributed capital and ending capital as shown in the the total column. (Note that the preclosing capital account balances are $45,000 [$40,000 + $5,000] for Ratcliffe and $32,000 [$35,000 − $3,000] for Yancey.)

Closing entries for the Ratcliffe and Yancey partnership at December 31, 19X2 are as follows:

December 31, 19X2

Revenue and expense summary	$34,500	
Ratcliffe capital		$20,700
Yancey capital		13,800

    To divide net income for the year 60% to Ratcliffe and 40% to Yancey.

December 31, 19X2

Ratcliffe capital	$ 6,000	
Yancey capital	9,000	
Ratcliffe drawing		$ 6,000
Yancey drawing		9,000

    To close partner drawing accounts to capital accounts.

RATCLIFFE AND YANCEY
STATEMENT OF PARTNERS' CAPITAL
FOR THE YEAR ENDED DECEMBER 31, 19X2

	60% Ratcliffe	40% Yancey	Total
Capital balances, January 1, 19X2	$40,000	$35,000	$75,000
Add: Additional investments	5,000	—	5,000
Deduct: Withdrawals	—	(3,000)	(3,000)
Deduct: Drawings	(6,000)	(9,000)	(15,000)
Net contributed capital	39,000	23,000	62,000
Add: Net income for 19X2	20,700	13,800	34,500
Capital balances, December 31, 19X2	$59,700	$36,800	$96,500

Exhibit 16–2 *Format for a Statement of Partners' Capital*

PROFIT AND LOSS SHARING AGREEMENTS

Partnership income may be divided equally among the partners, and equal division is required in the absence of a profit and loss sharing agreement. But partners may agree to share profits in a specified ratio, such as the 60:40 division illustrated for the Ratcliffe and Yancey partnership. The division of partnership income according to specified ratios is easy to comprehend and requires no further explanation, other than to note that profit sharing agreements also apply to the division of losses unless the agreement specifies otherwise.

Although agreements to share profits and losses equally or in specified ratios are common, other more complex profit sharing agreements are also encountered in practice. An equitable division of profits (and losses) frequently requires that consideration be given to the time that partners devote to the partnership business and the capital invested in the business by individual partners. If one partner manages the partnership, the partnership agreement may allow the managing partner a salary allowance equal to the amount he or she could earn in an alternative employment opportunity before remaining profits are allocated. *Such salary allowances are, of course, only provisions of the profit sharing agreement and are not expenses of the partnership.* Similarly, if one partner invests significantly more than another in a partnership venture, the agreement may provide an interest allowance on capital investments before remaining profits are divided. As in the case of salary allowances, *interest allowances are merely provisions of the partnership agreement and have no effect on the measurement of partnership income.*

Service Considerations in Profit and Loss Sharing Agreements

As mentioned previously, the equitable distribution of partnership income may require a salary allowance to a partner who devotes time to the partnership business while other partners work elsewhere. Salary allowances may also be used to provide a differential between the fair value of the talents of different partners, all of whom devote their time to the partnership. Another possibility for differentiation in the profit and loss sharing agreement is to provide salary allowances to active partners plus a bonus to the managing partner in order to encourage profit maximization. These alternatives are illustrated for the partnership of Bob, Gary, and Pete. Bob is the managing partner, Gary is the sales manager, and Pete works outside the partnership.

Salary Allowances in Profit Sharing Agreements   Assume that the partnership agreement provides that Bob and Gary receive salary allowances of $12,000 each, after which remaining income is allocated equally among the three partners. If parnership net income is $60,000 for 19X1 and $12,000 for 19X2, the income allocations would be as shown in Exhibit 16–3. The 19X1 allocation is $24,000 each to Bob and Gary and $12,000 to Pete. The 19X2 allocation is $8,000 income to both Bob and Gary and a $4,000 loss to Pete. Note that the partnership agreement has been followed in 19X2, even though the salary allowances of $24,000 exceeded partnership net income of $12,000. The income allocation schedule follows the order of the profit sharing agreement even when the partnership has a loss. Salary allowances, in that case, simply increase the loss to be divided equally.

Journal entries to distribute partnership income to individual capital accounts for 19X1 and 19X2 are as follows:

December 31, 19X1

Revenue and expense summary	$60,000	
Bob capital		$24,000
Gary capital		24,000
Pete capital		12,000

Partnership income allocation for 19X1.

INCOME ALLOCATION SCHEDULE—19X1

		Bob	Gary	Pete	Total
Net income	$60,000				
Salary allowances to Bob and Gary	(24,000)	$12,000	$12,000		$24,000
Remainder to divide	36,000				
Divided equally	(36,000)	12,000	12,000	$12,000	36,000
Remainder to divide	0				
Net income allocation		$24,000	$24,000	$12,000	$60,000

INCOME ALLOCATION SCHEDULE—19X2

		Bob	Gary	Pete	Total
Net income	$12,000				
Salary allowances to Bob and Gary	(24,000)	$12,000	$12,000		$24,000
Remainder to divide	(12,000)				
Divided equally	12,000	(4,000)	(4,000)	$ (4,000)	(12,000)
Remainder to divide	0				
Net income allocation		$ 8,000	$ 8,000	$ (4,000)	$12,000

( ) Deduction or loss.

Exhibit 16–3   *Salary Allowances in Profit Sharing Agreements*

December 31, 19X2		
Revenue and expense summary	$12,000	
Pete capital	4,000	
Bob capital		$ 8,000
Gary capital		8,000
Partnership income allocation for 19X2.		

Income allocation schedules such as those shown in Exhibit 16–3 can be used as explanations of the closing entries to distribute partnership income to individual capital accounts.

In partnership accounting, partner salary allowances are not expenses in the determination of partnership net income; instead, they are a means of achieving an equitable division of income among the partners based on time and talents devoted to partnership business. This point has already been established. However, there are situations in which calculations of income after salary allowances may be useful. These situations include performance comparisons and measurements of business success.

Calculating partnership income after salary allowances is appropriate in comparing the performance of a partnership business with similar businesses operated under the corporation form of organization. Stockholders who devote their time to corporate affairs are employees, and their salaries are deducted in measuring corporate net income. Failure to adjust partnership income for salary allowances may, therefore, result in invalid comparisons. Other adjustments, such as for corporate income taxes, also have to be made for valid comparisons.

Calculation of partnership income after salary allowances is also appropriate in assessing the success of a business. The financial success of a partnership business lies in its earning a fair return for the services performed by partners, for capital invested in the business, and for the risks taken. If partnership income is not greater than the combined amounts that active partners could earn by working outside of the partnership, then the business is not a financial success.

648

PARTNERSHIPS—
FORMATION,
OPERATIONS AND
CHANGES IN
OWNERSHIP INTERESTS

Income after salary allowances (or imputed salaries) should be sufficient to compensate for capital invested and risks undertaken.

Bonus and Salary Allowances   The partnership agreement of Bob, Gary, and Pete provides that Bob receive a bonus of 10 percent of partnership net income for managing the business; that Bob and Gary receive salary allowances of $10,000 and $8,000, respectively, for services rendered; and that the remaining partnership income be divided equally among the three partners. If partnership net income is $60,000 in 19X1 and $12,000 in 19X2, the partnership income is allocated as shown Exhibit 16–4.

INCOME ALLOCATION SCHEDULE—19X1

		Bob	Gary	Pete	Total
Net income	$60,000				
Bonus to Bob	(6,000)	$ 6,000			$ 6,000
Remainder to divide	54,000				
Salary allowances to Bob and Gary	(18,000)	10,000	$ 8,000		18,000
Remainder to divide	36,000				
Divided equally	(36,000)	12,000	12,000	$12,000	36,000
Remainder to divide	0				
Net income allocation		$28,000	$20,000	$12,000	$60,000

INCOME ALLOCATION SCHEDULE—19X2

		Bob	Gary	Pete	Total
Net income	$12,000				
Bonus to Bob	(1,200)	$ 1,200			$ 1,200
Remainder to divide	10,800				
Salary allowances to Bob and Gary	(18,000)	10,000	$ 8,000		18,000
Remainder to divide	(7,200)				
Divided equally	7,200	(2,400)	(2,400)	$ (2,400)	(7,200)
Remainder to divide	0				
Net income allocation		$ 8,800	$ 5,600	$ (2,400)	$12,000

( ) Deduction or loss.

Exhibit 16–4   *Bonus and Salary Allowances in Profit Sharing Agreements*

The allocation schedules illustrated follow the order of the profit sharing agreement in allocating bonus, salary allowances, and the remainder to individual partners. The bonus is computed on the basis of partnership net income as the concept of "partnership net income" is generally understood in accounting practice. Partners may, however, intend for salary allowances to be deducted in determining the base for computing the bonus. If this had been the intent, the bonus illustrated for 19X1 would have been $4,200 [($60,000 − $18,000) × 10 percent] rather than $6,000, and the final net income allocation would have been $26,800, $20,600, and $12,600 for Bob, Gary, and Pete, respectively. Sometimes the partners may intend for the bonus, as well as salary allowances to be deducted in determining the base for the bonus computation. Had this been the intent in the Bob, Gary, and Pete partnership agreement, the bonus would have been $3,818.18, computed as follows:

Let B = bonus
   B = 10% ($60,000 − $18,000 − B)
   B = $6,000 − $1,800 − .1B
1.1 B = $4,200
   B = $3,818.18

Check: $60,000 − $18,000 − $3,818.18   = $38,181.82 bonus base
   $38,181.82 × 10%   = $3,818.18 bonus

Since the intent of the partners may not be apparent when technical accounting terms are used, the partnership agreement should be precise in specifying measurement procedures to be used in determining the amount of a bonus based on operating performance.

Capital as a Factor in Profit Sharing Agreements

Capital is an important factor in the earning process of many businesses, and the capital contributions of partners are frequently considered in profit and loss sharing agreements. Total partnership income may be allocated on the basis of relative capital balances of the partners, or interest may be allowed on relative capital balances as one of several factors to be considered in achieving an equitable allocation of partnership net income.

If capital is to be considered in the division of partnership income, the profit sharing agreement should be specific with respect to the concept of capital to be applied. For example, capital may refer to beginning capital balances, ending capital balances, or average capital balances. In addition, several interpretations of average capital balances are possible, and capital balances may be determined before or after drawing accounts are closed to the partners' capital accounts. Thus, the precise concept of capital to be used should be designated in the partnership agreement.

When beginning capital balances are used in allocating partnership income, additional investments during the accounting period are discouraged because the partners making such investments are not compensated in the division of income until a later period. A similar problem arises when ending capital balances are used. Year-end investments are encouraged, but there is no incentive for a partner to make any investments before year-end. Also, there is no penalty for withdrawals if the amounts withdrawn are reinvested before period end. These considerations suggest that weighted average capital balances provide the most equitable basis for allocating partnership income, and a weighted average interpretation of capital should be assumed in the absence of evidence to the contrary. Average capital balances means weighted average unless another interpretation of average capital is specified in the agreement.

Usually the drawing allowances specified in a partnership agreement may be withdrawn without affecting the capital balances to be used in dividing partnership income. That is, drawing account balances up to the amounts specified in the agreement would not be deducted in determining average or year-end capital balances of the partners. Drawings in excess of allowable amounts would be charged against the partners' capital accounts in computing average or ending capital balances for purposes of dividing partnership income. Although excess drawings should be charged directly to the partner's capital account on a timely basis, drawing account balances may be excessive and, if so, they should be adjusted before average or ending capital is computed.

Income Allocated in Relation to Partnership Capital   The partnership of Ace and Butch was formed on January 1, 19X1, with each partner investing $20,000 cash. Changes in the capital accounts during 19X1 are summarized as follows:

650

PARTNERSHIPS—
FORMATION,
OPERATIONS AND
CHANGES IN
OWNERSHIP INTERESTS

	Ace	Butch
Capital balances January 1, 19X1	$20,000	$20,000
Investment, April 1	2,000	—
Withdrawal, July 1	—	−5,000
Investment, September 1	3,000	—
Withdrawal, October 1	—	−4,000
Investment, December 28	—	8,000
Capital balances December 31, 19X1	$25,000	$19,000

The beginning, ending, and average capital amounts for Ace and Butch for 19X1 are as follows:

COMPARISON OF CAPITAL BASES

	Beginning Capital Investment	Ending Capital Investment	Weighted Average Capital Investment
Ace	$20,000	$25,000	$22,500
Butch	20,000	19,000	16,500

Computations for the weighted average capital investments of Ace and Butch are shown in Exhibit 16–5. Actual investments are multiplied by the number of months outstanding to get dollar-month investment computations. Total dollar-month investments are divided by 12 to get weighted average annual capital balances. Ordinarily, computations to the nearest half-month are considered adequate, although the weighted average balances could easily be made on a weekly or even daily basis.

WEIGHTED AVERAGE CAPITAL CALCULATIONS

	Dollar-Month Investment	
Average Capital Investment of Ace		
$20,000 × 3 months (January 1 to April 1)	$ 60,000	
22,000 × 5 months (April 1 to September 1)	110,000	
25,000 × 4 months (September 1 to December 31)	100,000	
12 months	$270,000	
Ace's average capital investment ($270,000/12 months)		$22,500
Average Capital Investment of Butch		
$20,000 × 6 months (January 1 to July 1)	$120,000	
15,000 × 3 months (July 1 to October 1)	45,000	
11,000 × 3 months (October 1 to December 28)	33,000	
12 months	$198,000	
Butch's average capital investment ($198,000/12 months)		$16,500

Exhibit 16–5   *Computation of Weighted Average Capital Investment*

The Ace and Butch example can now be extended under the further assumption that partnership net income is to be divided on the basis of capital balances, and that net income for 19X1 is $100,000. Allocation of partnership income to Ace and Butch under each of the three capital bases would be:

Beginning Capital Balances:

Ace $100,000 × 20/40	$ 50,000
Butch $100,000 × 20/40	50,000
Total income	$ 100,000

Ending Capital Balances:

Ace $100,000 × 25/44	$ 56,818.18
Butch $100,000 × 19/44	43,181.82
Total income	$100,000.00

Average Capital Balances:

Ace $100,000 × 225/390	$ 57,692.31
Butch $100,000 × 165/390	42,307.69
Total income	$100,000.00

If the partnership agreement of Ace and Butch fails to specify how capital balances are to be computed, the weighted average computation is used and the $100,000 partnership income for 19X1 is allocated $57,692.31 to Ace and $42,307.69 to Butch.

Interest Allowances on Partnership Capital   Although capital investments may be used as the sole basis for income allocation, they may also be used as one of several income allocation provisions in a partnership agreement. For example, an agreement may provide for interest allowances on partnership capital in order to encourage capital investments, as well as salary allowances to recognize time devoted to the business. Remaining profits may then be divided equally or in any other ratio specified in the profit sharing agreement.

Consider the following information relating to the capital and drawing accounts of the Russo and Stokes partnership for the calendar year 19X1:

	Russo	*Stokes*
Capital Accounts		
Capital balances, January 1, 19X1	$186,000	$114,000
Additional investments, June 1, 19X1	24,000	36,000
Withdrawal, July 1, 19X1	—	−10,000
Capital balances, December 31, 19X1 (before drawings)	$210,000	$140,000
Drawing Accounts		
Drawing account balances,* December 31, 19X1	$ 10,000	$ 12,000

* Account titles may be partner salaries rather than partner drawings. In either case, the balances should be closed to partner capital accounts and not to the income summary.

The partnership agreement provides that the partnership income is to be divided equally after salary allowances of $12,000 per year for each partner, and after interest allowances at a 10 percent annual rate on average capital balances. Schedules showing the income allocations for 19X1 under this agreement are illustrated in Exhibit 16–6. The first schedule (Part A) assumes that partnership net income for 19X1 is $91,000, and the second schedule (Part B) assumes a partnership loss for 19X1 of $3,000.

652

PARTNERSHIPS—
FORMATION,
OPERATIONS AND
CHANGES IN
OWNERSHIP INTERESTS

PART A—PARTNERSHIP INCOME ASSUMED TO BE $91,000 INCOME ALLOCATION SCHEDULE

		Russo	Stokes	Total
Net income	$91,000			
Salary allowances	(24,000)	$12,000	$12,000	$24,000
Remainder to divide	67,000			
Interest allowances:				
$200,000 × 10%	(20,000)	20,000		20,000
$130,000 × 10%	(13,000)		13,000	13,000
Remainder to divide	34,000			
Divided equally	(34,000)	17,000	17,000	34,000
Remainder to divide	0			
Net income allocation		$49,000	$42,000	$91,000

PART B—PARTNERSHIP LOSS ASSUMED TO BE $3,000 INCOME ALLOCATION SCHEDULE

		Russo	Stokes	Total
Net loss	$ (3,000)			
Salary allowances	(24,000)	$12,000	$12,000	$24,000
Remainder to divide	(27,000)			
Interest allowances:				
$200,000 × 10%	(20,000)	20,000		20,000
$130,000 × 10%	(13,000)		13,000	13,000
Remainder to divide	(60,000)			
Divided equally	60,000	(30,000)	(30,000)	(60,000)
Remainder to divide	0			
Net income (loss) allocation		$ 2,000	$ (5,000)	$ (3,000)

( ) Deduction or loss.

Exhibit 16–6   *Interest and Salary Allowances in Profit Sharing Agreements*

The average capital balances for Russo and Stokes, as used in the exhibit, are computed as follows:

	Dollar-Month Investment	
Average Capital Investment of Russo		
$186,000 × 5 months	$ 930,000	
210,000 × 7 months	1,470,000	
12 months	$2,400,000	
Average capital ($2,400,000/12 months)		$200,000
Average Capital Investment of Stokes		
$114,000 × 5 months	$ 570,000	
150,000 × 1 month	150,000	
140,000 × 6 months	840,000	
12 months	$1,560,000	
Average capital ($1,560,000/12 months)		$130,000

Exhibit 16–6 shows that all provisions of the profit sharing agreement are used in allocating partnership income, regardless of whether the partnership

has net income or net loss. The full amount of salary allowances as provided in the agreement is included in the income division, even though Russo only withdrew $10,000 of the $12,000 allowable amount.

In Part A of Exhibit 16–6, partnership income of $91,000 was divided $49,000 to Russo and $42,000 to Stokes. The division of the $3,000 net loss in Part B was allocated as $2,000 income to Russo and a $5,000 loss to Stokes. In both cases, the partnership agreement provided for a $7,000 income allocation differential between the two partners. The amount of this differential was the same for the income and loss situations because the residual income amount was divided equally. A 60:40 division of income after salary and interest allowances, for example, would have resulted in a larger differential in Part A (that is, greater than $7,000) and a smaller differential in Part B (less than $7,000). One must be careful in making generalizations about the effect of various profit sharing provisions on final income allocations.

CHANGES IN PARTNERSHIP INTERESTS

The admission of a new partner or the withdrawal or death of an existing partner dissolves the existing legal partnership entity. But dissolution does not necessarily result in the termination of the partnership operations or of the partnership as a separate business and accounting entity. **Partnership dissolution** under the Uniform Partnership Act is simply "the change in the relation of the partners caused by any partner ceasing to be associated in the carrying on as distinguished from the winding up of the business" (Section 29 of the Act).

When a partnership is legally dissolved by the admittance of a new partner or by the retirement or death of an existing partner, a new partnership agreement is necessary for the continuing operations of the partnership business. A question arises as to whether the assets of the continuing partnership business should be revalued. Some argue that since legal dissolution terminates the old partnership, all assets transferred to the new partnership should be revalued in the same manner as if the assets had been sold to a corporate entity. Others argue that changes in partnership interests are not unlike changes in the stockholders of a corporation, and that private sales of ownership interests provide no basis for revaluation of the business entity. These alternative views reflect the concepts of the legal and business entities, respectively. Both views have merit, and this text does not emphasize either view. Instead, both views are discussed and illustrated in the following sections on changes in partnership interests. The revaluation approach is generally referred to as the **goodwill procedure**, while the absence of revaluation is referred to as the **bonus procedure**.

Assignment of an Interest to a Third Party

A partnership is not dissolved when a partner assigns his or her interest in the partnership to a third party because such an assignment does not in itself change the relations among partners. Such assignment only entitles the assignee to receive the assigning partner's interest in future partnership profits and in partnership assets in the event of liquidation. The assignee does not become a partner, however, and does not obtain the right to share in management of the partnership (Section 27 of the Act). If the assignee does not become a partner, the only change required on the partnership books is for transfer of the capital interest of the assignor partner to the assignee.

The assignment by Mark to Conn of his 25 percent interest in the Pilar-Mark partnership is recorded:

654

PARTNERSHIPS—
FORMATION,
OPERATIONS AND
CHANGES IN
OWNERSHIP INTERESTS

| Mark capital | XXX | |
| Conn capital | | XXX |

The amount of the capital transfer is equal to the recorded amount of Mark's capital at the time of the assignment, and it is independent of the consideration received by Mark for his 25 percent interest. If the recorded amount of Mark's capital is $50,000, then the amount of the transfer entry is $50,000, regardless of whether Conn pays Mark $50,000 or some other amount.

Admission of a New Partner

A new partner can be admitted with the consent of all continuing partners in the business. However, the old partnership is dissolved and a new agreement is necessary for the continuing operations of the partnership business. In the absence of a new agreement, all profits and losses in the new partnership are divided equally under the provisions of the Uniform Partnership Act.

A person may become a partner in an existing partnership *by purchasing an interest from one or more of the existing partners* with the consent of all continuing partners in the new partnership entity, or *by investing money or other resources in the partnership.* In either case, the partnership books should be closed to update the capital accounts in anticipation of a new partnership agreement. These situations are similar in the sense that the old partnership is legally dissolved, and capital and income interests will be based on a new partnership agreement. The situations are dissimilar in the sense that the partnership entity receives no new resources when a third party purchases an interest directly from existing partners, but it does receive new resources when a third party becomes a partner by direct investment in the partnership. Since the partners in the new agreement can agree upon any capital and profit sharing interests as they choose, the role of the accountant is largely one of advising the partners on matters concerning the equitable allocation of capital and income interests in the new agreement.

PURCHASE OF AN INTEREST FROM EXISTING PARTNERS

With the consent of all continuing partners, a new partner may be admitted into an existing partnership by purchasing an interest directly from the existing partners. The old partnership is dissolved, its books are closed, and a new partnership agreement governs the continuing business operations. If the capital accounts are aligned with the profit and loss sharing ratios before and after the admission of a new partner, the net assets of the old partnership are probably valued correctly.

For example, Alfano and Bailey are partners with capital balances of $50,000 each, and they share profits and losses equally. Cobb purchases one-half of Alfano's interest from Alfano for $25,000, and a new partnership of Alfano, Bailey, and Cobb is formed such that Alfano and Cobb each have a 25 percent interest in the capital and profits of the new partnership. The only entry required to record Alfano's transfer to Cobb is:

| Alfano capital | $25,000 | |
| Cobb capital | | $25,000 |

To record Cobb's admission into the partnership with the purchase of one-half of Alfano's interest.

In this case, the capital and income interests are aligned before and after the admission of Cobb, and the evidence indicates that the net assets of the old partnership were correctly valued. That is, Cobb's payment of $25,000 for a 25 percent interest in the capital and future income of the partnership implies a total valuation for the partnership of $100,000 ($25,000/.25), Since the net assets of the old partnership were recorded at $100,000, no basis for revaluation arises.

Now assume that Alfano and Bailey have capital balances of $50,000 and $40,000, respectively; that they share profits equally; and that they agree to take Cobb into the partnership with a payment of $25,000 directly to Alfano. The partners may agree that half of Alfano's capital balance is to be transferred to Cobb (as in the previous example); that the net assets are not to be revalued; and that future profits will be shared 25 percent, 50 percent, and 25 percent to Alfano, Bailey, and Cobb, respectively. Although it seems equitable, there is no compelling reason for such an agreement, since the capital and income interests were not aligned either before or after the admission of Cobb.

	Old Partnership			New Partnership		
	Capital Investment		Income Interest	Capital Investment		Income Interest
Alfano	$50,000	5/9	50%	$25,000	5/18	25%
Bailey	40,000	4/9	50%	40,000	8/18	50%
Cobb				25,000	5/18	25%
	$90,000			$90,000		

Also note that the $25,000 payment of Cobb to Alfano does not provide evidence as to the correct valuation of partnership net assets, since the payment was for five-eighteenths of the partnership net assets but 25 percent of future partnership profits. If revaluation is desirable, the asset value should be based on appraisals or evidence other than the amount of Cobb's payment to Alfano.

Revaluation/Goodwill Procedure

A third possibility is that Alfano and Bailey have capital balances of $50,000 and $40,000, respectively; that they share profits equally, and that Cobb is admitted to the partnership with a total payment of $50,000 directly to the partners. Cobb is to have a 50 percent interest in the capital and income of the new partnership. Alfano and Bailey will each have a 25 percent interest in future income of the partnership. Several additional questions of equity arise concerning the valuation of total partnership assets, the capital transfers to Cobb, and the division of the $50,000 payment between Alfano and Bailey. Cobb's $50,000 payment for a 50 percent interest in both capital and future income implies a $100,000 valuation for total partnership assets. If assets are to be revalued, the revaluation should be recorded prior to Cobb's admission to the partnership. The revaluation could be recorded:

Goodwill (or identifiable net assets)	$10,000	
Alfano capital		$5,000
Bailey capital		5,000

When assets are revalued and goodwill is recorded, goodwill should be amortized over a maximum of forty years in accordance with *APB Opinion No. 17*. If the assets are revalued and identifiable asset accounts are adjusted, the amount of the adjustments will be amortized or depreciated over the remaining asset lives. Although the revaluation procedure is commonly referred to as the goodwill procedure, goodwill should not be recorded until all identifiable assets have been adjusted to their fair values. Thus, the approach is comparable to the approach used to record business combinations under the purchase method or the acquisition of operating divisions or groups of assets.

The previous entry recording goodwill of $10,000 gives Alfano and Bailey capital balances of $55,000 and $45,000, respectively. If equal amounts of capital

656

PARTNERSHIPS—
FORMATION,
OPERATIONS AND
CHANGES IN
OWNERSHIP INTERESTS

are to be transferred to Cobb, the entry to record Cobb's admission to the partnership is:

Alfano capital	$25,000	
Bailey capital	25,000	
Cobb capital		$50,000

Since equal amounts of capital are transferred by Alfano and Bailey, it would seem equitable for Alfano and Bailey to share equally the $50,000 received from Cobb. The capital balances are summarized as follows:

CAPITAL BALANCES

	Before Revaluation	Revaluation	After Revaluation	Capital Transferred	Capital After Transfer	
Alfano	$50,000	$ 5,000	$ 55,000	$ −25,000	$ 30,000	(30%)
Bailey	40,000	5,000	45,000	−25,000	20,000	(20%)
Cobb				50,000	50,000	(50%)
	$90,000	$10,000	$100,000	$ 0	$100,000	

Alternatively, it may be desirable to realign the capital balances of Alfano and Bailey in the new partnership such that each will have a 25 percent interest in the capital and income of the new partnership. In this case, the admission of Cobb would be recorded:

Alfano capital	$30,000	
Bailey capital	20,000	
Cobb capital		$50,000

A division of the cash received from Cobb equal to the capital transfers ($30,000 and $20,000) would then seem equitable. In this case, the capital changes are as follows:

CAPITAL BALANCES

	Before Revaluation	Revaluation	After Revaluation	Capital Transferred	Capital After Transfer	
Alfano	$50,000	$ 5,000	$ 55,000	$ −30,000	$ 25,000	(25%)
Bailey	40,000	5,000	45,000	−20,000	25,000	(25%)
Cobb				50,000	50,000	(50%)
	$90,000	$10,000	$100,000	$ 0	$100,000	

Nonrevaluation/Bonus Procedure

If the assets of the new partnership are not to be revalued, but equal amounts of capital are to be transferred to Cobb, a single entry is adequate to record the transfer:

Alfano capital	$22,500	
Bailey capital	22,500	
Cobb capital		$45,000

Since equal amounts of capital and equal rights to future income are transferred by Alfano and Bailey to Cobb, an equal division of the $50,000 received from Cobb seems equitable. In this case, each of the old partners receives $2,500 in excess of the amount of capital transferred ($25,000 received less $22,500 capital transferred). This $2,500 excess for Alfano and Bailey represents half of the $10,000 unrecorded asset values that will accrue to the benefit of Cobb in future income allocations. The capital accounts before and after the admission of Cobb are as follows:

CAPITAL BALANCES

	Per Books	Capital Transferred	Capital After Transfer	
Alfano	$50,000	$ − 22,500	$27,500	(30.6%)
Bailey	40,000	− 22,500	17,500	(19.4%)
Cobb		45,000	45,000	(50.0%)
	$90,000	$ 0	$90,000	

Should Alfano and Bailey desire to equate their capital and income interests in the new partnership, Alfano would receive $30,000 of the amount paid by Cobb, and Bailey would receive $20,000. The entry to record the capital transfer in this case would be:

Alfano capital	$27,500	
Bailey capital	17,500	
Cobb capital		$45,000

The capital transfers of Alfano and Bailey are computed by deducting $22,500, the desired capital balances (25 percent of $90,000 total capital), from their existing capital balances of $50,000 and $40,000, respectively. As in the previous illustration where assets were not revalued, Alfano and Bailey each receive $2,500 more than the amount of capital transferred, again equal to their respective shares of unrecorded asset values that will accrue to the benefit of Cobb. A summary of the capital balances follows:

CAPITAL BALANCES

	Per Books	Capital Transferred	Capital After Transfer	
Alfano	$50,000	$ − 27,500	$22,500	(25%)
Bailey	40,000	− 17,500	22,500	(25%)
Cobb		45,000	45,000	(50%)
	$90,000	$ 0	$90,000	

The decision to revalue or not to revalue partnership assets when a new partner is admitted through payments to existing partners is less important than equity considerations surrounding capital transfers and cash distributions. Comparable treatment of all partners is the objective regardless of asset revaluation. Although the evidence supporting revaluation is not always convincing, a revaluation based on the price paid by an incoming partner does have the advantage of establishing a capital balance for that partner equal to the amount of his or her investment. For example, Cobb's capital credit was equal to his $50,000 payment to Alfano and Bailey when the assets were revalued. It was only $45,000 when the assets were not revalued. Also, the amounts of capital transfer and cash allocations are easier to determine when assets are revalued because gains and losses relating to the old partnership are formally recorded in the accounts.

INVESTING IN AN EXISTING PARTNERSHIP

A new partner may be admitted into an existing partnership by investing cash or other assets in the business, or by bringing clients or individual talents into the business that will contribute to future profitability. In this case, the old partnership is legally dissolved and the investment of the new partner is recorded under the provisions of the new partnership agreement. As in the case of a purchase of an interest, the net assets of the old partnership may or may not be revalued. But since new assets are being invested in the business, the basis for revaluation is not necessarily determined by the investment of the new partner. If the amount invested by the new partner implies that the old partnership has unrecorded asset values, a total valuation of the new business based on the investment of the new partner seems appropriate. On the other hand, if the capital interest granted to the new partner is greater than the amount of his or her investment and the identifiable assets of the old partnership are recorded at their fair values, there is an implication that the new partner is bringing goodwill into the business. In this case, the total valuation of the new business is determined by reference to the capital of the old partnership.

The evidence provided by the amount of an investment only relates to the total value of the business. Since values for identifiable assets have to be determined on an individual basis by appraisal or other valuation technique, it is assumed that the identifiable assets of the old partnership are recorded at their fair values, in the absence of evidence to the contrary. If identifiable assets of a partnership are to be revalued, the revaluation must be based on appraisals or other evidence relating to specific assets.

Partnership Investment at Book Value

Andrew and Boyles have capital balances of $40,000 each and share profits equally. They agree to admit Criner to a one-third interest in capital and profits of a new Andrew, Boyles, and Criner partnership for a $40,000 cash investment. Since Criner's $40,000 investment is equal to the capital interest that she receives [($80,000 + $40,000)/3], the issue of revaluation does not arise. Criner's investment is recorded on the partnership books:

Cash	$40,000	
Criner capital		$40,000

To record Criner's $40,000 cash investment for a one-third interest in partnership capital and income.

Partnership Assets Revalued
(Goodwill to Old Partners)

Now assume that Andrew and Boyles, who have capital balances of $40,000 each and share profits equally, agree to admit Criner to a one-third interest in the capital and profits of a new partnership for a cash investment of $50,000. Since Criner is willing to invest $50,000 for a one-third interest in the $80,000 recorded assets plus her $50,000 investment ($130,000 assets), there is an implication that the old partnership has unrecorded asset values. The amount of unrecorded assets is determined by reference to Criner's investment. By implication, total assets of the new partnership will be $150,000 ($50,000 ÷ ⅓) and the value of unrecorded assets must be $20,000, the excess of the $150,000 total value less the $80,000 recorded assets plus the $50,000 new investment. If the assets are revalued, the following entries are made:

Goodwill	$20,000	
Andrew capital		$10,000
Boyles capital		10,000

To revalue the assets of the old partnership based on the amount of Criner's investment.

| Cash | $50,000 | |
| Criner capital | | $50,000 |

To record Criner's investment in the partnership for a one-third interest in capital and income.

The $20,000 recorded as goodwill in the first entry is credited to the old partners in their old profit and loss sharing ratios. Conceptually, the revaluation constitutes a final act of the old partnership, and all further entries are those of the new partnership. The second entry merely records Criner's $50,000 cash investment and capital credit in equal amounts. A summary of the capital balances before and after the $20,000 revaluation and the investment of Criner is as follows:

CAPITAL BALANCES

	Before Revaluation	Revaluation	After Revaluation	New Investment	Capital After Investment	
Andrew	$40,000	$10,000	$ 50,000		$ 50,000	⅓
Boyles	40,000	10,000	50,000		50,000	⅓
Criner				$50,000	50,000	⅓
	$80,000	$20,000	$100,000	$50,000	$150,000	

Partnership Assets Not Revalued (Bonus to Old Partners)

If the partners decide against revaluation, the only entry required to record Criner's admittance into the partnership is as follows:

Cash	$50,000	
Andrew capital		$ 3,333
Boyles capital		3,333
Criner capital		43,334

To record Criner's investment in the partnership and to allow Andrew and Boyles a bonus due to unrecorded asset values.

In this case, partnership net assets are increased only by the amount of the new investment, the new partner's capital account is credited for her one-third interest in the $130,000 capital of the new partnership, and the difference between the investment and capital credit of the new partner is allocated to the capital accounts of the old partners in relation to the old profit sharing agreement. This situation is referred to as a *bonus to old partners* because the old partners receive capital credits for a part of the new partner's investment. The goodwill and bonus procedures are comparable in the sense that each partner would receive $50,000 if the business were immediately sold for $150,000. The capital balances before and after the admission of Criner are as follows:

CAPITAL BALANCES

	Per Books	Investment	Capital After Investment	
Andrew	$40,000	$ 3,333	$ 43,333	⅓
Boyles	40,000	3,333	43,333	⅓
Criner		43,334	43,334	⅓
	$80,000	$50,000	$130,000	

660

PARTNERSHIPS—
FORMATION,
OPERATIONS AND
CHANGES IN
OWNERSHIP INTERESTS

Partnership Assets Revalued
(Goodwill to New Partner)

Suppose that Andrew and Boyles agreed to admit Criner into the partnership *for a 40 percent interest* in the capital and profit with an investment of $50,000. In this case, there is an implication that Criner is bringing goodwill into the partnership. That is, Andrew and Boyles must be willing to admit Criner to a 40 percent interest in the $80,000 recorded assets plus her $50,000 investment (40% × $130,000 = $52,000) because they expect Criner's total contribution to exceed her cash investment. Accordingly, the total value of the partnership is determined by reference to the 60 percent interest retained in the new partnership capital and profits by Andrew and Boyles. Total capital of the new partnership is $133,333 ($80,000 old capital assumed to be fairly valued/.6), and the admisssion of Criner is recorded:

Cash	$50,000	
Goodwill	3,333	
Criner capital		$53,333

    To admit Criner to a 40% interest in capital and profits.

Total capital of the new partnership is $133,333 ($80,000 old capital + $50,000 new investment + $3,333 goodwill), and Criner has a 40 percent interest in that new capital. A summary of the capital balances before and after the admittance of Criner is as follows:

CAPITAL BALANCES

	Per Books	Investment plus Goodwill	Capital After Investment	
Andrew	$40,000		$ 40,000	30%
Boyles	40,000		40,000	30%
Criner		$53,333	53,333	40%
	$80,000	$53,333	$133,333	

Partnership Assets Not Revalued
(Bonus to New Partner)

Instead of allowing goodwill to the incoming partner, the bonus procedure can be used. Under this procedure the assets are not revalued, but the capital balances of Andrew and Boyles must be reduced to meet the 40 percent condition of the agreement. Total assets of the new partnership are $130,000, and Criner's 40 percent interest is $52,000. The $2,000 difference between Criner's capital credit of $52,000 and her $50,000 investment is considered a bonus to Criner. Since partnership assets are not revalued, the excess $2,000 credited to Criner's account must be charged against the capital accounts of Andrew and Boyles in relation to their old profit and loss sharing ratios. Criner's admittance to the partnership under the bonus procedure is recorded:

Cash	$50 000	
Andrew capital	1,000	
Boyles capital	1,000	
Criner capital		$52,000

    To record Criners investment of $50,000 for a 40% interest in the partnership
    and allow her a $2,000 bonus.

The capital accounts of the partnership before and after the admittance of Criner are as follows:

CAPITAL BALANCES

	Per Books	Investment	Capital After Investment	
Andrew	$40,000	$(1,000)	$ 39,000	30%
Boyles	40,000	(1,000)	39,000	30%
Criner		52,000	52,000	40%
	$80,000	$50,000	$130,000	

Basis for Revaluation

The revaluation/goodwill and nonrevaluation/bonus procedures are alternative approaches for recording changes in partnership interests through direct investments in an existing partnership. In deciding whether the goodwill or bonus relates to the old partners or the new partner the investment of the new partner is analyzed in terms of the nonrevaluation/bonus procedure. Under the nonrevaluation assumption, the capital credit of the new partner is determined by multiplying the new partner's capital interest by the net assets of the old partnership plus the investment. The analysis is as follows:

$$\text{If: } \frac{\text{Investment of}}{\text{new partner}} = \frac{\text{Capital credit}}{\text{of new partner}} \Rightarrow \text{No bonus (or goodwill)}$$

$$\text{If: } \frac{\text{Investment of}}{\text{new partner}} > \frac{\text{Capital credit}}{\text{of new partner}} \Rightarrow \begin{array}{l}\text{Bonus to old partners}\\ \text{(or goodwill to old partners}\\ \text{if assets are revalued)}\end{array}$$

$$\text{If: } \frac{\text{Investment of}}{\text{new partner}} < \frac{\text{Capital credit}}{\text{of new partner}} \Rightarrow \begin{array}{l}\text{Bonus to new partner}\\ \text{(or goodwill to new partner}\\ \text{if assets are revalued)}\end{array}$$

Since the amount of the old partnership capital provides no basis for revaluation of the old partners' capital, any revaluation relating to the old partners' capital should be based on the investment of the new partner. Similarly, the amount of the new partner's investment provides no basis for revaluation of the new partner's capital and, accordingly, any revaluation of the new partner's capital should be related to the old partnership capital retained. Application of this scenario prevents the downward adjustment of identifiable net assets of the old partnership that are assumed to be recorded at amounts equal to their fair values. If the evidence indicates an undervaluation or overvaluation of recorded net assets, adjustments should be made before comparing the new partner's investment and capital credit to identify bonus or goodwill.

A summary of the procedures used in the previous examples to compute the amounts of goodwill and bonus for Criner's investments is as follows:

	$50,000 Investment for a ⅓ Interest	$50,000 Investment for a 40% Interest
Nonrevaluation—Bonus		
Criner's investment	$ 50,000	$ 50,000
Criner's capital credit:		
$130,000 × ⅓	43,334	
$130,000 × 40%		52,000
Bonus to old partners ($50,000 > $43,334)	$ 6,666	
Bonus to Criner ($50,000 < $52,000)		$ 2,000

662

PARTNERSHIPS—
FORMATION,
OPERATIONS AND
CHANGES IN
OWNERSHIP INTERESTS

	$50,000 Investment for a ⅓ Interest	*$50,000 Investment for a 40% Interest*
Revaluation—Goodwill		
Total capital:		
$50,000 ÷ ⅓ (based on Criner's investment)	$150,000	
$80,000 ÷ .6 (based on old partnership capital)		$133,333
Book value of old partnership assets + Criner's investment	130,000	130,000
Goodwill (other identifiable assets) to old partners	$ 20,000	
Goodwill to Criner		$ 3,333

Conceptual Problems in Recording Partnership Investment

Since the partners can agree to any partnership valuation that they like, they can stipulate that partnership capital is to be determined by reference to old partnership capital or the investment of a new partner, regardless of whether the agreement implies bonus or goodwill to the old partners or the new partner. Certain conceptual problems do arise, however, when the conditions specified in the preceding section are not followed. The problems associated with a revaluation of old partnership assets based on the old partnership interest retained can be explained by reference to the previous examples. If a total valuation for the new partnership had been based on the two-thirds interest retained in the first example, the total partnership valuation would have been $120,000 ($80,000 ÷ ⅔). Criner's capital would have been one-third of this amount, or $40,000, and the $120,000 valuation would imply a $10,000 overvaluation of Criner's cash investment ($80,000 old assets plus $50,000 new investment − $120,000 total capital). The overvaluation must relate to Criner's investment, since the $80,000 capital of the old partners is used to determine the $120,000 total capital of the new partnership. Criner's willingness to invest $50,000 for a one-third interest also provides evidence to the contrary, since Criner is giving a bonus of $10,000 to the old partners. In spite of the conflicting evidence, the partners can agree to a $120,000 valuation of the new partnership capital, in which case Criner's admittance would be recorded:

Andrew capital	$5,000	
Boyles capital	5,000	
Other assets		$10,000
Cash	$50 000	
Andrew capital		$ 5,000
Boyles capital		5,000
Criner capital		40,000

In the second example where Criner invested $50,000 for a 40 percent interest, total partnership capital based on the amount of Criner's investment rather than the old partnership capital would have resulted in a total valuation for the new partnership of $125,000 ($50,000/.4). Such a valuation implies that the old partnership assets are overvalued by $5,000, since old partnership assets of $80,000 plus the $50,000 new investment totals $130,000. Unless the old partnership has unamortized goodwill on its books, this implied overvaluation contradicts the basic assumption of identifiable assets being equal to their fair values that underlies application of the revaluation approach. If the partners agree on a $125,000 total valuation, however, the admittance of Criner would be recorded as follows:

Andrew capital	$ 2,500	
Boyles capital	2,500	
Other assets		$ 5,000
Cash	$50 000	
Criner capital		$50,000

Even though there are conceptual problems with the valuations illustrated here, no inequity to the partners results because the relative profit and loss sharing ratios of the old partners remain unchanged in the new agreement. That is, Andrew and Boyles shared 50:50 before the admittance of Criner and equally after Criner's admittance. Inequities could result if the relative profit and loss sharing ratios of the old partners changed in the new partnership agreement. Similarly, inequities could result if the capital interest granted to the new partner is not aligned with the new partner's interest in future profits and losses.

DISSOLUTION OF A CONTINUING PARTNERSHIP THROUGH DEATH OR RETIREMENT

The retirement or death of a partner from a continuing partnership business dissolves the old partnership and requires a settlement with the retiring partner or with the estate of the deceased partner. In the absence of a partnership agreement to the contrary, the settlement is in accordance with Section 42 of the Uniform Partnership Act. This section provides that the retiring partner or the estate of a deceased partner "may have the value of his interest at the date of dissolution ascertained, and shall receive as an ordinary creditor an amount equal to the value of his interest in the dissolved partnership with interest." Since the valuation is at the date of dissolution, it follows that partnership books should be closed as of the date of death or retirement. When there is a time lag between death or retirement and final settlement, the capital balance of the deceased or retiring partner should be reclassified as a liability. Any interest (or other return) accruing on the liability up to the date of final settlement is considered an expense of the continuing partnership entity.

In recording the settlement, the accounting depends upon whether the retiring partner (or the estate of the deceased partner) receives an amount equal to the final balance of his or her capital account or something more or less than his or her final capital. If the retiring partner (or the estate of a deceased partner) is paid an amount equal to the final balance of his or her capital account, the only entry necessary is a charge to his or her capital account and a credit to cash for the amount paid. When the settlement with a retiring partner is more or less than the final capital account balance, the revaluation/goodwill and nonrevaluation/bonus procedures provide alternate methods of accounting for the settlement.

In order to illustrate the goodwill and bonus procedures, assume that Bonnie, Clyde, and Dillinger are partners with profit sharing percentages of 40 percent, 20 percent, and 40 percent, respectively, and that Dillinger decides to retire. The capital and income interests of the three partners on the date of Dillinger's retirement are as follows:

	Capital Balances	Percentage of Capital	Profit and Loss Percentage
Bonnie	$ 70,000	35%	40%
Clyde	50,000	25	20
Dillinger	80,000	40	40
Total capital	$200,000	100%	100%

664

PARTNERSHIPS—
FORMATION,
OPERATIONS AND
CHANGES IN
OWNERSHIP INTERESTS

Excess Payment to Retiring Partner

The partners agree that the business is undervalued on the partnership books and that Dillinger will be paid $92,000 in final settlement of his partnership interest. The excess payment to Dillinger can be recorded by three methods: (1) Dillinger may be granted a bonus, (2) partnership capital may be revalued to the extent of the excess payment to Dillinger, or (3) partnership capital may be revalued based on the amount implied by the excess payment.

Bonus to Retiring Partner   Dillinger's withdrawal from the partnership under the bonus procedure is recorded as follows:

Dillinger capital	$80,000	
Bonnie capital	8,000	
Clyde capital	4,000	
Cash		$92,000

This entry reflects the fact that Bonnie and Clyde granted a $12,000 bonus to Dillinger that was charged to their capital accounts in their 40:20 relative profit sharing ratios.

Goodwill Equal to Excess Payment Is Recorded   A second method of recording Dillinger's withdrawal is to record the $12,000 excess of cash paid to Dillinger over his capital account balance as goodwill:

Dillinger capital	$80,000	
Goodwill	12,000	
Cash		$92,000

Under this approach, goodwill is recorded only to the extent paid for by the continuing partnership. The problem with this approach is that it provides a revaluation of Dillinger's share of partnership assets, but it does not provide a revaluation of Bonnie and Clyde's capital interests. Thus, it is argued that this approach is inconsistent and logically unsound.

Revaluation of Total Partnership Capital Based on Excess Payment   A third approach for recording Dillinger's retirement is to revalue total partnership capital on the basis of the $12,000 excess payment. Under this method, total partnership capital is revalued as follows:

Goodwill (other assets)	$30,000	
Bonnie capital		$12,000
Clyde capital		6,000
Dillinger capital		12,000

The total undervaluation of the partnership is measured by the amount implied by the excess payment. In this case, the $30,000 is computed by dividing the $12,000 excess payment by Dillinger's 40 percent profit sharing percentage. Dillinger's retirement is then recorded:

Dillinger capital	$92,000	
Cash		$92,000

Total partnership capital implied by Dillinger's retirement settlement could have been computed by capitalizing the $92,000 payment to Dillinger to obtain a total partnership valuation of $230,000 ($92,000/40%). This approach is acceptable when the capital and income interests of the retiring (or deceased) partner are aligned. In the absence of such alignment, this alternate approach produces erroneous results. For example, assume the same facts as before except that Bonnie, Clyde, and Dillinger have capital balances of $70,000, $60,000, and

$70,000, respectively. Capitalizing the $92,000 payment to Dillinger by 40 percent produces a total partnership valuation of $230,000 and the same $30,000 good-will computation as before. But the results are erroneous because Dillinger's capital balance is only $82,000 after the goodwill is recorded [$70,000 + ($30,000 × 40%)]. The actual goodwill implied by the $92,000 payment to Dillinger is $55,000 [($92,000 − $70,000)/40%], and Dillinger's share is $22,000. Dillinger's capital account is increased to $92,000, the amount of the cash payment, when the implied goodwill is recorded.

Payment to Retiring Partner Less than Capital Balance

Suppose that Dillinger is paid $72,000 in final settlement of his capital interest. In this case, the three partners may have agreed that the business is worth less than its book value.

Overvalued Assets Written Down   A retirement payment to Dillinger of $8,000 less than his final capital balance implies that existing partnership capital is over-valued by $20,000 [($80,000 − $72,000)/40%]. If the evidence available supports this implication, the overvalued assets should be identified and reduced to their fair values. The revaluation and payment to Dillinger are recorded:

Bonnie capital	$ 8,000	
Clyde capital	4,000	
Dillinger capital	8,000	
Net assets		$20,000
Dillinger capital	$72,000	
Cash		$72,000

This method of recording Dillinger's withdrawal is appropriate if the $72,000 paid to Dillinger is the result of a valuation provided for under the Uniform Partnership Act. But it would not be appropriate if the $72,000 were determined by prior agreement of the partners without regard to total partnership capital at the time of withdrawal.

Bonus to Continuing Partners   If evidence indicates that partnership capital is fairly valued, the retirement of Dillinger would be recorded under the bonus procedure as follows:

Dillinger capital	$80,000	
Bonnie capital		$ 5,333
Clyde capital		2,667
Cash		72,000

This method of recording provides a bonus to Bonnie and Clyde. The bonus is measured by the excess of Dillinger's capital balance over the cash paid by the partnership for his 40 percent interest.

SUMMARY

Partnership accounting procedures are similar to those for other forms of business organization except for procedures relating to the measurement of partnership capital interests. Accounting measurements relating to the capital and income interests of partners are based on the partnership agreement, or in the absence of an agreement, on the Uniform Partnership Act except for partnerships in states that have not adopted the Act. The partnership agreement should be in writing and should cover matters relating to the amount and valuation of capital contributions, additional investments and withdrawals, loans to

666

PARTNERSHIPS—
FORMATION,
OPERATIONS AND
CHANGES IN
OWNERSHIP INTERESTS

partners, profit sharing arrangements, changes in partnership interests, and various other matters. These areas are discussed in the chapter, and related accounting concepts and procedures are illustrated.

Since partners can agree to value assets and divide income as they desire, a major role of the accountant is to advise the partners on the equitable allocation of capital and income interests in designing the partnership agreement. Once the agreement has been finalized, the role of the accountant is to interpret the agreement correctly and to account for partnership activities in accordance with the agreement.

ASSIGNMENT MATERIAL

QUESTIONS

1 Explain why the noncash investments of partners should be recorded at their fair values.

2 Is there a conceptual difference between partner drawings and withdrawals? A practical difference?

3 In the absence of an agreement for the division of profits, how are they divided under the Uniform Partnership Act? Does your answer also apply to losses? Does it apply if one partner invests three times as much as the other partners?

4 Why do some profit sharing agreements provide for salary and interest allowances?

5 Are partner salary allowances expenses of the partnership?

6 When a profit sharing agreement specifies that profits be divided in the ratio of capital balances, how should capital balances be computed?

7 Explain how a partner could have a loss from partnership operations for a period even though the partnership had net income.

8 The concept of partnership dissolution has a technical meaning under the provisions of the Uniform Partnership Act. Explain the concept.

9 If a partner sells his or her partnership interest directly to a third party, the partnership may or may not be dissolved. Under what conditions is the partnership dissolved?

10 If a partnership is dissolved with the death or retirement of a partner, how do you explain the fact that some partnerships have been in existence for fifty years or more?

11 How does the purchase of an interest from existing partners differ from acquiring an interest by investment in a partnership?

12 What alternative approaches can be used in recording the admission of a new partner?

13 Why is the goodwill procedure best described as a revaluation procedure?

14 Explain the bonus procedure for recording an investment in a partnership. When is the bonus applicable to old partners, and when is it applicable to new partners?

15 The goodwill procedure was used to record the investment of a new partner in the XYZ Partnership, but immediately thereafter, the entire business was sold for an amount equal to the recorded capital of the partnership. Under what conditions would the amounts received in final liquidation of the partnership have been the same as if the bonus procedure had been used?

16 Bob invests $10,000 cash for a 25 percent interest in the capital and earnings of the BOP Partnership. Explain how this investment could give rise to (a) the recording of goodwill, (b) the write-down of the partnership assets, (c) a bonus to old partners, and (d) a bonus to Bob.

EXERCISES

E 16-1 Mosely and Nelson enter into a used car partnership in which Mosely is to have a 40 percent interest in capital and profits and Nelson a 60 percent interest. Mosely contributes $20,000 cash and a used car inventory with a fair value of $60,000, and Nelson contributes $50,000 cash and land with a fair value of $70,000.

Mosely paid $48,000 for the used car inventory, and Nelson paid $80,000 for the land.

Required

1 Prepare journal entries to record the initial investments of Mosely and Nelson.
2 Calculate the inequity that would have resulted if the partnership had recorded noncash assets at cost rather than fair value.

E 16–2 The partnership agreement of Hish, Myers, and Jarrett provides for Hish to receive a salary of $30,000, for the partners to receive 10 percent interest on beginning of the year capital balances, and for remaining profits to be divided equally. The capital balances at January 1, 19X1 were $200,000, $220,000, and $180,000 for Hish, Myers, and Jarrett, respectively.

Required

1 Assume that the partnership has income of $120,000 for 19X1. Determine the income distribution to Hish, Myers, and Jarrett.
2 Assume instead that the partnership has a loss of $60,000 for 19X1. Determine the loss distribution to Hish, Myers, and Jarrett.

E 16–3 On December 31, 19X2 the total partnership capital (assets less liabilities) for the Bird, Cage, and Dean partnership is $372,000. Selected information related to the preclosing capital balances is as follows:

	Bird Capital	Cage Capital	Dean Capital	Total Capital
Balance January 1	$120,000	$ 90,000	$140,000	$350,000
Investments 19X2		20,000	20,000	40,000
Withdrawals 19X2	(30,000)		(30,000)	(60,000)
Drawings 19X2	(10,000)	(10,000)	(10,000)	(30,000)
	$ 80,000	$100,000	$120,000	$300,000

Required: Prepare a statement of partnership capital for the Bird, Cage, and Dean partnership for 19X2.

E 16–4 The capital accounts of the Saxon and Tolly partnership on September 30, 19X1 were:

Saxon capital (75% profit percentage)	$140,000
Tolly capital (25% profit percentage)	56,000
Total capital	$196,000

On October 1 Kuband was admitted to a 40 percent interest in the partnership when he purchased 40 percent of each existing partner's capital for $100,000, paid directly to Saxon and Tolly.

Required: Determine the capital balances of Saxon, Tolly, and Kuband after Kuband's admission to the partnership if goodwill is *not* recorded.

E 16–5 Bowen and Monita are partners in a retail business and divide profits 60 percent to Bowen and 40 percent to Monita. Their capital balances at December 31, 19X5 are as follows:

Bowen capital	$180,000
Monita capital	180,000
Total capital	$360,000

Partnership assets and liabilities have book values equal to fair values. The partners agree to admit Johnson into the partnership. Johnson purchases a one-third interest in partnership capital and profits directly from Bowen and Monita (one-third of each of their capital accounts) for $150,000.

Required: Prepare journal entries for the admission of Johnson into the partnership, assuming that partnership assets are revalued.

E 16–6 The capital balances and profit and loss sharing percentages for the Sprint, Telico, and Univar partnership at December 31, 19X1 are as follows:

Sprint capital (30%)	$80,000
Telico capital (50%)	$90,000
Univar capital (20%)	$70,000

The partners agree to admit Vernon into the partnership on January 1, 19X2 for a 20 percent interest in the capital and income of the business.

Required
1 Prepare the journal entry(s) to record Vernon's admission to the partnership assuming that he invests $50,000 in the partnership for the 20 percent interest and that partnership capital is *revalued.*
2 Prepare the journal entry(s) to record Vernon's admission to the partnership assuming that he invests $70,000 in the partnership for the 20 percent interest and that partnership capital is *revalued.*

E 16–7 The partnership of Lynn and Martin had capital account balances on December 31, 19X3 as follows:

Lynn capital	$45,000
Martin capital	35,000
Total capital	$80,000

On January 2, 19X4 Lynn and Martin agree to admit Nolan into the partnership with his investment of $38,000 for a one-fourth interest in the capital and earnings. Partnership assets are not to be revalued.

Required
1 Prepare the journal entry(s) to record Nolan's investment in the partnership.
2 Determine the capital balances for each partner after Nolan is admitted as a partner.

E 16–8 Capital balances and profit and loss sharing ratios for the Nixon, Mann, and Peter partnership on December 31, 19X1, just before the retirement of Nixon, are as follows:

Nixon capital (30%)	$64,000
Mann capital (30%)	$70,000
Peter capital (40%)	$80,000

On January 2, 19X2 Nixon is paid $85,000 cash upon his retirement.

Required: Prepare the journal entry(s) to record Nixon's retirement assuming that goodwill, as implied by the payment to Nixon, is recorded on the partnership books.

E 16–9 A summary balance sheet for the Jones, King, and Lamb partnership on March 31, 19X1, along with profit participation percentages is as follows:

Assets (at cost equal		Accounts payable	$ 40,000
to fair value)	$250,000	Jones capital (20%)	60,000
		King capital (30%)	70,000
		Lamb capital (50%)	80,000
			$250,000

On April 1, 19X1 King retires and is paid $91,000 for his entire partnership interest.

Required
1 Prepare the journal entry(s) to record the payment to King and King's retirement if no goodwill is recorded.
2 Prepare the journal entry(s) to record payment to King and King's retirement if implied goodwill is recorded.

E 16–10
1 Janice and Margaret formed a partnership on January 1, 19X5 with Janice contributing $20,000 cash and Margaret contributing equipment with a book value of $8,000 and a fair value of $6,000 and inventory items with a book value of $3,000 and fair value of $4,000. During 19X5 Janice made additional investments of $2,000 on April 1 and $2,000 on June 1, and on September 1, she withdrew $5,000. Margaret had no additional investments or withdrawals during the year. The average capital balances for 19X5 of Janice and Margaret were:
  a $19,000 and $11,000   **b** $21,250 and $10,000
  c $21,000 and $10,000   **d** $21,250 and $9,000

2 On January 1, 19X7 Janice and Margaret have capital balances of $25,000 and $20,000, respectively. On July 1, 19X7 Janice invests an additional $5,000 and Margaret withdraws $2,000. Profits and losses of the partnership are to be divided as follows:

- Margaret, the managing partner, receives a $20,000 salary and Janice receives $9,000.
- Both partners receive interest of 10 percent on their beginning capital balances.
- Remaining income is divided equally.

Income of the Janice-Margaret partnership for 19X7 is $12,000. Janice's share of partnership income is:
  a $11,500   **b** $10,750
  c $6,000   **d** $750

3 Thomas and Mark are partners having capital balances of $50,000 and $60,000, respectively. They admit Jay to a one-third interest in partnership capital and profits for an investment of $65,000. If the goodwill procedure is used in recording Jay's admission to the partnership:
  a Jay's capital will be $58,333
  b Total capital will be $175,000
  c Mark's capital will be $70,000
  d Goodwill will be recorded at $15,000

4 Shirley purchased an interest in the Tony and Olga partnership by paying Tony $40,000 for half of his capital and half of his 50 percent profit sharing interest. At the time Tony's capital balance was $30,000 and Olga's capital balance was $70,000. Shirley should receive a credit to her capital account of:
  a $15,000   **b** $20,000
  c $25,000   **d** $33,333

5 The balance sheet of the Freddie, Jenny, and Peggy partnership on December 31, 19X6, together with profit sharing ratios, revealed the following:

Cash	$240,000	Freddie capital (30%)	$200,000
Other assets	360,000	Jenny capital (30%)	170,000
		Peggy capital (40%)	230,000
	$600,000		$600,000

Jenny decided to retire from the partnership and the partners agreed that she should receive $200,000 cash as payment in full for her share of partnership assets. If the goodwill implied by the settlement with Jenny is recorded on the partnership books, total partnership assets after Jenny's withdrawal should be:
  a $566,667   **b** $500,000
  c $430,000   **d** $400,000

E 16–11
1 The Pete and Sells partnership has capital balances of $15,000 and $25,000, respectively, on January 1, 19X5. Pete withdraws $3,000 on January 3 and Sells withdraws $4,000 on April 2. Additional investments are $6,000 by Pete on August 29 and $2,000 by Sells on October 1, 19X5. The average capital investments of Pete and Sells, respectively, for the year 19X5 are:
  a $16,500 and $24,000   **b** $15,000 and $24,000
  c $14,000 and $22,500   **d** $13,500 and $22,833

2 Total partnership capital at December 31, 19X6 is $319,000 for the May and Sloan partnership. Information related to individual capital balances is as follows:

670

PARTNERSHIPS—
FORMATION,
OPERATIONS AND
CHANGES IN
OWNERSHIP INTERESTS

	May	Sloan
Capital balances January 1, 19X6	$185,000	$120,000
Additional investments 19X6	16,000	none
Withdrawals 19X6	5,000	8,000
Drawings 19X6	10,000	7,000

May's capital should be shown in the December 31, 19X6 balance sheet of the partnership at:

a $159,500 b $185,000

c $186,000 d $200,000

3 A profit and loss sharing schedule for the Hamilton and Hayes partnership for 19X2 includes the following information:

	Hamilton	Hayes
Salary to Hamilton	$12,000	—
Interest to the partners	3,000	$6,000
Remainder divided equally		

Hamilton's share of partnership profits of $15,000 for the year must be:

a $15,000 b $13,500

c $12,000 d $22,500

4 The capital account balances of the Cline and Daisy partnership at June 30, 19X6, together with profit sharing ratios, were as follows:

Cline capital (60%)	$420,000
Daisy capital (40%)	380,000

On that date they agreed to take Earl into the partnership for a 25 percent interest in capital and profits for a cash payment of $400,000. If partnership assets are revalued upon the admission of Earl, the balance of Cline's capital account after Earl's admission should be:

a $420,000 b $480,000

c $540,000 d $660,000

5 The December 31, 19X8 balance sheet of the Bennett, Carter, and Davis partnership is summarized as follows:

Cash	$100,000	Carter loan	$100,000
Other assets, at cost	500,000	Bennett capital	100,000
		Carter capital	200,000
		Davis capital	200,000
	$600,000		$600,000

The partners share profits and losses as follows: Bennett 20 percent, Carter 30 percent, and Davis 50 percent. Carter is retiring from the partnership and the partners have agreed that "other assets" should be adjusted to their fair value of $600,000 at December 31, 19X8. They further agree that Carter will receive $244,000 cash for his partnership interest exclusive of his loan which is to be paid in full and that no goodwill implied by Carter's payment shall be recorded.

After Carter's retirement, the capital balances of Bennett and Davis, respectively, will be:

a $116,000 and $240,000 b $101,714 and $254,286

c $100,000 and $200,000 d $73,143 and $182,857

6 Linkous and Quesenberry are partners with capital balances of $50,000 and $70,000, respectively, and they share profits and losses equally. The partners agree to take Duncan into the partnership for a 40 percent interest in capital and profits, while Linkous and Quesenberry each retain a 30 percent interest.

Duncan pays $60,000 cash directly to Linkous and Quesenberry for his

40 percent interest, and goodwill implied by Duncan's payment is recognized on the partnership books. If Linkous and Quesenberry transfer equal amounts of capital to Duncan, the capital balances after Duncan's admittance will be:

a Linkous $35,000, Quesenberry $55,000, Duncan $60,000
b Linkous $45,000, Quesenberry $45,000, Duncan $60,000
c Linkous $36,000, Quesenberry $36,000, Duncan $48,000
d Linkous $26,000, Quesenberry $46,000, Duncan $48,000

E 16-12   **[AICPA adapted]**

1 On May 1, 19X9, Cobb and Mott formed a partnership and agreed to share profits and losses in the ratio of 3:7, respectively. Cobb contributed a parcel of land that cost him $10,000. Mott contributed $40,000 cash. The land was sold for $18,000 on May 1, 19X9, immediately after formation of the partnership. What amount should be recorded in Cobb's capital account on formation of the partnership?

a $18,000   **b** $17,400
c $15,000   **d** $10,000

2 Arthur Plack, a partner in the Brite Partnership, has a 30 percent participation in partnership profits and losses. Plack's capital account had a net decrease of $60,000 during the calendar year 19X4. During 19X4 Plack withdrew $130,000 (charged against his capital account) and contributed property valued at $25,000 to the partnership. What was the net income of the Brite Partnership for 19X4?

a $150,000   **b** $233,333
c $350,000   **d** $550,000

3 Fox, Greg, and Howe are partners with average capital balances during 19X6 of $120,000, $60,000, and $40,000, respectively. Partners receive 10 percent interest on their average capital balances. After deducting salaries of $30,000 to Fox and $20,000 to Howe, the residual profit or loss is divided equally. In 19X6 the partnership sustained a $33,000 loss before interest and salaries to partners. By what amount should Fox's capital account change?

a $7,000 increase   **b** $11,000 decrease
c $35,000 decrease   **d** $42,000 increase

4 Beck, an active partner in the Beck and Cris partnership, receives an annual bonus of 25 percent of partnership net income after deducting the bonus. For the year ended December 31, 19X8, partnership net income before the bonus amounted to $300,000. Beck's 19X8 bonus should be:

a $56,250   **b** $60,000
c $62,500   **d** $75,000

E 16-13   **[AICPA adapted]**

1 Partners Allen, Baker, and Coe share profits and losses 50:30:20, respectively. The balance sheet at April 30, 19X5 follows:

Assets		Equities	
Cash	$ 40,000	Accounts payable	$100,000
Other assets	360,000	Allen capital	74,000
		Baker capital	130,000
		Coe capital	96,000
	$400,000		$400,000

The assets and liabilities are recorded and presented at their respective fair values. Jones is to be admitted as a new partner with a 20 percent capital interest and a 20 percent share of profits and losses in exchange for a cash contribution. No goodwill or bonus is to be recorded. How much cash should Jones contribute?

a $60,000   **b** $72,000
c $75,000   **d** $80,000

2 Elton and Don are partners who share profits and losses in the ratio of 7:3, respectively. On November 5, 19X8 their respective capital accounts were as follows:

Elton	$ 70,000
Don	60,000
	$130,000

672

PARTNERSHIPS—
FORMATION,
OPERATIONS AND
CHANGES IN
OWNERSHIP INTERESTS

On that date they agreed to admit Kravitz as a partner with a one-third interest in the capital and profits and losses upon his investment of $50,000. The new partnership will begin with a total capital of $180,000. Immediately after Kravitz's admission, what are the capital balances of Elton, Don, and Kravitz, respectively?

a $60,000, $60,000, $60,000   b $63,000, $57,000, $60,000
c $63,333, $56,667, $60,000   d $70,000, $60,000, $50,000

3 William desires to purchase a one-fourth capital and profit and loss interest in the partnership of Eli, George, and Dick. The three partners agree to sell William one-fourth of their respective capital and profit and loss interests in exchange for a total payment of $40,000. The capital accounts and the respective percentage interests in profits and losses immediately before the sale to William are:

Eli capital (60%)	$ 80,000
George capital (30%)	40,000
Dick capital (10%)	20,000
	$140,000

All other assets and liabilities are fairly valued, and implied goodwill is to be recorded prior to the acquisition by William. Immediately after William's acquisition, what should be the capital balances of Eli, George, and Dick, respectively?

a $60,000, $30,000, $15,000   b $69,000, $34,500, $16,500
c $77,000, $38,500, $19,500   d $92,000, $46,000, $22,000

4 The capital accounts of the partnership of Newton, Sharman, and Jackson on June 1, 19X7 are presented, along their respective profit and loss ratios:

Newton	$139,200	1/2
Sharman	208,800	1/3
Jackson	96,000	1/6
	$444,000	

On June 1, 19X7 Sidney was admitted to the partnership when he purchased, for $132,000, a proportionate interest from Newton and Sharman in the net assets and profits of the partnership. As a result of this transaction, Sidney acquired a one-fifth interest in the net assets and profits of the firm. Assuming that implied goodwill is *not* to be recorded, what is the combined gain realized by Newton and Sharman upon the sale of a portion of their interests in the partnership to Sidney?

a 0   b $43,200
c $62,400   d $82,000

5 James Dixon, a partner in an accounting firm, decided to withdraw from the partnership. Dixon's share of the partnership profits and losses was 20 percent. Upon withdrawing from the partnership, he was paid $74,000 in final settlement for his partnership interest. The total of the partners' capital accounts *before* recognition of partnership goodwill prior to Dixon's withdrawal was $210,000. After his withdrawal, the remaining partners' capital accounts, excluding their share of goodwill, totaled $160,000. The total agreed-upon goodwill of the firm was:

a $120,000   b $140,000
c $160,000   d $250,000

6 On June 30, 19X8 the balance sheet for the partnership of Williams, Brown, and Lowe, together with their respective profit and loss ratios, is summarized as follows:

Assets, at cost	$300,000	Williams loan	$ 15,000
		Williams capital (20%)	70,000
		Brown capital (20%)	65,000
		Lowe capital (60%)	150,000
			$300,000

Williams has decided to retire from the partnership, and by mutual agreement the assets are to be adjusted to their fair value of $360,000 at June 30, 19X8. It is agreed that the partnership will pay Williams $102,000 cash for his partnership interest exclusive of his loan, which is to be repaid in full. Goodwill is to be recorded in this transaction, as implied by the excess payment to Williams. After Williams's retirement, what are the capital account balances of Brown and Lowe, respectively?

a $65,000 and $150,000   **b** $97,000 and $246,000
c $73,000 and $174,000   **d** $77,000 and $186,000

E 16–14   The partnership agreement of Kray, Lamb, and Mann provides for the division of net income as follows:

    1 Lamb, who manages the partnership, is to receive a salary of $11,000 per year.
    2 Each partner is to be allowed interest at 10 percent on beginning capital.
    3 Remaining profits are to be divided equally.

     During 19X1 Kray invested an additional $4,000 in the partnership. Lamb withdrew $5,000 and Mann withdrew $4,000 during 19X1. No other investments or withdrawals were made during 19X1. On January 1, 19X1 the capital balances were Kray, $65,000; Lamb, $75,000; and Mann, $70,000. Total capital at year end was $252,000.

Required: Prepare a statement of partners' capital for the year ended December 31, 19X1.

E 16–15   After operating as partners for several years, Crosby and Chambers decided to sell one-half of each of their partnership interests to Chipper for a total of $65,000, paid directly to Crosby and Chambers.
     At the time of Chipper's admittance to the partnership, Crosby and Chambers had capital balances of $45,000 and $60,000, respectively, and shared profits 45 percent to Crosby and 55 percent to Chambers.

Required
    1 Calculate the capital balances of each of the partners immediately after Chipper is admitted as a partner.
    2 In designing a new partnership agreement, how should profits and losses be divided?
    3 If a new partnership agreement is not established, how will profits and losses be divided?

E 16–16   The Case, Donley, and Early partnership balance sheet and profit and loss percentages at June 30, 19X6 is summarized as follows:

Assets	$500,000	Case capital (30%)	$140,000
		Donley capital (30%)	175,000
		Early capital (40%)	185,000
	$500,000		$500,000

     On July 1, 19X6 the partners agree that Ms. Case is to retire immediately and receive $161,000 for her partnership interest.

Required: Prepare journal entries to illustrate *three* possible methods of accounting for the retirement of Ms. Case.

PROBLEMS

P 16–1   The partnership of Martin and Bosworth is being dissolved, and the assets and equities at book value and fair value and profit and loss sharing ratios at January 1, 19X1 are as follows:

	Book Value	*Fair Value*
Cash	$ 20,000	$ 20,000
Accounts receivable—net	100,000	100,000
Inventories	50,000	200,000
Plant assets—net	100,000	120,000
	$270,000	$440,000

674

PARTNERSHIPS—
FORMATION,
OPERATIONS AND
CHANGES IN
OWNERSHIP INTERESTS

	Book Value	Fair Value
Accounts payable	$ 50,000	$ 50,000
Martin capital (50%)	120,000	
Bosworth capital (50%)	100,000	
	$270,000	

Martin and Bosworth agree to admit Trent into the partnership for a one-third interest. Trent invests $95,000 cash and a building to be used in the business with a book value to Trent of $100,000 and a fair value of $110,000.

Required: Prepare a balance sheet for the Martin, Bosworth, and Trent partnership on January 2, 19X1 just after the admission of Trent assuming that the assets are to be revalued and goodwill recognized.

P 16–2 Ashe and Barbour are partners with capital balances on January 1, 19X6 of $40,000 and $50,000, respectively. The partnership agreement provides that each partner be allowed 10 percent interest on beginning capital balances; that Ashe receive a salary allowance of $12,000 per year and a 20 percent bonus of partnership income after interest, salary allowance, and bonus; and that remaining income be divided equally.

Required: Prepare an income distribution schedule to show how the $105,000 partnership net income for 19X6 should be divided.

P 16–3 The partnership agreement of Alex, Carl, and Erika provides that profits are to be divided as follows:
1 Alex is to receive a salary allowance of $10,000 for managing the partnership business.
2 Partners are to receive 10 percent interest on average capital balances.
3 Remaining profits are to be divided 30 percent, 30 percent, and 40 percent to Alex, Carl, and Erika, respectively.

Alex had a capital balance of $60,000 at January 1, 19X1 and had drawings of $8,000 during the year ended December 31, 19X1. Carl's capital balance on January 1, 19X1 was $90,000, and he invested an additional $30,000 on September 1, 19X1. Erika's beginning capital balance was $110,000, and she withdrew $10,000 on July 1 but invested an additional $20,000 on October 1, 19X1.

The partnership has a net loss of $12,000 during 19X1, and the accountant in charge allocated the net loss as follows: $200 profit to Alex, $4,800 loss to Carl, and $7,400 loss to Erika.

Required
1 A schedule to show the correct allocation of the partnership net loss for 19X1
2 A statement of partnership capital for the year ended December 31, 19X1
3 Journal entries to correct the books of the partnership at December 31, 19X1, assuming that all closing entries for the year have been recorded

P 16–4 A summary of changes in the capital account of the Kelly, Lynch, and Mister partnership for 19X2, before closing partnership net income to the capital accounts, is as follows:

	Kelly Capital	Lynch Capital	Mister Capital	Total Capital
Balance January 1, 19X2	$80,000	$80,000	$90,000	$250,000
Investment April 1	20,000			20,000
Withdrawal May 1		(15,000)		(15,000)
Withdrawal July 1	(10,000)			(10,000)
Withdrawal September 1			(30,000)	(30,000)
	$90,000	$65,000	$60,000	$215,000

Determine the allocation of the 19X2 net income to the partners under each of the following sets of independent assumptions:

1 Partnership net income is $48,000, and profit is divided on the basis of average capital balances during the year.

2 Partnership net income is $50,000, Kelly gets a bonus of 10 percent of income for managing the business, and the remaining profits are divided on the basis of beginning capital balances.

3 Partnership net loss is $35,000, each partner is allowed 10 percent interest on beginning capital balances, and the remaining profits are divided equally.

P 16-5 The partnership of Jones, Keller, and Glade was created on January 2, 19X6 with each of the partners contributing cash of $30,000. Reported profits, withdrawals, and additional investments were as follows:

	Reported Net Income	Withdrawals	Additional Investments
19X6	$19,000	$4,000 Keller 5,000 Jones	$5,000 Glade
19X7	$22,000	$8,000 Glade 3,000 Keller	$5,000 Jones
19X8	$29,000	$2,000 Glade 4,000 Keller	$6,000 Glade

The partnership agreement provides that partners are to be allowed 10 percent interest on the beginning-of-the-year capital balances, that Jones is to receive a $7,000 salary allowance, and that remaining profits are to be divided equally.

After the books were closed on December 31, 19X8, it was discovered that depreciation had been understated by $2,000 each year, and that the inventory taken at December 31, 19X6 was understated by $8,000.

Required
1 Calculate the balances in the three capital accounts on January 1, 19X9.
2 Calculate the balances that should be in the three capital accounts on January 1, 19X9.
3 Give the journal entry (one entry) to correct the books on January 1, 19X9.

P 16-6 The partnership of Burns and Cally is being dissolved, and its assets and equities at book value and fair value just prior to dissolution on January 1, 19X8 are as follows:

	Book Value	Fair Value
Assets		
Cash	$ 15,000	$ 15,000
Accounts receivable—net	45,000	40,000
Inventories	50,000	60,000
Plant assets—net	90,000	105,000
	$200,000	$220,000
Equities		
Accounts payable	$ 30,000	$ 30,000
Note payable (15%)	50,000	40,000
Burns capital (60%)	64,000	} 150,000
Cally capital (40%)	56,000	
	$200,000	$220,000

On January 2, 19X8 Burns and Cally take Dallas into the new partnership of Burns, Cally, and Dallas for a 40 percent interest in capital and profits.

Required
1 Prepare journal entries for the admission of Dallas into the partnership for an investment of $120,000, assuming that assets (including any goodwill) are to be revalued.

2 Prepare a balance sheet for the Burns, Cally, and Dallas partnership on January 2, 19X8, just after the admission of Dallas.

P 16–7 Capital balances and profit and loss sharing percentages for the Rake, Stan, and Tate partnership at December 31, 19X1 are as follows:

Rake capital	$ 80,000	50%
Stan capital	40,000	10%
Tate capital	80,000	40%
Total capital	$200,000	

Required: Prepare journal entries for Wilson's admittance into the partnership on January 1, 19X2 under each of the following independent assumptions:

1 Wilson purchases one-half of Rake's interest in the partnership for $50,000 paid directly to Rake.

2 Wilson purchases one-fourth of the capital and rights to future partnership profits from each of the partners for a total payment to the old partners of $60,000. The partnership capital is revalued.

3 Wilson invests $70,000 cash in the partnership for a 25 percent interest in the capital and profits, and partnership capital is revalued.

4 Wilson invests $45,000 in the partnership for a 20 percent interest in the capital and profits, and partnership capital is revalued to reflect Wilson's intangible contribution to the partnership.

5 Wilson invests $45,000 in the partnership for a 25 percent interest in the capital and profits, and partnership capital is not revalued.

P 16–8 Three partners, Pat, Mike, and Hay, have capital balances and profit sharing ratios at December 31, 19X3 as follows:

Pat	$144,000;	profit ratio ⅖
Mike	216,000;	profit ratio ½
Hay	90,000;	profit ratio ⅒

On January 1, 19X4 Con invests $85,080 in the business for a one-sixth interest in capital and income.

Required

1 Prepare journal entries giving *two* alternative solutions for recording Con's admission to the partnership.

2 Prepare journal entries giving *two* alternative solutions for recording Con's admission to the partnership if she purchased a one-sixth interest from each of the partners rather than paying the $85,080 into the business.

P 16–9 The AT Partnership was organized several years ago, and on January 1, 19X2 the partners agree to admit Carmen for a 40 percent interest in capital and earnings. Capital account balances and profit and loss sharing ratios at January 1, 19X2 before the admission of Carmen are as follows:

Aida (50%)	$500,000
Thais (50%)	280,000

Required: Prepare journal entries to record the admission of Carmen for a 40 percent interest in the capital and rights to future profits under the following independent assumptions.

1 Carmen pays $450,000 directly to Aida and Thais for 40 percent of each of their interests and the *bonus* procedure is used.

2 Carmen pays $600,000 directly to Aida and Thais for 40 percent of each of their interests and *goodwill* is recorded.

3 Carmen invests $450,000 in the partnership for her 40 percent interest, and *goodwill* is recorded.

4 Carmen invests $600,000 in the partnership for her 40 percent interest, and *goodwill* is recorded.

P 16–10 Gregg, Hill, and Price formed a partnership on January 1, 19X4, with each partner contributing $20,000 cash. Although the partnership agreement provided that Price receive a salary of $1,000 per month for managing the partnership business, Price has never withdrawn any money from the partnership. Gregg withdrew $2,000 in each of the years 19X4 and 19X5, and Hill invested an additional $8,000 in 19X4 and withdrew $2,000 during 19X5. Due to an oversight, the partnership has not maintained formal accounting records, but the following information as of December 31, 19X5 is available:

Cash on hand	$ 28,500
Due from customers	30,000
Merchandise on hand (at cost)	30,000
Delivery equipment—net of depreciation	35,000
Prepaid expenses	4,000
Assets	$127,500
Due to suppliers	$ 14,600
Wages payable	4,400
Note payable	10,000
Interest payable	500
Liabilities	$ 29,500

Additional Information

1 The partners agree that income for 19X4 was about half of the total income for the first two years of operations.
2 Although profits were not divided in 19X4, the partnership agreement provides that profits, after allowance for Price's salary, are to be divided each year on the basis of beginning-of-the-year capital balances.

Required: Prepare statements of partnership capital for the years ended December 31, 19X4 and December 31, 19X5.

P 16–11 The partnership of Drinkard and Boone was formed and commenced operations on March 1, 19X8, with Drinkard contributing $30,000 cash and Boone investing cash of $10,000 and equipment with an agreed-upon valuation of $20,000. On July 1, 19X8 Boone invested an additional $10,000 in the partnership. Drinkard made a capital withdrawal of $4,000 on May 2, 19X8 but reinvested the $4,000 on October 1, 19X8. During 19X8 Drinkard withdrew $800 per month and Boone, the managing partner, withdrew $1,000 per month. These drawings were charged to salary expense. A preclosing trial balance taken at December 31, 19X8 is as follows:

	Debit	Credit
Cash	$ 9,000	
Receivables—net	15,000	
Equipment—net	50,000	
Other assets	19,000	
Liabilities		$ 17,000
Drinkard capital		30,000
Boone capital		40,000
Service revenue		50,000
Supplies expense	17,000	
Utilities expense	4,000	
Salaries to partners	18,000	
Other miscellaneous expenses	5,000	
Total	$137,000	$137,000

Required

1 Journalize the entries necessary to close the partnership books assuming that there is no agreement regarding profit distribution.
2 Prepare a statement of partnership capital assuming that the partnership agreement provides for monthly salary allowances of $800 and $1,000 for Drinkard and Boone, respectively, and for the division of remaining profits in relation to average capital balances.
3 Prepare a profit distribution schedule for the Drinkard and Boone partnership

assuming monthly salary allowances of $800 and $1,000 for Drinkard and Boone, respectively; interest allowances at a 12 percent annual rate on average capital balances; and remaining profits divided equally.

P 16-12   A condensed balance sheet for the Peter, Quarry, and Sherel partnership at December 31, 19X7, and their profit and loss sharing percentages on that date are as follows:

CONDENSED BALANCE SHEET AT DECEMBER 31, 19X7

Cash	$ 15,000	
Other assets	185,000	
Total assets	$200,000	
Liabilities	$ 50,000	
Peter capital	75,000	50%
Quarry capital	50,000	30%
Sherel capital	25,000	20%
Total liabilities and capital	$200,000	100%

On January 1, 19X8 the partners decided to bring Tom into the partnership for a one-fourth interest in the capital and profits of the partnership. The following proposals for Tom's admittance into the partnership were considered:
1. Tom would purchase one-half of Peter's capital and right to future profits directly from Peter for $60,000.
2. Tom would purchase one-fourth of each of the partners' capital and rights to future profits by paying a total of $45,000 directly to the partners.
3. Tom would invest $55,000 cash in the partnership for a 25 percent interest in capital. Future profits would be divided 37½ percent, 22½ percent, 15 percent, and 25 percent for Peter, Quarry, Sherel, and Tom, respectively.

Required: Prepare journal entries with supporting computations to show Tom's admittance into the partnership under each of the above proposals assuming:
1. That partnership net assets are not to be revalued
2. That partnership net assets are to be revalued

APPENDIX

UNIFORM PARTNERSHIP ACT (1914)

(In 1981, the Uniform Partnership Act had been adopted in all U.S. states except Georgia and Louisiana.)

PART I
PRELIMINARY PROVISIONS

§ 1. Name of Act

This act may be cited as Uniform Partnership Act.

§ 2. Definition of Terms

In this act, "Court" includes every court and judge having jurisdiction in the case.
"Business" includes every trade, occupation, or profession.
"Person" includes individuals, partnerships, corporations, and other associations.
"Bankrupt" includes bankrupt under the Federal Bankruptcy Act or insolvent under any state insolvent act.
"Conveyance" includes every assignment, lease, mortgage, or encumbrance.
"Real Property" includes land and any interest or estate in land.

§ 3. Interpretation of Knowledge and Notice

(1) A person has "knowledge" of a fact within the meaning of this act not only when he has actual knowledge thereof, but also when he has knowledge of such other facts as in the circumstances shows bad faith.

(2) A person has "notice" of a fact within the meaning of this act when the person who claims the benefit of the notice:

(a) States the fact to such person, or

(b) Delivers through the mail, or by other means of communication, a written statement of the fact to such person or to a proper person at his place of business or residence.

§ 4. Rules of Construction

(1) The rule that statutes in derogration of the common law are to be strictly construed shall have no application to this act.

(2) The law of estoppel shall apply under this act.

(3) The law of agency shall apply under this act.

(4) This act shall be so interpreted and construed as to effect its general purpose to make uniform the law of those states which enact it.

(5) This act shall not be construed so as to impair the obligations of any contract existing when the act goes into effect, nor to affect any action or proceedings begun or right accrued before this act takes effect.

§ 5. Rules for Cases Not Provided for in This Act

In any case not provided for in this act the rules of law and equity, including the law merchant, shall govern.

PART II

NATURE OF A PARTNERSHIP

§ 6. Partnership Defined

(1) A partnership is an association of two or more persons to carry on as co-owners a business for profit.

(2) But any association formed under any other statute of this state, or any statute adopted by authority, other than the authority of this state, is not a partnership under this act, unless such association would have been a partnership in this state prior to the adoption of this act; but this act shall apply to limited partnerships except in so far as the statutes relating to such partnerships are inconsistent herewith.

§ 7. Rules for Determining the Existence of a Partnership

In determining whether a partnership exists, these rules shall apply:

(1) Except as provided by section 16 persons who are not partners as to each other are not partners as to third persons.

(2) Joint tenancy, tenancy in common, tenancy by the entireties, joint property, common property or part ownership does not of itself establish a partnership, whether such co-owners do or do not share any profits made by the use of the property.

(3) The sharing of gross returns does not of itself establish a partnership, whether or not the persons sharing them have a joint or common right or interest in any property from which the returns are derived.

(4) The receipt by a person of a share of the profits of a business is prima facie evidence that he is a partner in the business, but no such inference shall be drawn if such profits were received in payment:

680

PARTNERSHIPS—
FORMATION,
OPERATIONS AND
CHANGES IN
OWNERSHIP INTERESTS

(a) As a debt by installments or otherwise,

(b) As wages of an employee or rent to a landlord,

(c) As an annuity to a widow or representative of a deceased partner,

(d) As interest on a loan, though the amount of payment vary with the profits of the business,

(e) As the consideration for the sale of a good-will of a business or other property by installments or otherwise.

§ 8. Partnership Property

(1) All property originally brought into the partnership stock or subsequently acquired by purchase or otherwise, on account of the partnership, is partnership property.

(2) Unless the contrary intention appears, property acquired with partnership funds is partnership property.

(3) Any estate in real property may be acquired in the partnership name. Title so acquired can be conveyed only in the partnership name.

(4) A conveyance to a partnership in the partnership name, though without words of inheritance, passes the entire estate of the grantor unless a contrary intent appears.

PART III
RELATIONS OF PARTNERS TO PERSONS DEALING WITH THE PARTNERSHIP

§ 9. Partner Agent of Partnership as to Partnership Buiness

(1) Every partner is an agent of the partnership for the purpose of its business, and the act of every partner, including the execution in the partnership name of any instrument, for apparently carrying on in the usual way the business of the partnership of which he is a member binds the partnership, unless the partner so acting has in fact no authority to act for the partnership in the particular matter, and the person with whom he is dealing has knowledge of the fact that he has no such authority.

(2) An act of a partner which is not apparently for the carrying on of the business of the partnership in the usual way does not bind the partnership unless authorized by the other partners.

(3) Unless authorized by the other partners or unless they have abandoned the business, one or more but less than all the partners have no authority to:

(a) Assign the partnership property in trust for creditors or on the assignee's promise to pay the debts of the partnership,

(b) Dispose of the good-will of the business,

(c) Do any other act which would make it impossible to carry on the ordinary business of a partnership,

(d) Confess a judgment,

(e) Submit a partnership claim or liability to arbitration or reference.

(4) No act of a partner in contravention of a restriction on authority shall bind the partnership to persons having knowledge of the restriction.

§ 10. Conveyance of Real Property of the Partnership

(1) Where title to real property is in the partnership name, any partner may convey title to such property by a conveyance executed in the partnership name;

but the partnership may recover such property unless the partner's act binds the partnership under the provisions of paragraph (1) of section 9, or unless such property has been conveyed by the grantee or a person claiming through such grantee to a holder for value without knowledge that the partner, in making the conveyance, has exceeded his authority.

(2) Where title to real property is in the name of the partnership, a conveyance executed by a partner, in his own name, passes the equitable interest of the partnership, provided the act is one within the authority of the partner under the provisions of paragraph (1) of section 9.

(3) Where title to real property is in the name of one or more but not all the partners, and the record does not disclose the right of the partnership, the partners in whose name the title stands may convey title to such property, but the partnership may recover such property if the partners' act does not bind the partnership under the provisions of paragraph (1) of section 9, unless the purchaser or his assignee, is a holder for value, without knowledge.

(4) Where the title to real property is in the name of one or more or all the partners, or in a third person in trust for the partnership, a conveyance executed by a partner in the partnership name, or in his own name, passes the equitable interest of the partnership, provided the act is one within the authority of the partner under the provisions of paragraph (1) of section 9.

(5) Where the title to real property is in the names of all the partners a conveyance executed by all the partners passes all their rights in such property.

§ 11.   Partnership Bound by Admission of Partner

An admission or representation made by any partner concerning partnership affairs within the scope of his authority as conferred by this act is evidence against the partnership.

§ 12.   Partnership Charged with Knowledge of or Notice to Partner

Notice to any partner of any matter relating to partnership affairs, and the knowledge of the partner acting in the particular matter, acquired while a partner or then present to his mind, and the knowledge of any other partner who reasonably could and should have communicated it to the acting partner, operate as notice to or knowledge of the partnership, except in the case of a fraud on the partnership committed by or with the consent of that partner.

§ 13.   Partnership Bound by Partner's Wrongful Act

Where, by any wrongful act or omission of any partner acting in the ordinary course of the business of the partnership or with the authority of his co-partners, loss or injury is caused to any person, not being a partner in the partnership, or any penalty is incurred, the partnership is liable therefor to the same extent as the partner so acting or omitting to act.

§ 14.   Partnership Bound by Partner's Breach of Trust

The partnership is bound to make good the loss:
(a) Where one partner acting within the scope of his apparent authority receives money or property of a third person and misapplies it; and
(b) Where the partnership in the course of its business receives money or property of a third person and the money or property so received is misapplied by any partner while it is in the custody of the partnership.

682

PARTNERSHIPS—
FORMATION,
OPERATIONS AND
CHANGES IN
OWNERSHIP INTERESTS

§ 15. Nature of Partner's Liability

All partners are liable

(a) Jointly and severally for everything chargeable to the partnership under sections 13 and 14.

(b) Jointly for all other debts and obligations of the partnership; but any partner may enter into a separate obligation to perform a partnership contract.

§ 16. Partner by Estoppel

(1) When a person, by words spoken or written or by conduct, represents himself, or consents to another representing him to any one, as a partner in an existing partnership or with one or more persons not actual partners, he is liable to any such person to whom such representation has been made, who has, on the faith of such representation, given credit to the actual or apparent partnership, and if he has made such representation or consented to its being made in a public manner he is liable to such person, whether the representation has or has not been made or communicated to such person so giving credit by or with the knowledge of the apparent partner making the representation or consenting to its being made.

(a) When a partnership liability results, he is liable as though he were an actual member of the partnership.

(b) When no partnership liability results, he is liable jointly with the other persons, if any, so consenting to the contract or representation as to incur liability, otherwise separately.

(2) When a person has been thus represented to be a partner in an existing partnership, or with one or more persons not actual partners, he is an agent of the persons consenting to such representation to bind them to the same extent and in the same manner as though he were a partner in fact, with respect to persons who rely upon the representation. Where all the members of the existing partnership consent to the representation, a partnership act or obligation results; but in all other cases it is the joint act or obligation of the person acting and the persons consenting to the representation.

§ 17. Liability of Incoming Partner

A person admitted as a partner into an existing partnership is liable for all the obligations of the partnership arising before his admission as though he had been a partner when such obligations were incurred, except that his liability shall be satisfied only out of partnership property.

PART IV
RELATIONS OF PARTNERS TO ONE ANOTHER

§ 18. Rules Determining Rights and Duties of Partners

The rights and duties of the partners in relation to the partnership shall be determined, subject to any agreement between them, by the following rules:

(a) Each partner shall be repaid his contributions, whether by way of capital or advances to the partnership property and share equally in the profits and surplus remaining after all liabilities, including those to partners, are satisfied; and must contribute towards the losses, whether of capital or otherwise, sustained by the partnership according to his share in the profits.

(b) The partnership must indemnify every partner in respect of payments made and personal liabilities reasonably incurred by him in the ordinary and proper conduct of its business, or for the preservation of its business or property.

(c) A partner, who in aid of the partnership makes any payment or advance beyond the amount of capital which he agreed to contribute, shall be paid interest from the date of the payment or advance.

(d) A partner shall receive interest on the capital contributed by him only from the date when repayments should be made.

(e) All partners have equal rights in the management and conduct of the partnership business.

(f) No partner is entitled to remuneration for acting in the partnership business, except that a surviving partner is entitled to reasonable compensation for his services in winding up the partnership affairs.

(g) No person can become a member of a partnership without the consent of all the partners.

(h) Any difference arising as to ordinary matters connected with the partnership business may be decided by a majority of the partners; but no act in contravention of any agreement between the partners may be done rightfully without the consent of all the partners.

§ 19. Partnership Books

The partnership books shall be kept, subject to any agreement between the partners, at the principal place of business of the partnership, and every partner shall at all times have access to and may inspect and copy any of them.

§ 20. Duty of Partners to Render Information

Partners shall render on demand true and full information of all things affecting the partnership to any partner or the legal representative of any deceased partner or partner under legal disability.

§ 21. Partner Accountable as a Fiduciary

(1) Every partner must account to the partnership for any benefit, and hold as trustee for it any profits derived by him without the consent of the other partners from any transaction connected with the formation, conduct, or liquidation of the partnership or from any use by him of its property.

(2) This section applies also to the representatives of a deceased partner engaged in the liquidation of the affairs of the partnership as the personal representatives of the last surviving partner.

§ 22. Right to an Account

Any partner shall have the right to a formal account as to partnership affairs:

(a) If he is wrongfully excluded from the partnership business or possession of its property by his co-partners,

(b) If the right exists under the terms of any agreement

(c) As provided by section 21,

(d) Whenever other circumstances render it just and reasonable.

§ 23. Continuation of Partnership Beyond Fixed Term

(1) When a partnership for a fixed term or particular undertaking is continued after the termination of such term or particular undertaking without any express

684

PARTNERSHIPS—
FORMATION,
OPERATIONS AND
CHANGES IN
OWNERSHIP INTERESTS

agreement, the rights and duties of the partners remain the same as they were at such termination, so far as is consistent with a partnership at will.

(2) A continuation of the business by the partners or such of them as habitually acted therein during the term, without any settlement or liquidation of the partnership affairs, is prima facie evidence of a continuation of the partnership.

PART V
PROPERTY RIGHTS OF A PARTNER

§ 24. Extent of Property Rights of a Partner

The property rights of a partner are (1) his rights in specific partnership property, (2) his interest in the partnership, and (3) his right to participate in the management.

§ 25. Nature of a Partner's Right in Specific Partnership Property

(1) A partner is co-owner with his partners of specific partnership property holding as a tenant in partnership.

(2) The incidents of this tenancy are such that:

(a) A partner, subject to the provisions of this act and to any agreement between the partners, has an equal right with his partners to possess specific partnership property for partnership purposes; but he has no right to possess such property for any other purpose without the consent of his partners.

(b) A partner's right in specific partnership property is not assignable except in connection with the assignment of rights of all the partners in the same property.

(c) A partner's right in specific partnership property is not subject to attachment or execution, except on a claim against the partnership. When partnership property is attached for a partnership debt the partners, or any of them, or the representatives of a deceased partner, cannot claim any right under the homestead or exemption laws.

(d) On the death of a partner his right in specific partnership property vests in the surviving partner or partners, except where the deceased was the last surviving partner, when his right in such property vests in his legal representative. Such surviving partner or partners, or the legal representative of the last surviving partner, has no right to possess the partnership property for any but a partnership purpose.

(e) A partner's right in specific partnership property is not subject to dower, curtesy, or allowances to widows, heirs, or next of kin.

§ 26. Nature of Partner's Interest in the Partnership

A partner's interest in the partnership is his share of the profits and surplus, and the same is personal property.

§ 27. Assignment of Partner's Interest

(1) A conveyance by a partner of his interest in the partnership does not of itself dissolve the partnership, nor, as against the other partners in the absence of agreement, entitle the assignee, during the continuance of the partnership, to interfere in the management or administration of the partnership business or affairs, or to require any information or account of partnership transactions, or to inspect the partnership books; but it merely entitles the assignee to receive in accordance

with his contract the profits to which the assigning partner would otherwise be entitled.

(2) In case of a dissolution of the partnership, the assignee is entitled to receive his assignor's interest and may require an account from the date only of the last account agreed to by all the partners.

§ 28. Partner's Interest Subject to Charging Order

(1) On due application to a competent court by any judgment creditor of a partner, the court which entered the judgment, order, or decree, or any other court, may charge the interest of the debtor partner with payment of the unsatisfied amount of such judgment debt with interest thereon; and may then or later appoint a receiver of his share of the profits, and of any other money due or to fall due to him in respect of the partnership, and make all other orders, directions, accounts and inquiries which the debtor partner might have made, or which the circumstances of the case may require.

(2) The interest charged may be redeemed at any time before foreclosure, or in case of a sale being directed by the court may be purchased without thereby causing a dissolution:

(a) With separate property, by any one or more of the partners, or

(b) With partnership property, by any one or more of the partners with the consent of all the partners whose interests are not so charged or sold.

(3) Nothing in this act shall be held to deprive a partner of his right, if any, under the exemption laws, as regards his interest in the partnership.

PART VI
DISSOLUTION AND WINDING UP

§ 29. Dissolution Defined

The dissolution of a partnership is the change in the relation of the partners caused by any partner ceasing to be associated in the carrying on as distinguished from the winding up of the business.

§ 30. Partnership not Terminated by Dissolution

On dissolution the partnership is not terminated, but continues until the winding up of partnership affairs is completed.

§ 31. Causes of Dissolution

Dissolution is caused:

(1) Without violation of the agreement between the partners,

(a) By the termination of the definite term or particular undertaking specified in the agreement,

(b) By the express will of any partner when no definite term or particular undertaking is specified,

(c) By the express will of all the partners who have not assigned their interests or suffered them to be charged for their separate debts, either before or after the termination of any specified term or particular undertaking,

(d) By the expulsion of any partner from the business bona fide in accordance with such a power conferred by the agreement between the partners;

(2) In contravention of the agreement between the partners, where the cir-

686

PARTNERSHIPS—
FORMATION,
OPERATIONS AND
CHANGES IN
OWNERSHIP INTERESTS

cumstances do not permit a dissolution under any other provision of this section, by the express will of any partner at any time;

(3) By any event which makes it unlawful for the business of the partnership to be carried on or for the members to carry it on in partnership;

(4) By the death of any partner;

(5) By the bankruptcy of any partner or the partnership;

(6) By decree of court under section 32.

§ 32.   Dissolution by Decree of Court

(1) On application by or for a partner the court shall decree a dissolution whenever:

(a) A partner has been declared a lunatic in any judicial proceeding or is shown to be of unsound mind,

(b) A partner becomes in any other way incapable of performing his part of the partnership contract,

(c) A partner has been guilty of such conduct as tends to affect prejudicially the carrying on of the business,

(d) A partner wilfully or persistently commits a breach of the partnership agreement, or otherwise so conducts himself in matters relating to the partnership business that it is not reasonably practicable to carry on the business in partnership with him,

(e) The business of the partnership can only be carried on at a loss,

(f) Other circumstances render a dissolution equitable.

(2) On the application of the purchaser of a partner's interest under sections 28 or 29 [should read 27 or 28];

(a) After the termination of the specified term or particular undertaking,

(b) At any time if the partnership was a partnership at will when the interest was assigned or when the charging order was issued.

§ 33.   General Effect of Dissolution on Authority of Partner

Except so far as may be necessary to wind up partnership affairs or to complete transactions begun but not then finished, dissolution terminates all authority of any partner to act for the partnership,

(1) With respect to the partners,

(a) When the dissolution is not by the act, bankruptcy or death of a partner; or

(b) When the dissolution is by such act, bankruptcy or death of a partner, in cases where section 34 so requires.

(2) With respect to persons not partners, as declared in section 35.

§ 34.   Rights of Partner to Contribution from Co-partners after Dissolution

Where the dissolution is caused by the act, death or bankruptcy of a partner, each partner is liable to his co-partners for his share of any liability created by any partner acting for the partnership as if the partnership had not been dissolved unless

(a) The dissolution being by act of any partner, the partner acting for the partnership had knowledge of the dissolution, or

(b) The dissolution being by the death or bankruptcy of a partner, the partner acting for the partnership had knowledge or notice of the death or bankruptcy.

§ 35.   Power of Partner to Bind Partnership to Third Persons after Dissolution

(1) After dissolution a partner can bind the partnership except as provided in Paragraph (3).

(a) By any act appropriate for winding up partnership affairs or completing transactions unfinished at dissolution;

(b) By any transaction which would bind the partnership if dissolution had not taken place, provided the other party to the transaction

(I) Had extended credit to the partnership prior to dissolution and had no knowledge or notice of the dissolution; or

(II) Though he had not so extended credit, had nevertheless known of the partnership prior to dissolution, and, having no knowledge or notice of dissolution, the fact of dissolution had not been advertised in a newspaper of general circulation in the place (or in each place if more than one) at which the partnership business was regularly carried on.

(2) The liability of a partner under Paragraph (1b) shall be satisfied out of partnership assets alone when such partner had been prior to dissolution

(a) Unknown as a partner to the person with whom the contract is made; and

(b) So far unknown and inactive in partnership affairs that the business reputation of the partnership could not be said to have been in any degree due to his connection with it.

(3) The partnership is in no case bound by any act of a partner after dissolution

(a) Where the partnership is dissolved because it is unlawful to carry on the business, unless the act is appropriate for winding up partnership affairs; or

(b) Where the partner has become bankrupt; or

(c) Where the partner has no authority to wind up partnership affairs; except by a transaction with one who

(I) Had extended credit to the partnership prior to dissolution and had no knowledge or notice of his want of authority; or

(II) Had not extended credit to the partnership prior to dissolution and, having no knowedge or notice of his want of authority, the fact of his want of authority had not been advertised in the manner provided for advertising the fact of dissolution in Paragraph (1b II).

(4) Nothing in this section shall affect the liability under Section 16 of any person who after dissolution represents himself or consents to another representing him as a partner in a partnership engaged in carrying on business.

§ 36. Effect of Dissolution on Partner's Existing Liability

(1) The dissolution of the partnership does not of itself discharge the existing liability of any partner.

(2) A partner is discharged from any existing liability upon dissolution of the partnership by an agreement to that effect between himself, the partnership creditor and the person or partnership continuing the business; and such agreement may be inferred from the course of dealing between the creditor having knowledge of the dissolution and the person or partnership continuing the business.

(3) Where a person agrees to assume the existing obligations of a dissolved partnership, the partners whose obligations have been assumed shall be discharged from any liability to any creditor of the partnership who, knowing of the agreement, consents to a material alteration in the nature or time of payment of such obligations.

(4) The individual property of a deceased partner shall be liable for all obligations of the partnership incurred while he was a partner but subject to the prior payment of his separate debts.

§ 37. Right to Wind Up

Unless otherwise agreed the partners who have not wrongfully dissolved the partnership or the legal representative of the last surviving partner, not bankrupt,

688

PARTNERSHIPS—
FORMATION,
OPERATIONS AND
CHANGES IN
OWNERSHIP INTERESTS

has the right to wind up the partnership affairs; provided, however, that any partner, his legal representative or his assignee, upon cause shown, may obtain winding up by the court.

§ 38. Rights of Partners to Application of Partnership Property

(1) When dissolution is caused in any way, except in contravention of the partnership agreement, each partner, as against his co-partners and all persons claiming through them in respect of their interests in the partnership, unless otherwise agreed, may have the partnership property applied to discharge its liabilities, and the surplus applied to pay in cash the net amount owing to the respective partners. But if dissolution is caused by expulsion of a partner, bona fide under the partnership agreement and if the expelled partner is discharged from all partnership liabilities, either by payment or agreement under section 36(2), he shall receive in cash only the net amount due him from the partnership.

(2) When dissolution is caused in contravention of the partnership agreement the rights of the partners shall be as follows

(a) Each partner who has not caused dissolution wrongfully shall have,

I. All the rights specified in paragraph (1) of this section, and

II. The right, as against each partner who has caused the dissolution wrongfully, to damages for breach of the agreement.

(b) The partners who have not caused the dissolution wrongfully, if they all desire to continue the business in the same name, either by themselves or jointly with others, may do so, during the agreed term for the partnership and for that purpose may possess the partnership property, provided they secure the payment by bond approved by the court, or pay to any partner who has caused the dissolution wrongfully, the value of his interest in the partnership at the dissolution, less any damages recoverable under clause (2a II) of this section, and in like manner indemnify him against all present or future partnership liabilities.

(c) A partner who has caused the dissolution wrongfully shall have:

I. If the business is not continued under the provisions of paragraph (2b) all the rights of a partner under paragraph (1), subject to clause (2a II), of this section,

II. If the business is continued under paragraph (2b) of this section the right as against his co-partners and all claiming through them in respect of their interests in the partnership, to have the value of his interest in the partnership, less any damages caused to his co-partners by the dissolution, ascertained and paid to him in cash, or the payment secured by bond approved by the court, and to be released from all existing liabilities of the partnership; but in ascertaining the value of the partner's interest the value of the good-will of the business shall not be considered.

§ 39. Rights Where Partnership is Dissolved for Fraud or Misrepresentation

Where a partnership contract is rescinded on the ground of the fraud or misrepresentation of one of the parties thereto, the party entitled to rescind is, without prejudice to any other right, entitled.

(a) To a lien on, or a right of retention of, the surplus of the partnership property after satisfying the partnership liabilities to third persons for any sum of money paid by him for the purchase of an interest in the partnership and for any capital or advances contributed by him, and

(b) To stand, after all liabilities to third persons have been satisfied, in the place of the creditors of the partnership for any payments made by him in respect to the partnership liabilities; and

(c) To be indemnified by the person guilty of the fraud or making the representation against all debts and liabilities of the partnership.

§ 40.   Rules for Distribution

In settling accounts between the partners after dissolution, the following rules shall be observed, subject to any agreement to the contrary:

(a) The assets of the partnership are:

I. The partnership property,

II. The contributions of the partners necessary for the payment of all the liabilities specified in clause (b) of this paragraph.

(b) The liabilities of the partnership shall rank in order of payment as follows:

I. Those owing creditors other than partners,

II. Those owing to partners other than for capital and profits,

III. Those owing to partners in respect of capital,

IV. Those owing to partners in respect of profits.

(c) The assets shall be applied in the order of their declaration in clause (a) of this paragraph to the satisfaction of the liabilities.

(d) The partners shall contribute, as provided by section 18 (a) the amount necessary to satisfy the liabilities; but if any, but not all, of the partners are insolvent, or, not being subject to process, refuse to contribute, the other partners shall contribute their share of the liabilities, and, in the relative proportions in which they share the profits, the additional amount necessary to pay the liabilities.

(e) An assignee for the benefit of creditors or any person appointed by the court shall have the right to enforce the contributions specified in clause (d) of this paragraph.

(f) Any partner or his legal representative shall have the right to enforce the contributions specified in clause (d) of this paragraph, to the extent of the amount which he has paid in excess of his share of the liability.

(g) The individual property of a deceased partner shall be liable for the contributions specified in clause (d) of this paragraph.

(h) When partnership property and the individual properties of the partners are in possession of a court for distribution, partnership creditors shall have priority on partnership property and separate creditors on individual property, saving the rights of lien or secured creditors as heretofore.

(i) Where a partner has become bankrupt or his estate is insolvent the claims against his separate property shall rank in the following order:

I. Those owing to separate creditors,

II. Those owing to partnership creditors,

III. Those owing to partners by way of contribution.

§ 41.   Liability of Persons Continuing the Business in Certain Cases

(1) When any new partner is admitted into an existing partnership, or when any partner retires and assigns (or the representative of the deceased partner assigns) his rights in partnership property to two or more of the partners, or to one or more of the partners and one or more third persons, if the business is continued without liquidation of the partnership affairs, creditors of the first or dissolved partnership are also creditors of the partnership so continuing the business.

(2) When all but one partner retire and assign (or the representative of a

690

PARTNERSHIPS—
FORMATION,
OPERATIONS AND
CHANGES IN
OWNERSHIP INTERESTS

deceased partner assigns) their rights in partnership property to the remaining partner, who continues the business without liquidation of partnership affairs, either alone or with others, creditors of the dissolved partnership are also creditors of the person or partnership so continuing the business.

(3) When any partner retires or dies and the business of the dissolved partnership is continued as set forth in paragraphs (1) and (2) of this section, with the consent of the retired partners or the representative of the deceased partner, but without any assignment of his right in partnership property, rights of creditors of the dissolved partnership and of the creditors of the person or partnership continuing the business shall be as if such assignment had been made.

(4) When all the partners or their representatives assign their rights in partnership property to one or more third persons who promise to pay the debts and who continue the business of the dissolved partnership, creditors of the dissolved partnership are also creditors of the person or partnership continuing the business.

(5) When any partner wrongfully causes a dissolution and the remaining partners continue the business under the provisions of section 38(2b), either alone or with others, and without liquidation of the partnership affairs, creditors of the dissolved partnership are also creditors of the person or partnership continuing the business.

(6) When a partner is expelled and the remaining partners continue the business either alone or with others, without liquidation of the partnership affairs, creditors of the dissolved partnership are also creditors of the person or partnership continuing the business.

(7) The liability of a third person becoming a partner in the partnership continuing the business, under this section, to the creditors of the dissolved partnership shall be satisfied out of partnership property only.

(8) When the business of a partnership after dissolution is continued under any conditions set forth in this section the creditors of the dissolved partnership, as against the separate creditors of the retiring or deceased partner or the representative of the deceased partner, have a prior right to any claim of the retired partner or the representative of the deceased partner against the person or partnership continuing the business, on account of the retired or deceased partner's interest in the dissolved partnership or on account of any consideration promised for such interest or for his right in partnership property.

(9) Nothing in this section shall be held to modify any right of creditors to set aside any assignment on the ground of fraud.

(10) The use by the person or partnership continuing the business of the partnership name, or the name of a deceased partner as part thereof, shall not of itself make the individual property of the deceased partner liable for any debts contracted by such person or partnership.

§ 42.   Rights of Retiring or Estate of Deceased Partner When the Business Is Continued

When any partner retires or dies, and the business is continued under any of the conditions set forth in section 41(1, 2, 3, 5, 6), or section 38(2b) without any settlement of accounts as between him or his estate and the person or partnership continuing the business, unless otherwise agreed, he or his legal representative as against such persons or partnership may have the value of his interest at the date of dissolution ascertained, and shall receive as an ordinary creditor an amount equal to the value of his interest in the dissolved partnership with interest, or, at his option or at the option of his legal representative, in lieu of interest, the profits attributable to the use of his right in the property of the dissolved partnership; provided that the creditors of the dissolved partnership as against the separate creditors, or the representative of the retired or deceased partner, shall have priority on any claim arising under this section, as provided by section 41 (8) of this act.

§ 43. Accrual of Actions

The right to an account of his interest shall accrue to any partner, or his legal representative, as against the winding up partners or the surviving partners or the person or partnership continuing the business, at the date of dissolution, in the absence of any agreement to the contrary.

PART VII
MISCELLANEOUS PROVISIONS

§ 44. When Act Takes Effect

This act shall take effect on the _____ day of _____ one thousand nine hundred and _____ .

§ 45. Legislation Repealed

All acts or parts of acts inconsistent with this act are hereby repealed.

17

DISSOLUTION AND LIQUIDATION OF A PARTNERSHIP

The dissolution of a partnership is simply the change in the relationship of the partners that terminates the partnership as a legal entity. Upon dissolution, the partnership entity may continue under a new agreement, as discussed in Chapter 16, or the partnership may be terminated both as a legal and as a business entity. The termination of a partnership as a business entity involves winding up the affairs of the partnership business and is generally referred to as **partnership liquidation**. In this chapter, the focus will be on partnership dissolution that also involves liquidation of the partnership business.

THE LIQUIDATION PROCESS

In general, the liquidation of a partnership involves:

Converting noncash assets into cash
Recognizing gains and losses and liquidating expenses incurred during the liquidation period
Settling all liabilities
Distributing cash to the partners according to the balances in their capital accounts

This general description of the liquidation process assumes that the partnership is solvent in the sense that partnership assets exceed partnership liabilities. It also assumes that all the partners have equity in partnership net assets, that there are no partner loan balances, and that all assets are converted into cash before any cash is distributed to the partners. As these assumptions are relaxed, the liquidation process becomes more complex. Accordingly, this chapter begins with simple liquidations for solvent partnerships and proceeds to installment liquidations and liquidations of insolvent partnerships.

The rules for distributing assets in the liquidation of a partnership are covered in Section 40 of the Uniform Partnership Act. Section 40b gives the rank order of payment as follows:

I Amounts owed to creditors other than partners.
II Amounts owed to partners other than for capital and profits.
III Amounts due to partners with respect to their capital interests.

Although the Act lists profits as a fourth level of priority, all profits and losses and drawing balances should be closed to the capital accounts before any distributions are made. Since capital accounts are assumed to be updated before each distribution, the fourth level is not relevant to the discussion in this chapter. Additional comment on level II priority is also necessary because partnership property should never be distributed to a partner with a negative capital balance. Thus, partners' loan balances should be offset against capital balances in determining the amount of distributions to partners. Once the amount to be distributed to a particular partner is determined, that partner's loan balance should be charged before his or her capital account is reduced. This strategy is discussed further under the heading "Debit Capital Balances in a Solvent Partnership" and in conjunction with installment liquidations.

Simple Partnership Liquidation

A simple liquidation of a partnership refers to the conversion of all partnership assets into cash and a single distribution of cash to partners in final settlement of the affairs of the partnership. In order to illustrate a simple liquidation, assume that the balance sheet of Holmes and Kaiser at December 31, 19X1 is as follows:

HOLMES AND KAISER
BALANCE SHEET
AT DECEMBER 31, 19X1

Assets		*Liabilities and Equities*	
Cash	$ 10,000	Accounts payable	$ 40,000
Accounts receivable—net	30,000	Loan from Holmes	10,000
Inventory	30,000	Holmes capital	25,000
Plant assets—net	40,000	Kaiser capital	35,000
	$110,000		$110,000

Holmes and Kaiser share profits and losses 70 percent and 30 percent, respectively, and agree to liquidate their partnership as soon as possible after January 1, 19X2. The inventory items are sold for $25,000, plant assets are sold for $30,000, and $22,000 is collected in final settlement of the accounts receivable. As the final step in the partnership liquidation, the $87,000 available cash is distributed to the creditors and the partners.

	Order of Payment	
I	To creditors for accounts payable	$40,000
II	To Holmes for his loan balance	10,000
III	To Holmes for his capital balance	8,900
	To Kaiser for his capital balance	28,100
	Total distribution	$87,000

The amounts of cash distributed to the partners are equal to the partners' capital account balances after all losses on liquidation are recognized. Journal entries for the partnership during the liquidation period are shown in Exhibit 17–1. Losses during the liquidation period are charged directly to the capital accounts in the 70 and 30 percent profit sharing ratios. The established profit and loss sharing ratios are used during the liquidation period unless the partnership agreement specifies a different division of profits and losses during liquidation. In the case of agreements providing for salary and interest allowances, however, the residual profit and loss sharing ratios after such allowances would be applied during the liquidation period. This is because the gains and losses on liquidation are essentially adjustments of prior profits that would have been

Journal Entries to Record the Liquidation

Cash	$25,000	
Holmes capital	3,500	
Kaiser capital	1,500	
Inventory		$30,000

To record the sale of inventory items and the allocation of the $5,000 loss to the partners' capital accounts in their profit and loss sharing ratios.

Cash	$30,000	
Holmes capital	7,000	
Kaiser capital	3,000	
Plant assets—net		$40,000

To record the sale of plant assets and the allocation of the $10,000 loss to the partners' capital accounts in their profit and loss sharing ratios.

Cash	$22,000	
Holmes capital	5,600	
Kaiser capital	2,400	
Accounts receivable—net		$30,000

To record collection of $22,000 of acounts receivable and to write off the remaining $8,000 receivables as a loss charged to the partners' capital accounts in their profit and loss sharing ratios.

Accounts payable	$40,000	
Cash		$40,000

To record payment of nonpartner liabilities.

Loan from Holmes	$10,000	
Cash		$10,000

To pay loan from Holmes.

Holmes capital	$ 8,900	
Kaiser capital	28,100	
Cash		$37,000

To distribute cash to partners in final liquidation of the partnership.

Exhibit 17-1 *Simple Liquidation—Holmes and Kaiser Partnership*

shared in the residual profit sharing ratios if they had been recognized prior to dissolution.

A liquidating partnership should maintain a summary of transactions and balances during the liquidation stage. This summary of transactions and balances is provided for the Holmes and Kaiser partnership by the **partnership liquidation statement** shown in Exhibit 17–2. Liquidation statements are convenient references for use during the liquidation process, but, of course, they do not take the place of formal journalizing and posting during the phase-out period. In examining the liquidation statement for Holmes and Kaiser, note that assets are dichotomized into cash and noncash categories and that liabilities consist of priority (rank I or nonpartner) liabilities and partner (rank II) liabilities. Also note that all losses (and gains) are distributed to the partners' capital accounts as soon as they are recognized. With the capital accounts updated, the final distribution of cash to the partners is equal to the predistribution balances in the partners' capital accounts.

Debit Capital Balances in a Solvent Partnership

In liquidations of partnerships that are solvent, there will be sufficient cash to pay creditors and to distribute some cash to partners. But the process of liquidation may result in losses that force the capital accounts of some partners into debit balances. When this happens, those partners with debit balances have an

HOLMES AND KAISER PARTNERSHIP
STATEMENT OF PARTNERSHIP LIQUIDATION
FOR THE PERIOD JANUARY 1, 19X2 to JANUARY 31, 19X2

	Cash	Noncash Assets	Priority Liabilities	Holmes Loan	(70%) Holmes Capital	(30%) Kaiser Capital
Balances January 1, 19X2	$10,000	$100,000	$40,000	$10,000	$25,000	$35,000
Sale of inventory	25,000	30,000*			3,500*	1,500*
	35,000	70,000	40,000	10,000	21,500	33,500
Sale of plant assets	30,000	40,000*			7,000*	3,000*
	65,000	30,000	40,000	10,000	14,500	30,500
Collection of receivables	22,000	30,000*			5,600*	2,400*
	87,000	—	40,000	10,000	8,900	28,100
Payment of liabilities	40,000*		40,000*			
	47,000		—	10,000	8,900	28,100
Payment of Holmes loan	10,000*			10,000*		
	37,000			—	8,900	28,100
Final distribution to partners	37,000*				8,900*	28,100*
	—				—	—

* Deduct.

Exhibit 17–2   Statement of Partnership Liquidation

obligation to partners with credit balances, and they can be required to use their personal assets to settle their partnership obligations. If the partners with debit balances are without personal resources, the partners with equity will have to assume losses equal to the debit balances. Such losses would be shared in the relative profit and loss sharing ratios of the partners with capital.

Assume that the partnership of Jay, Jim, and Joe is in the process of liquidation and the partnership accounts have the following balances after all assets have been converted into cash and all liabilities have been paid:

	Debit	Credit
Cash	$25,000	
Jay capital (40%)	3,000	
Jim capital (40%)		$16,000
Joe capital (20%)		12,000
Total	$28,000	$28,000

If Jay is personally solvent, he should pay $3,000 into the partnership to eliminate his debit capital account balance. His payment of $3,000 will bring the partnership cash up to $28,000, which can then be distributed to Jim and Joe in final liquidation of the partnership. If Jay is unable to make his debit balance good, his debit balance represents a $3,000 loss to be charged to Jim and Joe in relation to their relative profit and loss sharing ratios. Jim's share of the loss is $2,000 ($3,000 × .4/.6), and Joe's share is $1,000 ($3,000 × .2/.6). In this case, the $25,000 is distributed $14,000 to Jim and $11,000 to Joe, and the partnership business is terminated.

When a partner with a debit capital balance has a loan receivable from the partnership, the rule of offset suggests that the loan be used to offset the debit capital balance up to the amount of the debit balance. For example, assume that the partnership of Jay, Jim, and Joe had account balances as follows:

	Debit	Credit
Cash	$25,000	
Loan from Jay		$ 5,000
Jay capital (40%)	8,000	
Jim capital (40%)		16,000
Joe capital (20%)		12,000
Total	$33,000	$33,000

Under the rule of offset, the loan from Jay would not be paid even though it has a higher priority ranking in liquidation than the capital interests of Jim and Joe. Instead it would be offset against Jay's debit capital balance, leaving Jay with a $3,000 obligation to Jim and Joe. If Jay is personally solvent, application of the rule of offset poses no problem. Jay simply pays $3,000 to the partnership so that Jim and Joe can receive the balances in their capital accounts in final liquidation. In this case, the rule of offset produces the same result as payment of the $5,000 loan balance to Jay, followed by the collection of $8,000 from Jay's personal assets.

If Jay is personally insolvent, however, the situation is changed considerably. In this case, Jay's personal creditors would have a prior claim on any money paid to Jay because personal creditors have a prior claim on personal assets. Under the rule of offset, $25,000 cash would be paid: $14,000 to Jim and $11,000 to Joe. Alternatively, if the $5,000 loan balance is paid directly to Jay, his personal creditors would be paid the amount of their claims up to $5,000, leaving less than $25,000 for distribution to Jim and Joe. Because of insufficient evidence that the rule of offset is generally accepted by the courts, it has been recommended that the rule not be applied without agreement from the partners, when a partner-creditor is personally insolvent.[1] Upon dissolution and subject to the rights of creditors, partners can agree to different property distributions than provided for under the Uniform Partnership Act.[2]

SAFE PAYMENTS TO PARTNERS

Ordinarily, the process of liquidating a business takes considerable time, and some cash may become available for distribution to partners after all liabilities are paid but before all noncash assets are converted into cash. If the partners decide to distribute available cash before all noncash assets are sold (and before all gains or losses are recognized), the question arises as to how much cash can be safely distributed to the individual partners. **Safe payments** are distributions that can be made to partners with assurance that the amounts distributed are not excessive, in other words, that the resources distributed will not have to be returned to the partnership.

The measurement of safe payments to partners is based on the following assumptions: (1) all partners are personally insolvent (that is, partners could not make any payments into the partnership), and (2) all noncash assets represent possible losses (that is, noncash assets should be considered losses for purposes of determining safe payments). In addition, when calculating safe payments the partnership may withhold specific amounts of cash on hand to cover liquidation expenses, unrecorded liabilities, and general contingencies. The amounts of cash withheld are contingent losses to the partners, and are considered losses for purposes of determining safe payments.

---

[1]Stephen A. Zeff, "Right of Offset vs. Partnershp Act in Winding-up Process," *Accounting Review* (January 1957), pp. 68–70.

[2]*Anderson* v. *Anderson*, 1958, 138 A.2d 880, 215 Md.–483.

Application of Safe Payments Schedule

Assume that the partnership of Buzz, Maxine, and Nancy is in the process of liquidation, and that its account balances are as follows:

Debits		Credits	
Cash	$ 80,000	Loan payable to Nancy	$ 20,000
Loan due from Maxine	10,000	Buzz capital (50%)	50,000
Land	20,000	Maxine capital (30%)	70,000
Buildings—net	140,000	Nancy capital (20%)	110,000
	$250,000		$250,000

All liabilities other than to partners have been paid, and the partners expect the sale of the land and buildings to take several months. Therefore, they agree that all cash on hand other than $10,000 to cover expenses and contingencies should be distributed immediately. Given this information, a schedule of safe payments is prepared to determine the amount of cash that can be safely distributed to each partner. A safe payments schedule for the Buzz, Maxine, and Nancy partnership is illustrated in Exhibit 17–3.

BUZZ, MAXINE, AND NANCY PARTNERSHIP
SCHEDULE OF SAFE PAYMENTS

	Possible Losses	Buzz Equity (50%)	Maxine Equity (30%)	Nancy Equity (20%)
Partners' equities (capital ± loan balances)		$50,000	$60,000	$130,000
Possible loss on noncash assets:				
Book value of land and buildings	$160,000	80,000*	48,000*	32,000*
		30,000*	12,000	98,000
Possible loss on contingencies:				
Cash withheld for contingencies, etc.	10,000	5,000*	3,000*	2,000*
		35,000*	9,000	96,000
Possible loss from Buzz:				
Buzz's debit balance allocated 60/40 to Maxine and Nancy		35,000	21,000*	14,000*
			12,000*	82,000
Possible loss from Maxine:				
Maxine's debit balance assigned to Nancy			12,000	12,000*
				$ 70,000

* Deduct or loss.

Exhibit 17–3 *Safe Payments Schedule*

The safe payments schedule begins with the equity of each partner shown on the top line. Partner equity is determined by combining the capital and loan balances for each of the partners. Possible losses are allocated to the partners in their profit and loss sharing ratios and are deducted from partner equity balances in the same manner that actual losses would be deducted. The possible losses shown in Exhibit 17–3 include the $160,000 book value of the land and buildings, the only noncash assets, and the $10,000 cash withheld from distribu-

698

DISSOLUTION
AND LIQUIDATION
OF A PARTNERSHIP

tion. After possible losses are deducted from the equity of each partner for purposes of safe payment calculations, some partners may show negative equity. If so, the negative amounts must be allocated to the partners with equity in their relative profit and loss sharing ratios. Allocations in the schedule are continued until none of the partners shows negative equity. At that point, the amount shown for partners with equity balances will be equal to the cash available for distribution. In the example shown in Exhibit 17–3, the allocations are continued until Nancy's equity shows a $70,000 balance and the equity of Buzz and Maxine is at zero. Thus, the $70,000 can be safely distributed to Nancy, but none of the $70,000 can be safely distributed to either Buzz or Maxine.

Note that the safe payments schedule is used only to determine the amount of advance distribution. That is, the safe payments schedule does not affect account balances or the statement of partnership liquidation. Actual cash distributed to Nancy is recorded in the usual fashion, with Nancy's loan balance being eliminated before her capital account is charged. The journal entry is:

Loan payable to Nancy	$20,000	
Nancy capital	50,000	
Cash		$70,000

After this entry is recorded, the account balances of the Buzz, Maxine, and Nancy partnership are as follows:

Debits		*Credits*	
Cash	$ 10,000	Buzz capital (50%)	$ 50,000
Loan due from Maxine	10,000	Maxine capital (30%)	70,000
Land	20,000	Nancy capital (20%)	60,000
Buildings—net	140,000		
	$180,000		$180,000

The partnership loan to Maxine can be charged to the capital balance of Maxine at any time, subject to the approval of the partners. Observe that the $10,000 loan to Maxine does not affect the determination of safe payments because the computations are based on the equity rather than the capital balances of the partners. Ordinarily, partnership loans to partners should be charged against partner capital balances at the beginning of the liquidation process.

Advance Distribution Requires Partner Approval

Any distribution to partners before all gains and losses have been realized and recognized requires the approval of all partners. Assume that Xavier, Young, and Zebula are partners sharing profits and losses equally, and that the partnership is in the process of liquidation with the following account balances after all nonpartner liabilities have been paid:

Debits		*Credits*	
Cash	$30,000	Xavier loan	$15,000
Equipment	45,000	Young capital	30,000
Xavier capital	10,000	Zebula capital	40,000
	$85,000		$85,000

If available cash is to be distributed, it should be paid $10,000 to Young and $20,000 to Zebula according to the following safe payment computations:

	Possible Losses	Xavier Equity	Young Equity	Zebula Equity
Partners' equities		$ 5,000	$30,000	$40,000
Possible loss on noncash asset:				
Equipment	$45,000	15,000*	15,000*	15,000*
		10,000*	15,000	25,000
Possible loss on Xavier's debit				
balance shared 50%/50%		10,000	5,000*	5,000*
Safe payments		—	$10,000	$20,000

Xavier may object to the immediate distribution of the $30,000 cash to Young and Zebula because his $15,000 loan to the partnership has a higher priority in liquidation than the capital balances of Young and Zebula. The objection simply means that the partners do not agree to the advance distribution of cash and, accordingly, all distributions are delayed until all assets are converted into cash and a final settlement can be made.

INSTALLMENT LIQUIDATIONS

An *installment liquidation* involves the distribution of cash to partners as it becomes available during the liquidation period and before all liquidation gains and losses have been realized. The alternative is a simple liquidation in which no cash is distributed to partners until all gains and losses on liquidation are realized and reflected in the partners' capital account balances.

General Principles of Installment Liquidation

An orderly liquidation of a solvent partnership may be carried out with distributions of available cash on a regular basis until all noncash assets are converted into cash. Liabilities other than those to partners must, of course, be paid before any distributions are made to partners. Once cash is available for distribution to partners, the amounts to be distributed to individual partners can be determined by the preparation of a schedule of safe payments for each installment distribution. A safe payments schedule will not be necessary, however, when the capital accounts at the start of the liquidation process are in the relative profit and loss sharing ratios of the partners, and there are no loan or advance balances with the partners. In this case, all distributions to partners will be made in the relative profit and loss sharing ratios.

When installment payments to partners are determined by reference to safe payments schedules, the order of distributions will be such that the remaining capital balances (equity balances if there are loans with partners) after each distribution will be ever closer to alignment with the profit and loss sharing ratios of the partners. Once all partners are included in an installment distribution, the remaining capital balances (equities) will be aligned and further installment payments will be in the profit sharing ratios. Thus, even though the capital accounts (equities) are not aligned at the start of the liquidation process, if all partners are included in the first installment, future installment payments to partners will be in the profit sharing ratios and additional safe payment schedules are not necessary.

Installment Liquidation Illustration

The partnership of Duro, Kemp, and Roth is to be liquidated as soon as possible after December 31, 19X1, and all cash on hand except for a $20,000 contingency balance is to be distributed at the end of each month until the liquidation is completed. Profits and losses are shared 50, 30, and 20 percent to Duro, Kemp, and Roth, respectively. A balance sheet of the partnership at December 31, 19X1 contains the following accounts and balances:

DURO, KEMP, AND ROTH
BALANCE SHEET
AT DECEMER 31, 19X1

Assets		Liabilities and Capital	
Cash	$ 240,000	Accounts payable	$ 300,000
Accounts receivable—net	280,000	Note payable	200,000
Loan to Roth	40,000	Loan from Kemp	20,000
Inventories	400,000	Duro capital (50%)	340,000
Land	100,000	Kemp capital (30%)	340,000
Equipment—net	300,000	Roth capital (20%)	200,000
Goodwill	40,000		
	$1,400,000		$1,400,000

A summary of liquidation events is as follows:

January 19X2—The loan to Roth is offset against his capital balance, the goodwill is written off, $200,000 is collected on account, inventory items that cost $160,000 are sold for $200,000, and cash is distributed.

February 19X2—Equipment with a book value of $80,000 is sold for $60,000, the remaining inventory items are sold for $180,000, liquidation expenses of $4,000 are paid, a liability of $8,000 is discovered, and cash is distributed.

March 19X2—The land is sold for $150,000, liquidation expenses of $5,000 are paid, and cash is distributed.

April 19X2—Additional equipment is sold for $150,000, the remaining equipment and receivables are written off, and all cash on hand is distributed in final liquidation of the partnership.

January Liquidation Events   The events of the Duro, Kemp, and Roth partnership during the month of January 19X2 are recorded as follows:

Roth capital	$ 40,000	
Loan to Roth		$ 40,000
To offset loan against capital.		
Duro capital	$ 20,000	
Kemp capital	12,000	
Roth capital	8,000	
Goodwill		$ 40,000
To write off goodwill.		
Cash	$200,000	
Accounts receivable		$200,000
To record collection of receivables.		
Cash	$200,000	
Inventories		$160,000
Duro capital		20,000
Kemp capital		12,000
Roth capital		8,000
To record sale of inventory items at a gain.		
Accounts payable	$300,000	
Note payable	200,000	
Cash		$500,000
To record payment of nonpartner liabilities.		

Loan from Kemp	$ 20,000	
Kemp capital	100,000	
Cash		$120,000

To record distribution of cash to Kemp.

In addition to being recorded in the accounts, each of the foregoing entries should be reflected in a statement of partnership liquidation, such as the one shown in Exhibit 17–4. A liquidation statement is a continuous record that summarizes all transactions and events during the liquidation period, and it will not be complete until the liquidation is finalized. Thus, the statement shown in Exhibit 17–4 for January events is really an interim statement. But interim liquidation statements are probably more important than the final liquidation statement, since interim statements show the progress that has been made toward liquidation to date and can provide a basis for current decisions as well as future planning. The completed liquidation statement can do little more than provide interested parties with an ability to check on what has been done. The partnership liquidation statement may be an acceptable legal document for partnerships that are liquidated through a bankruptcy court.[3]

DURO, KEMP, AND ROTH
STATEMENT OF PARTNERSHIP LIQUIDATION
FOR THE PERIOD JANUARY 1, 19X2 TO FEBRUARY 1, 19X2

	Cash	Noncash Asssets	Priority Liabilities	Duro Capital (50%)	Kemp Loan	Kemp Capital (30%)	Roth Capital (20%)
Balances January 1	$240,000	$1,160,000	$500,000	$340,000	$20,000	$340,000	$200,000
Offset Roth loan		40,000*					40,000*
Write-off of goodwill		40,000*		20,000*		12,000*	8,000*
Collection of receivables	200,000	200,000*					
Sale of inventory items	200,000	160,000*		20,000		12,000	8,000
Predistribution balances January 31	640,000	720,000	500,000	340,000	20,000	340,000	160,000
January distribution (see Exhibit 17–5)							
Creditors	500,000*		500,000*				
Kemp	120,000*				20,000*	100,000*	
Balances February 1	$ 20,000	$ 720,000	—	$340,000	—	$240,000	$160,000

* Deduct or loss.

Exhibit 17–4 *Interim Statement of Partnership Liquidation*

In the cash distribution that is made on January 31, 19X2 (see Exhibit 17–4), the partnership has $140,000 remaining after all nonpartner debts have been paid. Of this amount, $20,000 is retained by the partnership for contingencies, and $120,000 is available for distribution to the partners. The safe payments schedule that appears in Exhibit 17–5 shows that the full $120,000 should be distributed to Kemp. Since the partnership has a $20,000 loan payable to Kemp, the first $20,000 distributed to Kemp is applied to the loan, and the remaining $100,000 is charged to Kemp's capital account.

---

[3]When a partnership is liquidated under Chapter 7 of the Bankruptcy Act, court approval is required for all distributions.

DURO, KEMP, AND ROTH
SCHEDULE OF SAFE PAYMENTS
JANUARY 31, 19X2

	Possible Losses	Duro Capital (50%)	Kemp Capital and Loan (30%)	Roth Capital (20%)
Partners' equities January 31, 19X2 (see Statement of Liquidation)		$340,000	$360,000	$160,000
Possible loss on noncash assets (see Statement of Liquidation)	$720,000	360,000*	216,000*	144,000*
		20,000*	144,000	16,000
Possible loss on contingencies: cash withheld	20,000	10,000*	6,000*	4,000*
		30,000*	138,000	12,000
Possible loss from Duro: debit balance allocated 60:40		30,000	18,000*	12,000*
		—	$120,000	—

* Deduct or loss.

Exhibit 17–5 *First Installment—Safe Payments Schedule*

DURO, KEMP, AND ROTH
STATEMENT OF PARTNERSHIP LIQUIDATION
FOR THE PERIOD JANUARY 1, 19X2 TO MARCH 1, 19X2

	Cash	Noncash Assets	Priority Liabilities	Duro Capital (50%)	Kemp Loan	Kemp Capital (30%)	Roth Capital (20%)
Balances January 1	$240,000	$1,160,000	$500,000	$340,000	$20,000	$340,000	$200,000
Offset Roth loan		40,000*					40,000*
Write-off of goodwill		40,000*		20,000*		12,000*	8,000*
Collection of receivables	200,000	200,000*					
Sale of inventory items	200,000	160,000*		20,000		12,000	8,000
Predistribution balances January 31	640,000	720,000	500,000	340,000	20,000	340,000	160,000
January distribution (see Exhibit 17–5)							
Creditors	500,000*		500,000*				
Kemp	120,000*				20,000*	100,000*	
Balances February 1	$ 20,000	$ 720,000	—	$340,000	—	$240,000	$160,000
Equipment sale	60,000	80,000*		10,000*		6,000*	4,000*
Sale of inventory items	180,000	240,000*		30,000*		18,000*	12,000*
Liquidation expenses	4,000*			2,000*		1,200*	800*
Liability discovered			8,000	4,000*		2,400*	1,600*
Predistribution balances February 28	256,000	400,000	8,000	294,000		212,400	141,600
February distribution (see Exhibit 17–7)							
Creditors	8,000*		8,000*				
Partners	228,000*			84,000*		86,400*	57,600*
Balances March 1	$ 20,000	$ 400,000	—	$210,000		$126,000	$ 84,000

* Deduct or loss.

Exhibit 17–6 *Interim Statement of Partnership Liquidation*

February Liquidation Events   Journal entries to record the February 19X2 events of the Duro, Kemp, and Roth liquidation are:

Cash	$ 60,000	
Duro capital	10,000	
Kemp capital	6,000	
Roth capital	4,000	
Equipment—net		$ 80,000

To record sale of equipment at a $20,000 loss.

Cash	$180,000	
Duro capital	30,000	
Kemp capital	18,000	
Roth capital	12,000	
Inventories		$240,000

To record sale of remaining inventory items at a $60,000 loss.

Duro capital	$ 2,000	
Kemp capital	1,200	
Roth capital	800	
Cash		$ 4,000

To record payment of liquidation expenses.

Duro capital	$ 4,000	
Kemp capital	2,400	
Roth capital	1,600	
Accounts payable		$ 8,000

To record identification of an unrecorded liability.

Accounts payable	$ 8,000	
Cash		$ 8,000

To record payment of accounts payable.

Duro capital	$ 84,000	
Kemp capital	86,400	
Roth capital	57,600	
Cash		$228,000

To record distribution of cash to partners.

These entries are reflected in the liquidation statement that appears in Exhibit 17–6. The liquidation statement is for the period January 1, 19X2 to March 1, 19X2. Computations for the amount of cash distributed to partners on February 28, 19X2 are shown in Exhibit 17–7. Since all the partners are included in the

DURO, KEMP, AND ROTH SCHEDULE OF SAFE PAYMENTS FEBRUARY 28, 19X2	Possible Losses	Duro Capital (50%)	Kemp Capital (30%)	Roth Capital (20%)
Partners' equities February 28, 19X2 (see Statement of Liquidation)		$294,000	$212,400	$141,600
Possible loss on noncash assets (see Statement of Liquidation)	$400,000	200,000*	120,000*	80,000*
		94,000	92,400	61,600
Possible loss on contingencies: Cash withheld	20,000	10,000*	6,000*	4,000*
		$ 84,000	$ 86,400	$ 57,600
* Deduct or loss.				

Exhibit 17–7   *Second Installment—Safe Payments Schedule*

February 28 distribution, all future distributions will be in the profit and loss sharing ratios provided that the liquidation proceeds as planned.

Note that the plan of distribution can be upset by events such as the distribution of noncash assets to specific partners. In the liquidation of a medical practice partnership, for example, it might be expected that the doctors would withdraw equipment early in the liquidation process in order to continue their own practices. When noncash assets are distributed to partners, the fair value of such assets should be determined, and any difference between fair value and book value should be recognized as a partnership gain or loss. The distribution of noncash assets to specific partners and the valuation of the property distributed must be approved by all partners.

March and April Liquidation Events   By March 19X2 the liquidation of the Duro, Kemp, and Roth partnership has progressed to a point where partner capital balances are in their relative profit and loss sharing ratios. Journal entries for the events of March and April are as follows:

Entries for March

Cash	$150,000	
Duro capital		$ 25,000
Kemp capital		15,000
Roth capital		10,000
Land		100,000

To record sale of land at a $50,000 gain.

Duro capital	$ 2,500	
Kemp capital	1,500	
Roth capital	1,000	
Cash		$5,000

To record payment of liquidation expenses.

Duro capital	$ 72,500	
Kemp capital	43,500	
Roth capital	29,000	
Cash		$145,000

To record the March distribution of cash to partners.

Entries for April

Cash	$150,000	
Duro capital	35,000	
Kemp capital	21,000	
Roth capital	14,000	
Equipment—net		$220,000

To record sale of the remaining equipment at a $70,000 loss.

Duro capital	$ 40,000	
Kemp capital	24,000	
Roth capital	16,000	
Accounts receivable		$ 80,000

To record write-off of remaining receivables.

Duro capital	$ 85,000	
Kemp capital	51,000	
Roth capital	34,000	
Cash		$170,000

To record distribution of cash to partners in final liquidation.

These entries are reflected in a complete liquidation statement for the partnership in Exhibit 17–8. The complete liquidation statement covers the period January 1 to April 30, 19X2. Since the March and April cash distributions to partners are in the relative profit and loss sharing ratios, safe payment computations are not necessary. The $145,000 distributed to partners on March 31 is

DURO, KEMP, AND ROTH
STATEMENT OF PARTNERSHIP LIQUIDATION
FOR THE PERIOD JANUARY 1, 19X2 TO APRIL 30, 19X2

	Cash	Noncash Assets	Priority Liabilities	Duro Capital (50%)	Kemp Loan	Kemp Capital (30%)	Roth Capital (20%)
Balances January 1	$240,000	$1,160,000	$500,000	$340,000	$20,000	$340,000	$200,000
Offset Roth loan		40,000*					40,000*
Write-off of goodwill		40,000*		20,000*		12,000*	8,000*
Collection of receivables	200,000	200,000*					
Sale of inventory items	200,000	160,000*		20,000		12,000	8,000
Predistribution balances January 31	640,000	720,000	500,000	340,000	20,000	340,000	160,000
January distribution (see Exhibit 17–5)							
Creditors	500,000*		500,000*				
Kemp	120,000*				20,000*	100,000*	
Balances February 1	$ 20,000	$ 720,000	—	$340,000	—	$240,000	$160,000
Equipment sale	60,000	80,000*		10,000*		6,000*	4,000*
Sale of inventory items	180,000	240,000*		30,000*		18,000*	12,000*
Liquidation expenses	4,000*			2,000*		1,200*	800*
Liability discovered			8,000	4,000*		2,400*	1,600*
Predistribution balances February 28	256,000	400,000	8,000	294,000		212,400	141,600
February distribution (see Exhibit 17–7)							
Creditors	8,000*		8,000*				
Partners	228,000*			84,000*		86,400*	57,600*
Balances March 1	$ 20,000	$ 400,000	—	$210,000		$126,000	$ 84,000
Sale of land	150,000	100,000*		25,000		15,000	10,000
Liquidation expenses	5,000*			2,500*		1,500*	1,000*
Predistribution balances March 31	165,000	300,000		232,500		139,500	93,000
March distribution (50/30/20)	145,000*			72,500*		43,500*	29,000*
Balances April 1	$ 20,000	$ 300,000		$160,000		$ 96,000	$ 64,000
Sale of equipment	150,000	220,000*		35,000*		21,000*	14,000*
Write-off of receivables		80,000*		40,000*		24,000*	16,000*
Predistribution balances April 30	170,000	—		85,000		51,000	34,000
April distribution (50/30/20)	170,000*			85,000*		51,000*	34,000*
Liquidation completed April 30	—			—		—	—

* Deduct or loss.

Exhibit 17–8 Final Statement of Partnership Liquidation

determined by subtracting the $20,000 cash reserve from the $165,000 cash balance immediately before the distribution. All remaining cash is remitted to the partners in the final installment distribution on April 30, 19X2.

CASH DISTRIBUTION PLANS

Safe payment schedules are an effective method of computing the amount of safe payments to partners and preventing excessive payments to any partner. But the approach is inefficient if numerous installment distributions are made to partners because a safe payment schedule must be prepared for each distribution until the capital balances are aligned with the profit and loss sharing ratios. The safe payment schedule approach is also deficient as a planning device because it does not provide information that will help the partners project when they can expect to be included in cash distributions. These deficiencies of the safe payment approach can be overcome by preparing a cash distribution plan at the start of the liquidation process.

The development of a **cash distribution plan** (also referred to as a cash predistribution plan) for the liquidation of a partnership involves a ranking of the partners in terms of their vulnerability to possible losses, the use of the vulnerability ranking to prepare a schedule of assumed loss absorption, and the development of a cash distribution plan from the assumed loss absorption schedule. In illustrating the preparation of a cash distribution plan, the Duro, Kemp, and Roth example will be used.

Vulnerability Ranks

At the inception of the liquidation process, Duro, Kemp, and Roth had capital balances of $340,000, $340,000, and $200,000, respectively. But their equities (capital ± loan balances) were $340,000, $360,000, and $160,000, respectively. In determining their vulnerability to possible losses, the equity of each partner is divided by his or her profit sharing ratio to identify the maximum loss that the partner could absorb without reducing his or her equity below zero. **Vulnerability rankings** for Duro, Kemp, and Roth are determined as follows:

DURO, KEMP, AND ROTH VULNERABILITY RANKING

	Partner's Equity		Profit Sharing Ratio		Loss Absorption Potential	Vulnerability Ranking (1 most vulnerable)
Duro	$340,000	÷	.50	=	$ 680,000	1
Kemp	360,000	÷	.30	=	1,200,000	3
Roth	160,000	÷	.20	=	800,000	2

The vulnerability ranks indicate that Duro is most vulnerable to losses because his equity would be reduced to zero with a total partnership loss on liquidation of $680,000. Kemp, on the other hand, is least vulnerable because his equity is sufficient to absorb his share of liquidation losses up to $1,200,000. This interpretation helps explain why Kemp received all the cash distributed to partners in the first installment distribution in the previous illustration.

Assumed Loss Absorption

A **schedule of assumed loss absorption** is prepared as a second step in developing the cash distribution plan. This schedule starts with the preliquidation equities and charges each partner's equity with its share of the loss that would exactly eliminate the equity of the most vulnerable partner. The next step is to charge each remaining partner's equity with its share of the loss that would exactly eliminate the equity of the next most vulnerable partner. This process is continued until the equities of all but the least vulnerable partner have been reduced to zero. A schedule of assumed loss absorption for the Duro, Kemp, and Roth partnership is as follows:

DURO, KEMP, AND ROTH SCHEDULE OF ASSUMED LOSS ABSORPTION

	(50%) Duro	(30%) Kemp	(20%) Roth	Total
Preliquidation equities	$340,000	$360,000	$160,000	$860,000
Assumed loss to absorb Duro's equity (allocated 50%, 30%, 20%)	340,000*	204,000*	136,000*	680,000*
Balances	—	156,000	24,000	180,000
Assumed loss to absorb Roth's equity (allocated 60%, 40%)		36,000*	24,000*	60,000*
Balances		$120,000	—	$120,000

* Deduct.

The partnership loss that eliminates Duro's equity is $680,000, an amount computed in preparing the vulnerability ranks. After Duro's equity is reduced to zero in the first step, losses are divided 60 percent to Kemp and 40 percent to Roth until Roth's equity is reduced to zero. The additional partnership loss that reduces Roth's equity to zero is $60,000—Roth's $24,000 equity divided by his 40 percent profit sharing ratio after Duro is eliminated from consideration (in other words, it is assumed that Duro is personally insolvent). After Roth's equity has been reduced to zero, the equity of Kemp, the least vulnerable partner, stands at $120,000.

Cash Distribution Plan

Kemp should receive the first $120,000 distributed to the partners. A cash distribution plan for the Duro, Kemp, and Roth partnership is prepared from the schedule of assumed loss absorption as follows:

DURO, KEMP, AND ROTH CASH DISTRIBUTION PLAN

		Priority Liabilities	Kemp Loan	Duro	Kemp	Roth
First	$500,000	100%				
Next	20,000		100%			
Next	100,000				100%	
Next	60,000				60	40%
Remainder				50%	30	20

In developing the cash distribution plan, the first cash available for distribution goes to nonpartner creditors. These consist of the $300,000 accounts payable and the $200,000 note payable of the Duro, Kemp, and Roth partnership at December 31, 19X1. The next $20,000 goes to Kemp to settle his loan to the partnership, since partner loans have a higher priority than partner capital balances. The next $100,000 available is distributed to Kemp in consideration of his capital balance. This distribution aligns the capital and profit sharing ratios of Kemp and Roth. The next $60,000 is shared 60 percent and 40 percent between Kemp and Roth. This distribution completes the alignment of all capital balances and profit sharing ratios, and the remaining distributions are in accordance with the profit sharing ratios.

Kemp can analyze the cash distribution plan on January 1, 19X2 and determine that he will begin to receive cash after $500,000 has been paid to priority creditors. Similarly, Roth and Duro can use the plan to determine their chances of recovering some or all of their partnership equities. For example, if Duro expects $800,000 to be realized from all partnership assets, he can easily compute the amount he would receive [($800,000 − $680,000) × 50% = $60,000].

Cash Distribution Schedule

Further application of the cash distribution plan can be illustrated by assuming that the Duro, Kemp, and Roth partnership is liquidated in two installments, with $550,000 cash being distributed in the first installment and $250,000 in the second and final installment. Under these assumptions, the cash distribution plan would be used in preparing a **cash distribution schedule** such as the following one.

DURO, KEMP, AND ROTH CASH DISTRIBUTION SCHEDULE

	Cash Distributed	Priority Liabilities	Kemp Loan	Duro Capital	Kemp Capital	Roth Capital
First Installment						
Priority creditors	$500,000	$500,000				
Kemp loan	20,000		$20,000			
Kemp capital (remainder)	30,000				$ 30,000	
	$550,000	$500,000	$20,000		$ 30,000	
Second Installment						
Kemp capital	$ 70,000				$ 70,000	
Kemp and Roth (60/40)	60,000				36,000	$24,000
Remainder (50/30/20)	120,000			$60,000	36,000	24,000
	$250,000			$60,000	$142,000	$48,000

The $550,000 cash distributed in the first installment is allocated $500,000 to nonpartner liabilities and $20,000 to repay the loan from Kemp. The remaining $30,000 is paid to Kemp to reduce the balance of his capital account. In the second installment distribution, as shown in the cash distribution schedule, Kemp receives the first $70,000 in order to align his capital balance with that of Roth. The next $60,000 is allocated to Kemp and Roth in accordance with their 60:40 relative profit and loss sharing ratios, and the final $120,000 is allocated to Duro, Kemp, and Roth in their 50:30:20 relative profit and loss sharing ratios. The information from the cash distribution schedule is used in the same manner as information from safe payment schedules. That is, the cash payments indicated by the cash distribution schedules are entered in the statement of partnership liquidation and in the partnership records as cash distributions are actually made.

The preparation of a cash distribution plan is more time consuming than the preparation of a single safe payments schedule. But as shown here, the cash distribution plan provides a flexible and efficient means of determining safe payments to partners. In addition, the cash distribution plan serves a planning as well as a computational function.

INSOLVENT PARTNERS AND PARTNERSHIPS

The order for distributing assets in the liquidation of a partnership was listed early in this chapter as:

I Amounts owed to creditors other than partners
II Amounts owned to partners other than for capital and profits
III Amounts due to partners with respect to their capital interests

This order of distribution is specified in Section 40b of the Uniform Partnership Act. With respect to an insolvent partner, Section 40i of the Act gives the following rank order for claims against the separate property of a bankrupt partner:

I Those owing to separate creditors
II Those owing to partnership creditors
III Those owing to partners by way of contribution

These priority rankings have important implications for the liquidation of partnerships that are insolvent (partnership assets < partnership liabilities), and for the liquidation of partnerships that are solvent (partnership assets ≥ partnership liabilities), but one or more of the individual partners is insolvent (personal assets < personal liabilities). Partnership creditors must first seek recovery of their claims from partnership property, and the creditors of individual partners must first seek recovery of their claims from individual property. Thus, individual and partnership properties are marshaled separately in establishing the priority of claims.

Partnership Solvent—One or More Partners Personally Insolvent

In the liquidation of a solvent partnership, partnership creditors recover the full amount of their claims from partnership property. The partnership must be careful not to distribute partnership property to an insolvent partner because his or her personal creditors have a claim against partnership assets to the extent of the insolvent partner's equity in such assets. Also, if an insolvent partner has a credit capital balance and a solvent partner has an equal debit balance (that is, partnership assets = partnership liabilities = 0), the personal creditors of the insolvent partner have a claim against the personal assets of the solvent partner to the extent of the debit capital balance.

Even though the partnership is solvent, individual partners may have debit balances in their capital accounts at the time of dissolution, or they may end up with debit capital balances as a result of losses and expenses incurred during the liquidation process. Such partners are obligated to the partners with equity in the partnership for the amount of such debit balances. But if a partner with a debit capital balance is personally insolvent (personal assets < personal liabilities), the full amount of that partner's personal assets will go to his or her personal creditors (Rank I) under the Uniform Partnership Act, and amounts owing to partners by way of contribution (Rank III) will not share in distribution of that partner's personal assets. In those states that have not adopted the Uniform Partnership Act, however, it is possible under *common law or bankruptcy law* for the partners to share in the personal assets of an insolvent partner with a debit capital balance.[4]

To illustrate, West, York, and Zeff are partners sharing profits 30 percent, 30 percent, and 40 percent, respectively. West is personally insolvent with personal assets of $50,000 and personal liabilities of $100,000. The partnership account balances after all partnership liabilities have been paid are as follows:

	Case A	*Case B*	*Case C*
Cash	$60,000 dr	—	—
West capital (30%)	18,000 cr	$18,000 cr	$21,000 dr
York capital (30%)	18,000 cr	27,000 dr	9,000 cr
Zeff capital (40%)	24,000 cr	9,000 cr	12,000 cr

---

[4]A trustee in a partnership case under the Bankruptcy Act of 1978 has a claim against the estate of each general partner that is also a debtor in a bankruptcy case (11 U.S.C. paragraph 723[c]).

In case A, the $18,000 partnership equity of West should not be paid directly to West because her personal creditors have a prior claim against her $18,000 equity in partnership assets.

In case B, the personal creditors of West have a claim against the personal assets of York to the extent of the $18,000 that York owes West. Zeff also has a claim against York for $9,000.

In case C, West has a debit balance in her capital account and is insolvent. Under the provisions of the Uniform Partnership Act, York and Zeff are not allowed to share in the personal assets of West. Thus, they must share the $21,000 loss from West in their relative profit sharing ratios of 3/7 and 4/7.

Insolvent Partnership

When a partnership is insolvent, the cash available after all noncash assets have been converted into cash will not be sufficient to pay partnership creditors.[5] Partnership creditors will obtain partial recovery from partnership assets (Rank I) and will call upon individual partners to use their personal resources to satisfy remaining claims (Rank II). Although personal creditors have a prior claim (Rank I) on personal assets, partnership creditors can seek recovery of their claims from the personal assets of any partner who is personally solvent. Under the Uniform Partnership Act, partners are required to contribute the amounts necessary to satisfy partnership liabilities. The Act is specific in stating that a partner must contribute his or her share of the payment to satisfy the liabilities, as well as his or her relative share of the liabilities of any partners who are insolvent or who cannot or will not contribute their share of the payment to satisfy the liabilities (see Section 40b of the Act). A partner who pays more than his or her share of partnership liabilities does, of course, have a claim against partners with debit capital balances.

Rose, Faye, and Kate are partners sharing profits equally, and their partnership is in the process of liquidation. After all assets have been converted to cash and all available cash has been applied to the payment of partnership liabilities, the following account balances remain on the partnership books:

Liabilities	$90,000 cr
Rose capital (⅓)	30,000 dr
Faye capital (⅓)	30,000 dr
Kate capital (⅓)	30,000 dr

Provided that all partners have personal resources of at least $30,000, each partner should pay $30,000 into the partnership in full satisfaction of partnership liabilities. But the creditors may collect the full $90,000 deficiency from any one of the partners. For example, creditors may collect the $90,000 from Rose, in which case the remaining partnership balances would be:

Rose capital	$60,000 cr
Faye capital	30,000 dr
Kate capital	30,000 dr

If Faye and Kate can each pay $30,000 into the partnership, the fact that the creditors proceeded against Rose is of no great concern. But if the creditors proceeded against Rose because Kate is personally insolvent, and Faye's net personal assets are only $35,000, the situation is changed considerably. In this case, Rose and Faye share equally the $30,000 loss on Kate's insolvency, after which

---

[5]As used in this chapter, an insolvent partnership means that partnership liabilities exceed the fair value of partnership assets. Under the Bankruptcy Act of 1978, a partnership is insolvent if partnership liabilities exceed the fair value of partnership assets plus the excess of each general partner's personal assets over personal debts (11 U.S.C. paragraph 101[26]B).

Rose will have a $45,000 credit capital balance and Faye, a $45,000 debit capital balance. Since Faye's personal assets are only $35,000, Rose proceeds to collect the $35,000 from Faye, and the remaining $10,000 debit balance in Faye's capital account is written off as a loss to Rose.

The examples in this section illustrate some of the more general problems that arise in liquidations of partnerships that are insolvent or in which there are insolvent partners. Since many legal complications can arise in partnership liquidations, the accountant should not hesitate to seek legal counsel as the need arises.

SUMMARY

The liquidation of a partnership involves the conversion of noncash assets into cash, the recognition of gains and losses during the liquidation period, the payment of liabilities, and the distribution of cash to partners in final termination of the business entity. A simple liquidation refers to the conversion of all assets into cash before any distributions are made to partners.

A primary financial statement of a liquidating partnership is the statement of partnership liquidation, which summarizes all financial transactions and events during the liquidation period. This statement may also be used as a legal document for liquidations carried out under the jurisdiction of a court. When partnerships are liquidated by means of installment distributions to partners, cash is distributed to partners after liabilities have been paid but before all gains and losses on liquidation are recognized in the accounts. In order to prevent excessive payments to any partner, the amount of cash to be distributed is computed on the basis of two assumptions—that all partners are personally insolvent and that all noncash assets are actual losses. Under these assumptions, there are two primary approaches for computing the amounts that can be safely paid to partners in each installment distribution. The first approach is to prepare a safe payments schedule for each installment distribution, and the second approach is to prepare a cash distribution plan that can be used throughout the liquidation process.

The Uniform Partnership Act specifies priorities for the distribution of partnership assets in liquidations and for the distribution of the personal assets of insolvent partners. Partnership creditors rank first in recovering their claims from partnership property, and personal creditors rank first in recovering their claims from personal property. Priorities for other claims depend upon whether the partnership or the individual partners are insolvent, and each case requires separate analysis. Since the determination of property rights and creditor claims involves complex legal interpretations, competent legal advice is frequently needed and the accountant should not hesitate to seek legal counsel in matters relating to partnership liquidations.

ASSIGNMENT MATERIAL

QUESTIONS

1 How does the liquidation of a partnership differ from the dissolution of a partnership?
2 What is a simple partnership liquidation and how are distributions to partners determined?
3 The Uniform Partnership Act specifies a priority ranking for the distribution of partnership assets in liquidation. What is the ranking?
4 Under what conditions would partnership assets be distributed for partner capital interests before partner's loans to the partnership are paid?
5 What assumptions are made in determining the amount of distributions to individual partners prior to the recognition of all gains and losses on liquidation?

6 Why are partner equities rather than partner capital balances used in the preparation of safe payment schedules?

7 How do safe payment computations affect partnership ledger account balances?

8 What is a statement of partnership liquidation and how is the statement helpful to partners and other parties involved in the partnership liquidation?

9 If a partnership in liquidation has satisfied all of its nonpartner liabilities and has cash available for distribution to partners, under what circumstances would it be permissible to divide available cash in the profit and loss sharing ratios of the partners?

10 What are vulnerability ranks and how are they used in the preparation of cash distribution plans for partnership liquidations?

11 If a partnership is insolvent, how does one determine the amount of cash to distribute to individual partners?

12 When all partnership assets have been distributed in the liquidation of a partnership, some partners may have debit capital balances while others have credit capital balances. How are such balances disposed of if the partners with debit balances are personally solvent? If they are personally insolvent?

EXERCISES

E 17–1 The partnership of Dalby and Hill is in the process of liquidation. On January 1, 19X5 the ledger shows account balances as follows:

Cash	$10,000	Accounts payable	$15,000
Accounts receivable	25,000	Dalby capital	30,000
Lumber inventory	30,000	Hill capital	20,000

On January 10, 19X5 the lumber inventory is sold for $20,000 and, during January, accounts receivable of $21,000 are collected. No further collections on the receivables are expected. Profits are shared 60 percent to Dalby and 40 percent to Hill.

Required: Prepare a schedule showing how the cash available on February 1, 19X5 should be distributed.

E 17–2 After closing entries were made on December 31, 19X6, the ledger of Mike, Nancy, and Okey contained the following balances:

Cash	$39,000	Accounts payable	$ 5,000
Inventory	16,000	Mike capital (40%)	15,000
		Nancy capital (30%)	8,000
		Okey capital (30%)	27,000

Due to unsuccessful operations the partners decide to liquidate the business. During January some of the inventory is sold for $10,000, and on January 31, 19X7 all available cash is distributed. It is not known if the remaining inventory items can be sold.

Required: Prepare all the journal entries necessary to account for the transactions of the partnership during January 19X7.

E 17–3 The profit and loss sharing agreement of the partnership of Anita, Bernice, and Colleen provides that the partners are allowed 10 percent interest on their average capital balances for the year, Anita is allowed a $15,000 salary, and the remainder is divided 50 percent to Anita, 30 percent to Bernice, and 20 percent to Colleen. The December 31, 19X8 after-closing balances are as follows:

Net assets	$100,000	Anita capital	$ 40,000
		Bernice capital	35,000
		Colleen capital	25,000
			$100,000

In January 19X9 the partnership is preparing to liquidate the business and discovers that the year-end inventory was overvalued by $10,000, resulting in an error in calculating the 19X8 net income.

Required: Determine the correct capital balances of Anita, Bernice, and Colleen.

E 17-4 The trial balance of the Sandy, Tally, and Vassy partnership on December 31, 19X1 and the profit and loss percentages are as follows:

	Debit	Credit
Cash	$ 10,000	
Receivables—net	30,000	
Inventory	50,000	
Land and buildings—net	140,000	
Loan to Sandy	20,000	
Accounts payable		$ 40,000
Loan from Tally		10,000
Sandy capital (20%)		50,000
Tally capital (30%)		90,000
Vassy capital (50%)		60,000
	$250,000	$250,000

Early in January 19X2 the partners decide to dissolve their partnership and liquidate the business. During January, the land and buildings are sold for $100,000 cash, and $10,000 is collected on the receivables.

Required: If available cash is distributed on January 31, 19X2, how much will each of the partners receive?

E 17-5 A condensed balance sheet with profit sharing percentages for the Evers, Freda, and Grace partnership on January 1, 19X1 shows the following:

Cash	$100,000	Liabilities	$ 80,000
Other assets	500,000	Evers capital (40%)	100,000
		Freda capital (40%)	250,000
		Grace capital (20%)	170,000
	$600,000		$600,000

On January 2, 19X1 the partners decide to liquidate the business and during January they sell assets with a book value of $300,000 for $170,000.

Required: Prepare a safe payment schedule to show the amount of cash to be distributed to each partner if all available cash, except for a $10,000 contingency fund, is distributed immediately after the sale.

E 17-6 The partnership of Jerry, Joan, and Jill is in the process of liquidation. Its account balances on November 30, 19X8 are:

Cash	$ 8,000	Accounts payable	$ 4,000
Inventory	16,000	Due to Joan	4,000
Goodwill	8,000	Jerry capital	10,800
Receivable from Jerry	3,000	Joan capital	13,200
		Jill capital	3,000

Profits and losses are shared 40:50:10 to Jerry, Joan, and Jill, respectively.

Required: Prepare a statement of liquidation and a safe payments schedule for immediate distribution of all cash on hand.

E 17-7 The Shultz, Teachy, and Isaac Partnership became insolvent on January 1, 19X1, and the partnership is being liquidated as soon as practicable. In this respect the following information for the partners has been marshaled:

	Capital Balances	Personal Assets	Personal Liabilities
Shultz	$ 50,000	$80,000	$40,000
Teachy	(40,000)	30,000	50,000
Isaac	(30,000)	70,000	30,000
Total	$(20,000)		

Assume that residual profits and losses are shared equally among the three partners. Based on this information, calculate the *maximum* amount that Shultz can expect to receive from the partnership liquidation.

E 17-8   After all partnership assets were converted into cash and all available cash distributed to creditors, the ledger of the Ricke, Smith, and Tiller partnership showed the following balances:

	Debit	Credit
Accounts payable		$20,000
Ricke capital (30%)		10,000
Smith capital (30%)		60,000
Tiller capital (40%)	$90,000	
	$90,000	$90,000

The percentages indicated are residual profit and loss sharing ratios. Personal assets and liabilities of the partners are as follows:

	Ricke	Smith	Tiller
Personal assets	$50,000	$50,000	$100,000
Personal liabilities	45,000	40,000	40,000

The partnership creditors proceed against Tiller for recovery of their claims, and the partners settle their claims against each other in accordance with the Uniform Partnership Act.

Required: Prepare a schedule to show the phaseout of the partnership and the final closing of the books.

E 17-9   The partnership of Ace, Ben, Cid, and Don was dissolved on January 5, 19X1, and the account balances at June 30, 19X1, after all noncash assets are converted into cash, are as follows:

	Debits	Credits
Cash	$200,000	
Cid capital (20%)	170,000	
Don capital (10%)	80,000	
Accounts payable		$400,000
Ace capital (50%)		40,000
Ben capital (20%)		10,000
	$450,000	$450,000

Additional Information
  1 The percentages indicated represent the relevant profit and loss sharing ratios.
  2 Personal assets and liabilities of the partners at June 30, 19X1 are as follows:

	Personal Assets	Personal Liabilities
Ace	$600,000	$300,000
Ben	100,000	150,000
Cid	400,000	300,000
Don	100,000	20,000

  3 Ace pays $200,000 into the partnership, and partnership liabilities are paid on July 1, 19X1.

4 On July 15, 19X1 Cid pays $100,000 into the partnership and Don pays $80,000. No further contributions from either of these partners are possible.

5 Losses from the bankruptcy of Cid are divided among the solvent partners on July 15, 19X1.

6 Available cash is distributed and the partnership books are closed on July 31, 19X1.

Required: Prepare a liquidation statement for the Ace, Ben, Cid, and Don partnership for the period June 30, 19X1 to July 31, 19X1.

E 17-10 A trial balance of the David, Edwin, and Frank partnership on December 31, 19X1, including the profit and loss percentages, is as follows:

	Debit	Credit
Cash	$ 10,000	
Receivables—net	30,000	
Inventory	50,000	
Land and buildings—net	140,000	
Loan to David	20,000	
Accounts payable		$ 40,000
Loan from Edwin		10,000
David capital (20%)		50,000
Edwin capital (30%)		90,000
Frank capital (50%)		60,000
	$250,000	$250,000

Early in January 19X2 the partners decide to dissolve their partnership and liquidate the business. During January, the land and buildings are sold for $100,000, and $10,000 is collected on the receivables.

1 If available cash is distributed on January 31, 19X2, David, Edwin, and Frank should receive:

  a $24,000, $36,000, and $60,000, respectively

  b $8,000, $67,000, and $5,000, respectively

  c $16,000, $24,000, and $40,000, respectively

  d $28,000, $57,000, and $5,000, respectively

2 If available cash is distributed on January 31, 19X2 except for a $20,000 contingency cash fund, David, Edwin, and Frank should receive:

  a $20,000, $30,000, and $50,000, respectively

  b $12,000, $18,000, and $30,000, respectively

  c $2,000, $58,000, and 0, respectively

  d $4,000, $61,000, and $5,000, respectively

3 If a cash distribution plan is developed as of January 1, 19X2, the vulnerability ranks (1 is most vulnerable) for David, Edwin, and Frank, respectively, will be:

  a 1, 2, and 3   **b** 2, 3, and 1

  c 3, 2, and 1   **d** 3, 1, and 2

E 17-11 **1** In a partnership liquidation, the final cash distribution to the partners should be made in accordance with the:

  a Partners' profit and loss sharing ratios

  b Balances of the partners' capital accounts

  c Ratio of the capital contributions by the partners

  d Safe payments computations

2 In accounting for the liquidation of a partnership, cash payments to partners after all nonpartner creditors' claims have been satisfied, but before the final cash distribution, should be according to:

  a Their relative profit and loss sharing ratios

  b The final balances in partner capital accounts

  c Their relative share of the gain or loss on liquidation

  d Safe payments computations

3 After all noncash assets have been converted into cash in the liquidation of the Maris and DeMarco partnership, the ledger contains the following account balances:

	Debit	Credit
Cash	$34,000	—
Accounts payable	—	$25,000
Loan payable to Maris	—	9,000
Maris capital	8,000	—
DeMarco capital	—	8,000

Available cash should be distributed: $25,000 to accounts payable and:

a $9,000 to loan payable to Maris
b $4,500 each to Maris and DeMarco
c $1,000 to Maris and $8,000 to DeMarco
d $8,000 to Maris and $1,000 to DeMarco

4 The partnership of Gwen, Bill, and Sissy is in the process of liquidation and the ledger shows the following:

Cash	$ 80,000
Inventories	100,000
Accounts payable	60,000
Gwen capital (50%)	40,000
Bill capital (25%)	45,000
Sissy capital (25%)	35,000

If all available cash is distributed immediately:

a   Gwen, Bill, and Sissy should get $26,667 each.
b   Gwen, Bill, and Sissy should get $6,667 each.
c   Gwen should get $10,000, and Bill and Sissy should get $5,000 each.
d   Bill should get $15,000 and Sissy, $5,000.

5 The following balance sheet summary together with residual profit sharing ratios was developed on April 1, 19X6, the date on which the Dick, Frank, and Helen partnership began its liquidation:

Cash	$140,000	Liabilities	$ 60,000
Accounts receivable	60,000	Loan from Frank	20,000
Inventories	85,000	Dick capital, 20%	75,000
Plant assets—net	200,000	Frank capital, 40%	200,000
Loan to Dick	25,000	Helen capital, 40%	155,000
	$510,000		$510,000

If available cash except for a $5,000 contingency fund is distributed immediately, Dick, Frank, and Helen, respectively, should receive:

a $0, $80,000, and $15,000
b $16,000, $32,000, and $32,000
c $0, $70,000, and $5,000
d $0, $72,500, and $7,500

6 The partnership of Unsel, Vance, and Wayne was dissolved on June 30, 19X6, and the account balances after all noncash assets are converted to cash on September 1, 19X6, along with residual profit and loss sharing ratios, are:

Cash	$50,000	Accounts payable	$120,000
		Unsel capital (30%)	90,000
		Vance capital (30%)	(60,000)
		Wayne capital (40%)	(100,000)

Personal assets and liabilities of the partners at September 1, 19X6 are:

	Personal Assets	Personal Liabilities
Unsel	$ 80,000	$90,000
Vance	100,000	61,000
Wayne	190,000	80,000

If Wayne contributes $70,000 to the partnership to provide cash to pay the creditors, what amount of Unsel's $90,000 partnership equity would appear to be recoverable?

a $90,000   b $81,000
c $79,000   d None of the above

E 17-12   [AICPA adapted]

Use the following information in answering questions 1, 2, and 3. Q, R, S, and T are partners sharing profits and losses equally. The partnership is insolvent and is to be liquidated; the status of the partnership and each partner is as follows:

	Partnership Capital Balance	Personal Assets (Exclusive of Partnership Interest)	Personal Liabilities (Exclusive of Partnership Interest)
Q	$ 15,000	$100,000	$40,000
R	10,000	30,000	60,000
S	(20,000)	80,000	5,000
T	(30,000)	1,000	28,000
Total	$(25,000)		

Assume that the Uniform Partnership Act applies to these questions:

1 The partnership creditors:
   a Must first seek recovery against S because he is personally solvent and he has a negative capital balance.
   b Will *not* be paid in full regardless of how they proceed legally because the partnership assets are less than the partnership liabilities.
   c Will have to share R's interest in the partnership on a pro rata basis with R's personal creditors.
   d Have first claim to the partnership assets before any partner's personal creditors have rights to the partnership assets.

2 The partnership creditors may obtain recovery of their claims:
   a In the amount of $6,250 from each partner.
   b From the personal assets of either Q or R.
   c From the personal assets of either S or T.
   d From the personal assets of either Q or S for some or all of their claims.

3 If Q pays the full amount owed to partnership creditors from his personal assets, then:
   a Q's partnership loss will be increased by $25,000.
   b Q's partnership loss will be increased by $12,500.
   c Q will have a $40,000 total partnership loss.
   d Q's partnership loss will be the same as if S had paid partnership creditors from his personal assets.

4 X, Y, and Z have capital balances of $30,000, $15,000, and $5,000, respectively, in the XYZ partnership. The general partnership agreement is silent as to the manner in which partnership losses are to be allocated but does provide that partnership profits are to be allocated as follows: 40 percent to X, 25 percent to Y, and 35 percent to Z. The partners have decided to dissolve and liquidate the partnership. After paying all creditors, the amount available for distribution will be $20,000. X, Y, and Z are individually solvent. Under the circumstances, Z will:
   a Receive $7,000
   b Receive $12,000
   c Personally have to contribute an additional $5,500
   d Personally have to contribute an additional $5,000

PROBLEMS

P 17-1   Barnes, Nelson, and Gilbert are partners in a business that is in the process of liquidation. On January 1, 19X2, the ledger accounts show the balances indicated:

Cash	$15,000	Barnes capital	$62,000
Inventory	72,000	Nelson capital	28,000
Supplies	18,000	Gilbert capital	15,000

The cash is distributed to partners on January 1, 19X2. Inventory and supplies are sold for a lump-sum price of $81,000 on February 9, 19X2, and on February 10, 19X2, cash on hand is distributed to the partners in final liquidation of the business.

Required
1 Prepare the journal entry to distribute available cash on January 1, 19X2. Include proper explanation.
2 Prepare journal entries necessary on February 9, 19X2 to record the sale of assets and the distribution of the gain or loss to the partners' capital accounts.
3 Prepare the journal entry to distribute the cash on February 10, 19X2 in final liquidation of the business.

P 17-2 The December 31, 19X4 balance sheet of the Chan, Dickerson, and Grunther partnership, along with the partners' residual profit and loss sharing ratios, is summarized as follows:

Assets		*Equities*	
Cash	$ 60,000	Accounts payable	$ 90,000
Receivables	120,000	Loan from Dickerson	50,000
Inventories	150,000	Chan capital (20%)	95,000
Due from Chan	15,000	Dickerson capital (30%)	160,000
Other assets	255,000	Grunther capital (50%)	205,000
	$600,000		$600,000

The partners agree to liquidate their partnership as soon as possible after January 1, 19X5 and to distribute all cash as it becomes available.

Required: Prepare a cash distribution plan to show how cash will be distributed as it becomes available.

P 17-3 The assets, equities, and profit and loss sharing percentages of the Day, Easy, and Fox partnership at the beginning of its liquidation period on January 1, 19X2 are as follows:

Assets		*Equities*	
Cash	$120,000	Accounts payable	$110,000
Receivables—net	60,000	Loan from Fox	20,000
Inventories	120,000	Day capital (30%)	195,000
Land	50,000	Easy capital (30%)	75,000
Plant assets—net	150,000	Fox capital (40%)	100,000
	$500,000		$500,000

Required: Prepare a cash distribution plan for the phaseout period.

P 17-4 The partnership of Martin, Nelson, Oliver, and Pavlock is preparing to liquidate. Profit and loss sharing ratios are shown in the summarized balance sheet at December 31, 19X8 as follows:

Cash	$200,000	Other liabilities	$100,000
Inventories	200,000	Martin loan	100,000
Loan to Nelson	20,000	Martin capital (40%)	200,000
Other assets	380,000	Nelson capital (30%)	200,000
		Oliver capital (20%)	100,000
		Pavlock capital (10%)	100,000
	$800,000		$800,000

Required
1 The partners anticipate an installment liquidation. Prepare a cash distribution plan as of January 1, 19X9 that includes a $50,000 contingency fund to help the partners predict when they will be included in cash distributions.
2 During January 19X9, the inventories are sold for $100,000, the other liabilities are paid, and $50,000 is set aside for contingencies. The partners agree that loan balances should be closed to the capital accounts and remaining cash (less the contingency fund) should be distributed to partners. How much cash should each partner receive?

P 17-5 Jones, Smith, and Tandy are partners in a furniture store that began liquidation on January 1, 19X1, at which time the ledger contained the following account balances:

	Debit	Credit
Cash	$ 15,000	
Accounts receivable	20,000	
Inventories	65,000	
Land	50,000	
Buildings	100,000	
Accumulated depreciation—buildings		$ 40,000
Furniture and fixtures	50,000	
Accumulated depreciation—furniture and fixtures		30,000
Accounts payable		80,000
Jones capital (20%)		40,000
Smith capital (30%)		60,000
Tandy capital (50%)		50,000
	$300,000	$300,000

The following transactions and events occurred during the liquidation process:

January: Inventories were sold for $20,000 cash, collections on account totaled $14,000, and half of the amount due to creditors was paid.

February: Land costing $40,000 was sold for $60,000, the remaining land and buildings were sold for $40,000, and half of the remaining receivables were collected and the remainder were uncollectible.

March: The remaining liabilities were paid and available cash was distributed to the partners in final liquidation.

Required: Prepare a statement of liquidation for the Jones, Smith, and Tandy partnership.

P 17-6 The after-closing trial balance of the Link, Mack, and Nell partnership at December 31, 19X8 was as follows:

	Debit	Credit
Cash	$ 47,000	—
Receivables—net	25,000	—
Loan to Mack	8,000	—
Inventories	20,000	—
Plant assets—net	50,000	—
Accounts payable	—	$ 55,000
Loan from Link	—	15,000
Link capital (50%)	—	40,000
Mack capital (30%)	—	20,000
Nell capital (20%)	—	20,000
Total	$150,000	$150,000

Additional Information
1 The partnership is to be liquidated as soon as the assets can be converted into cash. Cash realized on conversion of assets is to be distributed as it becomes available, except that $10,000 is to be held to provide for contingencies during the liquidation period.
2 Profits and losses on liquidation are to be divided in the percentages indicated in the trial balance.

Required
1 Prepare a cash distribution plan for the Link, Mack, and Nell partnership.
2 If $25,000 cash is realized from the receivables and inventories during January 19X9, how should the cash be distributed at the end of January? (Assume that this is the first distribution of cash during the liquidation period.)

P 17–7 The balance sheet of Roger, Susan, and Tom, who share profits in the ratio of 30, 30, and 40 percent, respectively, included the following balances on January 1, 19X2 at the time of dissolution:

Cash	$ 20,000	Liabilities	$ 40,100
Other assets	130,000	Roger loan	5,000
Loan to Susan	10,000	Roger capital	9,900
		Susan capital	45,000
		Tom capital	60,000
	$160,000		$160,000

During January 19X2 part of the firm's assets are sold for $40,000. In February the remaining assets are sold for $21,000. Assume that available cash is distributed to the proper parties at the end of January and at the end of February.

Required: Prepare a statement of partnership liquidation with supporting safe payment schedules for each cash distribution. (It will not be possible to determine the actual gains and losses in January.)

P 17–8 The balance sheet of the Tucker, Gilliam, and Simpson partnership at December 31, 19X1 is as follows:

TUCKER, GILLIAM, AND SIMPSON PARTNERSHIP BALANCE SHEET ON DECEMBER 31, 19X1

Assets		*Liabilities*	
Cash	$120,000	Accounts payable	$ 65,000
Receivables—net	80,000	Due to Simpson	35,000
Due from Gilliam	10,000	Total liabilities	100,000
Inventories	90,000		
Land	50,000	*Capital*	
Buildings—net	120,000	Tucker capital (20%)	$130,000
Machinery—net	30,000	Gilliam capital (30%)	110,000
		Simpson capital (50%)	160,000
		Total capital	400,000
		Total liabilities and	
Total assets	$500,000	capital	$500,000

On January 1, 19X2, the partners agree to dissolve the partnership, distribute available cash immediately except for $10,000 to be held to cover contingencies, and liquidate the other assets as soon as possible. Profit sharing percentages are indicated in the balance sheet.

Required
1 Prepare a schedule showing the cash distribution on January 1, 19X2.
2 Prepare a cash distribution plan to show how all cash could be safely distributed to partners as it becomes available (assume no cash has been distributed).

P 17–9 The adjusted trial balance of the Jee, Moore, and Olsen partnership at December 31, 19X6 was as follows:

Cash	$ 50,000
Accounts receivable—net	100,000
Nonmonetary assets	800,000
Loan to Jee	50,000
Expenses	400,000
Total debits	$1,400,000

Accounts payable	$ 80,000
Loan from Olsen	20,000
Jee capital	300,000
Moore capital	450,000
Olsen capital	350,000
Revenue	200,000
Total credits	$1,400,000

Additional Information

1 Partnership profits are divided 20 percent, 40 percent, and 40 percent to Jee, Moore, and Olsen, respectively, after salary allowances of $25,000 each to Jee and Moore for time devoted to the business.
2 Due to the disastrous results of 19X6, the partners agreed to liquidate the business as soon as possible after January 1, 19X7, and to distribute available cash on a weekly basis.
3 During the first week in January, $85,500 was collected on the accounts receivable and cash was distributed on January 8, 19X7.

Required

1 Prepare the journal entries to close the partnership books at December 31, 19X6.
2 Develop a cash distribution plan for the partnership as of January 1, 19X7.
3 Prepare a cash distribution schedule for the January 8, 19X7 distribution of available cash.

P 17-10 The after-closing trial balances of the Beams, Plank, and Timbers partnership at December 31, 19X1 included the following accounts and balances:

Cash	$120,000
Accounts receivable—net	140,000
Loan to Timbers	20,000
Inventory	200,000
Plant assets—net	200,000
Trademarks	20,000
Total debits	$700,000
Accounts payable	$150,000
Notes payable	100,000
Loan from Plank	10,000
Beams capital (profit sharing ratio, 50%)	170,000
Plank capital (profit sharing ratio, 30%)	170,000
Timbers capital (profit sharing ratio, 20%)	100,000
Total credits	$700,000

The partnership is to be liquidated as soon as possible, and all available cash except for a $10,000 contingency balance is to be distributed at the end of each month prior to the time that all assets are converted into cash.

During January 19X2 $100,000 was collected from the accounts receivable, inventory items with a book value of $80,000 were sold for $100,000, and available cash was distributed.

During February 19X2 Beams received plant assets with a book value of $60,000 and a fair value of $50,000 in partial settlement of her equity in the partnership. Also during February, the remaining inventory items were sold for $60,000, liquidation expenses of $2,000 were paid, and a liability of $8,000 was discovered. Cash was distributed on February 28.

During March 19X2 the plant assets were sold for $110,000, the remaining non-cash assets were written off, final liquidation expenses of $5,000 were paid, and cash was distributed. The dissolution of the partnership was completed on March 31, 19X2.

Required: Prepare a statement of partnership liquidation for the Beams, Plank, and Timbers partnership for the period January 1, 19X2 to March 31, 19X2.

18

CORPORATE LIQUIDATIONS, REORGANIZATIONS, AND DEBT RESTRUCTURINGS FOR FINANCIALLY DISTRESSED CORPORATIONS

This chapter examines accounting and legal matters relating to financially distressed corporations.[1] Some corporations are able to recover from financial adversity through internal operating and policy changes, while others with more serious financial problems are forced to seek additional remedies. In general, these remedies are classified as direct agreements with creditors, reorganizations, and liquidations.[2]

A debtor corporation is considered insolvent when it is unable to pay its debts as they come due, or when its total debts exceed the fair value of its assets. The inability to make immediate payment is referred to as *equity insolvency*. Having total debts that exceed the fair value of total assets is referred to as *bankruptcy insolvency*. Debtor corporations that are insolvent in the equity sense may be able to avoid bankruptcy proceedings by negotiating an agreement directly with creditors. Debtor corporations that are insolvent in the bankruptcy sense will ordinarily be reorganized or liquidated under the supervision of a bankruptcy court.

A petition for relief can be filed with a bankruptcy court by either the debtor or the creditors. Therefore, a direct agreement between the parties can be reached only when both agree that resolving the matter out of court is in their own best interests.

BANKRUPTCY REFORM ACT OF 1978

The federal government has preempted legislation of state governments that deals with bankruptcies since 1898. The 1898 Bankruptcy Act and its numerous amendments were repealed when Congress enacted Title 11 of the United States

---

[1]Municipalities, railroads, stockbrokers, and commodity brokers are excluded from the discussion in this chapter. Bankruptcies of these entities are covered by special provisions of Title 11 of the United States Code.

[2]Dun & Bradstreet reports that there were 60,432 business failures in 1990 (up 20 percent over the previous year). Dun & Bradstreet defines business failure as a business that cannot pay creditors and ceases operations or goes into receivership or reorganization through legal proceedings. *The Wall Street Journal*, March 13, 1991, p. A2.

Code (U.S.C.), the Bankruptcy Act, that reflects the entire bankruptcy law and became effective October 1, 1979. The 1978 act, frequently referred to as the Bankruptcy Reform Act, provided a comprehensive law of bankruptcy as well as new bankruptcy judges and new bankruptcy courts (as separate but adjunct to each U.S. district court). The part of the 1978 act dealing with judges and courts provided that bankruptcy judges were to be appointed by the president for a period of fourteen years. This provision dealing with bankruptcy court judges was ruled unconstitutional in 1982 in the *Northern Pipeline* case because the bankruptcy judges were given the powers, but not the protection, of district court judges who were appointed for life. In response to this and other controversies, a series of amendments to the 1978 law were passed in 1984 and 1986. Bankruptcy judges are now appointed by federal appeals court judges. The 1986 law provided for 52 additional bankruptcy judges, bringing the total to 284.

Since its inception, the 1978 bankruptcy law has been used to protect firms from a variety of obligations. In 1983 several companies filed for bankruptcy in an attempt to have their collective bargaining contracts set aside (for example, Wilson Foods and Continental Airlines). Other companies threatened bankruptcy unless their employees agreed to substantial pay cuts or other concessions. Under pressure from organized labor, Congress passed a law in 1984 to clarify the Bankruptcy Code in relation to wage contracts. The law provides that a bankruptcy court can grant wage reductions only if they are "necessary."

In April 1985 the Wheeling-Pittsburgh Steel Corporation filed for protection from creditors under bankruptcy law, and two months later it asked the federal bankruptcy court to void its labor contract with United Steelworkers Union. The bankruptcy judge, ruling that Wheeling could void its labor contract, wrote that reduced wages were necessary for Wheeling-Pittsburgh to emerge from bankruptcy. The decision was upheld by a federal district judge, but was reversed in federal appeals court.

The labor contract controversy came up again in 1990 during Eastern Airline's bankruptcy court proceedings. Eastern, hoping to cut the pay of its pilots and change work rules, asked the bankruptcy court for permission to break the labor contract. The bankruptcy judge ruled in favor of management, explaining that bankruptcy law "gives debtors a 'breathing spell' from creditors' and labor's claims." This ruling was overturned by a U.S. district judge who ruled that the purpose of the 1984 change in the bankruptcy code was to prevent employers from using a bankruptcy filing "to obtain an automatic 'breathing spell' from their labor obligations."[3]

Other companies sought bankruptcy protection when they were sued for overwhelming amounts in damages. Manville, UNR Industries, and Amatex filed for bankruptcy because they were facing thousands of claims for asbestos-caused disease. A. H. Robins filed for bankruptcy law protection when thousands of Dalkon Shield users filed claims against the company. Companies in bankruptcy have generally been protected from environmental cleanup obligations incurred prior to the bankruptcy filing. In the LTV Corp. bankruptcy case, a U.S. district judge ruled that a company in bankruptcy proceedings cannot be required to pay cleanup costs incurred *after* a bankruptcy petition is filed if the costs relate to pollution that occurred *before* the filing, regardless of when the contamination was discovered.[4] In April 1987 Texaco filed for bankruptcy law protection to prevent seizure of its assets in settlement of a $10.3 billion judgment awarded to Pennzoil by the Texas state courts.

The jurisdiction of the bankruptcy court covers all cases under Title 11 of U.S.C. A case begins with the filing of a petition under which a debtor is initially brought into bankruptcy court. In general, the petition is filed in the district

---

[3] *The Wall Street Journal,* April 11, 1990, p. B3.
[4] *The Wall Street Journal,* March 22, 1990, p. A16.

724

CORPORATE
LIQUIDATIONS,
REORGANIZATIONS, AND
DEBT RESTRUCTURINGS
FOR FINANCIALLY
DISTRESSED
CORPORATIONS

where the debtor's principal place of business or principal assets have been located for at least 180 days. Either the debtor corporation or the creditors may file the petition. If the debtor corporation files the petition, the proceedings are termed a *voluntary bankruptcy proceeding*; if creditors file, it is an *involuntary bankruptcy proceeding*.

A petition commencing a case by or against a corporate debtor may be filed under either Chapter 7 or Chapter 11 of the Bankruptcy Act. *Chapter 7 of the Bankruptcy Act covers straight bankruptcy under which liquidation of the debtor corporation is expected,*[5] and *Chapter 11 of the Bankruptcy Act covers rehabilitation of the debtor and anticipates reorganization of the debtor corporation.* The bankruptcy court has the power (subject to various requests and conditions) to dismiss a case, to enter the order for relief (in other words, accept the petition), or to convert a Chapter 11 reorganization case into a Chapter 7 liquidation case or vice versa.

The Office of U.S. Trustee

The Bankruptcy Reform Act created the Office of U.S. Trustee to be responsible for the administrative duties of bankruptcy cases. Under the 1986 amendment to the Bankruptcy Act, the Attorney General is required to appoint one *U.S. trustee* in each of twenty-one regions for terms of five years. Districts not represented by a U.S. trustee are referred to as non-U.S. trustee districts. The duties of the U.S. trustee are to maintain and supervise a panel of private trustees eligible to serve in Chapter 7 cases, to serve as trustee or interim trustee in some bankruptcy cases (such as in a Chapter 7 case where a qualified private trustee is not available), to supervise the administration of bankruptcy cases, and to monitor appointed creditors' committees and preside over creditor meetings.

Duties of the Debtor Corporation

In addition to specific duties related to Chapter 7 liquidation cases and Chapter 11 reorganization cases, the debtor corporation is required to perform the following duties:

- File a list of creditors, a schedule of assets and liabilities, and a statement of debtor's financial affairs
- Cooperate with the trustee as necessary to enable the trustee to perform his duties
- Surrender all property to the trustee, including books, documents, records, and papers relating to the estate in cases involving a trustee
- Appear at hearings of the court as required

Duties of the Bankruptcy Judge

The role of the bankruptcy judge is judicial. The judge settles disputes that occur during the case and approves all payments of debts incurred before the bankruptcy filing, as well as other payments that are considered extraordinary.

The authority of bankruptcy judges to hear jury trials involving allegedly

---

[4]*The Wall Street Journal,* March 22, 1990, p. A16.

[5]Not all liquidations result from financial adversity. Voluntary liquidations are often based on the belief that the market value of the company's stock is less than the amount that could be realized by selling the company's assets. For example, in 1990 Prospect Group Inc. made plans to distribute its assets to stockholders over a three-year period and liquidate the company because it felt that the stock market did not recognize the value of Prospect's diverse assets. This type of liquidation does not involve restructurings or judicial remedies, and established accounting principles are applicable to winding up the company's affairs through liquidating dividends. For a discussion of voluntary liquidations, see Ronald J. Kudle, *Voluntary Corporate Liquidations* (Westport, CT: Quorum Books, Greenwood Press, 1988) or George E. Nogler and Kenneth B. Schwartz, "Financial Reporting and Auditors' Opinions on Voluntary Liquidations," *Accounting Horizons,* 3, 3 (September 1989), pp. 12–20.

improper transfers of the debtor's assets (such as fraudulent conveyance of assets[6] or preferential treatment of creditors) has not been established at the time of this writing. In February 1990 the federal appeals court in New York ruled that bankruptcy judges could preside over jury trials, but in May 1990, a federal appeals court in St. Louis ruled that the bankruptcy court was not authorized to hear jury trials, which must be tried in district court. District courts were formed by the Constitution; bankruptcy courts were created by Congress. A final decision may have to come from the U.S. Supreme Court.[7]

LIQUIDATION

A Chapter 7 liquidation case is commenced *voluntarily* when a debtor corporation files a petition with the bankruptcy court or *involuntarily* through filing by three or more entities[8] holding noncontingent, unsecured claims aggregating at least $5,000. A single creditor with an unsecured claim of $5,000 or more may also file a petition provided that there are fewer than twelve unsecured creditors. The court will grant the order for relief (accept the petition) under Chapter 7 if the creditors prove their claims, or if the debtor fails to contest the petition on a timely basis. The order for relief prevents creditors from seeking payment of their claims directly from the debtor. If the creditors fail to prove their alleged claims, the court will dismiss the case. The debtor may respond to the petition by filing for protection from creditors under Chapter 11.[9]

If an order for relief under Chapter 7 is granted, the U.S. trustee (or the court) will appoint an interim trustee to take possession of the debtor corporation's estate until a trustee is elected. (An interim trustee may be appointed at any time after commencement of a case if the court considers it necessary to preserve the property of the estate or prevent losses). The election for trustee takes place at a meeting of creditors and only unsecured creditors with undisputed claims are eligible to vote. A trustee will be elected if creditors holding a minimum of 20 percent in amount of claims vote for a candidate and one candidate obtains the votes of creditors holding a majority in amount of claims actually voting. If a trustee is not elected, the interim trustee serves as trustee. The unsecured creditors eligible to vote may also elect a creditors' committee of three to eleven members to consult with the trustee and to submit questions regarding the debtor's estate to the court.

Duties of the Trustee in Liquidation Cases

The filing of a case creates an estate. *The trustee takes possession of the estate, converts the estate assets into cash, and distributes the proceeds according to prioriy of claims, as directed by the bankruptcy court.* Other duties of the trustee in a liquidation case are:

---

[6]***Fradulent transfer*** is "a transfer of an interest or an obligation incurred by the debtor, within one year prior to the date the petition was filed, with the intent to hinder, delay, or defraud creditors or whereby the debtor received less than fair equivalent value and the debtor (1) was insolvent before or became insolvent as the result of such transfer, (2) was left with unreasonably small business capital, or (3) intended to incur debts beyond the ability to pay such debts as they matured. Fraudulent transfers may be voided." Grant W. Newton, *Bankruptcy and Insolvency Accounting*, 2nd ed. (New York: John Wiley & Sons, 1981) p. 636.

[7]*The Wall Street Journal*, May 11, 1990, p. B9.

[8]An entity under Title 11 means person, estate, trustee, or governmental unit. *Person* means individual, partnership, or corporation, but not a governmental unit.

[9]For example, on June 6, 1989 five unsecured creditors of Crazy Eddies, Inc., a New York electronics retailer, filed a petition under Chapter 7 to force the company into involuntary liquidation; and on June 20, the company responded by filing a *superseding* Chapter 11 petition. (Crazy Eddies' board subsequently changed its filing to Chapter 7 and sought liquidation.) *The Wall Street Journal*, March 1, 1990, p. B6.

726

CORPORATE
LIQUIDATIONS,
REORGANIZATIONS, AND
DEBT RESTRUCTURINGS
FOR FINANCIALLY
DISTRESSED
CORPORATIONS

- To investigate the financial affairs of the debtor.
- To provide information about the debtor's estate and its administration to parties in interest.
- To examine creditor claims and object to claims that appear improper.
- If authorized to operate the debtor's business, to provide periodic reports and summaries of operations, a statement of receipts and disbursements, and other information as the court specifies.
- To file final reports on trusteeship as required by the court.

The trustee has the power to avoid (invalidate) certain transfers of property of the debtor or certain obligations incurred by the debtor. These items are referred to as *preferences,* and those that a trustee can avoid are *voidable preferences.* A transfer is voidable only if the debtor was insolvent in the bankruptcy sense at the time of the transfer. When a transfer is voided, the trustee recovers the property or its value for the benefit of the debtor's estate.

Transfers made within ninety days of filing can be voided by the trustee. The time is extended to a year if the transfer is to an insider. A corporation's insiders are its officers and directors and their relatives, and the corporation's affiliates and the officers and directors of the affiliates and their relatives. A transfer in payment of a debt incurred in the ordinary course of business, made under ordinary terms, and paid within forty-five days of its incurrence is not voidable (utility bills, personal services, cash sales). But any transfer made within one year of filing can be voided if it is made with an intent to hinder, delay,

---

I. Secured Claims

Claims secured by valid liens.

II. Unsecured Priority Claims

1 Administrative expenses incurred in preserving and liquidating the estate including trustee's fees and legal and accounting fees.
2 Claims incurred between the date of filing an involuntary petition and the date a trustee is appointed.
3 Claims for wages, salaries, and commissions earned within 90 days of filing the petition and not exceeding $2,000 per individual.
4 Claims for contributions to employee benefit plans arising from services rendered within 180 days of filing the petition and limited to $2,000 per employee.
5 Claims of individuals not to exceed $900 arising from the purchase, lease, or rental of property that was not delivered or the purchase of services that were not provided by the debtor.
6 Claims of governmental units for income or gross receipts taxes, property taxes, employment taxes, excise taxes, and customs duties that originated within one to four years before filing (periods vary for different claims). Taxes collected or withheld for which the debtor is liable and penalties related to the foregoing are also included.

III. Unsecured Nonpriority Claims

1 Allowed claims that were timely filed.
2 Allowed claims where proof of claims was filed late.
3 Allowed claims (secured and unsecured) for any fine, penalty, or forfeiture, or for multiple, exemplary, or punitive charges arising prior to the order for relief or appointment of trustee.
4 Claims for interest on the unsecured priority claims or the unsecured nonpriority claims.

IV. Stockholders' Claims

Remaining assets are returned to the debtor corporation or its stockholders.

Exhibit 18–1 *Ranking of Claims in Chapter 7 Liquidation Cases*

or defraud any entity; or if the debtor was insolvent or becomes insolvent as a result of the transaction, and the debtor received less than equivalent value in the transaction.

Payment of Claims

Claims secured by valid liens are paid to the extent of the proceeds from property pledged as security. If the proceeds are insufficient to satisfy the claims of secured creditors, the amounts not satisfied are unsecured nonpriority claims (or general unsecured claims). Unsecured claims are divided into priority and nonpriority classes for Chapter 7 liquidation cases (see Exhibit 18–1). Unsecured priority claims are paid in full before any distributions are made to unsecured nonpriority claims. Further, claims within the unsecured priority claims class are ranked 1 through 6, such that claims in the first rank (administrative expenses) are paid in full before any distribution is made for claims in the second rank, and so forth. Within each of the six priority ranks, however, distributions are made on a pro rata basis when available cash is insufficient to pay all claims of that rank. Equivalent procedures apply to cash distributions in the four ranks included within the unsecured nonpriority class. Stockholders under a Chapter 7 liquidation are included in distributions only when all valid creditor claims have been fully satisfied.

ILLUSTRATION OF A LIQUIDATION CASE

Stilldown Corporation experienced a large operating loss in 19X1 and the first half of 19X2. By July 19X2 its accounts payable were overdue, and its accounts receivable had been pledged to support a bank loan that was in default. Stilldown's creditors were unwilling to extend additional credit or amend the terms of any of their loans, and on August 1, 19X2 Stilldown filed a voluntary petition for relief under Chapter 7 of the Bankruptcy Act.

A balance sheet prepared as of the date of filing is presented in Exhibit 18–2. Although the balance sheet shows stockholders' equity of $13,000 on a going concern basis, historical cost valuations are not good indicators of financial condition for a liquidating company.[10] An accounting statement that does provide relevant information for a liquidating company is the *statement of affairs.*

Statement of Affairs

The trustee's duties may include filing a statement of financial affairs with the bankruptcy court. This statement is a legal document prepared for the bankruptcy court. The accountant's **statement of affairs** is a financial statement that emphasizes liquidation values and provides relevant information for the trustee in liquidating the debtor corporation. It also provides information that may be useful to creditors and to the bankruptcy court.

A statement of affairs is prepared as of a specific date, and it shows balance sheet information with assets measured at expected net realizable values and classified on the basis of availability for fully secured, partially secured, priority, and unsecured creditors. Liabilities are classified in the statement of affairs as priority, fully secured, partially secured, and unsecured. Historical cost valuations are included in the statement for reference purposes.

An illustrative statement of affairs for Stilldown Corporation is presented in Exhibit 18–3. Information for the statement is derived from the balance sheet

---

[10]Generally accepted accounting principles are based on the assumption that a firm will continue to operate in the foreseeable future. But this going concern assumption is inappropriate for firms in serious financial difficulty. When available evidence contradicts the going concern assumption, independent auditors issue "going concern" qualifications (or disclaimers) in their audit reports.

728

CORPORATE
LIQUIDATIONS,
REORGANIZATIONS, AND
DEBT RESTRUCTURINGS
FOR FINANCIALLY
DISTRESSED
CORPORATIONS

STILLDOWN CORPORATION
BALANCE SHEET
AUGUST 1, 19X2

Assets

Current Assets		
Cash	$ 3,000	
Marketable securities (at market)	7,000	
Accounts receivable (net of estimated uncollectible accounts)	25,000	
Inventories	50,000	
Prepaid expenses	4,000	$ 89,000
Long-Term Assets		
Land	$ 15,000	
Building—net	40,000	
Equipment—net	30,000	
Intangible assets	6,000	91,000
Total assets		$180,000

Liabilities and Stockholders' Equity

Current Liabilities		
Accounts payable	$ 65,000	
Wages payable	13,000	
Property taxes payable	2,000	
Note payable—bank	25,000	
Notes payable—suppliers	5,000	
Interest payable	7,000	$117,000
Mortgage Payable		50,000
Total liabilities		167,000
Stockholders' Equity		
Capital stock	$200,000	
Retained earnings	(187,000)	
Total stockholders' equity		13,000
Total liabilities and stockholders' equity		$180,000

Exhibit 18–2   *Debtor Corporation's Balance Sheet at the Time of Filing a Petition with the Bankruptcy Court*

(see Exhibit 18–2) as of the filing date and other sources such as appraisals for the expected liquidation values of assets and contractual agreements with creditors concerning the security of their claims. The mortgage payable, together with $5,000 interest payable, is secured by the land and building. All accounts receivable are pledged as security for the bank loan, plus $2,000 unpaid interest that is included in interest payable.

It is expected that Stilldown's assets can be converted into cash within three months and that the realizable values will be as follows:

Cash	$ 3,000
Marketable securities	7,000
Accounts receivable	22,000
Inventories (net of selling expenses)	55,000
Prepaid expenses	none
Land and building	60,000
Equipment	12,000
Intangible assets	none
	$159,000

STILLDOWN CORPORATION
STATEMENT OF AFFAIRS—ON AUGUST 1, 19X2

Assets

Book Value			Realizable Values—Liability Offsets for Secured Creditors	Realizable Value Available for Unsecured Creditors
	Pledged for Fully Secured Creditors			
$ 55,000	Land and building—net		$60,000	
	Less: Mortgage payable	$50,000		
	Interest payable	5,000	55,000	$ 5,000
	Pledged for Partially Secured Creditors			
25,000	Accounts receivable		$22,000	
	Less: Note payable to bank	$25,000		
	Interest payable	2,000	27,000	0
	Available for Priority and Unsecured Creditors			
3,000	Cash			3,000
7,000	Marketable securities			7,000
50,000	Inventories			55,000
4,000	Prepaid expenses			0
30,000	Equipment—net			12,000
6,000	Intangible assets			0
	Total available for priority and unsecured creditors			$82,000
	Less: Priority liabilities			15,000
	Total available for unsecured creditors			67,000
	Estimated deficiency			8,000
$180,000				$75,000

Liabilities and Stockholders' Equity

Book Value		Secured and Priority Claims	Unsecured Nonpriority Claims
	Priority Liabilities		
$ 13,000	Wages payable	$13,000	
	Property taxes payable	2,000	
		15,000	
	Fully Secured Creditors		
50,000	Mortgage payable	50,000	
5,000	Interest payable	5,000	
		55,000	
	Partially Secured Creditors		
25,000	Note payable—bank	25,000	
2,000	Interest payable	2,000	
		27,000	
	Less: Accounts receivable pledged	22,000	$5,000
	Unsecured Creditors		
65,000	Accounts payable		65,000
5,000	Notes payable to suppliers		5,000
	Stockholders' Equity		
200,000	Capital stock		
(187,000)	Retained earnings		
$180,000			$75,000

Exhibit 18–3 Statement of Affairs

730

CORPORATE
LIQUIDATIONS,
REORGANIZATIONS, AND
DEBT RESTRUCTURINGS
FOR FINANCIALLY
DISTRESSED
CORPORATIONS

Assets pledged as security for creditor claims are offset against the claims of secured creditors in the asset section of the statement of affairs. Any excess of the realizable value of assets pledged over related claims is carried to the right-hand column of the statement to indicate the amount available for unsecured creditors. An excess of secured creditor claims over the realization value of assets pledged as security indicates that the claims are only partially secured. The unsecured portion is shown in the liability section of the statement as an unsecured nonpriority claim. (Note that the offset for partially secured creditors is shown in both the asset and the liability sections of the statement.)

The $8,000 estimated deficiency shown in the statement of affairs is a balancing figure that represents the excess of general unsecured claims over the total amount expected to be available to holders of such claims. Alternatively, the $8,000 estimated deficiency can be computed by subtracting the expected realizable value of assets from total liabilities ($167,000 − $159,000) or by deducting the $21,000 expected losses on assets ($180,000 book value − $159,000 realizable value) from the $13,000 stockholders' equity as shown in the historical balance sheet.

Trustee Accounting

A trustee in a Chapter 7 bankruptcy case takes over the assets of the debtor corporation. The trustee is accountable for those assets until being released by the bankruptcy court. The Bankruptcy Act does not cover procedural accounting details such as whether the trustee should create a new set of accounting records to establish accountability for the estate and show the eventual discharge of responsibility, or whether the corporation's existing accounting records should be continued under the direction of the trustee.

The trustee for Stilldown Corporation in this illustration creates a new set of accounting records. The assets are recorded on the trustee's books at recorded book values rather than at expected realizable values because of the subjectivity involved in estimating realizable amounts at the time of filing. Contra asset accounts are omitted from the trustee's books because they are not meaningful in a liquidation case and because it is desirable to keep the trustee accounts as simple as possible. The following entry could be prepared to open the trustee's books for Stilldown:

Cash	$ 3,000	
Marketable securities	7,000	
Accounts receivable	25,000	
Inventories	50,000	
Prepaid expenses	4,000	
Land	15,000	
Building	40,000	
Equipment	30,000	
Intangible assets	6,000	
Accounts payable		$65,000
Wages payable		13,000
Property taxes payable		2,000
Note payable—bank		25,000
Notes payable—suppliers		5,000
Interest payable		7,000
Mortgage payable		50,000
Estate equity		13,000

To record custody of Stilldown Corporation in liquidation

Subsequent to assuming custody of the estate, the trustee records gains and losses and liquidation expenses directly in the estate equity account. Any unrecorded assets or liabilities that are discovered by the trustee are also entered in the estate equity account. In order to distinguish assets and liabilities included in the initial estate and those acquired or incurred by the trustee, the assets and liabilities recorded after the trustee takes charge of the estate are identified as "new."

Transactions and events during the first month of Stilldown's trusteeship are described and journal entries to record them in the trustee's books are illustrated as follows:

1 A previously unrecorded utility bill for $500 is received.

Estate equity	$500	
Utilities payable—new		$500

2 Intangible assets are deemed worthless and are written off.

Estate equity	$6,000	
Intangible assets		$6,000

3 All inventory items are sold for $48,000, of which $18,000 is on account and $30,000 is in cash.

Cash	$30,000	
Accounts receivable—new	18,000	
Estate equity	2,000	
Inventories		$50,000

4 The equipment is sold for $14,200 cash.

Cash	$14,200	
Estate equity	15,800	
Equipment		$30,000

5 Wages and property taxes owed on August 1 (priority liabilities) are paid.

Wages payable	$13,000	
Property taxes payable	2,000	
Cash		$15,000

6 Land and building are sold for $64,000 cash, and the mortgage payable and related interest are paid.

Cash	$64,000	
Land		$15,000
Building		40,000
Estate equity		9,000
Mortgage payable	$50,000	
Interest payable	5,000	
Cash		$55,000

7 Insurance policies (included in prepaid expenses) are canceled, and a $1,000 cash refund is received.

Cash	$ 1,000	
Prepaid expenses		$ 1,000

8 Accounts receivable of $21,000 are collected from the amounts owed to Stilldown at August 1. The remaining $4,000 is uncollectible.

Cash	$21,000	
Estate equity	4,000	
Accounts receivable		$25,000

732

CORPORATE
LIQUIDATIONS,
REORGANIZATIONS, AND
DEBT RESTRUCTURINGS
FOR FINANCIALLY
DISTRESSED
CORPORATIONS

9 The $21,000 received on account is applied to the bank note payable and related interest.

Interest payable	$ 2,000	
Note payable—bank	19,000	
Cash		$21,000

10 Estate administration expenses of $3,000 are paid.

Estate equity	$ 3,000	
Cash		$ 3,000

11 Trustee fees of $2,000 are accrued.

Estate equity	$ 2,000	
Trustee's fee payable—new		$ 2,000

After the transactions and events through August 31 are entered on the trustee's books, financial statements can be prepared as needed to show progress toward liquidation and financial position as of August 31, 19X2.

Statement of Cash Receipts and Disbursements　The statement of cash receipts and disbursements is prepared directly from entries in the cash account which appears in summary form as follows:

CASH

Balance August 1, 19X2	$ 3,000	Wages and property taxes	$ 15,000
Inventory items sold	30,000	Mortgage and interest	
Equipment sold	14,200	payment	55,000
Land and building sold	64,000	Bank notes and interest	21,000
Insurance refund	1,000	Administrative expenses	3,000
Accounts receivable	21,000	Balance forward	39,200 √
	133,200		133,200
Balance August 31, 19X2	$ 39,200		

Exhibit 18–4 illustrates the Trustee's Interim Statement of Cash Receipts and Cash Disbursements for the period August 1 to August 31, 19X2. Since all disbursements require approval of the court, the statement should be a useful financial summary.

Statement of Changes in Estate Equity　Data contained in the estate equity account provide the basis for preparation of the **statement of changes in estate equity (or deficit).** That account appears in summary form as follows:

ESTATE EQUITY (DEFICIT)

Utility bill discovered	$ 500	August 1, 19X1 balance	$13,000
Intangibles written off	6,000	Land and building gain	9,000
Inventory loss	2,000		
Equipment loss	15,800		
Accounts receivable written off	4,000		
Administrative expenses	3,000		
Trustee's fee	2,000	Balance forward (deficit)	11,300 √
	33,300		33,300
August 31, 19X2 balance	$11,300		

Exhibit 18–5 illustrates the statement of changes in estate equity for Stilldown Corporation from August 1 to August 31, 19X2. Observe that the statement

STILLDOWN CORPORATION IN TRUSTEESHIP
STATEMENT OF CASH RECEIPTS AND DISBURSEMENTS
FROM AUGUST 1 TO AUGUST 31, 19X2

Cash balance, August 1, 19X2		$ 3,000
Add: Cash receipts		
Sale of inventory items	$30,000	
Sale of equipment	14,200	
Sale of land and building	64,000	
Refund from insurance policy	1,000	
Collection of receivables	21,000	
Total cash receipts		130,200
		133,200
Deduct: Cash disbursements		
Wages payable (priority claim)	$13,000	
Property taxes payable (priority claim)	2,000	
Mortgage payable and interest (fully secured)	55,000	
Bank note payable and interest (for secured portion)	21,000	
Administrative expenses (priority item)	3,000	
Total cash disbursements		94,000
Cash balance, August 31, 19X2		$ 39,200

Exhibit 18–4   *Trustee's Interim Statement of Cash Receipts and Cash Disbursements*

STILLDOWN CORPORATION IN TRUSTEESHIP
STATEMENT OF CHANGES IN ESTATE EQUITY
FROM AUGUST 1 TO AUGUST 31, 19X2

Estate equity August 1, 19X2		$13,000
Less: Net loss on asset liquidation		
(see schedule below)	$18,800	
Liability for utilities discovered	500	
Administrative expenses	3,000	
Trustee's fee	2,000	
Net decrease for the period		−24,300
Estate deficit August 31, 19X2		$11,300

SCHEDULE OF NET LOSSES ON ASSET LIQUIDATION

	Book Value August 1 −	Proceeds on Realization =	Gain or (Loss)
Accounts receivable	$25,000	$21,000	$ (4,000)
Inventories	50,000	48,000	(2,000)
Land and building	55,000	64,000	9,000
Equipment	30,000	14,200	(15,800)
Intangible assets	6,000	0	(6,000)
Net loss on liquidation of assets			$(18,800)

Exhibit 18–5   *Trustee's Statement of Changes in Estate Equity and Schedule of Net Losses on Asset Liquidation*

separates gains and losses on asset realization from expenses involved in liquidating the corporation.

Balance Sheet   A balance sheet is prepared directly from the ledger account balances of the trustee and is presented in Exhibit 18–6. Two key amounts that appear in the balance sheet—cash and estate deficit are supported by amounts

734

CORPORATE
LIQUIDATIONS,
REORGANIZATIONS, AND
DEBT RESTRUCTURINGS
FOR FINANCIALLY
DISTRESSED
CORPORATIONS

STILLDOWN CORPORATION IN TRUSTEESHIP BALANCE SHEET ON AUGUST 31, 19X2	
Assets	
Cash	$39,200
Marketable securities	7,000
Accounts receivable—new	18,000
Prepaid expenses	3,000
Total assets	$67,200
Liabilities and Deficit	
Accounts payable	$65,000
Utilities payable—discovered	500
Trustee's fee payable—new	2,000
Note payable—bank (unsecured portion)	6,000
Notes payable—suppliers	5,000
Total liabilities	78,500
Less: Estate deficit	11,300
Total liabilities less deficit	$67,200

Exhibit 18–6 *Trustee's Interim Balance Sheet During the Liquidation Phase*

from the statements of cash receipts and disbursements (Exhibit 18–4) and changes in estate equity (Exhibit 18–5). The statements presented in Exhibits 18–4, 18–5, and 18–6 are in a format familiar to accountants, but you will want to compare these financial statements with the traditional statement of realization and liquidation that is presented in Exhibit 18–7.

Statement of Realization and Liquidation The purpose of introducing the statement of realization and liquidation in this chapter is to make readers aware of the statement and its intended uses and limitations. The Bankruptcy Act does not require such a statement but rather allows the judge in a bankruptcy case to prescribe the form in which information is presented to the court.

A **statement of realization and liquidation** is an activity statement that is intended to show progress toward the liquidation of a debtor's estate. Its original purpose was to inform the bankruptcy court and interested creditors of the accomplishments of the trustee. A statement of realization and liquidation for Stilldown Corporation is presented in Exhibit 18–7. The statement is presented in its traditional format except for bracketed explanations of the various categories.

An examination of Stilldown's statement of realization and liquidation shows that the statement is complex and that its format is unusual. In addition, the logic of the statement's construction is not immediately apparent. These considerations, together with the fact that the statement does a poor job of showing progress toward liquidation, have resulted in the statement's decline in recent years. While a number of alternative formats for the statement have been proposed, many accountants feel that basic financial statements with supporting schedules provide more relevant information about liquidation activity.

Winding Up the Case

During September 19X2 the trustee for Stilldown Corporation collected the $18,000 accounts receivable, sold the marketable securities for $7,300, sold supplies (included in prepaid expenses) for $995 and wrote off the remaining prepaid expenses, and distributed cash in final liquidation of the estate. Journal entries on the trustee's books to record these transactions and events are as follows:

STILLDOWN CORPORATION IN TRUSTEESHIP
STATEMENT OF REALIZATION AND LIQUIDATION
AUGUST 1, 19X2 TO AUGUST 31, 19X2

Assets

Assets to Be Realized: [Noncash assets at August 1]			Assets Realized: [Proceeds from sale, disposal, or write-off]		
Marketable securities	$ 7,000		Accounts receivable	$21,000	
Accounts receivable	25,000		Inventories	48,000	
Inventories	50,000		Prepaid expenses	1,000	
Prepaid expenses	4,000		Land		
Land	15,000		Building	64,000	
Building	40,000		Equipment	14,200	
Equipment	30,000		Intangible assets	none	$148,200
Intangible assets	6,000	$177,000			

Assets Acquired: [New noncash assets received]			Assets Not Realized: [Noncash assets at August 31]		
Accounts receivable—new		18,000	Marketable securities	$ 7,000	
			Prepaid expenses	3,000	
			Accounts receivable—new	18,000	28,000

Liabilities

Liabilities Liquidated: [Amounts paid on liabilities]			Liabilities to Be Liquidated: [Liabilities at August 1]		
Wages payable	$13,000		Accounts payable	$65,000	
Property taxes payable	2,000		Wages payable	13,000	
Note payable—bank	19,000		Property taxes payable	2,000	
Interest payable	7,000		Note payable—bank	25,000	
Mortgage payable	50,000	91,000	Notes payable—suppliers	5,000	
			Interest payable	7,000	
			Mortgage payable	50,000	167,000

Liabilities Not Liquidated: [Liabilities at August 31]			Liabilities Incurred or Discovered: [Amounts incurred or discovered but unpaid at August 31]		
Accounts payable	$65,000				
Note payable—bank	6,000				
Notes payable—suppliers	5,000		Liability discovered for		
Liability discovered for			utilities	$ 500	
utilities	500		Trustee's fee payable—		
Trustee's fee payable—			new	2,000	2,500
new	2,000	78,500			

Income or Loss and Supplemental Items

Supplementary Expenses: [Expenses excluding asset losses and write-offs]			Supplementary Revenues: [Revenues excluding gains on assets or liability settlements]		
Liability discovered for			None		
utilities	$ 500				
Trustee's fee	2,000		Net Loss		24,300
Administrative expenses					
—new	3,000	5,500			
		$370,000			$370,000

Exhibit 18–7   *Statement of Realization and Liquidation*

736

CORPORATE
LIQUIDATIONS,
REORGANIZATIONS, AND
DEBT RESTRUCTURINGS
FOR FINANCIALLY
DISTRESSED
CORPORATIONS

Cash	$18,000	
Accounts receivable—new		$18,000
Collection of receivable in full.		
Cash	$ 7,300	
Marktable securities		$ 7,000
Estate equity		300
Sale of marketable securities for cash.		
Cash	$ 995	
Estate equity	2,005	
Prepaid expenses		$ 3,000
Sale of supplies and write-off of prepaid expenses.		

After these entries are entered in the trustee's records, the account balances are as follows:

	Debit	Credit
Cash	$65,495	
Accounts payable		$65,000
Utilities payable		500
Trustee's fee payable—new		2,000
Note payable—bank (unsecured portion)		6,000
Notes payable—suppliers		5,000
Estate equity	13,005	
	$78,500	$78,500

Since the trustee's fee is a priority claim, it is paid in full and the remaining claims of $76,500 (all first-rank unsecured creditors) receive 83¢ on the dollar ($63,495 ÷ $76,500) in final settlement of their claims. Entries to record the cash distributions are:

Trustee's fee payable—new	$ 2,000	
Cash		$ 2,000
To record payment of trustee's fee.		
Accounts payable	$53,950	
Utilities payable	415	
Note payable—bank	4,980	
Notes payable—suppliers	4,150	
Cash		$63,495
To record payment of 83¢ on the dollar to the general unsecured creditors.		

When the debtor is an individual, the court will grant a discharge voiding most existing liabilities or claims unless the debtor has (1) transferred, removed, destroyed, mutilated, or concealed property of the estate with intent to hinder, delay, or defraud; (2) made fraudulent statements under oath; (3) presented a false claim; (4) withheld information; or (5) failed to meet certain other conditions. But corporations are not eligible for discharge because their liabilities are limited to corporate assets. A case involving a corporation is closed when the estate is fully administered and the trustee is dismissed. The trustee makes the following entry in closing out the Stilldown Corporation case:

Accounts payable	$11,050	
Utilities payable	85	
Note payable—bank	1,020	
Notes payable—suppliers	850	
Estate equity		$13,005
To close the trustee's records.		

A Chapter 11 reorganization case is initiated voluntarily when a debtor corporation files a petition with the bankruptcy court, or involuntarily when creditors file a petition in accordance with the same $5,000 claim limitations applicable to Chapter 7 filings. The act of filing commences the case and initiates a hearing before the bankruptcy court. As mentioned earlier, the court may enter an order for relief under Chapter 11 (in other words, grant the petition for protection from creditors), convert the case to a Chapter 7 liquidation, or dismiss the case (for example, the case will be dismissed if the bankruptcy court believes that the filing was an act of bad faith). A U.S. trustee is appointed by the bankruptcy judge to be responsible for the administration of the Chapter 11 case.

Trustee or Debtor in Possession

In a Chapter 11 case, a trustee may be appointed for cause, but otherwise the debtor corporation is continued in possession of the estate. A trustee may be appointed in cases involving fraud, dishonesty, or gross mismanagement, or if the court rules that appointment of a trustee is in the best interest of creditors, equity holders, and other parties with an interest in the estate. For the most part, bankruptcy judges have been reluctant to appoint private trustees to operate businesses in reorganization cases because it is assumed that company managements are more qualified to operate and reorganize the companies.[11] If the debtor cannot remain in possession of the business, a private trustee is appointed by the U.S. trustee or by the bankruptcy court in non-U.S. trustee districts.

The duties of a trustee include:

- Being accountable for the property received from the debtor including operations of the debtor's business
- Filing a list of creditors, schedules of assets and liabilities, and a statement of financial affairs (if not filed by the debtor)
- Furnishing information to the court about the debtor's estate and its administration
- Examining creditor claims and objecting to claims that appear to be improper (normally, only the trustee can object)
- Filing a reorganization plan or reporting why he will not file a plan
- Filing final reports on the trusteeship as required by the court

A ***debtor in possession*** *performs the duties of a trustee.* It negotiates with the creditors, stockholders, and others in creating a plan of reorganization that will be confirmed by the bankruptcy court.

When a trustee is not appointed in a Chapter 11 case, an examiner will be appointed if loans to outsiders other than for goods and services exceed $5,000,000, or if the court concludes that such appointment is in the interests of the creditors, equity holders, or other parties with an interest in the estate. A primary function of the examiner is to value the debtor's assets and report such valuations to the court.

Committee Representation

Creditors' committees are responsible for protecting the interests of the creditors they represent and making sure that the assets of the debtor are preserved. The committees may review the debtor's transactions and object in bankruptcy court

---

[11]One notable exception was the Eastern Airlines bankruptcy case. In April 1990 the bankruptcy judge appointed a private trustee to operate Eastern because the company had lost $1.2 billion during the year it had been in bankruptcy and because Eastern's management had been unable to make reliable forecasts even in the short run. [*The Wall Street Journal*, April 20, 1990, p. A3.]

738

CORPORATE
LIQUIDATIONS,
REORGANIZATIONS, AND
DEBT RESTRUCTURINGS
FOR FINANCIALLY
DISTRESSED
CORPORATIONS

to those that they believe are not in the best interests of the creditors they represent. All negotiations between prepetition creditors and the debtor in possession must take place through the creditors' committees.

Unlike Chapter 7 cases, neither trustees nor creditors' committees are elected in Chapter 11 cases. A creditors' committee is *appointed by the U.S. trustee* as soon as practicable after the bankruptcy court grants an order for relief under Chapter 11. The creditors' committee (usually seven members) is selected from the largest unsecured creditors. Subsequently, the composition of that committee may be changed and other committees of creditors or equity holders may be appointed.

LTV Corporation's original creditors' committee included a representative from the United Mine Workers of America, a salaried retiree, and nineteen creditors representing different interest groups. The Pension Benefit Guarantee Corporation was an unofficial member that could not vote. In the Drexel Burnham Lambert Group, Inc., bankruptcy case, the Securities and Exchange Commission (SEC) asked to be a full voting member or a nonvoting member with full rights of participation on the unsecured creditors' committee. The SEC argued that Drexel owed the government $150 million, making it the largest unsecured creditor. The U.S. trustee opposed the SEC, arguing that government entities are barred from serving on creditors committees. The judge ordered the U.S. trustee and the SEC to work out a compromise. The SEC dropped its request for membership in the creditors' committee and aligned itself instead with a court-sanctioned group of securities-litigation claimants that were suing Drexel.[12] The California Public Employees' Retirement System also asked to be a nonvoting member of Drexel's creditors' committee in order to look out for their $25 million claim, and they lobbied to get the bankruptcy code changed to allow government agencies that are creditors to have full participation in creditors' committees.[13]

The selection of creditors' committees can be extremely important to the final disposition of a reorganization case. Creditor infighting can sabotage the most carefully designed reorganization plan. Allegheny International, Inc., filed for bankruptcy court protection in February 1988, expecting a fairly simple and timely reorganization. During the next twenty-six months, the company filed ten different reorganization plans, and creditor groups were suing each other.[14]

Operating Under Chapter 11

The Federal Office of Court Administration estimates that only one out of eight companies that seek reorganization under Chapter 11 reorganizes successfully.[15] Reorganization may take from six months to several years.[16] In the meantime, subject to restrictions of the Bankruptcy Code and the bankruptcy court, the debtor in possession continues operating the business while working out a reorganization plan that is acceptable to all parties concerned. On the day of the bankruptcy filing, the company's existing bank accounts and books are closed and new accounts and books reopened. For example, checks for $100 million had been mailed to vendors during the week before Federated Department Stores and Allied Stores Corp. filed for protection under Chapter 11. Vendors, realizing that the companies were financially distressed, hurried to cash their checks

---

[12]More than 400 lawsuits were pending against Drexel. Although not an official bankruptcy committee, the securities litigation group was approved by the bankruptcy court. It included the FDIC which had a large claim stemming from failed savings and loans companies. *The Wall Street Journal*, September 17, 1990, p. B6.

[13]*The Wall Street Journal*, March 23, 1990, p. B8.

[14]*The Wall Street Journal*, April 19, 1990, p. C5.

[15]*The Wall Street Journal*, January 16, 1990, p. A10.

[16]For example, Amatex Corporation operated under bankruptcy court protection for seven and one-half years before emerging in 1990. *The Wall Street Journal*, October 1, 1990, p. B2.

as soon as they arrived. Some vendors even flew to Delaware to cash the checks at the bank on which they were drawn. On Monday, January 15, 1990, banks were closed for Martin Luther King's birthday; however, the court accepted the bankruptcy filing and the bankruptcy judge halted payment on all commercial checks issued prior to the filing.[17]

Usually, the company will arrange a new line of credit with its banks to enable it to continue to operate. This is often referred to as debtor-in-possession financing. New financing agreements must be approved by the bankruptcy court.

Possible Benefits of Chapter 11 Protection to the Debtor in Possession With the bankruptcy court's approval, the company may be able to reduce its labor costs through layoffs or wage reductions, or by terminating its pension plans.[18] As mentioned earlier, it is now more difficult to use bankruptcy to break labor contracts than it was a few years ago. Also, with the bankruptcy court's approval, the company can reject certain executory contracts and unexpired leases. (***Executory contracts*** are those that have not been completely performed by both parties, such as purchase commitments.) Any claims for damages resulting from the cancellation of unfavorable contracts is treated as unsecured debt. Interest on unsecured debt stops at the time of filing. This can be a big factor for some companies. Interest of nearly $3 million a day was accruing on Pennzoil's $10.3 billion award from Texaco until the date of Texaco's Chapter 11 filing.

Creditors subject to the jurisdiction of the bankruptcy court may not commence or continue a lawsuit to take possession of the debtor's property without permission of the bankruptcy court; however, secured creditors may receive payments to protect their interest in collateral that the debtor continues to use in its operations. This is particularly applicable when the debtor continues to use collateralized property subject to depreciation, depletion, or amortization. Payments to the secured creditor may reduce the loan balance as the value of the collateral declines.

Financially distressed companies that find it necessary to restructure or swap debt may have difficulty gaining the necessary support from bondholders without filing for bankruptcy. A debt restructuring plan typically requires approval of 95 percent of each class of bondholders and a majority of stockholders. However, a debt restructuring under the bankruptcy court requires only two-thirds approval of each class of bondholders.[19]

Disadvantages of a Chapter 11 Filing A Chapter 11 filing creates the obvious disadvantage for the debtor corporation of losing the confidence of its lenders, suppliers, customers, and employees. Beyond this stigma of bankruptcy, there is the additional disadvantage of operating a business in competitive markets

---

[17]*The Wall Street Journal,* January 18, 1990, p. A3.

[18]LTV Corp. filed under Chapter 11 protection in July 1986 and in January 1987 the Pension Benefit Guaranty Corporation took over three LTV pension plans underfunded by $2 billion. LTV made a new contract with labor with benefits similar to the ones terminated. The new contract was approved by the bankruptcy court, but opposed by the PBGC. In September 1987, the PBGC, citing LTV's improved profitability and willingness to fund other employee benefits, reinstated the three pension funds (in other words, turned them back to LTV) and forced LTV to take charge of its $2 billion pension-fund shortfall. This reinstatement, the bankruptcy court reasoned, "violated the automatic-stay provision of the Bankruptcy Code, which forbids actions against debtor companies to the detriment of other creditors." In May 1989 a federal appeals court panel upheld a ruling in favor of LTV. The PBGC appealed and in June 1990, the Supreme Court reversed the lower court ruling and permitted the PBGC to reinstate the pension plans. Finally, in February 1991 LTV and the PBGC negotiated a preliminary settlement for restoring the pension plans. *The Wall Street Journal,* February 26, 1991, p. A3.

[19]For example, Community Newspapers, Inc., filed for Chapter 11 in February 1991 after failing to buy back its senior junk bonds for 75 cents on the dollar and its junior junk bonds for 27 cents on the dollar, even though it had 91 percent acceptance from senior bondholders and 89 percent acceptance from junior bondholders.

740

CORPORATE
LIQUIDATIONS,
REORGANIZATIONS, AND
DEBT RESTRUCTURINGS
FOR FINANCIALLY
DISTRESSED
CORPORATIONS

when capital expenditures, acquisitions, disposals of assets, borrowing money, and so on, require prior approval of the court. Depending on the circumstances of a particular case, the bankruptcy court may impose so many restrictions on company management that even day-to-day operations of the business become difficult. The company may have to sell off its profitable units to meet creditor demands for emerging from Chapter 11. Perhaps the biggest disadvantage to the debtor is the cost of the bankruptcy proceedings. Lawyers and other advisors are hired by the creditors' committees and the stockholders' committees, as well as by the debtor, but they are all paid from the debtor's assets.[20] Expenses of the creditors' committees may also be reimbursed. Soaring fees in bankruptcy cases have prompted some judges to cut fees that they think are unreasonable.

The Plan of Reorganization

The intent of debtor relief under Chapter 11 is reorganization, and the final objective of the court proceedings is confirmation of a ***reorganization plan*** that is "fair and equitable" to all interests concerned. Only the debtor corporation may file a plan during the first 120 days after the order for relief is granted. Subsequently, the debtor, the trustee, the creditors' committees, an equity security holders' committee, or other parties in interest may file plans.

To reduce bankruptcy expenses and shorten the time a debtor must operate under bankruptcy court restrictions, some firms file preapproved reorganization plans with the court at the same time they file under Chapter 11 (often called a prepackaged bankruptcy). In other words, the terms of the debt restructuring have been worked out with creditors, and some or all creditors have agreed to the plan before the bankruptcy filing.

Chapter 11 provisions stipulate that the plan of reorganization must:

- Identify classes of claims (except for the administrative expenses, claims arising after an involuntary filing but before the order of relief or appointment of a trustee, and certain tax claims which are given priority)
- Specify any class of claims that is not impaired (a class of claims is *impaired* unless the plan leaves unaltered the legal rights of each claim in the class)
- Specify any class of claims that is impaired
- Treat all claims within a particular class alike
- Provide adequate means for the plan's execution (such as retention of property by the debtor, merger, modification of a lien, and extension of maturity dates)
- Prohibit the issuance of nonvoting equity securities
- Contain provision for selection of officers and directors that is consistent with the interests of creditors, equityholders, and public policy

A reorganization plan may provide for sale of the debtor's property and distribution of the proceeds. Thus, it is possible for a debtor's estate to be liquidated under a Chapter 11 case. For example, in February 1990, the Drexel Burnham Lambert Group, Inc., filed for bankruptcy under Chapter 11 even though the firm's assets were to be liquidated and it would cease doing business. The firm selected a Chapter 11 liquidation so that management, rather than an outside trustee, could dismantle the company. (Drexel subsequently decided on a reorganization.)

Acceptance of a plan by a class of claims requires approval by at least two-thirds in amount and over half in number of claims. Classes of claims that are unimpaired are assumed to have accepted the plan, and classes that receive nothing are assumed to have rejected it without the necessity of a vote. In order for the bankruptcy court to confirm a plan, each class of claims must have accepted

---

[20]While Southmark Corporation was under bankruptcy court protection, lawyers, investment bankers, accountants, and other professionals, ran up fees of nearly $1 million a week for a year.

the plan or not be impaired under it. Within each class, each holder of a claim must either have accepted the plan or receive (or retain an interest) not less than that holder would receive if the debtor corporation were liquidated.

After the necessary approval has been obtained, the court holds a confirmation hearing to entertain objections to confirmation and to confirm that the plan is "fair and equitable." Confirmation by the court constitutes discharge of the debtor except for claims provided for in the reorganization plan.

The ranking of unsecured creditors in a large reorganization case is seldom simple and is often the result of negotiation rather than rule. Many reorganizations are complicated by professional investors who buy debt claims from the original holders at deep discounts and then push for settlements to turn a quick profit from their investment. In the Wheeling-Pittsburgh Steel Corp. bankruptcy case, the brokerage firm of Oppenheimer & Co. bought more than 20 percent of Wheeling's unsecured claims and threatened to hold up bankruptcy proceedings as long as they could if they did not get a better deal from senior creditors.[21] Similarly, Japonica Partners bought up enough bank claims at a discount to make it Allegheny International Inc.'s largest creditor, and when it blocked the company's reorganization plan, the other creditors asked the court to nullify Japonica's vote against the plan. The reorganization was eventually modified so that Japonica gained control of the company.

Shareholders have also become more aggressive in bankruptcies. One reason for the increased shareholder activism is the increase in investors that speculate in the stock of companies in Chapter 11. Another reason is the rise of lawyers and financial advisors that specialize in leading equity committees against creditors and management. When solvent companies seek bankruptcy reorganization (A. H. Robins and Texaco Inc., for example), shareholders have equity to protect.

The value of claims in a bankruptcy case can also be controversial. When a company is financially distressed, bondholders may give concessions to the debtor by swapping their bonds for new bonds issued at a discount. In the LTV Corp. case the bankruptcy judge ruled that bondholders filing claims must value their bonds at the "fair market value of property given in the exchange transaction." Bondholders that paid par for their bonds and did not participate in LTV's swap could claim par plus accrued interest.[22]

FINANCIAL REPORTING DURING REORGANIZATION

In 1990 the Accounting Standards Executive Committee (AcSEC) of the AICPA issued Statement of Position (SOP) 90-7, "Financial Reporting by Entities in Reorganization under the Bankruptcy Code," to provide guidance for financial reporting by firms during Chapter 11 reorganization and when they emerge from Chapter 11. Before issuance of the SOP, there was no prescribed accounting for a reorganization under Chapter 11, and practices were diverse. Since prepetition liabilities (those existing at the time of filing) are stayed, some firms classified them as long term while other firms classified them as current.

Under the SOP, the objective of financial statements prepared for a company operating under Chapter 11 is to reflect the financial evolution during the bankruptcy proceedings. Therefore, the financial statements should distinguish the transactions and events directly related to the reorganization from the ongoing operations of the business.

---

[21] *The Wall Street Journal*, September 18, 1989, pp. C1 and C10.
[22] *The Wall Street Journal*, January 31, 1990, p. A3.

742

CORPORATE
LIQUIDATIONS,
REORGANIZATIONS, AND
DEBT RESTRUCTURINGS
FOR FINANCIALLY
DISTRESSED
CORPORATIONS

Effects of Chapter 11 Proceedings on the Balance Sheet

The balance sheet should present prepetition liabilities that are subject to compromise separately from those that are not subject to compromise. *Prepetition liabilities subject to compromise* are the unsecured and undersecured liabilities incurred before the company entered Chapter 11 proceedings. A secured claim is undersecured if the collateral is worth less than the amount of the claim. The entire amount of an undersecured claim is included in prepetition liabilities subject to compromise. *Liabilities not subject to compromise* include fully secured liabilities incurred before the Chapter 11 filing and all postpetition claims. These claims should be classified as current or noncurrent in a classified balance sheet. *Postpetition liabilities* are those that are incurred after the filing of the Chapter 11 petition, and that are not associated with prebankruptcy events. (See SOP 90-7, Appendix C.)

Prepetition claims discovered after the Chapter 11 filing are included in the balance sheet at the allowed amount of the claims rather than the amount at which they may be settled. Claims that cannot be reasonably estimated should be disclosed in notes to the financial statements under the provisions of *FASB Statement No. 5,* "Accounting for Contingencies."

Effects of Chapter 11 Proceedings on the Income Statement and the Statement of Cash Flows

Professional fees and similar expenses related directly to the Chapter 11 proceedings are expensed as incurred. "Income, expenses, realized gains and losses, and provisions for losses that result from the restructuring of the business should be reported separately in the income statement as *reorganization items,* except for those required to be reported as discontinued operations" (SOP 90-7, paragraph 27).

Interest expense to be reported is the amount that will be paid during the proceedings, or the probable amount to be allowed as a priority, secured, or unsecured claim. Amounts by which reported interest expense differs from contractual interest is to be disclosed. Interest income earned as a result of bankruptcy proceedings is reported separately as a reorganization item. Generally, this includes all interest income.

Earnings per share for Chapter 11 companies should be reported as usual. If the issuance of common stock or common stock equivalents under a reorganization plan is probable, that fact should be disclosed.

Cash flow items relating to reorganization should be disclosed separately from cash flow items relating to the ongoing operations of the business in the statement of cash flows. The SOP recommends the direct method of presenting cash flows.

Supplementary Combined Financial Statements

The AcSEC concluded that consolidated financial statements that include one or more companies operating under Chapter 11 do not provide adequate information about the bankruptcy proceedings. Therefore, the SOP requires that *condensed combined financial statements* for all entities in reorganization proceedings be presented as supplementary information. Intercompany receivables and payables should be disclosed, with receivables written down if necessary. Consolidation may be inappropriate for some subsidiaries in bankruptcy, particularly if a trustee is appointed to operate the company in bankruptcy.

Ordinarily, a corporate reorganization involves a restructuring of liabilities and capital accounts, and a revaluation of the firm's assets. Participation of stockholders in the reorganized company depends upon whether they are deemed to have an equitable interest by the bankruptcy court. Many companies cannot emerge from bankruptcy as independent companies, and their reorganization plans include the sale of the company. In providing for the plan's execution, the debtor corporation typically amends its charter to provide for the issuance of new securities for cash or in exchange for creditor claims (that is, some creditors may become stockholders).

The financial condition of companies filing for bankrupcty court protection varies drastically. Occasionally, profitable corporations file for protection under Chapter 11. Settlements under a reorganization plan are influenced by the ability of the interested parties to negotiate and manipulate their relative positions through creditors' and equity holders' committees. Bankruptcy judges also have broad discretionary powers in bankruptcy settlements. A provision of the bankruptcy code known as the doctrine of equitable subordination allows judges to move unsecured creditors ahead of secured creditors in certain situations in the interest of "fairness."

Reorganization Value

Determining the reorganization value of the entity emerging from bankruptcy is an important part of the reorganization plan. The emerging entity's *reorganization value* approximates fair value of the entity without considering liabilities. In other words, it approximates the amount a willing buyer would pay for the assets of the entity at the time of the restructuring. Generally, the reorganization value is determined by discounting future cash flows for the reconstituted business, plus the expected proceeds from assets not required in the new business. The discount rates should reflect the business and financial risks involved. (See SOP 90-7, paragraph 9.)

Financial reporting by a company whose reorganization plan has been confirmed by the court is determined by whether the reorganized entity is essentially a new company that qualifies for fresh start reporting. The SOP provides two conditions that must be met for *fresh start reporting*:

1 The reorganization value of the emerging entity's assets immediately before the date of confirmation of the reorganization plan is less than the total of all post-petition liabilities and allowed claims.

2 Holders of existing voting shares immediately before confirmation of the reorganization plan receive less than 50 percent of the emerging entity. This loss of control must be substantive and not temporary.

When both of these conditions are met, the emerging entity is in effect a new company and it should adopt fresh start reporting.

Fresh Start Reporting

Fresh start reporting results in a new reporting entity with no retained earnings or deficit balance.

Allocating the Reorganization Value to Identifiable Assets   The reorganization value of the company should be allocated to tangible and identifiable intangible assets according to the purchase method of accounting for transactions as set

744

CORPORATE
LIQUIDATIONS,
REORGANIZATIONS, AND
DEBT RESTRUCTURINGS
FOR FINANCIALLY
DISTRESSED
CORPORATIONS

forth in *APB Opinion No. 16,* "Business Combinations."[23] Any amount of reorganization value not attributed to the tangible and identifiable intangible assets is reported as an unidentifiable intangible asset, "reorganization value in excess of amounts allocable to identifiable assets." The assumptions used in determining the excess during the allocation period should be consistent with the assumptions used in determining the reorganization value. (The maximum allocation period is 40 years, but a much shorter period is presumed.)

Reporting Liabilities   Liabilities, other than deferred income taxes, should be reported at their current value at the confirmation date of the reorganization plan. Deferred taxes are reported as required in the *FASB* Exposure Draft, "Accounting for Income Taxes." Benefits realized from prior net operating loss carryforwards are applied first to reduction of the reorganization value in excess of amounts allocable to identifiable assets and to other intangibles until exhausted, and finally, as a reduction of income tax expense.

Final Statements of Old Entity   The final statements of the old entity as of and for the period ending on the date of confirmation of the plan should disclose the effects of the adjustments on the individual asset and liability accounts resulting from adopting fresh start reporting. The statements should also show the effects of debt forgiveness. It is expected that the ending balance sheet of the old entity will be the same as the opening balance sheet of the new entity, including a zero retained earnings balance.

Disclosures in Initial Financial Statements of New Entity   Paragraph 39 of the SOP lists the following disclosures that should be included in notes to the initial financial statements of the new entity:

- Adjustments to the historical amounts of individual assets and liabilities
- The amount of debt forgiveness
- The amount of prior retained earnings or deficit eliminated
- Significant factors relating to the determination of reorganization value

Comparative Financial Statements   Fresh start financial statements of the new entity are not comparable with those prepared by the predecessor company before confirmation of the reorganization plan. If predecessor statements are required by the SEC or other regulatory agency, a clear distinction should be made between the fresh start statements of the new entity and the statements of the predecessor company.

Reporting by Entities
That Do Not Qualify
for Fresh Start

Companies emerging from reorganization that do not meet the criteria for fresh start reporting should report liabilities compromised at their present values as determined at appropriate interest rates under *APB Opinion No. 21,* "Interest on Receivables and Payables." Forgiveness of debt should be reported as an extraordinary item. Quasi-reorganization accounting should *not* be used for any entities emerging from bankruptcy court protection.

ILLUSTRATION OF A REORGANIZATION CASE

Baker Corporation files for protection from creditors under Chapter 11 of the bankruptcy act on January 5, 19X2. Baker is a debtor in possession, and at the time of filing, its balance sheet included the following items:

---

[23]See Chapter 1, "Business Combinations," for a discussion on assigning fair values to specific categories of assets, and then allocating the total purchase price, or in this case, the reorganization value, to those assets on the basis of the assigned fair values.

Current assets		
Cash	$ 50,000	
Accounts receivable—net	500,000	
Inventory	300,000	
Other current assets	50,000	$ 900,000
Plant assets		
Land	$ 200,000	
Building—net	500,000	
Equipment—net	300,000	
Goodwill	200,000	1,200,000
		$2,100,000
Current liabilities		
Accounts payable	$ 600,000	
Taxes payable	150,000	
Accrued interest on 15% bonds	90,000	
Note payable to bank	260,000	$1,100,000
15% bonds payable (partially secured with land and building)		1,200,000
Stockholders' deficit		
Common stock	$ 500,000	
Deficit	(700,000)	(200,000)
		$2,100,000

On the filing date, Baker's bank accounts and books are closed, and a new set of books is opened. The company is able to arrange short-term financing with the bank (with the bankruptcy court's approval) in order to continue operations while working out a reorganization plan.

During 19X2, no prepetition liabilities are paid and no interest is accrued on the bank note or the bonds payable. The bankruptcy court allows Baker Corporation to invest in $100,000 of new equipment in August 19X2. This new equipment has a use life of five years, and Baker uses straight-line depreciation calculated to the nearest half year. The building is being depreciated at a rate of $50,000 per year, and the old equipment at a rate of $60,000 per year. Goodwill amortization is $50,000 per year.

The $2,300,000 prepetition claims are included in the December 31, 19X2 balance sheet as a separate category, with a supplemental schedule to show details of the amount. Costs related to the bankruptcy, including all expenses of the creditor committees and the equity holder committee, are expensed as incurred and paid from cash.

Reclassification of Liabilities Subject to Compromise

At the beginning of 19X2, Baker reclassifies the liabilities subject to compromise into a separate account by that name. The entry to record the reclassification is as follows:

Accounts payable	$ 600,000	
Taxes payable	150,000	
Accrued interest on 15% bonds	90,000	
Note payable to bank	260,000	
15% bonds payable (partially secured)	1,200,000	
Liabilities subject to compromise		$2,300,000

To reclassify liabilities subject to compromise.

Disclosing Reclassified Liabilities in the Financial Statements   The balance sheet disclosures to report the reclassification in accordance with the provisions

746

CORPORATE
LIQUIDATIONS,
REORGANIZATIONS, AND
DEBT RESTRUCTURINGS
FOR FINANCIALLY
DISTRESSED
CORPORATIONS

of the AICPA's SOP 90-7 on financial reporting for entities in reorganization are included in Exhibit 18–8. The exhibit presents a combined income and retained earnings statement for 19X2, as well as a balance sheet at December 31, 19X2.

While the reclassification of liabilities subject to compromise poses no difficulties in preparing balance sheets and income statements, it does complicate the preparation of the cash flow statement. In particular, the year's changes in the account balances that are reclassified must be separated from changes that affect operations and cash flows for the period. Exhibit 18–9 presents a cash

---

**BAKER CORPORATION
INCOME AND RETAINED EARNINGS STATEMENT
FOR THE YEAR 19X2**

Sales	$ 1,000,000
Cost of sales	(430,000)
Wages and salaries	(250,000)
Depreciation and amortization	(170,000)
Other expenses	(50,000)
Earnings before reorganization items	100,000
Professional fees related to bankruptcy proceedings	(450,000)
Net loss	(350,000)
Beginning deficit	(700,000)
Deficit December 31, 19X2	$(1,050,000)

BALANCE SHEET AT DECEMBER 31, 19X2

Current assets		
Cash	$ 150,000	
Accounts receivable—net	350,000	
Inventory	370,000	
Other current assets	50,000	$ 920,000
Plant assets		
Land	$ 200,000	
Building—net	450,000	
Equipment—net	330,000	
Goodwill	150,000	1,130,000
		$2,050,000
Current liabilities		
Short-term borrowings	$ 150,000	
Accounts payable	100,000	
Wages and salaries payable	50,000	$ 300,000
Liabilities subject to compromise*		2,300,000
Stockholders' deficit		
Common stock	$ 500,000	
Deficit	(1,050,000)	(550,000)
		$2,050,000

* Liabilities subject to compromise:	
Partially secured 15% bonds payable plus $90,000 interest, secured by first mortgage on land and building	$1,290,000
Priority tax claim	150,000
Accounts payable and unsecured note to bank	860,000
	$2,300,000

Exhibit 18–8   *Balance Sheet and Income Statement During Chapter 11 Reorganization*

BAKER CORPORATION AND SUBSIDIARY
WORKING PAPERS FOR THE STATEMENT OF CASH FLOWS (DIRECT METHOD)
FOR THE YEAR ENDED DECEMBER 31, 19X2

	Year's Change	Reconciling Items		Cash Flow from Operations	Cash Flow—Investing Activities	Cash Flow—Financing Activities
		Debit	Credit			
Asset Changes						
Cash	100,000					
Accounts receivable—net	(150,000)	b 150,000				
Inventories	70,000		c 70,000			
Other current assets	0					
Land	0					
Buildings—net	50,000	e 50,000				
Equipment—net	30,000	e 70,000	g 100,000			
Goodwill	(50,000)	e 50,000				
Total asset changes	50,000					
Changes in Equities						
Accounts payable	(500,000)	c 100,000	a 600,000			
Taxes payable	(150,000)		a 150,000			
Accrued interest—15% bonds	(90,000)		a 90,000			
Short-term borrowings	150,000	f 150,000				
Note payable to bank	(260,000)		a 260,000			
Wages and salaries payable	50,000		d 50,000			
15% bonds payable	(1,200,000)		a 1,200,000			
Liabilities subject to compromise	2,300,000	a 2,300,000				
Common stock	0					
Deficit*	(350,000)					
Total equity changes	(50,000)					
Changes in the deficit*						
Sales	1,000,000		b 150,000	1,150,000		
Cost of goods sold	(430,000)		c 30,000	(400,000)		
Wages and salaries	(250,000)	d 50,000		(200,000)		
Depreciation and amortization	(170,000)		e 170,000			
Other expenses	(50,000)			(50,000)		
Professional fees paid for reorganization*	(450,000)			(450,000)		
Change in deficit**	(350,000)					
Proceeds from short-term borrowing			f 150,000			150,000
Purchase of equipment		g 100,000			100,000	
		3,020,000	3,020,000	50,000	100,000	150,000

* Requires separate disclosure in the cash flow from operating activities section.
** Deficit changes replace amounts in the deficit account for reconciling purposes.

Exhibit 18–9 *Working Papers for the Statement of Cash Flows*

flow working paper for Baker Corporation's 19X2 statement of cash flows, and Exhibit 18–10 presents the cash flows statement. Only the direct method of presenting the cash flow statement is illustrated because that is the format recommended in the SOP.

The cash flow working papers in Exhibit 18–9 show an initial reconciling entry to eliminate the effect of the entry that reclassified liabilities subject to compromise. This is necessary because a reclassification entry has no cash flow effects.

One other item in Exhibit 18–9 that is unique to firms in reorganization is professional fees relating to bankruptcy proceedings. While cash paid for these

748

CORPORATE
LIQUIDATIONS,
REORGANIZATIONS, AND
DEBT RESTRUCTURINGS
FOR FINANCIALLY
DISTRESSED
CORPORATIONS

items is classified as cash flows from operating activities, separate disclosure of operating cash flows *before* and *after* the operating cash flows from the professional fees of bankruptcy proceedings is recommended. This disclosure is illustrated in Exhibit 18–10 that presents the statement of cash flow for Baker Corporation for the year 19X2.

BAKER CORPORATION
STATEMENT OF CASH FLOWS
FOR THE YEAR ENDED DECEMBER 31, 19X2

Cash flows from operating activities		
Cash received from customers (sales $1,000,000 + decrease in accounts receivable $150,000)		$1,150,000
Cash paid to suppliers (cost of sales $430,000 + increase in inventory $70,000 – increase in accounts payable $100,000)		(400,000)
Cash paid to employees (wages and salaries $250,000 – increase in wages payable $50,000)		(200,000)
Cash paid for other expenses		(50,000)
Net cash flows provided by operating activities before reorganization items		500,000
Operating cash flows from reorganization		
Professional fees paid for services relating to bankruptcy proceedings		(450,000)
Net cash provided by operating activities		50,000
Cash flows from investing activities		
Capital expenditures	$(100,000)	
Net cash used in investing activities		(100,000)
Cash flows from financing activities		
Net short-term borrowings	$ 150,000	
Net cash provided by financing activities		150,000
Net increase in cash		$ 100,000
Reconciliation of net income to net cash provided by operating activities:		
Net loss		$ (350,000)
Adjutments to reconcile net loss to net cash provided by operations:		
Depreciation and amortization		170,000
Increase in postpetition payables (operating activities)		150,000
Decrease in accounts receivable		150,000
Increase in inventory		(70,000)
Cash provided by operating activities		$ 50,000

Exhibit 18–10   *Statement of Cash Flows During Chapter 11 Reorganization*

Operations Under Chapter 11

During the next six months, Baker continues to operate under Chapter 11 of the Bankruptcy Code while it works out a reorganization plan, and by June 30, 19X3, Baker has a plan. Balance sheet and income statement amounts reflecting operations for the first six months of 19X3 are summarized as follows:

COMPARATIVE BALANCE SHEETS 19X3

	January 1	June 30	Change
Cash	$ 150,000	$ 300,000	$150,000
Accounts receivable	350,000	335,000	(15,000)
Inventory	370,000	350,000	(20,000)
Other current assets	50,000	30,000	(20,000)
Land	200,000	200,000	—
Building—net	450,000	425,000	(25,000)
Equipment—net	330,000	290,000	(40,000)
Goodwill	150,000	125,000	(25,000)
Assets	$2,050,000	$2,055,000	5,000
Liabilities subject to compromise	$2,300,000	$2,300,000	—
Short-term loan	150,000	75,000	(75,000)
Accounts payable	100,000	125,000	25,000
Wages and salaries	50,000	55,000	5,000
Liabilities	2,600,000	2,555,000	(45,000)
Common stock	500,000	500,000	—
Deficit	(1,050,000)	(1,000,000)	50,000
Equities	$2,050,000	$2,055,000	$ 5,000

INCOME STATEMENT FOR SIX MONTHS ENDING JUNE 30, 19X3

Sales		$ 600,000
Cost of sales		(200,000)
Wages and salaries expense		(100,000)
Depreciation and amortization		
Building	$25,000	
Old equipment	30,000	
New equipment	10,000	
Goodwill	25,000	(90,000)
Other expenses		(30,000)
Earnings before reorganization items		180,000
Professional fees related to bankruptcy proceedings		(130,000)
Net income		50,000
Beginning deficit		(1,050,000)
Ending deficit		$(1,000,000)

The Reorganization Plan

After extensive negotiations among the parties of interest, a reorganization value of $2,200,000 is agreed upon, and a plan of reorganization is filed with the court. The terms of Baker's proposed reorganization plan include the following:

1 Baker's 15 percent bonds payable were secured with the land and building. The bondholders agree to accept $500,000 new common stock, $500,000 senior debt[24] of 12 percent bonds, and $100,000 cash payable December 31, 19X3.

2 The priority tax claims of $150,000 will be paid in cash as soon as the reorganization plan is confirmed by the bankruptcy court.

3 The remaining unsecured, nonpriority prepetition claims of $950,000 will be settled as follows:

---

[24]Senior debt takes precedence over other debts or has a prior claim on the company's assets in the event of liquidation.

750

CORPORATE
LIQUIDATIONS,
REORGANIZATIONS, AND
DEBT RESTRUCTURINGS
FOR FINANCIALLY
DISTRESSED
CORPORATIONS

  a Creditors represented by the accounts payable will receive $275,000 subordinated debt[25] and $140,000 common stock.

  b The $90,000 accrued interest on the 15 percent bonds will be forgiven.

  c The $260,000 note payable to the bank will be exchanged for $120,000 subordinated debt and $60,000 common stock.

4 Equity holders will exchange their stock for $100,000 common stock of the emerging company.

Fresh Start Reporting

The reorganization value is compared with the total postpetition liabilities and allowed claims at June 30 to determine if fresh start reporting is appropriate:

Postpetition liabilities	$ 255,000
Allowed claims subject to compromise	2,300,000
Total liabilities on June 30, 19X3	2,555,000
Less: Reorganization value	2,200,000
Excess liabilities over reorganization value	$ 355,000

The excess liabilities over reorganization value indicates that the first condition for fresh start reporting is met. Since the reorganization plan calls for the old equity holders to retain less than a 50 percent interest in the emerging company, the second condition is met, and fresh start reporting is appropriate. A summary of the proposed reorganized capital structure is as follows:

Postpetition liabilities	$ 255,000
Taxes payable	150,000
Current portion of senior debt, due December 31, 19X3	100,000
Senior debt, 12% bonds	500,000
Subordinated debt	395,000
Common stock	800,000
	$2,200,000

The plan is approved by each class of claims and confirmed by the bankruptcy court on June 30, 19X3. Baker Corporation records the provisions of the reorganization plan and the adoption of fresh start reporting in the books of the old entity as follows:

Accounts payable (prepetition)	$ 600,000	
Interest (prepetition)	90,000	
Bank note (prepetition)	260,000	
15% bonds payable (prepetition)	1,200,000	
12% senior debt		$500,000
12% senior debt—current		100,000
Subordinated debt		395,000
Common stock (new)		700,000
Gain on debt discharge		455,000

    To record settlement of the prepetition claims. [The summary account prepetition claims subject to compromise could have been used.]

---

[25]Subordinate debt ranks below senior debt.

Common stock (old)	$ 500,000	
Common stock (new)		$100,000
Additional paid-in capital		400,000

To record exchange of stock by equity holders.

Baker's assets that have fair values different from their recorded book values on June 30, 19X3 are summarized as follows:

	Fair Value	Book Value	Difference
Inventory	$ 375,000	$ 350,000	$ 25,000
Land	300,000	200,000	100,000
Buildings—net	350,000	425,000	(75,000)
Equipment—net	260,000	290,000	(30,000)
Goodwill	0	125,000	(125,000)
	$1,285,000	$1,390,000	$(105,000)

The entries to adjust Baker's assets for the fair value-book value differences and record the fress shart are:

Inventory	$ 25,000	
Land	100,000	
Loss on asset revaluation	105,000	
Buildings—net		$ 75,000
Equipment—net		30,000
Goodwill		125,000

To adjust Baker's assets to their fair values.

Reorganization value in excess of identifiable assets	$250,000	
Gain on debt discharge	455,000	
Additional paid-in capital	400,000	
Loss on asset revaluation		$ 105,000
Deficit		1,000,000

To eliminate the deficit and additional paid-in capital and to record the excess reorganization value and the fresh start.

Working papers to show the effect of the reorganization plan on Baker's balance sheet are presented in Exhibit 18–11.

The first column of the working papers reflects the balance sheet at June 30, 19X3, immediately before recognizing the terms of the reorganization plan and establishing fresh start reporting. Entries a through f in the adjustment columns adjust the identifiable assets to their reorganization value, which approximates fair value. Baker's goodwill is eliminated, and the excess reorganization value over the fair value of identifible assets is entered. Working paper entries g through k impose the terms of the reorganization plan.

Note that the last column, "reorganized balance sheet," is both the final balance sheet of the old entity and the opening balance sheet of the new emerging entity. Although the opening balance sheet of the new entity reflects the reorganization values of the assets, the SOP 90-7 states that the adjustments to historical cost should be disclosed in notes to the initial financial statements. The new emerging Baker Corporation should also disclose the amount of debt forgiveness, the deficit eliminated, and key factors used in the determination of the reorganization value.

BAKER CORPORATION
COMPARATIVE BALANCE SHEETS AT JUNE 30, 19X3

| | Preconfirmation Balance Sheet | Adjustments to Record Confirmation of Plan | | Reorganized Balance Sheet |
		Debits	Credits	
Assets				
Cash	$ 300,000			$ 300,000
Accounts receivable	335,000			335,000
Inventory	350,000	a 25,000		375,000
Other current assets	30,000			30,000
Land	200,000	b 100,000		300,000
Building	425,000		c 75,000	350,000
Equipment	290,000		d 30,000	260,000
Goodwill	125,000		e 125,000	—
Reorganization excess	—	f 250,000		250,000
	$2,055,000			$2,200,000
Equities **(postpetition claims)** Short-term bank loan	$ 75,000			$ 75,000
Accounts payable	125,000			125,000
Wages payable	55,000			55,000
(prepetition claims) Accounts payable—old	600,000	h 600,000		—
Taxes payable	150,000			150,000
Interest	90,000	i 90,000		—
Bank note	260,000	j 260,000		—
15% bonds payable	1,200,000	g 1,200,000		—
(stockholders' equity) Common stock—old	500,000	k 500,000		—
Deficit	(1,000,000)	c 75,000 d 30,000 e 125,000	a 25,000 b 100,000 f 250,000 g 100,000 h 185,000 i 90,000 j 80,000 k 400,000	—
(new equities) Current portion—bonds	—		g 100,000	100,000
12% senior debt	—		g 500,000	500,000
Subordinated debt	—		h 275,000 j 120,000	395,000
Common stock—new	—		g 500,000 h 140,000 j 60,000 k 100,000	800,000
Retained earnings—new	—			0
	$2,055,000			$2,200,000

Exhibit 18–11 *Working Papers to Show Confirmation of Reorganization Plan with Fresh Start Reporting*

TROUBLED DEBT RESTRUCTURINGS

The provisions of *FASB Statement No. 15,* "Accounting by Debtors and Creditors for Troubled Debt Restructurings," are primarily applicable to troubled debt restructurings arranged through direct negotiations between a debtor company and its creditors, and they do not apply to a general restatement of a debtor's liabilities under the bankruptcy act or in a quasi-reorganization. Settlements of specific liabilities adjudicated through federal bankruptcy or other courts are covered by *Statement No. 15,* provided that the settlements are not a part of a general liability restatement.

Concept of a Troubled Debt Restructuring

A *troubled debt restructuring* under *FASB Statment No. 15* occurs when a *creditor* "for economic or legal reasons related to the debtor's financial difficulties grants a concession to the debtor that it would not otherwise consider." Satisfaction of a debt by foreclosure, repossession, transfer of assets, or granting an equity interest in the debtor corporation is included in the term "troubled debt restructuring." It makes no difference whether the concession is negotiated between a debtor and a creditor or is imposed by law or a court.

Troubled debt restructurings are classified for accounting purposes as:

1 Transfer of assets in full settlement
2 The grant of an equity interest in full settlement
3 A modification of terms (for example, reduction of interest rates, extension of maturities, reduction in amounts of principal or interest)
4 Some combination of the above types

A debt restructuring is *not* a troubled debt restructuring if the fair value of assets received or equity interest transferred at least equals the carrying value of the creditor's receivable (creditor's viewpoint) or the debtor's payable (debtor's viewpoint). Since the carrying amounts of the debt (payable and receivable) may be different, a restructuring can be a troubled debt restructuring for the debtor but not for the creditor. Differences can stem from the write-down of a receivable to its expected net realizable value (either directly or through an allowance account) or from the sale of a receivable to a third party at an amount that reflects the debtor's financial difficulties.

In addition, a debt restructuring is *not* a troubled debt restructuring if an interest rate reduction reflects decreased market interest rates, if new debt securities are issued to the creditor that reflect current market rates of interest, or if the restructuring involves changes in lease agreements.

Debtor Accounting

A debtor that transfers third-party receivables, real estate, or other assets to a creditor in full settlement of a payable recognizes a gain on restructuring for the excess of the carrying value of the payable over the fair value of the assets transferred. The debtor also recognizes a gain or loss on the difference between the book value and fair value of assets transferred to the creditor (this is not a restructuring gain or loss). Foreclosures and repossessions are accounted for in the same manner as asset transfers.

When a debtor issues or grants an equity interest to a creditor in full settlement of a payable, the excess of the carrying value of the payable over the fair value of the equity interest is recognized as a gain on restructuring. The debtor accounts for the equity interest issued at its fair value, but legal fees or other direct costs of granting an equity interest reduce the carrying amount of the equity interest granted.

754

CORPORATE
LIQUIDATIONS,
REORGANIZATIONS, AND
DEBT RESTRUCTURINGS
FOR FINANCIALLY
DISTRESSED
CORPORATIONS

Modification of the terms of a debt includes adjustments such as reducing the stated interest rate, extending the maturity date, reducing the face amount or accrued interest on the debt, or some combination of these adjustments. The debtor in a troubled debt restructuring accounts for a modification of terms prospectively. The carrying amount of the payable does not change unless it exceeds total future cash payments under the new terms. In this case the payable is reduced to an amount equal to future cash payments (principal and interest), and a gain on restructuring is recognized. Subsequently, all cash payments are accounted for as reductions in the payable.

When total future cash payments under a modification of terms exceed the carrying value of the payable, the debtor does not reduce the payable or recognize a gain. Instead, the debtor calculates an effective interest rate that equates future cash payments and the carrying amounts of the payable and applies that rate in determining interest expense and principal components of future payments.

If a troubled debt restructuring involves a combination of asset transfers, granting an equity interest, and modification, the procedures are applied as described, but restructuring gains on asset transfers and equity interests granted are measured and recorded before the modifications are considered.

A debtor's individual gains on troubled debt restructurings are aggregated and reported as an extraordinary item on a net-of-tax basis if the effect is material. Direct costs incurred in a restructuring, other than those associated with granting an equity interest, are deducted in measuring gains on the restructurings of payables. Disclosures are required for aggregate gains on restructurings and related per share amounts, aggregate gains or losses on asset transfers, and principal changes and terms involved in each restructuring.

Creditor Accounting

Receivables of third parties, real estate, other assets, or equity securities received from a debtor in a troubled debt restructuring are recorded by the creditor at their fair values at the time of restructuring. The excess of the recorded amount of the receivable satisfied over the fair value of assets received is recorded as a loss. Creditor repossessions or foreclosures are accounted for in the same manner as other assets received from the debtor.

When the terms of a receivable are modified and total future cash receipts are less than the recorded amount of the receivable, the creditor reduces the receivable to reflect total future cash receipts and recognizes a loss on the writedown. Otherwise, the creditor uses the effective interest method in recognizing interest income from the receivable. The effective interest rate is determined by equating the recorded amount of the receivable with expected future cash receipts.

For troubled debt restructurings that involve a combination of asset transfers, equity interests, and modifications of terms, asset transfers and equity interests received by the creditor are measured and recorded before the modifications are considered. Otherwise, the procedures described are applicable.

A creditor's losses on restructuring are included in income in the period of restructuring, to the extent that they are not offset against allowances for uncollectible amounts. Legal fees and direct costs incurred by a creditor are treated as expenses when incurred. A creditor is required to disclose outstanding receivables whose terms have been modified in troubled debt restructuring and the amount of any commitments to loan additional funds to debtors owing amounts whose terms have been modified.

ILLUSTRATION OF A TROUBLED DEBT RESTRUCTURING

Slump Corporation is a financially distressed corporation with assets and liabilities as of January 1, 19X2 as follows:

		Book Value
Assets		
Cash		$ 5,000
Accounts receivable	$28,000	
Less: Uncollectible receivables	3,000	25,000
Inventory		60,000
Plant and equipment—net		360,000
Total assets		$450,000
Liabilities and Stockholders' Equity		
Accounts payable		$ 72,500
15% note payable—due December 1, 19X1		50,000
Interest on note payable		7,500
10% mortgage payable—due January 1, 19X3		100,000
Interest payable on mortgage		5,000
Capital stock, $100 par		200,000
Retained earnings		15,000
Total liabilities and stockholders' equity		$450,000

Transfer of Assets

Slump Corporation enters into an agreement with one of its suppliers, Kile Corporation, to transfer its accounts receivable (fair value $23,000) as payment in full for a $30,000 account payable owed to Kile. The concession was granted by Kile in order to make the best of a difficult situation. Slump and Kile record the troubled debt restructuring as follows:

Slump's Books

Loss on transfer of accounts receivable	$ 2,000	
Estimated uncollectible receivables	3,000	
Accounts receivable		$ 5,000
To restate receivables at fair value.		
Accounts payable—Kile	$30,000	
Accounts receivable		$23,000
Gain on restructuring of debt		7,000
To transfer receivables to Kile in full settlement of an account payable.		

Kile's Books

Investment in accounts receivable	$23,000	
Loss on settlement of receivables	5,500	
Estimated uncollectible receivables	1,500	
Accounts receivable—Slump		$30,000
To record acceptance of receivables of Slump in full settlement of account.		

The entries on Slump's books reflect a loss on transfer because the fair value of the receivables was less than book value at the time of restructuring. Slump also records a gain from cancellation of a $30,000 liability to Kile by transferring accounts receivable with a fair value of $23,000. This $7,000 gain is a gain from a troubled debt restructuring and is reported on Slump's income statement for 19X2 as an extraordinary item, if material when considered with other gains on restructuring.

Kile's entry to record the restructuring assumes that a $1,500 provision for uncollectible accounts receivable has been provided. Thus, Kile's loss is only $5,500, the $28,500 book value of the receivable from Slump less the $23,000 fair value of receivables accepted in full settlement. Kile's loss is included in its income for the period in accordance with *APB Opinion No. 30* tests for unusual nature and infrequency of occurrence.

756

CORPORATE
LIQUIDATIONS,
REORGANIZATIONS, AND
DEBT RESTRUCTURINGS
FOR FINANCIALLY
DISTRESSED
CORPORATIONS

Grant of an Equity Interest

Slump Corporation issues 500 shares of its stock to Equity Finance Company in full settlement of the 15 percent note payable and accrued interest. The shares have a fair value of $50,000 and the debt is carried at its $40,000 cost by Equity Finance, which purchased the note from the original payee. This restructuring is a troubled debt restructuring for Slump Corporation because it satisfies a $57,500 liability for an equity interest worth $50,000. Slump records the restructuring:

Slump's Books		
15% note payable	$50,000	
Interest on note payable	7,500	
Capital stock, $100 par		$50,000
Gain on restructuring of debt		7,500

To record grant of equity interest in full settlement of note.

The restructuring is not a troubled debt restructuring from the creditor's viewpoint because there is no loss to Equity Finance. Since the transaction is a reciprocal exchange that involves a monetary liability, Equity Finance should record a $10,000 gain and enter the equity investment at its fair value when received.

Modification of Terms

Bussy Bank, holder of Slump's 10 percent mortgage, agrees to a modification of terms such that the bank will accept $55,000 on December 31, 19X2 and December 31, 19X3 in full settlement of the debt, including interest. The carrying value of the debt on both Slump's books and Bussy Bank's books is $105,000.

Since total payments in the new agreement exceed $105,000, no gain or loss is recorded when the agreement is consummated. In accounting for the debt in subsequent periods, however, an effective interest rate has to be computed to equate the two future payments of $55,000 with the $105,000 carrying value of the debt. *Calculation* (P = present value of an annuity):

$$\$55,000 \times P \overline{_{2 \text{ years}}}_{\mid ? \text{ interest}} = \$105,000$$

$$\$105,000/\$55,000 = 1.9091 \text{ present value factor}$$

$$1.9091 = \text{annuity factor for two periods at } 3.16\% \text{ effective interest}$$

Payment and receipt of $55,000 at December 31, 19X2 and 19X3, are recorded by Slump and Bussy Bank as follows:

SLUMP BOOKS	19X2		19X3	
15% note payable	$46,682		$53,318	
Interest payable (January 1, 19X2)	5,000			
Interest expense	3,318		1,682	
Cash		$55,000		$55,000

To record payment of principal and interest:
19X2—$105,000 × 3.16% = $3,318
19X3—[$105,000 − ($55,000 − $3,318)] × 3.16% = $1,682

BUSSY'S BOOKS	19X2		19X3	
Cash	$55,000		$55,000	
15% note receivable		$46,682		$53,318
Interest receivable (January 1, 19X2)		5,000		
Interest income		3,318		1,682

To record receipt of payment for principal and interest:
19X2—$105,000 × 3.16% = $3,318
19X3—$53,318 × 3.16% = $1,682

The journal entries illustrated for Slump Corporation and Bussy Bank are symmetrical because the debt has a carrying value of $105,000 on both sets of books. If carrying amounts are different due to uncollectible account provisions or other adjustments, effective interest rates and interest expense and interest income will be different. As illustrated earlier, the differences can be so great that the modification is a troubled debt restructuring for the debtor corporation but not for the creditor.

SUMMARY

A debtor corporation that cannot solve its financial problems internally may be able to obtain relief by direct negotiation with creditors. Failing this, the debtor may seek protection from creditors by filing a petition for bankruptcy under Title 11 of the U.S.C. Either the debtor or the creditors can file a petition. A petition filed under Chapter 11 of the Bankruptcy Act covers reorganization of the debtor; a Chapter 7 filing covers liquidation of the debtor.

In a Chapter 7 liquidation case, a trustee and creditors' committee are elected by the unsecured creditors. The trustee takes possession of the debtor's estate, converts the assets into cash, and distributes the proceeds according to the priority of claims, as directed by the bankruptcy court.

In a Chapter 11 reorganization case, the U.S. trustee appoints a creditors' committee as soon as practicable after the filing. A trustee may be appointed for cause, but generally the debtor continues in possession. The debtor corporation continues operations while it works out a reorganization plan that is fair and equitable.

The AICPA's Statement of Position, "Financial Reporting by Entities in Reorganization Under the Bankruptcy Code," prescribes financial reporting for companies operating under Chapter 11. Some companies emerging from Chapter 11 are essentially new companies and qualify for fresh start reporting. Emerging companies that do not meet the criteria for fresh start reporting account for their liabilities in accordance with *APB Opinion No. 21,* "Interest on Receivables and Payables."

In a troubled debt restructuring, a creditor grants a concession to the debtor because of the debtor's financial troubles. For example, the creditor may accept assets or an equity interest from the debtor in full settlement of a debt, or the creditor may modify the terms of a debt by lowering interest rates, extending maturities, and so on. The concession may be negotiated directly between the debtor and creditor, or it may be imposed by a court. *FASB Statement No. 15* prescribes accounting procedures for troubled debt restructurings.

SELECTED READINGS

ALTMAN, EDWARD I. *Corporation Bankruptcy in America.* Lexington, MA: Heath Lexington Books, 1971.

ALTMAN, EDWARD I. *Corporation Financial Distress.* New York: John Wiley, 1983.

"Bankruptcy," Title 11 United States Code, 1978.

BRODSKY, MARK D., and JOEL B. ZWEIBEL. "Chapter 11 Acquisitions: Payoffs and Patience." *Mergers & Acquisitions 25,* (September/October 1990), pp. 47–53.

CASEY, CORNELIUS J., VICTOR E. MCGEE, and CLYDE P. STICKNEY. "Discriminating between Reorganized and Liquidated Firms in Bankruptcy." *The Accounting Review* (April 1986), pp. 249–262.

KUDLA, RONALD J. *Voluntary Corporate Liquidations.* Westport, CT: Quorum Books, Greenwood Press, 1988.

NEWTON, GRANT W. *Bankruptcy and Insolvency Accounting: Practice and Procedure,* 2nd ed. New York: John Wiley, 1981.

Organisation for Economic Co-operation and Development. *International Investment and Multinational Enterprises: Responsibility of Parent Companies for Their Subsidiaries.* Washington, D.C.: OECD Publications and Information Center, 1980.

758

CORPORATE
LIQUIDATIONS,
REORGANIZATIONS, AND
DEBT RESTRUCTURINGS
FOR FINANCIALLY
DISTRESSED
CORPORATIONS

PASTENA, VICTOR, and WILLIAM RULAND. "The Merger/Bankrutpcy Alternative." *The Accounting Review* (April 1986), pp. 288–301.

PARISER, DAVID B. "Financial Reporting Implications of Troubled Debt." *The CPA Journal* (February 1989), pp. 32–40.

ROBBINS, JOHN, AL GOLL, and PAUL ROSENFELD. "Accounting for Companies in Chapter 11 Reorganization." *Journal of Accountancy* (January 1991), pp. 74–80.

Statement of Financial Accounting Standards No. 15. "Accounting by Debtors and Creditors for Troubled Debt Restructurings." Stamford, CT: *Financial Accounting Standards Board, 1977.*

Statement of Position 90-7. "Financial Reporting by Entities in Reorganization under the Bankruptcy Code." Executive Committee of the Accounting Standards Division of the American Institute of Certified Public Accountants, 1990.

ASSIGNMENT MATERIAL

QUESTIONS

1 What is the distinction between *equity insolvency* and *bankruptcy insolvency?*

2 Is a Title 11 case under the Bankruptcy Act of 1978 the same as a Chapter 11 case? Discuss.

3 Bankruptcy proceedings may be designated as *voluntary* or *involuntary.* Distinguish between the two types, including the requirements for the filing of an involuntary petition.

4 Consider the following statement: "A bankrupt company is liquidated under Chapter 7 of the Bankruptcy Act, but a company that is not bankrupt will be rehabilitated under Chapter 11." Do you agree? Discuss.

5 What are the duties of the U.S. trustee under the Bankruptcy Act of 1978? Do U.S. trustees supervise the administration of all bankruptcy cases?

6 What obligations does a debtor corporation have in a bankruptcy case?

7 Is a trustee appointed in Title 11 cases? In all Chapter 7 cases? Discuss.

8 Do you agree with the following statement? "Trustees and creditor committees are appointed in Chapter 11 cases and elected in Chapter 7 cases."

9 Describe the duties of a trustee in a liquidation case under the Bankruptcy Act of 1978.

10 Which unsecured claims have priority in a Chapter 7 liquidation case? Discuss in terms of priority ranks.

11 Does the Bankruptcy Act of 1978 establish priorities for holders of unsecured non-priority claims (that is, general unsecured claims)?

12 What is the purpose of a statement of affairs and how are assets valued in this statement?

13 Does the Bankruptcy Act require a trustee to prepare a statement of realization and liquidation for the bankruptcy court?

14 Does filing a case under Chapter 11 of the Bankruptcy Act mean that the company will not be liquidated? Discuss.

15 What is a "debtor in possession reorganization case"?

16 When can a creditor committee file a plan of reorganization under a Chapter 11 case?

17 Discuss the requirements for approval of a plan of reorganization.

18 Does acceptance of a plan by two-thirds in amount and over half in number of claims constitute confirmation of a reorganization plan? Discuss.

19 Describe *prepetition liabilities subject to compromise* on the balance sheet of a company operating under Chapter 11 of the Bankruptcy Act.

20 The *reorganization value* of a firm emerging from Chapter 11 bankruptcy is used to determine the accounting of the reorganized company. Explain reorganization value as used in the AICPA's SOP 90-7, "Financial Reporting by Entities in Reorganization Under the Bankruptcy Code."

21 The SOP provides two conditions that must be met for an emerging firm to use fresh start reporting. What are these two conditions?

22 A firm emerging from Chapter 11 bankruptcy that does not qualify for fresh start reporting must still report the effect of the reorganization plan on its financial position and results of operations. How is debt forgiveness reported in the reorganized company's financial statements?

23 What is a troubled debt restructuring? Is it possible for an extinguishment of debt to be a troubled debt restructuring for the debtor corporation but not for the creditor?

24 When does the debtor corporation recognize a loss on the restructuring of debt?

25 If the terms of a debt are modified such that future payments of the debtor are greater than the carrying value of the debt, how does the debtor company account for the modification?

EXERCISES

E 18–1

1 If a debtor corporation is unable to pay its debts as they come due, its financial condition is one of:
a Bankruptcy
b Equity insolvency
c Bankruptcy insolvency
d Involuntary bankruptcy

2 A corporate reorganization under the Bankruptcy Act of 1978 is referred to as a (an):
a Chapter 7 case
b Chapter 11 case
c Involuntary case
d Voluntary case

3 A bankruptcy case in which creditors file the petition for liquidation of a corporate debtor might be referred to as a (an):
a Voluntary Chapter 7 case
b Voluntary Chapter 11 case
c Involuntary Title 11 case
d Voluntary Title 11 case

4 A voluntary petition for a Chapter 7 filing requires:
a Aggregate debt of $5,000
b Unsecured debt of $5,000
c Twelve or more unsecured creditors
d None of the above

5 Debtor in possession cases are most likely to stem from:
a Involuntary Chapter 7 petitions
b Voluntary Chapter 7 petitions
c Involuntary Chapter 11 petitions
d Voluntary Chapter 11 petitions

6 A single unsecured creditor with a $5,000 claim may file a petition to bring a corporate debtor into bankruptcy court if the debtor corporation has:
a Only 12 other creditors
b Only 12 other unsecured creditors
c Only 12 other secured and unsecured creditors
d Fewer than 12 unsecured creditors

7 A trustee in a Chapter 7 bankruptcy case is elected by the debtor corporation's:
a Creditors
b Unsecured creditors
c Secured creditors
d Creditors and stockholders

8 Preferences under the bankruptcy act relate to:
a Preferred stock of the debtor
b Unsecured priority claims
c Transfers of property by the debtor
d Ranking of claims by the court

9 Which one of the following is *not* included in the unsecured priority claims category in a liquidation case?
a Administrative expenses
b Wages, salaries, and commissions
c Contributions to employee benefit plans
d Interest on unsecured claims

10 Which of the following are elected in reorganization cases under the Bankruptcy Act of 1978?
a Debtor in possession
b Creditor committees
c Trustee
d None of the above

11 During the first 120 days after a court order for relief is granted in a Chapter 11 case, a plan of reorganization can only be filed by:
a The debtor corporation
b The trustee
c Creditor's committees
d Equity securityholders' committees

760

CORPORATE
LIQUIDATIONS,
REORGANIZATIONS, AND
DEBT RESTRUCTURINGS
FOR FINANCIALLY
DISTRESSED
CORPORATIONS

12 A plan of corporate reorganization under Chapter 11 of the Bankruptcy Act *may not:*
   a Provide for sale of the debtor's property
   b Treat claims within a particular class alike
   c Provide for issuance of nonvoting equity securities
   d Specify some classes of claims as unimpaired

13 In order to be finalized, a plan of reorganization under Chapter 11 of the Bankruptcy Act requires:
   a Discharge of liabilities
   b Confirmation by the court
   c Consent of all shareholders
   d Consent of all creditors

14 Which one of the following is *not* required for implementation of a plan of reorganization under Chapter 11 of the Bankruptcy Act?
   a A plan that is fair and equitable
   b Confirmation by the court
   c Acceptance by each class of claims that would be impaired by the plan
   d Approval of one-half in amount of all claims and two-thirds in number of holders of all claims

E 18-2

1 *FASB Statement No. 15,* "Accounting by Debtors and Creditors for Troubled Debt Restructurings," is applicable to:
   a Quasi-reorganizations
   b General liability restatements under the Bankrutpcy Act of 1978
   c Debt restructurings consummated through direct debtor-creditor negotiations
   d Interest rate changes resulting from escalator clauses in debt agreements

2 Classifications of troubled debt restructurings under *FASB Statement No. 15* do not include:
   a Transfer of assets
   b Adjudication of liabilities
   c Grant of an equity interest
   d Modification of terms

3 A debtor recognizes a gain on restructuring if:
   a Assets transferred at fair value exceed liabilities satisfied
   b Liabilities satisfied exceed the fair value of an equity interest granted to the creditor
   c Total future debt payments in a modification of terms exceed the carrying value of the restructured debt
   d Fair value of assets transferred to the creditor exceed their book value

4 A debtor corporation's gains on debt restructurings during a period are aggregated and, if material, are reported:
   a In income from continuing operations
   b In income before extraordinary items
   c As an extraordinary item on a net-of-tax basis
   d As a direct adjustment to stockholders' equity

5 In a troubled debt restructuring, a debtor's direct costs of restructuring, other than those of granting an equity interest, are:
   a Treated as expenses in the period incurred
   b Deducted in measuring gains on restructuring
   c Deferred and amortized over the restructuring period
   d Combined with gains or losses on assets transferred to the creditor

6 A creditor in a troubled debt restructuring:
   a Records assets received at the carrying value of the receivable satisfied
   b Recognizes a loss when the fair value of assets received is less than the carrying value of the receivable satisfied
   c Combines gains and losses on restructurings and reports the net amount as an extraordinary item on a net-of-tax basis
   d Reports losses on restructurings as uncollectible accounts expense in the period of restructuring

E 18-3 [AICPA adapted]

1 Bunker Industries, Inc., ceased doing business and is in bankruptcy. Among the claimants are employees seeking unpaid wages. The following statements describe the possible status of such claims in a bankruptcy proceeding or legal limitations placed on them. Which one is an incorrect statement?

a They are entitled to a priority.

b If a priority is afforded such claims, it cannot exceed $2,000 per wage earner.

c Such claims cannot include vacation, severance, or sick-leave pay.

d The amounts of excess wages not entitled to a priority are mere unsecured claims.

2 Merchant is in serious difficulty and is unable to meet current unsecured obligations of $25,000 to some fifteen creditors who are demanding immediate payment. Merchant owes Flintheart $5,000, and Flintheart has decided to file an involuntary petition against Merchant. Which of the following is necessary in order for Flintheart to validly file?

a Flintheart must be joined by at least two other creditors.

b Merchant must have committed a fraudulent act within one year of the filing.

c Flintheart must allege and subsequently establish that Merchant's liabilities exceed Merchant's assets upon fair valuation.

d Flintheart must be a secured creditor.

3 The federal Bankruptcy Act contains several important terms. One such term is *insider*. The term is used in connection with preferences and preferential transfers. Which among the following is not an insider?

a A secured creditor having a security interest in at least 25 percent or more of the debtor's property

b An affiliate of the debtor corporation

c A director of the debtor corportion

d The daughter of the president of the debtor corporation

4 Which of the following does not constitute a valid debt that may be proved and allowed against the debtor corporation's estate under the Bankruptcy Act?

a A workers' compensation award if the injury occurred before filing for bankruptcy

b An open account

c Contingent claims that are not capable of liquidation or of reasonable estimate

d Fixed liabilities evidenced by a written instrument absolutely owing but not due at the time of the filing of a petition

5 Marco Corporation owns all the shares of stock of Digits Corporation. Digits is currently short of cash and has had to default on some of its current liabilities. Marco loaned Digits $2,000 to tide it over its crisis and obtained a note from Digits for the amount of the loan. If Digits is petitioned into bankruptcy court, what is the status of Marco's loan?

a It is a provable and allowable claim against the debtor's estate which is superior to the claims of other general creditors.

b It is a provable and allowable claim against the debtor corporation's estate together with the claims of all other general creditors.

c It is invalid because the loan by Marco constituted a preferential transfer.

d It is worthless because Marco is liable for the debts of Digits, since it owns all of Digits's stock.

6 A voluntary bankruptcy proceeding is available to:

a All debtors provided they are insolvent

b Debtors only if the overwhelming preponderance of creditors have not petitioned for and obtained a receivership pursuant to state law

c Corporations only if a reorganization has been attempted and failed

d Most debtors even if they are *not* insolvent

7 An involuntary petition in bankruptcy:

a Will be denied if a majority of creditors in amount and in number have agreed to a common law composition agreement

b Can be filed by creditors only once in a seven-year period

c May be successfully opposed by the debtor by proof that the debtor is solvent in the bankruptcy sense

d If not contested will result in the entry of an order for relief by the bankruptcy judge

8 Lux Corporation has been suffering large losses for the past two years. Because of its inability to meet current obligations, Lux has filed a petition for reorganization under Chapter 11 of the Bankruptcy Code. The reorganization provisions under the Bankruptcy Code:

a Require that the court appoint a trustee in all cases

b Permit Lux to remain in possession of its assets

c Apply only to involuntary bankruptcy

d Will apply to Lux only if Lux is required to register pursuant to the federal securities laws

E 18–4 Likely Corporation is being liquidated under Chapter 7 of the Bankruptcy Act. After all noncash assets have been liquidated, $40,000 cash remains to pay the following approved claims:

Administrative expenses including trustee fees	$ 10,000
Salaries (not exceeding $2,000 per employee)	20,000
Property taxes	15,000
Claims between filing of the involuntary petition and appointment of the trustee	5,000
Accounts payable, unsecured	16,000
Notes payable, unsecured	30,000
Interest on unsecured notes payable	4,000
Total unpaid claims	$100,000

Required: Determine the amount to be paid to unsecured priority creditors in settlement of their claims.

E 18–5 Handyman Hardware, Inc., has been operating under Chapter 11 of the Bankrutpcy Code for the past 15 months. On March 31, 19X5, just before confirmation of its reorganization plan, Handyman's reorganization value is estimated at $2,000,000. A balance sheet for Handyman prepared on the same date is summarized as follows:

Current assets	$ 500,000	Postpetition liabilities	$ 800,000
Plant assets	2,000,000	Prepetition liabilities	
	$2,500,000	subject to compromise*	1,000,000
		Fully secured debt	600,000
		Capital stock	600,000
		Deficit	(500,000)
			$2,500,000

* Represents allowed claims. The reorganization plan calls for payment of $100,000, issuance of $200,000 notes, and $250,000 common stock in settlement of the prepetition liabilities.

Required: (1) On the basis of the reorganization value, does Handyman Hardware qualify for fresh start reporting? (2) What other condition must be met for fresh start reporting? Show calculations.

E 18–6 Worthy Corporation is being liquidated in an involuntary Chapter 7 case. All assets have been converted into cash, all secured creditors have been paid, and a total of $55,000 is available to cover the following claims:

Accounts payable ($5,000 was incurred between filing and the appointment of the trustee)	$30,000
Note payable—unsecured	20,000
Interest on note payable	2,000
Wages payable (earned within 90 days of filing and does not exceed $2,000 per individual)	8,000
Property taxes payable—current year	2,000
Administrative expenses incurred by the trustee	4,000

Required: Prepare a schedule showing the claims listed by priority rank in one column, the amounts to be paid in a second column, and the amounts to be written off in a third column.

E 18–7 Kassum Company experienced cash flow problems during 19X2 and on June 30, 19X2 was unable to pay principal and interest on a $50,000 debt to its principal supplier, Genair Corporation. In view of Kassum Company's distressed financial condition, Genair agreed to accept machinery with a book value of $52,000 and a fair value of $45,000 in full satisfaction of the $50,000 debt and $7,500 accrued interest.

Required: Prepare journal entries on the books of Kassum Company and Genair Corporation to record the troubled debt restructuring that was consummated on July 30, 19X2.

E 18–8 On January 1, 19X3 Second National Bank sold its $25,000, 15 percent note receivable from Milan Company to Stable Finance Company for $20,000, in anticipation of Milan's default on the loan. Stable did not accrue interest on the note during the first half of 19X3 because of the uncertain financial condition of Milan and the speculative nature of the investment. Milan Company was unable to pay the note and the $1,875 accrued interest on its June 30, 19X3 due date.

During August 19X3 Stable Finance and Milan negotiated an agreement under which Milan was to issue 1,000 shares of its $10 par common stock to Stable Finance in full satisfaction of the debt. The restructuring was consummated on August 31, at which time the stock had a fair value of $23,000, and accrued interest on the debt was $2,500 ($25,000 × 15% × ⅔ year).

Required
1 Is this a troubled debt restructuring? Discuss.
2 Prepare journal entries on the books of Milan Company to record the restructuring, assuming that it is a troubled debt restructuring.

E 18–9 Planter Corporation was unable to pay its $100,000, 12 percent note and $6,000 interest to Exchange Bank on September 30, 19X7. Due to the financially distressed condition of Planter, Exchange Bank agreed to extend the due date on the note for one year, and to reduce the interest rate from 12 to 3 percent, provided that the $6,000 accrued interest was paid immediately. This agreement was consummated on October 3, 19X7, on which date Planter paid the $6,000 interest due.

Required
1 Is this a troubled debt restructuring for Planter? For Exchange Bank?
2 Calculate the gain or loss on restructuring to be recorded on October 3, 19X7 by Planter and by Exchange Bank.
3 Prepare journal entries on the books of Planter and Exchange Bank to record the interest due on March 31, 19X8, and principal and interest due on September 30, 19X8.

E 18–10 [AICPA adapted]

1 On December 31, 19X3 Marsh Company entered into a debt restructuring agreement with Saxe Company, which was experiencing financial difficulties. Marsh restructured a $100,000 note receivable as follows:

Reduced the principal obligation to $70,000.
Forgave $12,000 of accrued interest.
Extended the maturity date from December 31, 19X3 to December 31, 19X5.
Reduced the interest rate from 12 to 8 percent. Interest was payable annually on December 31, 19X4 and 19X5.

In accordance with the agreement, Saxe made payments to Marsh on December 31, 19X4 and 19X5. How much interest income should Marsh report for the year ended December 31, 19X5?

a	$0	b	$5,600
c	$8,400	d	$11,200

2 Bricker Company is indebted to Springburn Bank under a $200,000, 16 percent, three-year note dated January 1, 19X1. Interest, payable annually on December 31, was paid on the December 31, 19X1 due date. During 19X2 Bricker experienced severe financial difficulties and was likely to default on the note and interest unless a concession was made by the bank. On December 31, 19X2 the bank agreed to settle the note and interest for 19X2 for $10,000 cash and a tract of land having a current market value of $140,000. Bricker's acquisition cost of the land is $100,000. Ignoring income taxes, what amount should Bricker report as extraordinary gain on the debt restructure in its income statement for the year ended December 31, 19X2?

a	$0	b	$50,000
c	$82,000	d	$122,000

3 During 19X2 Peterson Company experienced financial difficulties and is likely to default on a $500,000, 15 percent, three-year note dated January 1, 19X1, payable to Forest National Bank. On December 31, 19X2 the bank agreed to settle the note and unpaid interest of $75,000 for 19X2 for $50,000 cash and marketable securities

764

CORPORATE
LIQUIDATIONS,
REORGANIZATIONS, AND
DEBT RESTRUCTURINGS
FOR FINANCIALLY
DISTRESSED
CORPORATIONS

having a current market value of $375,000. Peterson's acquisition cost of the securities is $385,000. Ignoring income taxes, what amount should Peterson report as a gain from the debt restructuring in its 19X2 income statement?

a	$65,000	b	$75,000
c	$140,000	d	$150,000

Carr Company is indebted to Apex Company under a $700,000, 12 percent, four year note dated December 31, 19X1. Annual interest of $84,000 was paid on December 31, 19X2 and 19X3. During 19X4 Carr experienced financial difficulties and is likely to default on the note and interest unless concessions are made. On December 31, 19X4 Apex agreed to restructure the debt as follows:

Interest for 19X4 was reduced from $84,000 to $40,000 payable on January 31, 19X5.

Interest for 19X5 was waived.

The $700,000 principal amount was reduced to $600,000.

Ignoring income taxes, how much should Carr report as extraordinary gain on debt restructure in its income statement for the year ended December 31, 19X4?

a	$0	b	$60,000
c	$100,000	d	$144,000

5 Hull Company is indebted to Apex under a $500,000, 12 percent, three-year note dated December 31, 19X4. Because of Hull's financial difficultles developing in 19X6, Hull owed accrued interest of $60,000 on the note at December 31, 19X6. Under a troubled debt restructuring on December 31, 19X6, Apex agreed to settle the note and accrued interest for a tract of land having a fair value of $450,000. Hull's acquisition cost of the land is $360,000. Ignoring income taxes, on its 19X6 income statement Hull should report as a result of the troubled debt restructuring:

	Other Income	*Extraordinary Gain*
a	$200,000	$ 0
b	140,000	0
c	90,000	50,000
d	90,000	110,000

PROBLEMS

P 18–1 The balance sheet of Slim-Line Corporation appeared as follows on March 1, 19X2, when an interim trustee was appointed by the U.S. trustee to assume control of Slim-Line's estate in a Chapter 7 case.

Assets		*Liabilities and Stockholders' Equity*	
Cash	$ 2,000	Accounts payable	$25,000
Accounts receivable—net	4,000	Note payable—unsecured	20,000
Inventories	18,000	Revenue received in advance	500
Land	10,000	Wages payable	1,500
Buildings—net	50,000	Mortgage payable	40,000
Intangible assets	13,000	Capital stock	20,000
		Retained earnings deficit	(10,000)
Assets	$97,000	Liabilities and equity	$97,000

Additional Information
1 Creditors failed to elect a trustee, and accordingly the interim trustee became the trustee for the case.
2 The land and buildings are pledged as security for the mortgage payable.
3 In January 19X2 Slim-Line received $500 from a customer as a payment in advance for merchandise that is no longer marketed.

4 Activities of the trustee during March are summarized as follows:
   a $3,800 is collected on the receivables.
   b Inventories are sold for $9,700.
   c Land and buildings bring a total of $45,000.
   d Nothing is realized from the intangible assets.
   e Administrative expenses of $4,100 are incurred by the trustee.

Required
   1 Prepare a separate set of books for the trustee to assume possession of the estate and convert its assets into cash.
   2 Prepare financial statements on March 31 for Slim-Line in Trusteeship (balance sheet, cash receipts and disbursements, and changes in estate equity).
   3 Prepare journal entries on the trustee's books to distribute available cash to creditors and close the case.

P 18-2 Downing Corporation filed a petition under Chapter 7 of the Bankruptcy Act in January 19X6. On March 15, 19X6 the trustee provided the following information about the corporation s financial affairs.

	Book Values	Estimated Realizable Values
Assets		
Cash	$ 20,000	$ 20,000
Accounts receivable—net	100,000	75,000
Inventories	150,000	70,000
Plant assets—net	250,000	260,000
Total assets	$520,000	
Liabilities		
Liability for priority claims	$ 80,000	
Accounts payable—unsecured	150,000	
Note payable, secured by accounts receivable	100,000	
Mortgage payable, secured by all plant assets	200,000	
Total liabilities	$530,000	

Required
   1 Determine the amount expected to be available for unsecured claims.
   2 Determine the expected recovery per dollar of unsecured claims.
   3 Estimate the amount of recovery for each class of creditors.

P 18-3 Harder Corporation is a financially distressed corporation with assets and liabilities at June 30, 19X6 as follows:

Assets		Book Value	Liabilities	Book Value
Cash		$ 70,000	Accounts payable	$ 50,000
Accounts receivable	$50,000		15% note payable	100,000
Less: Uncollectible receivables	5,000	45,000	Interest on note payable	7,500
Inventory		80,000	15% mortgage payable	300,000
Plant and equipment—net		405,000	Interest on mortgage payable	22,500
Total assets		$600,000	Total liabilities	$480,000

Additional Information
   1 On July 1, 19X6 Kelly Supply Corporation, Harder's sole supplier, accepted all of Harder's accounts receivable with a fair value of $38,000 in full settlement of the accounts payable liability.

766

CORPORATE
LIQUIDATIONS,
REORGANIZATIONS, AND
DEBT RESTRUCTURINGS
FOR FINANCIALLY
DISTRESSED
CORPORATIONS

2 On July 5, 19X6 Belker Finance Corporation accepted 1,000 shares of Harder Corporation's $10 par common stock with a fair value of $80 per share in full settlement of the note payable and interest.
3 Also on July 5, 19X6 First National Bank agreed to accept $45,000 per year for eight years in full settlement of the mortgage payable and interest. The current interest rate on July 5 was 12 percent and the present value of the eight future payments on that date was $223,544.

Required: Calculate Harder Corporation's "gain or loss on restructuring" its debt in accordance with the provisions of *FASB Statement No. 15.*

P 18–4 Famous Fabrics Corporation is being liquidated under Chapter 7 of the Bankruptcy Act. All assets have been converted into cash and $352,400 cash is available to pay the following claims:

1 Administrative expenses of preserving and liquidating the debtor corporation's estate	$ 12,500
2 Merchandise creditors	87,000
3 Local government for property taxes	4,000
4 Local bank for unsecured loan (principal is $30,000 and interest is $4,500)	34,500
5 State government for gross receipts taxes	2,000
6 Employees for unpaid wages during the month before filing (includes $5,000 for the company president and under $2,000 for each of the other employees)	48,000
7 Customers for prepaid merchandise that was not delivered	900
8 Holders of the first mortgage on the company's real estate that was sold for $220,000 (includes $200,000 principal and $8,000 interest)	208,000

Assume that all the claims are allowed and that they were timely filed.

Required
1 Rank the claims according to priority under the Bankruptcy Act.
2 Show how the available cash will be distributed in final liquidation of the corporation.

P 18–5 Galax Corporation experienced financial difficulties during the current year and was able to obtain concessions from several of its creditors to enable it to continue operations. Information relating to each of the concessions is as follows:

1 Galax transfers inventory items with a normal selling price of $21,000 (cost $15,000) to Renner Corporation in full satisfaction of a $20,000 note and $3,000 accrued interest. The book value of the note and interest on Renner's books is $22,000 ($23,000 less a $1,000 allowance for uncollectible notes).
2 First Piedmont Finance Company accepts 3,000 shares of Galax Corporation's $10 par common stock in full satisfaction of a $50,000 note and $2,500 accrued interest. The stock has a book value of $60,000 and a fair value of $40,000. First Piedmont acquired the note and accrued interest for $35,000 flat just before the restructuring.
3 The First National Bank of Danville extends the $100,000 mortgage on Galax's plant for two years and reduces the interest rate from 15 percent to 6 percent in order to make the best of a difficult situation. In return, Galax pays the $3,750 accrued interest immediately.

Required: Prepare journal entries on the books of Galax Corporation and each of its creditors for the restructurings described.

P 18–6 The interim trustee developed the following information for Atlantic Corporation as of September 15, 19X8, four days after the company filed a petition under Chapter 7 of the Bankruptcy Act.

	Book Values	Estimated Realizable Values
Assets		
Cash	$ 40,000	$ 40,000
Accounts receivable—net	105,000	80,000
Inventories	100,000	105,000
Equipment—net	75,000	30,000
Land	25,000	45,000
Buildings—net	100,000	25,000
Intangible assets	5,000	—
	$450,000	$325,000
Equities		
Accounts payable	$200,000	
Wages payable	12,000	
Taxes payable	38,000	
Note payable	50,000	
Mortgage payable	100,000	
Interest payable on mortgage	2,500	
Capital stock	150,000	
Retained earnings (deficit)	(102,500)	
	$450,000	

Additional Information
1 The land and buildings are pledged as security for the mortgage payable and interest.
2 The accounts receivable are pledged as security for the note payable.
3 Wages payable, taxes payable, and $25,000 of the accounts payable (incurred between filing and appointment of the interim trustee) are priority items.
4 Expenses of converting the assets into cash and liquidating the corporation are expected to be $30,400.

Required: Prepare a schedule showing how the available cash will be distributed on October 1, 19X8 if the assets are liquidated at their estimated realizable values and the actual expenses of liquidating the corporation are equal to estimated expenses.

P 18–7 The unsecured creditors of Dawn Corporation filed a petition under Chapter 7 of the Bankruptcy Act on July 1, 19X6 to force Dawn into bankruptcy. The court order for relief was granted on July 10 at which time an interim trustee was appointed to supervise and liquidate the estate. A listing of assets and liabilities of Dawn Corporation as of July 10, 19X6, along with estimated realizable values, is as follows:

	Book Values	Estimated Realizable Values
Assets		
Cash	$ 80,000	$ 80,000
Accounts receivable—net	210,000	160,000
Inventories	200,000	210,000
Equipment—net	150,000	60,000
Land	50,000 ⎫	
Buildings—net	200,000 ⎬	140,000
Intangible assets	10,000 ⎭	—
	$900,000	$650,000

768

CORPORATE
LIQUIDATIONS,
REORGANIZATIONS, AND
DEBT RESTRUCTURINGS
FOR FINANCIALLY
DISTRESSED
CORPORATIONS

	Book Values	Estimated Realizable Values
Accounts payable	$400,000	
Note payable	100,000	
Wages payable (from June and July)	24,000	
Taxes payable	76,000	
Mortgage payable $200,000, plus $5,000 unpaid interest to July 10	205,000	
Capital stock	300,000	
Retained earnings deficit	(205,000)	
	$900,000	

Additional Information
1 Accounts receivable are pledged as security for the note payable.
2 No more than $1,000 is owed to any employee.
3 Taxes payable are a priority item.
4 Inventory items include $50,000 acquired on July 5, 19X6 and the unpaid invoice is included in accounts payable.
5 The mortgage payable and interest are secured by the land and buildings.
6 Trustee fees and other costs of liquidating the estate are expected to be $11,000.

Required
1 Prepare a statement of affairs for Dawn Corporation on July 10, 19X6.
2 Develop a schedule showing how available cash will be distributed to each class of claims assuming (a) the estimated realizable values are actually received and (b) the trustee and other fees of liquidating the estate are $11,000.

P 18-8 The balance sheet of Everlast Window Corporation at June 30, 19X1 contains the following items:

Assets	
Cash	$ 40,000
Accounts receivable—net	70,000
Inventories	50,000
Land	30,000
Building—net	200,000
Machinery—net	60,000
Goodwill	50,000
	$500,000

Equities	
Accounts payable	$110,000
Wages payable	60,000
Property taxes payable	10,000
Mortgage payable	150,000
Interest on mortgage payable	15,000
Note payable—unsecured	50,000
Interest payable—unsecured	5,000
Capital stock	200,000
Retained earnings deficit	(100,000)
	$500,000

The company is in financial difficulty and its stockholders and creditors have requested a statement of affairs for planning purposes. The following information is available:

1 The company estimates that $63,000 is the maximum amount collectible for the accounts receivable.
2 Except for 20% of the inventory items that are damaged and worth about $2,000, the cost of the other items is expected to be recovered in full.
3 The land and building have a combined appraisal value of $170,000 and are subject to the $150,000 mortgage and related accrued interest.
4 The appraised value of the machinery is $20,000.

5 The wages payable and property taxes payable are unsecured priority items and do not exceed any limitations of the Bankruptcy Act.

Required

1 Prepare a statement of affairs for Everlast Window Corporation as of June 30, 19X1.

2 Compute the estimated settlement per dollar of unsecured liabilities.

P 18-9 Lowstep Corporation filed for relief under Chapter 11 of the Bankruptcy Act on January 2, 19X2. A summary of Lowstep's assets and equities on this date, and at June 30, 19X2, is shown below. Estimated fair values of Lowstep's assets at June 30 are also shown.

	January 2, 19X2	June 30, 19X2	
		Per Books	Estimated Fair Value
Assets			
Cash	$ 200	$ 6,700	$ 6,700
Trade receivables—net	800	1,000	1,000
Inventories	2,000	1,600	2,000
Prepaid items	500	—	—
Land	1,000	1,000	2,000
Buildings—net	3,000	2,900	1,500
Equipment—net	2,000	1,800	1,800
Goodwill	4,500	4,000	0
	$14,000	$19,000	$15,000
Equities			
Accounts payable	$ 1,000	$ 3,000	
Wages payable	500	1,000	
Bank note payable (includes $500 interest)	5,000		
Long-term note payable (secured with equipment)	6,000		
Prepetition liabilities allowed		12,500	
Common stock	7,000	7,000	
Deficit	(5,500)	(4,500)	
	$14,000	$19,000	

The parties-in-interest agreed to a reorganization plan on July 1, 19X2, and a hearing to confirm that the plan is fair and equitable is scheduled for July 8. Under the reorganization plan, the reorganization value is set at $16,000, and the debt and equity holders will receive value as follows:

	To Receive Cash Consideration	To Receive Noncash Consideration
Post petition claims		
Accounts payable (in full)	$3,000	
Wages payable (in full)	1,000	
Prepetition claims		
Accounts payable (80%)	800	
Wages payable (80%)	400	
Bank note payable and interest (80%)		$ 2,000 note payable
		2,000 common stock
Long-term note payable (80%)		1,800 note payable
		3,000 common stock
Common stockholders*		2,000 common stock
	$5,200	$10,800

* Reorganization value over consideration allocated to creditors.

770

CORPORATE
LIQUIDATIONS,
REORGANIZATIONS AND
DEBT RESTRUCTURINGS
FOR FINANCIALLY
DISTRESSED
CORPORATIONS

The reorganization plan is confirmed on July 8, 19X2 under the new name of Highstep Corporation. There are no asset or liability changes between July 1 and July 8.

Required

1 Is the reorganization of Lowstep eligible for fresh start accounting? Show calculations.
2 Prepare journal entries to adjust Lowstep's accounts for the reorganization plan.
3 Prepare a fresh start balance sheet as of July 8, 19X2.

19

ACCOUNTING FOR STATE AND LOCAL GOVERNMENTAL UNITS—PART I

Accounting and reporting practices of business enterprises owned by individuals and having a primary objective of earning income for the private benefit of those owners are based on generally accepted accounting principles (GAAP). The pronouncements of the FASB and its predecessor organizations are the major sources of such accounting principles. In the nonbusiness area, however, the source of accounting principles is not nearly so well defined. This is largely because of the diverse nature of nonbusiness organizations, which include governmental units, hospitals, churches, colleges and universities, health and welfare organizations, professional associations, and many others. These organizations are commonly referred to as **nonprofit,** or **not-for-profit, entities** because they have neither individual ownership nor a private profit objective.

Ordinarily, the accounting and reporting systems of nonprofit organizations are maintained on a **fund basis.** That is, their financial information systems are divided (segmented) into separate financial and accounting entities (funds) corresponding to their diverse nonprofit objectives and to various restrictions on their operations and resources. Accounting principles have been developed to provide standards of accounting and reporting for particular types of nonprofit organizations. These include the *Codification of Governmental Accounting and Financial Reporting Principles,* published by the Governmental Accounting Standards Board (for state and local governmental entities); the *Chart of Accounts for Hospitals,* published by the American Hospital Association (for hospitals); *College and University Business Administration,* published by the American Council on Education (for colleges and universities); and a series of Industry Audit Guides prepared by committees of the AICPA for state and local governmental units, hospitals, colleges and universities, and voluntary health and welfare organizations. Because of the absence of accounting principles for numerous other types of nonprofit organizations, the AICPA issued an Audit and Accounting Guide in 1981 entitled *Audits of Certain Nonprofit Organizations.* The audit guide is applicable to audits of the financial statements of nonprofit organizations not covered by other authoritative pronouncements and it includes the AICPA's Statement of Position (SOP) 78-9 as an appendix. Thus, accounting guidance for nonprofit organizations comes from diverse sources and carries varying degrees of authoritative support.

The FASB issued its *Statement of Financial Accounting Concepts No. 4*, "Objectives of Financial Reporting by Nonbusiness Organizations," in 1980 and is currently working on a project for nonprofit organizations other than state and local governmental entities. State and local governmental entities fall under the jurisdiction of the Governmental Accounting Standards Board. A primary objective of the FASB project is to reduce the inconsistencies in accounting practices of the various nonprofit organizations that have evolved. The FASB expects to provide standards of accounting for contributions and depreciation, and for financial statement displays.

The objectives of this chapter and Chapter 20 are to summarize accounting and reporting principles for state and local governmental units and to illustrate fund accounting practices using a municipal accounting system as a model. Outside of the federal government, state and local governmental units constitute the largest single category of nonprofit organizations in terms of the dollar volume of annual expenditures.

HISTORICAL DEVELOPMENT OF ACCOUNTING PRINCIPLES FOR STATE AND LOCAL GOVERNMENTAL UNITS

The most important continuous source of accounting principles for state and local governmental units has been the Government Finance Officers Association[1] and its committees on governmental accounting. *Municipal Accounting and Auditing*, in 1951, and *Governmental Accounting, Auditing, and Financial Reporting (GAAFR)*,[2] in 1968, comprised more or less complete frameworks of accounting principles peculiar to governmental units. They also provided standards for evaluating the financial reports of governmental units, including audited financial statements that were issued in accordance with GAAP. *GAAFR* provided the most authoritative source of accounting principles for state and local governmental units from 1968 to 1974 when the AICPA issued its Industry Audit Guide, *Audits of State and Local Governmental Units*. The audit guide cited *GAAFR* as an authoritative source of accounting principles for state and local governmental units and noted that *GAAFR's* accounting principles constituted GAAP except where they were modified by the audit guide.

The AICPA's audit guide prompted the 1979 revision of *GAAFR* for purposes of updating and clarifying governmental accounting and financial reporting principles, and for incorporating pertinent aspects of the audit guide. The Government Finance Officers Association established a new committee, the National Council on Governmental Accounting (NCGA) for developing the 1979 *GAAFR* Restatement. As part of this project, the NCGA issued *Governmental Accounting and Financial Reporting Principles, Statement 1 (NCGA1)* in 1979. The following year, a new *GAAFR* was issued as a comprehensive volume to explain and illustrate the principles of *NCGA1*. Also in 1980, the AICPA issued *Statement of Position 80-2* that amended *Audits of State and Local Governmental Units* to recognize the principles of *NCGA1* as generally accepted accounting principles.

The Governmental Accounting Standards Board

In 1984 the Financial Accounting Foundation (parent of the FASB) formed the **Governmental Accounting Standards Board (GASB)** for the purpose of establishing and improving standards for governmental accounting and financial report-

---

[1]The Government Finance Officers Association was the Municipal Finance Officers Association before changing its name in 1985.

[2]Both publications were issued by the National Committee on Governmental Accounting, one of the governmental accounting committees of the Municipal Finance Officers Association.

ing. The AICPA Council declared that Rule 203 of Rules of Conduct applies to GASB's pronouncements and, therefore, CPAs are bound by those pronouncements for financial statements issued in accordance with GAAP.

In July 1984 GASB issued *GASB Statement No. 1, Authoritative Status of NCGA Pronouncements and AICPA Industry Audit Guide,* in which it affirmed that:

> All NCGA Statements and Interpretations heretofore issued and currently in effect are considered as being encompassed within the conventions, rules, and procedures referred to as "generally accepted accounting principles," and are continued in force until altered, amended, supplemented, revoked, or superseded.

The GASB integrated all effective accounting and reporting standards from these various sources into one publication in 1985 called *Codification of Governmental Accounting and Financial Reporting Standards.* The *Codification* was revised in 1987, with plans for additional revisions every two years.

GAAP Hierarchy for State and Local Government Entities

During the first five years of GASB's existence, some confusion developed about the jurisdiction of GASB and FASB over government-owned "special entities" such as hospitals, colleges and universities, and public utilities. In 1990 the Financial Accounting Foundation worked out an agreement for a GAAP hierarchy for state and local governmental units, including special entities. That agreement, modified slightly in 1991 by a proposed statement on auditing standards, lists the following categories, in descending order, as GAAP guidelines for state and local governments:[3]

1 *GASB statements and GASB interpretations.* This category also includes AICPA and FASB pronouncements that are made applicable to state and local governments by a GASB Statement or Interpretation.
2 *GASB technical bulletins.* This category also includes AICPA Industry Audit and Accounting Guides and Statements of Position that GASB declares are applicable to state and local governmental entities.
3 *Consensus positions* of GASB Emerging Issues Task Force (EITF) and "cleared" Accounting Standards Executive Committee practice bulletins made applicable by GASB.
4 *Pronouncements* issued by GASB staff and *practices* that are widely recognized and prevalent in state and local government.
5 *Other accounting literature.*

The Environment of Governmental Accounting

General governmental activities include providing goods and services to citizens on the basis of need, without regard to their ability to pay. The goods and services to be provided, and the level to be provided, are determined by the citizens through their elected officials or by mandate or persuasion from a higher government. General government activities are usually financed by taxes and by intergovernmental grants and subsidies, and there may be no relationship between the people receiving the services and those paying for them. Resource allocation involves restricting the use of funds to the various general governmental projects and programs. For example, taxes may be levied to finance a specific program, the state government may provide funds to finance a specific service at the local level, or borrowed funds may be restricted to a specific project. The existence of restrictions on resources is the primary reason for fund account-

---

[3]GASB, Action Report, June 1990, and Auditing Standards Board Exposure Draft, "The Meaning of 'Presents Fairly in Conformity with Generally Accepted Accounting Principles' in the Independent Auditor's Reports," 1991.

ing. **Fund accounting** is the use of multiple accounting entities (funds or account groups) to account for resources segregated according to purpose.

Some governmental entities also engage in business activities that provide services to users and finance those services through user charges.

OVERVIEW OF BASIC GOVERNMENTAL ACCOUNTING PRINCIPLES

Twelve basic accounting principles underlie accounting and reporting for governmental operations. Together, the principles form a model of fund accounting theory. The principles were set forth in the *NCGA 1,* identified as GAAP by GASB's *Statement 1,* and included in the GASB's *Codification of Governmental Accounting and Financial Reporting Standards.* The principles are summarized in this section.

Accounting and Reporting Capabilities
(Principle 1)

The first accounting principle specified in *Statement 1* is:

> A governmental accounting system must make it possible both: (a) to present fairly and with full disclosure the financial position and results of financial operations of the funds and account groups of the governmental unit in conformity with generally accepted accounting principles, and (b) to determine and demonstrate compliance with finance-related legal and contractual provisions. (GASB Cod. Sec. 1100.101)

This principle requires that the accounting system be sufficient to provide a basis for the preparation of external financial statements in accordance with GAAP. Further, the governmental accounting system must provide information necessary to show compliance with the numerous legal provisions and restrictions that come from constitutions, charters, resolutions, ordinances, intergovernmental grants, and other sources.

Fund Accounting Systems
(Principle 2)

The second principle requires the use of fund accounting for governmental units and defines a **fund:**

> Governmental accounting systems should be organized and operated on a fund basis. A fund is defined as a fiscal and accounting entity with a self-balancing set of accounts recording cash and other financial resources, together with all related liabilities and residual equities or balances, and changes therein, which are segregated for the purpose of carrying on specific activities or attaining certain objectives in accordance with special regulations, restrictions, or limitations. (GASB Cod. Sec. 1100.102)

Note that *a fund is both a fiscal and an accounting entity* and that it has a self-balancing set of accounts. The requirement for a self-balancing set of accounts means that the familiar debit and credit framework holds for the recording of transactions and events in the accounting system of each fund. But the requirement that a fund must be both a separate fiscal entity and a separate accounting entity indicates that the self-balancing feature is not adequate by itself. (Principle 5 recognizes the need for both a general long-term debt account group and a general fixed assets account group, each of which has a self-balancing set of accounts and equal debits and credits, but which are not funds because they are not *fiscal* entities that have transactions.)

Fund Categories   Governmental accounting uses three categories of funds, governmental, proprietary, and fiduciary. **Governmental funds** are those used to account for most general government functions that are basically different from those found in private enterprise. The governmental fund category includes the general fund, special revenue funds, capital projects funds, and debt service funds.

> Governmental funds are, in essence, accounting segregations of financial resources. Expendable assets are assigned to the various governmental funds according to the purposes for which they may or must be used; current liabilities are assigned to the fund from which they are to be paid; and the difference between governmental fund assets and liabilities, the fund equity, is referred to as "Fund Balance."
>
> The governmental fund measurement focus is on determination of *financial position and changes in financial position* (sources, uses, and balances of financial resources), rather than upon net income determination. The statement of revenues, expenditures, and changes in fund balance is the primary governmental fund operating statement. It may be supported or supplemented by more detailed schedules of revenues, expenditures, transfers, and other changes in fund balance.[4]

Proprietary funds are used to account for those ongoing activities that are similar to those of a business entity.

> All assets, liabilities, equities, revenues, expenses and transfers relating to the government's business and quasi-business activities—where *net income and capital maintenance are measured*—are accounted for through proprietary funds.[5]

GAAP for proprietary funds is similar to that for private business, except where GASB pronouncements have been issued. The measurement focus is on net income, financial position, and cash flows. The proprietary fund category includes enterprise funds and internal service funds.

Fiduciary funds "are used to account for assets held by a governmental unit in a trustee capacity or as an agent for individuals, private organizations, other governmental units, and/or other funds."[6] The appropriate accounting has to consider the fiduciary responsibilities of the governmental unit and the specific laws and restrictions applicable to each specific fund. The accounting measurement focus may be like governmental funds, proprietary funds, or strictly custodial. The fiduciary fund category includes trust funds and agency funds.

Types of Funds
(Principle 3)

Principle 3 as amended by *GASB Statement 6*, specifies seven types of funds that should be used by state and local governments. These funds are classified as governmental, proprietary, and fiduciary funds[7] (GASB Cod. Sec. 1100.103). Governmental funds include:

1 The **general fund**—to account for all financial resources except those required to be accounted for in another fund.
2 **Special revenue funds**—to account for the proceeds of specific revenue sources (other than expendable trusts or for major capital projects) that are legally restricted to expenditure for specified purposes.
3 **Capital projects funds**—to account for financial resources to be used for the acquisition or construction of major capital facilities (other than those financed by proprietary funds and trust funds).

---

[4]GASB Cod. Sec. 1300.102.

[5]Ibid.

[6]Ibid.

[7]Eight types of funds were recommended until January 1987 when *GASB Statement 6, Accounting and Financial Reporting for Special Assessments,* was issued to eliminate special assessment funds as a separate fund type.

4 **Debt service funds**—to account for the accumulation of resources for, and the payment of, general long-term debt principal and interest.

Proprietary funds include:

5 **Enterprise funds**—to account for operations (a) that are financed and operated in a manner similar to private business enterprises—where the intent of the governing body is that the costs (expenses, including depreciation) of providing goods or services to the general public on a continuing basis be financed or recovered primarily through user charges; or (b) where the governing body has decided that periodic determination of revenues earned, expenses incurred, and/or net income is appropriate for capital maintenance, public policy, management control, accountability, or other purposes.

6 **Internal service funds**—to account for the financing of goods or services provided by one department or agency to other departments or agencies of the governmental unit, or to other governmental units, on a cost-reimbursement basis.

Fiduciary funds include:

7 **Trust and agency funds**—to account for assets held by a governmental unit in a trustee capacity or as an agent for individuals, private organizations, other governmental units, and/or other funds. These include (a) expendable trust funds, (b) nonexpendable trust funds, (c) pension trust funds, and (d) agency funds.

Although each of these funds will be covered in more detail in a later section of this chapter and in Chapter 20, it is important to emphasize the broad classifications of funds—governmental, proprietary, and fiduciary—because other principles specify different accounting procedures for the different classifications.

Number of Funds (Principle 4)

The number of funds that should be used by a governmental unit is covered by the fourth principle:

> Governmental units should establish and maintain those funds required by law and sound financial administration. Only the minimum number of funds consistent with legal and operating requirements should be established, however, because unnecessary funds result in inflexibility, undue complexity, and inefficient financial administration. (GASB Cod. Sec. 1100.104)

Accounting for Fixed Assets and Long-Term Liabilities (Principle 5)

Matters related to accounting for fixed assets and long-term liabilities are explained in Principle 5 which distinguishes between **fund fixed assets** and **general fixed assets,** and **fund long-term liabilities** and **general long-term debt:**

> Fixed assets related to specific proprietary funds or trust funds should be accounted for through those funds. All other fixed assets of a governmental unit should be accounted for through the General Fixed Assets Account Group.
> Long-term liabilities of proprietary funds and trust funds should be accounted for through those funds. All other unmatured general long-term liabilities of the governmental unit, including special assessment debt for which the govermental unit is obligated in some manner, should be accounted for through the General Long Term Debt Account Group. (GASB Cod. Sec. 1100.105)

Fixed assets utilized in proprietary or trust fund activities are fund fixed assets. The assets are recorded in the accounts of proprietary funds because they are used in the production of goods and services that are sold to outside entities (enterprise funds) or sold to other governmental entities based on cost recovery through user charges (internal service funds). Bonds, notes, and other long-term liabilities expected to be paid from proprietary or trust funds are *fund* liabilities and should be included in the accounts of these funds.

Other fixed assets and long-term liabilities are considered *general* and are accounted for in the general fixed assets and the general long-term debt account groups. This is because general fixed assets relate to the general operations of the government as a whole, and unmatured general long-term debt is a liability of the general government, secured by the full faith and credit of the governmental unit.

Valuation of Fixed Assets and Depreciation of Fixed Assets (Principles 6 and 7)

Fixed asset valuation is explained in Principle 6, and depreciation on fixed assets is covered in Principle 7, as follows:

> Fixed assets should be accounted for at cost or, if the cost is not practically determinable, at estimated cost. Donated fixed assets should be recorded at their estimated fair value at the time received. (GASB Cod. Sec. 1100.106)
>
> Depreciation of general fixed assets should not be recorded in the accounts of governmental funds. Depreciation of general fixed assets may be recorded in cost accounting systems or calculated for cost finding analyses; and accumulated depreciation may be recorded in the General Fixed Assets Account Group.
>
> Depreciation of fixed assets accounted for in a proprietary fund should be recorded in the accounts of that fund. Depreciation is also recognized in those trust funds where expenses, net income, and/or capital maintenance are measured. (GASB Cod. Sec. 1100.107)

Note that depreciation expense is recorded on fund fixed assets of proprietary and trust funds, but not on general fixed assets. Although accumulated depreciation may be recorded in the general fixed assets account group, the related depreciation expense may not be recorded in the accounts of governmental funds. The reason is that governmental funds measure expenditures, not expenses. The acquisition of general fixed assets is a use of fund resources and it is recorded as an expenditure. When general fixed assets are sold, the proceeds are a source of funds for governmental funds. Depreciation expense is neither a use nor a source of funds, and it should not be recorded in any of the governmental funds.

Accrual Basis in Governmental Accounting (Principle 8)

The eighth principle explains the *accrual* and *modified accrual bases* of accounting and their application to governmental funds, proprietary funds, fiduciary funds, and interfund transfers:

> The modified accrual or accrual basis of accounting, as appropriate, should be used in measuring financial position and operating results.
>
> *Governmental fund* revenues and expenditures should be recognized on the modified accrual basis. Revenues should be recognized in the accounting period in which they become available and measurable. Expenditures should be recognized in the accounting period in which the fund liability is incurred, if measurable, except for unmatured interest on general long-term debt which should be recognized when due.
>
> *Proprietary fund* revenues and expenses should be recognized on the accrual basis. Revenues should be recognized in the accounting period in which they are earned and become measurable; expenses should be recognized in the period incurred, if measurable.

Fiduciary fund revenues and expenses or expenditures (as appropriate) should be recognized on the basis consistent with the fund's accounting measurement objective. Nonexpendable trust and pension trust funds should be accounted for on the accrual basis; expendable trust funds should be accounted for on the modified accrual basis. Agency fund assets and liabilities should be accounted for on the modified accrual basis.

Transfers should be recognized in the accounting period in which the interfund receivable and payable arise. (GASB Cod. Sec. 1100.108)

In *proprietary funds* where the operations are similar to those of a business enterprise, revenues and expenses are recognized on the accrual basis.

Governmental funds do not have operations like those of a business enterprise, and they do not have an income objective. Instead, they collect resources as necessary to cover the expenditures that have been approved by the legislative body (town council, city council, board of supervisors, state legislature, and so on). In measuring the revenues and expenditures (not expenses) of a governmental fund, a modified accrual basis of accounting is used. Under the modified accrual basis, revenues are recognized in the period in which they become available to cover expenditures approved for the same period, provided that they can be measured. Expenditures are recognized in the period in which the related liabilities are incurred, if measurable, except that interest on general long-term debt should be recognized when due.

The basis of accounting for *fiduciary funds* depends upon whether the funds are expendable or nonexpendable. **Expendable funds** are those in which resources can be expended as needed to meet the objectives of the fund. **Nonexpendable funds** are those that have a profit or capital maintenance objective. Thus, nonexpendable trust and pension trust funds are accounted for on the accrual basis, whereas expendable trust funds use the modified accrual basis.

Transfers between funds are recognized in the period in which the interfund receivable or payable arises.

Budgeting, Budgetary Control, and Budgetary Reporting (Principle 9)

The ninth principle of governmental accounting is concerned with budgeting and budgetary control:

> An annual budget should be adopted by every governmental unit. The accounting system should provide the basis for appropriate budgetary control.
>
> Budgetary comparisons should be included in the appropriate financial statements and schedules for govenmental funds for which an annual budget has been adopted. (GASB Cod. Sec. 1100.109)

Budgeting is considered especially important in governmental accounting, and the budget document is often considered more significant than the financial reports. Thus, the adoption of an annual budget is considered a basic principle of governmental accounting whether or not required by law. In addition, the accounting system is required to provide appropriate budgetary control either formally through the use of budgetary accounts (applies to the general fund, special revenue funds, and other governmental funds as needed) or informally through the maintenance of separate budgetary records and comparisons. Only the general fund and special revenue funds are *required* to use formal budgetary accounting practices. A comparison of actual and budgetary amounts is required to be included in the annual operating statements of all governmental funds for which an annual budget has been adopted.

Transfer, Revenue, Expenditure, and Expense Accounting Classification (Principle 10)

Principle 10 is concerned with classification of revenue, expenditures, and expense items and with interfund transfers. Interfund transfers and proceeds of general long-term debt must be clearly distinguished from fund revenues and expenditures or expenses in financial statements.

> Interfund transfers and proceeds of general long-term debt issues should be classified separately from fund revenues and expenditures or expenses.
>
> Governmental fund revenues should be classified by fund and source. Expenditures should be classified by fund, function (or program), organization unit, activity, character, and principal classes of objects.
>
> Proprietary fund revenues and expenses should be classified in essentially the same manner as those of similar business organizations, functions, or activities. (GASB Cod. Sec. 1100.110)

It is important not only to distinguish interfund transfers from fund revenues, expenditures, or expenses, but also to distinguish interfund transfers from other interfund transactions. Interfund loans and advances, quasi-external interfund transactions, and reimbursements are not interfund transfers. Accounting for the various types of interfund transactions depends on the nature of the transaction.

Interfund Loans and Advances   **Interfund loans** are loans that are made by one fund to another and must be repaid. The receivable and payable resulting from an interfund loan appear in different funds, and they must be disclosed in a combined balance sheet. The interfund receivable and payable are not eliminated as such balances would be in the consolidated financial statements of a parent company and subsidiary.

Quasi-External Transactions   **Quasi-external transactions** are those that would be treated as revenues, expenditures, or expenses if they involved organizations external to the governmental unit. Payments in lieu of taxes from a proprietary fund to the general fund, or internal service fund billings to departments are examples of quasi-external transactions. These transactions *are accounted for as revenues, expenditures, or expenses of the funds involved* even though they are not revenues, expenditures, or expenses of the governmental unit.[8] Any receivable and payable balances will appear on the balance sheets of the respective funds and should be disclosed in a combined balance sheet.

Reimbursements   A reimbursement is necessary when an expenditure applicable to one fund is made by a different fund. The **reimbursement interfund transaction** is recorded as *an expenditure or expense (as appropriate) in the reimbursing fund and as reductions of the expenditure or expense in the fund that is reimbursed.* This accounting assures that the revenue, expenditure, or expense appears only in the proper fund.

Interfund Transfers   Interfund transfers are classified as residual equity transfers and operating transfers. **Residual equity transfers** are nonrecurring and nonroutine transfers of equity between funds, such as an initial capital contribution from the general fund for organizing a fund or the transfer of a residual balance of a discontinued fund to the general fund or a debt service fund. All other interfund transfers are operating transfers. **Operating transfers** are legally authorized, recurring shifts of resources from one fund to another that do not

---

[8]GASB Cod. Sec. 1800.103 and 1800.104.

represent revenues and expenditures or expenses to the funds involved. For example, resources accumulated by the general fund are transferred to the debt service fund through which the money will be expended to service the debt.

Proceeds of General Long-Term Debt Issues   Proceeds of debt issues that are *not* fund liabilities (see Principle 5) should be reported as *bond issue proceeds,* or similar title, and shown as *other financing sources* in the operating statement of the recipient fund.

Classifications of Revenues, Expenses, and Expenditures   Revenues and expenses of proprietary funds are classified in the same manner as for similar business organizations, but Principle 10 prescribes rather precise classification requirements for the revenues and expenditures of governmental funds. **Governmental fund revenues** are increases in fund financial resources other than from interfund transfers and debt issue proceeds.

Sources of governmental fund revenues are taxes, licenses and permits, intergovernmental revenues, charges for services, fines and forfeits, and miscellaneous other sources. All the sources are reasonably self-explanatory except for intergovernmental revenue sources. *Intergovernmental revenues* include the following four sources of governmental financing:

> **Grants**—contributions or gifts from other governmental units (for example, state grants for highways) to be used for specified purposes. *Capital grants* are contributions or gifts restricted by the grantor for the acquisition or construction of fixed (capital) assets. Operating grants are contributions or gifts that are intended to finance operations or that may be used for either operations or capital outlays at the discretion of the grantee. (GASB Cod. Sec. G60.501–504)

By Fund	**By Activity (Line of Work to Perform a Function)***
Governmental Funds	Police Administration
General Fund (GF)	Traffic Control
Special Revenue Fund (SRF)	Street Cleaning
Capital Projects Fund (CPF)	
Debt Service Fund (DSF)	**By Organization Unit***
Proprietary Funds	City Council
Enterprise Fund (EF)	Police Department
Internal Service Fund (ISF)	Fire Department
	Planning Department
Fiduciary Funds	Nondepartmental
Trust Fund (TF)	
Agency Fund (AF)	**By Object of Expenditure**
	Current Expenditures
By Function (Broad Purposes)*	Personal Services
General Government	Supplies
Public Safety	Other Services and Charges
Highways and Streets	
Sanitation	*Capital Outlays*
Health and Welfare	Land
Culture and Recreation	Buildings
Education	Improvements Other than Buildings
	Machinery and Equipment
By Character Classification	Construction Work in Process
Current Expenditures	
Capital Outlays	*Debt Service*
Debt Service	Principal
	Interest

* Indicates that examples rather than complete classifications are provided.

Exhibit 19–1   *Summary of Expenditure Classifications*

Shared revenues—specific revenue sources shared with other govermental units (for example, shared gasoline taxes) in proportion to collections at the local level.

Entitlements—payments to which a state or local government is entitled as based on an allocation formula contained in applicable statutes (for example, payments of federal revenue-sharing funds to state and local governmental units).

Payments in lieu of taxes—amounts paid by one governmental unit to another for revenues lost because governmental units cannot tax each other (for example, payments by a state university to a town in which it is located).

Governmental fund expenditures are decreases in fund financial resources other than from interfund transfers. The expenditure classifications for governmental funds that are required by Principle 10 are summarized in Exhibit 19–1. *Only fund, character class, and function classifications are required for external financial reporting.*

Common Terminology and Classification (Principle 11)

Since the budget, the accounts, and the financial reports are essential elements of a governmental accounting system, the eleventh principle requires that consistent terminology and classifications be used throughout the accounting and reporting process:

> A common terminology and classification should be used consistently throughout the budget, the accounts, and the financial reports of each fund. (GASB Cod. Sec. 1100.111)

Interim and Annual Financial Reports (Principle 12)

The twelfth and final principle is concerned with financial reporting requirements. This principle covers the need for interim reports, the content of a comprehensive annual financial report, and the numerous requirements for external general-purpose financial statements when they are issued separately from the corresponding annual report:

> Appropriate interim financial statements and reports of financial position, operating results, and other pertinent information should be prepared to facilitate management control of financial operations, legislative oversight, and, where necessary or desired, for external reporting purposes.
>
> A comprehensive annual financial report covering all funds and account groups of the governmental unit—including . . . appropriate combined, combining, and individual fund statements; . . . schedules; narrative explanations; and statistical tables—should be prepared and published.
>
> General purpose financial statements may be issued separately from the comprehensive annual financial report. Such statements should include the basic financial statements and notes to the financial statements that are essential to fair presentation of financial position and operating results (and cash flows of proprietary-type funds and nonexpendable trust funds). (GASB Cod. Sec. 1100.112)

The basic financial statements that are essential to fair presentation (general purpose financial statements) are emphasized in this chapter and in Chapter 20.

A **budget** is "a plan of financial operation embodying an estimate of proposed expenditures for a given period and the proposed means of financing them."[9] Ordinarily, the preparation of a budget is the responsibility of the executive branch of government—the mayor, city manager, governor, and so on. Approval of a budget, however, is a legislative responsibility. A legislative body may approve a proposed budget as submitted by the chief executive, or it may amend the executive budget prior to approval. *When approved by the legislative body, the budget for expenditures becomes a spending ordinance that has the force of law. An approved revenue plan also has the force of law* because it provides the governmental unit with the power to levy taxes, to sell licenses, to charge for services, and so on, in the amount or at the rate approved.

Appropriations *are approved or authorized expenditures,* and they provide legislative control over the expenditure budget prepared by the executive. Such control may be in detail, as when the legislative body makes appropriations for each item included in the budget. The legislative body may, however, approve expenditures (make appropriations) by category (by department, for example), or in total. Line-item approval provides maximum control over the executive by the legislative branch because any change in the budget would have to be approved by the legislative body. If appropriations are made by department, however, the executive could allocate more resources to some items within a department (supplies, for example) and less to others (salaries, for example) without legislative approval of the change.

Appropriations may be restricted by allotments. **Allotments** are divisions of the appropriations authority by time period. In other words, the yearly appropriations are alloted to months or quarters to prevent expenditure of the appropriation too early in the year. Further, allotments may be necessary for coordinating revenues collected with payments for expenditures.

A current budget is normally for a one-year period, and it includes the operating budget as well as the capital budget for the current period. A capital budget should not be confused with a capital program. A **capital budget** simply represents the current portion of a capital program, whereas a **capital program** represents a plan of capital expenditures to be incurred each year over a fixed period of years.

Budgetary Approaches

Traditionally, the budgets of local governmental units have been prepared on a line-item basis in order to provide maximum control over expenditures. Although this approach does achieve its control objective in the sense of helping to avoid overspending of amounts appropriated, it is not a good approach for planning and evaluation. The fact that actual expenditures are in legal compliance with amounts appropriated does not provide assurance that expenditures are effective in meeting the needs of citizens or that resources are used efficiently in obtaining goods and services needed to carry out governmental programs.

Program and performance budgeting are alternative budgeting approaches that have been developed to improve the planning and evaluation functions of governmental budgets. A **program budget** organizes the proposed expenditure budget in terms of total cost of programs to be carried out or functions to be performed. Under this approach, the budget is organized into programs for public safety, health and welfare, recreation, ecology, public works, and so on (and the

---

[9]Municipal Finance Officers Association of the United States and Canada, *Governmental Accounting, Auditing, and Financial Reporting* (Chicago: Municipal Finance Officers Association of the United States and Canada, 1980), p. 56.

total cost of each program); rather than in terms of an object of expenditure classification including salaries, utilities, supplies, fringe benefits, insurance, automobiles, gasoline, repairs, and so on. The program approach permits the ranking of programs and the scaling of costs so that available resources are directed toward essential and high-priority programs before funds are appropriated for other programs. Program budgeting is considered a superior planning approach that can improve the *effectiveness* with which limited resources are allocated to fulfill the needs of the citizens.

A **performance budget** is one that emphasizes measurable performance of work programs and activities so that input costs can be compared with output benefits. Performance budgeting is primarily an evaluation approach, and it frequently involves cost accounting calculations such as the cost per mile of streets resurfaced, per ton mile of garbage hauled, per credit hour of instruction, and so on. Such information can be helpful in determining how *efficiently* resources are being used in providing public goods and services to citizens.

Another budgeting approach is **zero-base budgeting.** Under this approach, all appropriations are to be made without direct reference to prior years' programs or expenditures (that is, from zero base). The intent is to prevent appropriations for ineffective programs that might otherwise be approved year after year. Like the program approach, zero-base budgeting is primarily a tool for planning rather than for control or evaluation.

THE GENERAL FUND AND SPECIAL REVENUE FUNDS

The *general fund (GF)* is the entity used to account for all unrestricted resources except those required to be accounted for in another fund. In more descriptive terms, the GF is the entity that is used to account for the general operations of government including the revenue received and the expenditures made in providing public goods and services to the citizens. If a governmental unit has only one fund accounting entity, that fund is a general fund.

A *special revenue fund (SRF)* is the entity used to account for the proceeds of specific revenue sources (other than expendable trusts or for major capital projects) that are restricted by law or administrative action to expenditures for specified purposes. Although a government would have only one general fund, it could have many special revenue funds or none at all. If specific revenue sources are earmarked for education, a special revenue education fund should be utilized to account for the earmarked resources. Similarly, if a city receives state or federal funds specifically designated to be used for highway construction or maintenance, an SRF should be created to account for such funds.

Earmarked revenues are accounted for in separate special revenue funds in order to show compliance with legal or administrative requirements. Outside of this need to separate earmarked revenue sources, there is no essential difference between an SRF and a GF. Both types of funds are governmental funds, use the modified accrual basis, and are required to integrate their approved budgets into their accounting systems. Because the accounting requirements for special revenue funds are the same as for a general fund, only general fund accounting procedures are illustrated.

ACCOUNTING FOR THE GENERAL FUND

The after-closing trial balance of the Town of Blair General Fund at June 30, 19X1 shows the following ledger account balances:

Debits	
Cash	$31,000
Taxes receivable—delinquent	15,000
Accounts receivable	3,000
Supplies inventory	6,000
Total debits	$55,000

Credits	
Estimated uncollectible taxes—delinquent	$ 1,000
Vouchers payable	14,000
Note payable	15,000
Reserve for supplies	6,000
Reserve for encumbrances	9,000
Fund balance	10,000
Total credits	$55,000

Events for the year June 30, 19X1 to June 30, 19X2 of the Town of Blair include recording an approved budget, accounting for revenues from various sources, accounting for expenditures with encumbrance controls, preparing year-end adjusting and closing entries, and finally, preparing the general fund financial statements.

Revenues

Under the modified accrual basis of accounting, *revenues are recognized in the period in which they become available and are measurable.* Ordinarily, this means that revenue from property taxes is recognized when taxpayers are billed for the amount of taxes levied, and revenue from garbage collection and other city services is recognized when bills are rendered for services performed. But revenue from sales taxes, licenses, permits, fines, and the like cannot be measured objectively until cash is actually received. Therefore, revenue from these sources is not usually recognized until cash is collected. If taxes are collected in a period before they become available to finance expenditures, the amount received is recorded as a liability (deferred taxes), and it is not recognized as revenue until the succeeding period when it becomes available to cover expenditures.

Expenditures

Expenditures are decreases in the net financial resources of a governmental-type fund. Under modified accrual accounting *expenditures are normally recorded when the related liability is incurred.* This concept should not be confused with the expense concept because expenses are recognized when the related goods or services are used. Under modified accrual accounting, salaries, supplies, utilities, and fixed assets alike are recorded as expenditures when the related liabilities are incurred. In each of these cases, the net financial resources (assets minus liabilities) are reduced when the liabilities are incurred because the related resources are not recognized as assets of the general fund.

Encumbrances

Since expenditures in a period are limited by law to those for which appropriations have been made, it is extremely important to keep expenditures within authorized levels. A situation that could result in overspending appropriations arises when expenditures are approved without considering outstanding purchase orders or unperformed contracts. For example, assume that total appropriations for the year exceed actual expenditures to date by $4,000 and that an additional equipment purchase for $3,000 is approved. If $2,000 of supplies are on order, and expenditures are made for both the equipment and the supplies, actual expenditures for the period will exceed appropriations by $1,000. To prevent this type of situation, encumbrance accounting is used. *Encumbrance* means *commitment,* and **encumbrance accounting** records commitments made for goods on order and for unperformed contracts. Encumbrance accounting provides additional control over expenditures.

If the full amount of an appropriation is not expended during the period covered by the appropriation, a question arises as to whether the unexpended portion can be carried over as authorization for expenditures in the succeeding year. Although the laws of the governmental unit will cover this matter, a common position is that all appropriations lapse at the end of the year for which they are made, except that committed appropriations (that is, encumbrances outstanding) can continue to serve as authorizations for the items on order or under contract. Note that the after-closing trial balance for the Town of Blair includes a credit account "Reserve for Encumbrances" of $9,000. This account shows the amount of committed appropriations that is carried over to serve as authorization for the actual expenditures as they occur in the succeeding year. One of the first entries to be made in the year beginning July 1, 19X1 is to reclassify this account to identify it as a carryover from the prior year:

GF		
Reserve for encumbrances	$9,000	
Reserve for encumbrances—prior year		$9,000

The Budget

The Town of Blair has approved the following GF budget for the fiscal year July 1, 19X1 to June 30, 19X2.

TOWN OF BLAIR
GENERAL FUND BUDGET SUMMARY
FOR THE YEAR JULY 1, 19X1 TO JUNE 30, 19X2

Revenue Sources	
Taxes	$250,000
Licenses and permits	20,000
Intergovernmental revenue	40,000
Charges for services	60,000
Fines and forfeits	15,000
Rents and royalties	10,000
Miscellaneous revenues	5,000
Total budgeted revenues	$400,000
Expenditures	
Current services	
General government	$ 45,000
Public safety	140,000
Highways and streets	90,000
Sanitation	55,000
Health and welfare	20,000
Recreation	30,000
Capital outlays	15,000
Total appropriations	$395,000

The revenue categories used in the budget are the revenue sources illustrated by the NCGA in GAAFR. Budgeted expenditures as itemized in the general fund budget summary are organized by character class (current services, capital outlays, and debt service) and by function within the current services category. These are two of the classification schemes required by Principle 10 of *NCGA1*. Expenditures for each of the functions (for example, public safety) could be further divided into those applicable to specific departments or other organization units (such as police department and fire department). Expenditures in each of the organization units could also be presented in terms of the object of expenditure classification (personal services, supplies, and other services and charges). Exhibit 19–1 illustrated just some of the possibilities of expenditure classification.

Recording the Budget   On July 1, 19X1, the approved budget of Blair is recorded. The following general journal entry is made to record the budget in the accounts of the GF.

opening entry →

GF		
Estimated revenues	$400,000	
Appropriations		$395,000
Fund balance		5,000

To record the budget for the year July 1, 19X1 to June 30, 19X2.

The entry records total estimated revenues and total appropriations in the general ledger and credits the budgeted excess to the fund balance account. But *detailed subsidiary revenue and expenditure ledgers* are used to record line-item revenue and expense amounts, even if the budget is approved in terms of the broad categories reflected in the budget summary. In the case of legislative approval by category, however, the city manager (or chief executive) would have authority to authorize shifts from one line-item expenditure to another within the broad categories approved. The broad categories are used for budgeting and reporting purposes but not for accounting purposes. In other words, there is no account called Taxes or General Government, but the accounting system is organized to permit aggregation of the detailed items into these categories.

Subsidiary Ledgers   Details of the planned revenues (such as property taxes, sales taxes, and license revenue) are recorded in a *subsidiary revenue ledger,* and appropriation details (such as police supplies, mayor's office expenses, and maintenance of city hall) are recorded in a *subsidiary expenditure ledger*. By recording estimated revenues for individual items as debits in the subsidiary revenue ledger and actual revenue items as credits, the subsidiary account balances during the year will reveal differences between actual and budgeted revenue for each item to date, as well as the final excess or deficiency at year-end. Similarly, by recording actual expenditures as debits and appropriations as credits, the account balances shown in the individual accounts of the subsidiary expenditure ledger represent unexpended appropriations for each expenditure item. These subsidiary ledger techniques provide the means of achieving *formal budgetary control* over the items included in the approved budget.

The NCGA in *GAAFR* included the term control as part of the title of a control account (for example, revenue—control or expenditure—control). Since it is apparent that these accounts are control accounts for specific subsidiary ledger accounts such as property tax revenue or license revenue, the term *control* is not illustrated as part of the account title in this book. The control label may appear in some CPA examination questions to indicate that an account is a control account found in the general ledger.

Reporting the Budget in Financial Statements   Compliance with the approved budget is required for the general fund and for special revenue funds. To demonstrate compliance with the budget, a *statement of revenues, expenditures, and changes in fund balance—budget and actual* must be prepared as one of the required financial statements of governmental funds using formal budgeting procedures. As its title implies, the statement compares budgeted and actual operating results. This statement will be illustrated for the Town of Blair at the end of this section of the chapter.

Transactions for the Year

Accounting for Property Taxes   When the treasurer of Blair sends out property tax bills, revenue is recognized as follows:

GF

Taxes receivable—current	$200,000	
Estimated uncollectible taxes—current		$ 2,000
Revenue		198,000

To record the property tax levy.

This entry assumes that 1 percent of property tax levies will not be collectible. Therefore, revenue is recognized for 99 percent of the amount billed. Uncollectible taxes are not expenses in governmental accounting; instead they are revenue adjustments as illustrated. Like accounts receivable, taxes receivable is a control account for individual amounts owed. The *current* designation for taxes receivable is used to distinguish current taxes receivable from taxes that are past due. Any balances remaining in the "Taxes receivable—current" and "Estimated uncollectible taxes—current" accounts after the due date for payment are reclassified as "Taxes receivable—delinquent" and "Estimated uncollectible taxes receivable—delinquent." Note that the after-closing trial balance for the Town of Blair's general fund at June 30, 19X1, includes a debit account, "Taxes receivable—delinquent" of $15,000, and a credit account, "Estimated uncollectible taxes—delinquent," of $1,000.

Collections of property taxes are recorded in the usual manner for receivables as follows:

GF

Cash	$190,000	
Taxes receivable—current		$176,000
Taxes receivable—delinquent		14,000

To record collection of property taxes.

When a specific property tax bill is determined to be uncollectible, it is written off with the following entry:

GF

Estimated uncollectible taxes—delinquent	$ 1,000	
Taxes receivable—delinquent		$ 1,000

To record write-off of uncollectible account.

Charges for Services   Revenue is recognized when bills for garbage collection are sent out, and the entry is recorded:

GF

Accounts receivable	$ 60,000	
Revenue		$ 60,000

To record charges for garbage collection.

When customers pay their garbage bills that were recorded as revenue in the previous entry, the payment is entered as follows:

GF

Cash	$ 58,000	
Accounts receivable		$ 58,000

To record collection of receivables for garbage collection service.

Revenue from Other Sources   As previously mentioned, revenue from most other sources is recognized as cash is received. Thus, the collection of fees from business licenses is recorded:

GF

Cash	$ 20,000	
Revenue		$ 20,000

To record collection of business license fees.

Other revenues for the 19X1–19X2 fiscal year are recognized as cash is received. The amount in the followmg entry includes all revenue items not listed individually:

GF

Cash	$124,000	
Revenue		$124,000

To summarize other revenue items for the year.

Although the general ledger ordinarily includes only one revenue account, it is important to remember that the detailed revenue sources have to be recorded individually in a *subsidiary revenue ledger*.

Recording Expenditures   When the payroll for salaries is vouchered for payment, a GF entry is made as follows:

GF

Expenditures	$ 20,000	
Vouchers payable		$ 20,000

To record accrual of salaries.

Accounting for Encumbrances   During the year snow removal equipment that is expected to cost $15,000 is ordered. The following encumbrance entry is made at the time the purchase order is placed to recognize a commitment to pay for the equipment when it is received:

GF

Encumbrances	$ 15,000	
Reserve for encumbrances		$ 15,000

To record a purchase order for snow removal equipment estimated to cost $15,000.

This information helps prevent overspending because encumbrances can be deducted from unexpended appropriations to determine unencumbered appropriations (that is, maximum additional authorizations):

Appropriations (authorized expenditures)	$ _____
Less: Expenditures to date	_____
Unexpended appropriations	
Less: Encumbrances	_____
Unencumbered appropriations	$ _____

The remaining expenditure authority is reflected by the amount of unencumbered appropriations. When the snow removal equipment is received, the entry recording the encumbrance is reversed:

GF

Reserve for encumbrances	$ 15,000	
Encumbrances		$ 15,000

To reverse the encumbrance entry for snow removal equipment.

The entry to record the receipt of the equipment is unaffected by the encumbrance entries and is recorded for the actual amount of the invoice. Assuming that the actual cost of the equipment on order is $14,000, the expenditure is recorded:

GF

Expenditures	$ 14,000	
Vouchers payable		$ 14,000

To record the purchase of snow removal equipment.

Note that the amount of the encumbrance was an estimate of the actual cost, which was $1,000 less than the estimate. Like formal budgetary accounting, encumbrance accounting does not affect the recording of actual transactions and events.

The acquisition of fixed assets (such as the snow removal equipment) decreases net assets because fixed assets are not recorded as assets in the GF. Instead, they are recorded in a general fixed assets account group as explained further in Chapter 20.

In July 19X1 Blair received the equipment that had been ordered in the previous fiscal year and for which an encumbrance of $9,000 had been recorded. Recall that one of the first entries of the current year was to reclassify the reserve for encumbrances as reserve for encumbrances—prior year to show the authorization for items related to and chargeable against the prior year's appropriations. If the actual invoice is $8,500, the entry to record receipt of the equipment is:

GF

Expenditures—prior year	$ 8,500	
Vouchers payable		$ 8,500

To record receipt of equipment ordered during the prior year and chargeable against the prior year's reserve for encumbrances.

If the actual invoice had been more than the encumbered amount carried over from the prior year, the difference would have been charged to the current year's expenditures.

Supplies   Supply acquisitions are normally accounted for under the *purchase method* and are recorded as expenditures when the related liability is incurred. Under this method, the sequence of acquiring supplies is recorded:

GF

Encumbrances	$ 6,000	
Reserve for encumbrances		$ 6,000

To record the purchase order for operating supplies.

GF

Reserve for encumbrances	$ 6,000	
Encumbrances		$ 6,000

To reverse the encumbrance entry upon receipt of the supplies.

GF

Expenditures	$ 6,000	
Vouchers payable		$ 6,000

To record receipt of operating supplies.

Under the purchase method, this entry decreases the net assets of the general fund because supply purchases are recorded as expenditures rather than assets. (Accounting for supplies on hand requires a year-end adjusting entry that is explained shortly.)

When an additional $5,000 supplies are ordered, the entry is:

GF

Encumbrances	$ 5,000	
Reserve for encumbrances		$ 5,000

To record encumbrances for a purchase order for supplies.

These supplies have not been received at year-end June 30, 19X2.

A *consumption method* for the purchase of supplies is also acceptable if appropriations are made for supplies used rather than for supply purchases. The consumption basis is really accrual accounting for supplies. Supply purchases are recorded in the inventory account and supply usage is reported as a supply expenditure. Under this scheme, supplies on hand are appropriable assets, and a reserve for supplies should not be recorded.

Other Transactions for the Year   The note payable that was outstanding at June 30, 19X1 becomes due and is vouchered for payment:

GF

Note payable	$ 15,000	
Vouchers payable		$ 15,000

A summary entry to account for the rest of the various expenditures throughout the year is as follows:

GF

Expenditures	$348,040	
Vouchers payable		$348,040

Summary entry for accrual of salaries, purchase of supplies and fixed assets, etc.

GF

Vouchers payable	$403,000	
Cash		$403,000

To record payment of all vouchers for the year in summary form.

Year-end Procedures

Adjusting Entries   Recall that the entry to purchase supplies (purchase method) decreased net assets of the general fund because supply purchases are recorded as expenditures rather than assets. If supplies that cost $9,000 are on hand at the balance sheet date, however, the $6,000 beginning-of-the-period supplies on hand account would be adjusted by $3,000 at year-end, in other words, to a final balance of $9,000.

GF

Supplies inventory	$ 3,000	
Reserve for supplies inventory		$ 3,000

To adjust the supplies inventory and related reserve for supplies accounts.

This entry gives accounting recognition to a prepaid asset. Supplies-on-hand inventory is reported as an asset, while the reserve for supplies is intended to inform the users of the balance sheet that resources equal to the amount of the reserve are on hand, but that they are not available for appropriation, since they are tied up in resources that are not subject to appropriation. (Supplies on hand are not an appropriable resource because supply usage under the purchase method does not increase expenditures or reduce net assets.)

Assume that uncollected taxes on June 30, 19X2 are past due. Accordingly, the $24,000 taxes receivable—current and $2,000 estimated uncollectible taxes—current should be reclasslfied as delinquent. The entry for this reclassification is:

Taxes receivable—delinquent	$ 24,000	
Estimated uncollectible taxes—current	2,000	
Taxes receivable—current		$ 24,000
Estimated uncollectible taxes—delinquent		2,000

To reclassify past due taxes receivable as delinquent.

Blair's adjusted general fund trial balance at June 30, 19X2 includes the following accounts and balances:

Debits

Cash	$ 20,000
Taxes receivable—delinquent	24,000
Accounts receivable	5,000
Supplies inventory	9,000
Estimated revenues	400,000
Expenditures	381,500
Expenditures—prior year	8,500
Encumbrances	5,000
Total debits	$853,000

Credits

Estimated uncollectible taxes—delinquent	$ 2,000
Vouchers payable	16,000
Reserve for supplies	9,000
Reserve for encumbrances—prior year	9,000
Reserve for encumbrances	5,000
Fund balance	15,000
Appropriations	395,000
Revenues	402,000
Total credits	$853,000

Closing Entries   By year-end, the budgetary accounts will have served their purpose and they should be closed. The most direct method of closing budgetary accounts is to reverse the original entry to record the budget. At June 30, 19X2 the accounts for Blair could be closed as follows:

close →

GF		
Appropriations	$395,000	
Fund balance	5,000	
Estimated revenues		$400,000
To close the budgetary accounts.		

The advantage of this closing approach is that it emphasizes the fact that formal budgetary accounting does not affect actual revenues, expenditures, or any balance sheet account. When this entry is made to close the appropriations and estimated revenue accounts, the fund balance account is returned to its $10,000 beginning-of-the-year balance.

Actual revenues and expenditures are closed directly to the fund balance account. Under the assumption that committed appropriations can be carried over to the succeeding fiscal period to serve as authorization for items on order, any outstanding encumbrances at year-end would also be closed to the fund balance account. The adjusted trial balance shows that Blair had revenue of $402,000, expenditures of $381,500 for the current year, and encumbrances outstanding at June 30, 19X2 of $5,000. The entry to close these accounts is:

→

GF		
Revenues	$402,000	
Expenditures		$381,500
Encumbrances		5,000
Fund balance		15,500
To close revenue, expenditures, and encumbrances accounts.		

This entry relates to current year budgeted revenues and appropriations. Actual revenues exceeded expenditures by $20,500, of which $5,000 is committed for supplies ordered but not yet received. The $5,000 reserve for encumbrances account (that is, the credit related to the $5,000 closed out) is not closed at year-end, but rather is reflected in the fund equity section of the balance sheet. The uncommitted and unappropriated surplus is credited to fund balance. It is important to understand the difference between fund equity and fund balance. *Fund equity* is equal to the assets less liabilities of a fund. It consists of the balance of the fund balance account plus reserve accounts for encumbrances, supplies, and so on. Fund equity is frequently referred to as fund balance, but such designation is potentially confusing because fund balance is also used to indicate the balance of the fund balance account.

The $8,500 expenditure from the prior year's appropriations is charged against the prior year's reserve for encumbrances account.

GF

Reserve for encumbrances—prior year	$ 9,000	
Expenditures—prior year		$ 8,500
Fund balance		500

To close prior year reserve for encumbrances and related expenditures and credit the fund balance for the excess.

Financial Statements

The required general purpose financial statements for a general fund consist of a balance sheet, a statement of revenues and expenditures, a statement of changes in fund balance, and a statement comparing actual and budgeted amounts for revenues and expenditures. Ordinarily the statement of revenues and expenditures and the statement of changes in fund balance are combined into a single statement, as shown in Exhibit 19–2.

In examining the statement of revenues, expenditures, and changes in fund balance in Exhibit 19–2, note that the revenue and expenditure classifications

---

TOWN OF BLAIR GENERAL FUND
STATEMENT OF REVENUES, EXPENDITURES, AND
CHANGES IN FUND BALANCE
FOR THE FISCAL YEAR ENDED JUNE 30, 19X2

Revenues	
Taxes	$255,000
Licenses and permits	18,000
Intergovernmental revenue	40,000
Charges for services	62,000
Fines and forfeits	12,000
Rents and royalties	11,000
Miscellaneous revenue	4,000
Total revenues	402,000
Expenditures	
Current services:	
General government	$ 41,500
Public safety	136,000
Highway and streets	86,300
Sanitation	54,700
Health and welfare	19,500
Recreation	29,500
Capital outlays	22,500
Total expenditures	390,000
Excess of revenues over expenditures	12,000
Add: Decrease in reserve for encumbrances	4,000
Add: Unappropriated fund balance June 30, 19X1	10,000
Unappropriated fund balance June 30, 19X2	$ 26,000

Exhibit 19–2 *General Fund Statement of Operations*

TOWN OF BLAIR GENERAL FUND
BALANCE SHEET
AT JUNE 30, 19X2

Assets

Cash	$20,000	
Taxes receivable—delinquent (net of $2,000 estimated uncollectible taxes)	22,000	
Accounts receivable	5,000	
Supplies inventory	9,000	
Total assets		$56,000

Liabilities and Fund Equity

Vouchers payable		$16,000
Fund equity:		
Reserve for supplies	$ 9,000	
Reserve for encumbrances	5,000	
Fund balance (unappropriated) A–L–R	26,000	
Total fund equity		40,000 A–L
Total liabilities and fund equity		$56,000

Exhibit 19–3   *General Fund Balance Sheet*

are the same as those used in the budget presented earlier. This is required by principle eleven of NCGA *Statement 1,* which states that common terminology and classifications should be used consistently in the budget, the accounts, and the financial reports.

The statement of revenues and expenditures, and the statement of changes in fund balance, are combined by adding the $10,000 fund balance at the beginning of the year to the $12,000 excess of revenues over expenditures and adding the $4,000 decrease in reserve for encumbrances to get a $26,000 fund balance at June 30, 19X2. An excess of revenues over expenditures for a period increases the fund balance, and an excess of expenditures over revenues decreases the fund balance. Any change in the reserve for encumbrances also has to be considered in arriving at the ending fund balance. An increase in the reserve for encumbrances decreases the balance of the fund balance account, and a decrease increases it. The $3,000 increase in the reserve for inventories does not affect the fund balance account (unappropriated fund equity), but it does affect fund equity because an asset is recorded without a corresponding increase in liabilities.

As shown in the balance sheet for the Town of Blair in Exhibit 19–3, the **fund equity** of a governmental fund consists of the assets less the liabilities of the fund. The **fund balance,** however, consists of the assets less the liabilities and reserves of the fund. The difference between the fund equity and the fund balance concepts is important because only the amount represented by the fund balance is unrestricted and available for appropriation. Of the total $40,000 fund equity, $5,000 is committed to supplies on order and $9,000 is represented by supplies on hand. Conceptually, the remaining $26,000, as represented by the amount of the fund balance, is available for new authorizations and could be used to cover a budget deficit for the next period. In other words, appropriations could exceed estimated revenue by $26,000 during the next fiscal period, with the deficiency being covered by resources on hand.

Although not required for external reporting purposes, the following reconciliation of changes in fund equity is helpful in understanding the relationships between the fund balance account, reserve accounts, and fund equity. It can also be used as a problem-solving technique.

	Reserve for Encumbrances	Reserve for Supplies	Fund Balance	Fund Equity
Balance June 30, 19X1	$9,000	$6,000	$10,000	$25,000
Excess revenues over expenditures			12,000	12,000
Decrease in reserve for encumbrances	(4,000)		4,000	—
Increase in reserve for supplies		3,000		3,000
Balance June 30, 19X2	$5,000	$9,000	$26,000	$40,000

Required financial statements for general and special revenue funds include a statement that compares budgeted and actual amounts of revenues, expenditures, and changes in fund balance. The statement for the Town of Blair is presented in Exhibit 19–4. When the budget is prepared on a basis consistent with GAAP, the "Actual" column shows the same amounts as the statement of revenues, ex-

---

TOWN OF BLAIR GENERAL FUND
STATEMENT OF REVENUES, EXPENDITURES, AND
CHANGES IN FUND BALANCE
BUDGET AND ACTUAL
FOR THE YEAR ENDED JUNE 30, 19X2

	Budget	Actual (Budgetary Basis)	Variance Favorable (Unfavorable)
Revenues			
Taxes	$250,000	$255,000	$ 5,000
Licenses and permits	20,000	18,000	(2,000)
Intergovernmental revenue	40,000	40,000	—
Charges for services	60,000	62,000	2,000
Fines and forfeits	15,000	12,000	(3,000)
Rents and royalties	10,000	11,000	1,000
Miscellaneous revenue	5,000	4,000	(1,000)
Total revenues	400,000	402,000	2,000
Expenditures			
Current services:			
General government	$ 45,000	$ 44,500	$ 500
Public safety	140,000	138,000	2,000
Highways and streets	90,000	86,300	3,700
Sanitation	55,000	54,700	300
Health and welfare	20,000	19,500	500
Recreation	30,000	29,500	500
Capital outlays	15,000	14,000	1,000
Total expenditures	395,000	386,500*	8,500
Excess of revenue over expenditures	5,000	15,500	10,500
Add: Fund balance June 30, 19X1	10,000	10,000	—
Add: Excess prior year's encumbrance over actual expenditure		500	500
Unappropriated fund balance at June 30, 19X2	$ 15,000	$ 26,000	$11,000

* Actual expenditures on a budgetary basis includes the $5,000 supplies purchase commitment chargeable against the 19X2 appropriations, but excludes the $8,500 expenditure chargeable against the prior year's carryover appropriation.

Exhibit 19–4   *General Fund Comparison of Budget and Actual*

penditures, and changes in fund balances. The "Actual" column in Exhibit 19–4 differs from the data reflected in Exhibit 19–2 because the legally prescribed budgetary basis is assumed to include encumbered items. Thus, the budgetary comparison in Exhibit 19–4 includes actual data on the budgetary basis.

SUMMARY

Accounting principles for nonprofit organizations are not as well defined as for business enterprises. Even so, accounting principles for state and local governmental units have been developed through the efforts of the Government Finance Officers Association and its committees, and, more recently, the Governmental Accounting Standards Board. The *GASB Codification of Governmental Accounting and Financial Reporting* provides GAAP for the financial statements of state and local governmental units. Twelve basic accounting principles from *NCGA1* and included in the *GASB Codification* establish the objectives and underlying support for accounting and reporting practices of state and local governments.

Accounting requirements for general funds are the same as for special revenue funds, and the discussion of accounting procedures for the general fund applies equally to special revenue funds. The essential difference between a general fund and a special revenue fund lies in the fact that general fund revenues are available to finance the general needs of government, whereas the revenues of special revenue funds are restricted to specific uses. Only general fund and special revenue funds are always required to use formal budgetary accounting practices and to prepare statements comparing actual and budgeted revenues and expenditures. The basic accounting cycle for a general fund from recording the budget at the beginning of the year to the preparation of financial statements at year-end is illustrated.

SELECTED READINGS

Audits of State and Local Governmental Units, rev. ed. Audit and Accounting Guide. New York: American Institute of Certified Public Accountants, 1986.

BERRY, LEONARD EUGENE, and GORDON B. WARWOOD. *Governmental and Nonprofit Accounting: A Book of Readings.* Homewood, IL: Richard D. Irwin, 1984.

CARPENTER, VIVIAN L., and EHSAN H. FEROZ. "The Decision to Adopt GAAP: A Case Study of the Commonwealth of Kentucky." *Accounting Horizons* (June 1990), pp. 67–78.

Committee on Governmental Accounting of the New York State Society of CPAs. "Budgeting and Accounting in the Governmental Sector." *The CPA Journal* (November 1981), pp. 20–26.

DREBIN, ALLAN R., JAMES L. CHAN, and LORNA C. FERGUSON. *Objectives of Accounting and Financial Reporting for Governmental Accounting Units: A Research Study,* 9 volumes. Chicago: National Council on Governmental Accounting, 1981.

FALK, DAVID L., and MICHAEL H. GRANOF. "Internal Service Funds Are Beyond Salvation." *Accounting Horizons* (June 1990), pp. 58–66.

FREEMAN, ROBERT J., and CRAIG DOUGLAS SHOULDERS. "Defining the Governmental Reporting Entity." *Journal of Accountancy* (October 1982), pp. 50–63.

Governmental Accounting Standards Board. *Statement No. 1, Authoritative Status of NCGA Pronouncements and AICPA Industry Audit Guide.* Stamford, CT: Governmental Accounting Standards Board, 1984.

Governmental Accounting Standards Board. *Statement No. 6, Accounting and Financial Reporting for Special Assessments.* Stamford, CT: Governmental Accounting Standards Board, 1987.

Governmental Accounting Standards Board. *Statement No. 7, Advance Refundings Resulting in Defeasance of Debt.* Stamford, CT: Governmental Accounting Standards Board, 1987.

HOLDER, WILLIAM. *A Study of Selected Concepts for Governmental Financial Accounting and Reporting.* Chicago: National Council on Governmental Accounting, 1980.

HOLDER, WILLIAM. "Expenditure and Liability Recognition in Government." *Journal of Accountancy* (September 1983), pp. 79–84.

KIRK, DONALD J. "Commentary: Jurisdictional Conflicts and Conceptual Differences in Standard Setting: FASB and GASB." *Accounting Horizons* (December 1989), pp. 107–113.

MAUTZ, ROBERT K. "Monuments, Mistakes and Opportunities." *Accounting Horizons* (June 1988), pp. 123–128.

MILLER JOHN R., and PETER D. JACOBSON. "GASB After the Five-Year Structure Review." *Journal of Accountancy* (April 1990), pp. 85–91.

Municipal Finance Officers Association of the United States and Canada. *Governmental Accounting, Auditing, and Financial Reporting.* Chicago: Municipal Finance Officers Association of the United States and Canada, 1980.

National Council on Governmental Accounting. *Governmental Accounting and Financial Reporting Principles, Statement 1.* Chicago: Municipal Finance Officers Association of the United States and Canada, 1979.

National Council on Governmental Accounting. *Grant, Entitlement, and Shared Revenue Accounting and Reporting by State and Local Governments, Statement 2.* Chicago: Municipal Finance Officers Association of the United States and Canada, 1979.

O'DONOGHUE, C. KEVIN, and PATRICK F. HARDIMAN. "Governmental Accounting: Who's in Charge?" *The CPA Journal* (May 1989), pp. 28–35.

PALLOT, JUNE. "The Nature of Public Assets: A Response to Mautz." *Accounting Horizons* (June 1990), pp. 79–85.

PATTON, JAMES M. "An Experimental Investigation of Some Effects of Consolidating Municipal Financial Reports." *The Accounting Review* (April 1978) pp. 402–414.

Statement of Financial Accounting Concepts No. 4. "Ojectives of Financial Reporting by Nonbusiness Organizations." Stamford, CT: Financial Accounting Standards Board, 1980.

ASSIGNMENT MATERIAL

QUESTIONS

1 What organization provides GAAP for state and local governmental units? Explain.
2 Describe the concept of a fund as used in connection with governmental accounting. How many funds might be used by a single governmental unit? How many fund types?
3 Distinguish between governmental funds, proprietary funds, and fiduciary funds. Which funds are classified as governmental funds?
4 Why aren't fixed assets recorded in the accounts of a general fund? Explain.
5 What is the modified accrual basis and to which fund types is it applicable?
6 Are interfund transfers expenditures? Expenses? Explain.
7 What is an appropriation? How can budgetary approval be arranged to give the legislative body maximum control over the budget? How can it be arranged to give the executive maximum flexibility?
8 Distinguish between the line-item, program, performance, and zero-base approaches to budgeting.
9 What is included in the revenue source designated "intergovernmental revenues"?
10 Interpret the following general fund entry:

Estimated revenues	$100,000	
Fund balance	20,000	
Appropriations		$120,000

11 If revenue needed from property taxes to balance the budget is $115,640 and a 2 percent loss on uncollectible taxes is expected, at what amount should taxpayers be billed?
12 Assume that supplies on hand at the beginning of the year amount to $6,000, that supply purchases during the year are $40,000, that supplies on hand at year-end are $4,000, and that the purchase basis of accounting for supplies is used. What adjusting entry for supplies should be made at year-end?

13 What are encumbrances and how do encumbrance accounting practices help control expenditures?

14 Explain the concepts "fund equity" and "fund balance." How does the recording of supplies under the purchase method affect fund equity? The fund balance?

15 Why is a decrease in the reserve for encumbrances added to the excess of revenues over expenditures and other financing sources (uses) in determining the fund balance at year-end?

EXERCISES

E 19-1 **1** Which one of the following categories is included in the revenue and expenditure or expense classifications of a governmental unit?
    a Quasi-external transactions
    b Reimbursements
    c Operating transfers
    d Residual equity transfers

2 Budgeted expenditures should not exceed budgeted revenues unless:
    a Expected revenues are greater than expected expenditures
    b Fund assets are greater than fund liabilities
    c The fund balance account is greater than the budgeted deficit
    d The budgeted surplus is greater than the fund balance deficit

3 A capital budget, as used in governmental accounting, is:
    a The same as a capital program
    b Usually included as part of the current budget
    c A plan of capital expenditures to be incurred each year over a fixed period of years
    d A multiyear plan for capital expenditures

4 A debit balance in a subsidiary ledger revenue account on an interim date would indicate:
    a Negative revenue
    b An excess of actual over estimated revenue
    c An expected revenue deficiency in the current year
    d Budgeted revenues over actual revenues to date

5 *Payment* of notes payable by the general fund would not be recorded as an expenditure of the general fund if:
    a The notes were short term
    b The notes were long term
    c The notes were recorded as a general fund liability
    d The liability was created for services for another fund

6 A program budget emphasizes:
    a Unit costs   **b** Activity units
    c Total program costs   **d** Expenditure control

7 Performance budgeting:
    a Emphasizes efficiency evaluation and measurable performance of work programs
    b Is primarily a planning model
    c Is the same as program budgeting
    d Is organized on the basis of functions

E 19-2 **1** Maximum executive flexibility in administering an approved budget results when:
    a An appropriation is made for total expenditures
    b A program budgeting approach is used
    c The budget follows the line-item approach
    d The expenditure budget is approved on a departmental basis

2 A personal property tax levy is ordinarily:
    a Greater than budgeted revenue from property taxes
    b Equal to expected property tax receipts
    c Greater than personal property assessments
    d Equal to valuations of taxable personal property

3 When the *purchase basis* of accounting for supplies is used, the financial statements of the related fund entity:
    a Need not show material amounts of supplies on hand as an asset
    b Must disclose the cost of supplies used during the period
    c Should reflect the actual cost of supplies purchased in expenditures for the period
    d Need not disclose a fund balance restriction for material amounts of supplies on hand

4 When the *consumption basis* of accounting for supplies is used, the financial statements of the related fund entity:
  a Must show supply purchases as expenditures of the period
  b Must show a fund balance restriction for material amounts of supplies on hand
  c Must reflect the fact that perpetual inventory procedures have been used in accounting for supplies
  d Must show material amounts of supplies on hand as an asset

5 Depreciation should be recorded:
  a In the general fund   **b** On fund fixed assets
  c In governmental funds   **d** In capital projects funds

6 A general fund balance sheet that includes *estimated revenue less actual revenue* among its assets and resources:
  a Is most likely an interim statement
  b Is improperly prepared
  c Should also show *encumbrances less expenses* among liabilities and obligations
  d Is typical for governmental year-end statements

E 19–3 **[AICPA adapted]**

1 Authority granted by a legislative body to make expenditures and to incur obligations during a fiscal year is the definition of an:
  a Appropriation   **b** Allocation
  c Encumbrance   **d** Expenditure

2 Fixed assets donated to a governmental unit should be recorded:
  a As a memorandum entry only
  b At the donor's carrying amount
  c At estimated fair value when received
  d At the lower of donor's carrying amount or estimated fair value when received

3 For state and local governmental units, generally accepted accounting principles require that encumbrances outstanding at year-end be reported as:
  a Expenditures   **b** Reservations of fund balance
  c Deferred liabilities   **d** Current liabilities

4 The budgetary fund balance reserved for encumbrances account of a governmental fund type is increased when:
  a A purchase order is approved
  b Supplies previously ordered are received
  c Appropriations are recorded
  d The budget is recorded

5 Under the modified accrual basis of accounting for a governmental unit, revenues should be recognized in the accounting period in which they:
  a Are earned and become measurable
  b Are collected
  c Become available and measurable
  d Become available and earned

6 The estimated revenues control account balance of a governmental fund type is eliminated when:
  a The budgetary accounts are closed
  b The budget is recorded
  c Property taxes are recorded
  d Appropriations are closed

7 When a truck is received by a governmental unit, the truck should be recorded in the general fund as a debit to:
  a An appropriations control   **b** An encumbrances control
  c A fixed asset   **d** An expenditures control

E 19–4 **1** Public works, education, and recreation and culture are examples of expenditure classifications according to:
  a Function   **b** Character class
  c Activity   **d** Object-of-expenditure

2 The current expenditures of a municipal accounting department, if classified by function, would be found under the heading:
  a Public services   **b** General government
  c Public works   **d** Information systems

3 Street cleaning is an example of expenditure classification according to:

   a Activity   **b** Function

   c Character   **d** Organization unit

4 Repairs expenditures for maintenance of the town hall according to function would be classified under:

   a General fund   **b** General government

   c Current expenditures   **d** Other services and supplies

5 The category *public safety* in a municipal financial report would be used in classifying expenditures by:

   a Character class   **b** Organization unit

   c Object of expenditure   **d** Function

6 Expenditure classification by function would include the category:

   a Supplies   **b** Culture and recreation

   c Finance department   **d** Building inspection

E 19-5

1 Reserve accounts (reserve for encumbrances and reserve for supplies, for example) in a general fund balance sheet indicate:

   a Liabilities of the fund

   b That appropriations lapse

   c Liabilities of the fund that have not reached the payment stage

   d Fund assets on hand but not available for appropriation

2 When encumbrance accounting is used and payments are made for goods and services previously received and recorded, a debit entry is made to:

   a Encumbrances   **b** Accounts or vouchers payable

   c Goods and services   **d** Reserve for encumbrances

3 When a complete system of encumbrance accounting is used (in other words, all commitments are encumbered), the authorizations remaining available for expenditures at any interim date will be equal to:

   a Appropriations less encumbrances

   b Appropriations less expenditures

   c Appropriations plus encumbrances less expenditures

   d Appropriations less expenditures and encumbrances

4 A $15,000 reserve for encumbrances for a new police car appeared in the general fund balance sheet at year-end 19X1. This car was received in 19X2 and the actual cost was $15,000. This expenditure should be:

   a Charged against the reserve for encumbrances

   b Recorded as an expense in the operating statement for 19X1

   c Recorded as an expenditure in the operating statement for 19X2

   d Recorded as a general fund asset net of depreciation at year-end 19X2

5 A purchase order is encumbered in the amount of $4,500, but the actual expenditure is $4,750. The entry to record the expenditure includes:

   a A debit to reserve for encumbrances for $4,750

   b A debit to fund balance for $250

   c A credit to vouchers payable for $4,750

   d A credit to appropriations of $4,500

E 19-6 **|AICPA adapted|**

1 Of the items listed, those most likely to have parallel accounting procedures, account titles, and financial statements are:

   a Special revenue funds and trust funds

   b Internal service funds and debt service funds

   c The general fixed assets account group and the general long-term debt account group

   d The general fund and special revenue funds

2 What is the underlying reason for a governmental unit's using separate funds to account for its transactions?

   a Governmental units are so large that it would be unduly cumbersome to account for all transactions as a single unit.

   b Because of the diverse nature of the services offered and legal provisions regarding activities of a governmental unit, it is necessary to segregate activities by functional nature.

    c Generally accepted accounting principles require that not-for-profit entities report on a funds basis.

    d Many activities carried on by governmental units are short-lived, and their inclusion in a general set of accounts could cause undue probability of error and omission.

3 The *reserve for encumbrances—past year* account represents amounts recorded by a governmental unit for:

    a Anticipated expenditures in the next year

    b Expenditures for which purchase orders were made in the prior year but disbursement will be in the current year

    c Excess expenditures in the prior year that will be offset against the current-year budgeted amounts

    d Unanticipated expenditures of the prior year that become evident in the current year

4 Which of the following should be accrued as revenues by the general fund of a local government?

    a Sales taxes held by the state which will be remitted to the local government

    b Parking meter revenues

    c Sales taxes collected by merchants

    d Income taxes currently due

5 Harbor City's appropriations control account at December 31, 19X8 had a balance of $7,000,000. When the budgetary accounts were closed at year-end, this $7,000,000 appropriations control balance should have:

    a Been debited   **b** Been credited

    c Remained open   **d** Appeared as a contra account

6 Oro County's expenditures control account at December 31, 19X9 had a balance of $9,000,000. When Oro's books were closed, this $9,000,000 expenditures control balance should have:

    a Been debited   **b** Been credited

    c Remained open   **d** Appeared as a contra account

7 Fixed assets of an enterprise fund should be accounted for in the:

    a Enterprise fund but no depreciation on the fixed assets should be recorded

    b Enterprise fund and depreciation on the fixed assets should be recorded

    c General fixed asset account group but no depreciation on the fixed assets should be recorded

    d General fixed asset account group and depreciation on the fixed assets should be recorded

E 19-7   **|AICPA adapted|**

1 The following information pertains to Pine City's general fund for 19X9:

Appropriations	$6,500,000
Expenditures	5,000,000
Other financing sources	1,500,000
Other financing uses	2,000,000
Revenues	8,000,000

After Pine's general fund accounts were closed at the end of 19X9, the fund balance increased by:

    a $3,000,000   **b** $2,500,000

    c $1,500,000   **d** $1,000,000

2 At December 31, 19X9, Alto Township's committed appropriations that had not been expended in 19X9 totaled $10,000. These appropriations do not lapse at year-end. Alto reports on a calendar-year basis. On its December 31, 19X9 balance sheet, the $10,000 should be reported as:

    a Vouchers payable—prior year

    b Deferred expenditures

    c Fund balance reserved for encumbrances

    d Budgetary fund balance—reserved for encumbrances

3 When Rolan County adopted its budget for the year ending June 30, 19X8, $20,000,000 was recorded for estimated revenues control. Actual revenues for the year ended June 30, 19X8 amounted to $17,000,000. In closing the budgetary accounts at June 30, 19X8:

a Revenues control should be debited for $3,000,000
b Estimated revenues control should be debited for $3,000,000
c Revenues control should be credited for $20,000,000
d Estimated revenues control should be credited for $20,000,000

4 The following information pertains to Cobb City:

19X3 governmental fund revenues that became measurable and available in time to be used for payment of 19X3 liabilities	$16,000,000
Revenues earned in 19X1 and 19X2 and included in the $16,000,000 indicated	2,000,000
Sales taxes collected by merchants in 19X3 but not required to be remitted to Cobb until January 19X4	3,000,000

For the year ended December 31, 19X3, Cobb should recognize revenues of:

a $14,000,000   b $16,000,000
c $17,000,000   d $19,000,000

5 What would be the effect on the general fund balance in the current fiscal year of recording a $15,000 purchase for a new fire truck out of general fund resources, for which a $14,600 encumbrance had been recorded in the general fund in the previous fiscal year?

a Reduce the general fund balance $15,000
b Reduce the general fund balance $14,600
c Reduce the general fund balance $400
d Have no effect on the general fund balance

E 19-8

1 Intergovernmental revenue does not include:

a Shared taxes   b Interfund transfers
c Entitlements   d Payments in lieu of taxes

2 The six major source classifications of revenue recommended by the NCGA and included in the GASB's *Codification of Governmental Accounting and Financial Reporting Standards* are:

a Financial statement headings or classifications
b General ledger account titles
c Subsidiary ledger account titles
d Groupings that apply only to the statement of changes in fund balance

3 Many sources of governmental revenue are not accrued because they cannot be measured in advance. The following revenue classification is an exception to this observation:

a Licenses and permits   b Fines and forfeits
c Income taxes   d Property taxes

4 Newport Township determined that it needed $83,160 revenue from property taxes in order to balance its budget for 19X1. Total assessed valuation of taxable property in the township is $2,000,000 and a 1 percent loss on uncollectible taxes is expected. The 19X1 property tax rate for Newport should be:

a 4.117 percent   b 4.158 percent
c 4.198 percent   d 4.200 percent

5 Estimated uncollectible taxes are:

a Reported in the *reserve* section of a general fund balance sheet
b Credited when expenditures are debited for uncollectible taxes
c Recorded when property tax revenue is accrued
d Direct charges against the fund balance account

E 19-9 The following entry appeared in the general fund:

Taxes receivable—current	$100,000	
Revenues		$98,000
Estimated uncollectible taxes—current		2,000

1 The subsidiary revenue account involved would most likely be:

a Income taxes   b Property taxes
c Sales taxes   d Licenses and permits

2 The total tax levy must have been:

a $96,000   **b** $98,000

c $100,000   **d** $102,000

3 The recording of the receivable at gross and the revenue at net indicates:

a A budgetary appropriation for uncollectible tax expense of $2,000

b That responsibility for uncollectible taxes is a managerial function

c That the credit practices of commercial and governmental organizations are similar

d That uncollectible taxes are not included in budgetary appropriations

E 19–10   **|AICPA adapted|**

The following related entries were recorded in sequence in the general fund of a municipality:

Encumbrances	$12,000	
Reserve for encumbrances		$12,000
Reserve for encumbrances	$12,000	
Encumbrances		$12,000
Expenditures	$12,350	
Vouchers payable		$12,350

1 The sequence of the entries indicates that:

a An adverse event was foreseen and a reserve of $12,000 was created; later the reserve was canceled and a liability for the item was acknowledged.

b An order was placed for goods or services estimated to cost $12,000; the actual cost was $12,350 for which a liability was acknowledged upon receipt.

c Encumbrances were anticipated but later failed to materialize and were reversed. A liability of $12,350 was incurred.

d The first entry was erroneous and was reversed; a liability of $12,350 was acknowledged.

2 Entries similar to those for the general fund may also appear on the books of a municipality's:

a General fixed assets account group

b General long-term debt account group

c Trust fund

d Special revenue fund

3 Assuming appropriate governmental accounting principles were followed, the entries:

a Occurred in the same fiscal period

b Did not occur in the same fiscal period

c Could have occurred in the same fiscal period, but it is impossible to be sure of this

d Reflect the equivalent of a "prior-period adjustment" had the entity concerned been one operated for profit

4 Immediately after the first entry was recorded, the municipality had a balanced general fund budget for all transactions. What would be the effect of recording the last two entries?

a Not change the balanced condition of the budget

b Cause the municipality to show a surplus

c Cause the municipality to show a deficit

d Not affect the current budget but would affect the budget of the following fiscal period

E 19–11   **1** The fund equity reflected in the balance sheet of a general fund is a measurement of the fund's:

a Assets minus liabilities

b Assets minus (liabilities plus reserves)

c (Assets plus expected revenues) minus (liabilities plus appropriations)

d (Assets plus appropriations) minus (liabilities plus encumbrances)

2 The balance of the fund balance account in a preclosing trial balance of a general fund is most likely:

a The planned year-end balance

b The balance at the end of the prior year

c Available for appropriation in subsequent years

d Equal to fund assets less fund liabilities

3 The ledger of the Library Fund (a special revenue fund) at June 30, 19X4, after closing entries, included the following items:

Reserve for encumbrances	$ 4,000
Reserve for uncollectible taxes	6,000
Reserve for advance to enterprise fund	40,000
Reserve for supplies	15,000
Fund balance	35,000

At what amount should the fund equity be reported in the June 30, 19X4 balance sheet of the Library Fund?

   a $50,000   **b** $90,000

   c $94,000   **d** $98,000

4 The following information is from the preclosing trial balance of the town of Snowville on June 30, 19X5:

Fund balance	$ 12,000
Estimated revenues	116,000
Appropriations	120,000
Revenues	118,000
Expenditures	110,000
Encumbrances	9,000

During the fiscal year ended June 30, 19X5, an expenditure of $700 was charged directly to the prior year's reserve for encumbrances account and the excess of the prior year's reserve for encumbrances ($800) over the expenditure ($700) was closed to fund balance.

     The balance of the fund balance account on June 30, 19X4, after closing entries were made, must have been:

   a $7,900   **b** $8,000

   c $15,900   **d** $16,100

5 During the year ended June 30, 19X4, $80,000 cash was transferred from the general fund to other funds of the city of Huntsville. The $80,000 consists of:

- $18,000 to the Electric Utility Fund of which $16,000 was for current year services and $2,000 was for services received in the year ended June 30, 19X3
- $50,000 to the Central Purchasing Fund to provide initial capital for the fund
- $12,000 to the City Hall Capital Projects Fund to repay a temporary loan

In the statement of revenues, expenditures, and transfers of the general fund for the year ended June 30, 19X4, interfund transfers to other funds should be shown in the amount of:

   a $50,000   **b** $62,000

   c $68,000   **d** $78,000

E 19–12 Relate the terms given in the following two lists. Each letter should be used once and once only.

a Appropriations	**1** A control-centered budgeting approach
b Encumbrances	
c Payments in lieu of taxes	**2** A fiscal and accounting entity
d Grants-in-aid	**3** A budgetary account
e Program or performance, for example	**4** A type of intergovernmental revenue
f Fund	**5** A measurement of resources available for appropriation
g Line-item budget	
h Fund balance account balance	**6** Authorizations to spend
i Estimated revenues	**7** Roughly equivalent to levying taxes against governmental units
	8 Commitments
	9 Budgeting concepts

E 19-13 Classify each of the following general fund items by function according to the functional classifications illustrated on page 780. Classifications can be used more than once.
1. Repairs to garbage truck
2. City manager's salary
3. Fire truck
4. Park equipment
5. Highway work crew expenses
6. Classroom supplies
7. Police supplies
8. Welfare payments
9. Repairs to town hall
10. Teachers' salaries

E 19-14 Classify each of the following general fund items according to major revenue sources. Classifications can be used more than once.
1. City's share of gasoline taxes (collected by state)
2. 10 percent utility tax
3. Vehicle tax
4. State grant for police
5. Collections from traffic court
6. Garbage service fees
7. Parking meter collections
8. Proceeds from sale of city property
9. Building permits
10. Sales taxes—local options

E 19-15 Determine the property tax levy per $100 of assessed valuation from the following information:

Revenue needed for a balanced budget—$2,300,000

Total assessed value of taxable property—$13,000,000

Estimated revenue from nonproperty tax sources—$1,633,000

Anticipated percentage collection of property tax levies—98 percent

E 19-16 The Town of Blacksburg has purchase orders totaling $6,000 for supplies outstanding at June 30, 19X7, the close of its fiscal year.

What entries would be needed in the 19X7–19X8 fiscal year if the supplies are received on July 18, 19X7 at a cost of $5,800 and committed appropriations can be carried over to the next period?

E 19-17 A general ledger trial balance for Galax City contained the following balances at June 30, 19X7, just before closing entries were made:

Due from other funds	$ 600
Fund balance	3,000
Estimated revenues	18,000
Revenues	17,380
Appropriations	17,500
Expenditures—current year	16,450
Expenditures—prior year	1,900
Encumbrances	1,000
Reserve for encumbrances	1,000
Reserve for encumbrances—prior year	2,000

Required: Prepare closing entries.

E 19-18 The preclosing trial balance of the general fund of Pulaski County on June 30, 19X5 included the following:

Fund balance (unappropriated)	$ 250,000
Reserve for encumbrances	86,000
Expenditures	1,065,500
Appropriations	1,150,000
Estimated revenues	1,200,000
Encumbrances	80,000
Revenues	1,170,000

Expenditures include $5,500 chargeable to the prior year's reserve for encumbrances account. Encumbered appropriations of $6,000 were carried over from the prior year. Pulaski does not maintain separate reserve for encumbrances and expenditures accounts for current and prior years.

Required: Determine the unappropriated fund balance that will appear in the June 30, 19X5 balance sheet.

E 19–19   The city manager of Mason City has prepared a tentative expenditure budget of $960,000 for the coming fiscal year. Financing the planned expenditures is expected to come from (1) a $490,000 property tax levy; (2) shared revenues of $200,000; (3) a budget deficit of $40,000; and the remainder from (4) licenses and permits, fines and forfeits, and charges for services. A 2 percent loss on uncollectible property taxes is expected.

Required
  1 According to the city manager's plan, what is the total budgeted revenue amount?
  2 Calculate the expected revenue from property taxes.
  3 Calculate the expected revenue from licenses and permits, fines and forfeits, and charges for services.

E 19–20   The following accounts, among others, appeared in the ledger of the General Fund of the City of North Platte at June 30, 19X5:

Reserve for encumbrances—prior year	$ 1,000
Reserve for encumbrances—current year	20,000
Estimated revenues	2,000,000
Appropriations	1,980,000
Encumbrances	20,000
Revenues	1,990,000
Expenditures—current year	1,730,000
Expenditures—prior year	1,000
Transfers from other funds	10,000
Transfers to other funds	220,000
Fund balance	50,000

Required
  1 Prepare closing entries as of June 30, 19X5.
  2 Calculate the change in fund equity for the year.

E 19–21   A general ledger trial balance at June 30, 19X3 for Fortune City is as follows:

	Debits	Credits
Cash	$ 10,000	$ —
Taxes receivable	30,000	—
Allowance for uncollectible taxes	—	2,000
Due from other funds	3,000	—
Supplies inventory, June 30, 19X3	4,000	—
Estimated revenues	300,000	—
Expenditures	290,000	—
Expenditures—prior year	5,000	—
Encumbrances	6,000	—
Vouchers payable	—	15,000
Due to other funds	—	5,000
Reserve for encumbrances	—	6,000
Reserve for encumbrances—prior year	—	5,000
Fund balance	—	10,000
Appropriations	—	300,000
Revenue	—	305,000
	$648,000	$648,000

Fortune City uses a purchase basis in accounting for supplies.

Required: Prepare a general fund balance sheet as of June 30, 19X3.

E 19–22 The trial balance of the general fund of Idaho City before closing at December 31, 19X2 contained the following accounts and balances:

Fund balance	$ 25,000
Estimated revenues	100,000
Appropriations	95,000
Encumbrances	4,000
Reserve for encumbrances	4,000
Reserve for encumbrances—prior year	5,000
Revenues	101,000
Expenditures	94,000
Expenditures—prior year	4,800

Required

1 Prepare a statement of revenues, expenditures, and changes in the fund balance account for Idaho City's general fund in 19X2. (Details of revenue and expenditure accounts are omitted to simplify the requirement.)

2 Prepare a statement of revenues, expenditures, and changes in fund equity for Idaho City's general fund for 19X2. (Details of revenue and expenditure accounts are omitted to simplify the requirement.)

PROBLEMS

P 19–1 Prepare a statement of changes in unappropriated fund balance for Ekon City's General Fund for the fiscal year ended June 30, 19X7, from the following accounts and additional information:

Appropriations	$600,000
Estimated revenues	605,000
Encumbrances	20,000
Expenditures—current year	575,000
Expenditures—prior year	24,000
Revenues	615,000
Reserve for encumbrances	20,000
Reserve for encumbrances—prior year	25,000

The fund balance shown in the June 30, 19X7 trial balance is $65,000. Changes in the fund balance during the current year include an expenditure refund from 19X5 of $5,000, a charge for an increase in the "reserve for petty cash" account of $2,000, and the entry on July 1, 19X6 to record the budget.

(*Hint:* The fund is required to maintain a minimum cash balance level, and therefore amounts equal to petty cash are not available for appropriation. A reserve for petty cash is similar to a reserve for supplies and is treated the same in the financial statements.)

P 19–2 The preclosing trial balance for the General Fund of the Town of Valentine at June 30, 19X3 is as follows:

	Debits	Credits
Cash	$ 2,000	$ —
Taxes receivable	3,500	—
Allowances for uncollected taxes	—	500
Sundry accounts receivable	3,000	—
Vouchers payable	—	4,700
Fund balance	—	2,000
Reserve for encumbrances	—	2,000
Estimated revenues	52,000	—
Appropriations	—	50,000
Encumbrances	2,000	—
Expenditures	47,700	—
Revenues	—	51,000
	$110,200	$110,200

Required
1 Prepare closing entries.
2 Prepare a statement of changes in unappropriated fund balance.
3 Prepare a balance sheet.

P 19–3 Prepare entries in the general fund to record the following transactions and events:
1 Estimated revenues for the fiscal year were $250,000 and appropriations were $248,000.
2 The tax levy for the fiscal year, of which 99 percent is believed to be collectible, was $200,000.
3 Taxes collected were $150,000.
4 A loan of $15,000 was made to the special revenue fund.
5 Orders for supplies were placed in the amount of $18,000.
6 The items ordered in 5 were received. Actual cost was $18,150 and vouchers for that amount were prepared.
7 Materials were acquired from the Stores Fund (an internal service fund) in the amount of $800 (without encumbrance).
8 A $5,000 payment (transfer) was made to the debt service fund.
9 A cash payment of $15,000 was made for the purchase of equipment.
10 Licenses were collected in the amount of $3,000.
11 Taxes receivable in the amount of $900 became delinquent. It was estimated that one-third of this amount will not be collected.

P 19–4 The unadjusted trial balance of the General Fund of Alpine City at December 31, 19X2 was as follows:

	Debits	Credits
Cash	$ 32,500	$ —
Taxes receivable—delinquent	23,000	—
Allowance for uncollectible taxes—delinquent	—	3,500
Accounts receivable	18,500	—
Allowance for bad debts	—	1,500
Estimated revenues	150,000	—
Vouchers payable	—	30,000
Appropriations	—	170,000
Reserve for encumbrances	—	21,000
Fund balance	—	7,000
Revenues	—	153,000
Expenditures	147,000	—
Encumbrances	15,000	—
	$386,000	$386,000

Adjustment Information at December 31, 19X2
1 Salaries of $2,000 are owed to employees.
2 Supplies of $1,500 are on hand.
3 Of the $21,000 balance shown in the reserve for encumbrances account, $6,000 relates to carryover appropriations from 19X1. The $6,000 item applies to supplies that were purchased for $5,900 during 19X2.

Required
1 Adjusting entries
2 Closing entries
3 A statement of changes in unappropriated fund balance
4 A balance sheet

P 19-5 The after-closing trial balance of the city of Kearney's General Fund at June 30, 19X1 was as follows:

	Debits	Credits
Cash	$16,000	$ —
Taxes receivable	14,000	—
Due from utility fund	1,000	—
Supplies on hand	4,000	—
Accounts payable	—	2,000
Note payable	—	10,000
Reserve for supplies	—	4,000
Reserve for encumbrances	—	3,000
Fund balance	—	16,000
	$35,000	$35,000

During the fiscal year July 1, 19X1 to June 30, 19X2, the following transactions and events occurred:

1 The budget was recorded with estimated revenues of $85,000 and appropriations of $90,000
2 Cash collections for the year consisted of $84,000 from taxes and $6,000 from the utility fund for engineering services provided by General Fund employees.
3 Cash payments were as follows:

Wages and salaries	$24,000
Equipment	26,000
Supplies	16,000
Miscellaneous expenses	6,000
Note payable and interest	10,500

4 At June 30, 19X2 Kearney had $10,000 taxes receivable, a $2,000 receivable from the utility fund, and supplies on hand of $3,500. Accounts payable for supplies purchased were $4,000 at June 30, 19X2, and the balance of the reserve for encumbrances account was $2,000.

Required
1 Journal entries to summarize all the foregoing general fund transactions and events for the fiscal year ended June 30, 19X2.
2 Financial statements at and for the year ended June 30, 19X2.

P 19-6 The unadjusted account balances of the general fund of Whitestone City at fiscal year-end June 30, 19X8 are as follows:

	Debits
Cash	$ 265,000
Taxes receivable	170,000
Supplies on hand	30,000
Due from internal service fund	35,000
Estimated revenue	1,000,000
Current expenditures	905,000
Prior year expenditures	15,000
Operating transfer to capital projects fund	20,000
Encumbrances	60,000
	$2,500,000

	Credits	
Estimated uncollectible taxes	$	40,000
Vouchers payable		50,000
Due to capital projects fund		10,000
Notes payable		100,000
Reserve for encumbrances		60,000
Reserve for encumbrances—prior year		16,000
Reserve for supplies		30,000
Fund balance		194,000
Revenues		1,010,000
Appropriations		990,000
		$2,500,000

Information for Adjustments
1 Taxes receivable of $20,000 have been certified as uncollectible.
2 An inventory at June 30, 19X8 shows $40,000 supplies on hand.

Required
1 Prepare adjusting and closing entries on June 30, 19X8.
2 Prepare a statement of changes in unappropriated fund balance for the year ended June 30, 19X8.
3 Prepare a balance sheet at June 30, 19X8.

P 19-7 [AICPA adapted]

The comptroller of the City of Helmaville recently resigned. In his absence, the deputy comptroller attempted to calculate the amount of money required to be raised from property taxes for the General Fund for the fiscal year ending June 30, 19X7. The calculation is to be made as to January 1, 19X6, to serve as a basis for setting the property tax rate for the following fiscal year. The mayor has requested you to review the deputy comptroller's calculations and obtain other necessary information to prepare a formal statement for the General Fund which will disclose the amount of money required to be raised from property taxes for the fiscal year ending June 30, 19X7. Following are the calculations prepared by the deputy comptroller:

City resources other than proposed tax levy:		
Estimated General Fund working balance, January 1, 19X6	$	352,000
Estimated receipts from property taxes (January 1, 19X6–June 30, 19X6)		2,222,000
Estimated revenue from investments (January 1, 19X6–June 30, 19X7)		442,000
Estimated proceeds from sale of general obligation bonds in August 19X6		3,000,000
		$6,016,000
General Fund requirements:		
Estimated expenditures (January 1, 19X6–June 30, 19X6)		$1,900,000
Proposed appropriations (July 1, 19X6–June 30, 19X7)		4,300,000
		$6,200,000

Additional Information
1 The General Fund working balance required by the city council for July 1, 19X7 is $175,000.
2 Property tax collections are due in March and September of each year. Your review indicates that during the month of February 19X6 estimated expenditures will exceed available funds by $200,000. Pending collection of property taxes in March

19X6, this deficiency will have to be met by the issuance of thirty-day tax-anticipation notes of $200,000 at an estimated interest rate of 9 percent per annum.

3 The proposed general obligation bonds will be issued by the City Water Fund and will be used for the construction of a new water pumping station.

Required: Prepare a statement as of January 1, 19X6, calculating the property tax levy required for the City of Helmaville General Fund for the fiscal year ending June 30, 19X7.

P 19-8 **[AICPA adapted]**

The following summary of transactions was taken from the accounts of the Annaville School District General Fund *before* the books had been closed for the fiscal year ended June 30, 19X5:

	Postclosing Balances	Preclosing Balances
	June 30, 19X4	June 30, 19X5
Cash	$400,000	$ 700,000
Taxes receivable	150,000	170,000
Estimated uncollectible taxes	(40,000)	(70,000)
Estimated revenues	—	3,000,000
Expenditures	—	2,842,000
Expenditures—prior years	—	—
Encumbrances	—	91,000
	$510,000	$6,733,000
Vouchers payable	$ 80,000	$ 408,000
Due to other funds	210,000	142,000
Reserve for encumbrances	60,000	91,000
Fund balance	160,000	182,000
Revenues from taxes	—	2,800,000
Miscellaneous revenues	—	130,000
Appropriations	—	2,980,000
	$510,000	$6,733,000

Additional Information

1 The estimated taxes receivable for the year ended June 30, 19X5 were $2,870,000, and taxes collected during the year totaled $2,810,000.

2 An analysis of the transactions in the vouchers payable account for the year ended June 30, 19X5 follows:

	Debit (Credit)
Current expenditures	$(2,700,000)
Expenditures for prior years	(58,000)
Vouchers for payment to other funds	(210,000)
Cash payments during the year	2,640,000
Net change	$ (328,000)

During the year the General Fund was billed $142,000 for services performed on its behalf by other city funds.

On May 2, 19X5 commitment documents were issued for the purchase of new textbooks at a cost of $91,000.

Required: Based upon the data presented, reconstruct the *original detailed journal entries* that were required to record all transactions for the fiscal year ended June 30, 19X5, including the recording of the current year's budget. Do *not* prepare closing entries at June 30, 19X5.

The following information was abstracted from the accounts of the General Fund of the City of Rom after the books had been closed for the fiscal year ended June 30, 19X8:

	Postclosing Trial Balance June 30, 19X7	Transactions July 1, 19X7 to June 30, 19X8		Postclosing Trial Balance June 30, 19X8
		Debit	Credit	
Cash	$700,000	$1,820,000	$1,852,000	$668,000
Taxes receivable	40,000	1,870,000	1,828,000	82,000
	$740,000			$750,000
Allowances for uncollectible taxes	$ 8,000	8,000	10,000	$ 10,000
Vouchers payable	132,000	1,852,000	1,840,000	120,000
Fund balance:				
Reserve for encumbrances	—	1,000,000	1,070,000	70,000
Unreserved	600,000	140,000	60,000⎫ 30,000⎭	550,000
	$740,000			$750,000

Additional Information: The budget for the fiscal year ended June 30, 19X8 provided for estimated revenues of $2,000,000 and appropriations of $1,940,000.

Required: Prepare journal entries to record the budgeted and actual transactions for the fiscal year ended June 30, 19X8.

CHAPTER

20

ACCOUNTING FOR STATE AND LOCAL GOVERNMENTAL UNITS—PART II

The preceding chapter reviewed accounting standards for state and local governmental units and explained procedures relevant to accounting for the general fund and special revenue funds. These two governmental funds are the only funds of state and local governmental units that are *required* to use formal budgetary accounting practices. Other governmental funds integrate their budgets into their accounting systems only when an annual budget is legally adopted or when it is considered necessary for control purposes.

This chapter covers accounting procedures for those types of funds that do not ordinarily use formal budgetary accounting. The chapter includes those governmental funds not covered in the preceding chapter (capital projects funds and debt service funds), accounting procedures for the general fixed assets and the general long-term debt account groups, and accounting procedures applicable to proprietary-type funds (internal service funds and enterprise funds) and fiduciary-type funds (agency funds and trust funds).

While individual financial statements are illustrated in the sections that cover different funds and account groups, the actual statements that are essential for fair presentation in accordance with GAAP are combined statements presented in a columnar format with separate columns for the individual fund types and account groups. Thus, a final section of the chapter explains the process of combining the financial statements of similar funds into combined financial statements for each fund type, and the development of combined financial statements for all fund types and account groups for external reporting purposes.

CAPITAL PROJECTS FUNDS

The acquisition of minor general fixed assets from expenditures of annual appropriations are accounted for in the general fund or special revenue funds. But general fixed assets that cannot be financed through appropriations of these funds are accounted for in capital projects funds. The purpose of **capital projects funds (CPF)** is to account for resources segregated for the acquisition of major capital facilities other than those financed by trust and proprietary funds. Typical sources of financing include the proceeds of bond issues, grants and shared

812

revenues, transfers from other funds, and contributions from property owners. *GASB Statement No. 6* explains that when capital improvements are financed by special assessment debt, the proceeds from the special assessment debt should be described as contributions from property owners rather than bond proceeds.[1]

Capital projects funds are governmental funds that use modified accrual accounting and revenue and expenditure accounts. Ordinarily, a separate CPF is created to account for each major capital project. A CPF is created when it is legally authorized, and it exists for the life of the project. Formal budgetary accounting is not used unless numerous capital projects are financed through the same fund or facilities are being constructed with the governmental unit as the primary contractor.

The CPF may acquire fixed assets by purchase, construction, or capital lease agreements. Encumbrance accounting procedures are used to account for commitments made to contractors and for material and supply orders.

The next section illustrates the accounting and reporting for a CPF during a two-year construction project.

Accounting for a Capital Projects Fund

The City of Budding authorizes the construction of a new city hall on January 1, 19X1 in the amount of $1,000,000. Financing for the project is to be $500,000 from a 6½ percent serial bond issue, $400,000 from a federal grant, and $100,000 from the general fund (GF). Transactions and events during the life of the project are summarized as follows:

19X1

1 The city transfers $100,000 from the GF to the City Hall Capital Projects Fund (a CPF created for the construction).
2 Planning and architect's fees are paid in the amount of $40,000.
3 The contract is awarded to the lowest bidder for $950,000.
4 The bonds are sold for $502,000 (at a premium of $2,000).
5 The amount of the premium is transferred to the debt service fund.
6 The construction is certified to be 50 percent complete and a bill for $475,000 is received from the contractor.
7 Contracts payable, less a 10 percent retained percentage, is paid.
8 The books are closed and financial statements are prepared.

19X2

9 The amount due from the federal grant is received.
10 Construction is completed and the contractor is paid.
11 Closing entries are recorded.
12 Remaining cash is transferred to the GF.

Creation of the CPF   When the City Hall CPF is created, a memorandum entry is made in the CPF noting the $1,000,000 authorization.

CPF

Memorandum—City Hall Project authorization	$1,000,000

Interfund Transfer (1)   Interfund transfers of resources do not represent revenues and expenditures of the funds involved. The $100,000 transferred from the GF to the CPF is an *operating transfer* for the purpose of starting the CPF, and it requires an entry in both funds. The GF entry to record the transfer is:

GF

Transfer to City Hall CPF	$100,000	
Cash		$100,000
To record transfer to City Hall CPF.		

---

[1]Governmental Accounting Standards Board, *Statement 6, Accounting and Financial Reporting for Special Assessments* (GASB, 1987), paragraph 19.

The corresponding entry in the CPF to receive the $100,000 is:

CPF

Cash	$100,000	
Transfer from general fund		$100,000

To record receipt of funds from the GF.

Recording Expenditures (2)   Payments for planning and architect's fees are recorded:

CPF

Expenditures	$ 40,000	
Cash		$ 40,000

To record payments of planning and architect's fees.

Recording Encumbrances (3)   When the contract is awarded to a contractor, an encumbrance entry is made for the full amount of the contract:

CPF

Encumbrances	$950,000	
Reserve for encumbrances		$950,000

To record encumbrances for the amount of the contract.

Accounting for the Bond Proceeds (4 and 5)   Proceeds of bond issues are recognized in the CPF at the time the bonds are sold. The proceeds are recorded as *bond issue proceeds* or similar title, but not as revenue. Bonds to finance 50 percent of the cost of the City Hall project are sold at a premium. Although the full amount of the proceeds is recorded in the CPF, the premium is not available to finance the project because the premium is really an adjustment of the bond interest rate. Thus, the premium is transferred to the debt service fund through which the bond liability will be serviced. (The corresponding entry for the debt service fund is illustrated in the next section of this chapter.) Journal entries for the sale of bonds and transfer of the premium are:

CPF

Cash	$502,000	
Proceeds from bond issue		$502,000
To record sale of bonds.		
Transfer to debt service fund	$ 2,000	
Cash		$ 2,000

To transfer the premium to the City Hall Debt Service Fund.

If the bonds had been sold at a discount, the amount received would have been recorded as proceeds under the usual assumption that the sale of bonds at a discount reduces project authorization. Thus, even though a discount represents an adjustment of the interest rate in the same sense as does a premium, the two situations are usually treated differently. The practical reason for this is that the debt service fund will not have resources to cover the discount immediately. In addition it is not known at the time of bond sale if the additional resources equal to the amount of discount will be needed to complete the project.

Progress Payments and Retained Percentages (6 and 7)   A construction contract often provides that a portion of the contractor's remuneration be withheld until completion of the construction project and final inspection. Accounting entries for the amount owed on partial completion of the contract and the first progress payment on the contract are recorded:

CPF

Reserve for encumbrances	$475,000	
Encumbrances		$475,000

To reverse half of the amount encumbered.

Expenditures	$475,000	
Contracts payable		$427,500
Contracts payable—retained percentage		47,500

To record expenditure and a 10% retained percentage on the City Hall construction.

Contracts payable	$427,500	
Cash		$427,500

To record partial payment to the contractor.

Adjusting and Closing Entries (8)

At the end of the fiscal year, the CPF books are closed and financial statements are prepared. The City Hall construction project has not been completed and the statements for the CPF are interim statements.

Intergovernmental Revenue   The grant from the federal government is intergovernmental revenue. Under modified accrual accounting, revenue is recognized when it becomes "susceptible to accrual," which means measurable and available to finance expenditures of the fiscal period.[2] "Available" means collectible within the current period or soon enough thereafter to be used to pay liabilities of the current period.[3] The NCGA cautioned that "application of the 'susceptibility to accrual' criteria requires judgment, consideration of the materiality of the item in question, and due regard for the practicality of accrual, as well as consistency in application."[4]

Since the amount of the federal grant to the city hall project has not been received at the time the books are closed, it may be accrued provided that the commitment is firm. Failure to recognize revenue from the grant could make the CPF appear to be in financial difficulty for interim reporting purposes when, in fact, it has progressed as planned.

CPF (Adjusting Entry)

Due from federal grant	$400,000	
Revenue		$400,000

To accrue revenue from the federal grant.

Closing Entry—19X1   A closing entry for the CPF is recorded as follows:

CPF (Closing Entry)

Revenue	$400,000	
Transfer from general fund	100,000	
Proceeds from bond issue	502,000	
Expenditures		$515,000
Transfer to debt service fund		2,000
Encumbrances		475,000
Fund balance		10,000

To close the books at the end of 19X1.

---

[2]GASB Cod. Sec. G60.109.
[3]GASB Cod. Sec. 1600.106.
[4]Ibid.

Unissued Bonds at an Interim Statement Date   The bonds to finance the City Hall capital project have been issued by December 31, 19X1, but in some cases there will be authorized but unissued bonds at the interim reporting date. Unlike the federal grant, however, the existence of the unissued bonds would be disclosed only in a statement note. The reason is that the authorization of the bonds does not assure that they can be sold.

Required Financial Statements for the CPF

Required financial statements for capital projects funds include a statement of revenues and expenditures, a statement of changes in fund balance, and a balance sheet. The statement of revenues and expenditures and the statement of changes in fund balance can be combined as shown in Exhibit 20–1. As required by GAAP, the capital projects fund revenue from the federal grant is separated from transfers that are not revenue for the governmental entity as a whole. In the comprehensive statement of revenues, expenditures, and changes in fund balances, transfers

---

CITY OF BUDDING
CITY HALL CAPITAL PROJECTS FUND
STATEMENT OF REVENUES AND EXPENDITURES AND CHANGES
IN FUND BALANCE FOR THE YEAR ENDED DECEMBER 31, 19X1

Project authorization		$1,000,000
Revenues		
Revenue from federal grant		$ 400,000
Expenditures		515,000
Excess of expenditures over revenue		115,000
Other financing sources (uses)		
Bond proceeds	$502,000	
Operating transfer from general fund	100,000	
Operating transfer to debt service fund	(2,000)	600,000
Excess of revenue and other financing sources over expenditures and other uses		485,000
Less: Increase in encumbrances		475,000
Fund balance December 31, 19X1		$ 10,000

CITY OF BUDDING
CITY HALL CAPITAL PROJECTS FUND
BALANCE SHEET AT DECEMBER 31, 19X1

Assets		
Cash		$ 132,500
Due from federal grant		400,000
Total assets		$ 532,500
Liabilities		
Contracts payable—retained percentage		$ 47,500
Fund Equity		
Reserve for encumbrances	$475,000	
Fund balance	10,000	
Total fund equity		485,000
Total liabilities and fund equity		$ 532,500

Exhibit 20–1   *Financial Statements for Capital Projects Fund*

into a fund and proceeds from bond issues are separated from total revenues and reported as *other financing sources.* Similarly, transfers out of a fund are separated from total expenditures and are reported under the caption *other financing uses.*

Although the illustrations provided by the *GASB Codification* show other financing sources (uses) below the excess of revenues over expenditures (as shown in Exhibit 20–1), many municipal reports combine revenues and other financing sources to show the line-item *total sources of financial resources.* Similarly, expenditures and other financial uses are combined to show *total uses of financial resources.*

Entries for 19X2

Reinstatement of Encumbrances   At the start of year 19X2, the $475,000 encumbrance that was closed to the fund balance at the end of the year 19X1 is reinstated in the accounts as follows:

CPF

Encumbrances	$475,000	
Fund balance		$475,000

To reinstate the encumbrances previously closed to the fund balance.

Receipt of Grant (9)   When the federal grant is received, it is recorded:

CPF

Cash	$400,000	
Due from federal grant		$400,000

To record receipt of the federal grant.

Completion of the Project (10)   The journal entries to record completion of construction and payment to the contractor are as follows:

CPF

Reserve for encumbrances	$475,000	
Encumbrances		$475,000

To remove encumbrances when construction is complete.

Expenditures	$475,000	
Contracts payable		$475,000

To record expenditures on city hall construction.

Contracts payable	$475,000	
Contracts payable—retained percentage	47,500	
Cash		$522,500

To record final payment to contractor.

Closing Entries (11)   An entry is made to close expenditures to the fund balance:

CPF

Fund balance	$475,000	
Expenditures		$475,000

To close the expenditures to fund balance.

Residual Equity Transfer (12)   The transfer of the remaining fund balance to the general fund in final termination of the City Hall CPF is recorded as follows:

CPF

Residual equity transfer to GF	$ 10,000	
Cash		$ 10,000

To record transfer of cash to the general fund.

Fund balance	$ 10,000	
Residual equity transfer to GF		$ 10,000
To close City Hall CPF ledger.		

A corresponding entry is required in the general fund to receive the cash transferred. That entry is:

GF

Cash	$ 10,000	
Residual equity transfer from CPF		$ 10,000
To record receipt of cash from City Hall CPF.		

The $10,000 transfer to the general fund is a residual equity transfer. Residual equity transfers are presented separately as increases or decreases in the fund balance in the statement of revenues and expenditures and changes in fund balance.

Required Financial Statement (19X2)   Since the City Hall CPF was terminated in 19X2, it has no balance sheet items to report at the end of 19X2, and the only statement required is a statement of revenues and expenditures and changes in fund balance as follows:

CITY OF BUDDING
CITY HALL CAPITAL PROJECTS FUND
STATEMENT OF REVENUES AND EXPENDITURES AND CHANGES
IN FUND BALANCE FOR THE YEAR ENDED DECEMBER 31,19X2

Project authorization	$1,000,000
Revenues	None
Expenditures	$ (475,000)
Total expenditures over revenues	(475,000)
Add: Fund equity December 31, 19X1	485,000
	10,000
Less: Residual equity transfer to GF	(10,000)
Fund equity December 31, 19X2	$ 0

For *internal reporting purposes*, the statement of revenues and expenditures and changes in fund balance should be prepared to cover the entire term of the project from January 1, 19X1 through December 31, 19X2.

DEBT SERVICE FUNDS

Debt service funds (DSF) are governmental funds that are used to account for the receipt of resources from designated sources (such as taxes or transfers from the general fund) and to account for the use of these resources to make principal and interest payments on general long-term debt obligations. Ordinarily, a separate DSF is created to account for each general long-term debt issue. Although debt service funds make interest and principal payments on general long-term debt, the liability for general long-term debt is recorded in the general long-term debt (GLTD) account group and *not* in the DSF. Thus, the records of debt service funds and general long-term debt account groups have to be coordinated. As long-term debt is retired through expenditures in the DSF, the liability for the debt is reduced in the GLTD account group.

Revenues and expenditures of debt service funds are accounted for on the modified accrual basis. The GASB Codification (1600.121) contains an exception for interest on general long-term debt. Under modified accrual accounting, expenditures are ordinarily recognized in the accounting period in which related liabilities are incurred. But unmatured interest on general obligation long-term debt is recognized when due, rather than when the liability is incurred, unless resources have been provided to cover payments due within one year, in which case the expenditure may be accrued in the current period. This exception is made to avoid showing an expenditure and a liability for debt service in one period, and the transfer of resources from the general fund or other sources to pay the liability in the following period.

The operations of debt service funds for serial bond issues are much different than for term bond issues. In the case of a serial bond issue, where bonds are retired at regular intervals, resources are received as needed to service the debt and no significant balances are carried over from one period to the next. However, the operations of debt service funds for term bond issues have the objective of accumulating resources to retire all of the debt at maturity, as well as of making periodic interest payments. Thus, debt service funds for term bond issues involve sinking fund operations as well as operations for current debt service, and they are much more complex than for serial bond issues. Formal budgetary accounting is ordinarily needed for term bond issues but not for serial bond issues. Only serial bond debt service fund operations are illustrated in this chapter.

Accounting for the Debt Service Fund

Assume the $500,000, 6 ½ percent serial bond issue of the City of Budding that was issued for $502,000 on July 1, 19X1 has interest payment dates of January 1 and July 1 of each year. Principal amounts of $50,000 are due each year starting on July 1, 19X2, and cash for all debt service is to be provided by transfers from the general fund. Under these assumptions, the required journal entries for the City Hall Debt Service Fund for 19X1 and 19X2 are as follows:

DSF July 1, 19X1

Cash	$ 2,000	
Transfer from City Hall CPF		$ 2,000

To record receipt of issue premium from City Hall CPF.

DSF December 19X1

Cash	$14,250	
Transfer from general fund		$14,250

To record receipt of the January 1, 19X2 interest payment from the general fund, less the $2,000 already accumulated. ($500,000 × 6½% × ½ year) − $2,000 = $14,250.

DSF December 31, 19X1

Expenditures	$16,250	
Interest payable		$16,250

To record interest due on 6½% serial bond issue.

DSF January 1, 19X2

Interest payable	$16,250	
Cash		$16,250

To record payment of interest on bonds for first six months.

DSF June 19X2

Cash	$66,250	
Transfer from general fund		$66,250

To record receipt of $16,250 for interest payment plus $50,000 for the first serial payment due July 1, 19X2.

DSF July 1, 19X2

Expenditures	$66,250	
Cash		$66,250

To record payment of principal and interest on the serial bond issue.

DSF December 19X2

Cash	$14,625	
Transfer from general fund		$14,625

To record receipt of cash from GF for the January 1, 19X3 interest payment ($450,000 × 6½% × ½ year).

DSF December 31, 19X2

Expenditures	$14,625	
Interest payable		$14,625

To record interest due on 6½% serial bond issue.

Financial Statements for DSF

The financial reporting requirements for a debt service fund include the same statements as those required for other governmental funds. Comparative statements for the debt service fund of the City of Budding are shown in Exhibit 20–2. Since the general fund transfers are equal to the amounts necessary to cover debt service as payments come due, the debt service fund does not have

---

CITY OF BUDDING
CITY HALL DEBT SERVICE FUND
STATEMENT OF REVENUES AND EXPENDITURES
FOR THE YEARS ENDED DECEMBER 31, 19X2 and 19X1

	19X2	*19X1*
Transfers		
Transfer from City Hall Capital Projects Fund		$ 2,000
Transfers from General Fund	$80,875	14,250
Total transfers	80,875	16,250
Expenditures		
Interest payments	$30,875	$16,250
Principal payment	50,000	
Total expenditures	80,875	16,250
Excess of transfers over expenditures	0	0

CITY OF BUDDING
CITY HALL DEBT SERVICE FUND
BALANCE SHEET
AT DECEMBER 31, 19X2 AND 19X1

	19X2	*19X1*
Assets		
Cash	$14,625	$16,250
Total assets	$14,625	$16,250
Liabilities and Fund Balance:		
Interest payable	$14,625	$16,250
Fund balance	0	0
Total liabilities and fund balance	$14,625	$16,250

Exhibit 20–2   *Statements of the Debt Service Fund*

a fund balance at any statement date. Thus, a statement of changes in fund balance is not required.

Operating Transfers   The entries in December 19X1, June 19X2, and December 19X2 to record receipt of cash from the general fund are considered operating transfers that are made in connection with the normal operations of government. Operating transfers are not revenues or expenditures of either fund involved in the transaction. Instead, operating transfers are reported as "other financing sources (uses)." In this case, the $14,250 December 19X1 operating transfer for the payment of interest, the $66,250 operating transfer in June 19X2 for interest and the first serial payment, and the $14,625 operating transfer in December 19X2 for interest, are treated as other financing sources in the DSF and other financing uses in the GF.

Note that interest payable is accrued on December 31, 19X1 and 19X2 for interest payments due on January 1, 19X2 and 19X3. The interest is recorded because the amounts payable are due on January 1, and resources have been provided by transfers from the GF to cover the interest payments. Interest would *not* have been accrued at December 31 if the general fund transfers had been made on January 1 to pay interest on January 1.

SPECIAL ASSESSMENT ACTIVITIES

Public improvements deemed to benefit a limited group of property owners are frequently financed through special taxes levied against the property owners deemed to benefit from the improvements. These special tax levies are known as special assessment levies, or just **special assessments.** The more common types of special assessment projects include street paving, the construction of sidewalks, and the installation of sewer lines. Ordinarily, a special assessment project originates when property owners in an area petition the governmental unit to construct the improvements desired. If the project is authorized, the governmental unit obtains the financing, makes the improvement, and levies special assessments on the property owners for some or all of the cost incurred. The special assessments levied may be paid immediately, in which case the governmental unit is repaid for the resources it uses in constructing the improvement, and the special assessment project is terminated. In many cases, however, special assessment bonds are issued to pay the construction costs, and the special assessments are collected in installments over the term of the special assessment bond issue. Interest charged on the unpaid balances of special assessment receivables is used to cover the interest on the special assessment bonds. No serious problem of financing the special assessment project arises if special assessments are not paid as they come due. This is because the governmental unit has power to enforce collection through seizure of the real property against which special assessments are levied.

Traditionally, special assessment funds were used to account for the construction activities, financing, debt service, and any long-term debt relating to special assessment projects. A number of problems, both practical and conceptual, arose in connection with accounting for this "hybrid" fund. The GASB's solution to these problems was to eliminate special assessment funds entirely and transfer the functions to other funds or account groups. Thus, capital improvements related to special assessment projects are now accounted for in capital projects funds. Debt service on special assessment debt for which the government *is obligated in some manner* is accounted for in a debt service fund, and the related special assessment obligation is accounted for in the general long-term debt account group. Alternatively, the debt service on special assessment debt for which the governmental unit *is not obligated in any manner* is accounted for in an agency fund, and the related special assessment obligation is only disclosed in notes to the financial statements. These changes in accounting for special assessment activities are prescribed by *GASB Statement 6* that became effective in 1987.

ACCOUNT GROUPS

An account group has a self-balancing set of accounts and equal debits and credits, but account groups are not funds because they are not fiscal entities and they do not have transactions. Fixed assets that are assets of the general government and unmatured long-term liabilities that are liabilities of the general government are accounted for in account groups. Thus, a governmental unit needs two account groups—the general fixed assets account group and the general long-term debt account group.

GENERAL FIXED ASSETS ACCOUNT GROUP

General fixed assets of a governmental unit include all fixed assets other than those accounted for in proprietary funds (enterprise or internal service funds) or trust funds. Thus, they include fixed assets purchased by or through a general fund, special revenue fund, or capital projects fund as well as those acquired through donation, capitalized leases, and foreclosures. When fixed assets are acquired through a governmental fund, the purchase transactions are recorded as expenditures in the governmental funds, but the property acquired is recorded in the *general fixed assets (GFA) account group,* except for the purchase of *public domain* or *infrastructure fixed assets.* Public domain or infrastructure fixed assets consist of roads, curbs and gutters, and streets and sidewalks. The reporting of infrastructure fixed assets in the GFA account group is optional [GASB Cod. Sec. 1400.104].

General Fixed Asset Acquisitions

Fixed assets acquired by purchase are recorded at their cost, and those acquired by gift are recorded at their fair values at the time of receipt. (Fixed assets acquired by lease agreements are covered later in this chapter.) Depreciation on general fixed assets is not to be recorded in the accounts of governmental funds, but accumulated depreciation may be recorded (optional) in the GFA account group. Fixed asset classifications include the following:

> Land
> Buildings
> Improvements other than buildings
> Machinery and equipment
> Construction in progress

Entries in the GFA accounts are signaled by transactions in the governmental funds. Thus, expenditure transactions for capital outlays in governmental funds must be coordinated with general fixed asset records. If an entry is made in the general fund to record a $5,000 expenditure for a police car, the following entry is made in the GFA account group:

GFA Account Group

Machinery and equipment	$5,000	
Investment in general fixed assets—general revenue		$5,000

To record acquisition of police car through general revenue sources.

Similarly, if the capital projects fund records a $100,000 expenditure for a building acquired through a federal grant, the following entry in the GFA account group is made:

GFA Account Group

Buildings	$100,000	
Investment in general fixed assets—federal grant		$100,000
To record acquisition of a building through federal grant.		

The credit entry for recording fixed assets in the GFA account group is to the account "investment in general fixed assets" with the source of financing being specified.

Expenditures on incomplete construction projects of capital projects funds are recorded in the GFA account group as incurred rather than when construction is complete. Thus, partial payments on a building contract are recorded as expenditures in the CPF and as construction in progress in the GFA account group. Upon completion of the building, the amounts recorded as construction in progress in the GFA account group are reclassified as buildings.

CITY OF GOWER
STATEMENT OF CHANGES IN GENERAL FIXED ASSETS*
FOR THE FISCAL YEAR ENDED JUNE 30, 19X2

	Balance July 1, 19X1	Additions	Retirements	Balance June 30, 19X2
Assets by Function				
General government	$ 14,000	$ 7,500	$ —	$ 21,500
Public safety	33,000	—	—	33,000
Highways and streets	410,000	81,000	—	491,000
Sanitation	150,000	50,000	25,000	175,000
Health	50,000	—	10,000	40,000
Welfare	12,000	3,000	—	15,000
Culture and recreation	80,000	20,000	5,000	95,000
Education	1,000,000	300,000	75,000	1,225,000
Construction in progress	251,000	251,000	—	502,000
Total assets	$2,000,000	$712,500	$115,000	$2,597,500

*Footnote disclosure is acceptable.

CITY OF GOWER
STATEMENT OF GENERAL FIXED ASSETS [*BASIC STATEMENT*]
ON JUNE 30, 19X2

Assets	
Land	$ 280,000
Buildings	1,120,000
Improvements other than buildings	635,000
Equipment	497,000
Construction in progress	65,500
	$2,597,500
Investments in General Fixed Assets	
General revenues	$ 392,500
General obligation bonds	1,000,000
State shared revenues	250,000
Federal grants	500,000
State grants	300,000
Donations	155,000
	$2,597,500

Exhibit 20–3 *Financial Statements for General Fixed Assets Account Group*

Recording Accumulated Depreciation

Although the recording of accumulated depreciation in the GFA account group is optional, if it is recognized, the entry is recorded in the following format:

GFA Account Group
Investment in general fixed assets—(grants, donations,
  and so on)   XXX
    Accumulated depreciation—(buildings,
      equipment, and so on)   XXX

In this manner, accumulated depreciation is reflected in the accounts, but depreciation expense is never recorded.

Asset Dispositions

When general fixed assets are sold, retired, or abandoned, an entry is made debiting the investment in general fixed assets account and crediting the land, building, or other fixed assets account for its recorded amount (book value if accumulated depreciation is recorded). The entry in the GFA account group is independent of the amount received, if any, for the asset retired. Proceeds from the sale of general fixed assets are usually recorded as miscellaneous revenue in the general fund.

Financial Statements for the GFA Account Group

The financial statements prepared for the GFA account group are a statement of changes in general fixed assets and a statement of general fixed assets (balance sheet). These are illustrated in Exhibit 20–3. The statement of changes in general fixed assets could be expanded to include accumulated depreciation and the book value of general fixed assets where the optional accumulated depreciation is recorded. A statement of general fixed assets is a required basic statement, while the statement of changes in general fixed assets can be reported in statement form or in a financial statement note.

GENERAL LONG-TERM DEBT ACCOUNT GROUP

General long-term debt is defined by the GASB Codification as the *unmatured principal* of bonds, warrants, notes, special assessment debt for which the government is obligated in some manner, or other forms of noncurrent or long-term general obligation indebtedness that is not a specific liability of any proprietary fund or trust fund. Governmental-type funds do not record the obligations for general long-term debt in their accounts because such debt does not require current appropriation. But the obligations for general long-term debt are recorded in the **general long-term debt (GLTD) account group** where the debt is classified as term bonds, serial bonds, and other general long-term liabilities. *The amounts recorded for general long-term debt obligations (credit) are balanced by accounts that show the amounts available and to be provided for payment of the obligations (debits).*

Recording General Long-Term Debt Obligations

When a general obligation serial bond issue is sold, the proceeds received are recorded in a capital projects fund. At the same time, an entry for the bond liability is recorded in the GLTD account group. For example, the issuance of the serial bond issue for construction of the Budding City Hall (see page 814) would be recorded in the GLTD account group as follows:

GLTD Account Group

Amount to be provided for payment of serial bonds	$500,000	
Serial bonds payable		$500,000

As serial bonds are retired through the debt service fund, entries are made in the GLTD account group to reduce the recorded obligation. The July 1, 19X2 entry in the DSF for retirement of $50,000 par of the City Hall bonds (page 820) requires the following entry in the GLTD account group:

GLTD Account Group

Serial bonds payable	$50,000	
Amount to be provided for payment of serial bonds		$50,000

In the case of term bonds where resources are accumulated in the DSF to retire the full amount of the obligation at maturity, the sequence of recording in the GLTD account group is as follows:

1 Assume that $1,000,000 term bonds are issued with the proceeds being recorded in the CPF. The corresponding entry in the GLTD account group is:

GLTD Account Group

Amount to be provided for payment of term bonds	$1,000,000	
Term bonds payable		$1,000,000

2 If $50,000 is accumulated in the DSF for future retirement of these term bonds, the corresponding entry in the GLTD account group is:

GLTD Account Group

Amount available for payment of term bonds	$50,000	
Amount to be provided for payment of term bonds		$50,000

3 When bonds are retired through the DSF, the entry in the GLTD account group is:

GLTD Account Group

Term bonds payable	$1,000,000	
Amount available for payment of term bonds		$1,000,000

Financial Statements for GLTD Account Group

The financial statements that are usually prepared for general long-term debt are a statement of changes in general long-term debt and a statement of general long-term debt (balance sheet). These statements are illustrated in Exhibit 20–4. The statement of general long-term debt is a basic statement, but changes in general long-term debt may be disclosed in a statement as illustrated or in a statement note.

Defeasance of Debt

GASB Statement 7, "Advance Refundings Resulting in Defeasance of Debt," was issued to provide guidance in accounting for advance refundings of debt reported in the general long-term debt account group. Advance refundings usually result in the defeasance of debt in a legal sense or in substance. Legal defeasance occurs when the debt is legally satisfied even though the debt is not actually paid.

CITY OF RUTHERFORD
STATEMENT OF CHANGES IN GENERAL LONG-TERM DEBT*
FOR THE FISCAL YEAR ENDED JUNE 30, 19X2

	General Obligation		
	Serial Bonds	Term Bonds	Total
Bonds payable July 1, 19X1	$ 500,000	$2,000,000	$2,500,000
New bonds issued	1,000,000	—	1,000,000
	1,500,000	2,000,000	3,500,000
Bonds retired	200,000	—	200,000
Bonds payable June 30, 19X2	$1,300,000	$2,000,000	$3,300,000

*Footnote disclosure is acceptable.

CITY OF RUTHERFORD
STATEMENT OF GENERAL LONG-TERM DEBT [*BASIC STATEMENT*]
AT JUNE 30, 19X2

Amount Available and to Be Provided	
Term bonds:	
Amount available in Debt Service Fund	$ 770,000
Amount to be provided	1,230,000
Serial bonds:	
Amount to be provided	1,300,000
Total available and to be provided	$3,300,000
General Long-term Debt	
Term bonds:	
6% general obligation bonds due July 1, 19X9	$2,000,000
Serial bonds:	
5½% general obligation bonds due $100,000 annually	1,000,000
6% special assessment debt with government commitment due	
$60,000 annually	300,000
Total general obligation debt	$3,300,000

Exhibit 20–4 *Statements for General Long-Term Debt Account Group*

In-substance defeasance occurs when the debt is considered defeased for accounting and financial reporting purposes even though legal defeasance has not occurred. For accounting and financial reporting purposes, debt is defeased in substance if the debtor irrevocably places cash or other assets with an escrow agent in a trust to be used solely for satisfying payments of both interest and principal on the defeased debt, and the possibility of the debtor's having to make future payments on that debt is remote.

The accounting and reporting requirements of advance refundings that result in defeasance are covered in paragraphs 8 through 10 of *GASB Statement 7*. The proceeds from advance refunding that result in defeasance of debt reported in the GLTD account group are reported in the DSF as an other financing source called "proceeds of refunding bonds." Use of the proceeds to pay the escrow agent is reported as an other financing use under the title "payments to refunded bond escrow agent," and any payments to the escrow agent from other sources are reported as "debt service expenditures." Finally, the GLTD account group is adjusted for increases or decreases in the long-term debt.

ACCOUNTING FOR LEASES IN GOVERNMENTAL FUNDS

Lease agreements of state and local governments are accounted for under the provisions of *FASB Statement No. 13*, "Accounting for Leases," as amended and interpreted by *NCGA Statement 5*, "Accounting and Financial Reporting Principles for Lease Agreements by State and Local Governments." A lease agreement that is financed from general government resources must be accounted for under governmental fund accounting principles. [See GASB Cod. Sec. L20.]

Operating lease payments are typically recorded as rental expenditures.

When *capital leases* are used to acquire general fixed assets by purchase or construction, the asset is capitalized in the general fixed assets account group at the inception of the lease at the present value of future lease payments determined by *FASB Statement No. 13* criteria. For example, the entry might include the following:

GFA Account Group

Machinery and equipment	XXX	
Investment in general fixed assets—capital lease		XXX

At the same time, a liability in the same amount is recorded in the general long-term debt account group.

GLTD Account Group

Amount to be provided for payment of capital lease	XXX	
Capital lease payable		XXX

The governmental fund acquiring the general fixed asset through a capital lease records an expenditure and other financing source [GASB Cod. Sec. L20.111]. For example:

GF

Expenditures	XXX	
Other financing source—capital lease		XXX

Accounting for capital leases in the capital projects fund and debt service fund is not necessary unless legally mandated. Therefore, the entry usually would be recorded in the general fund or a special revenue fund. Observe that this entry is *memorandum* in the sense that it serves a disclosure objective, but does not affect the balance sheet or future period operating statements of the fund in which it is recorded.

PROPRIETARY FUNDS

Proprietary funds of the governmental unit are used to account for business activities that provide goods and services to users and finance those services by user charges. The objective of proprietary funds is to maintain capital and/or produce income, and full accrual accounting procedures are applicable. Thus, proprietary funds have revenue and expense, *not expenditure,* accounts. Revenues are recognized in the accounting period in which they *are earned and become measurable* and expenses are recognized in the period *incurred,* if measurable.

The fixed assets of proprietary funds are *fund fixed assets* and not general fixed assets. Liabilities incurred by a proprietary fund to be serviced from its revenues are *fund liabilities* and not general long-term obligations. Lease agreements of proprietary funds are accounted for under the provisions of *FASB Statement No. 13,* "Accounting for Leases."

The two types of funds within the proprietary fund classification are internal service funds and enterprise funds.

INTERNAL SERVICE FUNDS

Internal service funds (ISF) are proprietary funds that are used to account for the financing of goods and services provided by one department or agency to other departments or agencies of the governmental unit, or to other governmental units, on a cost reimbursement basis. Account classifications used by an ISF are those that would be used in accounting for similar operations of a private business enterprise.

The primary difference between an ISF and an enterprise fund lies in the user group for which the goods and services are intended. Enterprise funds provide goods and services to the general public, whereas internal service funds provide their goods and services to other departments or agencies within the same governmental unit (or occasionally to other governmental units). Even though the user groups for enterprise and internal service funds are different, the accounting is identical. Also, the financial statement requirements under the *GASB Codification* are the same.

Centralized purchasing, motor pools, and printing shops are among the more frequent operations accounted for through internal service funds at the state and local levels. Each of these activities offers potential efficiencies through economies of scale, improved services, and better control.

In many cases, the initial financing of an ISF is provided by a contribution of cash and/or operating facilities from the governmental unit after which the ISF is expected to be self-sustaining. Alternatively, the governmental unit may provide a long-term advance to the ISF to be repaid out of future operating flows of the fund. A contribution is classified as part of the fund equity of the ISF, whereas an advance is recorded as a liability of the ISF. Interfund advances are long-term liabilities and receivables. Short-term interfund loans are recorded as *due to Fund A, due from Fund B,* and so on.

Accounting for an Internal Service Fund

The City of Carlton creates a Central Motor Pool Fund with a cash contribution of $200,000 from the general fund and a contribution of existing motor vehicles with a fair value of $120,000. The cash contribution is recorded as a $200,000 residual equity transfer in the GF and is reported as a direct charge to the beginning fund balance of the GF [GASB Cod. Sec. 1800.107]. The equipment transferred is removed from the records of the general fixed assets account group at its original cost, or book value if accumulated depreciation has been recorded. In the records of the Central Motor Pool Fund, the capital contribution is recorded:

ISF		
Cash	$200,000	
Motor vehicles	120,000	
Contributed capital from Municipality		$320,000
To record contribution to establish the fund.		

A building is constructed on land owned by the city at a cost of $100,000, equipment is purchased for $50,000, and operating supplies are acquired for $20,000. These cash expenditures, in summary form, are recorded as follows:

ISF		
Building	$100,000	
Equipment	50,000	
Supplies on hand	20,000	
Cash		$170,000
To record purchase of building, equipment, and supplies.		

During the first year of operation, the Central Motor Pool Fund supplies motor pool vehicles to municipal departments and bills these departments at a predetermined rate based on miles driven. The rate is set to cover all costs of operating the motor pool and servicing the vehicles, including the cost of replacing worn-out vehicles. Journal entries to record revenue and expense transactions and year-end entries are shown in summary form as follows:

Due from general fund	$ 60,000	
Due from special revenue fund	30,000	
Due from enterprise fund	40,000	
Service revenue		$130,000
To charge user funds for vehicle services.		
Cash	$100,000	
Due from general fund		$ 60,000
Due from enterprise fund		40,000
To record collections from user funds.		
Salaries expense	$ 40,000	
Utilities expense	8,000	
Supplies expense	30,000	
Cash		$ 78,000
To record payments for expense items.		
Adjusting Entries		
Supplies expense	$ 5,000	
Supplies on hand		$ 5,000
To adjust supplies expense and supplies on hand accounts at year-end.		
Salaries expense	$ 4,000	
Accrued salaries payable		$ 4,000
To accrue salaries.		
Depreciation expense—building	$ 5,000	
Accumulated depreciation—building		$ 5,000
To record depreciation on building ($100,000/20 years).		
Depreciation expense—vehicles	$ 20,000	
Accumulated depreciation—vehicles		$ 20,000
To record depreciation on vehicles (200,000 miles driven × 10 cents per mile.)		
Depreciation expense—equipment	$ 10,000	
Accumulated depreciation—equipment		$ 10,000
To record depreciation on equipment ($50,000/5 years).		
Closing Entry		
Service revenue	$130,000	
Supplies expense		$ 35,000
Salaries expense		44,000
Utilities expense		8,000
Depreciation expense—building		5,000
Depreciation expense—vehicles		20,000
Depreciation expense—equipment		10,000
Retained earnings		8,000
To close revenue and expense accounts to retained earnings.		

Financial Statements of the ISF

Financial statements for the Central Motor Pool Fund are shown in Exhibits 20-5, 20-6, and 20-7. The required financial statements of an internal service fund include a balance sheet, an operating statement (or statement of revenues and expenses), a retained earnings statement, and a statement of cash flows.

```
CARLTON CENTRAL MOTOR POOL FUND
COMBINED STATEMENT OF OPERATIONS AND RETAINED
EARNINGS FOR THE YEAR ENDED DECEMBER 31, 19X1
```

Revenues		
Service revenues		$130,000
Expenses		
Supplies expense	$35,000	
Salaries expense	44,000	
Utilities expense	8,000	
Depreciation expense	35,000	
Total expenses		122,000
Net income		$ 8,000
Retained earnings, January 1, 19X1		0
Retained earnings, December 31, 19X1		$ 8,000

Exhibit 20–5   *Combined Statement of Operations and Retained Earnings for the ISF*

```
CARLTON CENTRAL MOTOR POOL FUND
BALANCE SHEET
AT DECEMBER 31, 19X1
```

Current Assets		
Cash	$ 52,000	
Due from special revenue fund	30,000	
Supplies on hand	15,000	
Total current assets		$ 97,000
Plant Assets		
Building (net of depreciation)	$ 95,000	
Vehicles (net of depreciation)	100,000	
Equipment (net of depreciation)	40,000	
Total plant assets		235,000
Total assets		$332,000
Liabilities and Fund Equity		
Accrued salaries payable		$ 4,000
Fund equity:		
Contributed capital from municipality	$320,000	
Retained earnings	8,000	
Total fund equity		328,000
Total liabilities and fund equity		$332,000

Exhibit 20–6   *Balance Sheet for the ISF*

CARLTON CENTRAL MOTOR POOL FUND
STATEMENT OF CASH FLOWS
FOR THE YEAR ENDED DECEMBER 31, 19X1

Direct Method

Cash Flows from Operating Activities

Cash received from customers		$ 100,000
Less: Cash paid to suppliers	$ (50,000)	
Cash paid for salaries	(40,000)	
Cash paid for utilities	(8,000)	(98,000)
Cash flows from operating activities		2,000

Cash Flows from Noncapital Financing Activities

Contributed capital from municipality	$ 200,000	
Cash from noncapital financing activities		200,000

Cash Flows from Capital and Related Financing Activities

Purchase of building	$(100,000)	
Purchase of equipment	(50,000)	
Net cash used in capital and related financing activities		(150,000)
Increase in cash for 19X1		$ 52,000

Indirect Method

Cash Flows from Operating Activities

Net income	$ 8,000	
Noncash expenses, revenues, losses and gains included in income:		
Depreciation	$ 35,000	
Due from special revenue fund	(30,000)	
Supplies on hand	(15,000)	
Accrued salaries payable	4,000	
Cash flows from operating activities		$ 2,000

Cash Flows from Noncapital Financing Activities

Contributed capital from municipality	$ 200,000	
Cash from noncapital financing activities		200,000

Cash Flows from Capital and Related Financing Activities

Purchase of building	$(100,000)	
Purchase of equipment	(50,000)	
Net cash used in capital and related financing activities		(150,000)
Increase in cash for 19X1		$ 52,000

Exhibit 20–7   *Cash Flow Statement for ISF (Includes Alternative Methods)*

Statement of Cash Flows for Proprietary and Nonexpendable Trust Funds

GASB Statement 9, "Reporting Cash Flows of Proprietary and Nonexpendable Trust Funds and Governmental Entities That Use Proprietary Fund Accounting," establishes standards for cash flow reporting for proprietary and nonexpendable trust funds and other governmental entities that use proprietary fund accounting, but it exempts public employee retirement systems and pension trust funds from the requirement. The objective of *GASB Statement 9* is to adapt the provisions of *FASB Statement No. 95,* "Statement of Cash Flows," more closely to the nature of governmental operations.

FAS 95 specifies a three section format for cash flow statements of business enterprises: operating activities, investing activities, and financing activities. *GASB Statement 9* recommends a cash flow statement with four separate sections for applicable governmental fund entities: cash flows from operating activities, cash flows from noncapital financing activities, cash flows from capital and related financing activities, and cash flows from investing activities. The content and application of these four sections are reviewed here:

Cash Flows from Operating Activities   Cash *inflows* of the operating activities section include:

> Receipts from sales of goods or services
> Receipts from quasi-external operating transactions
> Receipts from grants for operating activities
> Receipts from other funds for reimbursements of operating transactions
> All other receipts not included in one of the other three sections

Cash *outflows* of the operating activities section include:

> Payments for materials used in providing services or manufacturing goods for resale
> Principal payments to suppliers of those materials or goods on account or under short-term or long-term notes payable
> Payments to suppliers for other goods and services
> Payments to employees for salaries
> Payments to other governments as grants for operating activities
> Payments for taxes and in lieu of taxes
> All other cash payments not included in one of the other three sections

Cash Flows from Noncapital Financing Activities   Items to be considered cash *inflows* for the noncapital financing activities section include:

> Proceeds from bonds and notes not clearly related to the acquisition, construction or improvement of capital assets
> Receipts from grants and subsidies and receipts from other funds (except those restricted for capital purposes or operating activities)
> Receipts from property taxes and other taxes collected for the governmental enterprise and not restricted for capital purposes

Cash *outflows* for this section include:

> Repayments of amounts borrowed (including interest payments) other than those related to acquiring or constructing capital assets
> Amounts paid for grants and subsidies (except those for specific operating activities of the grantor government)
> Cash paid to other funds except for quasi-external transactions

Cash Flows from Capital and Related Financing Activities   Capital and related activities include acquiring and disposing of capital assets used in providing goods and services, including borrowing money and repaying it with interest. Cash *inflows* include amounts from capital grants, contributions, special assessments, insurance proceeds, and so on, as long as they are used to defray the cost of acquiring, constructing, or improving capital assets.

Cash *outflows* include amounts to acquire, construct, or improve capital assets, and to repay amounts borrowed (including interest) as long as the amounts are directly related to acquiring, constructing or improving capital assets.

Cash Flows from Investing Activities   Investing activities include making and collecting loans and acquiring and disposing of debt or equity instruments. Cash *inflows* include collections of loans and sales of investment securities (other than from cash equivalents) and the receipt of interest and dividends. Cash *outflows* include repayments of loans and payments to acquire investment securities (other than for cash equivalents). Cash equivalents are defined as short-term, highly liquid investments that are both readily convertible into known amounts of cash and so near their maturity that they present insignificant risk of changes in value because of changes in interest rates. Ordinarily, these include investments with original maturities of three months or less.

Direct or Indirect Method of Preparing Cash Flows Statement   The statement of cash flows can be prepared using either the direct or indirect method of presenting cash flows from operating activities. Both of these methods are illustrated in Exhibit 20–7 for the internal service fund. GASB encourages the use of the direct method. Only one method, direct or indirect, should be used in a combined or combining statement of cash flows.

ENTERPRISE FUNDS

Enterprise funds (EF) are used to account for proprietary types of operations that are financed and operated similarly to those of private business enterprises. The goods and services of enterprise funds are provided *to the general public on a continuing basis* with the costs being financed primarily through user charges. Since the objective of an enterprise fund is to maintain capital and/or generate net income, full accrual accounting procedures are applicable. Like internal service funds, enterprise funds are proprietary funds that use revenue and expense accounts, and accrual accounting practices similar to those of private business enterprises.

The fixed assets acquired and the long-term liabilities incurred by an EF are *fund fixed assets* and *fund long-term liabilities,* and they are recorded in the enterprise fund and not in the general fixed assets and general long-term debt account groups. Ordinarily, the long-term debt obligations are in the form of revenue bonds that are secured only by enterprise fund operations. However, if such bonds are also secured by the "full faith and credit" of the governmental unit, the contingent liability must be disclosed in a note to the statement of general long-term debt.

The GASB codification permits the use of enterprise fund accounting for any service for which there is a significant potential for financing through user charges. The types of operations accounted for through enterprise funds are about as diverse as those found in private enterprise. They range from the operation of electric and water utilities that are intended to produce income, to swimming pool and golf course operations where costs are intended to be recovered primarily from user charges.

Initial financing of an enterprise fund is typically the same as for an ISF. The governmental unit makes a capital contribution (a residual equity transfer in the general fund) or provides a long-term advance to the enterprise fund and future operations are expected to cover all costs, including depreciation on fund fixed assets, so that operations can continue indefinitely without further capital contributions.

The income or loss of an enterprise fund is closed to retained earnings, as in private business enterprises. Thus, a closing entry for an enterprise fund might appear as follows:

EF

Service revenue	$100,000	
Interest income	2,000	
Cost of supplies used		$40,000
Utility expense		16,000
Depreciation expense		20,000
Interest expense		6,000
Retained earnings		20,000

Customer Deposits Utility-type enterprise funds often require customer deposits to assure timely payment for services. Deposits are normally required before service starts and are refunded when service is terminated. Land developers may also be required to make good faith deposits to finance the cost of extending utilities service lines. Such assets should be segregated and reported as restricted assets in the enterprise fund balance sheet. Customer deposits remain in current liabilities until applied against unpaid billings or refunded to customers. Developer deposits are reclassified as contributed capital when they cease to be refundable. (*Audits of State and Local Governmental Units,* 1986, page 100.)

Required Financial Statements

Required financial statements for an enterprise fund consist of a balance sheet, an operating statement (or statement of revenues and expenses), a retained earnings statement (or statement of changes in fund balance), and a statement of cash flows. The financial statements of an enterprise fund differ only slightly from those of a business enterprise. Enterprise funds do not pay property taxes or income taxes, and these items are noticeably absent from the operating statement. In addition, an enterprise fund does not have capital stock and paid-in capital, and in place of stockholders' equity, its balance sheet shows a fund equity section, such as the following:

Fund Equity	
Contributed capital from municipality	$800,000
Retained earnings	150,000
Total fund equity	$950,000

One other difference from the statements of private businesses that may be found in the financial statements of an enterprise fund lies in such interfund account titles as due from general fund (for utility charges), due from internal service fund (for supply acquisitions), and advance from general fund (for long-term financing). Such items constitute only minor differences from private enterprise accounting.

COMBINING FINANCIAL STATEMENTS

A governmental unit may have a number of enterprise funds as well as numerous funds for all fund types other than the general fund. The funds of a given type are combined for basic financial reporting, but the GASB Codification recommends that combining financial statements also be included in a comprehensive annual report. Combining financial statements are used to aggregate individual fund account balances to produce relevant totals by fund type for basic reporting purposes.

The concept of combining financial statements is illustrated in Exhibit 20–8 for the balance sheets of the Town of Blacksburg, Virginia's three enterprise funds—Water and Sewer, Golf Course, and Transit System. Financial statement items for these individual enterprise funds are combined in the statement illustrated, and only the totals are used for basic financial reporting purposes. Similar

TOWN OF BLACKSBURG, VIRGINIA
ENTERPRISE FUNDS
COMBINING BALANCE SHEET
JUNE 30, 1990   Schedule 5

	Water and Sewer	Golf Course	Transit System	Total
Assets				
Current assets:				
Cash and temporary investments	$1,373,691	$ 17,654	$	$ 1,391,345
Cash with fiscal agent	115,450			115,450
Utilities receivable, net of allowance				
for uncollectibles	518,962			518,962
Accounts receivable, net	16,063	8	6,538	22,609
Accrued interest	9,077		1,742	10,819
Due from other funds	261,156			261,156
Receivable from other governments			602,609	602,609
Inventories, at cost		5,379	107,638	113,017
Total current assets	$2,294,399	$ 23,041	$ 718,527	$3,035,967
Property, plant and equipment:				
Land	7,514	376,947		384,461
Buildings		30,306	243,534	273,840
Water system—Plant	5,275,862			5,275,862
Sewer system—Plant	2,953,710			2,953,710
Equipment	494,574	88,088	3,268,675	3,851,337
Construction in progress	2,862		688,052	690,914
Total Property, Plant and				
Equipment	8,734,522	495,341	4,200,261	13,430,124
Less accumulated depreciation	(2,992,271)	(74,088)	(1,452,417)	(4,518,776)
Net property, plant and equipment	5,742,251	421,253	2,747,844	8,911,348
Total assets	$8,036,650	$444,294	$ 3,466,371	$11,947,315
Liabilities and fund equity				
Liabilities:				
Current liabilities:				
Accounts payable	$ 537,734	$ 1,997	$ 132,373	$ 672,104
Accrued expenses	55,207	9,037	13,552	77,796
Current maturities of long-term debt	250,000			250,000
Customer deposits	38,769			38,769
Due to other funds			261,156	261,156
Total current liabilities	881,710	11,034	407,081	1,299,825
Long-term debt	1,750,000			1,750,000
Total liabilities	2,631,710	11,034	407,081	3,049,825
Fund equity:				
Contributed capital	1,040,659	386,535	2,806,406	4,233,600
Retained earnings	4,364,281	46,725	252,884	4,663,890
Total fund equity	5,404,940	433,260	3,059,290	8,897,490
Total liabilities and fund equity	$8,036,650	$ 444,294	$ 3,466,371	$11,947,315

Source: Town of Blacksburg, Virginia, Comprehensive Annual Financial Report, June 30, 1990, Schedule 5

Exhibit 20–8   *Combining Balance Sheet*

combining statements for other fund types are needed to meet the requirements for a comprehensive annual report, although such statements are not required for a governmental unit's statements to be in accordance with generally accepted accounting principles.

FIDUCIARY FUNDS

Fiduciary fund types are used to account for assets held by a governmental unit as trustee or agent for individuals, private organizations, and other governmental units. The fiduciary grouping includes trust funds and agency funds, which are similar in the sense that the governmental unit acts in a fiduciary capacity for both types of funds. The accounting emphasis for trust and agency funds lies in showing how the government's fiduciary responsibilities have been met. A separate agency or trust fund is required for each agreement under which the governmental unit acts as agent or trustee.

The basis of accounting for fiduciary funds follows the nature and measurement objective of the fund. Agency funds are accounted for on the modified accrual basis because their operations are of a custodial nature. Expendable trust funds are accounted for on a modified accrual basis in the same manner as governmental funds because they have the same "source and use" measurement objective. Nonexpendable trust funds and pension trust funds have a capital maintenance or income objective and are accounted for in the same manner as proprietary funds.

AGENCY FUNDS

A local governmental unit acts as an **agent** for the federal government when it withholds income and social security taxes from employee payrolls. It acts as an agent for the state government when it collects sales taxes on goods and services sold to the public. But separate **agency funds (AF)** are not ordinarily used for such agency relationships because normal liability accounting procedures are adequate to show how the governmental unit's fiduciary responsibilities have been met.

The debt service transactions of a special assessment bond issue for which the government is *not obligated in any manner* are reported in an agency fund to reflect the fact that the government's duties are limited to acting as an agent for the assessed property owners and bondholders. Thus, the government acts as agent for the property owners in collecting special assessments and remitting the amounts collected to bondholders.

Agency funds are needed when the government's agency responsibilities involve numerous transactions, include several different governmental units, and/or do not arise from normal and recurring operations of any other fund. For example, if a county unit of government serves as a tax collection agency for all towns and cities located within the county, an agency fund is created to show the county's acceptance of responsibility for collecting taxes for other governmental units and the fulfillment of that responsibility.

Accounting for an Agency Fund

Assume that Wise County collects property taxes for its own purposes as well as for the cities of Ansley, Broken Bow, and Custer, and that total property tax levies for 19X1 are as follows:

Wise County	$100,000	50%
Ansley	50,000	25
Broken Bow	20,000	10
Custer	30,000	15
Total	$200,000	100%

When the tax levies are certified to the county for collection, a Tax Collection Agency Fund should be created. The county's custodial responsibility for collecting the taxes is recorded:

AF

Taxes receivable for local governmental units	$200,000	
Liability to Wise County		$100,000
Liability to Ansley		50,000
Liability to Broken Bow		20,000
Liability to Custer		30,000

If $180,000 of the levy is collected and $160,000 is remitted to the respective units of government during 19X1, the collection and remittance are recorded as follows:

AF

Cash	$180,000	
Taxes receivable for local governmental units		$180,000

To record collection of taxes receivable.

WISE COUNTY
TAX COLLECTION AGENCY FUND
STATEMENT OF CHANGES IN ASSETS AND LIABILITIES
FOR THE YEAR ENDED DECEMBER 31, 19X1

	Balance January 1, 19X1	Additions	Deductions	Balance December 31, 19X1
Assets				
Cash	—	$180,000	$160,000	$20,000
Taxes receivable	—	200,000	180,000	20,000
Total assets	—	$380,000	$340,000	$40,000
Liabilities				
Due to General Fund	—	$ 900	$ —	$ 900
Liability to Wise County	—	100,000	80,000	20,000
Liability to Ansley	—	50,000	40,450	9,550
Liability to Broken Bow	—	20,000	16,180	3,820
Liability to Custer	—	30,000	24,270	5,730
Total liabilities	—	$200,900	$160,900	$40,000

WISE COUNTY
TAX COLLECTION AGENCY FUND
BALANCE SHEET
ON DECEMBER 31, 19X1

Assets	
Cash	$20,000
Taxes receivable for local governmental units	20,000
Total assets	$40,000
Liabilities	
Due to General Fund	$ 900
Liability to Wise County	20,000
Liability to Ansley	9,550
Liability to Broken Bow	3,820
Liability to Custer	5,730
Total liabilities	$40,000

Exhibit 20–9 *Financial Statements for Agency Funds*

AF

Liability to Wise County	$ 80,000	
Liability to Ansley	40,000	
Liability to Broken Bow	16,000	
Liability to Custer	24,000	
Cash		$160,000

    To record remittance of taxes collected.

If Wise County charges Ansley, Broken Bow, and Custer a fee of 1 percent of taxes collected, the total charges would be $900 ($90,000 collected for these three cities times 1 percent), and the collection fees would be recorded:

AF

Liability to Ansley	$450	
Liability to Broken Bow	180	
Liability to Custer	270	
Due to general fund (of Wise County)		$900

    To charge cities a 1 percent fee for taxes collected for them.

Financial Statements for AF

Financial statements for the Tax Collection Agency Fund of Wise County are shown in Exhibit 20–9. Since agency funds do not have revenues and expenditures, the only statements included in the exhibit are a statement of changes in assets and liabilities and a balance sheet. The balance sheet is a required statement, whereas the statement of changes in assets and liabilities is optional.

TRUST FUNDS [TF]

Expendable trust funds are those in which trust fund assets can be expended as needed to meet the objectives of the trust. The accounting emphasis in such trust funds is on showing the source of resources received and the use of those resources in meeting the governmental unit's fiduciary responsibilities as trustee. Expendable trust funds are accounted for in the same manner as governmental-type funds. Thus, they account for their revenues and expenditures on a modified accrual basis, and their financial statement requirements consist of a balance sheet, a statement of revenues and expenditures, and a statement of changes in fund balance.

    Two significant differences between accounting for expendable trust funds and the governmental funds need to be recognized. First, any fixed assets relating to the operations of an expendable trust fund are *fund fixed assets* and are recorded in the accounts of the trust fund. Depreciation on such fixed assets is not recorded, however, because expendable trust funds do not have an income or capital maintenance objective.

    The second difference is that any long-term liabilities of an expendable trust fund are *fund long-term liabilities* and are accounted for as trust fund liabilities. Interest on such long-term liabilities is recorded when the liability is incurred.

    Nonexpendable trust funds are those for which the principal must be maintained intact in order to provide income to meet the purposes specified by the trust. The income may or may not be expendable. A trust fund in which the principal is nonexpendable but the income may be expended for purposes provided in the trust document is known as an **endowment trust fund.** An example of the endowment type of nonexpendable trust fund is a cemetery trust where some of the proceeds from the sale of cemetery lots are placed in trust to provide perpetual care of the cemetery. The trust principal is required to be maintained intact, but the income can be expended for maintenance of the cemetery. Alternatively, many student loan funds are nonexpendable both as to income and as to principal. In such trust funds, all amounts loaned to students are required to be repaid with interest and no part of the trust fund assets can be expended. Losses from bad debts can, of course, reduce trust fund assets.

All nonexpendable trust funds and pension trust funds are accounted for in the same manner as proprietary fund types. That is, they record their revenues and expenses on an accrual accounting basis including depreciation on their fund fixed assets and interest expense on their fund long-term liabilities. Required financial statements for nonexpendable trust funds are a balance sheet, an operating statement, a retained earnings (or fund balance) statement and a statement of cash flows.

Accounting for a Nonexpendable Trust Fund

On January 2, 19X1, the City of Plenty was named trustee for an apartment building that was placed in trust at the death of A. C. Olds. The trust document stipulated that the $250,000 trust fund principal be maintained intact, and that income be expended as needed to pay for recreational equipment and supplies for the city's parks, playgrounds, and recreation center. Transactions and events for the Olds Trust Fund for 19X1 are described, together with summary journal entries to record the items.

1 The trust fund principal consists of the apartment building with a fair value of $280,000, and land with a fair value of $70,000, less a $100,000, 7 percent mortgage payable to be serviced and retired from trust assets:

TF

Land	$ 70 000	
Apartment building	280,000	
7% Mortgage payable		$100,000
Trust fund principal		250,000

2 Rentals from the apartment building for 19X1 consist of $45,000 cash received and $5,000 rentals due on December 31, 19X1:

TF

Cash	$ 45,000	
Rent receivable	5,000	
Rental revenues		$ 50,000

3 Building maintenance costs for the year are $16,000, of which $2,000 remains unpaid at year-end:

TF

Maintenance expense	$ 16,000	
Accounts payable		$ 2,000
Cash		14,000

4 During 19X1, $3,500 mortgage interest is paid and $3,500 is accrued at year-end. In addition, a $10,000 principal payment on the mortgage is due January 1, 19X2:

TF

Interest expense	$ 7,000	
Interest payable		$ 3,500
Cash		3,500

5 Depreciation expense on the apartment building for 19X1 is $17,500 ($280,000/16 years):

TF

Depreciation expense	$ 17,500	
Accumulated depreciation—building		$ 17,500

6 Closing entries for the year are recorded:

TF

Rental revenues	$ 50,000	
Maintenance expense		$ 16,000
Depreciation expense		17,500
Interest expense		7,000
Retained earnings		9,500

7 Of the $9,500 income of the trust for the year, $5,000 is distributed to the general fund for recreational equipment:

TF

Retained earnings	$ 5,000	
Cash		$ 5,000

Financial Statements for a Nonexpendable Trust Fund

Financial statements for the Olds Trust Fund for the year ended December 31, 19X1, are shown in Exhibits 20–10, 20–11, and 20–12. Since the trust fund is classified as nonexpendable, a balance sheet, a combined statement of operations and retained earnings, and a statement of cash flows are required. Retained earnings accounts for trust funds are frequently designated *fund balance—earnings*.

CITY OF PLENTY
OLDS TRUST FUND
BALANCE SHEET
AT DECEMBER 31, 19X1

Assets		
Current assets:		
Cash	$ 22,500	
Rent receivable	5,000	
Total current assets		$ 27,500
Plant assets:		
Land	$ 70,000	
Apartment building (net of $17,500 depreciation)	262,500	
Total plant assets		332,500
Total assets		$360,000
Liabilities and Fund Equity		
Current liabilities		
Accounts payable	$ 2,000	
Interest payable	3,500	
Mortgage payable—current portion	10,000	
Total current liabilities	$ 15,500	
Long-term liabilities		
Mortgage payable—less current portion	90,000	
Total liabilities		$105,500
Fund equity:		
Fund balance—principal	$250,000	
Retained earnings	4,500	
Total fund equity		254,500
Total liabilities and fund equity		$360,000

Exhibit 20–10   *Balance Sheet for Nonexpendable Trust Fund*

CITY OF PLENTY
OLDS TRUST FUND
COMBINED STATEMENT OF OPERATIONS AND
RETAINED EARNINGS
FOR THE YEAR ENDED DECEMBER 31, 19X1

Rental Revenue		$ 50,000
Less: Costs and expenses		
Maintenance expense	$ 16,000	
Depreciation expense	17,500	
Interest expense	7,000	
Total costs and expenses		40,500
Net income		$ 9,500
Less: Income distributed		5,000
Retained earnings, December 31, 19X1		$ 4,500

Exhibit 20–11   *Combined Statement of Operations and Retained Earnings for Nonexpendable Trust Fund*

CITY OF PLENTY
OLDS TRUST FUND
STATEMENT OF CASH FLOWS
FOR THE YEAR ENDED DECEMBER 31, 19X1

Direct Method

Cash Flows from Operating Activities

Cash received from tenants		$ 45,000
Less: Cash paid for maintenance	$(14,000)	
Cash paid for interest	(3,500)	(17,500)
Cash flows from operating activities		27,500

Cash from Capital and Related Financing Activities

Distribution—recreational equipment	$ (5,000)	
Net cash used in capital and related financing activities		(5,000)

Cash Flows from Investing Activities

None	0	
Net cash used in investing activities		0
Increase in cash for 19X1		$ 22,500

Indirect Method

Cash Flows from Operating Activities

Net Income	$ 9,500	
Noncash expenses, revenues, losses, and gains included in income:		
Depreciation	$ 17,500	
Rent receivable	(5,000)	
Accounts payable	2,000	
Interest payable	3,500	
Cash flows from operating activities		$ 27,500

Cash from Capital and Related Financing Activities

Distribution—recreational equipment	$ (5,000)	
Net cash used in capital and related financing activities		(5,000)

Cash Flows from Investing Activities

None	0	
Net cash used in investing activities		0
Increase in cash for 19X1		$ 22,500

Exhibit 20–12   *Statement of Cash Flows for Nonexpendable Trust Fund*

Pension Trust Funds

Accounting and reporting for public employee retirement systems (PERS) is usually done through a pension trust fund. PERS are not subject to the regulations of ERISA (the federal government's Employee Retirement Income Security Act), and consequently, some governmental pension plans are fully funded, others are partially funded, while still others make *all* pension payments from current revenue.

Some public retirement systems are enormous. For example, in 1989 the California Public Employees Retirement System had pension fund assets of $54 billion, making it the nation's second largest pension fund. Of the 20 largest pension funds in 1989, public funds accounted for 13, and the retirement systems for state and local public employees were the fastest-growing pension funds.[5]

The GASB Codification recognizes three different approaches for accounting and reporting of defined benefit PERS[6] that are accepted until replaced by a new GASB standard. These approaches are based on the pension accounting principles found in the NCGA *Statement 1,* "Governmental Accounting and Reporting Principles," the NCGA *Statement 6,* "Pension Accounting and Financial Reporting: Public Employee Retirement Systems and State and Local Government Employer Entities," and *FASB Statement 35,* "Accounting and Reporting by Defined Benefit Pension Plans."

An Exposure Draft, "Accounting for Penisons by State and Local Government Employers," would require pension expense (or pension expenditure) for defined benefit pension plans to be determined using a systematic and rational actuarial approach, and recognizing a liability for the portion of the the expense that was not funded. Utilities, colleges and universities, and hospitals that use proprietary fund accounting could account for their pension plans under *FASB Statement No. 87,* "Employers' Accounting for Pensions," or the new GASB standard. If a final statement of the exposure draft is issued, it would be effective for financial statement periods beginning after June 15, 1994.

NCGA *Statement 1* identifies the pension trust fund as a proprietary fund that uses accrual accounting, has revenue and expenses, and determines net income. Fixed assets used in the plan may be recorded and depreciated. Because of the various legal, policy, and actuarial restrictions on pension plans, accounting for the pension plan emphasizes *accountability* for the financial resources contributed to and earned by the plan, and associating those resources with the proper interests.

GASB *Statement No. 5,* "Disclosures of Pension Information by Public Employee Retirement Systems and State and Local Government Employers" deals with disclosures for the financial statements of the pension fund and disclosures of the government employer. These disclosures are required for all pension plans, regardless of whether the plans are accounted for and reported under the provisions of *NCGA Statements 1* or *6,* or *FASB Statement No. 35.* The disclosures outlined in GASB *Statement 5* are in lieu of disclosures prescribed in the NCGA pronouncements. For plans accounted for under the provisions of *FASB Statement No. 35,* the disclosures are in addition to the *Statement 35* disclosures.

GASB *Statement 5,* paragraph 6, identifies the objectives of pension disclosures by governmental employers as follows: "To provide users with information needed to assess (a) the funding status of a PERS on a going-concern basis, (b) the progress made in accumulating sufficient assets to pay benefits when due, and (c) whether employers are making actuarially determined contributions." GASB *Statement 5* made it clear that unfunded pension plans must also meet the disclosure requirements for pension obligations.

---

[5]*The Wall Street Journal,* June 28, 1990, p. C–1.
[6]GASB Cod. Sec. Pe5.102.

Employer Disclosures   The disclosure requirements for employers are extensive under GASB *Statement 5*. A brief summary of the disclosures for a single employer PERS follows:[7]

1 A description of the plan including a statement about the employees covered, benefit provisions, eligibility and vesting requirements, and employee and employer obligations.
2 The employer's securities included in the PERS assets.
3 The fund status and progress including a description of the pension benefit obligation[8] and the portion applicable to retirees and beneficiaries and to current employees; the date the pension benefit obligation was determined; significant actuarial assumptions and changes therein; net assets available for benefits; and a calculation of the unfunded pension benefit obligation (pension obligations less net assets available for benefits).
4 Contributions required and contributions made including a statement of funding policy; a description of the actuarial method used; significant actuarial assumptions with reconciliation to those used to compute pension benefit obligations; contributions required and contributions made by employer and employees both in dollars and as a percent of current-year covered payroll;[9] and any current-year changes in any of the above factors. If contributions are not actuarially determined, that fact must be disclosed, along with a description of how the contribution requirement was determined, the amount of contribution requirement and the amount actually made by employees and employer in dollars and as a percent of current-year payroll. Current-year changes in methods used must also be disclosed.
5 Three year historical trend information, including
   a Net assets available for benefits, expressed as a percentage of the pension benefit obligation applicable to the entity's employees
   b Unfunded pension benefit obligation, expressed as a percentage of annual covered payroll
   c Employer contributions expressed as percentages of annual covered payroll
6 Ten year historical trend information, including
   a Net assets available for benefits (must be valued as of the date of the pension benefit obligation for PERS balance sheet purposes)
   b Pension benefit obligation
   c Net assets available for benefits as a percentage of the pension benefit obligation
   d Unfunded (assets in excess of) pension benefit obligation
   e Annual covered payroll
   f Unfunded pension benefit obligation as a percentage of annual covered payroll

If the ten-year historical trend information is available in the PERS report, it need not be repeated in the employer's statements. Otherwise, it should appear in the comprehensive annual financial report.

DISCLOSURES FOR POST RETIREMENT BENEFITS OTHER THAN PENSION BENEFITS

GASB *Statement 12,* "Disclosure of Information on Postemployment Benefits Other than Pension Benefits by State and Local Governments," provides disclosure

---

[7]GASB Cod. Sec. P20.123.

[8]*Pension benefit obligation* is defined as the actuarial present value of credited projected benefits, prorated on service, and discounted at a rate equal to the expected return on present and future plan assets. *Projected benefits* are the amounts expected to be paid at various future times under a particular set of actuarial assumptions. The portion of an individual's projected benefit allocated to service to date, determined in accordance with the terms of a pension plan and based on future compensation as projected to retirement, is the *credited projected benefit.* (GASB Cod. Sec. Pe6.528 and .530)

[9]Covered payroll includes all compensation paid to active employees covered by a PERS on which contributions are based.

requirements for state and local governmental employers (including governmental utilities, hospitals and universities) that provide postemployment benefits other than pension benefits. The statement does not alter accounting for these benefits.

The disclosures apply regardless of the fund-type used to report the employer's transactions, and they include:

1 A description of the benefits provided, employee groups covered, and employer and participant obligations to contribute
2 A description of the statutory, contractual, or other authority that establishes the benefits and obligations
3 A description of the accounting and financing or funding policies
4 The expenditures or expenses for the period and certain other financial information
5 A description of any significant changes in the plan that would affect comparability with the prior period disclosures

COMBINED FINANCIAL STATEMENTS

The financial statements illustrated up to this point have been those for individual funds. But individual financial statements are ordinarily impractical for external reporting purposes because of the large number of funds that may exist, even for a relatively small governmental unit. Except for the general fund, a governmental unit may have many individual funds within each type of fund.

When a governmental unit has more than one fund of a given type, the individual statements for that type of fund are usually combined for external reporting purposes. Thus, individual debt service fund balances would be combined into a single set of financial statements for all debt service funds. Similarly, all individual capital projects funds would be combined into a single set of financial statements for all capital projects funds. Expendable and nonexpendable trust funds are combined separately. This combining process continues until there is only one set of financial statements for each type of fund.

The statements for each type of fund are presented in combined financial statements for external reporting, with separate columns for each type of fund. Combined statements may or may not contain total columns. In this manner, the number of financial statements required for external financial reporting in accordance with GAAP is reduced to the following:

1 A combined balance sheet for all fund types and account groups,
2 A combined statement of revenues, expenditures, and changes in fund balances for all governmental fund types,
3 A combined statement of revenues, expenditures, and changes in fund balances— budget and actual—for general and special revenue fund types,
4 A combined statement of revenues, expenses, and changes in retained earnings for all proprietary fund types, and,
5 A combined statement of cash flows for all proprietary fund types.
(Notes to the financial statements are essential for fair presentation.)

Examples of the required statements are presented in Exhibits 20–13 through 20–17 to illustrate the basic financial reports for governmental units. The basic statements come from the 1990 *Comprehensive Annual Financial Report of the Town of Blacksburg, Virginia,* which also includes combining financial statements and other statistical information. Notes to the financial statements have been omitted from this reproduction.

Combined financial statements are used primarily for efficient presentation of data. The statements may contain horizontal column totals, but such columns are not required.

TOWN OF BLACKSBURG, VIRGINIA
COMBINED STATEMENT OF REVENUES, EXPENDITURES AND
CHANGES IN FUND BALANCES—ALL GOVERNMENTAL FUND TYPES
FOR THE FISCAL YEAR ENDED JUNE 30, 1990

	General	Debt Service	Capital Projects	Totals (Memorandum Only) 1990	1989
Revenues:					
Local taxes, licenses and permits	$4,525,939	$	$	$4,525,939	$3,868,921
Intergovernmental revenues	1,813,611		77,000	1,890,611	1,747,308
Charges for current services	1,127,168			1,127,168	1,075,317
Fines and foreits	136,294			136,294	97,188
Interest	119,072		64,727	183,799	188,632
Miscellaneous	298,372			298,372	128,058
Total revenues	8,020,456		141,727	8,162,183	7,105,424
Expenditures:					
Current:					
Legislative	115,563			115,563	103,080
Executive	346,983			346,983	295,850
Legal	105,616			105,616	96,227
Judicial	5,051			5,051	3,965
Finance	424,293			424,293	355,532
Police	2,278,572			2,278,572	2,007,686
Fire and rescue	281,419			281,419	241,262
Public works	2,251,247			2,251,247	2,066,107
Recreation	351,166			351,166	343,203
Planning, zoning, and economic development	294,418			294,418	241,758
Grants	22,939			22,939	3,336
Insurance	69,924			69,924	78,968
Miscellaneous	7,782			7,782	10,523
Capital outlay	438,720		442,481	881,201	1,213,908
Debt service:					
Principal retirement		400,000		400,000	400,000
Interest and fiscal charges		206,524		206,524	237,628
Total expenditures	6,993,693	606,524	442,481	8,042,698	7,699,033
Excess of revenues over (under) expenditures	1,026,763	(606,524)	(300,754)	119,485	(593,609)
Other Financing Sources (Uses):					
Operating transfers from other funds	32,476	606,524	769,832	1,408,832	811,705
Operating transfer to other funds	(1,328,913)		(58,348)	(1,387,261)	(765,428)
Capital lease					67,180
Net other financing sources (uses)	(1,296,437)	606,524	711,484	21,571	113,457
Excess of revenues and other sources over (under) expenditures and other uses	(269,674)		410,730	141,056	(480,152)
Fund balances at beginning of year	916,492		1,325,747	2,242,239	2,722,391
Fund balances at end of year	$ 646,818	$	$1,736,477	$2,383,295	$2,242,239

Source: Town of Blacksburg, Virginia, Comprehensive Annual Financial Report, June 30, 1990, Exhibit II

Exhibit 20–13 *Combined Statement of Revenues, Expenditures, and Changes in Fund Balances*

TOWN OF BLACKSBURG, VIRGINIA
COMBINED STATEMENT OF REVENUES, EXPENDITURES AND
CHANGES IN FUND BALANCES (NON-GAAP BUDGETARY BASIS),
BUDGET AND ACTUAL—GENERAL FUND
FOR THE FISCAL YEAR ENDED JUNE 30, 1990

	Revised Budget	Actual	Variance-Favorable (Unfavorable)
Revenues:			
Local taxes, licenses and permits	$ 4,705,900	$ 4,525,939	$(179,961)
Intergovernmental revenues	1,875,495	1,813,611	(61,884)
Charges for current services	1,174,942	1,127,168	(47,774)
Fines and forfeits	115,800	136,294	20,494
Interest	144,400	119,072	(25,328)
Miscellaneous	282,298	298,372	16,074
Total Revenues	$ 8,298,835	$ 8,020,456	$(278,379)
Expenditures:			
Current:			
Legislative	117,760	115,563	2,197
Executive	357,058	349,486	7,572
Legal	105,783	105,745	38
Judicial	5,059	5,051	8
Finance	431,963	424,293	7,670
Police	2,301,202	2,279,377	21,825
Fire and rescue	301,887	284,534	17,353
Public works	2,308,437	2,258,132	50,305
Recreation	363,689	351,166	12,523
Planning, zoning, and economic development	314,886	294,569	20,317
Grants		22,939	(22,939)
Insurance	75,300	69,924	5,376
Miscellaneous	48,896	7,782	41,114
Capital outlay	534,000	447,130	86,870
Total Expenditures	7,265,920	7,015,691	250,229
Excess of Revenues Over Expenditures	1,032,915	1,004,765	(28,150)
Other Financing Sources (Uses):			
Operating transfers from other funds		32,476	32,476
Operating transfers to other funds	(1,252,975)	(1,328,913)	(75,938)
Net Other Financing Sources (Uses)	(1,252,975)	(1,296,437)	(43,462)
Excess of Revenues and Other Sources Over (Under) Expenditures and Other Uses	(220,060)	(291,672)	(71,612)
Fund balances at beginning of year	916,492	916,492	
Fund balances at end of year	$ 696,432	$ 624,820	$ (71,612)

Source: Town of Blacksburg, Virginia, Comprehensive Annual Financial Report, June 30, 1990, Exhibit III

Exhibit 20-14 *Combined Statement of Revenues, Expenditures and Changes in Fund Balances—General Fund*

TOWN OF BLACKSBURG, VIRGINIA
COMBINED STATEMENT OF REVENUES, EXPENSES AND CHANGES
IN RETAINED EARNINGS—ALL PROPRIETARY FUND TYPES
FOR THE FISCAL YEAR ENDED JUNE 30, 1990

	Proprietary Fund Types		Totals (Memorandum Only)	
	Enterprise (Note 12)	Internal Service	1990	1989
Operating revenues:				
Charges for current services	$4,305,067	$386,541	$4,691,608	$4,516,773
Availability, installation, and connection fees	466,923		466,923	307,411
Miscellaneous	104,051		104,051	61,261
Total operating revenue	4,876,041	386,541	5,262,582	4,885,445
Operating Expenses:				
Personal services	1,002,198	125,836	1,128,034	1,039,589
Contractual services	2,214,855		2,214,855	1,862,292
Administraiton and other	1,402,717	264,170	1,666,887	1,400,799
Depreciation	689,084	5,094	694,178	608,697
Total operating expenses	5,308,854	395,100	5,703,954	4,911,377
Operating income (loss)	(432,813)	(8,559)	(441,372)	(25,932)
Nonoperating revenues (expenses):				
Interest on investments	180,148		180,148	145,444
Miscellaneous income	6,069		6,069	10,510
Gain/(loss) on sale of assets	(5,263)		(5,263)	37,369
Administrative assistance grant	244,725		244,725	206,668
Interest on serial bonds	(139,110)		(139,110)	(154,672)
Nonoperating revenues, net	286,569		286,569	245,319
Income (loss) before operating transfers	(146,244)	(8,559)	(154,803)	219,387
Operating transfers:				
From other funds	25,872		25,872	
To other funds	(47,443)		(47,443)	(46,277)
Net operating transfers	(21,571)		(21,571)	(46,277)
Net income (loss)	(167,815)	(8,559)	(176,374)	173,110
Add depreciation on fixed assets contributed by other governments which reduces contributed capital (Note 10)	368,341	2,954	371,295	317,956
Retained earnings at beginning of year	4,463,364	8,430	4,471,794	3,980,728
Retained earnings at end of year	$4,663,890	$ 2,825	$4,666,715	$4,471,794

Source: Town of Blacksburg, Virginia, Comprehensive Annual Financial Report, June 30, 1990, Exhibit IV

Exhibit 20–15   *Combined Statement of Revenues, Expenses and Changes in Retained Earnings—Proprietary and Similar Trust Funds*

TOWN OF BLACKSBURG, VIRGINIA
COMBINED BALANCE SHEET—ALL FUND TYPES AND ACCOUNT GROUPS
JUNE 30, 1990

	Governmental Fund Types		
	General	Debt Service	Capital Projects
Assets			
Cash and temporary investments	$ 363,649	$	$1,788,831
Cash with fiscal agents			
Assets held for employees for deferred compensation			
Receivables (net, where applicable, of allowances for uncollectibles):			
Delinquent taxes, including penalties	52,350		
Utilities			
Accounts	218,026		
Accrued interest	14,961		16,901
Due from other funds	2,712		
Due from other governments	357,314		
Inventories, at cost	123,413		
Land			
Buildings			
Water system—Plant			
Sewer system—Plant			
Equipment			
Construction in progress			
Accumulated depreciation			
Amount to be provided for retirement of general long-term debt			
Total assets	$1,132,425	$	$1,805,732
Liabilities and Fund Equity			
Liabilities:			
Accounts payable	$ 238,059	$	$ 69,255
Accrued expenditures and expenses	57,048		
Current maturities of long-term debt			
Customer depostis	102,318		
Due to other funds			
Deferred revenue	88,182		
Accured vacation payable long-term			
Obligation under capital leases			
Long-term debt			
Liability to agency			
Liability to employees for deferred compensation			
Total liabilities	485,607		69,255
Equity and other credits			
Investment in general fixed assets			
Contributed capital			
Retained earnings—Unreserved			
Fund balances:			
Reserved for encumbrances	21,998		
Reserved for central stores inventory	123,413		
Unreserved:			
Designated for subsequent years' expenditures	22,938		1,736,477
Undesignated	478,469		
Total equity and other credits	646,818		1,736,477
Total liabilities and equity and other credits	$1,132,425	$	$1,805,732

Source: Town of Blacksburg, Virginia, Comprehensive Annual Financial Report, June 30, 1990, Exhibit I

Exhibit 20–16   *Combined Balance Sheet—All Fund Types and Account Groups*

TOWN OF BLACKSBURG, VIRGINIA
COMBINED BALANCE SHEET—ALL FUND TYPES AND ACCOUNT GROUPS
JUNE 30, 1990

| Proprietary Fund Types | | Fiduciary Fund Type | Account Groups | | Totals (Memorandum Only) | |
Enterprise	Internal Service	Agency	General Fixed Assets	General Long-Term Debt	1990	1989
$ 1,391,345	$ 8,618	$107,657	$	$	$ 3,660,100	$ 3,778,440
115,450					115,450	118,100
		345,699			345,699	271,213
					52,350	61,043
518,962					518,962	562,751
22,609		46,062			286,697	196,626
10,819		3,792			46,473	21,628
261,156					263,868	1,257
602,609					959,923	533,339
113,017					236,430	188,739
384,461			1,684,492		2,068,953	2,058,953
273,840	126,889		4,929,339		5,330,068	5,305,943
5,275,862					5,275,862	5,199,256
2,953,710					2,953,710	2,951,426
3,851,337	19,722		3,825,731		7,696,790	6,758,147
690,914					690,914	34,260
(4,518,776)	(61,453)				(4,580,229)	(3,906,567)
				2,427,161	2,427,161	2,799,884
$11,947,315	$ 93,776	$503,210	$10,439,562	$2,427,161	$28,349,181	$26,934,438
$ 672,104	$ 6,154	$ 2,361	$	$	$ 987,933	$ 814,415
77,796	10,112	663			145,619	136,523
250,000					250,000	250,000
38,769					141,087	158,373
261,156		2,712			263,868	1,257
					88,182	77,799
				189,803	189,803	152,704
				57,358	57,358	67,180
1,750,000				2,180,000	3,930,000	4,580,000
		151,775			151,775	130,111
		345,699			345,699	271,213
3,049,825	16,266	503,210		2,427,161	6,551,324	6,639,575
			10,439,562		10,439,562	10,177,097
4,233,600	74,685				4,308,285	3,403,733
4,663,890	2,825				4,666,715	4,471,794
					21,998	67,710
					123,413	112,793
					1,759,415	1,480,747
					478,469	580,989
8,897,490	77,510		10,439,562		21,797,857	20,294,863
$11,947,315	$ 93,776	$503,210	$10,439,562	$2,427,161	$28,349,181	$26,934,438

Source: Town of Blacksburg, Virginia, Comprehensive Annual Financial Report, June 30, 1990, Exhibit I

Exhibit 20–16   *Combined Balance Sheet—All Fund Types and Account Groups (cont.)*

TOWN OF BLACKSBURG, VIRGINIA
COMBINED STATEMENT OF CASH FLOWS—ALL PROPRIETARY FUND TYPES
FOR THE FISCAL YEAR ENDED JUNE 30, 1990

	Proprietary Fund Types		Totals (Memorandum Only)	
	Enterprise	Internal Service	1990	1989
Operating Activities:				
Cash received from customers	$ 4,821,353	$ 386,586	$ 5,207,939	$ 4,771,294
Cash paid to suppliers	(3,535,447)	(268,831)	(3,804,278)	(3,223,369)
Cash paid to employees	(995,274)	(125,090)	(1,120,364)	(1,037,448)
Other operating revenue	104,051		104,051	61,261
Net cash provided (used) by operating activities	394,683	(7,335)	387,348	571,738
Noncapital Financing Activities:				
Operating transfers-out to other funds	(47,443)		(47,443)	(46,277)
Operating transfers-in from other funds	25,872		25,872	
Administrative assistance grant received	326,778		326,778	120,992
Miscellaneous income	6,069		6,069	10,510
Net cash provided (used) by noncapital activities	311,276		311,276	85,225
Capital and Related Financing Activities:				
Principal repayment of revenue bonds	(250,000)		(250,000)	(250,000)
Interest paid on revenue bonds	(142,625)		(142,625)	(158,125)
Acquisition and construction of capital assets	(1,457,196)	(343)	(1,457,539)	(365,471)
Proceeds from sale of property and equipment				46,528
Contributions of capital by other governments	772,656		772,656	76,149
Net cash provided (used) by financing activities	(1,077,165)	(343)	(1,077,508)	(650,919)
Investing Activities:				
Interest Income	178,444		178,444	148,171
Net cash provided (used) by investing activities	178,444		178,444	148,171
Net increase (decrease) in cash	(192,762)	(7,678)	(200,440)	154,215
Cash at beginning of year	1,699,557	16,296	1,715,853	1,561,638
Cash at end of year	$ 1,506,795	$ 8,618	$ 1,515,413	$ 1,715,853
Combined Reconciliation of Net Income to Net Cash Provided by Operating Activities:				
Operating income (loss)	$ (432,813)	$ (8,559)	$ (441,372)	$ (25,932)
Adjustments to reconcile operating income to net cash provided by operations:				
Depreciation	689,084	5,094	694,178	608,697
(Increase) decrease in utilities receivable	43,789		43,789	(107,774)
(Increase) decrease in accounts receivable	4,310	45	4,355	52,948
(Increase) decrease in inventory	(51,158)		(51,158)	12,416
Increase (decrease) in accounts payable	133,282	(4,661)	128,621	27,306
Increase (decrease) in accrued expenses	3,410	746	4,156	(1,312)
Increase (decrease) in customer deposits	1,264		1,264	1,936
(Increase) decrease in accrued interest	3,515		3,515	3,453
Net cash provided (used) by operating activities	$ 394,683	$ (7,335)	$ 387,348	$ 571,738

Source: Town of Blacksburg, Virginia, Comprehensive Annual Financial Report, June 30, 1990, Exhibit V

Exhibit 20–17   *Combined Statement of Cash Flows—All Proprietary Fund Types*

GOVERNMENTAL FUNDS—INTO THE FUTURE WITH GASB STATEMENT 11

In 1990 GASB issued Statement 11, "Measurement Focus and Basis of Accounting," that will change the way in which governmental type funds and expendable trust funds account for and report revenue and expenditures in their operating statements. GASB 11 is expected to be effective for periods beginning after June 15, 1994. Basically, the statement establishes (1) accrual accounting for governmental funds and (2) a financial resources measurement focus for the operating statements of governmental funds.

The accrual basis of accounting means that governmental funds will report expenditures when incurred, regardless of when paid. Revenues will be recognized when the underlying transactions or events occur. Tax revenues will be recorded when payment is demanded.

Statement 11 explains *measurement focus* as that which is expressed in reporting an entity's financial performance and position (in other words, which resources are being measured). The *basis of accounting* refers to when the effects of transactions and events are recognized. Operating results of governmental funds are to be expressed in terms of a flow of financial resources measurement focus. The basis of accounting should be the accrual basis. The *flow of financial resources measurement focus* measures how the financial resources obtained for a period compare to the claims incurred against those resources during the same period.

Two kinds of assets—financial resources and capital assets—are identified. Capital assets are long-lived, tangible assets, such as equipment, land, and infrastructure assets. Financial resources include:

> Cash
> Claims to cash (accounts receivable, taxes receivable)
> Claims to goods or services (prepaid items)
> Consumable goods (supplies inventories)
> Equity securities of other entities

Only financial resources are included in the measurement focus for governmental funds.[10] Financial resources are affected by transactions or events which include revenues, operating expenditures, interfund operating transfers, and residual equity transfers. Acquisition, disposition, and long-term financing of capital assets and certain other activities that have long-term economic benefits also affect financial resources.

The Objective Is Accountability

The most important objective of governmental financial reporting is accountability. Implicit in the need to be accountable is the need to report on the government's achievement of its goals. Statement 11 identifies the primary performance goal for state and local governments as "providing optimum services for their citizens within the limits of available resources."[11] The objective of accountability is served by a measurement of interperiod equity, the use of budgets, and the fund accounting structure.

Interperiod Equity Measurement One measure of financial performance for a period is the *interperiod equity measurement* which measures the extent to which

---

[10]The flow of financial resources measurement focus does *not* measure cost of services because depreciation is not considered.

[11]GASB Statement 11, paragraph 8. The performance goal for business enterprises is operating profit.

current-year revenues were sufficient to pay for current year services. Measuring interperiod equity involves the comparison of revenues obtained by the governmental unit with a financial measure of the services provided. In many instances, there will be little relationship between the services provided and the revenues obtained *except* for the time period basis of association. The operating statement therefore measures aggregate revenues and aggregate services for a time period to arrive at interperiod equity. Since interperiod equity cannot be measured completely within a single fund, each governmental fund is expected to contribute to the measurement of interperiod equity.

Accounting standards based on a concept of measuring interperiod equity emphasize results of operations, rather than financial position.

Use of Budgets   Governments establish financial performance goals for the period through the use of budgets. Budgets usually focus on *financing* the period's activities and are expressed in terms of financial resources. Budgetary laws and practices requiring a balanced budget are not consistent among governments, however, GASB believes that the intent of those laws is to prevent current-year citizens from shifting the burden of paying for current-year services to future-year taxpayers. The Board's emphasis on the measurement of interperiod equity reflects the spirit of governmental balanced budget laws.

Use of Fund Accounting   Statement 11 was developed under the existing funds structure which includes four types of governmental funds: general, special revenue, capital projects, and debt service. How funds should be reported or displayed is a separate project on financial reporting and is not included in GASB Statement 11.

Operating Debt   Operating debt is debt issued to finance operations or in anticipation of revenues.[12] Operating debt provides no benefit to future-year citizens, and therefore, it should not be recognized in the operating statement as an inflow of financial resources. Similarly, payments of operating debt principal should not be reported in the operating statement as an outflow of financial resources.

Effective Date

Statement 11 is effective for periods beginning after June 15, 1994. Earlier application is *prohibited* because Statement 11 provisions must be implemented simultaneously with future GASB pronouncements. The statement was issued early because its basic principles are needed for developing standards on other topics, and because state and local governmental units will need time to develop information systems necessary to implement Statement 11 provisions.

SUMMARY

Capital projects funds and debt service funds are governmental funds that use the modified accrual basis of accounting. Capital projects funds are used to account for the acquisition of major capital facilities, and debt service funds are used to account for the receipt and use of resources to service general long-term debt obligations. Neither capital projects funds nor debt service funds record fixed assets or depreciation in their accounts, nor do they account for general long-term debt in their accounts. General fixed assets and general long-term debt are recorded in separate self-balancing account groups.

Internal service funds, enterprise funds, and nonexpendable trust funds have operations that are similar to those of private business enterprises, and,

---

[12]Capital debt is debt issued for capital purposes. GASB Statement 11 refers to general long-term *capital* debt as liabilities that are expected to be paid from financial resources and that provide long-term financing to acquire capital assets or for certain other projects.

accordingly, the accounting and reporting requirements are quite similar to those of private businesses with the same or similar types of activities. Expendable trust funds have measurement objectives that are comparable with those of governmental funds, and their accounting requirements are essentially the same. Since the operations of agency funds are primarily custodial, agency fund assets and liabilities are accounted for on a modified accrual basis, but revenue and expenditure accounting is not applicable.

ASSIGNMENT MATERIAL

QUESTIONS

1 What is the purpose of capital projects funds? Are all general fixed assets of a governmental unit acquired through capital projects funds? Explain.

2 How are capital projects funds financed and when would a capital projects fund be terminated?

3 If bonds issued to finance a capital project are sold at a premium, is the amount of project authorization increased by the premium? Discuss.

4 When is it acceptable for a capital projects fund to recognize revenue prior to the time of actual receipt?

5 Are debt service funds used to account for debt service on all long-term obligations of a governmental unit? If not, which long-term debt obligations are excluded?

6 Describe a transaction that would affect the general fund, the debt service fund, and the general long-term debt account group at the same time.

7 Is interest paid through the debt service fund recorded on an accrual basis? Explain.

8 How do special assessment levies differ from general tax levies?

9 Which funds and/or account groups may be used to account for the activities of a special assessment construction project with long-term financing? Explain.

10 In which funds should the depreciation on general fixed assets be recognized?

11 Explain the account "investment in general fixed assets." When is the account balance increased and when is it decreased?

12 Is the account "amount provided for retirement of term bonds payable" an asset, a liability, or a fund equity account? Explain.

13 The first payment on a five-year capital lease for a street sweeper is recorded in the general fund on January 1, 19X1. What other funds and/or account groups might be affected? Discuss.

14 How are enterprise and internal service funds similar? How are they different?

15 Cite some governmental operations that might be accounted for through an internal service fund.

16 What financial statements are needed for an enterprise fund to meet the requirements for fair presentation in accordance with GAAP?

17 Are the accounts "capital contribution from municipality," "contributed capital from municipality," and "advance from municipality" alternatives? Discuss.

18 What fund types are included in the fiduciary fund category?

19 Compare the financial reporting requirements of expendable and nonexpendable trust funds.

20 Are all the agency responsibilities of a governmental unit accounted for through agency funds? Explain.

21 How many columns (not including total columns) are needed for a combined balance sheet of a governmental unit with a general fund, two special revenue funds, three internal service funds, four enterprise funds, and a general fixed assets account group? Explain.

EXERCISES

E 20-1 1 Assets financed through a capital projects fund should be capitalized and reported in annual reports:

  a Only when construction is completed

  b On the basis of expenditures to date

  c On the basis of expenditures and encumbrances to date

  d On the basis of amounts authorized for projects in progress

2 When capital projects funds are dissolved, any remaining assets are usually:
  a Transferred to other capital projects funds
  b Transferred to the general fund or the debt service fund
  c Appropriated for asset maintenance
  d Held indefinitely in a capital assets trust fund

3 The proceeds of an intergovernmental grant that are restricted to the construction of a municipal library should be recorded in:
  a The general fund   **b** A special revenue fund
  c A capital projects fund   **d** An agency fund

4 The city of Columbus issued general obligation serial bonds to finance the construction of a public health services center. This transaction requires recognition in the:
  a General fund
  b Capital projects fund and general fund
  c Capital projects fund and the general long-term debt account group
  d General fund and general long-term debt account group

5 During the fiscal year 19X3, Shawsville created a capital projects fund to account for the construction of a swimming pool which was financed 20 percent from taxes and 80 percent from the sale of long-term bonds at a premium. The swimming pool was completed and the excess of funds available over expenditures was transferred to another fund. Which of the following funds or accounting groups would not be affected by the activities of the capital projects fund?
  a General fund
  b Enterprise fund
  c Debt service fund
  d General fixed assets account group

E 20-2   **1** General obligation bonds of a governmental unit are frequently described as:
  a Mortgage bonds
  b Full faith and credit obligation bonds
  c Serial bonds
  d Tax anticipation bonds

2 If general obligation serial bonds are sold to finance a central purchasing facility for a city and the bonds are to be serviced through a debt service fund, the bond liability should be recorded in the:
  a General long-term debt account group
  b Central purchasing fund
  c Related enterprise fund
  d Debt service fund

3 On April 1, 19X1 the City of Greenspur sold an 8 percent, $100,000 serial bond issue with interest payment dates on April 1 and October 1. The related debt service fund received and paid out $4,000 during 19X1. If a balance sheet is prepared on December 31, 19X1:
  a It will show a fund balance deficit of $2,000
  b It should show interest payable of $2,000
  c Interest should not be accrued unless revenues are also accrued
  d Interest expense from October 1 to December 31 should be accrued according to the *GASB Codification*

4 Assume that $100,000 general obligation serial bonds are sold at a premium of $2,000. The entry required in the general long-term debt account group includes a:
  a Debit to cash of $102,000
  b Debit to amount to be provided for retirement of bonds, $100,000
  c Credit to bond premium, $2,000
  d Credit to amount provided for retirement of bonds, $100,000

5 Assume that assets are accumulated in the debt service fund during the current year to retire general obligation term bonds. This event:
  a Requires an entry in the general long-term debt account group
  b Is recognized in the debt service fund only
  c Would be recognized in both the general fund and the debt service fund
  d Would not affect the general long-term debt account group

6 The city's debt as reported in its general long-term debt account group is defeased through advance refunding under *GASB Statement 7* when:
  a An in-substance defeasance of the debt occurs
  b The refunding debt issue is sold

    c The proceeds of the refunding issue are deposited in an irrevocable trust with an escrow agent

    d The general long-term debt is actually paid

7 The liability for general long-term debt is recorded in the general long-term debt account group:

    a At par value less issuance discounts or plus issuance premium

    b At par value and discounts are reported as deferred charges and premiums are reported as deferred credits

    c At par or maturity value

    d At net present value and adjusted annually during the life of the debt issue

E 20–3 **[AICPA adapted]**

1 Which of the following funds of a governmental unit recognizes revenues in the accounting period in which they become available and measurable?

    a Capital projects funds   **b** Nonexpendable trust funds

    c Enterprise funds   **d** Internal service funds

2 The receipts from a special tax levy to retire and pay interest on general obligation bonds issued to finance the construction of a new City Hall should be recorded in a:

    a Debt service fund   **b** Capital projects fund

    c Revolving interest fund   **d** Special revenue fund

3 Lisa County issued $5,000,000 of general obligation bonds at 101 to finance a capital project. The $50,000 premium was to be used for payment of principal and interest. This transaction should be accounted for in the:

    a Capital projects fund, debt service fund, and general long-term debt account group.

    b Capital projects fund and debt service fund only

    c Debt service fund and the general long-term debt account group only

    d Debt service fund only

4 On December 31, 19X8, Park Township paid a contractor $4,000,000 for the total cost of a new police building built in 19X8. Financing was by means of a $3,000,000 general obligation bond issue sold at face amount on December 31, 19X8, with the remaining $1,000,000 transferred from the general fund. What amount should Park record as revenues in the capital projects fund in connection with the bond issue proceeds and the transfer?

    a $0   **b** $1,000,000

    c $3,000,000   **d** $4,000,000

5 In 19X8, Beech City issued $400,000 of bonds, the proceeds of which were restricted to the financing of a capital project. The bonds will be paid wholly from special assessments against benefited property owners. However, Beech is obligated to provide a secondary source of funds for repayment of the bonds in the event of default by the assessed property owners. In Beech's general-purpose financial statements, this $400,000 special assessment debt should:

    a Not be reported

    b Be reported in the special assessment fund

    c Be reported in the general long-term debt account group

    d Be reported in an agency fund

Use the following information in answering questions 6 and 7.

    On December 31, 19X7, Vane City paid a contractor $3,000,000 for the total cost of a new municipal annex built in 19X7 on city-owned land. Financing was provided by a $2,000,000 general obligation bond issue sold at face amount on December 31, 19X7, with the remaining $1,000,000 transferred from the general fund.

6 What account and amount should be reported in Vane's 19X7 financial statements for the general fund?

    a Other financing uses control, $1,000,000

    b Other financing sources control, $2,000,000

    c Expenditures control, $3,000,000

    d Other financing sources control, $3,000,000

7 What accounts and amounts should be reported in Vane's 19X7 financial statements for the capital projects fund?

    a Other financing sources control, $2,000,000; general long-term debt, $2,000,000

    b Revenues control, $2,000,000; expenditures control, $2,000,000

    c Other financing sources control, $3,000,000; expenditures control, $3,000,000

    d Revenues control, $3,000,000; expenditures control, $3,000,000

On March 2, 19X1, Finch City issued ten-year general obligation bonds at face amount, with interest payable March 1 and September 1. The proceeds were to be used to finance the construction of a civic center over the period April 1, 19X1 to March 31, 19X2. During the fiscal year ended June 30, 19X1, no resources had been provided to the debt service fund for the payment of principal and interest.

1 On June 30, 19X1, Finch's debt service fund should include interest payable on the general obligation bonds for:

   a zero months   **b** three months
   c four months   **d** six months

2 Proceeds from the general obligation bonds should be recorded in the:

   a General fund
   b Capital projects fund
   c General long-term debt account group
   d Debt service fund

3 The liability for the general obligation bonds should be recorded in the:

   a General fund
   b Capital projects fund
   c General long-term debt account group
   d Debt service fund

4 On June 30, 19X1, Finch's combined balance sheet should report the construction in progress for the civic center in the:

	Capital projects fund	General fixed assets account group
a	Yes	Yes
b	Yes	No
c	No	No
d	No	Yes

1 The *amount available in debt service funds* is an account of a govermental unit that would be included in the:

   a Liability section of the general long-term debt account group
   b Liability section of the debt service fund
   c Asset section of the general long-term debt account group
   d Asset section of the debt service fund

2 *Proceeds of general obligation bonds* is an account of a governmental unit that would be included in the:

   a Enterprise fund   **b** General fund
   c Capital projects fund   **d** Debt service fund

3 Equipment in general governmental service that had been constructed ten years before by a capital projects fund was sold. The receipts were accounted for as unrestricted revenue. Entries are necessary in the:

   a General fund and capital projects fund
   b General fund and general fixed assets account group
   c General fund, capital projects fund, and enterprise fund
   d General fund, capital projects fund, and general fixed assets account group

4 Cash secured from property tax revenue was transferred for eventual payment of principal and interest on general obligation bonds. The bonds had been issued when land had been acquired several years ago for a city park. Upon the transfer, an entry would *not* be made in which of the following:

   a Debt service fund
   b General fixed assets account group
   c General long-term debt account group
   d General fund

5 The following revenues were among those reported by Ariba Township in 19X9:

Net rental revenue (after depreciation) from a parking garage owned by Ariba	$ 40,000
Interest earned on investments held for employees' retirement benefits	100,000
Property taxes	6,000,000

What amount of the foregoing revenues should be accounted for in Ariba's governmental-type funds?

a $6,140,000   **b** $6,100,000

c $6,040,000   **d** $6,000,000

6 Kew City issued the following long-term obligations:

Revenue bonds to be repaid from admission fees collected from users of the city swimming pool	$1,000,000
General obligation bonds issued for the city water and sewer fund which will service the debt.	$1,800,000

Although these bonds are expected to be paid from enterprise funds, the full faith and credit of the city has been pledged as further assurance that the obligations will be paid. What amount of these bonds should be accounted for in the general long-term debt account group?

a $0   **b** $1,000,000

c $1,800,000   **d** $2,800,000

7 The following proceeds received by Grove City in 19X7 are legally restricted to expenditure for specified purposes:

Donation by a benefactor mandated to an expendable trust fund to provide meals for the needy	$300,000
Sales taxes to finance the maintenance of tourist facilities in the shopping district	900,000

What amount should be accounted for in Grove's special revenue funds?

a $0   **b** $300,000

c $900,000   **d** $1,200,000

8 In connection with Albury Township's long-term debt, the following cash accumulations are available to cover payment of principal and interest on:

Bonds for financing of water treatment plant construction	$1,000,000
General long-term obligations	400,000

The amount of these cash accumulations that should be accounted for in Albury's debt service funds is:

a $0   **b** $400,000

c $1,000,000   **d** $1,400,000

E 20-6   **1** Money to pay interest on special assessment bonds would likely come from:

      a Property taxes

      b Interest charges on deferred special assessment receivables

      c A debt service fund

      d Federal or state grants

   2 Assume that special assessment bonds are issued to finance a new sewer system. The construction activity should be accounted for in:

      a A special revenue fund

      b A capital projects fund

      c A debt service fund

      d A general fixed assets account group

   3 The proceeds from special assessment bonds to be repaid from special assessments against property owners should be recorded as:

      a Contributions from property owners

      b Bond proceeds

      c Special assessment revenues

      d Assessments receivable

   4 The collection of deferred special assessments and the remittance to the holders of special assessment bonds for which the governmental unit is not obligated in any manner should be accounted for in:

      a An agency fund

      b A capital projects fund

      c A debt service fund

      d A general long-term debt account group

5 The debt service on special assessment bonds serviced by liens on the assessed properties, but also backed by the full faith and credit of the governmental unit, should be accounted for in:
  a An agency fund
  b A capital projects fund
  c A debt service fund
  d A general long-term debt account group

E 20–7

1 A city provides initial financing for its enterprise fund with the stipulation that the amount advanced be returned to the general fund within five years. In recording the payment to the enterprise fund, the general fund should:
  a Debit the account *contribution to enterprise fund*
  b Debit the *expenditures* account
  c Credit a *due from enterprise fund* account
  d Credit a *reserve for advance to enterprise fund* account

2 During 19X4 the Electric Utility Enterprise Fund paid $10,000 interest and $100,000 principal payments in connection with general obligation bonds to be serviced from revenue derived from user charges from its customers. In which of the following funds or account groups would *entries* be required to account for these payments?
  a Debt service fund
  b General long-term debt account group
  c Internal service fund
  d None of the above

3 Revenue bonds were issued to finance construction of the Golden Age Housing Complex which was accounted for through the Golden Age Housing Fund, an enterprise fund. Which statement with respect to those bonds is correct?
  a Both the liability and the debt service should be accounted for in the Golden Age Housing Fund.
  b The liability should be accounted for in the Golden Age Housing Fund and the debt service should be accounted for through a debt service fund.
  c The debt service should be accounted for through a debt service fund and the bond liability should be accounted for in the general long-term debt account group.
  d The debt service should be accounted for through the Golden Age Housing Fund and the liability should be accounted for in the general long-term debt account group.

4 Internal service funds would *not* be used in accounting for goods and services provided to:
  a Enterprise funds
  b Other governmental funds
  c The public
  d Other departments within the same governmental unit

5 An internal service fund should *not* use:
  a Accrual accounting
  b The purchase basis in accounting for supplies
  c Encumbrance accounting
  d Flexible budgeting practices

6 If enterprise fund assets are financed through general obligation bonds, rather than revenue bonds, the debt:
  a Is not an enterprise fund liability
  b Must be serviced through a debt service fund
  c Is an enterprise fund liability if enterprise fund revenues are intended to service the debt
  d Is reported both as a fund long-term liability and a general obligation liability

7 Enterprise funds should be used in accounting for those government activities that involve:
  a Providing goods and services to the public
  b Providing goods and services subject to user charges
  c Providing goods and services to the public if a substantial amount of revenue is derived from user charges
  d Collection of money from the public

8 Which of the following would *not* be indicative of activities that should be accounted for through enterprise funds?
   a Incidental sales to the public
   b Self-supporting activities
   c Revenue bond financing
   d Provision of goods and services of a commercial type

E 20–8 **1** A governmental unit accounts for resources held in a trustee or agency relationship in

a Governmental funds	**b** Proprietary funds
c Fiduciary funds	**d** Custodial funds

2 Fiduciary funds include four different types of funds. Which of the following is *not* one of these types?

a Agency funds	**b** Tax collection funds
c Nonexpendable trust funds	**d** Pension trust funds

3 Agency funds maintain accounts for:

a Liabilities	**b** Revenues
c Expenses	**d** Fund balances

4 An example of a fiduciary fund that uses modified accrual accounting procedures is:

a An expendable trust fund	**b** An endowment fund
c A nonexpendable trust fund	**d** An employee retirement fund

5 A type of fiduciary fund in which principal is maintained intact and income is used for specified purposes is known as:

a An agency fund	**b** A corpus fund
c A pension trust fund	**d** An endowment fund

6 The focus of attention in accounting for trust and agency funds is on:
   a Fiduciary responsibility during a time period
   b Budget compliance during a time period
   c Project progress or completion
   d Maintaining captial

7 Which of the following is not a similarity of trust and agency funds?
   a Rarely incorporated into a government's operating budget
   b Involve a fiduciary relationship of the government
   c Likely to be in existence for long periods of time
   d Rarely subjected to formal budgetary control through accounting processes

8 Endowment funds are:
   a Agency funds
   b Expendable trust funds
   c All trust funds
   d Trust funds expendable for earnings only

E 20–9 **[AICPA adapted]**

1 Maple Township issued the following bonds during the year ended June 30, 19X8:

Bonds issued for the garbage collection enterprise fund that will service the debt	$500,000
Revenue bonds to be repaid with admission fees collected by the township zoo enterprise fund	350,000

What amount of these bonds should be accounted for in Maple's general long-term debt account group?

a $0	**b** $350,000
c $500,000	**d** $850,000

2 Lori Township received a gift of an ambulance having a market value of $180,000. What account in the general fixed assets account group should be debited for this $180,000 gift?
   a None (memorandum entry only)
   b Investment in general fixed assets from gifts
   c Machinery and equipment
   d General fund assets

3 Customers' security deposits that cannot be spent for normal operating purposes were collected by a governmental unit and accounted for in the enterprise fund. A portion of the amount collected was invested in marketable debt securities and a portion in marketable equity securities. How would each portion be classified in the balance sheet?

	Portion in Marketable Debt Securities	*Portion in Marketable Equity Securities*
a	Unrestricted asset	Restricted asset
b	Unrestricted asset	Unrestricted asset
c	Restricted asset	Unrestricted asset
d	Restricted asset	Restricted asset

4 Brockton City's water utility, which is an enterprise fund, transferred land and a building to the general city administration for public use at no charge to the city. The land was carried on the water-utility books at $4,000 and the building at a cost of $30,000 on which $23,000 depreciation had been recorded. In the year of the transfer, what would be the effect of the transaction?

a Reduce retained earnings of the water utility by $11,000 and increase the fund balance of the general fund by $11,000

b Reduce retained earnings of the water utility by $11,000 and increase the total assets in the general fixed assets account group by $11,000

c Reduce retained earnings of the water utility by $11,000 and increase the total assets in the general fixed assets account group by $34,000

d Have no effect on a combined balance sheet for the city

5 Brockton City serves as a collecting agency for the local independent school district and for a local water district. For this purpose, Brockton has created a single agency fund and charges the other entities a fee of 1 percent of the gross amounts collected. (The service fee is treated as a general fund revenue.) During the latest fiscal year, a gross amount of $268,000 was collected for the independent school district and $80,000 for the water district. As a consequence of the foregoing, Brockton's general fund should:

a Recognize receipts of $348,000

b Recognize receipts of $344,520

c Record revenue of $3,480

d Record encumbrances of $344,520

6 Through an internal service fund, Wood County operates a centralized data processing center to provide services to Wood's other governmental units. In 19X9, this internal service fund billed Wood's parks and recreation fund $75,000 for data processing services. What account should Wood's internal service fund credit to record this $75,000 billing to the parks and recreation fund?

a Operating revenues control

b Interfund exchanges

c Intergovermental transfers

d Data processing department expenses

E 20–10   **[AICPA adapted]**

Rock County has acquired equipment through a noncancelable lease-purchase agreement dated December 31, 19X1. This agreement requires no down payment and the following minimum lease payments:

December 31	Principal	Interest	Total
19X2	$50,000	$15,000	$65,000
19X3	50,000	10,000	60,000
19X4	50,000	5,000	55,000

1 What account should be debited for $150,000 in the general fund at inception of the lease if the equipment is a general fixed asset and Rock does *not* use a capital projects fund?
  a Other financing uses control
  b Equipment
  c Expenditures control
  d Memorandum entry only

2 What account should be credited for $150,000 in the general fixed assets account group at inception of the lease if the equipment is a general fixed asset?
  a Fund balance from capital lease transactions
  b Other financing sources control—capital leases
  c Expenditures control—capital leases
  d Investment in general fixed assets—capital leases

3 What journal entry is required for $150,000 in the general long-term debt account group at the inception of the lease if the lease payments are to be financed with general government resources?
  a Debit: Expenditures control
    Credit: Other financing sources control
  b Debit: Other financing uses control
    Credit: Expenditures control
  c Debit: Amount to be provided for lease payments
    Credit: Capital lease payable
  d Debit: Capital lease payable
    Credit: Amount to be provided for lease payments

4 If the lease payments are required to be made from a debt service fund, what account or accounts should be debited in the debt service fund for the December 31, 19X2 lease payment of $65,000?
  a Expenditures control, $65,000
  b Other financing sources control, $50,000, and expenditures control, $15,000
  c Amount to be provided for lease payments, $50,000, and expenditures control, $15,000
  d Expenditures control, $50,000, and amount to be provided for lease payments, $15,000

5 If the equipment is used in enterprise fund operations and the lease payments are to be financed with enterprise fund revenues, what account should be debited for $150,000 in the enterprise fund at inception of the lease?
  a Expenses control
  b Expenditures control
  c Other financing sources control
  d Equipment

6 If the equipment is used in internal service fund operations and the lease payments are financed with internal service fund revenues, what account or accounts should be debited in the internal service fund for the December 31, 19X2 lease payment of $65,000?
  a Expenditures control, $65,000
  b Expenses control, $65,000
  c Capital lease payable, $50,000, and expenses control, $15,000
  d Expenditures control, $50,000, and expenses control, $15,000

E 20–11 **[AICPA adapted]**

Elm City contributes to and administers a single-employer defined benefit pension plan on behalf of its covered employees. The plan is accounted for in a pension trust fund. Actuarially determined employer contribution requirements and contributions actually made for the past three years, along with the percentage of annual covered payroll, were as follows:

| | Contribution made | | Actuarial requirement | |
	Amount	Percent	Amount	Percent
19X9	$11,000	26	$11,000	26
19X8	5,000	12	10,000	24
19X7	None	None	8,000	20

1 What account should be credited in the pension trust fund to record the 19X9 employer contribution of $11,000?
  a Revenues control
  b Other financing sources control
  c Due from special revenue fund
  d Pension benefit obligation

2 To record the 19X9 pension contribution of $11,000, what debit is required in the governmental-type fund used in connection with employer pension contributions?
  a Other financing uses control
  b Expenditures control
  c Expenses control
  d Due to pension trust fund

3 In the notes to Elm's 19X9 financial statements, employer contributions expressed as percentages of annual covered payroll should be shown to the extent available for a minimum of
  a 1 year   **b** 2 years
  c 3 years   **d** 12 years

E 20–12 **1** Consider the following related journal entries:

Enterprise fund

Due from general fund	$ 5,000	
Accumulated depreciation	14,000	
Equipment		$19,000

General fund

Expenditures	$ 5,000	
Due to enterprise fund		$ 5,000

General fixed assets account group

Equipment	$ 5,000	
Investments in fixed assets—general revenue		$ 5,000

These entries indicate accounting procedures for:
  a An interfund sale and purchase of equipment
  b The retirement of equipment by a governmental organization
  c An unusual application of depreciation accounting
  d Intrafund transfers between expendable funds

2 Land acquired as a gift was recorded at $40,000 during 19X1. If the land is sold for $50,000 in 19X2, the appropriate entry in the general fixed assets account group would be a:
  a Debit to cash and a credit to land for $50,000
  b Debit to cash for $50,000, a credit to land for $40,000, and a credit to fund balance for $10,000
  c Debit to investment in fixed assets and a credit to land for $40,000
  d Debit to fund balance and a credit to land for $40,000

3 At June 30, 19X3 the nonexpendable loan fund trial balance contained the following:

Cash	$ 15,020
Loans receivable	86,070
Loan fund balance	$101,090

During the year July 1, 19X3 to June 30, 19X4 the following transactions and events took place:

Collections: Loans, $50,000 and interest, $2,000
New loans, $62,000
Write-off of uncollectible loans, $3,000

At June 30, 19X4 the unexpendable loan fund balance should be:
  a $98,090   **b** $100,090
  c $101,090   **d** $103,090

E 20–13 Prepare the journal entries that would be required in the general fixed assets account group to account for the following unrelated transactions and events.

1 A new fire truck was purchased for $50,000 cash. Financing was from general revenues.
2 Used police cars were sold for $4,500. These cars were purchased for $16,000 through state grant revenue and $10,000 accumulated depreciation was recorded on them.
3 A flood destroyed street cleaning equipment and $5,000 was received from insurance on the equipment. The cost of the equipment was $8,000 and no depreciation had been recorded.
4 Construction on the city hall was completed at a total cost of $680,000. The city hall project was financed by equal amounts of general obligation bond proceeds and federal revenue sharing funds. Expenditures in prior years were $460,000.
5 Land with a current value of $100,000 was donated to the city. The cost to the donor was $16,000.

E 20–14 The Police Complex Capital Projects Fund was established in 19X1 for construction in the authorized amount of $500,000. Financing was from a $400,000, twenty-year, term bond issue that was sold at par and from general fund transfers in the amount of $100,000. Amounts for repayment of the term bonds were transferred from a special revenue fund to a sinking fund, starting in 19X1.

The project was completed in 19X3 and the remaining fund balance was transferred to the fund responsible for servicing the long-term debt. A summary of revenues, expenditures, and encumbrances related to the project (but not including tranfers for debt service) is as follows:

	19X1	19X2	19X3
Bond proceeds and operating transfers	$500,000	none	none
Expenditures for the year	100,000	$250,000	$145,000
Encumbrances outstanding at December 31	400,000	150,000	none

Indicate which of the following funds or account groups are affected by activities related to the police complex in each of the three years, 19X1, 19X2, and 19X3.

1 General fund
2 Special revenue fund
3 Debt service fund
4 Capital projects fund
5 General fixed assets account group
6 General long-term debt account group

E 20–15 The City of Lite established a tax agency fund to collect property taxes for the City of Lite, Bloomer County, and Bloomer School District. Total tax levies of the three governmental units were $200,000 for 19X1 of which $60,000 was for the City of Lite, $40,000 for Bloomer County, and $100,000 for Bloomer School District.

The tax agency fund charges Bloomer County and Bloomer School District a 2 percent collection fee that it transfers to the general fund of the City of Life in order to cover costs incurred for agency fund operations.

During 19X1 the tax agency fund collected $150,000 of the 19X1 levies and remitted $100,000 to the various governmental units. The $100,000 includes $1,400 collection fees that were remitted to Lite's general fund.

Required: Prepare a balance sheet for the City of Lite Tax Agency Fund at December 31, 19X1.

E 20–16 Prepare all journal entries, other than adjusting and closing entries, to account for the activities described below that relate to the construction and financing of a new recreation center for the City of Unitas for the calendar year 19X1. Prepare entries for all funds and account groups affected and identify the fund or account group to which each journal entry relates.

March 1, 19X1—Sold $1,000,000 general obligation, 6 percent serial bonds at a premium of 1 percent to finance construction of a new recreation center. An additional $200,000 was received from a Federal grant to bring the total financing up to the $1,200,000 authorized expenditures for the project.

March 8, 19X1—The premium was transferred to another fund for debt service.

October 1, 19X1—The general fund transferred $20,000 to the debt service fund. This $20,000 together with the issue premium was used to pay the $30,000 interest that came due on the project during 19X1.

March 1 to December 31, 19X1—A contract for $1,150,000 was let for the recreation center. Contract expenditures of $500,000 were recorded and paid and engineering costs of $15,000, not under contract, were paid. Encumbrances of $650,000 relating to the construction contract were outstanding at December 31.

PROBLEMS

P 20–1   On June 15, 19X1, Loup City authorizes the issuance of $500,000 par of 6 percent serial bonds to be issued on July 1, 19X1 and to mature in annual serials of $100,000 beginning on July 1, 19X5. The proceeds of the bond issue are to be used to finance a new city hall.

During the fiscal year ended June 30, 19X2, the following events and transactions occurred:

July 1, 19X1—A contract for construction of the city hall is awarded to Kircher Construction Company for $480,000.

July 1, 19X1—$250,000 par value of the 6 percent serial bonds is sold at a premium of 2 percent.

December 20, 19X1—A bill is received from Kircher Construction Company for one-third of the contract price.

January 1, 19X2—Kircher Construction Company is paid for work completed to date, less a 10 percent retained percentage to ensure performance.

January 1, 19X2—Bond interest due is paid with funds transferred from the general fund and from the premium made available for interest payments.

June 30, 19X2—A bill is received from Kircher Construction Company for one-third of the contract price.

Required
1 Prepare journal entries to account for the transactions and events described above in each of the funds and account groups affected. Identify the fund or account group for each journal entry.
2 Prepare a closing journal entry for the capital projects fund at June 30, 19X2.

P 20–2   The City of Pilot sells a $1,000,000, 6 percent serial bond issue of general obligation bonds at par value on June 30, 19X4. Interest payment dates are December 31 and June 30. One-tenth of the bonds are to be retired annually with the first serial retirement to be made on June 30, 19X5.

A new fire station is to be constructed with the proceeds of the bond issue, and funds to service the debt are included in general fund appropriations on an annual basis beginning with the July 1, 19X4 to June 30, 19X5 fiscal year of Pilot. The first expenditure for the fire station occurs on August 1, 19X4.

Required
1 What funds and/or account groups are involved with the foregoing bond issue during Pilot's July 1, 19X3 to June 30, 19X4 fiscal year (involved to the extent that journal entries are required)?
2 What funds and/or account groups are involved with the foregoing bond issue during Pilot's July 1, 19X4 to June 30, 19X5 fiscal year (involved to the extent that journal entries are required)?
3 Prepare the journal entries required in Pilot's debt service fund during the fiscal year ended June 30, 19X5, assuming generally accepted accounting principles and contributions and expenditures according to the planned schedule.
4 Prepare a statement of general long-term debt for the city of Pilot as of June 30, 19X5, assuming that the bond issue described is Pilot's only long-term debt.

P 20-3 Comparative adjusted trial balances for the Motor Pool of Douwe County at June 30, 19X1 and June 30, 19X2 are as follows:

	June 30, 19X2	June 30, 19X1
Cash	$ 37,000	$ 44,000
Due from general fund	12,000	8,000
Due from electric fund	4,000	3,000
Supplies on hand	14,000	12,000
Autos	99,000	80,000
Supplies used	68,000	60,000
Salaries expense	25,000	20,000
Utilities expense	9,000	8,000
Depreciation	16,000	15,000
	$284,000	$250,000
Accumulated depreciation—autos	$ 56,000	$ 40,000
Accounts payable	11,000	10,000
Advance from general fund (current)	5,000	5,000
Contribution from general fund	50,000	50,000
Retained earnings	42,000	35,000
Revenue from billings	120,000	110,000
	$284,000	$250,000

Required: Prepare financial statements for the Motor Pool at and for the year ended June 30, 19X2. (The statement of cash flows is to be included.)

P 20-4 Selected activities relating to fixed assets of Progressive City for 19X3 are described in the following list. You are required to make journal entries for additions to and deletions from the general fixed assets account group using the five major classifications of assets recommended by the GASB.

General Fund

1 Office equipment is purchased for $6,000.
2 A new fire truck is purchased for $35,000.
3 Park equipment costing $8,000 is received and installed.
4 New radar equipment costing $8,000 is purchased and old radar equipment costing $4,000 is sold for $100. No depreciation had been recorded.
5 The roof on City Hall is replaced at a cost of $3,000.
6 $2,500 is received from the sale of buildings that cost $40,000 a number of years ago.

Motor Pool Fund

7 New automobiles are purchased for $15,000 and old automobiles costing $10,000 with $6,000 depreciation recorded are sold at $4,500.

Sewer Construction Fund

8 Initial expenditures on a new sewer system of $40,000 are vouchered during the year. The total cost of the system is estimated at $100,000 to be financed 50 percent by federal grants and 50 percent from a bond issue.

Street Paving Fund

9 Street paving costing $20,000 is completed for this special assessment project during the year. Expenditures of $6,000 had been recorded in the prior year.

Other

10 Land with a value of $20,000 is donated to the city during the year.

P 20-5 The accounts of the general fund, the debt service fund, the general fixed assets account group, and the general long-term debt account group of Ampora, Illinois were merged on June 30, 19X8 by an inexperienced bookkeeper. The combined account balances are included in a trial balance as follows:

TRIAL BALANCE
AMPORA, ILLINOIS
ON JUNE 30, 19X8

Cash ($8,000 belongs to the DSF)	$ 68,000	
Current taxes receivable	32,000	
Delinquent taxes receivable	8,000	
Land	30,000	
Buildings	90,000	
Construction in progress	35,000	
Investments	45,000	
Amount provided for payment of bonds	53,000	
Amount to be provided for payment of bonds	47,000	
Vouchers payable (GF)		$ 20,000
Due to internal service fund		4,000
Reserve for encumbrances		5,000
Bonds payable		100,000
Investment in general fixed assets—general revenue		55,000
Investment in general fixed assets—federal grant		100,000
Fund balance ($53,000 belong to DSF)		124,000
	$408,000	$408,000

Required: Prepare balance sheets for each of the funds or account groups involved. All account balances that apply to more than one fund or account group have been identified in the combined trial balance.

P 20–6 On January 1, 19X2 J. G. Monee created a Student Aid Trust Fund to which he donated a building valued at $40,000 (cost $25,000), bonds having a market value of $50,000, and $10,000 cash. The trust agreement stipulated that principal was to be maintained intact but earnmgs were to be used to support needy students. Consider gains on investments and depreciation as adjustments of earnings rather than of trust fund principal.

Activities for 19X2

1 During the year net rentals of $4,000 were collected for building rental (net rentals equal gross rentals less $12,000 out-of-pocket costs).
2 The bonds were sold for $55,000 on June 30, 19X2. Of the proceeds, $3,000 represented interest accrued from January 1 to June 30.
3 Stocks were purchased for $60,000 cash.
4 Depreciation on the building was calculated at $2,000 for the year.
5 Dividends receivable of $6,000 were recorded at December 31, 19X2.

Required: Prepare balance sheets for the Student Aid Principal Trust Fund and the Student Aid Earnings Trust Fund at December 31, 19X2.

P 20–7 Appros City maintains a cemetery trust fund that is expendable as to income but nonexpendable as to principal. Gains and losses and depreciation are adjustments to income. The trial balance of the cemetery trust fund at December 31, 19X1 contains the following accounts and balances:

Cash	$ 16,000 dr	
Investments	300,000 dr	
Equipment	25,000 dr	
Accumulated depreciation—equipment		$ 10,000 cr
Fund balance—principal		305,000 cr
Fund balance—earnings		26,000 cr

The following transactions and events occurred during 19X2:

1 Cash earnings of $15,000 are received from the investments.
2 Salaries for cemetery maintenance are $9,000.
3 Miscellaneous maintenance of $3,100 is paid.
4 Annual depreciation on the equipment is $3,000.
5 Investments that cost $18,000 are sold for $21,000.
6 Additional investments costing $24,000 are purchased.

Required: Prepare an after-closing trial balance for the Cemetery Trust Fund at December 31, 19X2. Note that trust fund principal and earnings are combined in a single fund.

P 20–8   [AICPA adapted]

In a special election held on May 1, 19X7, the voters of the City of Nicknar approved a $10,000,000 issue of 6 percent general obligation bonds maturing in twenty years. The proceeds of this sale will be used to help finance the construction of a new civic center. The total cost of the project was estimated at $15,000,000. The remaining $5,000,000 will be financed by an irrevocable state grant which has been awarded. A capital projects fund was established to account for this project and was designated the Civic Center Construction Fund. The formal project authorization was appropriately recorded in a memorandum entry.

The following transactions occurred during the fiscal year beginning July 1, 19X7 and ending June 30, 19X8:

1 On July 1 the General Fund loaned $500,000 to the Civic Center Construction Fund for defraying engineering and other expenses.
2 Preliminary engineering and planning costs of $320,000 were paid to Akron Engineering Company. There had been no encumbrance for this cost.
3 On December 1 the bonds were sold at 101. The premium on bonds was transferred to the Debt Service Fund.
4 On March 15 a contract for $12,000,000 was entered into with Candu Construction Company for the major part of the project.
5 Orders were placed for materials estimated to cost $55,000.
6 On April 1 a partial payment of $2,500,000 was received from the state.
7 The materials that were previously ordered were received at a cost of $51,000 and paid.
8 On June 15 a progress billing of $2,000,000 was received from Candu Construction for work done on the project. As per the terms of the contract, the city will withhold 6 percent of any billing until the project is completed.
9 The General Fund was repaid the $500,000 previously loaned.

Required

1 Prepare journal entries to record the transactions in the Civic Center Construction Fund for the period July 1, 19X7 through June 30, 19X8 and the appropriate closing entries at June 30, 19X8.
2 Prepare a balance sheet of the Civic Center Construction Fund on June 30, 19X8.

P 20–9   [AICPA adapted]

In compliance with a newly enacted state law, Dial County assumed the responsibility for collecting all property taxes levied within its boundaries as of July 1, 19X5. A composite property tax rate per $100 of net assessed valuation was developed for the fiscal year ending June 30, 19X6 and is as follows:

Dial County General Fund	$ 6.00
Eton City General Fund	3.00
Bart Township General Fund	1.00
	$10.00

All property taxes are due in quarterly installments and when collected are then distributed to the governmental units represented in the composite rate.

In order to administer collection and distribution of such taxes, the county has established a Tax Agency Fund.

Additional Information

1 In order to reimburse the county for estimated administrative expenses of operating the Tax Agency Fund, the Tax Agency Fund is to deduct 2 percent from the tax collections each quarter for Eton City and Bart Township. The total amount deducted is to be remitted to the Dial County General Fund.
2 Current-year tax levies to be collected by the Tax Agency Fund are as follows:

	Gross Levy	Estimated Amount to Be Collected
Dial County	$3,600,000	$3,500,000
Eton City	1,800,000	1,740,000
Bart Township	600,000	560,000
	$6,000,000	$5,800,000

3 $10,000 was charged back to Bart Township because of an error in the original computation of the current gross tax levy and the estimated amount to be collected.

4 As of September 30, 19X5 the Tax Agency Fund has received $1,440,000 in first-quarter payments. On October 1 this fund made a distribution to the three governmental units.

Required: For the period July 1, 19X5 through October 1, 19X5, prepare journal entries to record the transactions described for the following funds:

Dial County Tax Agency Fund
Dial County General Fund
Eton City General Fund
Bart Township General Fund

P 20–10 The City of Melborne authorized the construction of a new recreation center at a total cost of $1,000,000 on June 15, 19X7. On the same date, the city approved a $1,000,000, 8 percent, ten-year general obligation serial bond issue to finance the project. During the year July 1, 19X7 to June 30, 19X8, the following transactions and events occurred relative to the recreation center project.

1 On July 1, 19X7 the city sold $500,000 par of the authorized bonds, with interest payment dates on December 31 and June 30 and the first serial retirement to be made on June 30, 19X8. The bonds were sold at 102.

2 On July 5, 19X7 a construction contract for the recreation center was let in the amount of $960,000.

3 On December 15, 19X7 the contractor's bill for $320,000 was received based on certification that the work was one-third completed.

4 The contractor was paid for one-third of the contract less a 10 percent retained percentage to assure performance.

5 On December 30, 19X7 the GF transferred $10,000 to the fund responsible for servicing the serial bonds.

6 Interest on the serial bonds was paid on December 31, 19X7 with the money transferred from the GF and the CPF.

7 On June 15, 19X8 the contractor's bill for $320,000 was received based on certification that the work was two-thirds completed.

8 On June 28, 19X8 the GF transferred $70,000 to the fund responsible for servicing the serial bonds; $20,000 for interest and $50,000 for principal.

9 Interest and principal on the serial bonds was paid on June 30, 19X8.

10 On June 30, 19X8 the city sold the remaining $500,000 par of authorized bonds at par.

Required

1 Prepare all journal entries in the CPF necessary to account for the transactions and events given.

2 Identify the other funds or account groups affected by each of the transactions or events.

3 Prepare financial statements for the CPF for the year ended June 30, 19X8.

P 20–11 **[AICPA adapted]**

The following transactions represent practical situations frequently encountered in accounting for municipal governments. Each transaction is independent of the others.

1 The city council of Bernardville adopted a budget for the general operations of the government during the new fiscal year. Revenues were estimated at $695,000. Legal authorizations for budgeted expenditures were $650,000.

2 Taxes of $160,000 were levied for the special revenue fund of Millstown. One percent was estimated to be uncollectible.

3 a On July 25, 19X3 office supplies estimated to cost $2,390 were ordered for the city manager's office of Bullersville. Bullersville, which operates on a calendar year, does not maintain an inventory of such supplies.

b The supplies ordered July 25 were received on August 9, 19X3, accompanied by an invoice for $2,500.

4 On October 10, 19X3 the general fund of Washingtonville repaid to the utility fund a loan of $1,000 plus $40 interest. The loan had been made earlier in the fiscal year.

5 A prominent citizen died and left ten acres of undeveloped land to Harper City for a future school site. The donor's cost of the land was $55,000. The fair value of the land was $85,000.

6 a On March 6, 19X3 Dahlstrom City issued 4 percent special assessment bonds payable, due March 6, 19X8 at face value of $90,000. Interest is payable annually. Dahlstrom City, which operates on a calendar year, will use the proceeds to finance a curbing project. The city is secondarily liable to bond-holders of this issue.

b On October 29, 19X3 the full $84,000 cost of the completed curbing project was accrued. Also, appropriate closing entries were made with regard to the project.

7 a Conrad Thamm, a citizen of Basking Knoll, donated common stock valued at $22,000 to the city under a trust agreement. Under the terms of the agreement, the principal amount is to be kept intact; use of revenue from the stock is restricted to financing academic college scholarships for needy students.

b On December 14, 19X3 dividends of $1,100 were received on the stock donated by Mr. Thamm.

8 a On February 23, 19X3 the Town of Lincoln, which operates on the calendar year, issued 4 percent general obligation bonds with a face value of $300,000 payable in ten years, to finance the construction of an addition to the city hall. Total proceeds were $308,000.

b On December 31, 19X3 the addition to the city hall was officially approved, the full cost of $297,000 was paid to the contractor, and appropriate closing entries were made with regard to the project. (Assume that no entries have been made with regard to the project since February 23, 19X3.)

Required: For each transaction prepare the necessary journal entries for all the funds and account groups involved.

P 20-12 **[AICPA adapted]**

The city of Happy Hollow has engaged you to examine its financial statements for the year ended December 31, 19X1. The city was incorporated as a municipality and began operations on January 1, 19X1. You find that a budget was approved by the city council and was recorded, but all transactions have been recorded on the cash basis. The bookkeeper has provided an Operating Fund trial balance as follows:

Debits	
Cash	$238,900
Expenditures	72,500
Estimated revenues	114,100
	$425,500
Credits	
Appropriations	$102,000
Revenues	108,400
Bonds payable	200,000
Premium on bonds payable	3,000
Fund balance	12,100
	$425,500

Additional Information

1 Examination of the appropriation-expenditure ledger revealed the following information:

	Budgeted	Actual
Personal services	$ 45,000	$38,500
Supplies	19,000	11,000
Equipment	38,000	23,000
Total	$102,000	$72,500

2 Supplies and equipment in the amounts of $4,000 and $10,000, respectively, had been received, but the vouchers had not been paid at December 31.

3 At December 31 outstanding purchase orders for supplies and equipment not yet received were $1,200 and $3,800, respectively.

4 The inventory of supplies on December 31 was $1,700 by physical count. The decision was made to record the inventory of supplies. A city ordinance requires that expenditures are to be based on purchases, not on the basis of usage.

5 Examination of the revenue subsidiary ledger revealed the following:

	Budgeted	Actual
Property taxes	$102,600	$ 96,000
Licenses	7,400	7,900
Fines	4,100	4,500
Total	$114,100	$108,400

It was estimated that 5 percent of the property taxes would not be collected. Accordingly, property taxes were levied in an amount so that collections would yield the budgeted amount of $102,600.

6 On November 1, 19X1 Happy Hollow issued 8 percent general obligation term bonds with $200,000 face value for a premium of $3,000. Interest is payable each May 1 and November 1 until maturity fourteen years from the date of issuance. The city council ordered that the cash from the bond premium be set aside and restricted for the eventual retirement of the debt principal. The bonds were issued to finance the construction of a city hall, but no contracts had been let as of December 31.

Required

1 Prepare a worksheet showing adjustments and distributions to the proper funds or groups of accounts in conformity with generally accepted accounting principles applicable to governmental entities. (Formal adjusting entries are not required.)

2 Identify the financial statements that should be prepared for the general fund. (You are not required to prepare these statements.)

3 Draft formal closing entries for the general fund.

P 20–13 **[AICPA adapted]**

The City of Merlot operates a central garage through an Internal Service Fund to provide garage space and repairs for all city-owned and operated vehicles. The Central Garage Fund was established by a contribution of $200,000 from the general fund on July 1, 19X6, at which time the building was acquired. The after-closing trial balance at June 30, 19X8 was as follows:

	Debit	Credit
Cash	$150,000	
Due from General Fund	20,000	
Inventory of materials and supplies	80,000	
Land	60,000	
Building	200,000	
Accumulated depreciation—building		$ 10,000
Machinery and equipment	56,000	

	Debit	Credit
Accumulated depreciation—machinery and equipment		12,000
Vouchers payable		38,000
Contribution from General Fund		200,000
Retained earnings		306,000
	$566,000	$566,000

The following information applies to the fiscal year ended June 30, 19X9:

1 Materials and supplies were purchased on account for $74,000.
2 The inventory of materials and supplies at June 30, 19X9 was $58,000, which agreed with the physical count taken.
3 Salaries and wages paid to employees totaled $230,000 including related costs.
4 A billing was received from the Enterprise Fund for utility charges totaling $30,000, and was paid.
5 Depreciation of the building was recorded in the amount of $5,000. Depreciation of the machinery and equipment amounted to $8,000.
6 Billings to other departments for services rendered to them were as follows:

General Fund	$262,000
Water and Sewer Fund	84,000
Special Revenue Fund	32,000

7 Unpaid interfund receivable balances at June 30, 19X9 were as follows:

General Fund	$ 6,000
Special Revenue Fund	16,000

8 Vouchers payable at June 30, 19X9 were $14,000.

Required

1 For the period July 1, 19X8 through June 30, 19X9 prepare journal entries to record all the transactions in the Central Garage Fund accounts.
2 Prepare closing entries for the Central Garage Fund at June 30, 19X9.

21

COLLEGES AND UNIVERSITIES, HOSPITALS, AND VOLUNTARY HEALTH AND WELFARE ORGANIZATIONS

This chapter provides an introduction to accounting principles and reporting practices of nonprofit colleges and universities, hospitals, and voluntary health and welfare organizations. Each of these organization types is important for the resources it controls and for its impact on society.

The three organization types are alike in the sense that they are nonprofit organizations, have service objectives, and use fund accounting practices. But their service objectives, sources of financing, and degree of autonomy vary significantly, and these differences are reflected in different applications of fund accounting and in different accounting principles and reporting practices.

SOURCE OF ACCOUNTING PRINCIPLES FOR NONPROFITS

Outside of the governmental area, accounting principles and reporting practices for colleges and universities, hospitals, and voluntary health and welfare organizations are better established than for other types of nonprofit organizations. This is because separate accounting manuals for each of these organization types have been in existence for many years and because the AICPA has issued Industry Audit Guides in each of the three areas.[1] In addition, *FASB Statement No. 32*, "Specialized Accounting and Reporting Principles and Practices in AICPA Statements of Position and Guides on Accounting and Auditing Matters" (1979), cites the industry audit guides for colleges and universities, hospitals, and voluntary health and welfare organizations as sources of "preferable accounting principles" for purposes of applying *APB Opinion No. 20*, "Accounting Changes." In *Statement No. 32*, however, "the Board agreed to exercise responsibility for all specialized accounting and reporting principles and practices in the Guides and SOPs and after appropriate due process issuing them as FASB Statements."[2] *Specialized principles* refers to the current accounting principles and

---

[1] See AICPA Audit and Accounting Guide, *Audits of Certain Nonprofit Organizations*, 1981, for accounting and reporting standards applicable to other nonprofit organizations.

[2] *FASB Statement No. 32*, paragraph 2.

practices in the AICPA Guides and SOPs that were neither superseded by nor contained in ARBs, APB Opinions, FASB Statements, and FASB Interpretations.

Statements issued by the Financial Accounting Standards Board prescribing accounting principles for nonprofit organizations that issue GAAP financial statements and that are not a part of a governmental unit take precedence over other sources of accounting principles for nonprofits. In 1985 the Board issued *Concepts Statement No. 6,* "Elements of Financial Statements," which replaced *Concepts Statement No. 3,* "Elements of Financial Statements of Business Enterprises," in order to expand the scope of the statement to encompass nonprofit organizations.

SPECIALIZED ACCOUNTING AND REPORTING PRINCIPLES

The direction provided by Audit Guides and SOPs has been inconsistent in several key accounting principles. For example, before the issuance of *FASB Statement No. 93,* depreciation was recognized by hospitals and voluntary health and welfare organizations, but not by colleges and universities. In compliance with the respective audit guides, *restricted contributions* are accounted for as revenues in restricted funds by voluntary health and welfare organizations, but as direct additions to restricted fund balances for college and university accounting.

Recognition of Depreciation

FASB Statement No. 93, "Recognition of Depreciation by Not-for-Profit Organizations," requires all nonprofit organizations that issue general-purpose financial statements to record depreciation for long-lived assets, even if the assets are gifts. This statement did not eliminate all inconsistencies with regard to depreciation, however, because the Governmental Accounting Standards Board has no such requirement for government-supported colleges and universities. GASB instructed government-supported colleges and universities not to apply the provisions of *FASB Statement No. 93* in their financial statements.

Accounting for Contributions

Another area of inconsistent accounting principles is accounting for contributions. Contributions are an important part of the revenue of most nonprofit entities. Should contributions be recognized when they are pledged to a nonprofit organization or when the contribution is actually received? Do donor-imposed restrictions and conditions affect revenue recognition? Answers to these questions depend on the type of nonprofit organization.

In 1990 the FASB issued an Exposure Draft, "Accounting for Contributions Received and Contributions Made and Capitalization of Works of Art, Historical Treasures, and Similar Assets" that applies to all nonprofit organizations. The Exposure Draft deals with definition, recognition, and measurement of contributions received and contributions made. The FASB hopes to remove inconsistencies in the recognition requirements for contributions that currently exist in the *Audits of Providers of Health Care Services* (1990), *Audits of Colleges and Universities* (1973), *Audits of Voluntary Health and Welfare Organizations* (1974), and *Audits of Certain Nonprofit Organizations* (1981).

Recognizing Contributions Received *Contribution* is defined as "a transfer of cash or other assets to an entity or a settlement or cancellation of its liabilities from a voluntary nonreciprocal transfer by another entity acting other than as an owner."[3] Basically, the Exposure Draft requires that contributions received,

---

[3]Exposure Draft, "Accounting for Contributions Received and Contributions Made and Capitalization of Works of Art, Historical Treasures, and Similar Assets," paragraph 151.

874

COLLEGES
AND UNIVERSITIES,
HOSPITALS,
AND VOLUNTARY
HEALTH AND WELFARE
ORGANIZATIONS

including unconditional pledges,[4] be recognized as revenues in the period received, and reported as assets, decreases of liabilities, or expenses, depending on the form in which the benefits are received. Noncash contributions are measured at the fair values of the items received.

The Exposure Draft makes a clear distinction between *donor-imposed conditions* (the occurrence or failure to occur of an uncertain future event that releases the donor from its obligation) and *donor-imposed restrictions* (specifications of how the assets promised or received must be used). *Conditional pledges* are recognized as revenue after the conditions are removed; in other words, when they become *unconditional pledges.*

Contributions of Services   Under the Exposure Draft, contributions of services would be recognized as revenue if the services create or enhance other assets, are provided by entities that are normally paid for the service, or are the same as services normally purchased by the nonprofit organization.

Recognizing Contributions Made   The Exposure Draft also covers contributions that are to be recognized as expenses in the period in which the pledges are made and as corresponding asset decreases or liability increases. Contributions are measured at the fair values of the items given or the fair value of liabilities canceled.

Works of Art   Other provisions of the Exposure Draft relate to contributions of works of art, historical treasures, and similar items that should be recognized as revenue at their fair values if they will be sold, or if a market exists. Retroactive capitalization of assets not previously capitalized would also be required.

Financial Statement Implications   The financial statements of nonprofit entities should distinguish between contributions that increase permanently restricted net assets, temporarily restricted net assets, and unrestricted net assets. Contributions with permanent restrictions are those that the donor requires to be maintained permanently, but from which the recipient can use the income. Restrictions are deemed temporary if the donor permits the recipient organization to deplete the donated assets as specified, and the restriction is satisfied by the passage of time or by some action of the recipient.

At the time of this writing, it is unknown whether the Exposure Draft will become GAAP without further modification.

COLLEGES AND UNIVERSITIES

The usual objective of a college or university is to provide educational services to its constituents. As in governmental units, colleges and universities frequently provide their services on the basis of social desirability and finance them, at least in part, without reference to those receiving the benefits. The objectives of college and university accounting are to show the sources from which resources have been received and how those resources were utilized in meeting educational objectives. Fund accounting practices are used in achieving the accounting objectives.

Primary authority over accounting principles for private colleges and universities comes from the Financial Accounting Standards Board (FASB). The FASB accepts the provisions of the AICPA's Industry Audit Guide, *Audits of Colleges and Universities* as constituting generally accepted accounting principles for private colleges and universities except where those provisions have been superseded by FASB pronouncements. Similarly, the Governmental Accounting Standards

---

[4]A *pledge* is a written or oral promise to contribute cash or other asset to the organization. An *unconditional pledge* depends on the passage of time or demand by the nonprofit organization for performance. Unconditional pledges are recognized as receivables and revenues at their fair values when received.

Current Funds

Unrestricted Current Funds—to account for economic resources expendable for operating purposes in carrying out the objectives of the college or university (encompasses instruction, research, extension, and public service). This category includes auxiliary enterprises (such as resident halls, food services, intercollegiate athletics, college stores, and student unions), and separate subfunds may be used for each enterprise.

Restricted Current Funds—to account for economic resources expendable for operating purposes but restricted by donors or other outside agencies to a specific purpose.

Loan Funds

Individual Loan Funds—to account for resources available for student and faculty loans and related loan activity. Since resources may be restricted externally by donors or internally by the governing body, the accounting records must enable the sources and the restrictions to be identified.

Endowment and Similar Funds

Endowment Funds—to account for resources received from donors and outside agencies with the stipulation that principal be maintained in perpetuity and income be expended for general or specified purposes or added to principal.

Term Endowment Funds—to account for resources received from donors or outside agencies with the stipulation that principal may be expended after some time period or event.

Quasi-Endowment Funds—to account for resources designated by the governing board (internally designated) to be invested indefinitely with income being expended as directed.

Annuity and Life Income Funds

Annuity Funds—to account for resources acquired under the condition that the college or university make stipulated periodic payments to individuals as provided by agreement with the donor.

Life Income Funds—to account for funds contributed to the college or university under the requirement that the income be paid (usually until death) to a designated individual.

Plant Funds

Unexpended Plant Funds—to account for unexpended resources to be used for acquisition of physical property.

Renewal and Replacement Fund—to account for resources to be used for renewal or replacement of existing property.

Retirement of Indebtedness Funds—to account for resources set aside for debt service and debt retirements relating to institutional properties.

Investment in Plant Funds—to account for plant investments including land, buildings, improvements other than buildings and equipment (including books), and liabilities relating to plant assets.

Agency Funds

Individual Funds—to account for resources held by a college or university as custodian or agent for student or faculty groups.

Exhibit 21–1 *Fund Accounting Structure for Colleges and Universities*

Board (GASB) pronouncements apply to all governmental entities, including colleges and universities that are publicly owned and supported. Under the GASB Codification, *Audits of Colleges and Universities* constitute GAAP for government-supported colleges and universities, until the provisions are changed by GASB pronouncements or until GASB accepts a new FASB pronouncement. Thus, the AICPA's Industry Audit Guide is a primary source of accounting principles for

876

COLLEGES
AND UNIVERSITIES,
HOSPITALS,
AND VOLUNTARY
HEALTH AND WELFARE
ORGANIZATIONS

both private and publicly owned colleges and universities. Much of the material in the Industry Audit Guide comes from *College and University Business Administration,* an accounting manual prepared by the National Association of College and University Business Officers (NACUBO).

Fund Groupings

The accounting and reporting systems of colleges and unversities are divided into six fund groups. These groups are further divided into subgroups as needed for planning, control, decision making, and reporting purposes. This fund accounting structure is summarized in Exhibit 21–1, which also sketches the nature and scope of activities included in each group.

General Accounting and Reporting Matters

Colleges and universities are encouraged by NACUBO to prepare operating and capital budgets, but they are not required to integrate budgetary accounting into their accounting systems. If formal budgetary accounting is used, it can be applied in a manner similar to that used for governmental entities.

Basic financial statements for colleges and universities include a combined balance sheet for all fund groups, a combined statement of changes in fund balances for all fund groups, and a statement of revenues, expenditures, and other changes for the current funds grouping. Revenues are classified by source, and expenditures by function.

The Industry Audit Guide, *Audits of Colleges and Universities,* specifies that the accounts and reports be maintained on an accrual basis. This is interpreted to mean that revenues are recognized when earned and that expenditures are recognized when the related materials or services are received. *Accrual accounting,* as the term is used here, differs from its usage with respect to business entities, because colleges and universities do not report expenses or net income. Deferred expenses (supplies, for example) and accrued liabilities (salaries, for example) are reflected in the current funds balance sheet. Nonpublic colleges and universities report depreciation expense on capital assets in the statement of current funds revenues, expenditures, and other changes under the provisions of *FASB Statement No. 93.* Government-supported colleges and universities are guided by *GASB Statement 8,* "Applicability of *FASB Statement No. 93,* 'Recognition of Depreciation by Not-for-Profit Organizations,' to Certain State and Local Governmental Entities," and do not report depreciation. Expenditures for plant asset replacements and renewals are reported as current fund expenditures when acquired directly through current funds.

CURRENT FUNDS OF COLLEGES AND UNIVERSITIES

Only resources that are expendable for operating purposes are included in the **current funds grouping.** The current funds grouping contains two subgroups— one for unrestricted current funds and the other for restricted current funds. When expendable resources are restricted by donors or outside entities to expenditures for specific operating purposes, they are classified as **restricted current funds.** Otherwise, they are included in the **unrestricted current funds** subgroup. Since the current funds grouping encompasses resources received and expended for instruction, research, extension, and public service, as well as for the operation of **auxiliary enterprises** (student unions, dormitories, resident halls, intercollegiate athletics), it is an extremely important area of accounting for all educational institutions. By contrast, the scope and magnitude of activities accounted for through the other fund groupings vary widely from one institution to another.

Current Funds Revenues and Transfers

The term *revenue* is used only in accounting for current unrestricted funds and current restricted funds to the extent that equal amounts have been expended. Other fund groupings use the term *additions* to report activities that increase funds. The restricted current funds group has both revenue and additions. Current funds revenue control accounts include:

> Tuition and fees
> Appropriations (federal, state, and local)
> Government grants and contracts (federal, state, and local)
> Private gifts, grants, and contracts
> Endowment income
> Sales and services of educational activities
> Sales and services of auxiliary enterprises
> Sales and services of hospitals
> Other sources
> Independent operations

Transfers of unrestricted resources from other funds to the current funds are classified as nonmandatory transfers in the statement of revenues, expenditures, and other changes. Transfers are not included in revenue.

Revenue of Restricted Current Funds Group The restricted current funds group includes resources expendable for operating purposes that are *restricted by donors or other outside entities* for specific purposes. *Additions* to current restricted funds consist of restricted gifts, restricted endowment fund income, restricted contracts and grants from private organizations or governmental units, and income from investments of current restricted fund resources. *Revenue* of current restricted funds is recognized to the extent that such funds are expended during the period for current operating purposes. The timing of revenue recognition coincides with the removal of donor restrictions. Thus, the revenue of current restricted funds for a period is equal to current restricted fund expenditures for that period. Under the Exposure Draft, "Accounting for Contributions . . ." donor-restricted contributions would be recognized as revenue using the same guidelines as used for unrestricted revenue—in other words, in the period received.

Revenue of Auxiliary Enterprises The revenue of auxiliary enterprises includes amounts earned in providing facilities and services to faculty, staff, and students. It includes amounts charged for resident halls, food services, intercollegiate athletics, and college unions, as well as sales and receipts from college stores, barber shops, movie houses, and so on. The revenue of auxiliary enterprises does *not* include interdepartmental transactions of service departments.

Service Department Activities In accounting for the activities of service departments, such as storerooms, motor pools, and printshops, the accounting records are normally maintained on a cost-reimbursement basis, and no revenues or expenditures are recorded. Instead, the cost is reflected in the expenditures of the departments or divisions receiving the goods and services.

Revenue of Unrestricted Current Funds Group Revenue of unrestricted current funds includes unrestricted gifts, grants, and government appropriations, as well as unrestricted income earned from unrestricted resources. It also includes unrestricted income earned by endowment and similar funds, but it does *not* include net capital gains of endowment funds. Capital gains and losses from endowment fund investments are accounted for in those funds. If gains are used for current operating purposes, they are reported as *transfers* to current funds rather than revenue.

878

COLLEGES
AND UNIVERSITIES,
HOSPITALS,
AND VOLUNTARY
HEALTH AND WELFARE
ORGANIZATIONS

Current Fund Expenditures and Transfers

Expenditures   The term *expenditures* is used only in accounting for the current funds. Current fund expenditures include all expenses incurred in accordance with generally accepted accounting principles except expenditures for renewals and replacements of plant and equipment. For reporting purposes, current fund expenditures are classified broadly as *educational and general expenditures* and *expenditures of auxiliary enterprises*. Expenditures are classified on a functional basis in the statement of current funds revenues, expenditures, and other changes. Functional classifications include:

> Instruction—expenditures for the instruction program
>
> Research—expenditures to produce research outcome
>
> Public service—expenditures for activities to provide noninstructional services to external groups
>
> Academic support—expenditures to provide support for instruction, research, and publications
>
> Student services—amounts expended for admissions and registrar, and amounts expended for students' emotional, social, and physical well-being
>
> Institutional support—amounts expended for administration and the long range planning of the university
>
> Operation and maintenance of plant—expenditures of current operating funds for operating and maintaining the physical plant (net of amounts to auxiliary enterprises and university hospitals)
>
> Scholarships and fellowships—expenditures from restricted or unrestricted funds in the form of grants to students

Transfers   Sometimes current fund resources are transferred to other fund groups as directed by the governing board of a college or university or as stipulated in a binding agreement with outside entities. For example, the governing board may authorize transfers to a quasi-endowment fund to provide income for designated future purposes (board designated), a bond indenture may require amounts to be set aside for debt service or renewal or replacement of the educational plant (a binding agreement), or a gift agreement for a student loan fund may require matching transfers by the college or university (a binding agreement). Transfers of current funds resources to other funds under binding agreements are **mandatory transfers** and are so classified for reporting purposes. Discretionary or **board-designated transfers** are nonmandatory and are simply classified as transfers in the financial statements.

Sample Journal Entries
for the Unrestricted Current Fund

The journal entries presented here illustrate the recording of some typical events and transactions that would occur in the unrestricted current funds of colleges and universities. The examples are unrelated, and subsidiary account references are not included. The functional basis of classifying the expenditures and the revenue sources would be designated in the subsidiary accounts.

Tuition and Fees and Transfers   The full amount of tuition and fees (net of refunds) assessed against students for educational purposes is recognized as revenue. Tuition waivers for scholarships or staff benefits and estimated bad debts are recorded as expenditures.

When *some portion* of the tuition and fees is externally restricted for activities other than current operations, the full amount of the tuition and fees is recorded as revenue in the unrestricted current funds, and then the restricted amount is recorded as a mandatory transfer to the appropriate fund. When specific fees are assessed for legally or contractually restricted purposes (in other words, the *total* amount of the fees assessed is externally restricted), the fees are recorded directly as additions to the appropriate fund balance account.

Student tuition and fees for Northside College total $300,000. Ten percent of this amount is legally restricted for debt service on educational plant. Student tuition and fees also include $5,000 of tuition waivers provided under the fellowship program. Bad debts are estimated at 3 percent of gross revenue from student tuition and fees, or $9,000.

Accounts receivable	$300,000	
Revenues—educational and general		$300,000
To record tuition and fees.		
Expenditures—educational and general	$ 5,000	
Accounts receivable		$ 5,000
To record tuition waivers.		
Expenditures—educational and general	$ 9,000	
Allowance for uncollectible accounts		$ 9,000
To record allowance for uncollectible accounts.		
Mandatory transfer—principal and interest	$ 30,000	
Due to retirement of indebtedness funds		$ 30,000
To record legally binding transfer to plant funds to retire debt.		

In this example, only a portion of the fees are restricted. Therefore, the full amount of the revenue is reported in the unrestricted current funds subgroup, with the restricted portion being treated as a mandatory transfer to the plant funds.

If the governing board of Northside College had restricted a portion of the tuition and fees for nonoperating purposes, the full amount of tuition and fees would be recorded as revenue and the restricted portion would be treated as a nonmandatory transfer to the appropriate fund.

Appropriations from Federal, State, and Local Governments *Appropriations* include unrestricted amounts for current operations that are received, or made available, from legislative acts or from a local taxing authority. Restricted appropriations are classified as unrestricted if the governing board can change a restriction without going through a legislative process. Milton Junior College receives an appropriation from the state for current operations for $700,000.

Cash	$700,000	
Revenues—educational and general		$700,000
To record appropriations from the state government.		

Sales and Services of Educational Activities Unrestricted current funds revenue may be generated from sales of goods and services that are related incidentally to educational activities of the university. In other words, the goods and services sold are a by product of training or instruction. An example of this category of revenue is the dairy creamery of a land grant university that has $550 revenue from sales of its products.

Cash	$ 550	
Revenue—educational and general		$ 550
To record sales related to educational activities.		

Purchase of Supplies and Materials Because colleges and universities use accrual accounting, an expenditure is recognized when the supplies and materials are used. The purchase of supplies and materials increases an inventory account when the liability is incurred. The supplies inventory, if significant, is included in the financial statements as an asset (deferred charge or prepaid expense). For

880

COLLEGES
AND UNIVERSITIES,
HOSPITALS,
AND VOLUNTARY
HEALTH AND WELFARE
ORGANIZATIONS

example, Smithfield College purchases supplies and materials for $350,000 to be used in educational instruction. The purchase is recorded:

Supplies and materials inventory	$350,000	
Accounts payable		$350,000
To record purchase of supplies and materials.		

If Smithfield uses $320,000 of the supplies during the period, an entry is made as follows:

Expenditures—educational and general	$320,000	
Supplies and materials inventory		$320,000
To record utilization of supplies related to instructional purposes.		

If, however, an expenditure is recorded when the inventory is received and the liability incurred, an adjustment is made at the end of the period to recognize any significant inventory on hand as an asset (deferred charge) and decrease the expenditures amount.

Payment of Salaries and Wages　When salaries of $200,000 are paid in the unrestricted current funds, Smithfield College records payment as follows:

Expenditures—educational and general	$200,000	
Cash (salaries payable)		$200,000
To record expenditures for salaries.		

Sales and Services of Auxiliary Enterprises　Auxiliary enterprises are entities that exist to provide goods or services to students, faculty, and staff for fees related to the cost of those goods and services. All revenue directly derived from the operations of auxiliary enterprises is classified as *auxiliary revenue* and is reported in the current funds subgroups. All expenditures are classified as *auxiliary expenditures* and reported in the current funds. Fixed assets and long-term debt of auxiliary funds are accounted for in the plant fund.

The dining hall at Brighton College had sales of $60,800 and purchased $30,000 supplies during May. The supplies used by the auxiliary enterprise during the period amounted to $28,000. Salaries paid to auxiliary employees were $31,000. Summary entries are:

Cash	$ 60,800	
Revenues—auxiliary enterprises		$ 60,800
To record sales and services related to auxiliary enterprises.		
Supplies inventory	$ 30,000	
Cash (or accounts payable)		$ 30,000
To record purchase of supplies.		
Expenditures—auxiliary enterprises	$ 28,000	
Supplies inventory		$ 28,000
To record utilization of supplies related to auxiliary enterprises.		
Expenditures—auxiliary enterprises	$ 31,000	
Cash		$ 31,000
To record expenditures for salaries of auxiliary enterprises.		

Note that when a liability is incurred for the supplies, the inventory account is debited. The expenditure for supplies is not recognized until the supplies are used.

Mandatory Transfers for Loan Fund Matching Grants　Donors of gifts and grants for specific purposes may require that the college or university provide matching gifts under a binding agreement. For example, the federal government gives Cranwell University a $100,000 grant for student loans if Cranwell provides matching funds. Cranwell will record its matching gift to the student loan funds as a *mandatory transfer:*

Mandatory transfer—loan fund matching grant	$100,000	
Due to loan funds (or cash)		$100,000

To record mandatory transfer to loan fund under binding agreement to provide matching funds.

Nonmandatory Transfers   Funds transferred back to the unrestricted current funds from other funds are *nonmandatory transfers,* rather than revenue. Transfers made from unrestricted current funds to other funds at the discretion of the governing board of the college or university are also nonmandatory transfers. For example, the governing board of Highland College directs that $150,000 from unrestricted current funds be transferred to the student loan fund and that $200,000 be transferred to the renewal and replacement fund for the future renovation of the theater arts building:

Nonmandatory transfers to loan funds	$150,000	
Nonmandatory transfers to renewal and replacement fund	200,000	
Cash		$350,000

To record transfers to loan funds and renewal and replacement fund.

Expenditure for Plant Assets   Current funds expenditures may include the cost of minor plant assets provided that current funds are budgeted for and used by operating departments for the assets acquired. For more significant asset purchases, financial resources are transferred from the current funds to the plant funds making the purchase.

Redman Institute purchases equipment directly through unrestricted current funds in the amount of $35,000. The entry made in the unrestricted current funds grouping is:

Expenditures—educational and general	$ 35,000	
Accounts payable		$ 35,000

To record purchase of equipment.

A separate entry is made in the *investment in plant funds* to record the equipment:

Equipment	$ 35,000	
Net investment in plant		$ 35,000

To record purchase of equipment through current unrestricted funds.

Redman Institute purchases land as a building site for a new testing laboratory. The land costs $200,000, and the financial resources are available in the current unrestricted funds. For this purchase, however, the $200,000 is transferred to the investment in plant funds grouping for making the purchase. The entry in the current unrestricted funds is:

Nonmandatory transfer—investment in plant funds	$200,000	
Cash		$200,000

To transfer money to plant funds for the purchase of land.

Academic Year Different from Fiscal Year   Revenues and related expenditures of an academic year that falls within two different fiscal years should be recognized in the period in which classes are predominately conducted. Revenue received but not earned is reported in the balance sheet as *deferred credits.* Any prepaid expenditures are *deferred charges.* Adjusting entries might be as follows:

882

COLLEGES
AND UNIVERSITIES,
HOSPITALS,
AND VOLUNTARY
HEALTH AND WELFARE
ORGANIZATIONS

Revenues—educational and general
    Deferred credits (or deferred revenues)
  To defer revenue received but not earned.

Deferred charges
    Expenditures—educational and general
  To record prepaid expenses.

At the beginning of the next year, the entries are reversed to remove the liability and recognize revenue, and record the utilization of prepaid items.

Fund Balance Reserve Account   The governing board may set up a fund balance reserve account by a debit to *fund balances—unallocated* and a credit to *fund balances—allocated.* Such board–designated restrictions are included in unrestricted current funds. The fund balances—allocated account also includes equity in auxiliary enterprises and any reserve for encumbrances.

Closing Entries   At year-end, the revenues, expenditures, and mandatory and nonmandatory transfer accounts are closed to the fund balance account.

Sample Entries for Restricted Current Funds

Financial resources in the restricted current funds grouping are expendable for current operating purposes, but they are restricted by donors or other outside agencies to a specific purpose. When cash or other financial resources are received, they are recorded as increases in the fund balance. When the restrictions are removed and the cash is expended, the amount of the expenditure is recognized as revenue. In other words, revenues and expenditures are equal. (If the Exposure Draft, "Accounting for Contributions..." becomes a financial accounting standard, this procedure for recognizing revenue will change.)

An entry to record the receipt of cash that is restricted for specific purposes is as follows:

Cash	$500,000	
Fund balances—gifts		$200,000
Fund balances—grants		250,000
Fund balances—endowment income		50,000
To record receipt of cash.		

Expenditures are made during the period for the specific purposes designated by the donors and grantors:

Expenditures—educational and general	$400,000	
Expenditures—auxiliary enterprises	50,000	
Cash		$450,000
To record expenditures incurred.		

At the end of the period, revenue is recognized in the amount of the expenditures and the fund balances are adjusted:

Fund balances—gifts	$200,000	
Fund balances—grants	200,000	
Fund balances—endowment income	50,000	
Revenues—educational and general		$400,000
Revenues—auxiliary enterprises		50,000
To recognize revenue for the period.		

Statement of Current Funds Revenues, Expenditures, and Other Changes

A reporting format for current funds revenues, expenditures, and other changes of a state-supported university is illustrated in Exhibit 21–2. (The statement has

STATEMENT OF CURRENT FUNDS REVENUES, EXPENDITURES, AND OTHER CHANGES
FOR THE YEAR ENDED JUNE 30,19X2

	Unrestricted	Restricted	Total
Revenues			
Tuition and fees	$1,000,000		$1,000,000
State appropriations	1,200,000		1,200,000
Federal grants and contracts	50,000	$100,000	150,000
Private grants and gifts	400,000	250,000	650,000
Endowment income	75,000	20,000	95,000
Sales and services of educational departments	60,000		60,000
Sales and services of auxiliary enterprises	800,000		800,000
Total current revenues	3,585,000	370,000	3,955,000
Expenditures and Mandatory Transfers			
Educational and General			
Instruction	1,500,000	40,000	1,540,000
Research	600,000	250,000	850,000
Public service and extension	100,000		100,000
Academic support	50,000		50,000
Student services	40,000		40,000
Libraries	70,000	20,000	90,000
Operation and maintenance of plant	80,000		80,000
Scholarships and grants		60,000	60,000
General administration	90,000		90,000
Educational and general expenditures	2,530,000	370,000	2,900,000
Mandatory Transfers			
Principal and interest	40,000		40,000
Renewals and replacements	60,000		60,000
Loan fund matching grants	5,000		5,000
Total educational and general	2,635,000	370,000	3,005,000
Auxiliary Enterprises			
Expenditures	760,000		760,000
Total expenditures and mandatory transfers	3,395,000	370,000	3,765,000
Other Transfers and Additions (Deductions)			
Restricted receipts over transfers to revenues		30,000	30,000
Quasi-endowment fund created	(40,000)		(40,000)
Restricted resources refunded to grantor		(20,000)	(20,000)
Net increases in fund balances	$ 150,000	$ 10,000	$ 160,000

Exhibit 21–2 *College and University Operating Statement for Current Funds*

884

COLLEGES
AND UNIVERSITIES,
HOSPITALS,
AND VOLUNTARY
HEALTH AND WELFARE
ORGANIZATIONS

no relationship to the preceding unrelated sample entries.) Separate statement columns are used for unrestricted and restricted current funds subgroups. As expected, revenues and expenditures of restricted current funds are equal.

Although mandatory transfers are not expenditures, they are distinguished from nonmandatory transfers and are reported in a manner similar to that for expenditures. The mandatory transfers from current funds for principal and interest would be included in the combined statement of changes in fund balances for all fund groupings as a mandatory transfer to the *Retirement of Indebtedness* subgroup of the plant funds group. Similarly, the mandatory transfer for matching loan funds would be an addition to the loan funds group. Although Exhibit 21–2 does not illustrate mandatory transfers for auxiliary enterprises, mandatory transfers relating to dormitory bond indenture agreements are frequently found in the auxiliary enterprise category.

The "other transfers and additions (deductions)" section of Exhibit 21–2 shows $30,000 restricted receipts over transfers to revenues. This is a type of reconciling item that represents additions to the restricted current fund subgroup over amounts recognized as revenue. As explained earlier, revenue recognition of restricted current funds requires removal of donor restrictions through expenditures for specific operating purposes.

A statement of current funds revenues, expenditures, and other changes is the only separate statement for a fund group that is required for college and university reporting. Other statements (balance sheet and statement of changes in fund balances) are combined statements that include all fund groups.

OTHER FUND GROUPINGS OF COLLEGES AND UNIVERSITIES

Only current funds of colleges and universities have revenues and expenditures. Financial reporting of the other fund groupings is done through the balance sheet and the statement of changes in fund balances.

Loan Funds

Resources held by colleges and universities under agreements to provide loans to faculty, staff, and students are accounted for in the *loan funds group.* Fund assets consist of cash, loans, receivables, and temporary investments. Liabilities, if any, consist of amounts payable for operating expenses, loan refunds, and so on. Loan fund additions consist of gifts, bequests, gains on investments, interest on loans, and endowment fund income restricted to loans. Decreases result from loans written off, losses on investments, administrative expenses (if legally permitted), and refunds. Interest on student loans, if significant, must be accrued. Sources of loan funds available are disclosed, and restrictions are identified in presenting the loan fund balances in the combined balance sheet.

Endowment and Similar Funds

The *endowment fund group* consists of endowments, term endowments, and quasi-endowments. Annuity and life income funds, if insignificant, are also included in this group. The "similar funds" designation is used when annuity and life income funds are included.

A separate fund is used for each endowment. The usual assets are cash; certificates of deposit; and investments in securities, real estate, and so on. Liabilities typically consist of debts related to fund assets such as mortgage payable or taxes payable. Income measurement includes amortizing premiums and discounts on debt securities and depreciating fixed assets held as investments. Endowment fund income is

1 Credited to current restricted funds if restricted but expendable for current operating purposes, *or*

2 Credited to endowment, plant, or loan fund balances if so specified by the terms of the endowment agreement, *or*

3 Credited to revenue of unrestricted current funds if available for current expenditures without restrictions.

The assets and liabilities of endowment funds are combined for presentation in the balance sheet of the college or university, but separate fund balances are reported for endowments, term endowments, and quasi-endowments.

Annuity and Life Income Funds

The assets of annuity and life income funds consist of cash and various types of investments that are reported in a manner comparable to that used for endowment funds. Annuity fund liabilities consist of debts related to fund assets and the actuarial amount of annuities payable. Fund balances of annuity funds are increased by new gifts in excess of the present value of annuities payable (classified as additions) and decreased when remaining balances are transferred to other funds upon termination. Liabilities of life income funds consist of debts related to fund assets and life income payments currently due. Increases in the fund balances of life income funds consist of new gifts (additions) and investment gains less losses. (Income earned by a life income fund constitutes a payment currently due and does not increase the fund balance.) Decreases result from transfers to other funds when life income agreements are terminated.

Plant Funds

The *plant funds group* comprises four subgroups: unexpended plant funds, renewal and replacement funds, retirement of indebtedness funds, and investment in plant funds. The first three funds are used to account for the financial resources of the college or university. The last fund, the investment in plant funds, is used to account for the physical plant.

Unexpended Plant Funds and Renewal and Replacement Funds   *Unexpended plant funds* are used to account for resources held for additions and improvements to the physical plant, while *renewal and replacement funds* are used for resources held for renewal and replacements of the existing plant. Assets of unexpended plant funds and renewal and replacement funds include cash, receivables, and investments. Fund balance additions include gifts, donations,[5] investment income and gains, and transfers from other funds (including mandatory transfers for renewal and replacement funds). Deductions for unexpended plant funds include losses on investments and expenditures for new or improved facilities, and fund-raising costs. Renewal and replacement fund deductions consist of outlays for renovations, major repairs, and replacements. Separation of the fund balance into restricted and unrestricted (including board-designated) components is required for each subgroup.

Retirement of Indebtedness Fund   Assets of a *retirement of indebtedness fund* consist of liquid resources for current debt service and investments held for future debt retirement, including sinking fund investments. Fund balance additions include mandatory transfers, voluntary transfers, investment income and gains, gifts, and so on. Deductions consist of principal and interest payments, investment losses, and custodial expenses. Since the assets may consist of restricted and unrestricted resources, a separation of the fund balance into restricted and unrestricted components is essential.

Investment in Plant Fund   The assets of the *investment in plant funds* consist of the physical plant (land, buildings, improvements other than buildings, and

---

[5]See discussion of Exposure Draft, "Accounting for Contributions. . ." for possible changes in recognizing accounting for contributions.

886

COLLEGES
AND UNIVERSITIES,
HOSPITALS,
AND VOLUNTARY
HEALTH AND WELFARE
ORGANIZATIONS

equipment which includes library books). Assets acquired by purchase or construction are valued at cost, and those acquired by donation are valued at fair value. All liabilities relating to plant assets are also included in this category. The excess of assets over liabilities is designated as "net investment in plant," rather than fund balance. Additions arise from expenditures of unexpended plant funds, renewal and replacement funds, and current funds that require capitalization. Additions also result from gifts of books, equipment, and so on. Deductions in the net investment in plant arise from sales and other disposals and new indebtedness. Accumulated depreciation may be recorded on depreciable plant assets, and, if so, the charge is reported as a deduction in the net investment in plant account.

Financial statements of the four plant fund groups are included in the combined balance sheet and the combined statement of changes in fund balances for the college or university. Separate columns may be used for each plant fund subgroup, or a single column may be used for all subgroups provided that restricted and unrestricted fund balances for the subgroups are disclosed.

Agency Funds of Colleges and Universities

Agency funds are used to account for assets held by the college or university for individual students and faculty members and for their organizations. Transactions of agency funds only affect asset and liability accounts and do not result in revenues and expenditures. Agency fund assets and liabilities are included in a column of the college or university combined balance sheet, and no other financial statement presentations are required for basic reporting purposes.

FINANCIAL STATEMENTS OF COLLEGES AND UNIVERSITIES

The basic financial statements for colleges and universities are a balance sheet, a statement of changes in fund balances, and a statement of current funds revenues, expenditures, and other changes. This last statement was shown in Exhibit 21–2, and the other statements, which are combined financial statements, are shown in Exhibits 21–3 and 21–4. The balance sheet and statement of changes in fund balances are presented in a columnar format without separate columns for the four plant fund subgroupings. For alternative presentations that illustrate the details of the plant fund subgroups and a layered balance sheet format, the reader is referred to *College and University Business Administration* or the Industry Audit Guide *Audits of Colleges and Universities.*

HOSPITALS AND OTHER HEALTH CARE PROVIDERS

Hospitals and other health care providers constitute a significant area of nonprofit accounting both in terms of entities represented and in terms of cost of services provided. Although many such entities are voluntary nonprofit or government-owned organizations, some providers of health care are owned by investors and are operated on a proprietary basis. The unique features of accounting for investor-owned health care providers are not covered in this section, but the discussion is otherwise applicable to them because audited financial statements of all health care providers are required to be issued in accordance with generally accepted accounting principles except when such principles are inapplicable.

Accounting and reporting standards for health care providers are covered in the Audit and Accounting Guide, *Audits of Providers of Health Care Services* (AICPA, 1990). The audit guide also applies to the separate financial statements of state and local government-owned health care entities that use fund accounting and financial reporting principles. The provisions of the audit guide apply to a broad

BALANCE SHEET
ON JUNE 30, 19X2

	Current Funds		Loan Funds	Endowment and Similar Funds	Annuity and Life Income Funds	Plant Funds
	Unrestricted	Restricted				
Assets						
Cash	$ 95,000	$ 25,000	$ 4,000	$ 60,000	$150,000	$ 55,000
Investments	500,000	140,000	40,000	1,515,000	650,000	500,000
Accounts receivable (less allowances)	70,000					
Loans to students			50,000			
Unbilled charges		20,000				
Due from unrestricted funds						45,000
Inventories	170,000					
Prepaid expenses	15,000					
Deposits with trustees						200,000
Land						700,000
Improvements other than buildings						1,500,000
Buildings						8,000,000
Equipment						600,000
Library books						1,100,000
	$850,000	$185,000	$94,000	$1,575,000	$800,000	$12,700,000
Liabilities						
Accounts payable	$ 90,000	$ 55,000				$ 37,000
Accrued liabilities	40,000					
Students' deposits	25,000					
Due to other funds	45,000					
Annuities payable					$400,000	
Life income payable					30,000	
Notes payable						350,000
Bonds payable						2,100,000
Mortgages payable						5,200,000
Fund Balances						
Current funds	650,000	130,000				
Loan funds— restricted			$80,000			
Loan funds— unrestricted			14,000			
Endowment and similar funds:						
Endowment				$1,000,000		
Term endowment				100,000		
Quasi-endowment— unrestricted				475,000		
Annuity and life income funds:						
Annuity					270,000	
Life income					100,000	
Plant funds:						
Restricted						500,000
Unrestricted						63,000
Net investment in plant						4,450,000
	$850,000	$185,000	$94,000	$1,575,000	$800,000	$12,700,000

Exhibit 21–3   College and University Combined Balance Sheet

STATEMENT OF CHANGES IN FUND BALANCES
FOR THE YEAR ENDED JUNE 30, 19X2

	Current Funds		Loan Funds	Endowment and Similar Funds	Annuity and Life Income Funds	Plant Funds
	Unrestricted	Restricted				
Revenues and Other Additions						
Unrestricted current fund revenues	$3,585,000					
Expired term endowments—restricted						$ 10,000
State appropriations—restricted						20,000
Federal grants and contracts—restricted		$100,000				
Private gifts, grants, and contracts—restricted		250,000	$40,000	$ 500,000	$100,000	
Investment income—restricted		20,000	8,000			13,000
Realized gains on investments—restricted			1,000	15,000		
Interest on loans receivable			11,000			
Expended on plant facilities						300,000
Retirement of indebtedness						15,000
Matured annuity restricted to endowment				30,000		
Total revenues and other additions	3,585,000	370,000	60,000	545,000	100,000	358,000
Expenditures and Other Deductions						
Educational and general expenditures	2,530,000	370,000				
Auxiliary enterprises expenditures	760,000					
Refunded to grantors		20,000				
Loan cancellations and write-offs			8,000			
Administrative costs			3,000			
Expended for plant facilities						320,000
Retirement of indebtedness						15,000
Interest on indebtedness						5,000
Disposal of plant facilities						65,000
Expired term endowments restricted to plant				10,000		
Matured annuity restricted to endowment					30,000	
Total expenditures and other deductions	3,290,000	390,000	11,000	10,000	30,000	405,000
Transfers Among Funds—Additions (Deductions)						
Mandatory:						
Principal and interest	(40,000)					40,000
Renewals and replacements	(60,000)					60,000
Loan fund matching grant	(5,000)		5,000			
Restricted receipts over transfers to revenue		30,000				
Quasi-endowment fund created	(40,000)			40,000		
Net change—increase (decrease)	150,000	10,000	54,000	575,000	70,000	53,000
Fund balance—beginning	500,000	120,000	40,000	1,000,000	300,000	4,870,000
Fund balance—end of year	$ 650,000	$130,000	$94,000	$1,575,000	$370,000	$4,923,000

Exhibit 21–4 *College and University Combined Statement of Changes in Fund Balances*

range of health care providers including clinics, ambulatory care organizations, continuing care retirement communities, health maintenance organizations, home health agencies, hospitals, government-owned health care entities, and nursing homes that provide health care. The discussion in this chapter generally refers to hospitals as a matter of convenience, but note that the principles apply to other health care providers as well.

Although fund accounting is not *required*, many nonprofit health care entities use fund accounting to demonstrate compliance with donor and legislative restrictions. Fund accounting procedures are used in this chapter.

Fund Groupings

Hospital accounting systems that are maintained on a fund basis have major fund categories for restricted and unrestricted resources. These categories, including the major subgroups normally found in hospital accounting, are summarized in Exhibit 21–5 with notations of the general nature and scope of activities included in the subgroups.

General Funds

General Funds—to account for all unrestricted resources of the health care provider including assets whose use is limited, agency funds, and property, plant, and equipment, and related long-term debt, used in the general operations of the entity. Assets whose use is limited includes such items as resources that the governing board has set aside for specific purposes, proceeds of a debt issue that must be used in accordance with the indenture requirements, and assets that are restricted by agreements with outside entities other than a donor or grantor.

Restricted Funds

Temporarily Restricted:

Specific-Purpose Funds—to account for resources restricted by donors for specific operating purposes.

Plant Replacement and Expansion Funds—to account for donor-restricted resources for property, plant, and equipment, and revenue that third-party payors restrict to the replacement of property, plant and equipment.

Term Endowment Funds—to account for resources restricted by the donor for a specified period of time or until restrictions are satisfied.

Permanently Restricted:

Endowment or Pure Endowment Funds—to account for resources restricted indefinitely by endowment agreement. (Permanent restriction as to principal.)

Exhibit 21–5   *Fund Accounting Structure for Hospitals*

General Funds Category   The general funds category contains all unrestricted resources, including board-designated assets and other assets whose use is limited. *Board-designated funds* are included within the general (unrestricted) funds grouping because the governing board can rescind its own actions and direct the resources to general operating uses. The assets of the general funds include such items as cash, receivables, inventories, and prepaid expenses, as well as property, plant, and equipment used for the general operations of the hospital or other health care provider. Any related long-term debt is also included in the operating funds category.

Hospitals and other health care entities receive and hold resources of patients, residents, physicians, and others under agency relationships. In accepting an agent's responsibility for such resources, a hospital has a liability to return the resources to the principal or disburse them to another party on behalf of the principal. Such **agency funds** are included in general funds of hospitals, but receipts and disbursements of agency funds are not included in the results of operations.

Assets of the general funds also include proceeds of debt issues and funds deposited with trustees that are limited to use according to the trust agreement. (If the donor deposits the funds with the trustee and controls disposition of the trust, the assets are not included in the hospital's general fund.)

Donor-Restricted Funds Category   The *donor-restricted funds* category is used to account for resources restricted by donors or grantors and consists of three

890

COLLEGES
AND UNIVERSITIES,
HOSPITALS,
AND VOLUNTARY
HEALTH AND WELFARE
ORGANIZATIONS

subgroups that correspond to the donor or grantor restrictions. ***Specific-purpose funds*** are used to account for resources restricted by the donor for specific operating purposes. ***Plant replacement and expansion funds*** are used to account for resources that donors have restricted to acquisitions of property, plant, or equipment. The ***endowment funds*** *subgroups* consist of pure endowments (permanently restricted) and term endowments (temporarily restricted), and includes resources restricted by endowment agreements. Hospital endowment funds do *not* include quasi or board-designated endowments.

Accrual Accounting

The financial statements of health care entities should be prepared in accordance with generally accepted accounting principles. This means that ARBs, APB Opinions, and FASB Statements and Interpretations are applicable. Government operated health care entities are accounted for under GASB Statements and Interpretations, and the ARB, APB, and FASB pronouncements that the GASB says are applicable.

Hospitals use accrual accounting. Thus, hospitals measure and report revenues and expenses (rather than expenditures), use historical cost principles for asset valuations, and provide for depreciation on plant assets. Depreciation on minor equipment is determined on an inventory basis rather than by applying a depreciation formula.

Revenues, expenses, gains, and losses arising from providing health care services are classified as *operating*. Peripheral or incidental transactions result in *nonoperating* gains and losses.

Classification of Revenues and Gains

Revenue is reported in the period in which services are rendered. Hospital revenues consist of three major groupings—patient service revenues, other operating revenues, and nonoperating gains. Examples of items included within each of these groupings are given in Exhibit 21–6.

Patient Service Revenue   Patient service revenues include board and room, nursing services, and other professional services, and are recorded on an accrual basis at established (gross) rates as the services are being provided. Separate allowance accounts are used to record items that reduce gross patient service revenues to amounts ultimately collectible. These include:

> *Courtesy allowances*—discounts for doctors and employees
> *Contractual adjustments*—third-party payors (Medicare and Blue Cross, for example) frequently have agreements to reimburse at less than established rates

In hospital accounting, these allowance accounts are treated as deductions from patient service revenues rather than as operating expense.

Charity Care   Hospitals provide health care services free of charge to qualifying patients under a policy of ***charity care.*** Charity care is excluded from both gross patient service revenue and from expense. The hospital's policy for providing charity care and the level of charity care provided are disclosed in notes to the financial statements.

Other Operating Revenue   The *other operating revenues* classification includes tuition from schools operated by the hospital, rentals of hospital space, charges for preparing and reproducing medical records, room charges for telephone calls and television, and proceeds from cafeterias, gift shops, snack bars, and so on. Other operating revenue also includes donor-restricted grants and gifts for research, education, and other programs to the extent that expenditures have been made for the purposes specified. When the restricted gift or grant is received,

Patient Service Revenues	Other Operating Revenues

Routine care
Nursing
Delivery and labor rooms
Emergency room
Recovery rooms
Medical and surgical supplies
Laboratory—clinical and pathology
EKG–EEG
Radiation therapy
Pharmacy
Anesthesiology
Physical therapy
Respiratory therapy
Hemodialysis
Speech therapy
Ambulance
	Tuition from educational programs
	Research and specific purpose grants
	  (recognized only as expenditures are
	  made)
	Miscellaneous
	  Rental revenue for hospital space,
	    clinics, etc.
	  Gift shop, television rental,
	    telephone, cafeteria
	  Medical record transcripts
	  Donated medicine, linen, and office
	    supplies
	
	Nonoperating Gains
	
	Unrestricted gifts and grants
	  (including board-designated items)
	Unrestricted income from
	  endowments
	Investment income and gains from
	  unrestricted funds
	Gains on sale of plant assets
	Rentals received from property not
	  used in operations of the hospital
	Unrestricted funds from termination
	  of term endowments
	Donated services

Exhibit 21-6 *Examples of Hospital Revenue Classifications*

it is entered as an addition to a specific purpose fund or recorded as deferred revenue. When the restrictions are terminated through expenditures as specified by the donor, the specific purpose fund balance (or deferred revenue) is decreased and revenue is recorded in the operating fund.

Nonoperating Gains *Nonoperating gains* consist of gains that are not directly related to providing goods and services. This classification includes tax support, other subsidies, and all unrestricted gifts and grants, as well as those that are designated for specific purposes by the governing board. It also includes endowment income that is unrestricted, unrestricted resources from termination of term endowments, unrestricted pledges net of a provision for uncollectible amounts, and gains and losses on sales of hospital property.

   If donor contributions result from ongoing fund-raising activities that the hospital depends on to fulfill its basic health care services, the contributions would be classified as revenues instead of gains.[6] Similarly, tax support and other subsidies may be classified as revenues if they are major, ongoing sources of funds that the hospital depends on to fulfill its basic functions. Revenues and expenses are generally reported at gross amounts; gains and losses may be reported at net amounts.[7]

Classification of Operating Expenses

Operating expenses of hospitals are reported on an accrual basis and normally include functional categories for nursing services (medical and surgical, intensive care, nurseries, operating rooms), other professional services (laboratories,

---

[6]AICPA, *Audits of Providers of Health Care Services,* paragraph 12.5.

[7]AICPA, *Audits of Providers of Health Care Services,* paragraph 12.1.

892

COLLEGES
AND UNIVERSITIES,
HOSPITALS,
AND VOLUNTARY
HEALTH AND WELFARE
ORGANIZATIONS

radiology, anesthesiology, pharmacy), general services (housekeeping, maintenance, laundry), fiscal services (accounting, cashier, credits and collections, data processing), administrative services (personnel, purchasing, insurance, governing board), interest, and depreciation provisions.

Although accounts are maintained for employee and contractual allowances, these items are not expenses. As discussed earlier, they are revenue deductions that are subtracted from gross patient service revenues to show net patient service revenue in the statement of revenues and expenses. (See Exhibit 21–7.)

Provision for Bad Debts   The provision for bad debts is an expense. The difference between charity care and bad debts expense is that charity care results from the hospital's policy of providing health care to individuals who meet certain financial criteria and bad debt expense results from extending credit.[8] Health care services provided as charity care were never intended to provide cash flows.

Reporting Revenues and Expenses

All revenues and expenses of a nonprofit hospital are reported in the operating statement called a statement of revenues and expenses of general funds. For example, the income from the endowment funds should be reported in the operating fund as nonoperating revenue if it is unrestricted. It would be reported in a specific-purpose fund as an addition to fund balance if the income were restricted. In either case, it is not reported as revenue in the endowment fund. The same is true for specific-purpose funds. Assume that an individual donates funds to a hospital for AIDS research. As the research expenses are incurred, they are recorded in the operating funds. An amount equal to the AIDS research expenses is then transferred to the operating fund from the specific-purpose fund and recorded as *other operating revenue*.

Pledges   Pledges are reported in the period they are made, less an appropriate allowance for uncollectible amounts. If the pledged resources are to be used in a future period, they are reported in the general fund as *deferred revenue*. If the pledges are donor restricted in other ways, they are reported as additions to the restricted fund balance.

Donated Assets   Donated assets are recorded at fair value at the date of the gift. Unrestricted donated assets other than property and equipment are reported in the statement of revenues and expenses of the general fund. If restricted, they are reported as additions to the appropriate restricted fund balance.

Donated property and equipment, or donated assets restricted to the acquisition of property and equipment, are reported in restricted funds. A transfer to the general fund is reported when the property is placed in service or the assets are used to acquire property.

Donated Services   Donated services are reported as both an expense and revenue (contributions) *if* the services are significant, measurable, and the hospital controls the employment and duties of the donors.

Donated Funds Held In Trust

Resources that are held in a trust established by the donor, administered by outside fiscal agents, and not under the control of the hospital although the hospital receives income from the trust, should not be included in the balance sheet. The existence of the trust should be disclosed, however. Distributions from the trustee are reported on the accrual basis.

---

[8] AICPA, *Audits of Providers of Health Care Services*, Glossary.

Pooling of Investments

Investments applicable to several fund groups are often pooled for administrative efficiency. When investments are pooled, the pooled income should be assigned to individual funds on the basis of market value of investments contributed to the pool at the time of pooling.

Financial Reporting for Hospitals

Because hospitals are subject to generally accepted accounting principles except when such principles are inapplicable, their financial reporting requirements are similar to those for business enterprises. Basic financial statements for hospitals consist of (1) a balance sheet, (2) a statement of revenues and expenses of general funds, (3) a statement of changes in fund balances, and (4) a statement of cash flows of general funds. These basic statements are illustrated for a hospital in Exhibits 21–7, 21–8, 21–9, and 21–10. Either combined fund (aggregated) or layered fund (disaggregated) balance sheets are accepted. The layered balance sheet is illustrated in Exhibit 21–8. The statement of cash flows illustrated in Exhibit 21–10 is prepared using the indirect method. Although comparative current- and prior-year statements are not shown, most hospitals issue comparative statements.

CARE HOSPITAL
STATEMENT OF REVENUES AND EXPENSES OF GENERAL FUNDS
FOR THE YEAR ENDED DECEMBER 31, 19X2

Patient Service Revenues			
Inpatient services	$7,200,000		
Outpatient services	1,300,000		
Total patient service revenues		$8,500,000	
Deduct:			
Medicare contractual allowances	$ 710,000		
Employee allowances	50,000	760,000	
Net patient service revenues		7,740,000	
Other Operating Revenues (including $70,000 from Specific-Purpose Funds)		1,020,000	
Total operating revenues		8,760,000	
Operating Expenses			
Nursing services	$2,700,000		
Other professional services	1,800,000		
General services	1,500,000		
Fiscal services	500,000		
Administrative services	300,000		
Medical malpratice costs	180,000		
Provision for uncollectible accounts	600,000		
Provision for depreciation	400,000		
Total operating expenses		7,980,000	
Income from operations		780,000	
Nonoperating Gains			
Unrestricted donations	$ 150,000		
Unrestricted income from endowments	120,000		
Income from Board-Designated Funds	20,000		
Total nonoperating revenues		290,000	
Excess revenues over expenses		$1,070,000	

Exhibit 21–7   *Hospital Statement of Revenues and Expenses of General Funds*

CARE HOSPITAL
BALANCE SHEET AT DECEMBER 31, 19X2

General Funds

Current Assets			Current Liabilities		
Cash		$ 60,000	Accounts payable		$ 300,000
Accounts receivable-patients, less			Accrued interest		150,000
$120,000 estimated uncollectible			Accrued salaries		210,000
receivables		1,080,000	Payroll taxes payable		140,000
Accounts receivable—Medicare		400,000	Accrued pension expense		50,000
Receivable from limited use assets		100,000	Current portion of long-term debt		100,000
Inventories and prepaid items		170,000	Total current liabilities		950,000
Due from restricted funds		40,000			
Total current assets		1,850,000	Long-Term Debt		
			Notes payable		500,000
Assets Whose Use Is Limited			Bonds payable (net of current		
by Board for Capital Improvements:		230,000	portion)		900,000
			Mortgage payable		3,000,000
Property, Plant, and Equipment			Total long-term liabilities		4,400,000
Land		650,000			
Buildings	$5,000,000		Fund balance		3,080,000
Fixed equipment	2,000,000				
Movable equipment	1,500,000		Total liabilities and fund		
	8,500,000		balance		$8,430,000
Less: Accumulated					
depreciation	2,800,000	5,700,000			
Total property, plant,					
and equipment		6,350,000			
Total general assets		$8,430,000			

Donor-Restricted Funds

Specific-Purpose Funds					
Cash		$ 50,000	Due to unrestricted funds		$ 40,000
Investments		300,000	Fund balance		310,000
Total specific purpose assets		$ 350,000	Liabilities and fund balance		$ 350,000

Plant Replacement and Expansion Fund					
Cash		$ 10,000	Fund balance—donor restricted		$ 300,000
Investments		390,000	Fund balance—third party		
Pledges		30,000	restricted		130,000
Total plant replacement and					
expansion assets		$ 430,000	Total fund balance		$ 430,000

Endowment Fund					
Cash		$ 20,000	Fund balance—endowment		$1,420,000
Investments		1,500,000	Fund balance—term endowment		100,000
Total endowment assets		$1,520,000	Total fund balance		$1,520,000

Exhibit 21–8   *Hospital Balance Sheet*

```
┌─────────────────────────────────────────────────────────────────────┐
│ CARE HOSPITAL                                                         │
│ STATEMENT OF CHANGES IN FUND BALANCES                                 │
│ FOR THE YEAR ENDED DECEMBER 31, 19X2                                  │
├─────────────────────────────────────────────────────────────────────┤
```

General Funds

Fund balance January 1, 19X2		$1,990,000
Additions:		
Excess revenues over expenses	$1,070,000	
Transfer from plant replacement and		
expansion funds	220,000	1,290,000
Deductions:		
Transfers to plant replacement and expansion		
funds		(200,000)
Total general funds balances, December 31, 19X2		$3,080,000

Donor-Restricted Funds

Specific-Purpose Funds	
Fund balance, January 1, 19X2	$ 320,000
Restricted gifts and grants	80,000
Transfer to operating fund (other operating	
revenue)	(70,000)
Income from investments	20,000
Fund balance, December 31, 19X2	$ 350,000
Plant Replacement and Expansion Funds	
Fund balance, January 1, 19X2	$ 410,000
Income from investmnets	40,000
Transfer to general fund for equipment purchase	(220,000)
Transfer from general fund to reflect third-party	
restrictions	200,000
Fund balance, December 31, 19X2	$ 430,000
Endowment Funds	
Fund balance, January 1, 19X2	$1,470,000
Additions to term endowments	50,000
Fund balance, December 31, 19X2	$1,520,000

Exhibit 21–9 *Hospital Statement of Changes in Fund Balances*

CARE HOSPITAL
STATEMENT OF CASH FLOWS OF GENERAL FUNDS (*INDIRECT METHOD*)
FOR THE YEAR ENDED DECEMBER 31, 19X2

Cash Flows from Operating Activities and Gains and Losses		
Revenues and gains in excess of expenses and losses		$1,070,000
Adjustments to reconcile revenue and gains in excess of expenses and losses to net cash provided by operating activities and gains and losses		
Provision for depreciation	$ 400,000	
Provision for uncollectible accounts	600,000	
Decrease in amounts due from restricted funds	20,000	
Decrease in Medicare accounts receivable	40,000	
Decrease in unearned interest (limited-use assets)	15,000	
Increase in accounts payable and accrued expenses	60,000	
Increase in patient accounts receivable	(195,000)	
Increase in inventories and supplies	(40,000)	900,000
Net cash provided by operating activities and gains and losses		1,970,000
Cash Flows from Investing Activities		
Purchase of property, plant, and equipment	$(1,600,000)	
Transfer from donor-restricted fund for equipment	(50,000)	
Cash invested in limited use assets	(350,000)	
Net cash provided from financing activities		(2,000,000)
Cash Flows from Financing Activities		
Proceeds from long-term note payable	$ 500,000	
Repayment of bonds payable	(100,000)	
Repayment of mortgage note payable	(800,000)	
Payments from donor restricted funds	410,000	
Net cash provided from financing activities		10,000
Change in cash for 19X2		(20,000)
Cash and cash equivalents at beginning of year		80,000
Cash and cash equivalents at end of year		$ 60,000

Exhibit 21–10   *Hospital Statement of Cash Flows of General Funds*

Sample Journal Entries

The following *unrelated* situations describe some typical activities of a nonprofit hospital. The journal entries are provided to demonstrate how the concepts are implemented in the accounting system. Only general ledger accounts are shown.

Recording Patient Service Revenue   Gross charges at established rates for services rendered to patients of Giles Memorial Hospital amounted to $1,300,000. The hospital had contractual allowances with insurers and Medicare of $300,000. Hospital staff and their dependents received courtesy discounts of $9,000.

General fund		
Accounts receivable	$1,300,000	
Patient service revenue		$1,300,000
To record patient service charges at established rates.		
Courtesy allowances	$ 9,000	
Contractual allowances	300,000	
Accounts receivable		$ 309,000
To record courtesy allowances and contractual adjustments.		

Wages and Salaries   Colonial Nursing Center pays salaries and wages allocated to functional categories as follows: nursing services, $55,000; other professional services, $15,000; general services, $170,000; fiscal services, $12,000; and administrative services, $20,000.

General fund		
Nursing services expense	$ 55,000	
Other professional services	15,000	
General services	170,000	
Fiscal services	12,000	
Adminsitrative services	20,000	
Wages and salaries payable		$272,000
* To record accrual of payroll.*		

Purchase and Use of Supplies   The Indian Hills Clinic purchases materials and supplies for $130,000. The supplies usage by the major functional categories during the year is as follows: nursing services, $50,000; other professional services, $40,000; general services, $20,000; fiscal services, $5,000; and administrative services, $8,000.

General fund		
Inventory of materials and supplies	$130,000	
Cash (accounts payable)		$130,000
* To record purchase of supplies.*		
Nursing services expense	$ 50,000	
Other professional services expense	40,000	
General services expense	20,000	
Fiscal services expense	5,000	
Administrative services expense	8,000	
Inventory of materials and supplies		$123,000
* To record usage of materials and supplies.*		

Other Operating Revenues   Jackson County Hospital charges patient's rent for telephones and television in their rooms. Throughout the year, the hospital offers several health care courses for which tuition is charged. Revenue for television and telephone rental was $72,000 for the year, and the tuition charges for courses was $24,000.

General fund		
Cash (or accounts receivable)	$ 96,000	
Other operating revenue		$ 96,000
* To record revenue from television and telephone rentals and fees charged*		
* for health care courses.*		

Depreciation   County Hospital recognizes depreciation on its equipment, $50,000, and building, $20,000. County's movable (or minor) equipment is depreciated on an inventory basis and is determined to be $5,500.

General fund		
Depreciation expense	$ 75,500	
Accumulated depreciation—equipment		$ 50,000
Accumulated depreciation—building		20,000
Movable equipment		5,500
* To record depreciation on major equipment, building, and movable equipment.*		

Nonoperating Gains   Several years ago, Tuttle Memorial Hospital purchased a motel and a large office building near the hospital. The hospital operates the motel for patient's families, and the offices in the renovated building are rented to doctors. Revenue from motel operations was $150,000 for the year. Office

898

COLLEGES
AND UNIVERSITIES,
HOSPITALS,
AND VOLUNTARY
HEALTH AND WELFARE
ORGANIZATIONS

rentals were $800,000. Also, the hospital received unrestricted cash donations of $250,000.

General funds

Cash (receivables)	$950,000	
Nonoperating gains		$950,000

To record rental income from motel and office building operations.

Cash	$250,000	
Nonoperating gains		$250,000

To record receipt of unrestricted contributions.

Donated Assets   Fairview Hospital received marketable equity securities valued at $500,000 that were donor restricted (including any income from the securities) for the purchase of diagnostic equipment. The donation is recorded in a restricted fund until the funds are used to purchase the equipment.

Plant replacement and expansion fund (diagnostic equipment)

Marketable equity securities	$500,000	
Fund balance		$500,000

To record donation of securities.

Because income is donor restricted, dividends from the securities are recorded in the plant replacement and expansion fund as an increase in the fund balance. At the balance sheet date, the securities are grouped with other restricted securities and are reported at the lower of aggregate cost or market according to the provisions of *FASB Statement No. 12,* "Accounting for Certain Marketable Equity Securities."

At a later date, these securities that now have a book value of $550,000 are sold, and the proceeds used to purchase the diagnostic equipment that costs $560,000. The following entries might be made:

Plant replacement and expansion funds (diagnostic equipment)

Cash	$600,000	
Marketable equity securities		$550,000
Fund balance		50,000

To record sale of securities with a book value of $550,000.

Transfer to general fund	$560,000	
Cash		$560,000

To record transfer of proceeds from sale of securities to general fund for purchase of equipment costing $560,000. *This entry assumes that the gain from the sale is also restricted for the purchase of equipment. If the restriction was only for this particular equipment, the remaining $40,000 would also be transferred to the general fund.*

General fund

Equipment	$560,000	
Accounts payable (or cash)		$560,000

To record purchase of diagnostic equipment.

Cash	$560,000	
Transfer from plant replacement and expansion fund		$560,000

To record reimbursement for equipment from plant replacement and expansion fund.

This sequence of entries uses transfer accounts rather than direct increases and decreases of the fund balance. Transfer accounts are closed to the fund balance account at the end of the period, but they provide a convenient reference for preparing the statement of changes in fund balances.

Related Entity Disclosures

This section is primarily concerned with the separate financial statements of nonprofit hospitals or other health care providers. However, nonprofit entities may be related to other nonprofit entities in a way that would require disclosure in the financial statements. A nonprofit hospital is *related* to a separate organization if one of the following conditions is met:

1 The hospital controls the organization through contracts or legal documents. *Control* means the ability to direct the organization's activities, management, and policies.
2 The hospital is the sole beneficiary of the organization.

If the financial statements of the hospital and the related nonprofit organization are not consolidated or combined under with the provisions of *ARB No. 51*, as amended by *FASB Statement No. 94*, then the hospital's financial statement notes should include information about the assets, liabilities, results of operations, and changes in fund balance of the related organization.

Transfers Between Related Health Care Providers

A nonprofit hospital may diversify its operations by acquiring or creating various health care sidelines. Or the nonprofit hospital may purchase office buildings or other hospitals. The AICPA Technical Practice Aids Section 6400 (January 1991) provides guidance on accounting for transfers of resources between related, but separate, health care providers.

Creation of Affiliate   Central Municipal Hospital, a nonprofit hospital, creates a for-profit rehabilitation clinic by transferring equipment with a book value of $600,000 (fair value, $800,000) and $400,000 cash as initial start-up capital for the new clinic in exchange for the clinic's newly issued capital stock. Central records the $1,000,000 investment at book value:

Investment in Rehabilitation Clinic	$1,000,000	
Cash		$400,000
Equipment		600,000

To record investment of cash and equipment in rehabilitation clinic.

The clinic records the assets and the stock issued. Subsequently, Central will account for its investment in the clinic by the equity method.

Now assume that Central creates the rehabilitation clinic as a nonprofit entity with the same initial investment of $600,000 equipment and $400,000 cash. Because Central does not have a financial interest in the clinic, it cannot record an investment. Central records the book value of the assets transferred as a reduction of fund balance. The clinic records receipt of the assets as an increase in fund balance.

Transfers Between Not-for-Profit Related Entities   Accounting for the transfer of assets between *related* health care entities (entities under common control) depends on the purpose of the transfer—to provide additional capital, to provide a loan, or to transfer funds contributed by a third party. Generally, transfers between entities under common control should be made at book value rather than fair value.[9]

---

[9]*Interpretation No. 39 of APB Opinion No. 16,* "Transfers and Exchanges Between Enterprises under Common Control."

900

COLLEGES
AND UNIVERSITIES,
HOSPITALS,
AND VOLUNTARY
HEALTH AND WELFARE
ORGANIZATIONS

Belmont County Hospital, a nonprofit entity, has created or acquired several nonprofit health care entities, including the Belmont Nursing Home and the Family Medical Center. The hospital board of directors instructs Belmont Nursing Home to transfer $500,000 unrestricted cash to the Medical Center. The money will provide much-needed capital for the Medical Center and will not be repaid. Journal entries to record the transfer are:

Belmont Nursing Home—General Operating Fund

Fund balance	$500,000	
Cash		$500,000

To record transfer of cash to Family Medical Center.

Family Medical Center—General Operating Fund

Cash	$500,000	
Fund balance		$500,000

To record receipt of cash from Belmont Nursing Center.

Now assume that the hospital board instructs Belmont Nursing Home to loan $500,000 to the Family Medical Center. The Nursing Home creates an account or note receivable and Family Medical Center enters an account or note payable. If it later becomes apparent that the Family Medical Center will not be able to repay the loan, the receivable and payable should be transferred to the respective fund balances.

Finally, assume that Belmont Nursing Home receives a $50,000 donor-restricted contribution from an outside entity. The contribution is to be transferred to the Family Medical Center at a later date. The Nursing Home records an increase in the restricted fund balance at the time it receives the contribution and a corresponding decrease in the restricted fund balance when the cash is transferred to the Family Medical Center. The Medical Center increases its restricted fund balance by an equal amount.

Belmont Nursing Home—Specific-Purpose Fund

Cash	$ 50,000	
Fund balance		$ 50,000

To record receipt of donor-restricted contributions.

Fund balance	$ 50,000	
Cash		$ 50,000

To record transfer of donor-restricted contributions to the Family Medical Center.

If the original $50,000 was unrestricted, Belmont Nursing Home would recognize revenue when it received the contribution and would recognize an expense when it transferred the cash to the Family Medical Center. The medical center would recognize unrestricted contribution income.[10]

VOLUNTARY HEALTH AND WELFARE ORGANIZATIONS

Voluntary health and welfare organizations encompass a diverse group of nonprofit entities that are supported by and provide voluntary services to the public. They may expend their resources to solve basic social problems in the areas of health or welfare, or to alleviate such problems at the community level or on an individual basis. Accounting standards for these organizations are provided by the 1974 Industry Audit Guide of the AICPA, *Audits of Voluntary Health and Welfare Organizations.* The Industry Audit Guide states that the objective of financial

---

[10]*AICPA Technical Practice Aids,* Section 6400.27.

reporting for voluntary health and welfare organizations is "to disclose how the entity's resources have been acquired and used to accomplish the objectives of the organization." Other nonprofit organizations are not covered in this chapter, but the required accounting and reporting practices for other nonprofits described in the 1981 Industry Audit Guide *Audits of Certain Nonprofit Organizations* are very similar to those required for voluntary health and welfare organizations.

Fund Accounting

Most voluntary health and welfare organizations use fund accounting to segregate their restricted and unrestricted resources. The usual fund accounting structure is illustrated in Exhibit 21–11 with a brief description of the scope of activities accounted for in each fund.

Current Unrestricted Fund—to account for resources expendable at the discretion of the governing board including board-designated funds.

Current Restricted Funds—to account for resources expendable for current uses, but restricted by donors for specific operating purposes.

Land, Building, and Equipment Fund (or Plant Fund)—to account for the net investment in plant assets and unexpended resources restricted by donors to acquisition or replacement of plant assets. Liabilities related to plant assets are also included.

Endowment Funds—to account for gifts and bequests under endowment agreements with donors.

Custodian Funds—to account for assets received and to be held or disbursed on instructions of the person or entity from whom received.

Loan and Annuity Funds—to account for resources restricted by agreements with donors for loans or annuities (usually not significant for health and welfare organizations).

Exhibit 21–11 *Fund Accounting Structure for Voluntary Health and Welfare Organizations*

Current unrestricted and current restricted funds of voluntary health and welfare organizations are comparable to unrestricted current and restricted current fund groupings used in college and university accounting. Board-designated funds are included in the current unrestricted fund. The land, buildings, and equipment fund (plant fund) is used to account for plant assets and related liabilities and also donor-restricted resources for plant additions and replacements. Plant assets acquired through unrestricted current funds are recorded as additions to the plant fund balance. Unrestricted proceeds from the sale of plant assets are transferred to the current unrestricted fund. Endowment fund income is recorded as revenue of the current unrestricted fund if unrestricted, and it is credited to the applicable restricted fund if donor restricted. Custodian funds are essentially agency funds and involve only asset and liability accounting.

Accrual Basis

The financial statements of voluntary health and welfare organizations are subject to generally accepted accounting principles that include APB Opinions, FASB Statements, and other authoritative pronouncements except when such pronouncements are inapplicable. Thus, revenues and expenses are recorded as earned and incurred under the accrual basis of accounting. Financial statements prepared on the cash or modified accrual basis are acceptable only if the results are not materially different from statements prepared on an accrual basis.

902

COLLEGES
AND UNIVERSITIES,
HOSPITALS,
AND VOLUNTARY
HEALTH AND WELFARE
ORGANIZATIONS

Support and Revenue

Contributions and gifts of voluntary health and welfare organizations are classified as *support* or *public support* rather than revenue in order to distinguish resources received from voluntary contributions from those that result from the earning process. For reporting purposes, "support and revenue" is the basic statement classification with subclassifications for support and revenue. Support and revenue is reported in the fund grouping to which it relates.

Cash Donations and Pledges The major support for voluntary health and welfare organizations comes from cash donations and pledges. Such contributions are recorded as *support* when received unless specified by the donor for future periods. In this case, a deferred credit is recorded when the donation is received, and the deferred credit is reclassified as support in the period in which the resources may be used. Provisions for uncollectible pledges should be estimated and recorded.

Donated Securities Securities donated to the organization are recorded at their fair market values at the date of gift. Restricted contributions of securities are reported as *support* of the appropriate restricted fund, and unrestricted contributions of securities are reported in the current unrestricted fund.

Donated Materials and Services Donated materials, if significant, are recorded at their fair values when received, but donated services are *not* recorded unless the services are controlled by the organization, the amount of the *support* is clearly measurable, and the services would otherwise be performed by salaried personnel.

Investment Income and Realized Gains and Losses The income and net realized gains on investments of unrestricted funds are reported as *unrestricted revenue* of the current unrestricted fund. Income and net realized gains of restricted funds other than endowments are reported as *revenue of the restricted funds* unless legally available for unrestricted purposes, in which case they are included in revenue of the current unrestricted fund. Investment income (dividends and interest) of endowment funds is reported as revenue of the current unrestricted fund if unrestricted, and revenue of the appropriate restricted fund if restricted. But realized gains or losses on endowment fund investments are adjustments of the endowment fund principal unless the endowment agreement considers them as income. If investments of different funds are pooled, income should be allocated back to the individual funds by reference to the market values at the time the investments are pooled.

Exposure Draft, "Accounting for Contributions..." Revenue recognition under the Exposure Draft would require contributions to be recognized as revenue in the periods received. Similarly, unconditional pledges should be recognized as revenue when received.

Expenses

Expenses of voluntary health and welfare organizations are classified as *program services* and *supporting services* and are reported on a functional basis under these classifications. Program services relate to the expenses incurred in providing the organization's social service activities. Supporting services consist of administrative expenses and fund-raising costs. In reporting expenses in the statement of support, revenues and expenses, and changes in fund balances, the functional classifications might appear as follows:

Expenses

> *Program Services*
> Research
> Public education
> Professional education

Community services

Patient services

Supporting Services

Management and general

Fund raising

As in the case of support and revenues, expenses are reported in the funds to which they relate.

The functional basis of reporting expenses results in an informative but highly aggregated form of statement presentation. To overcome the limitations of aggregation, *Audits of Voluntary Health and Welfare Organizations* requires a separate statement of functional expenses. This statement reconciles the functional classifications with basic object-of-expenditure classifications such as salaries, supplies, postage, and awards and grants. (See Exhibit 21–13.)

Sample Journal Entries

The following journal entries provide examples of some typical accounting procedures for several fictitious, *unrelated* voluntary health and welfare organizations.

Contributions   Neighborhood Assistance Fund received unrestricted contributions in 19X3 of $11,800 in cash and $28,000 in pledges. An additional $9,000 in pledges were donor-restricted for a special project. Neighborhood's experience has been that 10 percent of the pledges will be uncollectible. Expenses of Neighborhood's fund-raising efforts were $550 that were paid in cash as incurred.

Current unrestricted fund

Cash	$11,800	
Support—contributions		$11,800
To record cash contributions.		

Current unrestricted fund

Pledges receivable	$28,000	
Allowance for uncollectible pledges		$ 2,800
Support—contributions		25,200

  To record pledges without donor specifications and to record allowance for bad debts
    for 10 percent of pledges.

Current restricted fund

Pledges receivable	$ 9,000	
Allowance for uncollectible pledges		$ 900
Support—contributions		8,100

  To record pledges restricted to special project and to record allowance for bad debts
    for 10 percent of pledges.

Deferred Contributions   In 19X2 a local voluntary health and welfare organization received unrestricted donations of $10,000 cash that were available for use in 19X2 and donations of $3,000 cash that were designated by the donors for use in 19X3. The journal entries to record the donation in 19X2 and to reclassify the deferred support in the following year are as follows:

Current unrestricted fund (19X2)

Cash	$13,000	
Support—contributions		$10,000
Deferred support—contributions		3,000

  To record cash contributions for use in 19X2 and cash contributions designated
    by donors for use in 19X3.

Current unrestricted fund (19X3)

Deferred support—contributions	$ 3,000	
Support—contributions		$ 3,000

  To reclassify deferred contributions when the resources can be used.

904

COLORED
COLLEGES
AND UNIVERSITIES,
HOSPITALS,
AND VOLUNTARY
HEALTH AND WELFARE
ORGANIZATIONS

Special Event Fund-Raisers   The Society for Better Nutrition held a fund raising event that featured a dinner of natural foods. Ticket sales for the dinner totaled $950 and expenses of the fund raiser amounted to $750. Proceeds of the special event are reported net of direct costs.

Current unrestricted fund		
Cash	$950	
Support—special event		$950
To record proceeds from a fund-raising event.		
Support—special event	$750	
Cash (or vouchers payable)		$750
To charge costs of fund-raising event against support from the event.		

Revenue from Membership Fees   Membership fees are revenue rather than contributions. The reason is that memberships give members certain benefits, such as the right to receive the organization's newsletters, and so on. If the organization has levels of memberships and the more expensive memberships do not entitle the members to additional benefits, the excess payments are classified as support. For example, the American Kidney Disease Foundation offers regular memberships for $10 and sustaining memberships for $50 and over. All members are entitled to the monthly newsletter and educational materials that are distributed periodically. The foundation received 4,000 regular memberships ($40,000) and 100 sustaining memberships ($15,000) that are recorded:

Current Unrestricted Fund		
Cash (or accounts receivable)	$55,000	
Revenue		$41,000
Support—contributions		14,000
To record revenue and support from the sale of memberships.		

Investment Income   Income earned on securities in The Food Pantry's endowment fund is unrestricted and available to pay for current operations of the voluntary health and welfare organization. Investment income is $3,700.

Current Unrestricted Fund		
Cash	$ 3,700	
Revenue—investment income		$ 3,700
To record investment income.		

Supplies   The Asthma Support Group had supplies on hand of $1,600 at January 1, 19X2. The organization purchased supplies for $1,500 during the year and received donations of supplies that had a fair value of $2,050. At the end of the 19X2 calendar year, the inventory on hand was $750. The supplies were allocated to public education programs, $2,000, and community service programs, $1,400; to fund raising expenses, $600; and to general administration, $400. Entries to summarize these events are:

Current unrestricted fund		
Materials and supplies inventory	$ 3,550	
Support—contributions		$ 2,050
Cash		1,500
To record donated materials and supplies and to record purchase of supplies.		
Expenses—management and general	$ 400	
Expenses—public education programs	2,000	
Expenses—community service	1,400	
Fund raising expenses	600	
Materials and supplies inventory		$ 4,400
To record allocation of supplies expense.		

Donated Services and Payment of Salaries An accounting firm donated its services to audit the books of the Society to Improve the Welfare of Children. The audit would have cost the Society $1,200 had the services not been donated. The Society paid salaries allocated to program services and administration as follows: public education programs, $6.000; community services, $4,000; management and general, $2,000.

Current unrestricted fund

Expenses—management and general	$ 1,200	
Support—donated services		$ 1,200

To record donated services allocated to management and general expenses.

Expenses—public education programs	$ 6,000	
Expenses—community services	4,000	
Expenses—management and general	2,000	
Payroll		$12,000

To record salaries allocated to program services and administration.

Depreciation Equipment owned by Action Against Poverty is accounted for in the plant, buildings, and equipment fund and is used in providing services to the organization's clients. The $8,000 depreciation expense on the equipment is allocated to the programs and general administration of the organization as follows:

Land, Buildings and Equipment Fund

Expenses—research programs	$ 1,000	
Expenses—public education programs	2,000	
Expenses—community services	4,000	
Expenses—management and general	1,000	
Accumulated depreciation		$ 8,000

To record depreciation allocated to programs and general administration.

Transfers Equipment costing $40,000 was purchased by the Heart Disease Research Institute. The equipment was financed by $30,000 in contributions accumulated for that purpose in the current restricted fund and $10,000 from general resources of the current unrestricted fund.

Current Unrestricted Fund

Transfer to land, buildings, and equipment fund	$10,000	
Cash		$10,000

To record payment for the purchase of equipment.

Current Restricted Fund

Transfer to land, buildings, and equipment fund	$30,000	
Cash		$30,000

To record payment for the purchase of equipment from donor-restricted resources.

Land, Buildings, and Equipment Fund

Cash	$40,000	
Transfer from current unrestricted fund		$10,000
Transfer from current restricted fund		30,000

To record receipt of cash from other funds.

Equipment	$40,000	
Cash		$40,000

To record acquisition of equipment.

Financial Reporting

The basic financial statements of a voluntary health and welfare organization consist of (1) a statement of support, revenues and expenses, and changes in fund balances; (2) a statement of functional expenses; and (3) a balance sheet.

906

COLLEGES
AND UNIVERSITIES,
HOSPITALS,
AND VOLUNTARY
HEALTH AND WELFARE
ORGANIZATIONS

Generally, a statement of cash flows is *not* required because the three basic statements are expected to include that information.

A national voluntary health and welfare organization may have financially interrelated local affiliates. Unless the local organizations are independent of the national organization, with separate purposes and separate governing boards, the financial statements of the national and local organizations are combined for reporting in accordance with generally accepted accounting principles.

Illustrative financial statements and accompanying statement notes for voluntary health and welfare organizations are presented in Exhibits 21–12, 21–13, 21–14, and 21–15. These statements are the audited financial statements of the Virginia Chapter of Arthritis Foundation, and are reprinted with permission. The Virginia Chapter is comprised of six local chapters, and it pays a portion of its revenues to the National Chapter of the Arthritis Foundation. The report also includes seven schedules containing supplementary information that are not reproduced here.

VIRGINIA CHAPTER OF ARTHRITIS FOUNDATION
BALANCE SHEET
DECEMBER 31, 1990 WITH COMPARATIVE FIGURES FOR 1989

Assets	1990	1989	*Liabilities and Fund Balance*	1990	1989
Current Funds					
Unrestricted					
Cash (including interest-bearing accounts of $24,932 in 1990 and $73,748 in 1989)	$ 27,674	$358,131	Accounts payable	$ 5,855	$ 5,667
			Accrued liabilities	13,627	12,681
			Due to National Chapter (Note 4)	18,313	21,552
Investments (note 3)	418,667	139,333	Total liabilities	37,795	39,900
Due from National Chapter	5,956	—			
Prepaid expenses	2,288	4,302	Fund balances:		
Other assets	3,214	3,117	Undesignated	420,004	310,650
			Designated for research purposes	—	154,333
				420,004	464,983
	$457,799	$504,883		$457,799	$504,883
Restricted					
	$ —	$ —		$ —	$ —
Endowment Funds					
Cash	$ 77,822	$ —	Fund balance—restricted	$ 77,822	$ —
Property and Equipment Fund					
Furniture and equipment (less accumulated depreciation of $38,209 in 1990 and $45,777 in 1989	$ 7,905	$ 12,143	Fund balance—expended	$ 7,905	$ 12,143

Source: Virginia Chapter of Arthritis Foundation, Financial Statements and Supplementary Schedules, December 31, 1990.

Exhibit 21–12   *Balance Sheet for Voluntary Health and Welfare Organization*

VIRGINIA CHAPTER OF ARTHRITIS FOUNDATION
STATEMENT OF SUPPORT, REVENUE AND EXPENSES AND CHANGES IN FUND BALANCES
YEAR ENDED DECEMBER 31, 1990 WITH COMPARATIVE TOTALS FOR 1989

	Current Funds		Endowment Funds	Property and Equipment Fund	Total all funds	
	Unrestricted	Restricted			1990	1989
Public Support and Revenue						
Public support:						
Contributions	$195,787	1,000	—	—	196,787	262,863
Membership contributions	64,623	—	—	—	64,623	78,887
Donated services and materials	13,948	—	—	—	13,948	24,022
Special events (net of direct costs of $38,644 in 1990 and $37,037 in 1989)	94,680	—	—	—	94,680	117,233
Legacies and bequests	82,404	—	77,822	—	160,226	14,277
Received from federated and nonfederated campaigns	72,932	—	—	—	72,932	75,776
Total public support	524,374	1,000	77,822	—	603,196	573,058
Revenue:						
Investment income	38,802	—	—	—	38,802	41,077
Miscellaneous	2,286	—	—	—	2,286	4,088
Total revenue	41,088	—	—	—	41,088	45,165
Total public support and revenue	565,462	1,000	77,822	—	644,284	618,223
Expenses						
Program services:						
Research	12,203	—	—	191	12,394	27,081
Public health and education	218,536	—	—	3,416	221,952	236,762
Professional education and training	20,876	—	—	326	21,202	18,599
Patient and community services	81,228	1,000	—	1,285	83,513	84,622
Total program services	332,843	1,000	—	5,218	339,061	367,064
Supporting services:						
Fund raising	96,875	—	—	859	97,734	73,606
Management and general	36,352	—	—	568	36,920	56,295
Total supporting services	133,227	—	—	1,427	134,654	129,901
Share due National Chapter (note 4)	141,964	—	—	—	141,964	148,149
Total expenses	608,034	1,000	—	6,645	615,679	645,114
Excess (deficiency) of public support and revenue over expenses	(42,572)	—	77,822	(6,645)		
Other changes in fund balances—property and equipment acquisitions	(2,407)	—	—	2,407		
Fund balances, beginning of year	464,983	—	—	12,143		
Fund balances, end of year	$420,004	—	77,822	7,905		

See accompanying notes to financial statements.

Source: Virginia Chapter of Arthritis Foundation, Financial Statements and Supplementary Schedules, December 31, 1990.

Exhibit 21-13   *Statement of Support, Revenues and Expenses, and Changes in Fund Balances for a Voluntary Health and Welfare Organization*

		Program Services			
	Research	Public Health and Education	Professional Education and Training	Patient and Community Services	Total
Salaries	$ 6,030	107,992	10,316	40,633	164,971
Employee benefits	872	15,619	1,492	5,877	23,860
Awards and grants	—	—	—	—	—
Professional fees	958	17,155	1,639	6,455	26,207
Telephone	525	9,402	898	3,538	14,363
Occupancy (note 5)	1,242	22,245	2,125	8,370	33,982
Postage and shipping	348	6,224	595	2,342	9,509
Office supplies	180	3,224	308	1,213	4,925
Printing and publications	768	13,748	1,313	5,173	21,002
Specific assistance to individuals	81	1,449	138	545	2,213
Dues and subscriptions	26	462	44	174	706
Rental and maintenance of equipment	120	2,152	206	810	3,288
Travel	680	12,186	1,164	4,585	18,615
Donated services and materials	165	2,954	282	1,112	4,513
Miscellaneous	208	3,724	356	1,401	5,689
Share due National Chapter (note 4)	—	—	—	—	—
Total expenses before depreciation	12,203	218,536	20,876	82,228	333,843
Depreciation	191	3,416	326	1,285	5,218
Total functional expenses	$12,394	221,952	21,202	83,513	339,061

VIRGINIA CHAPTER OF ARTHRITIS FOUNDATION
STATEMENT OF FUNCTIONAL EXPENSES
FOR THE YEAR ENDED DECEMBER 31, 1990 WITH COMPARATIVE FIGURES FOR 1989

See accompanying notes to financial statements.
Source: Virginia Chapter of Arthritis Foundation, Financial Statements and Supplementary Schedules, December 31, 1990

Exhibit 21–14 *Statement of Functional Expenses for a Voluntary Health and Welfare Organization*

VIRGINIA CHAPTER OF ARTHRITIS FOUNDATION
STATEMENT OF FUNCTIONAL EXPENSES
FOR THE YEAR ENDED DECEMBER 31, 1990 WITH COMPARATIVE FIGURES FOR 1989

| | Supporting Services | | | Share due National Chapter | Total Expenses | |
	Fund Raising	Management and General	Total		1990	1989
Salaries	27,166	17,964	45,130	—	210,101	219,550
Employee benefits	3,929	2,598	6,527	—	30,387	35,493
Awards and grants	—	—	—	—	—	20,067
Professional fees	46,217	2,854	49,071	—	75,278	61,554
Telephone	2,365	1,564	3,929	—	18,292	15,940
Occupancy (note 5)	5,596	3,700	9,296	—	43,278	43,245
Postage and shipping	1,566	1,035	2,601	—	12,110	13,779
Office supplies	811	536	1,347	—	6,272	6,162
Printing and publications	3,458	2,287	5,745	—	26,747	28,418
Specific assistance to individuals	365	241	606	—	2,819	2,304
Dues and subscriptions	116	77	193	—	899	969
Rental and maintenance of equipment	541	358	899	—	4,187	4,954
Travel	3,065	2,027	5,092	—	23,707	20,995
Donated services and materials	743	491	1,234	—	5,747	8,642
Miscellaneous	937	620	1,557	—	7,246	6,935
Share due National Chapter (note 4)	—	—	—	141,964	141,964	148,149
Total expenses before depreciation	96,875	36,352	133,227	141,964	609,034	637,156
Depreciation	859	568	1,427	—	6,645	7,958
Total functional expenses	97,734	36,920	134,654	141,964	615,679	645,114

See accompanying notes to financial statements.
Source: Virginia Chapter of Arthritis Foundation, Financial Statements and Supplementary Schedules, December 31, 1990

Exhibit 21–14   *Statement of Functional Expenses for a Voluntary Health and Welfare Organization (cont.)*

Notes to Financial Statements, December 31, 1990

1 *Organization*—The Virginia Chapter of Arthritis Foundation (the "Chapter") is a not-for-profit voluntary health agency established to help educate the public about arthritis and to raise funds to promote research into the causes and cures of arthritis. The Chapter is comprised of branches in Charlottesville, Norfolk, Roanoke, Warrenton, Newport News and Richmond. The Chapter is exempt from income taxes under Internal Revenue Code Section 501(c)(3).

2 *Summary of Significant Accounting Policies*—The Chapter reports in accordance with the American Institute of Certified Public Accountants' industry audit guide *Audits of Voluntary Health and Welfare Organizations*. Under the provisions of that Guide, the following accounting policies are prescribed:

  a The current unrestricted fund is used to account for all resources over which the governing board has discretionary control.

  b The property and equipment fund is used to account for the net investment in fixed assets and for unexpended resources restricted by donors or legal authorities for the acquisition of property and equipment for use in operations.

  c Depreciation of furniture and equipment used in operations is recorded in the property and equipment fund on a straight-line basis over the estimated useful lives of the assets (5 to 10 years).

  d Current restricted funds are used to account for funds restricted by donors to specific operating purposes or programs. Such funds are recognized as revenue when received unless specified for use in future periods.

  e Endowment funds represent the principal of contributions to be maintained intact in perpetuity.

  f Donated services and materials are recorded at the estimated fair market value of volunteer work received by the various branches for the performance of clerical work. It also includes the estimated fair market value of rent for the Warrenton branch, which currently uses the home of one of the directors as its office.

3 *Investments*—Investments are carried at cost and are comprised of the following at December 31, 1990 and 1989:

	December 31, 1990		December 31, 1989	
	Cost	*Estimated Market Value*	*Cost*	*Estimated Market Value*
Medium term bond fund	$128,417	$138,067	$139,333	$148,704
Managed bond fund	290,250	293,640	—	—
	$418,667	$431,707	$139,333	$148,704

4 *Share Due National Chapter*—The Chapter is required to pay the National Chapter of the Arthritis Foundation a portion of Chapter revenues ranging from 27% to 35% based on the source of revenue. The Chapter also benefits from the National Chapter of the Arthritis Foundation as it receives funds for its share of revenues generated from telethone and other federated contributions received by the National Chapter.

5 *Commitments*—The Chapter leases certain of its office space under operating leases expiring at various dates to 1994. Minimum future rental payments required under such leases that have initial or remaining non-cancellable lease terms in excess of one year as of December 31, 1990 are as follows:

Year ending December 31, 1991	$18,900
1992	20,700
1993	21,600
1994	22,950

Some of the Chapter's leases contain escalation clauses and renewal options. Total rental expense under operating leases approximated $43,200 in 1990 and $43,000 in 1989.

Source: Virginia Chapter of Arthritis Foundation, Financial Statements and Supplementary Schedules, December 31, 1990.

Exhibit 21–15   *Notes to the Financial Statements of a Voluntary Health Organization*

SUMMARY

Colleges and universities, hospitals, and voluntary health and welfare organizations use fund accounting practices and accrual accounting, but other accounting and reporting practices vary considerably. The operating statement of colleges and universities (the statement of current funds revenues, expenditures, and other changes) is a revenues and expenditures statement (except when depreciation is required) for current funds only.

Hospitals measure revenues and expenses including depreciation on an accrual basis, but their operating statement (statement of revenues and expenses of general funds) channels all revenues and expenses through the operating funds. Like hospitals, voluntary health and welfare organizations use accrual accounting and report revenues and expenses in their operating statements. But the operating statement of voluntary health and welfare organizations (statement of support, revenues and expenses, and changes in fund balance) includes all funds, such that support, revenues, and expenses are reported in the funds to which they relate.

Unlike colleges and universities and hospitals, voluntary health and welfare organizations include restricted gifts and grants in their operating statements as support and revenue in the period received.

Hospitals are required to prepare statements of cash flows of general funds in their audited financial statements. The cash flow statement is not a required statement of either colleges and universities or voluntary health and welfare organizations.

It is generally assumed that the accounting and reporting differences reflect different types of operating activities and levels of autonomy, and different financial statement users.

SELECTED READINGS

American Hospital Association. *Managerial Cost Accounting for Hospitals.* Chicago: American Hospital Association, 1980.

American Institute of Certified Public Accountants. *Audits of Colleges and Universities,* 2nd ed., Industry Audit Guide. New York: AICPA, 1975.

American Institute of Certified Public Accountants. *Audits of Providers of Health Care Services,* Audit and Accounting Guide. New York: AICPA, 1990.

American Institute of Certified Public Accountants. *Audits of Voluntary Health and Welfare Organizations,* Industry Audit Guide. New York: AICPA, 1974.

ANTHONY, ROBERT N. *Financial Accounting in Nonbusiness Organizations: An Exploratory Study of Conceptual Issues,* Research Report. Stamford, CT: Financial Accounting Standards Board, 1978.

ANTHONY, ROBERT N. and DAVID W. YOUNG. *Management Control in Nonprofit Organizations,* 3rd ed. Homewood, IL: Richard D. Irwin, Inc., 1984.

BASTABLE, C. W. "Collegiate Accounting Needs Re-evaluation." *Journal of Accountancy* (December 1973), pp. 51–57.

Chart of Accounts for Hospitals. Chicago: American Hospital Association, 1976.

College and University Business Administration, 4th ed. Washington, D.C.: National Association of College and University Business Officers, 1982.

EBEY, CARL F. "Why Don't Colleges Depreciate Fixed Assets?" *Management Accounting* (August 1983), pp. 13–17.

FETTERMAN, ALLEN L. "Update on Not-for-Profit Organizations." *The CPA Journal* (March 1990), pp. 26–30.

HENKE, EMERSON O., and LUCIAN G. CONWAY, JR. "A Recommended Reporting Format for College and University Financial Statements." *Accounting Horizons* (June 1989), pp. 49–65.

MAULDIN, ELAINE G. "How Not-for-Profit Organizations Should Value Investments." *Management Accounting* (November 1980), pp. 35–38.

MAUTZ, R. K. "Not-for-Profit Financial Reporting: Another View." *Journal of Accountancy* (August 1989), pp. 60–66.

912

COLLEGES
AND UNIVERSITIES,
HOSPITALS,
AND VOLUNTARY
HEALTH AND WELFARE
ORGANIZATIONS

MAUTZ, R. K. "Why Not-for-Profits Should Report Their Commitments." *Journal of Accountancy* (June 1990), pp. 92–98.

Proposed Statement of Financial Accounting Standards. "Accounting for Contributions Received and Contributions Made and Capitalization of Works of Art, Historical Treasures, and Similar Assets." Stamford, CT: Financial Accounting Standards Board, 1990.

Standards of Accounting and Financial Reporting for Voluntary Health and Welfare Organizations. New York: National Health Council, National Assembly of National Voluntary Health and Social Welfare Organizations, Inc., and United Way of America, 1975.

Statement of Financial Accounting Concepts No. 4. "Objectives of Financial Reporting by Nonbusiness Organizations." Stamford, CT: Financial Accounting Standards Board, 1980.

Statement of Financial Accounting Concepts No. 6. "Elements of Financial Statements." Stamford, CT: Financial Accounting Standards Board, 1985.

Statement of Financial Accounting Standards No. 93. "Recognition of Depreciation by Not-for-Profit Organizations." Stamford, CT: Financial Accounting Standards Board, 1987.

Statement of Position 74-8. "Financial Accounting and Reporting by Colleges and Universities." New York: American Institute of Certified Public Accountants, 1974.

ASSIGNMENT MATERIAL

QUESTIONS

1 What subgroups are included in the current funds grouping of college and university accounting systems?

2 Identify three types of endowment funds that may be included in the endowment and similar funds grouping of a university, and explain the differences in the three types.

3 Explain the differences that one would expect to find in the composition of the assets and liabilities of annuity and life income funds.

4 In which fund group and subgroup of a university would you expect to find an account or accounts for library books? Discuss how depreciation on library books would be reflected in the university's financial statements.

5 Explain why one of the financial statements of a university shows revenues and expenditures when colleges and universities are supposed to use the accrual basis of accounting.

6 Kepper College received $40,000 from federal grants for accounting research during 19X2. The college expended $25,000 in 19X2 and $12,000 in 19X3, and refunded $3,000 to the U.S. government in 19X4. In what fund or funds should the grant resources be recorded, and how should the grant activity be accounted for in each of the three years?

7 Is it true that revenue and expenditures of a university's service departments (centralized purchasing, for example) are excluded from the university's revenues and expenditures? Explain.

8 What is a *mandatory transfer* as the term is used in college and university accounting?

9 Assume that a university receives $5,000 of unrestricted income from endowment fund investments. Is this transaction recorded in the endowment fund? Explain.

10 Are board-designated funds of hospitals included in the general funds or the restricted funds category? Explain.

11 In which fund grouping of a hospital would medical equipment and related long term liabilities be recorded?

12 What fund grouping of hospitals corresponds to the restricted current funds grouping of colleges and universities?

13 How are net patient service revenues of hospitals measured, and in which hospital financial statement are they reported?

14 What are the three major revenue groupings of hospitals? Give an example of a revenue item that would be included in each grouping.

15 Are provisions for bad debts and depreciation of hospitals reported as expenses or expenditures? Explain.

16 Compare the basic financial statements required for colleges and universities, hospitals, and voluntary health and welfare organizations. Only statement titles need be included in the comparison.

17 Describe the nature of a land, building, and equipment fund of a voluntary health and welfare organization.

18 Would it ever be acceptable for a voluntary health and welfare organization to issue financial statements on a modified accrual basis? Explain.

19 Do voluntary health and welfare organizations recognize support and revenue from pledges when the pledges are received or when cash is received? Explain.

20 Expenses of voluntary health and welfare organizations include classifications for program services and supporting services. Explain these classifications.

21 What is the purpose of the combined statement of functional expenses of voluntary health and welfare organizations?

EXERCISES

E 21-1

1 The current funds grouping of a university accounting system includes:
   a Books
   b Unexpended research grants
   c Resources restricted for student loans by the governing board
   d Bonds payable

2 Which of the following subgroups of a university's accounting system is most likely to have resources free of external restrictions?
   a Term endowments   b Annuity funds
   c Restricted current funds   d Unexpended plant funds

3 Unrestricted current funds resources transferred to a university's renewal and replacement fund subgroup in accordance with the provisions of a bond indenture are classified as:
   a Mandatory transfers
   b Provisions for funded depreciation
   c Other transfers
   d Expenditures

4 Which of the following activities of a college or university would most likely be classified as an auxiliary enterprise?
   a Motor pool operations
   b Extension programs
   c Operation of a college store
   d Centralized purchasing

5 Select the statement that is most nearly correct with respect to college and university accounting.
   a Depreciation is only recorded in auxiliary enterprise funds.
   b Depreciation expense should be reported in the investment in plant funds subgroup.
   c Accumulated depreciation may not be reported in the investment in plant funds subgroup.
   d Replacement cost depreciation is a unique feature of university accounting.

6 A university recognizes revenue from a grant to supplement faculty salaries when:
   a The grant is awarded
   b Grant resources are received
   c Expenditures are made for the salary supplements
   d The amount of the grant is both measurable and available

7 Quasi-endowment funds of a university are:
   a Term endowments
   b Donor-restricted endowments
   c Grantor-restricted endowments
   d Board-designated resources accounted for as endowments

8 Unrestricted endowment fund income of a college or university should be recognized as revenue of:
   a Unrestricted current funds   b Endowment funds
   c Special-purpose funds   d Annuity funds

914

COLLEGES
AND UNIVERSITIES,
HOSPITALS,
AND VOLUNTARY
HEALTH AND WELFARE
ORGANIZATIONS

9 The subgroups of a university's plant fund grouping do not include:
   a Unexpended plant funds
   b Renewal and replacement funds
   c Retirement of indebtedness funds
   d Capital asset funds

10 The accrual basis of accounting is recommended for:
   a Colleges and universities, but not hospitals and voluntary health and welfare organizations
   b Hospitals, but not colleges and universities and voluntary health and welfare organizations
   c Voluntary health and welfare organizations, but not hospitals and colleges and universities
   d Colleges and universities, hospitals, and voluntary health and welfare organizations

E 21–2

1 Hospital accounting does not involve
   a Recording patient service revenue on a gross basis
   b Recognizing expenses on an accrual basis
   c Providing for depreciation on plant assets
   d Deducting uncollectible account provisions from patient service revenues

2 Discounts allowed to third-party payors in hospital accounting are recorded as
   a Charity care
   b Contractual allowances
   c Courtesy allowances
   d Mandatory discounts

3 Hospital long-term debt is accounted for in the grouping
   a General funds
   b Board-designated funds
   c Restricted funds
   d Plant replacement and expansion funds

4 Hospital room charges for telephone and television rentals should be classified as
   a Patient service revenues
   b Other operating revenues
   c Nonoperating gains
   d Miscellaneous income

5 A hospital bills patients at gross rates and provides for courtesy allowances for employees when they settle their accounts at less than gross rates. In accordance with this system, the journal entry to record courtesy allowances would appear
   a Debit—cash; debit—courtesy allowance; credit—accounts receivable
   b Debit—courtesy discount; credit—allowance for courtesy discounts
   c Debit—cash; debit—patient service revenue; credit—accounts receivable
   d Debit—accounts receivable; credit—courtesy allowances; credit—patient service revenue

6 Specific-purpose funds of hospitals are most like
   a Board-designated funds of colleges and universities
   b Custodian funds of colleges and universities
   c Restricted current funds of voluntary health and welfare organizations
   d Current restricted funds of governmental units

7 The restricted funds grouping recommended by *Audits of Providers of Health Care Services* does not include
   a Specific-purpose funds
   b Endowment funds
   c Plant funds
   d Plant replacement and expansion funds

8 Four basic financial statements are required to meet reporting standards of hospitals. Which of the following is not one of these statements?
   a Balance sheet
   b Statement of revenues and expenditures
   c Statement of changes in fund balances
   d Statement of cash flows

9 The functional categories recommended for operating expenses in *Audits of Providers of Health Care Services* do not include
   a Nursing services
   b Provision for depreciation
   c Transfers for plant replacement
   d Other professional services

10 Unrestricted income from a hospital's endowment fund investments should be reported in the statement of revenues and expenses of general funds as
   a Transfers to unrestricted funds
   b Other operating revenue
   c Nonoperating gains
   d None of the above

E 21–3 1 Voluntary health and welfare organizations include voluntary:
   a Hospitals
   b Health, welfare, and community service organizations
   c Social clubs
   d Fine arts association

2 Which of the following statements is *not* ordinarily required for voluntary health and welfare organizations that issue financial statements in accordance with GAAP?
   a Balance sheet
   b Statement of support, revenues and expenses, and changes in fund balances
   c Statement of functional expenses
   d Statement of cash flows

3 Pledges of voluntary health and welfare organizations are recognized as revenue and support in the period(s) in which:
   a The pledges are received
   b Cash is received from the pledges
   c All restrictions on pledged resources have been removed
   d Pledged resources are expended

4 Fund-raising costs of voluntary health and welfare organizations are classified as:
   a Functional expenditures   b Program services
   c Supporting services   d Management and general expenses

5 The property, plant, and equipment of a voluntary health and welfare organization is recorded in a (an):
   a Investment in fixed assets fund
   b Land, building, and equipment fund
   c Current unrestricted fund
   d General fixed assets account group

6 Program services of voluntary health and welfare organizations include:
   a Fund-raising costs
   b Administration expense
   c Cost of research programs
   d Accounting and data processing

7 Current unrestricted funds of voluntary health and welfare organizations include:
   a Plant assets   b Board-designated funds
   c Special-purpose funds   d Long-term liabilities

8 Net gains realized on investments by voluntary health and welfare organizations are reported as revenue in the current unrestricted fund if they:
   a Are from investments of unrestricted funds
   b Result from investments of restricted funds
   c Relate to endowment fund investments
   d Are legally available for specific operating purposes

E 21–4 **[AICPA adapted]**

1 What method of accounting should be used by colleges and universities?
   a Cash   b Modified cash
   c Restricted accrual   d Accrual

2 In the loan fund of a college or university, each of the following types of loans would be found *except:*
   a Student   b Staff
   c Building   d Faculty

3 Which of the following receipts is properly recorded as restricted current funds on the books of a university?
   a Tuition   b Student laboratory fees
   c Housing fees   d Research grants

916

COLLEGES
AND UNIVERSITIES,
HOSPITALS,
AND VOLUNTARY
HEALTH AND WELFARE
ORGANIZATIONS

4 Funds which the governing board of an institution, rather than a donor or other outside agency, has determined are to be retained and invested for other than loan or plant purposes would be accounted for in the:

  a Quasi-endowment fund   **b** Endowment fund

  c Agency fund   **d** Current fund—restricted

5 Funds established at a college by donors who have stipulated that the principal is nonexpendable but that the income generated may be expended by current operating funds would be accounted for in the:

  a Quasi-endowment fund   **b** Endowment fund

  c Term endowment fund   **d** Agency fund

6 An increase in Oak College's restricted current funds balance could be reported as an excess of:

  a Transfers to revenues over restricted receipts

  b Restricted receipts over transfers to revenues

  c Revenues over expenditures and mandatory transfers

  d Revenues and mandatory transfers over expenditures

E 21-5   **[AICPA adapted]**

1 Which of the following would be included in the general funds of a not-for-profit hospital?

  a Permanent endowments

  b Term endowments

  c Board-designated funds originating from previously accumulated income

  d Plant expansion and replacement funds

2 A gift to a voluntary not-for-profit hospital that is not restricted by the donor should be credited directly to:

  a Fund balance   **b** Deferred revenue

  c Operating revenue   **d** Nonoperating gains

3 Donated medicines which normally would be purchased by a hospital should be recorded at fair market value and should be credited directly to:

  a Other operating revenue   **b** Other nonoperating revenue

  c Fund balance   **d** Deferred revenue

Use the following information in answering questions 4, 5, and 6:

     Lori Hospital received a $300,000 unrestricted bequest and a $500,000 pure endowment grant in March 19X9. In April 19X9 a bank notified Lori that the bank received $10,000 to be held in permanent trust by the bank. Lori is to receive the income from this donation.

4 Lori should record the $300,000 unrestricted bequest as:

  a Nonoperating gains

  b Other operating revenue

  c A direct credit to the fund balance

  d A credit to operating expenses

5 The $500,000 pure endowment grant:

  a May be expended by the governing board only to the extent of the principal since the income from this fund must be accumulated

  b Should be reported as nonoperating revenue when the full amount of principal is expended

  c Should be recorded as a memorandum entry only

  d Should be accounted for as restricted funds upon receipt

6 The $10,000 donation being held by the bank in permanent trust should be:

  a Recorded in Lori's restricted endowment fund

  b Recorded by Lori as nonoperating gains

  c Recorded by Lori as other operating revenue

  d Disclosed in notes to Lori's financial statements

E 21-6   **[AICPA adapted]**

1 Voluntary health and welfare organizations, unlike some nonprofit organizations, recorded and recognized depreciation on fixed assets even before the issuance of *FASB Statement 93*. Why?

  a Fixed assets are more likely to be material in amount in a voluntary health and welfare organization than in other nonprofit organizations.

b Voluntary health and welfare organizations purchase their fixed assets and therefore have a historical cost basis from which to determine amounts to be depreciated.

c A fixed asset used by a voluntary health and welfare organization has alternative uses in private industry, and this opportunity cost should be reflected in the organization's financial statements.

d Contributors look for the most efficient use of funds, and since depreciation represents a cost of employing fixed assets, it is appropriate that a voluntary health and welfare organization reflect it as a cost of providing services.

2 A reason for a voluntary health and welfare organization to adopt fund accounting is that:

a Restrictions have been placed on certain of its assets by donors

b It provides more than one type of program service

c Fixed assets are significant

d Donated services are significant

3 Which basis of accounting should a voluntary health and welfare organization use?

a Cash basis for all funds

b Modified accrual basis for all funds

c Accrual basis for all funds

d Accrual basis for some funds and modified accrual basis for other funds

4 In a statement of support, revenue, and expenses and changes in fund balances of a voluntary health and welfare organization, depreciation expense should:

a Be included as an element of expense

b Be included as an element of other changes in fund balance

c Be included as an element of support

d Not be included

5 Which of the following funds of a voluntary health and welfare organization does not have a *counterpart fund* in governmental accounting?

a Current unrestricted   **b** Land, building, and equipment

c Custodian   **d** Endowment

6 A voluntary health and welfare organization received a pledge in 19X1 from a donor specifying that the amount pledged be used in 19X3. The donor paid the pledge in cash in 19X2. The pledge should be accounted for as:

a A deferred credit in the balance sheet at the end of 19X1, and as support in 19X2

b A deferred credit in the balance sheet at the end of 19X1 and 19X2, and as support in 19X3

c Support in 19X1

d Support in 19X2, and no deferred credit in the balance sheet at the end of 19X1

E 21-7   **[AICPA adapted]**

1 For the 19X7 summer session, Selva University assessed its students $300,000 for tuition and fees. However, the net amount realized was only $290,000 because of the following reductions:

Tuition remissions granted to faculty members' families	$3,000
Class cancellation refunds	7,000

How much unrestricted current funds revenues from tuition and fees should Selva report for the period?

a $290,000   **b** $293,000

c $297,000   **d** $300,000

2 The following information was available from Forest College's accounting records for its current funds for the year ended March 31, 19X8:

Restricted gifts received:	
Expended	$100,000
Not expended	300,000
Unrestricted gifts received:	
Expended	$600,000
Not expended	75,000

918

COLLEGES
AND UNIVERSITIES,
HOSPITALS,
AND VOLUNTARY
HEALTH AND WELFARE
ORGANIZATIONS

What amount should be included in current funds revenues for the year ended March 31, 19X8?

a $600,000   b $700,000

c $775,000   d $1,000,000

3 The following expenditures were among those incurred by Alma University during 19X7:

Administrative data processing	$ 50,000
Scholarships and fellowships	100,000
Operations and maintenance of physical plant	200,000

The amount to be included in the functional classification *institutional support* expenditures account is:

a $50,000   b $150,000

c $250,000   d $350,000

4 The following funds were among those on Kery University's books at April 30, 19X4:

Funds to be used for acquisition of additional properties for University purposes (unexpended at April 30, 19X4)	$3,000,000
Funds set aside for debt service charges and for retirement of indebtedness on University properties	5,000,000

How much of these funds should be included in plant funds?

a $0   b $3,000,000

c $5,000,000   d $8,000,000

5 During the years ended June 30, 19X3 and 19X4, Sanata University conducted a cancer research project financed by a $2,000,000 gift from an alumna. This entire amount was pledged by the donor on July 10, 19X2, although she paid only $500,000 at that date. The gift was restricted to the financing of this particular research project. During the two-year research period, Sanata's related gift receipts and research expenditures were as follows:

	Year Ended June 30	
	19X3	*19X4*
Gift receipts	$1,200,000	$ 800,000
Cancer research expenditures	900,000	1,100,000

How much gift revenue should Sanata report in the restricted column of its statement of current funds revenues, expenditures, and other changes for the year ended June 30, 19X4?

a $0   b $800,000

c $1,100,000   d $2,000,000

6 On January 2, 19X2, John Reynolds established a $500,000 trust, the income from which is to be paid to Mansfield University for general operating purposes. The Wyndham National Bank was appointed by Reynolds as trustee of the fund. What journal entry is required on Mansfield's books?

a Memorandum entry only

b Debit—cash, $500,000; credit—endowment fund balance, $500,000

c Debit—nonexpendable endowment fund, $500,000; credit—endowment fund balance, $500,000

d Debit—expendable funds, $500,000; credit—endowment fund balance, $500,000

E 21–8 [AICPA adapted]

1 Ross Hospital's accounting records disclosed the following information:

Net resources invested in plant assets	$10,000,000
Board-designated funds	2,000,000

What amount should be included as part of unrestricted funds?

a $12,000,000   **b** $10,000,000
c $2,000,000   **d** $0

2 Cliff Hospital, a voluntary institution, has a pure endowment fund, the income from which is required to be used for library acquisitions. State law and the donor are silent on the accounting treatment for investment gains and losses. In 19X2, Cliff sold 1,000 shares of stock from the endowment fund's investment portfolio. The carrying amount of these securities was $50,000. Net proceeds from the sale amounted to $120,000. This transaction should be recorded in the endowment fund as a debit to cash for $120,000 and as credits to:

a Endowment fund principal, $50,000 and endowment fund revenue, $70,000
b Endowment fund principal, $50,000 and due to general fund, $70,000
c Investments, $50,000 and endowment fund balance, $70,000
d Investments, $50,000 and endowment fund revenue, $70,000

3 Cedar Hospital has a marketable equity securities portfolio that is appropriately included in noncurrent assets in unrestricted funds. The portfolio has an aggregate cost of $300,000. It has an aggregate fair market value of $250,000 at the end of 19X7 and $290,000 at the end of 19X6. If the portfolio was properly reported in the balance sheet at the end of 19X6, the change in the valuation allowance at the end of 19X7 should be:

a $0   **b** A decrease of $40,000
c An increase of $40,000   **d** An increase of $50,000

4 Glenmore Hospital's property, plant, and equipment (net of depreciation) consist of the following:

Land	$ 500,000
Buildings	10,000,000
Movable equipment	2,000,000

What amount should be included in the restricted fund grouping?

a $0   **b** $2,000,000
c $10,500,000   **d** $12,500,000

5 During the year ended December 31, 19X1, Melford Hospital received the following donations stated at their respective fair values:

Employee services from members of a religious group	$100,000
Medical supplies from an association of physicians. These supplies were restricted for indigent care and were used for such purpose in 19X1	30,000

How much revenue (both operating and nonoperating) from donations should Melford report in its 19X1 statement of revenues and expenses of general funds?

a $0   **b** $30,000
c $100,000   **d** $130,000

6 On July 1, 19X1 Lilydale Hospital's Board of Trustees designated $200,000 for expansion of outpatient facilities. The $200,000 is expected to be expended in the fiscal year ending June 30, 19X4. In Lilydale's balance sheet at June 30, 19X2, this cash should be classified as a $200,000

a Restricted current asset   **b** Restricted noncurrent asset
c Unrestricted current asset   **d** Unrestricted noncurrent asset

E 21–9   [AICPA adapted]

Use the following information in answering questions 1, 2, and 3.

Ten years ago, Community Helpers, a voluntary health and welfare organization, received a bequest of a $100,000 certificate of deposit maturing in 19X8. The testator's only stipulations were that this certificate be held until maturity and that the interest revenue be used to finance salaries for a preschool program. Interest revenue for 19X8 was $8,000. When the certificate was redeemed, the board of trustees adopted a formal resolution designating $20,000 of the proceeds for the future purchase of equipment for the preschool program.

1 In regard to the certificate of deposit, what should be reported in the endowment fund column of the 19X8 statement of support, revenue, and expenses and changes in fund balances?

920

COLLEGES
AND UNIVERSITIES,
HOSPITALS,
AND VOLUNTARY
HEALTH AND WELFARE
ORGANIZATIONS

    a Legacies and bequests, $100,000

    b Direct reduction in fund balance for transfer to current unrestricted fund, $100,000

    c Transfer to land, building, and equipment fund, $20,000

    d Revenues control, $100,000

2 What should be reported in the current unrestricted funds column of the 19X8 statement of support, revenue, and expenses and changes in fund balances?

    a Investment income, $8,000

    b Direct reduction of fund balance for transfer to land, building, and equipment fund, $20,000

    c Direct addition to fund balance for transfer from endowment fund, $100,000

    d Public support, $108,000

3 What should be reported in the l9X8 year-end current unrestricted funds balance sheet?

    a Fund balance designated for preschool program, $28,000; undesignated fund balance, $80,000

    b Fund balance designated for purchase of equipment, $20,000; undesignated fund balance, $80,000

    c Fund balance designated for preschool program salaries, $8,000; undesignated fund balance, $80,000

    d Undesignated fund balance, $72,000

4 Lema Fund, a voluntary welfare organization funded by contributions from the general public, received unrestricted pledges of $200,000 during 19X3. It was estimated that 10 percent of these pledges would be uncollectible. By the end of 19X3, $130,000 of the pledges had been collected. It was expected that $50,000 more would be collected in 19X4 and that the balance of $20,000 would be written off as uncollectible. What amount should Lema include under public support in 19X3 for net contributions?

    a $200,000   **b** $180,000

    c $150,000   **d** $130,000

5 Cura Foundation, a voluntary health and welfare organization supported by contributions from the general public, included the following costs in its statement of functional expenses for the year ended December 31, 19X3:

Fund-raising	$500,000
Administrative (including data processing)	300,000
Research	100,000

Cura's functional expenses for 19X3 program services included:

    a $900,000   **b** $500,000

    c $300,000   **d** $100,000

6 Community Service Center is a voluntary welfare organization funded by contributions from the general public. During 19X3, Selma Zorn, a social worker on Community's permanent staff, earning $20,000 annually for a normal workload of 2,000 hours, contributed an additional 800 hours of her time to Community, at no charge. How much should Community record in 19X3 for contributed service expense?

    a $8,000   **b** $4,000

    c $800   **d** $0

PROBLEMS

P 21-1 The following data relate to Prince Winston University's current funds' grouping for the year ended December 31, 19X2:

Appropriations from state	$250,000
Auxiliary enterprise expenditures	195,000
Auxiliary enterprise revenues	215,000
Endowment income—restricted for salaries of researchers	20,000
Endowment income—unrestricted	40,000
Extension	100,000
General administration	60,000
Instruction	600,000
Libraries (including $30,000 for book purchases)	50,000
Operation and maintenance of plant	210,000

Private gifts and grants—restricted for library books	18,000
Private gifts and grants—unrestricted	300,000
Research (including research salaries of $15,000)	80,000
Transfer for plant replacements as required by bond indenture	20,000
Transfer for principal and interest payments as required by bond indenture	50,000
Transfer of unrestricted funds designated for student loans	10,000
Tuition and fees	400,000

Required: Prepare a statement of current funds revenues, expenditures, and other changes for 19X2.

P 21–2 The revenues and expenses of Hopeful Hospital for 19X2 were presented in the hospital's internal financial report as follows:

HOPEFUL HOSPITAL OPERATING STATEMENT FOR 19X2

	Debits	*Credits*
Administrative services	$ 200,000	
Cafeteria and gift shop income		$ 20,000
Contractual allowances	350,000	
Courtesy allowances	3,000	
Depreciation expense	150,000	
Fiscal services	300,000	
General services	900,000	
Medical malpractice costs	80,000	
Nursing services	1,400,000	
Other professional services	1,000,000	
Patient service revenue		4,200,000
Provision for bad debts	200,000	
Service charges for telephones and television		80,000
Unrestricted gifts		400,000
	$4,583,000	$4,700,000
Net income	117,000	
Total	$4,700,000	$4,700,000

Required: Prepare a statement of revenues and expenses of general funds for Hopeful Hospital in a form acceptable for external reporting.

P 21–3 At the beginning of 19X3, the citizens of North Pike created Share Shop, a voluntary health and welfare organization. Share receives donations of money, nonperishable groceries, and household items from contributors. The food and household items are distributed free of charge to families on the basis of need. Share allocates expenses 80 percent to community services and 20 percent to management and general services, unless otherwise noted.

Share has one paid administrator with a yearly salary of $14,600. Work is also done by regular volunteers whose services have a fair value of $8,000. The work of other volunteers cannot be measured.

A local transit company has provided warehouse space free of charge for the operations of Share Shop. Fair value of rent for the warehouse is $3,000 a year. Utilities of $1,800 are paid by Share for 19X3.

During the year, Share purchased supplies for $300. At December 31, 19X3, the supplies inventory was insignificant. Expenses incurred in determining which families were eligible for Share's services and other accounting and reporting expenses totaled $6,000.

Donated assets for 19X3 included nonperishable groceries at fair value, $60,000 and household items at fair value, $40,000. During the year, the Shop distributed three-fourths of the groceries and half of the household items. No portion of these distributions are allocated to management and general services.

In addition to the donated assets, Share received cash donations of $10,000 and pledges of $20,000. Share estimated that 10% of the pledges would be uncollectible.

At year end 19X3, $15,000 of the pledges had been collected, and Share estimates that only $1,000 of the remaining pledges will be uncollectible.

Town Council of North Pike made a $25,000 grant to Share Shop which will be paid in January 19X4.

Required: Prepare summary entries for Share Shop for the year 19X3.

P 21–4 |AICPA adapted|

A partial balance sheet of Rapapo State University as of the end of its fiscal year ended July 31, 19X2, is presented as follows:

RAPAPO STATE UNIVERSITY
CURRENT FUND BALANCE SHEET
JULY 31, 19X2

Assets		*Liabilities and Fund Balances*	
Unrestricted		*Unrestricted*	
Cash	$200,000	Accounts payable	$100,000
Accounts receivable—tuition and fees, less allowance for doubtful accounts of $15,000	360,000	Due to other funds	40,000
		Deferred revenue—tuition and fees	25,000
		Fund balance	435,000
Prepaid expenses	40,000		
Total unrestricted	600,000	Total unrestricted	600,000
Restricted		*Restricted*	
Cash	10,000	Accounts payable	5,000
Investments	210,000	Fund balance	215,000
Total restricted	220,000	Total restricted	220,000
Total current funds	$820,000	Total current funds	$820,000

The following information pertains to the year ended July 31, 19X3:
1 Cash collected from students' tuition totaled $3,000,000. Of this $3,000,000, $362,000 represented accounts receivable outstanding at July 31, 19X2, $2,500,000 was for current year tuition; and $138,000 was for tuition applicable to the semester beginning in August 19X3.
2 Deferred revenue at July 31, 19X2 was earned during the year ended July 31, 19X3.
3 Accounts receivable at July 31, 19X2, which were not collected during the year ended July 31, 19X3, were determined to be uncollectible and were written off against the allowance account. At July 31, 19X3 the allowance account was estimated at $10,000.
4 During the year, an unrestricted appropriation of $60,000 was made by the state. This state appropriation was to be paid to Rapapo sometime in August 19X3.
5 During the year, unrestricted cash gifts of $80,000 were received from alumni. Rapapo's board of trustees allocated $30,000 of these gifts to the student loan fund.
6 During the year, investments costing $25,000 were sold for $31,000. Restricted fund investments were purchased at a cost of $40,000. Investment income of $18,000 was earned and collected during the year.
7 Unrestricted general expenses of $2,500,000 were recorded in the voucher system. At July 31, 19X3 the unrestricted accounts payable balance was $75,000.
8 The restricted accounts payable balance at July 31, 19X2 was paid.
9 The $40,000 due to other funds at July 31, 19X2 was paid to the plant fund as required.
10 One quarter of the prepaid expenses at July 31, 19X2 expired during the current year and pertained to general education expense. There was no addition to prepaid expenses during the year.

Required

1 Prepare journal entries in summary form to record the foregoing transactions for the year ended July 31, 19X3.

2 Prepare a statement of changes in fund balances for the year ended July 31, 19X3.

P 21-5   [AICPA adapted]

Esperanza Hospital's postclosing trial balance at December 31, 19X6 appears as follows:

	Debit	Credit
Cash	$ 60,000	
Investment in U.S. Treasury bills	400,000	
Investment in corporate bonds	500,000	
Interest receivable	10,000	
Accounts receivable	50,000	
Inventory	30,000	
Land	100,000	
Building	800,000	
Equipment	170,000	
Allowance for depreciation		$ 410,000
Accounts payable		20,000
Notes payable		70,000
Endowment fund balance		520,000
Other fund balances		1,100,000
	$2,120,000	$2,120,000

Esperanza, which is a nonprofit hospital, did not maintain its books in conformity with the principles of hospital fund accounting. Effective January 1, 19X7, Esperanza's board of trustees voted to adjust the December 31, 19X6 general ledger balances and to establish separate funds for the general (unrestricted) funds, the endowment fund, and the plant replacement and expansion fund.

Additional Account Information

1 *Investment in corporate bonds* pertains to the amount required to be accumulated under a board policy to invest cash equal to accumulated depreciation until the funds are needed for asset replacement. The $500,000 balance at December 31, 19X6 is less than the full amount required because of errors in computation of building depreciation in the past years. Included in the allowance for depreciation is a correctly computed amount of $90,000 applicable to equipment.

2 *Endowment fund balance* has been credited with the following:

Donor's bequest of cash	$300,000
Gains on sales of securities	100,000
Interest and dividends earned in 19X4, 19X5, and 19X6	120,000
Total	$520,000

The terms of the bequest specify that the principal, plus all gains on sales of investments, are to remain fully invested in U.S. government or corporate securities. At December 31, 19X6 $400,000 was invested in U.S. Treasury bills. The bequest further specifies that interest and dividends earned on investments are to be used for payment of current operating expenses.

3 *Land* comprises the following:

Donation of land 16 years ago at appraised value	$ 40,000
Appreciation in fair value of land as determined by independent appraiser 6 years ago	60,000
Total	$100,000

4 *Building* comprises the following:

Hospital building completed 40 years ago from January 19X7 at cost (estimated useful life was 50 years when operations were started)	$720,000

924

COLLEGES
AND UNIVERSITIES,
HOSPITALS,
AND VOLUNTARY
HEALTH AND WELFARE
ORGANIZATIONS

Installation of elevator completed 20 years ago from January 19X7 at cost (estimated useful life was 20 years)	80,000
Total	$800,000

Required

1 Set up a worksheet to adjust the general ledger balances and establish separate funds as of January 1, 19X7. Enter the account titles and amounts from the trial balance in the first three worksheet columns, add debit and credit columns for adjustments, and columns for the general (unrestricted) funds, endowment fund, and plant replacement and expansion fund. Restate the ledger account balances properly.

2 Distribute the adjusted balances to establish the separate fund accounts. Supporting computations should be referenced to the worksheet adjustments.

P 21-6 [AICPA adapted]

Children's Agency, a voluntary health and welfare organization, conducts two programs: Medical Services Program and Community Information Services Program. It had the following transactions during the year ended June 30, 19X9:

1 Received the following contributions:

Unrestricted pledges	$800,000
Restricted cash	95,000
Building fund pledges	50,000
Endowment fund cash	1,000

2 Collected the following pledges:

Unrestricted	$450,000
Building fund	20,000

3 Received the following unrestricted cash revenues:

From theater party (net of direct costs)	$ 12,000
Bequests	10,000
Membership dues	8,000
Interest and dividends	5,000

4 Program expenses incurred (processed through vouchers payable):

Medical services	$ 60,000
Community information services	15,000

5 Services expenses incurred (processed through vouchers payable):

General administration	$150,000
Fund-raising	200,000

6 Fixed assets purchased with unrestricted cash $18,000

7 Depreciation of all buildings and equipment in the land, buildings, and equipment fund was allocated as follows:

Medical services program	$ 4,000
Community information services program	3,000
General administration	6,000
Fund-raising	2,000

8 Paid vouchers payable $330,000

Required: Prepare journal entries for the preceding transactions, using the following funds: current fund—unrestricted; current fund—restricted; land, buildings, and equipment fund; and endowment fund.

A

SEC INFLUENCE ON ACCOUNTING

The influence of the Securities and Exchange Commission (SEC) on the development of accounting and reporting principles is well recognized by accountants. Congress gave the SEC authority to establish accounting principles when it passed the Securities Exchange Act of 1934 under which the SEC was created. Initially, the administration of the Securities Act of 1933 was assigned to the Federal Trade Commission. But a year later, the 1934 act created the Securities and Exchange Commission and made it responsible for establishing regulations over accounting and auditing matters for firms under its jurisdiction. Thus, the SEC has the authority to prescribe accounting principles for entities that fall under its jurisdiction.

A combination of inadequate regulation of securities at the federal and state levels, the stock market crash of 1929, and the Great Depression of the 1930s all contributed to the enactment of new securities legislation in the early 1930s.

THE 1933 SECURITIES ACT

A primary objective of the Securities Act of 1933 was "to provide full and fair disclosure of the character of securities sold in interstate and foreign commerce and the mails, and to prevent fraud in the sale thereof. . ." (Securities Act of 1933). Another objective of the 1933 act was to protect investors against fraud, deceit and misrepresentation. There have been many amendments, but these objectives still constitute the primary thrust of the 1933 act.

The Securities Act of 1933 is often called the "truth in securities act." This is because *the SEC's objective is to prevent the issuers of securities from disclosing false, incomplete, or otherwise misleading information to prospective buyers of their securities.* The SEC emphasizes that its objective is not to pass judgment on the merits of any firm's securities. The SEC imposes severe penalties on firms and individuals that violate its disclosure requirements.

Issuance of Securities in Public Offerings

The Securities Act of 1933 is concerned with the issuance of specific securities to investors in public offerings. Such securities are required to be *registered with the SEC* and to be *advertised in a prospectus* prior to their being offered for sale to the public.

Exempt Security Issues   Certain security issuances are exempt from the 1933 act. A partial list of exempt securities includes those issued by governmental units, by not-for-profit organizations, by firms in bankruptcy and subject to court order, by firms in stock splits or in direct sales to existing shareholders (private placements), and by firms issuing intrastate securities with sales limited to residents of that state.

Issues of $5,000,000 or Less   *Regulation A* provides less restrictive registration procedures for security issuances not exceeding $5,000,000. Regulation A permits firms to use an *offering circular* rather than a prospectus as required for full registration.

The Prospectus   The **prospectus** is a part of the registration statement that provides detailed information about the background of the registrant firm, including its development, its business, and its financial statements. An **offering circular** is like a prospectus, but has fewer disclosure requirements. A copy of the prospectus is required to be presented to prospective buyers before the securities are offered for sale. A **preliminary prospectus** (also known as a *red herring prospectus*) is a communication that identifies the nature of the securities to be issued, states that they have not been approved or disapproved by the SEC, and explains how to obtain the prospectus when it becomes available.

THE SECURITIES EXCHANGE ACT OF 1934

The Securities Exchange Act of 1934 created the Securities and Exchange Commission and gave it authority to administer the 1933 act as well as regulate the trading of securities on national exchanges. Subsequently, the 1934 act was amended to include securities traded in over-the-counter markets, provided that the firms have total assets over $5 million and at least 500 stockholders. Firms that want their securities traded on the national exchanges, or in over-the-counter markets subject to the net asset and stockholder limitations, must file **registration statements** with the SEC. Form 10 is the primary form that is used for registering securities on national stock exchanges or in over-the-counter markets. This registration for trading purposes is required in addition to the registration prepared for new security issuances under the 1933 act.

Additional Periodic Reporting Requirements   Companies covered by the 1934 act also have periodic reporting responsibilities. These include filing 10-K annual reports, 10-Q quarterly reports, and 8-K current "material event" reports with the SEC. The information in these reports is publicly available so that company officers, directors, and major stockholders (insiders) will not be able to use it to gain an unfair advantage over the investing public. In other words, the objective is to provide full disclosure of all material facts about the company and thereby contribute to a more efficient and ethical securities market.

The SEC and National Exchanges   In addition to the registration and periodic reporting rules for companies whose stock is publicly traded, the Securities Exchange Act contains registration and reporting requirements for the national securities exchanges. The SEC has responsibility for monitoring the activities of the national exchanges and assuring their compliance with applicable legal provisions. The 1934 act also gave the SEC broad enforcement powers over stockbrokers and dealers and over accountants that are involved in SEC work.

Additional Responsibilities of the SEC

Subsequent to the Securities Exchange Act of 1934, the SEC acquired regulatory and administrative responsibilities under the Public Utilities Holding Company Act of 1935, the Trust Indenture Act of 1939, the Investment Company Act of

1940, the Investment Advisers Act of 1940, the Securities Investor Protection Act of 1970, and the Foreign Corrupt Practices Act of 1977. These acts are listed for identification purposes, but the SEC's responsibility under them is not discussed in this appendix.

THE REGISTRATION STATEMENT FOR SECURITY ISSUES

Firms issuing securities to the public under the Securities Act of 1933 are required provide full and fair disclosure of all material facts about those securities. The disclosures are provided in a registration statement that is filed with the SEC at least twenty days before the securities are offered for sale to the public. The twenty-day waiting period may be extended if the SEC finds deficient or misleading information in the registration statement. In addition, if an amendment to the registration statement is filed, the amended statement is treated as a new one for purposes of applying the twenty-day rule.

Security Registration

The registration of securities with the SEC is ordinarily a major undertaking for the registrant company. It involves developing a registration team consisting of financial managers, legal counsel, security underwriters, public accountants, and other professionals as needed. The team plans the registration process in detail, assigns responsibility for each task, coordinates the efforts of all team members, and maintains a viable timetable throughout each phase of the project. Because of its complexity, the coordination of efforts is sometimes referred to as a balancing act.

Registering Securities Under the Integrated Disclosure System

In 1980 the process of registering securities was changed when the SEC adopted an **integrated disclosure system** for almost all reports required by the 1933 and 1934 securities acts. The integrated system revised the registration forms and streamlined the process for filing with the SEC. As a result, the registration statement is now completed in accordance with instructions for the particular registration form deemed appropriate for a specific registrant company.

For example, Form S-1 is a general form to be used by firms going public (issuing securities to the public for the first time) and by firms that have been SEC registrants for fewer than three years. It is also a residual form to be used unless another form is specified. Forms S-2 and S-3 are forms with fewer disclosure requirements than S-1. They are used primarily for registrations of established firms that have been SEC registrants for over three years and that meet certain other criteria. Form S-4 is used for registering securities issued in a business combination. Firms issuing securities under *Regulation A* use Form 1-A. A number of other registration forms are applicable to selected types of security issues and firm situations.

THE INTEGRATED DISCLOSURE SYSTEM

The basic regulations of the Securities and Exchange Commission are *Regulation S-X,* which prescribes rules for the form and content of financial statements filed with the SEC, and *Regulation S-K,* which covers the nonfinancial statement disclosures of the registration statements and other periodic filings with the SEC. Prior to the 1980s, the two regulations sometimes had conflicting requirements and firms often had difficulty in identifying the appropriate rules and procedures for reporting to the SEC.

From 1933 to 1980 the SEC issued numerous *Accounting Series Releases (ASRs)*— official supplements to AICPA and FASB pronouncements, and *Staff*

Accounting Bulletins (SABs)—informal interpretations by the SEC staff on GAAP and S-X provisions. The issuance of these ASRs and SABs often increased the difficulty of complying with SEC regulations, because their provisions were sometimes inconsistent with GAAP or other SEC regulations.

Codification of SABs and ASRs

In implementing the integrated disclosure system, the SEC issued *SAB No. 40* to codify SABs 1 through 38. This was done to revise the content of the SABs to conform to GAAP, to eliminate duplicate material contained in some SABs, and in some cases to recognize FASB pronouncements as meeting the SEC's requirements. The SEC also codified the relevant accounting-related ASR s into *Financial Reporting Release (FRR) No. 1.* Thus, the current series consists of FRRs rather than ASRs.

Objectives of Integrated Disclosure System

The objectives of the integrated disclosure system are to simplify the registration process, to reduce the cost of compliance with SEC regulations, and to improve the quality of information provided to investors and other parties. *Under the integrated system, the disclosures included in SEC filings and those distributed to investors via prospectuses, proxy statements, and annual reports are essentially the same.*

Standardization of Audited Financial Statements

The integrated disclosure system amended Regulation S-X in order to standardize the financial statement requirements in most SEC filings. This permits the financial statements included in annual reports to shareholders to be the same as those included in the prospectus, the 10-K, and other reports filed with the SEC. It should be noted that the SEC's proxy rules govern the content of annual reports to shareholders. Under current rules, the content of the annual report to shareholders is the same as in 10-K filings. Form 10-K is the general form for the annual report that registrants file with the SEC. It is required to be filed within within 90 days after the end of the registrant company's fiscal year. The 10-K report must be signed by the chief executive officer, the chief financial officer, the chief accounting officer, and a majority of the company's board of directors.

The 10-K disclosures required by the SEC for public companies are summarized in Exhibit A-1. As shown in the exhibit, the SEC divides the disclosures into four groups. This is done in order to distinguish the information required to be disclosed in annual reports to shareholders, from the complete 10-K information package required for filings with the SEC. For example, the information included in Part II of the exhibit is primarily accounting information that is required for annual reports filed with the SEC as well as the annual reports distributed to the company's shareholders. The disclosure requirements summarized in Parts I, III and IV of the exhibit are only required for SEC filings, but they may be included in annual reports to shareholders.

In implementing its integrated disclosure system, the SEC eliminated a number of differences between reports filed with the SEC and those contained in annual reports to shareholders. This permitted public companies to meet many of the SEC filing requirements by reference to disclosures made in the annual reports to shareholders. That is, companies can include copies of their annual shareholder reports in their 10-K filings and satisfy many SEC disclosure requirements with one report. Information incorporated by reference to other reports is encouraged by the SEC and is not required to be duplicated. This "incorporation by reference" ruling has resulted in a substantial increase in the

SUMMARY OF REQUIRED DISCLOSURES UNDER SEC FORM 10-K

Part I
Item 1 Business (nature and history of the business, industry segments, etc.)
Item 2 Properties (location, description and use of property, etc.)
Item 3 Legal proceedings (details of pending legal proceedings)
Item 4 Voting by security holders (items submitted to shareholders for voting)

Part II
Item 5 Market for common equity (place traded, shares, dividends, etc.)
Item 6 Selected financial data (five-year trend data for net sales, income from continuing operations including EPS, total assets, long-term debt, cash dividends, etc.)
Item 7 Managements discussion and analysis (discussion of the firms' liquidity, capital resources, operations, financial condition, etc.)
Item 8 Financial statements and supplementary data (requirements include audited balance sheets for two years and audited income statements and statements of cash flows for three years. Also three-year and five-year summaries are required for selected statement items.)
Item 9 Changes in accountants and disagreements on accounting matters (changes in accountants and accounting changes, disagreements, disclosures, etc.)

Part III
Item 10 Directors and executive officers (names, ages, positions, etc.)
Item 11 Executive compensation (names, positions, salaries, stock options, etc.)
Item 12 Security ownership of beneficial owners and management (listing of insider owners of securities.)
Item 13 Certain relationships (business relations and transactions with management, etc.)

Part IV
Item 14 Exhibits, financial statement schedules, and 8-K reports (supporting schedules of securities, borrowings, subsidiaries, ratios, etc.)

Exhibit A–1 *Summary of Required Disclosures Under Form 10-K*

size of corporate annual reports and a corresponding decrease in the size of 10-K reports filed with the SEC.

Form 8-K Form 8-K is a report that requires registrants to inform the SEC about significant changes that take place regarding firm policies or financial condition. The report must be submitted within fifteen days (five days in some cases) of the occurrence of the event. Items that might be disclosed in Form 8-K include changes in management, major acquisitions or disposals of assets, lawsuits, bankruptcy filings, and unexpected changes in directors.

Form 10-Q Form 10-Q contains quarterly data prepared in accordance with GAAP. The form is filed within 45 days of the end of each of the registrant's first three quarters. Chapter 15 of this text describes and illustrates the SEC requirements for quarterly reports.

SEC DEVELOPMENTS

Regulation S The SEC issued **Regulation S** in 1990 to clarify the applicability of U.S. securities laws across national boundaries. Generally, the regulation provides that sales of securities outside the United States are not subject to the 1933 Securities Act. The regulation also provides "safe harbor" rules to exempt any U.S. companies that sell securities offshore from SEC registration requirements.

The EDGAR System One of the SEC's goals under the integrated disclosure system is to provide investors, analysts, and other interested parties with instant access to corporate information on file with the SEC. The **EDGAR** (Electronic Data Gathering, Analysis, and Retrieval) **system** will provide such information when it is fully operational. Some SEC registrants are expected to go on-line with electronic filing of SEC reports in 1991, and mandatory use of the EDGAR system is scheduled for essentially all SEC registrants by 1994.

SUMMARY

This appendix provides an overview of securities legislation related to financial accounting and reporting. It also explains the function of the Securities and Exchange Commission and its authority to prescribe accounting principles. SEC requirements that are relevant to particular topics are integrated into the chapters throughout this book. For example, in Chapters 4 and 12, the SEC's requirement to push down the purchase price of a subsidiary to the subsidiary's financial statements is discussed and illustrated; in Chapter 8, the SEC's position on recognizing gain on a subsidiary's stock sales is discussed; and in Chapter 15, the history of the SEC's efforts in requiring segment disclosures is traced and SEC requirements for interim reports are illustrated.

B

ESTATES AND TRUSTS

E state and trust accounting is frequently referred to as **fiduciary accounting** because estate and trust managers operate in a good-faith custodial or steward-ship relationship with the beneficiaries of the estate or trust property. A fiduciary is a person whom other people hold in particular confidence. Fiduciaries may be executors, trustees, administrators, and guardians, depending on the nature of their duties and the demands of custom.

In legal terms, *fiduciary* is an individual or an entity authorized to take posses-sion of the property of others. Upon taking possession of estate or trust property, the fiduciary (administrator of an estate or trustee of a trust, for example) has an obligation to administer it in the best interest of all beneficiaries. While similar practices are used in accounting for estates and trusts, there are a number of differences between the two types of entities. These include the manner in which the entities are created, the objectives of their activities, and the time spans of their existence. These differences are discussed and accounting practices for estates and trusts are reviewed and illustrated in this appendix.

CREATION OF AN ESTATE

An estate comes into existence at the death of an individual. If the deceased person (**decedent**) had a valid will in force at the time of death, he or she is said to have died **testate.**[1] In the absence of a valid will, the decedent is said to have died **intestate.** The estate consists of the property of the decedent at the time of death. Ordinarily, a **personal representative** of the decedent is appointed by a probate court to take control of the decedent's property, but some flexibility is provided if a valid will is in force at the time of death. In this case, the personal respresen-tative may leave real or tangible personal property under the control of the person presumably entitled to it under the terms of the will.

---

[1]People with sizable estates usually have lawyers draw up their wills. The lawyer can pro-vide for the eventual validation of the will and also help with estate planning so that property is distributed according to the client's wishes, and taxes are minimized.

PROBATE PROCEEDINGS

The personal representative of the deceased (or other interested party) files a petition with the appropriate probate court requesting that an existing will be **probated,** that is, for the will to be validated. The hearing of the probate court to establish validity is called a **testacy proceeding,** because its purpose is to determine whether the deceased died testate or intestate. Under the Uniform Probate Code [§1–201 (30)], the term *personal representative* includes both executor and administrator, as well as other designations for persons who perform the same functions.

Confirmation

A confirmation by a probate court that a will is valid means that the decedent died testate. Ordinarily, this leads to appointment of the personal representative named in the will as **executor** of the will. It also leads to the presumption that the estate property will be distributed in accordance with the provisions of the will, in the absence of extenuating circumstances.

A person dies intestate when he or she dies without leaving a will. Failure of the probate court to validate a will submitted for probate also means that the decedent died intestate. In either case, the court appoints an **administrator** to take control of the estate and supervise the distribution of estate assets in accordance with applicable state laws.

Uniform Probate Code

The state laws governing probate and distributions of estate property vary considerably, and do not provide a uniform basis for classifying the legal and accounting characteristics of estates. Therefore, the discussion and illustrations in this appendix are based on the 1974 edition of the Uniform Probate Code, which was approved by the National Conference of Commissioners on Uniform State Laws. The Uniform Probate Code has been approved by the American Bar Association, even though most states have not yet adopted it.

ADMINISTRATION OF THE ESTATE

The personal representative (executor or administrator) of the estate is a fiduciary who is expected to observe the standards of care applicable to trustees. Appointment by a probate court gives the executor authority to carry out the written instructions of the decedent, including the settlement and distribution of the estate. The executor is expected to perform this duty as expeditiously and efficiently as possible.

Within 30 days after appointment, the personal representative (executor or administrator) must inform the *heirs* and *devisees* of his or her appointment, and provide selected information about certain other matters. **Heirs** are the persons entitled to the property of the decedent under the statutes of intestate succession. **Intestate succession** is the order in which estate property is distributed to the surviving spouse, parents, children, and so on, if any estate property is not effectively distributed by will. **Devisees** are those persons designated in a will to receive a *devise* (a testamentary disposition of real or personal property). Under the Uniform Probate Code, "to devise" means to dispose of real or personal property by will. A specific devise is a gift of an object, while a general devise is a gift of money.

Inventory of Estate Property

The executor or administrator of a will is required to prepare and file an inventory of property owned by the deceased within three months of appointment. This inventory has to list the property in reasonable detail and show the fair market value on the date of death for each item of property. Any encumbrance on the property (such as a lien or other claim) must also be disclosed for each item. This inventory is filed with the probate court, and additional copies must be provided to interested persons on request. If appraisers are employed to assist in valuing the property, their names and addresses must accompany the property inventory. Subsequent discovery of property omitted from the inventory, or errors in valuing certain items, are corrected by preparing and filing a new or supplementary inventory of the estate property. Personal items of limited value are usually excluded from the inventory.

Exempt Property and Allowances

The Uniform Probate Code entitles the surviving spouse to a $5,000 *homestead allowance* which is exempt from, and has priority over, all claims against the estate. In the absence of a surviving spouse, the minor children would share the $5,000 equally. The surviving spouse also has an entitlement of up to $3,500 in household furniture, automobiles, and personal effects from the estate, depending on whether or not the property has been used to secure a loan. In the absence of a surviving spouse, the minor children share this property jointly.

The surviving spouse and minor children who were dependent on the deceased are also entitled to a *reasonable* family allowance to be paid out of the estate property during the period in which the estate is being administered. This family allowance is exempt from and has priority over all claims except the homestead allowance.

Claims Against the Estate

Under the Uniform Probate Code, the personal representative publishes a notice in a newspaper of general circulation in the county for three consecutive weeks. The purpose is to announce his or her appointment and to notify creditors to present their claims within four months of the date of first publication of the notice.

Claims against the estate *that arose before death* and were not presented within four months (three years, if the required notice to creditors was not published) are barred forever against the estate, the personal representative, the heirs, and the devisees [Uniform Probate Code, § 3–801–3].

All claims against the decedent's estate *that arose after death* are barred as claims against the estate, the personal representative, the heirs, and the devisees unless presented as:

1 A claim based on a contract with the personal representative within four months after performance is due and discharged, or
2 Any other claim within four months after it arises.

Classification of Claims   When estate assets are insufficient to pay all claims in full, payments are made as follows [Uniform Probate Code, § 3–805]:

1 Costs and expenses of administration of the estate
2 Reasonable funeral expenses and reasonable and necessary medical and hospital expenses of the last illness of the decedent
3 Debts and taxes with preference under federal or state law
4 All other claims

No preference is given for payment within a given class of claims.

Secured Claims   Payment of secured claims against the estate depends on the amount allowed if the creditor surrenders his security. But if the assets of the estate are encumbered by mortgage, pledge, lien, or other security interest, the personal representative may pay the encumbrance if it appears to be in the best interests of the estate [Uniform Probate Code, § 3–814].

ACCOUNTING FOR THE ESTATE

The executor (personal representative) records the inventory of estate property in a self-balancing set of accounts that show:

1 The property for which responsibility has been assumed.
2 The manner in which that responsibility is subsequently discharged.

Since the executor does not accept responsibility for the obligations of the decedent (testator), the liabilities of the estate are not recorded until paid.

Estate Principal and Income

The focus of fiduciary accounting lies in distinguishing between principal and income. That focus applies to accounting for both estates and trusts. Estates frequently realize income from various investments between the time that the property inventory is filed by the executor and the time the estate is fully administered. A primary reason for dividing estate principal and income is that the beneficiaries are likely to be different. For example, some devises specified in the will are distributed to the devisees from estate principal, while the income may accrue to the residual beneficiaries of the estate. **Residual beneficiaries** are those who are entitled to the remainder of the estate after all other rightful claims on the estate have been satisfied.

The National Conference of Commissioners on Uniform State Laws approved a Revised Uniform Principal and Income Act in 1978 to provide guidance in distinguishing between estate principal and income. That act provides that expenses incurred in settling a decedent's estate be charged against the principal of the estate. These expenses include debts, funeral expenses, estate taxes, interest and penalties, family allowances, attorney's fees, personal representative's fees, and court costs [Uniform Probate Code, § 5]

Alternatively, income (less expenses) earned after death on assets included in the decedent's estate is distributed to the specific devisee to whom the property was devised. Any remaining income that accrues during the period of estate administration is distributed to the devisees in proportion to their interests in the undivided (residual) assets of the estate.

Estate Income, Gains, and Losses

In accounting for the decedent's estate, the receipts due but unpaid at the date of death are a part of the estate principal. These include items such as interest, dividends, rents, royalties, and annuities due at the time of death. After death, earnings from income producing property are estate income, unless the will specifically provides otherwise. That is, amounts earned for the items listed would be classified as income, rather than principal, if they came due during the period of estate administration. In accounting for interest income on bond investments included in the estate inventory, no provision is made for amortization of bond issue premiums and discounts. This is because the bonds (and other securities) are included in the estate inventory at fair market value, and any gains or losses on disposal are adjustments of estate principal.

Depreciation is a related matter that requires interpretation under the Uniform Principal and Income Act [Uniform Probate Code, § 13 a(2) and c(3)]. The act provides that a reasonable allowance for depreciation be made on depreciable property of the estate, except that no depreciation is to be made on real property used by a beneficiary as a residence or on personal property held by a trustee who is not then making a depreciation allowance.

ILLUSTRATION OF ESTATE ACCOUNTING

On April 1, 19X2, Harry Olds entered the hospital with a terminal illness. He died May 1, 19X2, at the age of 70. Laura Hunt, Harry's only daughter, was appointed as executor of the estate by the probate court, which also confirmed that Harry had died testate. The will provided specific devises at estimated values to be awarded as follows:

Summer home to his daughter, Laura Hunt	$ 45,000
1973 Datsun 240Z to his grandson, Gary Hunt	8,000
200 shares of FFF stock to his friend, Michael Wallace	5,000
All other personal effects to Harry's widow, Gloria Olds	

The following general devises of cash were also provided:

Laura Hunt, in lieu of fees as executor	19,000
Sara Tyson, Harry's housekeeper	6,000
First Methodist Church	5,000
Humane Society	10,000
Gloria Olds is to receive the income in excess of expenses during the administration of the estate.	
The residue of the estate is to be placed in trust with the income used to support Harry's widow during her lifetime. Upon her mother's death, Laura gets the remainder of the estate.	

Laura informed the heirs and devisees of her appointment as executor of Harry's estate on May 19, 19X2, and at the same time, she placed the required notice to creditors in the newspaper. On June 15, 19X2, she filed the estate inventory that appears in Exhibit B–1 with the probate court.

HARRY OLDS, TESTATOR
INVENTORY OF ESTATE ASSETS
AS OF THE DATE OF DEATH ON MAY 1, 19X2

Description of Property	Fair Value
Cash in Commercial National Bank	$ 30,000
Cash in savings account at First National Bank	93,000
Certificate of deposit, 8%, 18 months, due August 1 (includes $10,000 accrued interest)	110,000
Certificate of deposit, 9%, one-year, due July 1 (includes $7,500 interest)	107,500
Note receivable plus $1,500 accrued interest from George Stein, 10%, due June 1	21,500
Rocky Mountain Power common stock, 1,000 shares	40,000
Southern Natural Gas common stock, 2,000 shares	30,000
Danville City 9%, $50,000 par municipal bonds	58,000
Interest on Danville City bonds, due June 1	1,875
Dividends receivable—utility stocks	1,500
Summer home	45,000
FFF common stock, 200 shares	5,000
1973 Datsun 240Z	8,000
Personal effects*	—
	$551,375

* The probate court permitted Laura to exclude Harry's personal effects other than specific devises from the inventory.

Submitted by Laura Hunt, executor on June 15, 19X2.

Exhibit B–1 Inventory of Estate Assets

Laura subsequently prepared the following entries to record transactions and events during the period of estate administration:

May 19, 19X2

Memorandum: Placed a notice in the Montgomery County News Messenger that creditors of the estate of Harry Olds should present their claims against the estate within four months.

June 15, 19X2 Recorded the inventory of estate assets as of May 1, 19X2:

Cash—principal	$ 30,000	
Savings account	93,000	
Certificate of deposit, due 8/1/X2	100,000	
Certificate of deposit, due 7/1/X2	100,000	
Note receivable—George Stein	20,000	
Rocky Mountain Power common stock	40,000	
Southern Natural Gas common stock	30,000	
FFF Company common stock	5,000	
Danville municipal bonds	58,000	
Summer home	45,000	
1973 Datsun 240Z	8,000	
Interest receivable on CDs	17,500	
Interest receivable—George Stein	1,500	
Interest receivable—municipal bonds	1,875	
Dividends receivable—common stock	1,500	
Estate principal		$551,375

June 16, 19X2 Cashed dividend checks received May 5 on utility stock:

Cash—principal	$ 1,500	
Dividends receivable—common stock		$ 1,500

June 18, 19X2 Collected interest of $2,250 on Danville City bonds. Interest of $375 was earned after the date of death:

Cash—principal	$ 1,875	
Cash—income	375	
Interest receivable—municipal bonds		$ 1,875
Estate income		375

June 23, 19X2 Funeral expenses of $4,500 were paid:

Funeral expenses	$ 4,500	
Cash—principal		$ 4,500

June 24, 19X2 Collected the $20,000 George Stein note and $1,650 interest. Interest of $150 was earned after the date of death:

Cash—principal	$ 21,500	
Cash—income	150	
Note receivable—George Stein		$ 20,000
Interest receivable—George Stein		1,500
Estate income		150

June 25, 19X2 Discovered and cashed a certificate of deposit that matured on April 15 and was excluded from the estate inventory. The proceeds were $10,800:

Cash—principal	$ 10,800	
Assets subsequently discovered		$ 10,800

June 28, 19X2 Paid hospital and medical bills in excess of amounts paid by Medicare and private health insurance policies:

Hospital and medical expenses	$ 19,000	
Cash—principal		$ 19,000

July 1, 19X2 Cashed the certificate of deposit that was due on June 1:

Cash—principal	$107,500	
Cash—income	1,500	
Certificate of deposit		$100,000
Interest receivable on CD		7,500
Estate income		1,500

July 12, 19X2 Paid cash to general devisees as provided in the will:

Devise—Laura Hunt	$ 19,000	
Devise—Sara Tyson	6,000	
Devise—First Methodist Church	5,000	
Devise—Humane Society	10,000	
Cash—principal		$ 40,000

August 1, 19X2 Recorded interest from savings account for the quarter ending July 31:

Cash—income	$ 1,395	
Estate income		$ 1,395

August 1, 19X2 Cashed in the certificate of deposit due August 1:

Cash—principal	$110,000	
Cash—income	2,000	
Certificate of deposit		$100,000
Interest receivable on CD		10,000
Estate income		2,000

August 5, 19X2 Received dividend checks on utilities stock:

Cash—income	$ 1,500	
Estate income		$ 1,500

August 15, 19X2 Paid a $500 mechanics bill on the Datsun 240Z that was incurred on April 10, 19X2 and submitted for payment on August 10:

Debts of decedent paid	$ 500	
Cash—principal		$ 500

August 25, 19X2 Delivered specific devises as provided in the will. Personal effects not included in the estate inventory were left with the widow, Gloria Olds:

Devise—summer home to Laura Hunt	$ 45,000	
Devise—1973 Datsun 240Z to Gary Hunt	8,000	
Devise—FFF stock to Michael Wallace	5,000	
Summer home		$ 45,000
1973 Datsun 240Z		8,000
FFF Company common stock		5,000

August 28, 19X2 Payment of attorney fees and court costs:

Attorney fees paid	$ 4,500	
Court costs paid	500	
Cash—principal		$ 5,000

August 31, 19X2 Distribution of estate income to Gloria Olds:

Distribution to Gloria Olds	$ 6,920	
Cash—income		$ 6,920

Closing Entries

Entries to close the nominal accounts to estate income and estate principal on August 31 are as follows:

Estate principal	$127,000	
Funeral expenses paid		$ 4,500
Hospital and medical expenses paid		19,000
Devises—Laura Hunt		64,000
Devise—Sara Tyson		6,000
Devise—First Methodist Church		5,000
Devise—Humane Society		10,000
Debts of decedent paid		500
Devise to Gary Hunt		8,000
Devise to Michael Wallace		5,000
Attorney fees paid		4,500
Court costs paid		500

Estate income	$ 6,920	
Distribution to Gloria Olds		$ 6,920
Assets subsequently discovered	$ 10,800	
Estate principal		$ 10,800

After these closing entries are made, the remaining account balances are as follows:

Cash—principal	$214,175
Savings account	93,000
Rocky Mountain Power common stock	40,000
Southern Natural Gas common stock	30,000
Danville municipal bonds	58,000
Estate principal	$435,175

August 31, 19X2   Laura Hunt transfers estate property to Ed Jones, Trustee for Gloria Olds, in accordance with the income trust established by Harry Olds' will:

Estate principal	$435,175	
Cash—principal		$214,175
Savings account		93,000
Rocky Mountain Power common stock		40,000
Southern Natural Gas common stock		30,000
Danville municipal bonds		58,000

Charge-Discharge Statement

The **charge-discharge statement** is a document prepared by the personal representative (executor or administrator) in order to show accountability for estate property received and maintained or disbursed in accordance with the will (or the probate court in intestate cases). A charge-discharge statement shows progress in the administration of the estate and termination of responsibility when the will has been fully administered. A final charge-discharge statement by Laura Hunt for her father's estate is shown in Exhibit B–2. The statement consists of two major parts: one for estate principal and one for estate income. The extent of detail is determined by the complexity of the estate, the number of devisees, and instructions from the probate court.

Income Taxes on Estate Income

Income on resources that are held by the estate while it is being settled is taxable, even though the inheritance may not be taxable to the beneficiary. The tax may be paid by the estate or by the beneficiary if estate property has already been distributed to the beneficiary. Estates and trusts file federal income tax returns on Form 1041, *U.S. Fiduciary Income Tax Return*. The beneficiary's share of income is reported on Schedule K-l of Form 1041.

For tax purposes, the beneficiary treats each item of income earned on estate property in the same way that it is treated by the estate. For example, if interest is earned on bonds held by the estate, the beneficiary classifies the income as interest. If the estate receives dividends from stock holdings, the beneficiary classifies the income as dividends. The fiduciary of the estate must provide this information to the beneficiary on Schedule K-1.

ACCOUNTING FOR TRUSTS

The will of Harry Olds resulted in the creation of an income trust for Gloria Olds. A trust created pursuant to a will is referred to as a **testamentary trust**. The fiduciary that administers a trust is the *trustee*. A trustee may be a business entity or a natural person. As in the case of estates, guidance in accounting for trusts

ESTATE OF HARRY OLDS
CHARGE-DISCHARGE STATEMENT
FOR THE PERIOD OF ESTATE ADMINISTRATION
MAY 1 TO AUGUST 31, 19X2

Estate Principal

I charge myself for:

Assets included in estate inventory	$551,375	
Assets discovered after inventory	10,800	
Total estate principal charge		$562,175

I credit myself for:

Funeral expenses paid	$ 4,500	
Hospital and medical expenses paid	19,000	
Mechanics bill paid	500	
Attorney fees and court costs	5,000	$ 29,000
Devises paid in cash to:		
Laura Hunt	$ 19,000	
Sara Tyson	6,000	
First Methodist Church	5,000	
Humane Society	10,000	40,000
Devises distributed in kind to:		
Laura Hunt (summer home)	$ 45,000	
Gary Hunt (Datsun 240Z)	8,000	
Michael Wallace (FFF stock)	5,000	58,000
Transferred to Ed Jones, trustee for Gloria Olds:		
Cash—principal	$214,175	
Savings account	93,000	
Rocky Mountain Power Company stock	40,000	
Southern Natural Gas Company stock	30,000	
Danville municipal bonds	58,000	435,175
Total estate principal discharge		$562,175

Estate Income

I charge myself for:

Estate income received during estate administration	$ 6,920

I credit myself for:

Payment of estate income to Gloria Olds as directed by the will	$ 6,920

Respectfully submitted: Laura Hunt, Estate Executor, August 31, 19X2.

Exhibit B-2   *Charge-Discharge Statement*

comes from state laws, the Uniform Trusts Act, the Uniform Probate Code, and the Revised Uniform Principal and Income Act.

The entry made by Ed Jones, the trustee, to open the books for the creation of the Gloria Olds Trust is as follows:

Cash	$214,175	
Savings account	93,000	
Rocky Mountain Power common stock	40,000	
Southern Natural Gas common stock	30,000	
Danville municipal bonds	58,000	
Trust fund principal		$435,175

To record receipt of property transferred from Laura Hunt, Executor.

A primary concern in accounting for trust entities is distinguishing between principal and income. This is especially true of income trusts such as the one created for Gloria Olds because the principal amount of the trust is to be maintained intact in order to provide income for Mrs. Olds's care until her death. Separate *trust fund principal* and *trust fund income* accounts are used to separate principal and income balances for accounting purposes. The use of separate principal and income cash accounts, however, is of limited value, and the practice is usually not necessary.

Chapter 20 of this book discusses trust funds of governmental units and illustrates accounting and reporting practices for them.

GLOSSARY

Acquisition: a business combination in which one corporation acquires control over the operations of another entity.

Actual Retirement of Bonds: the repurchase and retirement of bonds by the issuing affiliate.

Additions (Colleges and Universities): increases to the fund balance of fund groupings other than current unrestricted funds and current restricted funds to the extent that expenditures have not been made.

Administrator: the court appointed representative who takes control of the estate of a person who died intestate, and supervises the estate's distribution.

Affiliated: a subsidiary in a technical sense, although the term is sometimes used to refer to 20% to 50% owned equity investees.

Agency Funds (Colleges and Universities): a college and university fund type to account for resources held by the college or university as custodian or agent for student or faculty groups.

Agency Funds (Governmental Accounting): used to account for resources held by the governmental unit as agent for other funds, other governmental units, or individuals.

Agency Funds (Hospitals): used to account for resources owned by others but held by the hospital to be returned to the principal or disbursed to third parties.

Agency Theory: a theory of intercompany bondholdings that allocates constructive gains and losses to the issuing affiliate.

Allotments: divisions of the appropriation authority by time period.

Annuity Funds: a college and university fund type to account for resources acquired under the condition that stipulated periodic payments be made to individuals as directed by the donor of the resources.

Appropriations: approved or authorized expenditures.

Auxiliary Enterprises: a college and university grouping that encompasses student unions, dormitories, resident halls, and intercollegiate athletics, and is included in the current funds grouping.

Bankruptcy Insolvency: a condition in which an entity has total debts in excess of the fair market value of its assets.

Bonus Approach (Partnerships): the adjustment of partner capital balances as an alternative to revaluing partnership assets or recording goodwill.

Branch Operations: a company outlet that stocks goods, makes sales, maintains accounting records, and functions much like a separate business enterprise.

Budget: a plan of financial operations including proposed expenditures for a period and the means of financing them.

Business Combination: a uniting of previously separate business entities through acquisition by one entity of another entity's net assets or a majority of its outstanding voting common stock, or through an exchange of common stock.

Capital Budget (Governmental Accounting): the current portion of a capital program.

Capital Leases (Governmental Accounting): capitalized in the general fixed assets account group if used to acquire general fixed assets.

Capital Program (Governmental Accounting): a plan of capital expenditures by year over a fixed period of years.

Capital Projects Funds: to account for resources to be used for acquisition or construction of major capital facilities.

Cash Distribution Plan (Partnerships): a plan developed at the beginning of the liquidation period that shows how cash will be distributed throughout the phase-out period.

Cash Distribution Schedule (Partnerships): a schedule of cash distributions made to creditors and partners in a partnership liquidation.

Chapter 11 of the Bankruptcy Act: Chapter 11 covers rehabilitation of the debtor and anticipates a reorganization of the debtor corporation.

Chapter 7 of the Bankruptcy Act: Chapter 7 covers straight bankruptcy under which the debtor entity is expected to be liquidated.

Charge-Discharge Statement (Estates and Trusts): a document prepared by the executor or administrator of an estate to show accountability for property received and disbursed.

Conditional Pledge (Nonprofit Accounting): a pledge that is dependent upon the occurrence or failure to occur of an uncertain future event.

Conglomeration: the combination of firms in unrelated and diverse product lines and/or service functions.

Consolidation: (1) a business combination in which a new corporation is formed to take over two or more business entities that then go out of existence. (2) In a generic sense, it means the same as acquisition or merger. (3) The process of combining parent company and subsidiary financial statements.

Constructive Retirement of Bonds: the repurchase of bonds of one affiliate by another so that the bonds are held within the parent-subsidiary affiliation, and in effect retired.

Contemporary Theory: the current theory underlying consolidated financial statements. It reflects certain aspects of both entity and parent company theory.

Contribution (Nonprofit Accounting): a transfer of cash or other assets to an entity or a settlement or cancellation of its liabilities from a voluntary nonreciprocal transfer.

Conventional Approach of Accounting for Mutually Held Common Stock: parent company stock held by a subsidiary is accounted for as being constructively retired for consolidation purposes.

Corporate Joint Venture: a joint venture organized under the corporate form of business organization.

Cost Method (for Equity Investments): accounting for a common stock investment at its original cost and recording dividends received as income from the investment. Dividends over earnings since acquisition are returns of capital.

Current Funds: a college and university fund grouping to account for resources expendable for operating purposes. Includes unrestricted current funds and restricted current funds.

Current Rate Method: translation of all assets, liabilities, revenues, and expenses at current exchange rates.

Current Rate: the exchange rate in effect at the balance sheet date or the transaction date.

Current-Noncurrent Method: translation of current accounts at current exchange rates and noncurrent accounts at historical rates.

Current Restricted Funds (Voluntary Health and Welfare Organizations): to account for resources expendable for current uses, but restricted by donors for specific operating purposes.

Current Unrestricted Funds (Voluntary Health and Welfare Organizations): to account for resources expendable at the discretion of the governing board.

Custodian Funds (Voluntary Health and Welfare Organizations): to account for assets to be held or disbursed on instructions from the donor.

Debt Service Funds (Governmental Accounting): to account for the accumulation of resources and payment of principal and interest on long-term debt.

Debtor in Possession: a Chapter 11 case where the debtor corporation keeps control of the business and performs the duties of a trustee.

Decedent: a person that is deceased.

Denomonated: to denominate in a currency is to fix the amount in units of that currency.

Devisees: those persons designated in a will to receive real or personal property.

Direct Holdings: direct investments in voting stock of one or more investee companies.

Direct Quotation: the expression of an exchange rate in U.S. dollars (U.S. dollar equivalent).

Donor-Imposed Conditions (Nonprofit Accounting): the occurrence or failure to occur of an uncertain future event that releases the donor from its obligation.

Donor-Imposed Restrictions: specifications of how the assets promised or received must be used.

Downstream Sale: sales or other intercompany transactions from parent company to subsidiary.

Drawings (Partnerships): regular partner withdrawals as provided in the partnership agreement, and closed to partner capital at year end.

EDGAR System: the SEC's electronic data gathering, analysis, and retrieval system.

Encumbrance Accounting: recording commitments made for goods on order and for unperformed contracts to prevent overspending of amounts appropriated.

Endowment Funds (Nonprofit Accounting): to account for gifts and bequests received from donors under endowment agreements (hospitals and voluntary health and welfare organizations). A fund type for colleges and universities to account for resources received from donors or outside agencies with the stipulation that the principal be maintained in perpetuity and income be used as directed.

Endowment Trust Funds (Governmental Accounting): a trust fund in which the principal must remain intact but the earnings may be expended for authorized purposes.

Enterprise Funds (Governmental Accounting): to account for operations that are financed and operated in a manner similar to private enterprise.

Entitlements (Governmental Accounting): payments to which state or local governmental units are entitled based on an allocation formula.

Entity Theory: a theory under which consolidated financial statements are prepared from the view of the total business entity.

Equity Adjustment on Translation: an exchange gain or loss that is reported as a stockholders' equity adjustment.

Equity in Subsidiary Realized Income: the parent company or minority interests share of subsidiary income adjusted for intercompany gains and losses and amortization of cost-book value differentials.

Equity Insolvency: the inability of an entity to pay its debts as they come due.

Equity Method: accounting for a common stock investment on an accrual basis. Earnings increase the investment and dividends decrease it.

Exchange Rate: the ratio between a unit of one currency and the amount of another currency for which it can be exchanged.

Executory Contracts: contracts that have not been completely peformed by the parties to the contract (purchase commitments and leases, for example).

Executor: the court appointed representative who takes control of the estate of a decedent that died testate and supervises its distribution.

Expendable Funds: those in which resources can be expended to meet the objective of the fund.

Expendable Trust Funds: a trust fund in which the assets can be expended as needed to meet the fund's objectives.

Expenditures: (1) decreases in the net financial resources of a governmental type fund. (2) Also, the expenses of the current funds of a college or university.

Family Allowance: an allowance to a surviving spouse and minor children to be paid out of estate property during the period of estate administration.

Fiduciary Accounting: a term used to describe accounting for estates and trusts whose managers have a custodial or stewardship relationship with the trust or estate beneficiaries.

Fiduciary Funds: A category of funds to account for assets held by the government as trustee or agent. Includes expendable, nonexpendable, and pension trust funds and agency funds.

Fiduciary: an individual or entity authorized to take possession of the property of others.

Fixed Exchange Rates: exchange rates set by a government and subject to change only by that government.

Floating Exchange Rates: exchange rates that are market driven and reflect supply and demand factors, inflation, and so on. (Also free exchange rates.)

Foreign Currency Commitment: a contract or agreement that will result in a foreign currency transaction at a later date.

Foreign Currency Statements: the financial statements of a foreign subsidiary or other foreign entity and expressed in its local currency.

Foreign Currency Transactions: transactions whose terms are denominated in a currency other than the entity's functional currency.

Foreign Currency: a currency other than the entity's functional currency.

Foreign Transactions: transactions between entities in different countries.

Form 10-K: basic form for the annual report that firms file with the SEC.

Form 10-Q: form for quarterly reports that firms file with the SEC.

Form 8-K: form to disclose significant changes in firm policies, financial condition, etc. to the SEC.

Forward Exchange Contract (Futures): an agreement to exchange currencies at a specified future date and at a specified rate (the forward rate).

Free Exchange Rates: exchange rates that are market driven and reflect supply and demand factors, inflation, and so on. (Also, floating exchange rates.)

Fresh Start Reporting: accounting under a reorganization plan that meets prescribed conditions and enables the new entity to eliminate its prior deficit and report zero retained earnings.

Fund Accounting or Fund Basis: financial systems that are segmented into separate accounting and reporting entities (funds) on the basis of their objectives and restrictions on their operations and resources.

Fund Balance: the balance of the fund balance account. Also used to mean assets less liabilities of a fund.

Fund Equity: an amount equal to assets less liabilities of a fund.

Fund Fixed Assets (Governmental Accounting): fixed assets related to specific proprietary or trust funds and accounted for in those funds.

Fund Long-Term Liabilities (Governmental Accounting): long-term liabilities of proprietary and trust funds are designated fund long-term liabilities and accounted for in those funds.

Fund: a fiscal and accounting entity with a self-balancing set of accounts that records cash and other financial resources together with related liabilities and residual balances.

General Fixed Assets (Governmental Accounting): all fixed assets not classified as fund fixed assets. General fixed assets are accounted for in the general fixed assets account group.

General Fund (Governmental Accounting): to account for all financial resources not accounted for in another fund.

General Funds (Hospitals): to account for all unrestricted resources of a hospital.

General Long-Term Debt (Governmental Accounting): all unmatured general long-term liabilities other than fund long-term liabilities for which the governmental unit is obligated in some manner. Accounted for in the General Long-Term Debt Account Group.

General Partnership: an association in which each partner has unlimited liability.

Goodwill Approach (Partnerships): the adjustment of assets and liabilities to fair values and recording goodwill as an alternative to adjusting partner equity balances. (Also, a partnership revaluation approach.)

Governmental Accounting Standards Board (GASB): the standard setting body for governmental accounting and financial reporting.

Governmental Fund Expenditures: decreases in fund financial resources other than from interfund transfers.

Governmental Fund Revenues: increases in fund financial resources other than from transfers and debt issue proceeds.

Governmental Funds: a category of funds used to account for most governmental functions that are basically different from private enterprise. They include the general fund, special revenue funds, capital projects funds, and debt service funds.

Grants: contributions from other governmental units to be used for specific purposes.

Hedging Operations: purchase or sale of a foreign currency contract to offset the risks of holding receivables or payables denominated in a foreign currency.

Heirs: the persons entitled to the property of the decedent under the statutes of intestate succession.

Historical Rate: the exchange rate in effect at the time a specific transaction or event occurred.

Homestead Allowance: an allowance to a surviving spouse that has priority over all other claims against the estate.

Horizontal Integration: the combination of firms in the same business lines or markets.

Incomplete Application of the Equity Method: accounting for an equity investee without considering amortization of cost-book value differentials or intercompany profits. (Also called the simple equity method.)

Indirect Holdings: investments that enable an investor company to control an investee that is not directly owned through an investee that is directly owned.

Indirect Quotation: the expression of an exchange rate in foreign currency units (foreign currency per U.S dollar).

Industry Segment: a component of an enterprise engaged in providing goods and services primarily to unaffiliated customers for a profit.

Installment Liquidation (Partnerships): distribution of cash as it becomes available during the liquidation period.

Integrated Disclosure System: a system adopted by the SEC in 1980 to streamline its registration and reporting requirements.

Interfund Loans: loans made by one fund to another and that must be repaid.

Interim Financial Reports: unaudited financial reports that are issued for periods of less than a full year, and frequently called quarterly reports.

Internal Service Funds (Governmental Accounting): to account for financing goods and services provided by one department to other departments on a cost-reimbursement basis.

Intestate: having died without a valid will.

Investment in Plant Fund: used by colleges and universities to account for its physical plant which includes land, buildings, improvements other than buildings and equipment including library books.

Involuntary Bankruptcy Proceedings: the filing is involuntary if the creditors file the bankruptcy petition.

Joint Venture: a business entity that is owned, operated and jointly controlled by a small group of investors (venturers) for a specific undertaking. It may be temporary or relatively permanent, and it may be corporate or partnership.

Land, Building, and Equipment Fund (or Plant Fund) (Voluntary Health and Welfare Organizations): to account for net investment in plant assets and related liabilities, and unexpended resources restricted by donors for plant assets.

Leveraged Buyout: acquisition of a publicly-held company directly from its shareholders in a transaction financed primarily by debt.

Life Income Funds: a college and university fund type to account for resources acquired under the condition that the income be paid to a designated individual until death.

Limited Life: the legal life of partnerships terminates with the admission of a new partner, death or retirement of an old partner, etc.

Limited Partnership: an association in which one or more partners have limited liability and at least one partner has unlimited liability.

Loan Funds: a college and university fund grouping to account for resources available for student and faculty loans.

Local Currency: the currency of the country being referred to.

Local Transactions: transactions within a country that are measured in the currency of that country.

Mandatory Transfers (Colleges and Universities): transfers of resources under binding agreements with outside agencies or donors. A matching gift to a student loan fund, for example.

Measurement Focus (Governmental Accounting): that which is expressed in reporting an entity's financial performance and position.

Merger: a business combination in which one corporation takes over the operations of another entity and that entity goes out of existence. Also, a business combination or an acquisition in a generic sense.

Minority Interest: the stockholder interest in a subsidiary not owned by the parent company.

Monetary-nonmonetary Method: translation of monetary items at current exchange rates and nonmonetary items at historical rates.

Multiple Exchange Rates: fixed exchange rates with preferential rates set for different kinds of transactions.

Mutual Agency (Partnerships): each partner has the power to bind all other partners, in the absence of notification to the contrary.

Mutual Holdings: two or more affiliated companies that hold stock in each other.

Negative Goodwill: the excess of the fair market value of net assets acquired in a purchase business combination over the investment cost.

Nonexpendable Funds (Governmental Accounting): funds that have a profit or capital maintenance objective. Includes enterprise and internal service funds as well as nonexpendable trust and pension trust funds.

Nonexpendable Trust Funds: principal is maintained intact but income may or may not be expendable.

Nonmandatory Transfers (Colleges and Universities): funds transferred back to unrestricted current funds or transfers at the discretion of the governing board.

Nonprofit or Not-for-Profit Entities: nonbusiness organizations that have neither individual ownership nor private profit objectives.

Offering Circular: similar to a prospectus, but with fewer disclosure requirements.

Official Exchange Rates: exchange rates set by a government and subject to change only by that government.

One-line Consolidation: another name for the equity method of accounting. Under the equity method the investor's income and consolidated net income are equal.

Operating Leases (Governmental Accounting): lease payments are recorded as expenses or expenditures depending on the fund entity.

Operating Transfers (Governmental Accounting): legally authorized shifts of resources from one fund to another that are not revenues and expenditures or expenses.

Par Value Theory: a theory of intercompany bond holdings that allocates constructive gains or losses on the basis of issue and repurchase premiums and discounts.

Parent Company Theory: a theory under which consolidated financial statements are prepared from the view of parent company stockholders.

Parent-Subsidiary Relationship: a relationship that gives one corporation the power to control another corporation through its majority common stock ownership.

Partnership: an association of two or more persons to carry on as co-owners a business for profit.

Partnership Dissolution: the change in the relation of partners when any partner is no longer involved in carrying on the business.

Partnership Liquidation: the process of coverting assets into cash, settling all liabilities and distributing any remaining cash to partners.

Patient Service Revenue (Hospitals): revenue from board and room, nursing services, and other professional services and recorded on an accrual basis.

Payments in Lieu of Taxes: payments by one governmental unit to another for revenues lost because governments cannot tax each other.

Performance Budget: a budget that emphasizes measurable performance of work programs and activities.

Personal Representative: a person named by the probate court to take control of a decedent's estate.

Plant Funds: a college and university fund grouping to account for unexpended plant funds, renewal and replacement funds, retirement of indebtedness funds, and investment in plant funds. (Also used as another name for the land, building, and equipment fund of voluntary health and welfare organizations.)

Plant Replacement and Expansion Funds (Hospitals): a hospital fund group to account for donor-restricted resources for plant, property and equipment, and revenue restricted by third-party payors to replacing property, plant and equipment.

Pledges (Nonprofit Accounting): a written or oral promise to contribute cash or other assets to the organization.

Pooling of Interests Method: a business combination consummated through an exchange of common shares and accounted for on a book value basis.

Postpetition Liabilities: liabilities incurred after a Chapter 11 filing and not associated with prebankruptcy events.

Preacquisition Dividends: dividends paid on an equity investment prior to the date the investment was acquired during the year.

Preacquisition Earnings: income on an equity investment from beginning of the year up to the date the investment was acquired during the year.

Preliminary Prospectus: a preliminary communication about securities to be issued and explaining how to get a copy of the prospectus filed with the SEC.

Prepetition Liabilities Subject to Compromise: unsecured and undersecured liabilities incurred before a Chapter 11 bankruptcy filing.

Prepetition liabilities: liabilities of the debtor corporation at the time of a bankruptcy filing.

Probated: to probate a will is to validate a will.

Program Budget: an expenditure budget of the total cost of programs to be carried out or functions to be performed.

Proportionate or Pro Rata Consolidation: a practice in accounting for joint ventures in which each investor-venturer accounts for its share of assets, equities, revenues and expenses.

Proprietary Funds (Governmental Accounting): a category of funds to account for operations that are similar to those of private business enterprises. Includes enterprise funds and internal service funds.

Prospectus: information about an SEC registrant firm that includes its type of business, company background, and financial statements. It is a part of the SEC registration statement.

Purchase Method: a method of accounting for a business combination in which one corporation acquires a controlling interest in another entity. The acquisition is accounted for on a fair value basis.

Pure Endowments: endowments for which the principal is permanently restricted. (Quasi-endowments can be changed by the governing board.)

Push-Down Accounting: establishment of a new basis of subsidiary accounting based on the price paid by the parent company.

Quasi-Endowment Funds: a college and university fund type to account for resources designated by the governing board to be invested indefinitely, and with income being expended as directed.

Quasi-External Transactions: those that would be revenue and expenses for organizations external to the governmental unit.

Registration Statements: statements required for to be filed with the SEC for firms that issue securities to the public, and for firms whose shares are traded on national stock exchanges.

Regulation S: a 1990 regulation to clarify the applicability of security laws across national boundaries (SEC).

Remeasurement: the conversion of a foreign entity's financial statements from another currency into its functional currency.

Renewal and Replacement Funds (Colleges and Universities): to account for the resources held by colleges and universities for renewal and replacement of the physical plant.

Reorganization Plan: a plan for rehabilitation of the debtor corporation in a Chapter 11 case. To be confirmed, the plan must be fair and equitable to all interests concerned.

Reorganization Value: an approximation of the amount a willing buyer would pay for the assets of the corporation at the time of restructuring.

Reportable Industry Segment: an industry segment for which information is required to be reported.

Reporting Currency: the currency in which consolidated financial statements are prepared.

Residual Beneficiaries: those entitled to the remainder of an estate after all other rightful claims have been satisfied.

Residual Equity Transfer (Governmental Accounting): nonrecurring and nonroutine transfers of equity between funds.

Restricted Current Funds (Colleges and Universities and Voluntary Health and Welfare Organizations): encompasses resources expendable currently but restricted to expenditures for specified operating purposes.

Restricted Funds (Hospitals): a hospital fund grouping that includes specific purpose funds, plant replacement and expansion funds, and term endowment funds.

Retirement of Indebtedness Fund: used in college and university accounting for liquid resources held for current debt service, and investments held for future debt retirement.

Safe Payments (Partnerships): distributions that can be made to partners with assurance that the amounts are not excessive.

Salary allowances (Partnerships): partner salary allowances are drawings authorized in lieu of salaries, since partner rewards come from sharing in partnership earnings.

Sales Agency: a business office established to display merchandise and take customer orders, but not to fill orders or grant credit.

Shared Revenues (Governmental Accounting): specific revenue sources shared with other governmental units. Sales taxes, gasoline taxes and liquor taxes are examples.

Special Revenue Funds (Governmental Accounting): to account for proceeds from specific revenue sources that are legally restricted to specified purposes.

Specific Purpose Funds (Hospitals): a hospital fund group to account for resources restricted by donors for specific operating purposes.

Spot Rate: the exchange rate in effect for immediate delivery of the currencies exchanged.

Statement of Affairs: a financial statement that shows liquidation values of a bankrupt entity and provides estimates of possible recovery for unsecured creditors.

Statement of Functional Expenses (Voluntary Health and Welfare Organizations): a financial statement that shows the costs associated with the program services or other activities of the organization.

Statement of Revenues and Expenses for General Funds (Hospitals): includes all revenues and expenses with classifications for patient service revenues, other operating revenues, operating expenses and nonoperating gains.

Subsidiary: a corporation in which the controlling stockholders' interest lies with a parent company that controls its decisions and operations.

Temporal Method: translation of items carried at past, current, and future prices in a manner that retains their measurement bases.

Temporary Differences: Differences in taxable income and accounting income that originate in one accounting period and reverse in a later period.

Term Endowment Funds: a college and university fund type to account for resources received from donors or outside agencies with the stipulation that the principal may be expended after a period of time or the occurrence of some event.

Term Endowments: endowments for which the principal is temporarily restricted.

Testacy Proceeding: a hearing of a probate court to determine if the deceased died testate or intestate.

Testamentary Trust: a trust that is created pursuant to a will.

Translation Adjustment (Also Equity Adjustment on Translation): an exchange gain or loss that is reported as a direct stockholders' equity adjustment.

Translation: expressing functional currency measurements in the reporting currency.

Treasury Stock Approach: accounting for parent company stock held by a subsidiary as treasury stock in consolidated statements.

Troubled Debt Restructuring: occurs when a creditor grants a concession to a debtor because of the debtor's financial difficulties.

Trust and Agency Funds: to account for assets held in a trustee capacity or as agent for individuals, private organizations, and other governmental units.

Trustee: a lawyer appointed by the U. S. trustee or by the bankruptcy court to assume control of the debtor's estate, and coordinate its administration with the court.

Unconditional Pledge (Nonprofit Accounting): a pledge without restrictions or conditions.

Undivided Interest (Joint Ventures): an ownership arrangement in which two or more parties own property and title is held individually to the extent of each party's interest.

Unexpended Plant Funds: used by colleges and universities to account for resources held for additions and improvements to the physical plant.

Uniform Probate Code: a document prepared by the National Conference of Commissioners on Uniform State Laws that provides guidelines for estate and trust administration.

Unlimited Liability: Each partner is liable for all partnership debts, except for limited partners of partnerships that are allowed in some states.

Unrestricted Current Funds (Colleges and Universities): encompasses resources received and expended for instruction, research, extension, and public services, as well as auxiliary enterprises.

Upstream Sale: sales or other intercompany transactions from subsidiary to parent company.

U.S. Trustee: an administrative officer of the bankruptcy court; appointed by the attorney general for five year terms.

Venturers: The owner participants in a joint venture.

Vertical Integration: the combination of firms with operations in different but successive stages of production and/or distribution.

Voluntary Bankruptcy Proceedings: the filing is voluntary if the debtor files the bankruptcy petition.

Voluntary Health and Welfare Organizations: a diverse group of nonprofit entities that is supported by donations and seeks to solve basic social problems of health and welfare.

Vulnerability Ranking (Partnerships): a ranking of partners on the basis of the amount of partnership losses they could absorb without reducing their capital accounts below zero.

Zero-Base Budgeting: making budgetary appropriations without direct reference to prior years' programs or expenditure budgets.

INDEX

A

Accounting for equity investments [chart], 61
Accounting Principles Board:
  Opinion No. 9, 320
  Opinion No. 15, 397
  Opinion No. 16, 5–10, 17–20, 98, 450, 744
  Opinion No. 17, 655
  Opinion No. 18, 43, 318, 346, 363, 393,
    397, 458–460
  Opinion No. 21, 264, 744
  Opinion No. 22, 75
  Opinion No. 23, 405–406
  Opinion No. 28, 618–621
  Statement No. 2, 602
Accounting Research Bulletin No. 4, 517
Accounting Research Bulletin No. 40, 6
Accounting Research Bulletin No. 43, 18, 324,
    517, 566
Accounting Research Bulletin No. 51, 75, 172,
    179, 304, 359, 438, 441
Accounting Research Study No. 5, 8
Accounting Trends & Techniques, 23, 75, 91
Acquisition, 3–4
Affiliated companies, 73
Affiliation structure, 74, 346
Agency theory for allocating gains and
    losses on constructive bond
    retirement, 264
American Institute of Certified Public
    Accountants [AICPA] (*see also*
    specific publications):
  *Accounting Interpretation No. 1 of APB
    Opinion No. 18,* 173
  *Accounting Interpretation No. 2 of APB
    Opinion No. 18,* 459

*Accounting Interpretations of APB Opinion
    No. 16, Interpretation No. 25,* 100
  Issues Paper, "Accounting in
    Consolidation for Issuances of a
    Subsidiary's Stock," 320
  Issues Paper, "Joint Venture
    Accounting," 460
  Issues Paper, "Push-Down Accounting,"
    450
  Statement of Position 78–9, 460
  Statement of Position 90–7, 741–752 (*see
    also* Bankruptcy cases)
Alcoa, 460
Allegheny International, Inc., 738, 741
Allied-Signal Inc., 612, 614, 615, 617
Allied Stores Corporation, 738
Allison, Terry E., 412
American Express Co., 318
Arthritis Foundation, Virginia Chapter,
    906–910
Associated companies, 73
Assumptions for working problems, 60
Audits of Certain Nonprofit Organizations
    (AICPA), 873, 901
Audits of Colleges and Universities (AICPA),
    874
Audits of Providers of Health Care Services
    (AICPA), 886
*Audits of Voluntary Health and Welfare
    Organizations* (AICPA), 900, 903

B

Backer, Morton, 602
Bankruptcy Act, (*see* Bankruptcy cases)

952

INDEX

Bankruptcy cases:
  balance sheet prepared during
    reorganization, 742
  Bankruptcy Act of 1978, 722–723
  bankruptcy court created, 723
  bankruptcy court jurisdiction, 723, 725
  bankruptcy insolvency, 722
  bankruptcy judges, 723, 724
  Chapter 11 reorganizations, 724
  Chapter 7 liquidations, 724
  creditors' committees, 737–738
  debtor in possession, 737
  disclosures for subsidiaries in
    bankruptcy, 742
  disclosures in financial statements of
    new reorganized entity, 744
  doctrine of equitable subordination, 743
  emerging from Chapter 11, 744
  environmental cleanup costs, 723
  equity insolvency, 722
  examiner, 737
  fradulent conveyance of assets, 725
  fresh start reporting, 743, 750–752
  government agencies as creditors, 738
  income statement prepared during
    reorganization, 742
  insiders, 726
  involuntary bankruptcy proceedings, 724
  involuntary filing requirements, 725, 737
  labor contract controversy, 723
  noncomparability of financial statements
    of new and old entities, 744
  pension plans in reorganization, 739
  prepetition liabilities subject to
    compromise, 742, 745
  ranking of claims in liquidation [chart],
    726
  ranking of claims in reorganization, 741,
    743
  reasons for filing for bankruptcy, 723
  reorganization plan, 740
  reorganization value, 743–744
  reporting by entities that do not qualify
    for fresh start, 744
  statement of affairs, 727–730
  statement of cash flows prepared during
    reorganization, 742, 746–748
  statement of cash receipts and
    disbursements, 732–733
  statement of changes in estate equity,
    732–733
  statement of realization and liquidation,
    734–735
  Title 11 of U.S.C., 723
  trustee in liquidation, 725–726, 730–736
  trustee in reorganization, 737
  U.S. Trustee, 724, 737
  voidable preferences, 726
  voluntary bankruptcy proceedings, 724
  working papers for fresh start reporting,
    752
Beatrice Cos., 1, 2, 22

Blacksburg, Virginia financial statements,
    835, 844–850
Branch accounting:
  combining working papers illustrated,
    490, 491, 501
  compared with sales agencies, 483
  cost of sales computations, 488, 500
  excessive freight charges, 495–496
  expense allocations, 496–497
  foreign branch operations, 580–582
  freight charges, 494
  home office account, 486–487
  loading accounts, 492–494
  reciprocal accounts, 486
  reconciliation of home office and
    branch accounts, 497–498
  unrealized profits in branch inventory
    (loading), 492–494
Business combinations (*see also* Purchase
    business combination; Pooling of
    interests):
  accounting concept, 5, 72
  human cost, 3
  in restraint of trade, 2

C

California Public Employees' Retirement
    System, 738
California vs. American Stores Co., 2
Chevron Corporation, 59
College and university accounting (*see also*
    Nonprofit organizations):
  academic year different from fiscal year,
    881
  accrual accounting, 876
  additions to current restricted funds, 877
  agency funds, 886
  annuity and life income funds, 885
  appropriations, 879
  auxiliary enterprises, 876–878, 880
  board-designated (nonmandatory)
    transfers, 878, 881
  current funds grouping, 876
  depreciation, 876
  endowment and similar funds, 884
  expenditure classifications, 878
  financial statements, 883, 886–888
  fund accounting structure [chart], 875
  fund balance reserve account, 882
  loan funds, 884
  mandatory transfers, 878, 880, 884
  plant asset expenditures, 881
  plant funds, 885–886
  restricted current funds, 876, 882
  revenue classifications, 877
  source of GAAP, 874–875
  statement of current funds revenues,
    expenditures and other changes,
    883
  supplies, 879

College and university accounting (*cont.*)
transfers, 877–878
tuition, accounting for, 878–879
unrestricted current funds, 876, 878–882
College and University Business Administration, 876
Colley, J. Ron, 451
ConAgra, Inc., 1
Conglomeration, 1
Consolidated balance sheet, 76–88
compared with separate company
balance sheets, 76
compared under different consolidation
theories, 449
Consolidated earnings per share
dilutive securities of investee convertible
into parent shares, 399
dilutive securities of investee convertible
into subsidiary shares, 397
fully diluted EPS calculations [chart], 399
parent's equity in subsidiary realized
income, 397
primary EPS calculations [chart], 398
subsidiary options convertible into
parent common, 403
subsidiary options convertible into
subsidiary common, 401
subsidiary preferred convertible into
parent common, 401
subsidiary preferred convertible into
subsidiary common, 400
Consolidated financial statements (*see also*
specific statements):
purpose, 74
subsidiaries excluded from
consolidation, 74–75
Consolidated income statements, 88–91
compared with separate company
statements, 90
compared under different consolidation
theories, 449
Consolidated income taxes (*see* Income
taxes of consolidated entities)
Consolidated net income, 126
computations for indirect holdings, 350,
355
computation with intercompany sales, 180
computations for mutual holdings, 364, 371
Consolidated retained earnings, 126–127
Consolidated statement of cash flows, 91–96
direct method illustration, 95
dividends from equity investees, 93–94
income from equity investees, 93–94
indirect method illustration, 93
minority interest dividends, 93
working papers illustrated, 94, 96
Consolidated statement of cash flows with
foreign subsidiary, 577–580
goodwill, 578
individual translation adjustments
[chart], 578
intercompany transactions, 577–578
inventories, 578

Consolidation, 3
pooling of interests, 13, 16
Consolidation of parent and subsidiary
with different fiscal periods, 75
Consolidation policy, 74
disclosures, 75
Consolidation theories compared [chart],
439
Consolidation working papers:
adjustment and elimination entries, 78,
124–125
consolidated net income, 126
consolidated retained earnings, 126–127
cost to equity conversion schedule, 143
determining parent's method of
accounting, 130
entity theory, 446
indirect holdings, 351, 353, 357
locating errors, 143
minority interest income, 126
mutual holdings (conventional
approach), 366, 373
mutual holdings (treasury stock
approach), 362
parent company theory, 446
push-down accounting, 455–456
preferred stock in subsidiary capital
structure, 392, 395
real adjustments, 146
remeasurement of foreign subsidiary,
563
reciprocal accounts, 76, 125
separate income tax returns, 411
sequence of working paper entries,
125–126
subsidiary dividends, 125, 149
translation of foreign subsidiary, 559,
570
trial balance entries, 151
unamortized excess account, 85
Contemporary theory of consolidations,
437
Cost–book value differentials:
allocation of, 84, 144
allocation at gross fair value with
deferred taxes, 418
amortization in working papers, 87
entering in working papers, 85
foreign subsidiaries, 553, 557, 561, 567
under different consolidation theories, 442
Cost method of accounting for
investments, 43
compared to equity method, 44–46
cost to equity conversion schedule, 141,
192, 200, 242, 284, 354
dividends that are a return of capital, 43, 45
in consolidation working papers,
135–143, 193–194, 200–202,
240–244, 283, 286, 353
intercompany bond holdings, 271, 276
Cumulative-effect-type adjustments of
equity investees, 57

D

Dieter, Richard, 23
Drexel Burnham Lambert Group, Inc., 738

E

Earnings per share (*see* Consolidated
    earnings per share)
Eastern Airlines, 234, 723, 737
Eastman Kodak Co., 80
Emerging Issues Task Force (EITF)
    Consenses Issue No. 88–16, 455
Entity theory of consolidations, 438
Equity adjustment from translation
    account (*see also* Foreign currency
    financial statements and Hedge of
    net investment in foreign investee),
    556–558
Equity method of accounting for
    investments, 43:
  additional investment in investee, 55
  allocation of excess book values acquired
    over cost, 50–52
  allocation of excess cost over book
    values acquired, 47–48
  allocation of negative goodwill, 52
  amortization of excess book values
    acquired over cost, 52–53
  amortization of excess cost over book
    values acquired, 48–49
  compared to an incomplete equity
    method, 129
  compared to consolidation, 46, 79
  compared to cost method, 44–46
  cumulative-effect-type adjustments of
    investee, 57
  disclosures, 58
  extraordinary items of investee, 57
  indirect holdings, 349, 355
  interim acquisitions, 53
  mutual holdings, 363
  one-line consolidation, 46
  preferred stock of investee, 56
  recording the investment, 46
  related party transactions, 59
  relationship to *FASB Statement No. 94*
  restrictions from *FASB Statement No. 35*
  sale of an equity interest, 55, 312–317
  significant influence, 43
Estate accounting:
  charge-discharge statement, 938–939
  claims against the estate, 933
  classification of claims, 933
  creation of an estate, 931
  distinguishing between principal and
    income, 934
  family allowance, 933
  fiduciary relationship, 931, 934
  homestead allowance, 933
  income taxes on estate income, 938

  inventory of estate property, 932
  probating the will, 932
  Revised Uniform Principal and Income
    Act, 934, 939
  Uniform Probate Code, 932–934
Extraordinary items of equity investees, 57
Exxon Corporation, 58

F

Faludi, Susan C., 3
Federated Department Stores, 738
Financial Accounting Standards Board:
  Exposure Draft, Accounting for
    Contributions Received and
    Contributions Made and
    Capitalization of Works of Art,
    Historical Treasures, and Similar
    Assets, 873–874, 877, 902
  Exposure Draft, Accounting for Income
    Taxes, 405, 412
  Interpretation No. 4, 19
  Interpretation No. 18, 620
  Statement No. 1, 517
  Statement No. 3, 619, 621
  Statement No. 4, 265
  Statement No. 5, 742
  Statement No. 8, 517
  Statement No. 10, 8
  Statement No. 12, 43, 898
  Statement No. 14, 603–617
  Statement No. 15, 753
  Statement No. 18, 603
  Statement No. 21, 603
  Statement No. 32, 872
  Statement No. 35, 44
  Statement No. 38, 19, 842
  Statement No. 52, 516–523, 526–535, 548
  Statement No. 57, 59
  Statement No. 71, 219
  Statement No. 85, 397
  Statement No. 87, 19, 842
  Statement No. 93, 873, 876
  Statement No. 94, 74–75
  Statement No. 95, 91
  Statement No. 96, 405
Foreign currency (*see also* Foreign currency
    financial statements and Foreign
    currency transactions):
  change in functional currency, 550
  current rate, 521
  denominated in a currency, 519
  direct quotations of exchange rates, 520,
    522
  economic indicators of functional
    currency, 518
  exchange rates, 519
  fixed (or official) exchange rates,
    520–521
  floating (or free) exchange rates, 520
  foreign currency defined, 548

Foreign currency (*cont.*)
    functional currency concept defined, 518, 548
    Group of Seven (or G–7), 521
    historical rate, 521–522
    indirect quotations of exchange rates, 520, 522
    local currency defined, 548
    measured in a currency, 519
    multiple exchange rates, 521
    objectives of translation and *FAS 52,* 518
    spot rate, 521, 523
Foreign currency financial statements (*see also* Foreign currency and Foreign currency transactions):
    application of equity method, 556, 568, 573
    comparison of consolidated income statements under remeasurement and translation, 564
    consolidated statement of cash flows, 577–580
    cost–book value differentials, 553, 557, 561, 567
    current-noncurrent method, 517
    current rate method, 517, 519, 549–550
    disclosure of remeasurement gains and losses, 562
    equity adjustment from translation account, 556–558, 568–570, 572, 576
    exchange rates used for remeasurement and translation [chart], 551
    foreign currency defined, 548
    goodwill and goodwill amortization, 557, 569
    highly inflationary economies, 552
    intercompany transactions, 550–552, 554, 561, 571–573, 575
    local currency defined, 548
    lower-of-cost-or-market rule, 566
    minority interest in foreign subsidiary, 553, 569, 575
    monetary-nonmonetary method, 517
    objective of remeasurement, 549–550
    pooling of interests business combination, 553
    purchase business combination, 553
    remeasurement defined, 549
    remeasuring expenses of foreign investees, 562
    reporting currency defined, 548
    temporal method, 517, 519, 549
    translating statements when country has multiple exchange rates, 522
    translation defined, 549
Foreign currency transactions (*see also* Foreign currency and Foreign currency financial statements):
    discount to sell foreign currency, 530
    equity adjustment from translation (forward contracts), 533, 535
    exchange gains and losses, 523–528
    foreign transactions compared with foreign currency transactions, 522
    forward exchange contracts (futures), 526
    hedge of exposed net asset or liability position, 526, 527–530
    hedge of foreign currency commitment, 526, 530
    hedge of foreign currency commitment recorded on a net basis, 532
    hedge of net investment in a foreign investee, 526, 533
    hedging operations, 526
    premium to purchase foreign currency, 530
    speculation, 526
    summary of forward contracts [chart], 535
    year-end adjustments to current exchange rates, 524
Fuqua Industries, 79

G

General Cinema, 75
Goodwill, 20–23
    controversy, 22–23
    International Accounting Standards Committee, 23
Governmental accounting:
    account groups, 776–777, 822
    accrual accounting, 827
    accumulated depreciation on general fixed assets, 824
    agency funds, 776, 836–838
    allotments, 782
    appropriations, 782
    bond issue proceeds, 780, 814
    budgeting, 778, 782, 786, 791
    capital budget, 782
    capital program, 782
    capital projects fund, 775, 813–818
    cash flows statements, 831–833, 850
    combined financial statements, 844–850
    combining financial statements, 834
    common terminology and classifications in fund accounting systems, 781–793
    comprehensive annual report, 781, 816–817, 844
    consumption method of accounting for supplies in GF, 790
    customer deposits in EF, 834
    debt service fund, 776, 818–821
    defeasance of debt, 825–826
    developer deposits in EF, 834
    encumbrances, 784, 788–789
    endowment trust fund, 838
    enterprise fund, 776, 833–834
    entitlements, 781
    expendable trust funds, 778, 838
    expenditures, 779–781, 784

Governmental accounting (*cont.*)
expenses, 779
fiduciary funds, 775, 778, 836–843
fixed assets, 776–777
fund accounting systems, 774
fund categories, 774–775
fund equity vs. fund balance, 792–793
general fixed assets account group,
776–777, 822–824
general fund, 775, 783–795
general long-term debt account group,
776–777, 824–826
governmental funds, 774–775, 777–778
grants, 780, 815, 817
infrastructure fixed assets, 822
intergovernmental fund revenue, 780,
815
interfund loans and advances, 779
interfund transfers, 779, 813
interim financial reports, 781
internal service fund, 776, 827–831
interperiod equity measurement, 851–852
lease agreements in governmental fund
types, 827
line-item budgeting, 782
long-term liabilities, 776–777
measurement focus, 851–852
modified accrual accounting, 777, 813,
819, 838
nonexpendable trust funds, 778, 831,
838–841
operating transfers, 779, 813, 821
payments in lieu of taxes, 781
pension trust funds, 842–843
performance budget, 783
program budget, 782–783
property taxes, 785
proprietary funds, 775, 777, 827–835
public domain fixed assets, 822
purchase method of accounting for
supplies in GF, 789–790
quasi-external transactions, 779
reimbursement interfund transactions,
779
residual equity transfers, 779, 817–818,
828, 833
retained percentage on construction
contract in CPF, 814
revenues, 779–781, 784
shared revenues, 781
special assessments, 821, 836
special revenue funds, 775, 783
statement of revenues, expenditures, and
changes in fund balance-budget and
actual, 784, 846
subsidiary ledgers, 784
trust funds, 776
unissued bonds in CPF, 815
zero-based budgeting, 783
Governmental Accounting Standards Board
Statement No. 5, 842, 843
Statement No. 6, 813

Statement No. 7, 825
Statement No. 9, 831
Statement No. 11, 851–852
Statement No. 12, 843–844

H

Hallmark Cards, 263
Hendricksen, Eldon S., 437
H. J. Heinz Company, 609
Horizontal integration, 1
Hospitals, accounting for (*see also*
Nonprofit organizations):
agency funds, 889
bad debts, 892
board-designated funds, 889
charity care, 890, 892
donated assets, 892, 898
donated funds held in trust, 892
donated services, 892
donor restricted funds, 889
endowment funds, 890
expense classifications, 891
financial statements, 893–896
fund accounting structure [chart], 889
general funds, 889
investment pools, 893
nonoperating gains, 891, 897
other operating revenue, 890, 897
patient service revenues, 890, 896
plant replacement and expansion funds,
890
pledges, 892
related party disclosures, 899–900
revenue classifications, 890–891
source of GAAP, 886
specific purpose funds, 890
supplies, 897

I

Income taxation of consolidated entities:
advantages of filing consolidated tax
return, 404
affiliated group for tax purposes, 404
allocating gross fair value in business
combination, 418
consolidated income tax allocation, 412
consolidated tax return with downstream
sale, 413
consolidated tax return with upstream
sale, 416
consolidation working papers (separate
returns), 411
constructive gains and losses, 407
disclosures, 420
dividend deductions and exclusion, 404
elimination of unrealized profits on
gross basis, 407
income tax expense (separate returns), 409

Income taxation of consolidated entities (*cont.*)
  separate tax returns with downstream sale, 414
  separate tax returns with upstream sale, 417
  temporary differences, 405
  undistributed earnings, 405
  unrealized gains and losses, 407
Incomplete equity method, 129
  intercompany bond holdings, 271, 276, 282, 285
  intercompany inventory profits, 190, 198–199
  intercompany plant asset profits, 239
Indirect holdings:
  connecting affiliates relationship, 348
  consolidated net income computations, 350
  cost method, 352
  equity method, 349, 355
  father-son-grandson relationship, 348
  minority interest income computations, 350
Ingersoll Newspapers Inc., 263
Intercompany bond holdings:
  agency theory for allocating gains and losses, 264
  constructive gains and losses, 264
  constructive retirement of intercompany bonds, 263
  cost method of parent company accounting, 271, 276
  effective interest method, 264
  FASB Statement No. 4, 265
  incomplete equity method of parent company accounting, 271, 276
  minority interest computations, 274, 276, 277–278
  par value theory for allocating gains and losses, 264
  piecemeal recognition of constructive gain or loss, 267–270, 273
  reporting gains and losses from extinguishment of debt, 265
  summary illustration, 288
Intercompany borrowing, 263–264
Intercompany profit in inventories:
  consolidated net income computations, 180
  cost method, 192, 200
  downstream and upstream sales designations, 179
  elimination of intercompany purchases and sales, 173
  incomplete equity method, 190, 198
  minority interest computations, 180
  summary illustration, 203
  unrealized profit in beginning inventory, 176, 183, 185
  unrealized profit in ending inventory, 174, 181, 184
Intercompany profit in plant assets:
  FASB Statement No. 71, 219
  loss on intercompany sale, 234–235

  minority interest computation, 223, 233, 238
  piecemeal recognition through depreciation, 225–228, 238
  sale to outside entity, 224, 236
  year of intercompany sale, 225
Intercompany transactions with foreign subsidiary, 550–552, 554, 561, 571–575
Interim financial reports, 618
  advertising costs in interim reports, 619
  annual expenses in interim reports, 619
  computation of estimated annual effective tax rate, 620
  disclosures required, 621
  discrete theory, 621
  fourth quarter disclosures required in annual reports, 621, 622
  income taxes in interim reports, 620
  integral theory, 621
  interim inventory pricing using gross profit method, 619
  interim inventories under a standard cost system, 619
  inventory market declines, 619
  LIFO inventories, 619
  modifications of accounting procedures used in annual reports, 619–620
  SEC interim financial disclosures, 622–623
  segment disclosures, 618
  unaudited, 619, 622
International Accounting Standards Committee, 23, 24

J

Joint ventures:
  corporate joint ventures, 458
  defined, 457
  disclosures for joint ventures, 459, 460
  equity method, 458, 460
  established industry practice guidelines, 460
  general partnership, defined, 458
  limited partnership, defined, 458
  nature, 458
  proportionate consolidation, 460–461
  undivided interest, 458
  unincorporated joint venture, 459

K

Kimberly-Clark Corporation, 73

L

Leveraged buyouts, 454
Liquidation cases under the Bankruptcy Act (*see* Bankruptcy cases)
LTV Corp., 723, 738, 739, 741

M

Mautz, Robert K., 602
McFarland, Walter, 602
Merger, 3
    pooling of interests, 12, 15
Minority interest, 73
    changes in minority percent during
        period, 307, 311, 313, 315
    classification in balance sheet, 78
    computation with intercompany bond
        holdings, 274, 276–278
    computation with intercompany
        inventory sales, 180, 196–197
    computation with upstream depreciable
        assets, 233
    computation with upstream land sale,
        223, 225
    effects of unrealized profits, 179
    in cash flows statement, 93
    indirect holdings, 350, 355, 358
    in subsidiary's preferred stock, 391
    mutual holdings, 364, 371
    pooling of interests, 100
    valuation under different consolidation
        theories, 438–440, 450
Moonitz, Maurice, 438
Mutual holdings
    affiliation structures, 346
    allocation of mutual income, 364, 371
    conventional approach, 359, 362
    equity method, 363
    treasury stock approach, 359

N

National Council on Governmental Accounting
    Statement No. 1, 842
    Statement No. 6, 842
Negative goodwill, 20–22
Nonprofit organizations (*see also* specific
        nonprofit organizations, e.g.,
        Colleges and universities,
        Governmental accounting,
        Hospitals, and Voluntary health and
        welfare organizations):
    contributions, defined, 873
    contributions of services, 874
    depreciation, 873
    pledges, 874
    specialized principles, 872–873
    sources of GAAP for nonprofits, 872,
        874–875, 886, 900
Note to the Student, 10, 60
Nynex Corporation, 235

O

One-line consolidation (*see* equity
    method)

P

Paramount Communications Inc., 73
Parent company theory of consolidations,
    437
Parent-subsidiary relationship, 73
Partnerships:
    absence of profit sharing agreement,
        640, 646, 654
    additional investments, 643
    advance distribution in liquidation
        requires partners' approval, 698
    assignment of a partnership interest, 653
    assumed loss absorption schedule in
        liquidation, 706
    bankruptcy trustee, 709
    bonus and goodwill procedures
        compared, 661
    bonus on initial investment, 643
    bonuses in profit sharing agreements,
        648–649
    capital balances in profit sharing
        agreements, 649–653
    cash distribution plan in liquidation,
        706, 707
    cash distribution schedule in liquidation,
        708
    debit capital balances in liquidation,
        694–696
    dissolution of continuing partnership,
        663
    dissolution of partnership defined, 653
    division of losses, 646
    drawings, 643–644
    excess payment to retiring partner, 664
    financial statements, 644
    goodwill on initial investment, 643
    income allocation schedules, 647, 648,
        652
    insolvent partner, 709–710
    insolvent partnership, 709–711
    insolvent partnership as defined in
        Bankruptcy Act, 710
    installment liquidations, 699
    investment by new partner, 658–660
    limited life feature, 640
    loans to and from partners, 644
    mutual agency, 640
    noncash assets distributed to partners in
        liquidation, 704
    noncash investments, 641
    partnership agreements, 640
    partnership defined, 639
    partnership liquidation statements,
        694–695, 701–702, 705
    purchase of interest from partner, 654–657
    rank order for claims against separate
        property of insolvent partner, 709
    rank order of payment in liquidation,
        692, 693
    retiring partner paid less than capital
        balance, 665

Partnerships: (*cont.*)
   rules for distributing assets in
     liquidation, 692
   safe payments schedules in liquidation,
     697
   salary allowances, 643–644, 646–647
   simple partnership liquidation, 693
   statement of partnership capital, 645
   Uniform Partnership Act, 678–691
   unlimited liability, 640
   users of financial reports, 640
   vulnerability ranks in liquidation, 706
   weighted average capital balances, 649
   withdrawals, 643
Par value theory for allocating gains and
     losses on constructive bond
     retirements, 264
Pension Benefit Guarantee Corporation,
     738
Pooling of interests, 7
   acquisition of minority shares, 102
   change in accounting methods to
     conform pooled companies, 7
   combined operations, 15–16
   combining stockholders' equities, 11–15,
     99–102
   compared to purchase method, 23–27
   concepts underlying pooling, 7, 16
   conditions for, 8–9
   controversy, 6
   costs incurred to effect pooling, 7, 16, 25
   disclosure requirements, 27
   duplicate facilities, 9
   foreign subsidiary, 553
   intercompany stock holdings of
     combining companies, 14
   International Accounting Standards
     Committee, 24
   midyear pooling, 15–16, 307–309
   minority interest, 100
   reporting pooled retained earnings, 310
   separate equity accounts, 99
   substantially all test illustrated, 10
   treasury stock, 14
Preacquisition dividends, 305
Preacquisition earnings, 303, 311
   working paper adjustments and
     eliminations, 305–307
Preferred stock in investee's capital
     structure, 56, 389
   constructive retirement of subsidiary
     preferred stock, 393
   investment in preferred stock
     maintained on cost basis, 396
   minority interest, 391
Purchase business combination, 7
   acquisition of minority shares, 73
   allocation of cost, 18–20
   allocation of cost at gross fair value with
     deferred taxes, 418
   allocation period, 19
   compared with poolings of interests, 23–27

concepts underlying purchase method, 7,
   17
contingent consideration in purchase, 19
cost and fair values compared, 20
cost of acquired company, 17, 25
direct costs of combination, 17, 25
disclosure requirements, 27
duplicate facilities, 17
excess cost over fair value of interest
   acquired, 20–21
excess fair value over cost of interest
   acquired, 20, 21–22
foreign subsidiary, 553
goodwill, 20–23
identifiable intangible assets, 19
indirect costs of combination, 17
negative goodwill, 20, 21–22
pension plan asset or liability, 19
preacquisition contingency, 19
registration costs of securities issued,
   17–18, 25
Purchased income (*see* Preacquisition
   income)
Push down accounting, 97–98, 450–455

Q

Qualex, Inc., 79
Quantum Chemical Corporation, 73

R

Ralston Purina Company, 623–625
Reorganizations under the Bankruptcy Act
   (*see* Bankruptcy cases)
Revised Uniform Principal and Income
   Act, 934, 939
Rock, Robert H., 2–3

S

Securities and Exchange Commission:
   Accounting Series Release 236, 603
   areas of responsibility, 926
   codification of SABs and ASRs, 928
   EDGAR System, 929–930
   Financial Reporting Release (FRR) No. 1,
     928
   Form 8-K, 926, 929
   Form 10-K, 926, 928–929
   Form 10-Q, 622–624, 926
   integrated disclosure system, 927–930
   interim financial disclosures, 622–623,
     929
   offering circular, 926
   prospectus, 926
   proxy rules, 928
   registration statements, 926, 927
   Regulation A, 926, 927

Securities and Exchange Commission: (*cont.*)
    Regulation S, 929
    Regulation S–K, 927
    Regulation S–X, 75, 927
    reporting requirements under 1934
        Securities Act, 926
    Rule 3A–03, 75
    Securities Act of 1933, 925
    Securities Act of 1934, 926
    segment reporting requirements,
        602–603
    Staff Accounting Bulletin No. 40, 928
    Staff Accounting Bulletin No. 51, 321
    Staff Accounting Bulletin No. 54, 450
    Staff Accounting Bulletin No. 84, 321
Safeway Stores, Inc., 3
Sales agencies:
    accounting for, 484–486
    compared with branches, 483
Segment reporting:
    disclosures for export sales, 617
    disclosures for geographic operations,
        614–615
    disclosures for major customers, 617
    disclosures for reportable industry
        segments, 611–612
    dominant industry segment, 609
    foreign operations, tests for reporting, 609
    industry segment defined, 604
    nonpublic enterprises, 603
    reevaluation of reportable segments, 608
    reportable industry segment, 604
    restatement of segment information
        required, 612
    segment disclosures in interim reports,
        603, 618
    10% asset test, 607
    10% operating profit test, 604–606, 608
    10% revenue test, 607
    tests for disclosure under *FAS 14* [chart], 605
Sikora, Martin, 4
Skousen, K. Fred, 602
Subsidiary stock transactions, 318
    treasury stock transactions, 322
    stock dividends, 324
    stock splits, 323
Sun Company, 73, 612

T

Texas Air Corporation, 234
Texaco, 723, 739
Trial balance format for consolidation
    working papers, 149–152
Troubled debt restructurings, 753
    creditor accounting, 754
    debtor accounting, 753–754
    grant of equity interest, 753, 756

    modification of terms, 753, 756
    transfer of assets, 753, 755
Trust accounting:
    creation of income trust, 938
    distinguishing between principal and
        income, 939
    illustration of accounting for a trust
        fund, 839–841
    testamentary trust, 938

U

Unamortized excess account, 85
Uniform Partnership Act, 678–691
Uniform Probate Code, 932–934
Uniform Trusts Act, 939
Upjohn Company, 75

V

Vertical integration, 1
Voluntary health and welfare organizations
    (*see also* Nonprofit organizations):
    accrual accounting, 901
    contributions, 902, 903
    custodian funds, 901
    deferred contributions, 903
    donated materials, 902
    donated services, 902, 905
    expense allocation, 904–905
    expense classifications, 902
    financial statements, 905–910
    fund structure [chart], 901
    land, building and equipment fund, 901,
        905
    memberships, 904
    program services, 902
    revenue classifications, 902, 904
    special event fund-raisers, 904
    statement of functional expenses, 903,
        908–909
    support classifications, 902
    supporting services, 902
    transfers, 905

W

Wheeling-Pittsburgh Steel Corporation,
    723, 741
Whirlpool Corporation, 617, 618
Woolworth Corporation, 346, 564

Z

Zeff, Stephen A., 696